A

B O O K

The Philip E. Lilienthal imprint
honors special books
in commemoration of a man whose work
at the University of California Press from 1954 to 1979
was marked by dedication to young authors
and to high standards in the field of Asian Studies.
Friends, family, authors, and foundations have together
endowed the Lilienthal Fund, which enables the Press
to publish under this imprint selected books
in a way that reflects the taste and judgment
of a great and beloved author.

*The publisher gratefully acknowledges the generous contribution to this book provided by the Philip E. Lilienthal Asian Studies Endowment, which is supported by a major gift from Sally Lilienthal.*

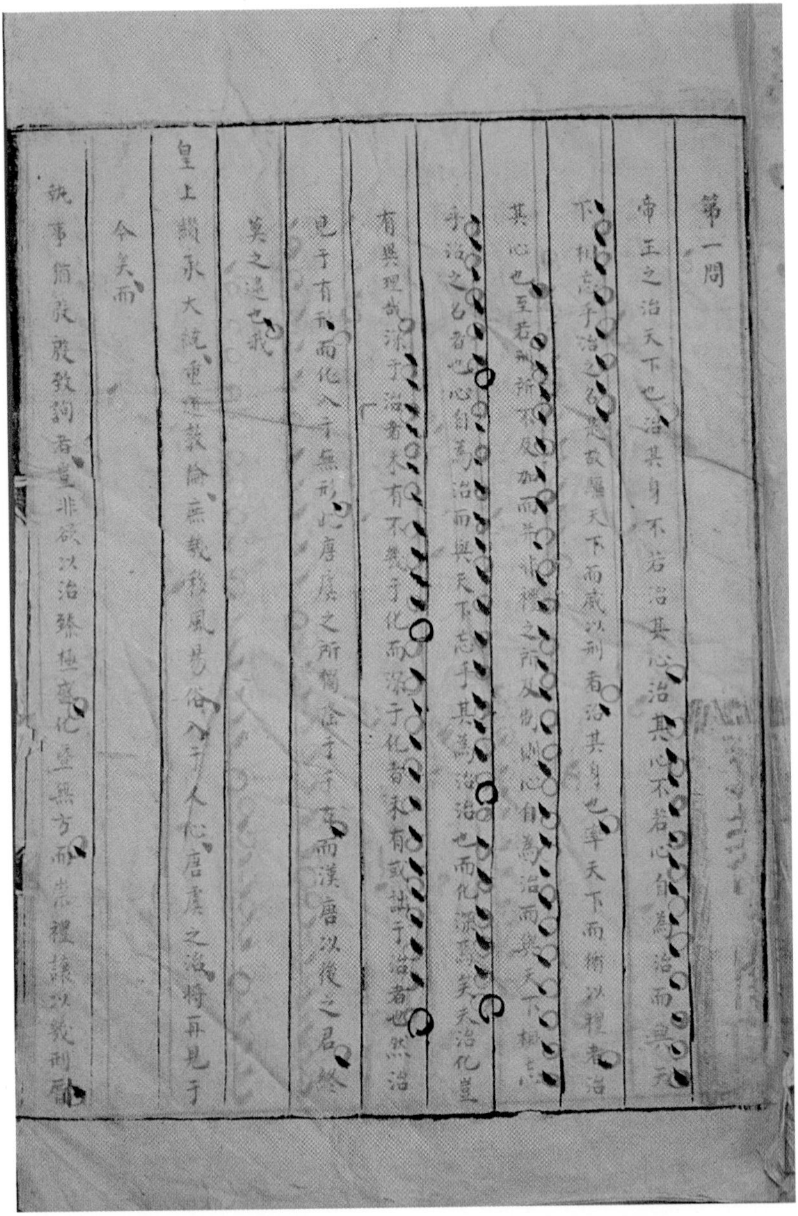

第一問
帝王之治天下也治其身不若治其心治其心不若心自爲治而與天
下相忘乎治之名是故驅天下而咸以刑者治其身也率天下而術以禮者治
其心也至若神所不及加而莫非禮之所及也則心自爲治而與天下相忘
乎治之名者也心自爲治而與天下忘乎其爲治治也而化深焉矣夫治化豈
有異理哉深于治者未有不幾于化而深于化者未有或詘于治者也然治
見于有形而化入于無形此唐虞之所獨[illegible]于千古而漢唐以後之君終
莫之逮也哉
皇上纘承大統重道敦倫無幾移風易俗入于人心唐虞之治將再見于
今矣而
執事循[illegible]殷致詢者豈非欲以治臻極盛化登無方而崇禮讓以教刑措


1667 Vermillion Ink Examination Paper. *Source:* Ming-Ch'ing Archives, Academia Sinica, Taiwan. Thanks are due Chang Wejen, the director, for permission to use these materials, and the Institute of History and Philology.

# A Cultural History of Civil Examinations in Late Imperial China

BENJAMIN A. ELMAN

UNIVERSITY OF CALIFORNIA PRESS

BERKELEY          LOS ANGELES          LONDON

University of California Press
Berkeley and Los Angeles, California

University of California Press, Ltd.
London, England

© 2000 by
The Regents of the University of California

Library of Congress Cataloging-in-Publication Data

Elman, Benjamin A.
    A cultural history of civil examinations in late imperial China /
Benjamin A. Elman.
        p.   cm.
    Includes bibliographical references.
    ISBN 0-520-21509-5 (alk. paper)
        1. Civil service—China—Examinations—History.   I. Title.
JQ1512.Z13E87277   2000                                          99-20628
351.51'0076—dc21                                                 CIP

Printed in the United States of America
9  8  7  6  5  4  3  2  1

Dedicated to Sarah (Ts'ai Su-erh 蔡素娥),
with love and affection

# CONTENTS

LIST OF ILLUSTRATIONS / ix
LIST OF TABLES / xi
PREFACE / xvii
ACKNOWLEDGMENTS / xxxvii

1. Rethinking the Historical Roots
of Late Imperial Civil Examinations / 1

2. Imperial Power, Cultural Politics,
and Civil Examinations in the Early Ming / 66

3. Institutional Dynamics and Mobilization of Elites
in Late Imperial Civil Examinations / 125

4. Examination Compounds and the Limits of Dynastic Power / 173

5. Classical Literacy and the Social Dimensions
of Late Imperial Civil Examinations / 239

6. Emotional Anxiety, Dreams of Success,
and the Examination Life / 295

7. The Cultural Scope of Civil Examinations
and the Eight-Legged Essay among Elites / 371

8. Examiner Standards, Literati Interpretation,
and Limits to the Dynastic Control of Knowledge / 421

9. Natural Studies, History, and Han Learning
in Civil Examinations / 460

10. Acceleration of Curricular Reform
under Ch'ing Rule before 1800 / 521

11. Delegitimation and Decanonization:
The Pitfalls of Late Ch'ing Examination Reform / 569

Appendix 1: Civil Examination Primary Sources, 1148–1904 / 627

Appendix 2: Civil Examination Primary Sources
in the Mormon Genealogical Library / 641

Appendix 3: Tables / 646

Appendix 4: Timelines for Civil Examination
Curriculum Change, 650–1905 / 729

Appendix 5: Major Types of Civil Examination Sources
besides Gazetteers / 738

BIBLIOGRAPHY OF PRIMARY
AND SECONDARY SOURCES / 741
INDEX / 797

# ILLUSTRATIONS

MAPS

1. Administrative Map of Late Imperial China      xviii

2. China during the Sung Dynasties      2

FIGURES

Frontispiece. A 1667 Vermillion Ink Examination Paper      ii

4.1. The Prefectural Examination Hall      176

4.2. The 1604 *Optimus* Drunk in an Examination Cell      178

4.3. The Nanking Provincial Examination Hall      179

4.4. The Shun-t'ien Provincial and Metropolitan Examination Hall      182

4.5. Main Entrance to the Nanking Examination Hall      183

4.6. Corridors to the Cells      183

4.7. Open Examination Cells      184

4.8. Cheating Shirt      186

4.9. Draft of 1685 Discourse Examination Essay      187

4.10. A 1685 Black Ink Examination Paper      188

4.11. The 1484 *Optimus* Paraded before Friends      192

4.12. The 1571 *Optimus* Dreams of an Official Placard      193

5.1. The 1430 *Optimus* Writes from Memory      262

5.2. The 1463 *Optimus* Learns Characters as a Child 264

5.3. The 1400 *Optimus* Reading as a Youth 271

5.4. The 1391 *Optimus* Reading at Home 274

6.1. Pointing to the Little Dipper in 1502 314

6.2. Using Bamboo Sticks to Divine Examination Success in Ch'ing Times 315

6.3. Sending Dog Meat in 1406 323

6.4. Three Heads Appear in a 1445 Dream-Vision 332

6.5. A Two-Headed Horseman Appears in a 1583 Dream-Vision 336

6.6. A Spirit Heralds the 1454 *Optimus* 337

6.7. Entering Heaven's Gate in 1544 338

6.8. Presenting a Goat's Head in 1451 340

6.9. A Yellow Crane Appears in 1505 341

6.10. An Immortal Presents Medicine in 1541 342

6.11. A Taoist Immortal Rides a Crane in 1559 344

6.12. Riding the Lotus Flower in 1553 345

6.13. Dreaming of an Auspicious Meeting at the Local Wen-ch'ang Temple in 1822 358

7.1. Writing Paraphernalia of the 1388 *Optimus* 378

11.1. Peasants Trashing a New School 623

# TABLES

1.1. Yuan *Chin-shih* Degrees by Year, 1315–1366 — 646

1.2. Annual Number of *Chü-jen* and *Chin-shih* in the Sung, Chin, Yuan, and Ming Dynasties — 647

1.3. *Chin-shih* by Reign Period during the Sung Dynasties — 648

1.4. *Chin-shih* by Reign Period during the Yuan Dynasty — 649

1.5. *Chin-shih* by Reign Period during the Ming Dynasty — 650

1.6. Establishment of Private Academies during the Sung and Ming Dynasties — 651

2.1. Provincial *Chü-jen* Quotas during the Ming Dynasty, 1370–1630 — 652

2.2. Ming Dynasty Ratio of Graduates to Candidates in Metropolitan Examinations, 1371–1601, with Comparisons to T'ang and Sung Ratios — 653

2.3. Ming Dynasty Frequency of Specialization on One of the Five Classics in Civil Metropolitan Examinations, 1371–1637 — 654

2.4. Ming Dynasty Frequency of Specialization on One of the Five Classics in Ying-t'ien Prefecture, 1399–1630 — 654

2.5. Ratios of Southern versus Northern Graduates on Early Ming *Chin-shih* Examinations — 655

2.6. Ranking of Prefectures Producing *Chü-jen* and *Chin-shih* during the Early and Mid-Ming Dynasty — 656

2.7. Ming-Ch'ing Provincial Quotas and Ch'ing *Chin-shih* Totals by Province — 656

2.8. Regional Breakdown of Top Three Finishers on Civil Palace Examinations and Top Finisher on Metropolitan Examinations during the Ming and Ch'ing Dynasties 657

2.9. Ratios of Early Ming Southern *Chin-shih* Graduates from Chiang-hsi and Che-chiang 658

3.1. Flow Chart of Civil Examinations and Degrees during the Ming and Ch'ing Dynasties 659

3.2. Local Civil Licentiate Quotas in T'ung-chou and Ching-hsiang, Chiang-su, 1645–95 660

3.3. Ming Dynasty Ratio of Graduates to Candidates in Ying-t'ien Prefecture (Chiang-nan) Provincial Examinations 661

3.4. Ming-Ch'ing Dynasty Ratio of Graduates to Candidates in Che-chiang Provincial Examinations 662

3.5. Ming-Ch'ing Dynasty Ratio of Graduates to Candidates in Shun-t'ien and Shan-tung Provincial Examinations 663

3.6. Ming-Ch'ing Dynasty Ratio of Graduates to Candidates in Other Provincial Examinations 664

3.7. Careers of Provincial *Chü-jen* Graduates from Shan-tung during the Ming Dynasty 666

3.8. Official Positions of *Chü-jen* Graduates from Shan-tung during the Ming Dynasty 667

3.9. Career Patterns of *Chin-shih* Graduates from Shan-tung during the Ming Dynasty 668

3.10. Civil Examination Officials on the 1465 Shan-tung Provincial Examination 669

3.11. Civil Examination Officials on the 1594 Shan-tung Provincial Examination 670

3.12. Examination Status of Chief and Associate Provincial Examiners during the Ming Dynasty, 1465–1639 671

3.13. Provincial Civil Examination Officials in Che-chiang during the Ming Dynasty 672

3.14. Examination Status of Chief and Associate Metropolitan Examiners during the Ming Dynasty 673

3.15. Metropolitan Civil Examination Officials during the Ming Dynasty 674

3.16. Palace Civil Examination Officials during the Ming Dynasty 676

3.17. Total Number of Fu-chien *Chü-jen* and *Chin-shih* by Prefecture, 1370–1634 — 677

3.18. *Chü-jen* Who Became *Chin-shih* from Fu-ch'eng, Fu-chien, 1370–1546 — 678

3.19. Profile of Civil Examination Success in Fu-chien during the Ming Dynasty, 1370–1636 — 679

3.20. Ch'ing Dynasty Ratio of Graduates to Candidates in Metropolitan Examinations, 1691–1850 — 680

3.21. Late Ming and Early Ch'ing *Chü-jen* in Shan-tung Who Received *Chin-shih* Degrees under Ch'ing Rule — 680

3.22. Date of *Chin-shih* Degree for High Civil Examination Officials during the Early Ch'ing Dynasty — 681

3.23. Provincial *Chü-jen* Quotas during the Ch'ing Dynasty, 1645–1900 — 682

4.1. Ming Dynasty Provincial Civil Examination Officials — 683

4.2. Ming Dynasty Metropolitan Civil Examination Officials — 684

4.3. Number of Wards by Classic in Ming Dynasty Civil Metropolitan Examinations — 685

4.4. Number of Wards by Classic in Ch'ing Dynasty Civil Metropolitan Examinations — 685

4.5. Metropolitan Civil Examination Officials during the Ch'ing Dynasty — 686

4.6. Percentage of Officials Becoming Local Officials through Civil Examination, *Yin* Privilege, or Purchase during the Ch'ing Dynasty — 687

4.7. Number of *Chien-sheng* Degrees Purchased and Amount Collected during the Tao-kuang Reign, 1821–50, by Province — 688

4.8. Quotas and Geographical Distribution of *Sheng-yuan* by Province before 1850 — 689

4.9. Quotas and Geographical Distribution of Civil *Sheng-yuan* by Province after 1850 — 690

5.1. Social Origins of Candidates in Ming-Ch'ing Provincial Civil Examinations — 691

5.2. Social Origins of Candidates for Ming-Ch'ing Metropolitan and Palace Civil Examinations — 691

5.3. *Chin-shih* from Special Statuses, 1371–1643 — 692

5.4. Geographical Distribution of *Chü-jen* Graduates by Examination in Ying-t'ien Prefecture (Nanking) during the Ming Dynasty — 693

5.5. Su-chou *Optimi* by Dynasty, 869–1874 — 693

5.6. Geographical Distribution of *Chü-jen* Graduates in the Shun-t'ien Capital Region during the Early Ch'ing Dynasty by Examination — 694

5.7. *Optimi* during the Ch'ing Dynasty by Province — 695

5.8. Geographic Distribution of *Chin-shih* in Ming Times — 696

5.9. Provincial Distribution of *Chin-shih* during the Ming Dynasty by Year, 1385–1622 — 697

5.10. Quotas and Actual Numbers of *Chin-shih* in Late Ch'ing Examinations — 698

5.11. Regional Distribution of *Chin-shih* in Early and Late Ch'ing — 699

5.12. Number of *Chin-shih* by Province per Million Mean Population — 700

5.13. Ming Dynasty Frequency of Specialization on One of the Five Classics in Che-chiang Province, 1370–1600 — 701

5.14. Ming Dynasty Frequency of Specialization on One of the Five Classics in Fu-chien Province, 1399–1636 — 701

5.15. Ch'ing Dynasty Frequency of Specialization on One of the Five Classics in Shun-t'ien Prefecture, 1654–1759 — 702

5.16. Ch'ing Dynasty Frequency of Specialization on One of the Five Classics in Chiang-nan, 1678–1747 — 702

5.17. Ch'ing Dynasty Frequency of Specialization on One of the Five Classics in Civil Metropolitan Examinations, 1655–1760 — 703

5.18. Age of *Chü-jen* on Provincial Examinations during the Ming Dynasty — 703

5.19. Age of *Chü-jen* on Provincial Examinations during the Ch'ing Dynasty — 704

5.20. Age of 47 Ming *Optimi* Attaining *Chin-shih* Degree — 705

5.21. Age of 67 Ch'ing *Optimi* Attaining *Chin-shih* Degree — 705

5.22. Age of *Chin-shih* on Palace Examinations during the Ming Dynasty — 706

5.23. Age of *Chin-shih* on Palace Examinations during the Ch'ing Dynasty — 706

8.1. Importance of the Four Books for Final Rankings during the Ming and Ch'ing Dynasties — 707

8.2. Importance of Policy Questions for Final Rankings during the Ming and Early Ch'ing Dynasties — 710

8.3. Sample of Rankings of 47 Palace Examination *Optimi* on Metropolitan and Provincial Civil Examinations during the Ming Dynasty, 1371–1610     716

8.4. Sample of Rankings of 60 Palace Examination *Optimi* on Metropolitan and Provincial Civil Examinations during the Ch'ing Dynasty, 1664–1852     717

8.5. Ming Dynasty Policy Questions Classified by Topic: Ying-t'ien Prefecture, 1474–1600     719

8.6. Ch'ing Dynasty Policy Questions Classified by Topic: Che-chiang Province, 1646–1859     720

8.7. Breakdown of 70 Imperially Selected Policy Questions for 1756–1762 Provincial Civil Examinations     721

8.8. Summary of Policy Questions for 1840 and 1849 Provincial Civil Examinations     722

10.1. Importance of Discourse Questions for Final Rankings during the Ming and Early Ch'ing Dynasties     723

10.2. Importance of Poetry Questions for Final Rankings during the Late Ch'ing Dynasty     724

10.3. Importance of Five Classics Questions for Final Rankings during the Late Ch'ing Dynasty     725

11.1. Total Upper and Lower Ch'ing Civil Examination Degree Graduates before and after the Taiping Rebellion     728

# PREFACE

In China since medieval times, imperial dynasties, gentry-literati elites, and classical studies were tightly intertwined in the operation of the civil service examinations.[1] All three dimensions were perpetuated during the late empire (1368–1911), and they stabilized for five hundred years because of their interdependence. When they fell in the twentieth century, they collapsed together, no longer connected to the political power and literary culture they had reinforced. To be properly evaluated, civil service examinations in premodern China should be combined with careful study of the primary sources that inform us of the educational, cultural, social, and political practices during Ming (1368–1644) and Ch'ing (1644–1911) times.

The complicated relationships among the imperial dynasty, local elites, and village peasants were transformed between 1400 and 1600. As China's population grew from approximately 65 million to 150 million, the reach of the imperial bureaucracy declined. Because the monetarization of the Ming economy during the "silver age" of 1550 to 1650 made inevitable the commutation of village and town labor tax services into cash levies, the imperial court and its bureaucracy lost control of their land and labor

---

1. In this volume, "gentry" refers to Han Chinese elites before 1900 who wielded local social and economic power as landlords or held provincial and empirewide political power as officials in the dynastic bureaucracy. "Literati" refers to selected members of the gentry who maintained their status as cultural elites primarily through classical scholarship, knowledge of lineage ritual, and literary publication. The cultural status of both the gentry at large and the literati in their midst correlated with their rank on the civil service examinations. Hence, because the terms overlap, they will frequently be presented together as "gentry-literati" or "scholar-gentry." In addition, during the late empire, gentry and merchants intermingled, with the latter becoming part of the gentry elite.

MAP I. Administrative Map of Late Imperial China. *Source:* Elman, *Classicism, Politics, and Kinship* (Berkeley: University of California Press, 1990), p. xxiv.

resources. The retreat of the dynasty from direct involvement in village affairs magnified the mediating role of the gentry-landlord elite in late Ming and Ch'ing politics and society. Under the umbrella of the central government, gentry and merchant elites in the Yangtzu delta and elsewhere diversified their hold on local power into expanded forms of profiteering based on land rent and commercial enterprises. They also monopolized positions in the imperial bureaucracy by translating their economic and social power into cultural and educational advantages that enabled mainly the sons of gentry and merchants to pass the civil examinations. Indeed, the civil examination system remained a tense bureaucratic arena, in which the imperial court gamely tried to maintain control of its elites, and the elites brazenly used the government to enhance their social status and economic assets.[2]

Any picture of late imperial government and society that presents their interaction as an unrelenting imperial hegemony is thus one-sided. So, too, any portrait of civil examinations as an unrelieved performance of despotic power misses the partnership between government and society. From medieval times in China, the examination market and its educational sites were maintained by both the dynasty and its evolving elites. Because the dynasty was the only legitimate "buyer" in this bureaucratized marketplace, however, the selection of elites for officialdom was represented as a tournament of talent. The dialogic aspects of the civil examinations accordingly were not conducive to a free marketplace of personnel. Both the court and gentry tried to influence this arena of transactions in their own favor.

Gentry and merchants got what they wanted, or, indeed, what they deserved, through the political system: confirmation of their beliefs, social status, political power, landed wealth. When legitimated by satisfied elites, the imperial court ruled through an elegant and sophisticated bureaucracy, which was filled with classically literate officials recruited from those very gentry and merchants on terms that their literati scholars prescribed. This remarkable partnership between late imperial dynasties and people of high social standing, often challenged since 1400, was unceremoniously eliminated in 1905. Literati-officials who were no longer satisfied with their lot convinced a naive and corrupt throne to abolish the very examinations that had helped hold the late empire together.

By carefully reviewing the primary examination sources that have be-

---

2. For discussion, see my *Classicism, Politics, and Kinship: The Ch'ang-chou School of New Text Confucianism in Late Imperial China* (Berkeley: University of California Press, 1990), pp. 16–19; and Richard von Glahn, *Fountain of Fortune: Money and Monetary Policy in China, 1000–1700* (Berkeley: University of California Press, 1996), pp. 113–41.

come available in the last fifteen years, this study shows that the late imperial examination system was not a premodern anachronism or an antimodern monolith. Classical examinations were an effective cultural, social, political, and educational construction that met the needs of the Ming-Ch'ing bureaucracy while simultaneously supporting the late imperial social structure, whose elite gentry and merchant status groups were defined in part by examination degree credentials. In addition, the late imperial cultural reconstruction of Sung dynasty (960–1279) *Tao-hsueh* 道學 (lit., "Tao Learning," but usually called "Neo-Confucianism")[3] as the orthodox classical curriculum for examination candidates after 1300 guaranteed the long-term prevalence of Sung moral philosophy in elite intellectual life until 1905.

Until very recently, most accounts of the late imperial civil service examination system were based on limited use of late imperial Chinese primary sources produced by officials and examiners serving in the examination bureaucracy (*Hsuan-chü* 選舉) in the Ministry of Rites (*Li-pu* 禮部) during the Ming and Ch'ing dynasties. Because local county, department, and prefectural compilers had limited access to *Li-pu* "records" (*lu* 錄) of the high-level provincial, metropolitan, and palace examinations, they derived much of their information on examination rolls in local and provincial gazetteers (*fang-chih* 方志) from "secondary" accounts available in their time. Compilers of local records were also swayed, for instance, by native-place loyalties and tended to include the names of degree-holders in their local lists even if such "native sons" had passed examinations under registrations elsewhere. This has resulted in much duplication of entries in local accounts of degree-holders. In addition, these *fang-chih* were widely acknowledged to be filled with errors and inaccurate information by the Ming and Ch'ing scholars who later had access to *Li-pu* sources and compiled the detailed studies of the examinations outlined in Appendix 1.[4]

---

3. See the essays in William Theodore de Bary and John W. Chaffee, eds., *Neo-Confucian Education: The Formative Stage* (Berkeley: University of California Press, 1989), passim, for recent views of "Neo-Confucianism." The editors present Neo-Confucian education as a liberal and progressive pursuit that went beyond earlier Confucian forms of education, but the degree to which Neo-Confucian educational ideals yielded progressive and liberal educational institutions in late imperial China is insufficiently demonstrated. For a critique see my "Education in Sung China," *Journal of the American Oriental Society* 111, 1 (January–March 1991): 83–93.

4. See, for example, the delineation of gazetteer errors in *Min-sheng hsien-shu* 閩省賢書 (Book about civil provincial examination worthies in Fu-chien), compiled by Shao Chieh-ch'un 邵捷春, late Ming edition, 2.3a, 5a, etc.; and *Nan-kuo hsien-shu* 南國賢書 (Book about civil provincial examination worthies in Ying-t'ien 應天 prefecture), compiled by Chang

Despite such limitations, late imperial gazetteers have long been used widely in Chinese and Western accounts as the main source for descriptions of the local and regional aspects of the civil selection process. Curiously, most contemporary accounts that have relied on such "secondary" gazetteer information have overlooked the hundreds of records of local, provincial, metropolitan, and palace examinations that survive from the Ming and Ch'ing dynasties and are now available in China, Taiwan, and the United States (see Appendix 2). This indifference to late imperial examination reports contrasts with the careful attention that the much sparser records of Sung dynasty (960–1279) civil examinations (see Appendix 1) have received from Edward Kracke and his successors, such as Robert Hartwell, Robert Hymes, John Chaffee, and Peter Bol.[5] Consequently, conclusions about the bureaucratic mechanics and cultural significance of the Chinese use of imperial examinations to select officials during the Ming and Ch'ing, when compared with Sung studies, have on the whole been partial and selective in the use of available primary sources. To redress these problems, many scholars in China are now making such sources more widely available.[6]

In addition, modern studies of Chinese civil examinations during the

---

Ch'ao-jui 張朝瑞, 1633 edition. Particularly for the late Ming and early Ch'ing, when many earlier examination reports had been lost, numerous errors accrued in later reissues of gazetteers and other related accounts of the examinations. See also Hans Bielenstein, "The Regional Provenance of *Chin-shih* during Ch'ing," *Bulletin of the Museum of Far Eastern Antiquities* (Stockholm) 64 (1992): 7.

5. E. A. Kracke, "Family vs. Merit in Chinese Civil Service Examinations during the Empire," *Harvard Journal of Asiatic Studies* 10 (1947): 103–23; Robert Hartwell, "Financial Expertise, Examinations, and the Formulation of Economic Policy in Northern Sung China," *Journal of Asian Studies* 30, 2 (1971): 281–314; Robert Hymes, *Statesmen and Gentlemen: The Elite of Fu-chou, Chiang-hsi, in Northern and Southern Sung* (Cambridge: Cambridge University Press, 1987); Chaffee, *The Thorny Gates of Learning in Sung China.* (Cambridge: Cambridge University Press, 1985); and Bol, "The Sung Examination System and the *Shih,*" *Asia Major* 3d ser., 3, 2 (1990): 149–71. Chaffee in particular has been tireless in his use of sources to document Sung examinations and their sociocultural significance.

6. See, for instance, Yang Hsueh-wei 楊學為 et al., *Chung-kuo k'ao-shih chih-tu shih tzu-liao hsuan-pien* 中國考試制度史資料選編 (Selected sources on the history of the Chinese civil service examination system) (Ho-fei, An-hui: Huang-shan shu-she, 1992); *Chung-kuo li-tai chuang-yuan tien-shih chüan* 中國歷代狀元殿試卷 (Palace examination papers over the dynasties in China), compiled by Teng Hung-p'o 鄧洪波 et al. (Hai-nan: Hai-nan Press, 1993); *Ch'ing-tai chu-chüan chi-ch'eng* 清代硃卷集成 (Ch'ing examination essays), 420 vols. (reprint, Taipei: Ch'eng-wen Publishing, 1993–94); and *Li-tai chin-tien tien-shih ting-chia chu-chüan* 歷代金殿試鼎甲硃卷 (Examination essays of the top three graduates of civil and palace examinations of several dynasties), compiled by Chung Kuang-chün 仲光軍 et al., 2 vols. (Shih-chia-chuang: Hua-shan Arts Press, 1995).

Ming and Ch'ing dynasties have been tied to specific ahistorical perspectives drawn from contemporary social science methodologies[7] or influenced by high-minded humanist convictions about which "great works" really matter in Chinese cultural and intellectual history. Scholars of philosophy, literature, and poetry often dismiss examination papers as student exercises not worthy of careful analysis, even when they acknowledge that provincial and metropolitan examination papers typically were produced by men in their twenties, thirties, forties, or fifties.[8] Others, based on late Ming accounts, decry rhetorically the irrelevance of policy questions and answers. They thereby disdain, and thus overlook, the value of these voluminous sources in gauging the issues that rulers and examiners were concerned with. Social scientists and historians usually build on the pioneering scholarship of Etienne Zi, Ssu-yü Teng, E. A. Kracke, Ping-ti Ho, Chung-li Chang, and Miyazaki Ichisada, who unlike their successors made extensive use of primary local, regional, and capital examination sources.[9]

In much of the recent scholarship about the late imperial civil service examination system, scholars still emphasize the social mobility, rather than the more limited circulation of elitics, which civil and military examinations permitted in a premodern society. In the same way, historians have evaluated the examination process in late imperial China from the perspective of the modernization process in early modern Europe and in world history. They have successfully exposed the failure of the examination systems in China, Korea, and Vietnam to advance the educational fronts of specialization and training in science deemed essential for nation-states to progress beyond their premodern institutions and autocratic polit-

7. For the classic works on the subject, see H. E. Dale, *The Higher Civil Service of Great Britain* (London: Oxford University Press, 1941); and Richard Bendix, *Higher Civil Servants in American Society* (Boulder: University of Colorado Press, 1949). See also Seymour M. Lipset and Richard Bendix, *Social Mobility in Industrial Society* (Berkeley: University of California Press, 1960).

8. See Alexander Woodside and Benjamin Elman, "Introduction," in Elman and Woodside, eds. *Education and Society in Late Imperial China, 1600–1900* (Berkeley: University of California Press, 1994), p. 11.

9. See Etienne Zi, *Pratique des examens littéraires en Chine* (Shanghai: Imprimerie de la Mission Catholique, 1894); Teng Ssu-yü 鄧嗣禹, *Chung-kuo k'ao-shih chih-tu shih* 中國考試制度史 (History of Chinese examination institutions) (Taipei: Student Bookstore, 1967); E. A. Kracke, "Family vs. Merit in Chinese Civil Service Examinations during the Empire," pp. 103–23; Ping-ti Ho, *The Ladder of Success in Imperial China* (New York: Wiley & Sons, 1962); Chung-li Chang, *The Chinese Gentry* (Seattle: University of Washington Press, 1955); and Miyazaki Ichisada 宮崎市定, *Kakyoshi* 科舉史 (History of the civil examination system) (Tokyo: Heibonsha, 1946; rev. ed. 1987). The less complete 1946 edition was the basis for the 1963 Japanese edition that Conrad Schirokauer translated under the title *China's Examination Hell* (New Haven: Yale University Press, 1981), which first appeared in English in 1976.

ical traditions. In my study I caution against such contemporary, ahistorical standards for political, cultural, and social formation, which have been exposed to recent criticism.[10] Such a priori judgments are often expressed teleologically when tied to the modernization narrative that still influences the historiography of Ming and Ch'ing dynasty China.[11]

The present work is based squarely on the newly available Ming-Ch'ing civil examination records, which I have compared with *fang-chih* records prepared by imperial contemporaries. The authoritative accounts by Zi, Teng, Ho, Chang, and Miyazaki, which pioneered the study of these primary sources when so few of them were initially available, will be assessed and revised based on these new sources. Appendices 1 and 2 have been prepared to give readers an idea of the range and magnitude of the 153 Ming dynasty and 869 Ch'ing official examination records used for this study. Appendix 3 presents tables of quantitative data that have been prepared based on these sources. Appendix 4 outlines the chronology of changes in the civil examination curriculum from the medieval to late empires. When compared with the two surviving Sung examinations and eighteen surviving Yuan (1280–1368) examination records, many only partial, these more than one thousand primary records from all levels of the late imperial civil examination bureaucracy allow us to delineate long-term patterns and changes that would be impossible for earlier periods. The over one thousand primary sources for the Ming-Ch'ing civil examinations are outlined by type, venue, and year in Appendix 1. They include eight major levels of local, provincial, metropolitan, and palace examination records (see Appendix 5).

## MAJOR ISSUES AND NEW PERSPECTIVES

This book presents a new cultural history of civil examinations in late imperial China that highlights the intersections between politics, society, economy, and intellectual life from 1400 to 1900. Its major theme is that both local elites and the imperial court continually influenced the govern-

10. See, for example, Naoki Sakai, "Modernity and Its Critique: The Problem of Universalism and Particularism," *South Atlantic Quarterly* 87, 3 (summer 1988): 475–504. See also Joyce Appleby et al., *Telling the Truth about History* (New York: Norton, 1994), pp. 198–235.

11. For a review of recent literature, see Ann Waltner, "Building on the Ladder of Success: The Ladder of Success in Imperial China and Recent Work on Social Mobility," *Ming Studies* 17 (1983): 30–36. For a bibliography, see Franklin Parker, "Civil Service Examinations in China: Annotated Bibliography," *Chinese Culture* (Taiwan) 27, 2 (June 1986): 103–110. For a corrective to modernist teleologies in recent assessments of the failures of the Ch'ing dynasty, see James L. Hevia, *Cherishing Men from Afar: Qing Guest Ritual and the Macartney Embassy of 1793* (Durham and London: Duke University Press, 1995), passim.

ment to reexamine and adjust the classical curriculum and to entertain new ways to improve the institutional system for selecting those candidates who were eligible to become officials. The chapters show how civil examinations, as a test of educational merit, served to tie the dynasty to literati culture bureaucratically. Civil examinations became a window on the larger literati culture because they were already penetrated by that culture through a political and social partnership between imperial interests and local elites that together shaped the classical curriculum.

As the book shows, civil examinations were a cultural arena within which diverse political and social interests contested each other and were balanced. The late imperial state, which was represented at different times by the emperor and his court, eunuchs, or officials in the bureaucracy, tried to control literati culture through the examinations. Literati groups inside and outside the government often evaded such control and successfully turned the tables by using the examinations to influence dynastic policy or revive literati values. Moreover, local elites were continually determined to use the lowest-level examinations in counties, prefectures, and townships to improve their status and enhance their family's standing in the community even if they never became officials. By giving a more nuanced discussion of the different functions of the civil examinations (cultural, political, intellectual, social, and bureaucratic) and showing the limits of the role imperial institutions could play in each arena, the book clarifies the historical significance of having an empirewide educational institution in late imperial China that served so many functions and brought diverse metropolitan, provincial, and local interests together in the carefully monitored examination marketplace.

Chapter 1 reconsiders exactly how the Tao Learning persuasion evolved among literati between 1240 and 1425, when imperial patronage was granted, and how Tao Learning became the curriculum for millions of examination candidates under the Ming.[12] Chapter 2 indicates that the victory of Tao Learning during the Yuan, Ming, and Ch'ing dynasties was not decided during the Southern Sung (1127–1279). Moreover, because the Mongol selection of *Tao-hsueh* as the core of the civil service examinations in 1313 was not complete, attention is given to early Ming and early Ch'ing appropriations of Tao Learning orthodoxy for civil examinations.

---

12. For critiques of overstated accounts of "Neo-Confucian orthodoxy" during the Sung dynasties, see Peter Bol, *"This Culture of Ours": Intellectual Transitions in T'ang and Sung China* (Stanford: Stanford University Press, 1992), pp. 1–31; and Hoyt Tillman, *Confucian Discourse and Chu Hsi's Ascendancy* (Honolulu: University of Hawaii Press, 1992), pp. 1–23. Bol notes, for example, "How could there be a Neo-Confucian orthodoxy before Chu Hsi in the absence of a Neo-Confucianism to be orthodox about?" See Bol, *"This Culture of Ours,"* p. 370, n129.

Each affected politically and socially how the Southern Sung triumph of *Tao-hsueh* literati learning would be interpreted and used in later dynasties. I contend that the Tao Learning scholars, who represented an intellectually diffuse movement in the Southern Sung dynasty and at times influenced the civil examinations, never created an empirewide orthodoxy for Sung civil examinations.[13] The creation of a single-minded and monocular *Tao-hsueh* orthodoxy, which built on Sung and Yuan precedents, was principally a Ming dynasty construction.

Chapters 1 and 2 build on Thomas Wilson's recent work, which has revealed how the seamless, ahistorical narrative of the triumph of the *Tao-hsueh* orthodoxy during the Sung-Yuan-Ming transition assumed an ideologically exclusionary conception of literati learning that highlighted Chu Hsi's 朱熹 (1130–1200) thought at the expense of other Sung currents of learning.[14] In addition, as is shown in Chapter 2, early Ming emperors were a significant political factor in the formation empirewide of a monocular and single-minded Tao Learning ideology in Ming civil examinations, which dissenting literati who remained out of politics often criticized.

A discussion of the advent of Han Learning (*Han-hsueh* 漢學) and evidential research (*k'ao-cheng-hsueh* 考證學) in the seventeenth and eighteenth centuries indicates that the late imperial Tao Learning civil examination curriculum did not merely carry on Sung intellectual trends. A remarkable turn from *Tao-hsueh*-style rationalism, typified by the philosophy of Chu Hsi, to a commitment to empirically based philological inquiry occurred in Ch'ing dynasty literati discourse.[15] This new classical learning of the

13. Hilde De Weerdt's dissertation, "The Composition of Examination Standards: *Daoxue* and Southern Sung Dynasty Examination Culture" (Ph.D. diss., Harvard University, East Asian Civilizations and Cultures, 1998), significantly revises past positions on this issue by stressing the role of *Tao-hsueh*-oriented literati in civil examination change after 1240.

14. See Thomas Wilson, *Genealogy of the Way: The Construction and Uses of the Confucian Tradition in Late Imperial China* (Stanford: Stanford University Press, 1995), passim. For the earlier "unfolding of Neo-Confucianism" position, see William Theodore de Bary et al., *The Unfolding of Neo-Confucianism* (New York: Columbia University Press, 1970), passim. See also de Bary, "Chu Hsi's Aims as an Educator," in de Bary and John W. Chaffee, eds., *Neo-Confucian Education: The Formative Stage,* pp. 186–218; and de Bary's recent "Confucian Education in Premodern East Asia," in Wei-ming Tu, ed., *Confucian Traditions in East Asian Modernity* (Cambridge: Harvard University Press, 1996), pp. 21–37.

15. See my "The Unravelling of Neo-Confucianism: From Philosophy to Philology in Late Imperial China," *Tsing Hua Journal of Chinese Studies,* n.s. 15 (1983): 67–89. For more recent research, see Hamaguchi Fujio 濱口富士雄, *Shindai kokyogaku no shisō shi teki kenkyō* 清代考據學の思想史的研究 (Research on the intellectual history of Ch'ing dynasty evidential studies) (Tokyo: Kokusho kankōkai, 1994); and Kinoshita Tetsuya 木下鉄矢, *Shindai koshō gaku to sono jidai* 清代考證學とその時代 (Ch'ing dynasty evidential research and its times) (Tokyo: Sōbunsha, 1995).

Ch'ing not only challenged "Sung Learning" (*Sung-hsueh* 宋學) among literati scholars but also penetrated the classical curriculum (see Chapters 9 and 10).

In contrast to their *Tao-hsueh* predecessors, Ch'ing *k'ao-cheng* scholars stressed exacting research, rigorous analysis, and collection of evidence drawn from ancient artifacts and historical documents and texts. Abstract ideas and a priori rational argumentation gave way as the primary objects of discussion among literati scholars to concrete facts, verifiable institutions, and historical events. This research program placed proof and verification at the center of the organization and analysis of the classical tradition. Concerned to restore native traditions in the precise sciences to their proper place of eminence, evidential scholars successfully incorporated technical aspects of Western astronomy and mathematics into their scholarship.[16] Unlike their Sung predecessors, Ch'ing evidential research scholars established a climate of criticism stimulated by their use of precise empirical methods to evaluate and verify knowledge drawn from a wide variety of sources. In general, they took Sung and Ming Tao Learning to be an obstacle to verifiable knowledge because it seemed to discourage empirical inquiry at the expense of moral cultivation.[17]

Unlike the studies of Sung examinations by John Chaffee and others, recent scholarship on the Ming and Ch'ing dynasties has underestimated the scale and magnitude of late imperial civil and military examinations. To remedy this oversight, Chapters 3, 4, and 5 analyze the examination compound as the venue for the personal identification, social organization, and political mobilization of manpower for dynastic service during the five centuries discussed in the present study. Entry into officialdom was the prerogative of a slim minority of degree candidates, however. As the door to official appointment, civil examinations also conferred social and cultural status on families seeking to become or maintain their status as local elites. In this way, the examination process confirmed social stability even when most candidates failed to gain political office.[18]

Local students were granted legal and tax benefits once they passed county or department licensing tests. Such young males had satisfied in part the cultural investments that had been made on their behalf, even if

16. See the recent findings of Chu Ping-yi, "Technical Knowledge, Cultural Practices and Social Boundaries: Wan-nan Scholars and Recasting of Jesuit Astronomy, 1600–1800" (Ph.D. diss., UCLA, History, 1994).

17. See my *From Philosophy to Philology: Social and Intellectual Aspects of Change in Late Imperial China* (Cambridge: Harvard University Council on East Asian Studies, 1984), passim.

18. For the Sung examinations and their extra-bureaucratic functions, see Peter Bol, "The Sung Examination System and the *Shih*," pp. 149–71.

they never achieved anything further. In this way, millions were mobilized biennially and triennially for the local county, township, and prefectural licensing and qualifying examinations. Several tens of thousands competed triennially in the fourteen to eighteen provincial examinations (more than 150,000 total in mid- and late Ch'ing provincial examinations), which yielded the final three to four thousand candidates for the triennial metropolitan and palace examinations in the capital. If, as we know, over fifty thousand men achieved the highest *chin-shih* 進士 (palace graduate, lit., "literatus presented to the emperor for appointment") degree during the Ming and Ch'ing dynasties,[19] and if, by a conservative estimate, one to two million men (two thousand per county with many repeaters), competed in biennial and triennial local examinations during these five hundred years, then the impact such mobilization had on daily life, individual hopes and anxieties, education priorities, and popular culture was widely experienced.[20] Recent attempts to situate empirewide examinations in the field of institutional and ritual practices are naive if such accounts assume civil examinations were of limited influence in intellectual and political life when compared with the role of Chinese rituals in the daily lives of Chinese before 1900.[21]

Almost all accounts of the role of the county magistrates and prefects in Ming-Ch'ing local governance (and the clerks beneath them) focus on their role in tax collection or court litigation, which suggests to many that the classical training they received and were tested on to become officials had little relevance for the execution of their actual duties once they received their appointments.[22] For magistrates or prefects, their legal

19. Ho, *The Ladder of Success in Imperial China*, p. 189, gives 51,341 for the total number of Ming-Ch'ing *chin-shih*.

20. For estimates of how many took the biennial local examinations, see Wolfram Eberhard, *Social Mobility in Traditional China* (Leiden: E. J. Brill, 1962), pp. 22–23; Frederic Wakeman, Jr., *The Fall of Imperial China* (New York: Free Press, 1975), pp. 22–23, 36n7; and Miyazaki,, *China's Examination Hell*, pp. 16–17. I give figures for specific local examinations in later chapters.

21. See, for example, Wilson, *Genealogy of the Way*, pp. 25–26, which usefully adds the canonization of the Classics and commentaries to our understanding of civil examinations. The recent focus on ritual by scholars of late imperial China, however, has tended to underestimate the magnitude of the role of civil examinations in dynastic ritual, which after all were under the Ministry of Rites.

22. John R. Watt, *The District Magistrate in Late Imperial China* (New York: Columbia University Press, 1972), pp. 78–98, stresses the role of classical theory on the magistrate's role but leaves out his role as examiner. James Cole, *Shaohsing: Competition and Cooperation in Nineteenth-Century China* (Tucson: University of Arizona Press, 1986), pp. 73–129, discusses the important role of subofficials in local society and their examination strategies for themselves, but he leaves unaddressed their role as clerks in the yamen when local civil and mil-

expertise and tax collection acumen were, it is commonly believed, their most practical skills, and if they lacked these skills, they could employ clerks and secretaries to provide them. In Chapter 3, a study of local civil examinations, which included both licensing and qualifying examinations, reveals that magistrates and prefects (and their clerks) spent a considerable amount of their time in their jurisdictions biennially supervising and grading civil licensing examinations. They also served as examiners for local triennial qualifying examinations, where they worked under the provincial education commissioner, and they were on the staffs of triennial provincial examinations, where beginning in the late Ming they served under Hanlin academicians and other capital officials.

In addition, although local magistrates and prefects were civil officials, they were also responsible for supervising and grading local licensing and qualifying examinations for the military bureaucracy—a demonstration of civilian oversight over military selection in local communities. This also illustrates, however, that the classically educated magistrate and prefect had to exhibit a mastery of the Chinese Military Classics dating from antiquity, as these were tested on the military examinations. Although military examinations cannot be discussed in any detail in this study,[23] it is clear from local records of examinations from the Pa-hsien 巴縣 County Archives in Ch'eng-tu and elsewhere (outlined in Appendix 1) that county and prefectural civil and military examinations were an important constituent of local governance. They were the core of the ritualistic and cultural repertoire of educational tools the bureaucracy employed for the impartial selection of talent by prefects, magistrates, and clerks, which balanced tax collection and penal judgments as forms of local social control. Indeed, as a cultural form of political selection (voluntary human talent for the bureaucracy), the examination system paralleled the extraction of

---

itary examinations were held. Similarly, recent studies of the local clerks' role in legal adjudication fail to mention the scope of their involvement in the examination process. But see the valuable work by Bradly Reed, "Scoundrels and Civil Servants: Clerks, Runners, and County Administration in Late Imperial China" (Ph.D. diss., UCLA, History, 1994).

23. Sam Gilbert's dissertation for the History Department at UCLA focuses on reevaluating the significance of the Ch'ing military examinations. See also Ralph Sawyer, trans., *The Seven Military Classics of Ancient China* (Boulder, Colo.: Westview Press, 1993). Although my account emphasizes the role of classical thought in the civil branch of Ming-Ch'ing government, the reader should keep in mind unresolved problems with notions of the civil service that follow longstanding literati civilian conceits and thereby slight the military service in such a definition. Cf. Winston Lo, "A New Perspective on the Sung Civil Service," *Journal of Asian History* 17 (1983): 121–35; and Alastair Johnston, *Cultural Realism: Strategic Culture and Grand Strategy in Chinese History* (Princeton: Princeton University Press, 1995), pp. 40–49.

local taxes (involuntary material resources for the dynasty). Examination graduates became the new examiners, who maintained the ceaseless cycle of examinations in county and prefectural towns, which kept so many young men busy studying at home or in schools.

The civil examination process during the Ming and Ch'ing dynasties, as indicated in Chapter 5, was not a system designed for increased social mobility. Instead, it served as an institutionalized system of inclusion and exclusion that publicly legitimated the impartial selection of officials.[24] Such selection represented a sophisticated, but not unmitigated or totalistic, process of social, political, and cultural reproduction of the status quo. As earlier work by Hilary Beattie has suggested, the overwhelming success of sons of literati and merchant elites in getting high examination rankings and thereby receiving official appointments through the civil selection process was not accidental or unearned.[25] The selection process permitted some circulation of elites, such as young men from military families, in and out of the total pool of examination candidates, but the educational curriculum and its formidable linguistic requirements effectively eliminated the lower classes from the selection process. In addition, an unstated gender ideology forbade all women from entry into the examination compounds even when, as talented writers, elite women demonstrated the curricular and linguistic talents required of their brothers.[26]

The study of Ming and Ch'ing civil examination primary sources from 1371 to 1904 allows a historicizing and revision of the "global" findings in the contemporary sociology of education about the monopolization of social and political status by credentialed elites. This account in turn exposes the weaknesses of structural, ahistorical accounts of educational institutions and their sociocultural impact.[27] Although their structural

24. Raymond Murphy, *Social Closure: The Theory of Monopolization and Exclusion* (Oxford: Clarendon Press, 1988), pp. 1–14. The classic statements of social reproduction achieved through education are by Emile Durkheim and Pierre Bourdieu. See Emile Durkheim, *Education and Sociology*, translated by Sherwood Fox (Glencoe, Ill.: Free Press, 1956); and Bourdieu and Jean-Claude Passeron, *Reproduction in Education, Society, and Culture*, translated by Richard Nice (Beverly Hills, Calif.: Sage Publications, 1977); and Michael Young, ed., *Knowledge and Control: New Directions for the Sociology of Education* (London: Collier Macmillan, 1971).

25. See Hilary Beattie, *Land and Lineage in China: A Study of T'ung-ch'eng County, Anhui, in the Ming and Ch'ing Dynasties* (Cambridge: Cambridge University Press, 1979).

26. On women writers in the Ming and Ch'ing, see Dorothy Ko, *Teachers of the Inner Chambers: Women and Culture in Seventeenth-Century China* (Stanford: Stanford University Press, 1994), pp. 179–218; and Susan Mann, *Precious Records: Women in China's Long Eighteenth Century* (Stanford: Stanford University Press, 1997).

27. Murphy, *Social Closure*, pp. 174–78, discusses the conceptual limits of using market

analysis is very useful as a functional description of educational institutions within a particular social and political setting, Pierre Bourdieu and Jean-Claude Passeron, for example, seriously undervalue how and why institutions, and the ideas that legitimize them, change.[28] Bourdieu and Passeron tend to overdetermine the functional link in education between the intentions of agents and the institutional consequences, even when the intentions and consequences in question are separated by long periods of time. They fail to consider the common finding that intentions and consequences over the long term are analytically distinct and that functionalism is not automatically linked to sinister intent.[29]

My study also points out the central role of language and classical literacy in culturally defining high and low social status in late imperial Chinese society. Chapter 5 addresses how education in private family homes and schools translated into linguistic and textual resources that enabled young men blessed with such training (there were no "public" schools in Ming-Ch'ing China) to pass the grueling biennial local licensing and renewal examinations more easily and thereby gain one of the places established by official quotas in the local dynastic school system in counties, townships, and prefectures. An official place in dynastic schools, where individual preparation for future examinations had long since displaced actual instruction, became the typical stepping stone to success in the final local qualifying examination, which was required for the triennial provincial examinations.

The general tendency to focus on social mobility since the T'ang dynasty (618–907) by researching the social status of civil examination graduates has meant that scholars have misunderstood how the monopolization of "cultural resources" by literati and merchant elites actually worked. Premised on a system of inclusion and exclusion based on tests of classical literacy that restricted the access of those in the lower classes (whose literacy was too vernacular to master the classical frames of language and writing tested in the local licensing examinations), the civil examinations concealed the resulting process of social selection. By requir-

---

metaphors such as "cultural capital" to describe "credential exclusion." For earlier positions, see the classic study by Randall Collins, *The Credential Society: An Historical Sociology of Education and Stratification* (Orlando: Academic Press, 1979), pp. 58–72, on the "cultural market."

28. Bourdieu and Passeron, *Reproduction in Education, Society, and Culture.*

29. See Boudon, *The Analysis of Ideology,* translated by Malcolm Slater (Chicago: University of Chicago Press, 1989), pp. 156–57, 223n26, 226n17. For discussion of the internal ideological process of educational change in the content of imperial civil service examinations, see Chapters 8–11 below.

ing linguistic mastery of nonvernacular classical texts, imperial examinations created a written linguistic barrier between those who were allowed into the empire's examinations compounds and those—the classically illiterate—who were kept out.

Chapter 6, which compares literati writings, popular accounts in novels and stories, and folklore traditions associated with the personal trials and tribulations of the examinees and examiners collected in several Ming and Ch'ing compendia, reveals more clearly why the civil examinations were central events in China's cultural history after 1400. It explores, for example, Ming-Ch'ing examination dreams and popular lore on Ming and Ch'ing palace examination *optimi*, whose success spawned a remarkable literature about the temples they visited, the dreams they or members of their family had, and the magical events in their early lives that were premonitions of their later success. These stories are treated as encoded cultural glosses given by late imperial literati, whose unconscious ties to a common culture and religion, encompassing both elites and popular culture, tempered their own understanding of what they considered the mantic forces of "fate" operating in the examination halls.

In past studies, the cultural significance of the civil and military examinations has typically been discussed as an aspect of elite society and literati culture far removed from the lives of the common people. The present work builds on more recent studies suggesting that the examinations represented a symbolic order transcending the social boundaries of gentry society and that this order had a significant role in popular culture and was in turn influenced by a popular religious mentality.[30]

Thousands of examination candidates congregated biennially at counties, townships, and prefectures, and triennially in provincial and national capitals, and these goings-on took on local significance as social, economic, cultural, and political events. Cultural paraphernalia, books of examination essays, charms from temples for good luck, soothsayers with otherworldly powers of intercession, parades of examiners, and policing checkpoints for candidates were all part of the market-fair atmosphere that accompanied the examinations, with the candidates marching into

---

30. See Richard Smith, *Fortune-Tellers and Philosophers: Divination in Traditional Chinese Society* (Boulder, Colo.: Westview Press, 1991), pp. 173–257, which presents the examinations in light of popular spirit mediums and spirit messages that were used by candidates to gauge their success and gain an advantage. See also Terry Kleeman's account and translation in *A God's Own Tale: The Book of Transformations of Wenchang, the Divine Lord of Zitong* (Albany: SUNY Press, 1994), pp. 73, 121, 290–92, which describes the intersection between religion and the fate of examination candidates. Liao Hsien-huei's dissertation at UCLA stresses the interaction between popular religion and the examination life of Sung dynasty literati.

and out of the prison-like examination compounds before and after each test session. Because it was virtually compulsory to participate in the civil examinations to be a member of the local elite, the examination hall was a way station to success for only a small minority of graduates. Given the limited success rates of elites at periodic examination tournaments, most candidates were locked inside examination cells for several days biennially or triennially until they were well into their thirties or forties.

Particularly in the provincial examinations of the south, where five to ten (and, by the eighteenth century, over fifteen thousand) candidates would gather every three years in the local capital of Nanking or Hang-chou, with the likelihood that only one in a hundred would pass, the intersection of commerce, political status, and social prestige produced an atmosphere of expectation and dread matched only by the frenzy of crowds at famous temples and shrines. Examination protests and riots were not uncommon, as candidates were given their only legal opportunity to gather in large groups. Fires, heavy rains, and corruption were periodic additions to the already terrible pressure on candidates, who ranged typically from under twenty to over sixty years of age.

Distrusted by the dynasty, which created and maintained an architecture of surveillance housing thousands of guards in the examination compound in addition to the candidates and their examiners, the candidates themselves were a hodgepodge of high and low, young sons of the famous and old men on their last try, savvy urban southerners and country bumpkins from northern small towns and villages. What they shared was years of preparation to compete for the few places that would separate them in their disparate futures. Success was alluring; failure was humiliating. Cheating became a cottage industry. What I describe as "male anxiety" and delineate through dreams, visions, and mental breakdowns was a by-product of this unrelenting cycle of tests and competitions. After centuries of implementation, the entire spectacle was so much a part of Chinese society that the bureaucracy and the society, the elites and the commoners, viewed it as a "natural" state of affairs, whose inequities were refracted through the lens of fate as much as corruption. One could finish first in the difficult southern provincial examinations and plummet to the bottom in the less competitive metropolitan examinations in Peking. Most test-takers failed several times at each level before achieving success.

The cultural and intellectual scope of the civil examinations is examined in Chapters 7 through 10. Most accounts of the intellectual content of the civil examinations have emphasized the dominating role of eight-legged literary essays in the examination curriculum. Historians have assumed that Ku Yen-wu 顧炎武 (1613–82) was correct when he contended that other parts of the examination, particularly the policy questions in session three, were not read carefully by the examiners.[31] These overstated views have had so much influence that a recent popular account summarized the tests as only requiring three essays on the Chinese Classics (actually the Four Books) and a poem.[32] This account's error may be exceptional, but a general theme in modern accounts has been the literary focus of the civil examinations and the unchanging nature of the classical disciplines tested. In contrast, I argue that the Ming examiners took greater care than the Ch'ing examiners and wrote much more copiously about how and why they chose the best answers to all three sessions of the provincial and metropolitan examinations.

Chapters 8 and 9 significantly revise these unbalanced literary accounts of the civil examinations by reconstructing historically the changing vicissitudes of the curriculum.[33] In particular, my analysis highlights the impor-

31. On Ku's position, which we will historicize later, see Lung-chang Young, "Ku Yen-wu's Views on the Ming Examination System," *Ming Studies* 23 (1987): 48–63. For recent acceptance of Ku's account of late Ming examinations that is uncritically applied to all examinations held during the Ming dynasty, see Wilson, *Genealogy of the Way*, pp. 52–53.

32. Valery M. Garrett, *Mandarin Squares: Mandarins and Their Insignia* (Oxford: Oxford University Press, 1990), p. 9. See also the facile account given in John Cleverley, *The Schooling of China: Tradition and Modernity in Chinese Education* (London: Allen and Unwin, 1985), pp. 10–13.

33. These vicissitudes have themselves been misrepresented in recent accounts that fail to grasp the limitations in late Ming Jesuit notice of Chinese civil examinations. See, for instance, Donald F. Lach and Edwin J. Van Kley, *Asia in the Making of Europe*, vol. 3, *A Century of Advance*, book 4, *East Asia* (Chicago: University of Chicago Press, 1993), p. 1639, which uncritically accepts Min-sun Chen's account of the discrepancy between the 1615 and 1642 accounts prepared by Nicolas Trigault and Alvarez Semedo of the number of examination essays required for the *chü-jen* provincial degree. Trigault described seven essays, three on the Four Books and four on the Classics, but he failed to add that this was only for the first of three sessions. Semedo reversed the number to four essays on the Four Books and three on the Five Classics, failing like Trigault to recognize that candidates prepared essays only on the Classics they had chosen to specialize on and that there were two other sessions. Min-sun Chen, "Three Contemporary Western Sources on the History of the Late Ming and the Manchu Conquest of China" (Ph.D. diss., University of Chicago, History, 1971), p. 75, had explained the discrepancy by claiming that both Trigault and Semedo were right and that there had been a change in practice between 1615 and 1642. There were no such curricular changes. Trigault was right when he related that of the seven essays required, three were on the Four Books and four were on the Five Classics. This practice remained in place until 1787. Lach and Van Kley also express their mystification over the role of calligraphy in civil examinations "when presumably the examiners only read copies of their [student] essays." See Lach and Van Kley, *Asia in the Making of Europe*, p. 1640n437. They fail to recognize that calligraphy mattered when the candidate's own papers were read at local licensing and qualifying examinations and at the palace and court examinations, but not at the provincial and metropolitan stages, when anonymous papers were graded.

tance of second-session discourse and third-session policy questions, which complemented the first-session literary essays based on the Four Books and Five Classics. Moreover, it accounts for the role of questions on documentary style and legal judgments, which lasted from 1384 until 1756. What is surprising is the constantly changing nature of the policy questions during the Ming and Ch'ing dynasties. Policy questions remained an important scholarly marker of literati interests even when their examination status was denigrated after the eight-legged essay took precedence in the late fifteenth century.

Chapter 8 documents the rise of "learning based on what can be ascertained" (k'ao-chü-hsueh 考據學) as a type of policy question that became common during the late fifteenth century. This finding of the first widespread use of this term as a scholarly category enables us to tie the emergence of "evidential research" (k'ao-cheng-hsueh 考證學) during the late Ming to the earlier evolution of civil examination policy questions. It also establishes a Ming precedent for the later revival, during the eighteenth and nineteenth centuries, of policy questions dealing with evidential research (also documented in Chapter 9). Finally, Chapter 8 elaborates on the historical significance of the abolition of poetry questions on civil examinations in the early Ming, a decision often mistakenly attributed to the Yuan dynasty. It then addresses the reasons for the revival, after 1756, of a poetry question on local, provincial, and metropolitan civil examinations under the Ch'ien-lung emperor, a much-misunderstood and understudied cultural event.[34]

Chapter 9 demonstrates that policy questions dealing with the natural world and unusual phenomena were very common during the Ming dynasty but disappeared almost entirely during the Ch'ing. The role of "natural studies" in the imperial examinations is reassessed based on this new finding, which defies our expectation that Ch'ing civil examinations would have had *more* questions on the natural world *after* the K'ang-hsi

---

34. Thomas Wilson in his otherwise succinct discussion of the civil examination system, for example, follows Miyazaki's account of late Ch'ing civil examinations (i.e., after 1787) and mistakenly concludes: "By the Ming-Ch'ing period poetry composition was required of all examination candidates. Poetry was usually part of the first session of the provincial examinations along with questions on the Four Books." See Wilson, *Genealogy of the Way*, p. 277n50. Too often, Miyazaki's ahistorical account of late Ch'ing examinations has been relied upon by others to describe periods it was not designed to cover. On this unfortunate tendency, see Wada Masahiro's 和田正廣 timely corrective in his "Mindai kakyo seidō no kamoku no tokushoku: bengo no donyū o megutte" 明代科擧制度の科目の特色：判語の導入をめぐって (Special characteristics of the Ming dynasty civil examination curriculum: concerning introduction of legal judgment questions), *Hōseishi kenkyō* 法制史研究 43 (1993): 274.

emperor eliminated the court enemies of the Jesuits.[35] Similarly, Chapter 9 explores how the policy questions on historical studies (*shih-hsueh* 史學) changed in tone and content from championing Tao Learning historical idealism during the Ming dynasty to favoring Han dynasty–style historical traditions associated with Ssu-ma Ch'ien 司馬遷 and Pan Ku 班固 in the Ch'ing.

It should be clear to anyone who reads Chapter 11 on delegitimation and decanonization that the Ch'ing dynasty, when it abrogated the civil and military examinations in the name of "Westernization" in 1904, effectively lost one of its key tools of social, political, and cultural influence. In the absence of viable educational replacements, the abrogation of civil examinations accelerated the demise of the Manchu dynasty and its eventual replacement by Han Chinese urban gentry-elites who championed republicanism. In other words, what has in the past been taken for granted as the long-overdue elimination of an outmoded and inefficient "late imperial" civil selection process in favor of a reformed educational system based on "modern" schools and educational models is turned on its head.[36] The abrupt demise of the civil examinations also suggests that the recurring elite criticism of the system since the Sung dynasties remained an important undercurrent before the system was challenged in the late nineteenth century.

The undoing of the traditional civil examination system in China in 1904–5 was not a simple substitution of the modern for the outmoded. Prasenjit Duara has described the failure of reformers in China to replace the traditional forms of political legitimacy in rural Chinese society at the end of the Ch'ing dynasty.[37] Others have noted the unforeseen consequences of the colonial zeal to replace "superstitious" religious beliefs in India and elsewhere.[38] Until modern forms of schooling and education took hold and penetrated as deeply into Chinese society as the civil examinations had, and until the new schools were widely understood and

35. On this question, see the recent dissertations by Chu Ping-yi, "Technical Knowledge, Cultural Practices and Social Boundaries"; and by Roger Hart, "Proof, Propaganda, and Patronage: A Cultural History of the Dissemination of Western Studies in Seventeenth-Century China" (Ph.D. diss., UCLA, History, 1997).

36. For the traditional view, see the still-insightful study by Wolfgang Franke, *The Reform and Abolition of the Traditional Chinese Examination System* (Cambridge: Harvard East Asian Monograph, 1960).

37. Duara, *Culture, Power, and the State: Rural North China, 1900–1942* (Stanford: Stanford University Press, 1988), pp. 242–57, notes that the state-building process modeled on westernization in the late Ch'ing destroyed the traditional bases of legitimation and was overwhelmed by the forces of delegitimation it unleashed.

38. Nicholas Dirks, *The Hollow Crown: Ethnohistory of an Indian Kingdom* (Cambridge: Cambridge University Press, 1987).

accepted as "natural" by millions of examination candidates, the sudden abrogation of the selection process was, for conservative Chinese gentry and Manchus, a *deus ex machina*, a blow from the outside that subverted and dismantled the cultural system built around the dynasty. The fall of the Ch'ing thus unleashed a parallel crisis in the established creedal system and compromised the social and political credentials the system had enforced.

Destruction of civil examinations, and of the Ministry of Rites that housed them, outpaced the construction of a replacement Ministry of Education and the recentering through school education of the social, political, and cultural functions that civil examinations had fulfilled for elite families and individuals for two dynasties. The new cultural and political institutions associated with the West and its "modernity" had less symbolic relevance and fewer cultural uses in the early twentieth century. In the end my study acknowledges the proven utility of premodern institutions, which were widely accepted for so long that they were naturalized into viable organizational forms, and the initial failure of unrealistic modern educational reforms, which sounded so inevitable but were unable to prevent the unforeseen and unintended consequences of decanonization and delegitimation after 1898.

# ACKNOWLEDGMENTS

This book has taken over ten years to complete. My research project initially was based on archival materials in the No. 1 Historical Archives in Peking, the Han Yü-shan Education Collection in the Department of Special Collections at UCLA,[1] and civil examination collections in Taiwan and Japan. In 1985 I began to identify and tabularize data (names, ages, lineages, social statuses, schools, examiners, curriculum changes, questions, answers, ranks, classical concentrations, etc.) in the uncataloged Ch'ing dynasty civil and military examination materials from the Peking Archives, which were then newly available on microfilm in the Mormon Genealogical Library.[2]

I was not surprised to see how contemporary assumptions about the content and form of the examinations had been colored by unrelenting animosity of many early-twentieth-century Chinese intellectuals toward the selection system, which their scholarly heirs have maintained into the late twentieth century.[3] Considering the educational resources and years of study needed to produce the demanding level of classical literacy required in the civil examinations, it is clear why so few artisans and peasants, and

1. See my "Ch'ing Dynasty Education Materials in the Department of Special Collections, UCLA," *Late Imperial China* 10, 2 (December 1989): 139–140. My thanks to James Lee for including this announcement in the journal.

2. See Melvin Thatcher, "Selected Sources for Late Imperial China on Microfilm at the Genealogical Society of Utah," *Late Imperial China* 19, 2 (December 1998): 111–29.

3. This is not to say that republican Chinese intellectuals were united on this question. For a corrective to the tendency to lump all May Fourth intellectuals as radicals, see Yen Chia-yen 嚴家炎, "Wu-ssu, wen-ko, ch'uan-t'ung wen-hua" 五四，文革，傳統文化 (May Fourth, cultural revolution, and traditional culture), *Erh-shih-i shih-chi* 二十一世紀 41 (1997): 11–18.

no women, could be found on the Ming and Ch'ing metropolitan and provincial civil examination rolls. It is more appropriate, I believe, to describe the educational function of Ch'ing civil examinations in terms of the social, political, and cultural reproduction of the late imperial status system (following Durkheim and Bourdieu on the sociology of education in Europe) than in light of social mobility.[4]

My research in Taiwan and Japan sponsored by Fulbright, Japan Foundation, and Taiwan National Science Council research grants from fall 1990 through fall 1991 revealed, however, that my chronological focus on the Ch'ing dynasty examination system was inadequate. When I discovered a great many sixteenth-century Ming dynasty examination sources in various rare book collections, I revised the time frame for the late imperial examinations from 1600–1900 to 1370–1904. Moreover, when I looked into the early Ming reigns in an article published in *T'oung Pao*,[5] I realized that the ideological and political link between the civil examinations and dynastic orthodoxy, which we usually associate with the earlier Southern Sung and Yuan dynasties, was in practice solidified empirewide only after the usurpation of the throne by the Yung-lo emperor 永樂 (r. 1402–24).

4. My theoretical argument was originally presented in "Social, Political, and Cultural Reproduction via Civil Service Examinations in Late Imperial China," *Journal of Asian Studies* 51, 1 (February 1991): 7–28. I was disappointed to discover that many concluded from that article that civil examinations represented a monolithic and unrelenting system of dynastic hegemony and that readers did not take into account my earlier work, which had documented numerous intellectual trends that were autonomous from the civil examination regime. For criticisms, see Hilde De Weerdt, "Aspects of Song Intellectual Life: A Preliminary Inquiry into Some Southern Song Encyclopedias," *Papers on China* (Harvard University) 3 (1994): 27; and Kai-wing Chow, "Writing for Success: Printing, Examinations, and Intellectual Change in Late Ming China," *Late Imperial China* 17, 1 (June 1996): 122. In this book, the theoretical arguments presented earlier have been adjusted and historically nuanced to detail the amount of criticism and resistance the relentless machinery of the civil examination regime received during the Ming and Ch'ing. In my view, the Sung dynasty may have been exceptional in its more diverse literati learning (as De Weerdt rightly argues), but the historical processes of social and political reproduction still operated in Sung China. Indeed, Bourdieu has shown how contemporary pluralism still serves to reproduce social elites via educational credentials. See his "Systems of Education and Systems of Thought," in Michael Young, ed., *Knowledge and Control: New Directions for the Sociology of Education* (London: Collier Macmillan, 1971), pp. 189–207. Nor was the late Ming the beginning of the "unlocking" of the reproduction process (as Chow argues). This process was effectively challenged only much later during the Taiping Rebellion and finally ended after the Boxer Rebellion. See Chapter 11.

5. See my "Where Is King Ch'eng? Civil Examinations and Confucian Ideology during the Early Ming, 1368–1415," *T'oung Pao* 79 (1993): 23–68.

Consequently, my study now focuses equally on the Ming dynasty as the landscape within which cutthroat provincial and metropolitan examination competitions were held triennially inside "cultural prisons" filled with thousands of candidates, examiners, copyists, woodblock cutters, guards, cooks, and doctors surrounded by a market-fair atmosphere and popular urban culture within which dreams, fate, and karma mattered to candidates as much as the classical curriculum. To complete the Ming dynasty portions of my research, I received a research grant from the Committee on Advanced Study in China (Committee for Scholarly Communication with China), sponsored by the National Academy of Sciences, to travel to Peking, Shanghai, Hang-chou, Nanking, and Ning-po in fall 1994 and summer 1995. There I completed study of rare early Ming civil examinations in Chinese libraries and archives. Expanding the project to include the Ming allowed me to add early documents that date from 1370 through 1500 and to include many provincial, metropolitan, and palace civil examinations not available anywhere else. Adding the Ming dynasty to my project of course delayed its expected completion, but I am convinced this added effort has made the study much stronger historically.

Along the way I have been fortunate in receiving research assistance and advice from graduate students who read various portions or helped me collect and computerize thousands of items of information. The students include Jeffrey Chang, Chu Ping-yi, Cong Xiaoping, Sam Gilbert, Huang Xincun, Karasawa Yasuhiko, Eugenia Lean, Lu Hanchao, Lü Miaw-fen, Meng Yue, Adam Schorr, David Wakefield, Yang Jui-sung, and Zhang Jinshu. Many have since completed or are about to complete their own important dissertations. Others have gone on in other fields, but their help on this research project, however brief, is greatly appreciated. UCLA Academic Senate research grants and China Center support funded some of these students as research assistants for several years beginning in 1987.

As noted earlier, research for this book was also funded by research fellowships in 1990–91 (eighteen months) and 1994–95 (four months) that enabled me to travel to archives and libraries in China, France, Hong Kong, Japan, and Taiwan. A Fulbright Foundation research fellowship for Taiwan during the 1990–91 academic year allowed me to study the examination holdings at the National Palace Museum, the National Central Library, the Ming-Ch'ing Archives (Academia Sinica), and the Fu Ssu-nien Rare Books Library (Academic Sinica). I especially want to thank Chang Wejen, who hosted me during my stay at the Ming-Ch'ing Archives. With his help, I was able to identify and catalog early Ch'ing dynasty examination sources and draft materials available nowhere else.

In return for such efforts, the UCLA East Asian Library received a copy of all material identified and organized. I also want to thank Angela Leung, Wu Jing-jyi, Tony Wang, Lin Ding-tzan, Chu Hung-lam, and Lin Ch'ing-chang for their encouragement while my wife, Sarah, and I were in Taiwan. President Wu Ta-yu of Academic Sinica kindly permitted us to rent research faculty housing in Nankang during our stay. My research in Taiwan was also supplemented by the Pacific Cultural Foundation and extended by the National Science Council, which appointed me as visiting research professor at the Institute of History, Tsing Hua University, during the fall 1991 semester. At Tsing Hua, Chang Yung-t'ang, Fu Dawie, and Huang Yilong were gracious hosts. I appreciated the chance to meet and exchange ideas with Chris Cullen (of London University) and Joseph Dauben (of City University of New York), also at Tsing Hua as visiting scholars.

A Japan Foundation fellowship in spring 1991 enabled me to carry out research at Kyoto and Tokyo universities. At the Institute for Humanistic Studies in Kyoto, Ono Kazuko and Hazama Naoki facilitated my research. At Tokyo University, the Chinese Philosophy Department was my official host in Japan. I want to thank professors Satō Shin'ichi and Mizoguchi Yūzō for their many kindnesses. In Hong Kong, I was able to report on my research at a December 1991 conference at Chinese University and as a visiting scholar at Hong Kong University in September, 1992, sponsored by the chair of the History Department, Adam Y. C. Lui. Professor Lui also facilitated my visit to the Fung Bing Shan Library and helped me during my kidney stone illness while there. I also received an appointment as Directeur d'Études at the Centre Recherches Linguistiques sur l'Asie Orientale, École des Hautes Études en Sciences Sociales, in September 1994, which enabled me to locate Chinese examination materials in the Bibliothèque Nationale and at the East Asian Library of the College de France. I want to thank Professors Alain Peyraube, Pierre-Etienne Will, Karine Chemla, Catherine Jami, Marianne Bastid, Ann Cheng, Georges Métailié, and Vivian Alleton for their hospitality.

A research fellowship from the Committee for Scholarly Communication with China permitted me to work on the project in Peking, Shanghai, Nanking, Ch'eng-tu, Hang-chou, and Ning-po in fall 1994 and summer 1995. My official and unofficial hosts were the Chinese Academy of Social Sciences (Institute of History), People's University (Ch'ing History Institute), and the Fudan University Library (Rare Books Division). I carried out research at the Rare Books Collections of the Nanking Library, Che-chiang Library, Peking Library, Shanghai Library, and the Pa-hsien Archives in Ch'eng-tu. I visited the T'ien-i ko Museum in Ning-po but was able to see only a few of the Ming examination records stored there. Fortunately, many early Ming records were also available in Shanghai. I want to express my deepest appreciation to Wang Junyi (CASS), Chen Zuwu (CASS), Wu Ge (Fudan), and Tang Zhijun (SASS) for their support. Cheng Chungde (People's University), Huang Aiping (People's University), Fang Zuyou (Ning-po University), Wu Guang (Hang-chou), Yang Xiangkui (CASS), Cai Fanglu (Ch'eng-tu Academy), Zhao Gang (Palace Museum), and Ma Xiaobin (Pa-hsien Archives) were also of great help to me while I was in China.

I should also acknowledge friends and colleagues at UCLA and elsewhere. Han Rogger, professor emeritus of Russian history, was kind enough to go over some Russian language translation examinations from the late Ch'ing dynasty with me, which were composed in frequently illegible Russian script. Joyce Appleby, professor of American history, commented on an earlier version of my arguments concerning cultural reproduction via examinations. Ron Mellor, a specialist on Rome, helped on Jesuit translations of eight-legged essays in Latin. Pauline Yu and David Schaberg in the East Asian Languages and Cultures Department gave me good advice about poetry translations. I would like to thank Richard Gunde of the UCLA China Center, Alex Woodside, Richard Smith, Roger Hart, Eugenia Lean, and Bruce Rusk for their comments on the portions of the manuscript they read.

A somewhat different version of Chapter 2 was presented at the Conference on Culture and the State in Chinese History, organized by Ted Huters, Pauline Yu, and R. Bin Wong at Laguna Beach in June 1992; it appears separately in the conference volume published in 1997 by Stanford University Press. Audiences at the April 1995 Harvard University Pre-modern China Seminar and at the October 1996 workshop "Reading Texts and Commentaries: Interpretive Strategies and Intellectual Authority in Chinese Classics," sponsored by the Center for Chinese Studies, University of California, Berkeley, where I presented various aspects of my research, also made many useful suggestions. I was also fortunate to attend the "Sung-Yuan-Ming Transitions" conference, organized by Paul Smith and Richard von Glahn at Lake Arrowhead, California, June 5–11, 1997, and sponsored by the American Council of Learned Societies, where a shorter version of Chapter 1 was discussed. Finally, appreciation is due James Cheng, former director of the East Asian Library at UCLA, Richard Gunde, assistant director of the UCLA Center for Chinese Studies, and Melvin Thatcher, then at the Hong Kong Mormon Genealogical Library, for their help in finding out about and gathering primary sources at UCLA.

After completing my research in China, I took a quarter of sabbatical leave while in residence at UCLA in spring 1996 to begin the final stages of preparing a manuscript suitable for publication; it was completed during the summer. Final revisions, based on recommendations by Peter Bol, Susan Naquin, Nathan Sivin, and two anonymous referees were completed in spring and summer 1997. Hilde De Weerdt and I exchanged views and information concerning her dissertation research on Sung examinations and my work on Ming-Ch'ing. She subsequently put me in touch with Charles Ridley, whose pioneering dissertation at Stanford in 1973 influenced my account of classical literacy. I have not always followed the advice of these readers, but their criticism was incisive and invaluable. The inevitable errors that remain in a project of this size are my responsibility. At the University of California Press, Sue Heinemann (project editor) and Sally Serafim and Carl Walesa (copy editors) did exceptional work on the manuscript; thanks are due to Sheila Levine and Laura Driussi for their encouragement. Thanks also to Albert Hoffstädt of E. J. Brill for his consideration. The UCLA International Studies and Overseas Programs office, through the kind auspices of Dean John Hawkins, provided a timely publication grant to help subsidize the production of this book and its many tables and illustrations.

CHAPTER ONE

# Rethinking the Historical Roots
# of Late Imperial Civil Examinations

This account of late imperial civil examinations begins by looking carefully at the historical conditions within which native and conquest dynasties appropriated the civil service and literati teachings (*ju-hsueh* 儒學, usually called Confucianism) in China before 1400. I hope thereby to avoid a starting point that predetermines an idealized and transcendental classical examination curriculum calling itself a *Tao-hsueh* orthodoxy and asserting itself effortlessly and bloodlessly in the hearts and minds of Han Chinese, Mongols, and Manchus during the Yuan, Ming, and Ch'ing dynasties.[1]

1. "Orthodoxy" here signifies what the multilayered late imperial government (represented by the asymmetrical interests of literati in the bureaucracy and the throne; i.e., "imperial interests") publicly authorized as "orthodox," which became the core of the civil service examination curriculum. Perennial in public and private life as a variegated form of elite discourse, *Tao-hsueh* moral philosophy was endorsed by the bureaucracy and the throne as the core of the education of a literatus during the Ming and Ch'ing dynasties. When moral philosophy entered the political arena of state examinations, however, its intellectual life was constricted into a system of "monocular" concepts, arguments, and beliefs endorsed by the dynasty "singlemindedly" for its larger political purposes. The educational content of civil examinations that resulted from that process of restrictive manipulation, by which concepts, arguments, and beliefs selectively served to legitimate political sovereignty and create a *Tao-hsueh* persuasion, is what I refer to as imperial "ideology." Peter Bol and William Theodore de Bary rightly stress the role of independent scholars in the formation of "orthodoxy." See Bol, "The Neo-Confucian Position in Chinese History, 1200–1600," paper presented at the Song-Yuan-Ming Transitions Conference (Lake Arrowhead, Calif., June 5–11, 1997); and de Bary, *Neo-Confucian Orthodoxy and the Learning of the Mind-and-Heart* (New York: Columbia University Press, 1981), pp. 1–66. See also the articles in Kwang-Ching Liu, ed., *Orthodoxy in Late Imperial China* (Berkeley: University of California Press, 1990), in which orthodoxy as a "mode of statecraft" (Chi-yun Chen, pp. 27–52) and "socio-ethics as orthodoxy" (K. C. Liu, pp. 53–100) are used to describe imperial efforts to promulgate literati doctrines and beliefs. The Tao Learning orthodoxy differs from its predecessors, however, by setting up a single vision of governance and society based on a coherent philosophical position drawn from classical learning as interpreted by *Tao-hsueh* scholars. Neither the Han nor the T'ang orthodoxy had placed such limits on imperial ideology.

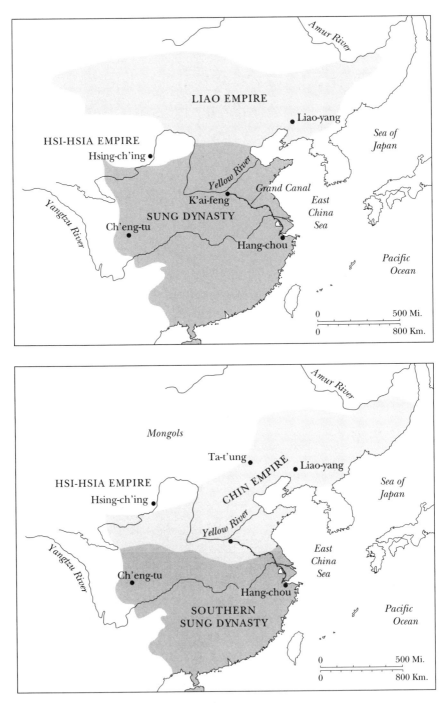

MAP 2. China during the Sung Dynasties.

The pioneering works by Hoyt Tillman and Peter Bol in particular have added historical perspective to earlier accounts of the intellectual evolution of Tao Learning during the Northern (960–1126) and Southern (1127–1279) Sung dynasties. This chapter examines exactly how the role in civil examinations of the Ch'eng-Chu (Ch'eng I 程頤 [1032–85] and Chu Hsi 朱熹 [1130–1200]) "school of principle" (li-hsüeh 理學) evolved between 1250 and 1450, even as the Sung imperium supporting it perished and was replaced by Mongol rulers, who waited until 1313 before granting imperial patronage to Tao Learning.[2]

The unrelenting wars among the Han Chinese, Tanguts, Khitan, Jurchen, and Mongol peoples for control of Sung China produced the conquest dynasties of Liao (907–1125), Hsi-hsia (990–1227), Chin (1115–1234), and Yuan (1280–1368). Faced with the competition of its northern, steppe neighbors, the T'ang and Sung were never able to reign supreme in East Asia after the An Lu-shan Rebellion (756–63). Competition among equally matched dynasties and the periodic shifts in the balance of power, as the Sung strategically allied with one of its enemies to hold the others in check, yielded an unstable political environment within which Han Chinese insiders and non-Han outsiders clashed over the meaning, significance, and future course of Sung culture and civilization and the role of civil examinations.[3] Indeed, Marco Polo in his *Travels* referred to south China as "Manzi," and he regarded it as a different kingdom from the north, which he called "Cathay." Military change in China between 960 and 1368 challenged Chinese state-society relations and produced new forms of cultural discourse, in which literati paid more attention to the roles of religion, art, literature, and entertainment in urban popular culture.[4]

James Liu and Conrad Schirokauer have provided useful lessons about the contested nature of "Sung China" and the Southern Sung political

2. Bol, "*This Culture of Ours*"; Tillman, *Confucian Discourse and Chu Hsi's Ascendancy*. On the Yuan and early Ming, see Thomas Wilson, *Genealogy of the Way*.

3. See David Wright, "Parity, Pedigree, and Peace: Routine Sung Diplomatic Missives to the Liao," *Journal of Sung-Yuan Studies* 26 (1996): 55–85, who stresses the "formal diplomatic parity" between the Sung and Liao. See also Morris Rossabi, ed., *China among Equals: The Middle Kingdom and Its Neighbors, 10th–14th Centuries* (Berkeley: University of California Press, 1983).

4. See Stephen West, "Mongol Influence on the Development of Northern Drama," in John Langlois, Jr., ed., *China under Mongol Rule* (Princeton: Princeton University Press, 1981), pp. 434–65; Valerie Hansen, *Changing Gods in Medieval China, 1127–1276* (Princeton: Princeton University Press, 1990); Ronald Latham, trans., *The Travels of Marco Polo* (Harmondsworth: Penguin Books, 1958), pp. 195–240; and Ruth Dunnell, *The Great State of White and High: Buddhism and State Formation in Eleventh-Century Xia* (Honolulu: University of Hawaii Press, 1996), pp. 3–26.

context within which Tao Learning was first labeled a heterodoxy, before it was refashioned into dynastic truth.[5] This chapter goes further and investigates the historical context for the Mongol selection of Tao Learning as the core curriculum of the civil examinations in 1313. It also inquires into the events of the early Ming dynasty, when, after the restoration of Han Chinese political rule, the Mongol Yuan *Tao-hsueh* orthodoxy was allegedly adopted in toto for Ming civil examinations. The Sung-Yuan-Ming transition from 1250 to 1450, as we shall see, greatly affected the political and social context within which Ch'eng-Chu learning became examination orthodoxy.

As the concluding remarks to this chapter emphasize, the different uses and timings of *Tao-hsueh* orthodoxy—which appeared very late in the Southern Sung dynasty; not at all under the Liao, Hsi-hsia, or Chin conquest dynasties; late again under the Yuan; and very early under Ming despots—tell us something about their asymmetrical historical significance. The Tao Learning vision was symbolically established by the Southern Sung court in 1240 and began to influence civil examinations thereafter, but it was not politically or educationally empowered as the official classical curriculum until 1313–14 under the Yuan dynasty.

Moreover, the events of 1240 under the Sung and 1313 under the Yuan, even when taken together, did not produce a seamless imperial *Tao-hsueh* orthodoxy that uniformly penetrated Han Chinese society and culture. This development coincided only with the return of native Han rule during the early Ming. Indeed, the construction of an empirewide, "monocular" imperial *Tao-hsueh* was possible only after the local and regional success among Sung-Yuan literati of much richer and more varied streams of Tao Learning, with both literary and philological components.[6] To a degree, *Tao-hsueh* clichés and arguments had become relatively standardized in the last examinations of the Southern Sung, but such examinations had diminished influence beyond the Hang-chou capital region after 1240.[7]

5. James T. C. Liu, "How Did a Neo-Confucian School Become the State Orthodoxy?" *Philosophy East and West* 23, 4 (1973): 483–505; and Schirokauer, "Neo-Confucians under Attack: The Condemnation of *Wei-hsueh*," in Haeger, ed., *Crisis and Prosperity in Sung China* (Tucson: University of Arizona Press, 1975), pp. 163–98.

6. For the instructive example of Tao Learning among literati in Wu-chou 婺州, see Bol, "The Neo-Confucian Position in Chinese History."

7. See De Weerdt, "Aspects of Song Intellectual Life," pp. 1–27. In her dissertation, De Weerdt argues for a growing homogenization in *Tao-hsueh* ideology in the last decades of the Southern Sung; see De Weerdt, "The Composition of Examination Standards."

## IMPORTANT VICISSITUDES IN THE
## CIVIL EXAMINATION CURRICULUM, 650–1400

The analysis here of continuity and change in the civil service curriculum between the T'ang and Ming dynasties reexamines the Yuan-Ming view that Sung China bequeathed a seamless *Tao-hsueh* orthodoxy to late imperial China. Institutionally speaking, there was no such imperial orthodoxy for most of the Sung dynasties. Nevertheless, to speak of Sung-Ming cultural continuity makes a certain degree of intellectual sense when referring to the literati currents of *Tao-hsueh* learning that first emerged in the Sung and later triumphed in the Ming. Thomas Wilson has already documented how the Sung origin of *Tao-hsueh* orthodoxy was culturally crafted in Sung, Yuan, and Ming times through a series of canon-making acts of institutional inclusion and exclusion, acts that recounted philosophically the seamless genealogy of *Tao-hsueh* truth.[8] In institutional terms, then, the Ming-Ch'ing civil examinations represented a decisive break with the actual classical curriculum used in the Sung civil service.

### *Han-T'ang Patterns*

Before the Northern Sung, the principal means of entry into the social and political elite was by official recommendation or kinship relations. During the Han dynasties, for example, textual expertise on a particular Classic was a prerequisite for appointment as an erudite (*po-shih* 博士) in the politically powerful Han Imperial Academy (*T'ai-hsueh* 太學). The academy had been formed to ensure the transmission of orthodox texts under imperial sponsorship, and each erudite was typically a specialist on one of the five Classics. After completing their course of study, disciples of erudites were orally examined and then granted government positions. Such tests of classical knowledge were first administered in 134 B.C. but not held regularly until A.D. 36. After A.D. 132 local officials recommended candidates for office, a practice giving the central government little control over the pool of qualified candidates. This tendency was enhanced after the fall of the Han in A.D. 220 because of the decentralization of power that ensued. In principle, this simple recruitment process was the forerunner of the elaborate imperial civil examinations set up during the T'ang and Sung dynasties.[9]

8. Wilson, *Genealogy of the Way*, pp. 23–143.

9. Franklin Houn, "The Civil Service Recruitment System of the Han Dynasty," *Tsinghua hsueh-pao* 清華學報, n.s. 1 (1956): 138–64. See also Patricia Ebrey, "Patron-Client Relations in the Later Han," *Journal of the American Oriental Society* 103, 3 (1983): 533–42.

Special civil examinations, which both qualified and appointed officials, began in the Western Han dynasty (206 B.C.–A.D. 8), when early emperors frequently questioned candidates orally using policy questions.[10] The Han origins of written policy questions can be traced to emperors "questioning by bamboo slips" (*ts'e-wen* 策問) candidates described as "men of wisdom and virtue" (*hsien-liang* 賢良) or "the upright and correct" (*fang-cheng* 方正). The candidates "answered using bamboo slips" (*tui-ts'e* 對策), based on their opinions concerning the most urgent problems of the day. The most famous of these Han dynasty examinations were the three questions Emperor Wu (r. 140–87 B.C.) in 134 B.C. asked the famous literatus Tung Chung-shu 董仲舒 (179–104 B.C.), who as a result of his persuasive answers (known as "Three Policy Answers of One Chosen Wise and Virtuous," or *Hsien-liang san-ts'e* 賢良三策) became an influential advisor.[11] Tung Chung-shu's articulation of a coherent and syncretic program for imperial statecraft in his policy answers remained influential into the late empire, and his policy answers also became stylistically praised and emulated. Overall, only thirty-six literati passed these special examinations during the Former and Later Han.[12]

After the fall of the Han, however, only the "nine-rank system" (*chiu-p'in kuan* 九品官) survived the social vacuum created by dynastic weakness and political decentralization. This rank system enabled literati families already established in government to control the process for recommending officials. From A.D. 220 until 583, when the system was abolished in the early Sui 隋 dynasty (581–618), the "arbiter's system" (*chung-cheng* 中正) for choosing the nine ranks in each province allowed the official class itself to control the selection of officials by determining the pool of candidates. In time, aristocrats maintained their power by ensuring that those eligible for office according to the nine ranks came from the local aristocracy. Until the Sui unification, the various northern and southern dynasties based appointments on the nine ranks.[13]

10. Sung accounts, following their Han and T'ang predecessors, traced the civil selection process back to the Chou 周 dynasty (1122?–221 B.C.), when the Classics claimed that Chou kings first used classical criteria to select meritorious officials. See, for example, *Yühai* 玉海 (Sea of jade), compiled by Wang Ying-lin 王應麟 (1223–1296), 1337 edition (facsimile, Taipei: Hua-wen Bookstore, 1964), 114.1a–5b. This view was maintained in the Ming and Ch'ing. See *Wu-li t'ung-k'ao* 五禮通考 (Comprehensive analysis of the five ritual texts), compiled by Ch'in Hui-t'ien 秦蕙田 (1702–64), 1761 edition, 173.1a–5b, which followed Sung sources closely.

11. The emperor's questions and Tung's answers are contained in *Han-shu* 漢書 (History of the Former Han dynasty), Pan Ku 班固, comp. (Peking: Chung-hua Bookstore, 1962), pp. 2495–2524.

12. Teng Ssu-yü 鄧嗣禹, *Chung-kuo k'ao-shih chih-tu shih* 中國考試制度史 (History of Chinese examination institutions), (Taipei: Student Bookstore, 1967), pp. 35–38.

13. See Miyazaki Ichisada 宮崎市定, *Kyūhin kan jinhō no kenkyū: kakyo zenshi* 九品官人法

In this way, the great aristocratic families of medieval China invoked the selection of officials by aristocratic privilege to ensure their local power in an era of political decentralization. The entrenched families of the Sui and T'ang dynasties were delegitimated in their official positions after the abrogation of the nine ranks in the Sui. Although the T'ang central government again controlled regular recruitment, aristocratic prerogative and domination of official ranks by the great families would remain a threat to centralized power and a reunified dynasty, which the revival of centrally controlled civil examinations was designed to redress.[14]

Under the T'ang emperors Kao-tsu (r. 618–26) and T'ai-tsung (r. 627–50), candidates first took qualifying examinations (chü 舉) demanding literary skills; then, to enter officialdom, they had to undergo a selection process (hsuan 選) that evaluated a candidate's character and determined the level of his appointment. Deportment, eloquence, calligraphy, and legal knowledge were used to select new officials from the pool of examination graduates.[15] As a result, the entire qualification and appointment process came to be called hsuan-chü 選舉, a term that encompassed selection and appointment to the civil service thereafter.[16]

Not until Empress Wu 則天吳后 (r. 684–704), however, did T'ang rulers discover that officials selected by open examinations served as a countervailing force to entrenched aristocrats in capital politics. The usefulness of this discovery was short-lived because court factions quickly developed around the patron-client relations between civil examiners and graduates eligible for office. Examiners were particularly powerful so long

---

の研究 : 科舉前史 (Research on the nine grades of civil officials: The early history of the civil examinations) (Kyoto: Dōbōsha, 1956), for the classic study of this takeover of the selection process by aristocrats; and Teng Ssu-yü, Chung-kuo k'ao-shih chih-tu shih, pp. 19–69. Cf. Charles Holcombe, In the Shadow of the Han: Literati Thought and Society at the Beginning of the Southern Dynasties (Honolulu: University of Hawaii Press, 1994), pp. 73–84, who draws on the work of Tanigawa Michio 谷川道雄. See, for example, Tanigawa, Medieval Chinese Society and the "Local Community," translated by Joshua Fogel (Berkeley: University of California Press, 1985).

14. John Lee, in "The Dragons and Tigers of 792: The Examination in T'ang History," T'ang Studies 6 (1988): 40–43, contends that the T'ang examination "had come to serve as an internal selection process for the aristocracy." T'ang examinations functionally shared more in common with medieval aristocratic trends than with imperial literati currents beginning in the Sung. See also P. A. Herbert, "T'ang Objections to Centralised Civil Service Selection," Papers on Far Eastern History 33 (1986): 81–83.

15. John Lee, "The Dragons and Tigers of 792," pp. 28, 32.

16. Robert des Rotours, Le traite des examens traduit de la nouvelle histoire des T'ang (Paris: Librairie Ernest Leroux, 1932), pp. 27–28, 42–43. See also P. A. Herbert, "Civil Service Recruitment in Early T'ang China: Ideal and Reality," in Chūgoku kankei ronsetsu shiryō 中國關係論説資料 28, 3B, I (1986): 30–36.

as both selection and appointment were under the control of the Ministry of Personnel (*Li-pu* 吏部). This changed in 737, though, when the Ministry of Rites took over the selection part of the process and gained control of the examiner-graduate rituals that had produced patron-client relations in the capital. The Ministry of Personnel thereafter controlled only official appointments.[17]

The great majority of literati officials during T'ang times, nonetheless, were not products of the examination system. Moreover, the examination system was a simple two-tiered process formally instituted only in the capital and based either on local recommendation of qualified candidates or on school attendance in capital schools. In addition, the T'ang was unique is permitting candidates for office to choose the prefecture from which they could be recommended. Many chose recommendation from the capital prefectures, where court patronage was most influential, a loophole that was lessened in the Sung and later dynasties. The Ming and Ch'ing dynasties required proof of local residency for all candidates.[18]

Emperor Wu's earlier use of policy questions during the Han dynasty to test men for official appointments became the precedent for later written palace examinations (*t'ing-shih* 廷試 or *tien-shih* 殿試), which during the T'ang, Sung, Yuan, Ming, and Ch'ing dynasties were the last hurdle for examination candidates seeking the exalted *chin-shih* 進士 (literatus presented to the emperor for appointment) degree required for high political appointments. After 690, when the palace examination was formally introduced by Empress Wu, the required questions reflected the literary turn toward *tsa-wen* 雜文 (belles lettres), which often included poetry, rhyme-prose, or eulogies (*shih-fu-sung* 詩賦頌). Such belles lettres had already been used in earlier T'ang dynasty civil examinations for the prestigious *chin-shih* degree.[19]

17. Herbert, "T'ang Objections to Centralised Civil Service Selection," pp. 89–93; and Oliver Moore, "The Ceremony of Gratitude," in Joseph P. McDermott, ed., *Court and State Ritual in China* (Cambridge: Cambridge University Press, 1998). Japanese scholars such as Araki Toshikazu and Miyazaki Ichisada, building on Naitō Kōnan's views, have overinterpreted such changes as reflecting in part the rise of late imperial autocracy. See Hisayuki Miyakawa, "An Outline of the Naito Hypothesis and Its Effects on Japanese Studies of China," *Far Eastern Quarterly* 14 (1954–55): 533–52.

18. Teng Ssu-yü, *Chung-kuo k'ao-shih chih-tu shih*, pp. 25–49, 77–134; Howard Wechsler, *Mirror to the Son of Heaven: Wei Cheng at the Court of T'ang T'ai-tsung* (New Haven: Yale University Press, 1974), pp. 57, 99; and Chaffee, *The Thorny Gates of Learning in Sung China*, pp. 14–15, 182. See also Oliver Moore, "The Ceremony of Gratitude."

19. In 685, Empress Wu had asked five policy questions on the palace examination, and then asked two in 689. See *Chung-kuo li-tai chuang-yuan tien-shih chüan*, pp. 1–16. See also Lo Lien-t'ien 羅聯添 *T'ang-tai wen-hsueh lun-chi* 唐代文學論集 (Collected essays on T'ang dynasty literature) (Taipei: Student Bookstore, 1989), pp. 379–95.

Questions requiring classical essays, which were similar to policy essays, were employed on the more popular T'ang *ming-ching* 明經 (clarifying the Classics) examinations, which paralleled the *chin-shih* as the top two tracks for civil selection. In fact, from 968 to 1070, Northern Sung dynasty palace examinations followed the T'ang precedent and included only poetry and rhyme-prose questions. After 1070, however, the palace examination was changed back to a single policy question requiring a long essay, which was administered, as in Han times, by the emperor to rank the candidates for official appointments. This single policy question format for palace examinations remained intact until 1904.[20]

Policy questions evolved during the T'ang and Sung dynasties as vehicles for addressing cultural, political, and institutional problems, sometimes including dissenting opinions, and they complemented the overriding literary focus on poetry and rhyme-prose in civil examinations during the middle empire.[21] The T'ang turn toward poetry questions and literary formalism in the curriculum for *chin-shih* examinations after 681, however, reflected a decisive change: stress on poetry, belles lettres, and culture

20. *Wu-li t'ung-k'ao*, 173.27b–31b, 174.3a–4a, 14b–15a. See, for example, the emperor's policy question in 1148, in *Shao-hsing shih-pa-nien t'ung-nien hsiao-lu* 紹興十八年同年小錄 (Minutiae for graduates of the 1148 civil examination), Ming edition (with 1491, 1595, and 1835 afterwords), pp. 5a–5b; see Appendix 1. Coming early in the Southern Sung (1127–1279), the 1148 palace question asked candidates to comment on the reasons why the Kuang-wu reign (A.D. 25–57), which followed the fall of the Former Han dynasty, was the most glorious era since antiquity: the question intimated that the Southern Sung headquartered in Hang-chou would also surpass its Northern Sung predecessor despite the fall of the north to the Jurchen Chin dynasty. This is one of the only two surviving Sung dynasty examination records (the other is for 1256), and it survives because Chu Hsi took his *chin-shih* on this examination, placing 90th in the third rank at the age of only nineteen. See p. 47a. See also Kracke, "Family vs. Merit in Chinese Civil Service Examinations during the Empire," pp. 103–23, which discusses the 1148 and 1256 examination lists. As we shall see in Chapters 8 and 9, policy questions during the late empire frequently did not involve current government "policy." Typically such questions were defined according to issues drawn from the "Classics, the Dynastic Histories, or practical affairs" (*ching-shih shih-wu ts'e* 經世時務策). On the historical importance of policy questions, see *Ch'ang-t'an* 常談 (Everyday discussions on the civil examinations), compiled by T'ao Fu-lü 陶福履, *Ts'ung-shu chi-ch'eng ch'u-pien* 叢書集成初編 edition (Shanghai: Commercial Press, 1936), pp. 21–24.

21. Examples of T'ang policy questions for both the *chin-shih* and *ming-ching* tests can be found in *Wen-yuan ying-hua* 文苑英華 (A gathering of masterpieces of literature), compiled by Li Fang 李昉, 1567 edition, *chüan* 卷 473–502; and Ch'üan Te-yü 權德輿, *Ch'üan Tsai-chih wen-chi* 權載之文集 (Collected essays of Ch'üan Te-yü), *Ssu-pu ts'ung-k'an* 四部叢刊 edition (Shanghai: Commercial Press, 1919–37), 40.3b–11b. See also des Rotours, *Le traité des examens traduit de la nouvelle histoire des T'ang*, pp. 292–347. Cf. David McMullen, *State and Scholars in T'ang China* (Cambridge: Cambridge University Press, 1988), pp. 23, 198.

among T'ang aristocratic elites, who were dissatisfied with the standards of classical learning (*ching-hsueh* 經學) adopted in the *ming-ching* civil selection curriculum. Essays for the *ming-ching* examinations were still important in the T'ang, and there were also specialty examinations (*chu-k'o* 諸科) in law, mathematics, paleography, ritual, Taoism, and history, but a student's ability to write in a variety of literary genres soon became the key cultural asset sought by T'ang literati.[22]

Typically, T'ang examiners tested students by covering phrases of a page from the Classics (*t'ieh-ching* 帖經) and requiring the candidate either to write the entire text from memory or to write the missing characters on tags placed over the text. Alternatively, they might require a candidate to supply the immediate phrase following the one read out loud, a testing technique known as *mo-i* 墨義 (literary meaning).[23] In addition to the Classics, the *Lao-tzu* 老子 was also tested during the T'ang dynasty, frequently as part of the policy questions, and a "degree in Taoism" (*Tao-k'o* 道科) was possible during the Sung from 1080 until 1120, which suggests that the final formation of a classical curriculum that eliminated Taoism from official literati thought was a Sung and Yuan invention and not a Han-T'ang policy.[24]

After the 680–81 shift in importance from *ming-ching* tests on the classical canon, which had included three policy questions, to the belles lettres on the *chin-shih* examinations, which still included a single policy question, literary criteria remained dominant in T'ang civil service selection until

22. See *Teng-k'o chi-k'ao* 登科記考 (Study of the records of ascension to civil degrees [during the T'ang]), compiled by Hsu Sung 徐松 (1781–1848) (reprint, Kyoto: Chūbun Press, 1982), 28.1a–56b. Cf. Araki Toshikazu 荒木敏一, *Sōdai kakyo seido kenkyū* 宋代科舉制度研究 (Study of the Sung dynasty civil service examination system) (Kyoto: Dōbōsha Press, 1969), pp. 356–57; Bol, *"This Culture of Ours"*, pp. 76–107; and McMullen, *State and Scholars in T'ang China*, pp. 88–94, 136–39, 197–99, 229–32. We have no figures for *ming-ching* degrees during the T'ang, but for *chin-shih* our figures allow us to calculate a total of 6,504 such degrees during the 289 years of T'ang rule, for an average of only 23 *chin-shih* per year. See Huang Kuang-liang, 黄光亮, *Ch'ing-tai k'o-chü chih-tu chih yen-chiu* 清代科舉制度之研究 (Research on the Ch'ing dynasty civil examination system) (Taipei: Chia-hsin Cement Co. Cultural Foundation, 1976), pp. 26–30. Ch'ing-lien Huang estimates 3,917 *chin-shih* during the T'ang based on incomplete figures from the *Teng-k'o chi-k'ao*. See Huang, "The Recruitment and Assessment of Civil Officials under the T'ang Dynasty" (Ph.D. diss., Princeton University, East Asian Studies, 1986), p. 29n38.

23. See Teng Ssu-yü, *Chung-kuo k'ao-shih chih-tu shih*, pp. 96–97.

24. See *Li-tai kung-chü chih* 歷代貢舉志 (Accounts of the civil examinations over several dynasties), compiled by Feng Meng-chen 馮夢禎 (Shanghai: Commercial Press, 1936), p. 3. See also Chao Hsin-i, "Daoist Examinations and Daoist Schools during the Northern Sung Dynasty," UCLA graduate seminar paper, 1994.

the end of the dynasty.[25] As the T'ang entry in Appendix 4 shows, however, there were frequent clashes of opinion in which the focus on belles lettres was called into question and a return to classical essays was briefly favored. In 752, for example, a compromise was worked out between the classicists and literary advocates whereby both classical learning and belles lettres were used on the *chin-shih* examinations, a compromise frequently emulated later during the Sung dynasties.

By 763 T'ang literati were calling for decentralized examinations and the complete elimination of the poetry and rhyme-prose questions. The role of literary examinations in the Hanlin Academy 翰林院, an imperial advisory institution that later evolved into the key group of ministers serving the emperor (see Chapter 3), was also debated. Moreover, policy questions on Taoism, which had begun in 675, were abrogated in 763, as literati, in the aftermath of the cultural crisis touched off by the An-lu Shan Rebellion, sought to base culture and writing on the Way. Some advocated that the higher examinations be replaced by the pre-T'ang system of recommendations from the provinces.[26]

In early T'ang court life, "writing as culture" had taken hold among literati, and literary composition was the most popular field of learned life. *Wen* 文 served as the literary core of a literati discourse that received the legacy of the sages and former kings and affirmed its relevance for the present. T'ang literati from Ch'üan Te-yü 權德輿 (759–818) to Han Yü 韓愈 (768–824) unintentionally helped undercut aristocratic culture in medieval China, according to Peter Bol, by introducing a "self-conscious inquiry and debate over ideas." The "new, creative, and variegated intellectual culture between 755 and 820," challenged the long-assumed unity between the *tao* of heaven and earth and the style and oeuvre of individual writers. This challenge resulted in reconfigurations of the relations between *wen* and *tao*.[27]

The centrality of belles lettres, except for a brief abrogation in 833–34, remained a key feature of T'ang literati culture, however. Denis Twitchett observes that the curriculum for T'ang civil examinations was very diverse

---

25. *Yü-hai*, 115.11b–16b. See also Stephen Owen, *The Great Age of Chinese Poetry: The High T'ang* (New Haven: Yale University Press, 1981), p. 5.

26. Herbert, "T'ang Objections to Centralised Civil Service Selection," pp. 98–105.

27. *Wu-li t'ung-k'ao*, 113.26a–33a; and McMullen, *State and Scholars in T'ang China*, pp. 88–95, 152, 230–31. On the "crisis of culture after 755," see Bol, *"This Culture of Ours"*, pp. 108–23; and Pulleyblank, "Neo-Confucianism and Neo-Legalism in T'ang Intellectual Life, 755–805," in Arthur Wright, ed., *The Confucian Persuasion* (Stanford: Stanford University Press, 1960), pp. 77–114.

throughout the dynasty. He also notes that there was no prescribed interpretation of the Classics that could be compared to the *Tao-hsueh* stress on Ch'eng-Chu interpretations during the Yuan and Ming. In fact, the notion of a rigid set of limits for classical scholarship was foreign to T'ang examinations, both in terms of content and style.[28] What did occur, nevertheless, during the transition from the northwestern, aristocratic literary culture of T'ang China to the ethical-philosophical discourse of Northern Sung was the demise of the aristocracy, or at least its redefinition, in the late T'ang and the social transformation of the *shih* 士 (gentry-literati) in the Sung.

### Northern Sung Debates

As we have seen, before 750 T'ang China, like Europe until the modern era, was dominated by a landed aristocracy. This aristocracy was organized into families and clans strategically located in the northwest, near the centers of political power in the Wei River Valley, the western and eastern capitals of Ch'ang-an and Lo-yang. By 1250, however, the transition to a central and southern-based Sung empire, whose capital was in the Yangtzu delta city of Hang-chou 杭州, symbolized the growing economic dominance of south China and the emergence of the bureaucratized *shih* as the "best and brightest" in the land.[29] Composition of the elite in China changed in revolutionary ways between 750 and 1100. Decline of the great aristocratic clans, which began in the years after the An Lu-shan Rebellion, coincided with the rise to prominence of southern literati in national politics in the late tenth century. The disruption of the continuity of the great families of medieval China was complete. The few

28. Denis Twitchett, "The Birth of the Chinese Meritocracy: Bureaucrats and Examinations in T'ang China," *The China Society Occasional Papers* (London) 18 (1974): 13.

29. On Europe, see J. H. Hexter, *Reappraisals in History: New Views on History and Society in Early Modern Europe* (Chicago: University of Chicago Press, 1979), pp. 45–70; Lawrence Stone, "The Educational Revolution in England, 1560–1640," *Past & Present* 28 (1964): 41–80; Stone, "Literacy and Education in England 1640–1900," *Past & Present* 42 (1969): 69–139; and Charles E. McClelland, "The Aristocracy and University Reform in Eighteenth-Century Germany," in Lawrence Stone, ed., *Schooling and Society: Studies in the History of Education* (Baltimore: Johns Hopkins University Press, 1976), pp. 146–73. On China, see Dennis Grafflin, "The Great Families of Medieval South China," *Harvard Journal of Asiatic Studies* 41 (1981): 65–74; and Robert Hartwell, "Demographic, Political, and Social Transformations of China, 750–1550," *Harvard Journal of Asiatic Studies* 42, 2 (December 1982): 365–442.

from the northwest that survived were forced to adapt to new social conditions they could no longer control.[30]

Fearing repetition of the centrifugal power of regional clans and military leaders after the reunification of China in 960, Northern Sung emperors promulgated anonymous civil service examinations as the measure of talent in the empire. They were faced with ruling an empire of extraordinary economic strength undergoing decisive demographic growth. As part of the process of developing a broad range of new institutional mechanisms by which to govern over 60 million subjects (perhaps 80 million by 1100), Northern Sung rulers chose civil service examinations to limit alternative military and aristocratic power centers and to draw into their government the sons of elites from newly emerging regions in south China. Deftly appropriating civilian values to legitimate the institution of fair and impartial bureaucratic channels to select officials, which were theoretically open to almost all Chinese, regardless of social background, Sung emperors put in place an examination system that, except during the Yuan and early Ming, occupied a central institutional position in Chinese government and society until 1904, when the civil service examinations were abolished.[31]

Winston Lo has shown that the Sung civil service operated in terms of a combination of position classification ("job description") and rank classification (personal "qualifications"). A personnel pool more than twice the size of actual positions was rendered tolerable by an equitable system of work rationing. In this way, all civil service graduates were guaranteed a minimal level of employment and remuneration. With the bureaucracy undergoing 100% turnover every three or four years, allocation of jobs and the accompanying remuneration was determined for the most part through position classification—that is, the importance of the position to be filled.[32]

30. Hymes, *Statesmen and Gentlemen*, pp. 29–61; Winston Lo, *An Introduction to the Civil Service of Sung China* (Honolulu: University of Hawaii Press, 1987), pp. 1–34; and Thomas Lee, *Government Education and Examinations in Sung China* (Hong Kong: Chinese University, 1982), pp. 287–97.

31. The best detailed analysis of the Sung examinations is in a series of articles by Chin Chung-shu 金中樞 entitled "Pei Sung k'o-chü chih-tu yen-chiu" 北宋科舉制度研究 (Research on the Northern Sung civil examination system), in *Sung-shih yen-chiu chi* 宋史研究集 (Taiwan) 11 (1979): 1–72; 13 (1981): 61–188; 14 (1983): 53–189; 15 (1984): 125–88; 16 (1986): 1–125. See also Eberhard, *Social Mobility in Traditional China*, pp. 22–25; E. A. Kracke, *Civil Service in Early Sung China* (Cambridge: Harvard-Yenching Institute, 1968), pp. 1–27; Thomas Lee, *Government Education and Examinations in Sung China*, pp. 19–45; and Chaffee, *The Thorny Gates of Learning in Sung China*, pp. 13–17, 182–88.

32. Winston Lo, *An Introduction to the Civil Service of Sung China*, pp. 115–70.

Rank classification during the Sung governed nominal salary, status, and fringe benefits for bureaucratic personnel. Work rationing provided considerable savings because appointments based on job classification were the real basis for remuneration; one's base pay, tied to rank, eventually became little more than token remuneration. Insufficient funding of the civil service was resolved by an elaborate system of ranks and assignments tied to definite terms of office. Because the civil service operated in an employer's market, work rationing inhibited the medieval (European as well as Chinese) tendency to regard office as a piece of private property to be sold or left to one's heirs.[33]

The years 600 to 1200 marked the transformation of the *shih* from men of good birth to men of culture. Significant changes occurred in the categories that were traditionally important for defining literati life: culture, birth, and office holding. Changes in the conception of the primary elite—for example, its new character ideals—played a part in redirecting their efforts to maintain their status as *shih*. Once the "commodity" of good birth ceased to be sufficient to define *shih* status, examination status and its correlates of culture and education became the sine qua non for literati identity. In the process, civilian governance by *shih* chosen through Sung examinations of unprecedented scope mitigated against the sort of military threat that had been so prevalent in the late T'ang and during the five Dynasties (907–60), although civil examinations were still in place in each of the five Dynasties.

Unquestioned loyalty to the ruling house was cemented by the decision of Emperor T'ai-tsu (r. 960–76) in the late tenth century (973) to require that the emperor himself administer the final "palace examination," testing all those who had successfully passed the highest-level capital examination. For all subsequent dynasties, the emperor in effect became the state's premier examiner, symbolically demanding oaths of allegiance from successful candidates for public office. In addition, a policy for covering up all candidates' names began at the palace examination in 992, in 1007 at the department examinations, and in the prefectures in 1032. Recopying of papers to prevent examiners from recognizing a candidate's calligraphy was initiated at the palace and department examinations in 1015 and in prefectures in 1037.[34]

33. During the Ming and Ch'ing, however, as provinces in the empire became full-fledged administrative units, the civil service dropped a fully functional dual rank system and depended mainly on position classification. Much of the responsibility for official appointments shifted from the capital to provincial governments. See Winston Lo, *An Introduction to the Civil Service of Sung China*, pp. 217–25.

34. See Araki, *Sōdai kakyo seido kenkyū*, pp. 243–64. During the Ming and Ch'ing, only

Because civil officials were drawn almost exclusively from the ranks of the literati, however, by 1100 the *shih* had accumulated enough independence and local power for their role as local elites to outshine their role as bureaucrats. Their domination of local society based on *shih* educational and cultural qualifications was one of the unforeseen outcomes of the court's enfranchisement of the *shih* in the Sung political order. Unlike T'ang aristocratic families, Sung gentry families were unable to monopolize official positions and thus could not perpetuate themselves in dynastic offices. Even the hereditary *yin* 陰 privilege could not accomplish this for elites. The high numbers of examination candidates (not equaled again until the mid-Ming dynasty) mitigated against any long-term monopoly of political status via examination success. Education geared toward passing examinations remained an important investment once the examinations also became a means to legitimate dominance in the local economy, institutions, and cultural activities.[35]

In intellectual terms, literati debates about the curriculum in Sung civil examinations, outlined in the Northern Sung entry in Appendix 4, continued to stress the controversy over belles lettres versus classical learning that had marked the late T'ang. Early Sung intellectual culture continued late T'ang meditations on the role of *ku-wen* prose when, according to Bol, literati such as Fan Chung-yen 范仲淹 (989–1052) and Ou-yang Hsiu 歐陽修 (1007–72) established "the role of the *ku-wen* writer as agitator for political and social transformation." A durable literary consensus did not emerge, however, and men such as Ch'eng I, who thought that *wen* was irrelevant to mastering the *tao* and its moral values, began the radical turn toward a solution that called itself appropriately Tao Learning. Nevertheless, Ch'eng I and his followers had little impact on Northern Sung civil examinations. Ou-yang Hsiu and Wang An-shih 王安石 (1021–86) had the most educational influence in this arena.[36]

Sung intellectual culture was initially dominated by the T'ang style literary (*shih-fu* 詩賦) requirements for the civil service *chin-shih* degree, which included a discourse essay (*lun* 論) based on quotations from the Classics, Histories, or pre-Han and Sung masters. *Ku-wen* scholars such as Fan Chung-yen tried to redress this focus on literary refinement by calling

---

answers for the provincial and metropolitan examinations had to be anonymous. For local examinations and palace examinations, the original papers themselves were graded.

35. Bol, *"This Culture of Ours"*, pp. 32–75.

36. Ibid., pp. 148–211. See also Yoshikawa Kōjirō, *An Introduction to Sung Poetry*, translated by Burton Watson (Cambridge: Harvard University Press, 1967), pp. 6–48; and Ronald Egan, *The Literary Works of Ou-yang Hsiu (1007–72)* (Cambridge: Cambridge University Press, 1984), pp. 12–29.

for educational reforms and by requiring *ku-wen* prose essays on the examinations.[37] Such views had already been prominent in 1029 court discussions about the classical curriculum. In 1044–45 debates over examination reform, for example, Ou-yang Hsiu suggested that policy questions be administered first so that candidates would immediately be tested on their knowledge of practical matters.[38] Those who passed this hurdle would be tested in later sessions on their literary ability, which would still determine their final rank. Thus, no one would be able to pass the *chin-shih* examination based on literary ability alone.[39]

Although Ou-yang's ideas were never put into effect, he subsequently caused an uproar as director of the 1057 examinations by passing only those candidates who had written essays in *ku-wen* prose. Despite the furor, *ku-wen* increasingly became influential as a movement, uniting in the 1050s even Ch'eng I, who stressed human nature as an innate endowment, and Su Shih 蘇軾 (1036–1101), who emphasized realistic responses to immediate human feelings and needs. Clearly, however, classical learning during the Northern Sung was starting to retake precedence from belles lettres on civil examinations. In the process, the *Analects* and the *Mencius* emerged as required texts in the classical curriculum, prefiguring the emergence in the Southern Sung of the Four Books as a discrete family of canonical texts.[40] Competing visions of the political order, all in the name of the *tao*, were invoked by *shih*, however, to reform the classical curriculum.

Wang An-shih and Ssu-ma Kuang 司馬光 (1019–86) represented the first opposing camps to emerge from the mid-eleventh-century *ku-wen* consensus. Both sought to address the proper relation between state and society. An activist, Wang found in antiquity his version of a universal political, social, economic, and cultural program, which he promulgated as the "New Policies" in the early 1070s. More conservative, Ssu-ma

37. See *Sung-shih* 宋史 (History of the Sung dynasty), compiled by T'o T'o 脫脫 (1313–55) et al. (Taipei: Ting-wen Bookstore, 1980), 5/3613 (*chüan* 卷 155).

38. For examples of the policy questions Ou-yang actually prepared for examinations, see *Ou-yang Wen-chung kung chi* 歐陽文忠公集 (Collection of Duke Ou-yang Hsiu) (Taipei: Commercial Press, 1967), vol. 2, 6.11–19 (*chüan* 卷 48).

39. *Wen-hsien t'ung-k'ao* 文獻通考 (Comprehensive analysis of civil institutions), compiled by Ma Tuan-lin 馬端臨 (Shanghai: Commercial Press, 1936), pp. 289–90. Cf. Araki, *Sōdai kakyo seido kenkyū*, pp. 365–80.

40. Uno Seiichi 宇野精一, "Gokyō kara Shisho e: keigakushi oboegaki" 五經から四書 へ: 經學史覺書 (From the Five Classics to the Four Books: Notes on the history of classical studies), *Tōyō no bunka to shakai* 東洋の文化と社會 2 (1952): 1–14. See also Daniel Gardner, "Principle and Pedagogy: Chu Hsi and the Four Books," *Harvard Journal of Asiatic Studies* 44, 1 (June 1984): 57–81.

Kuang attempted to install political reforms that would not require the reorganization of society. Except for a brief period between 1085 and 1093 when Ssu-ma Kuang and his followers were in charge, Wang An-shih's partisans dominated the Sung court until the fall of K'ai-feng.[41]

Wang An-shih sought to legitimate his agenda through a stress on schools and a unified and orthodox codification of select Classics that he placed at the core of the civil examination curriculum. For a brief period in the 1070s, as the chief minister of the Shen-tsung emperor (r. 1068–86), Wang An-shih tried to replace examination success with graduation from dynastic schools as the basis for selection of officials. However, in part because of the low prestige of schools vis-à-vis examination degrees (i.e., schools were a way station to such degrees and not valued independently), such reforms did not take hold, and examination success triumphed over formal training in imperial institutions of higher education. Despite considerable opposition to Wang's efforts to establish his version of classical orthodoxy, classical essays (ching-i 經義) for all chin-shih examinations replaced poetry and rhyme-prose in his educational regime. The ming-ching examinations were stopped, and all but the legal part of the specialty examinations were also eliminated.[42]

Ssu-ma Kuang, on the other hand, also opposed literary examinations, but he questioned the usefulness of anonymity as an examination procedure (he preferred knowing the moral character of the candidate).[43] He appealed instead to historical precedents in the Spring and Autumn Annals, which he emulated in his Comprehensive Mirror for Government (Tzu-chih t'ung-chien 資治通鑑), for understanding the political history of dynasties and the reasons for their rise and fall. As soon as Ssu-ma Kuang and his group were placed in positions of power, they restored belles lettres as an alternative chin-shih examination curriculum in 1089, thereby effecting a compromise between the competing demands of classicists and literary men. Seventy to eighty percent of the candidates for the chin-shih degree, however, preferred the literary over the classical path to public office. The

41. Araki, Sōdai kakyo seido kenkyū, pp. 346–64; and Bol, "This Culture of Ours", pp. 212–99.

42. Wang An-shih, "Ch'i kai k'o-t'iao chih cha-tzu" 乞改科條制劄子 (Directive to reform the civil curriculum), in Lin-ch'uan chi 臨川集 (Collection of Wang An-shih) (Taipei: Chung-hua Bookstore, SPPY, 1970), 42.4a–4b. See also Sung-shih, 5/3616–19 (chüan 卷 155).

43. Ssu-ma Kuang, "Ch'i i shih-k'o chü-shih cha-tzu" 乞以十科舉士劄子 (Directive for using ten types of examinations to select literati), in Wen-kuo Wen-cheng Ssu-ma kung wen-chi 溫國文正司馬公文集 (Collected essays of Duke Ssu-ma Kuang) (Shanghai: Commercial Press, 1920–22), 53.12a–13b. His other proposals on civil examinations can be found at 19.6a–8b, 21.5b–6a, 39.5a–14a. See also Sung-shih, 5/3620–21 (chüan 卷 155).

classical essay increasingly did take precedence. Until the fall of K'ai-feng in 1125, essay styles slowly evolved into the parallel-prose forms of writing later more stylized in the Ming-Ch'ing eight-legged essay ( *pa-ku-wen* 八股 文; see Chapter 7).[44]

Though at odds over policy, Wang An-shih and Ssu-ma Kuang agreed that political solutions were required to address the lack of unity in literati values and dislocations in the social order. When political reforms, whether activist or conservative, failed to fulfill their promise, those caught in the middle of the storm, such as Ch'eng I and Su Shih, were encouraged to search elsewhere for solutions to the problems of the age. Su questioned the need for any orthodoxy to unify literati values. He added, for example, that the key to selecting literati was to "know men" (*chih-jen* 知人) and to separate form from reality. Su noted that written examinations of any type were impractical measures of practical ability: "Speaking of them as literary pieces, discourse and policy questions are practical, whereas poetry and rhyme-prose questions are not. But speaking from the perspective of government, all written questions whether poetry, rhyme-prose, discourse, or policy are impractical."[45]

Ch'eng I stressed moral self-cultivation for all *shih* and thus fundamentally challenged the value of literary achievement and activist government service. His brother Ch'eng Hao 程顥 (1032–85) thought examinations an inadequate measure of ability and, as court censor in 1068, stressed schooling and teachers as the basis for social customs and political order.[46] When Ch'eng I claimed messianic authority for himself and for his brother Ch'eng Hao to speak for the *tao* of the sages lost after Mencius, they simultaneously gainsaid the literary culture of the T'ang and Sung and the classical legacy of the Han. In Ch'eng I's eyes, literary production was frivolous and political activism fundamentally misguided if they were not each centered on a fundamental moral understanding of the *tao*. Heavenly principles (*t'ien-li* 天理), not human artifice, were the way of heaven and earth. Moral principles that explained the raison d'être for human values and rituals became the guidelines for literati life.

The new discourse of *Tao-hsueh*, conservative politically and socially,

44. *Wu-li t'ung-k'ao*, 174.12a–16a.

45. Su Shih, "I hsueh-hsiao kung-chü chuang" 議學校貢舉狀 (Debates on schools and civil examinations), in *Tung-p'o ch'üan-chi* 東坡全集 (Complete collection of Su Shih), in *Ssu-k'u ch'üan-shu* 四庫全書 (Complete collection of the four treasuries) (reprint, Taipei: Commercial Press, 1983–86), 1107/699–701.

46. See Ch'eng Hao, "Ch'ing hsiu hsueh-hsiao tsun shih-ju ch'ü-shih cha-tzu" 請修學校尊師儒取士箚子 (A directive for building schools and honoring teachers and Confucians to select literati), in *Erh Ch'eng wen-chi* 二程文集 (Collected essays of the Ch'eng brothers) (Taipei: I-wen Press, n.d.), 7.2a–5a.

spoke to the beleaguered *shih* in philosophical and ethical terms. To know the *tao* through learning and cultivation required new character ideals and new models of enlightenment. Ch'eng I and his followers, particularly Chu Hsi, won the hearts of an influential minority of the *shih* in the twelfth century by convincing them to change the criteria of their identity so that their new learning could help them better fulfill their local ethical, cultural, and political responsibilities.[47] Eventually the old cultural-textual-literary tradition of *shih* learning was replaced by an ethical-philosophical perspective that resacralized the Classics and invented the Four Books as the repository of the truths taught by Confucius, Mencius, and their immediate disciples. Ch'eng I, Chu Hsi, and by extension their own followers became the direct disciples of Confucius and Mencius, leaving Han and T'ang literati out of the Tao Learning genealogy.

A minor group at first, *Tao-hsueh* eventually created the social, political, and intellectual conditions for its own increasingly influential standing in Southern Sung literati life.[48] In the north and even in the south, however, literary currents remained predominant among literati living under the Southern Sung or conquest dynasties where civil examinations still stressed belles lettres. The formation of *Tao-hsueh* orthodoxy, so clear in hindsight, was still a long way from completion, and poetry and prose remained important elements in the civilizing process that integrated Chinese and non-Chinese in a divided China after 1125. When we read the collected writings of venerable Northern Sung literati such as Ou-yang Hsiu and Wang An-shih, among many others, we find that poetry and rhyme-prose still had eminence of place in their oeuvre.

### Liao, Chin, Koryŏ, and Belles Lettres in North China and Korea

Political empowerment via civil examinations in Sung China was not uncontested. At the heart of the differences among Han Chinese, Tanguts, Khitan, Jurchen, Muslims, and Mongols initially lay the millennial social and cultural gulf between the nomadic warrior civilizations of the Eurasian steppe and the great agrarian grain and rice systems of imperial China.[49] Non-Han peoples, particularly the nomadic warriors of the

47. Bol, *"This Culture of Ours"*, pp. 300–342.

48. Tillman, *Confucian Discourse and Chu Hsi's Ascendancy*, pp. 1–23.

49. Herbert Franke and Denis Twitchett, eds., *The Cambridge History of China*, vol. 6, *Alien Regimes and Border States, 907–1368* (Cambridge: Cambridge University Press, 1994); and Denis Senor, ed., *The Cambridge History of Early Inner Asia* (Cambridge: Cambridge University Press, 1990). See also Thomas Barfield, *The Perilous Frontier: Nomadic Empires and China, 221 B.C. to A.D. 1757* (London: Blackwell, 1989); and Morris Rossabi, *Khubilai Khan* (Berkeley: University of California Press, 1988).

steppe, decisively challenged the Sung classical educational regime between 1100 and 1300. When both Han Chinese and nomadic peoples
found themselves living under a single ruler, dual organizations were
developed to administer the tribal military elites, on the one hand, and
Chinese bureaucratic styles of governance on the other—a precedent that
persisted in the dyarchy of Manchu and Han under the Ch'ing dynasty.
Civil examinations, when instituted, were subject to these centrifugal
forces.[50]

Hence, we can evaluate the continuity between Sung and late imperial
civil examinations by also taking note of the invention by literati of a
"barbarian break" between Sung and Ming China, when Han literati
insiders became a secondary elite in a primary elite world of non-Han
outsiders, some known collectively as the *se-mu* 色目 ("different category")
peoples. Although these social outsiders were themselves a myriad of peoples—Mongols, Tanguts, Khitan, Jurchen, Muslims, Tibetans, Persians,
Turks, Nestorians, Jews, Armenians, and so on—when placed within a
vast Han majority, they became part of the Mongol conquest elite. Before
the Mongol conquest, the Khitan and Jurchen warrior nobilities had ruled
as social outsiders who became political insiders during the Liao and Chin
conquest dynasties in the north and northwest. When a military group of
outsiders ruled over a society of insiders, the millennial civil bureaucracy
sometimes became expendable among such outsiders. At best, it was
always compromised by the dual political system that evolved to cater to
the conquering outsiders and their Han subjects. The Chin in particular
were adept in complementing Jurchen customary law with Han-style
administration. Conquest dynasties in general successfully allowed separate
laws and practices to be carried out among tribal constituencies.[51]

In order to defend the Han version of civilian culture, the Chinese
stereotyped such outsiders as "barbarians" because of their uncivilized
warrior ways and social manners. Levirate marriage, whereby a warrior
could inherit wives from his father and older male relatives, for instance,
was the rule among nomadic tribes. The Sung Chinese regarded such
relations as cases of incest. The *se-mu* outsider, unified socially only as a

50. Herbert Franke, "The Role of the State as a Structural Element in Polyethnic
Societies," in S. R. Schram, ed., *Foundations and Limits of State Power in China* (London:
University of London, 1987), pp. 87–112.

51. John K. Fairbank, *Trade and Diplomacy on the China Coast: The Opening of the Treaty
Ports, 1842–1854* (Stanford: Stanford University Press, 1969), pp. 4–41, 465–66. See Hoyt
Tillman, "An Overview of Chin History and Institutions," in Tillman and Stephen West,
eds., *China under Jurchen Rule* (Albany: SUNY Press, 1995), pp. 23–38; and Barfield, *The
Perilous Frontier*, pp. 167–84. The line between Han Chinese and "barbarian" was never as
clear as literati writers made it seem.

non-Han people, challenged and displaced the Han literati insider within the precincts of the government, while Chinese literati and commoners retreated within the environs of their immediate local society, exacerbating a social process that had started in the transition from Northern Sung political activism to Southern Sung localism.[52]

Civil examinations became a contested educational field within which classically literate Han elites initially fared poorly against their warrior conquerors, who had special examinations, lower requirements, and levirate rights of inheritance, until the warrior elites themselves were civilized via classical literacy in Chinese to compete directly with the Han majority for places in the conquest bureaucracy. This civilizing process occurred faster among the Khitan and Jurchen, who quickly domesticated themselves, using civil examinations early in their dynasties to quell tribal autonomy.[53] They also developed written versions of their own spoken languages, and some Jurchen warriors were adept in classical Chinese before the fall of the Sung.[54] The Mongols, however, proved more resistant to Han appeals for literate measures of political power in a civilian government, despite the repeated admonitions of Khitan literati such as the celebrated Yeh-lü Ch'u-ts'ai 耶律楚材 (1189–1243). To battle "not by wielding swords but by plying their writing brushes in supervised literary composition" represented an unacceptable threat to warrior illiterates.[55]

52. See Robert Hymes, *Statesmen and Gentlemen;* and the essays in Robert Hymes and Conrad Schirokauer, eds., *Ordering the World: Approaches to State and Society in Sung Dynasty China* (Berkeley: University of California Press, 1993).

53. See, for instance, Karl Wittfogel, "Public Office in the Liao Dynasty and the Chinese Examination System." *Harvard Journal of Asiatic Studies* 10 (1947): 13–40; Peter Bol, "Chao Ping-wen (1159–1232): Foundations for Literati Learning," in Tillman and West, eds., *China under Jurchen Rule*, pp. 115–44; and Jin Qicong, "Jurchen Literature under the Chin," in Tillman and West, eds., *China under Jurchen Rule*, pp. 216–237. Cf. Norbert Elias, *The Civilizing Process: The History of Manners* (Oxford: Blackwell, 1994), for discussion of the civilizing process as a transformation of individual personality structures.

54. The Jurchen general Wan-yen Tsung-han 完顏宗翰 (1080–1137), for example, supervised the classical language of submission submitted by the Sung emperor after the fall of K'ai-feng. See Winston Lo, "Wan-yen Tsung-han: Jurchen General as Sinologist," *Journal of Sung-Yuan Studies* 26 (1996): 87–89.

55. Igor de Rachewiltz, "Yeh-lü Ch'u-ts'ai (1189–1243): Buddhist Idealist and Confucian Statesman," in Arthur Wright and Denis Twitchett, eds., *Confucian Personalities* (Stanford: Stanford University Press, 1962), pp. 189–216. On the problems of using "sinification" or "sinicization" to describe the civilizing process, see Bol, "Seeking Common Ground: Han Literati under Jurchen Rule," *Harvard Journal of Asiatic Studies* 47, 2 (1987): 535–36. On "Confucianization," see John Dardess, *Conquerors and Confucians: Professional Elites in the Founding of the Ming Dynasty* (Stanford: Stanford University Press, 1973), pp. 2–3. See also Cyril Birch, trans., *Scenes for Mandarins: The Elite Theater of the Ming* (New York: Columbia University Press, 1995), p. 184.

Warrior elites on the steppe and in Korea and Japan contrasted most sharply with the civil official in China, although as the two character ideals came into contact throughout Asia, they began to overlap and share literary and military aspects. Since the T'ang dynasty, selection of bureaucrats by written examination had granted civil officials a literate status unmatched in the world of the warrior, where even popular literacy initially was the prerogative of shaman priests. The amateur ideal of the literatus, who was a member of a classically literate cultural aristocracy, challenged the battlefield prowess of the warrior from a largely illiterate military aristocracy until the warrior himself became socialized by literati standards.[56] After 1100, however, the warrior increasingly threatened the priority of the civil servant in wave after wave of military conquests in north and south China and in Korea and by becoming more and more literate.

First the Khitan and the Tanguts extended control over the northwest heartland of the T'ang and established the Liao and Hsi-hsia dynasties. Subsequently, the Jurchen subdued Liao (with Northern Sung encouragement) and then invaded the Sung in north China and established the Chin dynasty with its capital at Chung-tu 中都 ("Central Capital" at Peking). Thereafter, the Mongols defeated the Jurchen (with Southern Sung help) and extended their military sway over all of south China by 1280, establishing in turn the Yuan dynasty with the capital at Ta-tu 大都 ("Great Capital" at Peking). For an unprecedented span of time, lasting from 1125 to 1368, outsiders militarily enforced their political will on Han Chinese elites and commoners. The cultural, and hence political, dominance of Han Chinese literati was decisively overturned by nomadic warriors, under whom classical literacy alone no longer yielded political power. As we shall see, from the last years of the Southern Sung to the early fourteenth century, there were no civil examinations in China under conquest dynasties, and when there were, they favored the *se-mu* outsiders.[57]

The Khitan Liao dynasty was the first "conquest dynasty" (from the

56. On the aristocracy of culture, see Pierre Bourdieu, *Distinction: A Social Critique of the Judgement of Taste* (Cambridge: Harvard University Press, 1984), pp. 11–96, which derives in part from Joseph Levenson's description of the literati "amateur ideal" in his *Confucian China and Its Modern Fate: A Trilogy* (Berkeley: University of California Press, 1968), I:15–43.

57. For accounts of civil examinations under the Jurchen Chin dynasty, see Ching-shen Tao, "Political Recruitment in the Chin Dynasty," *Journal of the American Oriental Society* 94, 1 (January–March 1974): 24–33, which documents the greater scope of such examinations from 1123 to 1233. For the Hsi-hsia, see Dunnell, *The Great State of White and High*, pp. 27–83.

Han point of view) to inaugurate civil examinations based on Sung models, as the Liao and Chin entries in Appendix 4 reveal. From 977 to 983 the Liao curriculum had stressed T'ang-dynasty-style questions on identifying passages from the Classics (*t'ieh-ching* 帖經), followed by poetry and policy sessions. In 988 the Sung focus on belles lettres in the first session was adopted and a specialty session on law was included by the Liao in session two. Until 1011, however, the scope of the civil examinations was severely restricted, and only one to five *chin-shih* were chosen annually. The need to balance power among the Khitan noble lineages kept the hereditary prerogatives of the warrior elites intact. After 1011 the annual *chin-shih* quotas first increased to 70 to 80 and then to 100, which indicated that the Liao court had begun to incorporate Han Chinese as the largest group of non-tribal officeholders in the Liao's dual political system. Like the T'ang and Sung, the Liao also permitted the *yin* 蔭 privilege of sons succeeding their fathers in office to multiply, thereby restricting the effectiveness of the civil examinations as the route to high office.[58]

In addition, such literary trends carried over to the Korean Koryŏ 高麗 dynasty (918–1392), where, first under the conquering Mongols, civil examinations similarly stressed *shih-fu* rhyme-prose and poetry, and again early in the dynasty. Civil and military *yangban* 兩班 elites there also debated the introduction of the classical essay to the curriculum as long as the dynasty lasted. After 1392 both belles lettres and the classical essay were used in early Yi 李 dynasty (1392–1910) examinations.[59] The Korean aristocracy contrasted sharply with classically illiterate warrior elites in Japan, where civil examinations never penetrated Japanese society, except briefly for literary examinations among the Kyoto aristocracy in Heian times (794–1185) and classical essay examinations for Tokugawa retainers during and after the Kansei reign (1789–1800).[60]

When the Jurchen conquered north China, they initiated civil examinations that were based on both the Liao and Northern Sung curriculum, but they went well beyond the scope of the Liao by selecting 148 to 149

58. *Wu-li t'ung-k'ao*, 175.1a–1b. See also Wittfogel, "Public Office in the Liao Dynasty," pp. 1440. On the effects of the *yin* privilege in the Sung, see Chaffee, *The Thorny Gates of Learning*, pp. 108–13, and Peter Bol's review article "The Sung Examination System and the *Shih*," pp. 149–71.

59. *Koryŏ sa* 高麗史 (History of the Koryŏ dynasty) (Seoul: Yonsei University, 1955), 73.1a–3a. My thanks to John Duncan at UCLA for his information on this aspect of the Koryŏ-Yi dynasty transition in Korean history.

60. See Robert Backus, "The Relationship of Confucianism to the Tokugawa Bakufu as Revealed in the Kansei Educational Reform," *Harvard Journal of Asiatic Studies* 34 (1974): 125–35; and Ikuo Amano, *Education and Examination in Modern Japan*, translated by William K. Cummings and Fumiko Cummings (Tokyo: Tokyo University Press, 1990), chapter 1.

*chin-shih* annually. From 1115 to 1150, the Chin rulers emphasized poetry and rhyme-prose on examinations, but the Sung-dynasty Wang An-shih reforms stressing examination essays were also followed until 1139. After that, the required curriculum was divided geographically, with belles lettres questions the norm in the north, where Jurchen and Chinese competed with each other, and with the classical essay the criterion in the south, where Han Chinese were the vast majority. In 1151, however, the Chin followed educational currents of the Southern Sung and unified the civil examination curriculum, with poetry and rhyme-prose the key to the selection process in the north and south. The triumph of belles lettres lasted only until 1188, however, when the classical essay (*ching-i* 經義) was restored to parity with poetry and rhyme-prose.[61]

By 1180 the Jurchen had also developed their own writing system based on hieroglyphics (*ta-tzu* 大字) and phonetics (*hsiao-tzu* 小字)[62] and were administering policy questions in Jurchen for their military elites. Parallel Jurchen-language examinations, designed for the warrior minority, and classical examinations for the Han Chinese lasted for the remainder of the dynasty. This dualistic practice was accompanied by an extraordinary increase in quotas for *chin-shih*. Tao Ching-shen has documented how the annual average for *chin-shih* under the Chin increased from 59 initially (1123–36) to over 200 (1188–1233) by the end of the dynasty. The latter quota generally exceeded that of the Sung (see Table 1.3), except during the Hui-tsung (1101–1125), Kuang-tsung (1190–94), and Li-tsung (1225–64) reigns. Hereditary selection and protection of Jurchen nobles, however, granted them easier access and greater advancement to high posts than Han Chinese.[63]

Neither the Liao nor the Chin incorporated any aspects of the Tao Learning movement into their civil examinations. For both conquest dynasties and the Sung, belles lettres or the classical essay remained the sine qua non marking the tens of thousands of men, who as literati or warrior nobles jointly competed for places in the bureaucracy and high standing in local society. Han Chinese literati in the north certainly followed the classical trends emerging in the Southern Sung, but the impact

---

61. See *Chin-shih* 金史 (History of the Chin dynasty), compiled by Toghto (T'o T'o) 脱脱 (1314–55) et al. (Peking: Chung-hua Bookstore, 1965), 51.1130; *Wu-li t'ung-k'ao*, 175.1b–9a. See also Hoyt Tillman, "An Overview of Chin History and Institutions," pp. 23–38, and "Confucianism under the Chin and the Impact of Sung Confucian Tao-hsueh," pp. 71–114, both in Tillman and West, eds., *China under Jurchen Rule*; and Bol, "Chao Ping-wen (1159–1232)," pp. 115–44.

62. *Wu-li t'ung-k'ao*, 175.5a–6a; and Winston Lo, "Wan-yen Tsung-han," p. 100n35.

63. Tao, "Political Recruitment in the Chin Dynasty," p. 28. See also Bol, "Seeking Common Ground," pp. 469–79.

of *Tao-hsueh* was still limited to a select group of literati. Most of the *Tao-hsueh* "fellowship," as Hoyt Tillman aptly calls them, were not yet dominant in the south either.[64]

Living in the north under the Chin, distinguished literati such as Chao Ping-wen 趙秉文 (1159–1232) and Yuan Hao-wen 元好問 (1190–1257) continued to stress the cultural values of the Northern Sung, with *wen* and *tao* as their chief categories of intellectual concern.[65] Their literary perspective meant that northern literati had more in common with the belles lettres and ancient-style prose (*ku-wen*) traditions emanating from Northern Sung "men of culture" (*wen-jen* 文人) such as Su Shih than with the transcendental moralism of Ch'eng I and Ch'eng Hao, whose home areas in the northwest fell under first Liao and then Chin control.[66]

Hoyt Tillman has shown that Chin literati were certainly aware of the *Tao-hsueh* fellowship in the south and the increasing Southern Sung popularity of Ch'eng I's metaphysical views, but even if Chao Ping-wen and others were sympathetic with aspects of *Tao-hsueh*, others such as Wang Jo-hsu 王若虛 (1174–1243) still kept their distance from the movement in favor of the cultural pluralism that marked Northern Sung literary concerns.[67] As we shall see, the need for ideological unity in the Southern Sung came later and depended on the wars with the Mongols after 1234, when, during the Li-tsung reign, the *Tao-hsueh* fellowship began its march toward imperial orthodoxy.[68]

### Southern Sung Belles Lettres and Chu Hsi's Attack

Mongol rule in north China from 1234 to 1271 created a dilemma for the Southern Sung. Chin institutions were at times used by the Mongols, but they remained highly suspicious of civil examinations as the way to choose

64. Tillman, *Confucian Discourse and Chu Hsi's Ascendancy*, pp. 2–5.
65. See Bol, "Chao Ping-wen," pp. 115–44.
66. Bol, "Seeking Common Ground," pp. 488–93.
67. Tillman, "Confucianism under the Chin," pp. 71–114. Tillman successfully refutes Yoshikawa Kōjirō's view that Chin literati all followed Su Shih, but he errs by concluding that unlike Yoshikawa "it would be better to focus on the writings of the principal literary giants," than "on the culture of the examination system." See p. 114n9. Yoshikawa had a keen sense of the overlap between T'ang-Sung belles lettres and literati culture. See Yoshikawa 吉川幸次郎, "Shushigaku hokuden zenshi" 朱子學北傳前史 (Early history of the spread north of Chu Hsi studies), in *Uno Tetsuto sensei byakuju shukuga kinen Tōyō gaku ronsō* 于野哲人先生百壽祝賀記念東洋學論叢 (Tokyo: Honoring Committee for Uno Tetsuto, 1974). Cf. Bol, "Seeking Common Ground," pp. 495–511, on "examination learning" under the Chin.
68. Tillman, *Confucian Discourse and Chu Hsi's Ascendancy*, pp. 231–50, presents the years 1202–79 as the fourth phase in the growth of the Tao Learning fellowship. See also Tillman, "Confucianism Under the Chin," p. 111.

officials.[69] The Southern Sung, however, substantially expanded quotas for civil examinations beyond earlier limits. As the dynasty shrank, its numbers of *chin-shih* increased (see Table 1.3), although not dramatically. Using John Chaffee's calculations, for example, more than 19% (7,570) of all Sung *chin-shih* degrees (39,711) were awarded between 1225 and 1279, a period of 54 years that made up 17% of the reign in time. Before 1240, however, more than 35,000 Sung *chin-shih* had never been required to master the views of Ch'eng I or Chu Hsi.[70] They remained masters of *shih-fu* poetry and *ku-wen* prose, which were complemented by classical and historical studies. *Tao-hsueh* penetration of Southern Sung civil examinations did occur, however, in the less important sessions on discourse (*lun* 論) and policy (*ts'e* 策) questions.[71]

In terms of the official curriculum, however, the Southern Sung chronology in Appendix 4 shows how the Southern Sung civil examinations initially swung back to the belles lettres of the T'ang-Sung literary tradition. Then the official pendulum returned to the centrist position in 1143–45, when literary style and classical learning were again balanced against each other for *chin-shih* degrees. The attack on literary examinations, however, was now joined by *Tao-hsueh* literati such as Chu Hsi, who vehemently called for the complete abrogation of poetry and rhyme-prose from all civil examinations. Chu's followers attacked the moral irrelevance of literary measures of literati culture. In the process, *Tao-hsueh* views

69. The Mongols' use of Chin institutions and officials is described in Igor de Rachewiltz, "Personnel and Personalities in North China in the Early Mongol Period," *Journal of the Economic and Social History of the Orient* 9, 1–2 (1966): 88–144. See also Tao Ching-shen, "The Influence of Jurchen Rule on Chinese Political Institutions," *Journal of Asian Studies* 30, 1 (1970): 121–30.

70. Chaffee, *The Thorny Gates of Learning*, pp. 132–33, gives 39,605 total *chin-shih* during the Sung dynasties and presents them by circuit and by overlapping reigns. On pp. 192–95 he presents the annual number of Sung *chin-shih* degrees, which totals 39,711 degrees. I use this latter number. See also Huang Kuang-liang, *Ch'ing-tai k'o-chü chih-tu chih yen-chiu*, pp. 41–51, for his Sung figures of 42,852 total *chin-shih* from the *Ku-chin t'u-shu chi-ch'eng* 古今圖 書集成 (Synthesis of books and illustrations past and present) encyclopedia, 1728 edition, *chüan* 71. A total of 4,335 are facilitated degrees granted during the Li-tsung reign; subtracting those yields 38,517 regular *chin-shih* degrees awarded during the Sung. Although neither Huang (except for the years between 1241–62) nor Chaffee includes facilitated degree-holders (*t'e-tsou-ming chin-shih* 特奏名進士) in their counts of Sung *chin-shih*, because the facilitated degree did not automatically carry with it official status, their figures for *chin-shih* are roughly comparable in aggregate and by reign. See also Table 1.2.

71. For examples of *Tao-hsueh* impact on Southern Sung examinations, see *Ku-chin yuan-liu chih-lun* 古今源流至論 (The best discourse essays past and present), compiled by Lin Chiung 林駉 and Huang Lü-weng 黃履翁, early Ming edition (reprint, Taipei: Hsin-hsing Bookstore, 1970), 2/1–22, 2/115–30.

began to influence the civil curriculum in the 1220s. Such influence peaked in the 1260s, when the required discourse essays increasingly reflected Ch'eng-Chu teachings.[72]

Although Chu's commentaries to the Classics and Four Books were made official between 1211 and 1212 in the curriculum of the Dynastic School for literati and the *Tao-hsueh* founders of the Northern Sung were honored with sacrifices in the official temple honoring Confucius, their views on the examinations were implemented slowly and in piecemeal form.[73] Even when the Li-tsung emperor canonized five *Tao-hsueh* masters in 1241, Chu Hsi's "subtle thought and brilliant analysis" remained a minority voice in the civil examinations themselves. As late as 1264, seven years before the demise of all civil examinations in China until 1314, there were still calls for reforming the curriculum based on the Ch'eng brothers' emphasis on moral behavior and personal cultivation. Further additions of *Tao-hsueh* worthies to the official temple had to wait until 1267. *Tao-hsueh* views were left hanging in symbolic arenas and practiced in the lesser precincts of the large-scale Southern Sung *chin-shih* competitions. The political career of Wang Ying-lin 王應麟 (1223–96), who was castigated for his failure to become a Southern Sung martyr, suggests that the politics of the late Sung were so wracked by factions that in the face of the Mongol wars, the dynasty and its officials were not operating in an intellectual vacuum but in a period of military and political collapse.[74]

Although private views that were never sent to court, Chu Hsi's reform proposals, outlined in Appendix 4 under the Southern Sung chronology, give us a clearer idea of where the *Tao-hsueh* fellowship stood circa 1200 on the issue of classical learning versus belles lettres. Chu Hsi's personal recommendations were not a self-serving set of proposals that exclusively favored the *Tao-hsueh* view of classical learning. Remarkably precise and technical, Chu's views on the subject stressed three areas: (1) increasing quotas for competitive southern regions; (2) recommendation of moral

---

72. *Wu-li t'ung-k'ao*, 174.18b–21b, *Yü-hai* 116.34a–41a, *Hsu wen-hsien t'ung-k'ao* 續文獻通考 (Comprehensive analysis of civil institutions, continuation), compiled by Wang Ch'i 王圻, in *Shih-t'ung* 十通 (Ten comprehensive encyclopedias) (Shanghai: Commercial Press, 1936), 34.3141–45: and *Sung-shih*, 5/3625–29 (*chüan* 卷 156). See De Weerdt, "The Composition of Examination Standards."

73. Richard Davis, in *Wind against the Mountain: The Crisis of Politics and Culture in Thirteenth-Century China* (Cambridge: Harvard University Council on East Asian Studies, 1996), pp. 63–69, notes that the 1,600 students in the Hang-chou Dynastic School did have considerable political influence in the capital, however.

74. Charles B. Langley, "Wang Yinglin (1223–1296): A Study in the Political and Intellectual History of the Demise of the Sung" (Ph.D. diss., Indiana University, East Asian Languages and Cultures, 1980), pp. 273–74. Cf. Tillman, *Confucian Discourse and Chu Hsi's Ascendancy*, pp. 232–33; and Wilson, *Genealogy of the Way*, pp. 42–47.

candidates; and (3) a comprehensive curriculum. His chief concerns were creating regional equity in the selection process, ensuring that virtuous men would be recommended for office, and requiring full mastery of the classical legacy by all literati.[75]

When compared with the literary versus classical swings of the examination curriculum pendulum during the more than two centuries of the Sung dynasties preceding him, however, Chu's recommended curriculum was far from practical. Rather than a *Tao-hsueh* manifesto, his proposals affirmed the entire classical and historical repertoire of texts that had accrued in the literati tradition since antiquity. If this was orthodoxy, it was one that no practical administrator or reigning monarch could have implemented, even if Chu Hsi had submitted them for action. The *Tao-hsueh* persuasion was dissolved into a myriad of canonical texts and commentaries, which would take a cycle of ten to twelve years of examinations to complete. Unafraid to make the Classics as well as their commentaries legitimate objects of individual interpretation, Chu's proposals challenged both literati and the government to make classical studies superior to literary expertise, an agenda that he shared with Wang An-shih.

In Chu's four-part scheme, classical essays were required for three examination fields scheduled on the Five Classics, along with essays on the other classical field later known as the Four Books. Discourse essays on pre-Han (*chu-tzu* 諸子) philosophical fields, and policy essays for the specialty fields of history and policy rounded out the curriculum. This would be the core curriculum. The Five Classics, Four Books, pre-Han masters, Dynastic Histories, and institutional encyclopedias were the foundation of the required reading list. Students would take examinations on the Classics beginning in their first year. Over the course of the next decade, they would prepare to take several additional examinations to complete their studies. Rather than have students simply learn from the *Tao-hsueh* masters of the Northern Sung, Chu recommended that they start by mastering the scholia (*chu-shu* 注疏) tradition derived from Han and T'ang commentaries for the Classics. Han commentators, despite their considerable theoretical flaws, should be the beginning point for classical studies. Sung scholars such as Ou-yang Hsiu, Wang An-shih, Hu Yuan 胡瑗 (993–1059), and the *Tao-hsueh* masters could then be profitably studied.

---

75. Chu Hsi, "Hsueh-hsiao kung-chü ssu-i" 學校貢舉私議 (Personal proposals for schools and civil examinations), in *Chu-tzu ta-ch'üan* 朱子大全 (Complete collection of Master Chu Hsi) (Shanghai: Commercial Press, 1920–22), 69.18a–26a. For the approximate dating of Chu's proposals see *Sung-shih*, 5/3633–34 (*chüan* 卷 156), which places them between 1187 and 1190. See also Daniel Gardner, "Transmitting the Way: Chu Hsi and His Program of Learning," *Harvard Journal of Asiatic Studies* 49, 1 (June 1989): 141–72.

Although Chu's appreciation of ancient classical studies should not be overstated, his ecumenical curriculum gave no hint of the future split between Sung *Tao-hsueh* (known later as Sung Learning, *Sung-hsueh* 宋學) and "Han Learning" (*Han-hsueh* 漢學), which would become more definitive when *Tao-hsueh* became orthodox empirewide in the Yuan and Ming dynasties.[76]

On one point, however, Chu was eminently clear and highly practical: "The reason why poetry and rhyme-prose should be eliminated [from civil examinations] is that they are empty words that were useless to educate people and insufficient to select literati [for office]." In this proposal, Chu Hsi spoke to his followers unequivocally. Belles lettres were anathema for the *Tao-hsueh* fellowship.[77] The slow evolution of the Northern and Southern Sung denigration of poetry also entailed Sung reinterpretations of the great T'ang poets such as Tu Fu 杜甫 (712–70); these moralized their literary achievements and allowed their poetry to remain esteemed for the themes of political loyalty and concern for the plight of the people in them.[78]

During the remainder of the Southern Sung, however, the *chin-shih* degree-holders still trafficked in classical studies or belles lettres. In addition to *Tao-hsueh* penetration of civil examinations in the 1260s, what helped force the shift from belles lettres to classical studies was that the civil examinations themselves, which had balanced poetry/rhyme-prose and the classical essay from 681 to 1271—almost six hundred years—were abrogated between 1237–38 and 1314, unintentionally ceding to literati in local communities the cultural autonomy to decide the fate of their sacred doctrines and teachings outside the precincts of the dynastic rulers.

### Tao-hsueh *and* Civil Examinations *under the* Yuan

Left without imperial support or an examination road to officialdom, Han Chinese literati under the Yuan dynasty did not disappear.[79] Lacking

76. Chu Hsi, "Hsueh-hsiao kung-chü ssu-i," 69.24b–25a. On the reading list for *Tao-hsueh* studies compiled by Ch'eng Tuan-li 程端禮 (1271–1345), who worked in local government schools under the Yuan, see *Ch'eng-shih chia-shu tu-shu fen-nien jih-ch'eng* 程氏家塾讀書分年日程 (Daily and yearly reading schedule in the Cheng clan school), *Pai-pu ts'ung-shu* 百部叢書 edition (reprint, Taipei: I-wen Press), 2.20a–24b, which was remarkably consistent with Chu Hsi's ecumenical curriculum, unlike the Yuan examination curriculum's stress on *Tao-hsueh* orthodoxy.

77. Ch'eng Tuan-li, *Ch'eng-shih chia-shu tu-shu fen-nien jih-ch'eng*, 69.23a.

78. Eva Shan Chou, *Reconsidering Tu Fu: Literary Greatness and Cultural Context* (Cambridge: Cambridge University Press, 1995), pp. 20–27.

79. Bol, "Seeking Common Ground," pp. 520–38.

insider status in a conquest dynasty, many turned to alternative careers in medicine, literature, and art, and, although not the first to pursue such careers, they made them increasingly respectable.[80] The impact of the Yuan unification of north and south China was especially marked in Chinese painting. By overcoming the north-south polarization of regional tastes after 1127, the political unification achieved under the Mongols after 1279 brought about a cultural merger in the flow of artistic themes and ideas in Chinese painting. An intense antiquarianism was provoked in south China when the Northern Sung imperial collection of antiquities was broken up into private collections and became available to literati in the south.[81]

The revival of northern amateur-scholar traditions in calligraphy, painting, and literature competed with *Tao-hsueh* moral philosophy for the attentions of increasingly apolitical Yuan literati. Out of direct dynastic control, for example, both art and literature achieved unprecedented autonomy under Mongol rule. James Cahill has described how Chinese painting "underwent a major revolution, the most decisive in all its history."[82] The demise of the Sung imperial academy of painting meant that imperial power could not dictate taste to literati painters. Scholar-amateur painting during the Yuan superseded the professional artisan-painters in Hang-chou associated with the Painting Academy of the Southern Sung. The varieties of archaism painted by literati painters no longer depended on imperial taste for their popularity. One of the unforeseen benefits of political disenfranchisement under the Mongols was the cultural autonomy of Han Chinese literati and merchant elites.[83]

Similarly, the Mongols and their *se-mu* "outsiders" initially never saw any need for ideological control or used education to channel Han "insiders" into acceptable career paths. Civil examinations were at first feared by warriors as the haven of literate foes and quickly eliminated. Chin advisors prevailed upon the Mongols to treat literati as a privileged group, like Buddhists and Taoists, who should be exempt from labor tax and

80. See Robert Hymes, "Not Quite Gentlemen? Doctors in Sung and Yuan," *Chinese Science* 7 (1986): 11–85; and West, "Mongol Influence on the Development of Northern Drama," pp. 434–65. On the Southern Sung roots of such currents, see Jacques Gernet, *Daily Life in China on the Eve of the Mongol Invasion, 1250–1276* (Stanford: Stanford University Press, 1962), pp. 219–42.

81. Marilyn Wong Fu, "The Impact of the Re-unification: Northern Elements in the Life and Art of Hsien-yu Shu (1257?-1302) and Their Relation to Early Yuan Literati Culture," in Langlois, ed., *China under Mongol Rule*, pp. 371–433.

82. James Cahill, *Hills beyond a River: Chinese Painting of the Yuan Period, 1279–1368* (New York: Weatherhill, 1976), p. 3.

83. See John D. Langlois, Jr., "Introduction," in Langlois, ed., *China under Mongol Rule* (Princeton: Princeton University Press, 1981), pp. 16–17.

physical punishment. The only time before 1313 that examinations were promulgated was in 1237–38, when the Mongols designed a series of localized tests on belles lettres to identify the members of official literati households (*ju-hu* 儒戶). Over 4,000 men passed the examinations, but this only permitted them to establish "literati" households that were exempt from some tax obligations. Few were ever appointed to office.[84]

Under such benign neglect, classical education thrived privately under the Yuan. Academies were created in larger numbers, and Han Chinese lineages intensified their localist activities of the Southern Sung. Lineages such as that of Ch'eng Tuan-li 程端禮 (1271–1345), who worked in local government schools under the Yuan, organized themselves to transmit literati learning and maintain their standing in local communities.[85] In addition, it was still possible for literati households to translate their social status into political influence by becoming government clerks and local education officials. Hsiao Ch'i-ch'ing estimates that clerks represented 85% of all ranked officials during the Yuan. As in the Chin dynasty, the recruitment of literati through the clerical service was a viable alternative to the cessation of the Sung civil examination process. Robert Hymes contends, for example, that the category of literati households reinforced the established status of Han Chinese elites who had served the Southern Sung. Under the Yuan they acted as important intermediaries between the Mongol and *se-mu* outsiders and local Chinese society.[86]

A classical education remained the most respectable route for southern Chinese literati to follow, particularly after 1291 when the Mongols began regulation of local dynastic schools and private academies. Although few educational officials attained prominence during the Yuan, this career

84. On Yuan literati as an elite status group, see Hsiao Ch'i-ch'ing 蕭啟慶, "Yuan-tai te ju-hu—ju-shih ti-wei yen-chin shih-shang te i-chang" 元代的儒戶—儒士地位演進史上的一章 (Yuan dynasty literati households—a chapter in the historical change in status of literati), *Tung-fang wen-hua* 東方文化 16, 1–2 (1978): 151–70.

85. See Ch'eng Tuan-li, *Ch'eng-shih chia-shu tu-shu fen-nien jih-ch'eng;* and John Dardess, "The Cheng Communal Family: Social Organization and Neo-Confucianism in Yuan and Early Ming China," *Harvard Journal of Asiatic Studies* 34 (1974): 7–53. Cf. Hsiao Ch'i-ch'ing, "Yuan-tai te ju-hu—ju-shih ti-wei yen-chin shih-shang te i-chang," pp. 165–67, and Hsiao, "Yuan-tai k'o-chü yü ching-ying liu-tung" 元代科舉與菁英流動 (Yuan dynasty civil examinations and elite mobility), *Han-hsueh yen-chiu* 漢學研究 5, 1 (June 1987): 129–60.

86. Hsiao Ch'i-ch'ing, "Yuan-tai te ju-hu—ju-shih ti-wei yen-chin shih-shang te i-chang," pp. 162–65. Cf. Robert Hymes, "Marriage, Kin Groups, and the Localist Strategy in Sung and Yuan Fu-chou," in Patricia Buckley Ebrey and James L. Watson, eds., *Kinship Organization in Late Imperial China* (Berkeley: University of California Press, 1986), pp. 108–13; and Bol, "Seeking Common Ground," pp. 480–81, 537.

path remained respectable locally through the Sung-Yuan-Ming transition until the late sixteenth century, when Ming dynasty local education officials were displaced by centrally appointed *chin-shih* degree-holders to supervise local and provincial civil examinations (see Chapter 3).[87] Moreover, the popularity of poetry and prose among literati seems to have been intensified by the Yuan suspension of civil examinations. Chao Meng-fu 趙孟頫 (1254–1322), a scion of the Sung imperial line who served the Mongol court after 1276, and other Yuan literati complained that in the absence of civil examinations that had required classical erudition to pass, poetry in particular had become the rage among southern literati.[88] The comments of such southern literati show how far the Ch'eng-Chu fellowship still had to go before Chu Hsi's private guidelines for literati education could be widely accepted or enforced in civil examinations.

The focus on belles lettres during the Yuan, however, concerned Ch'eng-Chu followers. As the Yuan chronology in Appendix 4 reveals, northern *Tao-hsueh* literati in the 1260s were opposed to the reconstitution of civil examinations in the north because they feared that such examinations would again test *shih-fu* poetry and rhyme-prose. The 1237–38 examinations to determine literati households, for example, had tested both the Classics and belles lettres, following Chin dynasty precedents.[89] In 1275 the Ch'eng-Chu scholar Yang Kung-i 楊恭懿 (1225–94) proposed to the Yuan court that the civil examination curriculum should be based on the Classics, replacing the belles lettres of the T'ang and Sung dynasties. Thereafter (as in 1284), Ch'eng-Chu scholars supported on their terms the general literati demand for restoration of civil examinations, but their call was not heeded by the Mongols until 1313, when Mongol rule over south China had been consolidated.[90]

In the absence of examinations in the north after 1238, however, belles lettres slowly but surely lost their institutional hold in the north China

87. Yan-shuan Lao, "Southern Chinese Scholars and Educational Institutions in Early Yuan: Some Preliminary Remarks," in Langlois, ed., *China under Mongol Rule*, pp. 111–12.

88. Yan-shuan Lao, "Southern Chinese Scholars and Educational Institutions in Early Yuan," pp. 108–11. Such poetry was not always social or escapist, however. See, for instance, Stephen West, "Yuan Hao-wen's Poems of Death and Disorder, 1233–1235," in Tillman and West, eds., *China under Jurchen Rule*, pp. 281–303.

89. *Wu-li t'ung-k'ao*, 1229.9b.

90. Ibid. See also Yuan-chu Lam, "On Yuan Examination System: The Role of Northern Ch'eng-Chu Pioneering Scholars," *Journal of Turkish Studies* 9 (1985): 202–03; and Yao Ta-li 姚大力, "Yuan-tai k'o-chü chih-tu te hsing-fei chi ch'i she-hui pei-ching" 元代科舉制度的行廢及其社會背景 (The social background and promulgation of the civil examination system in the Yuan period), *Yuan-shih chi pei-fang min-tsu shih yen-chiu* 元史及北方民族史研究 5 (1982).

bureaucracy and their literati constituency there, leaving the field open to *Tao-hsueh* champions who opposed all literary examinations in the 1260s unless they tested the Ch'eng-Chu version of classical learning. *Tao-hsueh* literati in local society had gained control of the examination debate while the Mongols hesitated to reinstate examinations for fear of the vast Han majority. In effect, the examination system, by its very absence as an institutional bulwark of conservatism favoring belles lettres, had become irrelevant to the battle over its future content. Its reconstitution by the Mongols in 1313 would eventually accommodate their most influential literati constituency of the time, the *Tao-hsueh* fellowship. What Chu Hsi and his followers could not fully accomplish in Sung times, their later disciples achieved under the watchful eye of a Mongol court seeking literati support for its legitimacy. The Yuan dynasty wisely accommodated itself to the shifts in the mainstream of northern and southern *shih* learning.[91]

If we look carefully at the civil examination curriculum actually promulgated for Han Chinese after 1313, however, we can see that even under the Mongols the victory of classical studies and Ch'eng-Chu orthodoxy over the regime of T'ang-Sung belles lettres was still incomplete. The Four Books now clearly stood out in the examination curriculum as canonical texts equal in stature to the Five Classics, a change that Chu Hsi had favored, but the second session of the provincial and metropolitan examinations for Chinese still required the genre of ancient-style rhyme-prose (*ku-fu* 古賦). Candidates were also required to prepare official documents in decree or memorial style. Poetry had been dropped, but literary ability was still tested on examinations between 1314 and 1366.[92]

Even when the Mongols, at the urging of their Han Chinese and Jurchen ministers, finally approved the civil examinations in 1313, after decades of debate and ambivalence,[93] they limited their scope and made sure that quotas for Han Chinese would be balanced by an equal quota for Mongol and *se-mu* candidates. With only 3% of the registered house-

---

91. Yao Ta-li 姚大力, "Chin-mo Yuan-ch'u li-hsueh tsai pei-fang de ch'uan-po" 金末元初理學在北方的傳播 (The transmission of the school of principle in the north during the late Chin and early Yuan), *Yuan-shih lun-ts'ung* 元史論叢 2 (1983).

92. *Wu-li t'ung-k'ao*, 1229.10b–12b. See also the *Hsu wen-hsien t'ung-k'ao*, 34.3150–51, which overstates the claim that T'ang-Sung belles lettres were dropped in the Yuan. See also Stephen West, "Rewriting Text, Inscribing Ideology: The Case of *Zaju* Comedy," paper presented at the Song-Yuan-Ming Transitions Conference (Lake Arrowhead, Calif., June 5–11, 1997), for evidence from Yuan drama that literary criteria remained important in Yuan civil examinations.

93. Dardess, *Conquerors and Confucians*, pp. 35–74.

holds, Mongols and other non-Han candidates occupied 50% of the quota for all degrees until 1366 and 30% of all official positions.[94] Only about 350 *chü-jen* 舉人 (provincial graduate, lit., "raised candidate") degrees were awarded triennially between 1315 and 1366. Moreover, as Table 1.1 shows, only 16 metropolitan examinations were held under the Yuan, and only 1,136 of the highest *chin-shih* degrees were awarded between 1315 and 1368, an average of only 21 per annum.

Under the Jurchen, 45 triennial metropolitan examinations were held between 1123 and 1233 in north China, yielding a total of 16,484 *chin-shih* degrees (see Table 1.2), or 148 to 149 annually, although the Chin rulers used hereditary selection and protection to give Jurchen elites priority over Han Chinese in filling the most important positions in the bureaucracy. During the Northern Sung the average number of *chin-shih* degrees per annum had been 115, and during the Southern Sung 135 *chin-shih* degrees had been awarded annually.[95] Not until the fifteenth century would the scope and magnitude of the civil examinations again approach the levels of the Sung and Chin dynasties.

If we look at the 1333 *Yuan-t'ung yuan-nian chin-shih lu* 元統元年進士錄 (Palace *chin-shih* roll), for instance, we see that the quotas for the 100 *chin-shih* were divided equally among four ethnic groups: (1) Mongols, (2) *se-mu*, (3) Han Chinese in north China, and (4) southerners. The Mongol and *se-mu* candidates answered different and shorter policy questions than did their Han counterparts. The top Mongol *chin-shih*, for example, answered a policy question on classical models for protecting the empire (*pao t'ien-hsia* 保天下), while the top Han Chinese *chin-shih* answered a question calling for a full assessment of the classical forms of imperial power, par-

94. Based on the 1290 Yuan dynasty census, Murakami Masatsugu 村上正二, estimates a total population of one million Mongols and an equal number of *se-mu*, 10 million northern Chinese, and 60 million southern Chinese. See his *Chūgoku no rekishi 6: Yuboku minzoku kokka: Gen* 中國の歷史 6: 游牧民族國家：元 (Chinese history 6: Nomadic tribal nations: The Yuan) (Tokyo: Kodansha, 1977), p. 142. We should add that the census figures show a precipitate drop in north China under Mongol rule. A Chin census of 1195 counted a population of about 50 million in north China alone. The first Mongol census of 1235–36 showed only 8.5 million in the north. Cf. Ho Ping-ti, "An Estimate of Total Population of Sung-Chin China," in Françoise Aubin, ed., *Études Sung en Memorium Etienne Balazs* (Paris, 1970), pp. 3–53; and Hans Bielenstein, "Chinese Historical Demography, A.D. 2–1982," *Bulletin of the Museum of Far Eastern Antiquities* 59 (1967): 85–88.

95. Tao, "Political Recruitment in the Chin Dynasty," pp. 28, 33, gives 193–94 *chin-shih* annually for the Northern Sung and 148–49 for the Southern Sung from 1123 to 1233. His figures are based on averages per examinations from Araki, *Sōdai kakyo seido kenkyū*, pp. 450–61. Tables here are based on available *chin-shih* totals for the entire Sung period.

ticularly those associated with the emperor (*huang-ti* 皇帝) and those associated with kings and hegemons (*wang-pa* 王霸).[96]

For the provincial and metropolitan civil examinations, Mongols and *se-mu* had fewer sessions and answered fewer questions than Han candidates, giving them a further advantage in the limited competition. In the former, there were two sessions in the metropolitan examinations: in the first session, questions were drawn from the Four Books (one essay) and Five Classics (five quotations), with answers based on the Ch'eng-Chu commentaries; in the second, candidates answered a single policy question. As John Dardess has noted, this "scrapped the traditional Sung examination, with its emphasis upon metrical composition."[97]

What Dardess and others failed to recognize, however, is that the same examinations for Han Chinese had three sessions and that metrical composition (called *tz'u-chang* 詞章 *tz'u-fu* 詞賦, or *ku-fu* 古賦, all forms of ancient-style rhyme-prose) was still required on the second session. The heralded Yuan dynasty break with Sung civil examinations, which became a major theme in the early Ming dynasty, then, was incomplete for Han Chinese, for whom T'ang-Sung forms of literary composition remained extremely important.[98]

When we consider that only about 2% of the ranked bureaucracy was chosen from the *chin-shih* graduates, we can see how recommendation and hereditary privilege also confirmed Mongols and *se-mu* in their dominant position at the upper levels of the Mongol government. Significant numbers of Han Chinese literati turned to occupations outside the civil ser-

96. *Yuan-t'ung yuan-nien chin-shih lu* 元統元年進士錄 (1333 palace *chin-shih* roll) (photolithograph reproduction; see Appendix 1), B.1a–11b, gives T'ung T'ung's 同同 policy answer for the palace examination question. B.15a–24b gives Li Ch'i's 李齊 answer as the top southern Han graduate.

97. Dardess, *Conquerors and Confucians*, p. 36.

98. We have records beginning with the 1314 provincial examination and extending to 1366 that on the provincial and metropolitan examinations a prose-poem was required of all Han candidates. The T'ang poetic model known as metrical poetry (*lü-shih* 律詩 was dropped, however. See the *Chiang-hsi hsiang-shih lu* 江西鄉試錄 (Chiang-hsi civil provincial roll): 1314; *Hui-shih lu* 會試錄 (Civil metropolitan roll): 1315, 1317, 1321, 1324, 1327, 1330, 1333; *T'ing-shih chin-shih wen* 廷試進士問 (Civil palace question): 1315, 1318; *Yuan-t'ung yuan-nien chin-shih lu* 元統元年進士錄 (Civil palace *chin-shih* roll): 1333; *Yü-shih ts'e* 御試策 (Civil palace question and answers): 1334; *Hu-kuang hsiang-shih lu* 湖廣鄉試錄 (Hu-kuang civil provincial roll): 1335; *Shan-tung hsiang-shih t'i-ming-chi* 山東鄉試題名記 (Shan-tung civil provincial roll): 1350; *Chin-shih t'i-ming-chi* 進士題名記 (Civil *chin-shih* roll): 1351; *Kuo-tzu-chien kung-shih t'i-ming-chi* 國子監貢士題名記 (Imperial School Civil *chin-shih* roll): 1360, 1366; *Shan-tung hsiang-shih t'i-ming pei-chi* 山東鄉試題名碑記 (Civil provincial roll): 1362.

vice, for example, when faced with alien rule, first under the Jurchen after the fall of the Sung dynasty capital K'ai-feng in 1127, and continuing under the Mongols after 1235, when civil examinations were stopped.[99] The Chiang-hsi literatus Chieh Hsi-ssu 揭傒斯 noted, for example, that "since the civil examinations were abrogated, the sons and brothers of literati engaged either in agriculture, crafts, or commerce."[100] Their reinstatement, he implied, would draw Han Chinese back to government careers, a prospect that frightened many Mongols and se-mu, who as outsiders feared their special privileges over the Chinese would diminish.

In contrast, Mongol warrior elites were preserved fairly intact by employing Muslim and Tibetan outsiders to rule the Han Chinese during the thirteenth and fourteenth centuries, a tactic that directly confronted the millennial civilian ideals of the classically inspired bureaucracy and its use of civil examinations to select literate officials.[101] Later the seventeenth-century Manchu conquering elite, following the lead of their Jurchen predecessors, who had successfully ruled in north China by employing civil examinations for themselves and Han Chinese before the Mongol conquest,[102] quickly adapted to the Han Chinese stress on civil examinations and successfully accommodated the civilian ideal. At the same time they tried vainly to maintain their elite warrior traditions in Manchu, Mongol, and Chinese banners garrisoned throughout the empire. The cultural demise of Manchus in the twentieth century epitomizes the bureaucratic civilizing process and its long-term effects on warrior culture, which began in earnest after the demise of the Northern Sung dynasty and only fully triumphed in the nineteenth century.[103] Such hindsight allows us to better understand the political tensions and rhetorical ambiguities that marked Yuan dynasty debates about restoring civil

99. Dardess, *Conquerors and Confucians*, p. 36; Tillman and West, eds., *China under Jurchen Rule;* and Langlois, ed., *China under Mongol Rule.* See also Frederick Mote, "Confucian Eremitism in the Yuan Period," in Arthur Wright, ed., *The Confucian Persuasion* (Stanford: Stanford University Press, 1960), pp. 202–40; and John Langlois, Jr., "Chinese Culturalism and the Yuan Analogy: Seventeenth-Century Perspectives," *Harvard Journal of Asiatic Studies* 40, 2 (December 1980): 355–98. Similar career patterns for Han gentry later briefly recurred under the Manchus after 1644.

100. See *Chieh Wen-an kung ch'üan-chi* 揭文安公全集 (Complete collection of Chieh Hsi-ssu) (Shanghai: Commercial Press, *Ssu-pu ts'ung-k'an* 四部叢刊, 1920–22), 9.84. Cf. Dardess, *Conquerors and Confucians*, pp. 64–65.

101. Morris Rossabi, "The Muslims in the Early Yuan Dynasty," pp. 258–295; and Herbert Franke, "Tibetans in Yuan China," pp. 296–328, both in Langlois, ed., *China under Mongol Rule.*

102. Tillman, "An Overview of Chin History and Institutions," pp. 23–38.

103. Pamela K. Crossley, *Orphan Warriors: Three Manchu Generations and the End of the Ch'ing World* (Princeton: Princeton University Press, 1990), pp. 13–73.

examinations, a debate that extended from 1237 to 1313, before the examinations were belatedly restarted on a small scale.[104]

It was not, however, until the first Ming provincial and metropolitan examinations, given consecutively in 1370 and 1371, that the T'ang-Sung emphasis on poetry in the examinations finally ended. Included only at the end of the Yuan format above, the Ming session-one curriculum required two classical essays, one a composite essay on the Four Books discussing several quotations, and the other an essay on a quotation from the specialty Classic (*chuan-ching* 專經) that the student had designated. As during the Yuan, Ming classical essays relied on Ch'eng-Chu commentaries for the correct interpretation of the passages cited by the examiners. In sessions two and three, a discourse essay, now dealing with a quotation from the Classic of Filial Piety (*Hsiao ching* 孝經), and a policy answer were required in turn. These written tests were then followed by physical and mental tests of the "five arts" of ancient literati, which the first Ming emperor saw as an antidote to purely bookish learning.[105]

The most fundamental change in literati examination life and the classical curriculum during the Sung-Yuan-Ming transition, then, was the complete elimination of poetry from the civil examination curriculum. That this epochal change was due in part to the influence of Chu Hsi and the *Tao-hsueh* fellowship during the Yuan and Ming dynasties is manifest. Their views had swung the pendulum of dynastic support for the examination curriculum away from T'ang literature and toward the Sung classical essay and *Tao-hsueh* topics on discourse and policy questions. To the Northern Sung reforms of Wang An-shih was added the exclusive focus on the Four Books and Ch'eng-Chu commentaries for a degree of orthodoxy that even Chu Hsi had not advocated.

The complete removal of poetry by the Ming examination bureaucracy lasted from 1370, long after the fall of the Sung, to 1756, when the examination curriculum pendulum swung decisively back to balance the essay with a poetry question again (see Chapter 10). Sung *Tao-hsueh* found more fertile ground for its anti-poetry views under the Mongols and the Ming than under the Sung. But this new examination policy never really hindered the popularity of poetry and literary flair among literati groups during the Ming dynasty, which demonstrates the cultural limits of the classical curriculum in influencing literati intellectual life. The relative

104. *Hsu wen-hsien t'ung-k'ao*, pp. 3150–53. See also *Wu-li t'ung-k'ao*, 175.9b–16b.

105. See *Huang Ming t'ung-chi chi-yao* 皇明通紀集要 (Collection of essentials to the Comprehensive Accounts of the August Ming dynasty), compiled by Ch'en Chien 陳建, and appended by Chiang Hsu-ch'i 江旭奇, late Ming edition (reprint, Taipei: Wen-hai Press), 4.32a.

autonomy of gentry and merchant elites enabled them to use their partnership with the imperial government to contest and limit the full impact of imperial educational policies outside the precincts of the examination halls. Poetry might be banned in the dynasty's "cultural prisons" after 1370, but in spite of—or perhaps because of—that ban, poetry and belles lettres survived as popular genres in private poetry societies. Both were usually included in collections of late imperial literati writings.

## Ming Documentary Tests and Legal Judgments

Anxious to gain the support of Han literati, the first Ming ruler, Chu Yuan-chang 朱元璋 (1328–98), officially acknowledged in 1369 the classical vision whereby "the educational transformation of the people was the prerequisite for the ordering of the nation and...schools were the basis for such transformation." He ordered all prefectures and counties to establish official schools, where, according to the literati ideal, future officials would be trained and provide governance via education (cheng-chiao 政教). Officials would in turn nourish the people's material needs and help them form healthy customs (yang-min ch'eng-su 養民成俗). A year before he ascended the throne in 1368, Chu had already announced his plans to hold civil and military service examinations to recruit officials into his administration. In addition, Chu reestablished the Hanlin Academy and the Imperial School for literati. The message was clear: the civilian literatus would again be actively recruited for public service:

> Those who participate in civil examinations will be scrutinized in light of their words and deeds to observe their virtue. They will be tested on classical techniques to observe their expertise. They will be tested on calligraphy, numerical calculations, horsemanship, and archery to observe their abilities. Then they will be tested on policy questions dealing with the Classics, the Histories, and practical affairs to observe their political acumen. Those who participate in military examinations will first be evaluated according to their knowledge of planning and strategy and then according to their military arts. For both we will seek [those proficient in] practical [matters] at the expense of empty literary [arts].[106]

Fresh from his victories over his rivals in the Yangtzu delta, Chu Yuan-chang had in mind a government under the emperor balanced between a civil and military bureaucracy. During the early reigns of the Ming

---

106. See ibid., 4.32a; and *Huang Ming kung-chü k'ao* 皇明貢舉考 (Survey of civil examinations during the Ming dynasty), compiled by Chang Ch'ao-jui 張朝瑞, Ming Wan-li edition, 1.17b.

dynasty, it was by no means certain that the civil bureaucracy would automatically retake precedence over its military counterpart. Moreover, there was no mention yet of what shape the written content of the civil and military examinations would take. Would the Ming civil examinations, for example, follow the literary focus of Southern Sung and Chin dynasty tests? Or would they continue the Yuan precedent, which adapted the personal recommendations of Chu Hsi, and scrap the Sung balance between metrical composition and classical essays?[107]

According to the Yuan literatus Yü Chi 虞集 (1272–1348), the official recognition granted the Ch'eng-Chu "school of principle" had been one of the dynasty's major accomplishments.[108] Through the intervention particularly of Liu Chi 劉基 (1311–75), who had passed the 1333 Yuan *chin-shih* examination and subsequently became one of Chu Yuan-chang's most trusted advisors, the emperor had chosen Yuan models based on *Tao-hsueh* for testing candidates for office. Until 1380 state-building in Ming China "replicated Yuan institutions with an almost slavish fidelity." In 1370 Chu Yuan-chang, now the Hung-wu emperor (r. 1368–98), announced the commencement of civil examinations to select literati for government service:

> The system for selection of literati for the civil service during the Han, T'ang, and Sung [dynasties], each had its set institutions; however, each gave priority to literary studies and thus failed to select men on the basis of the comprehensiveness of the six arts. Coming to the previous Yuan [dynasty], the establishment of the selection system was based on antiquity to receive superlative literati as influential and powerful officials.... Beginning from the eighth month of the third year of the Hung-wu reign [1370], I have established special civil examinations to select literati who harbor talent and preserve virtue, are resolute in the illumination of the Classics and cultivation of moral behavior, are broad in their knowledge of antiquity and penetrating in its application to today, achieve a balance between form and substance, and whose fame and reality are combined. Those who are selected from among these candidates will then be personally given a policy question from me to answer in the palace so I can observe their knowledge, determine their final rank, and make their official assignment.[109]

107. *Yuan-shih* 元史 (History of the Yuan dynasty) (reprint, 7 vols., Taipei: Ting-wen Press, 1982), 81.2015–12.

108. See Yü Chi, *Tao-yuan hsueh-ku lu* 道園學古錄 (Record of the study of antiquity in the garden of the Way) (Shanghai: Commercial Press, *Kuo-hsueh chi-pen ts'ung-shu* 國學基本叢書, 1929–41), 35.588–89.

109. John Dardess, *Confucianism and Autocracy: Professional Elites in the Founding of the Ming Dynasty* (Berkeley: University of California Press, 1983), p. 195. For Chu's remarks, see *Huang Ming kung-chü k'ao*, 1.18a–b.

Following the Yuan model for the civil and military service, the first Ming emperor reconstituted a selection and appointment process that governed the civilian and military bureaucracy and enabled the imperial dynasty to control its human resources. Chu Yuan-chang's government effectively replaced Mongol rule and established bureaucratic channels that penetrated down to counties and prefectures in the search for classically literate men to enter the elite world of officialdom. In addition, Chu enlarged the local scope of the Sung and Yuan civil examination selection process by instituting county and prefectural licensing examinations (see Chapter 3).[110]

In the regulations and format for the civil examinations, which were appended to Chu Yuan-chang's announcement, it was also made clear that the Ch'eng-Chu school of Tao Learning was required for the proper mastery of the Four Books and Five Classics curriculum. Accordingly, the political, social, and cultural regulations of the civil examination system favored classical norms of governance under post-Yuan historical conditions. The civil service process—its curriculum, forms of testing, and routines for official appointment—made it one of the key institutions that bridged the Mongol era and permitted Southern Sung Tao Learning to make the transition from a regionally based literati movement to a dynastic orthodoxy that flourished even more widely in late imperial China. The early Ming government required mastery of Ch'eng-Chu learning of its dominant social elites.[111] As we have seen, however, not only was the Yuan the model for the Ming, but the Chin had also served as a model for the Yuan. The early Ming link to the Southern Sung examinations was thus mediated through two conquest dynasties.

Tao Learning, called heterodox shortly after its inception, but a widespread literati persuasion by the thirteenth and fourteenth centuries, was declared the Ming orthodoxy.[112] Li T'iao-yuan 李調元 (1734–1803) later contended that the institutional form of the Ming civil examinations was indebted to the Yuan dynasty, not the Sung.[113] Such views cast doubt on the typical view of Sung-Ming continuity. Actual widespread use of the Ch'eng-Chu orthodoxy on civil examinations, consequently, was not a Sung phenomenon but rather a series of Yuan-Ming political and educa-

---

110. *Ming-shih*, 3/1724–25.

111. See *Ch'ang-t'an*, pp. 24–25. See also Abe Takeo, *Gendaishi no kenkyū*, pp. 10–11.

112. See also Conrad Schirokauer, "Neo-Confucians under Attack," pp. 163–96.

113. See Li's preface to his *Chih-i k'o-so chi* 制義科瑣記 (Collection of fragments about the crafted eight-legged essays for civil examinations), *Ts'ung-shu chi-ch'eng ch'u-pien* 叢書集成初編 edition (Shanghai: Commercial Press, 1936), p. 2a. Li argued, less plausibly, that even the eight-legged essay derived from the Yuan and not the classical essays of Wang An-shih's time.

tional events. The Yuan stress on Chu Hsi's works and collected commentaries to prepare examination essays, for example, became the core curriculum for Ming (and Ch'ing) civil examinations.[114]

Provincial and metropolitan examinations during the early Ming mirrored the education administered in dynastic schools. The first high-level Ming civil examinations were in three parts (outlined in the 1370–71 examination format given in Appendix 4). Each session was administered separately, and candidates were initially required to prepare an essay of at least 500 graphs on one of the Five Classics and another of at least 300 graphs on the Four Books (see Chapter 7). Next, a discourse (*lun* 論) of at least 300 graphs based on a text from the Classic of Filial Piety was required, as well as writings in correct documentary style. The Ming *lun* essay initially represented a significant departure from its Sung counterpart, which had been based on quotations from the Classics, Histories, or pre-Han and Sung masters. Later, quotations from Tao Learning were added. The increasing penetration of *Tao-hsueh* themes in *lun* essays during the last years of the Southern Sung eventually was regularized into an official doctrinal orthodoxy in the Ming. Finally, the candidate had to prepare an answer in at least 1,000 graphs to a practical question on an aspect of public policy (*ts'e* 策). Those who passed this stage were tested again in ten days for their physical prowess in horsemanship and archery, and their mental prowess in calligraphy, mathematics, and penal law.[115]

Cultural production of Tao Learning as imperial orthodoxy (e.g., the use of the Four Books and Five Classics as interpreted by Southern Sung literati) and the core examination curriculum dated from the Yuan; its massive reproduction through civil examinations from the Ming. Despite the hiatus in examinations between 1372 and 1384 (see Chapter 2), the epochal break with purely literary examinations and their stress on poetry and belles lettres, which occurred in Ming civil examinations, was accompanied by additional changes in 1384 that incorporated T'ang-Sung traditions in legal studies and Han-T'ang documentary style. The following format list outlines that in session two of Ming and Ch'ing (up to 1757) provincial and metropolitan examinations imperial examiners stressed administrative essay writing of Han imperial patents (*chao* 詔), T'ang imperial proclamations (*kao* 誥), and Sung dynasty style edicts (*piao* 表), which indicates that the turn away from poetry and rhyme-prose was not

114. See *Chih-i ts'ung-hua* 制藝叢話 (Collected comments on the crafting of eight-legged civil examination essays), compiled by Liang Chang-chü 梁章鉅 (1775–1849), 1859 edition (reprint, Taipei: Kuang-wen Bookstore, 1976), 1.5b.

115. *Ming-shih*, 3/1694. See also Liang Chang-chü, *Chih-i k'o-so chi*, 1.5–6.

only promulgated in terms of the *Tao-hsueh* agenda. The *piao* in particular represented a continuation of the Sung dynasty ceremony of gratitude immediately after the civil examinations. Parading at the head of all *chin-shih* graduates, each Ming and Ch'ing *optimus* presented the emperor with a "memorial of gratitude" (*hsieh-piao* 謝表), which was the form the session-two *piao* question usually took, as his first act as an imperial official.[116]

FORMAT OF PROVINCIAL AND METROPOLITAN CIVIL SERVICE
EXAMINATIONS DURING THE MING DYNASTY, 1384–1643

| Session No. | No. of Questions |
| --- | --- |
| ONE | |
| 1. Four Books 四書 | 3 quotations |
| 2. Change 易經 | 4 quotations |
| 3. Documents 書經 | 4 quotations |
| 4. Poetry 詩經 | 4 quotations |
| 5. Annals 春秋 | 4 quotations |
| 6. Rites 禮記 | 4 quotations |
| TWO | |
| 1. Discourse 論 | 1 quotation |
| 2. Documentary style 詔誥表 | 3 documents |
| 3. Judicial terms 判語 | 5 terms |
| THREE | |
| 1. Policy questions 經史時務策 | 5 essays |

NOTE: On session one, all candidates were expected to specialize (*chuan-ching* 專經) on one of the five Classics and write essays for only that Classic. This format lasted until 1756.

Legal essay questions called *p'an* 判 (judgments) had been common during the T'ang and Sung as specialty examinations before the *chin-shih* degree became paramount in the selection process.[117] The degree in law (*ming-fa* 明法) had been one of six different degrees in Sui-T'ang times

116. On these documentary styles, which go back to Sung dynasty polymath examinations (*po-hsueh hung-tz'u* 博學宏詞), see Langley, "Wang Yinglin," pp. 151–79. On *piao*, see Moore, "The Ceremony of Gratitude," who notes that the Sung revised the T'ang ceremony of thanks to focus on the emperor and not the examiners.

117. For examples of T'ang legal essays called *p'an* 判, see *Po Chü-i chi-chien chiao* 白居易集箋校 (Collated notes to the collected writings of Po Chü-i) (Shanghai: Ku-chi Press, 1988), 6/3561–652. For discussion, see P. A. Herbert, *Examine the Honest, Appraise the Able: Contemporary Assessments of Civil Service Selection in Early T'ang China* (Canberra: Australian National University, 1988), pp. 31–34.

that Sung reformers such as Wang An-shih continued to stress in the Northern Sung dynasty, when his followers had attacked belles lettres as the criterion for selection of officials. During the Northern Sung, particularly after 1071, even *chin-shih* could be tested on the dynasty's legal statutes. Such tests of legal expertise had focused on penal laws in two key areas: prescriptive administrative laws and proscriptive penal laws. The penal code itself was the key in such legal examinations. A candidate for office was expected to demonstrate his knowledge of the actual content of statutes and ordinances in the code.[118]

Although the *ming-fa* examination had been abolished in 1102, some revival of legal tests occurred in the Southern Sung.[119] Thereafter, however, the specialty examinations of medieval China were abandoned in favor of *chin-shih* tests balancing classical erudition with literary performance. Consequently, when the judicial terms (*p'an-yü* 判語) were introduced in 1384 provincial and 1385 metropolitan civil examinations, this reform represented a conscious effort to heed the Hung-wu emperor's call for "practical learning" (*shih-hsueh* 實學), which had its precedent in the *ming-fa* examinations of T'ang and Sung. One of the reasons Chu Yuan-chang stopped all examinations in 1372 (see also Chapter 2), for instance, had been his dissatisfaction with the continued literary focus on the 1370–72 examinations he had inaugurated. Chu suddenly suspended all examinations in 1373 because, he claimed, the graduates who took office were not practically trained. In his early 1373 ban, Chu Yuan-chang complained:

> I established the civil examinations to search for worthy men. I tried hard [as I announced] "to get literati whose illumination of the Classics, cultivation of moral behavior, and balance between form and substance" would be the criteria to appoint them to official positions. Today, what the examiners for the most part select are naive and immature youths. In observing their prose and words it appears as if they can be useful, but when they are tried out they cannot carry out the many affairs of government. I have sought out worthy men based on my practical mindedness, and the empire responds to me by presenting me with empty writings. This does not accord

118. See Hsu Tao-lin 徐道鄰, *Chung-kuo fa-chih-shih lun-chi* 中國法制史論集 (Collected essays on China's legal-institutional history) (Taipei: Cheng-chung Bookstore, 1961), pp. 188–217. See also Brian McKnight, "Mandarins as Legal Experts: Professional Learning in Sung China," in de Bary and Chaffee, eds., *Neo-Confucian Education: The Formative Stage*, pp. 493–516. Cf. Chaffee, *The Thorny Gates of Learning in Sung China*, pp. 15, 189.

119. See, for example, *Lu Chiu-yuan chi* 陸九淵集 (Collected writings of Lu Chiu-yuan) (Taipei: Ch'i-hai Press, 1981), pp. 363–65, for Lu Chiu-yuan's policy answers to the 1162 provincial examination, one of which asked candidates what they thought of specialty examinations on law.

with my intent to take responsibility for practical affairs and search for worthy men.

From today all civil examinations will be temporarily stopped. I have separately ordered examiners to observe and select men of worth and talent. The basis for this is to be moral behavior. Literary talent is of secondary importance. When the scholars in the empire are directed to emulate the capable and the virtuous, then the training of literati will return to stress the basics [of moral behavior].[120]

As in the T'ang and Sung, the five terms chosen by examiners after 1384 for candidates to identify and explain in brief essays were chosen from the legal code, which Chu and later Ming emperors wanted all *chü-jen* and *chin-shih* degree-holders to be familiar with. The Ming code had first been compiled in 1373, revised in 1376, and completed in 1389. As early as 1381, Chu Yuan-chang had ordered all students in the dynastic schools to study Ming laws and regulations (*lü-ling* 律令).[121] Thereafter, from 1384 until 1643, all Ming provincial and metropolitan civil examinations included *p'an-yü* as identification questions on session two.[122] This testing regime continued until 1756, when the Ch'ing dynasty decided to abandon legal questions in favor of reviving the metrical poetry requirement of T'ang and Sung (see Chapter 10).

Wada Masahiro has explained the epochal nature of this shift from medieval poetry and belles lettres on T'ang-Sung civil examinations to documentary and legal questions on Ming-Ch'ing tests in light of the increasingly unified call by both literati and emperors for an end to the medieval regime of poetry as the educational measure of the literatus-official. In this decisive shift, both the *Tao-hsueh* fellowship and Ming rulers put together a late imperial examination model that (1) tested the Four Books and Five Classics in light of Ch'eng-Chu moral philosophy, (2) expected candidates to write administrative documents in ancient forms and to master the dynasty's legal code, and (3) required policy essays based on contemporary affairs. Accordingly, the shift away from belles lettres as the measure of the cultural and political style of the scholar-official can be only partially explained by appealing to the long-term influence of Chu Hsi and his Southern Sung followers. The Han tradition of policy questions and the Sui-T'ang-Sung tradition of specialty examinations, both of which preceded the rise of the classical essay, were revived along with Ch'eng-Chu classical learning, and all remained a constant feature of

---

120. *Huang Ming kung-chü k'ao*, 1.19a. See also *Ting-chia cheng-hsin lu* 鼎甲徵信錄 (Record of verified and reliable information concerning the top three candidates for the civil examinations), compiled by Yen Hsiang-hui 閻湘慧, 1864 edition, 1.1a.

121. *Huang Ming kung-chü k'ao*, 1.92a.

122. Wada, "Mindai kakyo seido no kamoku no tokushoku," pp. 271–308.

triennial provincial and metropolitan civil examinations from 1384 until 1757.[123]

Consequently, in the haste to map the complicated road leading to the triumph of the *Tao-hsueh* persuasion during the Sung-Yuan-Ming transition, a triumph that may not have been as total as is often assumed, scholars have usually overstated the demise of *wen* in post-Sung literati discourse and correspondingly overdetermined the centrality of Ch'eng-Chu philosophy in late imperial civil examinations. While *Tao-hsueh* certainly became the centerpiece of official literati discourse after the Yuan dynasty, legal studies and *wen* nevertheless remained extremely important forms of cultural and political expression. The judicial terms requirement initially guaranteed that the Ming legal code would be an important part of the education of an examination candidate. The removal of legal questions in favor of metrical poetry in 1756 suggests that the archaic themes of Han Learning in the eighteenth century, and its efforts "to return to antiquity" (*fu-ku* 復古), were important factors in the conscious decision to undo the examination model worked out in the Yuan and early Ming.

In addition, we know that the ability to compose *wen* remained a clear marker of elite social status during the Ming and Ch'ing dynasties. One has only to think of the centrality in later years of the infamous "eight-legged essay," for which Ch'eng-Chu learning was the required content in a literary exercise testing stylistic form (see Chapter 7), to realize how incomplete the *Tao-hsueh* victory over T'ang-Sung belles lettres really was. Ming-Ch'ing civil examination essays were judged explicitly on their content (principles, i.e., *li* 理) and their form (style, i.e., *wen* 文). And poetry, although no longer the rage it had been in T'ang and Sung times, remained a mark of the "man of culture" (*wen-jen* 文人) into the twentieth century. Unless we can fully appreciate the literati ardor for *wen*, we will never really understand why literary style loomed so large in medieval and late imperial civil examinations.

The narrative of Chinese intellectual history since the Sung has only recently included the political, social, and cultural context within which Sung forms of literati thought, Taoism, Buddhism, and Islam emerged and how these currents interacted with conquest dynasties and non-Han peoples. Since the Sung-Yuan-Ming transition, native accounts stressed the seamless development of triumphant Sung "moral philosophy" (*li-hsueh* 理學, lit. "studies of moral principles"), which unfolded from the Sung to the late empires, tended to overlook Sung China as a venue of

---

123. Ibid. Cf. Wejen Chang, "Legal Education in Ch'ing China," in Elman and Woodside, eds., *Education and Society in Late Imperial China, 1600–1900*, pp. 294–96, 323n7, 325n26, 326n27.

intellectual conflict, cultural tension, social upheaval, and political failure. The Sung instead became the vibrant spring from which late imperial China and its scholastic *Tao-hsueh* orthodoxy emerged empirewide in full force, as discussion of the T'u-mu 土木 incident of 1448–49 below will show.

When framed in philosophical glory, the intellectual history of the Sung dynasty typically underestimated its political and military debacles. Rather than being treated as an account of several historical dynasties competing for cultural legitimacy and political power, Chinese intellectual history from 960 to 1280 was idealized. The Khitan, Tanguts, Jurchen, Mongols, Muslims, and Tibetans were written out of the main plot of this story, appearing only on the margins as bit players in the destiny of the "Middle Kingdom." They were the barbarian outsiders who occasionally ruined the high-minded literati plot, the uncivilized military hordes that extinguished the civilian and cultural glory of the great capitals of K'ai-feng and Hang-chou under the Sung.

What needs to be added is how Sung China became the sacred keeper of the literati flame of doctrinal transmission from Northern to Southern Sung *Tao-hsueh* masters and how that sacred vision was integrated as a cultural and political ideology into the civil examination curriculum during the Sung-Yuan-Ming transition. One clue to the invention of "Sung China" is the Ming civil examination system, which as an institution of unprecedented scope and magnitude emulated the Sung dynasties.[124] The triumph and unfolding of *Tao-hsueh* was intertwined with political struggles over the educational curriculum that ensued during the Sung, Chin, and Yuan dynasties.

## SE-MU "BARBARIANS," HAN "CHINESE," AND SUNG-MING IMPERIAL HISTORIOGRAPHY

With the loss of the Han and T'ang dynasty ancient "homelands" in the northwest and north, first to the Khitan and Jurchen in the eleventh and twelfth centuries, and then to the Mongols in the thirteenth, native Han Chinese living after 1000 expressed through orthodox and heterodox forms of moral theory and practice significant intellectual unease about the outsiders in their midst, whom they considered "barbarians" (*i* 夷).[125]

124. Chaffee, *The Thorny Gates of Learning in Sung China.*

125. Wang Gungwu, "The Rhetoric of a Lesser Empire: Early Sung Relations with Its Neighbors," in Morris Rossabi, ed., *China among Equals: The Middle Kingdom and Its Northern Neighbors, 10th–14th Centuries* (Berkeley: University of California Press, 1983), pp. 47–65.

Of course, neither the category of "insider" nor that of "outsider" was fixed. Both Han "Chinese" and non-Han "barbarians" were mutually dependent terms describing a fluid social and political continuum, particularly in northwest and north China, since the early empire. The reconstruction of fixed identities known as Han versus barbarian by Sung literati and their Yuan successors represented efforts to transcend the social realities of the non-Han outsiders, known collectively as the *se-mu* peoples, in their midst. They grounded their political and cultural discourse in essentialized categories, which we should not accept at face value.[126]

The triumph of Ch'eng-Chu Tao Learning in the Southern Sung, for example, can in part be interpreted in light of this continual unease. During both the Northern and Southern Sung dynasties, the themes of "honoring the ruler" (*tsun-wang* 尊王) and "driving out the barbarians" (*jang-i* 攘夷) were important concepts in Sung interpretations of Confucius' *Spring and Autumn Annals,* one of the Five Classics.[127] Such themes reflected the threats from northern "barbarians" that materialized with the collapse of the Northern Sung and the formation of the Southern Sung. Until the Mongol triumph in 1280, Sung rulers and ministers remained preoccupied with the "barbarian problem." The Southern Sung's 1234 military campaign in Lo-yang, for example, was in part sponsored by Tao Learning luminaries in the Li-tsung court who sought to take advantage of Jurchen weakness in the face of Mongol threats. When repulsed by Mongols, the Southern Sung realized that the dream of recovering the north was unattainable.[128]

In an influential work entitled *Ch'un-ch'iu tsun-wang fa-wei* 春秋尊王發微 (Bringing to light the honoring of the ruler in the *Spring and Autumn Annals*), Sun Fu 孫復 (992–1057), who served in the Northern Sung imperial court, had already compared the barbarian threats confronting the Sung dynasty to the chaos in Warring States (403–221 B.C.) times, and not to the great unifications of Han and T'ang. Just as the contentiousness of the feudal lords had threatened the ancient Chou dynasty (1122?–221 B.C.), so the barbarian threats of the eleventh century threatened the Sung dynasty. What was required, Sun contended, was to strengthen the imperial institution. "Honoring the ruler" was the doctrinal means to unite the empire

126. See Michael Brose, "Uighur Elites in Yuan and Ming: A Case of Negotiated Identity," paper presented at the Song-Yuan-Ming Transitions Conference (Lake Arrowhead, Calif., June 5–11, 1997).

127. On the uses of the *Annals* in classical discourse, see my *Classicism, Politics, and Kinship*, pp. 147–85.

128. Charles Peterson, "Old Illusions and New Realities: Sung Foreign Policy, 1217–1234," in Rossabi, ed., *China among Equals*, pp. 229–30.

and bring an end to internal divisiveness. In addition, Sun Fu called for "driving out the barbarians."[129]

Sung literati saw in the *Annals* principles for behavior that governed relations with barbarian dynasties. The stability of the Northern Sung dynasty depended on successful relations with the Khitan and Jurchen tribes that encroached on the north China plain, but Sun Fu and his followers took a hard line. They called instead for military action to attack the intruding "barbarians" and defend the dynasty. Themes of "imperial majesty" (*wei* 威) that would overawe foreigners were now stressed. Chinese forms of dynastic loyalty, sometimes mislabeled as Sung "proto-nationalism," became a rallying point for anti-barbarian sentiments. Chinese culturalism (the appeal to literati culture rather than particularistic appeals to the dynasty) did not automatically restrict the development of such forms of nativist identity in the imperial dynasty. The tensions between what was Han and what was barbarian during the Sung dynasties permitted interesting forms of nativism, with the *Annals* providing a convenient locus classicus for the articulation of such sentiments.[130]

In addition to Sun Fu, Hu An-kuo 胡安國 (1074–1138), also a Northern Sung imperial courtesan, composed an important commentary to the *Annals* that carried further Sun Fu's themes of "honoring the ruler and driving out the barbarians." Such views became slogans of the hard-liners on the "barbarian question," who tried to rally support around the Sung emperor and then move to retake lands in north China already lost to the Khitan Liao and Jurchen Chin dynasties. Like Sun Fu, Hu An-kuo thought that the plight of the Sung dynasty resulted from failure to obey the values encoded in the *Annals*. After the Spring and Autumn period, according to Hu, Chinese and barbarians had culturally mingled to the detriment of both. Hu An-kuo and others called for "revenge" (*fu-chiu* 復仇) against the "barbarians" after the fall of all of north China to the Jurchen in the twelfth century.[131] Clearly, he did not dare compare the Sung to the Han or T'ang dynasties.

---

129. Sun Fu, *Ch'un-ch'iu tsun-wang fa-wei*, in *T'ung-chih-t'ang ching-chieh* 通志堂經解 (T'ung-chih Hall's exegesis of the Classics), 1676 edition (reprint, Taipei), 1.1a–2a, 1.13a–b, 1.16a–b, 2.3b, 12.8a–b. For discussion, see Mou Jun-sun 牟潤孫, "Liang-Sung Ch'un-ch'iu-hsueh chih chu-liu shang" 兩宋春秋學之主流上 (Main currents in studies of the *Annals* during the two Sung dynasties, part 1), *Ta-lu tsa-chih* 大陸雜志 5, 4 (August 1952): 113–15.

130. Rolf Trauzettel, "Sung Patriotism as a First Step toward Chinese Nationalism," in John Haeger, ed., *Crisis and Prosperity in Sung China* (Tucson: University of Arizona Press, 1978), pp. 199–213.

131. On Hu An-kuo's commentary, see Mou Jun-sun, "Liang Sung Ch'un-ch'iu-hsueh chih chu-liu hsia," 兩宋春秋學之主流下 (Main currents in studies of the *Annals* during the two Sung dynasties, part 2), *Ta-lu tsa-chih* 大陸雜志 5, 5 (September 1952): 170–72. See also

Hu's nativist reading of the *Annals* was influential enough to inspire in the young Lu Chiu-yuan 陸九淵 (Hsiang-shan 象山 [1139–92]), later Chu Hsi's main intellectual antagonist, the resolve at age sixteen to become a soldier and help drive the barbarians out of the Chinese heartland in the north. Classical scholarship and Han nativism were interwoven to form an anti-barbarian political position, which proved unsuccessful in the long run. For many Southern Sung literati, such as Ch'en Liang 陳亮 (1143–94), the need to drive the Jurchen from northern China and restore it to native rule became a political obsession. Ch'en Liang's patriotism invoked Confucius and the latter's *Annals* as the proper "way of civilized people" (*jen-tao* 人道), in contrast to the barbarians, who violated Chinese norms of ritual, social, and ethical behavior.[132] Ch'en Liang's sense of national peril led him to enunciate in particularistic terms the lessons Confucius had encoded in the *Annals*. According to Chen's reading, Chinese and barbarians had separate Ways, which should not be mixed. Ch'en attributed the decline of the Chou to its failure to keep barbarians out of the Chinese heartland, a failure he also saw in the Sung.[133]

Hu An-kuo's commentary to the *Annals* became so prominent after the fall of the Sung dynasty that during the Yuan, when the civil examinations were restored in 1313, and under the Ming, when Chinese Han rule was restored in 1368, it was formally known as one of the "four commentaries," standing on a par with the more ancient "three commentaries" (*Tso* 左, *Kung-yang* 公羊, and *Ku-liang* 穀梁), dating from the Han dynasties. Imperial authority was perceived by leading literati as the key to

---

Sung Ting-tsung 宋鼎宗, "Sung-ju Ch'un-ch'iu jang-i shuo" 宋儒春秋攘夷説 (The theory of repelling the barbarians in the Spring and Autumn Annals among Sung literati), *Ch'eng-kung ta-hsueh hsueh-pao* 成功大學學報 18 (March 1983): 7–20, On Hu An-kuo's commentary, see John D. Langlois, Jr., "Law, Statecraft, and *The Spring and Autumn Annals* in Yuan Political Thought," in Hok-lam Chan and Wm. Theodore de Bary, eds., *Yuan Thought: Chinese Thought and Religion under the Mongols* (New York: Columbia University Press, 1982), pp. 124–25; and Schirokauer, "Neo-Confucians under Attack," pp. 165–66.

132. For discussion, see Ch'en Ch'ing-hsin 陳慶新, "Sung-ju Ch'un-ch'iu tsun-wang yao-i te fa-wei yü ch'i cheng-chih ssu-hsiang" 宋儒春秋遵王要義的發微與其政治思想 (Propagation of the key meaning to honor the ruler in the Spring and Autumn Annals by Sung literati and their political thought), *Hsin-ya hsueh-pao* 新亞學報 1A (Dec. 1971): 269–368. Cf. Hoyt Tillman, *Utilitarian Confucianism: Ch'en Liang's Challenge to Chu Hsi* (Cambridge: Harvard University Council on East Asian Studies, 1982), pp. 31, 108, 166–67; and Tillman, "Proto-Nationalism in Twelfth-Century China? The Case of Ch'en Liang," *Harvard Journal of Asiatic Studies* 39, 2 (December 1979): 403, 423.

133. Ch'en Liang, *Lung-ch'uan wen-chi* 龍川文集 (Collected essays of Ch'en Liang), *Ssu-pu pei-yao* 四部備要 edition (Shanghai: Chung-hua Bookstore, 1927–35), 4.5b–6b. See also Tillman, "Proto-Nationalism in Twelfth-Century China?," pp. 410–11.

maintain domestic solidarity and repel external threats. Such nativist versus barbarian issues carried over to the development of a notion of "legitimate succession" (*cheng-t'ung* 正統) during the Northern Sung, which shifted the criteria of legitimate succession from theories of yin-yang and the
five evolutive phases, which Former Han literati had used in their political
cosmology, to issues of moral legitimacy and political unification.

Ou-yang Hsiu and Chu Hsi formulated a theory of legitimate succession that eventually became a prominent historiographical principle for
the writing and interpretation of Chinese history under conquest dynasties. Ou-yang Hsiu's official histories of the T'ang dynasty and the Five
Dynasties period left him sensitive to the ambiguities of writing on periods
when political legitimacy was contested. Rather than using the evolving
configurations of the five phases to determine legitimate succession, Ou-
yang measured degrees of political unification as the key determinant of
legitimacy. His single political criterion provided a fixed, universal historiographical guideline for evaluating changes in dynasties, which allowed
Ou-yang to elaborate on the theme of "magnifying universal rule" (*ta i-
t'ung* 大一統).[134]

These views were allegedly completed by Chu Hsi in the late-twelfth-
century *Tzu-chih t'ung-chien kang-mu* 資治通鑑綱目 (Outline of the Comprehensive Mirror for Aid in Government; actually Chu Hsi only prepared
the guidelines for this condensation—see Chapter 9), which eventually
became a textbook of political ethics. Although Chu Hsi thought the
theme of kingship in the *Annals* was more important than the issue of relations with barbarians, nevertheless he admitted that the *Annals* favored
keeping China and the barbarians in separate inner and outer zones. In
contrast to Ch'en Liang, however, Chu Hsi distinguished between restoring north China to Sung control and long-term revenge against the barbarians. Dynastic unity was thus a more important reason for dealing with
the barbarian menace for Chu Hsi than the particularistic emotions that
the issue evoked for Ch'en Liang and others.

Chu Hsi's guidelines were based on chronicles completed in 1084 and
entitled *Comprehensive Mirror for Aid in Government*, in which Ssu-ma Kuang
had used Confucius' *Annals* as a model to cover historically the period
from the Eastern Chou (when the *Annals* left off) to the Five Dynasties
(907–959). They were later amplified, classifying the imperial regimes of
the Chinese past as either legitimate or illegitimate. Ssu-ma Kuang had

134. Richard L. Davis, "Historiography as Politics in Yang Wei-chen's 'Polemic on
Legitimate Succession,'" *T'oung Pao* 69, 1–3 (1983): 33–39. See also Hok-lam Chan,
"Chinese Official Historiography at the Yuan Court: The Composition of the Liao, Chin,
and Sung Histories," in Langlois, ed., *China under Mongol Rule*, pp. 68–71.

refused to do so, indicating that Chu Hsi was responding to political pressures in the thirteenth century that were very different from those of the eleventh.[135] The contrasting ideals of Northern Sung notions of political legitimacy (*chih-t'ung* 治統, lit., "legitimate transmission of governance") and Southern Sung views of cultural legitimacy (*tao-t'ung* 道統, lit. "legitimate succession of the Way"; see Chapter 2) reveal that political and dynastic forms of succession were stressed in the former while moral *cum* cultural succession was emphasized in the latter.[136]

Issues of legitimate succession continued unabated during the Mongol Yuan dynasty, when "Han nativism" was replaced by "Sung loyalism." Literati scholars charged by the Yuan court to compile dynastic histories of the earlier Liao, Chin, and Sung dynasties became embroiled in heated discussions over the legitimacy of these dynasties. All emperors, whether theirs was a native or a conquest dynasty, compiled the records of their predecessors to justify their own legitimacy. Consequently, dynastic historiography remained a politically charged vocation, particularly when outsiders were the rulers. To interpret the past (Sung, Liao, Chin) was to affirm the present (Yuan). Conquest emperors thus employed native scholars to write them into Chinese history.

Efforts by literati under Mongol rule to formulate acceptable principles for legitimate dynastic succession, such as from Sung to Yuan, were further complicated by the fact that the Liao and Chin were each alien conquerors, while Yuan rulers, sponsors of the history projects, were also of foreign origin and had destroyed a legitimate Han Chinese dynasty, the Southern Sung. For Han Chinese, it was imperative to defend the legitimacy of the Sung, even in the face of Mongol pressure to grant the Liao and Chin dynasties legitimacy in classical historiography. For its part, the Yuan government refused to accede to Chinese scholar-official demands that the Sung be accorded primacy simply because it was a native Chinese dynasty. Debate was so intense that the writing of official histories was paralyzed, and the Yuan History Bureau became little more than a storehouse for documents.

135. See Ssu-ma Kuang's preface to the *Tzu-chih t'ung-chien* 資治通鑑 (Comprehensive mirror for aid in government) (Taipei: Hung-shih Press, 1980, 11 vols.), 1/33–34; and Hoklam Chan, *Theories of Legitimacy in Imperial China* (Seattle: University of Washington Press, 1982), p. 69. Cf. Davis, "Historiography as Politics," pp. 40–42. See also Robert Hartwell, "Historical-Analogism, Public Policy, and Social Science in Eleventh- and Twelfth-Century China," *American Historical Review* 76, 3 (June 1971): 690–95.

136. See Ellen Neskar, "The Cult of Confucian Worthies" (Ph.D. diss., Columbia University, East Asian Languages and Cultures, 1994), pp. 303, 332.

Yang Wei-chen 楊維楨 (1296–1370), in his "Polemic on Legitimate Succession" (*Cheng-t'ung p'ien* 正統篇), composed sixty years after Sung rule had been eliminated, reveals that political legitimacy for the pre-Yuan period was very much in dispute during the Yuan. Yang Wei-chen was an ardent spokesman for traditional literati values and defender of the imperial historiographical tradition. Yang's dilemma centered around his efforts to demonstrate that Northern Sung legitimacy had been transmitted to the Southern Sung and then to the Yuan. This scheme bypassed the Liao and Chin as legitimate dynasties. Yang connected philosophical orthodoxy to political legitimacy through the *Tao-hsueh* concept of *tao-t'ung*, which had earlier been employed by Chu Hsi and his Northern Sung predecessors to affirm the true transmission of literati values from the time of Confucius and Mencius to the Sung dynasty.

From this angle, China's spiritual center, and thus its political values, had followed the Northern Sung court south when the north fell to the Jurchen in 1126. Although Yang Wei-chen accepted the Yuan as a legitimate, not an alien, dynasty, his flagrant display of Han nativism led the Yuan court to ban Yang's essay because of its disparaging remarks about the Khitan and Jurchen "barbarians." Such ethnic bias aroused the court's suspicion that he was implicitly criticizing the Mongols as well.[137]

When the Ming dynasty succeeded the Yuan, however, its rulers declined any political accommodation with the Mongols and their nomadic neighbors, a policy that lasted from 1368 until 1570. As Chapter 2 details, Ming literati, following the lead of Yang Wei-chen and others, successfully unified the themes of Northern Sung political continuity (*chih-t'ung* 治統) and Southern Sung cultural transmission (*tao-t'ung* 道統) to herald the sagely *Tao-hsueh* qualities of early Ming emperors. Ming ministers invariably saw in accommodationist tendencies, which included possible diplomatic and commercial relations, one of the reasons for the fall of the Sung to the steppe barbarians. As a result of its more narrow-minded defensive and punitive measures, the Ming faced continual threats from its Mongol neighbors on the steppe. During its first century of rule, for example, the "perennial problem of the Mongol menace" became so acute for the Ming that its literati advisors misperceived in all warning signs from the steppe the possibility for a repeat reconquest of China by the Mongols.[138]

137. Hok-lam Chan, *Theories of Legitimacy in Imperial China*, pp. 71–88; and Davis, "Historiography as Politics," pp. 45–51.

138. Henry Serruys, *Sino-Mongol Relations during the Ming*, in *Mélanges chinois et bouddhiques*, vol. 1, *The Mongols in China during the Hung-wu Period, 1368–1398* (Brussels: Institut Belge des Hautes Études Chinoises 1959), and vol. 2, *The Tribute System and the Diplomatic Missions* (1967), p. 8. Cf. Barfield, *The Perilous Frontier*, pp. 229–50.

The infamous T'u-mu 土木 debacle of 1448–49, for instance, began when the Oirats, who had reunified Western Mongol forces north of the rebuilt Great Wall, captured the reigning Cheng-t'ung emperor (r. 1436–49) after he led a Ming military campaign against them. In the climactic battle, the Ming army lost half of its army of over 500,000 soldiers. Rather than capitulate to the ensuing Oirat extortionist demands for ransom or move the capital from Peking back to Nan-ching (Nanking 南京), the Ming court under the leadership of Yü Ch'ien 于謙 (1398–1457) and others chose to replace the captured emperor with his younger brother, who was then enthroned as the Ching-t'ai emperor (r. 1450–1456) and led the successful defense of Peking. The proposal to retreat to the south reminded Ming officials too much of the disastrous experiences of the Southern Sung when it had moved its capital from K'ai-feng to Hang-chou.[139]

The crisis continued when the Cheng-t'ung emperor, a worthless hostage by then, was returned by the Oirats in 1450. After several years as a prince he retook the throne in 1457 as the T'ien-shun emperor (r. 1457–64) during the coup d'état of 1457 in which Yü Ch'ien and other officials, who had sacrificed their emperor in 1449, were accused of treason and executed. After 1457 the Ming pulled its army back from the Inner Mongolian steppe, and what eventually was the Great Wall became in the sixteenth century the only immediate barrier separating the capital Peking from Mongol tribes.[140] And in the 1460s, the Ming court gave up naval expeditions to Southeast Asia and the Indian Ocean, which had been especially prominent from 1403 to 1434, in favor of a strictly coastal navy. The T'ien-shun emperor, who as the Cheng-t'ung emperor had already suppressed the great "Treasure Ships" of the Ming navy before his capture by the Oirats, maintained a military vigil on his northern borders after returning to power. In 1474 only 140 warships of the 400 ships in the main fleet remained. Thereafter, all seagoing ships of more than two masts were scrapped and used as lumber, while the court attended to military campaigns against the Mongols and rebellious southeastern tribes.

139. See Philip de Heer, *The Care-Taker Emperor: Aspects of the Imperial Institution in Fifteenth-Century China as Reflected in the Political History of the Reign of Chu Ch'i-yü* (Leiden: E.J. Brill, 1986); and Frederick W. Mote, "The T'u-mu Incident of 1449," in Frank Kierman, Jr., and John Fairbank, eds., *Chinese Ways in Warfare* (Cambridge: Harvard University Press, 1974), pp. 243–72. Cf. L. Carrington Goodrich et al., *Dictionary of Ming Biography* (New York: Columbia University Press, 1976), p. 1609; and Johnston, *Cultural Realism*, pp. 195–97.

140. Arthur Waldron, *The Great Wall of China: From History to Myth* (Cambridge: Cambridge University Press, 1990), pp. 79–86, notes how the Yung-lo emperor had begun to withdraw Ming forces from steppe garrisons as early as 1403–10.

This northern border focus on steppe defenses lasted until the mid-six-teenth century, when the Wo-k'ou 倭寇 pirate menace loomed in the Yangtzu delta and the southeast.[141] Ku Yen-wu 顧炎武 (1613–82) would later note that this strategic retreat of the Ming military from the steppe after the loss at T'u-mu cost the dynasty strategic garrisons that earlier had served as an outer defensive barrier. Frederick Mote has noted that even Wang Fu-chih's 王夫之 (1619–92) dark, perhaps racist fulminations against barbarian rule after the Manchu quest, which he made a major part of his work entitled *Huang-shu* 黃書 (Yellow book), reveal the mark of a strident anti-foreignism among Chinese literati dating from the early Ming dynasty.[142]

The T'u-mu crisis and the dilemmas it provoked marked a turning point in Ming history that elicited a wave of intense anti-Mongol senti-ment among Ming Han Chinese.[143] Literati scholars after 1449 discarded the relatively benign portrait of the Yuan painted by the Ming founding emperors, whose Chin-hua advisors had freely adapted Yuan institutions to their immediate needs. Early Ming wholesale adoption of the Yuan civil examination curriculum, for instance, has been seen as evidence of Yuan-Ming continuity.[144] The anti-Mongol tone in the fifteenth-century

141. On the Ming fleets and their forays into the Indian Ocean, see Joseph Needham, *Science and Civilisation in China* (Cambridge: Cambridge University Press, 1954–), vol. 4, part 3, pp. 477–553. On Ming relations with Southeast Asia, see Wang Gungwu, *Community and Nation: China, Southeast Asia and Australia* (St. Leonards, Australia: Allen and Unwin, 1992), pp. 77–146. See also Lo Jung-pang, "The Decline of the Early Ming Navy," *Oriens Extremus* 5, 2 (1958): 147–68.

142. Mote, "The T'u-mu Incident of 1449," pp. 267–72. See also Frederick Mote and Denis Twitchett, eds., *The Cambridge History of China*, vol. 7, part 1, *The Ming Dynasty, 1368–1644* (Cambridge: Cambridge University Press, 1988), pp. 316–340, 376–402, 466–79, 490–505. See Wang Fu-chih's study of Sung dynasty rulers entitled *Sung-lun* 宋論 (Discus-sions of the Sung) (Shanghai: Chung-hua Bookstore, *Ssu-pu pei-yao* 四部備要, 1927–35), 8.5a–9a, in which he contended that barbarian outsiders were not entitled to rule the Central Kingdom. Cf. Arthur Hummel et al., *Eminent Chinese of the Ch'ing Period* (reprint, Taipei: Ch'eng-wen Bookstore, 1972), pp. 817–18. On the early sixteenth-century threats from the steppe that the Ming faced, see Waldron, *The Great Wall of China*, pp. 122–39.

143. On the T'u-mu debacle as a turning point, see Meng Sen 孟森, *Ming-tai shih* 明代史 (History of the Ming period) (Taipei: Chung-hua ts'ung-shu wei-yuan-hui, 1967), p. 133. See also Waldron, *The Great Wall of China*, pp. 91–107, who links the early building of stone border walls to this period. For discussion of Ming strategic choices, see Johnston, *Cultural Realism*, pp. 184–85, 234–35, and passim.

144. John Dardess, "Ming T'ai-tsu on the Yuan: An Autocrat's Assessment of the Mongol Dynasty," *Bulletin of Sung and Yuan Studies* 14 (1978): 6–11, shows that Chu Yuan-chang did not deny legitimacy to his Mongol predecessors. See also Dardess' *Confucianism and Autocracy*, pp. 194–95.

calls for renewed Ming efforts to rewrite the history of the Sung dynasty and grant it legitimacy over the Liao and Chin was inspired by the T'u-mu debacle. Indeed, the famous cult of the Southern Sung general Yueh Fei 岳飛 (1103–41) as the model military leader who had opposed the alien Jurchen invasions was inaugurated officially by the Ming just after the T'u-mu debacle.[145]

The strong anti-Mongol bias of Ming historiography in the early sixteenth century exemplified a cultural response to the humiliations visited on the Ming court by the Oirat wars. Thereafter, many Ming scholars no longer granted political legitimacy to the alien Yuan dynasty either. In the late fifteenth century, the historian Wang Chu 王洙 (fl. ca. 1521), for example, completed an influential work entitled *Sung-shih chih* 宋史質 (Verified history of the Sung Dynasty), in which he refuted the legitimacy of the Mongol rulers by placing the Ming line in direct succession to the Sung house. Accounts of the Liao and Chin were relegated to the "monographs on foreign countries." Other Ming literati such as K'o Wei-ch'i 柯維騏 (1497–1574) and Wang Wei-chien 王惟儉 (fl. ca. 1595) reasserted the supremacy of Han Chinese rule over all alien conquerors in China's past. "Sung loyalism" was reconfigured into Ming "Han nativism."[146] The superiority of "Sung China" was reinvented by the Ming after the T'u-mu debacle.[147]

One example of this ahistorical narrative was the view that the late imperial civil service examinations were, in content, simply a tribute to Sung moral philosophy and political discourse. Past accounts of the triumph and unfolding of Ch'eng-Chu orthodoxy, beginning in the North-

145. Li Tse-fen 李則芬, *Yuan-shih hsin-chiang* 元史新講 (New lectures on Yuan history), 5 vols. (Taipei: Chung-hua Bookstore, 1978); and Hok-lam Chan, "Chinese Official Historiography at the Yuan Court," pp. 96–97. Cf. Mote, "The T'u-mu Incident of 1449," p. 271. On the formation of the Yueh Fei cult, see James T. C. Liu, "Yueh Fei (1103–1141) and China's Heritage of Loyalty," *Journal of Asian Studies* 31 (1972): 291–97; and Hellmut Wilhelm, "From Myth to Myth: The Case of Yueh Fei's Biography," in Twitchett and Wright, eds., *Confucian Personalities*, pp. 146–61.

146. Hok-lam Chan, "Chinese Official Historiography at the Yuan Court," pp. 95–105. Post-Manchu accounts of conquest dynasties such as the Yuan and Ch'ing, written by Republican historians since the May Fourth Movement, have added modern layers of anti-foreign interpretation to the Ming invention of "Sung China" as "China" since the T'u-mu Incident.

147. Langlois, "Chinese Culturalism and the Yuan Analogy," pp. 355–97, describes how the Sung victory over the Yuan on the battlefield of literati culture was analogized to the Manchu Ch'ing dynasty by seventeenth-century Han Chinese elites after the fall of the Ming in 1644 to a second wave of barbarians. Culturalism, the universality and continuity of Chinese culture, permitted Han accommodation with the Manchus, if the latter honored the symbolic supremacy of the Sung Tao Learning orthodoxy.

ern Sung, wrongly assumed that the Yuan and Ming appropriation of Tao Learning as orthodox moral philosophy simply continued Sung dynasty intellectual and cultural trends, which unfolded for the remainder of the imperial era.[148] As we have seen, however, the civil examination curriculum continually changed, and those changes reflected the interests of both the imperial government and its literati elites.

The early Ming appropriation of Ch'eng-Chu orthodoxy for civil examinations from the local to the provincial and national levels affected how Sung *Tao-hsueh* would be politically interpreted and socially used. The triumph of a single-minded Ch'eng-Chu orthodoxy empirewide, which was only partially defined in Sung China but never became official until the Yuan, was principally a Ming dynasty construction.

## ANALYSIS OF *CHIN-SHIH* DEGREES FROM THE SUNG TO THE MING

It is worth reiterating that there were no civil examinations in north China between 1238 and 1314, and none were held in south China from 1274 to 1314. Between 1315 and 1400 only 2,179 *chin-shih* degrees were awarded, an average of only 34 per year. Most high positions in the bureaucracy from 1279 to 1450 were filled by recommendation or other similar means.[149] In addition, Mongols and other non-Han candidates occupied 50% of the *chü-jen* and *chin-shih* quotas from 1314 to 1366, even though they made up only about 3% of all registered households.[150]

Table 1.2 reveals, for instance, that the average number of *chin-shih* dropped from 124 a year during the Sung dynasties, when approximately 39,711 such degrees were awarded, to 13 annually under the Yuan, when only a total of 1136 *chin-shih* degrees were given out. Until 1450, the Ming dynasty annually granted only 31 to 76 *chin-shih*, and it was not until the period beginning 1451–1505 that about 100 such degrees were annually awarded. For the entire Ming period, 24,594 *chin-shih* degrees were granted over 276 years (89 annually), about 37% fewer than were awarded during the Sung. For the period of 960–1904, when an approximate total of 108,672 *chin-shih* degrees were presented, the Sung accounted for 36% of that total, the Yuan only 1%, and the Ming 23%. What should be espe-

148. See de Bary, ed., *The Unfolding of Neo-Confucianism.* On the Mongol role, see de Bary's *Neo-Confucian Orthodoxy and the Learning of the Mind-and-Heart,* pp. 38–60.

149. See Rafe de Crespigny, "The Recruitment System of the Imperial Bureaucracy of Later Han," *Chung Chi Journal* 6, 1 (November 1966): 71, on *fang-cheng* 方正 (sincere and upright) candidates recommended for office since the Han, a pattern of selection that persisted in the middle and late empires.

150. John W. Dardess, *Conquerors and Confucians,* pp. 64–69, 161–62.

cially noted, however, is that a conquest dynasty, the Chin, granted some 16,484 *chin-shih* degrees (15% of the total), or 149 annually, a degree-granting rate that exceeded even the Sung. In this part of China from 1115 to 1234, there was no official Tao Learning orthodoxy at all. Poetry and prose based on T'ang models were the rage in the north, as they were in the south (see below). *Tao-hsueh* remained an important literati persuasion during this time, however, and its champions actively successfully promoted their fellowship in local society.[151]

A Tao Learning imperial orthodoxy, although symbolically important in 1240 and 1313, and although more pervasive in civil examination questions administered in southern departments beginning under the Li-tsung emperor (r. 1225–64), when 16% of all Sung *chin-shih* degrees (32% of Southern Sung *chin-shih* degrees) were awarded (see Table 1.3), did not yet achieve empirewide influence as a monocular ideology outside the imperial schools, private academies, or Hang-chou capital region examinations until 1450, when the ratios of candidates to graduates for *chin-shih* degrees again began to approach the high levels of the Sung and Chin dynasties. The diffuse *Tao-hsueh* penetration of civil examinations in the waning years of the Southern Sung, while growing, was not yet a single-minded orthodoxy.[152] If we look closely at the added information in Tables 1.3–1.5, we can see that between 1064 and 1125, usually over 150 *chin-shih* degrees were granted annually. This pace continued in the Southern Sung, especially from 1163 to 1265, which included an increase in *chin-shih* quotas to 164 annually during the Li-tsung reign. It was not unusual during the Southern Sung to award 500 or more *chin-shih* degrees at a single metropolitan civil examination, something that never happened during either the Ming or the Ch'ing.

*Chin-shih* quotas dropped precipitously during the Yuan, when the maximum number of *chin-shih* diminished to 100 for each metropolitan examination. Because that quota was rarely met (only in 1333 were there 100 *chin-shih;* see Table 1.4), the Yuan annual average was just 13 *chin-shih*. From 1315 to 1368, when examinations were held, there were only 21 per year, a drop of 83% from average Sung quotas, and a drop of 87% from late Sung quotas. Moreover, those who held *chin-shih* degrees under the Mongols after 1315 usually held only local posts in county administration or judicial matters.[153]

---

151. Bol, "Seeking Common Ground," pp. 461–538.

152. De Weerdt, "The Composition of Examination Standards," documents the increased influence of Tao Learning on the discourse (*lun* 論) and policy questions (*ts'e* 策) during the Southern Sung. See also *Ku-chin yuan-liu chih-lun*, passim.

153. Yang Shu-fan 楊樹藩, "Yuan-tai k'o-chü chih-tu" 元代科舉制度 (The Yuan civil service examination system), *Sung-shih yen-chiu chi* 宋史研究集 14 (1983): 210–16.

During the early Ming from 1370 to 1402, *chin-shih* quotas remained at the low level of the Yuan dynasty. Despite an increase to 84 annual *chin-shih* during the Yung-lo reign, not until 1465 did the annual quota reach 100, where it stayed for the remainder of the dynasty. During the first century of the Ming, only 44 *chin-shih* were granted per year. For the next two centuries, the quota more than doubled to 109 annually. This rate, which was about the same during the Ch'ing dynasty, was still well below the Chin quota of 149 and the Sung quota of 124. Between 1271 and 1465, for almost two centuries, the Sung-Yuan-Ming bureaucracy was not reproduced by civil examinations. Recommendation, purchase, and other special means were used to appoint local, provincial, and metropolitan officials. During this transition of two hundred years, a Ch'eng-Chu orthodoxy was still not the sine qua non for official status, although literati were increasingly sympathetic to its teachings in the Li-tsung reign, when between 1241 and 1262 over 7,700 *chin-shih* degrees overall were awarded, 3,479 of them regular *chin-shih* degrees and more than 50% of them facilitated degrees (*t'e-tsou* 特奏).

To the analysis of the wider scope and greater magnitude of Sung and Chin dynasty literary civil examinations, when compared with the smaller-scale but more Ch'eng-Chu–oriented curriculum of the Yuan and early Ming, we can add inverse evidence from the documented numbers of private academies (*shu-yuan* 書院) during the Sung and Ming dynasties (see Table 1.6). Based on the estimates of Sung historians, there were at least 56 to 73 such academies during the Northern Sung, and about 260 to 317 of them during the Southern Sung, with another 108 to 125 Sung academies whose origins are unclear. The total of between 425 and 515 Sung academies, however, is far fewer in toto than during the Ming, when, depending on the source, some 926 to 1,962 were created and maintained.[154] The range of the per year index for academies during the Southern Sung was 1.64–2.07. The overall Sung index of between 1.33–1.61 was at least doubled in the Yuan, when 320 to 406 academies probably were in existence, and perhaps even quintupled in the Ming, particularly during the sixteenth century. The estimates for the number of late Ch'ing dynasty private or semi-official academies are usually three per

154. See John Chaffee, "Chu Hsi and the Revival of the White Deer Grotto Academy, 1179–81," *T'oung Pao* 71 (1985): 46–47; and Linda Walton-Vargo, "Education, Social Change, and Neo-Confucianism in Sung-Yuan China: Academies and the Local Elite in Ming Prefecture (Ningpo)" (Ph.D. diss., University of Pennsylvania, History, 1978), pp. 244–245; and Tillman, *Confucian Discourse and Chu Hsi's Ascendancy*, p. 110. On the difficulties in obtaining figures for Sung academies, see Pai Hsin-liang 白新良, *Chung-kuo ku-tai shu-yuan fa-chan shih* 中國古代書院發展史 (History of academy development in ancient China) (T'ien-chin: T'ien-chin University Press, 1995), pp. 271–73.

county. With 1,350 counties in late imperial times, that would mean there were approximately 3,000 in mid-Ch'ing and 4,000 to 4,365 academies in the last centuries of the Ch'ing period, two to four times that of the Ming and eight to ten times that of the Sung.[155]

No one has yet demonstrated that most Sung academies, even during the Southern Sung, were part of the Tao Learning fellowship that Hoyt Tillman has carefully studied. If we accept Tillman's generous estimate that 10% of the 63 to 71 million Sung Chinese he counts were Han literati, it remains clear that in the absence of an empirewide and highly competitive Tao Learning–based civil examination selection process before 1450, those literati with clear loyalties to *Tao-hsueh* were a vocal but elite fellowship in a sea of six to seven million gentry-landlords with multifaceted literati, Taoist, and Buddhist interests and concerns. Certainly, as Hilde De Weerdt shows, *Tao-hsueh* was penetrating less important sessions of the Southern Sung civil examinations, but it was not yet a dynastic orthodoxy required of all officials.[156] By way of contrast, most Ming and Ch'ing academies were completely or partially oriented toward Ch'eng-Chu learning because of the civil examination curriculum.

After 1202, as Neskar and De Weerdt demonstrate, the *Tao-hsueh* fellowship increased in numbers, and public commemorations of Chu Hsi multiplied, before Sung China succumbed first to the Jurchen and then to Mongols.[157] The evidence studied to date, however, indicates that Ch'eng-Chu moral philosophy was not as pervasive empirewide during the Southern Sung as it would become during the Ming and Ch'ing. Making Chu Hsi's commentaries orthodox in Southern Sung imperial schools, where enrollments were limited, influenced but did not yet transform an educational environment in which the required literary curriculum of Southern Sung civil examinations in the dynastic schools continued to stress T'ang-style poetry and prose. When *Tao-hsueh* penetrated the less important discourse and policy questions in civil examinations after 1260, the examiners' impact in a declining dynasty was not empirewide.[158]

155. See also Chung-li Chang, *The Income of the Chinese Gentry* (Seattle: University of Washington Press, 1962), pp. 105–06. Before the nineteenth century there were likely only two academies per county. Pai Hsin-liang in his *Chung-kuo ku-tai shu-yuan fa-chan shih*, pp. 271–73, gives 4,365 for the number of Ch'ing academies, but many were formed in the nineteenth century. See Table 1.6.

156. De Weerdt, "The Composition of Examination Standards."

157. See also De Weerdt, "Aspects of Song Intellectual Life," pp. 1–27; and Neskar, "The Cult of Confucian Worthies," chapters 7–8.

158. See Ihara Hiroshi 井原弘, "Chūgoku chishikijin no kisō shakai—Sōdai Onshū Yōka gakuha o rei to shite" 中國知識人の基層社會—宋代溫州永嘉學派を例として (The social basis of Chinese intellectuals: The Sung dynasty Wen-chou and Yung-chia scholarly traditions as examples), *Shisō* 思想 802 (April 1991): 82–103.

Some 50,000 Ming-Ch'ing *chin-shih* mastered the Ch'eng-Chu orthodoxy, not to mention the millions of candidates for local, provincial, and metropolitan civil examinations. How many of the 39,000 Sung and 16,500 Chin dynasty *chin-shih* mastered Ch'eng I's or Chu Hsi's philosophy is debatable.[159] Not a majority, since over 30,000 Sung *chin-shih* degrees were awarded before the Li-tsung reign, when after 1240 *Tao-hsueh* questions increasingly penetrated Southern Sung civil examinations. In addition, Chu Hsi's own private recommendations for a model curriculum (see above) did not advocate his views as examination orthodoxy. Lu Chiu-yuan, for instance, in policy questions he prepared while director in 1182 of the Dynastic School (*Kuo-tzu-chien* 國子監; also called *T'ai-hsueh*, "Imperial Academy") for literati, gave no hint of his role in the evolution of *Tao-hsueh*. In one question that focused on the problem of heterodoxy (*i-tuan chih shuo* 異端之說), Lu simply pointed to the moral superiority of the literati values taught by Confucius in antiquity and the dangers of Buddhism since the T'ang dynasty.[160] The same holds for candidates for Chin and pre-1240 Sung prefectural qualifying examinations. Most, as Bol and others have shown, were also masters of *wen* 文, the poetic and prose styles that marked a man of letters before the Yuan dynasty, not simply champions of *Tao-hsueh* orthodoxy.[161]

By the 1250s, however, the penetration of Ch'eng-Chu themes was more manifest. In the famous 1256 palace examination, for instance, both the imperial question by Emperor Li-tsung and the 10,000-character answer composed by the *optimus* Wen T'ien-hsiang 文天祥 (1236–83) focused in part on the *Tao-hsueh* metaphysical notions of the "Ultimate-less" (*wu-chi* 無極) and "Great Ultimate" (*t'ai-chi* 太極), which had set in motion the natural processes of yin-yang and the five phases. Wen's rambling essay on the "unity of the *tao* in heavenly and human affairs" has been read by succeeding generations as the last testament of a stout Sung loyalist who later chose starvation and death rather than serve the victorious Mongols after Hang-chou fell.[162] It should also be read as an example of the penetration of *Tao-hsueh* themes in late Sung civil examinations.

159. Wada Masahiro 和田正廣, "Mindai kyojinzō no keisei katei ni kan suru ichi kō satsu" 明代舉人層の形成過程にする 一考察 (A study of the formative process of the *chü-jen* class in the Ming dynasty), *Shigaku zasshi* 宋學雜志 83.3 (March 1978): 36–71.

160. See *Lu Chiu-yuan chi*, pp. 287–98 (*chüan* 卷 24).

161. In addition to Bol's *"This Culture of Ours"*, pp. 148–211, see also Ronald C. Egan, *Word, Image, and Deed in the Life of Su Shi* (Cambridge: Harvard University Council on East Asian Studies, Harvard-Yenching Institute Monograph Series 39, 1994), pp. 169–351.

162. See both the emperor's question and Wen's policy answer in the 1522 edition of the *Pao-yu ssu-nien teng-k'o-lu* 寶祐四年登科録 (1256 palace examination *chin-shih* roll), pp. 1a–7a, 104a–129b.

Until the Ming, then, there was no widespread official orthodoxy that emphasized Ch'eng-Chu Learning. Moreover, the civil examinations between 1250 and 1450 did not recruit adequate numbers of candidates and thus could not produce an official *Tao-hsueh*-oriented elite until the fifteenth century. The *chin-shih* totals we have examined support both of these conclusions.

## FINAL COMMENTS

In a declining Sung dynasty surrounded by powerful barbarian enemies, the civil examinations performed different political, social, and cultural functions from those during the rise of the Ming imperium, which successfully drove the Mongols and their allies out of south and north China. In summary, a cultural apotheosis of millennial proportions began in the twelfth and thirteenth centuries, when a vocal number of Han literati lost faith in imperial politics and increasingly turned to social and cultural initiatives for local solutions in a time of warfare and dynastic decline.[163] As the boundaries of the Northern and Southern Sung dynasties diminished, as the capital was moved first from T'ang Lo-yang (in the northwest corridor) to Sung K'ai-feng (on the northern plain) in 960 and then to the seaport town of Hang-chou (in the southern heartland) in 1127, Sung literati, in search of higher moral ground, retreated conceptually from politics to culture in tandem with their army's retreats on the battlefields and the vast Han migrations from north to south China.[164] The changes in the classical curriculum and scope of civil examinations traced above were part of this millennial shift.

Appeals to political activism diminished. Sung irredentism, which political realists and *Tao-hsueh* idealists had agreed upon after the loss of the north to the Jurchen, eventually was replaced by purely cultural appeals and moral visions that transcended the failures on the battlefield. The epochal turn from the literary concerns of *wen* 文 to the metaphysical focus on the Way (*tao* 道), which Peter Bol has described for the literati during the T'ang-Sung transition,[165] became more poignant in the thir-

163. Hymes and Schirokauer, eds., *Ordering the World*, passim. See also James T. C. Liu, "How Did a Neo-Confucian School Become the State Orthodoxy?," pp. 483–505; and Tillman, *Confucian Discourse and Chu Hsi's Ascendancy*, passim.

164. John W. Haeger, "1126–27: Political Crisis and the Integrity of Culture," pp. 143–60; Schirokauer, "Neo-Confucians under Attack," pp. 163–96; Charles Peterson, "First Sung Reactions to the Mongol Invasion of the North, 1211–17," pp. 215–51, all in John Haeger, ed., *Crisis and Prosperity in Sung China* (Tucson: University of Arizona Press, 1975). See also Hartwell, "Demographic, Political, and Social Transformations of China," pp. 365–442.

165. Bol, *"This Culture of Ours."*

teenth century as Southern Sung literati retraced the embattled steps of Confucius at Kuang: "When under siege in K'uang, the Master said, 'With King Wen dead, is not culture (*wen*) invested here in me? If heaven intends culture to be destroyed, those who come after me will not be able to have any part of it. If heaven does not intend this culture to be destroyed, then what can the men of K'uang do to me.'"[166]

Military and political defeats during the thirteenth century at the hands of outsiders whom the Sung Chinese considered barbarians were transmogrified by later Yuan and Ming literati, particularly after the Yung-lo usurpation (see Chapter 2) and the T'u-mu debacle (see above), into a moral and cultural victory on the plane of classical morality and heavenly *Tao-hsueh* visions of the highest truths. Early in the thirteenth century, the teachings of Chu Hsi had been rescued by his loyal followers from political charges of cultural heterodoxy and moral deception. Literati in the Southern Sung court had feared the growing influence of what seemed to them a strange group of self-righteous literati with no practical experience.[167]

Slowly but surely the views of Chu Hsi, coupled with the teachings of Ch'eng I to form a formidable theoretical vision, became a cultural front behind which the faltering Southern Sung appealed to its spiritual superiority in the wake of barbarian invasions. But a monocular *Tao-hsueh* imperial ideology had not yet been constructed. Moral victory was plucked from the jaws of military defeat by turning that cultural front into a fortress of local literati after the Sung dynasty had been defeated.[168] Even before their defeat by the Mongols, for example, many Southern Sung literati had lived to see the Jurchen support T'ang and Sung styles of classicism and viewed with alarm how the Mongols gained literati support in north China by also championing the views of Chu Hsi. Symbolic compensation paid to the Han Chinese literati insiders seemed a small price for the outsiders to pay for political legitimacy. This "triumph" was then commemorated where it mattered most, among literati themselves and in the reproduction of classical orthodoxy in civil examinations based on Southern Sung transcendental truths.

If the Mongol warrior became civilized by literati standards, the Han Chinese literatus who served him drew on the social consequences of the conquest to put into practice Sung societal ideals that had never been

---

166. *Lun-yü yin-te* 論語引得 (Concordance to the Analects) (reprint, Taipei: Chinese Materials and Research Aids Service Center, 1966), 16/9/5; D. C. Lau, trans., *Confucius: The Analects* (Harmondsworth: Penguin Books, 1979), p. 96.

167. Schirokauer, "Neo-Confucians under Attack," pp. 163–96.

168. Tillman, *Confucian Discourse and Chu Hsi's Ascendancy*, pp. 231–263; and Wilson, *Genealogy of the Way*, pp. 35–47.

widespread under Sung rulers. Bettine Birge has shown, for example, how the Mongol military conquest of Southern Sung China made levirate marriage acceptable among even Han Chinese after the Sung legal code was officially abrogated in 1271. The social consequences of extending levirate marriage to all people, made legal by the direct order of Khubilai Khan (r. 1264–94), unintentionally yielded a literati reaction led by *Tao-hsueh* scholars in government positions dealing with legal cases, which transformed Chinese marriage and property laws during the thirteenth and fourteenth centuries. The Mongol era thus made a decisive cultural difference in social relations and educational curriculum.[169]

These complicated processes of give and take, influence and reaction, are usually adumbrated in light of the concepts of "Confucianization" and "sinification," but the cultural ambivalences for "Chinese" in a "barbarian" political world, and for Jurchen and Mongols in a "Han Chinese" social world, were not so easily resolved or set aside. The civilizing process cut both ways, and Chinese had to stare military defeat in the face and experience its tragedies firsthand before they could envision cultural triumph under the rule of their enemies. Meanwhile, the victorious outsiders willingly endured the cutting edges of classical literacy and bureaucracy in their quest to become legitimate rulers of the vast and wealthy Chinese empire. Each side learned to make a virtue out of necessity.[170]

Such ambivalences were especially poignant when warrior societies such as the Mongols and later the Manchus accepted a monocular version of the heralded *Tao-hsueh* persuasion of their defeated Sung and Ming Chinese foes to legitimate their own rule over the empire.[171] Debates over what should be taught and how literati values should be defined and practiced under native and conquest dynasties indicate that the late empire of Ming and Ch'ing was for Han Chinese a period of emotional turmoil. In light of their own intellectual debates over the threat of barbarian warrior culture, whether Khitan, Tangut, Jurchen, Mongol, or Manchu, to the millennial integrity of Han Chinese values and civilized forms and institutions, literati eventually came to terms with the lessons of the demise of the Sung dynasty. Their dynasty could be conquered from without by force of arms, but their culture could endure and triumph in the end as political forms and cultural symbols.[172] Civil examinations were one aspect

169. Birge, *Holding Her Own: Women, Property and Confucian Reaction in Sung and Yuan China (960–1368)* (Cambridge: Cambridge University Press, 1997).

170. Bol, "Seeking Common Ground," pp. 534–538; and Birge, *Holding Her Own,* show the difficulties in viewing Sung-Chin-Yuan cultural change simply as processes of "Confucianization" and "sinification."

171. Hok-lam Chan, *Theories of Legitimacy in Imperial China.*

172. Langlois, "Chinese Culturalism and the Yuan Analogy," pp. 355–98.

of this single-minded triumph, which Khitan, Tanguts, Jurchen, Mongols, and Manchus adopted sooner or later to draw expert Chinese into their governments and to make their own warriors more suitable for political offices.

Lurking within the classical debate and criticism of Sung *Tao-hsueh* in later times lay the dangerous political stratum of anti-barbarian feeling. At the same time, however, outsiders became insiders whenever Han literati accepted Jurchen, Mongols, and Manchus as legitimate emperors ruling over the dynasty. The affinity of the conqueror for the government and its military raison d'être was balanced by the literatus and his ties to local society and its local Han civilization. In a complicated process, the Khitan, Tangut, Jurchen, Mongol, and Manchu warrior became civilized enough to gain the political legitimacy that only the literati historian in the civil bureaucracy could grant.[173]

Behind the literati facade of cultural omniscience (voiced through elite education and the cut-throat competition for success on the civil service examinations after 1450) lurked a deep-seated realization that the very continuity of Han Chinese culture had been threatened in the post-Sung empires. Behind the veil of political arrogance (expressed by the dragon throne and its mandarins) lurked a disquieting sense that Han Chinese often served a hostile barbarian dynastic family that had co-opted classical discourse as its own but attempted to minimize the full implications of the Han civilizing process by granting their military elites special status outside the bureaucratic civil system.

Consequently, memorization as a mental technology to internalize exactly the required classical curriculum tested in examinations was a heroic, cultural act of great meaning for Han Chinese insiders and the warrior outsiders who became insiders (see Chapter 5). As in early modern Europe, where stress on order and conformity ensured that rote learning (e.g., the catechism) played a fundamental role in the educational process, late imperial dynastic educators prized orthodoxy and the rote reception of that orthodoxy by insiders and outsiders alike. Repetition as a habit of learning was the key to developing the memory as a pedagogic tool to produce uniformity by education.[174] The inculcation of classical literacy confirmed Han Chinese preeminence over the warrior in the precincts of the bureaucracy and on the higher ground of political ideology and moral truth. As long as their military power was not threatened by such social and political dynamics, the Khitan, Tangut, Jurchen, Mongol, and Man-

---

173. Hok-lam Chan, "Chinese Official Historiography at the Yuan Court."

174. R. A. Houston, *Literacy in Early Modern Europe: Culture and Education, 1500–1800* (New York: Longman, 1988), pp. 56–58.

chu warrior elites begrudgingly granted Han literati the ideological space that guaranteed their complicity in the conquest dynasty. A monocular version of Ch'eng-Chu Tao Learning best filled that ideological space for three dynasties, under the Mongol Yuan, Chinese Ming, and Manchu Ch'ing, from 1315 to 1905.

As Chapter 10 clarifies, even the Oboi Regents, who represented the Manchu conquering elite in its truest warrior colors, backed down from their efforts in the early 1660s to denigrate the Four Books and Five Classics in civil examinations when Han Chinese challenged such curricular reforms.[175] Rulers, officials, and examiners generally believed or, as we shall see in the next chapter, became convinced that the pious recital of the Four Books and Five Classics by Han Chinese students represented an act of faith in literati moral values and submission to imperial sovereignty. Inculcation of the classical language to instill a model set of ideas and facts by mastering verbatim canonical ancient texts in effect promised an acceptable mind-set that was structured by classical attitudes, concepts, and beliefs.

Jurchen, Mongols, and Manchus seeking political legitimacy and Ming Chinese searching for cultural superiority could find common ground in a "classical memory" as the educational source for reproduction of classical ideals and political loyalty. Such ideals of cultural control were impossible to realize fully. In the realm of public rhetoric, however, before such doctrines could be subverted in practice, even those who privately disparaged and resisted such goals of hegemony had to voice agreement with the doctrines of the Tao Learning orthodoxy to gain official office. The political construction of Ming dynastic power was indelibly tied to efforts to reinvent empirewide a Ming vision of the Sung and Yuan civil examination regime.

175. Robert Oxnam, *Ruling from Horseback: Manchu Politics in the Oboi Regency* (Chicago: University of Chicago Press, 1975), pp. 84–89.

CHAPTER TWO

# Imperial Power, Cultural Politics,
# and Civil Examinations
# in the Early Ming

In an imperial government balanced since the early empire between an emperor and his bureaucracy, the interests of the dynasty were never uniformly decided in favor of the ruler or his officials. Nor was there ever an essentialized "state" that merely served the whims of the emperor and his court without any resistance from the bureaucracy and the scholar-officials who served there. Given the asymmetrical overlap between imperial interests and literati values, each dynasty defined itself in terms of a partnership between the ruler and his gentry-officials in the bureaucracy. This dynamic partnership made Chinese political culture vital and adaptive. In the first reigns of the Ming, however, the balance of power between the ruler and his bureaucracy tilted briefly in favor of the ruler and altered the peaceful story of the traditional contest between imperial interests and literati ideals.[1]

Early Ming rulers enforced policies of terror that curtailed the executive branches of the bureaucracy and for a time between 1380 and 1402 carried out bloody political purges that made it seem to many literati contemporaries as if emperors were at last all-powerful in government. Ming "autocracy," as it has since been called, was not the end of the partnership between state and society, however. It is curious, for example, that simultaneous with the growth of the Ming court's power over the bureaucracy after 1380, literati were still able to prevail on early Ming emperors

---

1. The late imperial Chinese government was in important ways separate (that is, semi-autonomous) from the gentry-officials who filled its bureaucratic precincts. The ruling house maintained its private pedigrees for a royal aristocracy whose interests were at times asymmetrical with the class-based interests of gentry elites. Especially during conquest dynasties, court interests serving the aristocratic elite did not always correlate exactly with the interests of bureaucratic or local elites.

to enhance the role of Ch'eng-Chu Tao Learning in government. Some have interpreted this enhancement of *Tao-hsueh* simply as the political legitimation of Ming autocracy by literati at court. But why choose Ch'eng-Chu learning then? Legitimation is only part of the story, and we would do well to remember that Ming emperors still needed their officials to rule effectively and used the civil examinations to choose them. Hence, even in the early Ming the tenuous partnership between the ruler and his bureaucracy was never severed, despite misgivings on both sides. Ming rulers made the values and ideas of their gentry elites the sacred doctrines of the dynasty because, in part, that is what Ming elites themselves believed.[2]

How and why Sung dynasty Ch'eng-Chu doctrine became imperial orthodoxy in late imperial China is a complicated historical question. In raising this question, this chapter moves from the timeless integrity of educational and philosophic positions to the political, social, and economic contingency of ideas in particular historical contexts. How ideas inform and authorize action is a question that carries us outside the scholarly domain of "pure" philosophy and the traditional history of ideas. Instead of interrogating ideas in "texts" for their universal "meaning," cultural historians decipher the particular "contexts" of those whose actions were informed and served by references to those ideas. In the contemporary turn from the "history of ideas" to "cultural history," our role as intellectual historians adds to our study of the ideals of philosophy their historical uses.

The Tao Learning orthodoxy in court politics and elite society has been evaluated by intellectual historians in light of its sophisticated and multidimensional set of metaphysical doctrines and moral teachings, which emerged during the Sung dynasties and were systematized by Chu Hsi, arguably the greatest philosopher in Chinese history. For the cultural historian, however, the Ch'eng-Chu school of Tao Learning also had its political uses as a dynastic ideology. Sung Tao Learning philosophy and imperial politics, as we have seen, became dubious partners during the Mongol Yuan dynasty, when the classical interpretations of Ch'eng I and Chu Hsi were made the orthodox guidelines for the imperial examination system belatedly resumed in 1314.

During the first Ming reign, however, the reproduction of the bureaucracy per se was not premised on the mastery of Tao Learning moral philosophy, although *Tao-hsueh* was still orthodox in the 1370–71 civil

---

2. For differing views, which we will try to reconcile, see F. W. Mote, "The Growth of Chinese Despotism," *Oriens Extremus* 8, 1 (Aug. 1961): 1–41; and de Bary, *Neo-Confucian Orthodoxy and the Learning of the Mind-and-Heart*, pp. 158–68.

examinations. Chu Yuan-chang, the first Ming ruler, feared its Mencian political message and held the civil examinations in check until 1384. But besides its still-limited educational function as an examination curriculum, the Ch'eng-Chu persuasion provided the cultural language of imperial power for emperors such as Chu Yuan-chang, Chu Ti 朱棣 (1360–1424), and their successors, who all claimed the mantle of the sage-kings for themselves. They each repossessed the "orthodox transmission of the Tao" (*tao-t'ung* 道統), and thus reestablished their "political legitimacy" (*chih-t'ung* 治統, lit., "legitimate transmission of governance") in the eyes of their cherished literati.[3]

Tseng Ch'i 曾棨 (1372–1432), the *optimus* for the 1404 palace examination, for instance, began the tradition in examination essays of referring to Ming emperors in Tao Learning terms:

> Your humble servant recognizes that the emperor's mind is the mind of the Yellow Emperor, Yao, and Shun. Those sages before and after have all had this mind. The Paramount Ancestor [i.e., Chu Yuan-chang], as sage and worthy, [wisely] wielded both civil and military power. The exalted Ming was set in motion, and its great virtue was accomplished. He was the esteemed ruler who unified heaven and magnified filial piety and thereby exemplified in reality this mind-heart. That is why your majesty has felicitously followed the intentions of the people and spoken of their affairs. How can [the needs of] this age and this people be disregarded?[4]

Tseng Ch'i added to his palace answer the doctrine of the method of the mind (*hsin-fa* 心法) and its centrality for imperial governance. The sagely mind (聖者此心也) had its locus classicus in the *Documents Classic*, especially the "sixteen-character transmission" (*shih-liu tzu ch'uan* 十六子傳) concerning the famous bifurcation between the "mind of the Tao" (*tao-hsin* 道心) and the "human mind" (*jen-hsin* 人心).[5] In particular, Tseng Ch'i

---

3. Curiously, in Ming examination papers, the *tao-t'ung* was more frequently paired with the *chih-t'ung* than with the earlier T'ang and Sung notion of orthodox political legitimacy called the *cheng-t'ung* 正統, a concept that Jao Tsung-i 饒宗頤 has detailed in his *Chung-kuo shih-hsueh shang chih cheng-t'ung lun* 中國史學上之正統論 (Theories of orthodox political legitimacy in Chinese historiography) (Hong Kong: Lung-men Bookstore, 1977).

4. *Huang-Ming chuang-yuan ch'üan-ts'e* 皇明狀元全策 (Complete set of policy questions prepared during the Ming dynasty by *optimi* for the palace civil examination), 1591 edition, 2.18a–19b, 36a–b. Although composed at imperial behest in the public precincts of an imperial examination, such formulaic descriptions of Ming emperors also demonstrate that emperors were willing to adopt *Tao-hsueh* rhetoric to gain literati support.

5. See my "Philosophy (*I-li*) versus Philology (*K'ao-cheng*): The *Jen-hsin Tao-hsin* Debate." *T'oung Pao* 59, 4–5 (1983): 175–222.

cited the parts of the sixteen-character passage that stressed that the ruler must "have absolute refinement and singleness of purpose to hold stead-fastly to the mean" (惟精惟一，允執厥中).[6] Significantly, however, Tseng had established the precedent for linking the *Tao-hsueh* focus on the moral cultivation of the mind to discussion of the sagely qualities of Ming emperors, in this case the Hung-wu emperor. It was a precedent that would be reproduced over and over again in examination essays, becom-ing in the Ch'ing dynasty a mantra about the emperor's cultural prestige.[7]

By the mid-Ming, emperors were said by civil service candidates to have not only unified the *tao-t'ung* and *chih-t'ung*. The emperor also took precedence over his literati in reestablishing the "orthodox transmission of the Tao," a position never granted publicly by literati in Sung or Yuan times. Hu Cheng-meng 胡正蒙, the *tertius* in 1547, wrote on his palace essay, for example, that "the rulers in Han, T'ang, and Sung had posi-tions but no learning, while Chou Tun-i [周敦頤, 1017–73], Ch'eng I, Ch'eng Hao [程顥, 1032–85], and Chu Hsi as the four Sung masters had learning but no achievements. That was why in the preceding hundreds and thousands of years the transmission of the *tao-t'ung* had been inter-rupted" (夫漢唐宋之諸君，有其位而無其學。周程朱之四子，有其學而無其功。此上下千數百年之間，道統之傳所以不續也。). Only the early Ming emperors had for the first time successfully combined *tao-hsueh* morality and imperial governance simultaneously.[8]

The fragile early Ming partnership between emperors and literati in turn led to a long-term political and cultural relationship, which was con-summated in a formal wedding between Tao Learning classical teachings and imperial power during the Ming and Ch'ing dynasties. Han-Chinese Ming and Manchu Ch'ing emperors, like their Mongol predecessors, believed that the Ch'eng-Chu school provided the cultural and political justification for their rule. When emperors selected Ch'eng-Chu learning as the verbal machinery of their rule, they in effect tied the "constitution-ality" of their dynasty to that philosophy and committed the bureaucracy to its educational propagation in schools and on civil examinations. This selection was a major concession to the state-society partnership in place.

---

6. *Huang-Ming chuang-yuan ch'üan-ts'e*, 2.19a–20a.

7. Chin-shing Huang, *Philosophy, Philology, and Politics in Eighteenth-Century China* (Cam-bridge: Cambridge University Press, 1995), pp. 157–68, documents the Ch'ing aspects of the "unity of the tradition of the way and that of governance." I document the early Ming roots of this political and cultural homology.

8. See *Chin-shih teng-k'o-lu* 進士登科錄 (Record of the ascension to *chin-shih* rank on the civil palace examination), 1547: 3b–6b, for the imperial palace question. For the portions of the three top answers dealing with the issue of moral and political transmission of legitima-cy, see 8a–b, 19b–22b, and 24a–33b.

At times, such as during the Southern Sung dynasty, the dynastic orthodoxy was diffuse and came from wider literati circles; at other times, such as in the early Ming, it was narrower and was made the core of the civil service examination curriculum, thereby influencing the evolution of future literati culture. Thus, Tao Learning moral philosophy, while an autonomous field of inquiry with its own inherent intellectual integrity and growth, also provided a system of concepts, arguments, and beliefs endorsed and manipulated by both rulers and officials in the Ming dynasty for their political purposes. The linguistic products of that process of manipulation—when concepts, arguments, and beliefs selectively served to legitimate political sovereignty—are what I refer to as imperial "ideology."

I intend to show how late imperial dynasties successfully incorporated Tao Learning philosophy into the civil service examination system to train and select loyal officials who would share power with the ruler and serve the larger interests of the dynasty. The political coherence of imperial ideology derived from its intimate ties to and selective reproduction of Ch'eng-Chu learning. That ideological coherence, however, was as much "extracted from" as "reflective of" the philosophical doctrines on which it was based. Dynastic ideology may have had many elective affinities with Tao Learning moral philosophy, but the political purposes to which those affinities were applied were determined by the needs of the dynasty rather than the integrity of the philosophy. The emperor (or those who spoke for him) and the bureaucracy, not the philosopher Chu Hsi, had the final say on how Ch'eng-Chu concepts, arguments, and beliefs were put into educational practice via civil examinations.

As a carefully crafted literati disguise worn by the participants in an autocratic but not yet totalitarian political culture, Tao Learning translated into imperial ideology, and as an ideology it helped justify, that is, induce, public acceptance of the social, bureaucratic, and military forms of power on which the late empires of Ming and Ch'ing were largely based. This chapter locates the origins of the political and cultural uses of that imperial disguise in the required educational curriculum of civil service examinations in the early Ming. Many literati helped to create it. Many saw through the disguise. After 1425 most, fortunately, never had to face cruel but charismatic "sage-kings" like the Hung-wu emperor, Chu Yuan-chang, or his son, the Yung-lo emperor, Chu Ti (r. 1402–24). Hence, they could live with the disguise and, once again, modify it to serve literati needs.

## EARLY MING CIVIL EXAMINATIONS

Late imperial institutions for selecting candidates for the Chinese civil service took their final form in early Ming China. In an effort to bridge the civilian, cultural, and racial gaps in the imperial system that had emerged under Jurchen and Mongol governance during the Chin and Yuan dynasties, Chu Yuan-chang invited literati in 1368 to recommend local talents for appointment as prefects and magistrates. An early adept of the millenarian White Lotus Buddhist sects that had revolted against Mongol rule, whose themes and symbols he continued to use to justify the new dynasty to the people, the Hung-wu emperor was also persuaded by literati elites from Chin-hua, Che-chiang, where his forces had sojourned for a time between 1355 and 1360, to don the ideological garb of a classical sage-king in order to reunify the literati of the empire and rekindle the orthodox legacy of the Sung dynasties.[9]

Central to his political and cultural legitimation was the emperor's ability to recruit talented men and assign them positions in the bureaucracy and local governance. Under Mongol rule, Han Chinese, as we have seen, were third-class subjects in their own land, continually subjected to arbitrary decisions that granted Mongols and other *se-mu* peoples privileged status in the *Pax Mongolica* of the day. Chinese chafed under the symbolic and material forms of violence used by the Machiavellian Mongols to maintain control as a minority over the massive numbers of Han people in north and south China. Many disgruntled or impecunious literati scholars, generally prevented from joining the Yuan dynasty as high officials, turned to alternative careers, ranging from medicine to the literary and theatrical arts.[10]

Besides the long-term hiatus in imperial examinations, which were comparable in scale and frequency to those of the Sung and Chin dynasties, literati eremitism, a legitimate Chinese response to alien rule, meant

9. John Dardess, "The Transformation of Messianic Revolt and the Founding of the Ming Dynasty," *Journal of Asian Studies* 29, 3 (1970): 539–58; John D. Langlois, Jr., "Political Thought in Chin-hua under Mongol Rule," in Langlois, ed., *China under Mongol Rule*, pp. 137–85, at pp. 184–85; and Romeyn Taylor, "The Social Origins of the Ming Dynasty (1351–1360)," *Monumenta Serica* 22 (1963): 1–78. On early Ming state-building, see Chang I-shan 張奕善, *Chu-Ming wang-ch'ao shih-lun wen-chi—T'ai-tsu, T'ai-tsung p'ien* 朱明王朝史論文輯—太祖太宗篇 (Collected historical essays on the Chu's Ming dynasty—Emperors T'ai-tsu and T'ai-tsung) (Taipei: Kuo-li pien-i kuan, 1991), pp. 14–19, 40–48.

10. See Hymes, "Not Quite Gentlemen?" pp. 11–85; and West, "Mongol Influence on the Development of Northern Drama," pp. 435–42. Tao, "Political Recruitment in the Chin Dynasty," pp. 24–34; and Bol, "Seeking Common Ground," pp. 469–79, 495–501, describe how different the Jurchen Chin dynasty had been.

that when the Ming dynasty officially replaced the Yuan, the new ruler would have to find ways to attract local scholars into government service.[11] Such voluntary eremitism came in different forms, however, and these scholars, especially those who lived in the north, where a Han Chinese emperor had not ruled since 1126, could not be expected automatically to shift their allegiance to the Ming dynasty, especially during its early years, when the Mongol throne in the north still retained a measure of legitimacy. To gain the support of local literati the first Ming emperor appealed to the precedents of the ancient empires that had preceded the Mongol conquest.

> I have heard that in high antiquity when they established their rule the [three] emperors and [five] kings used the military to pacify the world. When it came time to preserve their accomplishments, they spoke of the military to spread awe throughout the world. Putting into effect government principles and policies, however, depends on civilian officials. Of these two, one must not favor one over the other.... Accordingly, I wish to emulate the institutions of antiquity by establishing two systems of selection for military and civilian affairs and thereby broadly search for worthies in the world [to serve me].[12]

To fill the bureaucracy with new officials, provincial civil examinations for all pacified provinces were held yearly between 1370 and 1372.[13] In 1370, for example, a total of 500 graduates were selected according to a provincial quota of 100 for the capital region, 40 for large provinces, and 25 for smaller ones.[14] Table 2.1 reveals that it was not until after 1440 that provincial quotas increased substantially, by 38% and then by another 55% after 1453.

11. On Yuan Confucians as an elite status group, see Hsiao Ch'i-ch'ing, "Yuan-tai te Ju-hu—Ju-shih ti-wei yen-chin shih-shang te i-chang," pp. 151–70.

12. *Ming-shih*, 3/1686, 3/1711; and *Huang-Ming kung-chü k'ao*, 1.18a. Cf. Mote, "Confucian Eremitism in the Yuan Period," pp. 229–236. See also Yan-shuan Lao, "Southern Chinese Scholars and Educational Institutions in Early Yuan," pp. 131–33.

13. There is some question whether the provincial examinations were held in 1371. See *Huang-Ming kung-chü k'ao*, 2.7b–8b. The *Chih-i k'o-so chi* by Li T'iao-yuan, 1.1, indicates that provincial examinations were held in 1371.

14. *Huang-Ming san-yuan k'ao* 皇明三元考 (Study of the provincial, metropolitan, and palace civil examination *optimi* during the Ming dynasty), compiled by Chang Hung-tao 張弘道 and Chang Ning-tao 張凝道, late Ming edition (after 1618), 1.1a–2a. This source indicates that, in addition to 1370 and 1372, 1371 provincial examinations did take place; see 1.4a–5a. For Ming provincial quotas from 1370 to 1573, see Tilemann Grimm, *Erziehung und Politik in konfuzianischen China der Ming-Zeit* (Hamburg: Gesellschaft fur Natur- und Volkerkunde Ostasiens e.V., 1960), pp. 61–64. Grimm gives 510 provincial graduates for 1370, increasing to 550 in 1425, and then to 1,195 in 1573.

Fortunately, we have some of the questions and answers from the 1370 Chiang-hsi 江西 provincial examination, which confirm that the first Ming civil examinations generally followed the Yuan system of classical essays, although, as we saw in Chapter 1, the poetry question had been retained for Han Chinese candidates under the Mongols. For instance, one of the special characteristics of Yuan examinations was that in the first session the questions from the Five Classics took precedence over those from the Four Books. Moreover, the question on the Four Books was known as a clarification of "doubts on the Four Books" (*Ssu-shu i* 四書疑), and, unlike earlier Sung and later Ming questions (requiring students to identify and elucidate separately several quotations from the Four Books), it demanded that candidates write an essay clarifying the interrelation among the Four Books. Wu Po-tsung 吳伯宗 (n.d.), the top finisher in the Chiang-hsi competition, for instance, prepared an essay of over 650 characters describing the reasons for differences in four quotations (one each from the *Great Learning* and *Doctrine of the Mean* and two from the *Mencius*) that advocated bringing peace and order to the world (*t'ien-hsia p'ing* 天下平).[15]

Session two consisted of a single "discourse" (*lun* 論) essay, along with three types of documents, and session three of a single policy question (*ts'e* 策). Legal questions were not yet required on the civil examinations (see Chapter 1). The discourse question required students to explain "how the rites could bring peace to the ruler and order to the people" (禮以安上治民), an essay topic that paraphrased Confucius' words cited in the *Records of Rites* (*Li-chi* 禮記) to the effect that "Nothing was superior to the rites in bringing peace to the ruler and order to the people" (孔子曰，安上治民，莫善於禮).[16]

The policy question focused on why the "six arts" (*liu i* 六藝) of antiquity should be revived to "produce men of talent in the military and civilian arts." Wu's policy answer pointed out that neither the Han nor T'ang dynasty had put into practice the six arts, favoring instead belles lettres. Wu added that the Ming had now successfully restored the ancient program for selecting literati for office. In essence, Wu's policy answer recapitulated Chu Yuan-chang's criticism of earlier Han, T'ang, and Sung stress on literary achievements and Chu's preference (noted in his 1367 policy announcement above) for the six arts for more practical all-around

15. See Wu Po-tsung, *Jung-chin chi* 榮進集 (Collection from the glorious *chin-shih*), SKCS, 1233.218–21. Cf. *Huang-Ming kung-chü k'ao*, 2.2a–3b.

16. See *Li-chi yin-te* 禮記引得 (Concordance to the Record of Rites) (reprint, Shanghai: Ku-chi Press, 1983), 26/3.

qualifications for office.[17] The turn from literary to classical examinations was consciously heralded in the 1370 provincial examination.

The first metropolitan civil examination was convened in Nanking in 1371. Under the supervision of the chief examiner Sung Lien 宋濂 (1310–81), one of Chu Yuan-chang's early Chin-hua advisors, 120 (including one Korean) out of 189 candidates (including three Koreans and one Vietnamese) were selected (64.5%), perhaps the least competitive metropolitan examination in late imperial history.[18] Table 2.2 shows that during the Ming dynasty overall, less than one in ten candidates usually passed the metropolitan examinations, especially after 1450, when the number of candidates for *chin-shih* degrees increased steadily.

As in the Yuan, candidates were expected to choose one of the Five Classics for specialization (*chuan-ching* 專經). Of the 120 graduates in 1371, we know the specializations for all: 21 (17.5%) on the *Change Classic*, 24 (20%) on the *Documents*, 28 (23.3%) on the *Poetry*, 40 (33.3%) on the *Spring and Autumn Annals*, and 7 (5.8%) on the Rites.[19] Compared with later Ming dynasty rates of specialization, the 1371 metropolitan examination was remarkable for the inordinately high number of *chin-shih* graduates who specialized on the *Annals*, which was generally true for much of the early Ming, when the *Annals* was popular among candidates. Table 2.3 describes how after 1400, typically 30% of all *chin*-shih candidates would specialize on the *Change*, 20% on the *Documents*, 30% on the *Poetry*, but only 6% to 7% on the *Annals* and about the same on the *Record of Rites*.[20] Table 2.4,

---

17. See Wu Po-tsung, *Jung-chin chi*, 1233.218–25. See also Li T'iao-yuan, *Chih-i k'o so-chi*, 1.4.

18. See Sung Lien, "Hui-shih chi-lu t'i-tz'u" 會試紀錄題辭 (Remarks on records of the metropolitan examination), in *Sung Wen-hsien kung ch'üan-chi* 宋文憲公全集, *Ssu-pu pei-yao* edition (Shanghai: Chung-hua Bookstore, 1927–37), 2.18b–19a. Sung noted the emphasis on practical matters in the tests rather than literary themes. See also *Huang-Ming san-yuan k'ao*, 1.2a–3a; and *Ming-tai wei-k'o hsing-shih lu* 明代魏科姓氏録 (Record of names on the highest examinations during the Ming dynasty), compiled by Chang Wei-hsiang 張惟驤, Ch'ing edition (reprint, Taipei: Ming-wen Bookstore, *Ming-tai chuan-chi ts'ung-k'an*, 1991), A.1a. Cf. Li T'iao-yuan, *Chih-i k'o so-chi*, 1.1. The *Huang-Ming kung-chü k'ao*, 2.3b, indicates that 72 out of the 500-plus graduates of the 1370 provincial examinations were granted appointments even though they did not compete in the 1371 metropolitan examinations.

19. *Chin-shih teng-k'o lu* 進士登科録 (Record of the ascension to *chin-shih* rank on the palace examination), 1371 palace civil examination, in *I-hai chu-ch'en* 藝海珠塵 (Dust from pearls of writing in the literary world), Ch'ing edition, *ko-chi* 革集 collection, pp. 4a ff. See also *Hui-shih lu* 會試録 (Record of the metropolitan civil examination), 1371: 13a–19b.

20. Frequencies of specialization have also been tabularized for Chapter 5 and are discussed in Chapter 9 in light of historical and natural studies. A full explanation for why candidates favored different classics at different times must await future research, but the

drawing on figures from Nanking (then in Ying-t'ien prefecture), reveals similar currents for *chü-jen* graduates of Ming dynasty provincial examinations.

Although he did not finish first (Yü Yu-jen 俞友仁 [n.d.] from Che-chiang did), Wu Po-tsung at age thirty-eight successfully passed the 1371 metropolitan examination; he ranked number 24, with a specialization on the *Documents Classic*. Like the 1370 provincial examination, the 1371 metropolitan examination also followed the three-session format established during the Yuan dynasty. Most notable perhaps was that the single policy question for session three focused on the relationship between rituals and laws in public governance, which would become a common feature of Ming dynasty policy questions and prefigured the addition of legal *p'an-yü* questions to session two in provincial and metropolitan examinations starting in 1384 (see Chapter 1). The 1371 policy question was in fact a series of questions that initially asked for a delineation of how the sage-kings had "established penal laws and regulations" to order the world. Then candidates were asked to explain how rituals and music, especially through schooling, could be used "to correct customs."[21]

Wu Po-tsung's answer reaffirmed the classical paradigm for governance enunciated during the Han dynasty, after the failure of purely Legalist policies during the Ch'in dynasty (221–207 B.C.).[22] He noted that the "Way of accomplished governance" (致治之道) was irrevocably tied to the "laws of governance" (為治之法). Consequently, "the law is always part of the Tao" (法亦未嘗不囿於道之內).[23] As the first metropolitan policy question and answer during the Ming dynasty, both were thereafter frequently cited, and subsequent civil examinations reproduced this moral-legal paradigm as required learning. Literati protestations that morality and principle based on Ch'eng-Chu teachings alone sufficed to rule the world was not the sort of political theory that was tested in the Ming civil selection process, although laws were contained and thus constrained within the Tao.[24] By 1384–85, the Hung-wu emperor expected all provincial and

---

linguistic aspects of such choices are given in Chapter 5. I should add that the Sung Hu An-kuo commentary to the *Annals* allowed for literati critiques of past emperors.

21. Wu Po-tsung, *Jung-chin chi*, 1233.225–30.

22. On the Han dynasty synthesis of rituals and laws, see my *Classicism, Politics, and Kinship*, pp. 257–66.

23. Wu Po-tsung, *Jung-chin chi*, 1233.230–33.

24. For examples during the early Ming see the 1397, 1411, 1415, 1421, 1427, 1430, 1436, 1448, 1460, 1472, 1475, and 1487 palace examination questions and answers in *Huang-Ming chuang-yuan ch'üan-ts'e*. For late Ming examples, see the 1571, 1577, 1598, and 1604 metropoli-

metropolitan candidates for civil service degrees to be conversant with the statutes in the recently completed Ming legal code.[25]

In the climactic 1371 policy question that Chu Yuan-chang personally presented in the palace for the final 120 candidates for the *chin-shih* degree, the emperor asked about how to select talented officials and what general policies to follow:

> In past dynasties, the personal policy questions [asked by emperors] all invoked the duties of "respecting heaven" and "working diligently for the people." Of those kings and emperors who in antiquity respected heaven and diligently worked for the people, which of them can we use as models today?...
>
> Looking at it from the past as something applicable today, nothing has been more urgent than [human] relations and [people's] customs. How do we clarify the [five cardinal] relations? How can we encourage the flourishing of [proper] customs? Since the Three Dynasties, only the customs of literati of the Eastern Han and the principles for [human] relations of the Chao's Sung [dynasty] approximated the ideal. When all is said and done, by which way can we reach the ideal? You must have something to say about such matters. Please write down [your views] on the paper [provided] without being cursory or incomplete.[26]

We are fortunate also to have the number-one-ranking policy answer to Chu Yuan-chang's palace examination question, which was prepared by Wu Po-tsung. It turned out that Wu, who was the number-one Chiang-hsi candidate, also was the first palace *optimus* (*chuang-yuan* 狀元) of the Ming dynasty and was thus celebrated thereafter.[27] Answering the emperor's questions point by point, as was the Ming-Ch'ing pattern for palace examinations, Wu first presented an eloquent and later often cited defense of written tests to judge the merits of candidates for office, about which, as we will see, the emperor remained suspicious. Invoking Yang Hsiung's

tan policy questions in *Huang-Ming ts'e-heng* 皇明策衡 (Weighing civil policy examination essays during the Ming dynasty), compiled by Mao Wei 茅維, Wu-hsing edition (1605). The latter also contains legal policy questions asked on 1552, 1582, 1588, 1594, 1600, and 1603 provincial examinations. Cf. Dardess, *Confucianism and Autocracy*, pp. 197–202.

25. See Edward Farmer, "Social Order in Early Ming China: Some Norms Codified in the Hung-wu period," in Brian McKnight, ed., *Law and the State in Traditional East Asia* (Honolulu: University of Hawaii Press, 1987), pp. 6–10.

26. *Teng-k'o lu*, 1371: 1a–1b.

27. See *Ming Chuang-yuan t'u-k'ao* 明狀元圖考 (Illustrated survey of *optimi* during the Ming dynasty), compiled by Ku Ting-ch'en 顧鼎臣 and Ku Tsu-hsun 顧祖訓, 1607 edition, 1.4a–4b. Wu Ch'eng-en 吳承恩 and Ch'eng I-chen 程一楨 added materials that brought it up to 1604. Materials for 1607–28 were later added by unknown compilers.

揚雄 (53 B.C.–A.D. 18) famous phrase that "words are the sound of the mind" (言者心之聲也), Wu wrote:

Your servant has heard that words are the sound of the mind. People hide their mind, and it cannot be fathomed. But the strengths and weaknesses of their words permit us to observe the depravity and correctness inherent in their mind. Words are not hard, but actions alone are. Thus those who can speak [moral words] do not go against [their words] in their actions. In this manner, the ancient kings and emperors in observing people had them set forth official memorials so they could observe their profundity. They had them tested for their abilities and examined the results. Afterwards, they could select from among the candidates the practical strengths of those worthy.[28]

In addition, Wu Po-tsung presented the proven classical cultural program for social and political harmony. Schools were the key to the social and political order:

Your servant has heard that since long ago emperors and kings were most concerned in their governance with clarifying human relations and fostering social customs. And the means by which human relations are clarified and social customs are enriched all derive from encouraging schools in order to transform the people via learning and that's all. If the transformation through learning is put into effect, then the minds of the people will be correct. Human relations will then be clarified, and social customs will be enriched. This principle is absolute.[29]

Although Wu Po-tsung lost his life in the political purges later carried out by the Hung-wu emperor, Wu's views on written tests and education were repeatedly referred to by later examiners. For example, during the early Ch'ing, facing suspicions of the Manchu conquest elite, Han Chinese examiners justified the use of written examinations to test students by reference to Wu's citation of Yang Hsiung's memorable phrase "words are the sound of the mind."[30] They thereby hoped to use the early Ming precedent for civil examinations to justify their usefulness in the early Ch'ing. In this effort, Han examiners prevailed but not before the Oboi

---

28. Wu Po-tsung, *Jung-chin chi*, 1233.233–34. For the locus classicus of Wu's answer, see Yang Hsiung, *Fa-yen* 法言 (Model words), in *Yang Tzu-yun chi* 揚子雲集 (Collection of Yang Hsiung), compiled by Cheng P'u 鄭樸, late Ming Wan-li edition, 1.15b.

29. Wu Po-tsung, *Jung-chin chi*, 1233.233–34.

30. See the prefaces ("Hsu" 序) and afterwords ("Hou-hsu" 後序) for the *Shun-t'ien-fu hsiang-shih-lu* 順天府鄉試錄 (Records of the provincial civil examinations during the Shun-chih reign held in Shun-t'ien prefecture), 1654, 1657, 1660 editions.

Regents tried for a time (1664–67) to rid the civil examinations of the infamous eight-legged essays, which had emerged in the late fifteenth century as the formalist basis for the first session of the examinations (see Chapters 7 and 10).

Chu Yuan-chang was pleased with Wu's policy answer, hence Po-tsung's ranking as *optimus*. The emperor was not impressed, however, with Wu Po-tsung's defense of written tests to select men for public office. As we have seen, after holding the 1372 provincial examinations, Chu suspended all examinations in 1373 because graduates who took office were "naive and immature youths." Although the emperor was clearly upset with the results of the first civil examinations and the job performance of the first group of *chin-shih*, there were cultural and political matters at stake.

Earlier accounts of Ming T'ai-tsu typically have uncritically linked his use of civil examinations to the unrelenting growth of Ming despotism.[31] Such accounts have overlooked early Ming imperial fears that the selection system might actually undercut the power of the emperor and give southern constituencies in the bureaucracy too much political power. We turn first to the Mencian classical threat Chu Yuan-chang thought he faced, which demonstrates the limits of automatically linking the civil examinations to Ming imperial power. The first Ming emperor's actions in this case also suggest that Sung *Tao-hsueh* teachings, which drew on Mencius' views of human nature as universally good for their inspiration, had to be politically circumscribed and domesticated to fit in with Ming imperial ideology. Even so, they still represented literati values long established in classical teachings.

## MENCIUS AND MING CIVIL EXAMINATIONS

Literati during the early Ming, in contrast to their predecessors during the Mongol Yuan dynasty, were again at the heart of political life. They hoped that the Hung-wu emperor's revival of the civil examinations, his uses of classical rituals to balance legal norms, the increased reliance during the early Ming on scholars appointed to the Hanlin Academy, and imperial authorization of Ch'eng-Chu moral theory for the new dynasty would revive Sung cultural ideals betrayed or disregarded by the Yuan. Chu Yuan-chang, however, perceived as necessary a descending view of

31. For example, see Yao Lo-yeh 姚樂野, "Ming-Ch'ing k'o-chü chih yü chung-yang chi-ch'uan te chuan-chih chu-i" 明清科舉制與中央集權的專制主義 (The Ming-Ch'ing civil examination system and despotism via the centralization of power), *Ssu-ch'uan ta-hsueh hsueh-pao* 四川大學學報 1 (1990): 98–104.

political power, dating from the early and middle empires but solidified under Mongol rule, whereby power descended from the ruler and then was transmitted to his officials and subjects.[32] The Ming founder thus tolerated no public threat to his political legitimacy or overt classical limits placed on his personal power.

Untutored in the Classics, the peasant-soldier become emperor sought legitimation of his rule by initially relying on his Chin-hua advisors. The activist institutions and rituals presented in the *Rituals of Chou*, a text associated with reformist traditions since the Wang Mang 王莽 interregnum (A.D. 9–23) and later used by Wang An-shih to authorize his reform program during the Northern Sung, were also frequently cited in the early Ming. Ming dynasty rural control systems for village tax collection and household registration, for instance, had their locus classicus in the *Rituals of Chou*. Chu Yuan-chang thus used activist models for his autocratic policies.[33] According to the same logic, the emperor had been persuaded by the Yuan scholar-official Liu Chi that the classical Canon as interpreted by the Tao Learning Ch'eng-Chu tradition would best serve the Ming dynasty—as it had the Yuan—as the civil examination curriculum.[34]

After the 1370–72 provincial, metropolitan, and palace civil examinations, however, Chu Yuan-chang, now a student of the Canon himself,[35] became particularly angered by the political philosophy of Mencius, whom the Ch'eng-Chu school had enshrined as Confucius' doctrinal successor in the *tao-t'ung* lineage of orthodox teachings.[36] What infuriated the Hung-wu emperor was the passage in the *Mencius* (one of Chu Hsi's Four Books and hence part of session one of the Yuan and early Ming provincial and metropolitan civil examinations) in which Mencius defended an ascending view of political sovereignty based on the people and drew limits to the loyalty an official owed his ruler: "When the ruler regards his officials as the ground or the grass, they regard him as a robber and an enemy." Such questioning of the bonds between the ruler and his officials

32. On imperial power in China, see the many useful essays in S. R. Schram, ed., *Foundations and Limits of State Power in China* (London: University of London, 1987), passim.

33. On the links between the *Rituals of Chou* and classical Legalism, see Elman, *Classicism, Politics, and Kinship*, pp. 125–26.

34. On the role of "Chin-hua advisors" in giving the emperor the authoritarian ideological tools he required, see Dardess, *Confucianism and Autocracy,* passim.

35. See the *Huang-Ming t'ung-chi shu-i* 皇明通紀述遺 (Additions to the Comprehensive Accounts of the August Ming dynasty), compiled by Ch'en Chien 陳建, and appended by P'u Shih-ch'ang 卜世昌 and T'u Heng 屠衡, 1605 edition (reprint, Taipei: Student Bookstore, 1972), 2.14a, 2.17a, for examples of Chu Yuan-chang's efforts to become classically literate.

36. See *Huang-Ming t'ung-chi chi-yao*, 9.5b–6a.

was tied to Mencius' claim that the ruler served the people: "Mencius said: 'The people are the most important element [in a polity]; the spirits of the land and grain are the next; the sovereign is the least important.'"[37]

In fact Mencius cited Confucius for his position on tyranny: "Confucius said: 'The Way has only two courses, that of benevolence and that of malevolence. One who carries the oppression of his people to the highest pitch will himself be slain, and his kingdom will perish. If [such a ruler] does not carry oppression to an extreme, his life will still be in jeopardy, and his kingdom will be weakened. He will be called [a tyrant] as Yü [r. 781–770 B.C.] and Li [r. 878–827] [in antiquity] were.'"[38] Such classical parables, Chu Yuan-chang discovered, challenged the Ming dynasty's sovereignty, based since the early empire of the Legalists on a descending view of power emanating from the ruler. Instead, for Mencius, the polity derived its power from the "ascending" will of the people. During the Former Han dynasty, the ascending view had at times still evoked voluntarist strains that legitimated Confucius as an "uncrowned king" and decried false kings.[39] These threats to his dynasty's sovereignty were more than Chu Yuan-chang could tolerate. While pondering whether to abolish the civil examinations, he demanded of his ministers that the text of the *Mencius* be removed from the reading list for civil examination candidates because of its lèse-majesté (非臣子所宜言), thus effectively compromising the canonical stature of the Four Books. In addition, Chu called for removing Mencius from the sacrificial ceremony performed for Confucius and the official pantheon of sages, scholars, and martyrs.[40]

Chu's chief ministers, particularly Ch'ien T'ang 錢唐 (fl. ca. 1368–73), tried to head off these dangerous precedents, which threatened Ch'eng-Chu intellectual orthodoxy, by agreeing to remove those passages in the *Mencius* that the emperor found objectionable, that is, all those guilty of lèse-majesté, but successfully prevailed on him to keep the remaining text

---

37. See T'u Shan 涂山, *Ming-cheng t'ung-tsung* 明政統宗 (Chronicle of Ming government), ca. 1615 edition (reprint, Taipei: Ch'eng-wen Bookstore, 1971), 5.11a; and *Meng-tzu yin-te* 孟子引得 (Concordance to the Mencius) (Peking: Harvard-Yenching Publication, 1941), 56/7B/14. Cf. James Legge, trans., *The Four Books* (reprint, New York: Paragon, 1966), p. 985.

38. *Lun-yü yin-te*, 23/12/7. Cf. Lau, trans., *Confucius: The Analects*, p. 693.

39. See Elman, *Classicism, Politics, and Kinship*, pp. 205–13. Recent studies have questioned how prominent such views were, even in the Former Han. See Michael Nylan, "The *Chin Wen/Ku Wen* Controversy in Han Times," *T'oung Pao* 80 (1994): 83–136.

40. *Huang-Ming kung-chü k'ao*, 1.85b. See also T'u Shan, *Ming-cheng t'ung-tsung*, 5.11a; and Yun-yi Ho, *The Ministry of Rites and Suburban Sacrifices in Early Ming* (Taipei: Shuang-yeh Bookstore, 1980), p. 95.

as required reading for the civil examination system. Because the examinations were stopped in 1373, this brouhaha became a moot point until 1384. Later a censored version of the *Mencius* was used in the civil examinations, after Chu had successfully purged his enemies from the civil and military bureaucracies.[41]

Subsequently, Liu San-wu 劉三五 (1312–99?), who entered the Hanlin Academy by recommendation in 1384, was entrusted in 1394 with preparation of a formal edition of the *Mencius* that deleted eighty-eight sections that Chu Yuan-chang had found objectionable. The expurgated version was then entitled the *Meng-tzu chieh-wen* 孟子節文 (Abridged text of the Mencius).[42] The censored edition of the *Mencius* was the standard text for civil examination candidates until 1414–15, when the original was curiously restored (see below) during the Yung-lo reign. Chu Yuan-chang succeeded, however, in removing Mencius' tablet from Confucius' ancestral temple in Ch'ü-fu, thereby making it clear that the Ming dynasty stood opposed to Mencian "ascending" notions of the priority of the people over the ruler. Later, the Yung-lo emperor also restored Mencius' tablet as part of his efforts to patronize literati.

In a work entitled "Essay on the Great Sacrifice," Chu Yuan-chang emphasized that he considered the ruler, not the people, the key to world

41. *Ming-shih*, 139.398; and *Huang-Ming t'ung-chi chi-yao*, 9.5b–6a. Cf. Chia Nai-lien 賈乃謙, "Ts'ung Meng-tzu chieh-wen chih Ch'ien-shu" 從孟子節文致潛書 (From the Abridged text of the Mencius to the Submerged writings), *Tung-pei shih-ta hsueh-pao* 東北師大學報 2 (1987): 43–44, which suggests that because the "Veritable Records of the Hung-wu Reign" makes no mention of these events, it likely has been tampered with. During the Ch'ing dynasty, Chu I-tsun 朱彝尊 (1629–1709), among others, thought the story of Chu Yuan-chang's censorship of Mencius untrue because there were insufficient records of it. See Chu I-tsun, *P'u-shu-t'ing chi* 曝書亭集 (Collection from the Pavilion for Honoring Books) (Shanghai: Commercial Press, *Ssu-pu ts'ung-k'an*, 1919–37), 69.8b–9b.

42. See the "Foreword" by Liu San-wu to the *Meng-tzu chieh-wen*, 1395 edition, p. 1a, in *Pei-ching t'u-shu-kuan ku-chi chen-pen ts'ung-k'an* 北京圖書館古籍珍本叢刊 (Peking: Shu-mu Press, 1988), vol. 1. My thanks to Adam Schorr for checking the excisions, which in general are similar to the passage of lèse majesté cited above. A full discussion of all the excised passages would be useful, but such a detailed account here would carry us too far afield. See also Chu Ron-Guey 朱榮貴, "Ts'ung Liu San-wu Meng-tzu chieh-wen lun chün-ch'üan te hsien-chih yü chih-shih fen-tzu chih tzu-chu-hsing" 從劉三梧孟子節文論君權的限制與知識分子之自主性 (Limits on the ruler's power and the autonomy of intellectuals as viewed from Liu San-wu's Abridged text of the Mencius), *Chung-kuo wen-che yen-chiu chi-k'an* 中國文哲研究集刊 6 (1995): 173–95, for the claim that the case demonstrated a literati (= modern intellectuals?) victory in imperial politics. The case really demonstrates that the partnership between imperial and literati interests had survived the Hung-wu purges.

ordering: "When people multiplied in great number, they could not be tamed without rulers. Therefore, heaven produced a ruler to establish order for the people."[43] For Chu, without the ruler the rancorous masses, led on by disputatious officials, would devolve into chaos. He filled his own edicts, orders, and essays, which were first collected and published in 1374 and later expanded, with accounts of the centrality of the ruler and his special mediating role in the cosmos.[44] In essence he sided with the long-standing Legalist view of political power, which justified sovereignty by presenting the ruler as the catalyst that brought public order by ameliorating contending selfish interests. Chu would not permit mention of legitimate "dynastic revolution," particularly in the precincts of the civil service. Apparently he felt that the Ming house had the mandate to rule in perpetuity.

Although the succeeding but too brief reign of Chien-wen (1399–1402) was much less autocratic than that of Chu Yuan-chang, the tenor of imperial policy toward officials and subjects had been set.[45] And, unfortunately, Ming despotism yielded another brief reign of terror immediately after the Prince of Yen 燕王 in Pei-p'ing 北平 (Peking), Chu Ti, ousted the Chien-wen emperor by force and took the throne.[46] An appraisal of Ming China as an unrelieved despotism is too narrow an assessment, given the logistical limitations of the premodern Chinese government, but the power of Ming emperors and their officials and eunuchs to manipulate the raison d'être of the empire was ideologically grounded in an anti-Mencian despotism bequeathed by Chu Yuan-chang that threatened to dissolve the literati partnership with the dynasty.

Such court autocracy was institutionally strengthened in 1380 when

43. Translated in Ho Yun-yi, *The Ministry of Rites and Suburban Sacrifices in Early Ming*, p. 229. The Yung-lo emperor, on the other hand, granted the Mencian view that dynasties lasted only as long as their moral mandate. See Chu Ti's 1409 *Sheng-hsueh hsin-fa* 聖學心法 (The method of the mind in the sages' teachings) (1409; *Chung-kuo tzu-hsueh ming-chu chi-ch'eng* 中國子學名著集成 reprint, Taipei, 1978), "Hsu" 序, pp. 27a–27b.

44. See *Ming T'ai-tsu yü-chih wen-chi* 明太祖御製文集 (Collected writings of Chu Yuan-chang) (reprint, Taipei: Student Bookstore, 1965), which collects the Hung-wu emperor's edicts, orders, essays, palace examination questions, and poetry together from earlier editions of his work.

45. See Kobayashi Kazumi 小林一美, "Shū Genchō no kobu seiji" 朱元璋の恐怖政治 (Chu Yuan-chang's reign of terror), in *Yamane Yukio kyōju taikyū kinen Mindaishi ronshū jō* 山根幸夫教授退休紀念明代史論叢上 (Tokyo: Kyoko shoin, 1990), pp. 40–43.

46. On the Chien-wen reign, see Hok-lam Chan, "The Chien-wen, Yung-lo, Hung-hsi, and Hsuan-te Reigns, 1399–1435," in Frederick W. Mote and Denis Twitchett, eds., *The Cambridge History of China*, vol. 7, part 1, *The Ming Dynasty, 1368–1644* (Cambridge: Cambridge University Press, 1988), pp. 184–93.

Chu executed his prime minister Hu Wei-yung 胡惟庸 (d. 1380), who had been chief councilor from 1378 to 1380, for alleged treason. Fearing repetition of such ministerial efforts to usurp imperial power, the emperor liquidated all executive positions in the bureaucracy and placed all civilian and military offices in the bureaucracy under his immediate control. The bloody purges of 1380 were repeated in 1390–93. Estimates vary, but by Chu Yuan-chang's own estimate perhaps 50,000 to 70,000 people were executed.[47] In a policy question that the emperor prepared for his court after executing Hu and his clique, Chu Yuan-chang made it clear that even the Legalist Ch'in dynasty had not been authoritarian enough:

> Long ago the Ch'in emperor eliminated the feudal system [of lords and vassals] and differentiated the Three Dukes in order to unify the feudal states under heaven into administrative commanderies and counties. In the imperial court, he established a senior and junior minister who accepted the ruler's orders and managed the general affairs of the hundred offices. When he established laws and institutions during this time, none of them derived from the Way of the former sages and worthies. After the establishment of prime ministers, officials expanded their own power at the expense of the ruler's majesty and largesse.[48] Disorder began with the Ch'in. The power of prime ministers became very strong, as in the case [of the eunuch Chao Kao's 趙高 (d. 207 B.C.) using treachery] by calling a stag a horse [to test the loyalty of Ch'in officials and later executing those who had disagreed with him]. Since the Ch'in, all who became rulers under heaven have not reflected on the calamity of establishing prime ministers. Ministers succeeded each other and the ruler authorized them. Over and over, abuses affected the ruler and the dynasty. Is this state of affairs because [ministers] have usurped the ruler's majesty and largesse? Or is it due to the ruler's neglect of governance that they occur? Having read [and thought] about this for a long time, I am still confused and have especially posed this imperial query for you.[49]

47. See Thomas Massey, "Chu Yuan-chang, the Hu-Lan Cases, and Early Ming Confucianism," paper presented at the Columbia University Neo-Confucian Seminar, pp. 53–54.

48. Here Chu Yuan-chang is citing the "Great Plan" ("Hung-fan" 洪範) chapter of the *Documents Classic* on *tso-fu tso-wei* 作福作威, which James Legge translates as "confer favors" and "display the terrors of majesty." See Legge, *The Chinese Classics*, vol. 3, *The Shoo King or The Book of Historical Documents* (reprint, Taipei: Wen-shih-che Press, 1972), p. 334.

49. See Chu's question under the title "Ch'ih-wen wen-hsueh chih shih" 敕問文學之士 (Imperial question for civil literati), in *Ming T'ai-tsu yü-chih wen-chi*, 11.4a–b. For the Chao Kao affair, see Ssu-ma Ch'ien 司馬遷, *Shih-chi* 史記 (Records of the official historian) (Peking: Chung-hua Press, 1972), 1/273 (*chüan* 6).

By tracing the institution of prime ministers back to the Legalist Ch'in dynasty, the Hung-wu emperor was thereby able in good conscience to eliminate an alternative venue for political power that rivaled the emperor's by claiming that the imperial ruler—not the balancing role of the minister—represented the Way of the sages and worthies. Here, of course, the emperor was having it his own way, completely ignoring the tradition associated with the Duke of Chou of a chief minister serving the ruler.[50] During the T'ang dynasty, high officials had sat with the emperor as social equals. Starting with the Sung dynasties, they stood in front of a seated emperor. Beginning under the Ming and continuing under the Ch'ing, officials were required to prostrate themselves and kneel (kowtow 磕頭) before him. Changes in the rites of audience corresponded to the growing authoritarian nature of dynastic power, which reached its peak in the early Ming.[51]

The Mencian ideal of the people as the final locus of political sovereignty was censored. Instead of Mencius' ascending view of power, the dynasty came first, and the prerogatives of the ruler were championed in very un-Mencian ways. Late imperial orthodoxy, which drew so much of its theoretical vision from Mencius, was for a time curtailed when appropriated by Chu Yuan-chang and his Hanlin advisors as the civil service curriculum.[52] In the early Ming in particular, authoritarian political ideals ("descending" views of power) triumphed over classical forms of Mencian voluntarism ("ascending" views of power) in the official rhetoric of the dynasty. During the Hung-wu reign, in particular, the Mencian view of political power was seriously curtailed.[53]

Mencian political idealism survived, however. When the civil examinations were restored in 1384–85, Chu Yuan-chang discovered that Mencian-inspired literati critics of his treatment of officials remained. But from among them the emperor selected two dedicated and uncompromising officials in the 1385 palace examination: Lien Tzu-ning 練子寧 (d. 1402) and Huang Tzu-ch'eng 黃子澄 (d. 1402). Another, Ch'i T'ai 齊泰

50. See my "Ming Politics and Confucian Classics: The Duke of Chou Serves King Ch'eng" 明代政治與經學：周公相成王, in the *International Conference Volume on Ming Dynasty Classical Studies* 國際明代經學研討會 (Nankang, Taiwan: Institute of Chinese Literature and Philosophy, Academia Sinica, 1996), pp. 95–121.

51. Tilemann Grimm, "State and Power in Juxtaposition: An Assessment of Ming Despotism," in S. R. Schram, ed., *The Scope of State Power in China* (London: School of Oriental and African Studies, 1985), pp. 27–50.

52. Chia Nai-lien, "Ts'ung Meng-tzu chieh-wen chih Ch'ien-shu," pp. 43–50.

53. Ojima Sukema 小島祐馬, *Chūgoku no shakai shisō* 中國の社會思想 (Social thought in China) (Tokyo: Chikuma Bookstore, 1967), pp. 75–92.

(d. 1402), was selected in 1388.[54] All were martyred in 1402 when they remained loyal to the Ch'ien-wen emperor and refused to acknowledge Chu Yuan-chang's son, the Prince of Yen, as the Yung-lo emperor.[55] Imperial power could never eliminate literati dissent.

When examinations were reinstated in 1384–85, the requirements for the provincial and metropolitan examinations changed. In session one the Four Books (minus portions of the *Mencius*) now took priority over the Five Classics, thus giving Chu Hsi's required commentaries to the *Analects, Mencius, Great Learning,* and *Doctrine of the Mean* unquestioned preeminence in the selection process. Moreover, candidates were required to answer five policy questions in session three, in place of only one on the 1370–72 examinations. And, as noted in Chapter 1, the Hung-wu emperor's stress on laws and administration had translated into required documentary essays and legal questions that were added to the second session. This venture accorded with Chu Yuan-chang's efforts to give his own imperial orders and announcements (*chao* 詔 and *kao* 誥) canonical status by making his own "Great Announcement" ("Ta-kao" 大誥) required on the civil examinations.[56] For the palace examination, however, a single policy question prepared by the emperor remained the rule. In addition, for the first time the top finishers were usually entitled to enter the Hanlin Academy, a policy that lasted until the end of the Ch'ing dynasty and made Hanlin advisors the key insiders in the imperial court.[57]

54. The *Dictionary of Ming Biography,* p. 224, apparently following the *Huang-Ming kung-chü k'ao,* 2.9a, account, contends that Ch'i T'ai received his *chin-shih* in 1385 using the name Ch'i Te 齊德 and finished first on the 1384 Ying-t'ien provincial examination. The *Huang-Ming san-yuan k'ao,* 1.13a, lists Ch'i as a distinguished official who received his *chin-shih* in 1388. On 1.7a, the latter source corrects the former by giving the name of Liao Meng-chan 廖孟瞻 for the number-one finisher on the 1384 Ying-t'ien examination.

55. *Huang-Ming san-yuan k'ao,* 1.6b–11a. Huang and Ch'i, in particular, were responsible for the Chien-wen emperor's policy of "reducing the feudatories" (*hsiao-fan* 消藩), which threatened Chu Ti's position as the Prince of Yen in Peking. See Chang I-shan, *Chu-Ming wang-ch'ao,* pp. 215–26.

56. *Ming T'ai-tsu shih-lu,* p. 212.3; and *Ming T'ai-tsu yü-chih wen-chi, chüan,* 1–4. Chu Yuan-chang's "Great Announcement" mimicked the "Great Announcement" in the *Documents Classic* usually attributed to the Duke of Chou when he acted as prime minister for the Chou king. See Legge, *The Chinese Classics,* vol. 3, p. 362. On the curriculum, see also *Huang-Ming kung-chü k'ao,* 1.21a–21b, and the comments of Ch'iu Chün 丘濬 (1420–95), which are cited on p. 22a. Ch'iu concludes that the 1384–85 civil examinations were "the first in several hundred years to put into practice Master Chu [Hsi]'s intentions" for reform of the examination curriculum. We have seen in Chapter 1 that Chu Hsi had never intended to base the civil examination curriculum on a single tradition of classical learning.

57. *Ming-tai wei-k'o hsing-shih lu,* A.1b–2a. On the centrality of the Hanlin under the Ming, and the emergence of later "Grand Secretaries" from their midst, see Yun-yi Ho,

In the metropolitan examination of 1385, Huang Tzu-ch'eng finished first and Lien Tzu-ning second. Huang had finished second on the Ying-t'ien provincial examination in Nanking the year before. On the palace examination, however, Lien finished second and Huang third, both behind the *optimus* Ting Hsien 丁顯 from Fu-chien, who had initially been ranked lower by the examiners but was declared with some controversy *optimus* by the emperor because Ting's name corresponded with a dream the emperor had earlier (see Chapter 6) and because the examiners' choice, Hua Lun 花綸, was too young.[58] Career-wise, both Ting Hsien and Hua Lun were overshadowed by Lien Tzu-ning and Huang Tzu-ch'eng.

What was memorable from the 1385 examinations, however, was the audacious, "Mencian" answer Lien Tzu-ning prepared for Chu Yuan-chang's policy question on the palace examination. The Hung-wu emperor's question stressed his devotion to models of antiquity in setting up the Ming dynasty:[59]

> Since I replaced the Yuan [dynasty] and united all the peoples in the empire, officials have respected ancient institutions, and a penal code that emulates that of old regulations has been put in place. I have energetically tried to seek worthy men but after several tries none has been appropriate. Those of ability I have delegated to obey my heart, but while outwardly they follow me, in intent they are quite different.... What can be done to achieve order?

Lien Tzu-ning—whose father, a diarist in the imperial court, had earlier offered stern advice to Chu Yuan-chang, for which he was demoted—

---

*The Ministry of Rites*, pp. 99–100; Charles Hucker, *The Ming Dynasty: Its Origins and Evolving Institutions* (Ann Arbor: University of Michigan, Center for Chinese Studies, 1978), pp. 89–91; and my "Imperial Politics and Confucian Societies in Late Imperial China: The Hanlin and Donglin Academies," *Modern China* 15, 4 (1989): 383–86.

58. *Chuang-yuan t'u-k'ao*, 1.5a–5b; *Huang-Ming san-yuan k'ao*, 1.6b–11a; and *Huang-Ming kung-chü k'ao*, 2.9a–11a. Only the *Huang-Ming san-yuan k'ao*, 1.7a, gives someone other than Hua Lun as *optimus* for the 1384 Chekiang examination. There is also some question about Huang Tzu-ch'eng's ranking third on the palace examination in 1385; see L. Carrington Goodrich, "Who Was T'an-hua in 1385," *Ming Studies* 3 (1976): 9–10.

59. Both the emperor's question and Lien's answer have been preserved in Lien's *Lien Chung-ch'eng Chin-ch'uan chi* 練中丞金川集 (Collection of Lien Tzu-ning from Chin-ch'uan), 1762 edition, 2.1a–7a. For discussion, see *Huang-Ming kung-chü k'ao*, 1.75a; Langlois, "The Hung-wu Reign," in Frederick W. Mote and Denis Twitchett, eds., *The Cambridge History of China*, vol. 7, part 1, *The Ming Dynasty, 1368–1644* (Cambridge: Cambridge University Press, 1988), p. 150; and Dardess, *Confucianism and Autocracy*, p. 263.

boldly transferred the blame for misgovernment from officials to the emperor. He accused the Hung-wu emperor of creating a political atmosphere in which the ancient Legalist "schemes of Kuan Chung and Shang Yang" and the devious "practices of Shen Pu-hai and Han Fei" were dominant and whose result was a betrayal of the very ideals of the sage-kings that the emperor wished to put into effect. How could the emperor expect to gain effective officials in such a political whirlwind?

> The Way of the ruler lies in knowing men [of talent]. The work of officials lies in taking responsibility for matters [of state]. If the ruler is enlightened about knowing men, then officials will be practical in taking responsibility for matters.... It is not that your majesty's intentions in criticizing their shortcomings have been superficial. Nor has your intent in delegating responsibility to them been excessively cavalier. Yet the results in their repaying the dynasty have been as bewildering as one's catching the wind. Can the fruits of all [officials] be so insufficient in achieving order? The reason [for this state of affairs] is that everyone is concerned with appearances, and no one searches for the reality.
>
> Accordingly, the employment of men in antiquity was based on [the ruler's] constant concern for whether the person [appointed] was worthy of taking on each responsibility. In this manner responsibility was conferred on an official, and there were no doubts. Today it is not like this. Men are rapidly advanced owing to some small merit, and rapidly executed owing to some small fault. This is why men of talent disappoint you despite your earnest search for them. Moreover, the production of talent is very hard, but the nurturing of talent is even harder. Because you know how hard it is to produce such talented men, how can you bear to mutilate and execute them for trivial reasons?... How can you bear to murder and slay them and still say "I can use the talented men of the empire"?[60]

Miraculously, Lien Tzu-ning, a student of the "praise and blame" traditions in the *Spring and Autumn Annals* that were popular among literati in the early Ming, survived his daring display of classical remonstrance. Clothing his views within an examination essay that he knew the emperor would read, Lien had demonstrated that the classical way of governance was still not the monopoly of the ruler. Chu Yuan-chang had already executed thousands of officials for seeking power and alleged corruption. Perhaps he recognized in Lien an incorruptible literati voice, the very kind of official he had sought to work with him. Not only did he spare Lien, but the emperor and his examiners awarded Lien with second place in the palace examination, and he was appointed to the Hanlin Academy. Instead of taking office, however, Lien returned home to deal with family

60. *Lien Chung-ch'eng Chin-ch'uan chi*, 2.1b–7a.

matters. When he later returned to the Ming capital in Nanking, he rose instead through the bureaucracy as a censor and subsequently served as one of the Chien-wen emperor's chief advisors. Lien Tzu-ning was a vice-censor when his fateful confrontation with Chu Ti, the Prince of Yen, took place (see below). Between 1385 and 1402, Lien's literati idealism hadn't changed, but Chu Ti's political agenda, unlike his father's, required Lien's capitulation or his death.

Returning to the reasons Chu Yuan-chang had second thoughts about the usefulness of the civil examination system, however, we should add to Chu's strong aversion to Mencian elements in the classical Canon his long-standing distrust of southern Chinese literati, whose wealth and cultural prestige contrasted sharply with his own humble beginnings in rural An-hui province. For Ming and Ch'ing rulers, the "south" represented a difficult but essential region to integrate into the Chinese empire.[61] Moreover, if the civil examination process were allowed to function without regional quotas, southern literati would dominate the competition for official positions. How to keep the bureaucracy from becoming hostage to southerners became an important imperial goal in the early Ming, a policy that lasted until 1904, when the last dynasty relinquished quotas in educational administration (see Chapter 11).

## THE NORTHERN VERSUS SOUTHERN QUOTA ISSUE

Because the civil examinations tested classical learning based on ancient texts drawn from antiquity, they were essentially tests administered in a written language that diverged from vernacular Chinese and the myriad dialects of Ming China that had been influenced, particularly in the north, by interaction with non-Chinese *se-mu* outsiders.[62] To acquire the cultural training necessary to qualify for the civil service, most students preparing for the examinations had to master a written language (classical Chinese) whose linguistic terseness, thousands of unusual written graphs, and archaic grammatical forms required memorization and constant attention from childhood to manhood.[63]

---

61. On the immoral "lure of the South" as perceived by emperors during the Ch'ing, see Silas Wu, *Passage to Power: K'ang-hsi and His Heir Apparent, 1661–1722* (Cambridge: Harvard University Press, 1979), pp. 83–105; and Philip Kuhn, *Soulstealers: The Chinese Sorcery Scare of 1768* (Cambridge: Harvard University Press, 1990), pp. 187ff.

62. See Hashimoto Mantarō 橋本萬太郎, "Hoppogo" 北方語 (Northern Chinese language), in *Gengogaku daijiten* 現語學大辭典, vol. 3: *Sekai gengo hen* 世界語言編, Part 2–1 (Tokyo: Sanseido Press, 1992), pp. 1088–89, 1091–92.

63. See Chapter 5 for detailed discussion of this point.

Since Sung times a classical education, with its empowering literacy, had been perceived as a partial guarantor of civil service success.[64] A perennial feature of the civil examinations since the Northern Sung had been the cutthroat competition among candidates for the limited number of degrees, particularly the highly coveted *chin-shih* degree, which alone guaranteed high official appointment. A ratio of 1 to 10 was not unusual for a candidate's likelihood of succeeding in the final *chin-shih* competition. In 977, for instance, 5,200 candidates competed for 500 *chin-shih* degrees, a ratio of almost 10 to 1.[65] Because of the south's higher economic productivity and larger population, Chinese living in the southern provinces initially faced an even higher hurdle to leap in the provincial examinations.[66] Ou-yang Hsiu noted, for example, that in the civil examinations of his day, the competition for successful places in the provincial examinations was 100 to 1 in the southeast and only 10 to 1 in the northwest.[67]

Ou-yang Hsiu added, however, that because of superior cultural resources, southern candidates for the *chin-shih* examination were better able to prepare the florid poetry and literary answers for belles lettres required by the examiners. Hence, it was no surprise that a "cult of literary style" (*hao-wen* 好文) emerged in the south, while northern literati "emphasized substance" (*shang-chih* 尚質), that is classical learning, according to Ou-yang. Given a choice, as Sung candidates had (see Chapter 1), southerners opted for literary talent and northerners focused on classical studies.[68] Such regional disparities reappeared when the Hung-wu emperor revived the civil examinations in 1370, principally because the north had been ruled for over two centuries by non-Han rulers and had become even more culturally distinct from the south, which was tenuously unified with the north only after 1280. It should be recalled, for instance, that one of the reasons Chu Yuan-chang had turned to the Yuan examination curriculum was to get away from the purely literary criteria for selection of imperial officials used during the T'ang, Sung, and Chin dynasties. One of the emperor's chief complaints in 1369 had been that "the ancients practiced literature to illuminate morality or to penetrate worldly matters," whereas "today's litterateurs did not study morality or take into

64. On empowering literacy, see Harvey Graff, *The Legacies of Literacy: Continuities and Contradictions in Western Culture and Society* (Bloomington: Indiana University Press, 1987), pp. 2–5, 384–86.

65. *Wen-hsien t'ung-k'ao*, 30.284.

66. See Hartwell, "Demographic, Political, and Social Transformations of China," pp. 365–442.

67. *Wen-hsien t'ung-k'ao*, 30.292.

68. Ibid.

account worldly affairs." Such men of culture were fixated on empty literary concerns, the emperor contended.[69]

Southern dominance in the early civil examinations of 1370–72 became
a ticklish problem for the Hung-wu emperor and his successors. Danjō
Hiroshi has discussed the 1373 suspension of examinations and has concluded that Chu Yuan-chang's efforts to limit the domination of the civil
examinations, and thus appointment to political office by southerners,
influenced him to suspend the examinations. The emperor's critique of literary talent (*wen-tz'u* 文詞) was a direct attack on southern literati cultural
superiority and his praise of practical studies and moral behavior (*te-hsing*
德行) referred to the less culturally developed north.[70] In effect, Chu
Yuan-chang, in his efforts to find a political means to appear fair and at
the same time keep the examination market from becoming a southern
monopoly, was echoing the cultural distinction between the "refinement"
of the southeast and the "simplicity" of the northwest drawn by Ou-yang
Hsiu three centuries earlier.[71]

During the 1371 metropolitan examination (see Table 2.5), for example,
89 of the 120 graduates (74%) came from southern provinces while only 31
(26%) were from the north. Part of the political landscape to the early
examinations, then, was the Hung-wu emperor's efforts to avoid a bureaucracy dominated by southerners. When we add to Danjō's account the
Hung-wu emperor's well-known animosity toward the Chiang-nan 江南
elite, which had supported the claim of his arch-enemy Chang Shih-
ch'eng 張士誠 (d. 1367) to the throne of the state of Wu 吳 in final military campaigns lasting from 1365 to 1367, we see more clearly the political
linkage between closing the civil examinations and economic policy in the
early Ming.[72]

69. *Huang-Ming t'ung-chi shu-i*, 1.6b–7a.

70. Danjō Hiroshi 檀上寬, "Mindai kakyo kaikaku no seijiteki haikei—nanbokuken no
sōsetsu o megutte" 明代科舉改革の 政治的背景— 南北卷の 創設をめぐって (The political
background to Ming dynasty reform of the civil service examination—concerning the establishment of quotas for northern and southern candidates), *Tōhō gakuhō* 東方學報 58 (1986):
499–524, stresses geographical fairness as the reason for early Ming attention to the north-
south division.

71. See Danjō, "Mindai nanbokuken no shisō teki haikei" 明代南北卷の思想的背景
(The intellectual background to the northern versus southern examination papers case during the Ming dynasty), in Kotani Nakao 小谷仲男 et al., *Higashi Ajiashi ni okeru bunka denpa
to chihōsa no shosō* 東アジア史における 文化傳播と 地方差の 諸相 (Fuyama University,
1988), pp. 55–67.

72. On Chiang-nan support for Chu's rival, see Cheng K'o-ch'eng鄭克晟, *Ming-tai
cheng-cheng t'an-yuan* 明代政爭探源 (Inquiry into the origins of political struggle during the
Ming dynasty) (T'ien-chin: T'ien-chin ku-chi Press, 1988), pp. 16–24.

To prevent the amassing of land by Chiang-nan landlords (as well as to avenge himself), Chu Yuan-chang had already confiscated much of the land of Chiang-nan landlords and converted it into dynastic property farmed by government tenants. He deliberately imposed punitive tax levels in Chiang-nan, which were not eased until 1380 and again in 1393. Su-chou prefecture provided almost 10% of all land tax receipts, Sung-chiang prefecture over 4%.[73] The Hung-wu emperor had also prohibited appointment of Su-chou or Sung-chiang natives to the post of Minister of Revenue, which was intended to prevent natives of these wealthy prefectures from gaining control of the fiscal administration and granting special favors to their native place at the expense of the national treasury.[74]

Efforts to control Chiang-nan economic resources thus were paralleled by the emperor's efforts to thwart their translation into cultural resources leading to southern examination success. It is therefore not surprising that in the six metropolitan examinations during the thirty years of the Hung-wu reign, only four literati from Su-chou achieved *chin-shih* status. Given Su-chou's examination success during later reigns, it appears that Chu Yuan-chang's animosity toward the Su-chou elite carried over into the examination process. Another factor may have been the phenomenal success of Chiang-hsi candidates, such as Wu Po-tsung (*optimus* in 1371), in early Ming examinations (see also Table 2.6).[75]

The Chien-wen and Yung-lo emperors both surrounded themselves with advisors from Chiang-hsi. Danjō Hiroshi has noted that the Chien-wen reign represented an important shift toward southern literati—except those from Chiang-nan—in leadership positions in the court. In addition to Chiang-hsi, many court officials, such as Fang Hsiao-ju 方孝孺 (1357–1402), were associated with "Eastern Che-chiang" scholarly traditions.[76] For example, 200 men from the southern province of Che-chiang received *chin-shih* degrees under the Hung-wu emperor (141 from Chiang-hsi; see Table 2.9), but only 59 from all of Chiang-nan, then the Metropolitan Region. Only when the Chien-wen and Yung-lo emperors reigned did

73. Ibid., pp. 28–37, details these policies.

74. *Huang-Ming t'ung-chi chi-yao*, 7.11b–12a.

75. For example, in 1400, the top five on the palace examination were all from Chiang-hsi province, and Chiang-hsi candidates took seven of the top ten places. See the *Tien-shih teng-k'o lu* 殿試登科錄 (Record of the ascension to *chin-shih* rank on the palace examination), 1400: 1/11–16, in *Ming-tai teng-k'o-lu hui-pien* 明代登科錄彙編 (Compendium of Ming dynasty civil and military examination records) (reprint, 22 vols., Taipei: Student Bookstore, 1969).

76. Danjō Hiroshi, "Minsho Kenbunchō no rekishi teki ichi" 明初建文朝の歷史的位置 (The historical position of the Chien-wen court in the early Ming), *Chūgoku—bunka to shakai* 中國—文化と社會 7 (1992): 167–75.

Chiang-nan totals approach and surpass those of Che-chiang (but still not Chiang-hsi's). Chapter 5 discusses some of the reasons for the later decline of Chiang-hsi elites in the examination market.[77]

As Tables 2.5 and 2.6 reveal, the less affluent north with its relatively poorer families and lineages was at a cultural disadvantage in a civil service competition that still tested the literary aspects of classical learning.[78] Dominant gentry lineages and nouveau riche merchant families in the culturally ascendant Lower Yangtzu region maintained their high local status through the superior facilities they provided for their talented male children. Lineage schools in the south became jealously guarded private possessions through which the elites of southern society, particularly in Chiang-nan, competed with each other for social, political, and academic ascendancy. Corporate estates thus played a central role in perpetuating an economic and political environment in which southern gentry and merchants were, from Sung times, educationally dominant. By the late Ming, schools for sons of merchants also emerged in the Yangtzu delta.[79]

Was such a sophisticated understanding of southern educational advantages behind the Hung-wu emperor's civil examination policies? Not consciously, as the long-term success of the south shown in Table 2.6 demonstrates. But in 1381, for instance, the emperor presented sets of the Four Books and Five Classics to schools in north China, noting at the time that "since the chaos and destruction of the civil war in the north, books on the classics had been destroyed and were scarce, and thus scholars there have no way to become enlightened even if they possessed admirable traits of simplicity."[80] Moreover, southern dominance of the civil examination competition remained a perennial imperial problem in the early Ming.

Until 1384, for nine years, the Ming government chose its candidates for office by testing those recommended by local officials. In 1382 the 3,700 officials who were appointed had been recommended by local

77. See Danjō, "Mindai kakyo kaikaku," p. 514. On Su-chou see Chien Chin-sung 簡錦松, Ming-tai wen-hsueh p'i-p'ing yen-chiu 明代文學批評研究 (Research on Ming dynasty literary criticism) (Taipei: Student Bookstore, 1989), p. 109; and Ping-ti Ho, The Ladder of Success in Imperial China, pp. 227, 246.

78. On the historical roots of the economic disparity between north and south China, see Philip Huang, The Peasant Economy and Social Change in North China (Stanford: Stanford University Press, 1985), pp. 54–66; and Huang, The Peasant Family and Rural Development in the Yangzi Delta, 1350–1988 (Stanford: Stanford University Press, 1990), pp. 40–43.

79. See Evelyn Rawski, Education and Popular Literacy in Ch'ing China (Ann Arbor: University of Michigan Press, 1979), pp. 28–32, 85–88; and Elman, Classicism, Politics, and Kinship, pp. 36–73.

80. Huang-Ming t'ung-chi chi-yao, 7.15a.

officials for a special examination in Nanking. When this proved ineffective, the civil examinations were officially restarted in 1384, but only after Chu Yuan-chang's liquidation of the executive organs of the bureaucracy and the execution of thousands of officials, whom the emperor implicated in the alleged 1380 and 1390 plots led by prime minister Hu Wei-yung or his clique. Recommendation remained an important road to official success until the palace coup of 1457, when the restored Ying-tsung emperor closed down this channel of recruitment. The emperor blamed ministers from Chiang-hsi, who had risen through recommendation, for earlier choosing his brother to rule in his place while he was held captive by Oirat Mongols (see Chapter 1).[81]

Hence, in the 1385 metropolitan examination, 472 candidates received *chin-shih* degrees, indicating that Chu no longer feared the civil examination process and that he needed immediate replacements for the officials he had slain.[82] This was the highest total of graduates during the Ming, matched only by the 472 (some sources say 470) passed in 1404 by the Yung-lo emperor, who also needed loyal officials as soon as possible in his first civil examination (see below). Moreover, quotas for the 1384 provincial civil examinations had also increased by 6%.[83] Of the 472 graduates in 1385, 340 (72%) still came from southern provinces, while 132 (28%) were from the north. If the emperor had meant to keep southern literati from monopolizing the civil examinations, he had clearly failed.

Although regional quotas were not yet set for the metropolitan examinations, as they had been for provincial examinations, Chu Yuan-chang remained concerned about the "southern problem." In an interesting exchange in 1389 with Chu Yuan-chang, in which the emperor was discussing public governance, Liu San-wu spoke of the differences between northerners and southerners:

*Liu:* The customs of south and north are different. For [southerners], transformation through moral training suffices; for [northerners] one has to use [imperial] majesty to control them [by force].

81. Chang I-shan, *Chu-Ming wang-ch'ao*, pp. 78–104. See also de Heer, *The Care-Taker Emperor*, passim.

82. For example, the death penalty was the fate of 68 of the 120 earlier *chin-shih*. See Langlois, "The Hung-wu Reign," pp. 148–55.

83. *Huang-Ming kung-chü k'ao*, 1.32b. Cf. Danjō, "Mindai kakyo kaikaku," p. 514; and Ikoma Shō 生駒晶, "Minsho kakyo gokakusha no shushin ni kan suru ichi kōsatsu" 明初科舉合格者の出身に關する一考察 (A study of birthplaces of successful examination candidates during the early Ming), in *Yamane Yukio kyōju taikyū kinen Mindaishi ronshū* 山根幸夫教授退休紀念明代史論叢上 (Tokyo: Kyoko shoin, 1990), p. 48.

*Emperor:* The earth has a north and a south, but the people do not have two hearts. The kings and emperors [in the past] saw them all as the same in humanity. Can there really be this sort of mutual distinction between them? You say that public morals of southerners are weak. Therefore, they can be transformed through morality. Public morals of northerners are too set in their ways. Therefore one uses [imperial] majesty to control northerners [by force]. However, what part of the earth lacks both gentlemen and petty people? The gentleman embraces morality, while the petty person embraces majesty [through fear]. Each can properly cultivate themselves when put to the test. How can you summarize things in one word?[84]

Chu Yuan-chang objected to the notion that southerners had a monopoly on gentlemen.

Furthermore, in the spring 1397 metropolitan and palace examinations, the Hung-wu emperor discovered during the palace examination that all 52 graduates for that year were southern literati.[85] The emperor asked Liu San-wu, the chief examiner from the Hanlin Academy, to reread the failed papers from the metropolitan examination to ascertain possible favoritism. Liu, a southern literatus from Hu-kuang, and the readers reported back that no changes in ranking or regional representation were necessary. Liu explained: "In our selection there has been no division between northerners and southerners. It is just that south of the great Yangtzu there are many outstanding literati. Northern literati themselves just don't compare to southerners." The emperor angrily replied: "Can it be as you say that there are no outstanding literati north of the Yangtzu?"

Outraged, Chu Yuan-chang had two, perhaps more, of the readers executed (some dismembered in public), although he spared Liu San-wu for his past service. Chu Yuan-chang then read the metropolitan examination papers himself. After ranking the papers, he held a second palace examination. Ironically, the subject for the second palace examination was the emperor's complaint that after thirty years in power he still needed to complement civil rule with penal measures. Under such imperial pressure, the metropolitan and palace rolls of 1397 *chin-shih* were reissued with 61 graduates, all northerners.[86] Thereafter, examiners took careful note of the

---

84. *Huang-Ming t'ung-chi chi-yao,* 9.1b–2a; and *Ming-shih chi-shih pen-mo* 明史紀事本末 (Record of the beginning and end of recorded events in Ming history), compiled by Ku Ying-t'ai 谷應泰, San-min Bookstore version of the 1658 edition (Taipei, 1969), pp. 153–54.

85. *Huang-Ming t'ung-chi chi-yao,* 10.6a–6b.

86. See *Huang-Ming kung-chü k'ao,* 2.37b–38a; *Chuang-yuan t'u-k'ao,* 1.11a–11b; *Ming-tai wei-k'o hsing-shih lu,* A.2b–3a; and *Huang-Ming san-yuan k'ao,* 1.20a–20b. This is the only year with two sets of metropolitan and palace examination rosters, thus yielding two *chuang-yuan,* and so on.

geographical background of *chin-shih* candidates. A bureaucratic pigeon-hole was devised to identify the geographical origins of examination papers; anonymous papers thereafter were designated for grading as either a "northern paper" (*pei-chüan* 北卷) or a "southern paper" (*nan-chüan* 南卷).

Despite the Hung-wu emperor's intervention in 1397, he did not set a permanent quota for *chin-shih* degrees. He did successfully raise the issue for official scrutiny. Southern domination of the *chin-shih* rolls continued at above the 80% level until a regional quota was set by the Hung-hsi emperor in 1425, which granted northern candidates 40% of all places in the metropolitan examinations, but no metropolitan examinations were held in 1425 or 1426. Later in the 1427 examination during the Hsuan-te reign (1426–35), the first metropolitan examination under a regional quota system, the quota was slightly revised to grant northerners 35%, southerners 55%, and those from the "central region" 10% of all places. The central region quota was established in 1427 to solve problems of determining whether marginal areas should be placed in the northern or southern quota. After 1489 this ratio was followed until the late Ming and, as Table 2.7 reveals, reiterated in the Ch'ing.[87]

The *chin-shih* quotas did set absolute limits on the degree of dominance southern gentry could achieve in the competition for selection of officials. Nevertheless, quotas could not equalize the competition for the highest rankings in the palace examinations, which determined whether a graduate was appointed to the court, to the metropolitan and provincial bureaucracy, or to local prefectures and counties. As Table 2.8 indicates, the highest-ranked *chin-shih* generally came from the south and consequently were more likely to be appointed to the Hanlin Academy or other high capital positions.

In the 1424 metropolitan examination, for example, 125 graduates (84.5%) came from the south and 8 (5.4%) from the central region, while only 15 (10.1 %) came from the north (see Table 2.5). The *Veritable Records* (*Shih-lu* 實錄) from the Hung-hsi reign (1425) noted that typically only 10% of the metropolitan graduates were northerners. Clearly they kept track. The 1425 quota reform claimed that literary talent (i.e., addressing candidates from the south) was insufficient as a measure for selecting officials

87. The north included five provinces: the Northern Chih-li capital region, Shan-tung, Shan-hsi, Ho-nan, and Shen-hsi. The south comprised the eastern prefectures belonging to the Southern Chih-li capital region, Che-chiang, Chiang-hsi, Fu-chien, Hu-kuang, and Kuang-tung. For the central region, Ssu-ch'uan, Kuang-hsi, Yun-nan, Kuei-chou, and the western prefectures and townships of the Southern Chih-li region were counted together. See *Ming-shih*, 3/1686–87, 3/1697. See also Danjō, "Mindai kakyo kaikaku," pp. 499–507.

and that practical and moral aspects (i.e., addressing candidates from the north) must also be taken into account. The 6:4 quota, and later the 1427 revision to 55:35:10, guaranteed northerners sufficient access to the lower levels of the civil service.[88]

The quota system for *chin-shih* degrees was established ten years after the Yung-lo emperor began to move the capital to Peking in 1415, a process that was completed, with second thoughts, in 1421.[89] Such a policy represented farsighted efforts to reunify northerners and southerners after two centuries of separation and to equalize the chances of the north vis-à-vis the south at a time when the change in capitals further cemented the importance of the north in imperial politics. For instance, the institutionalization of the Peking dialect as the official spoken language of "Mandarins," with its Mongol and Jurchen hybrid accretions, meant that after 1425 the dominant values, ideas, questions, and debates that prevailed in court and among officials would be articulated in a classical language whose pronunciation was shrewdly based on the hybrid Mandarin dialect of the capital region in north China and not on the Han Chinese dialects of the more populous and prosperous south, as had been the case when the capital had been in Nanking from 1368 to 1415. China was divided into linguistic units to give special advantages to one group, northerners. Southern Chinese whose native dialects differed from the dominant, official language of Mandarin were still able to overcome their linguistic disadvantages through the translation of their greater wealth into superior educational resources and facilities, but at the price of relegating their native southern dialects below Mandarin in importance.

The chief method the Hung-wu emperor had used to deal with these problems, however, was to stop altogether or to limit the scope of the civil examination process. Thus, during the first Ming reign the examinations were not the chief means of official recruitment. A total of only 930 *chin-shih* degrees were awarded in the thirty years Chu Yuan-chang was in power. This worked out to only about 31 per year, about the same rate as during the Yuan (see Chapter 1), such a low number that the bureaucracy

---

88. See Danjō, "Mindai kakyo kaikaku," pp. 508–10. On pp. 511–18, Danjō uses ancillary Ming writings to establish the 1427 date. The *Huang-Ming chuang-yuan ch'üan-ts'e*, 3.46a, corroborates 1427 as the date for the beginning of tripartite quotas, but Tung Ch'i-ch'ang 董其昌 (1555–1636) in his *Hsueh-k'o k'ao-lueh* 學科考略 (Brief overview of civil examination studies) (Shanghai: Commercial Press, *Ts'ung-shu chi-ch'eng ch'u-pien*, 1936), p. 6, gives 1425 for the beginning of tripartite quotas.

89. On the process of switching the capital, see Aramiya Manabu 新宮學, "Nankei kando" 南京還都 (Restoring the capital to Nanking), in *Wada Hakutoku kyōju koki kinen: Minshin jidai no hō to shakai* 和田博德教授古稀記念：明清時代の法と社會 (Tokyo: Kyuko shoin, 1993), pp. 59–89.

was not significantly reproduced via this avenue of selection.[90] Thereafter, the yearly production of *chin-shih* increased, but for the early reigns the civil examinations remained only one small avenue to high office. Their regional bias was simply unacceptable to the Hung-wu and Yung-lo emperors. Only after 1450, when an acceptable regional quota system for *chin-shih* degrees was in place, did civil examinations become the chief route to high office.[91]

## FROM USURPER TO SAGE: THE YUNG-LO REIGN

The Yung-lo reign began in 1402 with a bloodbath after a divisive civil war. It ended in 1424 with Chu Ti, the Prince of Yen, declared in civil examinations essays (see below) a sage-king in the line of Yao, Shun, and Yü.[92] Unlike Han and T'ang emperors, who had not received the transmission of "political legitimacy" (*chih-t'ung*) from the sages, the Yung-lo emperor claimed that he and his father had repossessed the "orthodox transmission of the Tao" (*tao-t'ung*).[93] He could not have accomplished this feat without literati support. Nor could he have succeeded without relieving the troubled marriage between Ch'eng-Chu Tao Learning and the Hung-wu emperor, which enabled Chu Ti to restore the dynasty's partnership with literati by expanding the scope and magnitude of the civil service examination curriculum beyond the limits his father, Chu Yuan-chang, had imposed. But before we can grasp how the *Tao-hsueh* persuasion increasingly permeated political life during the Ming dynasty and how the court-bureaucracy partnership was restored, we must first reconstruct the tragic imperial bloodletting of literati that the narrative of Ming Tao Learning orthodoxy has written out of its genealogy.

When Chu Ti, then Prince of Yen in "Pei-p'ing" (北平, "Northern Peace"), installed himself by force as the Yung-lo (永樂, "Eternal Happiness") emperor in 1402, he personally asked the eminent literati-scholar Fang Hsiao-ju and then capital vice-censor Lien Tzu-ning to serve him. A

---

90. Danjō, "Mindai kakyo kaikaku," p. 514; and Ikoma, "Minsho kakyo gokakusha no shushin ni kan suru ichi kōsatsu," pp. 48.

91. Wolfgang Franke notes that the average number of *chin-shih* rose from about 150 every three years between 1388 and 1448, to 290 between 1451 and 1505, and then to 330 from 1508 to 1643. See Franke, "Historical Writing during the Ming," in Frederick W. Mote and Denis Twitchett, eds. *The Cambridge History of China*, vol. 7, part 1, *The Ming Dynasty, 1368–1644* (Cambridge: Cambridge University Press, 1988), p. 726. Compare this with Tables 1.1–1.4.

92. See the palace examination questions by the Yung-lo emperor and the best essays dating from 1404–24 in *Huang-Ming chuang-yuan ch'üan-ts'e*, 2.18a–52b, 3.1a–40a.

93. See Chu Ti's "Hsu" 序 (Preface) to his *Sheng-hsueh hsin-fa*.

controversial *secundus* (*pang-yen* 榜眼) in the 1385 palace examination, who had berated Chu Yuan-chang in his palace essay for Chu's execution of ministers and officials, Lien had loyally served both the founding Hung-wu and succeeding Chien-wen emperors. When Lien refused and rebuked the prince for his usurpation, Chu Ti had Lien's tongue cut off to silence him. The Prince of Yen then justified his occupation of the Ming capital and ascension to the throne in place of the Chien-wen emperor by saying: "My only desire was to emulate the Duke of Chou, who came to support young King Ch'eng."[94] It is said that Lien put his finger to his mouth and using his blood traced on the ground the sentence: "Where is King Ch'eng?"[95]

In Fang Hsiao-ju's case the confrontation with imperial majesty was equally chilling. The Prince of Yen, politely at first, demanded that Fang, a confidant of the Chien-wen emperor and likely the last official to see him still alive, draft the announcement of the prince's succession. When Fang refused and labeled Chu Ti a criminal, the two men got into a heated argument:

94. For the locus classicus of the Duke of Chou's sagely behavior as regent in assisting the infant son, King Ch'eng (r. 1042/35–1006 B.C.), of his brother King Wu (r. 1049/45–1043 B.C.), see *Shang-shu cheng-i* 尚書正義 (Orthodox meanings in the Documents Classic), compiled by K'ung Ying-ta 孔穎達 (547–648) et al., in *Shang-shu lei-chü ch'u-chi* 尚書類聚初集 (Taipei: Hsin-wen-feng Press, 1984), vol. 1, 198–202. See also Ssu-ma Ch'ien, *Shih-chi*, 33/1518.

95. See the account in *Ming-shih chi-shih pen-mo*, p. 209. See also the 1609 preface by Kuo Tzu-chang 郭子章 to the *Lien Chung-ch'eng kung wen-chi* 練中丞公文集 (Collected writings of Lien Tzu-ning), late Ming Wan-li edition, p. 3a; and the 1762 preface by Chou Huang 周煌 to the *Lien Chung-ch'eng Chin-ch'uan chi*, pp. 1a–4a. Lien's collected writings were first put together in 1491 by Wang Tso 王佐 (1440–1512) under the title *Chin-ch'uan yü-hsieh chi* 金川玉屑集 (Collection of exquisite writing from Chin-ch'uan). Later Wang was able to add writings by Lien called "Tzu-ning i-kao" 子寧遺稿 (Bequeathed drafts of Lien Tzu-ning) that had been hidden by one of Lien's townsmen. The collection was republished in 1543. Li Meng-yang 李夢陽 (1473–1529), when he served as an education official in Chiang-hsi in 1511, prepared a shrine near Lien's birthplace and also helped print his writings. See Li's "Lien-kung i-shih" 練公遺事 (Remaining affairs of Master Lien), appended to *Lien Chung-ch'eng kung wen-chi*, pp. 17a–17b. For different versions of this confrontation, which generally confirm the version translated, see *Chien-wen ch'ao-yeh hui-pien* 建文朝野彙編 (Compendium of unofficial records on the Chien-wen reign), compiled by T'u Shu-fang 屠叔方, Wan-li edition, 10.15a–31a, in *Pei-ching t'u-shu-kuan ku-chi chen-pen ts'ung-k'an*, vol. 11 (Peking: Shu-mu Press, 1988). Late Ming and early Ch'ing biographies of Lien accept this version of the events. See Li Chih 李贄 (1527–1602), *Hsu ts'ang-shu* 續藏書 (A book to be hidden away, continuation) (Taipei: Chung-hua Bookstore, 1974), pp. 283–85; and the *Ming ming-ch'en yen-hsing-lu* 明名臣言行錄 (Record of words and actions of famous Ming officials), compiled by Hsu K'ai-jen 徐開任, Ch'ing edition (reprint, Taipei: Ming-wen Bookstore, 1991), 10.4a–7b.

*Prince:* I modeled myself on the Duke of Chou who served King Ch'eng and no more.

*Fang Hsiao-ju:* Where is King Ch'eng?

*Prince:* He burned himself to death [in the palace].

*Fang:* Why don't you establish King Ch'eng's son as emperor?

*Prince:* The nation requires a mature ruler.

*Fang:* Then why don't you establish King Ch'eng's younger brother as ruler?

*Prince:* These are my family's affairs and that's all.[96]

The prince became agitated and gave Fang Hsiao-ju the writing brush to prepare the announcement of his accession. Fang threw the brush to the ground and in tears scornfully continued the argument:

*Fang:* If I must die, then so be it. I will not write the draft for the announcement.

*Prince* (loudly): How can you expect to die so suddenly? In dying are you not concerned about your relatives to the ninth degree?

*Fang:* What does it matter to me if you make it to the tenth degree?

The Prince of Yen, realizing that Fang Hsiao-ju—who knew what happened to the Chien-wen emperor—would never acknowledge him as the new emperor, ordered his attendants to use knives to slit open Fang's mouth on both sides up to his ears. Then, Fang was tossed back into prison, where his friends and followers were brought to him one by one. When Fang refused to see them, they were killed. It is said that Fang was in agony for seven days, but until his death he continued to mock Chu Ti for his pretensions and left a famous lyric for posterity.[97]

"King Ch'eng," that is, the Chien-wen emperor, was probably dead. Only the remains of the empress and their eldest son were found in the fire debris. A funeral service for the fallen ruler was carried out by the

---

96. *Huang-Ming t'ung-chi shu-i,* 3.66a–66b. For unofficial late-Ming versions, again see *Chien-wen ch'ao-yeh hui-pien,* 7.1a–28b. See also *Ming-shih chi-shih pen-mo,* pp. 206–07; Li Chih, *Hsu ts'ang-shu,* pp. 287–88; and Robert Crawford, Harry Lamley, and Albert Mann, "Fang Hsiao-ju in Light of Early Ming Society," *Monumenta Serica* 15 (1956): 305–07.

97. Given the close overlap in the accounts of Lien Tzu-ning's and Fang Hsiao-ju's defiance, it is likely that the accounts have become conflated. In the *Yü-p'i li-tai t'ung-chien chi-lan* 御批歷代通鑑輯覽 (Imperially approved collection of mirrors for aid in government over several dynasties), Ch'ien-lung edition (reprint, Taipei: n.p., n.d.), 101.21b–22a, for instance, the King Ch'eng story is associated only with Fang Hsiao-ju.

Prince of Yen on July 20, one week after the fall of Nanking on July 13, although rumors that the Chien-wen emperor had escaped the burning palace continued throughout the Ming dynasty.[98] Lien Tzu-ning was executed, along with his entire family and lineage. From the latter, over 150 people were murdered, some only distantly related (the ninth or tenth degree of kinship). Several hundred were banished. In Fang Hsiao-ju's case some 873 of his relatives were executed. Besides Fang and Lien, the kin of other Chien-wen loyalists were also eliminated, with some estimates going as high as ten thousand for the total number of officials and members of their families who were murdered in 1402.[99]

The Chien-wen reign was expunged from the historical records, becoming instead the 31st to the 35th years of the long-since-dead (d. 1398) Hung-wu emperor.[100] "Veritable Records" of the early reigns were twice tampered with, and in the final version of the Hung-wu reign the "Veritable Records" were doctored with falsehoods to confirm Chu Ti as the legitimate and sole successor to his father.[101] As the "Eternal Happiness" (Yung-lo) emperor, Chu Ti became a powerful monarch, known posthumously as "T'ai-tsung" 太宗 (Paramount scion) and "Wen huang-ti" 文皇帝 (Emperor of culture), the latter an ironic if savvy choice given the military means Chu Ti had used to remove his nephew, the "Establisher of Culture" (Chien-wen), from the throne in 1402. After 1538, the Yung-lo emperor was granted the additional temple name "Ch'eng-tsu" 成祖 (Formative ancestor) by the then-reigning Chia-ching emperor (r. 1522–66), who, like Chu Ti, established a new line of imperial succession.[102]

98. For an account of these rumors, Chu Ti's unwillingness to quash them, and how the Ch'ing dynasty *Ming History* project handled them, see *Yü-p'i li-tai t'ung-chien chi-lan,* 101.21a–21b; and Harold Kahn, *Monarchy in the Emperor's Eyes: Image and Reality in the Ch'ien-lung Reign* (Cambridge: Harvard University Press, 1971), pp. 14–46.

99. See *Ming-shih chi-shih pen-mo,* pp. 206–19.

100. See the *Chien-wen ch'ao-yeh hui-pien,* 20.24a.

101. See Hok-lam Chan, "The Rise of Ming T'ai-tsu (1368–98): Facts and Fictions in Early Ming Historiography," *Journal of the American Oriental Society* 95 (1975): 679–715. See also Romeyn Taylor, trans., *Basic Annals of Ming T'ai-tsu* (San Francisco: Chinese Materials Center, 1975), p. 10; and Wolfgang Franke, "The Veritable Records of the Ming Dynasty," in W. G. Beasley and E. G. Pulleyblank, eds., *Historians of China and Japan* (Oxford: Oxford University Press, 1961), pp. 60–77. The *Basic Annals,* compiled in the Ch'ing, restored the Hung-wu emperor's plea for future obedience to his "Imperial Grandson."

102. On the Chia-ching emperor's decision, see Carney Fisher, *The Chosen One: Succession and Adoption in the Court of Ming Shizong* (Sydney: Allen & Unwin, 1990); and Adam Schorr, "The Trap of Words: Political Power, Cultural Authority, and Language Debates in Ming Dynasty China" (Ph.D. diss., UCLA, East Asian Languages and Culture, 1994), pp. 263–86.

In effect, Chu Ti was the second founder of the Ming dynasty (he moved the capital to Pei-ching 北京 [Peking] between 1415 and 1421), after his father, Chu Yuan-chang, who was called "T'ai-tsu" 太祖 (Paramount ancestor), had established the first Ming capital in Nanking. Following the usurpation, Chu Ti actively promoted classical studies, especially the literati persuasion known as Tao Learning. Chu's own *Sheng-hsueh hsin-fa* 聖學心法 (The method of the mind in the sages' teachings), completed in 1409 and presented to his designated successor, was emblematic in his mind of the unity of the *tao-t'ung* (orthodox transmission of the Tao), which he and his successors successfully linked to the *chih-t'ung* (transmission of political legitimacy) that Ming emperors claimed for their reigns.[103]

The "sagely Duke of Chou" became a "sage-king," a paragon of Sung dynasty Ch'eng-Chu ideals, which linked him doctrinally to the sagely rulers of antiquity, just as Sung Tao Learning masters were linked to the teachings of Confucius and Mencius. We shall see in Chapter 8 how this uniquely late imperial cultural and political homology played out in the precincts of the expanded scope of Ming and Ch'ing civil examinations after 1425. For the Ming, both Chu Yuan-chang and Chu Ti were canonized as the imperial successors of Yao and Shun, just as Ch'eng I and Chu Hsi succeeded Confucius and Mencius. A typical refrain in prefaces prepared for officials' reports by examiners such as Wu Ch'i 吳啟 (1456 *chin-shih*), chief examiner for the 1465 Shan-tung provincial examination for instance, went: "His highness has modeled himself on his imperial ancestors and ruled [the dynasty] by basing it all on the *Tao* of the various [sages] such as Yao, Shun, Yü, T'ang, King Wen, King Wu, the Duke of Chou and Confucius. None has been more glorious than today's [rulers] in applying the *Tao* of scholars to rule the empire" (我皇上法祖宗而為治，一皆本諸堯舜禹湯文武周公孔子之道，以儒道君天下，莫盛於今日。).[104]

103. See Chu Ti's preface to his *Sheng-hsueh hsin-fa*, pp. 1a–28a. Cf. *Huang-Ming kung-chü k'ao*, 1.82a. For a summary of Chu Ti's "image building," see Cheuk-yin Lee 李焯然, "Chih-kuo chih Tao—Ming Ch'eng-tsu chi ch'i Sheng-hsueh hsin-fa" 治國之道—明成祖及其聖學心法 (The art of rulership—the Ming Emperor Ch'eng-tsu and his *The Method of the Mind in the Sages' Teachings*), *Han-hsueh yen-chiu* 漢學研究 17 (1991): 211–25. Lee's account glosses over the murders of 1402. For a more balanced discussion, see Chu Hung 朱鴻, *Ming Ch'eng-tsu yü Yung-lo cheng-chih* 明成祖與永樂政治 (The Ming Emperor Ch'eng-tsu and politics in the Yung-lo reign) (Taipei: Teacher's College Institute of History Monograph, 1988), pp. 81–129. Cf. Wilson, *Genealogy of the Way*, pp. 88–97, 229–36.

104. See Wu Ch'i's "Hsu" 序 (Preface), pp. 4b–5a, for the *Shan-tung hsiang-shih lu* 山東鄉試錄 (Record of Shan-tung provincial civil examinations), 1465, in *Ming-tai teng-k'o-lu hui-pien*, vol. 2.

To become such a moral paragon, however, Chu Ti had to submit symbolically to certain classical constraints, namely the Mencian strain of political idealism that had cost both Fang Hsiao-ju and Lien Tzu-ning their lives but had also apotheosized them into literati martyrs. Having usurped the throne from the Chien-wen emperor, whom he accused of incompetence and heresy, and whose officials he described as traitorous vermin (*chien-ch'en* 姦臣), Chu Ti stood to gain from Mencius' legitimation of regicide. He himself had just removed an emperor whom he accused of corruption and immorality, and thus the "change in heaven's mandate" conveniently served his political needs in ways that his father, as we have seen, foresaw and vehemently opposed.[105]

In fact, perversely, what had offended Chu Yuan-chang about Mencius' words could now be welcomed, although unofficially, by Chu Ti as justification for his military action. His nephew, a ruler who had not been worthy of the office, had been rightfully forced out. As early as 1404, Chu Ti decided that Mencius should be restored to the imperial curriculum for rulers (*ti-wang chih hsueh* 帝王之學), although the expurgated *Meng-tzu chieh-wen* was still used as the official text through the 1409 metropolitan examination.[106] In 1409 Chu Ti had included in his preface to the *Sheng-hsueh hsin-fa* a full and public capitulation to the Mencian view that "the people were the basis of the dynasty" (民者國之本也). Indeed, the Yung-lo emperor added: "A sagely king always preserves his common people as his children. If they have nothing to eat, he first considers their hunger. If they have no clothing, he first thinks about their feeling cold. If the people want life, then I will accord with their wishes. If the desires of the people hate luxury, then I will get rid of such excesses."[107] Chu Ti had learned that emperors could have it both ways—both hide and reveal their true intentions—through the Canon if they conceded the moral high ground to the "people" and restored the partnership between literati and the court to gain public support.[108]

In this way, Tao Learning moral philosophy was utilized in part as political ideology in an attempt to draw attention away from the events of 1402.[109] But the "Chien-wen martyrs," however suicidal in their actions, were also motivated by morally compelling literati political ideals that had

105. *Huang-Ming t'ung-chi chi-yao*, 11.8a, 12.17b; and *Ming-shih chi-shih pen-mo*, 16.193.

106. *Huang-Ming t'ung-chi shu-i*, 4.8b–9b; and Li T'iao-yuan, *Chih-i k'o-so chi*, 1.29–30.

107. *Sheng-hsueh hsin-fa*, "Hsu," p. 10a.

108. Mao P'ei-chi 毛佩琦, "Ts'ung Sheng-hsueh hsin-fa k'an Ming Ch'eng-tsu Chu Ti te chih-kuo li-hsiang" 從聖學心法看明成祖朱棣的治國理想 (A view of Ming Ch'eng-tsu Chu Ti's ideals of ordering the dynasty from his *The method of the mind in the sages' teachings*), *Ming-shih yen-chiu* 明史研究 1 (1991): 119–30.

109. See Hok-lam Chan, "The Chien-wen, Yung-lo, Hung-hsi, and Hsuan-te Reigns," pp. 214–21.

preceded but were still part of Tao Learning in the tumultuous early years of the fifteenth century. At the same time, however, the political usurper, Chu Ti, culturally appropriated Tao Learning moral philosophy and became a great Ming sage-emperor. Both sides claimed classical orthodoxy. Chu Ti was the victor in the world of political power, but Lien Tzu-ning and Fang Hsiao-ju remained frightening legends.

The martyrdom of loyal officials and the sageliness of the new emperor were both woven into the historical tapestry known as the Ming dynasty. Who were the real upholders of classical ideals? Chu Ti? Fang Hsiao-ju? Who had the right to judge? Was Chu Ti's support for Tao Learning merely a ploy? Or was it a way to cleanse himself and his officials psychologically after the period of bloodletting he had ordered and gain literati support? Historians, in contrast to philosophers, must deal with both sides. The seamless narrative of Chu Yuan-chang's and Chu Ti's sageliness, despite their execution of thousands of officials, was continually reproduced in the civil examinations, where the early Ming dynasty could control the public record of its political and cultural legitimacy by determining the official interpretations of the Classics. I emphasize here the early Ming cultural idealization of Ming sage-kings, because Chu Ti's successful usurpation of power in 1402 was later studied and emulated by the early Manchu emperors of the Ch'ing dynasty to justify their conquest of the Ming and right to rule over "China" (see Chapter 11).

Most Mandarins, as we shall see, were indispensable partners in the wedding between Tao Learning and imperial autocracy during the Hung-wu and Yung-lo reigns. Moreover, the repeated ideological uses of Tao Learning by Ming and Ch'ing rulers were not fortuitous. The classical Canon and its commentators had since the Han and T'ang dynasties been supported by and in turn been supportive of the imperial system. Li Shih-min 李世民 (r. 626–49), for instance, had assassinated his brother, the chosen successor, in 626 and then forced his father, Emperor Kao-tsu (r. 618–26), to abdicate in his favor. Later in 638, as Emperor T'ai-tsung, Li Shih-min authorized compilation of the *Wu-ching cheng-i* 五經正義 (Orthodox meanings in the Five Classics) to provide the definitive textual basis for classical learning in civil examinations during the T'ang dynasty. As we have seen, however, no definitive "T'ang orthodoxy" emerged. Instead T'ang emperors such as Li Shih-min were content to accept the literary and classical trends that literati created—as long as imperial power was not challenged. Changes in the T'ang civil examinations resulted from the shifting balance among literati involved in the debates over belles lettres versus classical learning in the curriculum.[110]

110. Howard J. Wechsler, "T'ai-tsung (reign 626–49) the Consolidator," in Denis Twitchett, ed., *The Cambridge History of China*, vol. 3, part 1 (Cambridge: Cambridge

After the fall of the Sung dynasty, however, Yuan, Ming, and Ch'ing rulers wisely chose Tao Learning to serve this ideological function. When compared with the alternatives offered by Buddhism, Taoism, and popular religion, which Mongol, Han Chinese, and Manchu emperors also used effectively to assert dynastic legitimacy among commoners,[111] the appeal to Ch'eng-Chu Tao Learning put these rulers in touch with their most lettered and influential elite, the Han Chinese literati.[112] In Weberian terms, a natural "elective affinity" between the Ming dynasty (the ruler and his bureaucracy) and literati thought (Tao Learning) was exploited by both sides to a degree that Yuan dynasty rulers and literati had never achieved.

In particular, we should note the hidden affinity that united the moral values of Tao Learning and the social values of local Han gentry elites, an affinity that, as we saw in Chapter 1, gathered covert strength during the Yuan dynasty when Han Chinese were marginalized under Mongol rule. When Mongol rulers in the early fourteenth century turned somewhat from coercive to cultural forms of control vis-à-vis Han Chinese, they reproduced a structure of political relationships which during the Sung had empowered Han elites via the civil service examinations in the bureaucracy. By the early Ming, the cultural values of the dynastic educational system reflected the Tao Learning sympathies of local gentry elites. The latter thereby held an advantage in their quest for prestige and status because the civil examinations tested what they took as their cultural birthright, mastery of Tao Learning. A profound marriage of cultural and political convenience between the ruler and his literati elites lurked beneath the tumultuous events of 1402.[113]

On the other side were the martyrs like Fang Hsiao-ju and Lien Tzu-ning, who defied both political ideology and social status to choose instead

University Press, 1979), pp. 182–87, 214–15. For the Hung-wu emperor's interest in Li Shih-min, see Chia Nai-lien, "Ts'ung Meng-tzu chieh-wen chih Ch'ien-shu," p. 45.

111. See Romeyn Taylor, "Official and Popular Religion and the Political Organization of Chinese Society in the Ming," in Kwang-ching Liu, ed., Orthodoxy in Late Imperial China, pp. 126–57. See also K'o-k'uan Sun, "Yü Chi and Southern Taoism during the Yuan Period," in Langlois, ed., China under Mongol Rule, p. 212–53; and James Watson, "Standardizing the Gods: The Promotion of T'ien Hou ('Empress of Heaven') along the South China Coast," in David Johnson, Andrew Nathan, and Evelyn Rawski, eds., Popular Culture in Late Imperial China (Berkeley: University of California Press, 1985), pp. 292–324.

112. On the literatus (shih 士), see Bol, This Culture of Ours, pp. 32–75.

113. See also the discussion in Chapter 7. Cf. Pierre Bourdieu and Monique de Saint-Martin, "Scholastic Values and the Values of the Educational System," in J. Eggleston, ed., Contemporary Research in the Sociology of Education (London: Metheun, 1974), pp. 338–71.

martyrdom. Tao Learning served both sides. The raison d'être for both imperial power and literati idealism was located, selectively to be sure, in the classical Canon. An analysis of the precise cultural content of imperial ideology in early Ming China enables us to grasp how Ch'eng-Chu philosophy simultaneously served imperial purposes and elite interests after 1402. At the same time, however, the legends of Lien Tzu-ning and Fang Hsiao-ju eluded contextualization and leapt from historical contingency to timeless martyrdom.

The actions of the "Chien-wen martyrs" were never part of the Ming civil examination curriculum nor an object of official study until the eve of the fall of the dynasty in the seventeenth century. Their legends lived on, however, as millions of Ming and Ch'ing dynasty examination candidates, generation after generation, relearned in the *Documents Classic* the sagely model set by the Duke of Chou in dutifully serving his brother's son, King Ch'eng. The chasm between public writing, which the dynasty could and did monitor, and private reading, which was beyond the reach of late imperial government, could not be bridged after the political usurper Chu Ti achieved sage-king status. If the early Ming is a frightening period in Chinese history because of the slaughter of officials by the Hung-wu and Yung-lo emperors, it is also frightening because a few literati were willing to die, and sacrifice almost all their kin, rather than submit to them.

## ESTABLISHING A LATE IMPERIAL
## *TAO-HSUEH* CLASSICAL CURRICULUM

If the suppressed memories of Lien Tzu-ning and Fang Hsiao-ju lived on as legend, the cultural work needed to augment Chu Ti's legitimacy and to domesticate politically orthodox Ch'eng-Chu Tao Learning was carried out by men who made the transition from serving the Chien-wen emperor to submitting to the Yung-lo emperor with few public qualms of conscience. For every Lien Tzu-ning there were many others like Hanlin academician Yang Jung 楊榮 (1371–1440), who greeted the Prince of Yen when he entered Nanking and felicitously chose to serve the new ruler. Yang changed his name from Tzu-jung 子榮 to commemorate the occasion. Yang Jung had taken his *chin-shih* in 1400, placing sixth, under the tutelage of the Chien-wen emperor.[114] The examiners and 110 graduates of the 1400 *chin-shih* examination were representative of the fact that most of the Chien-wen emperor's officials did not heed the classical injunction

114. *Tien-shih teng-k'o lu*, 1400: 1/14.

held by some later literati that once having served the Chien-wen emperor they could not very well serve his murderer (*pu erh-ch'en* 不二臣).[115]

### Early Ming Literati Collaborators

Records from the palace examination of 1400, for example, show that Fang Hsiao-ju was one of the Chien-wen emperor's readers for the examination, while Hsieh Chin 解縉 (1369–1415) was one of the officials in charge of collecting the candidates' papers. Both were Hanlin academicians. Rather than martyr himself in 1402, Hsieh Chin, a *chin-shih* of 1388, chose the path of least resistance. For his loyalty, Chu Ti reappointed Hsieh to the Hanlin Academy and immediately delegated him in 1402 to go through the Chien-wen emperor's papers and remove anything that might be used to challenge the usurpation. Next, and still in 1402, the Yung-lo emperor put Hsieh Chin in charge of the first revision of Chu Yuan-chang's "Veritable Records," which were altered to confirm Chu Ti as emperor and denigrate the Chien-wen emperor as illegitimate. Among the changes introduced was the claim that Chu Ti was born to the Empress Ma (he was likely born of a concubine). The version of history that Chu Ti had Hsieh Chin help prepare (there was a second revision; see below) thus presented Chu as the eldest surviving son of Chu Yuan-chang. Chu Ti rightfully should have been designated the heir apparent in 1392, when his older brother died, but as a result of unscrupulous advisors who later served the Chien-wen emperor, the heir became instead the unqualified "imperial grandson."[116]

Hu Kuang 胡廣 (1370–1418) was selected as *optimus* for the 1400 palace examination. Like Lien Tzu-ning, Hu was one of the Chiang-hsi elite so prominent in the Chien-wen emperor's court. Hu finished eighth on the metropolitan examination of the same year and second in an earlier Chiang-hsi provincial competition. Curiously, the Chien-wen emperor had Hu change his name to Ching 靖 before he entered the Hanlin Academy because the original was the same name as that of a Han dynasty official.[117]

Another Chiang-hsi native who took his *chin-shih* degree in 1400 was

---

115. Ibid., 1400: 1/1–68. In this case, literati were not caught in the dilemma of choosing between dynasties, such as Sung or Yuan and Ming or Ch'ing, but of serving two consecutive rulers of the same dynasty. The rhetoric of *pu-erh-ch'en* was more muted when dealing with rulers in the same dynasty.

116. *Tien-shih teng-k'o lu*, 1400: 1/3. On Hsieh's career, see his biography in *Ming-shih*, 147.4115–23. The process of fabrication is detailed in Hok-lam Chan, "The Rise of Ming T'ai-tsu," pp. 688–91.

117. *Huang-Ming san-yuan k'ao*, 1.34a–b.

Chin Yu-tzu 金幼孜 (1368–1431), who finished seventh on the palace examination and thirteenth on the metropolitan. Earlier he had finished ninth on the Chiang-hsi provincial examination.[118] Chin was Lien Tzu-ning's townsman. They grew up together and as young men studied Confucius' *Spring and Autumn Annals* in preparation for the civil examinations.[119] After 1402 both Hu Kuang and Chin Yu-tzu served the Yung-lo emperor. They had not conspired against the Chien-wen emperor and saw collaboration with his conquering uncle as a way to strike a public peace with a ruler in vital need of literati support.

By conceding the moral high ground of Tao Learning to his officials, Chu Ti did not have to worry about any regional opposition from Lien's cohorts. Hu immediately changed his name back to Kuang. Changing names perhaps mitigated the moral dilemmas Hu faced.[120] Reappointed by Chu Ti as a Hanlin academician, he was later in 1414 placed in charge of the *Wu-ching Ssu-shu ta-ch'üan* 五經四書大全 (Great collection [of commentaries] for the Five Classics and Four Books) project that the Yung-lo emperor authorized to augment the Tao Learning orthodoxy. Chin Yu-tzu joined Hu Kuang and Yang Jung on this influential cultural project.[121]

In addition to ordering changes in the "Veritable Records of the Hung-wu Reign," whose first revision was completed in 1403, Chu Ti also instructed Hsieh Chin in 1404 to employ some 147 scholars to bring together all extant classical, literary, and historical writings in a single collection; when completed in 1404, the emperor named it the *Wen-hsien ta-ch'eng* 文獻大成 (Great collection of written documents). In some ways this project picked up from similar such projects initiated during the T'ang and Northern Sung dynasties. During Chu Yuan-chang's reign, for example, Hsieh Chin had in 1388 suggested to the Hung-wu emperor that he authorize a compilation of essential Tao Learning writings on the Classics. Previously, in 1373–74, Chu Yuan-chang had already indicated his interest in copying Li Shih-min, T'ang T'ai-tsung (see above), in compiling definitive records of classical learning and ancient institutional works. At that time a work entitled *Ch'ün-ching lei-yao* 群經類要 (Classified essentials

118. *Tien-shih teng-k'o lu*, 1400: 1/11, 15.

119. There is a story that Lien told Chin that Chin was destined to be a "famous official," while Lien himself would be a "loyal official." See *Chien-wen ch'ao-yeh hui-pien*, 10.15a–15b.

120. *Chuang-yuan t'u-k'ao*, 1.13a. See also the discussion in Chapter 6 about the cultural significance of name changing.

121. See Lin Ch'ing-chang 林慶彰, "Wu-ching ta-ch'üan chih hsiu-tsuan chi ch'i hsiang-kuan wen-t'i t'an-chiu" 五經大全之修纂及其相關問題探究 (Inquiry into the compilation of the Complete Collection [of commentaries] for the Five Classics and related issues), *Chung-kuo wen-che yen-chiu chi-k'an* 中國文哲研究集刊 1 (1991): 366–67.

of the Classics) was prepared to explicate the Four Books and Five Classics.[122]

The haste with which the Yung-lo project was undertaken, so soon after the usurpation, and the fact that Hsieh Chin, who had just completed an initial whitewashing of the "Veritable Records," was chosen to collect and edit the materials suggest that Chu Ti had political as well as cultural motives in mind when he said to Hsieh: "The world's affairs and matters from antiquity to today are scattered throughout many books. They are not easy to examine or read. I want to gather all affairs and matters recorded in each book and unify all the various compilations by using a phonetic classification scheme to facilitate study. Whatever contains words dealing with the techniques and crafts of the classics, histories, philosophers, litterateurs, the hundred schools, astronomy, geography, yin-yang, prognostication, medicine, Buddhism, and Taoism should all be collected into a single work."[123]

In addition to collecting documents, the compilers could ferret out materials damaging to the legitimacy of Chu Ti's accession to the throne. It is likely, then, that the compilation had its darker side, political shadows that would reach deep into the eighteenth century, when the Ch'ien-lung emperor (r. 1736–95), who understood Chu Ti's motives well and was very familiar with the records of the Yung-lo reign, authorized in the 1770s and 1780s the voluminous *Ssu-k'u ch'üan-shu* 四庫全書 (Great collection of the four treasuries) project, in part to ferret out anti-Manchu writings.[124]

The political implications of the project are clearer when we take into account that Chu Ti proved unhappy with the *Wen-hsien ta-ch'eng* when it was completed in 1404.[125] In 1405 the Yung-lo emperor instructed his close confidant Yao Kuang-hsiao 姚廣孝 (1335–1418) to undertake the project. A staff of 2,169 compilers, including Buddhists and medical specialists, was placed at Yao's disposal to comb through all known works and copy them for the project. A Buddhist monk somewhat critical of Tao Learning,[126] Yao had been instrumental in encouraging Chu Ti to

122. *Ming-shih,* 147.4115–16; *Huang-Ming kung-chü k'ao,* 1.76a–81b; and *Huang-Ming t'ung-chi chi-yao,* 6.10b. See also Ch'iu Han-sheng 邱漢生, "Ming-ch'u Chu-hsueh te t'ung-chih ti-wei" 明初朱學的統治地位 (The hegemony of Chu Hsi learning in the early Ming), *Chung-kuo che-hsueh* 中國哲學 14 (1988): 142–43.

123. *Huang-Ming kung-chü k'ao,* 1.81b. See also Shang Ch'uan 商傳, *Yung-lo huang-ti* 永樂皇帝 (The Yung-lo emperor) (Peking: Peking Press, 1989), pp. 140–47; and Chang Ch'en-shih 張忱石, "Yung-lo ta-tien shih-hua" 永樂大典史話 (Historical remarks on the Great compendium of the Yung-lo era), in *Ku-tai yao-chi kai-shu* 古代要籍概述 (Peking: Chung-hua Bookstore, 1987), pp. 187–92.

124. See Kahn, *Monarchy in the Emperor's Eyes,* pp. 44–46.

125. *Huang-Ming kung-chü k'ao,* 1.81b; and *Huang-Ming t'ung-chi chi-yao,* 13.9a.

126. Shang Ch'uan, *Yung-lo huang-ti,* p. 147.

revolt against the Chien-wen emperor and remained until Yao's death one of the emperor's closest advisors. Moreover, shortly after completing this encyclopedic project in 1407, which became known as the *Yung-lo ta-tien* 永樂大典 (Great compendium of the Yung-lo era), Yao was put in charge of a second revision of the Hung-wu emperor's "Veritable Records," lasting from 1411 to 1418. All copies of the first revision by Hsieh Chin, like copies of the original completed earlier, were completely eradicated, leaving only Yao's second revision.[127]

When we note that there were 472 graduates on the 1404 metropolitan civil examination, the first under the Yung-lo emperor, and that this was the highest number since 1385, when Chu Yuan-chang needed to fill his depleted bureaucracy after the Hu Wei-yung affair, then we can agree with Danjō Hiroshi that the sudden increase in *chin-shih* passed on the palace examination reflected the emperor's need to reproduce, immediately, literati loyal to him and not the Chien-wen emperor. When asked by examiners what quota to set in 1404, the emperor replied that he wanted to set it initially to its highest level to date but that this quota should not be continued thereafter.[128] After completion of the palace examination, the emperor further ordered that all candidates who had earlier failed the metropolitan examination should be reexamined in a special literary examination. In this way, another 60 "loyal" students were chosen to enter the Imperial School to prepare for the next metropolitan examination.[129]

Hsieh Chin, an examiner in 1400 under Chien-wen, was again chosen examiner in 1404 under Yung-lo.[130] The *optimus* for the 1404 palace examination was Tseng Ch'i from Chiang-hsi (discussed above). In fact, the top seven places all went to candidates from Chiang-hsi, the top three from Chi-shui 吉水, Hsieh Chin's and Hu Kuang's own home county. As in 1400, Chiang-hsi graduates quickly filled the Hanlin Academy. In total (see Table 2.9), 24% of the 470 graduates (some sources give 472) came from Chiang-hsi, compared with 18% from Che-chiang and 15% from Chiang-nan (not in Table 2.9).

127. See Hok-lam Chan, "The Rise of Ming T'ai-tsu," pp. 689–90; and Chang Ch'en-shih, "Yung-lo ta-tien shih-hua," p. 188.

128. See Danjō, "Mindai kakyo kaikaku," pp. 499–514. Provincial examinations were held in 1403 rather than 1402 because of the civil war and because they had been held in 1402 under the Chien-wen emperor. Similarly the metropolitan examination was delayed to 1404 instead of 1403. See *Huang-Ming san-yuan k'ao*, 2.1a–2b; and *Huang-Ming kung-chü k'ao*, 2.47–48a. Peking was officially designated the "Northern Capital" for the 1403 provincial examination. Recommended candidates were also selected for appointment in 1403. See Shang Ch'uan, *Yung-lo huang-ti*, p. 153.

129. *Huang-Ming t'ung-chi chi-yao*, 13.6a.

130. Ibid., 13.4b.

In 1406, 25% of the *chin-shih* came from Chiang-hsi; in 1411 it was up to 32%.[131] Later in 1404 Hsieh Chin was promoted to the rank of Grand Secretary,[132] confirming that loyalty to the new emperor, particularly among the Chiang-hsi elite, was quickly rewarded. In one account of Chu Ti's meeting with his seven top advisors, most of whom were from Chiang-hsi (including Hsieh Chin, Hu Kuang, Yang Jung, and Chin Yu-tzu), he praised them all for their support since he took power in 1402. Throughout the Yung-lo reign, Chiang-hsi natives took 25% to 30% of the triennial *chin-shih* degrees, a figure that began to diminish in the sixteenth century (see Chapter 5).[133]

### Early Ming Examination Ideology

Not surprisingly, the palace examination policy questions and answers for the 1404 and 1406 examinations, and thereafter, made no mention of the Chien-wen reign or even that there had been a civil war. As in the "Veritable Records," the Chien-wen reign simply disappeared. Chu Ti himself prepared the 1404 palace policy question. In 1404 the emperor asked candidates to explain the different institutional systems of antiquity; in 1406 he required them to comment on the changes in schooling during the Han, T'ang, and Sung dynasties. His focus in 1404 was on the political order; in 1406 the emphasis was the role of education in ordering society.[134]

We have seen above that Tseng Ch'i's number-one-ranked policy answer for the 1404 palace examination simply conceded that "the emperor had received the mandate to rule and now occupied the position of a sage."[135] Lin Huan 林環, the top graduate in 1406, who went on as a Hanlin compiler to work on the *Yung-lo ta-tien* project, similarly made the ruler's mind the central theme of his palace policy answer:

> Sages in ordering the world never failed to take the examining of antiquity as the Way. Moreover, when have sages not based the occurrence of order on the mind? Only the Paramount Ancestor [Chu Yuan-chang], as sage and worthy, [wisely] wielded both civil and military power. The exalted

131. *Huang-Ming chin-shih teng-k'o k'ao* 皇明進士登科考 (Study of the accession to *chin-shih* status during the august Ming dynasty), compiled by Yü Hsien 俞憲, 1548 edition, 3.2a, in *Ming-tai teng-k'o lu hui-pien*. Cf. Ikoma, "Minsho kakyo gokakusha no shushin ni kan suru ichi kōsatsu," p. 48.

132. *Huang-Ming t'ung-chi chi-yao*, 13.7b.

133. *Huang-Ming t'ung-chi shu-i*, 4.12a.

134. *Huang-Ming chuang-yuan ch'üan-ts'e*, 2.18a–44a; and *Huang-Ming chin-shih teng-k'o k'ao*, 3.1a–20b.

135. *Huang-Ming chuang-yuan ch'üan-ts'e*, 2.18a–19b, 36a–b.

Ming was set in motion, and its great virtue was accomplished. He was the esteemed ruler who unified heaven and magnified filial piety. He initiated the building of the broad foundation, taking care that the [ancient] six schools would be united and the political unification would last ten thousand generations. His achievement has been rarely duplicated. Your highness has succeeded with precious intent in thoughtfully forging ahead of past glories, and continuing the beautiful plans [of before] and opening tomorrow's glory.[136]

Lin's verbatim duplication in his 1406 policy answer of part of the pledge of loyalty prepared by Tseng Ch'i in 1404 (see above) indicates that such pledges in policy questions, which were not expected in classical essays, had political as well as cultural meaning. Initially, the Hung-wu emperor was given eminence of place in establishing the "political legitimacy" of the dynasty, but the direct transmission of that legitimacy to the Yung-lo emperor, despite his usurpation, was part of the idealized political narrative acceptable in public discourse. Throughout the Ming, formulaic paeans to the early Ming emperors became a major aspect of the civil examinations (see Chapter 8). In the Yung-lo emperor's case, such rhetoric papered over his 1402 usurpation of power.

Moreover, a significant intellectual tension was introduced into imperial Tao Learning beginning in the Yung-lo reign. As Peter Bol has noted, an important feature of the position taken by Ch'eng-Chu followers since the Southern Sung had been the claim that "latter-day rulers are not sages" and that the "authority of the sage-kings" had been transferred to scholars since Confucius.[137] During the Ming, this position was continued by dissenting literati who were critical of the Yung-lo reign (see below). In the imperial precincts of the civil examination compound, however, Chu Yuan-chang and Chu Ti, the founders of the Ming, were anointed with sage-king status linking them directly back to the enlightened rule of antiquity, which had been lost since the time of Confucius. In effect, Ming emperors co-opted the sagehood ideal of their *Tao-hsueh* followers and in public rhetoric displaced the literati as the pivot of moral orthodoxy. Nevertheless, the private writings of dissenting literati continued to stress the priority of the literatus over the ruler in the cultural life of the dynasty. These two streams of official and unofficial interpretation lasted to the end of the Ming, one in and the other out of power.

Imperial focus on the unified "mind" of the emperor in 1404 and 1406, which thereafter became one of the most widely wielded slogans in Ming and Ch'ing civil examinations, dated from the Yung-lo reign, when Chu

136. Ibid., 2.36b–43b, especially 36b–37a.
137. See Bol, "The Neo-Confucian Position in Chinese History," pp. 46–48.

Ti successfully used this Tao Learning image of "mind transmission" (*ch'uan-shou hsin-fa* 傳授心法) after the "terror of 1402" to co-opt classical legitimacy. The *hsin-fa* (methods of mind) of the sage-kings had been a frequent subject in literati writings to that point, but it was during the Yung-lo reign that this philosophic doctrine was turned into imperial ideology on the civil examinations. From 1371 to 1400, not a single palace policy question had addressed the "sage-kings' methods of the mind."[138] After the 1404 and 1406 palace examinations, the subject also appeared repeatedly in Ming metropolitan and provincial policy questions, from which we have provided some examples above.[139] In the 1547 palace examination, for a final example, the policy question attributed to the Chia-ching emperor (r. 1522–66) opined that both the Hung-wu and Yung-lo emperors had "continued the orthodox transmission of the Way of the [ancient] kings and emperors" (眞有以上繼皇王道統之正).[140]

Chu Ti's *Sheng-hsueh hsin-fa*, completed with the help of his Hanlin academicians in 1409 and presented to the heir (the future Hung-hsi emperor, r. 1425) for his moral cultivation, also preached the unity of the "orthodox transmission of the Way" and "political legitimacy."[141] A prelude to the Tao Learning compendium known as the *Hsing-li ta-ch'üan* 性理大全 (Great collection of works on nature and principles), which was later compiled from 1414 to 1415, Chu Ti's selection of classical commentaries represented reauthorization of Ch'eng-Chu Learning as cultural and philosophic orthodoxy. Chu Ti's elucidation of the famous "mind of the Tao" passage in the *Documents Classic* serves as a representative example. Citing Chu Hsi and his Sung disciples, the emperor demonstrated that he was in complete agreement with Chu Hsi that the "mind of Tao," as the venue for moral principles, should be the master, while the human mind, venue for selfish desires, should take its orders from the former. The emperor, in effect, appropriated Chu Hsi's commentary to educate his son and his subjects.[142]

---

138. See *Huang-Ming chuang-yuan ch'üan-ts'e*, 2.1a–17a. On earlier uses of *hsin-fa*, see de Bary, *Neo-Confucian Orthodoxy and the Learning of the Mind-and-Heart*, pp. 1–73.

139. For further early Ming examples, see the palace examination of 1412 in *Tien-shih teng-k'o lu*, 1412: 1/275–285, which links the "mind of the emperors and kings" with their political governance, and the palace examination of 1521 in *Tien-shih teng-k'o lu*, 1521: 6/2993ff, both in *Huang-Ming teng-k'o lu hui-pien*. See also *Hui-shih lu*, 1547: 10a–b, 50-a–57, for a policy question and answer that stresses the sageliness of the Yung-lo emperor.

140. *Chin-shih teng-k'o lu*, 1547: 1b–8b.

141. *Huang-Ming kung-chü k'ao*, 1.82a.

142. See Chu Ti, *Sheng-hsueh hsin-fa*, pp. 2b–3a. For discussion see my "Philosophy (*I-li*) versus Philology (*K'ao-cheng*)," pp. 177–80.

Perhaps by 1409 the Yung-lo emperor had put behind him his brutal actions in 1402, but the almost obligatory use of the *hsin-fa* doctrine as early as the 1404 and 1406 palace examinations suggests that more than just imperial conversion to Tao Learning orthodoxy was involved. As a sage-king, Chu Ti could have it both ways: he used Ch'eng-Chu learning for political legitimacy, and at the same time he became the greatest imperial patron of Sung Tao Learning. His literati supporters could have it both ways as well: they used *Tao-hsueh* to restore literati influence in the government, and simultaneously they saw to it that Ch'eng-Chu learning prevailed in official rhetoric.

But Chu's preface to the *Sheng-hsueh hsin-fa* had some ambiguous elements. Speaking of the principles of loyalty the ruler expected his officials to live up to, Chu Ti wrote:

> When the ruler becomes a ruler like Yao and Shun, the people become like the people of Yao and Shun. As for illustrious officials such as Kao [Yao], K'uei, [Hou] Chi, and Hsieh,[143] can they not be called glorious? Therefore, in upholding high principles without submitting to threats, nothing is greater than loyalty. Those who receive their positions and salaries from the ruler should concern themselves with the dynasty as they do their families. They should forget about themselves and follow the dynasty. They should not avoid difficulties or dangers. Nor should they make plans according to their own benefit. They should strengthen their resolve and ascertain that their resolve is unchangeable.[144]

Lien Tzu-ning, Fang Hsiao-ju, and the Chien-wen martyrs had lived up to this ideal, more than Chu Ti's well-placed collaborators such as Hsieh Chin or Hu Kuang. But mention of the former remained anathema in public life, although the emperor did on occasion, as in 1413, wish that Lien Tzu-ning had submitted to him. On the other hand, Hu Kuang, when he died in 1418, was greatly honored for his service. Earlier, however, Hsieh Chin, hated by the Yung-lo emperor's designated successor for Hsieh's opposition to him, was eventually thrown into prison in 1411 on charges of lèse-majesté where he died in 1415.[145]

### *The* Tao-hsueh *Canon*

In addition to the "correction" of the historical record, Chu Ti's regime required educational legitimation to reproduce that record. The Yung-lo

143. Kao Yao and K'uei served Emperor Shun; Hou Chi and Hsieh served Emperor Yao.

144. Chu Ti, *Sheng-hsueh hsin-fa*, "Hsu," pp. 24b–25a.

145. See *Huang-Ming t'ung-chi chi-yao*, 14.11b, 14.18b. For Hsieh's fall from grace, see *Huang-Ming t'ung-chi shu-i*, 4.17a–17b.

emperor wished to "appear as sage ruler, a teacher of his people, and a patron of learning."[146] These cultural endeavors were brought to a climax in 1415 by publication and dissemination of three classical projects, the *Ssu shu ta-ch'üan* 四書大全 (Great collection [of commentaries] for the Four Books), *Wu-ching ta-ch'üan*, and *Hsing-li ta-ch'üan* 性理大全 (Great collection [of commentaries for study] of nature and principle), whose purpose was to define and print for use the sources candidates should use to prepare for the civil examinations in all government schools down to the county level.

Scholars in the Hanlin Academy first prepared two major publishing projects, which enshrined the Ch'eng-Chu *Tao-hsueh* school as imperial orthodoxy. Entitled the *Great Collection [of Commentaries] for the Five Classics and Four Books,* these two collections were compiled in great haste. It took only nine months, from 1414 to 1415, for Hu Kuang and his staff to prepare and blend the Sung and Yuan scholia into a coherent passage-by-passage commentary for the Five Classics and Four Books. The haste with which the commentaries were compiled, perhaps to add cultural luster to the events surrounding the imminent move of the court to Peking in 1415, elicited later criticism for lack of comprehensiveness.[147] Because the three collections were compiled by Hanlin academicians who had previously been employed in revising the "Veritable Records of the Hung-wu Reign" and had also helped edit the *Yung-lo ta-tien,* later scholars also suspected that the real purpose of the *San-pu ta-ch'üan* 三部大全 trilogy was to eliminate the Chien-wen reign from classical learning. Ch'ing literati such as Ku Yen-wu frequently blamed the Yung-lo projects and their pervasive examination influence for the decline of classical studies during the Ming dynasty:

> The ruler [that is, Chu Ti] lied to the court, and those below [that is, the bureaucracy] swindled the literati. Was there ever anything like this in

---

146. Hok-lam Chan, "The Chien-wen, Yung-lo, Hung-hsi, and Hsuan-te Reigns," p. 221.

147. There are currently several studies under way to review the sources used in these early Ming projects. See, for example, Ch'en Heng-sung 陳恆嵩, "Shu-chuan ta-ch'üan ch'ü-ts'ai lai-yuan t'an-chiu" 書傳大全取材來源探究 (Inquiry into the sources selected for the *Complete Collection of Commentaries for the Documents Classic*); and Yang Chin-lung 楊晉龍, "Shih-chuan ta-ch'üan ch'ü-ts'ai lai-yuan t'an-chiu" 詩傳大全取材來源探究 (Inquiry into the sources selected for the *Complete Collection of Commentaries for the Poetry Classic*), both in Lin Ch'ing-chang 林慶彰, ed., *Ming-tai ching-hsueh kuo-chi yen-t'ao-hui lun-wen chi* 明代經學國際研討會論文集 (Taipei: Institute of Chinese Literature and Philosophy, Academia Sinica, 1996).

T'ang or Sung times? Did they not compromise honest and upright officials while replacing the Chien-wen emperor? Moreover, when the writing of [eight-legged] examination essays began, literati all at once discarded the "practical learning" transmitted since the Sung and Yuan dynasties. Those above and below were mutually gullible and became fixated on careerist interests, never stopping to ask why. Alas! The demise of classical studies in reality began from this.[148]

Other Ch'ing scholars also frequently blamed the Yung-lo projects and their pervasive influence on examinations for the decline of classical studies during the Ming dynasty. The Ch'ing compilers of the *Ming History* had similar complaints.[149]

Such intent becomes clearer when we read the preface Chu Ti prepared when the last of the trilogy, the *Hsing-li ta-ch'üan*, was completed and all three works were officially authorized for printing. Chu wrote in 1415 that upon succeeding to the throne, all sage-kings had "used the Way to order the world." Hence, he himself, "as successor to the illustrious foundations established by the great emperor, the Paramount Ancestor," had ordered his Hanlin academicians to prepare the three works "to include whatever had clarified the meaning of the Classics and to exclude whatever was contrary to the lessons of the Classics."[150] In their own statement, Hu Kuang and the compilers (including Yang Jung and Chin Yu-tzu from Chiang-hsi) echoed Chu Ti's pretense that the Chien-wen emperor had never existed and that Chu was the legitimate successor by praising him in no uncertain terms: "Never before has there been a ruler of such great action, who has been able to clarify the Way of the Six

148. *Huang-Ming kung-chü k'ao*, 1.82a–82b. See also Ku Yen-wu 顧炎武, *Jih-chih lu* 日知錄 (Record of knowledge gained day by day), in *Ssu-k'u ch'üan-shu* 四庫全書 (Complete collection of the four treasuries) (reprint, Taipei: Commercial Press, 1983–86), 858.801. On the other hand, the compilation of the three series was facilitated by the earlier completion of the *Yung-lo ta-tien* that readily supplied whatever material was necessary for the 1415 trilogy. Tim Brook contends that Ku never suggested "a conspiracy was afoot to alter the texts in such a way as to favor the rule of the Ming house." See Brook, "Edifying Knowledge: The Building of School Libraries in Ming China," *Late Imperial China* 17, 1 (June 1996): 105.

149. See the 1780s accounts of the *Ssu-shu ta-ch'üan* and *Hsing-li ta-ch'üan* by the editors of the *Ssu-k'u ch'üan-shu* project in the *Ssu-k'u ch'üan-shu tsung-mu* 四庫全書總目 (Catalog of the complete collection of the four treasuries), compiled by Chi Yun 紀昀 et al. (reprint, Taipei: I-wen Press, 1974), 36.13b–14b, 93.7b–9a. See also *Ming-shih*, 282.7222. Cf. Ch'iu Han-sheng, "Ming-ch'u Chu-hsueh te t'ung-chih ti-wei," pp. 147–53; and Lin Ch'ing-chang, "Wu-ching ta-ch'üan chih hsiu-tsuan," pp. 377–81.

150. Chu Ti, "Yü-chih Hsing-li ta-ch'üan hsu" 御製性理大全序 (Imperial preface to the official presentation of the *Great Collection of Works on Nature and Principle*), in *Hsing-li ta-ch'üan*, 1415 edition (reprint, Kyoto: Chūbun Press), pp. 1a–3b.

Classics and continue the [dynastic] unity from our previous sages like this."[151]

The *Great Collection of Works on Nature and Principle* represented curricular support for Sung Tao Learning and was required for the local, provincial, and metropolitan civil examinations for the duration of the Ming dynasty. As noted above, it included a full and unexpurgated version of the *Mencius*, Chu Ti having nothing to fear from legitimation of regicide.[152] Because of this concession, the *Ta-ch'üan* collections represented the changing political circumstances within which the Five Classics and Four Books were studied and interpreted. Both the emperor and his literati advisors collaborated to produce one of the most famous classical compendia of the late empire. As a textual monument, the *Great Collection* trilogy transcended its historical context and became a record of the post–Chu Hsi commentarial tradition that rivaled Han-T'ang scholia for eminence of place.[153]

The early Ming compilers of the *Great Collection of the Four Books*, for example, highlighted for examination candidates Chu Hsi's explication of the *Great Learning, Analects, Mencius,* and *Doctrine of the Mean.* The collected commentaries that were used became the basic imperial texts of the Four Books for almost five hundred years. The Ming government saw to it that these editions of the *Tao-hsueh* Canon were placed in county schools empirewide. No such definitive collection had existed empirewide during the Sung or Yuan dynasties. As we saw in Chapter 1, Chu Hsi was more ecumenical in his private recommendations that candidates for degrees be required to master Han and T'ang commentaries, as well as Sung masters, in the civil examination curriculum.[154]

Now such Han-T'ang commentaries were dropped as discrete works and were only selectively cited in the Sung and Yuan commentaries chosen for inclusion in the *San-pu ta-ch'üan* projects. Ming Hanlin academicians overdetermined, for example, the rigorous moralism that derived from the Ch'eng-Chu bifurcation of heavenly principles from human desires. They were later accused by Ch'ing dynasty Han Learning advocates of presenting a Buddhistic vision of good versus evil, which was more formalistic than the more nuanced dualism that Chu Hsi himself

---

151. See Hu Kuang et al., "Chin-shu piao" 進書表 (Words on presenting the [three] books), in *Hsing-li ta-ch'üan,* p. 3b. See also *Ta-Ming T'ai-tsung Wen huang-ti shih-lu* 大明太宗文皇帝實錄 (Veritable records of the Yung-lo emperor), Ming edition (reprint, Taipei: Academia Sinica), 158.2a–4a.

152. *Huang-Ming t'ung-chi chi-yao,* 11.8a, 12.17b; and *Ming-shih chi-shih pen-mo,* 16.193.

153. Ch'iu Han-sheng, "Ming-ch'u Chu-hsueh te t'ung-chih ti-wei," pp. 144–47.

154. See Brook, "Edifying Knowledge," pp. 106–07.

had enunciated.[155] When they chose commentaries on the text of the *Mencius*, for example, the early Ming Hanlin scholars working on the *Great Collection of the Four Books* selected notes that set limits to Mencius' discussion of the legitimate grounds for officials and the people to oppose an evil ruler. For the passages in the *Mencius* that had enraged the Hung-wu emperor but were tolerated by Chu Ti, Hu Kuang chose commentators who stressed that Mencius' words applied only to the chaotic historical situation of the Warring States period. Accordingly, Mencius stood as a guide to the past, not as a model for the present. His criticism of ancient tyrants could not be translated into a precedent for the enlightened age of the Ming. Moreover, the commentaries chosen, which cited the Yuan literatus Hu Ping-wen 胡炳文 (1250–1333), indicated that Mencius himself had set limits in his attack on evil rulers:

> Without Mencius' theories, there would have been no way to warn those who during later generations served as rulers of the people.... However, "Mencius said: if one has the moral integrity that I Yin [renowned advisor of the first Shang ruler, ca. 1766–1753 B.C.] had [in urging banishment of the ruler], then it is permissible [to do so]. If, however, one does not have the moral integrity of an I Yin, then a person [who speaks in this way] must be a usurper."[156]

The Yung-lo emperor's personal legitimacy and his dynasty's sovereignty, despite the important concessions made to Mencian political theory, were still based on a descending view of political power that had been demonstrated on the battlefield by force of arms. Loyalty to the ruler and his dynasty determined the limits of political criticism. If literati dissented from policies of their ruler, the forms of their dissent were politically circumscribed. Although high moral ground had been granted the ruler, even one who had fought a civil war to take power, the throne and its officials together determined the acceptable limits in practice of Mencius' theories in the civil examinations. By restoring the complete and unexpurgated version of the *Mencius*, the Yung-lo emperor had disclaimed his

155. For an example of such dualism, see the Sung-Yuan notes selected by Hu Kuang et al. on "benevolence" in the *Lun-yü chi-chu ta-ch'üan* 論語集注大全 (Great collection of the collected notes to the *Analects*), 12.4b–5a, in *Ssu-shu ta-ch'üan* (SKCS edition). See also my "Criticism as Philosophy: Conceptual Change in Ch'ing Dynasty Evidential Research," *Tsing Hua Journal of Chinese Studies*, n.s., 17 (1985): 165–98.

156. *Meng-tzu chi-chu ta-ch'üan* 孟子集注大全 (Great collection of the collected notes to the Mencius), 2.28a–29b (quotation from Hu Ping-wen), 8.5b–8b, 10.34a–35b, in *Ssu-shu ta-ch'üan*. See also *Meng-tzu yin-te*, 52/7A/31; and Lau, trans., *Mencius*, p. 189. Cf. Yun-yi Ho, "Ideological Implications of Ming Sacrifices in Early Ming," *Ming Studies* 6 (spring 1978): 55–67.

direct authority over the interpretation of any classic. Indeed, some late Ming literati outside the bureaucracy challenged the court's descending view of power at the same time that they rehabilitated the historical record of the Chien-wen emperor, Fang Hsiao-ju, and Lien Tzu-ning.[157]

Furthermore, the concern for moral self-cultivation, so prominent in the writings of Sung literati such as Ch'eng I and Chu Hsi, and so heralded by the Yung-lo emperor after 1402, probably did play an important part in granting literati some political autonomy and moral prestige, which was institutionalized through the avenue of moral remonstrance. Remonstrance as a form of political dissent, exemplified best in the careers of Lien Tzu-ning and Fang Hsiao-ju, in turn served to measure the ruler according to universal classical standards of *Tao-hsueh*. Chu Ti seems to have understood this after the 1402 Nanking massacre, even if his motives for supporting Tao Learning had an opportunistic side. During the Ming and Ch'ing, however, rulers frequently closed this avenue of dissent or diverted it into a form of bureaucratic surveillance.[158]

Although the complete *Mencius* was rehabilitated in 1415, the passages that had troubled Chu Yuan-chang in 1372 were rarely chosen by examiners for essay topics in provincial or metropolitan civil examinations. An interesting exception, which confirmed the rule, is the famous quotation "The people should be valued most" (*min wei kuei* 民為貴) from the *Mencius,* which was chosen by examiners for the 1624 Chiang-hsi provincial examination to express their dissatisfaction with eunuch power.[159] The answer by Ai Nan-ying 艾南英 (1583–1646) was highly prized (see Chapter 7 for a translation); however, because of his remarks in answering a politically indiscreet policy question for the same provincial examination, said to be critical of the powerful eunuch Wei Chung-hsien 魏忠賢 (1568–1627), Ai was barred from taking the metropolitan examinations for three periods. Never a *chin-shih* degree-holder, Ai became a model examination essay writer and a leading voice among late Ming literati who reassessed the legitimacy of the early Ming in light of the tragic events of 1402. The brief victory of imperial power during the early Ming was increasingly muted by literati inside and outside the government.[160]

157. On the late-Ming rehabilitation of the Chien-wen martyrs, see my "Where Is King Ch'eng," pp. 64–67. Cf. my "Imperial Politics and Confucian Societies in Late Imperial China," pp. 393–402.

158. See Hucker, "Confucianism and the Chinese Censorial System," in David S. Nivison and Arthur Wright, eds., *Confucianism in Action* (Stanford: Stanford University Press, 1969), pp. 182–208.

159. See Andrew Lo, trans., "Four Examination Essays of the Ming Dynasty," *Renditions* 33–34 (1990): 176–78.

160. See Ai Nan-ying, *T'ien-yung-tzu chi* 天傭子集 (Collection of the Heavenly Hired Hand), 1699 edition (reprint, Taipei: I-wen Press, 1980), p. 49 ("Biography" 傳, A.1a), and 10.16a–18a. See also *Ming-shih,* 288.7402.

As we shall see, such Mencian passages were not raised very often in Ming-Ch'ing civil examinations. In uncensored form (a major concession by Chu Ti to his officials), Mencius was allowed to speak to his readers, most of whom were candidates for the examinations. The *Ta-ch'üan* trilogy was printed and distributed to all county and prefectural schools after all. A sage-king like Chu Ti was the beneficiary of all that the classical Canon could offer. Even its dissenting portions turned in his favor, as long as he restored a working relationship with his literati elites and heeded their moral values.

## THE YUNG-LO LEGACY

The Yung-lo emperor, after moving the capital of the Ming dynasty to Peking between 1415 and 1421, eventually became one of the most expansive rulers in Chinese history. Some have linked the move to Chu Ti's desire, in part, to get away from Nanking, where the memories of the 1402 martyrs still lingered.[161] Moreover, after 1425, the civil examinations became the principal means for filling higher offices in the bureaucracy. Only with the 1385 and 1404 metropolitan examinations, discussed above, had early Ming civil examinations ever approached in scope and magnitude the level of Sung civil service appointments to the bureaucracy via examinations.

Accordingly, although it was important symbolically that Tao Learning had been ritually honored by the Southern Sung court in 1241 and had even become civil examination orthodoxy under the Yuan in 1313, these were preliminary steps in the triumph of Ch'eng-Chu Tao Learning in Ming cultural and political life, when for the first time the government put Tao Learning into practice empirewide as imperial ideology. By becoming the principal road to official appointment after 1425, the civil examinations thereafter guaranteed that the dynastic curriculum established in 1415 based on Tao Learning and the *Ta-ch'üan* trilogy, which became the key texts in the curriculum, would be studied and mastered by millions of civil examination candidates. The cultural reproduction of Tao Learning in this manner was institutionalized for half a millennium (see Chapter 7).

Although many Ch'eng-Chu believers had been killed by the Hung-wu and Yung-lo emperors, Tao Learning and its literati supporters overall had benefited from the sometimes tepid support of Chu Yuan-chang and the "unswerving faith" of Chu Ti—so much so that Ch'ing literati such as Chu I-tsun 朱彞尊 (1629–1709) and Ch'üan Tsu-wang 全祖望 (1705–55) naively believed early Ming emperors to be enviable stalwarts of ortho-

---

161. See Chang I-shan, *Chu-Ming wang-ch'ao*, pp. 280–93.

doxy.[162] But the triumph of Tao Learning as imperial ideology during the early Ming was achieved at a price. In the process, the linkage between autocratic power and Ch'eng-Chu philosophic discourse was consummated in a bittersweet wedding between perhaps the most powerful emperor in Chinese history, Chu Ti, and officials who championed Tao Learning moral ideals based on personal self-cultivation.

Despite the restoration of a partnership between the imperial court and the government, the memory of Chu Ti's violent usurpation weighed heavily on the conscience of the Ming. A Chiang-hsi literatus, Wu Yü-pi 吳與弼 (1392–1469), for instance, refused to participate in the civil examinations because he was unwilling to serve the Yung-lo emperor, whom he regarded as an usurper. This act alienated him from his father Wu P'u 吳溥 (1363–1426), who had ranked first on the 1400 metropolitan examination (he was fourth on the Chien-wen palace examination) and had by 1403 become involved in revising and reissuing the "Veritable Records of the Hung-wu Reign" (for which the Yung-lo emperor quickly promoted him a grade in the Hanlin Academy). Wu P'u then served as a deputy chief compiler for the *Yung-lo ta-tien*. Wu Yü-pi's personal integrity influenced his Chiang-hsi disciple, Hu Chü-jen 胡居仁 (1434–84), who also refused to take Ming civil examinations, even though the Yung-lo emperor was dead. Hu appealed indirectly in his writings to the Mencian injunction against political usurpation. Both Wu and Hu became model Tao Learning scholars honored for both their apolitical integrity and their moral cultivation by later Ming Confucians.[163]

Troubling legends of the heroism of Lien Tzu-ning and Fang Hsiao-ju remained and their question "Where is King Ch'eng?" was still unanswered. Chu Ti himself only relented in his persecution of the families of the "Chien-wen martyrs" in 1416, when he learned from Hu Kuang, who had just returned from Chiang-hsi to attend his mother's funeral, that the people there were finally pacified.[164] Pardons were granted in succeeding reigns for surviving family members of the Chien-wen emperor's executed officials. In 1425, for example, thousands of Fang Hsiao-ju's descendants were rehabilitated by the Hung-hsi emperor.[165] The next year, the Hsuan-

162. Chia Nai-lien, "Ts'ung Meng-tzu chieh-wen chih Ch'ien-shu," pp. 43–44.

163. Hu Chü-jen, *Chü-yeh-lu* 居業錄 (Record of the enterprise of sitting in reverence), SKCS, 714.36–44. See also Wing-tsit Chan, "The Ch'eng-Chu School of Early Ming," in William Theodore de Bary et al., *Self and Society in Ming Thought* (New York: Columbia University Press, 1970), pp. 45–46.

164. *Ming-shih*, 147.4125.

165. Chiao Hung 焦竑, *Kuo-ch'ao hsien-cheng lu* 國朝獻徵錄 (Record of verified documents during the Ming dynasty), 1616 Wan-li edition (reprint, Taipei: Student Bookstore, 1984), 20.56a–56b.

te emperor (r. 1426–35) pardoned Lien Tzu-ning's surviving kin.[166] But it was not until 1573 that all the "Chien-wen martyrs" were pardoned.[167]

Universal "truth," legitimated in late imperial official and educational life by the Ming dynasty in the form of Ch'eng-Chu philosophy, drew the Classics and Four Books into the government's conservative political agenda. A "descending" view of political power remained entrenched, but elites increasingly transmitted their interests to the court. Early in the Hung-chih reign (1488–1505), for example, literati in government attempted to eliminate what they considered "immoral shrines" (*yin-tz'u* 淫祠). Early in his reign, as we have seen, Chu Yuan-chang alone had wanted Mencius' tablet removed from the official sacrifices. This action was not unprecedented, for followers of Tao Learning in the Southern Sung had sought to add *Tao-hsueh* masters into the official temple for literati and remove Wang An-shih, but Chu Yuan-chang had acted on his own without literati support.

What was new in the mid-Ming policy was that the proposal to remove both images commemorating Confucius' disciples and all tablets of Han dynasty literati from the official Ch'ü-fu Temple was actively debated by literati and recommended to the court. This proposal was successfully mitigated by Ni Yueh 倪岳 (1444–1501), who as Minister of Personnel contended that Han literati had been invaluable in preserving and transmitting the Classics. In 1530, however, the tablet commemorating the Later Han classicist Cheng Hsuan 鄭玄 (127–200) was successfully removed from the Ch'ü-fu Temple. Removal of Cheng Hsuan's tablet revealed the degree to which the Ch'eng-Chu Tao Learning orthodoxy during the Ming had begun to sanctify itself through policies of ritual exclusion, but these sanctifications were literati driven and not imperially inspired.[168]

Tao Learning moral philosophy became a fixture as late imperial ideology and civil examination orthodoxy were woven together through a web of interconnected political, moral, and institutional threads into their final,

166. See the emperor's order, pp. 1a–3a, which is part of the "Lien-kung i-shih" appended to *Lien Chung-ch'eng kung wen-chi*.

167. See the "Lien-kung i-shih," for the 1573 imperial pardon, pp. 4a–5b, appended to *Lien Chung-ch'eng kung wen-chi*.

168. *Ming Shih-tsung shih-lu* 明世宗實錄 (Veritable records of the Ming dynasty Shih-ts'ung reign) (reprint, Taipei: Academia Sinica, 1965), 119.3b–4a. See also *Huang-Ming kung-chü k'ao*, 1.88b–89a. Cheng Hsuan, who would become a "patron saint" of the Han Learning revival in the eighteenth century, had his tablet reinstated in the official temple in 1724. See *Ta-Ch'ing Shih-tsung Hsien (Yung-cheng) huang-ti shih-lu* 大清世宗憲雍正皇帝實錄 (Veritable records of the Great Ch'ing dynasty Yung-cheng emperor Hsien's reign) (reprint, Taipei: Hua-wen Bookstore, 1964), 20.18b–20a.

imperial form by the Yung-lo emperor and his literati collaborators. Even if Emperor Wu (r. 140–87 B.C.) of the Han, T'ai-tsung of the T'ang, and T'ai-tsu of the Sung (r. 960–76) were his historical predecessors in such imperial *cum* classical cultural endeavors, and even if Emperor Li-tsung (r. 1225–64) during the Southern Sung and Jen-tsung (r. 1312–20) during the Yuan had already placed Tao Learning on the imperial pedestals of first ritual and then civil examination orthodoxy, Chu Ti and his government still left a legacy for the Ming and Ch'ing dynasties that overshadowed them. The imperial dynasty and its Ch'eng-Chu orthodoxy, which collapsed in the late nineteenth century, drew its cultural lineage directly— Sung and Yuan precedents notwithstanding—from the early Ming.

When the Manchu K'ang-hsi emperor (r. 1662–1722), who was arguably half-Mongol, had his Hanlin scholars compile the Tao Learning tract entitled the *Hsing-li ching-i* 性理精義 (Essentials of works on nature and principles; issued in 1715), and the *Ku-chin t'u-shu chi-ch'eng* 古今圖書集成 (Synthesis of books and illustrations past and present) encyclopedia (revised and printed in 1728 under the Yung-cheng emperor, r. 1723–35), he and his government were taking a page out of the Yung-lo reign to present the ruler as a Tao Learning sage-king working in partnership with his elites. The same could be said of the Ch'ien-lung emperor and his officials, who in 1773 ordered the compilation of the greatest bibliographic project in Chinese history, the *Ssu-k'u ch'üan-shu*, which was designed in part to ferret out anti-Manchu writings and thereby control, like its predecessor the *Yung-lo ta-tien*, the official version of acceptable knowledge.

Already, the 1673 K'ang-hsi emperor's "Preface" for the reissuing of the Ming version of the *Hsing-li ta ch'üan*, for a final example, linked early Ch'ing political legitimacy, the *chih-t'ung*, to the *Tao-hsueh* cultural policies of the Hung-wu and Yung-lo emperors and based that legitimacy on the "method of the mind" *(hsin-fa)* transferred from the early sage-kings to their Ch'ing peers, who had reappropriated the Way as receivers of the *tao-t'ung*. Ch'ing emperors, like their Ming predecessors, became enlightened Ch'eng-Chu sage-kings too.[169] Ming and Ch'ing emperors and their ministers appealed to the Way of the sage-kings, which since antiquity had been the model for contemporary governance. They claimed, moreover, that the moral principles of antiquity had been transmitted, mind to mind, from the sage-kings to the present emperor through Ch'eng-Chu teachings. Thereafter, emperors, Mandarins, and Tao Learning shared affinities

169. See the K'ang-hsi preface, in *Ssu-k'u ch'üan-shu*, 710.1–2; and for discussion, see Huang Chin-shing, *Philosophy, Philology, and Politics in Eighteenth-Century China*, pp. 157–68.

suitable to each. They had worked together to fashion the ideological mortar of the late imperial civil examinations.

Accordingly, civil examinations in late imperial China were politically part of the administrative process of selecting, evaluating, promoting, and punishing officials that balanced imperial interests and literati values. Viewed in isolation, the *Tao-hsueh* curriculum of the Ming and Ch'ing dynasties is often perceived as a cultural field of philosophical and historical discourse tied simply to the Four Books, Five Classics, and Dynastic Histories. That cultural field was championed by local literati, to be sure, but the "examination life," its rituals of preparation, and its stages of success were also tied to the complex and interrelated processes of political, social, and cultural reproduction.[170] Functioning as social and political litmus tests, licensing examinations, as we shall see in the next chapter, stood as a purposive barrier sealing in at best semi-literate masses from fully classically literate elites who were full partners in maintaining the imperial system.

What was unique about this conscious effort by the Ming government to expand Yuan dynasty instruments for political efficacy was its remarkable success in accomplishing the goals for which it was designed. Seen in terms of its own essential functions, the civil service recruitment process effectively restructured the complex relations between social status, political power, and cultural prestige for five centuries. More often than not, examinations in late imperial China were simply recognized for what they were, one of several tools in the repertoire of the government to maintain public order and political efficacy. From the point of view of the dynasty, reproduction of well-trained and loyal literati officials remained the prime concern. Imperial support of education and examinations was contingent on the success of the examination process in supplying talented and loyal men for the empire to employ.

Because elite education became closely identified with the dynasty's primary goal of selection, it is missing the point to evaluate the examination system, as so many contemporaries have, solely according to its economic or scientific sterility. Nor can we simply assume that the selection process served imperial interests alone. Chinese elites were able to gain enough social and cultural recognition and autonomy through the selection process that the emperor and his court could not dictate the intellectual and moral terms of the selection of gentry as officials.

170. Cf. Bourdieu and Passeron, *Reproduction in Education, Society, and Culture,* pp. 194–210. See also Martin Carnoy, "Education, Economy, and the State," in Michael Apple, ed., *Cultural and Economic Reproduction in Education* (London: Routledge & Kegan Paul, 1982), pp. 79–126.

Once set in place and granted full legitimacy in the mid-Ming, the civil service recruitment system achieved for education in late imperial China a degree of empirewide standardization and local importance unprecedented in the premodern world. Writing in 1878, John Henry Gray noted: "The system of competitive examination, and the fact that literary attainments are necessary qualifications for the highest political appointments, prove an immense stimulus to national education."[171] The social habits, political interests, and moral values inherited by officials since the Yuan and Ming dynasties were officially reproduced (with much unofficial and official dissent) through a system of dynastic schooling and civil examinations that took their mature form during the early fifteenth century and lasted until 1905.

171. See John Henry Gray, *China: A History of the Laws, Manners, and Customs of the People* (London: Macmillan, 1878), p. 166.

# CHAPTER THREE

# Institutional Dynamics
# and Mobilization of Elites
# in Late Imperial Civil Examinations

From a narrative account of the origins of the Ming civil examination regime in Chapter 2, we move in Chapter 3 to an institutional analysis of the structure and process of late imperial examinations from 1450 to 1850. The hallmark of the Ming system was its extraordinary elaboration of Sung-Yuan civil examination models. We will find that after the middle of the Ming, because of the interrelated impact of the intense commercialization of the Ming economy and slow but steady demographic growth reaching 150 million subjects by 1600, the history of the civil service was, on the one hand, a story of the expansion and intensification of its institutional machinery from the capital to all 1,200 counties. On the other hand, the secular upsurge in numbers of candidates, which continued under the Ch'ing dynasty, led to the increasing dominance of a declining number (vis-à-vis population growth) of *chin-shih* over an ever-increasing number of local degree-holders and provincial graduates.

In this and the next chapters, discussion of the sociohistorical consequences of the Ming expansion is limited principally to the examination regime and its testing sites. Later chapters (6 to 9) describe the interaction between the examination marketplace and elite cultural history outside its precincts. For specialized readers, the details of the examination regime presented in this and following chapters will not be new. Nevertheless, both the general reader and specialized scholar will find, I think, that the nitty-gritty aspects of the examination process and its institutional evolution are better understood when discussed in a comprehensive fashion that represents the civil examinations from top to bottom. Although in purely functional terms the institutional parts formed the whole selection process, that process produced unforeseen social, political, and cultural consequences that a functional analysis alone cannot explain. The historical consequences of the examination regime are analytically distinct from its intended function.

With exceptions, such as the pioneering work by Ping-ti Ho, studies of late imperial civil examinations have usually dismissed them as an institutional obstacle to modernization in imperial China.[1] A more comprehensive view, which I commend as more incisive than the current view emphasizing its most recent history during a process of decline after 1860, reveals that there were no a priori reasons that the members of the gentry-official managerial elite reproduced by the examination regime before 1850 were by definition inefficient as political and social "managers" in a pre-industrial society. In fact, a classical education based on nontechnical classical moral and political theory was as suitable for selection of elites in China to serve the dynasty at its highest echelons of power as humanism as a classical education was for elites in the nation-states of early modern Europe.[2]

If we evaluate literati education solely in light of modern goals of academic specialization and economic productivity, then the social and political dynamics of this cultural and institutional enterprise are misrepresented. Hence, our analysis of civil examinations here is an account of success, not failure. Where developments are comparable for both the Ming and Ch'ing dynasties, I shall describe events and processes that tell us about both dynasties, while at the same time highlighting notable differences. Where the Ch'ing significantly altered the Ming civil service, or its practice after 1644 significantly changed, that analysis will be saved for the end of this chapter and elaborated in Chapters 10 and 11, which focus on the last stages of development during the Ch'ing dynasty and the final demise of the imperial civil service system in 1905.

## POLITICAL REPRODUCTION OF OFFICIALS

The Ming dynasty represented the mature forms of civil governance that turned post-Mongol China into a discrete temporal unit known as the "late empire." Its bureaucracy reproduced itself through a selection and appointment system (hsuan-chü 選舉), which according to the official Ming-shih 明史 (Ming history) had four major components: (1) dynastic schools

1. See the work of Ping-ti Ho, Etienne Zi, Miyazaki Ichisada, and others cited in the Preface.

2. See Liang Ch'i-ch'ao, Intellectual Trends in the Ch'ing Period, translated by Immanuel Hsu (Cambridge: Harvard University Press, 1959), p. 28. Cf. Anthony Grafton and Lisa Jardine, From Humanism to the Humanities: Education and the Liberal Arts in Fifteenth- and Sixteenth-Century Europe (Cambridge: Harvard University Press, 1986), pp. 161–220.

(*hsueh-hsiao* 學校), (2) civil and military examinations (*k'o-mu* 科目), (3) recommendation (*chien-chü* 薦舉), and (4) appointment (*ch'üan-hsuan* 銓選). This organizational presentation modified the presentation by the *Sung-shih* 宋史 (Sung history) of the Sung selection and appointment process, which had six aspects: (1) examinations, (2) schools, (3) appointment, (4) protection privilege (*pu-yin* 補廕), (5) sponsored appointment (*pao-jen* 保任), and (6) evaluation (*k'ao-k'o* 考課). Although the Ming and Ch'ing maintained a merit-rating review process comparable to that of the Sung, other aspects, such as the protection policy and sponsored appointment, were curtailed in the late empire.[3]

During the Ming and Ch'ing dynasties, those that held office by virtue of their degrees (*k'o-mu ch'u-shen* 科目出身) were part of a larger administrative process involving the Ministry of Rites for education and the Ministry of Personnel for appointment and evaluation (*k'ao-chi* 考績). Unlike during the T'ang and Sung, when the level of assignments and the classification of ranks were fluid, during the Ming the civil service was governed by a strict correspondence between the two (i.e., an official could be appointed only to a position appropriate to his rank). At the same time, Sung traditions of hereditary privilege, which had compromised the fairness of Sung civil examinations, were significantly pared down.[4]

The civil service examinations in turn engendered a dynastic school system down to the prefectural level during the Sung and further down to counties in the Ming and Ch'ing dynasties.[5] These high-level dynasty-run schools initially prepared candidates for the written tests devised by appointed examiners. Despite their initial success as an empirewide school network, dynastic schools eventually were absorbed into the examination system and during the Ming and Ch'ing dynasties remained schools in name only. Some actual teaching took place in them, but they simply became quota-based way stations for students to prepare on their own for civil service examinations and receive stipends for their efforts.[6]

Moreover, entry into dynastic schools presupposed classical literacy. Because training in both vernacular and classical literacy was left to the private domain, dynastic schools in imperial China never entertained

3. See *Sung-shih*, 5/3604; and *Ming-shih*, 3/1675.

4. See also Chaffee, *The Thorny Gates of Learning in Sung China*, pp. 95–115; and Winston Lo, *An Introduction to the Civil Service of Sung China*, pp. 30–31, 141–70.

5. The Sung school system had also extended down to the county level, but local examinations there were not controlled by the prefecture (= Ming province) or department (= Ming metropolitan region) authorities.

6. Teng Ssu-yü, *Chung-kuo k'ao-shih chih-tu shih*, pp. 140–48; and Thomas Lee, *Government Education and Examinations in Sung China*, pp. 55–137.

goals of mass education until the twentieth century. Designed to recruit talent into what Ping-ti Ho has aptly described as the "ladder of success" in imperial China, a classical education became the sine qua non for social and political prestige in national and local affairs. Oriented to antiquity and classicism themselves, imperial rulers recognized elite education based on the Classics as an essential task of government, and Chinese gentry perceived a classical education as the correct measure of their moral and social worth. Both believed that ancient wisdom, properly generalized and inculcated, tempered men as leaders and prepared them for wielding political power in the central and provincial bureaucracy and in local yamens.[7]

Imperial control over elite education was premised on the dynasty's prerogative to select and promote officials. In fact, the government was more concerned with organizing and codifying examination competitions than it was with setting up schools or training teachers. After creating functional units in officialdom to be filled through competitive selection, the government was willing to allow the actual process of education in classical Chinese and training for the examinations to drift out of dynastic schools into the private domain of tutors, academies, or lineage schools.

The examination process by 1500 drew millions of young and old males into its selection process. Beginning with biennial local examinations and concluding with triennial provincial and metropolitan examinations (the latter followed by a palace test), the Ming civil service successfully mobilized its human resources through the relentless machinery of an institutional matrix within which, despite centuries of repeated criticism and constant efforts at reform (see Chapter 4), the "examination life,"[8] like death and taxes, became one of the fixtures of elite society and popular culture.

More important for the dynasty, under good or bad emperors, despots or incompetents, the civil selection machinery ensured that every three years a new group of classically literate and generally well-read male adults entered the government service. Freshness and new energy, however ultimately routinized, kept the Ming and Ch'ing bureaucracies from succumbing completely to corruption, absolutism, or irrelevance.[9] After

7. Alexander Woodside, "Some Mid-Qing [Ch'ing] Theorists of Popular Schools," *Modern China* 9, 1 (1983): 3–35; and Ping-ti Ho, *The Ladder of Success in Imperial China*, pp. 255–66.

8. See Chung-li Chang, *The Chinese Gentry*, pp. 165–209. For the Sung, see Chaffee, *The Thorny Gates of Learning in Sung China*, pp. 3–9, 166–81.

9. Frederick Mote in his "Introduction," in Frederick W. Mote and Denis Twitchett, eds., *The Cambridge History of China*, vol. 7, *The Ming Dynasty* (Cambridge: Cambridge

1384, Ming provincial and metropolitan civil examinations, for example, were organized like clockwork, hardly ever missing a bureaucratic beat. Ch'ing provincial and metropolitan examinations similarly took place every three years. To celebrate imperial birthdays or auspicious events Manchu emperors frequently authorized an extra number of special "imperial grace" examinations (en-k'o 恩科) during the Ch'ing.[10]

The Ming and Ch'ing bureaucracies affirmed the rule of seniority as an ideological bulwark of bureaucratic autonomy. Strict bureaucratic procedure was supposed to prevail over personal taste in appointments and promotions. Such relative autonomy from imperial fiat, which revived after the decisive interventions of the early Ming reigns under T'ai-tsu and T'ai-tsung (see Chapter 2), reduced, but did not eliminate, the capricious leverage of the ruler in public affairs. Through fixed personnel rules, literati officials achieved a modicum of self-respect appropriate to their status as imperial partners with the ruler, which was determined by impartial examination success. In effect, the dynasty accommodated elite interests, and "the elite in turn provided the dynasty with political legitimation and trained manpower."[11]

Given low bureaucratic densities in imperial government and steadily increasing population, strict quotas for local, provincial, and metropolitan examination competitions were utilized by the dynasty to limit the numbers of candidates to acceptable levels.[12] G. William Skinner has noted that the Ming-Ch'ing examination system also integrated systems of local towns and cities within provinces because the "ascent up the regular acad-

University Press, 1988), pp. 6–7, rightly stresses the advantages of a self-regulating bureaucracy in Ming China that was reproduced by competitive examinations. The Cambridge volume on the Ming never details how the examinations actually worked, however.

10. During the Ming dynasty, there were 89 metropolitan and palace examinations or one every 3.1 years. During the Ch'ing, there were 112 metropolitan and palace examinations (once every 2.4 years), for example, of which 84 were regularly scheduled examinations (cheng-k'o 正科), 2 added examinations (chia-k'o 加科), and 27 imperial grace examinations. See Huang Kuang-liang, Ch'ing-tai k'o-chü chih-tu chih yen-chiu, pp. 137–52. Iona Man-cheong, "The Class of 1761: The Politics of a Metropolitan Examination" (Ph.D. diss., Yale University, History, 1991), pp. 329–30, gives 25 grace examinations during the Ch'ing, with 5,555 chin-shih degrees granted, or 21% of the total number of Ch'ing chin-shih.

11. Winston Lo, An Introduction to the Civil Service of Sung China, pp. 19–22, 217–8; Dardess, Confucianism and Autocracy, pp. 13–84; and Thomas Metzger, The Internal Organization of Ch'ing Bureaucracy (Cambridge: Harvard University Press, 1973), pp. 397–417.

12. Susan Naquin and Evelyn Rawski, Chinese Society in the Eighteenth Century (New Haven: Yale University Press, 1987), pp. 106–14, 123–27, 224–25, suggest, however, that historians have underestimated the expanding size of imperial Chinese administration.

emic ladder recapitulated the hierarchy of administrative capitals."[13] Local county and prefectural dynastic schools, and even private academies, were effectively mobilized into feeder institutions for the imperial bureaucracy and the creation of a local and empirewide literati elite.[14] The nested hierarchy of local towns and cities in all provinces correlated exactly with the dynasty's control over local civil and military degrees granted by its magistrates, prefects, and provincial education commissioners.[15]

Although the stability in the number of county seats in imperial China (1,180 in Han; 1,235 in T'ang; 1,230 in Sung; 1,115 in Yuan; 1,385 in Ming; and 1,360 in Ch'ing) is illusory, due to the consolidation of counties as population grew,[16] it does reveal that the number of positions for magistrates and prefects in the bureaucracy remained relatively constant at the same time that the number of candidates for such positions increased dramatically after 1500 (see below). The concomitant "secular decline in governmental effectiveness" resulted from an increasingly lower degree of bureaucratic intensity in the administration (4,000 county seats in 1585, and 8,500 in 1850, would have been required to keep pace with the early imperial density of local officials). As population rose to an estimated 150 million in the sixteenth century and then to 400 to 450 million in the nineteenth, direly affecting the dynasty's ability to regulate its tax and legal systems, the civil service selection process remained an important exception to and bulwark against this secular process of administrative decline until the Taiping Rebellion (1850–64).[17]

An almost constant tug-of-war existed between local elites seeking to expand their influence through civil examinations and educational officials hoping to keep the "valve" of elite circulation under political control. Calls for lowering of quotas after a period of unusual expansion in numbers of licentiates were a constant feature in educational policy debates. Ch'ing rulers, for instance, equated high numbers of licentiates with the fall of the Ming dynasty.[18] In addition, after 1425, as we have seen in

13. See Skinner, "Introduction: Urban and Rural in Chinese Society," in Skinner, ed., *The City in Late Imperial China* (Stanford: Stanford University Press, 1977), p. 272.

14. See Tilemann Grimm, "Academies and Urban Systems in Kwangtung," in Skinner, ed., *The City in Late Imperial China*, pp. 487–90, 496–98.

15. See Skinner, "Cities and the Hierarchy of Local Systems," in Skinner, ed., *The City in Late Imperial China*, pp. 338–39.

16. See Skinner, "Introduction: Urban Development in Imperial China," in Skinner, ed., *The City in Late Imperial China*, pp. 19–20.

17. Ibid., pp. 21–23.

18. Oxnam, *Ruling from Horseback*, pp. 84–89: and Lawrence Kessler, *K'ang-hsi and the Consolidation of Ch'ing Rule* (Chicago: University of Chicago Press, 1976), pp. 154–58. Cf. William Ayers, *Chang Chih-tung and Educational Reform in China* (Cambridge: Harvard University Press, 1971), pp. 44–50.

Chapter 2, the Ming dynasty applied an additional regional quota for metropolitan examinations in the capital to seek geographical balance.

Because of economic advantages in south China (especially the Yangtzu delta but including Fu-chien and later Kuang-tung provinces in the southeast), candidates from the south were always performing better on the metropolitan examinations than candidates from less prosperous regions in the north (north China plain), northwest (Wei River valley), and southwest (Yun-nan and Kuei-chou). To keep the south's domination of the examinations within acceptable bounds, court officials eventually settled on an official ratio of 55:10:35 (north:central:south) for allocations of the highest *chin-shih* degrees to candidates from the south versus the north.[19]

It is interesting that the autonomy of education from political and social control rarely became an issue of contention in the late empire, although Ming and Ch'ing emperors and their officials frequently tried to set limits on the proliferation of private academies outside the dynastic school system.[20] In the minds of both rulers and subjects, the connection between education and public order rarely was a matter of doubt. Whether for idealistic ends or as a realistic means of control, rulers and elites equated social and political order with moral and political indoctrination through education. Remonstrating censors might challenge imperial prerogative but not imperial control of examinations, although at times a few dissenters unsuccessfully challenged the entire examination regime (see Chapter 4).

A frequent bone of contention, however, was the differing views literati had of the kind of education best suited for the fulfillment of their social and political roles. High-minded officials and local literati often appealed for the relative autonomy of education and self-cultivation, called "learning for the sake of one's self" (*wei-chi chih hsueh* 為己之學), in private academies or at home as an antidote to the warping of classical educational goals by the cutthroat examination process. During the late Ming, for example, private academies briefly became centers for dissenting political views. These challenges were themselves institutionally channeled through examination success into the civil service before factional infighting and eunuch political power precipitated the fall of the dynasty (see Chapter 4).[21]

19. Chaffee, *The Thorny Gates of Learning in Sung China*, pp. 119–56; and Ping-ti Ho, *The Ladder of Success*, pp. 222–54. See also Chapter 1 above.

20. See my "Imperial Politics and Confucian Societies in Late Imperial China," pp. 387–93.

21. See John Meskill, *Academies in Ming China: A Historical Essay* (Tucson: University of Arizona Press, 1982), pp. 66–138; de Bary, "Chu Hsi's Aims as an Educator," pp. 195–97; Mizoguchi Yūzō 溝口雄三, "Iwayuru Tōrinha jinshi no shisō" いわゆる東林派人士の思想

Even in its most stridently expressed form, however, literati dissent rarely challenged the process of social selection that the civil service produced or the right of the government to determine social hierarchies through educational policies. Education was premised on social distinctions between men and women and between literati, peasants, artisans, and merchants (*shih, nung, kung, shang* 士農工商), in descending order of rank and prestige. Until the Ming, for instance, sons of merchants were not legally permitted to take the civil service examinations. Furthermore, occupational prohibitions, which extended from so-called mean peoples to all Taoist and Buddhist priests, kept many others out of the civil service competition. When this social vision became out of sync with reality, the dynasty's vision of education changed only enough in the late fourteenth century to enfranchise sons of merchants in the examination competition. Although Koreans and Vietnamese occasionally participated in civil examinations during the Ming dynasty, the Ch'ing dynasty steadfastly refused to allow the classically fluent son of then customs inspector Sir Robert Hart (1835–1911) to take an early Kuang-hsu (r. 1875–1908) provincial examination in the capital region (Shun-t'ien) because of the protest by literati the request engendered against foreigners.[22]

Before 1860, positions in the civil administration carried more prestige, power, and remuneration than corresponding positions in commerce, craft guilds, or the army. Entering officialdom became the goal of all who could afford the educational time and expenses required to prepare for the civil examinations. The government's minimum requirement that the educational system help to inculcate and reinforce the political, social, and moral values of Tao Learning to maintain the dynasty coincided with literati rhetoric exalting the sanctity of Ch'eng-Chu learning and affirming the priority of civilian values as the measure of social and moral worth.

The dynasty's monopoly of those legitimate cultural symbols that were defined publicly in light of classical learning enabled the ruler to justify the institutional conditions necessary for staffing his government. The examination hierarchy in effect reproduced acceptable social hierarchies by redirecting wealth and power derived from commerce or military success into the civil service. Because so few could succeed in becoming officials, however, political legitimation transmitted through education

---

(The thought of the members of the so-called Tung-lin faction), *Tōyō bunka kenkyūjo kiyō* 東洋文化研究所紀要 75 (March 1978): 111–341; and Ono Kazuko 小野和子 "Tōrin tō kō (ichi)" 東林黨考一 (Study of the Tung-lin party, part 1), *Tōhō gakuhō* 東方學報 52 (1980): 563–594; and Ono, "Tōrin tō kō (ni)" 東林黨考二 (Study of the Tung-lin party, part 2), *Tōhō gakuhō* 東方學報 55 (1983): 307–15.

22. Hsu K'o, *Ch'ing-pai lei-ch'ao* 清稗類鈔 (Classified jottings on Ch'ing dynasty unofficial history) (Shanghai: Commercial Press, 1920), 21.85.

could succeed only because enhanced social status was an important by-product of the examination competition at all levels and not because of naked imperial power.

## MOBILIZATION: THE DYNAMIC SCOPE AND MAGNITUDE OF LOCAL EXAMINATIONS

Under the Ming, bureaucratic channels of selection by examination for the first time penetrated beyond the imperial and provincial capitals down to all counties and prefectures in the search for classically literate men to enter the elite world of officialdom.[23] During the T'ang, for instance, civil examinations had been held only in the imperial capital. As in Han and Sui times, a candidate was recommended by local elites.[24] Under the Sung, the examinations were expanded to two levels, one in the prefectures (called *chieh-shih* 解試; lit., "dispatched examination") and one at the capital (*sheng-shih* 省試, "department examination").[25] Although some local examinations were held, recommendation was still the rule for local students. The limited scope of Yuan local examinations, as we have seen, meant that they were not yet an effective conduit to high office.[26]

As the flow chart of civil examinations in Table 3.1 shows, under the Ming, biennial *sui-k'ao* 歲考 (licensing tests; lit., "tests by year") and triennial *k'o-k'ao* 科考 (qualifying tests) were regularly held in county, department, and prefectural yamens to choose eligible candidates for the triennial provincial examinations (now called *hsiang-shih* 鄉試).[27] In theory, two

23. *Ming-shih*, 3/1724–25. See also William Rowe, "Success Stories: Lineage and Elite Status in Hanyang County, Hupeh, c. 1368–1949," in Joseph Esherick and Mary Rankin, eds., *Chinese Local Elites and Patterns of Dominance* (Berkeley: University of California Press, 1990), pp. 51–81.

24. See Seo Tatsuhiko 妹尾達彦, "Tōdai no kakyo seido to Chōan no gokaku giri" 唐代の科舉制度と長安の合格儀禮 (The T'ang civil service system and graduate rituals in Ch'ang-an), in *Ryūreisei—Chūgoku Chōsen no hō to kokka* 律令制—中國朝鮮の法と國家 (Tokyo: Kyūko shoin, 1986), pp. 239–74.

25. See Ch'ing-lien Huang, "The Recruitment and Assessment of Civil Officials under the T'ang Dynasty," pp. 24–28; and Twitchett, *The Birth of the Chinese Meritocracy*, p. 12. On the Sung prefectural and department examinations, see Hymes, *Statesmen and Gentlemen*, pp. 29–30; and Chaffee, *The Thorny Gates of Learning in Sung China*, pp. 23–24.

26. On local examinations during the Southern Sung and Chin dynasty, see *Hsu wen-hsien t'ung-kao*, 41.3185. In 1406, the Ming still followed Sung-Yuan recommendation policies for recruiting local talent. Later formal examinations of youths (*t'ung-shih* 童試) were instituted.

27. To maintain tradition, however, the number-one finisher in provincial examinations was still called the *chieh-yuan* 解元 (dispatched *optimus*), following the name for Sung dynasty prefectural, *chieh-shih* 解試, forwarding examinations.

local examinations were held every three years by the magistrate, prefect, or provincial education commissioner.[28]

The provincial examinations were then followed by the metropolitan (*hui-shih* 會試) and palace examinations (*tien-shih* 殿試), which as before remained the final stage of the process in the dynasty's capital. Normally, candidates would take the provincial examinations in the fall (eighth lunar month) and if successful move on to the metropolitan examinations in Nanking (up to 1421) or Peking (from 1415) in the spring (third lunar month) of the following year.[29] A final palace examination for all metropolitan graduates was administered by the emperor himself as a personal litmus test to ensure political loyalty to him and fair and impartial final rankings. This final stage represented a Sung change from T'ang examinations when loyalty to examiners had outweighed loyalty to the ruler. The Sung government abrogated ceremonies of gratitude to examiners and focused examination ritual on the palace test, with the emperor as chief examiner (see Chapter 4).[30] Systematic quotas were established at the local and provincial levels (see Tables 2.1 and 2.7), while northern, central, and southern quotas were established for the capital *chin-shih* degree. In general, this three-tiered arrangement remained in force until 1905, although the questions for each session were frequently changed during the Ch'ing period (see Chapter 10).

## Licensing Examinations

Unlike the longer and more bureaucratic format used in provincial and metropolitan examinations, in which candidates prepared anonymous papers and participated in all three sessions (see below), biennial local examinations consisted of a series of single-day tests to appoint new candidates as dynastic school students, which also conveniently doubled as *sui-shih* 歲試 (or *sui-k'ao* 歲考) tests to renew the status of past licentiates (*sheng-yuan;* that is, those candidates licensed to participate in higher-level civil service examinations) who had not become *chü-jen.* New students were first chosen by magistrates and prefects in preliminary county (*hsien-k'ao* 縣考), department (*chou-k'ao* 州考), and prefectural (*fu-k'ao* 府考) tests. All new candidates and renewal students were in their turn asked to write two

28. Shang Yen-liu 商衍鎏, *Ch'ing-tai k'o-chü k'ao-shih shu-lueh* 清代科舉考試述略 (Summary of civil examinations during the Ch'ing period) (Peking: San-lien Bookstore, 1958), pp. 1–21, summarizes the Ch'ing dynasty organization of local examinations, which derived from the Ming. See also Zi, *Pratique des examens littéraires en Chine,* pp. 35–80.

29. Li T'iao-yuan, *Chih-i k'o-so chi,* 1.29–30.

30. See Moore, "The Ceremony of Gratitude."

essays, one based on a passage from the *Four Books* and another one from the *Five Classics*. In addition policy questions were given, and after 1756 a poetry question was required (see Chapter 10). During the Ch'ing, the local authorities also designated "apprentice candidates" known as *t'ung-sheng* 童生, who had never been students in dynastic schools.[31]

At the insistence of the Hung-wu emperor, early Ming local candidates were also expected to demonstrate mastery of his "Great Announcement" (*Ta-kao* 大誥), a tract of moral and legal admonishments (see Chapter 2). Later the *Ta-kao* was replaced by memorization of T'ai-tsu's *Sheng-yü liu-yen* 聖諭六言 (Sacred edict in six maxims), which succeeding Ming emperors thought necessary to lessen the literary aspects of civil examinations.[32] These additions became the precedent for using first the K'ang-hsi emperor's 1670 *Sacred Edict* (*Sheng-yü* 聖諭) and then the Yung-cheng emperor's 1724 *Amplified Instructions* (*Sheng-yü kuang-hsun* 聖諭廣訓) in Ch'ing local examinations and moral lectures by local officials (*hsiang-yueh* 鄉約).[33]

After the candidates' and students' own papers were reviewed for their

31. See Sheang [Shang] Yen-liu, "Memories of the Chinese Imperial Civil Service Examination System," translated by Ellen Klempner, in *American Asian Review* 3, 1 (spring 1985): 54–56. Etienne Zi's *Pratique des examens littéraires en Chine*, pp. 35–69, upon which both Kamo Naoki's (see below) and Miyazaki Ichisada's (see below) accounts are based, records the curriculum of the nineteenth century, taking no note of the changes in curriculum before 1860 that we will stress here. Cf. Victor Purcell, *Problems of Chinese Education* (London: Kegan, Paul, Trench, Trubner, 1936), pp. 27–28, which describes classical and poetry questions in local examinations during the late Ch'ing. Later *t'ung-sheng* also meant "licentiates."

32. See Omura Kōdō 大村興道, "Shinchō kyōiku shisōshi ni okeru Seigo kōkun ni tsuite" 清朝教育思想史に於ける聖諭廣訓について (Concerning the Amplified Instructions of the Sacred Edict in the history of educational thought in the Ch'ing dynasty), in Hayashi Tomoharu 林友春, ed., *Kinsei Chūgoku kyōikushi kenkyū* 近世中國教育史研究 (Tokyo: Kokutosha, 1958), pp. 233–46. See also Miyazaki Ichisada, *Kakyoshi*, p. 90.

33. See Ch'en Wu-t'ung 陳梧桐, *Chu Yuan-chang yen-chiu* 朱元璋研究 (Study of Chu Yuan-chang) (T'ien-chin: People's Press, 1993), pp. 156–70. The *Ch'in-ting Ta-Ch'ing hui-tien shih-li* 欽定大清會典事例 (Collected statutes and precedents in the great Ch'ing) (Taipei: Chung-hua Bookstore, 1968), 386.2b, notes that in the reexamination of *t'ung-sheng* for the *sui-k'ao*, they must write a question on a section of the *Sheng-yü kuang-hsun*. On the *Sacred Edict* and its successor, see Victor Mair, "Language and Ideology in the Written Popularizations of the *Sacred Edict*," in David Johnson, Andrew Nathan, and Evelyn Rawski, eds., *Popular Culture in Late Imperial Culture*, pp. 325–59. Until about 1670, local Ch'ing examinations continued to require the Ming imperial maxims. For examples in actual examinations, see *Ssu-ch'uan sheng tang-an-kuan Pa-hsien tang-an*, "Wen-wei" 四川省檔案館巴縣檔案, "文衞" (Cultural and health materials in the Ssu-ch'uan Provincial Archives, Pa-hsien County Archives), Tao-kuang 道光 microfilm, reel 13, document no. 984 (1850); and Kuang-hsu 光緒 microfilm reel 55, document no. 6199 (1888). See also Kamo Naoki 狩野直喜, *Shinchō no seido to bungaku* 清朝の制度と文學 (Ch'ing institutions and literature) (Tokyo: Misuzu Bookstore, 1984), pp. 380–83; and Justus Doolittle, *Social Life of the Chinese* (New York: Harper & Brothers, 1865), pp. 392–93.

calligraphy, style, and content by yamen clerks, who were themselves not allowed to take such examinations but could rise through meritorious local service, they were graded.[34] Those that passed were then subjected to a second and third series of similar questions, a process that continued for several days until most were weeded out. The eminent Shanghai 上海 county painter and calligrapher Tung Ch'i-ch'ang 董其昌 (1555–1636), for instance, finished second on his first prefectural examination in Sung-chiang at the age of seventeen. When Tung inquired why his cousin had been chosen number one ahead of him, he was told—ironically, given the later fame of his painting and writing style—that while his essays were outstanding in content they were poorer in calligraphy. Tung apparently then made up his mind to practice his calligraphy.[35] The candidates who had survived the repeated ordeals were divided into six ranks based on their style and content (*wen-li* 文理), which were evaluated in light of Ch'eng-Chu *Tao-hsueh* teachings.[36]

After the screening by magistrates and prefects, the successful new candidates then gathered in the prefectural capital for a final licensing examination (*yuan-k'ao* 院考), which sometimes also doubled conveniently as a triennial qualifying examination (*k'o-k'ao*) for past licentiates. There the provincial education commissioner (called a *Ti-hsueh-kuan* 提學官 during the Ming, a *Tu-hsueh-tao* 督學道 from 1644 to 1684, and a *Hsueh-cheng* 學政 thereafter), as he traveled on his regular testing schedule through the province, determined who would become the new licentiates and enter the dynastic schools. If appropriate that year, the commissioner also chose the select few, group by group, from among the new and old licentiates who could go on to compete in the provincial examination. For both the licensing (*yuan-k'ao*) and qualifying (*k'o-k'ao*) examinations, the education commissioner repeated the same testing format and curriculum used in the preliminary county, department, and prefectural tests.

34. On the magistrate's use of yamen advisors and clerks to grade local examinations, see Kamo, *Shinchō no seido to bungaku*, p. 376. See also Lu Shen 陸深, *K'o-ch'ang t'iao-kuan* 科場條貫 (Rules in the examination compound), in *Chi-lu hui-pien* 紀錄彙編, compiled by Shen Chieh-fu 沈節甫, Ming Wan-li edition (lithograph, Shanghai: Commercial Press, 1938), 136.4a. On clerical promotion, see Dardess, *A Ming Society: T'ai-ho County, Kiangsi, in the Fourteenth to Seventeenth Centuries* (Berkeley: University of California Press, 1996), pp. 146–49.

35. Hummel, ed., *Eminent Chinese of the Ch'ing Period*, p. 788.

36. For regulations and standards used in Ming local examinations, see *Liang-Che hsueh-cheng* 兩浙學政 (Education commissioners in western and eastern Che-chiang), 1610 edition, pp. 2b–5b, 23b–25a, and passim.

## Qualifying Examinations

Gaining a place in the county, department, or prefectural school meant that as a *sheng-yuan* the former candidates (including *t'ung-sheng*) could now take the triennial qualifying examination (*k'o-k'ao*), also supervised by the education commissioner, for the privilege of traveling to the provincial capital and taking the triennial provincial examination. Given the small prefectural quotas allotted, however, most usually remained behind. Those who failed the provincial examinations also returned to compete again in the next renewal (*sui-k'ao*) and qualifying (*k'o-k'ao*) examination cycles.

Because, as we shall see, few licentiates ever became *chü-jen*, the Ming dynasty required licentiates to keep taking local renewal examinations to maintain their legal status. Thus, the local *sui-k'ao* renewal test usually also doubled as a county, department, or prefectural licensing test, which was required of both youthful candidates (usually under twenty) hoping to become new *sheng-yuan*, and old *sheng-yuan* (anywhere from twenty to sixty years old) seeking to keep their status. Earlier accounts of local examinations have assumed that there was no overlap in the separate local examinations, but it was logistically inconceivable for local magistrates, prefects, and education commissioners to supervise so many different examinations every other year, given their other political responsibilities. Table 3.2, based on early Ch'ing sources, shows that local examinations in T'ung-chou 通州 (also called Nan-t'ung 南通), a typical example, did frequently overlap.[37]

When possible, new candidates and past licentiates were tested together, though they were usually divided by age, with twenty as the dividing line. Different questions, using the same format, were assigned to each group. Similarly, there was an overlap of new and old licentiates when the qualifying examination (*k'o-k'ao*) was held simultaneously with the final licensing examination (*yuan-k'ao*).[38] In fact, the records of local examinations that survive from the early Ch'ing dynasty reveal that whenever pos-

37. See Miyazaki, *China's Examination Hell,* pp. 18–38, for an overly idealized account, which is based on Etienne Zi's too literal, step-by-step description of local examinations, in *Pratique des examens littéraires en Chine,* pp. 35–99. Indeed, if there had been no doubling up of local civil and military examinations, magistrates and prefects would have had to hold and supervise tests continuously. In many cases, candidates for civil and military *sheng-yuan* degrees were convened together by local officials, rather than tested separately, as has long been assumed.

38. See *Kuo-ch'ao Yü-yang k'o-ming-lu* 國朝虞陽科名錄 (Record of civil service graduates in Yü-yang under the Ch'ing dynasty), compiled by Wang Yuan-chung 王元種, 1850 edition, 4.1a–33b, which contains early Ch'ing *sui-k'ao* and *k'o-k'ao* records for Ch'ang-shu 常熟 county that are comparable to those of the late Ming. See also Kamo, *Shinchō no seido to bungaku,* p. 378.

sible, licensing, renewal, and qualifying examinations were held together (*sui-k'o ping-shih* 歲科併試 or *sui-k'o ping-ju* 歲科併入).[39] The young (*wei-kuan* 未冠) and old (*i-kuan* 已冠) were brought together in such joint examinations and tested group by group over several consecutive days.[40]

## Quotas

The number of new licentiates, usually aged between seventeen and thirty-seven in Ch'ing times,[41] was based on established yearly quotas for each county, department, and prefecture. Each licentiate was given a stipend paid in rice, and his family was granted tax service exemptions.[42] Ming quotas for the total number of licentiates in an area were initially set at 40 candidates per prefecture and 30 candidates per county and department. During the Hsuan-te reign (1426–35), these limits were increased to 60 for the capital prefectures in Nanking and Peking, although they remained at 40 for other prefectures. In 1392, the quota for new students was limited to two annually in the prefectural school, one annually in county schools, and only two every three years for department schools. These guidelines for quotas remained on the books into the sixteenth century, but by then were ignored.[43]

For example, T'ung-chou, which included Ching-hsiang 靜庠 during the Ming dynasty, generally had a total pool of 2,080 *sheng-yuan* after 1465. Eight new licentiates normally entered dynastic schools via each licensing

39. See *T'ung-Hsiang t'i-ming lu* 通庠題名錄 (Record of civil service graduates in T'ung-chou and Ching-hsiang), compiled by Li Yun-hui 李芸暉, 1895 edition, 2.5b–8a, for joint examinations in 1661, 1662, 1668, 1672, 1674, and 1676 in T'ung-chou; and *Ching-hsiang t'i-ming lu* 靜庠題名錄 (Record of civil service graduates in Ching-hsiang), compiled by Li Yun-hui 李芸暉, 1895 edition, 1.2b, for a joint examination in 1656. For confirmation of these findings, see also *Sung-chiang-fu shu li-k'o ts'ai-ch'in lu ch'u-pien* 松江府屬歷科采芹錄初編 (Preliminary compilation of the record of civil selection over several examinations in Sung-chiang prefecture) (Shanghai: Kuo-kuang photolithograph, 1939), 1.1a–10b, which shows that local renewal and qualifying examinations were jointly held in 1661–75.

40. See *Kuo-ch'ao Yü-yang k'o-ming-lu*, 4.2a–5a, for examples.

41. See Charles Ridley, "Educational Theory and Practice in Late Imperial China: The Teaching of Writing as a Specific Case" (Ph.D. diss., Stanford University, Education, 1973), pp. 150–53.

42. Ku Yen-wu, *Jih-chih lu chi-shih* 日知錄集釋 (Record of knowledge gained day by day, collected notes) (Taipei: Shih-chieh Bookstore, 1962), 17.392–97. For discussion, see Makino Tatsumi 牧野巽, "Ko Enbu no seiin ron" 顧炎武 生員論 (Ku Yen-wu's "Essay on Licentiates"), in Hayashi Tomoharu 林友春, ed., *Kinsei Chūgoku kyōikushi kenkyū* 近世中國教育研究 (Research on education in early modern China) (Tokyo: Kokutosha, 1958), pp. 221–29.

43. See *Ming-shih*, 3/1680–81.

examination there after 1490 (when records become available), although 33, an unusually high number, were added in 1503. In the late Ming, the T'ung-chou school quota went up to 27. During the T'ien-ch'i reign (1621–27), the quota increased to 36 new licentiates, with as many as 18 purchasing degrees (*chien-sheng* 監生) in 1626 and 12 in 1627.[44] Figures for Fu-ch'eng city in Fu-chien province, between 1370 and 1546, indicate that the prefectural school there triennially usually added 7 to 12 new students, with a low of 3 in 1399, 1408, and 1543, and a high of 20 in 1453. The three county schools regularly took in between 1 to 10 new students, with a high of 14 in the Min 閩 county school in 1471.[45]

Quotas for local and provincial examinations represented dynastic efforts to control its selection of elites on the basis of talent, just as tax quotas had been set to equalize the extraction of material resources. When compared to the Ming tax system, which was designed to extract material wealth and labor from local society, the Ming selection of literati (*ch'ü-shih* 取士) was longer lasting and more effective in drawing on its gentry elites for political appointments. The Ming dynasty lost control of its material resources in the sixteenth century, when the tax burden increasingly fell on commoners who received none of the generous exemptions granted official families, many of whom hid their true wealth. Despite early Ch'ing dynasty efforts to curtail the degree of tax evasion prevalent in south China, for example, the late imperial government never regained full control of its material resources.[46] In contrast, political selection of elites through local selection quotas and the hierarchical civil appointment process remained relatively effective until massive peasant rebellions, unprecedented demographic growth, and widespread sale of degrees to raise funds in the mid–nineteenth century seriously compromised the efficiency and integrity of the civil service (see Chapter 11).[47]

44. *T'ung-Hsiang t'i-ming lu*, A.1a. 1.1a–29a, gives local *sheng-yuan* rolls from 1368–1643. After 1725 T'ung-chou and Ching-hsiang were split into two. Ping-ti Ho, *The Ladder of Success in Imperial China*, p. 177 (Table 20), presents these figures under "Nan-t'ung."

45. *Fu-ch'eng hsiang-chin-shih t'i-ming chi* 福城鄉進士題名記 (Record of graduates of local, provincial, and palace examinations from Fu-ch'eng, Fu-chien) (ca. 1546 mss), pp. 1a–61b.

46. Ray Huang, *Taxation and Governmental Finance in Sixteenth-Century Ming China* (Cambridge: Cambridge University Press, 1974), pp. 313–23; and Huang Ch'ing-lien, "The *Li-chia* System in Ming Times and Its Operation in Ying-t'ien Prefecture," *Bulletin of the Institute of History and Philology* (Academia Sinica, Taiwan) 54 (1983): 103–55.

47. *Huang-ch'ao hsu wen-hsien t'ung-kao* 皇朝續文獻通考 (Comprehensive survey of state documents during the Ch'ing dynasty, continuation), compiled by Liu Chin-tsao 劉錦藻 (Shanghai: Commercial Press, 1936), pp. 8452–53. See *Yang-ch'eng Tien T'ai-shih ch'üan-kao* 陽城田太師全稿 (Complete drafts of T'ien Ts'ung-tien from Yang-ch'eng), 1722 edition, 1.32a, in which T'ien Ts'ung-tien (田從典, 1649–1726) explicitly compares the government's extraction of wealth to its selection of talent.

Establishing quotas based on the ratio between successful and failed candidates, which had begun in 997, demonstrated that the Ming dynasty saw access to the civil service as an institutional means to confine and regulate the power of elites. Government intervention in elite composition through control of civil and military selection was most keenly felt at the initial stages of the examination competition: licensing at the prefecture (Sung) and county (Ming and Ch'ing) levels for the privilege of entering the examination selection process.[48]

Gentry social status and official political position were dual products of the Ming decision to reinstitutionalize civil service examinations empirewide in Chinese society after a hiatus of two centuries. Political reproduction of officials coincided with social reproduction of local gentry (see also Chapter 5). The dynasty in effect legitimated its elite and granted them their preferred curriculum to master. Despite the rhetoric of impartiality and egalitarian classical ideals that successfully suppressed the reality of the unequal chances of candidates in the exclusive civil service, success on the civil examinations evolved as a prerogative of the wealthy and powerful in local communities. In the contest for local quotas and examination success, artisans, peasants, and clerks were poorly equipped to take advantage of the theoretical openness of the civil service. It was therefore no accident that during the late empire only 1.6% to 1.9% of the total population of China achieved gentry status.[49]

## The Civil Examination Market

By 1500, there were some 30,000 licentiates (*sheng-yuan*) out of an approximate population of 65 million, a ratio of almost 1 licentiate per 2,200 persons.[50] By comparison, in 1700, there were perhaps 500,000 licentiates in a total population of 150 million, or a ratio of 1 licentiate per 300 persons. While the ratio of licentiates to population became higher over time, the

---

48. Thomas Lee, "The Social Significance of the Quota System in Sung Civil Service Examinations," *Journal of the Institute of Chinese Studies* (Chinese University of Hong Kong) 13 (1982): 287–318.

49. Wolfram Eberhard, *Social Mobility in Traditional China*, pp. 22–23; Winston Lo, *An Introduction to the Civil Service of Sung China*, pp. 22–34; and Frederic Wakeman, Jr., *The Fall of Imperial China* (New York: Free Press, 1975), p. 22, 36n7.

50. Wang Ao 王鏊 (1450–1524), *Chen-tse ch'ang-yü* 震澤長語 (Common sayings of Wang Ao) (Taipei: Commercial Press, 1965), A.20 (卷上), gives 35,820 *sheng-yuan* since the early Cheng-te reign (1506–21).

likelihood that licentiates would pass higher examinations entitling them to civil appointments became, as we shall see, lower. In fact, in Ch'ing times licentiate status was much less rare or special and had become a social necessity to remain a member of the elite.[51]

Nevertheless, beginning in the fifteenth century, each stage of the Ming civil service selection process eliminated the vast majority of candidates, and the odds for success in all stages of the selection process was perhaps only slightly better than the 1 in 6,000 (.01%) during the Ch'ing. Wada Masahiro rightly sees Ming dynasty ratios of local licentiates to higher-degree holders as a key to understanding the social dynamics of the elite degree-holding gentry during the Ming dynasty. In the early Ming, the ratio of *chin-shih* to *chü-jen* to dynastic school students (*chien-sheng*) was 1:3:6, a ratio that lasted until 1570.[52] This ratio later became 1:3:9 after 1570, showing a decided increase of 50% in *chien-sheng* in late Ming dynastic schools. Thus during the Ming there were about 24,450 *chin-shih*, 73,150 *chü-jen*, and 220,050 dynastic school students. Adding the half million licentiates (from Ku Yen-wu's estimate) into the framework,[53] Wada concludes that by the late Ming the ratio from top to bottom degree holders was 1:3:9:21. We can extrapolate that while only 14% of all *sheng-yuan* passed the provincial civil examinations and became *chü-jen*, far fewer (4.8%) ever achieved *chin-shih* status under the Ming.[54]

As population increased during the late empire, however, the concomitant increasing roll of potential candidates for a much more slowly enlarging number of metropolitan, provincial, and local positions (20,400 civil positions circa 1500; 24,680 circa 1625)[55] meant that the vast majority of licentiates who were never appointed to a position could pose a local secu-

51. Ku Yen-wu, *Jih-chih lu chi-shih*, 17.392–97, on *sheng-yuan* quotas. Ping-ti Ho, *The Ladder of Success in Imperial China*, pp. 173–83; and Mi Chu Wiens, "Lord and Peasant: The Sixteenth to the Eighteenth Century," *Modern China* 6, 1 (1980): 9–12.

52. Wada Masahiro, "Mindai kyojinzō no keisei katei ni kan suru ichi kōsatsu," pp. 36–71. Wada's figures from the *Chang-chou fu-chih* 漳州府志 (Prefectural gazetteer of Chang-chou) in the Wan-li era (1573–1615), which confirm this ratio, are on p. 64.

53. William S. Atwell, "From Education to Politics: The Fu She," in Wm. Theodore de Bary, ed., *The Unfolding of Neo-Confucianism* (New York: Columbia University Press, 1975), p. 338, estimates there were about six hundred thousand *sheng-yuan* in the late Ming.

54. Wada, "Mindai kyojinzō no keisei katei ni kan suru ichi kōsatsu," p. 37. We should add that until the nineteenth century, these ratios were comparable during the Ch'ing dynasty, when there were 25,779 *chin-shih*. John Dardess' mathematical analysis of "promotion in hierarchical systems" is similar to Wada's analysis. See Dardess, *A Ming Society*, pp. 166–67.

55. Wang Ao, *Chen-tse ch'ang-yü*, A.20; and Dardess, *A Ming Society*, p. 140.

rity problem, in terms of both unfulfilled expectations leading to rebellion and unscrupulous manipulation of fiscal tax exemptions from the required labor service. Officials also feared that an overproduction of licentiates would lead to a loss of local discipline, heterodox views of literati learning, and a weakening of local paternalism. In a recent study, for example, Lü Miaw-fen contends that the main audience for Wang Yang-ming's 王陽明 (Shou-jen 守仁; 1472–1528) new views of *Tao-hsueh* was the larger number of *sheng-yuan* in the fifteenth century who were sympathetic to his criticism of Ch'eng-Chu teachings and unhappy with the increasingly competitive examination market that enshrined them.[56]

There were good reasons that provincial and metropolitan examination compounds looked more like prisons than schools (see Chapter 4). Unlike contemporary Europe and Japan, however, where absolute social barriers between nobility and commoners prevented the translation of commercial wealth into elite status, landed affluence and commercial wealth during the Ming and Ch'ing dynasties were intertwined with examination status, thereby releasing some of the potential for class-based revolt in China.

## *CHÜ-JEN* AS A NEW POLITICAL GROUP

During the Cheng-t'ung reign (1436–49), provincial examination quotas for residents in the dual capital regions of Peking and Nanking were set at 100 candidates, with populous provinces allowed 65 candidates and less populated provinces progressively less. The quotas were increased until at the end of the Ming, dual-capital quotas reached 130 and the number for populous provinces was raised to 100 candidates. Competition for both the civil *chü-jen* and *chin-shih* degrees increased dramatically after 1450 and became for the first time logistically comparable to the formidable Sung dynasty civil examination competition levels.[57]

56. See Lü Miaw-fen, "Practice as Knowledge: Yang-ming Learning and *Chiang-hui* in Sixteenth Century China" (Ph.D. diss., UCLA, History, 1997), chap. 1.

57. Over 15,000 (in 992) and 17,000 (in 1124) candidates typically had competed for *chin-shih* degrees. Eight hundred passed (4.7%) in 1124. See *Wu-li t'ung-kao*, 174.5b and 174.18b. On Sung provincial examinations (*chieh-shih*) for *chü-jen* degrees, success ratios ranged from only 0.5% (1/200) in the Southern Sung, to quotas unrealistically set as high as 50% in the Northern Sung. Usually only 10% to 20% passed the *chieh-shih* before 1100. Competition in Fu-chou 福州, the leading Southern Sung producer of *chin-shih*, rose from 3,000 for 40 *chü-jen* places (1.3% = 1/75) in 1090 to 18,000 for 54 places (0.3% = 1/333) in 1207. See Chaffee, *The Thorny Gates of Learning in Sung China*, pp. 35–41.

*Levels of Competition*

Residualism—that is, repeated failures—became a typical feature of the "examination life" for candidates of both the *chü-jen* and *chin-shih* degrees, documented in more detail later. Wada Masahiro estimates that the number who failed in Ming provincial examinations had risen from 850 per examination in 1441, to 3,200 in 1495, and then to 4,200 in 1573, a four-fold increase in 132 years.[58] The levels of competition in provincial civil examinations during the fifteenth and sixteenth centuries increased so much that a late Ming popular song in the Yangtzu delta declared that in Nanking (Ying-t'ien) provincial examinations "gold went to the *chü-jen*, and [only] silver to the *chin-shih*" (金舉人，銀進士), because the competition was so much keener for *chü-jen*.[59] By 1630, about 49,200 candidates empirewide, 45% less than in the "High Ching," triennially competed for 1,278 *chü-jen* degrees. Only 2.6% would succeed.[60]

During the Ch'ing dynasty, approximately 2 million candidates sat for county licensing and qualifying examinations held twice every three years. Of these only 30,000 (1.5%) achieved licentiate status. Earlier estimates that 1,500 of the latter (5%) would pass the triennial provincial examinations, and that of these 300 (20%) would pass the triennial metropolitan examinations, were far too generous.[61] Instead, 89,600 is a better, conservative estimate for the total number of the eligible *chü-jen* degree candidates in all seventeen provinces before 1850, of whom less than 1,300 (1.5%) passed.[62]

As Tables 3.3 and 3.4 demonstrate, the number of *sheng-yuan* candidates qualified to compete in southern provincial examinations in Nanking (Ying-t'ien) and Hang-chou (Che-chiang) increased from under 2,000 before 1465 to 4,000–4,500 by 1550 and then went up to 7,500 in Nanking in 1630. *Chü-jen* success rates dropped from 5–10% to 2%, a tendency that

58. See Wada, "Mindai kyojinzō no keisei katei ni kan suru ichi kōsatsu," p. 43.

59. See Ku Kung-hsieh 顧公燮, *Hsiao-hsia hsien-chi chai-ch'ao* 消夏閑記摘抄 (Selected notes jotted in leisure to pass the summer), ca. 1797 edition, in *Han-fen-lou mi-chi* 涌芬樓秘笈 (Shanghai: Commercial Press, 1917), *erh-chi* 二集, B.2a.

60. This estimate is derived from a composite of information from the tables in Appendix 3 mentioned below.

61. These very generous ratios are drawn by Wakeman, *The Fall of Imperial China*, pp. 21–23. The figures in Ichisada Miyazaki, *China's Examination Hell*, pp. 121–22, are somewhat more reliable, because Miyazaki includes both the Ming and Ch'ing examinations in his estimates. Cf. Allan Barr, "Pu Songling [P'u Sung-ling] and the Qing [Ch'ing] Examination System," *Late Imperial China* 7, 1 (1986): 92–103.

62. Chung-li Chang, *The Chinese Gentry*, p. 168. See also T. L. Bullock, "Competitive Examinations in China," in James Knowles, ed., *Nineteenth Century* (London), 36 (July 1894): 91.

became increasingly alarming during the Ch'ing, when less than one in a hundred candidates passed southern provincial examinations. Table 3.5 shows that this secular trend was also true in north China, and Table 3.6 summarizes information available on all other Ming provinces, which affirms the same trend throughout the dynasty.

### Chü-jen *Identity*

A new social dynamic in Ming times resulted from the significant difference between the provincial *chü-jen* degree and corresponding middle-level degrees during the T'ang, Sung, and Yuan dynasties. Before the Ming, if a candidate failed the equivalent of the regional or provincial examination preceding the capital and palace levels of tests, then he returned to his home area and was required to start over again with the regional examination before he could qualify for the *chin-shih* or *ming-ching* competition again.[63] In the early Ming, this requirement was changed to permit *chü-jen* who failed in the *chin-shih* competition to maintain their hard-earned provincial degree status; thus they automatically qualified for future metropolitan civil examinations, in addition to remaining eligible for lower-level official appointments. Moreover, they were allowed to enter the Imperial School (*Kuo-hsueh* 國學, later called *Kuo-tzu chien* 國子監) to continue their progress toward the *chin-shih* degree.[64]

According to Wada Masahiro, this meant that, unlike the Sung and Yuan, during the Ming a *chü-jen* class of degree-holders emerged with its own special social status and political prerogatives, with three main divisions: (1) *fu-pang* (second-class provincial graduates) who qualified for local educational posts, (2) *chü-jen* who entered the Imperial School to continue their studies and thus were eligible for possible lower-level appointments, and (3) *chü-jen* who returned to their home areas to prepare for the next *chin-shih* examinations. Increasingly, the provincial graduates chose to return home rather than to enter the Imperial School, and the government initiated unsuccessful policies to get them back into the school. Because of the increasing importance of the *chin-shih* degree (documented

---

63. See Chaffee, *The Thorny Gates of Learning in Sung China,* pp. 30–34, on Sung *chü-jen.* Chaffee points out that although Sung *chü-jen* who failed to become *chin-shih* were not merely licentiates again, their semi-official status was ambiguous. Their degree granted them higher prestige in local ceremonies, and many were granted exemptions to take capital examinations again without again qualifying on the provincial examinations. Such exemptions were granted when a candidate had been a *chü-jen* for fifteen years or more, however, and they were not considered officials until they passed the capital examination.

64. Wada, "Mindai kyojinzō no keisei katei ni kan suru ichi kōsatsu," pp. 38–39.

below), provincial graduates increasingly preferred to take their chances at the metropolitan examination rather than serve the dynasty in a minor capacity. This development suggests that only at the highest levels was a career in government acceptable to elites. Many literati who had the means preferred to stay at home rather than enter the stream of candidates in the Imperial School.[65]

The failure of the school education system to gain an independent status went back to the period 1383–96, when a system of grade levels and points per level, which had copied earlier such educational standards for government school students during the Sung dynasty, was in place. Most school students opted to follow the examination path for advancement, with local dynastic schools a venue of last resort. Because dynastic schools became part of the examination system and were not independent, Imperial School students received no social or political benefits that were commensurate with the *chin-shih* track. Consequently, many *chü-jen* opted for the civil examinations rather than attend the Imperial School system and wait there for an official appointment. Indeed, the schools increasingly were filled with candidates who had repeatedly failed higher examinations and had nowhere else to go. Because civil service examinations became the most prestigious channel for the selection of officials, the civil degree curriculum itself became the basis for the dynastic school system that extended down from the Imperial School to dynastic schools at the prefectural ( *fu-hsueh* 府學), county (*hsien-hsueh* 縣學), and department (*chou-hsueh* 州學) levels of administration. In effect, schools became testing centers.[66]

Seasonal and monthly examinations were administered in dynastic schools to check the progress of licensed students. Foreigners or Chinese from abroad, principally from the Ryukyu Islands, Japan, Korea, Vietnam, and Siam (Thailand), were also permitted according to the terms of the imperial tributary system to study in dynastic schools as tribute students. Although Chinese candidates continued to take advantage of the recommendation, inheritance ( *yin* 廕), and purchase (*chüan-na* 捐納) provisions of the selection and appointment process, most high-level civil officials in Ming and Ch'ing China were selected on the basis of their success on local, provincial, and metropolitan examinations, particularly after

65. Ibid., pp. 37–63.

66. Watari Masamitsu 和田正廣, "Minsho no kakyo fukkatsu to kensei" 明初の科舉復活と監生 (Early Ming revival of the civil service examination system and Imperial School students), *Shūkan tōyō gaku* 集刊東洋學 49 (1983): 19–36. See also *Ch'ang-t'an*, p. 33. On Sung Imperial School students, see Chaffee, *The Thorny Gates of Learning in Sung China*, pp. 30–31.

1459, when the Ming dynasty abolished the recommendation process in the aftermath of the T'u-mu debacle (see Chapters 2 and 5).[67]

Mongol rulers had raised the level of entry in the official hierarchy for *yin* claimants from the seventh to the fifth rank, which favored the sons of its *se-mu* elite over those of the few Han Chinese in the government. In 1467, the Ch'eng-hua emperor (r. 1465–88) limited the claim to the *yin* prerogative to officials within the three highest ranks only, a policy that contrasted with the Mongol precedent of granting hereditary privilege to members of all ranks above the two lowest. Unlike during the Sung, when hereditary statuses compromised the fairness of the degree market,[68] in Ming times the *yin* prerogative assured the holder access only to a minor position in the central government or prefect in the provinces.[69]

## Levels of Appointment

So important were examination credentials that by the Chia-ching reign (1522–57), the imperial school system had been overshadowed by the very examinations the schools were designed to prepare students for. Education in dynastic schools counted for little if the student failed to pass the higher civil examinations. Doomed to lives as minor functionaries, students who remained in dynastic schools too long had little chance for success in imperial politics. In fact, by the late Ming it became difficult for candidates who only got as far as the provincial *chü-jen* degree to gain reputable government positions.[70]

SHAN-TUNG. Table 3.7 shows that the rate of provincial graduates who became officials in Shan-tung province, for example, increased to almost 50% between 1369 and 1474. After 1500, however, the percentage who based on their *chü-jen* degrees alone became officials declined steadily, reaching 33% in 1600 and declining further to 17–19% in the late Ming. Paralleling this decline, as Table 3.7 shows, was the increasing rate of *chü-jen* who became *chin-shih* over the course of the Ming. After an initially high rate of *chü-jen* becoming *chin-shih* in 1369 (27%) and 1384 (36%), the percentage declined to 10% in 1450. During this time, *chü-jen* stood a good

---

67. For discussion of the recommendation channel and tribute in Ming times, see Dardess, *A Ming Society*, pp. 142–46, 160–61.

68. Chaffee, *The Thorny Gates of Learning in Sung China*, pp. 108–13.

69. *Ming-shih*, 3/1675–76, 1677–78, 1679, 1682, 1713; and *Ch'ing-shih kao* 清史稿 (Draft history of the Ch'ing dynasty), Chung-hua Press edition, 40 vols. (Peking, 1977), 11/3108. See Wittfogel, "Public Office in the Liao Dynasty," pp. 38–39.

70. *Ming-shih*, 3/1717.

chance of gaining a prestigious official appointment. After 1474, the percentage becoming *chin-shih* climbed regularly. From 1549 to 1642, the rate was generally between 38% and 46%.

As we can see in Table 3.8, provincial graduates made up 13% to 24% of high local officials in 1369 and 1400, respectively. By 1501 this rate had gone up to 44%, with 27% of *chü-jen* from that year becoming county magistrates. Thereafter, the number of *chü-jen* attaining such local offices declined to 30% in 1549 and to 15% in 1624. They were replaced in such positions by the increasing number of *chü-jen* who went on to take the metropolitan examination and became *chin-shih*. Overall, 29% of the 842 Ming dynasty *chü-jen* in Shan-tung for whom we have information held important local offices, but the majority of them served between 1450 and 1600.

Early in the Ming dynasty, then, provincial degree-holders were conspicuous in administration, but they were eventually displaced by the increasing number of metropolitan *chin-shih* degree-holders.[71] Of the three routes of career advancement—namely, metropolitan graduates, provincial graduates, and clerical officials (*li-yuan* 吏員) chosen locally for yamen service—the *chin-shih* degree became the sole guarantee of high political position and elite social esteem.[72] Table 3.9, which traces the highest offices held by *chin-shih* degree-holders in Shan-tung province from 1404 to 1643, reveals that while many held high office in the central and provincial bureaucracy, as expected, after 1500 many others were appointed to local positions as magistrates, prefects, and various levels of yamen aides. Particularly after 1574, the tendency for *chin-shih* degree-holders to become prefects or magistrates became pronounced. In 1574, 26% of Shan-tung *chin-shih* held such offices. In 1601, 17% became magistrates or prefects. This rate increased to 19% in 1625 and returned to 17% in 1643.

*CHÜ-JEN* AND *CHIN-SHIH* AS EDUCATION OFFICIALS. *Chü-jen* initially also served as prefecture, county, and department education officials, which entitled them to act as provincial examination officials in the early and mid-Ming. Because of their length and complexity, the triennial provincial and metropolitan examinations in particular required a full complement of examination officials to administer. Although examination officials had been important since medieval times, the full bureaucratization of education and examination officials from the county to the metro-

---

71. Dardess, *A Ming Society*, p. 158, attributes the changes in *chü-jen* appointments to changes in "assignment policy," but fails to see the connection to increasing *chin-shih* rolls.

72. *Ming-shih*, 3/1680, 3/1715, 1717. See Dardess, *A Ming Society*, pp. 146–49.

politan and palace levels did not become formalized until the middle of the fifteenth century.[73]

"Education intendants" (t'i-hsueh kuan 提學官 or t'i-tiao kuan 提調官) evolved during the late fourteenth century from regional supervisors of dynastic schools into a specialized permanent office responsible for local and provincial education and examinations. As "education commissioners," their jurisdictions and influence straddled the middle ground between prefects and magistrates in local society and provincial governors. In particular, they had the final say in licensing and qualifying candidates in all counties, departments, and prefectures in their province. Local literati were called on to help in the selection process.[74]

Under the provincial education commissioners, three categories of Ming local education officials (hsueh-kuan 學官 or chiao-kuan 教官) were designated to be in charge of dynastic schools. In prefectural schools, the supervising faculty consisted of a low-ranking or unranked "instructors" (chiao-shou 教授, the twentieth-century term for "professor") and four "assistant instructors" (hsun-tao 訓導). In county schools the instructor was classified as a chiao-yü 教諭, and he was complemented by two assistants. At the department school, the instructor was called a hsueh-cheng 學正 (not to be confused with the education commissioner 學政 of Ch'ing times), and he had three assistant instructors under him. If we use late Ming figures (140 prefectures, 193 departments, and 1,138 counties), then empirewide there were 1,471 instructors and 3,415 assistant instructors at the local level (not counting education officials in Ming garrison schools, wei-hsueh 衛學), who were supervised by education commissioners in thirteen provinces and the two capital regions in Nanking and Peking.[75]

In 1385, emulating the Yuan practice,[76] all chü-jen who had failed the metropolitan examination that year were appointed as instructors in local

---

73. See Tilemann Grimm, "Ming Education Intendants," in Charles Hucker, ed., *Chinese Government in Ming Times: Seven Studies* (New York: Columbia University Press, 1969), pp. 130–39.

74. See Grimm, *Erziehung und Politik in kunfuzianischen China der Ming-Zeit*, pp. 85–88.

75. *Ming-shih*, 2/882, 3/1686. See also Wu Chih-ho 吳智和, *Ming-tai te ju-hsueh chiao-kuan* 明代的儒學教官 (Education officials in literati schools during Ming times) (Taipei: Student Bookstore, 1991), pp. 19–20, 267–69. Dardess, *A Ming Society*, p. 161, gives figures up to the sixteenth century from the *Ming shih-lu*: 5,244 teaching posts, 1,564 instructors, and 3,680 assistant instructors. Figures for the Ming in Chang Chien-jen 張健仁, *Ming-tai chiao-yü kuan-li chih-tu yen-chiu* 明代教育管理制度研究 (Research on the educational review system of the Ming dynasty) (Taipei: Wen-chin Press, 1991), are roughly comparable: 159 prefectures; 234 departments, 1,171 counties; 1,564 dynastic schools.

76. *Wu-li t'ung-k'ao*, 175.16b. See also Hsiao Ch'i-ch'ing, "Yuan-tai te ju-hu—ju-shih ti-wei yen-chin shih-shang te i-chang," pp. 165–67.

schools, indicating that the provincial degree was still deemed appropriate for education officials. Also recommended by prefects and magistrates, local education officials by the late fourteenth century increasingly came from the surplus of dynastic school students (*chien-sheng*) who had not been successful in higher examinations but were able to maintain their status as licentiates (*sheng-yuan*). In addition, during the early Ming it was not considered unusual to appoint *chin-shih* degree-holders as local education officials. By the mid–fifteenth century, however, many ambitious literati saw education positions as dead ends.[77]

For example, the *optimus* on the 1433 palace examination, Ts'ao Nai 曹 鼐 (1402–44), had served as an assistant instructor after initially failing an earlier metropolitan examination, but he petitioned for another appointment before taking the metropolitan examination again. Until 1464 education officials were discouraged from leaving their posts to take the metropolitan examination in Peking. After 1487, special examinations were organized every six years to select education officials for the metropolitan examination. Later, the Ming tried to encourage *chü-jen* to become education officials by allowing them to take the metropolitan examination if their students passed the provincial examinations.[78]

By the late sixteenth century, local education officials had been significantly down-classed, and *chin-shih* dominated most prestigious appointments of metropolitan, provincial, and local significance. As we have seen, they were increasingly appointed as magistrates and prefects, but *chin-shih*, for reasons detailed below, also took over most appointments as education commissioners, the only education appointment that survived the sharp drop in status of local education officials. Even *chü-jen* avoided low-level education appointments so that they could continue to compete for the *chin-shih* degree.

The Ming government had tried in 1394 to recruit *chü-jen* from the newly created supplementary list of provincial graduates (*fu-pang* 副榜) to serve as local education officials, but this was also unsuccessful in an academic climate within which the *chin-shih* degree became the priority for

77. Gazetteers typically included lists of *chü-jen* and *chin-shih* degree-holders from local areas. The Chia-ching edition of the *K'un-shan hsien-chih* 昆山縣志, 1538: 7.1a–14b, for example, gives lists of *chü-jen* in this Yangtzu delta county. During the early Ming, many of those listed as provincial graduates held positions as education officials in outside provinces.

78. See *Ming T'ai-tsu shih-lu*, 73.4b; *Huang-Ming kung-chü k'ao*, 1.40a; and *Ming-shih*, 69.1679–80. See also Wu Chih-ho, *Ming-tai te ju-hsueh chiao-kuan*, pp. 25–32; and Tai-loi Ma, "The Local Education Officials of Ming China, 1368–1644," *Oriens Extremus* 22, 1 (1975): 11–27.

licentiates and *chü-jen*. To fill education positions, the Ming government began in 1450 to appoint annual tribute students (*sui-kung* 歲貢) as local education officials, which solved the problem of finding local men to take the positions but doomed the positions to the lower level of the civil service.[79] Lü K'un 呂坤 (1536–1618), writing in the early seventeenth century, attacked the complete bankruptcy of the Ming system of local education officials: "What do instructors in prefectural schools (*chiao-shou*) transmit (*shou* 授) as teachings? What do department school instructors (*hsueh-cheng*) have to show for their correcting (*cheng* 正) others? What affairs have instructors in county schools (*chiao-yü*) proclaimed (*yü* 諭)? What have the assistant instructors (*hsun-tao*) provided direction (*tao* 導) for?"[80] The implication was that in terms of the "rectification of names" (*cheng-ming* 正名), Ming education officials were unworthy of their titles. Not until the Yung-cheng emperor's reign (1723–34) would there be another attempt to improve the examination standing and institutional efficacy of local education officials (see Chapter 4).[81]

THE 1580S DISPLACEMENT OF *CHÜ-JEN* AS EXAMINERS. The selection of civil examination officials during the Ming generally followed this down-classing trend as well. Table 3.10 reveals that *chü-jen* represented almost 50% of all the Shan-tung civil examination officials in 1465 and that of the top twelve examiners they held seven places (58%). Moreover, local education officials from outside provinces were appointed as the seven chief and associate examiners, and all these were instructors (four were assistants) with *chü-jen* degrees. Only four *chin-shih* (13%) were assigned to the 1465 examination, and their roles were as senior supervisors. Six county magistrates and two assistants, as outsiders serving in Shan-tung province, were also assigned to this provincial examination, but they were all given minor appointments as clerks (2), collectors (1), sealers (2), copyists (1), proofreaders (1), or suppliers (1). Six of the latter eight were *chü-jen*, and two were *chien-sheng*. As of 1465, then, lower-degree holders, especially *chü-jen*, stood a good chance of appointment as education officials and as examiners in the provincial examinations.

79. Tai-loi Ma, "The Local Education Officials of Ming China," pp. 17–21; and Wu Chih-ho, *Ming-tai te ju-hsueh chiao-kuan*, pp. 26–28, 80–93, 256–57.

80. See Lü K'un, "Chiao-kuan chih chih" 教官之制 (The institution of education officials), in *Ming-tai chiao-yü lun-chu hsuan* 明代教育論著選, compiled by Kao Shih-liang 高時良 (Peking: People's Press, 1990), pp. 532–36.

81. Araki Toshikazu 荒木敏一, "Yōsei jidai ni okeru gakuchin sei no kaikaku" 雍正時代に於ける學臣制の改革 (The reform of education officials in the Yung-cheng age), in *Yōsei jidai no kenkyū* 雍正時代の研究 (Kyoto: Tōmeisha, 1986), pp. 503–18.

Tables 3.11 and 3.12 reveal that the 1465 Shan-tung pattern for provincial examinations remained in place until about 1585. Until then most of the chief (*chu-k'ao* 主考) and associate examiners (*t'ung-k'ao* 同考) assigned to the civil provincial examinations after 1465 were chosen from the pool of 4,200 education officials assigned to dynastic schools throughout the empire (eliminating by law of avoidance those who came from the province in which the examination took place), and most of them held *chü-jen* degrees.[82] The pre-1585 Ming practice of *chü-jen* first becoming education officials and then serving as outside chief and associate provincial examiners meant that local *chin-shih* degree-holders were often placed under *chü-jen* in the provincial examination compound. In the 1549 Che-chiang provincial examination, for instance, many *chin-shih* served as clerks, collectors, and sealers while *chü-jen* occupied all ten places as chief and associate examiners.[83] Similarly in 1567, all six associate examiners were still outside *chü-jen,* and although the two chief examiners were *chin-shih* degree-holders, they were both prefectural school instructors from outside provinces.[84] After 1585, however, the policy for selecting provincial examiners changed dramatically, as Tables 3.10 through 3.13 reveal. In 1583, for instance, the Wan-li emperor (r. 1573–1619) began to assign Hanlin academicians from the capital as chief examiners in provincial examinations, signaling that the court wished to exert more direct control in the provinces.[85] Previously, Hanlin members had been assigned chiefly to metropolitan and palace civil examinations and generally only to the provincial examinations in the capital prefectures of Ying-t'ien and Shun-t'ien.[86] In Shan-tung, for example, the number of *chin-shih* selected as chief and associate examiners went up dramatically in 1585 and 1594. In 1594, only 22% of all examination officials were *chü-jen,* down from 50% in 1465. By the last years of the Ming, *chin-shih* degree-holders had displaced *chü-jen* as the vast majority of examiners in provincial examinations. In Chiang-hsi in 1567, all twelve chief and associate examiners were both *chü-jen* degree-holders and education officials. By 1627, all seventeen examiners were *chin-shih*. In 1639, eleven of the fourteen chief and associate examiners in Shen-hsi provincial examinations were *chin-shih,* and only three remained *chü-jen*. In 1567, all seven had been *chü-jen* serving as education officials elsewhere.

---

82. *Ming-shih,* 3/1688, gives 4,200 for the total of education officials, which includes those in prefectures, counties, townships, and garrisons. Our earlier figures left out garrisons.

83. *Che-chiang hsiang-shih lu,* 1549: 1a–6b.

84. Ibid., 1567: 1a–6b.

85. *Wu-li t'ung-kao,* 175.20a–b, 23b.

86. *Huang-Ming kung-chü k'ao,* 1.41a.

Furthermore, after 1585 the *chin-shih* chosen as examiners usually no longer were education officials. In 1585, three of the fourteen associate examiners for Shan-tung were *chin-shih* serving as county magistrates from other provinces, and two were outside judges (*t'ui-kuan* 推官). In 1627 Chiang-hsi, eleven of the fifteen *chin-shih* associate examiners were magistrates, and the other four were *chin-shih* serving as *t'ui-kuan*. For the 1639 Shen-hsi provincial examination, eight associate examiners were magistrates, one was a judge, and only three were still prefectural education officials holding *chü-jen* degrees. The gathering of outside county magistrates triennially for the provincial examinations was a chance for them to renew their classical training and interests, apart from their legal and tax responsibilities. It meant that their knowledge of classical learning was continually renewed for local and provincial examinations and not merely tossed aside once they took office.

Consequently, three simultaneous and related processes were operating politically and socially in Ming times after 1585: (1) *chin-shih* were replacing *chü-jen* as chief and associate examiners on provincial examinations; (2) outside prefects and magistrates were replacing outside dynastic school instructors as the key provincial examiners; (3) competition levels for *chü-jen* were becoming so intense that only 2% to 3% (see Tables 3.3 to 3.6) of the candidates could expect to pass the provincial examinations. As *chin-shih* degree-holders, because of their increasing numbers, took over most higher-level positions as prefects and magistrates in the Ming bureaucracy, they left in their political wake *chü-jen* and education officials. *Chin-shih* also took control of the selection of *chü-jen* candidates. Before 1585, *chü-jen* degree-holders serving as education officials and examiners had selected who would become their peers. By the end of the Ming they were displaced from positions of power and influence by *chin-shih* degree-holders, a social down-classing that carried over into the Ch'ing dynasty.

The generalized down-classing of *chü-jen* degree-holders and education officials represented a major change in the social conditions of political recruitment in late imperial China that would last from 1600 to 1900, when late-Ch'ing *chin-shih* degrees were stigmatized by reformers in the early twentieth century (see Chapter 11). The precipitous increase in Ming civil examination candidates, based in part on commercial development and population growth, produced a decided devaluation of all degrees but the highest *chin-shih* for high-level appointments. A product of this political down-classing of *chü-jen* was the increasing disparity between individual and family expectations for lower-degree holders and their realistic political opportunities. Of the 24,680 positions in the late Ming bureaucracy, the top ones as ministers, governors, education commissioners, or prefects and magistrates were taken by *chin-shih* degree-holders. The remainder were left for *chü-jen* (see the account of Li Chih 李贄 [1527–1602] below), tribute students, and recommended *sheng-yuan*.

After 1600, fewer *chü-jen* would achieve political success, which meant that they would have to lower their expectations and take advantage of the surviving benefits of their lowered status and take lower-level jobs as functionaries in local governance. For many, a *chü-jen* degree became a social end in itself, a required way station on the road toward the coveted *chin-shih* that most never got. These fifteenth- and sixteenth-century developments ruptured the early Ming harmony between the youthful dreams of millions of candidates and the likelihood of success for more than a very few. The social and legal benefits given to licentiates and *chü-jen* sufficiently compensated candidates for their degrees despite their increasing exclusion from higher public office, but at a great psychological cost. The pressures of failure, however, produced personal and family anxieties that were sublimated into dreams and nightmares, which Ming and Ch'ing elites clinically recorded and religiously commented upon with both curiosity and dread (see Chapter 6).

CHANGES IN METROPOLITAN AND PALACE EXAMINATION OFFICIALS. In metropolitan civil examinations, *chin-shih* degree-holders had early on been appointed as the chief and associate examiners. Table 3.14 indicates that for the seventeen examinations between 1371 and 1622 not a single *chü-jen* had been appointed as a higher examiner in Peking. What did occur, however, was that an overabundance of *chin-shih* in the late Ming examination market, which had generated *chü-jen* down-classing, also affected negatively the pool of *chin-shih* degree-holders who passed in the second or third tier (*chia* 甲) of graduates. Initially, those who finished in the first or at the top of the second tier entered the Hanlin Academy and served as the emperor's secretaries (see below). The few who were appointed as metropolitan examiners in the period from 1371 to 1415 served as the chief examiners only. After 1478, however, Hanlin academicians usually comprised 80% or more of the positions of both chief and associate metropolitan examiners.

The policy change favoring Hanlin members as metropolitan associate examiners was recommended in 1453 by the chief minister of Rites, Hu Ying 胡濙 (1375–1463), who disapproved of education officials taking such posts, and was put into practice for the 1454 metropolitan examination.[87]

87. See Lu Shen, *K'o-ch'ang t'iao-kuan*, 136.1b–2b; and Li T'iao-yuan, *Chih-i k'o-so chi*, p. 33. See also *Ming-shih*, 3/1698–99. Actually, the practice had already started by at least 1445. See *Hui-shih lu*, 1445: 1a–1b, in *Ming-tai teng-k'o lu hui-pien*, vol. 1, where both chief examiners and four of the eight associate examiners were Hanlin members.

In 1527, the policy of appointing Hanlin academicians was applied to chief examiners in the provincial civil examinations as well (see Table 3.12). In 1504 such positions had been upgraded from *chü-jen* education officials to *chin-shih* degree-holders. After 1523, most *chü-jen* served as lower-level examination paper collectors, sealers, copyists, or proofreaders (see Table 3.15).[88]

Although the 1527 change was briefly reversed in 1534, the "Hanlin club" of highest-ranking *chin-shih* degree-holders (described at the end of this chapter) was by the sixteenth century firmly in control of the key examiner positions in the palace (see Table 3.16) and metropolitan examinations. Their appointment as chief examiners in provincial examinations was increasingly conspicuous as well. We shall later see that during the Ch'ing, Hanlin academicians were also appointed as associate examiners for provincial civil examinations, thus taking complete charge of *chü-jen* and *chin-shih* selection in the name of the imperial court and Ministry of Rites. Beginning in the sixteenth century, then, the political center in Peking—the emperor and his inner court of ministers—directly controlled the middle and top levels of the empirewide examination market.[89]

This trend accelerated in the early K'ang-hsi era (1662–1722) of the Ch'ing dynasty, when the responsibilities of Hanlin academicians increased vis-à-vis the civil service and provincial education. Members of the Hanlin were now sent out (*san-kuan* 散官) and assigned as educational commissioners in the Chih-li capital region in 1680, and in Che-chiang and Chiang-su provinces in 1681. Hanlin academicians were also routinely assigned to monitor special "repeat" (*fu-shih* 覆試) examinations in the capital for *chü-jen* in 1699, before such graduates, typically from southern provinces such as Chiang-su, were allowed into the compound for the metropolitan examinations. In addition, the tradition of assigning the palace *chuang-yuan* 狀元 to provincial examinations began in 1669. Before then, the *optimus* usually had been assigned to serve as an associate examiner on the metropolitan examinations.[90]

FU-CHIEN. If we look at Fu-chien province in the southeast, we have further evidence that during the Ming dynasty the *chin-shih* degree was outpacing *chü-jen* status in the degree market. Table 2.6 has already shown

88. *Huang-Ming kung-chü k'ao*, 1.43b–44a. See also, for example, the *Hui-shih lu*, 1502: 1a–4b, in *Ming-tai teng-k'o lu hui-pien*, vol. 5.

89. The *Chih-i k'o so-chi*, 1.11–33, discusses the main officials that were employed for Ming examinations from 1385 to 1454.

90. See *Tan-mo lu*, 3.18b–19b. Cf. *Ch'ing-pai lei-ch'ao*, 21.13. In the Chia-ch'ing era (1796–1820), the *chuang-yuan* could also be appointed as Chiang-su provincial education commissioner. See *Kuo-ch'ao Yü-yang k'o-ming lu*, 4B.62b; and *Chih-i k'o-so chi*, 4.137.

INSTITUTIONAL DYNAMICS AND ELITES / 155

us that Fu-chou prefecture had 1,852 *chü-jen* in the early Ming along with 479 *chin-shih*. Hsing-hua prefecture had 1,096 *chü-jen* and 349 *chin-shih*. Fu-chou ranked second nationally for prefectures producing *chü-jen* in the early Ming and fourth in producing *chin-shih*, while Hsing-hua was sixth in both. Thus two prefectures in a single province had achieved remarkable success in the provincial and metropolitan examinations.[91]

Table 3.17 gives the prefectural breakdown in Fu-chien province for all *chü-jen* and *chin-shih* degrees from the early to late Ming. Along with Fu-chou and Hsing-hua, the prefectures of Ch'üan-chou and Chang-chou also produced an inordinate number of *chü-jen* and *chin-shih*. Overall, we find that 26% (2,327) of Fu-chien's total number of Ming (to 1634) *chü-jen* (8,808) gained *chin-shih* degrees. This means that 6,481 Fu-chien provincial graduates never gained the highest degree and had to compete with each other to gain whatever offices were not taken by palace graduates. With a surplus of provincial graduates in every province, the likelihood was that *chü-jen* could gain only local appointments, such as educational officials (see above), while *chin-shih* were appointed nationally.

Among those in Fu-chien province who had to make due with only a *chü-jen* degree was the infamous Ming literatus Li Chih 李贄 (1527–1602), from Ch'üan-chou prefecture, who finished twenty-second on the 1552 Fu-chien provincial examination. As one of ninety (= 3%) graduates out of three thousand candidates, Li Chih initially had been a third-class prefectural school student (*fu-hsueh-sheng* 附學生) whose family had purchased his student status for him. He had specialized on the *Documents Classic* in his studies for the *chü-jen* degree, but his family's financial plight prevented him from ever taking the metropolitan examination for the *chin-shih* degree.[92]

Known for his iconoclasm and criticism of Ch'eng-Chu orthodoxy later in his life, Li Chih at the time of the 1552 provincial examination showed by passing a conventional test at age twenty-five that he had obediently mastered the required interpretations of the Classics that he would later attack. With only a provincial degree in hand, Li could not gain an important office, but in 1555 he was fortunate to get a post as a county director of studies (*chiao-yü* 教諭) in Ho-nan province, which as we saw above remained one of the few appointments a *chü-jen* could still aspire to in the sixteenth century. In 1561 he traveled to Peking, where he waited for about two years for a place in the Imperial School, the last resort for

91. See Chien Chin-sung, *Ming-tai wen-hsueh p'i-p'ing yen-chiu*, pp. 115–19. Cf. Ping-ti Ho, *The Ladder of Success in Imperial China*, pp. 246–47.

92. *Fu-chien hsiang-shih lu* 福建鄉試錄 (Records of the Fu-chien provincial civil examination), 1552: 17a, in *Ming-tai teng-k'o lu hui-pien*, 12/6015; and *Min-sheng hsien-shu*, 5.15a.

unemployed provincial graduates, but had to resign from that when he learned of the death of his grandfather.[93]

Subsequently Li Chih returned to Peking and found a minor position there in the Ministry of Rites. From 1571 to 1576 he served in offices of the Ministry of Justice in Nanking. In 1578, Li Chih finally gained the post of prefect in Yun-nan province, a position he resigned from after serving three years, which effectively ended his undistinguished official career. The post of prefect, of course, was a position that a *chin-shih* degree-holder qualified for early in his career. The trials and tribulations Li Chih faced were typical of Ming *chü-jen*, most of whom did not gain his level of fame or ignominy. Later, in an essay entitled "Preamble to the Sages' Teachings" ("Sheng-chiao hsiao-yin" 聖教小引), Li described how far he had come intellectually from his student days: "When I was young I read the sages' teachings but did not understand them. I honored Confucius but did not know why Confucius deserved honor. I was 'like a short man watching a play behind a tall man,'[94] who followed along with others' research and simply chimed in. Hence before I was fifty I was just like a hunting dog who started barking because other dogs were barking. If you asked why I was barking, I would be speechless and have to laugh at myself."[95]

Table 3.18 further confirms how hard it became to get the *chin-shih* degree in Ming times. Fu-ch'eng city in Fu-chou prefecture, which ranked so high nationally in aggregate figures, produced a total of 306 *chin-shih* degree-holders from 1370 to 1546. Over those 176 years, however, the average number of *chin-shih* was less than 2 annually. If the 24.9% to 75.1% ratio of Ming *chin-shih* to *chü-jen* in Fu-chou prefecture is applied to Fu-ch'eng city, then approximately 1,227 *chü-jen* came from there, or only 7 a year.

The celebrity status of *chin-shih* when compared to *chü-jen* in Fu-chien province can be assessed from Table 3.19. Highly successful regions in the examination market usually kept records to document their local prestige. Such information was then included in local gazetteers and in provincial records. Below we see that Fu-chien could claim 92 Hanlin academicians in Ming times (through 1636), with 33 Fu-chien *chin-shih* degree-holders

93. See *Dictionary of Ming Biography*, pp. 807–08.

94. Here Li Chih is referring to Chu Hsi's remarks in the *Chu-tzu yü-lei* 朱子語類 (Conversations with Master Chu [Hsi] classified topically), 1473 edition (reprint, Taipei: Chung-cheng Bookstore), 116.14a, to the effect that "It's like a short man watching a play. When he hears others praise it, he also praises it."

95. See Li Chih, *Hsu fen-shu* 續焚書 (Continuation to a book destined to be burned) (Peking: Chung-hua Bookstore, 1975), p. 66 (卷 2).

finishing among the top 3 in the palace examination and 53 finishing among the top 5. Family success was also highlighted in such records.

What is clear, however, is that except for those who finished number one on the Fu-chien provincial examination (*chieh-yuan*), which was recorded by prefecture, and a family that had over three generations produced the *chieh-yuan* each time, the examination records cited here were strongly biased toward *chin-shih* degrees. Few *chü-jen* successes were recorded, indicating how commonplace this degree had already become in Fu-chien during the Ming dynasty. Fame in this record came only to the number-one finisher on the provincial examination, although *chü-jen* degree-holders overall remained important enough to be recorded in most provincial gazetteers honoring local elites. Such inclusion in gazetteers indicates that while examination records were biased toward *chin-shih*, local gazetteers still valorized *chü-jen* status and often included the names of licentiates in local communities.

## *CHIN-SHIH* AND THE HANLIN "CLUB"

Political reproduction through the egalitarian selection of literati officials was cemented by a final "palace examination" administered by the emperor himself to test all those who had successfully passed the highest-level capital examination. Since the T'ang and Sung, the emperor in effect was the dynasty's premier examiner, symbolically demanding oaths of allegiance from successful candidates for public office. Beginning in the Ming, the ruler was acknowledged as a Ch'eng-Chu sage-king. To be an official of more than one dynasty thus represented a moral breach of this ideal, though often broken, code of loyalty. Political legitimation of the imperial order by civil examinations in fact presupposed social recognition of the legitimacy of the selection process itself. In a convoluted but tightly woven ideological canvas of loyalties encompassing the partnership between state and society, even emperors became educated in the classical rationale for their imperial legitimacy by tutors selected from the civil service examinations.[96]

### Chin-shih *Quotas and Rankings*

Absolute quotas for metropolitan examinations were not set, although the general number of successful *chin-shih* in a triennial examination usually was around 300 to 350 candidates after 1475. The quotas fluctuated widely, however, particularly during the volatile years of the early Ming. In 1385, for instance, only 32 *chin-shih* were passed, while 472 names appeared on

96. Kahn, *Monarchy in the Emperor's Eyes*, pp. 115–81.

the 1406 roll of successful candidates—the low and high for the Ming dynasty. Figures frequently moved between 100, 200, 250, and 350 candidates, although Ping-ti Ho has estimated that during the Ming as a whole an average of 89 names per annum (289 per examination) were passed in the metropolitan examinations.[97]

Table 2.2 revealed that after 1450 typically 3,000 to 4,000 chü-jen competed triennially in the metropolitan examination for 250 to 350 places, which meant that only 7.5% to 10% received chin-shih degrees. After 1550, the number of candidates increased to between 4,500 and 4,700. With no significant changes in the number of chin-shih the degree ratio declined to 6.4% in 1601. In the late Ming, over 62,000 chü-jen competed for about 4,200 places on the fourteen metropolitan examinations held between 1549 and 1589.[98] Table 3.20 shows that the competition in civil metropolitan examinations during the Ch'ing dynasty, following long-term Ming-Ch'ing demographic trends, increased by 100% in the eighteenth century, as success rates dropped further, to 3.5%.

The top-ranking chin-shih were chosen for the Hanlin Academy beginning in 1385, a practice that was confirmed in 1404 by the Yung-lo emperor when he selected 29 chin-shih as Hanlin bachelors (Shu-chi-shih 庶吉士) to serve in the court.[99] This practice was maintained thereafter during the Ming and Ch'ing dynasties.[100] Normally the top 3 finishers were appointed as Academicians (Hsueh-shih 學士), while the top 20 to 40 chin-shih were eligible to become bachelors.[101] Because it represented the most prestigious academic institution during the late empire, as well as the training ground for the highest echelon of officialdom, the Hanlin Academy enabled those who passed the civil service examinations with honors to reach the forefront of the Ming and Ch'ing political world.[102]

### The Hanlin Academy and the Court

The origins of the Hanlin Academy as an imperial society of scholar-officials can be traced back to the T'ang dynasty, when medieval emper-

97. Ping-ti Ho, *The Ladder of Success in Imperial China*, p. 189.

98. Wada Masahiro estimates that the average triennial pool of Ming candidates for the metropolitan examination increased from 420 in the early Ming (1370–1414) to 3,500 in the mid-Ming (1450–1505), and then to over 4,500 in the late Ming (1549–89). See Wada, "Mindai kyojinzō no keisei katei ni kan suru ichi kōsatsu," p. 69.

99. *Ming-tai wei-k'o hsing-shih lu*, A.1b; *Wu-li t'ung-k'ao*, 175.21b.

100. Adam Y. C. Lui, *The Hanlin Academy: Training Ground for the Ambitious, 1644–1850* (Hamden, Conn.: Shoe String Press, Archon Books, 1981).

101. *Ming-shih*, 3/1695.

102. Jerry Dennerline, *The Chia-ting Loyalists: Confucian Leadership and Social Change in Seventeenth-Century China* (New Haven: Yale University Press, 1981), pp. 18–21.

ors granted personal favorites an honored place as special advisors within the court. Not yet regarded as full members of the bureaucracy, Hanlin academicians initially served as personal advisors to T'ang and Sung emperors, who chose them as much for their moral reputations as for their academic or political qualifications. In time, Hanlin scholars also became involved in drafting imperial documents for Sung emperors. As the latter's private secretaries, Hanlin members, through their proximity to the throne, successfully garnered a degree of political power from the bureaucracy, and members of the academy assumed substantive posts for the first time.

During the Sung dynasty, the functions of Hanlin academicians shifted increasingly from political matters to cultural affairs. Hanlin readers were assigned to take charge of the required classical and historical discussions with the emperor. This shift in emphasis marked the first extension of the Hanlin Academy's influence into literary and educational fields. Although the Hanlin Academy had considerably diminished political influence under the Yuan dynasty, whose Mongol rulers regularly favored military over bureaucratic forms of rule and chose *se-mu* peoples over Han Chinese, Hanlin appointees were still assigned to deal with cultural matters, particularly the preparation of Han and non-Han dynastic histories discussed in Chapter 1.[103]

When the Ming dynasty restored Han Chinese civilian rule, the Hanlin Academy became a fully developed government institution. Its political functions increased under the Hung-wu emperor after the purge of Hu Wei-yung and the elimination of all executive offices in the bureaucracy. In the fifteenth century, Hanlin duties included supervision of palace, metropolitan, and provincial civil examinations (see above), publication of literary works, work on special cultural projects such as the *Yung-lo ta-tien* and *San-pu ta-ch'üan* (see Chapter 1), participation in classical and historical discussions with the emperor, and performance of temporary assignments as imperial envoys. When compared to their T'ang and Sung predecessors, the role of Ming Hanlin academicians in policy making declined as they increasingly became the Grand Secretaries (*Ta-hsueh-shih* 大學士) serving the emperor as his handles on the bureaucracy and examination market. Their cultural and educational influence, as we have seen, increased immensely.[104]

103. See Yamamoto Takayoshi 山本隆義, "Gendai ni okeru Kanrin gakushi in ni tsuite" 元代に於ける翰林學士院について (Concerning the Hanlin Academy during the Yuan period), *Tōhōgaku* 東方學 11 (1955): 81–99.

104. See also Peter Ditmanson, "Intellectual Lineages and the Early Ming Court," *Papers on Chinese History* (Harvard University) 5 (1996): 1–17.

## Hanlin Career Patterns

The views of Hanlin academicians and bachelors thus were not the idle thoughts of marginal literati. They were the opinions of highly placed metropolitan and palace examination graduates, who had the ear of the emperor and inner court and were destined to become officials with empirewide impact. Increasingly, the academy became an important stepping-stone to political influence in the court and bureaucracy at the apex of the civil examination process, and its cultural influence through appointees to the Ministry of Rites was significant.[105] An *optimus, secundus,* or *tertius* on the palace examination, for example, followed a career pattern typical of a Hanlin academician. This Ming-Ch'ing pattern entailed close links between the Hanlin Academy, the Ministry of Rites, and the Grand Secretariat (*Nei-ko* 內閣). A Hanlin career represented a late imperial model for political advancement through these complementary and overlapping governmental bodies. The compilers of the official *Ming History* noted: "Only *chin-shih* could enter the Hanlin. Only Hanlin [members] could enter the inner court. Only Hanlin could serve as the minister or vice-minister of Rites in the north and south, or as minister of the right of personnel." After 1646 all top finishers on the metropolitan and provincial examinations, once they became *chin-shih*, could also enter the Hanlin Academy.[106]

The Ming functions and structure of the Ministry of Rites, for example, remained similar to those of earlier dynasties, but without any executive positions after 1380, the emperor and his immediate staff increasingly became the key coordinators of educational affairs and examination matters in the realm. Although the name "Ministry of Rites" sounds peripheral to the center ring of political power, in Ming China its ministers and functionaries were on the main stage. The Bureau of Ceremonies, for example, was charged with all ceremonial affairs, but the latter included administration of the empirewide Imperial School system, as well as supervision of the civil examination system from the county, prefecture, and provincial levels to the metropolitan level in Peking. In effect, the Ministry of Rites controlled the imperial education system and the examination market. In part, it was a "Ministry of Education." As we have seen, by 1600 Hanlin members effectively supervised the upper levels of the civil selection process for the emperor and the ministry.

105. On the cultural activities of the Hanlin academicians and bachelors, see *Kuo-ch'ao li-k'o Han-lin kuan k'o* 國朝歷科翰林館課 (Series of examinations for Ming dynasty Hanlin academicians), 1603 edition, passim.

106. See *Ming-shih,* 3/1702, for the comment. See also *Chih-i k'o-suo chi,* 4.131–32.

In addition, the Bureau of Receptions had as its charge the management of foreign relations under the tributary system in effect in China since the Yung-lo emperor had reinitiated contact with his "vassals" in Southeast Asia and invaded Vietnam.[107] In other words, the Ministry of Rites had as its portfolio two major functions of government: education/examinations and tribute/foreign affairs. The classical training of all *chin-shih* thus yielded a post-Mongol view of the world inculcated through the rigorous examination system and practiced in the arena of foreign affairs. The top graduates became the new examiners.

By taking care of both imperial sacrifices via the Bureau of Sacrifices and imperial family matters via the Court of the Imperial Clan, the Ministry of Rites during the Ming dynasty had the further distinction of being the only ministry to be a member of the inner court of the emperor and at the same time a full-fledged member of the outer court bureaucracy. It thus had access to the inner sanctum of imperial prerogative and could effect its policies through the education and examination bureaucracy down to all county levels outside Peking. The academy lay at the heart of the political partnership between the court and the bureaucracy until the early eighteenth century, when the Manchu inner court insulated itself from both the Hanlin Academy and the Ministry of Rites by creating the Ch'ing dynasty's Grand Council (*Chün-chi chu* 軍機處).[108]

The most important members of the inner court during the Ming dynasty came from the Hanlin Academy, the Grand Secretariat, and the palace eunuchs. After 1380, the Grand Secretariat increasingly coordinated and supervised the six ministries, and the Ministry of Rites, because it straddled the middle ground between inner and outer echelons of power, also became more important. When later Ming emperors, especially during the sixteenth and seventeenth centuries, delegated much of their authority to members of the inner court, the close links between the Grand Secretariat and Ministry of Rites became more intimate and produced career patterns of major political and institutional consequences not only for the Ming but also for the Ch'ing bureaucratic system.

Statistical study of this phenomenon reveals that a majority of the Grand Secretaries during the Ming originated from the Ministry of Rites.[109] Close links between the Ministry of Rites and the Grand

---

107. Wang Gungwu, *Community and Nation*, pp. 77–146.

108. Yun-yi Ho, *The Ministry of Rites*, pp. 60–75. On the Grand Council, see Beatrice S. Bartlett, *Monarchs and Ministers: The Grand Council in Mid-Ch'ing China, 1723–1820* (Berkeley: University of California Press, 1991), pp. 2–7, 17–64.

109. Otto Berkelbach von der Sprenkel, "High Officials of the Ming: A Note on the Ch'i Ch'ing Nien Piao of the Ming History," *Bulletin of the School of Oriental and African Studies* 14 (1952): 98–99.

Secretariat had another distinctive feature. Most Grand Secretaries had also been members of the Hanlin Academy early in their official careers. During the Ming dynasty, for example, 75% (124) of all (165) Grand Secretaries had earlier been members of the Hanlin Academy. Moreover, 109 of these 165 Grand Secretaries (66%) had also served in the Ministry of Rites, and 93 of the latter (56% of 165) went directly from the Ministry of Rites to the Grand Secretariat.[110]

We see the Hanlin Academy, Ministry of Rites, and Grand Secretariat all converging in Ming political life. In a typical Ming bureaucratic career, then, a successful *chin-shih* graduate (normally with high honors) of the palace examination was first appointed to the Hanlin Academy, where he served the court as a compiler, editor, provincial examiner, or personal secretary to the emperor. From there he went on to serve in a variety of possible positions but eventually became a fixture in the Ministry of Rites, often as a palace or metropolitan examination official. The Ministry of Rites then served as a springboard for promotion to the Grand Secretariat, which until the early eighteenth century remained the highest advisory body in the bureaucratic apparatus. Thereafter, the Grand Council was added to the inner court, and its members replaced Grand Secretaries as key court figures in the outer bureaucracy and greatly influenced the metropolitan and palace examinations.[111]

The top *chin-shih* finishers were guaranteed entry into the Hanlin Academy, although others could be chosen for various extenuating reasons. For example, during the Ch'ing between 1646 and 1659 all first-place finishers on the metropolitan examination *hui-yuan* were automatically placed in the Hanlin Academy regardless of their finish on the palace examination. Later, those who finished first on the provincial examinations (*chieh-yuan*) were honored this way as well. In fact, from 1673 until 1685, if the same person finished first on both the palace and metropolitan examinations, then all first-place finishers on the provincial examinations for that year's *chin-shih* competition were also placed into the Hanlin Academy.[112]

---

110. Yun-yi Ho, *The Ministry of Rites*, p. 16. Cf. Ku Hung-ting, "Upward Career Mobility Patterns of High-Ranking Officials in Ch'ing China, 1730–1796," *Papers on Far Eastern History* (Australia), 29 (1984): 45–66.

111. Yun-yi Ho, *The Ministry of Rites*, pp. 16–19. See also Lui, *The Hanlin Academy: Training Ground for the Ambitious, 1644–1850*, pp. 29–44. Lui divides the functions of the Hanlin into three categories relating to the emperor, relating to literary projects, and special temporary functions, which represents Ch'ing continuation of a Ming pattern. On the impact of the Grand Council, see Iona Man-cheong, "Fair Fraud and Fraudulent Fairness: The 1761 Examination Case," *Late Imperial China* 18, 2 (December 1997): 58–66.

112. See *Chih-i k'o so-chi*, 4.131–32.

Those Hanlin bachelors who did well in the academy's own three-year program in its Institute of Advanced Studies (*Shu-ch'ang-kuan* 庶常館) were "released from the Institute" (*san-kuan* 散館) and took a special literary examination that tested classical erudition and rhyme-prose. Interestingly, although belles lettres had been eliminated from the regular examinations since the early Ming, they were still the mainstay of the Hanlin examinations. If bachelors did well on this Hanlin examination, they were retained in the academy (*liu-guan* 留館) as compilers. If not, they were "released into officialdom" from the academy to take up appointments in the central bureaucracy or as local officials.[113] Either way, their time in the academy had enabled them to become the elite of *chin-shih* degree-holders. Members of this exclusive club became a special community of scholars from whom candidates for the Ming and Ch'ing dynasties' most important positions were drawn.[114]

## ROLES OF HAN CHINESE AND MANCHUS DURING EARLY CH'ING CIVIL EXAMINATIONS

Under Manchu military and political control, the Ming civil and military service system was reinstated soon after the Ch'ing dynasty was formed in Peking in 1644.[115] The first *optimus* and *chin-shih* classes were chosen in 1646. This was considered a very outstanding group of 373 palace examination graduates, many of whom went on to hold high positions in the Manchu government.[116] Following Ming precedent, the fourfold division of the selection and evaluation process for officials remained: (1) schools, (2) examinations, (3) recommendation, and (4) appointment.

113. For examples of *san-kuan* examinations testing Hanlin bachelors, see the Ch'ing dynasty examination papers (翰林散館試卷) of O-min 鄂敏 (1730 *chin-shih*), and Han Yen-tseng 韓彥曽 (1730 *chin-shih*) in the Rare Books Collection of Fudan University in Shanghai, nos. 3852 and 3853. My thanks to Wu Ge 吳格, the director of the Rare Books Section, for his help in viewing these materials.

114. For discussion, see Chang Chung-ju 章中如, *Ch'ing-tai k'ao-shih chih-tu* 清代考試制度 (Ch'ing civil examination system) (Shanghai: Li-ming Bookstore, 1931), pp. 41–42.

115. Manchu examination policy took into account earlier Chin dynasty models for Jurchen and Han Chinese examinations that had evolved between 1123 and 1189. Chin examinations, based on the Southern Sung stress on poetry and prose, were models for the Yuan dynasty's first civil examination in 1238. See Chapter 1.

116. See *Tan-mo lu* 淡墨錄 (Record of skilled civil examination papers), by Li T'iao-yuan 李調元, in *Han-hai* 函海 (Seas of writings) (1881 collectanea), compiled by Li T'iao-yuan, 1.6a–8a.

*Manchu-Han Relations in Early Civil Examinations*

Important changes, especially in the schooling system for the enlarged empire, were made, however. For example, in addition to the Imperial School system, special dynastic schools were also established for the eight military banners (composed of Manchus, Mongols, and Chinese military families) as well as a school (*tsung-hsueh* 宗學) for the Manchu imperial family.[117] The Manchu court had initiated examinations for Manchus, Mongols, and Chinese banners in their native languages in Manchuria as early as 1634, after establishing a Ming-style bureaucracy in 1627. The first Han bannerman *chin-shih* in Sheng-ching 盛京 (Shen-yang, Manchuria), for example, was Shen Wen-k'uei 沈文奎, whose family was originally from Chiang-hsi.[118]

The touchy issue of Manchu-Han relations was raised by the regent Dorgon (1612–50) and other advisors of the then eight-year-old Shun-chih emperor (r. 1644–62), in the very first Ch'ing dynasty palace examination in 1646. In this question passed by the 373 metropolitan graduates, the emperor's regent wanted information to enable the dynasty to bring Manchu and Han officials and people together for a common purpose (今如何為政而後能使滿漢官民同合志歟？). The dynasty's first *optimus*, Fu I-chien 傅以漸 (1609–65) from Shan-tung, replied that Manchus and Chinese could surely work together to improve the new dynasty, but the cultural content of that initiative had to come from a sagely ruler who understood that "the order of the two emperors and three kings was based on the Way, and their Way was based on the mind" (二帝三王之治本於道，二帝三王之道本於心), a Ch'eng-Chu moral cum political mantra that Ming literati had successfully fashioned into orthodoxy (see Chapter 2).[119]

In the 1649 palace examination, the emperor again inquired about how best to deal with Manchu versus Han Chinese quotas on civil examinations. He asked the metropolitan graduates to describe "how Manchus and Han Chinese could be unified so that their hearts were the same and they worked together without division" (今欲聯滿漢為一體，使之同心，合力勸然無間，何道而可民為邦？). The top answer by the second *chuang-yuan* under the Ch'ing, Liu Tzu-chuang 劉子壯, argued for cultural unity instead of a special palace quota for Manchus versus Han candidates. Again, that cultural unity was defined in light of the moral cultivation ideals transmitted to the Ming and Ch'ing by the Sung dynasty Tao Learning school.

117. *Ch'ing-shih kao*, 11/3099–3100.
118. *Tan-mo lu*, 1.3a–6a, and 1.15b–16a; and *Ch'ing-pai lei-ch'ao*, 21.8.
119. *Chuang-yuan ts'e* 狀元策 (Policy essays by *optimi*), compiled by Chiao Hung 焦竑, Wu Tao-nan 吳道南, et al., 1733 edition, 8.1a–5b.

Liu applied the long-standing distinction drawn between northern and southern literati to the differences between Manchus and Chinese: "I would say that the Manchus stress substance (*chih* 質), so we should use culture (*wen* 文) to complement this trait. Han people emphasize culture, so we should use substance to complement this trait." The caricature of the moral northern bumpkin versus the superficial southern litterateur of Sung and Ming times was now translated into a stereotype defining Manchus as the equivalent of moral northerners and all Han Chinese as cultured southerners.[120]

As during the Mongol era, the Manchu conquest elite initially felt that northern Chinese were more reliable subjects than southerners. Table 3.21 shows, for instance, that in Shan-tung province, in the last two Ming provincial examinations in the province, 19 of 85 (22%) *chü-jen* graduates in 1639, and 31 of 90 (34%) *chü-jen* in 1642, went on to take their *chin-shih* degrees under Manchu auspices in Ch'ing civil examinations starting with the 1646 metropolitan and palace examination. The Manchu regime was clearly anxious to accommodate such crossovers. In the 1646 metropolitan examinations, for example, 53% of the Shan-tung *chü-jen* from the previous year's 95 graduates on the first Ch'ing provincial examination in Shan-tung quickly passed and received *chin-shih* degrees. The Ch'ing policy of relying on northern collaborators, so successful in military and political terms after 1644, was also a major feature of early Ch'ing civil examinations.[121]

To this end, the court also appointed civil examiners with great care. Manchu and Han bannermen were appointed chief examiners in metropolitan examinations ahead of Han Chinese, as Table 3.22 shows. Most of the Ming *chin-shih* degree-holders who were appointed as chief or associate examiners in metropolitan examinations were northerners until 1658 (18 out of 20 associate examiners in 1649), when enough loyal *chin-shih* graduates had been produced under the Ch'ing dynasty to fill the available positions in the examination bureaucracy. In 1649, for example, two southern examiners were appointed for the first time as metropolitan examiners. In 1658, all 22 chief and associate examiners were Han Chinese. Thirteen of the twenty 1658 associate examiners were 1655 *chin-shih*, and many of them were southerners.[122]

Similarly, the percentage of northerners serving as provincial examiners was very high (over 70%) in the initial 1645, 1646, and 1648 provincial

120. Ibid., 8.1a–10a. See also *Tan-mo lu*, 1.16a.

121. Cf. Wakeman, *The Great Enterprise: The Manchu Reconstruction of Imperial Order in Seventeenth-Century China* (Berkeley: University of California Press, 1985), pp. 1129–1135, on "twice-serving ministers."

122. See *Kuo-ch'ao Yü-yang k'o-ming lu*, 1.2a–2b, for the 1649 metropolitan examination. See also *Hui-shih lu*, 1658: 1a–2b.

examinations. From 1651 to 1660, however, the percentage of southern examiners slowly increased from 47% in 1651 to 69% in 1657. According to Frederic Wakeman, Jr., this evolution represented the "revival of literati networks," particularly those from the south. The gradual revival of late Ming southern literati networks, after initial northern dominance, also occurred among the 1646–58 palace examination graduates. After the initial dominance of northerners in 1646, southern dominance in the *chin-shih* rolls from 1647 to 1658 again paralleled Ming geographical distributions (see Chapter 5) for metropolitan and palace examination graduates.[123]

In the early Ch'ing, a 4:6 Manchu-to-Han quota had been in effect for the palace examination, a ratio that had been borrowed from the northern versus southern quotas of Ming times to apply to Manchu-Han relations. Two separate groups of candidates (i.e., Manchu/Mongol and Han Chinese bannermen) had been channeled via these quotas toward *chin-shih* degrees until 1655, which was the last examination to maintain the division of candidates according to the 4:6 ratio. In 1652 and 1655, for instance, completely separate metropolitan and palace civil examinations were held for Han Chinese and bannermen, but they were recombined in 1658. Furthermore, a ten-point quota of 4:2:4 (Manchu, Mongol, and Chinese) was set for bannermen seeking the *chin-shih* degree in 1652 and 1655. After 1655, no Manchu bannerman ever finished among the coveted top three *chin-shih* places in the palace examination until 1883. Thereafter, Han examination officials such as Hung Ch'eng-ch'ou 洪承疇 (1593–1665), who was one of the first Ming officials from the south (Fu-chien) to serve the Manchus as a metropolitan and palace examination chief supervisor (*tsung-tsai* 總裁) in 1649, were blamed (or praised) for never allowing Manchus the rank of *chuang-yuan* in the civil examinations.[124]

Special examinations for Manchu bannermen were also established in 1651, which were separate from those for Han banners. Those Manchus who did not know classical Chinese were permitted to take the tests in their own language (Ch'ing-wen 清文). During the K'ang-hsi reign, these special examinations were formalized into "translation examinations" (*fan-i hsiang-shih* 翻譯鄉試) at the provincial level, whereby Manchus could choose to take examinations in their language. (Such privileges were

123. Wakeman, *The Great Enterprise*, pp. 886–90.

124. *Tan-mo lu*, 1.10b–13a; and *Kuo-ch'ao Shan-tung li-k'o hsiang-shih*, on the 1649 metropolitan examination. See also Bielenstein, "The Regional Provenance," pp. 6, 28. Thus, during the Ch'ing there were 114 *chuang-yuan* (one Han and one Manchu in 1652 and 1655), etc., but only 112 metropolitan and palace examinations. Cf. Wang Chen-main, *Hung Ch'eng-chou* (Tucson: University of Arizona Press, 1999), 8:24 of draft ms.; and *Ch'ing-pai lei-ch'ao*, 21.9, and 21.127.

extended to Mongols in 1735.) Subsequently in 1697, Manchus related to the imperial family were encouraged to take the civil examinations with other Manchus. As we shall see in Chapter 4, cheating was common among bannermen taking military examinations.[125]

Initially, Manchu and Mongol translation examinations were administered in a single session with one question based on documentary style and another on an essay topic based on a quotation from either the Four Books or Five Classics. Later, during the Ch'ien-lung reign (1736–95), the requirements were tightened, and Manchus and Mongols were encouraged to take examinations in classical Chinese in an effort to unite civilian and military training. Questions in Chinese based on Sung dynasty classicism and philology (hsiao-hsueh 小學) were introduced, but most Manchus still did not compete with the Chinese in provincial and metropolitan examinations. Additionally, translation examinations were required in the specialized translation bureaus, which dated back to the early Ming and were placed under the jurisdiction of the Hanlin Academy. These bureaus were responsible for ritual communication in foreign affairs with Siam, with Islamic peoples, and later, during the early Ch'ing, with Russia.[126]

In addition, Chinese who passed the palace and the court (after 1723) examinations with highest honors and entered the Hanlin Academy, where they served as imperial secretaries, were required to learn Manchu, a practice that began in 1647.[127] In 1688, a Chinese candidate from Hang-chou, Ling Shao-wen 凌紹雯, answered the policy question on the palace examination in both classical Chinese and Manchu and was appointed as a compiler to the Hanlin Academy based on his bilingual ability, even

125. These banner examinations and their quotas are spelled out in detail in *Tan-mo lu*, 1.1a–3a, and 1.14a–15b. Eventually by 1660, the Han banner examinations were the same as ordinary Han examinations, that is, much more difficult than examinations for Manchus and Mongols. See also the discussion in *Chih-i ts'ung-hua*, 1.5b, of Mongolian examination questions and their stress on Chu Hsi's interpretations for the Four Books and Five Classics. Cf. *Ch'ing-pai lei-ch'ao*, 21.7; Man-kam Leung, "Mongolian Language and Examinations in Peking and Other Metropolitan Areas during the Manchu Dynasty in China (1644–1911)," *The Canada-Mongolia Review* 1 (1975): 29–44; and Oxnam, *Ruling from Horseback*, pp. 122–24.

126. For examples of translation examinations, see *Fan-i hui-shih lu* 翻譯會試錄, 1739, 1809, 1811, which are in the Ming-Ch'ing Archives, Academia Sinica, Taiwan. See also the translation examinations in Russian, Latin, Arabic, and Siamese from Ch'ing dynasty translation bureaus in the same collection. The UCLA East Asian Library has copies of these materials. Cf. Pamela Crossley, "Structure and Symbol in the Role of the Ming-Qing Foreign Translation Bureaus (*Siyiguan*)," *Central and Inner Asian Studies* 5 (1991): 38–70. She notes that the translation bureaus date to medieval times.

127. See *Tan-mo lu*, 1.9b–10a.

though Ling finished at the bottom of the second tier of *chin-shih* graduates.[128] Special essay tests in Manchu and translation questions from classical Chinese to Manchu were administered to Hanlin academicians in the palace to ensure that documents and memorials were accurately recorded in the dual official languages.[129] In 1748, the Ch'ien-lung emperor reproached both Ch'ien Wei-ch'eng 錢維城 (1720–72) and Chuang Ts'un-yü 莊存與 (1719–88), who as *optimus* and *secundus* on the 1745 palace examination had entered the Hanlin Academy, for their poor performances in learning Manchu.[130]

The Ch'ing dynasty was also concerned that other minorities in the enlarged empire should receive appropriate attention in local educational affairs. The P'eng 棚 people in Chiang-hsi province, to this end, were incorporated as a minority group by the education commissioner there in 1762 when he created a *sheng-yuan* quota for the P'eng, which allowed them one place for each fifty candidates. In 1763 the Chiang-hsi provincial governor, T'ang P'in 湯聘, who was concurrently the education commissioner, argued for establishing local licentiate quotas for the P'eng people in order to encourage them to settle down and discard their nomadic pattern of life, a policy that he sought support for in a 1731 precedent that went back to the Yung-cheng reign.[131]

Such minority quotas, however, became the targets of Han people seeking local status in the southwest. In 1767, a memorial from the Kuang-hsi provincial education commissioner, Mei Li-pen 梅立本 (d. 1767), noted that in five prefectures Han Chinese were using the easier native quotas instead of their own more competitive quotas in local examinations to become licentiates. Mei added that it was hard to verify

---

128. Ibid., 6.10b.

129. *Ch'ing-shih kao*, 11/3169. See also *Huang-ch'ao hsu wen-hsien t'ung-k'ao*, 1/8424–25, 8429, 8433, 8440, 8447, 8450. Manchu-language examinations administered to Hanlin members are part of the Han Yü-shan Special Collection in the UCLA University Research Library, Department of Special Collections. Thanks are due Pamela Crossley of Dartmouth College, who identified and classified the Manchu-language materials in the collection. Cf. Cheryl M. Boettcher, "'To Make Them Ready for Official Employment': Literacy in Manchu and the Hanlin Cohort of 1655," UCLA History Department Writing Seminar Paper, winter-spring 1993.

130. See Hummel, *Eminent Chinese of the Ch'ing Period*, p. 158.

131. See the "Chiang-hsi hsueh-cheng tsou" 江西學政奏 (Memorial by the Chiang-hsi provincial education commissioner) by Chou Huang 周煌 (d. 1785), in *I-hui ch'ao-chien* 移會 抄件 (Copied memoranda items), 1762, 8th month, 19th day in the Ming-Ch'ing Archives, Academia Sinica, Taiwan. See also the *Li-pu i-hui* 禮部移會 (Memoranda from the Ministry of Rites), 1763, 4th month, also in the Ming-Ch'ing Archives, which asked to set up *t'ung-sheng* (= licentiates) quotas for the P'eng people in Chiang-hsi province.

authentic native people (*t'u-chi* 土籍) as native.[132] Similarly, a 1785 memorial from the governor-general of Shen-hsi and Kan-su provinces in the northwest, Fu-k'ang-an 福康安 (d. 1796), a member of the Yellow Banner, discussed the need to establish schools for orthodox literati studies to flourish among Muslims there. Fu-k'ang-an, an experienced Manchu military leader who had helped lead Ch'ing forces in Kan-su successfully against Muslim separatists in 1784, clearly perceived the civil examinations as a way to incorporate the *Hui-min* 回民 (Chinese Muslims) into the empire's mainstream. He recommended that the official quotas for Muslims be increased to four places on both local civil and military *sui-shih* examinations.[133]

Other frequent memorials and edicts dealt with the special requirements of the minorities in southwest China, which had been described by the education reformer Ch'en Hung-mou 陳宏謀 (1696–1771), who had served in Yun-nan province from 1733 to 1738.[134] In an 1807 memorial, the provincial education commissioner in Hu-nan province, Li Tsung-han 李宗瀚 (1769–1831), requested that Miao 苗 candidates taking provincial examinations be granted quotas of their own so that they would not have to compete for places with better-prepared Han Chinese. Li was quick to add, however, that local officials would have to be wary of those, notably Han Chinese, who would falsely claim Miao heritage to fill the latter's more easily attained quotas. Again, the goal was to assimilate the Miao into the literati mainstream via local quotas for the examinations.[135]

### Early Manchu Civil Examination Policies

After initially higher *chü-jen* and *chin-shih* rolls in the 1640s and 1650s, early Manchu rulers deliberately set lower quotas in 1660 (see Table 3.23), which lasted into the eighteenth century, for local and provincial examinations in Han Chinese provinces, perceiving in the late Ming high quotas the government's loss of control over gentry, merchant, and military families in local society. The total number of triennial *chü-jen* degrees was nearly cut in half from over 1,400 in 1645 to 796 in 1660, rising only to

132. See the "Kuang-hsi hsueh-cheng tsou" 廣西學政奏 (Memorial of the Kuang-hsi education commissioner), in *I-hui ch'ao-chien* 移會抄件 (Copied memoranda items), 1767, 7th month, which includes the memorial dated 7th month 28th day.

133. See the memorials in *Li-pu i-hui nei-ko* 禮部移會內閣 (Memoranda from the Ministry of Rites for the Inner Court), 1785, 1st month, 26th day.

134. See Rowe, "Education and Empire in Southwest China: Ch'en Hung-mou in Yunnan, 1733–38," in Elman and Woodside, eds., *Education and Society in Late Imperial China*, pp. 421–33.

135. *Huang-ch'ao hsu wen-hsien t'ung-k'ao*, p. 8438.

about 1,000 in 1700. The second-class *chü-jen* list (*fu-pang* 副榜), which had existed since Ming times and padded local *chü-jen* lists by up to 10%, was abolished in 1662. After *fu-pang* status was restored in the eighteenth century, however, it was seen as an unacceptable route to the *chin-shih* degree. Literati such as Wang Ming-sheng 王鳴盛 (1722–98), for example, chose to compete again for the *chü-jen* degree in the 1747 Chiang-nan provincial examination even though he already held second-class status there. Moreover, local quotas for licentiates were decreased to twenty in a large prefecture, fifteen in a large county, and only five in a small county.[136]

More stringent policies in education to regain control of the dynasty's human resources correlated with Manchu efforts in the 1660s to crack down on tax evasion by gentry families in the Yangtzu delta and recover material resources for dynastic use. In addition, because of the large number of Manchus and Han bannermen in the central bureaucracy, fewer positions were now available for civilian Han Chinese, although Manchu appointments were less conspicuous in provincial and local administration. The total number of *chin-shih* degrees awarded triennially declined 61% from a high of 399 in 1645 to 155 in 1667, and then declined another 30% to 109 in 1676, after briefly rising to 299 in 1670.[137]

Provincial quotas were somewhat more generous in number early in the Shun-chih reign, when, for example, Chiang-nan (An-hui and Chiang-su provinces) and the capital region of Shun-t'ien each were permitted over 160 successful candidates to compete in the metropolitan examinations. In the late Ming 100 had been permitted. In 1660, however, provincial quotas there were more drastically cut to about 60 in large provinces. Although gradually increased during the K'ang-hsi reign (1662–1722), the numbers remained far below late Ming quotas even though by 1700 the population in the empire reached over 200 million.[138] As late as 1765, the An-hui provincial education commissioner sent a memorial requesting an increase in provincial quotas for the Yangtzu delta provinces of Che-chiang, Chiang-su, and An-hui and justified the request by indicating that local civil and military quotas for such a prosperous region were still too low.[139]

136. *Ch'in-ting Ta-Ch'ing hui-tien shih-li*, 348.1a–b, 348.5a–b, 350.2b, 370.1a–b. See also Huang Kuang-liang, *Ch'ing-tai k'o-chü chih-tu chih yen-chiu*, pp. 377–425, on local licentiate quotas. On Wang Ming-sheng, see *Chiang-nan hsiang-shih lu*, 1747: 26a. Cf. Ping-ti Ho, *The Ladder of Success in Imperial China*, pp. 179–81.

137. Kessler, *K'ang-hsi and the Consolidation of Ch'ing Rule*, pp. 30–39. See also Oxnam, *Ruling from Horseback*, pp. 87–88, 101–08.

138. *Ch'ing-shih kao*, 11/3157–58.

139. See "An-hui hsueh-cheng t'i-pen" 安徽學政題本 (Memorial of the An-hui education commissioner), 1765, 7th month, 26th day, in the Ming-Ch'ing Archives, Academia Sinica, Taiwan.

As in the Ming, no absolute limits were set on the number of metropolitan graduates permitted, although regional quotas were still in effect. In 1646, when 399 *chin-shih* were graduated, 58% came from the south, 38% were from the north, and 4% came from central portions of the empire. These figures roughly corresponded to the 55:35:10 regional ratio worked out during the Ming dynasty. Eventually, a ratio of 60:40, south to north (see Table 2.5), was worked out, with the quota for the central portions divided up between them. Quotas were established for the southwestern provinces of Yun-nan, Ssu-ch'uan, Kuei-chou, and Kuang-hsi (two for Yun-nan and Ssu-ch'uan, one for Kuei-chou and Kuang-hsi). Southwestern quotas were doubled by the emperor in 1700 for the 1701 metropolitan examination.[140]

The number of metropolitan and palace examination graduates tended to be around 300 *chin-shih* for the triennial examinations, with a range of 110 (for a low in 1789) to 406 (a high in 1730). Ping-ti Ho has calculated that for the Ch'ing period as a whole there were 239 graduates per examination (down 50 from the Ming) or approximately 100 per annum (up 11 from the Ming). The number of per annum graduates was actually higher during the Ch'ing because of the frequent use of special examinations (*chih-k'o* 制科) such as the *po-hsueh hung-tz'u* 博學宏詞 (search for broad learning and extensive words) special examinations of 1679 and 1736.[141] In addition, the Manchu throne frequently deviated from the regular triennial schedule of examinations and scheduled special "grace examinations" to commemorate the longevity of reigns or to celebrate imperial birthdays.[142]

To be properly evaluated, the structure and process of civil service examinations in late imperial China described in this chapter should not be disaggregated from their educational, social, and political forms of practice during Ming and Ch'ing times. By understanding the long-term institutional aspects of civil examinations in Ming and Ch'ing times, we learn how civil examinations successfully mobilized elites during the late empire and prioritized the Tao Learning domain of classical knowledge for them. We also perceive the increasing preeminence of a small number of *chin-*

---

140. See *Tan-mo lu*, 3.19b–20a.

141. *Ch'ing-shih kao*, 11/3099, 3158–59. See also Ping-ti Ho, *The Ladder of Success in Imperial China*, p. 189.

142. See note 8 above. Of the 112 metropolitan/palace examinations given during the Ch'ing, 75% were "regular examinations." Metropolitan/palace "grace examinations" were held in 1659, 1713, 1723, 1737, 1752, 1761, 1771, 1780, 1790, 1795, 1796, 1801, 1809, 1819, 1822, 1832, 1836, 1841, 1845, 1852, 1860, 1863, 1876, 1890, 1894, 1901–1902 (held in 1903), and 1904. See Huang Kuang-liang, *Ch'ing-tai k'o-chü chih-tu yen-chiu*, pp. 137–52. For a different count, see Man-cheong, "The Class of 1761," pp. 329–31.

*shih* degree-holders, who monopolized the upper levels of the imperial bureaucracy after 1580, over the vast number of provincial and local graduates, not to mention the millions of candidates for county examinations. Their preeminence meant that the partnership between literati and the court was increasingly limited after 1600 to an ever more exclusive group of literati, usually from the wealthiest households and lineages.

The few of the local elite that gained the prestigious *chin-shih* degree represented the interests of their gentry peers to the court, but they also transmitted the imperial power that had blessed them with success, whether of Han Chinese Ming emperors or Manchu rulers, to their less successful cohorts. A late imperial aristocracy of culture and status had been fashioned around the much coveted *chin-shih* degree, the difficulty of acquiring which surpassed that of the Yuan and early Ming dynasties. In time, even the Sung prestige of a *chin-shih* degree was surpassed in the Ch'ing examination market when in the eighteenth century only 1% of the ever-growing number of candidates could even pass a given provincial examination to gain the lesser *chü-jen* degree. Most literati, then, had to deal with examination failure, and such failures produced a variety of forms of resistance to the examination regime.

The next chapter further elaborates on the political dynamics of this remarkable premodern regime of civil examinations, and explores more fully the intense public resistance they generated. The focus will be on how the examination compounds actually worked and why they represented a venue of struggle and compromise between imperial and literati interests. We shall see that the *chü-jen* and *chin-shih* career goals, described above, represented the pinnacle of a pyramid of success and failure that had at its base a series of county, department, and prefectural yamen halls and provincial testing compounds. These examinations sites conveyed successful graduates up the ladder of success, but they also delivered imperial power and influence down to local towns and communities. In the process, both rulers and local elites tried to ensure that the examination regime served their different political and social agendas.

# CHAPTER FOUR

# Examination Compounds
# and the Limits of Dynastic Power

Understanding the competitive tensions in the examination market, as described in Chapter 3, helps explain the police-like rigor of the civil service examinations as a systematic and stylized educational form of cultural practice that Han Chinese insiders in the Ming and warrior outsiders in the Ch'ing could both support. It was not a given that after the Mongol era, when civil examinations were not the rule or widespread, the Ming dynasty would automatically reproduce and expand a Sung-inspired system into an empirewide array of examination halls. Political forces and cultural fears pushed Han Chinese and their non-Han rulers to agree publicly on a particular ancient moment when sages had ordered the empire and then claim the Tao Learning view of that cultural order as the source of knowledge and behavior for its bureaucratic elites.

Imperial and bureaucratic authority in late imperial China was conveyed in part through the accredited cultural institutions of the Ministry of Rites, the Hanlin Academy, and civil examinations, which in turn transmitted the moral teachings of Ch'eng-Chu Tao Learning. Government interference with its elites could try to thwart their free associations with undesirable social and political types and thereby alter the social conditions of their development. In other words, the ruler could try to transform his elite into a service class, although in the end a partnership was usually the result. Miyazaki Ichisada has described how T'ang rulers saw this process: "After an examination, while observing the splendid sight of the new *chin-shih* leaving the government building in a triumphant column, [T'ang] T'ai-tsung [r. 627–50] exclaimed, 'The heroes of the empire are all in my pocket!'" A powerful emperor who had seized the throne by force, T'ai-tsung exaggerated his preeminence over the medieval bureaucracy. The dynastic school curriculum, after all, continually reflected literati values and culture in medieval and late imperial times.[1]

Moreover, examination halls empirewide were supervised by literati officials, who were in charge of the military and police apparatus needed when so many men were brought together to be tested at a single place. The expense of maintaining the civil examinations was very high and made it difficult for the court to increase the number of assigned personnel (see Chapter 3). Examiners in charge of the 1756 metropolitan examination in Shun-t'ien prefecture, for example, described the number of officials and the budget required for a total of 35 days to convene the metropolitan examination there. They listed 86 readers on the job for 27 days, and 706 copyists, most of whom worked for 26 days. The total cost of the operation was 4,089 taels of silver. Later that year, Ch'en Hung-mou 陳宏謀 (1696–1771), then serving in the court as a Grand Secretary, described the need for enhanced funding given the increase to over 2,000 candidates for the metropolitan examination. In the 1763 metropolitan examination, Ch'en noted, 1,738 taels had sufficed, but for the 1766 examination 2,204 taels of silver were needed, an increase of 27%, which the Ch'ien-lung emperor approved.[2]

The limits of late imperial dynastic power were also revealed through the examination regime. Forms of resistance to imperial prerogative emerged among examiners, and widespread dissatisfaction and corruption among the candidates at times triumphed over the high-minded goals of some of the examiners in charge of the classical examinations. The examination hall became a contested site, where the political interests of the dynasty, the social interests of its elites, and the cultural ideals of Tao Learning were worked out in practice more than in theory.

## EXAMINATION COMPOUNDS
## AS "CULTURAL PRISONS"

The local, provincial, and capital testing sites were each a social and political microcosm of the late imperial cultural regime for ensuring that officials had mastered the Tao Learning orthodoxy undergirding the cul-

1. See Miyazaki, *China's Examination Hell*, p. 113. See also Moore, "The Ceremony of Gratitude," for an account of T'ang examination ceremony. Cf. Philip Rieff, *The Feeling Intellect: Selected Writings* (Chicago: University of Chicago Press, 1990), pp. 221–22, 247–48.

2. See "Shun-t'ien fu t'i-pen" 順天府題本 (Memorials from Shun-t'ien prefecture), 1767, 5th month, 26th day. See also the *Kung-pu t'i-pen* 工部題本 (Memoranda including memorials from the Ministry of Works) 7th month, 11th day. Both are in the Ming-Ch'ing Archives, Academia Sinica, Taiwan. One tael equaled 1.32 silver dollars.

tural legitimacy of the Ming and Ch'ing dynasties. I make no claim here that such reproduction was uniform. Many privately resisted on the outside what was publicly tested inside the examination compound, but the machinery of examinations went on regardless. Public commitments to the late empire's system of cultural prestige were first reproduced empirewide in the civil examinations under Ming rulers and lasted until 1904. Such commitments to the teachings of the ancient sages and their Ch'eng-Chu interpreters implied that the classical curriculum was the civilian ideal that literati stood for and that the civil examinations measured the literatus (*tsao-shih* 造士) suitable for public office by standards that literati themselves had devised.[3]

Such protestations belied, however, the anxiety felt by many Han Chinese in a "barbarian"-threatened world. It also disguised the personal anxiety felt by millions of candidates during the late empire as they entered the biennial and triennial stream of candidates at local, provincial, and capital testing sites. Such anxiety was not resolved by the results of the competition, because nearly all failed many times before proving their mettle as literati acceptable for office (see Chapter 6). Most never went beyond the licensing examinations that the Ming dynasty promulgated in all counties and prefectures of the empire. For many candidates, a local degree yielded enough of a tax break and legal privileges (see Chapter 3) to keep them relatively contented.

Residualism—that is, repeated failures—was more characteristic of the selection process than success. Famous failures became part of the lore of examinations. When the novelist Wu Ching-tzu 吳敬梓 (1701–54) was a candidate for a 1729 local licensing examination, for example, he offended the examiner by appearing for the *sui-k'ao* obviously drunk. His literary talents were recognized, but his moral character was suspect. Several examination failures later, he translated his failures into short literary spoofs of the examinations that he included in his widely read novel *Ju-lin wai-shih* 儒林外史 (The scholars), which represented an accepted literary form of public protest and entertainment in Ming and Ch'ing times.[4]

### *Examinations as Public Spectacle and Private Experience*

Lacking special county, department, or prefectural examination sites, magistrates and prefects convened licensing and qualifying examinations in the

---

3. See *Wu-li t'ung-k'ao*, 173.3a–b, for the ancient ideal of "measuring the literatus" enunciated in the *Li-chi* 禮記 (Record of rites) classic.

4. See Paul Ropp, *Dissent in Early Modern China* (Ann Arbor: University of Michigan Press, 1981), pp. 67–68. *Ju-lin wai-shih* is of course much more than a spoof of examinations.

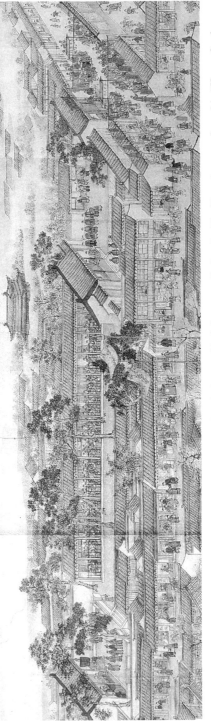

FIGURE 4.1. The Prefectural Examination Hall. *Source:* Scroll painting entitled *Prosperous Suzhou*, by Xu Yang in 1759, from his "Ku-su fan-hua t'u" 姑蘇繁華圖 (Hong Kong: Commercial Press, 1990), 14th and 15th leaves.

heart of the town within their local yamen. Typical late Ming prefectural examinations had between four and five thousand candidates.[5] The prefectural yamen in Su-chou, illustrated in Figure 4.1 during a mid–eighteenth century local examination, for example, had two courtyards. Outside the right archway were shops selling examination supplies. The gates were heavily guarded while the examination took place, and a crowd was usually milling outside. Clerks stood in the outer courtyard with horns and gongs to beat when the examination commenced or ended. The inner courtyard was bounded by two corridors that normally served as offices for the six official yamen departments (paralleling the Six Ministries), where long tables in the halls for Rites, Revenue, and Personnel, and so forth were used temporarily by candidates for the examination. At the back of the inner courtyard there was a hall built on a high platform. The chief examiner would sit there after calling the roll, checking over the list of guarantors, issuing answer sheets, and preparing the questions. He was flanked by two rows of officials standing on both sides of him, all overlooking the candidates at the yamen tables in the courtyard. Each candidate was part of a mutual guarantee group of usually four students to prevent cheating, and all were monitored even when they went to the latrines inside the yamen.[6]

Since the T'ang, the ceremonies of cultural prestige were most celebrated at the palace examination in the imperial capital,[7] but pomp and ceremony were noticeable at all levels, especially at Ming-era provincial examination sites. There, once the special examination halls and their thousands of individual cubicles were swept and cleared of filth and rub-

5. See Lach and Van Kley, *Asia in the Making of Europe*, vol. 3, book 4, p. 1639, citing Nicolas Trigault's 1615 *De christiana expeditione apud Sinas*.

6. See Hsu Yang's 徐揚 1759 "Ku-Su fan-hua t'u" 姑蘇繁華圖 (Painting of prosperous Su-chou) (Hong Kong: Commercial Press, 1988, 1990), Section 8. Students are depicted at the prefectural examination in Su-chou sitting in rows behind long tables lined up horizontally behind each other. Photographs of local examination compounds are also given in Shang Yen-liu 商衍鎏, *Ch'ing-tai k'o-chü k'ao-shih shu-lueh* 清代科舉考試述略 (Summary of civil examinations during the Ch'ing period) (Peking: San-lien Bookstore, 1958), pp. 10–11. See also Sheang [Shang] Yen-liu, "Memories of the Chinese Imperial Civil Service Examination System," pp. 54–62.

7. Rituals for palace examinations are described in *Chuang-yuan ts'e*, 1733 edition, pp. 1a–2a (for the Ch'ing), pp. 2b–3a (for the Ming). Ranks and numbers of examination officials are also given. See also John Meskill, "A Conferral of the Degree of *Chin-shih*," *Monumenta Serica* 23 (1964): 351–71; and Sheang [Shang] Yen-liu, "Memories of the Chinese Imperial Civil Service Examination System," pp. 75–78, who describes the impressive *chin-shih* induction ceremonies in the Ch'ing palace in 1667 and 1904 respectively. On Sung examination ceremony, see Chaffee, *The Thorny Gates of Learning in Sung China*, pp. 158–61. On T'ang ceremony, see Moore, "The Ceremony of Gratitude."

FIGURE 4.2.   The 1604 *Optimus* Drunk in an Examination Cell.
*Source: Ming chuang-yuan t'u-k'ao* 明狀元圖考 (Illustrated survey of *optimi* during the Ming dynasty). Compiled by Ku Ting-ch'en 顧鼎臣 and Ku Tsu-hsun 顧祖訓. 1607 edition.

bish that had accumulated in prior years, a festive market atmosphere prevailed outside the compound. Transformed every three years, the provincial compounds became venues simultaneously for cultural rituals, the deployment of police, and the testing of Ch'eng-Chu learning. Inside the halls there would be five to ten thousand candidates and a large retinue of examiners, clerks, printers, cooks, guards, and suppliers. Besides the list of Ming provincial and metropolitan examiners outlined in Tables 4.1 and 4.2, locals were assigned to sit in examination cells with the candidate, as shown in Figure 4.2. There were also clerks to copy the test papers, woodblock cutters to prepare them for the printers, cooks to feed the examiners and their staffs, and suppliers to provide water for the candidates. The Nanking examination compound, one of the largest in Ming and Ch'ing times, could hold 7,500 candidates in 1630 (17,000 in 1850), for example, and all told there were some twelve to fifteen thousand people

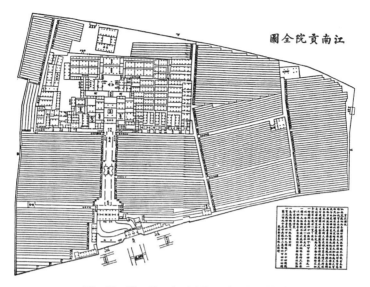

FIGURE 4.3. The Nanking Provincial Examination Hall. *Source:*
Etienne Zi, *Pratique des examens littéraires en Chine* (Shanghai: Imprimerie
de la Mission Catholique, 1894), foldout. See also Miyazaki Ichisada
宮崎市定, *Kakyoshi* 科舉史 (History of the civil examination system)
(Tokyo: Heibonsha, 1987 revision of 1946 edition), pp. 136–37.

housed inside during the three Ming sessions of examinations (see Figure
4.3). To keep pace with the expansion of candidates the number of Ming
overseers was increased, but the sum total of candidates continually outpaced the government's personnel.[8]

Candidates for *chü-jen* degrees could enter the provincial compound,
usually in the eastern part of the city, only the night before each of the
three day-long sessions commenced. To ensure their eligibility, licentiates,
accompanied by their servants, usually appeared in the provincial capital
a week in advance of the August–September (the lunar eighth month) triennial date to register and present their county credentials, which guaranteed their identity, and documented their immediate family lineage, their
social status, and that they were not in mourning for a parent. Once

8. Ku Yen-wu's *Jih-chih lu chi-shih*, pp. 376–419 (*chüan* 卷 16–17), gives a detailed account
of many aspects of the Ming examinations compounds, as does the *Huang-ch'ao ching-shih
wen-pien* 皇朝經世文編 (Collected writings on statecraft from the Ch'ing dynasty), edited by
Wei Yuan 魏源, 1827 and 1873 editions (reprint, Taipei: World Bookstore, 1964), 57.1a–20a.
See also *Lu-chuan chi-shih* 臚傳紀事 (Autobiography and record of occurrences), compiled by
Miu T'ung 繆彤 (Shanghai: Commercial Press, *Ts'ung-shu chi-ch'eng ch'u-pien*, 1936), pp. 1–6,
which is an account by the 1667 *optimus* of provincial, metropolitan, and palace civil examination procedures then in effect.

approved for admission, candidates had to prepare their own stock of writing paraphernalia, to purchase blank writing paper stamped with an official seal, and to take the necessary precautions for food provisions and toilet facilities while waiting for the provincial governor and examiners to enter the compound first.[9] Shops catering to the candidates abounded outside the main gates of the examination compounds (see Figure 4.1), carrying store names such as "Examination supplies for the *optimus*" (*Chuang-yuan kao-chü* 狀元考具) and "Famous writing brushes for three examinations" (*San-k'ao ming-pi* 三考名筆). The entertainment districts of provincial capitals such as Nanking also welcomed the male candidates into a ribald world of prostitution and drinking games in which the men ranked the women for their beauty according to degree titles and the courtesans acted out the roles of Hanlin examiners.[10]

Rice and gruel would be provided for candidates inside the compound, but most preferred to furnish their own, which the candidate could cook in a portable coal furnace. Custom also dictated that friends and relatives would present candidates with small gifts of food as they entered the southern gate of the compound. Many friends and relatives would stay as close to the examination site as possible, heightening the triennial fair-like atmosphere of commerce and activity in the city.[11] Candidates also provided their own candles if they expected to write at night, though the result was frequent fires in the examination hall. In 1438, for instance, a fire raged through the examination hall during a provincial examination in Shun-t'ien, the capital prefecture. Another account claims that in the fall of 1463 over one thousand perished in the Shun-t'ien hall in a metropolitan examination fire, although two other versions claim that that fire killed only some ninety *chü-jen* and that there was another fire when the examination was rescheduled for the following spring. One of the candidates in 1463, Lo Lun 羅倫 (1431–78), escaped the fire, but because of his father's death Lo had to wait until 1466 to retake the metropolitan examination. He was the 1466 *optimus* on the palace examination.[12]

9. Gray, *China*, pp. 172–73. For examples of the registration forms, required paper, etc., see Zi, *Pratique des examens littéraires en Chine*, pp. 20, 37, 61, 90–91, 112, 126, 129. See also Birch, trans., *Scenes for Mandarins*, p. 207.

10. See Hsu Yang's 1759 "Ku-Su fan-hua t'u," Section 8, for the shops outside the prefectural examination site in Su-chou. See also Dorothy Ko, "The Written Word and the Bound Foot: A History of the Courtesan's Aura," in Ellen Widmer and Kang-i Sun Chang, eds., *Writing Women in Late Imperial China* (Stanford: Stanford University Press, 1997), pp. 82–90.

11. For late-nineteenth-century accounts that confirm late-Ming versions, see James Knowles, "Competitive Examinations in China," *The Nineteenth Century: A Monthly Review* 36 (July–December 1894): 87–99.

12. See *Chih-i k'o-so-chi*, 1.13a, for this early Ming policy. The candle policy was fre-

After entering the main gate in the south, the official overseers followed the main road north to their official yamens, where both they and their staff would remain in residence for the three weeks that were needed to complete the three sessions and grade and rank the candidates. The inner overseers (*nei-lien kuan* 內簾官) determined the questions (or the detailed text if the questions were set by the emperor), and they took charge of supervising the grading and ranking process; outer overseers (*wai-lien kuan* 外簾官) handled all administrative matters involving supplies and surveillance.[13] Special rooms for sleeping, cooking, reading, and printing made up the central command post, around which on the east, west, and south sides the myriad small rooms or cells for the candidates were arranged. As the number of candidates rose, the shape of the compounds sometimes changed from a rectangle (as in Shun-t'ien prefecture; see Figure 4.4) to the misshapen triangle in Nanking (see Figure 4.3). North remained the examiners' preserve, however, and no cells could be placed there, although in Nanking some cells began to appear on the northeast and northwest when some 15,000 to 17,000 candidates took the examination during the eighteenth and nineteenth centuries.[14]

The commercial bustle outside the examination hall contrasted with the stark, tawdry atmosphere inside the double walls that surrounded the grounds and was invisible to the public. The individually divided cells for the candidates radiated out east and west from the main south-to-north entry passage in a series of parallel rows that were separated by alleys no more than four feet wide (see Figure 4.5).[15] Large earthenware water jars were placed at the entrances to the rows of parallel cells (see Figure 4.6) for boiling and in case of fire. The end cells were usually close to the public latrines, where the stench was often unbearable. Candidates

---

quently reconsidered because of the fire hazard in Peking in particular, due to the dry weather and strong winds there. See *Chuang-yuan t'u-k'ao*, 2.17b; *Wu-li t'ung-k'ao*, 1229.25a; and *Chih-i k'o-so-chi*, 1.32, 1.46–47; and on Lo Lun see *Dictionary of Ming Biography*, p. 984. See also the *Ch'in-ting Ta-Ch'ing hui-tien shih-li*, 386.15a, which stipulates that candidates taking local reexaminations should not be permitted to use candles during the examination.

13. Huang Kuang-liang, *Ch'ing-tai k'o-chü chih-tu chih yen-chiu*, pp. 280–93, presents the Ch'ing system of inner and outer examiners, which was based on the Ming.

14. On the metropolitan examination hall in Peking, see Katsumata Kenjirō 勝又憲治 郎, "Hokukei no kakyo jidai to kōin" 北京の科舉時代と貢院 (The examination hall and Peking in the age of civil examinations), *Tōhō gakuhō* 東方學報 (Tokyo) 6 (1936): 203–39.

15. See Zi, *Pratique des examens littéraires en Chine*, pp. 102, 104, 106, 139, 143. Diagrams of the cells are also reproduced in the special civil examination issue of the *Ku-kung wen-wu yueh-k'an* 故宮文物月刊 (Palace Museum Monthly) 88 (July 1990): 35, 51.

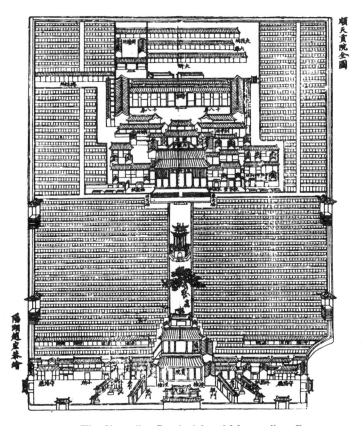

FIGURE 4.4. The Shun-t'ien Provincial and Metropolitan Examination Hall. *Source: Shun-t'ien fu-chih* 順天府志 (Shun-t'ien prefectural gazetteer), 1885 edition.

described such a location as one of the "six agonies" inside the compound.[16]

The entry to each cell was open from top to bottom for easier surveillance from a single pavilion raised high above ground level; thus rain and sunlight could easily enter the cells (see Figure 4.7). Stories of candidates' papers destroyed by fire or blown away by the wind abound in popular accounts. A 1640 candidate, for example, dreamt that because fire had destroyed his examination papers they had to be rewritten.[17] Candidates

16. See Sheang [Shang] Yen-liu, "Memories of the Chinese Imperial Civil Service Examination System," pp. 66–67.

17. See *Ch'ien-Ming k'o-ch'ang i-wen-lu* 前明科場異聞錄 (Recording unusual matters heard in the earlier Ming examination grounds), Wei-ching-t'ang shu-fang 味經堂書坊 edition (Canton; reprint, Ch'ien-t'ang, 1873), B.45b. Another had his paper blown away in the palace examination of 1451, but was given paper and allowed to finish. See *Chih-i k'o-so-chi*, 1.47.

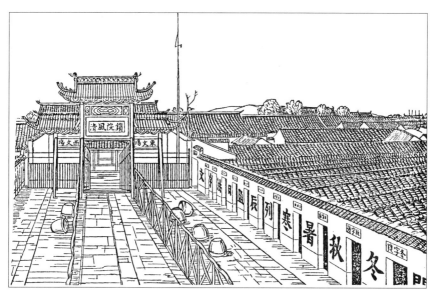

FIGURE 4.5.    Main Entrance to the Nanking Examination Hall. *Source:* Etienne Zi, *Pratique des examens littéraires en Chine* (Shanghai: Imprimerie de la Mission Catholique, 1894), p. 104.

FIGURE 4.6.    Corridors to the Cells. *Source:* Etienne Zi, *Pratique des examens littéraires en Chine* (Shanghai: Imprimerie de la Mission Catholique, 1894), p. 106.

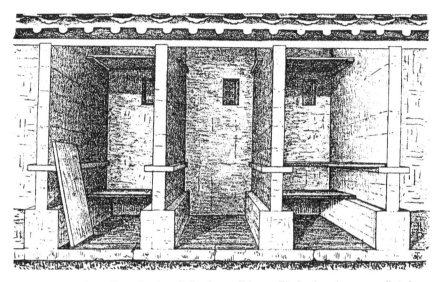

FIGURE 4.7. Open Examination Cells. *Source:* Etienne Zi, *Pratique des examens littéraires en Chine* (Shanghai: Imprimerie de la Mission Catholique, 1894), p. 141.

consequently had to bring a light oilcloth screen with them to protect themselves, their toilet facilities, and their ink stone, brushes, and paper from rain, wind, and fire, in addition to having a padded quilt for sleeping in an exposed room. Such screens also helped against mosquito attacks in southern examination compounds such as Kuang-chou.[18]

To prevent cheating, the examiners required provincial candidates before they entered the hall to gather by prefecture at a prescribed hour outside the main gate, where they and the basket of supplies each carried on his back were searched by inspectors and clerks. The infamous rough body searches were a rude awakening to the vexing sanitary and surveillance conditions inside and have been recorded by outraged literati ever since the T'ang dynasty. Some candidates in each dynasty were so appalled by the dehumanizing conditions that they immediately left for home.[19]

Those who made it through the searches were subject to strict surveillance inside as well. All provisions and clothing were frequently searched, and no printed or written material was allowed inside the compound.

18. See Sheang [Shang] Yen-liu, "Memories of the Chinese Imperial Civil Service Examination System," p. 67.

19. Wu Ching-tzu, *The Scholars*, translated by Yang Hsien-yi and Gladys Yang (Peking: Foreign Languages Press, 1957), pp. 465–66, describes the late-Ming opening of the gates in the Nanking provincial compound. See also Zi, *Pratique des Examens Litteraires en Chine*, p. 18; and Moore, "The Ceremony of Gratitude," which describes T'ang conditions.

Those caught wearing inner gowns with the classics inscribed on them in small print (see Figure 4.8), for instance, were expelled and punished, usually by a ban on their taking the next cycle(s) of the provincial examinations or by losing their licentiate status altogether.[20] Once past the initial checkpoints set up on the eve of each session at the main gate, candidates entered the examination hall and located their assigned alleys, which were classified according to the characters in the *Thousand Character Text* (*Ch'ien-tzu wen* 千字文), and then found the number of their cell in that alley (see figures 4.5 and 4.6). Students from the same prefecture (or province, in the case of metropolitan examinations) were placed in pre-established alleys assigned them. The search for one's cell recapitulated the candidate's youthful training in the classics, for all had begun as children to learn to read and write by memorizing the *Thousand Character Text* and *Three Character Classic* (*San-tzu ching* 三字經) primers (see Chapter 5).[21]

Once inside, all candidates and overseers were cut off from the outside. No one was allowed in or out during the next two nights and three days. If a candidate died or became seriously ill in the compound, his body was passed through an opening in the walls by the guards.[22] The cells contained two movable planks, which when placed in proper positions could serve as seat, desk, and bed (see Figure 4.7). When writing, candidates sat with their backs to the wall of their cell and faced north toward the open entrance to enable the guards to watch them (see Figure 4.2). Once the gates closed, guards waited until the following morning, when the calling of the roll began and it was ascertained that all candidates were in their assigned cells. The themes for each session (see Chapter 1) were then given out as printed slips of paper and posted as *piao* (表 posters) in the compound.[23]

For each of the three sessions, candidates had two full days to complete their essays. Normally, they prepared a draft of their answers in cursive or running script before recopying them in regular script (see Figure 4.9). Many finished early, but some worked to the last minute, often requesting a candle to work if they had not brought one with them.[24] By dusk of the third day, all papers were collected. The candidates were then ushered

20. *Huang-Ming kung-chü k'ao*, 1.48a–b.

21. See Ch'eng Tuan-li, *Ch'eng-shih chia-shu tu-shu fen-nien jih-ch'eng*, 1.1a–15b. Cf. Ridley, "Educational Theory and Practice in Late Imperial China," pp. 386–94.

22. See "Competitive Examinations in China: A Chapter of Chinese Travel," *Edinburgh Magazine* (London) 138 (July–December 1885), p. 481.

23. The Ming-Ch'ing Archive at Academia Sinica, Taiwan, contains twenty-five of these "posters," which I was able to copy and examine. They date from 1699 to 1851. Of these, nine are from provincial civil examinations, and seven are from metropolitan civil examinations.

24. *Huang-Ming kung-chü k'ao*, 1.55a, dates this practice from 1384.

FIGURE 4.8. Cheating Shirt (with detail). *Source:* Gest Oriental Library and East Asian Collections, Princeton University. My thanks to Martin Heijdra for his help in obtaining this image (although this shirt may not have actually been used for cheating).

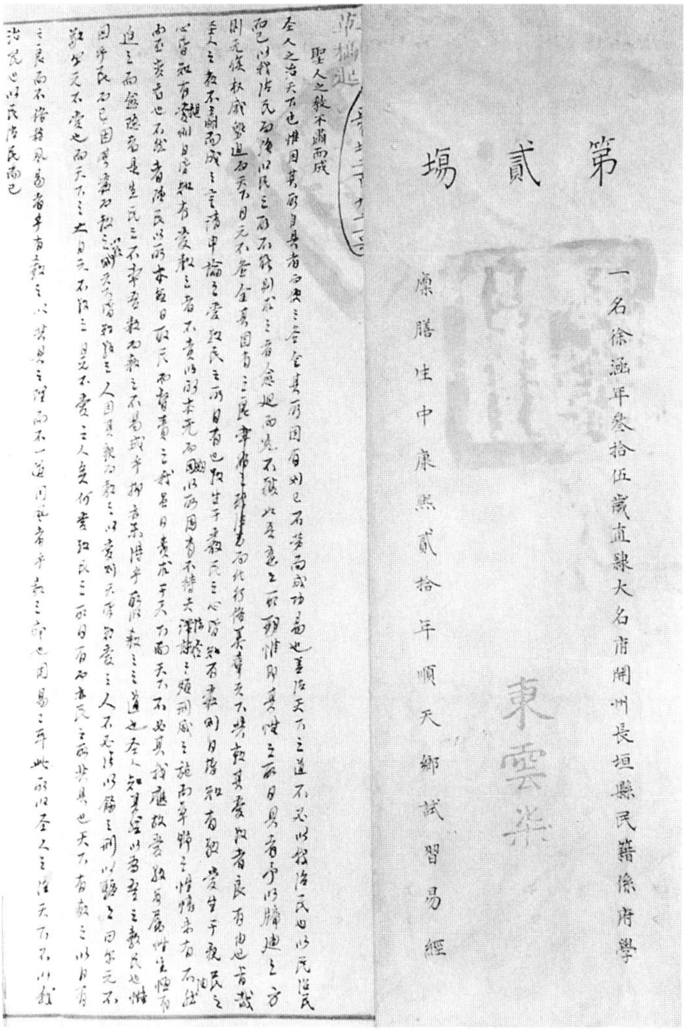

FIGURE 4.9. Draft of 1685 Discourse Examination Essay. *Source:*
Ming-Ch'ing Archives, Academia Sinica, Taiwan.

out of the compound by prefectural group (or by province in metropolitan
examinations), after spending two nights inside the provincial examination compound. Between the second and third sessions, candidates were
allowed one full day and night of rest before reentering the compound to
complete all three sessions.[25]

25. See *Lin-wen pien-lan* 臨文便覽 (Overview for writing down essays), 1875 edition, *t'iao-
li* 條例 (regulations), for the rules for writing down essays on provincial, metropolitan, and
palace examinations.

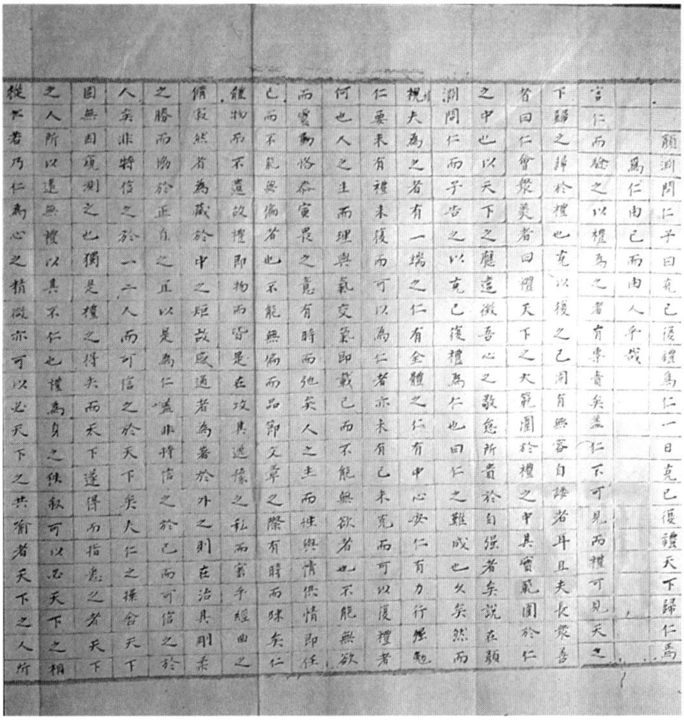
顏淵問仁子曰克己復禮為仁一日克己復禮天下歸仁焉
為仁由己而由人乎哉

FIGURE 4.10. 1685 Black Ink Examination Paper. *Source:* Ming-Ch'ing Archives, Academia Sinica, Taiwan.

Examination papers prepared by the candidates, which were composed using black ink (*mo-chüan* 墨卷; see Figure 4.10), were then stamped according to the assigned examination ward, where they would be graded, and checked over for form, calligraphy, and possible violations (smudge marks, too many changes, use of banned characters, etc.). They were then passed on to some two to three hundred copyists, who recopied all the papers using red ink (*chu-chüan* 硃卷; see Frontispiece) and assigned a secret code to each of the copies to preserve the anonymity of all candidates.[26] Another hundred or so proofreaders checked the copies with the originals to ensure accuracy, and passed the red-ink versions to the appropriate associate examiners to begin the process of reading the anonymous papers. Ming examiners sometimes used green ink (*ch'ing-pi* 青筆) to mark the red papers for balance and form.[27]

26. *Chih-i k'o-so-chi,* 1.13.

27. *Huang-Ming kung-chü k'ao,* 1.53a. I have not seen green markings on Ch'ing examinations.

For grading purposes on both the provincial and metropolitan examinations, the papers were divided (*fen-chüan-chih* 分卷制) first according to which of the Five Classics a candidate had chosen for his specialization (*chuan-ching* 專經). As Tables 4.3 and 4.4 show, each Classic had at least one examination wardroom (*fang* 房; the *Change, Documents,* and *Poetry* Classics had several wards), where the papers for each were graded separately by the associate examiner assigned to that wardroom. The top examination paper from each of the Five Classics (known as *wu-k'uei* 五魁 or *ching-k'uei* 經魁) was certain then to be placed among the top five names for the entire examination.[28] Each specialization group, in other words, determined one of the top five places in the provincial and metropolitan competition. Provincial examinations had a minimum of five wards, one for each Classic, while the metropolitan examination had up to twenty wards, depending on the specialization rates of candidates.[29]

Ever since the T'ang dynasty, such wards had created teacher-student loyalties among the examiners and graduates (see below). Such ties were especially strong in the Ming dynasty, when the initiation rites that created mentor-mentee solidarity between examiners and examination candidates became a matter of political concern. The Chia-ching emperor (r. 1522–66), for example, decreed that students could not carry out any special rites of respect toward their ward head after the examination. During the Wan-li era (1573–1619) teacher-student groups based on ward loyalties were particularly evident. Later, between 1658 and 1679 under the Ch'ing, the ward as a unit of examination organization was abolished to prevent teacher-student cliques from developing. Even though the ward was reintroduced in 1679, the K'ang-hsi emperor (r. 1662–1722) still decreed that no special rites of respect toward the ward head could be carried out by candidates.[30] The scholar-official Ch'ien Ta-hsin 錢大昕 (1728–1804) later criticized examination followers who treated their examiners as patrons rather than teachers. Similarly, Ch'in Ying 秦瀛 (1743–1821) linked so-called examination teachers to the increasing corruption among candidates in the eighteenth century (see below).[31]

28. Ibid., 1.63a–b, dates this practice from 1385.

29. Ibid., 1.41b, gives 1450 as the date associate examiners were regularly assigned to specialize on one of the Five Classics. See also Ku Yen-wu, *Jih-chih lu chi-shih,* 16.382, which describes the eighteen metropolitan wards of the late Ming. For an example of a Ming examination report based on seventeen wards, see *Hui-shih t'ung-nien shih-chiang lu* 會試同年世講錄 (Record of same year metropolitan graduates), 1556: 13/6567–6570, in *Ming-tai teng-k'o-lu hui-pien.*

30. *Chih-i k'o-so-chi,* 4.130.

31. See *Ch'ing-tai ch'ien-ch'i chiao-yü lun-chu hsuan* 清代前期教育論著選 (Selections of writings on education from the early Ch'ing period), edited by Li Kuo-chün 李國鈞 et al. (Peking: People's Education Press, 1990, 3 vols.), 3/147–48, 3/256–57.

It was the job of the chief examiners to review the rankings of passing (*chien-chüan* 薦卷) and failing (*lo-chüan* 落卷) papers made by the associate examiners in the wards and recommend the final list of names that would be posted outside the hall. Given the thousands of rolls of paper (*chüan* 卷) that were produced and recopied, it took the associate and chief examiners about twenty days to complete the final ranking list of graduates.[32] In the 1466 palace examination, for instance, the eventual *optimus*, Lo Lun 羅倫 (1431–78), wrote a lengthy policy answer that required thirty rolls to complete. He had asked the examiners for extra paper to complete his answer. The story went that an elderly examiner could not rise from his kneeling position after reading all the rolls Lo had prepared and required help to stand. Thereafter, a limit of thirteen rolls was set for the palace examination policy answer.[33]

Limits were also established for essay lengths in Ming provincial and metropolitan examinations. Early Ming examination questions based on the Four Books required a short essay answer of at least 200 written graphs in length. A brief essay of at least 300 graphs elucidating the "meanings" (*ching-i*) of one of the Five Classics was the standard for classical studies. Despite the increasing number of examination readers, however, the pressure to read and grade within a prescribed period all papers inevitably meant that the questions administered during the first session were given the most attention by the examiners and thus the students as well. These were the infamous eight-legged essays (*pa-ku-wen* 八股文) written on the Four Books and Five Classics, which after 1475 became the benchmark for the civil examinations as a whole (see Chapter 7). In addition, the length of answers gradually increased until a typical eight-legged essay contained 700 graphs in the eighteenth century.[34] During the Ch'ing dynasty, all of the copied red papers from provincial examinations were sent to the capital for the Ministry of Rites to review for errors or irregularities.[35]

32. Huang Kuang-liang, *Ch'ing-tai k'o-chü chih-tu chih yen-chiu*, pp. 292–93, indicates that in the early Ch'ing two weeks were required to grade papers for the provincial and metropolitan examination. Five days were added by imperial order in 1687, and another ten days in 1711, thus giving examiners a month to complete their rankings.

33. *Chih-i k'o-so-chi*, 1.51–52.

34. See *Ch'ing-shih kao*, 11/3152.

35. See *Ch'in-ting mo-k'an t'iao-li* 欽定磨勘條例 (Imperially prescribed guidelines for post-examination review of civil examination papers), late Ch'ien-lung (1736–95) edition, 1.1b–2a. Review of examinations began after 1701 and was reaffirmed in 1736. Examination reports and materials survive in the No. 1 Historical Archives in Peking and in the Ming-Ch'ing Archives in Academia Sinica, Taiwan. Portions are available in Japan, Europe, and the United States.

Candidates and their friends and relatives waited for the rankings to be posted outside the examination hall. Indeed, a famous painting from the late Ming entitled "Looking at Examination Results" ("Kuan-pang t'u" 觀榜圖),[36] by Ch'ou Ying 仇英 (ca. 1490–1552), chose as its theme anxious candidates going over the examination results after they were posted. Hawkers would write down the names of successful candidates and sell them on the streets. Those few who became *chü-jen* in the provincial examination were then invited to the governor's yamen for a celebration and decorated with an embroidered collar. Formal and informal festivities followed, and as word was passed from the province to the home prefecture, county, and department, the graduate made his way home with much fanfare.[37] Such fanfare for *chü-jen*, however eventful in the provinces, paled in comparison to the reception received by *chin-shih* degree-holders in the capital and at home (see Figure 4.11). Beginning in 1388, the *optimus* was permitted to build a memorial arch (*p'ai-fang* 牌坊) at home, and in 1404, inscribed stelae containing the names of all *chin-shih* in order of final rank were triennially placed in the grounds of the Imperial School in Nanking, a tradition that lasted from 1416 until 1904 in Peking. Later, Ming *chü-jen* and *chin-shih* degree-holders regularly erected memorial flagpoles or plaques in front of their homes or ancestral hall to mark their achievements (see Figure 4.12).[38] The vast majority of candidates failed, however, and most failed several times in their quest for the *chü-jen* and *chin-shih* degrees. They were, however, allowed to see their failed papers and learn from the examiners' comments.[39]

## Political Architecture of Surveillance and Control

As a natural, although sometimes contested, form of selection that marked the educational divide separating Han Chinese from their Mongol or Manchu rulers, and Han elites from their less-advantaged commoners, civil examinations generally elicited voluntary compliance within the ritual regime supervised by the Ministry of Rites. Literary competition was more civilized than warrior hegemony. Those literati who passed demonstrated

36. The painting is in the National Palace Museum, Taiwan. For a portion of the painting that has been published in an English work, see Wakeman, *The Great Enterprise*, p. 121. More detailed reprints are reproduced in the special issue of the *Ku-kung wen-wu yueh-k'an*, pp. 4–5, 6–7, 8, 25, 26–27, 28.

37. See Sheang [Shang] Yen-liu, "Memories of the Chinese Imperial Civil Service Examination System," p. 68. Doolittle, *Social Life of the Chinese*, pp. 412–20, describes the festivities in the nineteenth century.

38. *Chih-i k'o-so-chi*, 1.18, 1.22, 1.134–35.

39. Huang Kuang-liang, *Ch'ing-tai k'o-chü chih-tu chih yen-chiu*, p. 293.

FIGURE 4.11. The 1484 *Optimus* Paraded before Friends.
*Source: Ming chuang-yuan t'u-k'ao* 明狀元圖考 (Illustrated survey
of *optimi* during the Ming dynasty). Compiled by Ku Ting-
ch'en 顧鼎臣 and Ku Tsu-hsun 顧祖訓. 1607 edition.

their mastery of the Sung Ch'eng-Chu values that had survived the
Mongol era and the classical texts upon which they were based. Examination halls thus were not prisons in the literal sense, a site where alleged
criminals were held against their wills until their cases were decided or
their sentences were executed. Formal prisons mandated compliance
according to the provisions of the penal code. Late imperial elites publicly
complied with the requirements of continuous registration for examination
and reexamination and personally acquiesced to the perpetual assessments

FIGURE 4.12. The 1571 *Optimus* Dreams of an Official Placard.
*Source: Ming chuang-yuan t'u-k'ao* 明狀元圖考 (Illustrated survey of
*optimi* during the Ming dynasty). Compiled by Ku Ting-ch'en
顧鼎臣 and Ku Tsu-hsun 顧祖訓. 1607 edition.

and classifications that determined the winners and losers in the examination market.

Describing the examination halls as "cultural prisons,"[40] although a
somewhat imprecise metaphor, indicates that in China civil and military

40. I use this term with some misgivings. The "cells" in the examination compound
could just as easily be compared to the monastic cave retreats and mountain pavilions of
temples that Buddhist monks often retired to for meditation. Once locked into the examina-

candidates were voluntarily locked into such compounds, which kept unauthorized people out of the examinations, in contrast to a penal prison that involuntarily locked alleged criminals in. The irony is that sons of elites competed with each other to enter the examination compounds while the sons of peasants and artisans could only dream of gaining entry to the cells as candidates, although they might on occasion enter as agents of surveillance. Such social acceptance of a regime of political control tells us how different "cultural prisons" were from jails and why they could be glorified as "civilized" reinventions after the barbarian era had passed. In this sense, the examination cells had more in common with monastic life than with penal law. Indeed, the spectacles of Buddhist temple celebrations, with large numbers of celibate monks and merit-making laypeople participating, represent a symbolic order of public life directly parallel to the political displays at civil examinations. During the T'ang dynasty, for example, the civil examination graduation ritual known as the "ceremony of gratitude" directly paralleled ordination rites in Buddhist temples by relying on Buddhist vocabulary, gestures, and objects.[41]

When not in use, the specially constructed examination compounds that dotted the landscape of provincial capitals and the imperial capital resembled ramshackle prisons without inmates. Repainted and restored periodically according to the relentless pace of biennial and triennial examinations empirewide, the compounds in effect became "cultural prisons" when each of the tens of thousands of cells in the provinces and capital contained a candidate for civil office.[42] The continuous registration requirements, the regimented surveillance procedures, and perpetual assessments orchestrated empirewide, which mobilized millions of candidates and thousands of overseers within examination halls, signaled a coercive technology within which at first sight docile individuals were objectified

---

tion compound, however, candidates, unlike monks, could not exit, and their behavior was carefully policed by guards and clerks. My thanks to Marianne Bastid for her advice on this matter.

41. Jacques Gernet, *Buddhism in Chinese Society: An Economic History From the Fifth to the Tenth Centuries,* translated by Franciscus Verellen (New York: Columbia University Press, 1995), p. 240. See also Moore, "The Ceremony of Gratitude."

42. Curiously, neither Ming-Ch'ing prisons (*chien* 監) nor jails (*yü* 獄) were built on the scale of examination compounds, which suggests that the late imperial state could achieve a modicum of social stability without large penal colonies or huge gulags. See L. Carrington Goodrich, "Prisons in Peking, *circa* 1500," *Tsing-hua hsueh-pao* 清華學報, n.s.,10 (1973): 45–53; Henry Brougham Loch, *Personal Narrative of Occurrences during Lord Elgin's Second Embassy to China in 1860* (London, 1900), pp. 110–22; and Derk Bodde, "Prison Life in Eighteenth Century Peking," *Journal of the American Oriental Society* 89 (April–June 1969): 311–33. Bodde estimates that the Ch'ing prison in the eighteenth century held about 2,500 inmates.

into atomized candidates who willingly competed anonymously with each other. Their identity became their anonymously written papers. The process inside the examination compound temporarily stripped them of their names, family, and social rank. As candidates they were presumed to be equal literates in the gaze of the examiners.

The historical specificity of police surveillance inside Ming-Ch'ing examination compounds has generally been slighted. Most accounts of the selection process have highlighted its role in social mobility and selection of talent or just assumed that the imperial surveillance system was uniform since the T'ang or Sung dynasty. The Ch'ing scholar-official Chao I 趙翼 (1727–1814) noted in his historical studies, however, that examination surveillance procedures in T'ang and Sung were lax when compared to the strict policing in Ming and Ch'ing examination halls.[43] Examination of the actual operation of examinations, as opposed to their idealized history, reopens the role of the dynasty in policing virtue in such short-lived and artificial examination halls.

The spatial nesting of hierarchies of civilian and military surveillance, the machinery of control whereby candidates were enclosed, grouped, and separated into cells according to a predetermined economy of time depending on the level of the examination, and the careful observance of protocol and behavior all suggest that the civil examinations were an exercise in cultural and educational might unmatched in coercive magnitude by any other educational institution.[44] Only death and taxes, and perhaps legal cases, affected more people during the late empire.

## FORMS OF RESISTANCE
## TO THE EXAMINATION REGIME

The guards were there to prevent cheating, corruption, and irregularities. Table 4.5 reveals that two doctors (*i-kuan* 醫官) were added to the regular yamen staff inside Ch'ing provincial and metropolitan examination compounds after 1800. As more problems arose, more and more overseers were also needed for "special assignments" (*wei-kuan* 委官). As anonymous individuals, candidates were assigned physical places within a sophisticated political architecture of surveillance and control.

43. Chao I, *Nien-erh shih cha-chi* 廿二史箚記 (Reading notes to the twenty-two dynastic histories) (Taipei: Kuang-wen Bookstore, 1974), pp. 433–35 (*chüan* 卷 25).

44. See Michael Dutton, *Policing and Punishment in China* (Cambridge: Cambridge University Press, 1992), pp. 97–184, for an account of the role of prisons in the regime of punishment and the role of households in the policing of virtue. Cf. Michel Foucault, *Discipline and Punish: The Birth of the Prison,* translated by Alan Sheridan (New York: Vintage Books, 1979), pp. 170–228.

Special guards were always on the watch within the alleys to keep candidates from passing notes to each other. Other watchmen were posted atop the central examiners' yamen or on towers at the corners of the walls to watch for outsiders passing materials in or insiders passing information to each other. The levels of cheating and corruption that occurred represented insubordination to the premeditated surveillance, whether the cheaters were simply attempting to get ahead or protesting the strict oversight of their behavior. The candidates were not as docile as they appeared and had devised numerous tactics to counteract what they perceived as the oppressiveness of the process. Most simply sought personal advantage, but some occasionally attempted to counter power that was, in their eyes, masquerading as orthodox knowledge.[45]

## Cheating and Irregularities

Cheating dated back to the inception of the civil examinations. T'ang and Sung examiners had regularly discussed the problem and devised procedures to deal with it. In 1225, for example, cheating problems in Southern Sung examinations were endemic, and examination irregularities such as plagiarism were noted in the 1230s and 1240s.[46] In Ming times, the time-honored techniques of cheaters, which at times depended on the collusion of examiners, were well known: (1) impersonation—that is, either "assuming someone else's name" (*ting-ming* 頂名) or "sitting in someone else's cell" (*ch'iang-t'i* 槍替; also called "a scallion" *i-t'iao-ts'ung* 一條蔥), in which an experienced, usually older, essay writer entered the cell in place of the actual, more youthful, candidate; (2) after the questions were announced, passing essays composed by someone inside or outside the compound to the candidate in his cell (*ch'uan-ti* 傳遞); (3) secretly carrying materials on or in one's clothing[47] into the examination cell (*huai-hsia* 懷挾; see Figure 4.8); (4) bribing the examiners (*kuan-chieh* 關節); (5) signaling one's anonymous paper to a bribed examiner by leaving blank pages (*i-pai-ko-chüan* 曳白割卷) or including a secret code of two or three graphs agreed upon in advance; and (6) buying the questions in advance (*mai-t'i* 賣題) from an

---

45. See *Ch'ing-pai lei-ch'ao*, 21.73, which recounts how a thousand candidates in Shunt'ien were kicked out for bringing in notes. Cf. Rieff, *The Feeling Intellect*, pp. 272–73.

46. *Hsu wen-hsien t'ung-k'ao*, 34.3141–42.

47. Lucille Chia notes the popularity of cheap "kerchief albums" that candidates smuggled into examination halls, which were "small books with characters as minute as the heads of flies." See Chia, "*Mashaben:* Commercial Publishing in Jianyang, Song-Ming," paper presented at the Song-Yuan-Ming Transitions Conference (Lake Arrowhead, Calif., June 5–11, 1997), p. 13.

examiner or clerk.[48] Cheating was taken for granted in the popular imagination and in the novels, plays, and stories of the time, which were usually written by those who failed.[49] The popular tragic heroes were those
who failed time after time, and sometimes succumbed to cheating their
way to success. The heartless villains became the examiners, inverting in
the popular imagination the prestige system of those who passed legiti-
mately and the examiners who passed them.

Examiners and clerks had devised numerous devices to deal with such
irregularities. Shortly after the questions were announced, for example,
clerks would check each cell and mark each paper with a seal to keep the
scroll of paper currently being written on from being replaced by another
or someone else's scroll. In addition, clerks would regularly make the
rounds of all cells and check the admission slips of all candidates with the
cell number they currently occupied. If there were any discrepancies in
the seals stamped on the paper or on the admission slips, the candidate's
paper was stamped as disqualified. P'u Sung-ling, for instance, was automatically failed in the 1687 Shan-tung provincial examination, which he
had failed several times previously, because he had inadvertently (or so he
claimed) skipped a page in his answer sheets while writing out one of his
essays.[50] Another technique to control cheating included seating the best
candidates, based on the lists from local qualifying examinations, in rows
of cells closer to the yamen examiners. Thus "honored," they would have
less of a chance to communicate with lesser talents in the compound.[51]

Gatherings of thousands of candidates in examination compounds
could get ugly, overturning the characteristic decorum of docile candidates
"writing essays in the place of the sages" (*tai sheng-jen li-yen* 代聖人立言)
under the watch of their "teachers." Fires, as we have seen, and epidemics

48. These are enumerated for the Ming in *Chih-i k'o-so-chi*, 2.48, 2.54, 3.87; and *Huang-Ming kung-chü-k'ao*, 1.53b–54a. For the Ch'ing, see *Ch'ing-pai lei-ch'ao*, 21.18–20, 33–34. For discussion see Chung-li Chang, *The Chinese Gentry*, pp. 188–97. For example, slips of paper called *t'iao-tzu* 條子, which had holes cut into them, were one device to alert examiners of a candidate's identity. When laid over a page of the examination paper, the holes would reveal a set of characters that had been prearranged.

49. See Wu Ching-tzu, *The Scholars;* and P'u Song-ling, *Strange Tales from Liaozhai*, trans-lated by Lu Yunzhong, Chen Tifang, Yang Liyi, and Yang Zhihong (Hong Kong: Commercial Press, 1988). See also Birch, trans., *Scenes for Mandarins*, pp. 200–06, where the tricks of the trade were played out in scene five of Wu Ping's 吳炳 *Lü mu-tan* 綠牧丹 (The green peony). For the original, see Wu Ping's play in Wu Mei 吳梅, ed., *She-mo t'a-shih ch'ü-ts'ung* 奢摩他室曲叢 (Shanghai: Commercial Press, 1928), vol. 19, A.9a–12b.

50. Barr, "Pu Songling and the Qing Examination System," p. 89.

51. Doolittle, *Social Life of the Chinese*, pp. 421–28, gives a nineteenth-century account of these procedures.

could easily threaten the entire examination hall, which brought so many outsiders together for several days in one confined place in the provincial and dynastic capital. Second, riots sometimes occurred when the candidates acted on rumors of irregularities in the proceedings or instances of examiner corruption. Even a mistaken character in the question could lead to strikes and protests against the examiners.[52]

In the Nanking examination compound in 1567, for example, the civilian candidates for the provincial *chü-jen* degree rioted when they learned that the quota for graduates had been significantly reduced. They also verbally abused the chief examiners.[53] Later, in 1603, an examination riot broke out in Su-chou. The local licentiates were irate that the local prefect supervising the prefectural examination there allegedly had tampered with the papers of some candidates, and as a result the latter were purposely failed. When the next round of the local examination began, some candidates inside the yamen protested, and one of them was beaten by order of the prefect. In the ensuing melee, candidates and the crowd milling outside the yamen began to riot by throwing rocks and bricks, thus turning the examination protest into a public riot. The prefect was attacked physically, and he later was allowed to resign his office.[54]

During the Ch'ing dynasty, protests by candidates also deteriorated into riots. In the 1699 Shun-t'ien provincial examination, for example, there were reports of irregularities, and the chief examiners, although innocent, were initially punished. In 1705, the provincial candidates in Shun-t'ien paraded through the streets and symbolically beheaded two straw images of the chief examiners. Subsequently in 1711, an examination riot occurred in Yang-chou prefecture when disappointed candidates saw the final results and accused the chief examiner Gali 噶禮 (d. 1714), a Manchu, of selling degrees to the sons of salt merchants. The rioters marched through the streets, posted their grievances, and broke into the prefectural school, where they kept the education official there hostage. Gali and the Chinese governor of Chiang-su, Chang Po-hsing 張伯行 (1652–1725), impeached each other over the case, and the scandal dragged on into 1712, when the K'ang-hsi emperor dismissed both Chang and Gali from office.[55] In 1711, two *chü-jen* candidates in Chiang-nan were discovered to be illiterate (*wen-li pu-t'ung* 文理不通), and following a 1657 precedent the chief examiners

52. *Ch'ing-pai lei-ch'ao*, 21.24–25, gives an example in which the character *yen* 焉 on a question was mistaken for *ma* 馬 by a clerk supervising a county examination.

53. Yuan Tsing, "Urban Riots and Disturbances," in Jonathan Spence and John Wills, eds., *From Ming to Ch'ing: Conquest, Region, and Continuity in Seventeenth-Century China* (New Haven: Yale University Press, 1979), p. 286.

54. Ibid., pp. 292–93.

55. Ibid., pp. 301–02.

were fired. Investigators later learned that the candidates had buried written material inside the examination compound some time before the provincial examination commenced in August. Even the governor of Chiang-nan was implicated in the case, which became a precedent for similar cases thereafter.[56]

In addition, cheating was notorious among bannermen taking military examinations in the eighteenth and nineteenth centuries. In 1758, the emperor's personal advisor, Chuang Ts'un-yü 莊存與 (1719–88), a Chiang-nan literatus, was almost sacked when his stringent surveillance provoked a bannerman riot in the Peking examination compound. Initially he was held responsible for the case, but the Ch'ien-lung emperor bailed him out and pointed the finger at the notorious behavior of the bannermen in such circumstances: "If they [the eight Manchu banners] want to study the Chinese language, however, they must also devote their minds to oral recitations. [In this way,] they will have the strength to take the examinations. If they cannot compose the written answers by themselves, and can only cheat by passing slips of paper containing the answers, or by secretly carrying notes or books into the examination room, thereby through reckless luck achieving an honored name, then the time spent in studying Chinese can be seen as a deleterious means for taking laws and regulations lightly and indulging in corrupt practices."[57]

### Bribery and Its Consequences

Clerks and guards, because they were usually commoners of lower social status and wealth than the candidates for civil degrees, could also be bribed by the candidates themselves, who often came from wealthy families. The social discrepancy between clerks and candidates was a serious problem, particularly because the male children of clerks were forbidden since 1384 from taking the civil examinations and were doomed to local hereditary sinecures in official yamens, which they perceived as an inadequate reward for their services.[58] In some cases, a clerk's son successfully

56. See Huang Kuang-liang, *Ch'ing-tai k'o-chü chih-tu chih yen-chiu*, pp. 262–64, for the 1711 case.

57. *Shang-yü tang* 上諭檔 (Imperial edict record book) (Ch'ing archives in the Palace Museum, Taiwan), pp. 038–050, under Ch'ien-lung 23, 2nd month. See also my *Classicism, Politics, and Kinship*, pp. 107–108.

58. See Lu Shen, *K'o-ch'ang tiao-kuan*, 136.4a, and *Huang-Ming kung-chü-k'ao*, 1.106b–107a. See also Dardess, *A Ming Society*, pp. 146–149. The Ming and Ch'ing government tried to set up separate examinations for clerks. See *Ch'ing-pai lei-ch'ao*, 21.164. For discussion, see T'ung-tsu Ch'u, *Local Government in China under the Ch'ing* (Stanford: Stanford University Press, 1962), pp. 36–55.

took the provincial examinations by entering false information on the required recommendation forms, which were transmitted to the provincial level after the magistrate was bribed and allowed the son to take the county licensing examination.[59] If clerks could bribe magistrates in this way, then the local elite could similarly see to it that their sons were also ranked highly on the provincial candidate's list. Indeed, the legalized sale of Imperial School degrees (chien-sheng) during both the Ming and Ch'ing dynasties, because it equated official status with financial means, made the difference between bribery and legal purchase a matter of social position and wealth.[60]

The most serious problem to the dynasty, however, was bribery of the chief and associate examiners, because this usually involved large sums of money and could lead to riots in the compounds if other candidates learned about it. The provincial education commissioner was the most susceptible to such overtures because he served in the provincial capital for three years and had regularly made the rounds of all prefectures, counties, and departments in his jurisdiction supervising the final licensing and qualifying examinations. Prefects and magistrates might also as a favor to a relative or friend place certain licentiates from the local qualifying examinations at the top of the provincial examination list of names.[61]

Because, after 1580, the chief and associate examiners in the provincial examination yamen were chin-shih outsiders specially appointed by the Ministry of Rites to monitor the examinations, they were harder to influence in the provinces. Some of the latter came directly from the court or the Hanlin Academy and would be more difficult to approach by local candidates without well-placed relatives or friends.[62] Critics noted, however, that when a Hanlin academician received his assignment to be a provincial examiner, his supplies and travel requirements were paid by the counties, departments, and prefectures he passed through. In addition, a Hanlin examiner could expect gifts from local officials and local literati before and after the examinations.[63]

In the metropolitan examination, moreover, the pressure on Hanlin examiners could also come from the court. The most famous case of a high official who influenced examiners during the Ming dynasty involved

59. Ch'ing-pai lei-ch'ao, 21.126–27.

60. Literati took advantage of fiscal crises during the Ming to get around "tribute student" policies whenever the dynasty permitted the direct purchase of degree status. See Dardess, A Ming Society, pp. 163–64. For the Ch'ing, see further below.

61. Doolittle, Social Life of the Chinese, pp. 425–28.

62. For Ming cases in which the examiners were accused of bribery, see Chih-i k'o-so-chi, 2.48–49, 2.55, 2.72–73. See also Doolittle, Social Life of the Chinese, pp. 26–27.

63. Chung-li Chang, The Chinese Gentry, pp. 194–95.

the senior minister Chang Chü-cheng 張居正 (1525–82), who allegedly tried to influence the metropolitan examiners in 1574 to reconsider when his first son was not selected for the palace examination that year. Later his second son took his *chin-shih* degree, in 1577, and a third passed as the *optimus* in the 1580 palace examination. It was plausible to many that Chang could influence the examiners because the Wan-li emperor had left day-to-day executive matters in his hands, although such charges were never proven.[64]

Because it was structural, corruption continued in the eighteenth and nineteenth centuries empirewide. In 1741, the Ch'ien-lung emperor (r. 1736–95) issued an edict demanding that examiners prevent irregularities in provincial examinations.[65] Later in 1752, a proctor in that year's Shun-t'ien provincial examination was shown to have accepted a bribe from one of the candidates, who turned out to be the proctor's nephew. The candidate was deprived of his *chü-jen* degree, and his uncle was dismissed and lowered in rank by two steps.[66] The Ch'ien-lung emperor also feared that Grand Secretaries and even members of the Grand Council were able to influence the outcomes of the metropolitan and palace examinations in favor of their kin. Lu Hsun's 魯迅 (Chou Shu-jen 周樹人, 1881–1936) grandfather, Chou Fu-ch'ing 周福清, a Hanlin academician and the first important scholar in the Chou family from Shao-hsing, was arrested for attempting to bribe an examiner assigned to the 1893 Che-chiang provincial examination. The scandal affected Lu Hsun's family both financially and socially, and Lu was forced to leave his lineage school.[67]

An increasing number of "avoidance laws" in the eighteenth century were applied to cases in which officials from distinguished lineages were expected to refuse service as examiners if this would favor their relatives.

64. *Ming-shih*, 3/1702, 7/5650; and *Chih-i k'o-so-chi*, 2.63–64. Cf. Ray Huang, *1587: A Year of No Significance* (New Haven: Yale University Press, 1981), pp. 9–26, 33–41. In 1577, officials tried to impeach Chang for not retiring to observe the required period of mourning on the death of his father. After 1582, his wealth and the wealth of his brothers and sons were confiscated.

65. See the Ch'ien-lung emperor's 1741 edict on cheating and bribery in the Shun-t'ien provincial examinations, in *Ch'ing-tai ch'ien-ch'i chiao-yü lun-chu hsuan*, 3/7–8.

66. Huang Kuang-liang, *Ch'ing-tai k'o-chü chih-tu chih yen-chiu*, pp. 270–71.

67. See *Ch'ing-pai lei-ch'ao*, 21.87; and Howard Boorman and Richard Howard, eds., *Biographical Dictionary of Republican China* (New York: Columbia University Press, 1967), p. 417. For the case details, see Mary Buck, "Justice for All: The Application of Law by Analogy in the Case of Zhou Fuqing," *Journal of Chinese Law* 7, 2 (fall 1993): 118–27. Mancheong, "Fair Fraud and Fraudulent Fairness," pp. 52–58, describes mid-Ch'ing avoidance examinations and the civil examination avoidance law in light of how kin members mobilized their political influence as examiners.

In addition, laws treating corruption and bribery in civil examinations were included under a statute in the Ch'ing legal code called "Partiality in the examination of candidates for degrees." The statute stipulated the number of blows of the heavy bamboo meted out to officials who passed unworthy candidates or prevented worthy candidates from passing. Such guidelines descended from the Ming penal code. Penalties were considerably augmented if bribery of officials was involved. Such penalties began at seventy blows of the heavy bamboo for accepting an ounce of silver and increased for every additional five ounces to reach temporary and permanent banishment, and ended with death by strangulation for bribes of more than eighty ounces of silver. One of the Ch'ing substatutes on collusion among provincial and metropolitan examiners ordered the immediate decapitation of the guilty parties. Although the severity of such punishments was mitigated in practice, as in the case of Chou Fu-ch'ing cited above (he was never executed for his collusion and languished in prison until 1901), the legal code made it clear that the Ministry of Personnel was committed to upholding the integrity of the civil examinations.[68]

### Charges and Protests by Candidates

Examinations were the only opportunity for the current and future elites of imperial China to gather in one place as a large group. Competition separated candidates from each other, but corruption and cheating brought them together, especially when examiner favoritism or unfairness was manifest to some.[69] The consequences were serious for all involved if the alleged corruption of examiners led to a riot within the compound. Because such accusations were frequently made by disgruntled candidates who feared failure, the court had to be careful. In 1457, accusations that the readers had been unfair (*yueh-chüan pu-kung* 閱卷不公) in the Shunt'ien examination, where the sons of high officials empirewide often took provincial examinations, enraged the T'ien-shun emperor (r. 1457–64), who used the 1397 precedent of the Hung-wu emperor to order that the candidates be reexamined. In 1460, similar charges were made against metropolitan examiners but were found to be unsubstantiated (*ssu-nien* 私念).[70]

68. Mary Buck, "Justice for All," pp. 127–37.

69. Regulations for examiners and candidates were laid out in detail in the *Ch'in-ting k'o-ch'ang t'iao-li* 欽定科場條例 (Imperially prescribed guidelines for the civil examination grounds), 1832 edition. See also Shang Yen-liu, *Ch'ing-tai k'o-chü k'ao-shih shu-lueh*, pp. 325–50; and Huang Kuang-liang, *Ch'ing-tai k'o-chü chih-tu chih yen-chiu*, pp. 258–275, for accounts of corruption cases involving the civil examinations.

70. *Chih-i k'o-so-chi*, 2.48–49.

Ming examination records are filled with famous literati who were charged successfully or unsuccessfully with corruption on the civil examinations when they were assigned as examiners. Appointed as one of the chief examiners for the 1499 metropolitan examination, Ch'eng Min-cheng 程敏政 (1466 *secundus*) was imprisoned after the examination on the charge of selling essay themes in advance.[71] Chiao Hung 焦竑 (1541–1620), the *optimus* in 1589, was assigned from the Hanlin Academy to act as assistant chief examiner on the 1597 Shun-t'ien civil examination. Because certain Taoist phrases appeared on some examination papers as a possible code for the examiner to recognize the author of the answer, Chiao was charged with corruption and dismissed from the court and demoted to associate magistrate in Fu-ning department in Fu-chien province.[72]

Similarly, though at a lower level, the famous painter Tung Ch'i-ch'ang, when serving as provincial education commissioner in Hu-kuang, was faced with a student demonstration at a local examination he administered in 1605. An investigation of the matter exonerated him, but Tung resigned his appointment and went home to live in retirement for seventeen years.[73] T'ang Pin-yin 湯賓尹 (b. 1568), who finished first on the 1595 metropolitan and third on the palace examination,[74] was frequently but unsuccessfully accused of favoritism during his career. As an associate examiner for the 1610 metropolitan examination, for example, he allegedly retrieved the already failed paper of Han Ching 韓敬, the eventual top name on metropolitan list, and put it before the chief examiner to rank as number one. Han Ching wound up as the palace *optimus* as well, one of only eight Ming *chin-shih* who was both *hui-yuan* and *chuang-yuan*.[75]

Ch'ien Ch'ien-i 錢謙益 (1582–1664) finished third (*t'an-hua* 探花) on the same 1610 palace examination but retired from office when his father died. When he resumed his career ten years later he was assigned as an examiner in Che-chiang in 1621. At the time of the examination, Ch'ien reported an irregularity whereby a candidate had ended his essays with characters that if linked together seemed to produce an insulting sentence

71. See Ku Chieh-kang, "A Study of Literary Persecution during the Ming," translated by L. Carrington Goodrich, *Harvard Journal of Asiatic Studies* 3 (1938): 282–85.

72. *Chih-i k'o-so-chi*, 2.78–79.

73. See Hummel, ed., *Eminent Chinese of the Ch'ing Period*, p. 787.

74. *Chin-shih t'ung-nien hsu-ch'ih pien-lan* 進士同年序齒便覽 (Overview of *chin-shih* graduates in the same year), 1595: 242–43.

75. *Ch'ien-Ming kung-chü k'ao-lueh* 前明貢舉考略 (Brief study of civil examinations in the earlier Ming dynasty), compiled by Huang Ch'ung-lan 黃崇蘭, 1834 edition, 2.32a–b. Cf. *Chih-i k'o-so-chi*, 2.72–77; and *Chuang-yuan ts'e*, 1733 edition, A.6a.

perhaps meant to signal his identity to an examiner. When the coded language was uncovered, the candidate tried to bribe the examiners, but they immediately reported it to Ch'ien as their chief supervisor. Ch'ien in turn reported the incident to the Ministry of Rites and was mildly punished because he had not prevented the event from occurring. Seven years later, in 1628, while serving as the examiner for the metropolitan examination and a candidate for senior Grand Secretary, he was charged by his opponents with bribery in the 1621 provincial examination and dismissed from office. Ch'ien retired to his home in Ch'ang-shu county outside Su-chou and devoted himself to his private collection of books.[76]

Similar cases occurred during the early Ch'ing, when the Manchu and Han bannerman conquest elite tried to control cheating among southern candidates for degrees. In the 1657 Chiang-nan provincial examination, for instance, a near-riot among failed candidates resulted when the examiners that year were charged with corruption. The candidates had learned that some of the original papers supposedly prepared by candidates had no names on them and might have been prepared in advance for candidates the examiners favored. Candidates congregated at the local literary temple (wen-miao 文廟) dedicated to Lord Wen-ch'ang 文昌 (see Chapter 6), where they wailed and sang angry songs slandering the examiners.

After a review carried out by the censor, the emperor immediately dismissed the chief and associate examiners from all offices and asked that candidates involved in the corruption be taken to Peking for further investigation. In addition, the emperor ordered a reexamination (fu-shih 覆試) in 1658 for all the unimplicated candidates in the Yangtzu delta. The 1657 Chiang-nan examination scandal also precipitated the need for the reexamination of provincial graduates from the capital region in Shun-t'ien prefecture, because many southerners also registered for the provincial examination there.

Subsequently, although the chief examiners were fired, their lives were spared because of previous meritorious service. Some of the associate examiners in Nanking were executed, and eight 1657 graduates had their chü-jen degrees revoked. Such severe sentences for the examiners reminded many of the examiner executions associated with the 1397 palace examination (see Chapter 2) during the early Ming.[77] Repeat examinations were also required for metropolitan examination graduates before the palace

76. *Tien-shih teng-k'o lu* 殿試登科錄, 1610. Cf. *Chih-i k'o-so-chi*, 3.103–04. See also Ku Chieh-kang, "A Study of Literary Persecution during the Ming," pp. 291–93; and Wakeman, *The Great Enterprise*, pp. 124–25.

77. See *Tan-mo lu*, 2.8b–10a. See also Huang Kuang-liang, *Ch'ing-tai k'o-chü chih-tu chih yen-chiu*, pp. 259–61, on the 1657–58 case.

examination could be administered. The Ch'ing court also responded by stopping local examinations.[78]

The problems, because they were endemic, continued, however. In 1754, a process for outside review of provincial examinations was reinstated. The process of review had started in 1701 (1702 for the provincial examinations) and was reaffirmed in 1736, and thereafter. The reviews set guidelines for errors committed by examination officials and staff and the appropriate punishments.[79] In 1768, the emperor received memorials describing the need for added supervision of military examinations and for measures to keep the questions secret. Two Chinese and two Manchu censors were added to the examiner list by the emperor.[80]

Numerous other cases dealing specifically with local examination irregularities are cited below to show how endemic such problems had become before 1850. Indeed, the Taiping Rebellion, which centered in the Yangtzu delta, may simply have exacerbated a crisis of trust in the examination regime that had been building since the late Ming (see Chapter 11).

## CIVIL EXAMINATIONS, POLITICAL GROUPS, AND ORGANIZED DISSENT

Since the T'ang dynasty, the ritual conventions of civil examinations had become enmeshed in factional politics at court. Ceremonies celebrating examination graduates had soon led to a social and intellectual solidarity between the graduates and their examiners that exacerbated the very political factions at court that the meritocratic examinations had been promulgated to prevent. To counter the impact of the local "wine-drinking ceremony" for their patrons, which candidates attended before leaving for higher examinations, and the capital "ceremony of gratitude" (hsieh-en 謝恩) in building patron-client relationships between examiners and gradu-

---

78. See Ch'in-ting Ta-Ch'ing hui-tien shih-li, 382.13b. See also Ch'ing li-ch'ao hsiu-ts'ai lu 清歷朝秀才錄 (Record of local licentiates [in Su-chou] during Ch'ing reign periods) (late Ch'ing manuscript), pp. 14b–15b, for the break in local renewal and qualifying examinations there in 1661–62. Beginning in 1881, repeat examinations were required only for those who had ranked in the second or third tier of graduates. First-grade students were excused.

79. See Tan-mo lu, 14.10b–11b; and Ch'ang-t'an, pp. 37–38. See also Ch'in-ting mo-k'an t'iao-li, 1.1b–2a, for details of the review process for provincial and metropolitan civil examination papers.

80. See the memorials for 1768, 7th month, 26th day, and another on the 9th month, 29th day, in the Ping-pu t'i-pen 兵部題本 (Memoranda including memorials from the Ministry of Military Personnel), in the Ming-Ch'ing Archives, Academia Sinica, Taiwan.

ates, the court beginning in the late T'ang forbade the ceremony of gratitude.[81]

Although unsuccessful in the late T'ang, this policy was revived during
the Five Dynasties and Northern Sung when the focus of the examination
ceremony shifted from the examiners to loyalty and affection for the
emperor. To demote the literati examiners, the Sung government also
focused *chin-shih* examination ritual on the palace examination, with the
emperor as chief examiner, and required the graduates to attend the ceremony of gratitude for him before attending the ceremony to Confucius
inside the Imperial Academy. This capital ceremony of gratitude performed by graduating *chin-shih* to the emperor became increasingly grand
during the Ming and Ch'ing dynasties, but even with the main focus on
the ruler, the devotion of graduates to their examiners was never overcome (see above). In the late Ming, for example, Matteo Ricci (1552–1610)
observed examination graduates weeping before their examiners and
noted the lifelong friendships sealed on such occasions. Out of such well-
placed friendships emerged political alliances and examination corruption
that also bedeviled the Ming and Ch'ing dynasties.[82]

In addition, local politics or national emergencies could divert attention
from the timeless principles in classical quotations chosen as topics for
examination essays, and examiners and candidates had to be careful that
their questions and answers not be read as political allegories of the present. A tenuous balance was maintained, despite the centrifugal social and
political forces that tugged at the examination regime, which politically
tracked the graduates. Failing to avoid certain sensitive issues, or using
banned words in examination essays, could lead to personal disaster. A
frequent cause of failure on examinations was a candidate's use of taboo
characters in an essay. In 1456, the Hanlin chief examiners in charge of
the Shun-t'ien provincial examination were charged with selecting themes
that violated the taboo against using characters identical to imperial
names. The examiners, Liu Yen 劉儼 (1394–1457) and Huang Chien 黃諫
(1442 *t'an-hua*), were also charged with allowing cheating inside the examination compound. Similarly, in 1537 the two chief examiners of the Ying-
t'ien provincial examination in Nanking were accused of lèse-majesté in
their questions for the candidates.[83]

Such charges frequently hid the special interests of those who made the

81. Moore, "The Ceremony of Gratitude."

82. See Pasquale M. d'Elia, S.J., ed., *Fonti Ricciane: documenti originali concernenti Matteo Ricci e la storia delle relazioni tra l'Europe e la Cina* (Rome: Libreria dello Stato, 1942), vol. 1, p. 49, cited in Moore, "The Ceremony of Gratitude."

83. See Ku Chieh-kang, "A Study of Literary Persecution during the Ming," pp. 279–90; and Wakeman, *The Great Enterprise*, p. 358n127.

charges. In 1456, for example, the Grand Secretaries Ch'en Hsun 陳循 (1385–1462) and Wang Wen 王文 (1393–1457) were angry that their sons Ch'en Ying 瑛 (b. 1431) and Wang Lun 綸 (fl. ca. 1465–87) had failed the 1456 Shun-t'ien provincial examination, and they blamed the chief examiners, who were their political enemies, for the low rankings. After initially siding with the accusers, the soon-to-be-deposed Y'ing-t'ai emperor (r. 1450–56) exonerated the examiners but took no action against their accusers. As we shall see in Chapter 8, Wang Wen was executed and Ch'en Hsun was exiled by the T'ien-shun emperor when he retook the throne in 1457, and Wang Lun had to wait until the Ch'eng-hua reign beginning in 1465 before he was permitted to take the provincial examination again.[84]

In 1586, one of the future leaders of the Tung-lin Academy 東林書院 in Wu-hsi county, Ku Yun-ch'eng 顧允成 (1554–1607), took the metropolitan and palace examination. In his palace policy answer, he was explicitly critical of Chang Chü-cheng's role until his death in 1582 as chief minister under the Wan-li emperor: "Chang had misled the ruler and advanced his private interests for himself and his followers. He did not deserve to be trusted" (張居正罔上，行私階下，不足信). Remarkably, Ku still finished low in the third tier of candidates, despite his remarks, suggesting examiner sympathies with his criticism of Chang, which echoed criticism of Chang's alleged interference in the 1574 and 1577 metropolitan examinations cited above. The case deserves careful attention because Tung-lin followers would later use civil examination success to gain entry as a faction of literati via the Hanlin Academy to the central court.[85]

During Chang Chü-cheng's rise to Grand Secretary and chief minister, a series of examination riots had broken out between 1567 and 1572 in several prefectures in the Yangtzu delta. In 1567, the student rioters had accused the provincial examiners of corruption when irregularities in the numbers attached to the anonymous examination papers were discovered. The role of dissatisfied *sheng-yuan* degree-holders in these riots has been linked to late Ming urban demonstrations against unpopular officials and excessive taxation, which many of the Tung-lin partisans supported.[86] Chang Chü-cheng's hard-line policies in the Ming court were in part a

84. See *Dictionary of Ming Biography*, pp. 970–71.

85. *Chih-i k'o-so-chi*, 2.71–72. On the Tung-lin faction's battle with Wei Chung-hsien, see my "Imperial Politics and Confucian Societies in Late Imperial China," pp. 393–96. The definitive study is now Ono Kazuko 小野和子, *Minki dōsha kō* 明季黨社考 (Study of Ming dynasty factions and societies) (Kyoto: Dōhōsha, 1996).

86. Fu I-ling 傅衣凌, *Ming-tai Chiang-nan shih-min ching-chi shih-t'an* 明代江南市民經濟試探 (Exploration of the urbanite economy in Chiang-nan during the Ming period) (Shanghai: People's Press, 1957), pp. 111–12. On the 1567 examination riot in Ch'ang-chou prefecture, see Wakeman, *The Great Enterprise*, pp. 105–07, 107n59.

response to these local disturbances among southern lower degree-holders.

Shih Kuan-min (fl. ca. 1565), then prefect in Ch'ang-chou prefecture, where a 1567 disturbance had occurred, was subsequently accused of wrongfully collecting private funds since 1572 to construct the Lung-ch'eng 龍城 Academy in Wu-chin county. For his indiscretion, Shih was dismissed as prefect, but alarmingly, an accompanying imperial edict was issued abolishing private academies, especially those in the Yangtzu delta, where most such academies existed. Academy grounds were ordered returned to their local communities, and the buildings were to be turned into government yamens. Public gatherings were forbidden (except for examination purposes), and regional censors and education commissioners were ordered to supervise local education more carefully.[87]

Using the misappropriation of private funds for the Lung-ch'eng Academy as a pretext, Chang Chü-cheng was able to force the conversion of sixty-four private academies in the Yangtzu delta to official control. What had turned Chang against private academies, in addition to the examination riots their members participated in, was their uproar in 1577 over his failure to go into full mourning upon the death of his father. According to ritual precedent, government officials were expected to resign and spend three years (actually twenty-seven months) in mourning. High-minded literati, enraged by Chang's flouting of established ritual to stay in office, demanded his impeachment for improperly fulfilling the requirements for filial piety. Chang exacted his revenge by closing down the academies that served as the organizational nexus for his opponents. Out of this ritual controversy emerged the Tung-lin and other activist groups of the late Ming.[88]

In 1603, Ku Hsien-ch'eng 顧憲成 (1550–1612), Ku Yun-ch'eng's elder brother, decided at the suggestion of his friend and townsman Kao P'an-lung 高攀龍 (1562–1626) to rebuild the Tung-lin Academy in Wu-hsi county and restore it to cultural prominence. Ku's prestige as an exemplary literatus who had been ousted from the court and reduced to commoner status in 1601 for his outspoken views on corruption in the selection of Grand Secretaries drew large gatherings to the meetings of the Tung-lin Academy. Moreover, he called on sympathetic officials to join together in a common cause. The literati associated with the Tung-lin

87. John Meskill, "Academies and Politics in the Ming Dynasty," in Charles Hucker, ed., *Chinese Government in Ming Times: Six Studies* (New York: Columbia University Press, 1966), pp. 160–63; Ray Huang, *1587: A Year of No Significance,* pp. 60–67; and Robert Crawford, "Chang Chü-cheng's Confucian Legalism," in William Theodore de Bary et al., *Self and Society in Ming Thought* (New York: Columbia University Press, 1970), pp. 367–404.

88. *Ming-shih,* 8/5647–48.

Academy quickly became the leading voice for moral leadership and political reform in the late Ming.[89]

Besides the scholarly meetings that attracted hundreds of concerned literati to the Tung-lin Academy in Wu-hsi, scholarly meetings were also organized at the Ching-cheng-t'ang 經正堂 (Hall of classical correctness), the chief lecture room in the Lung-ch'eng Academy in nearby Wu-chin county, which had provoked Chang Chü-cheng's prohibitions against private academies. Additional meetings were held in I-hsing county at the Ming-tao Academy 明道書院 and in nearby prefectures. Hence, the Tung-lin partisans were centered in the major county seats of Chang-chou prefecture.[90]

Representing a late Ming convergence between literati moral rhetoric and political activism, the Tung-lin partisans at their apogee of influence commanded the attention of literati empirewide by successfully getting examiners to place their members via the civil service examinations into the Hanlin Academy. For a time between 1620 and 1623, members of the Tung-lin, after initial setbacks, were strategically placed in the Peking imperial bureaucracy. With the Hanlin Academy serving as a convenient gateway to political power and influence within the court and outer bureaucracy (see Chapter 3), many key posts were held by Tung-lin partisans in early 1624. Political intrigue and court infighting led to disaster for the Tung-lin group, however. They suffered a series of reverses that coincided with the rise of the eunuch Wei Chung-hsien 魏忠賢 (1568–1627), who became the youthful T'ien-ch'i emperor's (r. 1621–28) intimate advisor. Despite their high place in the imperial court, and in part because of it, the Tung-lin partisans were gradually undermined by Wei's followers at court and eventually dismissed from office.

89. See Ku Hsien-ch'eng, "Tung-lin hui-yueh fu" 東林會約附 (Addition to the statutes for meetings at the Tung-lin), in *Ku Tuan-wen kung i-shu* 顧端文公遺書 (Bequeathed writings of Ku Hsien-ch'eng), Ch'ing dynasty K'ang-hsi edition, vol. 4, pp. 14a–15b. See also *I-hsing hsien-chih* 宜興縣志 (Gazetteer of I-hsing county), 1869: 4.44a–45a; and Charles Hucker, "The Tung-lin Movement of the Late Ming Period," in John K. Fairbank, ed., *Chinese Thought and Institutions* (Chicago: University of Chicago Press, 1973), pp. 147–50. For the social context, see Richard von Glahn, "Municipal Reform and Urban Social Conflict in Late Ming China," *Journal of Asian Studies* 50, 2 (1991); and Yuan Tsing, "Urban Riots and Disturbances," pp. 280–313.

90. See Ku Hsien-cheng, "Ching-cheng-t'ang shang-yü" 經正堂商語 (Discussions at the Hall of Classical Correctness), in *Ku Tuan-wen kung i-shu*, vol. 5, 1.1a–7a. See also Chu T'an 朱倓, *Ming-chi she-tang yen-chiu* 明季社黨研究 (Research on Ming dynasty societies and parties) (Ch'ung-ch'ing: Commercial Press, 1945); and Mizoguchi Yūzō 溝口雄三, "Iwayuru Tōrinha jinshi no shisō" いわゆる東林派人士の思想 (The thought of the so-called members of the Tung-lin group), *Tōyō bunka kenkyūjo kiyō* 東洋文化研究所紀要 75 (1978): 111–49.

In summer 1625, Wei's purge of the Tung-lin partisans climaxed. Arrests and deaths by torture of Tung-lin leaders were accompanied by imperial denunciations of private academies as politically subversive organizations. The halls of the Tung-lin Academy, partially destroyed in 1625, were completely torn down after Kao P'an-lung committed suicide in Wu-hsi in 1626. Sun Shen-hsing 孫慎行 (1565–1636), a Tung-lin partisan from Wu-chin county who had entered the Hanlin Academy after finishing third on the 1595 palace examination,[91] was kept out of office by Wei after 1621 and banished in 1627, a sentence that was not carried out when Wei's group precipitously fell from power.[92] A special imperial order was sent out to destroy all academies assumed to be part of the Tung-lin network.[93]

We shall see in more detail in Chapter 7 that the controversial Ai Nan-ying 艾南英 (1583–1646) was banned from Ming provincial examinations in 1624 for answering a question in the Chiang-hsi test in a way that was critical of eunuch power in the capital. For neither the first time nor the last, examiners, many of whom were by then Tung-lin followers, brought their court politics with them to the provinces. In like fashion, examiners sent to Nanking and Hang-chou for the 1624 provincial examinations allegedly did not pay proper homage to the eunuch leader Wei Chung-hsien, who was on the verge of eliminating the Tung-lin group. As a result they were dismissed and lost their right to register in their local areas (*hsiao ch'i chi* 消其籍).[94]

Wei Chung-hsien's use of terror failed to rein in the political forces of late Ming literati. After Wei fell from power in 1627, private academies and associations reemerged. Among the most successful and best-organized group of literati were those associated with the Fu-she 復社 (Return to antiquity society), which centered on Su-chou, then the leading cultural and commercial center in the Yangtzu delta. A formidable organization formed in 1629 and dedicated to supporting its members in the factional struggles of the day, the Fu-she represented the largest political interest group ever organized within a dynasty.[95]

---

91. *Chin-shih t'ung-nien hsu-ch'ih pien-lan*, 1595: 49a.

92. Sun Shen-hsing, *En-hsu chu-kung chih lueh* 恩卹諸公志略 (Brief account of several dukes whose blood flowed as tribute), in *Ching-t'o i-shih* 荊駝遺史, compiled by Ch'en Hu 陳湖, Tao-kuang edition (1820–49), I.2a.

93. For contemporary lists of Tung-lin martyrs, see Chin Jih-sheng 金日升, *Sung-t'ien lu-pi* 松天臚筆 (Display of writings in praise of heaven), 1633 edition, vol. 1, 1a–24a; and "Tung-lin pieh-sheng" 東林別乘 (Separate records of Tung-lin) (Kuang-chou 1958 transcription).

94. *Ch'ien-Ming kung-chü k'ao-lueh*, 2.38b. Cf. Ai Nan-ying, *T'ien-yung-tzu chi*, A.1a (p. 49); and Ku Yen-wu, *Jih-chih lu chi-shih*, 16.388.

95. Atwell, "From Education to Politics," pp. 333–67.

Civil examination success was the time-honored route to power that the Fu-she partisans also followed. In the 1630 Ying-t'ien provincial examination, for example, thirty Fu-she members passed, including Chang P'u 張溥 (1602–41), the founder of the association (he placed number thirty), and Ch'en Tzu-lung 陳子龍 (1608–47), who finished seventy-first. This remarkable total represented 20% of the 150 *chü-jen* degrees granted that year in Nanking out of the total of 7,500 candidates. In the 1631 metropolitan examination in Peking, this success story was repeated, when 62 (18%) of the 347 graduates were Fu-she members. Two years after its founding, several Fu-she partisans were selected by palace examiners to enter the Hanlin Academy and thereby gain influence over the provincial and capital selection process for *chü-jen* and *chin-shih*.[96]

This penetration of Fu-she members into the late Ming court climaxed in 1643, when the top three places out of four hundred graduates on the civil palace examination went to its members. All were eligible to enter the Hanlin Academy. Since 1631, several Fu-she members had served as Ming Grand Secretaries. With the fall of the Ming dynasty to Manchu conquerors, however, the Fu-she ceased to function, although some of its members did pass Ch'ing dynasty civil examinations.[97] Ming-style factionalism disappeared, and the reasons for the fall of the Ming were in part attributed to the debilitating impact of political groups such as the Tung-lin and Fu-she, which had allegedly tried to press their agendas through the precincts of the civil examinations.

During the Ch'ing dynasty, Manchu rulers at first were able to prevent the recurrence of literati factions using the civil examinations to further their political influence. Instead, individual cases of sedition periodically surfaced. In the 1726 Chiang-hsi provincial examination, for example, the provincial education commissioner Cha Ssu-t'ing 查嗣庭 (1664–1727) was accused of the crime of lèse-majesté because the first and last characters of the four-character subject he chose from the *Great Learning* (*wei-min so-chih* 維民所止, "where the people rest") for the topic of an eight-legged essay on session one, when combined as *wei-chih* 維止, suspiciously looked like the graphs for the Yung-cheng 雍正 reign title with the head of each character lopped off, implying regicide. To the outside observer, such concern seems the height of imperial paranoia, but in an environment of classically literate Han Chinese and somewhat less literate Manchu overlords, the role of language was a touchy issue for the ruler and his court.

Sure enough, when an investigation revealed seditious literature in his possession and in Ch'a's poetry, the emperor ordered Ch'a put in jail,

96. *Ying-t'ien hsiang-shih lu* 應天鄉試錄, 1630: 19b–22a. Cf. Atwell, "From Education to Politics," p. 341; and Wakeman, *The Great Enterprise*, pp. 113–26.

97. Wakeman, *The Great Enterprise*, pp. 230–31, 279–80, 890–91.

where he died the next year. His body was ordered dismembered. The paranoia had been justified, and examinations were halted in Che-chiang province, where Cha Ssu-t'ing came from. His two older brothers were also arrested. No *chü-jen* from Che-chiang were permitted to take the 1727 metropolitan examination.[98] The succeeding education commissioner was able to convince the court to hold the 1729 provincial examination in Che-chiang on schedule, however, after a thorough investigation produced no evidence of lingering sedition.[99]

In a 1740 case, the Ch'ien-lung emperor grew concerned about possible seditious content in the commentaries to the Five Classics and Four Books that the 1712 *chin-shih* degree-holder from Kuang-hsi, Hsieh Chi-shih 謝濟 世 (1689–1756), had prepared. Hsieh had been a Hanlin academician under the K'ang-hsi emperor. While serving as censor in 1726 under the Yung-cheng emperor, he was sentenced to death but then exiled to Mongolia for making false charges against an imperial favorite. Hsieh's exile writings, particularly his annotations of the *Great Learning*, were scrutinized by the military commander and found to impugn the orthodox commentary by Chu Hsi. Some of Hsieh's statements were interpreted to imply oblique criticism of the throne. Although again sentenced to death, he was released in 1730 and pardoned in 1735 by the Ch'ien-lung emperor upon the latter's accession to the throne.

Hsieh then had the audacity in a 1736 memorial to attack the civil palace examination for the rigidity of its content and criticized the examiners' exclusive reliance on fixed literary principles and styles of calligraphy. When he was again investigated in 1740 while serving as an intendant in Hu-nan and found to have included unorthodox views in his recent classical works that deviated from the Ch'eng-Chu persuasion (與 程朱違悖牴牾), all of Hsieh Chi-shih's publications and woodblocks were ordered destroyed. The governor-general in charge of the investigation reported that Hsieh had repented his crime. Otherwise he would have been sentenced to death a third time.[100]

For final examples, we should note the 1876 local examination in Tung-hsien in Ssu-ch'uan province and the 1895 metropolitan protest led by K'ang Yu-wei 康有為 (1858–1927), in which large groups of candidates

---

98. Bielenstein, "The Regional Provenance," pp. 23–24. The province made up for this loss by graduating 71 *chin-shih* in 1730 and 43 in 1733, which were higher unofficial quotas than Che-chiang had received in the 1723 (24) or 1724 (36) palace examinations.

99. See Shang Yen-liu, *Ch'ing-tai k'o-chü k'ao-shih shu-lu*, pp. 327–28. Cf. Hummel, ed., *Eminent Chinese of the Ch'ing Period*, p. 22.

100. See the Ch'ien-lung emperor's 1740 edict on Hsieh's case, in *Ch'ing-tai ch'ien-ch'i chiao-yü lun-chu hsuan*, 3/8. Cf. Hummel, ed., *Eminent Chinese of the Ch'ing Period*, pp. 306–07.

used the gathering of examination candidates to protest contemporary issues. A local demonstration reminiscent of late Ming urban protests, it arose because examination candidates in Tung-hsien were unhappy with the violent means used by local officials to deal with tax protests in the 1870s. They addressed their dissatisfaction to Chang Chih-tung 張之洞 (1837–1909), who was then serving as education commissioner in Ssu-ch'uan province, by writing complaints on their examination papers rather than preparing essays on the required quotations from the Four Books and Five Classics. A high-placed court official, Chang Chih-tung memorialized the throne about the causes of the tax protest as he saw them, which influenced the final decision in the case against the entrenched local officials.[101] On the national level, the 1895 protest in Peking before the metropolitan civil examination was unprecedented and signaled the weakening of the throne in political matters and the increasing power of literati dissent (see Chapter 11).

## LATE MING CRITIQUES OF EXAMINATIONS AND CALLS FOR REFORM

The failure of the examination system to accomplish its stated goal—to select literati (*shih*) of worth and talent for public office—had been frequently claimed during the T'ang, Sung, and Ming dynasties. Candidates for office "study things they will never use and later use what they have never studied" (*so-hsi fei so-yung so-yung fei so-hsi* 所習非所用，所用非所習), a sentiment first enunciated by the T'ang literatus Chao K'uang 趙匡 (fl. ca. 770), was the most frequently heard refrain.[102] But reform was generally inconceivable unless the goals of reformers were articulated within a framework of change that would take into account how reforms would deliver a better civil service than that in place. Without a viable means to improve the civil examinations, reforms could be entertained but not enacted. From the very beginning and at the very end, reformers presented schools as a viable alternative to civil examinations to select men for official positions (see Chapter 1).[103]

Dissatisfaction among Ming literati began in the fifteenth century, when after the Yung-lo reign civil examinations again approached the

101. See Guangyuan Zhou, "Illusion and Reality in the Law of the Late Qing," *Modern China* 19, 4 (October 1993): 442–43.

102. Tu Yu 杜佑 (d. 812), *T'ung-tien* 通典 (Comprehensive institutions) (Shanghai: Commercial Press, 1936), vol. 1, 17.97. Cf. Pulleyblank, "Neo-Confucianism and Neo-Legalism in T'ang Intellectual Life," pp. 91, 104–05.

103. Cf. David Hamilton, *Towards a Theory of Schooling* (New York: The Falmer Press, 1989), p. 151.

scale they had reached during the Sung. Ch'en Chen-ch'eng 陳真晟 (1411–74), who failed the Fu-chien provincial examinations repeatedly before devoting himself to classical scholarship instead as a form of resistance to the examination regime, pointed to the unnatural contradiction between the lofty ideals of Ch'eng-Chu learning and the constrained Ch'eng-Chu orthodoxy in the civil examination curriculum:

> Although the civil examinations allegedly tested "studies of principles" to select the worthy and talented, yet in reality they wearied them. The [curriculum] mimicked "orthodox studies," but forced later candidates to progress too late, consumed as they were by competition and insincerity. The real reason literati values have greatly declined is due to the civil examinations. That is why Master Chu [Hsi] added: "Human talent has not been stimulated and literati values are unattractive because of the ways of the civil examinations." Who today would not believe him? Didn't our first emperor T'ai-tsu, being wise and sagacious, also realize this?

Civil examinations, Ch'en Chen-ch'eng concluded, "were originally not the way of the early sage-kings. But already implemented for generations they would be difficult to eradicate completely. If examinations are not abrogated, however, then orthodox teachings will not be put into practice." Ch'en was in effect a Ch'eng-Chu follower critical of both the examinations and the early Ming's use of Tao Learning as imperial orthodoxy, in the tradition of Wu Yü-pi and Hu Chü-jen (see Chapter 2).[104]

Even those who praised the selection system saw much room for improvement. Ch'iu Chün 丘濬 (1420–95) and Wang Ao 王鏊 (1450–1524) each affirmed examinations and the Ch'eng-Chu curriculum, but they also thought that the classical specialization policy was adversely affecting classical studies. Both thought that the policy questions should receive more attention. Wang Ao—ironically, because his examination essays became models for eight-legged essays after the mid-Ming, as we shall see in Chapter 7—felt that too much emphasis had been placed on the classical essay, which satisfied examiner requirements but demonstrated little learning.[105] Policy debates concerning civil examinations reached a startling level of seriousness in the late Ming, when, just before the fall of the dynasty, a number of literati called for the abrogation of the entire apparatus of civil examinations.

Those associated with the Fu-she society in the Yangtzu delta, for instance, actively debated 1636 proposals to the throne by Ch'en Ch'i-hsin

---

104. Ch'en Chen-ch'eng, "Ch'eng-shih hsueh-chih" 程氏學制 (Study system of Master Ch'eng), in *Ming-tai chiao-yü lun-chu hsuan*, pp. 134–36.

105. *Huang-Ming kung-chü k'ao*, 1.22b–25a, 41b–42a, 45a–46b. See also *Hsu wen-hsien t'ung-k'ao*, 35.3158.

陳啟新 (n.d.), then a military examination official from Huai-an, who called for abrogating the civil examinations in favor of a recommendation procedure to select officials. About the same time, the governor of Ho-nan memorialized suggesting gradual diminution of the scope of the civil examinations and their replacement by the process of guaranteed recommendation ( *pao-chü* 保舉) similar to that of the Sung.[106]

Both Ch'en Ch'i-hsin and the governor appealed for precedents to the Ming founder, Chu Yuan-chang, who temporarily stopped civil examinations in 1373. The emperor in his early 1373 ban had complained that the graduates were immature youths unqualified for office (see Chapter 2). The Ho-nan governor's call for change was premised on the need to produce a new generation of local officials able to cope with the increasing breakdown of late Ming law and social order. He suggested that the emperor temporarily stop the civil examinations. If the recommendation procedure did not produce more men of talent, then the examinations could be reinstituted. If recommendation did the job, then the examinations should be permanently stopped.[107]

Given his view of the decline of the Ming military, Ch'en Ch'i-hsin was not willing to consider the gradual solution offered by the Ho-nan governor. Ch'en outlined three major "illnesses" in Ming institutions:

1. The use of literary examinations to select good men as officials was a fundamental problem. Such tests had produced men whose morality and learning was little more than "empty talk on paper" (*chih-shang k'ung-t'an* 紙上空談);

2. The rigid reliance on *chin-shih* qualifications to appoint officials kept out many men of talent. The early Ming had been well served by numerous lower degree-holders, but after the Chia-ching reign (1522–66) those who held important offices were limited to higher degree-holders;

3. The use of overlapping county and judicial officials (*t'ui-chih*, i.e., the judge, *t'ui-kuan* 推官; and county magistrate, *chih-hsien* 知縣) for local positions was superfluous.

Given *chin-shih* domination of almost all official posts such as magistrate, which were described in Chapter 3, the positions of overlapping judicial officials were now a dead end and should be eliminated, according to Ch'en. As solutions Ch'en Ch'i-hsin called for immediate elimination of civil examinations, promotion of all moral candidates (*hsiao-lien* 孝廉; lit.,

---

106. *Fu-she chi-lueh* 復社紀略 (Abridged records of the Return to Antiquity Society) (unpaginated late Ming ms.), B.7–9.

107. Ibid., B.7–9.

"filial and incorruptible") regardless of degree status, and elimination of the post of local judicial officials.[108]

The Ch'ung-chen emperor (r. 1628–44) carefully considered this proposal to "return to the selection process advocated by the founding Hung-wu emperor." It provoked, however, a vigorous rejoinder from the emperor's high civil officials, all *chin-shih*, who accused Ch'en, as an inexperienced military official from Huai-an, of harboring deep-seated jealousy toward the civil service. While admitting that not everyone selected for officialdom via literary examinations was worthy, the censor Chan Erh-hsuan 詹爾選 (1631 *chin-shih*) quickly listed outstanding literati since the Sung such as Wen T'ien-hsiang 文天祥 (1236–1283), Wang Yang-ming 王陽明 (1472–1529), and Yü Ch'ien 于謙 (1398–1457), among others, who had demonstrated their talents through the civil selection process. As the coup de grâce for their point-by-point rebuttal, the court officials also accused Ch'en of harboring anti-literati sentiments, which they compared to the infamous policy of "burning books and burying alive literati" (*fen-shu k'ang-ju* 焚書坑儒) during the Legalist Ch'in dynasty. If the emperor were to use such proposals, they concluded, "it would be admitting that Confucius and Mencius were not worth emulating."[109]

Depressed at the results, Ch'en Ch'i-hsin could do little else to oppose court officials. Given the level of self-righteous rhetoric that they leveled at him and the factional political environment of the late Ming, Ch'en was lucky that he was not singled out for prosecution. The episode demonstrated, however, the ideological obstacles that reformers of the civil examinations would have to face, and such incidents were repeated in the 1660s when civil examination reforms under the Manchus were first entertained (see Chapter 10). Lurking within the late Ming court's defense of civil examinations was an unspoken effort to keep low officials like Ch'en Ch'i-hsin, who were outside the official *chin-shih* mainstream, from opening wide the path to wealth and status (*fu-kuei* 富貴). In the end the Ch'ung-chen emperor was praised by his court for "destroying Ch'i-hsin's false prejudices" (破啟新之假騙).[110]

We should note that some of the leaders of the massive peasant rebellions that brought the Ming to its knees in 1644 were candidates who had repeatedly failed late Ming civil examinations. The debate over Ch'en Ch'i-hsin's proposal also suggests that eighteenth-century policy changes that permitted more fluid movement between civil and military candidates

108. Ibid., B.11–19.

109. Ibid., B.18–28. See also *Ch'ung-chen shih-lu* 崇禎實錄 (Veritable records of the Ch'ung-chen reign) (reprint, Taipei: Academia Sinica Institute of History and Philology, 1967), 9.3a–b.

110. *Fu-she chi-lueh*, B.23, B.38.

in local examinations (see below) were a response to civil-military developments that were already a problem in the late Ming.[111]

At the end of its reign, the Ming court faced continued pressure to
reform civil examinations. Huang Ch'un-yao 黃淳耀 (1605–45), who took
his *chin-shih* degree in 1643 in the last Ming metropolitan and civil examination, also saw the examinations as a colossal misuse of talent. He took a
mediating position in his detailed analysis of the problems inherent in the
examination process.[112] Rather than memorialize the Ch'ung-chen emperor,
Huang chose instead to address the literati community in a series of essays
entitled "K'o-chü lun" 科舉論 (On the civil examinations). Huang's assessment became the starting point for early Ch'ing efforts to deal with
deficiencies in the use of written examinations to test candidates for
office.[113]

In the preface, Huang Ch'un-yao summarized the history of the selection process, saying that nothing was better than the recommendation system used during the Han and nothing worse than the poetry-prose belles
lettres examinations of the T'ang. Huang noted that Sung literati such as
Wang An-shih had tried to correct the overly literary focus in T'ang
examinations by substituting essays on "classical meanings." Early Ming
emperors had similarly stressed the "meanings and principles" (*i-li* 義理)
of Sung Tao Learning and Han-T'ang scholia for classical learning for the
examination curriculum. In addition, there had been avenues for promotion of officials outside the examination process. But after 1465 only the
civil examinations provided a sure path to "wealth and status." The path
was mainly marked, however, by a candidate's ability to compose eight-
legged style essays with quotations from the Four Books and Five Classics
on the first session of the examination proceedings.[114]

Seeking a middle ground between those like Ch'en Ch'i-hsin who
advocated abolishing the civil examinations and others like Chan Erh-
hsuan who wanted to preserve them intact, Huang Ch'un-yao saw both as
unrealistic extremes. If properly reformed, the examinations could still
serve their purpose. To this end, Huang proposed three major changes in
the late Ming civil selection system: (1) replace the literary focus of *ching-i*
style essays with a concern for more practical learning (*shih-hsueh* 實學); (2)
reinstitute the recommendation system of the Han dynasty as an alternative avenue for selection of officials; and (3) reform the Imperial School

111. Cf. Hummel, ed., *Eminent Chinese of the Ch'ing Period*, p. 492.

112. *Ming-shih*, 10/7258–59.

113. Huang Ch'un-yao, *T'ao-an chi* 陶菴集 (Collection of Huang Ch'un-yao), Chia-ting
edition (1676), 3.1a–14b. See also 2.14b, 2.36a.

114. Huang Ch'un-yao, *T'ao-an chi*, 3.1a–2b.

system so that local schools were more than just venues for examination preparation.[115]

On the first point, Huang stressed that the goal of the classical essay had been to test comprehension of classical techniques for governance (*ching-shu* 經術). Unfortunately, the *ching-i* essay had become a "useless form of empty words" (*wu-i chih k'ung-yen* 無益之空言) that required literati to "waste their spirit" (*lao ching-shen* 勞精神) on literary forms. Huang proposed cutting the number of eight-legged essays required for session one from seven to five. More attention should be given to questions on the second and third sessions of the provincial and metropolitan examinations. The historical, legal, and policy questions of session three deserved higher priority from the examiners.[116]

Revival of Han dynasty recommendation procedures for nominating outstanding men for public office, Huang argued, would also prevent "words on paper" (*yen-tz'u* 言詞) alone from determining who could serve the dynasty. In the name of "practical learning," a constant refrain among Ming reformers, Huang called for selection of "men of wisdom and virtue" (*hsien-liang* 賢良) à la Han, men who would be recommended by local officials. The latter would be punished if their recommendations were tinged with favoritism. Men recommended in this manner would be tested on policy and discourse questions and thus could avoid the formalistic requirements of literary tests. In the early Ming, the Hung-wu emperor had demoted civil examinations in importance and stressed recommendation, a policy that Huang maintained should be reinstituted. In this manner, literati would again "prioritize moral behavior and relegate literary technique" (先德行而後文藝). No longer left out, local worthies could then climb the "ladder of success."[117]

With dynastic schools mainly serving as testing venues, according to Huang, "the bringing forth of human talent today was difficult because it depended on one's own ability to rise." The stress on literary examinations at the expense of schools had been deleterious. It had prevented students in the dynastic schools, from the Imperial School to county, department, and prefectural schools, from performing their function in "transforming the empire via teaching" (*chiao-hua t'ien-hsia* 教化天下). Biennial and triennial examinations empirewide had produced an examination-oriented life among literati seeking public office that kept them from attending to their roles as local leaders and educators. Huang proposed that local licensing and qualifying examinations should be com-

115. Ibid., 3.3a–11b.
116. Ibid., 3.3a–5a.
117. Ibid., 3.5a–8a.

bined so that local scholars would have more time for their other social roles in society. We have seen in Chapter 3 that the combination of local examinations became more common during the Ch'ing dynasty.[118]

In his concluding remarks, Huang Ch'un-yao emphasized that without civil examination reform, "human talent would be daily lost" (人材之日沒也). What the court would get in return, he continued, would be "strange literati" (ch'i-shih 奇士) and not "balanced people" (chung-jen 中人), suggesting the high psychological cost, diagnosed as "stasis," that the examination regime had imposed on young men (see Chapter 6). Huang wrote: "If a classical essay can trouble a balanced person, how much more so a strange literatus." He wondered out loud whether any "balanced people" were among the 300 triennial chin-shih degree-holders. Men who "study things they will never use and later use what they have never studied" (citing Chao K'uang) seemed to him to be the only product of the civil examinations. Huang continued: "Times and circumstances change. Each day is new, and each lunation is different. Is it not painful to say that regarding the great matters of the empire alone we should stick to the way things are?"[119]

Neither Huang, who perished in the Chia-ting massacre of 1645, nor the Ming survived long enough for such proposals to be implemented. In fact, even the interim rebel leader Li Tzu-ch'eng 李自成 (1605?–45), when he captured Peking in 1644, held provincial examinations on the Ming model.[120] Late Ming literati such as Ai Nan-ying and Ku Yen-wu delineated the police-like rigors of the civil examinations in great detail for a literati audience. Ai described in vivid detail the horrors that licentiates faced in local examinations.[121] Ku Yen-wu, in addition to his biting criticism of the memorization of examination essays that became pandemic in late Ming civil examinations, traced the police-like atmosphere of the examination compound to the T'ang dynasty. The result, Ku thought, was a surveillance and control system that was replete with minutely detailed punishments for irregularities but had lost sight of its goal of searching for talent.[122]

Many others such as Huang Tsung-hsi also protested the surveillance excesses of the examination compound and its intimidation of literati, but

118. Ibid., 3.8a–11b.

119. Ibid., 3.11b–14b.

120. Vincent Shih, *The Taiping Ideology: Its Sources, Interpretations, and Influences* (Seattle: University of Washington Press, 1967), pp. 376–77.

121. See *Chih-i k'o-so-chi*, 3.104–113, for Ai Nan-ying's comments; and Lung-chang Young, "Ku Yen-wu's Views," pp. 52–56.

122. Ai Nan-ying, *T'ien-yung-tzu chi,* 3.3a–10a, 28a–30a; and Ku Yen-wu, *Jih-chih lu chih-shih,* 17.406–07. Cf. Lung-chang Young, "Ku Yen-wu's Views," pp. 48–57.

did not overtly challenge imperial control of the examination mechanism.[123] The organization of centralized surveillance linked the autocratic power of the emperor to the lowest levels of power in Chinese society via the bureaucracy and its literati collaborators. As anonymous instruments of this mechanism, sons of elites in effect became the bearers of the power relations undergirding the late empire, which allowed a few of them to enter its political precincts as officials. The Tung-lin and Fu-she successes were noteworthy, however, because for the first time groups of literati had openly targeted the process for the advancement of their political fortunes as a defined group. Before the Tung-lin group, and after the demise of the Fu-she, the literati "partnership" with the throne was premised on the illegality of gentry factions in the government.[124]

What is interesting, nevertheless, is how many of the examination reform themes enunciated in the late Ming were again proposed in the early Ch'ing dynasty. Soon after Ch'ing armies conquered Peking, civil examinations were held in 1645–46 and on a regular basis thereafter. Surprisingly, the Manchu court paid close attention to calls for reform of the civil examinations. Between 1663 and 1787, in particular, the court threw its weight behind efforts to modify the civil examinations along the lines outlined by late Ming critics (see Chapter 10).

## CH'ING EFFORTS TO CONTROL
## LOCAL CANDIDATES, 1650–1850

During the Ch'ing dynasty, the Manchu throne felt perennial uncertainty about how to control the recruitment of *t'ung-sheng* 童生 candidates who took dynastic school entry examinations in local counties and departments. As the first step of the process of selection, the local examinations were also the furthest away from the direct control of the court in Peking. With the decline of education officials in the late Ming, only the provincial education commissioners and the prefects and magistrates were reliable tools for monitoring local education. The chronology of Manchu policy toward this unfolding difficulty is presented to highlight how much local resistance there was to Ch'ing control of examination spectacles. The court also realized that its policies were under constant assault.[125]

123. David Nivison, "Protest against Conventions and Conventions of Protest," in Arthur Wright, ed., *The Confucian Persuasion* (Stanford: Stanford University Press, 1960), pp. 177–201. See also William Theodore de Bary, trans., *A Plan for the Prince: Huang Tsung-hsi's Ming-i tai-fang lu* (New York: Columbia University Press, 1993), pp. 111–121.

124. See my "Imperial Politics and Confucian Societies in Late Imperial China," pp. 390–93.

125. For discussion, see Makino Tatsumi 牧野巽, "Ko Enbu no seiin ron," pp. 227–28.

*Illiteracy*

In 1652, during the Shun-chih reign (1644–61), for instance, the emperor decreed that local candidates should be registered in groups of five to take the local examination and that the five should be checked for accurate registration as a group. Thus not only would the government hold the candidate, his family, and his recommenders responsible for his actions inside the yamen compound; in addition, groups of candidates would serve as mutually responsible units to monitor each other's behavior. This borrowed a page from the *li-chia* 里甲 local responsibility units created during the Ming to collect taxes and supervise local corvée labor.[126] In addition, it was stipulated that those who were illiterate in the grammar and principles (*wen-li pu-t'ung che* 文理不通者; see Chapter 5 for discussion of what constituted classical literacy) of the Classics should not be permitted to enter official schools. Those who presented false registration papers, bribed education officials, and so forth were to be immediately prosecuted.[127]

In 1700, during the K'ang-hsi reign (1662–1722), the court decreed that if there were examination papers that were illiterate (*huang-miu pu-t'ung* 荒謬不通; i.e., "preposterous"), then the county and prefecture examinations should both be sent to the education commissioner for immediate review. It was becoming clear that local education officials were being bribed to permit classically illiterate commoners into the yamen compounds. In the early eighteenth century, then, the Ch'ing court no longer trusted its magistrates alone to select the candidates eligible to become licentiates.

This problem remained unresolved in 1723, when the Yung-cheng emperor (r. 1723–35) ordained that *t'ung-sheng* examination papers had to be reevaluated by the prefecture and education commissioner before licentiate status could be granted. Those who were immoral (*pu-tuan chih shih* 不端之士) must not be granted such status. The Yung-cheng emperor also ordered that for both the local licensing and qualifying examinations, the education commissioner must explain on the papers that were not passed why they were not selected. To further augment local morality, the court commanded in 1725 that when *t'ung-sheng* were reexamined for the licensing and qualifying examinations, they must write from memory a section of the *Sheng-yü kuang-hsun* (Amplified Instructions for the Sacred Edict), a practice that had been required since the K'ang-hsi era for licensing examinations (see Chapter 1).[128]

126. Huang Ch'ing-lien, "The *Li-chia* System in Ming Times and Its Operation in Ying-t'ien Prefecture," *Bulletin of the Institute of History and Philology* (Academia Sinica, Taiwan) 54 (1983): 103–155.

127. *Ch'in-ting Ta-Ch'ing hui-tien shih-li*, 386.1a–2a.

128. Ibid., 386.2a.

*Local Military Examination Candidates*

Beginning in 1731, however, a new problem began to bedevil the court. Although local magistrates and prefects were civil officials, they were also responsible for supervising and grading local licensing and qualifying examinations for the military bureaucracy (*wu-chü* 武舉). This required literati oversight of military guard selection in local communities. Provincial education commissioners, magistrates, and prefects thus had to master the Chinese military Classics dating from antiquity, which were tested as required texts on the military examinations.[129]

In this regard, interestingly, the classical literacy levels of local candidates for civil and military degrees were becoming roughly the same, and candidates were legally permitted since 1713–14 during the K'ang-hsi reign to cross over and take either examination for licentiate status.[130] Although this privilege was revoked in 1741, the Ch'ien-lung emperor in 1744 required all local education officials to call all civil and military licentiates together each month to recite together the expanded version of the Sacred Edict. In some cases, civil candidates had been permitted to take the military versions of the provincial and metropolitan examinations for the *chü-jen* and *chin-shih* degrees, which represented successful maneuvering by lower elites within the system to satisfy their interests.[131]

The permission for *t'ung-sheng* and *sheng-yuan* to cross over legally and take either examination made the process of checking the identity of candidates in local examinations doubly difficult, however. Correct registration for the examination of military *t'ung-sheng* in the outdoor (physical) and indoor (written) sessions at the yamen was needed to prevent fraud. Already in 1723, the court complained that some "civil and military licentiates are premeditated murderers" (*mou-sha ku-sha* 謀殺故殺) and ordered that their crimes must be punished. In 1727, the K'ang-hsi policy was reversed by the Yung-cheng emperor and military students were again forbidden to take civil exams.[132]

The language of the court in 1733 showed how far local degree candidates were from the ideal, refined literatus. Now "gentry bullies" (*hao-shen* 豪紳) were singled out as a type to prohibit from taking the licensing examination. In 1735, the court prescribed local education officials up to the education commissioner to supervise the civil and military *t'ung-sheng* more carefully to prevent wrongdoing. In 1736, the first year of the Ch'ien-lung reign, this policy was expanded to include an order that at the renewal examination for civil and military licentiates, the education

129. See Sawyer, trans., *The Seven Military Classics of Ancient China*, pp. 16–18.
130. *Ch'ing-pai lei-ch'ao*, 21.6–7.
131. Ibid., 20.167–70. See also *Ch'in-ting Ta-Ch'ing hui-tien shih-li*, 382.5a.
132. *Ch'in-ting Ta-Ch'ing hui-tien shih-li*, 383.4a, 386.2b; and *Ch'ing-pai lei-ch'ao*, 20.169.

commissioner for each province should report on each licentiate's behavior. Those who committed transgressions had to be removed. Too many undesirables were gaining access to the civil and military selection process.[133] Later, in 1820, the sons and grandsons of yamen clerks were no longer permitted to take civil examinations for civil appointment, which had been briefly granted. Instead they were permitted to take only local military examinations for military guard positions. The narrowing of social statuses between literati elites, commoner clerks, and military families was becoming difficult to prevent when each group was to some degree classically literate.[134]

Although the long-standing civilian triumph over military men through examination prestige was generally accepted by Han Chinese, this goal was complicated by the fact that the Manchu conquering elite came from warrior banners that had eliminated the Ming dynasty and placed the Han military directly under its command. Even though bannerman examinations had been held for Han Chinese in the banners as early as 1629, bannermen initially were not allowed to take the civil examinations after the Ming dynasty was defeated, in order to maintain their martial traditions and prevent their changing from military men to civilian officials.[135]

After 1652, however, bannermen were permitted to compete in the regular civil examinations, although following 1665 they could also opt to take translation examinations.[136] The prestige of the former, however, meant that many bannermen who became classically literate preferred the regular path to office to taking military slots kept for the banners.[137] Nonetheless, most bannermen remained military men, and corruption in the bannerman translation examinations in the capital, where the Manchu, Mongol, and Han banners were entrenched, was rife.[138] In addition, between 1655 and 1904 only one Manchu bannerman (in 1883) was ever ranked high enough by the usually Han Chinese chief and associate examiners to finish among the top three finishers on the metropolitan or palace examination.[139]

133. *Ch'in-ting Ta-Ch'ing hui-tien shih-li*, 383.3a–b, 383.15a.

134. Ibid., 386.14a.

135. *Ch'ing-pai lei-ch'ao*, 20.8–9.

136. Ibid., 21. 65–66. Such translation examinations were stopped between 1698 and 1718. They were dropped again in 1838 and resumed in the 1870s.

137. Wakeman, *The Great Enterprise*, pp. 888–89, 1041, 1041n99.

138. *Ch'ing-pai lei-ch'ao*, 21.57–58. See, for example, the 1758 bannermen examination, in which a riot broke out when the Hanlin examiner prevented Manchu candidates from passing information or using hidden notes on the examination, which is described in my *Classicism, Politics, and Kinship*, pp. 107–08.

139. *Ch'ing-pai lei-ch'ao*, 21.127. Shang Yen-liu 商衍鎏, a Chinese bannerman, finished third in the 1904 palace examination. See *Hui-shih t'ung-nien ch'ih-lu* 會試同年齒錄 (Record of same year metropolitan graduates), 1904: 1a. There was one Mongol *optimus* in 1865.

## Ch'ien-lung Era Developments

Throughout the Ch'ien-lung reign, a reformist period for the civil examinations (highlighted in Chapter 10), the court complained that required procedures in the local licensing examinations were regularly abused. The complaints for the most part repeated those made in the Ming. In 1738, education officials were told to watch for cases where a candidate had someone else take the examination for him. Again in 1743, the issue of fraud where someone else took the candidate's place in the examination was raised. Now, however, the court decided that physical punishment for imposters was required. If caught, such people should get eighty blows.[140]

The increasing numbers of local candidates was also causing concern. To alleviate the pressure on local officials, the Ch'ien-lung emperor in 1743–44 considered eliminating t'ung-sheng quotas in prefectural examinations. Selection was to be based solely on the quality of candidates' papers (wen-feng kao-hsia 文風高下). The rationale for this change referred back to a 1700 precedent for removing t'ung-sheng quotas. Instead, it was recommended that, for each place in the prefectural school, officials would select fifty candidates from civil and twenty from military examinations. Fearing the practical effects of removing quotas, the court stressed that those papers that were classically illiterate must not be selected.[141]

Nevertheless, examination fraud remained evident. In 1745 in Chiang-su province, some candidates took the sui-k'ao examinations in several places; some sold examination papers. Again, the court asked for more careful supervision of candidate registration by education officials. In 1746, the court reemphasized that the registration information of candidates must be carefully checked in county and department examinations. Those t'ung-sheng caught using false names would have their status removed and would be prosecuted. In 1749, no reexamination was permitted after the formal examination in counties and departments. Papers that were classically illiterate (see Chapter 5) would be thrown away.[142]

The court's litany of transgressions continued in 1752. Candidates were handing in papers using false names; clerks were collecting duplicate papers, sometimes three to four times or four to five times more than the number of candidates. The education commissioner had to report such flagrant cases to the governor for action. The court later noted in 1764 and 1766 that in t'ung-sheng examinations, the registration forms often indicated that the candidate was a youth and yet the person taking the examination was sometimes forty or fifty years old. At the time of registration

---

140. Ch'in-ting Ta-Ch'ing hui-tien shih-li, 386.4a.
141. Ibid., 386.4a–5a.
142. Ibid., 386.5b–6b.

and entry, education officials must compare the forms to the person entering to take the examination to prevent fraud. Education commissioners
had to scrutinize the appearance of candidates more carefully.[143]

To streamline the process, the court in 1758 allowed some local examinations to be consolidated beyond the periodic practice of combining *sui-
k'ao* and *k'o-k'ao* (see Chapter 3). Normally each county held its own examination for *t'ung-sheng*. In cases where two counties were in the same city,
such as Yang-hu and Wu-chin in Ch'ang-chou, then they could hold the
licensing and qualifying examinations together. Because the county was
the beginning of the selection of the literatus, and local examination
papers were sent to the prefecture and then to the education commissioner for review to prevent fraud, this new procedure meant that the education commissioner, and his staff of clerks and advisors, could supervise
examinations in two counties at once.[144]

### The Spread of Corruption to 1820

Beginning in 1767, another set of problems beset the court. Candidates
were changing their names after registration, and names no longer agreed
with their previous examination papers. The officials advising the Ch'ien-
lung emperor correctly perceived that the examination papers were being
tampered with by the examiners themselves, who were colluding with candidates to overcome the rules preventing the latter's pursuit of their private interests. To remedy this crime, the emperor ordered that local education officials should not be permitted to read local examination papers,
a procedure the Yung-cheng emperor had reinstituted (see Chapter 3).
Nor should local academy heads be invited to read examination papers in
the yamen. By 1792, reports noted that the reading and grading of local
county and prefectural examination papers were full of problems.
Everywhere the members of an official's staff (*mu-yu* 幕友) were becoming
the de facto examiners by reading and evaluating papers for the magistrate and prefect, and illiterate papers were routinely accepted. This practice of allowing one's yamen staff to read papers had to be corrected and
those involved punished.[145]

Given the increase in *t'ung-sheng* candidates (e.g., the number of candidates in Chiang-hsi province competing in 1803 for a single place was
now several hundred), irregularities in the local examinations increased.[146]

143. Ibid., 386.7a–9a.
144. Ibid., 386.7a–8a.
145. Ibid., 386.9a–11b.
146. Ibid., 386.12a–19a. In 1829, for example, candidates who were caring for their parents and thus unable to participate in local examinations were permitted to purchase licentiate degrees.

One legitimate loophole that had existed since Ming times was partially closed in 1807. In the Ming, sons of officials had been granted the privilege of taking local and provincial examinations in the capital region, if their fathers were serving away from their home province. By the late Ming, this avenue was frequently followed by southern families, whose sons faced stiffer odds passing civil examinations in the more populous and culturally advanced provinces in the Yangtzu delta and southeast coast. After 1807, those registering in Shun-t'ien prefecture for local examinations were expected to have resided there for an appropriate time (usually twenty years) before such registration could be granted. Moreover, such special registrations would supposedly be checked, and fraudulent candidates would be punished.[147]

But the procedures to monitor the registration of degree candidates could also lead to false charges, as in the 1819 case in which a man accused his elder cousins of dual registration and then purchasing a degree in a locality other than where they had been born. The two cousins, although eventually exonerated, became overwrought emotionally and allegedly died as a result of the case.[148] After 1820, the Tao-kuang court (1821–50) sought to enforce the rules in place without taking any major new initiatives. A notice that those who tampered with or rearranged the official ranking list after an examination would be punished suggested that after the papers had been graded, the final rankings were sometimes ignored. Cases of imposters taking examinations for candidates were still frequent, and in 1824 the court stipulated that candidates taking the licensing reexamination would not be permitted to extend their time using candles on the examination. Here, the court was adding a time distinction between the regular licensing examination and the frequent reexaminations (*fu-shih* 覆試), which were instituted at all levels in the nineteenth century (see Chapter 10). When results were in doubt, the tendency was to repeat the examination.[149]

The need to correct irregularities in the registration process for the local examinations was repeated in 1826. In 1827, the court appealed to local officials not to engage in immoral behavior such as adultery. Such behavior not only was immoral but could easily compromise their impartiality in the examination process. That same year a request to allow sons and grandsons of yamen clerks to take the military examinations, as granted earlier in 1820, was approved in an imperial edict. This policy can be

147. Ibid., 386.12a–12b.
148. Derk Bodde and Clarence Morris, *Law in Imperial China* (Philadelphia: University of Pennsylvania Press, 1973), p. 408.
149. *Ch'in-ting Ta-Ch'ing hui-tien shih-li*, 386.13b–15a.

interpreted as an effort to reduce the dependency of clerks on bribes and payoffs from examination candidates. In addition, for the first time yamen clerks were permitted to purchase lower degrees. Although the door to local degrees was widening to include clerks, the court in 1829 made it clear that anyone legally indicted could not take civil or military licensing examinations. In addition, merchant influence in Canton examinations due to illicit profits made in the opium trade became a new source of worry.[150]

## Purchase of Local Degrees to 1850

Between 1837 and 1848, the regulations for local purchase of licensing degrees were clarified. In the middle of the nineteenth century, the Ch'ing dynasty entered a second protracted period (the first since the 1670s)[151] when the court used the sale of local degrees to pay for military campaigns. In 1815, commoners were already allowed to purchase local degrees in their place of birth to raise funds for the court. In 1824, the sons and grandsons of those in An-hui province who donated supplies for military campaigns in the middle Yangtzu region were permitted to purchase degrees. In 1829, this policy was expanded to include permission for those caring for their parents (and thus unable to take examinations) to purchase degrees.[152]

Table 4.6 demonstrates the secular trends that were affecting the Ch'ing bureaucracy in the eighteenth and nineteenth centuries as a result of these changes. As the regular degree route in this representative sample of officials' qualifications decreased by over 25%, from 73% in 1764 to 44% in 1871, the percentage of officials who purchased their initial degrees increased precipitously by 27%, from 22% in 1764 to 51% in 1871. Table 4.7 gives figures for the number of dynastic school degrees by province that were purchased before 1850. The average cost for *chien-sheng* status was more than one hundred taels, and nine provinces sold over ten thousand such degrees in the first half of the Tao-kuang reign. This declined to six provinces selling more than ten thousand degrees in the period from 1836–50.

What these two tables reveal, however, is the degree to which the government succumbed to the pressures of outside fund-raising that it had fought against in its detailed rules and enforced regulations against corruption inside examination compounds. The sale of 315,000 degrees in

150. Ibid., 386.16a–18a. See also Hsu K'o, *Ch'ing-pai lei-ch'ao*, 21.86.

151. *Kuo-ch'ao Yü-yang k'o-ming-lu*, 4A.19a–24, describes how many degrees were sold for approximately one hundred taels each in a local area between 1678 (34 purchased) and 1682 (45 purchased). A peak of 106 degrees were purchased in Yü-yang in 1679.

152. *Ch'in-ting Ta-Ch'ing hui-tien shih-li*, 386.13a, 15b, 18a, 19a–b.

1820–50 resulted in a lowering of classical standards, which Chang Chih-tung, then Hu-pei education commissioner, noted in an 1868 memorial to the throne. Errors in the *t'ung-sheng* examination papers were so common that Chang counted over fifty papers on one examination alone that were classically illiterate. Chang noted that this was in part the result of the ravages of war. In addition, cheating was still rampant, according to Chang, who emphasized to the court the need to return to rigorous standards of earlier periods. The irony was not missed: an education commissioner was now lecturing the court about public morality and examination discipline, which had been compromised by the sale of licentiate and dynastic school degrees.[153]

As the court tried vainly after 1800 to stem the tide of foul play in its examination halls, the increasing tendency for the government to sell licentiate degrees to raise funds in an era of military troubles served to exacerbate the demographic nightmare that was fueling the resistance to the dynasty's increasingly rhetorical appeal to fairness and morality in the examination market. Bribery in the yamen compounds between candidates and examiners was now replaced by the legitimate purchase of degrees. In the Tao-kuang era, what earlier was deemed corruption was now legalized in the flurry to sell degrees to raise money. Efforts to counteract this pernicious trend were only partially successful during the T'ung-chih Restoration (1862–74), one of whose priorities was the abolition of the sale of degrees.[154] Feng Kuei-fen 馮桂芬 (1809–74), then a leading reformer and a Hanlin academician since 1840, noted correctly:

> In the past ten years [the 1850s], sales of rank have been frequent, and civil government has therefore been weakened. When civil government is weakened, social ferment becomes critical; when social ferment becomes critical, the public revenues are strained; when the public revenues are strained, there is increased sale of rank. This is the way in which one rebellion leads to another. In discussion of present-day governance, I consider the abolition of sale of rank to be the first principle.[155]

## CONTROLLING LOCAL LICENTIATES, 1650–1800

If monitoring some 2 million to 3 million *t'ung-sheng* candidates for biennial local examinations empirewide was increasingly futile by 1800, the Ch'ing court's efforts to supervise and control its half-million licensed

153. Ibid., 386.19b–20b.

154. See Mary Wright, *The Last Stand of Chinese Conservatism: The T'ung-chih Restoration, 1862–1874* (Stanford: Stanford University Press, 1957), pp. 79–87.

155. Feng Kuei-fen, *Chiao-pin-lu k'ang-i* 校邠廬抗議 (Protests from the hut of revision), 1897 edition (reprint, Taipei: Wen-hai Press), 1.17b–19a. Translated in Mary Wright, *The Last Stand of Chinese Conservatism*, p. 85.

degree-holders was equally difficult. In 1651, during the Shun-chih reign, the court consciously tried to use the levers of promotion and demotion to keep lower-degree holders in line. Local officials were commanded to abrogate licentiate status for those who committed crimes. Their examination papers at the renewal examinations would be dismissed unread.[156]

Furthermore, the emperor, fearing resurgence of late Ming–style political dissent among degree-holders, forbade in 1651 any further establishment of academies, to prevent Tung-lin or Fu-she style factions from recurring. This fear continued into the early years of the K'ang-hsi reign. The emperor noted in 1662 that local licentiates should be concerned with their "training to become a literatus" (shih-hsi 士習) and should not be involved in forming factional alliances. In 1663, the K'ang-hsi emperor added that local officials were not reporting mediocre students in dynastic schools, and educational commissioners were lax in their duties.[157]

### The Character Question and Yung-cheng Reforms

By 1723, during the Yung-cheng reign, the court deliberately changed its policy toward sheng-yuan. When evaluating examination papers of licentiates, educational commissioners were now told to note both the literary (wen-li 文理) and moral qualities (p'in-hsing 品行) of the candidate. In 1726, the Yung-cheng emperor appealed to all licentiates to recognize that they were the top of the "four classes" (ssu-min chih shou 四民之首) and should set an example, rather than deluding others and betraying the sages' teachings. If literati training were immoral (shih-hsi pu-tuan 士習不端), then "how could one expect the customs of the people to become correct?" (民風何由而正).[158]

Accompanying this effort at moral suasion, the court revealed that although it would reward examination success with political status, the government would also punish those licentiates who were not acting properly by removing that official status. The language of criticism that the Yung-cheng emperor addressed to his licentiates in 1726 contrasted sharply with his high-minded moral appeals. He contended that literati were now setting a bad example and bullying the people, thus ruining public morals. It was the job of local education officials to punish those transgressing what was right and to restore public morality. The Yung-cheng emperor's efforts to revive the official status of lowly education officials (see Chapter 3) by appointing provincial chü-jen and low-ranking

156. Ch'in-ting Ta-Ch'ing hui-tien shih-li, chüan 卷 383, presents efforts to control local sheng-yuan 生員. See 383.1a–2a.
157. Ibid., 383.2a–3a.
158. Ibid., 383.3b–4b.

*chin-shih* graduates to such posts must be seen in light of the court's efforts to find new ways to control what it perceived as the wayward tendencies of myriad licentiates who failed to move up the ladder of civil or military examinations.[159]

What troubled the court was that examination officials took the grading of anonymous papers as their chief responsibility and did not pay enough attention to the immorality of the literati or the collapse of public morals. One way to improve public morals, the Yung-cheng emperor contended, was to charge the provincial governor and education commissioner with monitoring each other's activities in educational activities. In addition, the court reverted to the Ming pattern of appointing provincial education commissioners from the Hanlin Academy.

In the early Ch'ing, most commissioners had been selected by the ministries or by the censorate. As early as the K'ang-hsi period in 1684, it became normal policy to appoint Hanlin academicians as education commissioners. The Yung-cheng emperor firmly reinstated this policy to transmit imperial influence directly down to local educational and examination levels. By appointing men from the Hanlin, the Yung-cheng emperor tried to use the position of provincial education commissioner to carry out the reforms he planned to control local licentiates.[160]

Among his reformist plans, the emperor initiated a special examination for those licentiates recommended by the educational commissioner for their moral behavior (*jen-p'in tuan-fang* 人品端方), after each commissioner completed his three-year term in the province. Commissioners could recommend four to five candidates in a large province or two in a small province. The emperor would personally test such candidates in a special examination in the capital. This policy represented a return to the Han dynasty precedent for recommendation of outstanding local talents (see Chapter 1), which was now meant to complement the formal system for examination and reexamination of local candidates.[161]

In 1727, the emperor prepared an edict stressing the imperial version of the social mobility myth that was at the heart of the civil selection mystique since antiquity. Citing the *Documents Classic,* he noted that the

159. Ibid., 383.5a–5b. On the Yung-cheng era rehabilitation of education officials, see Araki Toshikazu 荒木敏一, "Chokusho kyōgaku no sei o tsujite kantaru Yōsei chika no bunkyō seisaku" 直省教學の制を通じて觀たる雍正治下の文教政策 (Yung-cheng era educational policies viewed through the provincial education system), in *Yōsei jidai no kenkyū* 雍正時代の研究 (Kyoto: Tōmeisha, 1986), pp. 284–308.

160. *Ch'in-ting Ta-Ch'ing hui-tien shih-li,* 383.5b. See Araki, "Yōsei jidai ni okeru gakuchin sei no kaikaku," pp. 503–18.

161. Ibid., 383.6a–6b. See also Feng Meng-chen 馮夢禎, *Li-tai kung-chü chih* 歷代貢舉志 (Accounts of the civil examinations over several dynasties) (Shanghai: Commercial Press, 1936), pp. 1–3.

dynasty's search for talent had successfully reached to the lowest levels of society and brought order to all the regions (野無遺賢，萬邦咸寧).[162] Yet the number of candidates recommended for their moral qualities had been very low. The Yung-cheng emperor wondered out loud: "How from among the hundreds of licentiates and tribute students in local schools,...no candidates of high moral quality were recommended?" The emperor stressed that he preferred practical men over those with only literary talent. He reiterated that the same moral standards should hold for the Manchu, Mongol, and Han bannermen recommended for office.[163]

From 1728 until 1730, the Yung-cheng court kept up its pressure to improve the moral character of its degree-holders. Yet it was duly noted that the educational commissioners still had not recommended many local licentiates for their moral qualities. Outstanding students should be selected to enter the Imperial Schools, while those of inferior talent had to be removed, the court repeated. All licentiates should take the understanding of principles (*i ming-li wei-chu* 以明理為主) as their task, and all immoral words (*wang chih yü* 妄之語) should be eliminated.[164]

In 1729, the court complained that education officials continued to value literary talent over moral qualities. As a result, those inferior in virtue were not punished, and those superior were not rewarded. To drive its point home, the Yung-cheng court drew on the 1652 precedent for registering *t'ung-sheng* candidates in groups of five (see above) and set up local groups of five licentiates who would be monitored together to evaluate their moral qualities and behavior and held responsible for the transgressions of any one of them. The emperor also decreed that in the renewal examinations, the local records should note any immoral behavior of these groups of licentiates. Those deficient should lose their status and privileges. In 1730, the emperor complained that although the provinces had finally started to recommend men of moral character for entry into the Imperial School, the recommendations still did not document any actual deeds that merited such recommendations.[165]

## The 1733 Boycott

The Yung-cheng era of reformism closed, however, with a local examination boycott that highlighted the tensions between local licentiates and the court's reformers. In 1733, local licentiates throughout Kai-feng prefecture

162. See *Shang-shu t'ung-chien* 尚書通檢 (Concordance to the Documents Classic) (reprint, Peking: Ch'ao-jih wen-hsien Press, 1982), p. 2 (03:0050).

163. *Ch'in-ting Ta-Ch'ing hui-tien shih-li*, 383.7a–7b.

164. Ibid., 383.9a–10a.

165. Ibid., 383.10b–12a.

in Ho-nan province boycotted the renewal and qualifying examinations in their counties because the new education commissioner had been overly strict in efforts to prevent absenteeism (*ch'ueh-k'ao* 缺考) or examination skipping (*pi-k'ao* 避考) in the prefecture. By 1700, most local examiners had given up trying to keep track of every licentiate who was supposed to appear at the biennial *sui-k'ao* renewal or triennial *k'o-k'ao* qualifying examination. The boycott represented the only public means by which licentiates could protest the return to an unrelenting examination regime. They refused to enter the compound.[166]

The court commented on the case in 1734 by noting that local problems with licentiates had reached such a sorry state that licentiates now dared to boycott examinations to protest the government's efforts to control their examination behavior. This betrayed the dynasty's largess toward literati in setting up the evaluation process to select them for office, the emperor wrote in an edict. Candidates should have voiced their protests to the appropriate officials and not have used the examinations to stage a protest. It was decreed that all those who out of selfish concerns (*ssu-hsin chih fen* 私心之忿) boycotted civil examinations in Ho-fei and Ho-nan should not be permitted to take future examinations. Moreover, if groups united to boycott future examinations, as occurred in 1733, the civil and military examinations would be stopped altogether in that area. Education officials who incited candidates to such acts would be dismissed from their posts.[167]

### Ch'ien-lung Era Reformism

Reformist zeal continued during the Ch'ien-lung reign. In 1736, the education commissioner for each province was asked to report on each candidate's behavior at the renewal examination for civil and military licentiates. Those who committed transgressions should be removed. But in 1739, cases of illegal behavior by local students in the Chih-li capital region, and in Hu-nan and Fu-chien provinces, were again brought to the court's attention. The emperor wrote that such acts betrayed the confidence that the dynasty had placed in literati, many of whom no longer were models for the people to emulate. Local officials were once more exhorted to be more vigilant in handling such cases. In addition, a new policy advocated by Ch'en Hung-mou 陳弘謀 (1696–1771), then a

166. See Araki Toshikazu 荒木敏一, "Yōsei ninen no hikō jiken to Ten Bunkei" 雍正二年の罷考事件と田文鏡 (T'ien Wen-ching and the 1725 examination boycott), *Tōyōshi kenkyū* 東洋史研究 15, 4 (March 1957): 100–104. Araki also attributes the boycott to efforts to get *sheng-yuan* to fulfill their corvee labor obligations. See pp. 104–10.

167. *Ch'in-ting Ta-Ch'ing hui-tien shih-li*, 383.12b–13a.

provincial official, sought in 1741 to require all *chin-shih* and *chü-jen* candidates to provide written proof that they had no unburied corpses of relatives at home or in temporary burial. The recommended statute was not adopted because court officials deemed it unenforceable and likely to become the pretext for baseless charges against legitimate candidates.[168]

As Chapter 10 relates, the 1740s represented a period of major reassessment of the civil examinations by the Ch'ien-lung court. Irregularities and crimes in the provincial examination halls and local yamens had reached a level that already threatened the viability of the selection process. In 1741, for instance, an examination scandal surfaced in Shan-hsi province in which the Manchu education commissioner there had been selling both civil and military *sheng-yuan* degrees since 1740. After an investigation led by the Manchu governor of Shan-hsi, it was determined that the education commissioner should be sacked. Two prefects were implicated in the crimes and dismissed, but to show its generosity the court retained their services for a period of probation (*ko-chih liu-jen* 革職留任).[169]

In 1745, the perennial problem noted since the Ming dynasty of traveling candidates who did not appear at the dynastic school was addressed. Such licentiates had to inform local education officials if they would not be in attendance; otherwise they would be removed from the roster of names eligible for the renewal and qualifying examinations. In 1746, the issue was again literati behavior, which continued to be distressing for the court. Ritual impropriety (*pu-chih li-i* 不知禮義) was invoked by the emperor as a sign of the decline of public morality. In 1747, the court reiterated that unsavory licentiates had to be investigated and removed if the case warranted it.[170]

In 1750 another bribery scandal rocked the court, one that involved the education commissioner of Ssu-ch'uan province. As in 1741, the case again involved a Hanlin academician who had been sent out to the provinces to serve as education commissioner. The scale of the sale of local licentiate degrees was carefully investigated, and the Ch'ien-lung court learned that both *sheng-yuan* and *chien-sheng* slots were being sold by the commissioner for four to five thousand taels of silver. The demand for degrees was driving the corruption. The emperor noted in his 1752 edict about the case that corruption had reached the precincts of even the palace examination in the inner court. The Ssu-ch'uan case had palace implications, because the accused education commissioner, Chu Ch'üan 朱荃 of Che-chiang

---

168. Ibid., 383.15a–19a. See also Norman Kutcher, "Death and Mourning in China, 1550–1800" (Ph.D. diss., Yale University, History, 1991), who discusses the bureaucratization of mourning practices in the eighteenth century.

169. Huang Kuang-liang, *Ch'ing-tai k'o-chü chih-tu chih yen-chiu*, pp. 266–67.

170. *Ch'in-ting Ta-Ch'ing hui-tien shih-li*, 383.20a–21a.

province, was the son-in-law of Chang T'ing-yü 張廷玉 (1672–1755), an important court minister under both the Yung-cheng and Ch'ien-lung emperors, who had finally retired in 1750. Unhappy with the implications that the court had known about Chu Ch'üan's actions, the Ch'ien-lung emperor decided to allow Chu to expiate his crimes through official work.[171]

Such complaints moved from the plane of moral exhortation to the nitty-gritty problem of gaining mastery over a huge constituency of licentiates that was increasingly outside the government's control. The emperor in 1742 had already contended that local examiners had to get away from purely literary evaluation of examination papers and focus more on moral character.[172] The 1750s and 1760s witnessed a constant barrage of court orders badgering local education officials: (1) they must report on the evaluation of licentiate behavior; (2) local officials must review more carefully the sale of civil degree titles; (3) the moral character of licentiates must be reviewed; (4) those licentiates who lived more than one hundred *li* 里 (1 Chinese mile = 0.555 kilometer) away had to report to local county and department education officials. And again in 1769, the Ministry of Rites set up a special examination for candidates of high moral character who were recommended by education commissioners after completing their three-year term in a province. This time, the Ch'ien-lung emperor established a regular quota for such moral paragons.[173]

Because of earlier corruption cases, scrutiny of provincial education commissioners and local education officials was heightened. For instance, Weng Fang-kang 翁方綱 (1733–1818), a Hanlin member since 1752, had frequently been appointed by the court as a provincial examiner beginning in 1759. Later, in 1764, he was sent out to serve as commissioner of education in Kuang-tung province. After two terms there, however, he was accused of submitting a report on licentiates enrolled in dynastic schools in which the ages of some of the students were wrongly entered. Given the likelihood that foul play was involved, this finding was sufficient to have Weng removed from office, even though he was still technically a Hanlin reader. Weng lived in retirement for a year before he was permitted to return to the Hanlin Academy.[174]

The evaluation process of those of high moral character took hold, finally, in the 1770s and 1780s as education commissioners filled their tri-

171. Huang Kuang-liang, *Ch'ing-tai k'o-chü chih-tu chih yen-chiu*, pp. 268–70.
172. *Ch'in-ting Ta-Ch'ing hui-tien shih-li*, 383.19a.
173. Ibid., 383.21b–24b.
174. Hummel, ed., *Eminent Chinese of the Ch'ing Period*, p. 856.

ennial quotas for special court examinations. In 1789, however, Weng Fang-kang, who had returned to grace and was then commissioner of education in Chiang-hsi province, noted that the recommendation of licentiates of high moral character from the lists of those taking the biennial renewal examination (*sui-k'ao*) had diminished the value of the triennial qualifying examination (*k'o-k'ao*) because moral character was still not evaluated during the latter. The latter was still seen as having little relevance for the special selection of men of moral character but remained the path to high office via the provincial examination. Weng recommended that the evaluation of moral character should take place for both local examinations equally.[175] Things became so difficult that Juan Yuan 阮元 (1764–1849), while education commissioner in Che-chiang province from 1795 to 1798, prepared policy questions for senior licentiates (*yu-hsing sheng-yuan* 優行生員) asking for their recommendations on how to prevent cheating.[176]

## THE SHEER NUMBERS OF LICENTIATES TO 1850

After 1800, beginning with the Chia-ch'ing reign (1796–1820), the court remained on the alert but no longer took an activist stance concerning its local constituency of *sheng-yuan*. In 1811, for example, the court tried to redress the unforeseen consequences of establishing a regular quota for candidates of high moral character by limiting to three the number of such candidates an education commissioner could name when leaving to take another post. In 1819, the court stipulated that licentiates who had their status abolished and wished to reapply to restore that status had to have their case reviewed by local officials. Clearly, one of the consequences of the Yung-cheng- and Ch'ien-lung-era reforms was to remove many licentiates from the local dynastic school rolls.[177]

During the Tao-kuang era (1821–50), the court again tried vigilantly to keep up the local review of licentiates and the increasing number for whom reinstatement was required. In 1824, the court sought to regularize the process of removing or reinstating licentiates by appealing to public standards (*ch'ing-chieh chih kung-ssu* 情節之公私) as the only way to decide such cases. The court correctly perceived that new irregularities were penetrating this poorly supervised path back to respectability by many who had not really reformed their behavior. In 1825, the Tao-kuang emperor

175. *Ch'in-ting Ta-Ch'ing hui-tien shih-li*, 383.25a–b.
176. See *Ch'ing-tai ch'ien-ch'i chiao-yü lun-chu hsuan*, pp. 356–57.
177. *Ch'in-ting Ta-Ch'ing hui-tien shih-li*, 383.26a–27a.

issued an edict that rebuked the literati, the head of the "four classes," for failing to live up to their role as models for the people.[178]

The degree to which the selection of candidates of high moral character had been regularized in the early nineteenth century was clear in an 1829 order. The court took to task those education commissioners who were reporting candidates of high moral character by dividing them into first- and second-class examples of moral excellence. This degree of the bureaucratization of morality the court thought disingenuous. In 1835, the emperor decreed that social customs and moral minds went hand in hand and advised local officials to use practical guides to evaluate the status of licentiates and not rely purely on the literary aspects of examinations.[179]

In 1851, however, another local examination boycott occurred, this one in Nan-hai county, in Kuang-tung. Students from the Hsi-hu Academy 西湖書院 had protested against a local prefect, whom they had pressured to favor them on the local examination. When this failed, they refused to allow anyone to enter the yamen to take the examination, hoping thereby to implicate the prefect as the object of the general boycott. The court was furious and ordered that all involved should be punished by not allowing any of them ever to take any more local examinations. This decision followed the 1734 precedent set by the Yung-cheng emperor concerning the 1733 boycott in Kai-feng. On the eve of the Taiping Rebellion (1850–64), the politicization of the civil examinations had become more common, a legacy that was duly noted in an 1856 edict by the Hsien-feng emperor (r. 1851–61).[180]

The sheer numbers of local candidates and licentiates had by 1850 overwhelmed the dynasty's capacity through its education and examination officials to maintain the fairness of the civil selection process. The examination and yamen compounds were filled to the brim, as more and more candidates sought to pass examinations and try at least to gain licentiate status. Table 4.8 reveals, for example, that before 1850 there were over half a million civil licentiates and over two hundred thousand military *sheng-yuan* that local education officials and the provincial educational commissioner had to keep track of. In addition there were more than three hundred fifty thousand dynastic school students (*chien-sheng*) who had achieved licentiate status through irregular means such as purchase of a lower degree.

With a constituency of about 1.1 million degree-holders empirewide, of whom only 2.2% were higher civil and military *chü-jen* and *chin-shih*

178. Ibid., 383.27a–b.
179. Ibid., 383.28a–29a.
180. Ibid., 383.30a–31b. Similar boycotts occurred in 1886 in Hu-nan and An-hui provinces. See 383.35a–b.

degree-holders, the Ch'ing dynasty had its hands full keeping the machinery of county, department, prefectural, provincial, and metropolitan civil and military examinations operating fairly and efficiently.[181] As the population of China rose from perhaps 150–200 million in 1700 to 300 million in 1800, the levels of competition in the cultural prisons of the dynasty became unbearable. Over 3 million t'ung-sheng candidates strained to enter the biennially open doors of local examinations.

After 1850, however, the examination doors were closed in the Yangtzu delta during the Taiping Rebellion (see Chapter 11), and Ch'ing dynasty total population was by then about 450 million. Table 4.9 discloses that degreed literati after 1850 had reached almost 1.5 million, an increase of 36% over pre-Taiping estimates, at a time when the general population had increased about 50%. Almost 650,000 were civil licentiates and another 260,000 were military sheng-yuan. The largest pool of examination candidates were licentiates and irregular students, who were all roughly comparable in classical literacy by 1850. When the more than 2 million non-degreed local candidates for local examinations are added to the total, the Ch'ing dynasty had perhaps up to 3 million classically literate males before 1850, which increased to some 4 million to 5 million after the Taiping Rebellion.

The events after 1850 should not be used as a simple-minded gauge of the successes and failures of a system of bureaucratic reproduction that lasted intact in its late imperial form from 1400 to 1900. Our response to a cultural and educational regime that so many millions of Han Chinese and thousands of Mongols and Manchus before 1905 willingly submitted to, that thousands of others rebelled against, and that many cheated their way into should be more cautious. That fifty thousand to seventy-five thousand or more licensed but nervous male candidates, usually ranging in age from fifteen to fifty, appeared empirewide every three years at the gates of the seventeen provincial examination compounds, when in all likelihood during the late Ming and Ch'ing dynasties only 1% to 3% would graduate, remained unprecedented until the twentieth century, when national examinations became the rule rather than the exception.

A proper assessment of the historical significance of this educational regime and its examination machinery requires a thorough sociocultural study that does not take the nitty-gritty machinery of the late imperial selection process for granted. The "thick description" in this and the pre-

181. Chung-li Chang, *The Chinese Gentry*, pp. 122–41. See also Table 11.1 in Appendix 3; and Carsey Yee, "The Shuntian Examination Scandal of 1858: The Legal Defense of Imperial Institutions" (manuscript, n.d.).

vious chapter about how the civil examinations operated is meant to counteract earlier dismissive scholarly accounts. Otherwise it remains impossible to grasp why it lasted so long. Millions of male Chinese from childhood to old age, as well as their families and kin, dreamed of the chance to enter the examination compounds.

# CHAPTER FIVE

# Classical Literacy
## and the Social Dimensions
## of Late Imperial Civil Examinations

One of the new issues examined in this study is the central role of the official language of the bureaucracy (*kuan-hua* 官話) and classical literacy (*t'ung wen-li* 通文理) in defining social status in late imperial Chinese society. In addition to exploring the social and geographical origins of civil examination graduates, by building on the findings of Ping-ti Ho and others, this chapter delineates how, in the absence of any "public" schools in Ming-Ch'ing China, education in private lineage schools, charity and temple schools, or at home transmitted the classical training needed by young men to pass local licensing and renewal examinations and thereby enter local dynastic schools in counties, townships, or prefectures. An official place in dynastic schools became the typical stepping-stone to further success in provincial and metropolitan examinations.

Past tendencies to research the social status of graduates of the civil examinations, while valuable, have yielded a general misunderstanding of how the monopolization of cultural resources by gentry and merchant elites was put to use. As we shall see, the civil service concealed the process of social selection that resulted from an examination regime designed to measure the merits of literati by testing classical learning in general and Tao Learning in particular. The educational requirement to master nonvernacular classical texts created a linguistic barrier between those licensed to compete in the empire's examination compounds and those who were kept out because they were classically illiterate. In this way, the partnership between imperial interests and the bureaucracy was monopolized almost exclusively in local society by fully literate gentry-merchant elites with some level of degree success.

## SOCIAL REPRODUCTION OF GENTRY ELITES

If the imperial dynasty stressed political reproduction of loyal officials to share power in the bureaucracy, those who participated in the examination process as loyal subjects perceived the system as the most prestigious means to achieve personal, family, and lineage success. Such success, however, required substantial investments of time, effort, and training. For families, clans, and lineages, the dynasty's mechanisms for political selection from the pool of examination candidates translated into targets of local strategies for social reproduction. Accordingly, those who could afford the financial and labor sacrifices (read "investments") needed to prepare young men for the examinations did so without question. The linkage between filial piety and examination success is exemplified in the historical record over and over again by "sacrificing" families and hardworking sons who passed the examinations and rewarded the efforts of their elders. Careerism usually won out over individual idealism among talented young men who occasionally were forced to choose between their social obligations to their parents and relatives and their personal aspirations.[1]

The dynastic school system was limited to candidates already socialized through schooling and family traditions in *kuan-hua* (Mandarin; i.e., the dialect spoken by officials, first based on Nanking in the early Ming and later on Peking after the capital moved there between 1415 and 1422) and literate in classical Chinese. Presuming the ability to read and write already, dynastic schools thus were oriented mainly to examination preparation and not reading, writing, or other more elementary tasks.[2] Initial stages in training and preparing a son for the civil service became the private responsibility of lineages seeking to attain or maintain elite status as gentry families. The civil examinations in particular represented the focal point toward which imperial interests, family strategies, and individual hopes and aspirations were directed. In the absence of alternative careers of comparable social status and political prestige, the goal of becoming an official took priority.

Clear boundaries were erected in elite families to demarcate male education from female upbringing. Women were barred from the examination compounds (except in novels and stories where they posed as men),

---

1. Nivison, "Protest against Conventions and Conventions of Protest," pp. 177–201; and Willard Peterson, *Bitter Gourd: Fang I-chih and the Impetus for Intellectual Change* (New Haven: Yale University Press, 1979), pp. 44–63.

2. See Ridley, "Educational Theory and Practice in Late Imperial China," pp. 145–206.

even though this practice was only culturally enforced and never legally questioned. Although many women were literate since Sung times, this gender split in family literacy remained intact until the seventeenth century, when education of women in elite families became more widespread.[3] Many elite sons received their early classical lessons from their mothers.[4]

The famous Hsu 徐 brothers (Hsu Ch'ien-hsueh 乾學 [1631–94], Ping-i 秉義 [1633–1711], and Yuan-wen 元文 [1634–91]) in K'un-shan 崑山 county, for example, were all educated by their mother early on.[5] Similarly, male members of the New Text "school" of classical learning centered on the Chuang 莊 lineage in Ch'ang-chou prefecture, Chiang-su province, during the late eighteenth century were educated by their mothers.[6] Education for men and women thus meant different things, although the differences were not absolute, especially among elites, and depended on a diffuse Han Chinese gender ideology granting boys competitive access via civil examinations since the T'ang and Sung dynasties to political, social, and economic leadership in society, while at the same time defining women in subordinate roles as wives, mothers, and matriarchs.[7]

State office and local social prestige were monopolized by degree-holders only after 1450, while the uncredentialed, such as merchants, artisans, and peasants, were excluded from high office unless they somehow gained, through testing or purchase,[8] a lower degree. If a degree-holder never held office, nonetheless enhanced social status, labor tax benefits (exemption from corvée labor in the Ming), and legal privileges (commutation of punishments) were important by-products of the selection and

3. For an account of examinations for women in scholar-beauty romances, see Stephen Roddy, *Literati Identity and Its Fictional Representations in Late Imperial China* (Stanford: Stanford University Press, 1998), pp. 172–75, 282n5. For Sung aspects, see Beverly Bossler, "Women's Literacy in Song Dynasty China: Preliminary Inquiries," paper presented at the Song-Yuan-Ming Transitions Conference (Lake Arrowhead, Calif., June 5–11, 1997).

4. Hsiung Ping-chen, "Constructed Emotions: The Bond between Mothers and Sons in Late Imperial China," *Late Imperial China* 15, 1 (June 1994): 97–99.

5. *Ch'ing-pai lei-ch'ao*, 20.33–34, 20.36, also indicates that the Han Learning scholar Chang Hui-yen 張惠言 (1761–1802) was taught by his mother, and also describes "instructions for women" (*nü-shun* 女訓). See also Ko, *Teachers of the Inner Chambers*, pp. 29–67.

6. See my *Classicism, Politics, and Kinship*, pp. 57–59. See also Mann, *Precious Records*.

7. Patricia Ebrey, *The Inner Quarters: Marriage and the Lives of Chinese Women in the Sung Period* (Berkeley: University of California Press, 1993), pp. 21–44.

8. See *Huang-Ming kung-chü k'ao*, 1.104a, on the sale of degrees in the mid-fifteenth century to raise funds to deal with border dangers resulting from the T'u-mu debacle. See also Arthur H. Smith, *Chinese Characteristics* (Port Washington, N.Y.: Kennikat Press, 1894), p. 28, on how the purchase of degrees did not "dampen the ardor of any student."

exclusion process.[9] Even if higher-level provincial and metropolitan examinations were insurmountable hurdles for a young man, achievement of licentiate status in local county-level competition was sufficient social reward to merit the investment of family resources for the required training.[10]

As well-organized kinship groups within gentry society, local lineages, for example, were able to translate social and economic strength into civil service examination success, which in turn correlated with their dominant control of local cultural and educational resources.[11] John Dardess has noted that since the early Ming the Hsiao family 蕭 in T'ai-ho 泰和 county, Chiang-hsi, for example, had maintained a "primary school" exclusively for the tutoring of its children. He concludes: "It was not wealth, not high office, but education that perpetuated a patriline."[12] Later, an increasing number of higher-order lineages empirewide but particularly dense in the south, which were built around corporate estates that united a set of component local lineages, required classically literate and highly placed leaders who moved easily in elite circles and could mediate on behalf of the kin group with county, provincial, and national leaders. Economic surpluses produced by wealthy lineages, particularly in the prosperous Yangtzu delta, enabled members of rich segments of such lineages to gain better access to a classical education and success on civil examinations, which in turn led to increased political and economic power outside the lineage.[13]

In an earlier study, which was based on extensive use of genealogical sources, I was able to document how members of two powerful lineages, the Chuangs 莊 and Lius 劉, in Ch'ang-chou prefecture, Chiang-su province, were able during the Ming and Ch'ing dynasties to foster educational resources for the wider elite socialization of their children in the official vernacular, particularly when as officials their families lived in other provinces, and at the same time how they were able to provide more rigorous schooling at home for both boys and girls in the required classical canon than most families could afford. The success of their young

9. See Bol, "The Sung Examination System and the *Shih*," pp. 155–71; and Murphy, *Social Closure*, pp. 1–14.

10. Maurice Freedman, *Chinese Lineage and Society: Fukien and Kwangtung* (London: Athlone Press, 1971), pp. 68–96; and Chung-li Chang, *The Chinese Gentry*, pp. 32–51.

11. See my *Classicism, Politics, and Kinship*, pp. 22–25, 52–59, for a detailed account of the Chuang and Liu lineages and their educational success in Ch'ang-chou prefecture from the late Ming to late Ch'ing.

12. See Dardess, *A Ming Society*, pp. 56–57, 117.

13. Joseph Esherick and Mary Rankin, eds., *Chinese Local Elites and Patterns of Dominance* (Berkeley: University of California Press, 1990), passim. See also Dardess, *A Ming Society*, p. 70, which notes that the increasing use of silver for financial transactions in the late Ming required local scribes, some of whom acted on behalf of endowed lineages.

men on civil examinations from 1600 to 1800 and their daughters in literature was extraordinary but based on a typical sociocultural pattern.[14]

The Chuangs and Lius accomplished this feat by building on the social and political advantages provided by their complex kinship organizations, the long-term intermarriage strategies between their two successful lineages, and increased corporate investments in lineage land that remained tax-exempt. They were typical of literati families empirewide in their use of their financial resources and charitable estates to further their educational strategies. This cultural approach used by local literati gave such lineages significant schooling advantages when competing with others in the examination market. Indeed, I argue that the Chuangs and Lius in particular possessed the proper linguistic tools and schooling facilities for mastering the official classical canon. The translation of their greater economic assets into superior educational resources was the underlying structural reason why the two lineages became an affinally related "professional elite" whose remarkable success in the imperial bureaucracy in the eighteenth century, although unprecedented, was still an important marker of the overlap in economic wealth, cultural resources, examination success, and political prestige in late imperial China.

Joseph McDermott has shown in his recent research that such educational strategies also played an important role in Hui-chou lineages. McDermott documents how by mid-Ming times lineages in Ch'i-men 祁 門 county, An-hui province, built a hall to worship their ancestors and also set up schools to educate their sons. Such higher-order lineages, because of their corporate responsibilities for component local lineages, required classically literate men and, in some cases, women to socialize with and influence local and empirewide officials and gentry. In Hui-chou, for instance, the leadership of local lineages slowly devolved by late Ming times into the hands of members of the lineage who had achieved licentiate status. Unable to attain public office with just a lower-level degree, such *sheng-yuan* increasingly became the de facto managers of their lineage estates.[15] Economic surpluses produced by wealthy lineages, particularly in

14. For discussion of the Chuangs and Lius, see my *Classicism, Politics, and Kinship*, pp. 36–73. My findings are perhaps unique to the Chuangs and Lius, but the overall cultural strategy they used is still analogous to the earlier findings presented by many others such as Hilary Beattie in *Land and Lineage in China*, passim. Cf. Harriet Zurndorfer, "Local Lineages and Local Development: A Case Study of the Fan Lineage, Hsiu-ning *hsien*, Hui-chou, 800–1500," *T'oung Pao* 70 (1984): 18–59. For discussion of many other relevant primary sources and secondary scholarship, which for reasons of space I cannot cite here, see my *Classicism, Politics, and Kinship*, pp. 15–35.

15. Joseph McDermott, "Land, Labor, and Lineage in Southeast China," paper presented at the Song-Yuan-Ming Transitions Conference (Lake Arrowhead, Calif., June 5–11, 1997), pp. 15, 31–32.

the prosperous Yangtzu delta, thus enabled members of rich segments of such lineages, such as the Yaos 姚 and Fangs 方 in T'ung-ch'eng prefecture, An-hui province, the Wangs 王 and Lius 劉 in Yang-chou prefecture, Chiang-su province, and the Huis 惠 in Su-chou prefecture, Chiang-su province, to have better access to a classical education and success on civil examinations, which in turn led to sources of political and economic power outside the lineage.[16]

Success over time depended on economic resources needed to provide or pay for the protracted education in ancient versions of classical Chinese required of bright young male members of the lineage. Relying on families with a strong tradition of classical scholarship and Mandarin-speaking credentials as a result of office-holding, many "super-lineages" in the Yangtzu delta thus had inherent local advantages for future social and political advancement, when compared with lesser families and lineages. Education was not simply a marker of social status. Within a broader society of illiterates and those only semi-literate or "primer-literate" in vernacular Mandarin Chinese or other regional dialects, control over the spoken word in official life and the written word in classical documents had political advantages.

In a new book, David Wakefield has documented in detail how gentry in Fu-chien province maintained what he has called an "education orientation," in addition to a family and lineage orientation, to execute their private responsibilities in the provision of educational resources and thereby maintain their local social and political dominance. According to Wakefield, the evidence from Fu-chien and Taiwan during the Ch'ing dynasty indicates that even families of modest means established tax-exempt trusts to foster education and examination success. When a family had sufficient financial assets, it set aside income to support young men in the family in their quest for a civil or military degree. The amount set aside for each son was higher for those who competed for advanced degrees such as *chü-jen* and *chin-shih* titles, and substantially less for licentiates.

Citing a 1797 family contract in Fu-chien, for example, Wakefield relates how a certain family there surnamed Han decided, upon the death of the father, to establish an educational trust by investing what remained

16. Patricia Ebrey and James Watson, eds., *Kinship Organization in Late Imperial China 1000–1940* (Berkeley: University of California Press, 1986). See also Beattie, *Land and Lineage in China*, p. 51; and Kai-wing Chow, "Discourse, Examination, and Local Elite: The Invention of the T'ung-ch'eng School in Ch'ing China," in Elman and Woodside, eds., *Education and Society in Late Imperial China*, pp. 197–205; and my *Classicism, Politics, and Kinship*, pp. 6–15.

from his personal retirement trust (*yang-lao* 養老) after paying funeral expenses. The contract stated: "We feel that study can raise social status and that such honors can bring glory to our ancestors.... The educational trust is designed to encourage the grandchildren to succeed [in the examinations] in order to become officials above and bring honor to our homes below." Shares were given out in increasing numbers to family members competing for the higher degree.

A typical trust such as the Han educational trust was designed as an incentive to reward the most successful students in the family. Much less was allocated for those studying for preliminary licentiate examinations. Individual families were expected to provide support for childhood training. Educational trusts were designed to entice adult males to strive for the provincial and metropolitan examinations. *Chü-jen* and *chin-shih* degree-holders, moreover, received the added trust income for the rest of their lives, although they could not pass that income on to their children upon death. Furthermore, when the educational property of the family was divided (*fen-chia* 分家), not only was the income of the educational trust divided among the sons but so were the books, rooms, and other assets.[17]

So successful were the civil service examinations in capturing the fancy of ambitious men and their families that one of the defining characteristics for gentry status became examination success. Social advantages could be easily transmuted into academic advantages (what Pierre Bourdieu would label "symbolic capital" but I call "cultural resources" instead).[18] Wealth and power provided the resources for adequate linguistic and cultural training that would in turn legitimate and add to the wealth and power of a successful candidate in the examination cycle. Once legally enfranchised to compete, merchant families as much as official families saw in the civil service the route to greater wealth and orthodox success and power. As the sine qua non for long-term lineage prestige, success on the imperial examinations and subsequent office-holding conferred direct power and prestige on those most closely related to the graduate and the official. The flow of local prestige went further afield, however, following diverse agnatic routes within the lineage and among affines, if one married into a lineage that had traditionally monopolized local examination quotas.[19]

17. See David Wakefield, *Fenjia: Household Division and Inheritance in Qing and Republican China* (Honolulu: University of Hawaii Press, 1998), pp. 174–78.

18. For discussion, see Elman, *Classicism, Politics, and Kinship*, p. xix.

19. Denis Twitchett, "The Fan Clan's Charitable Estate, 1050–1760," in David Nivison and Arthur Wright, eds., *Confucianism in Action* (Stanford: Stanford University Press, 1959), pp. 122–23; and Rubie Watson, *Inequality among Brothers: Class and Kinship in South China* (Cambridge: Cambridge University Press, 1985), pp. 7, 98, 105, 175.

Merchants, artisans, and other commoners, however, frequently lacked access to the proper linguistic training and educational facilities for mastering literati political and moral discourse. To address this problem, charitable schools (*i-hsueh* 義學), some within but most outside lineages, increasingly were created. They represented the intermingling of gentry charitable institutions, elementary education, and local philanthropy, and complemented "community schools" (*she-hsueh* 社學) set up by the dynasty to deliver instruction to deserving local commoners. In such semi-official charitable institutions, "primer literacy" could commence for an elementary student from a poor family or one from a poorer segment of a well-off lineage. Buddhist temple schools also fulfilled this function. Typically the curriculum in such schools was divided between beginners (*meng-kuan* 蒙館) and more examination-oriented classical instruction (*ching-kuan* 經館).

Lineage-endowed schooling also provided more opportunities for lesser families in the lineage to advance than would have been possible where lineages were not prominent. Corporate descent groups as a whole benefited from any degree-holding member of the lineage, no matter how humble in origins. Accordingly, the failure of families in a lineage to maintain their status as degree-holders for several generations could be offset by the academic success of other agnates or affines. The social mobility of lineages, when taken as a corporate whole, was thus distinct from that of individual families.[20]

Dominant lineages and nouveau riche merchant families in the culturally ascendant Yangtzu delta maintained their high local status through the superior facilities they provided for their talented male children. Lineage schools and merchant-financed academies (in Yang-chou, for example, academies were established by salt merchants for their sons) became jealously guarded private possessions, whereby the elite of local society competed with each other for social, political, and academic ascendancy. Successful corporate estates thus played a central role in perpetuating an economic and political environment in which gentry and merchants, once legally enfranchised, were dominant. The rhetoric of kinship

20. For a detailed discussion of the scope and influence of lineage and charity schools, see Ōkubo Eiko 大久保英子, *Min-Shin jidai shoin no kenkyū* 明清時代書院の研究 (Research on academies in the Ming-Ch'ing period) (Tokyo: Kokusho kankōkai, 1976), pp. 339–49; and Angela Ki Che Leung, "Elementary Education in the Lower Yangtzu Region in the Seventeenth and Eighteenth Centuries," in Elman and Woodside, eds., *Education and Society in Late Imperial China*, pp. 382–91, who stresses their role in elementary instruction. For the role of charitable schools in border provinces such as Yun-nan, see Rowe, "Education and Empire in Southwest China," pp. 427–43.

when translated into local philanthropy favored those already entrenched in local society.[21]

Artisan or peasant mothers and fathers generally could not afford the luxury of years of training for their sons in a classical language divorced from vernacular grammar and native speech. The occasional poor student who toiled in the fields by day and read by oil lamp late into the night in order to pass the examinations was celebrated precisely because he was so rare. Although the civil service competition was theoretically open to all, its content linguistically excluded over 90% of China's people from even the first step on the ladder to success. Unequal social distribution of linguistic and cultural resources based on a Tao Learning curriculum meant that those from families with limited traditions of literacy were unable to compete successfully in the degree market with those whose family traditions embraced classical literacy. The examinations were designed to test the merits of young men, most of whom came from literati or merchant backgrounds.[22]

Rare successes by a few humble candidates helped mystify the examination process. The educational mortality of the lower classes was ideologically legitimated by obtaining from them (with the exceptions of Taoists and Buddhists) the recognition that a classical education represented legitimate grounds for the examination success of literati. Those commoners who were legally eligible but in fact linguistically excluded from the selection process were asked to acknowledge that their lesser fates were due to their lack of classical training. The classically trained elites in turn could blame the classically illiterate for their ignorance.

## SOCIAL ADVANTAGES AMONG GENTRY

Social mobility in late imperial China occurred mainly within the strata of Chinese with the cultural and linguistic resources to prepare their sons for the rigors of an examination cycle based on memorization of ancient texts in archaic classical Chinese. Edward Kracke and Ping-ti Ho have estimated that officials whose immediate male ancestors had commoner status for

21. Evelyn Rawski, *Education and Popular Literacy in Ch'ing China* (Ann Arbor: University of Michigan Press, 1979), pp. 28–32, 85–88.

22. David Johnson, "Communication, Class, and Consciousness in Late Imperial China," in Johnson, Andrew Nathan, and Evelyn Rawski, eds., *Popular Culture in Late Imperial China* (Berkeley: University of California Press, 1985), p. 59, estimates there were at least 5 million classically educated male commoners in Ch'ing times, or roughly 5% of the adult male population in 1800, 10% in 1700. Such rates were likely lower during Ming times, when private schools were less common. See Ōkubo Eiko, *Min-Shin jidai shoin no kenkyū*, pp. 78–85.

at least three generations before they passed the metropolitan examinations comprised 53%, 49.5%, and 37.6% respectively of the Sung, Ming, and Ch'ing *chin-shih* examination rolls they studied. Recent studies suggest, however, that these figures are inflated because they overlook or undervalue the number of those commoners who had officials as relatives from collateral lines in a lineage or from affinal ties to other families. Such collaterals or affines could be decisive in determining the likelihood of academic success of those who at first sight seem to be commoners.[23]

The anonymous character of civil examinations persuaded rulers, elites, and commoners of the viability of the literati dream (and nightmare—see Chapter 6) of public success and social advancement, thereby misrepresenting its objective consequences. As an institution that since the Sung dynasties demanded anonymity for provincial and metropolitan test papers while they were being graded by examiners, and which renounced the arbitrary privilege of hereditary transfer of social and political status, the examination system diverted attention from the de facto elimination that took place prior to examinations.

Measurement of social mobility through examinations by Kracke, Ho, and others thus contains an unforeseen trap. By isolating those who were graduates from the larger pool of examination candidates, and then proceeding to reconstruct the social backgrounds of only the former, this analysis leaves us with a skewed population of "survivors" in the examination process. It would be more useful to stress the role of examinations in creating a broad class of classically literate males that included all who competed in the selection process, including the failures. Earlier analysis missed the relation between examination licentiates and those who were excluded because of their inferior education or legal status. The gatekeeping function of the civil service examinations was an unspoken social goal of the process of selection.[24]

Exclusion of those who lacked sufficient cultural and linguistic resources for training their sons was successfully defended by the imperial ideal of open competition to select the "best and the brightest" in the empire to serve the emperor. The social neutrality of the dynasty was a fiction (the court and its literati in the bureaucracy were partners), and the cultural autonomy of private schools and academies (as long as they did not meddle in politics) was illusory. With such misperceptions most literati refracted the reality of the social structure of classical literacy during the

23. Kracke, "Family vs. Merit in Chinese Civil Service Examinations during the Empire," pp. 103–23; Ping-ti Ho, *The Ladder of Success in Imperial China*, pp. 70–125, especially Table 10 on p. 114; and Hymes, *Statesmen and Gentlemen*, pp. 34–48.

24. Etienne Balazs, *Chinese Civilization and Bureaucracy*, translated by H. M. Wright (New Haven: Yale University Press, 1964), pp. 6–7. Cf. Bourdieu and Passeron, *Reproduction in Education, Society, and Culture*, pp. 141–67.

Ming and Ch'ing dynasties. Examination selection effected an elimination process using classical learning as the criterion for exclusion that was more thorough the less advantaged the social class. The Ming court recognized this phenomenon but tried only to redress the advantages southern elites had over their northern counterparts (see Chapter 2).[25]

Because those who could not qualify to meet the difficult minimal requirements for passing even the lowest-level, three-tiered licentiate examinations (county, department, prefecture) were not randomly distributed among the different social classes in Ming-Ch'ing society, the examination process presented social selection as the selection of talent. Moreover, the stringent requirements of examination and reexamination at the county and department levels to gain admission to prefectural qualifying examinations meant that families dependent on the productive labor of sons in agriculture, crafts, and trade could not provide them with the years of training needed to keep up in the examination process. Moreover, many poorer literati who were burdened with corvée responsibilities in tax or grain collection could not compete in the examination market either.[26]

Excluding the masses of peasants, artisans, clerks,[27] Buddhist and Taoist priests—not to mention all women—from the licensing stage of the selection process ensured that those in the competition were a self-selected minority of young men from literati or merchant families, lineages, or clans with sufficient linguistic and cultural resources to invest in their male children. Gentry monopoly of the cultural and linguistic resources required by the dynasty enabled families of wealth and power to continue to monopolize those resources over several generations. The hereditary transmission of cultural resources during the Ming and Ch'ing replaced the medieval hereditary transmission of official status of the T'ang and Northern Sung (see Chapter 1).

## SOCIAL ORIGINS OF EXAMINATION GRADUATES

In the early Ming, the Hung-wu emperor had ordered the Ministry of Revenue to complete a registration of all households (hu-t'ieh 戶帖) in the realm. The so-called yellow registers (huang-ts'e 黃冊) contained household

25. Cf. Kenneth Lockridge, *Literacy in Colonial New England. An Enquiry into the Social Context of Literacy in the Early Modern West* (New York: Norton, 1974), pp. 3–7; and Bourdieu and Passeron, *Reproduction in Education, Society, and Culture*, pp. 1–27.

26. Eberhard, *Social Mobility in Traditional China*, pp. 22–23. On the impact of the labor services tax on Ming literati, see my *Classicism, Politics, and Kinship*, p. 45.

27. Clerks were banned from participating in Ming examinations in 1384. See Lu Shen, *K'o-ch'ang t'iao-kuan*, 136.4a. Sons of clerks were occasionally permitted to take local licensing examinations during the late Ch'ing. See Chapter 4.

and population records, and the "fish-scale maps and books" (*yü-lin t'u-ts'e* 魚鱗圖冊) comprised the land survey. Tax quotas were established in 1381 for each county and prefecture. Revised in 1391, this massive undertaking aimed at measuring the economic resources under Ming control, equalizing the distribution of the land tax (paid in kind), and obtaining fair labor services from all households. The register reflected the dynasty's assessment of its material and labor resources.[28]

One of the important ways the Ming dynasty was able to measure access to the civil and military examinations, for example, was to use the official classifications of the entire population into social and economic categories (*chi* 籍) determined by the government. These classifications, such as households of commoners, military men, artisans, and merchants, reflected the initial status of each family in the society and how much labor service they had to provide. Each category of household was assigned a specific labor service it had to perform for the bureaucracy, and these tasks were organized according to the *li-chia* 里甲 village-family units of 110 households in each community. A merchant household was expected to supply merchandise or goods on demand; a military family had to provide at least two soldiers for service; an artisan household provided one worker for imperial workshops; and so forth.[29]

The land registers were supposed to be revised every ten years, and each family was required to perform its labor service in perpetuity. The wide gap between the theory and practice of tax collection, however, greatly diminished the dynasty's control of the economy by the sixteenth century. Regional markets gradually turned to a silver currency out of the direct control of the government, confirming the dynasty's weakened hold over its agrarian tax resources.[30] Geared to a village commodity economy circa 1400, the tax system became increasingly obsolete as Ming population rose from 65 million to 150 million and the Ming economy became more commercialized. By 1600, the Ming government had bowed to the inevitable and through the Single Whip Reforms allowed the land tax and

28. Wang Yuquan, "Some Salient Features of the Ming Labor Service System," *Ming Studies* 21 (spring 1986): 1–44.

29. See Langlois, "The Hung-wu Reign," pp. 123–24; and Edward Farmer, "Social Regulations of the First Ming Emperor," in Kwang-Ching Liu, ed., *Orthodoxy in Late Imperial China* (Berkeley: University of California Press, 1990), pp. 116–123. Cf. Ray Huang, *Taxation and Government Finance in Sixteenth-Century China* (Cambridge: Cambridge University Press, 1974), pp. 1–6. Wang Yuquan, "Some Salient Features of the Ming Labor Service System," pp. 26–29, presents forty-seven categories of service households during the Ming.

30. Mi Chu Wiens, "Changes in the Fiscal and Rural Control Systems in the Fourteenth and Fifteenth Centuries," pp. 53–69.

service labor systems to be commuted into a single monetary payment in silver. In terms of its labor resources, however, the early Ming classification of the entire population into social categories remained in existence but not in force.[31]

In addition to determining the tax and labor service obligations of each family, these social classifications provided a partial basis for recording each family member's standing in the legal system and social status in the civil and military examinations. We have seen in Chapter 3, for example, that sons of merchants were for the first time enfranchised during the Ming dynasty to participate in the examination process, while the so-called mean peoples still were not. The goal was to classify individuals in families according to their initial social standing when the dynasty had come to power. In the eighteenth century, the emancipation of labor made such classifications demarcating society moot.[32]

Although not a caste system as such, because it did not legally enforce social statuses on the population, the Ming hereditary categories of "official," "scholar," "commoner," "merchant," "military," and "artisan" families meant that Ming candidates for officialdom were classified according to the original occupations of their families, even when their immediate parents no longer pursued that occupation.[33] Such social classifications, which were supposed to describe a person's official hereditary lot (*fen* 分) and local status but often were out-of-date, were duly recorded in all documents that permitted sons of eligible families to take licensing examinations for the civil service market.

As they proceeded up the "ladder of success," those who came from eligible families still were classified according to their family's social status in the labor service register, even when their families had already entered the upper elite as bona fide literati. In other words, in the late imperial period, society was much more fluid than the Ming classification of corvée labor sources pretended it was, and early Ming social classifications had by the late Ming become anachronistic. This is one of the reasons why the succeeding Ch'ing dynasty stopped keeping track of family status in its registration documents for civil examinations.

31. Ray Huang, *Taxation and Government Finance in Sixteenth-Century Ming China*, pp. 112–33; and von Glahn, *Fountain of Fortune*.

32. In 1771 it was decreed that only in the fourth generation after emancipation could those from previously outcast background take civil examinations. See *Ta-Ch'ing hui-tien shih-li*, 158.32, for the decree of 1771. See also Philip Kuhn, *Soulstealers*, pp. 34–36, on the emancipation of labor in the 1720s.

33. On "literati" as a fiscal category, see Dardess, *Confucianism and Autocracy*, pp. 14–19. On Ming enforcement of social categories, see Ping-ti Ho, *The Ladder of Success in Imperial China*, p. 67.

In 1765, for instance, the Manchu Grand Secretary Fu-heng 傅恒 (d. 1770), among others, prepared memorials specifically requesting that the long-standing distinction between "military officer examination papers" (*kuan-chüan* 官卷) and "commoner papers" (*min-chüan* 民卷) be dropped because sons of military officers were finding the competition among themselves too keen and increasingly were entering the commoner examination group (see also Chapter 4). This indicates that since the early Ch'ing, papers had been divided into separate social categories and graded according to the quota for each social group. In the interest of fairness (*kung-p'ing* 公平), the memorial called for change because this division had outlived its relevance.[34]

Ming non-enforcement of legal barriers to occupational and status mobility had made such official information out-of-date by 1600. By the eighteenth century, the *yin* privilege, whereby sons of officials could inherit their student ranking without taking any examinations, had also receded in social importance when compared to the Sung period. Such appointments, when made, were confined to minor positions in the central government or appointments as subprefect or magistrate.[35] In the early Ch'ing, quotas were set in each province for the number of merchant sons (not sons of commoners who had become merchants) who could take the civil examinations. For every ten such places, only one graduate was allowed, although in the early years the quota was not reached.[36]

Furthermore, after reviewing a 1786 case in Hang-chou, the court reiterated that education officials should not distinguish between those from commoner and merchant families for admission to dynastic schools, solidifying a policy begun in the early Ming, when sons of merchants were for the first time enfranchised to take the civil examinations.[37] In the 1786 case, the examination papers of candidates for provincial examinations from merchant families were placed together with those of commoners.[38] What mattered in the Ch'ing registration process was what official positions a candidate's family had held in the preceding three generations.[39]

34. See the memorials in *Li-pu t'i-pen* 禮部題本 (Memoranda including memorials from the Ministry of Rites), 1765, 5th month, by Grand Secretary Fu-heng et al., collected in the Ming-Ch'ing Archives, Academia Sinica, Taiwan.

35. Wittfogel, "Public Office in the Liao Dynasty," p. 39.

36. See *Ch'in-ting hui-tien shih-li*, 381.1a–3a.

37. *Ch'ing-shih kao*, 11/3150–51; *Ming-shih*, 3/1694; and *Huang-ch'ao hsu wen-hsien t'ung-k'ao*, 1/8423. See also James J. Y. Liu, *The Art of Chinese Poetry* (Chicago: University of Chicago Press, 1962), pp. 26–29.

38. See *Ch'in-ting hui-tien shih-li*, 381.8a–8b.

39. Ping-ti Ho rightly argues that "in Ming times there was a great deal of occupational mobility which eventually resulted in status mobility." See Ho, *The Ladder of Success in*

Table 5.1, for example, presents the social origins of graduates of provincial examinations from the late Ming to the early Ch'ing dynasty. About half of all *chü-jen* in these provinces were of commoner social origins (*min-chi* 民籍), which meant that their families had not been classified as upper elites in the early Ming. By 1552, however, many were de facto part of the upper literati elite. "Commoner" status was also a social rubric for other occupational groups that included literati, farmers, traders, and merchants.[40] For instance, Wang Yang-ming 王陽明 (1472–1528), the renowned military general and moral philosopher of the mid-Ming, came from a Che-chiang family originally classified as "commoners," but his father, Wang Hua 王華 (1453–1522), had been the palace examination *optimus* in 1481 and had risen to become minister of personnel in 1507. Wang's family had long been members of the local elite in Yü-yao 餘姚 county in Ning-po prefecture in spite of their "commoner" status.[41]

The numbers of *chü-jen* from official, artisanal, and merchant families were extremely small, except for the 16% of *chü-jen* who came from special families in the 1591 Che-chiang provincial examination. From 1591 to 1648, the number of *chü-jen* from "special" families declined steadily, down to only 2% in the 1648 Shan-tung provincial examination. Although few families had been officially categorized as "merchant" in the early Ming, by the sixteenth century, those engaged in trade and commerce were still classified according to their family's early social status as commoner, military, or artisan. Interestingly, however, around 20% of the Ming provincial graduates came from military families, whether or not their families were by the late Ming still occupied with military matters. Military officer families were also producing up to 7% of Che-chiang *chü-jen*.

Table 5.2 gives us comparable figures for the social origins of Ming *chin-shih*, which also reveal that except for the early Ming period between 1411 and 1436 (when 76% to 83% came from commoner families) and early Ch'ing (in 1649), usually 55% to 64% of *chin-shih* were commoners. Again, those from special families constituted less than 10%, while over 25% of the *chin-shih* in our sample during the Ming were of military family origins. Usually another 3% to 4% were from military officer families that dated back to the early Ming. Under the Manchus, this group of *chin-shih*

---

*Imperial China,* p. 71. However, such occupational mobility was not a product of the civil examination process, which tended to reward those with educational and cultural resources, regardless of their family's early-Ming occupational status. On the Ch'ing registration for civil examinations, see Zi, *Pratique des examens littéraires en Chine,* pp. 19–21.

40. Ping-ti Ho, *The Ladder of Success in Imperial China,* pp. 70–71.

41. *Tien-shih teng-k'o lu* 殿試登科録 (Record of the civil palace examination), 1499: 9b.

from military families declined substantially, to 13% in 1649 and to only 9% in 1651. Graduates with military officer backgrounds also declined. Ch'ing examinations records, as noted above, thereafter stopped keeping track of such information, in part because the Manchu banners had become the new military elites.

These findings are confirmed by Ping-ti Ho's analysis of *chin-shih* from special statuses during the Ming dynasty, summarized in Table 5.3.[42] Here we see that the military family category, which Ho included in his category of "special" statuses, usually constituted between 17% and 31% of all Ming civil *chin-shih* degree-holders. If we add those who came from military officer families, the percentage of Ming military families producing *chin-shih* increases over time from 18% to 36% of the total.[43] It is noteworthy that only 160 Ming *chin-shih* (0.7%) came from "literati-scholar" ( *ju* 儒) families (usually translated as "Confucians"), while in Ho's pool of 22,604 graduates about 14,500 (56% to 80% over time; 64% overall) usually came from commoner families. Commoners thus became the largest category of *chü-jen* and *chin-shih* degree-holders, even though such "commoners" were usually already members of local literati elites.[44]

Yü Chih-chia 于志嘉 has noted that the Ming differed from the Yuan by permitting sons of military families to register for civil examinations, although there is evidence that this change had commenced in the Yuan. He is also critical of earlier research in China and Taiwan that has underestimated the social status and fluidity of Ming military households. Scholars had argued that during the Yuan dynasty, military sons were permitted to become yamen clerks only if they no longer performed military duties. Such scholars contended that during the Hung-wu reign in the early Ming, the policy toward military households changed only enough to allow sons of military families to take local examinations and attain licentiate status.[45]

42. On the occupational and status mobility of military families, see Ping-ti Ho, *The Ladder of Success in Imperial China*, pp. 59–62.

43. See Table 9 in Yü Chih-chia, "Mindai gunko no shakai teki chi i ni tsuite" 明代軍戶の社會的地位について (The social status of military households in the Ming dynasty), *Tōyō gakuhō* 東洋學報 71, 3–4 (March 1990): 122.

44. On this issue of examinations and social mobility, see the parallel evidence for the Sung dynasty in Hymes, *Statesmen and Gentlemen*, pp. 29–61. Elite social status usually preceded examination success, which confirmed and heightened that status. Ping-ti Ho, *The Ladder of Success in Imperial China*, p. 73, thus overstates the case for social mobility by arguing that "examination became the most important channel of social mobility" since the Sung dynasty.

45. Yü Chih-chia, "Mindai gunko no shakai teki chi i ni tsuite," pp. 91–129. See also Hsiao Ch'i-ch'ing, "Yuan-tai te ju-hu—ju-shih ti-wei yen-chin shih-shang te i-chang," pp. 151–70.

To refute this position, Yü has studied in detail the social standing of the 302 *chin-shih* who passed the 1610 palace examination. The list of graduates is incomplete, but of these, about eighty-eight came from military or military officer families, thus constituting at least 29% of the total of *chin-shih* in 1610. The surviving historical records from that metropolitan and palace examination provide us with reliable information about seventy-seven (25%) of those *chin-shih* who came from military or military officer families. One interesting finding is that among these graduates the designation that they were from military households contrasted with family background information in other palace examinations, in which their brothers or fathers were classified as commoners when the latter became *chin-shih*. Such errors in the *chin-shih* records indicate that by 1610, the categories of commoners and military were not that far apart. Indeed, the *chuang-yuan* in 1610 was Han Ching 韓敬, who came from a Che-chiang military family. His father had been a 1571 *chin-shih*. Despite following in a direct descent line of three generations of Ming officials, Han's family was still listed as a military household.[46]

The records from this examination also reveal that commoner households such as the Chuang lineage in Ch'ang-chou prefecture, from which two brothers became *chin-shih* in 1610, remained classified as commoner households despite their transition to the status of an upper gentry lineage in the late Ming. In the Ming, the Chuangs produced a total of six *chin-shih* degree-holders. In the Ch'ing, the Chuangs became a "super-lineage" that produced twenty-seven *chin-shih* and altogether ninety-seven degree-holders. Eleven Chuangs entered the Hanlin Academy. Of these, two were brothers: one was an *optimus* in 1754 (Chuang P'ei-yin 莊培因 [1723–59]), and another finished third on the 1745 palace examination (Chuang Ts'un-yü 莊存與 [1719–88]). As a combination of literati families of immense wealth and prestige, they remained technically a commoner lineage.[47]

The importance of military families, who had been bequeathed land and wealth in the early Ming by thankful rulers, in the civil service can be traced, at least initially, to the successful translation of their early eco-

46. Yü Chih-chia, "Mindai gunko no shakai teki chi i ni tsuite," pp. 96–106. See also *Wan-li san-shih-pa-nien keng-hsu k'o hsu ch'ih-lu* 萬曆三十八年庚戌科序齒錄 (Record of graduates of the 1610 palace examination), in *Ming-tai teng-k'o-lu hui-pien*, vol. 21, p. 11931; and *Tien-shih teng-k'o lu*, 1610: 1a. On the same examination, the distinguished scholar Ch'ien Ch'ien-i 錢謙益 (1582–1664), who came from a family of scholars, was listed as a commoner in social origins.

47. *Wan-li san-shih-pa-nien keng-hsu k'o hsu ch'ih-lu*, pp. 11727–964, especially p. 11755 on Chuang Ch'i-yuan 莊起元 (1559–1633) and p. 11776 on Chuang T'ing-ch'en 莊廷臣 (1559–1643). For discussion, see my *Classicism, Politics, and Kinship*, pp. 52–54.

nomic resources as military families into sufficient educational resources for their sons to compete successfully in the civil degree market. In addition, military families relied on the Ming military examinations to maintain their social status, although many chose the civil examinations to gain higher status and civilian office. Many men from military households rose to high office in the central bureaucracy, and several, such as Chang Chücheng (see Chapter 4), became Grand Secretaries in the imperial court.[48]

Because tax obligations had to be fulfilled by at least one member of an assigned family, the official statuses used to classify and measure Ming civil service candidates were obsolete by 1600. They do tell us, however, how much had changed after 1400, confirming the existence among merchants and gentry of considerable occupational fluidity and substantial circulation of elites in the examination market.

## GEOGRAPHICAL DISTRIBUTIONS
## OF EXAMINATION GRADUATES

Despite local and provincial quotas for the *sheng-yuan* and *chü-jen* degrees, and regional quotas for *chin-shih*, the Ming and Ch'ing bureaucracies, like that of the Sung, were never able to offset the financial advantages of particular prefectures and counties in the south, which they could translate into superior educational preparation for the civil examination market. Table 5.4 indicates that in the Yangtzu delta province of Chiang-su, for instance, Su-chou and Ch'ang-chou prefectures usually ranked first and second in the Nanking provincial examinations, with Su-chou frequently taking as many as 20% of the places in the most competitive ("gold goes to the *chü-jen*") examinations in the empire. This despite the efforts by the first Ming emperor (see Chapter 2) to curtail Su-chou's preeminence in the late fourteenth century, a repressive policy that was successful until the mid–fifteenth century.

Su-chou produced fifty top-ranked *chin-shih* graduates from the T'ang to the late Ch'ing, as Table 5.5 reveals. Of these, nine Su-chou *chuang-yuan* came during the Ming and twenty-six in the Ch'ing. Nine times (1562, 1622, 1659, 1673, 1676, 1712, 1715, 1811, 1852), Su-chou *chin-shih* took two of the top three places in the palace examination. In particular, its four counties of Yuan-ho 元和, Wu-hsien 吳縣, Ch'ang-chou 長洲, and Ch'ang-shu 常熟 had outstanding success on both provincial and metropolitan examinations.[49]

48. Yü Chih-chia, "Mindai gunko no shakai teki chi i ni tsuite," pp. 106–21.

49. *Su-chou chuang-yuan* 蘇州狀元 (*Optimi* from Su-chou), compiled by Li Chia-ch'iu 李嘉球, pp. 261–334. Cf. *Chih-i k'o-so-chi*, 4.125.

In the northern capital region, it was not only local candidates who competed for degrees; the sons of officials from other provinces were also allowed to compete in the civil examinations there. This registration flexibility for children of officials was especially exploited by southerners until this loophole was limited somewhat in the Ch'ing. Competition rates in their home provinces were prohibitive, and the number of classically literate candidates there was much higher than in the north.[50] Table 5.6 tells us that during the early Ch'ing dynasty, a sizable number of candidates from other provinces received their *chü-jen* degrees in Peking. In 1654, for example, graduates from southern provinces (Chiang-nan, Che-chiang, and Fu-chien) took 20% of the degrees in Shun-t'ien; in 1657, they took 28%; and in 1660, 19% of the northern capital region's provincial quota went to candidates registered in the south. Table 5.4 reveals that outsiders made up a very small percentage of *chü-jen* in the southern capital region during the Ming dynasty. The spillover of southern candidates from southern provincial examinations to the Shun-t'ien examination in Peking not only increased the number of southern *chü-jen* but also increased the south's potential for *chin-shih* degree-holders.

Table 5.7 shows that for the dynasty as a whole, men from Chiang-su province constituted 43% of all *chuang-yuan* in the Ch'ing, with Su-chou alone accounting for over half of those, or 23% of all *optimi*. During the early Ming, candidates from Chiang-hsi and Che-chiang provinces had outpaced Chiang-su in the *chin-shih* market (see Table 2.9), but by the mid-Ming, the Yangtzu delta took the lead in producing *optimi*. Table 2.8 confirmed that overall, for both the Ming and Ch'ing dynasties, men from the Yangtzu delta had a commanding lead in taking the top places in the metropolitan and palace examinations in the capital.

These trends for the geographical origins of *chuang-yuan* are verified in Table 5.8, which presents the provincial distribution of all *chin-shih* for whom we have information (93%) during the Ming. The Yangtzu delta provinces of Chiang-su and An-hui, when taken together as "Chiang-nan" 江南 in the civil examinations, ranked first in *chin-shih* production from the mid-Ming (1473–1571) on, taking 16% of all places. Che-chiang finished second throughout the Ming, taking 14% of the *chin-shih* places, although it would have ranked first if the figures for An-hui were not added to those of Chiang-su. Chiang-hsi province, which had been so prominent during the Sung-Yuan-Ming transition in both political and cultural life (see Chapter 2), had produced 17% of *chin-shih* during the early Ming (1371–1472), ranking first in that century. During the mid-Ming, the percentage of Chiang-hsi *chin-shih* declined to 10%, and for the

50. Bielenstein, "The Regional Provenance," p. 17.

late Ming it fell further, to 8%, less than half the rate in the early Ming. Curiously, however, Chiang-hsi became a stronghold for Wang Yang-ming learning after Wang successfully led military campaigns between 1517 and 1519 against rebels there.[51]

One of the most telling secular trends in the civil examinations was the decline of Chiang-hsi in cultural eminence after the early Ming, a trend that accelerated during the Ch'ing. John Dardess has studied the puzzle of Chiang-hsi's precipitous decline during the Ming in terms of a single county, T'ai-ho. Compelling social changes in Chiang-hsi beginning in the Ch'eng-hua reign (1465–87) partly account for this decline. Dardess documents the "contraction" of the local upper class due to increased downward mobility in the late fifteenth century. He also notes that emigration to other provinces seems to have increased, and that many native sons increasingly passed provincial examinations outside Chiang-hsi. Others entered dynastic schools via county quotas in other areas. Moreover, bureaucratic infighting based on regional cliques, such as the battles between Chiang-hsi men and Shan-tung men in court politics, may have lessened Chiang-hsi's influence and played a part in the decline of bureaucratic recruitment via the recommendation process in the province. In particular, the Ying-tsung emperor (r. 1457–64) in part blamed Chiang-hsi men for his predicament after his 1449 capture by the Oirats, when the Ming court's response was to enthrone his brother in his place. When the Ying-tsung emperor again took the throne in 1457, he supported efforts to root out the recommendation channel, which took effect in 1459. Chiang-hsi natives no longer could exploit this avenue to official positions.[52]

Dardess describes the "shining sense of optimism" of early Ming literati in T'ai-ho county and contrasts that with the lack of such optimism in literati writings from T'ai-ho in the sixteenth century. Local elites, according to Dardess, increasingly turned to issues of empirewide political and intellectual change and away from local developments, an apparent reverse of the Sung trends toward regionalism and localism that had enriched Chiang-hsi's political and cultural status during the Sung-Yuan-Ming transition (see Chapter 1).[53] Moreover, the Yangtzu delta provinces of Chiang-su, An-hui, and Che-chiang became the hub of Ming commerce, which included an elaborate network of rivers, canals, and lakes that linked the Yangtzu River east and west and the Grand Canal north

51. For early Ming trends, see Ikoma Shō, "Minsho kakyo gokakusha no shushin ni kan suru ichi kōsatsu," pp. 45–71. See also Lü Miaw-fen, "Practice as Knowledge: Yang-ming Learning and *Chiang-hui* in Sixteenth Century China," chapter 1.

52. See de Heer, *The Care-Taker Emperor*, passim; and Dardess, *A Ming Society*, pp. 105–06, 110–11, 144–45, 167–69, 202–03. On p. 203, Dardess cautions, however, that political cliques were "fuzzily bounded."

53. Dardess, *A Ming Society*, pp. 248–53.

and south. They took advantage of their strategic location in an interregional trading area linking north and south China to the middle and upper Yangtzu regions. Chiang-hsi slowly became a provincial backwater where scarcer economic resources translated into fewer educational resources for Chiang-hsi families and lineages.

Table 5.9 displays this secular trend in more detail by documenting the provincial distribution on eight palace examinations between 1385 and 1622. Again, Chiang-nan regularly outpaced Che-chiang and Chiang-hsi in the sixteenth century, after the latter's dominance in 1385 (34% for both) and 1442 (41% for both). While Che-chiang recovered its second-place ranking for producing *chin-shih* from Fu-chien in 1547 and thereafter, Chiang-hsi fell behind both Fu-chien and Shan-tung. This trend continued in the Ch'ing.[54]

Hans Bielenstein has presented the most comprehensive statistical assessment of the "regional provenance of *chin-shih*" during the Ch'ing dynasty. Except for the early Ch'ing, when high numbers of *chin-shih* degree-holders between 1646 and 1661 came from the more pacified northern provinces (95% of the *chin-shih* in 1646, for instance, came from the northern capital region, Shan-tung, Ho-nan, or Shan-hsi province), the south in general maintained its dominance in the examination market despite the Ch'ing reimposition of the 55 south/10 central/35 north regional quota that had been in effect for *chin-shih* degrees since 1427 (see Chapter 2 and Table 5.10).[55]

The quota system was gradually altered in the eighteenth century to increase the number of degree-holders in lesser provinces, particularly frontier areas, and to lessen the success of southern provinces. The evidence for this change comes from Bielenstein's comparison of regional quotas for *chin-shih* during the first century of Manchu rule and those in place in the last century. Table 5.11 reveals that although the rankings of provinces in producing *chin-shih* did not shift dramatically, the percentages of *chin-shih* coming from the leading provinces during the Ming and early Ch'ing declined by about 2% to 3% in the late Ch'ing. In contrast, frontier provinces in the late Ch'ing such as Kan-su in the northwest tripled their quota, while Kuei-chou in the southwest almost quadrupled the number of its *chin-shih* degree-holders. Bielenstein notes that the increase of *chin-shih* from outer provinces was especially noticeable among the lists of first- and second-class graduates, while southerners were increasingly found in the third rank.[56]

54. See Ping-ti Ho, *The Ladder of Success in Imperial China*, p. 228 (Table 28: Geographic Distribution of *Chin-shih* in Ch'ing Times). Fu-chien also saw a substantial drop in its *chin-shih* rate under the Ch'ing.

55. Bielenstein, "The Regional Provenance," pp. 6–178.

56. Ibid., pp. 17–18, 30, 32, 33.

Table 5.12, which correlates the percentage of *chin-shih* by province with population figures for both the Ming and Ch'ing, also confirms the long-term centrality of the Yangtzu delta, along with Che-chiang, in the late imperial examination market, but the figures also divulge the unique success of the southeastern province of Fu-chien in producing top candidates during the Ming dynasty in particular. In the late Ch'ing, Fu-chien's fortunes revived, when the number of its *chin-shih* increased 18%. Two prefectures in the province became the two leading producers of *chin-shih* degree-holders in the period from 1776 to 1904. None had ranked among the top ten prefectures in the early and mid-Ch'ing.[57]

Table 5.12 also graphically reveals, however, how much all provinces were affected by population increases during the Ch'ing dynasty. For Chiang-nan, the number of *chin-shih* per mean population declined 63%; in Che-chiang the decline was 58%; Fu-chien experienced a remarkable 73% drop. Only frontier provinces in the southeast (Kuei-chou and Kuang-hsi) and Liao-ning in the northeast, where educational opportunities were expanding, showed statistical increases.[58]

Such geographical trends translated into power and influence in imperial politics. The higher percentage of southerners in official life became a perennial problem in Ming politics, as we saw in Chapter 2, and the Ch'ing changes in the quota system had merely offset the educational advantages of the south over other regions in the empire, not eliminated them. It is possible to calculate the figures given above because the Ming and Ch'ing government itself kept judicious track of the numbers of graduates by province in its efforts to keep the examination market reasonably fair and open to all candidates empirewide.[59] Nevertheless, at the very top of the pinnacle of power, only *chin-shih*, particularly those who finished at the top of their class and entered the Hanlin Academy (see Chapters 3 and 4), could transmit their local and regional interests to the imperial bureaucracy.

## MEMORIZATION AND THE CULTURAL SOCIOLOGY OF CLASSICISM BEFORE 1900

Civil examinations in late imperial China were a social spectacle in villages and towns from start to finish, which complemented the political spectacle inside and outside examination compounds. Frequently the rites

57. Ibid., pp. 21, 30, 77–78.

58. See William Rowe, "Education and Empire in Southwest China," pp. 417–57.

59. Danjō Hiroshi, "Mindai nanbokuken no shisō haikei," pp. 55–66, contends that officials viewed "fairness" in the examination competition as the sine qua non for its success.

of passage from childhood to young adult in wealthy families were measured by the number of classical texts a boy had mastered at a particular age. "Capping" of a young boy between the ages of sixteen and twenty-one, for example, implied that he had mastered all of the Four Books 四書 and one of the Five Classics 五經—the minimum requirement before 1787 for any aspirant to compete in local civil service examinations.[60] But this was not an age-graded educational system. Graduates as peers differed in ages substantially, as we shall see. The social and cultural effects of forming alliances between graduates of a particular examination who differed widely in age meant that neither the young nor the old could seek solidarity in their own age group. A *t'ung-nien* 同年 (same year of graduation) reunion would be far different from a college reunion in the West.

Although Tao Learning scholars such as Chu Hsi and others had since the Sung dynasty criticized the uselessness of rote learning for moral self-cultivation and intellectual awakening, one of the ironies of the late imperial examination regime was that it required careful memorization of Ch'eng-Chu annotations of the Classics to succeed in the degree market. Such rote learning tended to cut against the grain of moral cultivation, because the examinations had no means to measure morality directly or determine whether the memorization of *Tao-hsueh* doctrine brought with it increased intellectual awakening. It was simply assumed that good writing was the mark of a cultivated literatus, but there were enough counterexamples to challenge that bland educational notion.

### Memorization as a Mental Technology

A common Ming saying was: "To bequeath a case full of gold does not compare to teaching a son one Classic."[61] The written traditions of composition in imperial China were rehearsed orally in a student's ability to recall verbatim a classical text. The oral and the written went together in the examination regime, enhancing both literacy and memory (see Figure

60. John Dardess, "The Management of Children and Youth in Upper-Class Households in Late Imperial China," paper presented at the summer 1987 meetings of the Pacific Coast Branch of the American Historical Association (Pasadena, Calif., Occidental College). Capping seems to have been less prevalent in north China during the Ch'ing dynasty. In more recent work, Dardess reaches the conclusion that "there is little common ground between members of successive generations," and that "irreconcilable philosophical differences" marked the Ming Chiang-hsi literati he studied. By leaving the classical language out of his analysis, Dardess overlooks the linguistic continuity that undergirded classical debates. See Dardess, *A Ming Society*, p. 173.

61. Cited in Wu Han 吳晗, *Chu Yuan-chang chuan* 朱元璋傳 (Biography of Chu Yuan-chang) (Peking: San-lien Bookstore, 1949), p. 235.

FIGURE 5.1. The 1430 *Optimus* Writes from Memory. *Source: Ming chuang-yuan t'u-k'ao* 明狀元圖考 (Illustrated survey of *optimi* during the Ming dynasty). Compiled by Ku Ting-ch'en 顧鼎臣 and Ku Tsu-hsun 顧祖訓. 1607 edition.

5.1).[62] Classical literacy was formed through a three-stage learning process: (1) memorization of Chinese graphs; (2) reading the Four Books, one of the Five Classics (until 1786, when all the Classics had to be memorized), and the Histories; (3) and composition.

62. Ridley, "Educational Theory and Practice in Late Imperial China," pp. 150–52, Willard Peterson, *Bitter Gourd*, pp. 44–47. Cf. Jack Goody, *The Interface between the Written and the Oral* (Cambridge: Cambridge University Press, 1987), pp. 59–77, 86–91, 234–43.

The ability to write elegant examination essays was the crowning achievement for educated men (and women). This creative learning process began with rote memorization during childhood, continued with youthful reading, and concluded with mature writing. As a graded sequence of learning, its foundation was long hours of oral memorization spent by children aged three to eight *sui* 歲 (Chinese counts of age added an extra year if one was born just before the lunar new year). Premodern Chinese literati, such as the Ming loyalist turned educator Lu Shih-i 陸世 儀 (1611–72), believed that the memory (*chi-hsing* 記性) was strongest at an early age, while understanding (*wu-hsing* 悟性) was a gradual achievement that derived from mastering the literary language and its moral and historical content. Lu thought students were educable at age five or six, but mature learning could commence only when they reached fifteen *sui*.[63]

First children learned written graphs (see Figure 5.2). Usually before they entered clan or temple schools at age eight, students had already memorized the *Thousand Character Text* (*Ch'ien-tzu wen* 千字文) and *Hundred Surnames* (*Pai-chia hsing* 百家姓) primers, which both dated from the Sung. In addition, they mastered the *Three Character Classic* (*San-tzu ching* 三字經), which was a *Tao-hsueh* tract attributed to Wang Ying-lin 王應麟 (1223–96) of the early Yuan.[64] Altogether these three famous primers contained about 1,500 different written characters within the total of 2,636 graphs in them. Pre-school sessions at home, often under the guidance of their mothers,[65] enabled students to memorize the important sequences and combinations of written graphs that were peculiar to the classical written language.[66] The memorization of primers was reinforced by calligraphy

63. See Lu Shih-i's essays distinguishing elementary (*hsiao-hsueh* 小學) from advanced (*ta-hsueh* 大學) education, in *Ch'ing-tai ch'ien-ch'i chiao-yü lun-chu hsuan*, 1/129–44.

64. The attribution of the *San-tzu ching* to Wang Ying-lin began in 1666 by the commentator Wang Hsiang 王相, although recent scholarship challenges the assumption that a polymath such as Wang Ying-lin would have produced such an ideologically biased classical primer. See Michael Fish, "Bibliographical Notes on the *San Tzu Ching* and Related Texts" (master's thesis, Indiana University, 1968), pp. 26–34. Cf. Langley, "Wang Ying-lin," pp. xix–xx. See also Hoyt Tillman, "Encyclopedias, Polymaths, and *Tao-hsueh* Confucians," *Journal of Sung-Yuan Studies* 22 (1990–92): 89–108. For a translation, see Herbert Giles, trans., *San Tzu Ching: Elementary Chinese* (1910; reprint, Taipei: Wen-chih Press, 1984). Cynthia Brokaw, "Commercial Publishing in Late Imperial China: The Zou and Ma Family Businesses of Sibao, Fujian," *Late Imperial China* 17, 1 (June 1996): 74, gives evidence for the "large number of editions of the *Three Character Classic*" in Fu-chien province in Ming times.

65. Ko, *Teachers of the Inner Chambers*, p. 128.

66. See Chang Chih-kung 張志公, *Ch'uan-t'ung yü-wen chiao-yü ch'u-t'an* 傳統語文教育初 探 (Preliminary inquiry into traditional language education) (Shanghai: Education Press, 1962), pp. 3–86; and Angela Ki Che Leung, "Elementary Education in the Lower Yangtzu Region," pp. 393–96; and Rawski, *Literacy and Popular Literacy in Ch'ing China*, pp. 136–39.

FIGURE 5.2. The 1463 *Optimus* Learns Characters as a Child.
*Source: Ming chuang-yuan t'u-k'ao* 明狀元圖考 (Illustrated survey
of *optimi* during the Ming dynasty). Compiled by Ku Ting-
ch'en 顧鼎臣 and Ku Tsu-hsun 顧祖訓. 1607 edition.

practice.[67] The Reverend Justus Doolittle described the situation he found
in 1865:

67. See Sheang [Shang] Yen-liu, "Memories of the Chinese Imperial Civil Service
Examination System," pp. 49–52.

Pupils do not study, in school, books on mathematics, geography, and the natural sciences, but the writings of Confucius and Mencius. These they are required to commit to memory, and recite with their backs toward the book. This is called "*backing the book*" [*pei-shu* 背書]. They are not taught in classes, but each studies the book he pleases, taking a longer or shorter lesson according to his ability. They all study out loud, oftentimes screaming at the top of their voices. They first learn the sounds of the characters, so as to recite them *memoriter*. After years of study they acquire an insight into their meaning and use. They commence to write when they begin going to school, tracing the characters given them as patterns on paper by means of hair pencil and China ink. It requires an immense amount of practice to write the language correctly and rapidly.[68]

Educators as diverse as Ch'eng Tuan-li 程端禮 (1271–1345) in the Yuan and the 1821 *chü-jen* Wang Yun 王筠 (1784–1854) in the Ch'ing, for example, emphasized tracing all the characters in primers as the best way to improve calligraphy. Ch'eng thought that students should over time increase their tracing from 1,500 to 4,000 characters a day.[69] In his discussion of methods for teaching youths, Wang Yun noted, for example, that the knowledge of characters (*shih-tzu* 識字) was the primary constituent of classical literacy. Reading and writing could begin only after about 2,000 different graphs had been committed to memory:

Explanations are possible only after more than one thousand characters have been learned; reading is possible only after mastering two thousand characters.... When a student is learning characters, he should concentrate on learning characters. He should not make plans to read the Classics. When the student is reading the Classics, that's all he should do. He should not make plans to write essays. With regard to the characters, however, the Classics are nothing more than the characters turned into sentences, which in turn have been combined into chapters.[70]

68. See Doolittle, *Social Life of the Chinese*, pp. 377–78. John Henry Gray in his *China: A History of the Laws, Manners and Customs of the People*, pp. 167–68, describes the "din which arises from a Chinese schoolroom" in the 1870s, made by students "committing their lessons to memory" by reading aloud.

69. Ridley, "Educational Theory and Practice in Late Imperial China," pp. 391–92. On Sung dynasty primers, which included the *Ch'ien-tzu wen* and *Pai-chia hsing*, see Thomas H. C. Lee, "Sung Schools and Education before Chu Hsi," in de Bary and Chaffee, eds., *Neo-Confucian Education*, pp. 130–31.

70. See Wang Yun, "Chiao t'ung-tzu fa" 教童子法 (On teaching youthful students), in *Ch'ing-tai ch'ien-ch'i chiao-yü lun-chu hsuan*, 3/484–92.

Next began the memorization of the Four Books and, during the Ming dynasty, one of the Five Classics (all five were required after 1786). If minimal classical literacy (what I call "primer literacy") required mastery of 2,000 different characters, students generally increased that total steadily to the over 10,000 common characters in the Classics, which were required for fully empowering classical literacy.[71] Poetry, which was an important part of classical literacy in T'ang-Sung examinations, was restored to the civil examinations after 1756. The paleographical dictionary *Shuo-wen chieh-tzu* 説文解字 (Analysis of characters as an explanation of writing), compiled during the Later Han dynasty by Hsu Shen 許慎 (58–147), for example, contained 9,373 different characters arranged according to 530 radicals (*pu-shou* 部首), a framework that despite modification remained the basic organization in most premodern classical dictionaries.[72]

Because of requirements to compose poetry, rhyme-prose, and belles lettres (see Chapter 1), rhyming and pronunciation dictionaries were produced as examination aids during both the T'ang and Sung dynasties. Lu Fa-yen's 陸法言 (fl. ca. A.D. 601) *Ch'ieh-yun* 切韻 (Rhymes by syllabic transcription), for instance, contained about 12,000 different characters. Subsequently in the Northern Sung, Ch'en P'eng-nien 陳彭年 (961–1017) enlarged the *Ch'ieh-yun* to include 26,194 graphs; he and his compilers entitled their edition the *Kuang-yun* 廣韻 (Expansion of rhymes). It was then enlarged under the title *Chi-yun* 集韻 (Collected rhymes) to include over 50,000 graphs.[73] The Southern Sung polymath Cheng Ch'iao 鄭樵 (1104–62) analyzed over 24,000 characters in his *T'ung-chih* 通志 (Comprehensive encyclopedia). During the Ch'ing dynasty, the *K'ang-hsi tzu-tien* 康熙字典, completed in 1716, grouped 47,030 different characters under 214 radicals. Altogether there were about 48,000 different characters in late imperial times, but many of them were simply variants.[74]

Estimates of the total number of graphs per Classic have been disputed, but literati educators did schedule the memorization process according to the number of graphs in each. Many characters of course frequently repeated. Wang Ch'ang 王昶 (1725–1806), a private academy teacher in the heyday of Han Learning during the eighteenth century when all of

71. On literacy and empowerment, see Graff, *The Legacies of Literacy*, pp. 10–11.

72. See my *From Philosophy to Philology*, pp. 213–15.

73. Thomas H. C. Lee, "Sung Schools and Education before Chu Hsi," pp. 131–32.

74. For discussion, see T. H. Tsien, *Written on Bamboo and Silk* (Chicago: University of Chicago Press, 1962), p. 24; S. Robert Ramsey, *The Languages of China* (Princeton: Princeton University Press, 1987), pp. 116–24; John DeFrancis, *The Chinese Language: Fact and Fantasy* (Honolulu: University of Hawaii Press, 1984), pp. 82–85; and Tillman, "Encyclopedias, Polymaths, and *Tao-hsueh* Confucians," pp. 94–98.

the Five Classics were required in the civil examinations, told incoming students at his academy in Nan-ch'ang, Chiang-hsi, in 1789 that the number of repeating graphs (or repeating "words") in each Classic totaled 40,848 in the *Poetry Classic*, 27,134 in the *Documents*, 24,437 in the *Change*, 98,994 in the *Record of Rites* (which included the *Great Learning* and the *Doctrine of the Mean*), and 15,984 in the *Spring and Autumn Annals*. Wang enthusiastically predicted that it would take students only 690 days, if they were diligent, to recite from memory the more than 200,000 words in these five texts.[75]

Using the "Thirteen Classics" of the T'ang and Sung dynasties as his base line, Miyazaki Ichisada has given us an approximate character count for words that includes the Four Books, Five Classics, and commentaries to the *Spring and Autumn Annals*. He suggests that candidates for T'ang-Sung civil examinations had to memorize about 570,000 repeating graphs. I have added a note about examination requirements to Miyazaki's list:[76]

| | | |
|---|---|---|
| *Analects* | 11,705 characters | Required in Ming-Ch'ing |
| *Mencius* | 34,685 | Required in Ming-Ch'ing |
| *Filial Piety* | 1,903 | Required until 1787 |
| *Change* | 24,107 | Optional in Ming-Ch'ing |
| *Documents* | 25,700 | Optional in Ming-Ch'ing |
| *Poetry* | 39,234 | Optional in Ming-Ch'ing |
| *Tso Commentary* | 196,845 | Optional in Ming-Ch'ing |
| *Kung-yang chuan* | 44,075 | Optional in Ming-Ch'ing |
| *Ku-liang chuan* | 41,512 | Optional in Ming-Ch'ing |
| *Rites of Chou* | 45,806 | Not required |
| *Decorum Ritual* | 56,624 | Not required |
| *Record of Rites* (includes *Great Learning* and *Doctrine of the Mean*, which were required) | 99,010 | Optional in Ming-Ch'ing |
| Total (correcting Miyazaki's totals) | 621,206 characters (470,000 optional) | 518,000 required after 1786; Four Books: about 75,000; Five Classics: about 470,000 |

75. Wang Ch'ang, *Ch'un-jung-t'ang chi* 春融堂集 (Collection from the Hall of Cheerful Spring), 1807 edition, 68.9a–b. The total number of words in the Five Classics was 207,397, according to Wang. Cf. Alexander Woodside and Benjamin A. Elman, "The Expansion of Education in Ch'ing China," in Elman and Woodside, eds., *Education and Society in Late Imperial China*, p. 534.

76. See Miyazaki, *Kakyo*, pp. 294–97, for his account of the "Thirteen Classics" in late imperial China, which is based on the *Tu-shu fen-nien jih-ch'eng* 讀書分年日程 (Yearly sched-

Based on this formidable, although somewhat anachronistic, list, Miyazaki estimates that at the rate of 200 characters a day it would have taken six years to memorize about 400,000 characters, even when most were characters that repeated, a less sanguine view than Wang Ch'ang's estimate of 690 days for 200,000 words.[77] Wang's optimistic account is confirmed by Shang Yen-liu 商衍鎏, the last Ch'ing *tertius*, on the 1904 civil palace examination, who wrote:

> Before I reached the age of twelve, my course of studies to prepare for the examinations consisted of the above-mentioned [classical] program. When one comes to think of it, wouldn't it seem too much to ask of a five- to twelve-year-old boy to not only study so many texts, including the Four Books and Five Classics, but to memorize them and to expect him to understand and explain them as well? In actuality, as long as one studied every day without interruption, this could be achieved—there was nothing strange or miraculous about it.[78]

Repetition as a habit of learning based on reciting and copying was the key to developing the memory as a pedagogic tool to produce shared linguistic conventions by education. The child's ability to memorize was thus highly prized among literati and in popular culture. Legends of men who as youths had committed prodigious amounts of information to memory were often recounted. Ni Heng 禰衡 from Shan-tung province during the Later Han dynasty was remembered for his ability on his travels to memorize at a single glance all the characters of the Seven Classics officially inscribed by Ts'ai Yung 蔡邕 (133–92) on hundreds of stone stelae. Ni failed to recite only two graphs, which were those missing from the stelae themselves. Hsing Shao 邢邵 (d. ca. 560), a northerner living during the

---

ule for reading books), 1796 edition. Miyazaki notes that he has excluded the *Erh-ya* (one of the T'ang "Thirteen Classics") from his calculations, although we will see below that it was still a much-studied etymological dictionary. During the T'ang, Sung, and Yuan, and from 1370 until 1786, all candidates (with some exceptions) specialized on one of the Five Classics. After that, until 1900, they had to master all of them. Cf. the shortened list in Miyazaki, *China's Examination Hell*, p. 16, which presents character counts for the Four Books (two are in the *Record of Rites)* and Five Classics. On the *Annals*, Miyazaki gives figures for the *Tso* 左, *Ku-liang* 穀梁, and *Kung-yang* 公羊 commentaries in *Kakyo*. In *China's Examination Hell*, only the *Tso Commentary* is listed. Neither account gives us figures for the Sung dynasty Hu An-kuo commentary to the *Annals* (see Chapter 1), which was required during the Ming and Ch'ing dynasties until 1793 when it was dropped (see Chapter 10).

77. Miyazaki, *China's Examination Hell*, p. 16.

78. Sheang [Shang] Yen-liu, "Memories of the Chinese Imperial Civil Service Examination System," p. 52.

Northern and Southern dynasties period (386–588), was able to memorize the entire text of the *History of the Former Han Dynasty* in just five days.[79]

During the T'ang, Lu Chuang-tao 盧莊道 was said at age thirteen to be able to recite works he had memorized both forward and backward. His fame spread until T'ang T'ai-tsung called him to court for a personal examination, after which the emperor declared, "This is my precocious son," and appointed Lu to his personal guard. In the Sung, Hu I 胡沂 became famous for memorizing the entire Five Classics at the age of six. This feat was almost replicated in the Yuan when Tseng Lu 曾魯 (1319–72) reportedly recited the Five Classics without error at the age of seven *sui*. Later in the Ming, Sang Yueh 桑悅, who took his *chü-jen* degree in 1465 and became a local education official, when asked why he would throw away or burn his books, would reply that he had always been able memorize any book that caught his eye. "It's already inside me," he would exclaim.[80]

For those without photographic memories, instruction in mnemonic skills was part of the classical teaching repertoire in imperial China, where oral recitation was aided by rhyming characters, four-character jingles, and the technique of writing matching and balanced, antithetical pairs of characters known as *shu-tui* 屬對. Wang Yun and most educators made the memorization of the latter two-character phrases a major building block of a classical memory. After the poetry question was added in 1756, which required candidates to compose T'ang dynasty regulated verse, the demands of balance, symmetry, and antithetical lines became even more pronounced.[81]

To facilitate the ability of candidates to compose classically literate essays, the K'ang-hsi emperor ordered the *P'ei-wen yun-fu* 佩文韻府 (Thesaurus arranged by rhymes) to be compiled in 1704. It was completed and printed in 1711 and again in 1720. This sophisticated reference work classified phrases and allusions according to the rhyme of over ten thousand different characters used as the last character in a passage. Under each entry, the editors illustrated its literary uses. One of the key aspects of the *Thesaurus* was that it conveniently organized pairs of parallel phrases for examination candidates, which could be easily memorized.[82]

79. These stories are recounted in *Ku-chin t'u-shu chi-ch'eng*, vol. 606, 112.32a–34a. Cf. Tsien, *Written on Bamboo and Silk*, pp. 73–76.

80. *Ku-chin t'u-shu chi-ch'eng*, vol. 606, 112. 34b. Cf. Jonathan Spence, *The Memory Palace of Matteo Ricci* (New York: Viking Penguin, 1985), pp. 156–57.

81. Wang Yun, "Chiao t'ung-tzu fa," p. 486.

82. See Ssu-yü Teng and Knight Biggerstaff, comps., *An Annotated Bibliography of Selected Chinese Reference Works*, 2nd edition (Cambridge: Harvard University Press, 1971), pp. 97–98. For discussion, see James J. Y. Liu, *The Art of Chinese Poetry*, pp. 146–50.

Writing in 1923, the chancellor of Peking University, Ts'ai Yuan-p'ei 蔡元培 (1868–1940), who passed the special 1890 civil metropolitan examination ranked eighty-first and entered the Hanlin Academy in 1892,[83] described such learning techniques in his memoirs:

> Balanced, antithetical clauses [*tui-chü* 對句] are a technique for constructing phrases that started with one character and extended to four characters. Writing five character phrases or more would have been writing poetry [not essays]. This allowed for free construction without having to present model phrases first. Using antithesis, not only nouns, verbs, and adjectives were paired, but among nouns, animals, plants, minerals, utensils, and homes, and among adjectives, colors, qualities, and numbers could also be matched....Other cases were obtained through analogy. In addition, when we composed antithetical clauses, we also discriminated among the four tones. Characters in even tone, for example, were paired with others of even tone.[84]

When it became known that the Jesuit missionary Matteo Ricci (1552–1610) had a prodigious memory, based on the European art of remembering the order of things (what Jonathan Spence calls the "memory palace"), he was able to present his mnemonic devices to the literati world of the late Ming. For instance, the governor of Chiang-hsi province, Lu Wan-kai 陸萬垓, who took his *chin-shih* ranked twenty-fourth in 1568, invited Ricci to teach his memory-enhancing techniques to his three sons then preparing for the civil examinations. In addition to his use of astronomy and geography, Ricci used his memory skills to enhance literati interest in Christianity. Seeing the usefulness of such memory techniques and printed primers to convey vocabulary and doctrine, the Jesuits constructed their own classical primer, which was entitled *T'ien-chu sheng-chiao ssu-tzu ching* 天主聖教四字經 (The Catholic four-character classic), as a means of creating a popular classical catechism to spread the foreign faith in seventeenth-century China.[85]

83. *En-k'o hui-shih lu* 恩科會試錄 (Grace civil metropolitan examination), 1890: 27b.

84. *Ts'ai Yuan-p'ei ch'üan-chi* 蔡元培全集 (Complete works of Ts'ai Yuan-p'ei) (Tainan: Wang-chia Press, 1968), p. 462. Cf. Ridley, "Educational Theory and Practice in Late Imperial China," pp. 404–05.

85. Spence, *The Memory Palace of Matteo Ricci*, pp. 3–4, 140–41, 160–61. See also Eugenio Menegon, "The Catholic Four-Character Classic (*Tianzhu Shengjiao Sizijing*): A Confucian Pattern to Spread a Foreign Faith in Late Ming China," University of California, Berkeley, seminar paper, fall 1992. For discussion of European memory arts that derive from Greek and Latin sources, see Frances Yates, *The Art of Memory* (New York: Penguin, 1969).

FIGURE 5.3. The 1400 *Optimus* Reading as a Youth. *Source: Ming chuang-yuan t'u-k'ao* 明狀元圖考 (Illustrated survey of *optimi* during the Ming dynasty). Compiled by Ku Ting-ch'en 顧鼎臣 and Ku Tsu-hsun 顧祖訓. 1607 edition.

## Scope of the Classical Curriculum

Although the curriculum he recommended was still tied to Southern Sung educational traditions, Ch'eng Tuan-li, who had extensive experience working in local government schools during the Yuan dynasty, prepared a reading schedule for his Ch'eng clan school, which remained widely influential as a model classical curriculum during the Ming and Ch'ing (see Figure 5.3). Because it was widely emulated, it is worth detailing the classical reading regime that Ch'eng formulated for youths by the time they were fifteen to master the Ch'eng-Chu orthodoxy and prepare for civil examinations:[86]

PRE-SCHOOL CLASSICAL READINGS (BEFORE THE AGE OF EIGHT *SUI*)

*Hsing-li tzu-hsun* 性理字訓 (Glosses for characters on nature and principles)
　Optional alternative: *Thousand Character Text* or other primers such as
　the *Meng-ch'iu* 蒙求 (Search for knowledge by children).

*T'ung-tzu hsu-chih* 童子須知 (What all local youthful candidates should know)
　A primer by Chu Hsi.

CLASSICAL READINGS IN SCHOOL (AFTER THE AGE OF EIGHT UNTIL FOURTEEN OR FIFTEEN)

*Hsiao-hsueh* 小學 (Elementary learning)
　An anthology of classical selections compiled by Chu Hsi.[87]

Four Books in order (required at all levels of civil examinations):
　*Great Learning:* text and commentaries
　*Analects:* text only
　*Mencius:* text only
　*Doctrine of the Mean:* text only

Seven Classics 七經 in order (one required at all levels of civil examinations):[88]
　*Filial Piety* 孝經 (required for Ming-Ch'ing "discourse" questions)
　*Change* 易經: complement with Sung Tao Learning commentaries
　*Documents* 書經: text only
　*Poetry* 詩經: text only
　*Decorum Ritual* 儀禮 and *Record of Rites* 禮記: text only
　*Rituals of Chou* 周禮: text only
　*Spring and Autumn Annals* 春秋: text and three Han commentaries

ADVANCED CLASSICAL TRAINING (AFTER THE AGE OF FIFTEEN)

　*Ta-hsueh chang-chü* 大學章句 (Parsing of phrases in the Great Learning), by Chu Hsi.
　*Lun-yü chi-chu* 論語集注 (Collected notes to the Analects), by Chu Hsi.
　*Meng-tzu chi-chu* 孟子集注 (Collected notes to the Mencius), by Chu Hsi.
　*Chung-yung chang-chü* 中庸章句 (Parsing of phrases in the Doctrine of the Mean), by Chu Hsi.

86. See Ch'eng Tuan-li, *Ch'eng-shih chia-shu tu-shu fen-nien jih-ch'eng*, 1.1a–15b.
87. See M. Theresa Kelleher, "Back to Basics: Chu Hsi's *Elementary Learning (Hsiao-hsueh)*," in de Bary and Chaffee, eds., *Neo-Confucian Education*, pp. 219–51.
88. During the T'ang and Sung, the Classics were often organized as the "Seven," "Nine," or "Thirteen Classics." Beginning in the Yuan and Ming, the "Five Classics" became the basic texts referred to as "Classics" in the civil examinations, although publications during both the Ming and Ch'ing dynasties often unofficially referred to the "Seven" and "Thirteen" Classics. For discussion, see Chapter 1.

*Lun-yü huo-wen* 論語或問 (Questions on the Analects), by Chu Hsi:
compare with *Lun-yü chi-chu*.
*Meng-tzu huo-wen* 孟子或問 (Questions on the Mencius), by Chu Hsi:
compare with *Meng-tzu chi-chu*.
Review original text of Classics by copying out portions (*ch'ao-fa* 鈔法)
from memory.
Take three to four years to master the six rules of character formation
(*shu-fa liu-t'iao* 書法六條).[89]

Except for its focus on the "Thirteen Classics," Ch'eng's curriculum
was emulated in the Ming and early Ch'ing civil examination curriculum,
which emphasized mastery of the Four Books and one of the Five
Classics. From 1645 until 1757, the curriculum for provincial and metropolitan examinations was exactly as it had been during the Ming dynasty
from 1384 to 1643. I have presented the Ming format in Chapter 1. Below
I represent the Ch'ing format for the examination curriculum. If a student
could cope with such intense rote training, he could try his hand at passing the licensing examinations as early as age fifteen, although, as we will
see below, most young men rarely achieved licentiate status before age
twenty-one.

FORMAT OF PROVINCIAL AND METROPOLITAN CIVIL SERVICE
EXAMINATIONS DURING THE EARLY CH'ING DYNASTY, 1646–1756

| *Session No.* | *No. of Questions* |
| --- | --- |
| ONE | |
| 1. Four Books 四書 | 3 quotations |
| 2. Change 易經 | 4 quotations (optional) |
| 3. Documents 書經 | 4 quotations (optional) |
| 4. Poetry 詩經 | 4 quotations (optional) |
| 5. Annals 春秋 | 4 quotations (optional) |
| 6. Rites 禮記 | 4 quotations (optional) |
| TWO | |
| 1. Discourse 論 | 1 quotation |
| 2. Documentary style 詔誥表 | 3 documents |
| 3. Judicial terms 判語 | 5 terms |
| THREE | |
| 1. Policy questions 經史時務策 | 5 essays |

NOTE: On session one, all candidates were expected to specialize on one of the
Five Classics (*chuan-ching* 專經) and write essays for only that Classic.

89. See my *From Philosophy to Philology*, pp. 212–13.

FIGURE 5.4. The 1391 *Optimus* Reading at Home. *Source: Ming chuang-yuan t'u-k'ao* 明狀元圖考 (Illustrated survey of *optimi* during the Ming dynasty). Compiled by Ku Ting-ch'en 顧鼎臣 and Ku Tsu-hsun 顧祖訓. 1607 edition.

In perhaps the best-documented case of a late imperial "examination life," Chang Chien 張謇 (Chi-chih 季直, b. 1853), the 1894 palace examination *chuang-yuan* at the age of forty-one *sui*, had begun at the age of four (three years old in Western chronology because a year was added at the first lunar new year after Chang was born) to learn the *Thousand Character Text* from his father and at the age of sixteen was ready to take the county licensing examination in 1868 requiring classical essays and regulated verse, which he passed (see also Figure 5.4).[90]

If we compare Ch'eng Tuan-li's early-fourteenth-century list with the classical curriculum that Chang Chien followed on his quest to become a *chin-shih* degree-holder in the late nineteenth century, we find many parallels, despite differences, which demonstrate the educational integrity (except for poetry) of the classical curriculum for elites from 1315 to 1756, when the curriculum was significantly revamped. The major difference was the return of poetry, particularly T'ang regulated verse (*lü-shih* 律詩), to the civil examinations in the middle of the Ch'ien-lung reign and thereafter (see Chapter 10). The content of Chang's education is listed below by the age in *sui* at which he studied a particular text:[91]

| AGE | TEXT |
|---|---|
| 4–5: | *Thousand Character Text* |
| 5–11: | *Three Character Classic* |
| | *Hundred Surnames* 百家姓 |
| | Works on poetry (required on civil examinations since 1756) |
| | *Filial Piety Classic* |
| | *Great Learning* |
| | *Doctrine of the Mean* |
| | *Analects* |
| | *Mencius* |
| | *Poetry Classic* |
| | Classical writing primers[92] |
| 12: | Recite Four Books from memory |
| 13: | Review Four Books and Five Classics |
| | *Erh-ya* 爾雅 (Progress toward correctness) dictionary |
| | Poetry exercises[93] |
| 14: | *Record of Rites* |
| | *Spring and Autumn Annals* |
| | *Tso Commentary* 左傳 |

90. Ridley, "Educational Theory and Practice in Late Imperial China," pp. 153–56, 346–50, 376–77.

91. Ibid., pp. 376–79.

92. For writing primers, see Chang Chih-kung, *Ch'uan-t'ung yü-wen chiao-yü ch'u-t'an*, pp. 87–92; and Ridley, "Educational Theory and Practice in Late Imperial China," pp. 64–85.

93. See Chang Chih-kung, *Ch'uan-t'ung yü-wen chiao-yü ch'u-t'an*, pp. 92–106.

AGE     TEXT
        Composition exercises[94]

15:     *Rites of Chou*
        *Decorum Ritual*

17:     Historical collections such as *Tzu-chih t'ung-chien kang-mu* 資治通鑑綱
        目 (Condensation of the Comprehensive Mirror of History), attrib-
        uted to Chu Hsi (see Chapter 9).

The chronology of Chang Chi-chih's readings represented an ordered
arrangement from elementary texts to the more difficult Four Books and
the Five Classics (all of which were required in Chang's time; see below).
Composition (*tso-wen* 作文), defined as the dual ability to write well about
the Four Books and Five Classics using classical Chinese forms and the
ability to compose poetry in regulated verse, represented the culmination
of the transition from childhood to the young *t'ung-sheng* student.[95] The
historical readings were needed to handle policy questions in provincial,
metropolitan, and palace examinations (see Chapters 8 and 9).

By his sixteenth birthday, Chang Chien passed the local *t'ung-sheng*
examination in his home county of T'ung-chou 通州 in Chiang-su
province, although he ranked below number 200 on the final roll. The
same year, Chang passed the prefectural licensing examination to become
a licentiate, and two years later he finished in the first tier on the qualifying examination. At the age of eighteen, young but not unusually young,
Chang Chien proceeded to the next level of examinations at the provincial capital, where he would have a much harder time (see below).[96]

### Essay Writing and Formation of a Writing Elite

Apart from the obvious differences in the social status and political power
of the audiences, one of the key cultural differences between the elite examination audience for works requiring full classical literacy in late imperial
China and those for whom more popular works exhibiting vernacular literacy were intended was that among the former the ability to write took
precedence. The regimen for reading described above for civil examination candidates was not intended to make them members of a "reading
public," although a "reading elite" certainly was a by-product of their
training. They were in training, via memorization and calligraphy practice, to become members of a "writing elite" whose essays would mark
each as a classically trained literatus who could write his way to fame, for-

94. See ibid., pp. 118–43.
95. See Ridley, "Educational Theory and Practice in Late Imperial China," pp. 440–58,
on the teaching of writing.
96. Ibid., p. 155.

tune, and power via essays on the local, provincial, metropolitan, and palace examinations.[97]

Composition, then, was the final stage of a classical education. Reading alone was insufficient in such a cultural context. To write classical Chinese well was to perform a literary art whose cultural expectations were limited to and appreciated by an elite audience that could not only read the product but also understand and reproduce the prosodic rules that underlaid the score. The limitation, control, and selection of the "writing elite," not the enlargement of the "reading public," was the dynasty's goal in using civil examinations to select officials.

Reading, consequently, was subsumed as an ancillary task needed to reach the final goal. To write with technical proficiency and aesthetic sensibility was the sine qua non of the literatus as a man of culture, the terms of which are described in more detail in Chapter 7. From the point of view of the court and the bureaucracy, classical composition was a means to ensure common linguistic traits and classical memories in officialdom. From the angle of the literatus, however, to write was to engage in a form of *wen* 文 (culture) that allowed him to reach back to the ancients and enunciate the truths of his scholarly predecessors. Both the needs of Ming and Ch'ing imperial orthodoxy and the acute cultural sensibilities of educated men were met and compromised in the examination regime. It was not a one-way imperial hegemony based simply on political or social power. Nor was it an autonomous field of literati authority.

The task was to train youths to think and write properly in classical forms once they had memorized and read the minimum requirements for classical literacy. To write about the Four Books and Five Classics required a literatus "to speak in the place of the sages" (*tai sheng-jen li-yen* 代聖人立言). A child could memorize characters, chant poetry lines, and master balanced, antithetical phrases, but a full classical education required a level of understanding and thinking that only a young adult could bring to fruition and project into an essay.[98] For example, Chang

---

97. For discussion, see Chang Chih-kung, *Ch'uan-t'ung yü-wen chiao-yü ch'u-t'an*, 118–34. Recent studies of publishing and print culture in Ming and Ch'ing times have been so hasty in applying Roger Chartier's seminal studies of books, publishing, and passive reading in early modern French cultural history that they missed the active role of writing in literati culture. See Chartier, "Gutenberg Revisited From the East," *Late Imperial China* 17, 1 (1996): 1–9; and the several essays packaged in the latter as a "Special Issue: Publishing and the Print Culture in Late Imperial China." These very informative essays invoke, uncritically, European cultural practices for refracting Ming and Ch'ing forms of reading and writing. In his *oeuvre*, Chartier never reveals how early modern Europeans, actively, learned to write, for example. For similar limitations, see Alberto Manguel, *A History of Reading* (New York: Viking Press, 1996), passim.

98. Liang Chang-chü, *Chih-i ts'ung-hua*, 1.10b.

Hsueh-ch'eng 章學誠 (1738–1801), who spent much of his career teaching classical writing at academies such as Lien-ch'ih 蓮池 in Pao-ting in 1785, while waiting for an official appointment, described the transition from child to adult among elites in terms of writing: "Today, when I have a boy compose an essay, even if it is just a string of several words, he should complete the sentence.... It should proceed from small to large, from brief to long, to enable him to grasp that even a three- or five-word phrase is not too little and that several hundreds and thousands of words are not too many. It's just like an infant whose organs and bones are already complete, and he grows into a man."[99]

Chang Hsueh-ch'eng and other Ch'ing educators contended that as youths grew in writing skills they would be able to write longer and more complicated essays. Chang was of a mind that the whole essay mattered more than its parts. Focus on the latter represented a piecemeal approach, which Chang thought a child could successfully mimic but not necessarily understand. Most others, however, saw the parts as the means to prepare for the whole essay as the boy reached maturity. They trained children to write parts of the eight-legged essay (*pa-ku-wen* 八股文) separately before they could link the parts together into a coherent essay. Both sides were agreed, however, that young children were incapable of writing meaningful essays. Numerous writing primers were devised to try to facilitate the transition from reading to writing.[100]

Wang Yun thought a student was ready to write essays at the age of sixteen *sui*. Like Chang Hsueh-ch'eng, he used a metaphor of physical growth and maturation to describe how a child progressed from early memorization to the adult ability to compose essays. Prosodic rules could be learned mechanically, but the aesthetic sensibility needed to appreciate style and moral content took time and ultimately depended on the student himself. Because of the demands of the civil examinations, even those like Chang Hsueh-ch'eng who expressed doubts about the usefulness of the eight-legged essay form (see Chapter 7) chose the examination essay to teach writing.[101]

99. See Chang Hsueh-ch'eng, "Lun k'o-meng hsueh wen-fa" 論科蒙學文法 (On teaching students to write), in *Chang-shih i-shu* 章氏遺書 (Bequeathed works of Mr. Chang Hsueh-ch'eng) (reprint, Shanghai: Commercial Press, 1936), "Pu-i" 補遺 (Supplement), p. 3a.

100. See Chang Chih-kung, *Ch'uan-t'ung yü-wen chiao-yü ch'u-t'an*, pp. 139–43, on teaching the eight-legged essay. For the different views of training writing, see Ridley, "Educational Theory and Practice in Late Imperial China," pp. 447–49. For an overview of Ch'ing classical writing primers, see pp. 64–83.

101. Wang Yun, "Chiao t'ung-tzu fa" 教童子法 (On teaching youthful students). In *Ch'ing-tai ch'ien-ch'i chiao-yü lun-chu hsuan*, pp. 485–86. Cf. Ridley, "Educational Theory and Practice in Late Imperial China," pp. 449–57.

The transition from glib childhood phrases to serious adult essays was mediated by the use of grammatical particles (*hsu-tzu* 虛字), which enabled the prose writer to navigate from the balanced pieces of literary form to a thematically tightly conceived classical essay. Ch'eng Tuan-li noted the importance of such particles for writing during the Yuan dynasty in his sophisticated account of the phonological, paleographical, and etymological moorings of the classical essay and how such techniques had to be used to produce a sophisticated essay worthy of respect and emulation.[102] The *Chu-tzu pien-lueh* 助字辨略 (Discerning the use of particles), prepared by Liu Ch'i 劉淇 in the early Ch'ing, provided teachers and students with a systematic dictionary of particles and their usage, which Li maintained complemented "concrete words" (*shih-tzu* 實字) as the two pillars of a good classical essay.[103]

Many teachers of writing, both Wang Yun and Chang Hsueh-ch'eng included, saw the eight-legged essay as a necessary evil, but they challenged the usual methods for teaching this mechanical form by first showing students how to emulate ancient-style prose essays of the great T'ang and Sung masters, which were then undergoing a revival.[104] These *ku-wen* pieces were thought by many in the Ch'ing to be the prose origins of the eight-legged essay form in the Sung before the examination essay took a more mechanical, rule-like direction in the Ming (see Chapter 7). Chang Hsueh-ch'eng considered the eight-legged essay too difficult for most beginning students and recommended starting with smaller sections.[105]

Throughout the late empire, however, prose composition remained trapped between the ideals of classical educators such as Chang Hsueh-ch'eng and the reality of the centrality of the classical essay (and regulated poetry in Chang's time) for personal, family, and lineage success.[106] Few students could separate the classical essay as a literary form from its careerist political and social context. The many that railed against it, as we shall see in Chapter 7, eventually took matters into their own hands and made a virtue out of necessity by inscribing the mid-Ming inspired

102. See Ch'eng Tuan-li, *Ch'eng-shih chia-shu tu-shu fen-nien jih-ch'eng*, "Hsueh tso-wen" 學作文 (Studying how to write essays), 2.5b–9a; ibid., "Tso k'o-chü wen-tzu chih fa" 作科舉文字之法 (Rules for writing characters in the civil examinations), 2.9b–12b; and ibid., "I-lun t'i" 議論體 (Style for arguments), 2.17b–20b.

103. See Ridley, "Educational Theory and Practice in Late Imperial China," pp. 458–61.

104. See Theodore Huters, "From Writing to Literature: The Development of Late Qing Theories of Prose," *Harvard Journal of Asiatic Studies* 47, 1 (June 1987).

105. Wang Yun, "Chiao t'ung-tzu fa," pp. 491–92; and Chang Hsueh-ch'eng, "Lun k'o-meng hsueh wen-fa," pp. 1b–2a.

106. On these issues, see Nivison, "Protest against Conventions and Conventions of Protest," pp. 195–201.

"eight-legged essay" with a degree of literary seriousness in the eighteenth century, which would grant it respectability for a time among literati as a proud emblem of classical literacy and ancient-style prose.

### ꞏ Classical Specialization during the Ming and Ch'ing

In their studies, candidates for Ming and Ch'ing civil examinations were permitted to specialize on one of the Five Classics (*chuan-ching* 專經). The tradition of classical specialization went back to the Han dynasty, when the court assigned specialists as *po-shih* 博士 (learned literatus) to the Imperial Academy (*T'ai-hsueh* 太學). This tradition of specialization dated specifically from the reign of Han Wu-ti 漢武帝 (140–87 B.C.), who appointed the "Learned literati of the Five Classics" (*wu-ching po-shih* 五經 博士) to the academy.[107] During the T'ang and Sung, along with specialty examinations in law, calligraphy, and mathematics, specialization examinations on the Classics were continued. Under the Yuan, specialization on one of the Five Classics was reinitiated in 1314.[108]

Until 1787, when all of the Five Classics became required (see below), licentiates and *chü-jen* degree-holders wrote essays on session one of the provincial and metropolitan examinations using quotations from the Four Books and the Classic of their choice. In 1370–71, *chü-jen* and *chin-shih* candidates prepared one essay of 500 characters on the Classic of their choice and one essay of 300 characters on the Four Books. In 1384, the requirements were increased to three short essays (200 characters each) on the Four Books and four essays (now 300 characters each) on one of the Five Classics. These length requirements gradually changed, and in Ch'ing times essays on the Four Books and one of the Five Classics were required to have an increasing number of characters: 550 graphs in 1646; 650 in 1681; and 700 in 1778.[109]

Registration records noted beforehand which of the Five Classics a candidate had selected, and clerks in the provincial and metropolitan examination compounds assigned his papers to the appropriate wardroom in which the associate examiner graded papers for that particular Classic (see Chapter 4). Wang Yang-ming, for example, registered as one of the 2,200 candidates for the 1492 Che-chiang provincial examination at the age of only twenty *sui*. Wang passed on his first try as one of the 4% who became *chü-jen* from Che-chiang that year, although he finished a disap-

---

107. See T'ang Chih-chün 湯志鈞 et al., *Hsi-Han ching-hsueh yü cheng-chih* 西漢經學與政 治 (Classicism and politics in the Western Han) (Shanghai: Ku-chi Press, 1994), pp. 61–82.

108. *Wu-li t'ung-k'ao*, 173.26a–27a, 174.14a, 174.16a.

109. See *Chih-i k'o-so-chi*, 1.4, 1.10. See also *Ch'ing-shih kao*, 11.3151–52 (*chüan* 108).

pointing number seventy out of ninety graduates. In addition, he was one of the nine *chü-jen* specialists (10%) on the *Record of Rites* (*Li-chi*). Assuming the graduate quotas per Classic reflected the pool of candidates as well, then 610 (28%) candidates specialized on the *Change Classic*, 490 (22%) on the *Documents*, 760 (34%) studied the *Poetry Classic*, 120 (5.5%) specialized on the *Spring and Autumn Annals*, and 220 (10%) on the *Li-chi*.[110]

This registration information tells us that by the time he passed local examinations in Yü-yao county, Wang Yang-ming had probably memorized 145,000 repeating graphs, two-thirds of which came from the *Record of Rites*. Given its length (only the *Tso Commentary* to the *Annals* was longer), Wang was making a minority choice when he selected the lengthy *Li-chi* for memorization, although that choice was made easier by the fact that two of the Four Books came from its midst. Nevertheless, Wang Yang-ming was among a small group of candidates. Eighty-five percent of the others studied either the *Change, Documents,* or *Poetry Classic*. Competition in the wardrooms of these Classics was very intense; for the *Li-chi* and *Annals*, however, it was much less. What was lost in the longer amount of time needed to memorize the *Record of Rites* was made up for by the lower levels of competition (one out of 220) within that classical ward.

In the 1499 metropolitan examination, Wang Yang-ming, then twenty-eight, was one of the twenty-two (7.3%) graduates (out of 300) who had chosen the *Rites* for their classical essays. Wang's metropolitan essays were graded by the associate examiners assigned to the wardroom for that Classic, Liu Ch'un 劉春 (1487 *chin-shih*) and Lin T'ing-yü 林廷玉 (1454–1532; 1484 *chin-shih*), both of whom had also specialized on the *Li-chi*. Wang Yang-ming's essay on one of the *Li-chi* quotations, which dealt with ritual and music (*li-yueh* 禮樂), was chosen as the best essay out of a total of about 255 candidates who were *Li-chi* specialists and recorded in the official *Hui-shih lu* 會試錄 (Record of the metropolitan examination). This high finish in a less competitive examination ward enabled Wang eventually to finish second overall on the 1499 metropolitan examination, which classified him as one of the *wu-k'uei* 五魁, the top five finishers (one chosen from each classical ward) for the Five Classics.[111] Had he specialized on the *Poetry Classic,* for instance, he would have had to compete with about 1,285 candidates, for the *Change* 875, and for the *Documents* 840 competitors. Wang Yang-ming then finished ninth on the palace examination, which required a single policy essay on the uses of ritual and music to bring order to society.[112]

110. *Che-chiang hsiang-shih lu,* 1492: 16a–21a.

111. *Huang-Ming kung-chü k'ao,* 1.63b–64a. Cf. *Ch'eng-wei lu,* 24.27a–b.

112. See *Hui-shih lu,* 1484 (unpaginated), 1487: 6b, and 1499: 5a–11b; and *Tien-shih teng-k'o lu,* 1499: 9b (examination roll), 1a–6a (imperial question).

Table 5.13 places Wang Yang-ming's individual choice of classical specialization in 1492 within the context of Che-chiang provincial examinations throughout the Ming dynasty (see also Tables 2.3 and 2.4). We can see that in terms of classical quotas 1499 was a typical mid-Ming provincial examination in Che-chiang. Secular trends in the choice of classical specialization by young literati allow us to describe changes in classical studies during the Ming dynasty, which future studies of literati intellectual currents may be able to contextualize more appropriately than we can do here. We know that the number of examination wards in provincial and metropolitan examinations waxed and waned based on the changing specialization rates for the Five Classics.

For example, one of the reasons for the popularity of the *Annals* in the early Ming was its patronage by the Hung-wu emperor in 1395 as the most comprehensive Classic in the official canon, which contained the "great pattern and model of the sages" (求聖人大經大法).[113] In addition, we know that in the early Ming, the Sung dynasty Hu An-kuo commentary was favored over the much longer and more ancient Han dynasty commentaries to the *Annals*. Thus, early Ming students did not have to memorize the 280,000 graphs in the three Han commentaries. When questions from the *Tso Commentary* were used, however, most candidates began to choose other Classics to master, leaving the *Annals* as the choice of specialization for only about 6% to 8% of the candidates after 1500.[114]

Over the course of the Ming dynasty, two major trends in Che-chiang provincial examinations are discernible: (1) the decline in popularity of the *Spring and Autumn Annals* among civil examination candidates from a high of 28% in 1370 to a low of 5.6% in 1501; (2) the dramatic increase in the specialization rates for the *Change Classic* from 10% in 1403 to 42% in 1576. Briefer trends include: (1) the fifteenth-century popularity of the *Documents Classic*, peaking in 1423 at 38%; (2) the slow decline of specialization rates for the *Poetry Classic* in the late Ming from 36% in 1501 to 27% in 1600; and (3) the fifty-year upward spike in rates for the *Li-chi* to over 10% from 1423, which lasted in Che-chiang until 1492, when Wang Yang-ming chose the *Li-chi* in the provincial examination there.

These trends are confirmed by Table 5.14, which gives us specialization trends in Ming Fu-chien provincial examinations. When further compared with Table 2.3 on Ming civil metropolitan examinations and Table 2.4 on the Ming Ying-t'ien capital region examinations, we can conclude that empirewide there was a remarkable consistency in the popularity of the

113. *Huang-Ming kung-chü k'ao*, 1.72b–73a.
114. Ridley, "Educational Theory and Practice in Late Imperial China," p. 210.

*Poetry Classic.* About 30% to 35% of young literati consistently chose it for their specialization. If 50,000 to 75,000 licentiates competed in late Ming triennial provincial examinations, then our specialization figures tell us that 15,000 to 22,500 of them had chosen the 40,000 graphs in the *Poetry* to memorize, in addition to the 75,000 graphs in the Four Books. Besides its more reasonable length (the *Poetry* was the third shortest Classic), its song-like quality when coupled to its immediately available mnemonic devices such as rhymes and parallel phrases made it a favorite among examination candidates to chant during the Ming dynasty.

The *Documents* and *Change* Classics remained perennial favorites among Ming examination candidates. As the two shortest Classics with about 25,000 graphs in each, the *Change* and *Documents* initially had specialization rates of over 20%, and such rates rose to over 30% for each, although at different times. Whereas the popularity of the *Documents Classic* peaked in the early fifteenth century and then declined back to a specialization rate of 20% in the late Ming, the *Change* reached 30% in the mid-Ming and stayed at that high level, challenging the *Poetry Classic* as first choice in the civil examination market, at times drawing 40% of the candidates.

During the Ch'ing dynasty, the rates of specialization remained remarkably consistent. In 1645, the 171 *chü-jen* quota in the Shun-t'ien capital region provincial examination was set according to classical specialization: forty-nine graduates on the *Change Classic* or 28.7%; sixty on the *Poetry* or 35.1%; thirty-six on the *Documents* or 21.1%; fifteen on the *Annals* or 8.8%; and eleven on the *Rites* or 6.4%. Other provinces were expected to conform, more or less, to these percentages, which tables 5.15 and 5.16 confirm. The quota was adopted to ensure that there would be *chü-jen* and *chin-shih* graduates from all the Classics, despite the popularity of the *Change, Poetry,* and *Documents* Classics among the candidates. Officials feared that if Ming dynasty trends continued, the three shortest Classics would eventually surpass the 85% allotment granted to them as a whole, and almost no one would study the *Annals* or *Record of Rites.*[115]

There were also reports in 1723 that because candles were not authorized for local examinations held in the winter, when daylight hours were shorter, the required essay question on the Classics was often omitted. Local examiners by custom only assigned winter *t'ung-sheng* candidates and licentiates the two required essays on quotations from the Four Books. This custom meant that many licentiates, particularly those who sought only local degree status, were not bothering to master even one of the Five Classics. To resolve this, the Yung-cheng emperor decreed that dur-

115. See *Ch'eng-wei lu,* 114.27a–b.

ing the winter one essay each on both the Four Books and Five Classics would be required on local licensing and renewal examinations.[116]

Seventeenth-century literati such as Ku Yen-wu had already critiqued Ming classical learning for its superficiality and blamed this problem in part on the popularity of certain Classics due to the classical specialization policy, which resulted in fewer candidates having a comprehensive knowledge of the Classics. Others such as Huang Tsung-hsi were also part of this broader wave in literati learning that encouraged a reemphasis on the Five Classics. In the 1681 Chiang-nan provincial examination, for instance, Chu I-tsun 朱彝尊 (1629–1709) served as examiner. One of the policy questions he prepared tested the candidates on the *chuan-ching* 專經 requirement, which he traced back to the Sung and Yuan dynasty, when Sung commentaries first took precedence over Han and T'ang dynasty scholia (*chu-shu* 注疏).[117] A consensus among literati began to emerge slowly in the eighteenth century that mastery of only one Classic was insufficient. Eventually the Ch'ing government was convinced by this consensus that all the Classics should be learned by all candidates.[118]

As the tables in Appendix 3 reveal, early in the Ch'ien-lung reign a special category already existed for *chü-jen* and *chin-shih* who had mastered all of the Five Classics. This category dated from 1724 during the Yung-cheng reign, when the emperor had added five such graduates to the regular *chü-jen* quota for most provinces. Such special "Five Classics" candidates were encouraged to write all twenty essays on the four quotations from each of the Classics, instead of only four on a single Classic. If they did this successfully on the first session, in addition to preparing the mandatory three essays on the Four Books, then they were exempted from all but the documentary questions on the second and third sessions of provincial and metropolitan examinations.[119] Table 5.15 reveals that 8.2% of the candidates in the 1735 Shun-t'ien examination chose this new path, which required memorizing 470,000 repeating graphs compared to the typical 100,000 to 115,000 memorized by those who wrote essays on the Four Books and one of the three shortest Classics. Table 5.16 indicates that less than 5% in Chiang-nan followed this new educational path in the

---

116. Ridley, "Educational Theory and Practice in Late Imperial China," p. 214.

117. See Chu I-tsun 朱彝尊, *P'u-shu t'ing-chi* 曝書亭集 (Collection from the Pavilion for Honoring Books), *Ssu-pu pei-yao* edition, 60.10a–b.

118. Ku Yen-wu, *Jih-chih-lu chi-shih*, pp. 471–73 (*chüan* 19). For discussion, see my *From Philosophy to Philology*, pp. 113–18.

119. *Kuo-ch'ao liang-Che k'o-ming lu* 國朝兩浙科名錄 (Record of examinations in Che-chiang during the Ch'ing dynasty), 1857 edition (Peking), p. 139a; and Liang Chang-chü, *Chih-i ts'ung-hua*, 1.2a–2b.

1740s, a figure that is confirmed in Table 5.17 for the 1742 metropolitan examination in Peking. The distinguished Chia-ting county classicist Wang Ming-sheng 王鳴盛 (1722–98), for instance, took advantage of this option in the 1747 Chiang-nan provincial examination.[120]

Reforms to encourage classical studies on the civil examinations were completed in three stages over three decades between 1756 and 1786 (see Chapter 10 for a detailed account). In 1787, the court decided to move the new (in 1756) poetry question from session two to session one to balance the Four Books, a move that infuriated Ch'ing literati who still supported Sung and Yuan Tao Learning examination essay reforms (again, see Chapter 10). The addition of regulated verse to the curriculum entailed that all candidates, from all local to the metropolitan examinations, also had to master the famous collections of T'ang and Sung ancient-style poetry (*ku-shih* 古詩), most notably the *T'ang-shih san-pai-shou* 唐詩三百首 (Three hundred T'ang poems).[121]

At the same time, the emperor decided to phase in gradually over five years from 1788 to 1793 the requirement that all literati must master each of the Five Classics. Given the formidable length (about 470,000 repeating characters) of the Five Classics, it was impossible to change the memorization habits of students overnight. After 1793, therefore, the classical memorization requirements for *chü-jen* and *chin-shih* degrees increased over fourfold for young candidates, to which must be added the requirement since 1756 that candidates must also learn hundreds of T'ang and Sung ancient-style poems (*ku-shih* 古詩). Miyazaki Ichisada's ahistorical portrait of an "examination hell" based on memorization in China therefore can be dated from 1793 to 1898, the last century of the institution.[122] Such changes affected literati by increasing the number of years of classical study required to master the examination curriculum, which translated into older degree graduates.

---

120. See *Chiang-nan hsiang-shih lu,* 1747: 26a. Those that specialized had to answer only the *piao* document question. Those who chose to master all Five Classics were required to prepare all three documents: *chao, kao,* and *piao.* See the *T'i-mu* 題目 (Questions) posters for 1724 metropolitan and 1741 Shun-t'ien provincial examinations, in the Ming-Ch'ing Archives, Academia Sinica, Taiwan.

121. See Weng Fang-kang 翁方綱 (1733–1818), "Tzu-hsu" 自序 (Personal preface) to his *Shih-chou shih-hua* 石洲詩話 (Poetry talks from rock islets), in *Ch'ing shih-hua hsu-pien* 清詩話續編 (Ch'ing works on poetry discussions, continuation), compiled by Kuo Shao-yü 郭紹虞 (Shanghai: Ku-chi Press, 1983), p. 1363, which describes how in 1765–68 when serving as provincial examiner and education commissioner, Weng discussed the addition of poetry to the curriculum with all county yamen staffs.

122. See Li T'iao-yuan, *Tan-mo lu,* 16.10a–12a. Cf. Miyazaki, *China's Examination Hell,* pp. 111–29.

## THE AGE OF *CHÜ-JEN* AND *CHIN-SHIH* AT TIME OF DEGREE

One of the most distinguishing features of the late imperial civil examination system was its lack of overt discrimination against the elderly. In a society in which filial piety and respect for elders was a foundation of public and private morality, it made eminent sense to rulers, examiners, and candidates that all ages should be eligible to take civil examinations as many times as they could afford to and as long as their social and linguistic credentials remained intact. In fact, however, the examinations could alter perceptions of one's social status in remarkable ways. Elderly licentiates, for example, would grovel before youthful *chü-jen* degree-holders because of their differentiated political status, which augmented the social status of the successful young man and diminished that of the failed elderly. Old failures contrasted with youthful prodigies within a public ideology that honored the elderly but left room for unofficial stress on youth and mental vitality.

In his satirical novel *Ju-lin wai-shih* 儒林外史 (The scholars), the eighteenth-century novelist and examination failure Wu Ching-tzu 吳敬梓 (1701–54) exploited this theme in his depiction of a 1487 meeting between a younger licentiate who had passed the prefectural qualifying examination and an older village teacher in the temple school who was over sixty and had not yet qualified to try for the *chü-jen* degree: "Ming dynasty scholars called all those who passed the prefectural examination 'classmates,' and those who only qualified for this examination 'juniors.' A young man in his teens who passed was considered senior to an unsuccessful candidate, even if the latter were eighty years old. It was like the case of a concubine. A woman is called 'new wife' when she marries, and later 'mistress'; but a concubine remains 'new wife' even when her hair is white."[123] Yet, in theory at least, all competed in the examination market on an equal footing within the examination compound.

Table 3.19, which profiles civil examination success in Fu-chien province during the Ming dynasty, also curiously records the wide range in the ages of candidates who passed the civil examinations, as if success on the relentless examinations were a mark of both precociousness and endurance. Over forty degree-holders in Ming Fu-chien were between thirteen and nineteen *sui*, which is not surprising given how early young men began to memorize the Four Books and one of the Five Classics. More than eighty Fu-chien graduates were over eighty, however, with some over one hundred *sui* when they entered the examination com-

123. Wu Ching-tzu, *The Scholars*, pp. 17–18. For discussion, see Ropp, *Dissent in Early Modern China*, pp. 61–75.

pounds. One, Lin Ch'un-tse 林春澤, was appointed as prefect at the age of one hundred four![124]

Given the prodigious memorization requirements, less before 1756 and considerably more after 1793, boys who achieved *chü-jen* status before age twenty were heralded as prodigies. Wang Shih-chen 王世貞 (1526–90) was said to have memorized a prodigious number of characters by the age of six and gained his *chü-jen* degree at age seventeen. In 1547 at the age of only twenty-one, Shih-chen passed the metropolitan and palace examinations and went on to literary fame and high position.[125] T'ang Hsien-tsu 湯顯祖 (1550–1616), who became one of the most celebrated scholar-playwrights of the seventeenth century, received his licentiate degree at the precocious age of thirteen in his Chiang-hsi hometown. Taught by his grandfather in early childhood, T'ang then studied in his family school, where he was instructed by Lo Ju-fang 羅汝芳 (1515–88), a follower of Wang Yang-ming. Skilled at an early age in the composition of eight-legged essays, T'ang Hsien-tsu passed the 1570 Chiang-hsi provincial examination at the age of only twenty, the first in his family to receive the *chü-jen* degree. After starting out in 1571 at age twenty-one with four unsuccessful attempts (the others were in 1574, 1577, and 1580) to pass the metropolitan examination, however, T'ang had to wait until 1583 before he was able to gain the *chin-shih* degree on his fifth try at age thirty-three.[126]

Weng Fang-kang's 翁方綱 (1733–1818) reputation as a distinguished scholar-official, for example, derived in part because of his fame for becoming a licentiate at the very unusual age of eleven *sui* in 1744. He took his *chü-jen* degree in Fu-chien province at the unheard-of age of fourteen in 1747, and gained his *chin-shih* at nineteen in 1752, both when a candidate still was only required to master one of the Five Classics. In 1754, when he was twenty-one, Weng Fang-kang capped his precipitous career rise and became a Hanlin bachelor. Weng was particularly influential in the wider use of the poetry question on the examinations after 1756.[127]

The Mongol bannerman and scholar-official Fa-shih-shan 法式善 (1753–1813), whose *Ch'ing-mi shu-wen* 清秘述聞 (Gleanings on Ch'ing secrets) detailed Ch'ing official examiners in seventeenth- and eighteenth-century civil examinations, became a licentiate at the age of twenty-six *sui*

---

124. *Min-sheng hsien-shu*, 1.38a–42a.

125. *Dictionary of Ming Biography*, pp. 1399–1400.

126. See Cyril Birch, trans., *Scenes for Mandarins*, pp. 10–13; and Hummel, ed., *Eminent Chinese of the Ch'ing Period*, pp. 708–09.

127. See Weng Fang-kang, "Tzu-hsu" to his *Shih-chou shih-hua*, p. 1363. Cf. Hummel, ed., *Eminent Chinese of the Ch'ing Period*, p. 856.

in 1778. He owed such early success to having been adopted into a Mongol household of a bannerman who had married a Han Chinese woman with considerable poetic and classical talent. She trained him in the Classics. The next year, as a non-Han prodigy, Fa-shih-shan passed the provincial examination, and two years later in 1780, at the age of only twenty-eight, he entered the Hanlin Academy, despite a *chin-shih* degree ranking at the bottom of the third tier. He became one of the most distinguished classicists of his time.[128]

Similarly, the late Ch'ing literatus Chang Chih-tung 張之洞 (1837–1909) accomplished the feat of passing the 1852 Shun-t'ien provincial examination at the age of fifteen *sui*, a remarkable accomplishment when it is recalled that the requirements now included all of the Five Classics, and he finished first besides. His essays on the Four Books, and both his poetry answer and essay for the first policy answer, were included in the official record of the examination as model writings. They were recopied and emulated in subsequent examinations. Eleven years later, at the still relatively young age of twenty-six, Chang passed the metropolitan examination for the *chin-shih* degree, ranking third on the 1863 palace examination. He then entered the Hanlin Academy, from where he was later sent out to supervise provincial examinations in Che-chiang, Hu-pei, and Ssu-ch'uan from 1867 to 1877.[129]

One was considered old if by the age of forty *sui*, he was still taking local qualifying examinations, though there was a report of a man in Hu-pei who was over seventy when he took a local examination. Indeed, old men were known to explain classical passages to younger candidates in the examination compound in exchange for essays written by the younger man in the latest styles.[130] Authorities frequently noted that in licensing examinations for the youngest candidates (*t'ung-sheng*), the registration forms often indicated that the candidate was a youth and yet the person taking the examination was sometimes forty or fifty. To prevent fraud at the time of registration and false entry into the examination compound, as we have seen, examination officials scolded education officials for not comparing the forms more carefully to the person actually entering to take the examination.[131]

---

128. Fa-shih-shan 法式善, *Ch'ing-mi shu-wen* 清秘述聞 (Gleanings on Ch'ing secrets) (Peking: Chung-hua Bookstore, 1982). Cf. Hummel, ed., *Eminent Chinese of the Ch'ing Period*, p. 227. Hummel mistakenly gives sixteen for Fa-shih-shan's age when he became a licentiate.

129. *Shun-t'ien hsiang-shih-lu* 順天鄉試錄 (Record of the Shun-t'ien provincial civil examination), 1852: 44a. Chang's essays for all the quotations from the *Four Books* 四書文 are on pp. 31a–38b. His poem is on pp. 38b–39b, and his policy answer on pp. 53a–56.

130. See *Ch'ing-pai lei-ch'ao*, compiled by Hsu K'o, 21.25, 21.38, 21.42.

131. For a 1741 example, see *Ch'in-ting Ta-Ch'ing hui-tien shih-li*, 386.8b.

The few who went on to pass the prohibitively competitive Ming and Ch'ing dynasty provincial examinations, in which less than 5% usually graduated, were usually in their mid- to late twenties. Table 5.18 discloses that in the sixteenth century, for instance, most provincial graduates (63%) in Ying-t'ien prefecture were aged between twenty-one and thirty, and only 26% were between thirty-one and forty. The youngest graduate was fifteen *sui*, while the oldest was fifty. When we compare such Ming provincial results in Nanking with those empirewide in the Ch'ing period in Table 5.19, we find that the age at which candidates typically became *chü-jen* in the nineteenth century increased. The 21–30 *sui* group now decreased to 42% in 1834 and 1851, whereas the 31–40 *sui* group constituted 37% in 1834 and 36% in 1851, compared to 26% in 1531. Moreover, during the Ming only 7% to 8% had been over forty, with none over fifty *sui*, while in the Ch'ing 15% to 17% were over forty. Over 3% of all *chü-jen* in 1835 and 1851 were over fifty. This age shift can be directly tied to the end of the custom of classical specialization in 1787, and the sudden increase after 1793 in the amount of material that had to be mastered, which clearly took candidates much more time.

The 1894 *chuang-yuan* Chang Chien, who, as we have seen, qualified in 1871 at the youthful age of eighteen for the Chiang-nan provincial examination, failed at this level five times over the next ten years (1870, 1873, 1875, 1876, and 1879) before finally passing in 1885, ranked second at the age of thirty-three. This age of passing was typical for 20% of the provincial candidates. During these ten years Chang had been required to take and pass several renewal and requalifying examinations to remain eligible for the *chü-jen* degree. After his belated success in the provincial examination, it took Chang five tries (1886, 1889, 1890, 1892, and 1894) before he successfully passed the metropolitan examination nine years later at the age of forty-two. Although he only ranked sixtieth on the *hui-shih*, Chang placed tenth on a reexamination, and he finished first on the 1894 palace examination. He immediately entered the Hanlin Academy as a compiler. His subsequent fame as an *optimus* rested on almost twenty years of examination failure in Chang Chien's life, during which he persevered under the pressure to succeed.[132]

When old men in their eighties qualified for the provincial examinations, as became more common in the late Ch'ing, they were typically rewarded with *fu-pang* 副榜 (secondary list) honors, even when they again failed. In the 1852 provincial examinations, there were thirteen men over ninety *sui*, for example, and they were awarded the *chü-jen* degree. In addition, the sixty-five candidates over eighty were granted *fu-pang* status.

132. Ridley, "Educational Theory and Practice in Late Imperial China," pp. 154–56.

There were seventeen candidates over ninety in 1853, with seventy-nine over eighty *sui*.[133]

Those who passed the metropolitan and palace examinations in the capital ranged in age from their twenties to their fifties and sixties, although most were in their mid- to late thirties or early forties when they received the cherished *chin-shih* degree. Tables 5.20 and 5.21 compare the ages of the top-ranked civilian *chin-shih* (called *chuang-yuan*) for both the Ming and Ch'ing dynasties. We see that in the Ming about 13% of all *optimi* for whom we have information were under twenty-five *sui*. In the Ch'ing this percentage decreased to 6%. Over half of the fifty-five Ming *chuang-yuan* were aged between twenty-six and thirty-five; in the Ch'ing this remained roughly the same. For the Ming, 83% of the *optimi* were age twenty-six to forty-five, for the Ch'ing 86%. Older *chuang-yuan* (over forty-six) increased from only 4% in the Ming to about 8% in the Ch'ing. The range in Ming times was from nineteen (1487) to fifty-one *sui* (1589), and in the Ch'ing from twenty-four (1737 and 1778) to fifty-nine *sui* (1703). In general, fewer youths and more older men were chosen as *chuang-yuan* as we move from the Ming to the Ch'ing dynasty, with the average age moving from thirty-three to thirty-six. Consequently, we can see that Chang Chien was a fairly typical, although somewhat older, *optimus* in 1894. Most, like him, had failed provincial and metropolitan examinations several times over ten to twenty years of their adult lives before they arrived at the pinnacle of the examination system. The emotional costs of such delayed success will be assessed in Chapter 6.

Tables 5.22 and 5.23 tell us a bit more about the general age divisions among all *chin-shih* graduates, not simply those such as Chang Chien who finished first. In the figures for the palace examinations of 1472 and 1529, we see that very few were under twenty and that most *chin-shih* were between twenty-six and forty-five *sui* (94% in 1472 and 82% in 1529). A greater number (16%) were twenty-five or under in 1529, however. During the Ch'ing, 72% of all *chin-shih* were between twenty-six and forty-five in 1835, 80% in 1868, and 86% in 1894—figures that are roughly comparable to the Ch'ing *chuang-yuan* totals shown above.

Unlike the figures for *chuang-yuan*, however, younger (twenty-five *sui* and under) metropolitan graduates increased during the nineteenth century, suggesting that while the average age of *chin-shih* at the time of degree increased from the Ming to the Ch'ing, the number of younger *chin-shih*

133. *Ch'ing-pai lei-ch'ao*, 21.95. In 1736, the Ch'ien-lung emperor rewarded all old men who took the metropolitan examination that year. See also *Hsu-tseng k'o-ch'ang t'iao-li* 續增科場條例 (Continuation to the Imperially prescribed guidelines for the civil examination grounds), 1855 edition, pp. 9a, 27b–28a, 40a–41a, 50b–52b.

was also growing, though fewer became *optimi*. In 1868, 15% of all *chin-shih* were twenty-five or under; in 1894 the rate was 11%. Only 6% of *chuang-yuan* during the Ch'ing were under twenty-five. As the number of candidates for the *chü-jen* degree increased in the Ch'ing, their average age also increased (see Table 5.19), but on the metropolitan examinations for the *chin-shih* degree younger *chin-shih* were doing better than older ones. The percentage of those over fifty *sui* declined from 5% in 1835 to less than 1% in 1894. Perhaps, younger candidates were more in tune with the stylistic changes associated with late Ch'ing examination essay trends (see Chapter 7). Perhaps the reintroduction of poetry questions in the late eighteenth century also made a difference. Whatever the reason, more older candidates were failing than in the past.

Examiners reported the unusual increase in older candidates, often with great concern, because they realized that such old men had failed the examinations over and over again at a time when population increase had prohibitively outpaced examination places. In the 1699 Shun-t'ien provincial examination, for example, Huang Chang-pai 黃章百, a Kuang-tung literatus of over 100 *sui*, was led into the Peking examination compound (*kung-yuan* 貢院) at night with full pomp and circumstance by his great-grandson, who held a lantern and a placard with the words "a hundred year-old in the examination compound" (*pai-sui kuan-ch'ang* 百歲觀場) to commemorate the event of both taking the examination.[134] At the other extreme, the Ch'ien-lung emperor also commanded examiners in 1770 to pass two youths, one eleven and the other thirteen *sui*, at the Shun-t'ien provincial examination in order to encourage them as young prodigies to qualify for the metropolitan examinations.[135]

In 1784, the increase in elderly candidates for the *chin-shih* became very alarming. A memorial by Chuang Ts'un-yü noted that among the metropolitan candidates that year, one was over ninety, twenty were over eighty, and five were over 70 *sui*. The Ch'ien-lung emperor ordered officials to give them special awards, even though they had not passed the examination.[136] In 1826, a 104-year-old candidate, again from Kuang-tung,

134. *Kuo-ch'ao kung-chü k'ao-lueh* 國朝貢舉考略 (Summary of Ch'ing civil examinations), compiled by Huang Ch'ung-lan 黃崇蘭, 1834 edition, 1.30b; and *Ch'ing-pai lei-ch'ao*, 21.67–68.

135. See *Li-pu t'i-pen*, 1770, 10th month, 5th day, in the Ming-Ch'ing Archives, Academia Sinica, Taiwan. The *Li-pu t'i-pen* of the same date also discusses giving one candidate who is eighty-five and another of eighty the *chü-jen* degree, if they do not pass on their own merits.

136. See the memorial Chuang Ts'un-yü prepared after the 1784 metropolitan examination in *Li-pu t'i-pen*, 1784, third month, 29th day.

failed the metropolitan examination but was assigned to the Imperial School as symbolic compensation.[137]

Such alarming trends were confirmed by contemporary Western observers: "In what land but China would it be possible to find examples of a grandfather, son, and grandson all competing in the same examination for the same degree, age and indomitable perseverance being rewarded at the age of eighty years by the long-coveted honor?"[138]

By its duration and elaboration from the Ming to Ch'ing, the late imperial civil examination system became a dynamic force in reproducing the character of Chinese society on terms of state and society that each dynasty and its cooperating literati set for themselves. Classical learning, literati prestige, dynastic power, and cultural practice were accommodated to this testing system to such a degree that the examination system in the Ming-Ch'ing era functioned as a measurable arbiter of elite culture, politics, and society. Civil examinations could not dictate to the society; literati dictated the curriculum to the government. In educational terms, the examinations were one of the main institutions communicating educational authority from one generation to the next.[139]

Despite shortcomings in fairness due to special facilitated degrees for licentiates, hereditary privileges for some officials, or purchase of degrees by the wealthy, and disparities in the geography of success, whether regional or rural-urban in form, the civil service examinations remained the main avenue to wealth and power in late imperial China until the late nineteenth century. The overlap between officials and gentry culture that resulted disguised, through the appearance of fairness and openness, the de facto elimination from officialdom of the lower classes. As a political, social, and cultural institution, the educational curriculum designed for the civil service in China served to defend and legitimate the differentiation

---

137. *Kuo-ch'ao kung-chü k'ao-lüeh*, 3.26b.

138. See Arthur H. Smith, *Chinese Characteristics*, p. 29; and E. L. Oxenham, "Ages of Candidates at Chinese Examinations; Tabular Statement," *Journal of the China Branch of the Royal Asiatic Society*, n.s., 23 (1888): 286–87, which gives age groups on ten sites for the 1885 provincial examinations. Oxenham noted: "One peculiarity of the examination system in China is the absence of any limit of age for intending competitors. Children of 12 to 15 and dotards of 80 can all equally compete at the same examination. The veterans rarely if ever succeed, but nearly every list of successful candidates contains the names of two, three, or four youthful prodigies under 20 years of age." See also Doolittle, *Social Life of the Chinese*, p. 398, on the honors bestowed on octogenarians competing for degrees.

139. Rieff, *The Feeling Intellect*, pp. 234–45.

of Chinese society into aristocratic rulers (even if non-Chinese in origin), gentry-officials, and illiterate or non–classically literate commoners.[140]

In general, the social dimensions of the literati and merchant groups who competed in the Ming-Ch'ing civil examination market described in this chapter were constantly under demographic pressure. By 1850, the institutions designed in the early Ming had not changed enough to keep pace with the society at large (see Chapter 3). As population trebled in Ch'ing times from 150 million in 1700 to 450 million in 1850, the number of *chü-jen* and *chin-shih* remained relatively stagnant. Competition for degrees at all levels, from the county to the capital, became prohibitive. The resulting ever higher memorization standards that became required in the late eighteenth century were a response to increased competition in the examination market.[141]

By focusing on the nineteenth century, most of my scholarly predecessors structured their usually negative assumptions about the late imperial civil service, its classical content, and the literary form of the examinations within a historical context that was too brief and exceptional. Moreover, interpretation of that institutional content and form has been colored by the animosity of early twentieth-century Chinese intellectuals toward the selection system. I suggest they were driven by historical agendas that we no longer share with them, while at the same time I acknowledge the emotionalism of their critiques and the partial validity of their hindsight.

My goal in this study is not to rehabilitate the imperial examination system of Ming and Ch'ing times. Instead, almost a century after its demise, we can gain a sense of how a carefully balanced and constantly contested piece of educational and social engineering had been worked out by cooperation between the imperial dynasty and its gentry-dominated society. The partnership worked relatively successfully until 1850, when the cataclysmic decline of both literati culture and imperial institutions began. Civil institutions for the social and political circulation of elites in effect served as a flawed but well-oiled "educational gyroscope" whose intense, self-centered motion every two or three years within examination compounds was the sine qua non for gentry officials and aristocratic rulers to maintain their proper balance and direction vis-à-vis the society at large. After 1850 that gyroscope was calibrated by a dynasty that increasingly lost its bearings. Instead of recognizing the demographic sources of their dynastic failure, the court and its officials eventually threw that gyroscope out the door (see Chapter 11).

---

140. Hsiao Kung-chuan, *Rural China: Imperial Control in the Nineteenth-Century* (Seattle: University of Washington Press, 1960), pp. 67–72.

141. See also Bielenstein, "The Regional Provenance," p. 11.

In the next chapters, I turn from the external, institutional, social, and political analysis of civil examinations in practice, which I engaged in in Chapters 3 to 5, to the internal, popular, literary and classical forms of knowledge that informed the examination curriculum and late imperial literati culture. The next object of analysis will be those cultural dimensions that existed outside the precincts of late imperial civil examinations. The cultural forms and popular images we will specify were not mere epiphenomena, hollow rhetoric, or superstitious belief that grew out of an autocratic political regime wedded to a savvy literati elite. Had they been empty cultural forms, the examination process would not have lasted very long, nor would it have voluntarily drawn into its "cultural prisons" the best and brightest of the empire.

# CHAPTER SIX

# Emotional Anxiety, Dreams of Success, and the Examination Life

Because the young and the old competed "equally" in the examination market, youths and old men brought different personal experiences into the examination compound. The rituals of success looked alluring to the young, while the tortures of failure were the common denominator of older men still seeking an elusive degree. For all, however, their emotional tensions, based on years of preparation for young boys, and even more years of defeat for old men, were the human response to the dynasty's examination regime. Its venues were places of opportunity for the young who succeeded and "cultural prisons" for the old who never made it out.[1] The pressure to succeed molded their individual characters. For most, persistence, symbolized by the career of *optimus* Chang Chien 張謇 (see Chapter 5), became a way of life. Others sublimated their frustrations into cultural symbols of elite and popular expression and, occasionally, political resistance to the cultural prisons that tormented them.

The institutional mechanisms of the civil examinations mediated between elite intellectual discourse and the everyday lives of literati. Emotional tensions, which brought a few fame and fortune but left most dealing with despair or disappointment, were the catalysts in their lives.[2] This chapter documents how often literati turned to religion and the mantic arts in their efforts to channel their emotional responses to the classical

1. See Fang I-chih's 方以智 (1611–71) account of "Seven Solutions" ("Ch'i-chieh" 七解), written in 1637, which presented options for a young man from a family of means, one of them being the "examination man"; translated in Willard Peterson, *Bitter Gourd*, pp. 44–47.

2. See Nivison, "Protest against Conventions and Conventions of Protest," pp. 177–201. Cf. Walter Abell, *The Collective Dream in Art* (Cambridge: Harvard University Press, 1957), pp. 57–66.

regime of competitive local, provincial, and metropolitan examinations. Shang Yen-liu 商衍鎏, the last Ch'ing *tertius*, on the 1904 civil palace examination, wrote about his examination experiences: "In 1891 at the age of twenty, my [brilliant] cousin passed the provincial examination and became a *chü-jen*. However, upon his return the following year to Kuang-chou [Canton], from the metropolitan examination in Peking, he fell ill and died soon after. My mother said to me, 'Too much intelligence short-ens one's life—better be a bit stupid like you.' " [3]

Popular novels such as Wu Ching-tzu's (1701–54) *The Scholars* and sto-ries by P'u Sung-ling 蒲松齡 (1640–1715) were usually written in the ver-nacular by those who failed classical examinations and therefore mocked the selection process in a popular idiom. Such fictional accounts were not "transparent texts." Their narratives must be read as cultural construc-tions that frame the examination process from the point of view of the failures. Because such works appealed to both elites and non-elites as a "popular" audience, I intentionally problematize the "popular-elite" dichotomy below and show the complex and fluid interaction between both poles. [4] Recorded dreams and auspicious events were manifest, nonofficial accounts of the underlying, collective mental tensions of the examination candidates that publicly explained their individual success or failure. [5]

Hence, the anxiety produced by examinations was a historical phenom-enon, which was experienced most personally and deeply by boys and men, given the gender ideology of their patriarchal society. Fathers and mothers, sisters and extended relatives, were not immune to this anxiety. They shared in the experience and offered comfort, solace, and encour-

3. Sheang [Shang] Yen-liu, "Memories of the Chinese Imperial Civil Service Examination System," p. 52. My thanks to Tom Metzger for telling me about this source.

4. See Robert Hegel, "Distinguishing Levels of Audiences for Ming-Ch'ing Vernacular Literature: A Case Study," in David Johnson, Andrew Nathan, and Evelyn Rawski, eds., *Popular Culture in Late Imperial China*, pp. 125–26; and Ropp, *Dissent in Early Modern China*, pp. 18–32. Cf. Miyazaki, *China's Examination Hell*, pp. 58–60. Because an exclusive dichotomy between "popular culture" and "elite discourse" will not explain adequately how the civil examination regime penetrated both elite and non-elite cultural life, I use "popular" to mean "nonofficial" rather than "non-elite." Hence, I mean by "popular" those techniques that elites and non-elites used to mediate fate and invoke religion to deal with their lives. My thanks to Eugenia Lean for her advice on this question.

5. See Judith Zeitlin, *Historian of the Strange: Pu Songling and the Chinese Classical Tale* (Stanford: Stanford University Press, 1993), pp. 132–81, on the use of dreams in late Ming literature. For Sung examinations and literati dreams of success, see Chaffee, *The Thorny Gates of Learning in Sung China*, pp. 177–81.

agement, but the direct, personal experience of examination success or failure belonged to the millions of male examination candidates who, as we have seen, competed with each other against increasingly difficult odds. A deep chasm of social and political making separated the official classical standards of the examiners (see Chapter 8) from the religious strategies candidates were willing to appropriate therapeutically to assuage their fears and emotions.

The frustration of literati in civil examinations was a common theme since Sui and T'ang times.[6] The required levels of memorizing characters, wide reading in classical works, and years of training needed to write classical essays (and regulated verse after 1756) entailed a childhood and young adulthood that sons of elites shared over time across generations and empirewide across linguistic and geographic barriers. Those who short-circuited the educational regime by mastering model examination essays and leaving the task of memorization to others were nonetheless classically literate if they hoped to get beyond the local licensing and qualifying examinations and enter officialdom.

Classical illiteracy was common in local tests, as we saw in the account of t'ung-sheng and sheng-yuan in Chapter 4, but the classically illiterate were generally weeded out in provincial examinations, where corruption inside the examination compound and examiner bribery were more telling alternate routes for classical literates to gain chü-jen and chin-shih degrees. In a triennial provincial examination market with 50 to 75 thousand candidates in Ming times, and 100 to 150 thousand in the Qing, the challenge was not to demonstrate classical literacy, which was the cultural divider for boys in local examinations, but to write elegant eight-legged essays that would stand out in a sea of essays by youths and old men who had honed their writing skills for decades. An attempt by a classically illiterate candidate to buy a lower degree was exposed quickly enough when such a young man bribed his way into office and was found out. The Ch'ing court in particular was always on the watch for such consequences.[7]

Examination success usually meant career success, although the terms of such success changed dramatically from Ming to Ch'ing (see Chapter 3). All but chin-shih degree-holders were downclassed by the late Ming, and in the Ch'ing even chin-shih degree-holders frequently had to wait years to gain appointment as a magistrate or prefect if they finished in the bottom

---

6. *T'ang-Sung k'o-ch'ang i-wen-lu* 唐宋科場異聞錄 (Recording unusual matters heard in the T'ang and Sung examination grounds), Wei-ching-t'ang shu-fang 味經堂書坊 edition (reprint, Canton: Ch'ien-t'ang, 1873). See also Chaffee, *The Thorny Gates of Learning in Sung China*, pp. 169–77.

7. See *Ch'in-ting mo-k'an t'iao-li*, 1.1a–19b.

tier of graduates. Enough local social prestige, legal privileges, and corvée labor exemptions continued to accrue to both *sheng-yuan* and *chü-jen*, however, to keep most young and old men from elite families competing in the examination market. The diminishing opportunities for success via civil examinations by the nineteenth century, however, severely exacerbated the human tensions that had been autochthonous to the market since the expansion of civil examinations during the T'ang and Sung dynasties. No dynasty had faced a demographic expansion of elites commensurate with the Ch'ing.[8]

Growing up as a male member of an elite family in Ming and Ch'ing times presupposed long-standing patterns of socialization. Adults defined childhood for millions of young men in terms of a regimen for daily examination preparation. Male anxiety and literati frustrations went hand in hand. What I call "male anxiety" was an elite social and intellectual phenomenon generated by the historical experiences of men in individual and family life. Indeed, as Judith Zeitlin has noted, Ming doctors had diagnosed a particular form of "emotional stasis" (*yü* 鬱), whose discernible symptoms of anxiety (*ssu-yü* 思鬱) they associated with failed examination candidates continually frustrated in their quest for success. There was no single response to this emotional pressure any more than there was an autonomous gentry-merchant elite to dictate that response. There were, however, discernible patterns in how Chinese elites dealt with the historical reality of male anxiety in the examination life, its relentless institutional machinery, and the diverse mental tensions the process engendered.[9]

8. In this regard, see the career of Chang Hsueh-ch'eng in the late eighteenth century, described by David Nivison in *The Life and Thought of Chang Hsueh-ch'eng (1738–1801)* (Stanford: Stanford University Press, 1966); and my *From Philosophy to Philology*, pp. 130–31. See also David Johnson, "Communication, Class, and Consciousness in Late Imperial China," pp. 50–67.

9. For earlier use of the concept of "male anxiety," see T'ien Ju-k'ang, *Male Anxiety and Female Chastity: A Comparative Study of Chinese Ethical Values in Ming-Ch'ing Times* (Leiden: E. J. Brill, 1988), pp. 83–89, which usefully links the frustrations of Ming scholars to the prohibitive level of competition in civil examinations. T'ien, however, delimits "male anxiety" to a single, unmediated response common to all literati in the Yangtzu delta and thereby overdetermines its scope as the only explanation for the rise of the ideal of female chastity in the late empire. For a critical review of *Male Anxiety and Female Chastity*, see Ropp, pp. 605–06, in *Journal of Asian Studies* 48, 3 (August 1989). See also Martin Huang, *Literati and Self-Re/Presentation: Autobiographical Sensibility in the Eighteenth-Century Chinese Novel* (Stanford: Stanford University Press, 1995), pp. 26–27, for an account of the "problematic literati self," which usefully describes the intellectual tensions reflected in mid-Ch'ing novels. For the illness associated with examination candidates, see Chang Chieh-pin 張介賓, *Ching-yueh ch'üan-shu* 景岳全書 (Complete works of physician Chang) (Shanghai: Science and Technology Press, 1984), pp. 357–59. Women with unfulfilled sexual longing were also likely victims of such "emotional stasis." My thanks to Judith Zeitlin for photocopying and send-

## RELIGION AND THE POPULAR VALORIZATION
## OF EXAMINATIONS

In the popular imagination, "fate" (*ming* 命) typically was used to explain away the inherent social and cultural inequalities at the heart of the selection process. Many accepted their success or failure because they believed that the gods had determined the final ranks beforehand.[10] Members of the elite, when unsuccessful in the examination competition themselves, could therapeutically invoke fate to explain why others succeeded when in fact they were not superior in any way.[11] Faced with the uncertainties of daily life, many Chinese, whether elite or peasant, had turned to gods, temples, and local religious practices to negotiate the terms of their normality. One of the ironies of literati life was that an educational regime that tested the generally areligious classical canon of the Four Books and Five Classics, and had forbidden Taoist and Buddhist monks from entering the examination hall and their patrologies from inclusion in the official curriculum, was imbued with so many outside religious sensibilities that there were no clear markers between religious and examination life (see also Chapter 8). In the T'ang dynasty, for instance, an imperial decree commanded that official examination candidates should be lodged at the Kuang-chai Temple 光宅寺 if they were unable to return home after an examination that lasted into the evening. During the Sung dynasty, literati temples honoring Confucius may have been venues of prayer before examinations.[12]

---

ing this source to me. She discusses "stasis" as an illness in her forthcoming article entitled "Making the Invisible Visible: Images of Desire and Constructions of the Female Body in Chinese Literature, Medicine, and Art."

10. See C. K. Yang, *Religion in Chinese Society* (Berkeley: University of California Press, 1967), pp. 265–68. For a late Ming example of fate deciding rank, see *Ch'ien-Ming k'o-ch'ang i-wen-lu*, B.31a. On the belief in the futility of bribery because fate determined success, see B.53a–b. Miyazaki Ichisada relied on this and similar sources for the many anecdotes in his *China's Examination Hell*, translated by Schirokauer, but unfortunately Miyazaki did not subject the stories to systematic analysis. For the Sung, see Chaffee, *The Thorny Gates of Learning in Sung China*, pp. 177ff.

11. Ropp, *Dissent in Early Modern China*, pp. 91–119; and Barr, "Pu Songling [P'u Sung-ling] and the Qing [Ch'ing] Examination System," pp. 103–9. When compared with the "fatalistic" ideologies common among Buddhist or Hindu peasants in South and Southeast Asia, for example, the Chinese ideology of social mobility through examination success did affect peasant beliefs in the usefulness of education and created a climate of rising expectations among low-level licentiates who dreamed of examination glory but frequently rebelled politically when their hopes were repeatedly dashed.

12. See Gernet, *Buddhism in Chinese Society*, p. 226. Liao Hsien-huei is currently preparing a Ph.D. dissertation in History at UCLA, tentatively entitled "Praying for a Revelation:

To cope with the educational and examination pressures, candidates since the T'ang and Sung dynasties had appealed to local deities for moral support. Such forms of religious practice were designed to redirect the candidate's anxieties about success and to help him in the examination market. The Taoist cult of Wen-ch'ang 文昌, the patron deity of the literary arts in medieval times, had by the Southern Sung dynasty become an object of veneration associated with the deity's predictions of examination success. Official recognition came to the cult under the Yuan. Yü Chi 虞集 (1272–1348), who had supported the Mongol reestablishment of civil examinations in 1314–15 (see Chapter 1), described Wen-ch'ang's appeal to literati:

> When the Sung perished, Shu [Ssu-ch'uan province] was ravaged and not one of the inhabitants survived. The offerings to the gods were suspended. After the examination had been abolished for more than forty years we heard of no supernatural feats from Wen-ch'ang. In 1314, when the Son of Heaven made an especially sagacious decision and, clearly summoning all within the empire, selected officials through the examinations, the people of Shu gradually began to offer sacrifice to Wen-ch'ang again.[13]

The "Cinnamon Record" (*Kuei-chi* 桂籍) in the deity's 1181 revelation of the *Hua-shu* 化書 (Book of transformations) stipulated Wen-ch'ang's spiritual influence in civil examinations:

> The Cinnamon Record of scholars is administered by the Heavenly Bureau.
> Success or failure, glory or decline, none escape their fate.
> Dreams reveal the examination topic according to the degree of one's sincerity.
> Hidden Merit determines one's position on the placard of successful candidates.
> A man of humble heritage may bring his wife enfeoffment and his son an assured office;
> An official trailing purple, a golden seal at his waist, begins as a white-robed candidate.
> To repay the student who works sleepless nights in the study
> I have strived in literary and moral refinement, not recoiling at toil!

---

The Mental Universe of the Song Examination Candidates, 960–1276," which investigates the Sung aspects of civil examinations and popular religion. See also Valerie Hansen, *Changing Gods in Medieval China*, passim; and Julia K. Murray, "The Temple of Confucius and Pictorial Biographies of the Sage," *Journal of Asian Studies* 55, 2 (May 1996): 269–300.

13. See Terry Kleeman, "Introduction," pp. 49, 73–75, in Kleeman, trans., *A God's Own Tale*.

Because of my unstinting devotion to the classics through many incarnations as a scholar, the Thearch commanded me to take charge of the Cinnamon Record in the Heavenly Bureau. All local and national examinations, rankings, colors of clothing, salaries, and enfeoffments were memorialized to me and even promotions and demotions within the civil and military bureaucracies were under my supervision.[14]

Wen-ch'ang's efficacy was concretely demonstrated in a story included in the 1194 continuation of the *Hua-shu* about Li Teng 李登, a talented candidate who had consulted with a Taoist priest to find out why after four decades he had still not gotten the *chin-shih* degree. The priest checked with Wen-ch'ang and learned:

When Li Teng was first born he was bestowed a jade seal and was fated to place first on the district examinations at eighteen and be *optimus* at the palace examinations at age nineteen. At thirty-three he should have reached the rank of chancellor of the right. After being selected he spied on a neighbor woman, Chang Yen-niang. Although the affair had not been resolved, he had her father, Chang Ch'eng, bound and thrown into jail. For this crime his success was postponed ten years, and he was demoted to the second group of successful examinees. After being selected at the age of twenty-eight, he encroached upon and seized the dwelling of his elder brother, Li Feng, and this resulted in litigation. For this his success was postponed another ten years, and he was demoted to the third group of graduates. After being selected at the age of thirty-eight, he violated in his room in Ch'ang-an Madame née Cheng, the wife of a commoner, then framed her husband, Pai Yuan, for a crime. For this his success was postponed a further ten years, and his standing was demoted to the fourth group. After being selected at the age of forty-eight, he stole Ch'ing-niang, the maiden daughter of his neighbor Wang Chi. As an unrepentant evil-doer, he has already been erased from the records. He will never pass.

Such moral rigor in religious discourse about the examinations attached an easily understood level of popular meaning and ethical significance to the literary examinations, which rationalized and explained the examiners' rankings in light of cosmological justice, not classical essay content or technique.[15]

In the Ming dynasty, the Wen-ch'ang cult flourished as never before. Fifteenth-century accounts of examination candidates frequently mentioned their visits to Wen-ch'ang temples (*Wen-ch'ang she* 文昌社) in their community or on their way to the provincial or metropolitan examina-

14. Kleeman, trans., *A God's Own Tale*, pp. 290–91.
15. See C. K. Yang, *Religion in Chinese Society*, pp. 270–71.

tions in larger cities. Licentiates, for example, paid a group visit to a T'ai-yuan 太原, Shan-hsi, Wen-ch'ang temple in 1441. In 1454 the heralded Ming scholar-official Ch'iu Chün was still preparing for the metropolitan examinations ten years after he had finished first on the Kuang-tung provincial examination. In a dream Ch'iu spoke with Wen-ch'ang, who praised Ch'iu for his sincerity in studies and promised that Ch'iu would pass the upcoming examination and receive his *chin-shih* degree ranked one of the top graduates. It became de rigueur for Ming candidates, such as the Wang Yang-ming follower Yang Ch'i-yuan 楊起元 (1547–99), who was known to insert Ch'an doctrine into his examination essays (see Chapter 7), to claim that they passed only after consulting the "Divine Lord Wen-ch'ang" (文昌帝君).[16]

An example of a religious cult for a deified historical figure frequently invoked by Ming and Ch'ing examination candidates was that of Kuan-ti 關帝, the god of war and sometimes wealth. Kuan-ti had been apotheosized in medieval times from the loyal warrior-official Kuan Yü 關羽, who was romanticized in the novel *Romance of the Three Kingdoms*, to Lord Kuan 關公, a deity who took pity on humans and granted merchants economic wealth and literati examination success.[17] His empirewide cult "glorified the loyal and rewarded the good" by measuring human acts according to the "standards of merit and evil." Under the Ch'ing, the Yung-cheng emperor organized the Kuan-ti cult into a hierarchy of temples throughout the empire that the court appropriated as official guardians of the dynasty.[18]

In 1547, for example, it was noted that Kuan-ti repaid an examination candidate, Chang Ch'un 張春, with provincial and metropolitan success, after he asked Chang in the latter's dream to treat his ear illness. Chang was staying in a temple that had an image of Kuan-ti, and after awakening, Chang discovered that the ear on the image was plugged with honey, which he removed. The next night Chang again dreamed that Kuan-ti had thanked him for his cure and that he would not forget Chang's kind act. In the late Ming, a chronically ill licentiate dreamed that Kuan-ti had

---

16. See *Ch'ien-Ming k'o-ch'ang i-wen-lu*, A.14a, for the visit of licentiates to the T'ai-yuan temple, A.17a–b, on Ch'iu Chün, and B.13a, on Yang Ch'i-yuan. For discussion, see Angela Leung (Liang Ch'i-tzu 梁其姿), *Shih-shan yü chiao-hua: Ming-Ch'ing te tz'u-shan tsu-chih* 施善與教化：明清的慈善組織 (Performing merit and transforming through culture: charitable institutions in Ming and Ch'ing) (Taipei: Lien-ching Press, 1997), pp. 132–34.

17. Kuan Yü was honored first as a "lord" (*kung* 公), before later becoming a "king" (*wang* 王), and then in late Ming times he became an "emperor" (*ti* 帝).

18. See C. K. Yang, *Religion in Chinese Society*, pp. 159–61; and Prasenjit Duara, "Superscribing Symbols: The Myth of Guandi, Chinese God of War," *Journal of Asian Studies* 47, 4 (November 1988): 783–85.

told him he would recover and pass the next examination, but later, because of his avarice after recovering, he failed, according to Kuan-ti, in order that "heaven's principles" (*t'ien-li* 天理) would not be harmed. Kuan-ti explained himself when the candidate came to the temple and used bamboo sticks (*ch'iu-ch'ien* 求籤) to divine why he had failed the examination. In 1619 eight graduates of that year's metropolitan examination were said to have been on a list of graduates that Kuan-ti had presented in a dream.[19]

Another prominent late imperial examination cult to a historical figure was devoted to the early Ming official Yü Ch'ien 于謙 (1398–1457). During the Oirat campaign and T'u-mu debacle, Yü and others in the court had replaced the Cheng-t'ung emperor (r. 1436–49), when he was ransomed by the Oirats, with his younger brother (see Chapter 1). The new Ching-t'ai emperor (r. 1450–56) then led the successful defense of Peking. After returning and spending several years as a prince, the former emperor retook the throne in 1457 in a coup d'état, after which Yü Ch'ien and other officials, who had sacrificed their emperor in 1449, were accused of treason and executed. Yü Ch'ien's name was rehabilitated in 1466, and his son petitioned in 1489 to establish a memorial shrine for his father in his native Hang-chou near Ch'ien's grave site. Yü Ch'ien's posthumous title was later, in 1590, changed to Chung-su 忠肅, which became the name for his shrine. Another shrine was erected in Peking.[20]

Yü Ch'ien's grave site and shrine, known as the "Yü Chung-su tz'u" 于忠肅祠, became in late Ming and Ch'ing times a popular venue for Che-chiang examination candidates to stop on their way to the provincial and metropolitan examinations, where they would implore the spirit of Yü Ch'ien for guidance and signs of future examination success. As with Kuan-ti, Yü Ch'ien represented a historical figure whose loyal acts had transcended his times and whose pure spirit could affect the fates of others, but the Yü Ch'ien cult was localized and not empirewide. Many candidates associated their subsequent successes with dreams while staying in the Hang-chou shrine. The 1652 *optimus*, Tsou Chung-i 鄒忠倚, for example, although he was from Wu-hsi in Chiang-su province, conjoined his success with a visit to the Yü Chung-su shrine as a boy; there he had dreamed of seeing Yü Ch'ien, who told him his future ranking.[21]

19. *Ch'ien-Ming k'o-ch'ang i-wen-lu*, A.46a, B.30a–31a, and B.32b–33a.

20. *Dictionary of Ming Biography*, pp. 1608–11.

21. See *Ch'ing-pai lei-ch'ai*, 74.91–92, 74.95. See also *Kuo-ch'ao k'o-ch'ang i-wen lu* 國朝科場異聞錄 (Recording unusual matters heard in the Ch'ing examination grounds), Wei-ching-t'ang shu-fang 味經堂書坊 edition (reprint, Canton: Ch'ien-t'ang, 1873), 1.15b–16a. The Yü Ch'ien Shrine in Hang-chou is now under repair. When I visited it in August 1995, it was closed to the public, but Professor Wu Kuang 吳光 of the Che-chiang Academy of Social Science and I were permitted to walk through it.

## Popular Lore and Religion

These religious cults were honored in Ch'ing times with visits by countless numbers of examination candidates. Many of their experiences in seeking the intervention of Wen-ch'ang, Kuan-ti, and Yü Ch'ien were published in two collections of *I-wen lu* 異聞錄 (Records of unusual matters heard in the examination grounds), which were based on accounts of Ming and Ch'ing examination candidates and emphasized the otherworldly and mysterious aspects of the examination market. As a subgenre of the *chih-kuai* 志怪 (records of anomalies) collections that had proliferated since medieval times, the Ming and Ch'ing *I-wen lu* were continuations of earlier T'ang and Sung records of unusual events in the civil examinations, and they represented the popular perceptions of Chinese that reverberated inside and outside the examination compounds.[22] But given the expansion of the examinations to counties, departments, and prefectures on a regular basis, and the increase in the number of candidates empirewide, the numbers of such accounts increased dramatically during the Ming, so much so that, as we shall see, examiners made such anomalies a frequent object of questioning in the examinations themselves.[23]

In addition to such late imperial cults, both Buddhist and Taoist temples served as spiritual sites to help literati cope with the mental and emotional demands of the civil examinations. Usually, the temples overlapped with the empirewide Wen-ch'ang and Kuan-ti shrines. Kuan-ti, for example, had already been appropriated as a Buddhist deity in the T'ang, and during the late empire Kuan-ti's forbidding statue stood guard at the gate of most Buddhist temples.[24] In 1550, for instance, a Buddhist monk used the technique of physiognomy (*hsiang* 相) to predict the success of Hsu Chung-hsing 徐中行 (1517–78) in the forthcoming 1550 metropolitan examination. The monk told Hsu that he was destined to remain a *chü-jen* degree-holder for the rest of his life and never hold a higher office than county magistrate. When Hsu indicated displeasure with his fate, the

22. See Kenneth DeWoskin, "The Six Dynasties *Chih-kuai* and the Birth of Fiction," in Andrew Plaks, ed., *Chinese Narrative* (Princeton: Princeton University Press, 1977), pp. 21–52; and Glen Dudbridge, *Religious Experience and Lay Society in T'ang China* (Cambridge: Cambridge University Press, 1995), p. 64. For discussion of how popular culture "reverberated" in elite society, see Paul Katz, *Demon Hordes and Burning Boats: The Cult of Marshall Wen in Late Imperial Chekiang* (Albany: SUNY Press, 1995), pp. 113–15.

23. See the *Ch'ien-Ming k'o-ch'ang i-wen-lu* and *Kuo-ch'ao k'o-ch'ang i-wen lu*, both cited above.

24. See Timothy Brook, *Praying for Power: Buddhism and the Formation of Gentry Society in Late-Ming China* (Cambridge: Harvard-Yenching Institute Monograph Series, 1993), pp. 288–90.

monk told him that "hidden virtue" (*yin-te* 陰德) was required to escape the "fixed regularities" (*ting-shu* 定數) of his physiognomy. Hsu nodded in agreement, and although he was very poor, he collected thirty taels of gold from his writing talents and secretly dropped the gold into Lake T'ai for the fish. When the monk saw Hsu again, he immediately saw hidden virtue in Hsu's countenance, and declared that he would become a *chin-shih* the next year.

Because Hsu Chung-hsing also became a high court official, the story of his changing his fate was a parable about the examination market in the silver age.[25] This clear moral inversion of the corrupt uses of gold and silver to buy examination success by paying off examiners could also take the form of "spirit-money" used in temples and shrines to honor the dead and to redeem one's moral debts. In Hsu's documented case of karmic "good deeds," the gold, like spirit-money, translated into a spiritual "payment" that yielded worldly success. Just as cultural resources invested in a classical education were the linguistic key to a candidate's examination success, so too the investments in shrines and temples and faith in spiritual matters brought with them peace of mind, hope, and solace in the face of likely examination failure.[26]

Similarly in 1594, a Taoist scolded Chang Wei-yen 張畏巖, who, after seeing the results posted, attacked the civil examiners for failing him on a 1594 provincial examination. The Taoist priest had laughed at Chang and claimed that he could tell from Chang's physiognomy that his essays were not outstanding enough. When Chang angrily asked the priest how he knew his essays were inadequate, the Taoist replied that essay writing required spiritual peace and equanimity (作文貴心氣和平). Chang's commotion over his failure demonstrated that his mind was not at peace, the priest added.

Chang then asked for guidance, and the Taoist told him that heaven established one's fate based on good works. Chang replied that he was a poor literatus and could not afford to practice good deeds, to which the Taoist appealed to a notion of "hidden merit" (*yin-kung* 陰功) that emanated from the mind. Such unlimited merit was not based on wealth but on emotional maturity and spiritual peace, the Taoist contended, and Chang had simply wasted his energies by attacking his examiners. At this, Chang became enlightened. Later, in 1597, Chang dreamed that the

25. See Richard von Glahn, "The Enchantment of Wealth: The God Wutong in the Social History of Jiangnan," *Harvard Journal of Asiatic Studies* 51, 2 (December 1991): 695–704.

26. *Ch'ien-Ming k'o-ch'ang i-wen-lu,* A.47a–b. For the roots of Buddhist soothsayers in the Sui and T'ang, see Gernet, *Buddhism in Chinese Society,* pp. 250–53, 286–97.

provincial examination roster for that year was still missing one name for someone who could accumulate virtue and avoid error. Chang fulfilled the requirement and passed the 1597 provincial examination ranked number 105.[27]

Internal, mental well-being was the spiritual correlate to the external pressures and educational requirements to succeed in late imperial examinations. In this episode, the Taoist ideals of spiritual enlightenment were made available in passing to a high-strung candidate who clearly had spent years preparing for the provincial examination and could not accept his failure when he saw the final list of graduates. Again, not only were religion and morality the proper way to deal with failure without blaming the examinations themselves, but success was ultimately tied to spiritual enlightenment and emotional maturity. Religion and literati life had together created a remarkably healthy psychological haven from the cruel realities of the examination compound.

Morality was the typical ad hoc measure of examination success. Before the 1481 metropolitan examination, for example, Wang Yang-ming's father, Wang Hua 王華, was staying with a wealthy family, whose master was sonless although he had many concubines. One evening the master sent one of the concubines to Wang's room with a note saying that this was his idea so that he might have an heir. Wang refused the liaison, writing in reply that this would "alarm the heavens" (k'ung-ching t'ien-hsia 恐驚天下). The next day a Taoist was invited into the house to pray for the ancestors, but he fell into a deep sleep in the middle. On awakening, the priest related that he had attended an examination in heaven, where the chuang-yuan was announced. The Taoist, upon questioning, didn't dare divulge the name of the optimus, but he remembered that in the dream the procession in front of the man was carrying a banner that read "alarm the heavens."[28]

Karma and retribution were also cultural constructs used in late imperial times to elucidate the examination market. Yuan Huang 袁黃 (1533–1606), one of the leaders of late Ming efforts to link Taoism, Confucianism, and Buddhism (san-chiao 三教), encouraged the use of morality books (shan-shu 善書) to measure an individual's societal status and worth. Yuan contended that "success in the examinations depends entirely on secret virtue." He also maintained that examination success did not rest on a candidate's ability but rather on his ancestors' store of merit. "Ledgers of merit and demerit," as Yuan Huang and his moral bookkeep-

27. Ch'ien-Ming k'o-ch'ang i-wen-lu, B.24b–25a.
28. See ibid., A.24b. See also Miyazaki, China's Examination Hell, pp. 96–97, although the translation strays from the original.

ing followers called them, became literati equivalents to the popular religious notions of good works, moral rebirth, and worldly success.[29]

In an examination market in which most candidates for the *chü-jen* and *chin-shih* degrees in particular regarded their levels of classical literacy and memory as roughly equivalent (they rarely blamed themselves for their failures), most sought the explanation for why one failed while another passed in religious terms. The impact of Buddhism and Taoism in the mental life of literati who mastered Ch'eng-Chu learning for the examinations was widespread.[30] At times, such as the late Ming, the doctrines of Chinese religion, particularly those of Ch'an Buddhism, entered the actual content of the examination essays (see Chapter 7), but for the most part, the candidates were able to keep to the required Tao Learning curriculum in their classical essays at the same time that their mental lives betrayed much wider sources of personal inspiration and moral support.

Many literati believed in reincarnation. In the 1642 provincial examinations, a candidate received prior information about the questions from an auspicious woman who appeared in his dreams and turned out to have died the day the candidate was born.[31] Some claimed that certain coincidences in the life of the 1659 metropolitan *hui-yuan* Chu Chin 朱錦, for instance, indicated that he was reincarnated from a century earlier.[32] As a young boy of three and four, Ch'en Yuan-lung 陳元龍 had dreamt of Buddhist chants, but his mother urged him toward literati studies (*ju-hsueh* 儒學) instead, claiming that the teachings of Buddhism were not worth following. When she passed away, Ch'en refused to take any examinations due to her death. The head of the 1679 special *po-hsueh hung-tz'u* examination encouraged Ch'en to accept an invitation to participate, but to no avail. Ch'en subsequently finished third on the 1685 palace examination and held high office. The tensions of Buddhism versus an official life had taken Ch'en Yuan-lung several decades to resolve.[33]

Despite the obvious advantages seen in the life of an official, Ming-Ch'ing religious literature also offered young men a distinct path separate from the examination life. In the values spread through *pao-chüan* 寶卷

---

29. For discussion, see Cynthia Brokaw, *The Ledgers of Merit and Demerit: Social Change and Moral Order in Late Imperial China* (Princeton: Princeton University Press, 1991), pp. 17–27, 68, 231–32.

30. See the account of a 1595 dream that the *optimus* must come from a family that for three generations has not eaten beef (三代不食牛肉), in *Ch'ien-Ming k'o-ch'ang i-wen-lu*, B.24a. See also Hsu K'o, *Ch'ing-pai lei-ch'ao*, 74.99, which relates how in 1750 Kuan-yin 觀音 predicted examination success.

31. *Chih-i k'o-so-chi*, 3.97–98.

32. Ibid., 4.119–20.

33. *Ch'ing-pai lei-ch'ao*, 21.91–92.

(precious scrolls) scriptures dating from the early Ming, which recorded the efforts of moral persons who attain salvation, the combination of popular Buddhist notions of karma and literati aspirations for enlightenment sometimes presented the examination road to fame and fortune as the way to perdition. The contest between this-worldly success and other-worldly enlightenment could also challenge the family values of daily life. Buddhist and Taoist clergy were also models encouraging men and women to steer clear of social entanglements and follow a life of celibacy.[34]

Even when this religious ideal was compromised, a heroine such as Hsiang-nü 香女 ("Fragrance") in the *Liu Hsiang pao-chüan* 劉香寶卷 (Liu Hsiang's precious scroll), first published in the eighteenth century, could dismiss her husband's examination aspirations by saying, "What's the use of reading books?...It's better to study the Way; profit lies therein. To be an official for one life is to gain enemies for ten thousand lifetimes. I am pointing out to you the path to the Western Land. I urge you, husband, to take the earliest opportunity to practice spiritual discipline." Fragrance's mother-in-law, enraged, forbade her son from seeing Fragrance and ordered him to prepare for the examination. Eventually he became an *optimus*, but his and his family's fate was an early death ordained by the Jade Emperor.[35] Fragrance, on the other hand, became a sainted religious leader who overcame every worldly obstacle placed in her path.

On the dark side of these uplifting tales of success or escape were the alleged criminal reasons for examination failure. A son dreamed of his dead mother, who told him that his crime of three lives past had come to light. He could not enter school and learn to read until he had expiated his past crimes, which eventually he did. Inside the examination compound, ghosts and apparitions of the past would appear before candidates to remind them of their past transgressions. In the stories, many such young men went crazy or died on the spot.[36] In fact, many candidates accepted gossip about a custom that had supposedly developed among examination proctors to unfurl black and red banners after the roll call inside the compound while they called out: "Wrongs will be righted; those aggrieved will take revenge."[37]

34. See Daniel Overmyer, "Values in Chinese Sectarian Literature: Ming and Ch'ing *Pao-chüan*," in Johnson, Nathan, and Rawski, eds., *Popular Culture in Late Imperial China*, pp. 219–54.

35. Ibid., pp. 245–50.

36. *Hsiao-shih i-wen-lu* 小試異聞錄 (Recording unusual matters heard in the local examination grounds), Ch'ien-t'ang, 1873 edition, pp. 3a–4b, 12a–b. See also *Ch'ien-Ming k'o-ch'ang i-wen-lu*, A.38b–39a.

37. See Sheang [Shang] Yen-liu, "Memories of the Chinese Imperial Civil Service Examination System," pp. 65–66.

Spirits and ghosts could also play tricks with a candidate's mind, testing his emotional mettle. Wen-ch'ang could just as easily predict that a candidate's papers in the 1640 metropolitan examination would catch fire from the small stove in his cell and would be destroyed, and order him to prepare two copies and keep one in reserve. The candidate obeyed, a fire did burn up his papers, and because of his reserve copy he passed.[38] A spirit could give a candidate the wrong questions for an examination in order to ensure that he would be unprepared and that someone else would come out number one.[39]

Spirits could likewise affect the examiners, as in 1726, when Chang Lei 張壘 allegedly relied on the spirits to ferret out the best paper with "hidden virtue" in the Chiang-nan provincial examination.[40] In the 1783 Chiang-hsi provincial examination, the examiners were reported to have chosen the top paper based on a dream of one of the examiners. In 1804 a spirit appeared in a provincial examiner's dream and explained the classical merits of a particular essay to him. The spirit pointed out that the candidate had successfully used the *Erh-ya chu-shu* 爾雅注疏 (Scholia to the progress toward correctness) etymological dictionary for one of the sections of his eight-legged essay (see Chapter 5).[41]

In 1657 a candidate in the provincial examinations had completed his essays and was waiting in his cell for them to be collected when the god of literature (*k'uei-hsing* 魁星) danced in before his eyes and said that he would be the *chuang-yuan* on this cycle of civil examinations. The spirit asked the candidate to write the two characters for *chuang-yuan* on its own piece of paper. The candidate was elated at this auspicious news and began to write the first character *chuang* 狀, when suddenly the god tipped over his ink-stone and left. Because of the smudges on his official papers, the candidate was disqualified from consideration.[42]

In an earlier, 1618 provincial examination, the ending was different. A candidate was ill inside the examination compound and fell into a deep sleep without writing any of his essays. After handing in a blank paper to the collection clerks, the candidate assumed he had of course failed, but later he learned that his name was on the final list of graduates. When he looked at his examination papers supplied to him by the examiners, he discovered that the essays had been written in proper, regular script, which he attributed to a helpful spirit in his cell.[43]

38. *Ch'ien-Ming k'o-ch'ang i-wen-lu*, B.45a–b.
39. Ibid., B.54b.
40. *Ch'ing-pai lei-ch'ao*, 74.124–25.
41. Ibid., 74.102–03, 74.105.
42. *Chih-i k'o-so-chi*, 4.118.
43. *Ch'ien-Ming k'o-ch'ang i-wen-lu*, B.30a.

A profligate life usually led to failure. In 1664 a candidate awaiting the results of the metropolitan examination got drunk and passed out. In his stupor, he recalled his past unfilial behavior toward his mother and father, and of course on awakening discovered he had failed.[44] During the 1849 Chiang-nan provincial examination, a candidate from the illustrious Hsu family of K'un-shan county, which had garnered several *chin-shih* degrees early in the dynasty, went drinking after the second session, thinking that his high ranking had already been sealed by the essays on the Four Books and Five Classics he had completed. He drank himself drunk and was unable to meet the roll call for entering the compound to complete the third session's required policy questions. The examiners' initially had ranked his eight-legged essays ahead of the eventual *chieh-yuan,* but because his papers for the third session had not been handed in, he was disqualified.[45]

A reformed life, however, would lead to success. In a great turnabout, Chang Chih-tung 張之洞 (1837–1909), gave up his heavy drinking as a youth after one of his elders in his lineage, Chang Chih-wan 張之萬 (1811–97), finished as the empire's *optimus* in 1847. Determined to emulate Chih-wan, Chang finished first on the Shun-t'ien provincial examination in 1852, but only finished third as *t'an-hua* on the 1863 palace examination. Despite his success, Chih-tung's failure to win the coveted status of *optimus* was attributed to his early addiction to drinking.[46]

Sexual promiscuity also loomed large in the popular view of examination success. The candidate who abstained from sex the night before the 1612 Chiang-nan provincial examination, for instance, was rewarded with the highest examination honors, and the one who indulged lost out.[47] A jilted woman often returned to haunt a candidate in his examination cell, dooming him to eternal failure. Or, if she committed suicide, she could return as a temptress, seduce her tormentor, and leave him for dead.[48] Another common theme was possession, in which a fox-fairy (*hu* 狐) invaded the candidate's body and took over his mind. In 1879, for instance, a fairy began speaking in a Chiang-hsi dialect through the mouth of a candidate from Hang-chou and had to be appeased with watermelons before she would depart, taking the form of a young wife as she left.[49]

44. *Chih-i k'o-so-chi,* 4.140–41.

45. *Ch'ing-pai lei-ch'ao,* 21.82.

46. Ibid., 21.107.

47. *Ch'ien-Ming k'o-ch'ang i-wen-lu,* B.27a.

48. For a 1633 revenge story of a jilted woman, see *Chih-i k'o-so-chi,* 3.88–89. For another in 1639, see *Ch'ien-Ming k'o-ch'ang i-wen-lu,* B.44a 45a. See also Miyazaki, *China's Examination Hell,* pp. 46–47.

49. *Ch'ing-pai lei-ch'ao,* 74.168. See also Zeitlin, *Historian of the Strange,* pp. 174–81.

These stories and anecdotes reveal how the complex institutional machinery and rigorous curricular content of the civil examinations typically were elided in popular culture as morality tales that fit in with the themes of fairness and justice in government and society. We need not accept the historicity of these entertaining *chih-kuai* collections "recording unusual matters heard in the examination grounds." Such records do reveal, however, a general sense that during the late empire elites and commoners both accepted the civil examinations as a natural part of life and infused them with a religious and cosmological narrative that fully accepted the examination regime and legitimated its place in the emotional life of the candidates and their families.[50] The therapeutic uses of religion in Ming morality books, which Judith Berling has described as the "management of moral capital," carried over to the examination life. The reorganization of one's emotional experiences as an examination candidate accompanied changes in character ideals to deal with panic and the emptiness of failure. These religious tales of examination success or failure also legitimated the literati examinations as venues for Taoist and Buddhist parables. Popular religion and faith in some compelling symbolic of self-integrating communal purpose helped men cope with their travails and understand themselves better.[51]

### Techniques for Examination Prediction

To cope better with the pressures of the civil examinations and thereby gain an insight into the nitty-gritty workings of the next examination, candidates and their families also used time-honored techniques of communication with the other world to predict success or failure, to gather clues about the possible quotations from the Four Books that might be selected by examiners, or to divine the riddle that a fortune-teller or dream had elicited from the gods, spirits, and ancestors. "Reading fate" (*k'an-ming* 看命) became an obsession among Ming-Ch'ing examination candidates as they sought some auspicious sign for their prospects in the prohibitive examination market.[52]

Mantic techniques for analyzing civil examinations took many cultural forms, the chief among them being fate prediction (*suan-ming* 算命) using

---

50. See C. K. Yang, *Religion in Chinese Society*, pp. 267–68.

51. See Judith Berling, "Religion and Popular Culture: The Management of Moral Capital," in *The Romance of the Three Teachings,*" in Johnson, Nathan, and Rawski, *Popular Culture in Late Imperial China*, pp. 208–12. See also Philip Rieff, *The Triumph of the Therapeutic* (New York: Harper & Row, 1968), pp. 1–27.

52. Richard Smith, *Fortune-Tellers and Philosophers*, p. 173.

the *I-ching*, physiognomy (*k'an-hsiang* 看相),[53] spirit-writing (*fu-chi* 扶乩),[54] deciphering of written words (*ch'ai-tzu* 拆字 or *ts'e-tzu* 測字), dream inter-pretation (*chan-meng* 占夢), sighting of portents (*chao* 兆), and geomancy (*feng-shui* 風水). Each was practiced in a variety of ways, as Richard Smith's rich account of late imperial fortune-tellers makes clear.[55] The remarkable degree to which popular culture, Buddhist and Taoist religion, and elite intellectual life interacted in these mantic devices, however, tells us how far off the historical mark our earlier accounts of "Confucian agnosticism" or elite areligiosity have been.[56] As we shall see, the late imperial examiners tried to set intellectual limits to such popular tech-niques. However, even in the policy questions they devised for civil exami-nations that were designed to show the folly of blindly accepting a strict correlation between earthly and supernatural events, they were trying to influence a world of discourse largely outside their control.

Fate prediction was on the minds of many examination candidates. Based on their acceptance of the Buddhist and Taoist doctrines of karma and moral retribution, which had become an accepted part of Ming examination life, they tried to discern how their "individual fates" (*yuan-fen* 緣分, lit., "karmic allotments") could be calculated using the methods of fate extrapolation (*t'ui-suan* 推算), auspicious versus inauspicious day selection (*chi-hsiung* 吉凶), or the eight-characters (*pa-tzu* 八字) of a per-son's birth. Astrology (*chan-hsing* 占星), complete with Chinese "horo-scopes," was widely used by fortune-tellers and Buddhist monks and Taoist priests. It included milfoil divination based on the *Change Classic* (*I-ching*) and numerical systems designed to discern numerological patterns.[57]

53. Chu P'ing-yi 祝平一, *Han-tai te hsiang-jen shu* 漢代的相人術 (The technique of phys-iognomy in the Han period) (Taipei: Hsueh-sheng Bookstore, 1990), presents the roots of this mantic approach.

54. See Terence Russell, "Chen Tuan at Mount Huangbo: A Spirit-writing Cult in Late Ming China," *Asiatische Studien* 44, 1 (1990): 107–40.

55. Richard Smith, *Fortune-Tellers and Philosophers*, pp. 131–257. See also Wang Ming-hsi-ung 王明雄, *T'an-t'ien shuo-ming* 談天説命 (On heaven and fate) (Taipei: Huang-kuan Magazine Press, 1988), which presents an overview of all of these techniques as used today.

56. See, for an example, Herrlee Creel, *Confucius and the Chinese Way* (New York: Harper & Row, 1960). For a continuation of this theme, which contends that "Neo-Confucians had much in common with their Puritan contemporaries" and thereby underdetermines the place of cults, gods, and popular culture in literati life, see Pei-yi Wu, *The Confu-cian's Progress: Autobiographical Writings in Traditional China* (Princeton: Princeton University Press, 1990), p. 230. For a more nuanced account, see Martin Huang, *Literati and Self-Re/Presentation*, pp. 143–52.

57. See *Ch'ing-pai lei-ch'ao*, 73.100–19, for Ch'ing examples of reading fate for examina-tion candidates. On the theory behind the practice, see Richard Smith, *Fortune-Tellers and Philosophers*, 174–86; and Wang Ming-hsiung, *T'an-t'ien shuo-ming*, pp. 87–102, on specifically Buddhist techniques.

During the Ming dynasty, for example, fate calculations were so common that an illustrated seventeenth-century record of all Ming *chuang-yuan* to 1640 included the eight-character, stem-branch (*t'ien-kan ti-chih* 天干地 支, lit., "heavenly stems and earthly branches") combinations for dating each's birth by year, month, day, and hour according to the conventional divination method. The four pairs of stem-branch characters used in the orthodox calendar (*huang-li* 皇曆) and in all almanacs (*t'ung-shu* 通書) were known as the "four pillars" (*ssu-chu* 四柱) of one's fate, and they correlated with one's future official position, wealth, and social standing.[58] The compilers of the Ming collection added information for each *chuang-yuan*, such as bureaucratic rank, punishments received, and early death, where appropriate, to show the correlations between their birth dates and their fates. The compilers also added a commentary ("Chuang-yuan ming-tsao p'ing-chu" 狀元命造評註) to explain the fate calculations for many of the *optimi*.[59]

Fortune-tellers also employed star-based techniques for reading fate (*hsing-ming* 星命) to link an individual's personal fate to the heavens and the likelihood of his examination success. These techniques usually incorporated astrological signs, each identified with one of twelve animals (rat, ox, tiger, rabbit, dragon, snake, horse, sheep, monkey, rooster, dog, and pig), which correlated with the twelve earthly branches. For example, an illustration by Huang Ying-ch'eng 黃應澄 (see Figure 6.1)—included in the Ming collection entitled *Ming chuang-yuan t'u-k'ao* 明狀元圖考 (Illustrated survey of *optimi* during the Ming dynasty), initially compiled by Ku Ting-ch'en 顧鼎臣 (1453–1540) and completed by others—shows a diviner pointing out to the 1502 *optimus* K'ang Hai 康海 (1475–1541) that the southern dipper in the heavens has guaranteed his examination success.[60]

58. On *pa-tzu* methods for reading fate, see Chao Wei-pang, "The Chinese Science of Fate-Calculation," *Folklore Studies* 5 (1946): 313; and Wang Ming-hsiung, *T'an-t'ien shuo-ming*, pp. 67–72.

59. *Chuang-yuan t'u-k'ao*, 6.38a–42b, 6.43a–48b. See also Richard Smith, *Fortune-Tellers and Philosophers*, pp. 43, 176–77; and his *Chinese Almanacs* (Hong Kong and Oxford: Oxford University Press, 1992), pp. 25–33.

60. *Chuang-yuan t'u-k'ao*, 2.36b–37b. The collection was begun by Ku Ting-ch'en, himself a 1505 *optimus* (see below), and continued by his grandson Ku Tsu-hsun 顧祖訓 and called *Ming chuang-yuan t'u-k'ao*. Their version covered Ming *chuang-yuan* from 1371 to 1571. Wu Ch'eng-en 吳承恩 and Ch'eng I-chen 程一楨 added materials that brought it up to 1604. Materials for 1607–28 were later also added by unknown compilers. We will discuss Ch'ing *optimi* included in the continuation called *Chuang-yuan t'u-k'ao* and compiled by Ch'en Mei 陳枚 and Chien Hou-fu 簡侯甫, who added materials covering 1631–82 to the Ming collection, below. I have benefited from the research paper on the collection prepared by Chiang Chu-shan 蔣竹山 for my winter 1990 seminar at Tsing Hua University, Hsin-chu, Taiwan. In addition, I have relied on both editions, although I usually cite the Ch'ing version below.

FIGURE 6.1.  Pointing to the Little Dipper in 1502. *Source: Ming chuang-yuan t'u-k'ao* 明狀元圖考 (Illustrated survey of *optimi* during the Ming dynasty). Compiled by Ku Ting-ch'en 顧鼎臣 and Ku Tsu-hsun 顧祖訓. 1607 edition.

The diviner used the positions of the moon and constellations on the ecliptic of the celestial sphere to confirm that the little dipper's location on the lower equatorial was very auspicious for K'ang. According to the diviner, the god of literature was then residing in a place more favorable to a candidate from the northwest, and since K'ang Hai was from Shen-hsi his fortune was more auspicious than that of the metropolitan *hui-yuan* and others who came from the south. The god of literature was associated

FIGURE 6.2.   Using Bamboo Sticks to Divine Examination
Success in Ch'ing Times. *Source: Tien-shih-chai hua-pao* 點石齋畫
報 (The Tien-shih Pavilion's Pictorial), serial 2, vol. 11 (1897),
*ch'ou* 丑, pp. 57b–58a. Reprinted by Yang-chou: Chiang-su Rare
Books, 1983.

with the little dipper (*tou-su* 斗宿) in the southern skies, and K'ang Hai's
fortune was read in accordance with the traditional mantic view that the
southern dipper (*nan-tou* 南斗) guaranteed high official position, reward as
a *chin-shih* degree-holder, and a high salary.[61]

*I-ching* divination was widely practiced by fortune-tellers, and candidates
often consulted the *Change Classic* for hints about their future success.
Frequently such divinations took place in Kuan-ti temples (*Kuan-ti miao* 關
帝廟) where bamboo sticks were used for divination to determine auspicious years for candidates that were related to their eight-character birth
information (see Figure 6.2).[62] Fortune-tellers formed judgments based on

61. Ibid. See also *Chin-shih* (金史), p. 301. My thanks to Chris Cullen for his help in elucidating this figure and the fortune associated with the southern dipper.

62. *Ch'ien-Ming k'o-ch'ang i-wen-lu*, B.39a–b.

drawing randomly one of the sixty-four hexagrams and then determining the multivalent symbolism contained in the patterns among the lines, trigrams, and the hexagrams—relationships that were thought to be the keys to making the correct prognostication (*chan* 占). Mantic techniques for divination using the *I-ching* were based on milfoil stalks or their substitutes. Typically bamboo sticks were shaken to select one in fate calculations dealing with examinations.[63]

The Ch'ing scholar-official Wang Chieh 王杰 (1725–1805), the *optimus* of the 1761 palace examination, for example, had his fate calculated by Ch'en Hung-mou 陳宏謀 (1696–1771) before the 1759 Shen-hsi provincial examination. Ch'en was then governor in Shan-hsi province in the northwest, and Wang was serving on his secretarial staff. Ch'en told Wang that the divination had revealed an auspicious result (*chia-chao* 佳兆) was in store for him.[64] Ch'en Hung-mou also told Wang Chieh that the bamboo slips (*chu-ch'ien* 諸籤) had revealed Wang's rank, but he wanted to wait until after the Shen-hsi examination to confirm the prediction.

Surprisingly, Wang did not do well on the 1759 provincial examination and was placed on the *fu-pang* list of supplementary *chü-jen*. Ch'en Hung-mou, it turned out, had correctly seen in the bamboo slips that Wang would be the eighth-ranking *fu-pang*. This ranking did not seem auspicious enough to Wang, and the next year he took the special 1760 Shen-hsi provincial examination. This time Ch'en Hung-mou guaranteed success, and he turned out to be right, as Wang finished seventh. By coincidence, the 1760 *chieh-yuan* had the same given name Chieh as Wang's, which the second divination had also predicted.

When Wang Chieh traveled to Peking to take the metropolitan and palace examinations, he again consulted with the *Change Classic* using bamboo slips and learned that he would not finish in the top ten on the metropolitan examination but that his fortune was unlimited for the palace. Ch'en Hung-mou concurred and told Wang that the calculations confirmed (*yu-shu tsai* 有數在) Wang's likely final rank as *chuang-yuan*. Chao I 趙翼 (1727–1814), a Ch'ang-chou 常州 literatus who would become a distinguished military leader and historian, was Wang's chief competitor for top honors in 1761. Chao finished first in the metropolitan examination, while Wang, as predicted, finished eleventh.

In the palace rankings, the examiners initially ranked Chao number one again and Wang rose to third. The Ch'ien-lung emperor, however, looked over the final list, saw that Wang Chieh was from Shen-hsi, a

---

63. See Richard Smith, *Fortune-Tellers and Philosophers*, pp. 94–119.

64. *Ch'ing-pai lei-ch'ao*, 73.77–78. Cf. Richard Smith, *Fortune-Tellers and Philosophers*, pp. 108–19, for other cases of *I-ching* prognostication.

province that had not produced a single *optimus* under the Ch'ing, while Chao I came from a prefecture in Chiang-su province with a rich tradition of *chuang-yuan,* and he reversed their positions, placing Wang first and Chao third. Based on the dynasty's long tradition of regional quotas, the emperor's intervention made legitimate political sense. But in light of Wang's reliance on the *I-ching* and his mentor's divinations, the reversal of ranks was also viewed by Wang and Ch'en as a legitimate act of fate. The emperor had acted to confirm the prescience of the other world.[65]

Indeed, Chao I's remarkable equanimity in the face of this sudden reversal was also read as a sign of his acceptance of his fate, although Chao himself considered his ties to the Grand Council, where he had clerked, as the political reason he had been demoted. Chao bemoaned the fact that he had been too well connected. He maintained that the Chi'enlung emperor had not wanted to show favoritism toward a clerk of the prestigious grand councilors. In 1754 there had been an example of someone who had not so rationalized his fate. Ch'ü Li-chiang 瞿麗江, whose family also lived in Ch'ang-chou prefecture in Chiang-su province, had ranked third on the metropolitan and was preliminarily named the *optimus* on the palace examination. However, when the chief examiner suddenly switched Ch'ü's name with the third name on the palace list, his fellow townsman Chuang P'ei-yin 莊培因 (1723–59), Ch'ü became so distressed that he died on the spot, allegedly from aggravation. If Ch'ü, unlike Chao I, was emotionally unable to accept his sudden reversal of fortune, the Chuangs, also from Ch'ang-chou prefecture, had earlier proven that they had paid their moral dues to the demons of fate in the examination marketplace.[66]

Earlier in the 1745 palace examination, for example, Chuang Ts'un-yü 莊存與 (1719–88) had finished second to his hometown, Wu-chin 武進 county, rival Ch'ien Wei-ch'eng 錢維城 (1720–72). Ch'ien Wei-ch'eng later was one of the senior examiners in the 1754 palace examination, and it was likely due to Ch'ien's intervention that Ts'un-yü's younger brother P'ei-yin finished first that year, in part, according to popular lore, to make up for Ts'un-yü's second-place finish in 1745 (莊存與之胞弟).[67] The secret, internal examiner politics for ranking candidates in 1754 were thus read publicly in light of earlier events in 1745 and rationalized as an act of retribution for the Chuangs and repayment for their earlier loss. The fact that such an intervention was patently unfair by the allegedly impartial

65. *Ch'ing-pai lei-ch'ao,* 73.78. See also Hummel, ed., *Eminent Chinese,* p. 75.

66. *Kuo-ch'ao k'o-ch'ang i-wen lu,* 7.32b. On Chao I's ties to the Grand Council, see Mancheong, "Fair Fraud and Fraudulent Fairness," pp. 66–75.

67. *Hui-shih lu,* 1754; and *Kuo-ch'ao k'o-ch'ang i-wen lu,* 5.29a–b.

standards of the examinations themselves was overlooked and translated instead into a story of fate and delayed success.

Furthermore, earlier in 1727, Ts'un-yü's and P'ei-yin's father, Chuang Chu 莊柱 (1670–1759), had initially been ranked the *optimus* after the palace examination, but later his name was switched with the tenth-place finisher, P'eng Ch'i-feng 彭啟豐 (1701–84) from Su-chou, who had been the metropolitan *hui-yuan*. The Yung-cheng emperor had directly intervened in the final rankings because on recent palace examinations Chiang-su graduates had dominated the top rankings for *chin-shih*, and he wanted to select an *optimus* from a border province instead. He mistakenly thought that someone with the surname of P'eng was likely from outside the Yangtzu delta. When he discovered that P'eng Ch'i-feng was from Su-chou, the cultural center of the Yangtzu delta, the Yung-cheng emperor declined to make another change and decided he could still use the occasion to honor P'eng as the grandson of an earlier *chuang-yuan*, P'eng Ting-ch'iu 彭定求 (1645–1719), the *optimus* in 1676.[68]

What made Chuang Chu's fate more emotionally tolerable for him and his disappointed family, however, was that his mother had already dreamed of three celestial spirits, who appeared before her and assessed the Chuang lineage's chances of success vis-à-vis the P'engs in the upcoming palace examination. With regard to "hidden virtue," the three spirits found the Chuangs and P'engs to be equal. It was only in their "cherishing of written characters" (*hsi-tzu* 惜字) that the P'engs surpassed the Chuangs. Because the P'eng lineage had properly collected, cleansed, and burned in a special furnace all abandoned paper with written characters that they found, they had properly worshiped the Divine Lord Wen-ch'ang, the patron saint of letters and deserved P'eng Ch'i-feng's elevation to *optimus*. This revelation explained the switch in results for the Chuangs. Thereafter, the P'eng lineage in Su-chou and the Chuang lineage in Ch'ang-chou frequently intermarried, and the Chuangs became avid supporters of "Societies for Cherishing Written Characters," which of course explained Chuang Ts'un-yü's and P'ei-yin's later examination success as *pang-yen* in 1745 and *chuang-yuan* in 1754.[69]

The civil examination success of the P'engs and Chuangs was linked in the popular imagination to their lineages' good works and support of pop-

---

68. *Kuo-ch'ao k'o-ch'ang i-wen lu*, 4.6a. See also Hummel, ed., *Eminent Chinese*, pp. 616–17.

69. *Kuo-ch'ao k'o-ch'ang i-wen lu*, 4.6a. See also Liang Ch'i-tzu 梁其姿 (Angela Leung), "Ch'ing-tai te hsi-tzu hui" 清代的惜字會 (Societies for cherishing written characters during the Ch'ing dynasty), *Hsin shih-hsueh* 新史學 (Taiwan) 5, 2 (June 1994): 83–113; and my *Classicism, Politics, and Kinship*, pp. 52–59.

ular religion, which were deemed more important than the cultural resources they had invested in a classical education for their sons. This tale of good works and moral retribution later carried over to the previously unfortunate Ch'ü lineage in Ch'ang-chou prefecture as well. Before the 1814 metropolitan examination, for instance, Ch'ü Jung 瞿溶 (Chi-chien 給諫), a grandson of the tragic Ch'ü Li-chiang, dreamed that Chuang P'ei-yin had appeared before him and presented Jung with a stem of apricot blossoms saying, "We are returning to your family something that belongs to them." This auspicious offering implied that the Chuangs were repaying Ch'ü Jung for the events of sixty years earlier that had led to his grandfather's unexpected death.[70] As a result, Ch'ü finished first on the metropolitan and fifth overall on the palace examination. Moral retribution was also served by Ch'ü Jung's finishing ahead of Liu Feng-lu 劉逢祿 (1776–1829), the last important scion by his mother of the distinguished Chuang tradition of New Text (chin-wen 今文) classical learning in Ch'ang-chou, who ranked only thirty-sixth. In this cautionary tale of trial and tribulation for the competitive sons of illustrious lineages in Ch'ang-chou, closure had been reached. All their allotments of fate had been spent, and good works had triumphed.[71]

The rituals of spirit-writing (fu-chi 扶乩), in which a spirit medium passively transmitted spirit messages by means of a divining instrument, had been applied to civil examinations since the T'ang and Sung dynasties. During the Sung, fu-chi involved the composition of poetry and other literary forms, which required mediums to be masters of the poetic forms used in the belles lettres portions of the examinations.[72] By the late Ming, although the civil examinations no longer required poetry, this method of communicating with the other world was also used to produce books of moral teachings authored by the spirits themselves. It was both "natural" and culturally acceptable for examination candidates on their way to a local, provincial, or metropolitan civil examination to visit temples known to be auspicious and to ask the medium there for advance notice of the examination questions. Often the interrogator and the spirit exchanged poetic couplets to demonstrate their classical erudition and poetic flair. It

70. See Wolfram Eberhard, *Lexikon chinesischer Symbole* (Cologne: Eugen Diederichs Verlag, 1983), p. 23.

71. *Kuo-ch'ao k'o-ch'ang i-wen lu*, 7.32b. For discussion, see my *Classicism, Politics, and Kinship*, pp. 59–73.

72. See Hsu Ti-shan 許地山, *Fu-chi mi-hsin te yen-chiu* 扶乩迷信的研究 (Research on spirit-writing superstition) (Ch'ang-sha, 1941), pp. 49–50. Russell, "Chen Tuan at Mount Huangbo," pp. 108–16, emphasizes how prevalent *fu-chi* was in popular culture and religious life and the importance of poetry for the mediums.

was also common for the audience to assume that the spirit who wrote through the planchette was a famous poet or writer from the past.[73]

For example, a candidate on his way to the 1688 metropolitan examination in Peking stopped to ask a medium to communicate with the "writing spirit" (*pi-shen* 筆神) and ask it to predict the upcoming quotations from the Four Books that would appear on the first session of the examination. The spirit replied via the medium by writing on the planchette the two characters for "I don't know" (*pu-chih* 不知). The candidate then asked the spirit: "How is it that the spirits and worthies have no way of knowing?" The medium then recorded the spirit's second reply: "I don't know. I don't know. And again I don't know" (不知，不知，又不知).

Meanwhile, a crowd had gathered in the temple, which probably included other examination candidates. They were all amused at the spirit's apparent profession of ignorance and remained unenlightened. When the candidate was in his examination cell, however, he suddenly realized that the spirit had indeed correctly predicted what the first quotation from the Four Books would be. It was taken from the last chapter of Confucius' *Analects*, which included three "I don't knows" in the quotation: "Confucius said, 'Not knowing fate, a man has no way of becoming a gentleman; not knowing the rites, he has no way of taking a stand; not knowing words, he has no way of judging people'" (孔子曰，不知命，無以為君子也。不知禮，無以立也。不知言，無以知人。). The required quotation for the first eight-legged essay, of course, included the phrase "*pu-chih*" three times. The failure of the candidate to recognize what the spirit was telling him also demonstrated his deficiencies as a gentleman who did not know his own fate.[74]

Among the interesting cultural developments that set the classical and literary context for sessions of spirit-writing were changes in the actual curriculum of the civil examinations over the centuries. In the turn from T'ang-Sung belles lettres to Ming-Ch'ing classical essays, described in Chapter 1, not only did candidates have to adjust their study of the classical canon, but spirits (particularly their mediums!) also had to keep up with the classical curriculum if they hoped to provide the proper guidance when implored for a prediction of examination questions. Hence, from 1370 until poetry testing was resumed in 1756, it made little linguistic sense for mediums to transmit specific poetry lines when queried about the

73. See *Ch'ing-pai lei-ch'ao*, 73.13–14. See also Overmyer, "Values in Chinese Sectarian Literature," p. 221; Richard Smith, *Fortune-Tellers and Philosophers*, pp. 226–28; and Judith Zeitlin, "Spirit-writing and Performance in the Work of You Tong (1618–1704)," November 1995 draft, pp. 1–2.

74. *Ch'ing-pai lei-ch'ao*, 73.16. See *Lun-yü yin-te*, 42/20/3. See also Lau, trans., *Confucius: The Analects*, p. 160.

examinations. Their opinions on most matters, however, still were expressed using poetic forms.[75]

Ironically, one way to trace the changes in the examination curriculum from Sung through Ch'ing times is to follow the changes in the content of the responses spirits "wrote out" on planchettes for candidates. In a local temple, for instance, a candidate once asked the medium there to predict the questions for the upcoming 1843 Che-chiang provincial examination. Suddenly Kuan-ti took hold of the medium and wrote out on the planchette a reply that alluded to the likely questions, but Kuan-ti also added: "I do not read the *Spring and Autumn Annals.*" The candidate didn't know what this meant until, while taking the second session of the provincial examination, which after 1787 required candidates to master all of the Five Classics (see Chapter 5), he noted that Kuan-ti had successfully predicted the quotations from the *Change, Documents, Poetry,* and *Rites* classics. Only the quotation from the *Annals* was missing from Kuan-ti's prediction, which suggested that Kuan-ti (or the medium) had preferred it when the curriculum had allowed candidates to specialize on one of the Classics. Before 1756, few candidates, like Kuan-ti, had mastered the *Annals* because of the length of its commentaries (see Tables 5.16 and 5.17).[76]

As we shall see in Chapter 10, the period after 1740 was replete with changes in the civil examination curriculum, including the addition of a required poetry question in T'ang regulated verse in 1756. Judith Zeitlin has described, for example, the bafflement of the Han Learning scholar Chi Yun 紀昀 (1724–1805) when he and a group of scholars consulted a spirit-writing medium near West Lake in Hang-chou in the late eighteenth century. The poem that appeared through the medium alluded to a famous medieval courtesan and poet whose grave site was nearby and who they thought was probably the actual spirit writing the poem.[77]

What troubled Chi Yun was that the poem the spirit composed was written in T'ang regulated verse (*lü-shih* 律詩), a form that had not been invented during the Southern Ch'i dynasty (479–502), when the spirit had actually lived. "How is it you are able to compose regulated verse?" Chi Yun asked. The spirit-poet replied that spirits also kept up with the times even though they lived in the other world. Chi Yun then asked the spirit-poet to compose lines in the Southern Ch'i dynasty style, which she successfully did via the medium. Still not convinced that the spirit they were communicating with was the actual Six Dynasties courtesan "Little Su" (蘇小小), Chi Yun concluded, curiously, that it was more likely that she

75. Russell, "Chen Tuan at Mount Huangbo," p. 123.

76. *Ch'ing-pai lei-ch'ao,* 73.22.

77. Zeitlin, "Spirit-writing and Performance," p. 3.

was being impersonated by an unknown ghost from a later period, one who knew T'ang regulated verse very well. And, we might add, one who could provide late eighteenth-century examination candidates with predictions of the lines of T'ang verse needed for the new poetry question.[78]

Similar to spirit-writing, the technique known as "deciphering written words" (*ch'ai-tzu* 拆字 or *ts'e-tzu* 測字), which came from a medium or appeared in a dream, replicated the six paleographical rules of written graph formation. In use in China since the *Shuo-wen chieh-tzu* 説文解字 (Analysis of characters as an explanation of writing) by Hsu Shen 許慎 (58–147), the rules had classified almost ten thousand different characters by sound and structure according to 530 radicals (*pu-shou* 部首). Such philologically technical word analysis was appropriated in popular culture by fortune-tellers and diviners to decipher the cryptic messages often received via spirit-writing.[79]

The semantic, radical component of a graph and its complementary, phonetic component, which had been used together by classical scholars to determine the ancient meaning of the graph, could be turned inside out by clever predictors of fate, who broke characters down into their structural components and then recombined them in efforts to fathom the secret message or pun that was being transmitted through them. In 1406, for example, the Fu-chien literatus Lin Huan 林環 dreamed (see Figure 6.3) that when he was about to take the spring metropolitan and palace examinations, his friend sent him some dog meat (*ch'üan-jou* 犬肉). Later, Lin realized that this had been an auspicious omen (*hsien-chao* 先兆) and that he had been destined by fate to become the 1406 *optimus*.

When the character *ch'üan* 犬 for dog was analyzed by Lin and his Hanlin colleagues, they saw first that it was the right side of the character for *chuang* 狀 in *chuang-yuan* 狀元 (*optimus*). Second, the character for dog was itself both the organizing radical and the first character under the radical for *chuang* 狀. These two methods of *ch'ai-tzu* confirmed that Lin Huan had been assured of becoming the *chuang-yuan*. In essence, this approach gave free rein to the imagination to construct plausible, ad hoc "dissections" of characters to suit the immediate needs of the interpreter.[80]

This technique could also be used to predict future success or failure. Chi Yun, for example, approached a famous "word analyst" from Che-

78. See Chi Yun, *Yueh-wei ts'ao-t'ang pi-chi* 閲微草堂筆記 (Note-form writings from the straw hut for reading subtleties) (Shanghai: Ku-chi Press, 1980), 18.451–52.

79. *Ch'ing-pai lei-ch'ao*, 73.90–91. See also Richard Smith, *Fortune-Tellers and Philosophers*, pp. 43, 201; and Wolfgang Bauer, "Chinese Glyphomancy," in Sarah Allan and Alvin Cohen, eds., *Legend, Lore, and Religion in China* (San Francisco: Chinese Materials Center, 1979), pp. 71–96.

80. *Chuang-yuan t'u-k'ao*, 1.15a–b.

FIGURE 6.3. Sending Dog Meat in 1406. *Source: Ming chuang-yuan t'u-k'ao* 明狀元圖考 (Illustrated survey of *optimi* during the Ming dynasty). Compiled by Ku Ting-ch'en 顧鼎臣 and Ku Tsu-hsun 顧祖訓. 1607 edition.

chiang province after the 1754 metropolitan examination, which he had passed, but before the palace examination, to find out what his final *chin-shih* rank would be. Chi Yun wrote down the character for black ink (*mo* 墨) for the man to analyze and determine Chi's rank. The Che-chiang man replied that there was no hope for Chi Yun to finish in the top tier (*i-chia* 一甲) of three *chin-shih* graduates because the top part of the character for *mo* was similar to the character *li* 里, which if turned upside down was the equivalent of *erh-chia* 二甲, or the second tier of *chin-shih* graduates.

However, the analyst went on, Chi was destined to enter the Hanlin Academy because the four dots 丶丶丶丶 under *li* 里 in the graph *mo* 墨 were the same as the four dots that formed the feet of the character *shu* 庶. The bottom graph of *t'u* 土, also in *mo*, was close to the graph *shih* 士. The latter *shih* was the head for *chi* 吉, and when *shu*, *chi*, and *shih* were put together as *shu-chi-shih* 庶吉士, this was the official title for a Hanlin Academy probationer. Chi Yun finished seventh in the second tier and entered the Hanlin Academy as a *shu-chi-shih*.[81]

Because so much in fate calculations depended on one's birth date and identity, another common technique that candidates used was to change their fates or escape an inauspicious spirit-writing session by modifying their names. A name change served candidates as an identity change, which could reconfigure their karmic allotments. Or the change could allow them to take advantage of an auspicious fate awaiting someone who met the criteria of a particular surname or given name. To dream of the "heavenly rankings" (*t'ien-pang* 天榜), as many candidates did, was to see the final earthly rankings in advance.[82] In many cases, the change of name was simply a strategic decision based on a prophetic dream or a political decision to avoid possible misunderstandings if one's name carried double meanings.

For example, Yuan Huang, who believed that "success in the examinations depends entirely on secret virtue," failed the 1577 metropolitan examination when he registered under his given name of Yuan Liao-fan 袁了凡. Later he dreamed that someone named Yuan Huang 袁黃 was destined to be the *hui-yuan*, so Liao-fan changed his name to Huang. On the 1586 palace examination, as "Yuan Huang," he indeed gained his *chin-shih* degree ranked number 190, but he was only ranked 185th behind the top two finishers on the metropolitan examination, Yuan Tsung-tao 袁宗道 (1560–1600) and Huang Ju-liang 黃汝良. The dream, it turned out, had correctly predicted the surnames of the top two metropolitan finishers, Yuan and Huang. Yuan Tsung-tao, like Yuan Huang, was also a practitioner of Taoist and Buddhist cultivation techniques.[83]

In 1690 Lu Tsu-yü 陸祖禹 was told by an examiner to change his name if he expected to pass under Manchu rule, because his earlier name, Hsi-man 餼滿 ("present plentiful gifts"), was slightly embarrassing and could imply "to use Manchus for sacrifice." Because of this, Lu's name

81. *Ch'ing-pai lei-ch'ao*, 73.92, which mistakenly gives 1748 for the date of the metropolitan examination.

82. For a Ming example of the "heavenly rankings" for the 1619 metropolitan examination, see *Ch'ien-Ming k'o-ch'ang i-wen-lu*, B.30a–b, and passim.

83. *Chih-i k'o-so-chi*, 2.66; and *Hui-shih lu*, 1586: 18a–36b, in *Ming-tai teng-k'o lu hui-pien*, vol. 20.

was not placed on the official *chü-jen* roll, although the examiner had wanted to rank him one of the top five finishers. Lu had also dreamed that someone else had told him to change his name if he hoped to gain a higher degree. As a *fu-pang* alternate, Lu was able to compete in higher examinations successfully after changing his name to Tsu-yü.[84]

In another case, the great-great-grandson of Ch'en Hung-mou, Ch'en Chi-ch'ang 陳繼昌, took his *chü-jen* degree ranked number one under the name Shou-jui 守叡, but for the 1820 metropolitan examination, based on a dream, he changed his name to Chi-ch'ang. The result was that he finished first on both the metropolitan and palace examinations. Based on an auspicious dream, Ch'en became one of only two Ch'ing literati (see Chapter 7) to finish first on all provincial and capital examinations (under the name Chi-ch'ang). He also was ranked number one on his three local examinations (under the name Shou-jui) and thus was known as holder of "greater and lower" (*ta-hsiao* 大小) "three firsts" (*san-yuan* 三元).[85]

For a final example, consider the case of Wei Yun-ko 魏芸閣, who dreamed he saw the heavenly rankings (*t'ien-pang* 天榜) for the 1821 Che-chiang provincial examination. The first name on the roll was a literatus from Hang-chou with the name Wei Shih-lung 魏士龍. After checking to see that there was no one registered from Hang-chou with the name Shih-lung, Wei Yun-ko changed his name to correspond to the heavenly rankings. The heavenly rankings had not indicated what year the roll referred to, however, so, as Wei Shih-lung, Wei Yun-ko failed the 1821 provincial examination. He had to wait until 1844 for the prophecy to come true, and as Wei Shih-lung he finally finished as the Che-chiang *chieh-yuan* that year. Hsu K'o, as compiler of such records, which he labeled as "*mi-hsin*" 迷信 (confused belief), questioned whether the twenty-four-year wait had been worth it.[86]

Disappearances and replacements were another variation to the theme of changing one's fate. Ann Waltner has related the interesting story of Chou K'o-ch'ang 周克昌, by P'u Sung-ling, in which a young boy disappeared and was secretly replaced by his ghost. Diligent, the ghost Chou grew up and passed the examinations. Although he married, as a ghost he never consummated his marriage and was berated by his mother for not providing the family with an heir. When the "real" Chou reappeared, a second exchange was arranged with the merchant who had adopted him. The real Chou then replaced the ghost and fathered an heir, and the Chou family was thereby granted double success: "success in the examina-

---

84. *Ch'ing-pai lei-ch'ao*, 74.84.

85. Ibid., 74.54. Here the year for the provincial examination is 1813, but later in 74.109, the year 1819 is given for Ch'en's achievement as *chieh-yuan*.

86. *Ch'ing-pai lei-ch'ao*, 74.111.

tions and bliss in the bedroom" (科第閨幃福). Although studious, the ghost had outlived his usefulness. Such stories reflected the practical uses of identity change, in which the other world was brought into this world as an ally to achieve examination success.[87]

Similarly, the use of geomancy (*feng-shui* 風水) to locate auspicious sites for tombs, houses, and temples was applied to the examination market. Famous geomancers were much sought after because of their success in selecting auspicious ancestral lands. Such grave sites were thought to yield examination success as well, given the carryover between the generations that was assumed in the practice of ancestor worship. We have seen that Yuan Huang, for instance, taught that examination success did not depend on a candidate's ability but rather on his ancestors' store of merit. Clearly, late imperial literati saw many pragmatic and therapeutic reasons to draw on such techniques, which added to the repertoire of popular religion in appealing to Han and non-Han ruling elites.[88]

## DREAMS AND ASPIRATIONS
## OF MING *CHUANG-YUAN*

As shown above, perhaps the most representative form of communication between this and the other world since antiquity in China was the dream.[89] Dream interpretations (*chan-meng* 占夢) and the sighting of portents (*chao* 兆) in the dreams of examination candidates, common in medieval China,[90] became sophisticated cultural forms widely reported in Ming times.[91] Even Chu Yuan-chang, the first emperor of the Ming, had recorded one of his own dreams ("Chi-meng" 紀夢), which was collected in his imperial writings. In the dream, Chu relived his life one year before becoming emperor, in which there had been several signs that he was des-

87. See P'u Sung-ling 蒲松齡, *Liao-chai chih-i* 聊齋志異 (Strange tales of Liao-chai) (Shanghai: Ku-chi Press, 1962), 3/1067–68. See also the cover of Ann Waltner's *Getting An Heir: Adoption and the Construction of Kinship in Late Imperial China* (Honolulu: University of Hawaii Press, 1990).

88. See Richard Smith, *Fortune-Tellers and Philosophers*, pp. 131–59.

89. See Yao Wei-chün 姚偉鈞, *Shen-mi te chan-meng* 神秘的占夢 (Mysteries of dreams) (Kuang-hsi: People's Press, 1991), pp. 3–18. On Sung examination dreams, see Chaffee, *The Thorny Gates of Learning in Sung China*, pp. 179–80.

90. See Liu Wen-ying 劉文英, *Chung-kuo ku-tai te meng-shu* 中國古代的夢書 (Dream books from ancient China) (Peking: Chung-hua Bookstore, 1990), pp. 1–65; and Roberto Ong, *The Interpretation of Dreams in Ancient China* (Bochum: Studienverlag Brockmeyer, 1985), pp. 8–46. See also Carolyn Brown, ed., *Psycho-Sinology: The Universe of Dreams in Chinese Culture* (Lantham, Md.: University Press of America, 1988).

91. Lien-che Tu Fang, "Ming Dreams," *Tsing Hua Journal of Chinese Studies*, n.s., 10, 1 (June 1973): 61–70.

tined to unite China under his military forces. The signs for his success were laid out in his dream as they were in popular religion and literati life. First a fairy crane sent by the immortals appeared in Chu's dream and led him into visions of Buddhist guardians and Taoist priests. The priests presented him with a crimson robe and a sword. They then told him to move on. The dream in effect legitimated the rags-to-riches tale of a peasant boy who was designated by the other, darker world to become the founder of a new, "bright" (*ming* 明) dynasty in the visible world.[92]

As spontaneous reflections of the anxiety in their lives, produced under the enormous mental and physical pressures of the civil examination regime and, for them, its "cultural prisons," the visions that late imperial literati projected in dreams provide us with a unique window to gauge their mental world, as they recalled it, through language and visual imagery for interpretation by fortune-tellers, diviners, shamans, and Buddhist and Taoist priests. The dream market for examinations, which involved "sleep meditation" as a religious form, was a faithful replica of the cultural constructions that accompanied the social and political dynamics of the examination market.[93] Frequently, these exchanges, which resulted in personal gains and losses, were expressed in humorous terms.

For instance, the poet and calligrapher Ho Shao-chi 何紹基 (1799–1873), some time before the 1820 metropolitan examination in Peking, had a dream in which he reached a market where there were many *man-t'ou* 饅頭 (steamed rolls). After choosing one roll to eat and finishing it, he took another, when suddenly a stranger came by and stole it from him. Later, Ho realized that the *man-t'ou* thief was none other than the 1820 *optimus* Ch'en Chi-ch'ang 陳繼昌, who, as we have seen, changed his name after taking first place in the provincial examination and thereby was assured of finishing first on both the palace and the metropolitan examinations. Ho realized that he had met his match, as the dream had suggested. Ho finished first on the 1835 provincial examination, which counted for the *man-t'ou* he had eaten in the dream, but in the 1836 metropolitan and palace examinations he could not duplicate Ch'en Chi-ch'ang's feat of "three firsts," two under the name Chi-ch'ang. The second *man-t'ou* went to Ch'en.[94]

92. See *Ming T'ai-tsu yü-chih wen-chi*, 16.8a–14b. See also Romeyn Taylor, "Ming T'ai-tsu's Story of a Dream," *Monumenta Serica* 32 (1976): 1–20.

93. See Michel Strickmann, "Dreamwork of Psycho-Sinologists: Doctors, Taoists, Monks," in Carolyn Brown, ed., *Psycho-Sinology: The Universe of Dreams in Chinese Culture*, pp. 25–46; and Russell, "Chen Tuan at Mount Huangbo," p. 122. See also Kathleen Kelleher, "Seems Taking a Final Exam Is Everyone's Worst Nightmare," in *Los Angeles Times*, Tuesday, May 28, 1996, E-1 and E-4.

94. *Ch'ing-pai lei-ch'ao*, 74.109. Here the year for the provincial examination that Ch'en passed is 1819, but earlier in 74.54, the year 1813 is given for Ch'en's achievement as *chieh-*

Since antiquity, Han Chinese had regarded the dream as a message from the spirit-world, which complemented fate prediction, spirit-writing, geomancy, physiognomy, and deciphering written words in communicating with that world.[95] To "pray for dreams" (*ch'i-meng* 祈夢) and engage in "sleep meditation" was a common goal for those who visited temples overnight. Temple dreams invoked by prayer were thought to be the best means to communicate with Wen-ch'ang, Kuan-ti, or other gods and worthies associated with a particular temple. At times, the hypnotic arts (*ts'ui-mien-shu* 催眠術) were added to "map out dreams" (*t'u-meng* 圖夢) and lay bare the meanings of what people said they saw in their visions. The Hang-chou temple to the martyred Ming minister, Yü Ch'ien, for instance, became a center for sleep meditation and dream incubation, an examination tradition that lasted into the twentieth century, and one that will likely be revived in the twenty-first when Yü's temple is rebuilt in Hang-chou.[96]

Dreams as a therapeutic device were commonly used outside the examination market as a sign of healing and the restoration of health.[97] Chang Feng-i 張鳳翼 (1527–1613), for example, compiled a collection entitled *Meng-chan lei-k'ao* 夢占類考 (Classified studies of dream interpretations) after recovering from an unsuccessful trip to Peking in 1565 to pass the metropolitan examination. Despondent and prone to drinking, he remained very ill until late in 1567, when he dreamed of visiting the Eight Immortals of the Ch'üan-chen 全真 sect of Taoism. In the dream, Lü Tung-pin 呂洞賓 took Chang's pulse and gave him a white pill, which eventually helped him to recover. Chang failed the metropolitan examination four times altogether, and retired to a healthier life of leisure and writing operas in his native Su-chou. His collection of dream interpretations was based on his 1565–67 tribulations.[98]

*yuan*. For a recent collection of strange stories and humorous anecdotes from the civil examinations, see Wang Chih-tung 王志東, *Chung-kuo k'o-chü ku-shih* 中國科舉故事 (Stories about the Chinese civil examinations) (Taipei: Han-hsin Cultural Enterprises, 1993). Pages 212–86 deal with the Ming and Ch'ing dynasties.

95. Yao Wei-chün, *Shen-mi te chan-meng*, pp. 19–35, discusses the chief techniques used in dream interpretation since ancient times in China.

96. *Ch'ing-pai lei-ch'ao*, 73.55. See also Ong, *The Interpretation of Dreams in Ancient China*, pp. 36–46; and Richard Smith, *Fortune-Tellers and Philosophers*, pp. 245–46.

97. On the therapeutic role of dreams, see C. G. Jung, *Dreams* (Princeton: Princeton University Press, 1974), pp. 39–41, 73–74. Jung calls this the "processes of psychic compensation."

98. See Chang Feng-i, "Hsu" 序 (Preface), *Meng-chan lei-k'ao*, late Ming edition, pp. 1a–b. See also Lien-che Tu Fang, "Ming Dreams," pp. 59–60; and Ong, *The Interpretation of Dreams in Ancient China*, pp. 165–66.

Ch'en Shih-yuan's 陳士元 1562 compilation entitled *Meng-chan i-chih* 夢占逸旨 (Remaining points on dream interpretation) laid out in rich historical detail the two major traditions of dream interpretation in imperial China: (1) the dream as prophecy (*chao* 兆) and (2) the dream as illusion (*huan* 幻). In the examination market, unlike the literary world, the dream functioned mainly as a form of communication with the other world. Although different, dreams and conscious perception (*chueh* 覺) were forms of realization that added to human knowledge (*chih* 知) of fate and prognostication. In Ch'en's view, "there were early auspicious signs for all examination rankings and salary grades" (科甲爵品莫不有前兆). He then traced the written evidence from the T'ang through Ming times for dreams as auspicious signs of examination success.[99]

At least five Ming emperors reputedly relied on dreams to choose the *optimus*, for example, in the palace examination. In 1385 the Hung-wu emperor, whose own famous dream was recorded as an autobiographical account of his fated ascent to power, dreamed of nails (*ting* 釘) and silk thread (*ssu* 絲) and therefore chose Ting Hsien 丁顯 as the *chuang-yuan*. The reasoning was: (1) Ting's surname was the same sound as the character for nails and (2) the character for silk thread formed part of Hsien's name.[100] In 1421, the Yung-lo emperor reportedly dreamed of a crane (*ho* 鶴), a symbol for Taoist immortals, before the palace examination. Based on this omen, he selected Tseng Ho-ling 曾鶴齡 as the *optimus* because Tseng's name included the graph for a crane.

Later in 1448, the Cheng-t'ung emperor dreamed of meeting a literatus, a Taoist, and a Buddhist before the palace examination. He then chose the top three *chin-shih* based on their intellectual backgrounds: The *chuang-yuan* P'eng Shih 彭時 (1416–75) was registered from a hereditary literatus family (*ju-chi* 儒籍); the *pang-yen* Ch'en Chien 陳鑑 (1415–71) had once been a student of music in a Taoist temple; and the *t'an-hua* Yueh Cheng 岳正 (1418–72) had served in a Buddhist temple. In 1544, the Chia-ching emperor chose a candidate with the character "thunder" 雷 in his name because of a dream in which the emperor heard thunder. Ch'in Ming-lei 秦鳴雷 (1518–93, lit., "noise of thunder") from Che-chiang province was the beneficiary of the dream.[101]

99. See Ch'en Shih-yuan, *Meng-chan i-chih* (*Pai-pu ts'ung-shu* 百部叢書 reprint, Taipei: I-wen Publishing Co., 1968), 1.1a, 1.5a, 1.6a, 6.1a–7a, 8.9a–11b. The "Hsu" 序 (Preface) dates from 1562.

100. *Chuang-yuan t'u-k'ao*, 1.5b. See also Lien-che Tu Fang, "Ming Dreams," p. 60; and Rudolph Wagner, "Imperial Dreams in China," in Carolyn Brown, ed., *Psycho-Sinology: The Universe of Dreams in Chinese Culture*, pp. 11–24.

101. *Chuang-yuan t'u-k'ao*, 1.21a; *Chih-i k'o-so-chi*, 1.39; and *Ch'ien-Ming k'o-ch'ang i-wen lu*, A.45a–b. See also Lien-che Tu Fang, "Ming Dreams," pp. 60–61.

In a discourse that narrated communications between temporal emperors and the gods and ghosts of the other world, it was impossible to verify accounts of imperial dreams. Many were imperial fabrications; others were imputed to the ruler; but even as fabrications, the dreams represented cultural accounts that drew on historical events and molded them to the morality tale being told. It was reported, for instance, that Yü Ch'ien had appeared as a ghost before his banished wife and asked to borrow her eyes so that he could appear normal before the emperor and plead his case. In the morning Yü's wife became blind, while Yü himself appeared before the emperor as an image in a fire that broke out in the imperial palace. Realizing the injustice done to Yü in 1457, the emperor pardoned his wife. It was patently a false dream, however; the Ch'eng-hua emperor could not have pardoned her, because Yü's wife had passed away years before while in exile. He did rehabilitate the Yü name and allow the son of Wang Wen 王文 (1393–1457), also martyred in 1457, to take the civil examinations in 1465 (see Chapter 8). The fabrication of the dream did, however, explain that policy decision and right the wrong done to Yü Ch'ien, and thus it is useful to us historically as a lie about how things ideally should have appeared.[102]

We also know that dream interpretation played a significant role in the lives of more than half of all *chuang-yuan* during the Ming dynasty.[103] Dreams were interpreted as human "counterparts" (*hsiang* 象; see Chapter 9) to the other world that could be diagrammed (*t'u* 圖) and analyzed to understand a person's character and behavior and divine his fate. The *Ming chuang-yuan t'u-k'ao* 明狀元圖考 (Illustrated survey of *optimi* during the Ming dynasty), for example, was a collection that diagrammed and discussed the dreams of *optimi* from 1371 to 1571. Initially compiled by Ku Ting-ch'en, a 1505 *optimus* (see above), and continued by his grandson Ku Tsu-hsun 顧祖訓, it retold the foreordained achievements of all Ming *chuang-yuan*. Wu Ch'eng-en 吳承恩 and Ch'eng I-chen 程一楨 later added materials that brought it up to 1604. This semiofficial work, for which there is a later, 1607 edition was honored with a new preface by the late Ming Hanlin academician and imperial grand secretary Shen I-kuan 沈一貫 (1531–1615), who thereby granted it an imperial imprimatur as an

102. See Lien-che Tu Fang, "Ming Dreams," pp. 69–70; and Hegel, "Heavens and Hells in Chinese Fictional Dreams," pp. 1–10.

103. For a recent collection of dreams, stories, and anecdotes about all *chuang-yuan* in Chinese history, see Tsou Shao-chih 鄒紹志 and Kuei Sheng 桂勝, *Chung-kuo chuang-yuan ch'ü-wen* 中國狀元趣聞 (Interesting things heard about Chinese *optimi*) (Taipei: Han-hsin Cultural Enterprises, 1993). Pages 1–144 cover stories before the Ming.

acceptable biographical record of the dreams of success of great men that was in vogue during the Ming.[104]

Such premonitory dreams of success were widely written about and were illustrated in the uniquely Ming woodblock form of portraying dreams graphically as a "vision" of consciousness that emanated from the mind while the body was asleep.[105] Astrological signs such as the southern dipper, auspicious omens such as dog meat, and unusual coincidences fed into the Ming belief that the mind at rest tended to weave a cultural matrix of visual images and symbols whose surface aspects could be studied for the manifest content they implied. These dream-visions may be interpreted as historical constructions and not as actual dreams whose riddles need deciphering. It is likely that all were ad hoc constructions and not manifest dreams, as they were presented. It is worth making the Ming solutions to the riddle of the dreams the object of analysis to see how such dreams and their cultural interpretations functioned in the examination market.[106]

For our purposes, the "manifest content" of this cultural matrix was channeled in part by the male anxiety and motivating psychological tensions that the examination life entailed. Although the "latent dream-thoughts" of *chuang-yuan* will never be transparent to us because they were always encoded, transposed, revised, and distorted in the manifest cultural discourse peculiar to Ming China, we can begin to decode some external aspects of the interrelation between the psychological makeup of the men and families who claimed to have had such dreams and their sociohistorical experiences and pressures. Their repressions and sublimations were far different from those we can intuit today because the cultural terms of their conscious acceptance and rejection of their thoughts were defined by their times and not ours. Indeed, to call their mental streams of consciousness "streams," "repressions," or "sublimations" tells us more about ourselves than about Ming literati, given the historical changes that have occurred in the conscious and unconscious internalization of human agency over time and from culture to culture.[107] Nevertheless, through

104. See the "Fan-li" 凡例 (Overview) in the *Chuang-yuan t'u-k'ao*, pp. 1a–b, and Shen I-kuan's preface, pp. 1a–b. See also note 60 above for discussion of the Ch'ing edition called the *Chuang-yuan t'u-k'ao* and discussion of Ming printing in Chapter 7.

105. Judith Zeitlin, in her *Historian of the Strange*, pp. 137, 173, describes this woodblock print technique of illustrating dreams as a "dream bubble."

106. *Chuang-yuan t'u-k'ao*, passim.

107. On the historicization of human agency, see Friedrich Nietzsche, *On the Genealogy of Morals*, translated by Francis Golffing (Garden City, N.Y.: Anchor Books, 1956), passim; and Nietzsche's "Preface" to *Beyond Good and Evil*, translated by Walter Kaufmann (New York: Vintage Books, 1966). See also Jung's discussion of "taking up the context" to determine the associations made in a dream, in *Dreams*, pp. 71–72.

FIGURE 6.4.    Three Heads Appear in a 1445 Dream-Vision.
*Source: Ming chuang-yuan t'u-k'ao* 明狀元圖考 (Illustrated survey of
*optimi* during the Ming dynasty). Compiled by Ku Ting-ch'en
顧鼎臣 and Ku Tsu-hsun 顧祖訓. 1607 edition.

their graphically recorded "dream-visions," we do get a vivid sense of
what preyed on their minds as they lived out the grueling days of the premodern examination life in examination cells, which, thankfully, we can
never again reproduce verbatim.[108]

108. Abell, *The Collective Dream in Art*, pp. 62–70. The classic, if simplistic, examples of
dreams as "an attempt at the fulfillment of a wish" are to dream of food while starving or

Figure 6.4 presents a late Ming woodblock illustration prepared by Huang Ying-ch'eng for the *Ming chuang-yuan t'u-k'ao* in which three heads (*jen-shou san k'o* 人首三顆) appear in a 1445 dream-vision. The print represents a dream, actually a "day-dream," that Shang Lu 商輅 (1414–86) reportedly had while a young man reading the classics in his family's study (*hsueh-she* 學舍), probably sometime before 1435. The published account of it indicates that his teacher, a man named "literatus Hung" 洪士, had been living with him in his room, helping him prepare for the civil examinations. The elegant setting of the study, his neat reading desk complete with the writing paraphernalia required of all calligraphers (see Chapter 5), and the fact that he had a live-in tutor all indicate that Shang's Che-chiang family was one of substantial means and could provide him the time and cultural resources needed to devote to his classical studies. This was not a rags-to-riches story.[109]

In the illustration, however, Shang Lu is not pictured hard at work, which would have been the usual image of his mental preparations on the road to classical literacy and future examination success. Instead, he is portrayed asleep while studying, his teacher is absent, and from Shang's head emanates a dream-vision of a man holding three heads laced together by their hair, which the man presents to Shang. We should explore a little further the cultural overlap between "three heads" and "three firsts," which in both Chinese and English are homologous. Curiously, the Chinese term for head used in the dream is *shou* 首 and not *t'ou* 頭, the more physical image of the head attached to the body, although both were used to describe notions of coming in first, being on top, or referring to the leader. Accordingly, it is not a gory scene (no blood is depicted, for instance), nor one that would evoke immediate horror, but nonetheless three bodiless heads are being presented as trophies to Shang, who will triumph over many others. Shang Lu rests peacefully, so we are assured that this is a wishful dream, not one driven directly by overt anxiety or punishment.

Clearly, however, the stakes are very high, and some sense of the sacrifice of the body is evoked by the powerful images of the three heads held in one hand by the mysterious man. We might speculate that war-

---

to dream of water while thirsty. Cf. Sigmund Freud, *New Introductory Lectures on Psychoanalysis*, translated by James Strachey (New York: Norton, 1964), pp. 7–30, particularly pp. 43–44 on Freud's account of curing a student preparing for his doctoral examinations of "mental exhaustion," which leads Freud to a discussion of "dreams and occultism."

109. On Shang Lu's life, see *Ming-shih*, 7/4687–91; and *Dictionary of Ming Biography*, pp. 1161–63.

riors in imperial China, not students, typically severed the heads of their enemies and presented them to their leader as a trophy to confirm total victory in battle. Or, we might note that decapitation was a legal measure the Ming dynastic code enforced in capital cases if the crime were determined to be a "heavy" one, as opposed to a "lighter" one, which would entail death by strangulation or slicing. Perhaps the military and legal readings of Shang Lu's dream have some very limited relevance in evoking the examination market, where to compete and win meant that others had to fail. Lacking the detailed information that would tell us more about the dream's latent characteristics, however, we are left with its placid manifest content as pictured by the late Ming compilers. It is by Ming cultural standards definitely not a troubling dream, and we should not read too much blood and gore into it.[110]

Upon awakening, Shang Lu immediately related the manifest content of the dream to his teacher, who instead of scolding him for falling asleep while studying tells him that it is an "auspicious dream" (chi-meng 吉夢). The "three heads" are a vision into the future of Shang's life as a candidate for the civil examinations. With hindsight, of course, the dream at face value is easy enough to decipher. Shang's preordained success was corroborated when, at the age of twenty-one, he passed the 1435 Che-chiang provincial examination ranked first. He followed that up ten years later as the number-one graduate on the metropolitan, and received the final of his "three heads" by being named chuang-yuan on the 1445 palace examination. Shang was to that point the only literatus who had achieved "three firsts" (san-yuan 三元) on the Ming civil examinations. Because of his own influence as an examiner, Shang would see to it that another aspiring challenger, Wang Ao 王鏊 (1450–1524), would not duplicate the feat, and for the Ming, only Shang Lu attained this exclusive civil examination height (see Chapter 7).

Read with hindsight as ad hoc rationalization, Shang Lu's dream presents his success as a natural outcome of fate. The hard work and classical memory required to achieve such unprecedented success are elided in favor of a smooth path to fame, fortune, and high political office.[111] Read more historically, however, the placid dream covers up what must have been the considerable worries Shang had when, after passing the 1435 provincial examination, he probably failed the 1436, 1439, and 1442 met-

110. See Bodde and Morris, Law in Imperial China, pp. 133–34, 552.

111. See Sheang [Shang] Yen-liu, "Memories of the Chinese Imperial Civil Service Examination System," p. 52, which describes the hard work as follows: "In actuality, as long as one studied everyday without interruption, this [that is, so much memorization] could be achieved—there was nothing strange or miraculous about it."

ropolitan examinations. Given that he was over twenty in 1435, Shang probably also had failed the highly competitive Che-chiang provincial examination a couple of times, in addition to failing the metropolitan examination perhaps three times. Like most candidates (see Chapter 5), then, Shang had to wait until he was in his thirties before he received the coveted *chin-shih* degree and entered the civil service.

The story of preordained success becomes more problematic when the failures are added to the record. Forgotten are the childhood years of memorization (Shang specialized on the *Documents Classic*, for example) and youthful days spent in the study reading widely and practicing examination essays. In fact, the metropolitan record of the 1445 examination indicates that Shang's eight-legged essays were not particularly outstanding. Not one of his three essays on the Four Books was picked as the best. Only one of his four essays on quotations from the *Documents* was selected. Shang made his mark by writing the best discourse and documentary papers on session two, and one of his policy essays on session three was also chosen as the best on that question. For the late Ming audience, the single dream-vision replaced those hours, days, months, and years of hard work and disregarded the closeness of the competition for the high honors that Shang had been very fortunate to win.[112]

A similar dream, recorded by the 1583 *optimus* Chu Kuo-tso 朱國祚, is depicted as a dream-vision in Figure 6.5. In their commentary, the late Ming compilers of the *Chuang-yuan t'u-k'ao* noted that as a young candidate Chu had been on his way home from a local examination in T'ung-chou when a friend invited him on his boat, and they began drinking. Later at a stop along the way, the friend dragged Chu into a wine house filled with prostitutes. Alarmed, Chu ran out the door and without stopping walked the twenty *li* back to T'ung-chou. Later, when Chu took the provincial examination, he had a dream in his studio, again a daydream, in which a two-headed horseman appeared before him. Chu thought this strange, and in his dream he urged on the horse he was riding so that he was in front of the two-headed horseman.

The virtuous behavior Chu Kuo-tso had demonstrated was a moral backdrop for the dream-vision he experienced. The real meaning of the dream was not clear until after the rankings for the palace examination. Chu had not finished first on the provincial or metropolitan examination, so his status as *optimus* was equivalent to only "one head." The manifest meaning of the dream became clear, however, when Chu realized that on the palace examination he had finished ahead of Li T'ing-chi 李廷機, who had been first on both the provincial and metropolitan examinations,

---

112. See *Hui-shih lu*, 1445: 14a, in *Ming-tai teng-k'o lu hui-pien*, vol. 1.

FIGURE 6.5.   A Two-Headed Horseman Appears in a 1583
Dream-Vision. *Source: Ming chuang-yuan t'u-k'ao* 明狀元圖考
(Illustrated survey of optimi during the Ming dynasty).
Compiled by Ku Ting-ch'en 顧鼎臣 and Ku Tsu-hsun 顧祖訓.
1607 edition.

and was thus a man with "two heads" (*shuang-t'ou-jen* 雙頭人). By passing
ahead of Li in the dream, Chu had assured himself of finishing ahead of a
man who had "two firsts" to his credit. "One head," in this case at least,
was better than two.[113]

The dreams typical of Ming *chuang-yuan*, which reflected the religious
beliefs of the compilers, were wish-fulfillment dreams of becoming number

113. *Chuang-yuan t'u-k'ao*, 3.33a–34a.

FIGURE 6.6. A Spirit Heralds the 1454 *Optimus. Source: Ming chuang-yuan t'u-k'ao* 明狀元圖考 (Illustrated survey of *optimi* during the Ming dynasty). Compiled by Ku Ting-ch'en 顧鼎臣 and Ku Tsu-hsun 顧祖訓. 1607 edition.

one in the palace examination. In Figure 6.6, for instance, a spirit appears in a dream-vision and heralds the future 1454 *optimus* Sun Hsien 孫賢 at the gate in front of his home while Sun dozes over a book with a cup and pot of tea nearby on his desk in a pleasant studio. The herald carries a yellow pennant with the graphs for *chuang-yuan* on it, and he is dressed in the formal imperial garb of one who is responsible for announcing the

FIGURE 6.7. Entering Heaven's Gate in 1544. *Source: Ming chuang-yuan t'u-k'ao* 明狀元圖考 (Illustrated survey of *optimi* during the Ming dynasty). Compiled by Ku Ting-ch'en 顧鼎臣 and Ku Tsu-hsun 顧祖訓. 1607 edition.

final ranking lists (*chin-pang* 金榜) to the public. The compilers tell us that Sun's success also had several auspicious dreams associated with it.[114]

Similar wish-fulfillment dreams were reported by many Ming *chuang-yuan* or members of their families. Ch'in Ming-lei 秦鳴雷 frequently had dreams of storming the imperial Gate of Heaven (*T'ien-men* 天門) before

114. Ibid., 2.11b–13a.

he became the 1544 *optimus*. Figure 6.7 shows a dream-vision emanating from the second floor of an elegant pastoral pavilion overlooking water and mountains where Ch'in is daydreaming. In the dream he whips his horse upward toward a closed gate to a high-walled city. Civil examinations were usually viewed as the means to enter the gate of officialdom, but Ch'in's dream was specifically oriented toward the gate forbidding entry to the walled imperial city, where the emperor resided. As an *optimus*, he would enter that gate in triumph and serve in the court as a Hanlin academician. Another version of this dream was to ride the dragon, as the 1472 *optimus* Wu K'uan 吳寬 (1436–1504) did, before the palace examination.[115]

Sumptuous meals and hobnobbing with the rich and powerful were another feature of candidates' dreams. Figure 6.8 shows K'o Ch'ien 柯潛 (1423–73) asleep on a carpet in front of an altar in his home. He is dreaming that he is seated at the head of a table eating with friends at a temple. Auspiciously, one of his friends presents a goat's head (*yang-t'ou* 羊頭) as one of the delicacies. Using the technique of deciphering written words (*ch'ai-tzu*), those at the banquet cleverly figure out what this augurs for K'o. The year 1451 was known as the *hsin-wei* 辛未 year, according to the lunar sexagenary cycle of keeping track of time using the twelve heavenly stems and ten earthly branches. The graph for goat 羊 resembled the bottom of the character for *hsin* 辛 in the sexagenary cycle; 1451 was the year of the goat; and moreover, the head itself implied finishing first that year.[116]

Wish-fulfillment dreams often recorded auspicious omens tied to popular culture and religion, which affirmed the hopes and aspirations of the candidates and members of their families. Usually the omens that were described in such dreams were straightforward symbols from local cults or the Taoist and Buddhist pantheon of worthies and deities. A dream-vision that the 1505 *optimus* Ku Ting-ch'en, the initial compiler of the *Ming chuang-yuan t'u k'ao*, included in the collection was one in which a yellow crane (*huang-ho* 黃鶴) descended to get a better look at him (see Figure 6.9). The crane, an auspicious bird associated with Taoism, also represented the relationship between father and son. Ku had faithfully burned incense every evening to honor his father, who was over fifty when Ting-ch'en was born, and prayed for his father's long life. In appearing before Ku Ting-ch'en, the crane was auspiciously communicating not only Ku's future examination success but also that that success would be shared with his father. His filiality was rewarded when at the age of eighty, Ting-

115. Ibid., 3.12b–13b, and 2.21b–22b. The "dragon's head" (*lung-t'ou* 龍頭) and "dragon-spirit" (*lung-shen* 龍神) also appeared in auspicious dreams for the 1478 (2.24b–25b) and 1526 (3.4a–b) *chuang-yuan*.

116. *Chuang-yuan t'u-k'ao*, 2.10b–11a. See also 3.14a–15a, for a depiction of a meal honoring the 1547 *optimus*.

FIGURE 6.8.    Presenting a Goat's Head in 1451. *Source: Ming chuang-yuan t'u-k'ao* 明狀元圖考 (Illustrated survey of *optimi* during the Ming dynasty). Compiled by Ku Ting-ch'en 顧鼎臣 and Ku Tsu-hsun 顧祖訓. 1607 edition.

ch'en's father saw his son become the empire's *chuang-yuan,* and Ku went on to collect records of all such auspicious events to show that his fate was not unique.[117]

117. Ibid., 2.38a–39a. See Eberhard, *Lexikon chinesischer Symbole,* pp. 163–64. See also Ong, *The Interpretation of Dreams in Ancient China,* p. 112, which relates Su Shih's dream in the famous prose-poem on Red Cliff, in which Su equates the crane with a Taoist immortal.

FIGURE 6.9.   A Yellow Crane Appears in 1505. *Source: Ming chuang-yuan t'u-k'ao* 明狀元圖考 (Illustrated survey of *optimi* during the Ming dynasty). Compiled by Ku Ting-ch'en 顧鼎臣 and Ku Tsu-hsun 顧祖訓. 1607 edition.

Shen K'un 沈坤 (d. 1560?), the 1541 *optimus*, had what appeared initially to be an auspicious dream while asleep in his bedroom (illustrated in Figure 6.10). Out of Shen's bedroom flows a dream-vision in which a Taoist immortal (*hsien* 仙) presents Shen with medicine in the form of a round elixir. The elixir, known as "Awakening the Nine Foods" (*chiu-shih chih hsing* 九食之醒), was expected to activate the stomach as if there were

FIGURE 6.10. An Immortal Presents Medicine in 1541. *Source: Ming chuang-yuan t'u-k'ao* 明狀元圖考 (Illustrated survey of *optimi* during the Ming dynasty). Compiled by Ku Ting-ch'en 顧鼎臣 and Ku Tsu-hsun 顧祖訓. 1607 edition.

something inside. A strange, incense-like smell would then envelop the room and inflame one's nostrils. In the dream, Shen clearly accepted the elixir, which apparently enabled him to become the first *chuang-yuan* from his native place in the Huai-an region 淮安郡 in northern Chiang-su.

The full effects of the elixir, however, were not clear until eighteen years later in 1559, when Ting Shih-mei 丁士美 became the second *opti-*

*mus* from Huai-an. What was growing inside Shen K'un's stomach turned out to be another *optimus* from Huai-an. By the time Ting became the *optimus*, however, Shen K'un's political fortunes had declined, and he was arrested, tried, and executed based on false charges, which no one opposed because of Shen's notorious behavior and detested character. The popular version of what happened was that "a new *chuang-yuan* had entered the court, while the old one had entered prison" (新狀元入朝，舊狀元入獄). The compilers added their view that Shen K'un's glorious success and calamitous ending had been set by ingesting the elixir (榮辱禍福事皆前定).[118]

Curiously, however, in Figure 6.11, depicting Ting Shih-mei's own dream, prior to his becoming the 1559 *optimus*, a female Taoist immortal descends toward him riding a crane to deliver a yellow flag. As she descends, a group of heavenly fairies are seen in the sky, producing the music of the immortals by playing on classical instruments. After the yellow flag, announcing the auspicious selection of Ting by the gods, is placed in front of the gate to his home, the immortal remounts the crane and returns to the heavens. There is no mention in Ting's dream narrative of any connection to the trial and execution of Shen K'un. We are told only of his sympathies for Taoism. The doors to the other world are not interlocking, revealing that the dream narratives are themselves fragmented, cultural constructions appropriate to a specific story line.[119]

Although most of the dreams and mantic arts reviewed here in light of the examination market were tied to popular cults and religious Taoism, the influence of Buddhism was clear in the case of the 1553 *optimus* Ch'en Chin 陳謹 (1525–66), in our final example of a dream-vision illustrated by Huang Ying-ch'eng for the *Ming chuang-yuan t'u-k'ao* collection. In the dream, which floats above the roofs of three elegant buildings in a compound, Ch'en Chin is shown sitting on a lotus flower in a meditating "lotus position" surrounded by three people (see Figure 6.12). All are floating on a cloud in the sky, and the dream scene takes precedence over the earthly world seen from above. The three personages floating on the cloud dropping from the sky are an immortal, a young man, and a woman. The three had invited Ch'en to mount the lotus, and he has obliged them. As they entered the clouds, Ch'en became afraid, but the immortal presented him with a gold cap and crimson official robe, both symbols that he would become the *optimus* and formally appear before the emperor.

118. *Chuang-yuan t'u-k'ao*, 3.11a–12a. See also *Dictionary of Ming Biography*, p. 924.
119. Ibid., 3.20a–21a.

FIGURE 6.11. A Taoist Immortal Rides a Crane in 1559. *Source: Ming chuang-yuan t'u-k'ao* 明狀元圖考 (Illustrated survey of *optimi* during the Ming dynasty). Compiled by Ku Ting-ch'en 顧鼎臣 and Ku Tsu-hsun 顧祖訓. 1607 edition.

Sitting like a Buddha in meditation but dressed in the garb of a literatus, Ch'en Chin appears in the dream-vision at peace and in control, after having put aside his initial fears. The illustration projects an image of order and inevitability, which of course clashes with our historical portrayal of the examination market as a venue of furious competition, widespread corruption, and male anxiety. Sitting on a lotus in Buddhist-style meditation, Ch'en has floated to the other world and received its blessing

FIGURE 6.12. Riding the Lotus Flower in 1553. *Source: Ming chuang-yuan t'u-k'ao* 明狀元圖考 (Illustrated survey of *optimi* during the Ming dynasty). Compiled by Ku Ting-ch'en 顧鼎臣 and Ku Tsu-hsun 顧祖訓. 1607 edition.

for success in this world. Again, there is no mention of the years of hard work, memorization, and essay writing that any young boy from a family of means would have endured. A therapeutic victory over the trials and tribulations of the Ming examination market has been achieved.[120]

120. Ibid., 3.17b–18a.

## RESISTANCE TO THE MANTIC ARTS
## IN CIVIL EXAMINATIONS

When mantic techniques failed to produce the expected effects, however, profound disillusionment often followed. Many assailed the pervasive uses of divination, geomancy, and dream interpretation in the examination market as misplaced reliance on the other world. Similar sentiments were repeated inside Ming examination halls. The reign of cults, gods, spirits, and the mantic techniques to communicate with them was challenged by many metropolitan and provincial examiners, who used the political precincts of the dynasty's "cultural prisons" to place limits on elite belief in popular notions of fate and communication with the other world. The institutional regime of examinations enforced examiner power to elide nonofficial beliefs.[121] For instance, in the third-session policy questions (whose range of content is detailed in Chapter 9), examiners at times raised the issue of natural anomalies (*tsai-i* 災異) and asked students how to account for such events.[122]

*The 1558 Shun-t'ien Provincial Examination*
*and Interpretation of Natural Anomalies*

Representative of the elite trend to profess publicly its distance from popular religion and the mantic arts, the 1558 policy question on anomalies, which were usually seen as inauspicious natural disasters, was administered by examiners in charge of the Shun-t'ien provincial examination in the northern capital region.[123] Of the more than 3,500 candidates who took this examination, only 135 (3.86%) passed. For the five policy ques-

121. For background, see Deborah Sommer, "Confucianism's Encounter with the Evil Arts of Herodoxy: Ch'iu Chün's (1420–1495) Visions of Ritual Reform," paper presented at the University Seminar on Neo-Confucian Studies (New York: Columbia University, December 7, 1990). Ch'iu was an influential mid-Ming examination official. For his prefaces to Ming civil examination reports, see *Ssu-k'u ch'üan-shu*, 1248.163–192.

122. For policy questions on anomalies in 1558, 1561, 1573, 1582, 1588, 1594, 1597, 1603, and 1604, in provincial and metropolitan examinations, see *Huang-Ming tse-heng*, which covers the broad range of policy questions from 1504 to 1604 that dealt with heterodoxy, astrology, the five phases, heavenly bodies, and strange artifacts. See also *Ying-t'ien fu hsiang-shih lu*, 1597: 5a–6b, 34a–42b, for a policy question and answer on heaven's mandate (*t'ien-ming* 天命) and anomalies; and *Hui-shih chu-chüan* 會試硃卷 (Metropolitan examination essays), 1604: 26a, for a question on "eternal fate" (*yung-ming* 永命).

123. *Shun-t'ien hsiang-shih lu* 順天鄉試錄 (Record of the 1558 Shun-t'ien prefecture provincial civil examination), 1558: 12a–13a. See also the policy questions on *tsai-i* from the 1594 Shun-t'ien and 1597 Chiang-hsi, Hu-kuang, and Yun-nan provincial examinations in *Huang-Ming ts'e-heng, chüan* 12, 15, and 16.

tions on session three, the examiners selected two dealing directly or indirectly with the natural world (*tzu-jan* 自然): (1) "Serving Heaven" (which included discussion of astronomy and governance), (2) "Establishing officials," (3) "Employing talent," (4) "Disaster and inauspicious events" (which discussed the resonance between the realms of Heaven and people), and (5) the "Four Barbarians." That over 3,500 candidates had to be prepared to answer two policy questions on natural studies indicates that the provincial examinations in the late Ming exerted a broad influence on students preparing for the examinations by having them study aspects of the "Chinese sciences" (see Chapter 9).[124]

The examiners began their question by addressing the overlap between the heavenly and human realms and the subtle principles underlying this overlap. Citing the "Hung-fan" 洪範 (Great plan) chapter of the *Documents Classic* as the locus classicus, the examiners asked candidates to explain how the "five matters" (*wu-shih* 五事) in human affairs corresponded to the "five phases" (*wu-hsing* 五行) in the heavenly order. In many other civil examinations, these issues were raised by focusing on the five phases themselves.[125]

Since antiquity, literati as officials had debated the role of natural disasters in society and their impact on politics. Discussion of this issue usually lay within the limits of the boundaries first demarcated by Hsun-tzu 荀子 in the Warring States era and later substantially revised by Tung Chung-shu 董仲舒 (179–104 B.C.), who, as a result of his persuasive examination policy essays (*hsien-liang san-ts'e* 賢良三策), became one of the most influential advisors in the Former Han.[126] For Hsun-tzu, the spheres of heaven and man interacted, but the latter's destiny depended on man's own abilities to govern effectively. Anomalies were odd (*kuai chih k'o yeh* 怪之可也) but not to be feared (*erh wei chih fei yeh* 而畏之非也).[127] Tung Chung-shu, on the other hand, regarded anomalies in nature as "omens"

---

124. *Huang-Ming ts'e-heng*, 2.24a. See also the "Hsu" 序 (Preface) to the *Shun-t'ien-fu hsiang-shih lu*, 1558: 2b. For the policy questions see pp. 8a–14b.

125. The second policy question in the 1582 Ying-t'ien provincial examination in the southern capital region, for example, dealt with the five phases as a correspondence system (*shih-ying* 事應) between people and Heaven. See *Huang-Ming ts'e-heng*, 7.26a; and *Nan-kuo hsien-shu*, 4.37a–42a. A policy question on the five phases was repeated in the 1597 Honan provincial examination. See *Huang-Ming ts'e-heng*, 16.73a.

126. The emperor's questions and Tung's answers are contained in *Han-shu*, pp. 2495–2524. In the eighteenth century, the Ch'ien-lung emperor made Tung's famous *ts'e* one of the guiding elements in the emperor's notions of statecraft and world-ordering. See Chun-shu Chang, "Emperorship in Eighteenth-Century China," *The Journal of the Institute of Chinese Studies of the Chinese University of Hong Kong* 7, 2 (December 1974): 554–56.

127. *Hsun-tzu chi-chieh* 荀子集解 (Collected notes to the Hsun-tzu) (Taipei: Hua-cheng Bookstore, 1979), pp. 209–13.

(*ch'ien* 譴) arising from errors in the dynasty (*fan tsai-i chih pen chin sheng yü kuo-chia chih shih* 凡災翼之本菫生於國家之失).[128] In this 1558 question, the examiners were asking candidates to define what the "overlap between heaven and people" (*t'ien-jen chih chi* 天人之際) meant for contemporary Ming literati.

What was at stake here were the dangers of indulging too readily in the arts of communication between the real and unseen worlds. The 1558 examiners asked:

> How can the resonance between the five phases and five matters be demonstrated? To observe the overlap, some use the year, others the moon, and still others the day. How does one divide things up like this? Next, Confucius in preparing the *Spring and Autumn Annals* recorded calamities as inauspicious, but why didn't he record the corresponding events? In commenting on this some have said that Confucius feared that if there was no overlap then others would not have believed in the overlap. Is this right or wrong?[129]

Here the examiners were referring to Ou-yang Hsiu's 歐陽修 (1007–72) discussion of anomalies in the *Annals* in his *Hsin T'ang-shu* 新唐書 (New history of the T'ang dynasty). There, Ou-yang described Confucius as very cautious in his efforts to links events on earth to the heavens. Confucius regarded disasters (*tsai* 災) and inauspicious events (*i* 翼) as omens (*ch'ien* 譴), according to Ou-yang Hsiu, which rightfully instilled fear and the need for moral cultivation (*k'ung-chü hsiu-hsing* 恐懼修省). Ou-yang noted that Confucius also recognized the need to be circumspect (*kai shen chih yeh* 蓋慎之也) about omens and did not try to link all anomalies to human events (*t'ien-tao yuan fei chun-chun i yü jen* 天道遠非諄諄以諭人).[130] Candidates were asked to assess the interpretation of anomalies given by one of the greatest Sung literati.

Finally, the question turned to the manipulation of calamities as inauspicious political events by Han dynasty officials during the first century B.C., when prognostication and prophecy based on *ch'en-wei* 讖緯 (apocrypha) were popular at court. The role of portents in political culture during the Han has been explored in detail by Wolfram Eberhard, and the function of astronomy, astrology, and meteorology has been described as

128. *Ch'un-ch'iu fan-lu i-cheng* 春秋繁露義證 (Proofs of meanings in [Tung Chung-shu's] The Spring and Autumn's Radiant Dew), compiled by Su Yü 蘇輿 (Kyoto: Chūbun Press, 1973), 8.24a–24b.

129. *Shun-t'ien-fu hsiang-shih lu*, 1558: 12a–12b.

130. Ou-yang Hsiu and Sung Ch'i 宋祁, *Hsin T'ang-shu* (New history of the T'ang dynasty) (Peking: Chung-hua Bookstore, 1971), 34.873.

"purely political."[131] Believing in the conjuncture between abnormal natural phenomena and sociopolitical life, Han officials used this belief as an ideological weapon in the political struggles of the times. While Eberhard overstates the case and overlooks the technical achievements made by Han calendrical specialists in determining lunations and accurately predicting lunar eclipses, it is nonetheless clear that the Ming examiners were exposing this Han predilection for omens to ask students what they thought of the effort to link politics to anomalies in imperial governance.[132]

Among the examples the Ming examiners raised were those of Kung-sun Hung 公孫弘 (d. 121 B.C.), Kung-sun Ch'ing 公孫卿, Ching Fang 京房 (79–37 B.C.), and I Feng 翼奉, all high officials who had been questioned by Han emperors about the meaning of natural calamities or anomalies. When asked why floods had occurred in Yü's 禹 reign (tr., 3rd mill. B.C.), for example, Kung-sun Hung had replied that virtue and anomalies were mutually exclusive and that "if one accorded with heaven's virtue then harmony arose, if one opposed it, calamity struck" (天德無私親，順之和起，逆之害生).[133]

Likewise the Han official Kung-sun Ch'ing had explicated the reasons why natural disasters such as droughts occurred, while Ching Fang, who was exiled for his alleged crimes as a Han minister, predicted a great deluge and was imprisoned and executed when his prediction came to pass.[134] I Feng had replied to an emperor concerned about calamities during his reign that "heaven's heart determined whether the kingly way was peaceful or endangered" (考天心言王道之安危).[135] Most of these views could be discredited (pu tsu ch'eng 不足稱), the examiners implied in their question, but the students were asked if there was anything of note to some of the pronouncements (so-yen yu ho-tao che yü 所言有合道者歟). Some principle must explain such things, the examiners concluded.[136]

The examiners then brought up the nine years of recorded floods under Emperor Yao 堯 (tr., r. 3rd mill. B.C.) and the seven years of drought under Emperor T'ang 湯 (tr., r. 2nd mill. B.C.) as examples of inauspicious events for the candidates to evaluate. Was it possible that

131. Eberhard, "The Political Function of Astronomy and Astronomers in Han China," in John K. Fairbank, ed., Chinese Thought and Institutions (Chicago: University of Chicago Press, 1957), pp. 33–70.

132. See Nathan Sivin, "Cosmos and Computation in Early Chinese Mathematical Astronomy," T'oung Pao 55 (1969): 53–54n1.

133. Han-shu, 58.2617.

134. Shih-chi, 12.472–73; Han-shu, 75.3162.

135. Han-shu, 75.3171–72.

136. Shun-t'ien-fu hsiang-shih lu, 1558: 13a.

later eras, for which no such inauspicious events were recorded, could be considered superior to the reigns of the sage-kings Yao and T'ang? If heaven had no aims (*wu-i* 無意), then why should one fear inauspicious events? If indeed heaven had its purposes (*yu-i* 有意), then its heart would be in favor of life. Yet if heaven had its purposes, then how could calamities serve its goal of favoring life?

When viewed in light of the mantic arts then prevalent in Ming cultural life, the 1558 Shun-t'ien examiners were cutting against the grain of public culture in Peking and elsewhere that surrounded the examination compound in which the question was delivered. The popular correlate to the role of anomaly interpretation by Han officials criticized by the examiners was the effort by examination candidates to divine their futures via the mantic arts. The way the collected dreams of *optimi*, which reflected popular lore in the sixteenth and seventeenth centuries, were honored as biographical sources indicates that literati communication with the other world was more tolerated in government and society than in the halls and cells of the civil examinations.

Since the Han, the records of "anomalies" had been featured in a variety of private and official writings that sought to domesticate the other world by fixing its unusual impact on everyday life within a taxonomy known as *chih-kuai* 志怪 (recording unusual events). Indeed, following the fall of the Han in A.D. 220, anomaly records were shifted from the "small writings" (*hsiao-shuo* 小説) section in the canon of "philosophers" (*tzu-pu* 子部) to the section on "histories" (*shih-pu* 史部). After the T'ang, when the civil examinations were reconstituted and expanded, the accounts in many *i-wen lu* 異聞錄 (records of unusual matters) that we discussed above focused on the examination compounds and the mental life of candidates, which in effect became an important subgenre in the *chih-kuai* category.[137]

These accounts mounted in number and by Sung times were widely prevalent in encyclopedias such as the *T'ai-p'ing kuang-chi* 太平廣記 (Expanded records of the T'ai-p'ing era), completed in 977, and in "note-form literature" (*pi-chi* 筆記). Daiwie Fu has examined the evolution of the anomaly accounts in Northern Sung times and found that in general there was a tendency among Sung literati such as Shen Kua 沈括 (1031–95) to revise the T'ang categorization of natural anomalies by distancing themselves from such records of ghosts and divine spirits. In his *Meng-hsi pi-t'an* 夢溪筆談 (Brush talks from the dream book), for instance,

137. See Dudbridge, *Religious Experience and Lay Society in T'ang China*, pp. 31–42; and Robert F. Campany, *Strange Writing: Anomaly Accounts in Early Medieval China* (Albany: SUNY Press, 1996), pp. 28–29, 150–55, which revises earlier findings in DeWoskin, "The Six Dynasties *Chih-kuai* and the Birth of Fiction," pp. 21–52.

Shen Kua retained the Han-T'ang style of fascination with marvels and anomalies but, according to Fu, also sought to dispel the "supernormal aura of ghosts." In Fu's view, Sung literati sought to create an official intellectual position that would distance elites from the popular lore associated with Han-T'ang aristocratic culture and recorded in *chih-kuai* accounts.[138]

Yiyi Wu has described, for instance, how Northern Sung literati-officials adopted an attitude of what Wu calls, a bit too teleologically, "pragmatic agnosticism" toward astral anomalies and thereby triumphed over career bureaucrats in the Directorate of Astronomy between the 1006 sighting of a supernova (*k'o-hsing* 客星) and the 1066 discovery of a comet (Halley's) in the heavens. Fan Chung-yen 范仲淹 (989–1052) was extremely circumspect in viewing astral anomalies such as the supernova of 1006 or the meteor shower of 1038 as evidence of heaven's interaction with human and political affairs. In a like manner, Ou-yang Hsiu attacked then-popular sky-reading traditions and attempted to separate politics from astral anomalies. The Sung literati position, which the Ming examiners tried to reproduce, stressed human agency in the political world. Hsun-tzu's classical position of distancing heaven from human affairs was preferred to Tung Chung-shu's Han interpretation of anomalies as omens of political failure.[139]

Representative of this Sung effort was Hung Mai 洪邁 (1123–1202), whose collection of anecdotes and stories of unusual events, like Shen Kua's *Meng-hsi pi-t'an*, entertained elites with a wide array of Sung popular lore concerning the mantic arts. Hung preferred to record such materials for posterity in his *I-chien chih* 夷堅志 (Record of I-chien), but when politics became involved he was careful to diagnose the cause of political failure as the activities of rulers and not impute celestial phenomena as the ultimate reason for such events. Astral omens had supposedly heralded the rise of Wang An-shih, but, according to Hung Mai, such auspicious sightings had not prevented the dynasty from collapsing in 1127 to the Jurchen Chin onslaught, which Hung attributed to Wang's disastrous reform polices. For Hung, "treating the real as unreal and treating the unreal as real" were both confused.[140]

138. See Daiwie Fu, "A Contextual and Taxonomic Study of the 'Divine Marvels' and 'Strange Occurrences' in the *Mengxi bitan*," *Chinese Science* 11 (1993–94): 3–35.

139. See Yiyi Wu, "Auspicious Omens and Their Consequences: Zhen-ren (1006–1066) Literati's Perception of Astral Anomalies" (Ph.D. diss., Princeton University, History, 1990), pp. 131–63, 171–252. See also Yung Sik Kim, "The World-View of Chu Hsi (1130–1200): Knowledge about the Natural World in 'Chu-tzu ch'üan-shu'" (Ph.D. diss., Princeton University, History, 1980), pp. 14–40, 147–216.

140. Hung Mai, *Jung-chai sui-pi* 容齋隨筆 (Miscellaneous jottings from Jung Studio) (Shanghai, Ku-chi Press, 1978), 1/218. See Yves Hervouet, ed., *A Sung Bibliography* (Hong

Accordingly, we can see that by invoking Ou-yang Hsiu's cautious position on linking events on earth to the heavens, the 1558 Ming examiners in Shun-t'ien were appealing to a classical (Hsun-tzu) and Sung (Ou-yang Hsiu) ideal that tolerated records of anomalous events but also sought to set limits to how seriously such speculations should be taken. In addition, by explicitly attacking the role of Han officials in manipulating omens and anomalies for political purposes, the Shun-t'ien examiners were also trying to control the impact of the mantic arts in official life, if not in personal life, by stressing instead Tao Learning notions of human responsibility and moral cultivation.

The 1558 policy question on anomalies sought to reproduce the Sung sense of prudence and care about overinterpreting the linkages between this and the other world. The answer they selected as most outstanding, and thus the one that best reflected their cosmological perspective, was written by Wu Shao 吳紹, an imperial student from Chia-hsing county in Che-chiang province who finished third overall in the Shun-t'ien provincial examination. His answer was rated by the examiners as a model for "fathoming the principles" (ch'iung-li 窮理) that mediated between heaven and people. In the opening to his answer, Wu Shao agreed with the examiners that the interaction between Heaven and man was subtle and hard to discern. Nonetheless, Wu contended, heaven had "concrete principles" (shih-li 實理), and man had "concrete affairs" (shih-shih 實事). Heaven's "concrete principles" were based on the operations of yin and yang; "concrete affairs" were brought to completion under the control of men. Accordingly, Wu Shao concluded: "Those who say that heaven has planned out calamities to accord with earthly affairs are slandering heaven. Similarly, those who say that people have planned earthly affairs to accord with calamities are slandering men. These are all instances of seeking the principles unsuccessfully and twisting words to misconstrue things. Would the gentlemen select such views?"[141]

Because heaven and people were unified in principle, the gentleman could seek principles to fathom successfully the workings of heaven and earth, according to Wu Shao. Confucius' *Spring and Autumn Annals* exemplified this approach. His chronicle of events and calamities did not link heaven and humans to explain inauspicious events; rather, because his standpoint was for the public good and because he resided in correct prin-

Kong: Chinese University Press, 1978), pp. 304–05. For discussion, see Yiyi Wu, "Auspicious Omens and Their Consequences," pp. 268–70; Zeitlin, *Historian of the Strange*, pp. 190–91; and Valerie Hansen, *Changing Gods in Medieval China*, passim.

141. *Shun-t'ien-fu hsiang-shih lu*, 1558: 68a–69b; and *Huang-Ming ts'e-heng*, 2.24b.

ciples, he did not force events to fit the notion that calamities were preordained. Wu further explained: "Therefore, I think those who discuss calamities and inauspicious events must use the *Annals* as their standard. Confucius' intent was true, and his words were straight. The chronicle was verified according to unchanging principles."[142]

Coming to the part of the question dealing with the calamities that had beset the sage-kings Yao and T'ang, Wu Shao noted that the lack of such calamities in later reigns did not mean that Yao or T'ang were deficient in morality. Rather, the problem lay in the operations of *ch'i* 氣 (the material/spiritual world of matter and energy), which was unified in its operations between heaven and earth. Sometimes it acted in harmony with people; at other times it went against them. Even a sage-king such as Yao or T'ang could not control the operations of *ch'i* when they went against the ruler's will. Later reigns were more fortunate in living in a time when the operations of *ch'i* were more harmonious. Rather than fear such events, according to Wu Shao, the gentleman understood that "heaven has its Way, and men have their efficacy." Fear of the workings of the universe could be tamed and brought within the framework of self-control and self-scrutiny in the realm of human affairs.[143]

To explain why calamities occurred (*so-i-jan* 所以然), Wu Shao appealed to the subtle revolutions of the heavenly Way, which were beyond the ken of humans. The great virtuous power of heaven favored life, but even heaven could not stand in the way of the workings of the Way, when heaven's heart was moved by the plight of men caught up in calamities. To blame heaven for the calamity was to slander heaven and misrepresent its support of life. The prediction of calamities by ancients such as Ching Fang did not confirm heaven's intentions but merely demonstrated the various purposes imputed by men to heaven when calamities occurred. The actual causes for such calamities were never really fathomed.

Wu Shao compared the calamities of heaven to the diseases of humans. Just as an illness must be identified and dealt with by testing one's pulse, so too an anomaly or calamity in the heavens is revealed in light of the "arcane aspects of correspondence" (*hsiang-wei* 象緯). On earth they are revealed in mountains and streams. In things, calamities and anomalies are revealed in supernatural birds, animals, plants, and trees. Among humans, they are seen in villains. When the causes are properly examined, then both illness and calamities can be handled and treated. Just as a doctor and medicine are required to treat an illness and restore the

142. *Huang-Ming ts'e-heng*, 2.24b–26a.
143. Ibid., 2.26a–27a.

inborn vitalities (*yuan-ch'i* 元氣) of the body, the cultivation of moral standards and judgments based on laws and regulations are needed to cope with a calamity and restore the original vitality of the dynasty.[144]

Wu Shao concluded his policy answer by declaring that those who sought to bring order to the world did not make plans depending on whether there would be calamities. They simply concerned themselves with whether their plans were complete. Yao handled nine years of floods and T'ang seven years of drought by making the appropriate plans to deal with such calamities. Those who did not have to face calamities never had to come up with the plans to deal with such events. Thus Yao and T'ang were great sage-kings, according to Wu Shao, precisely because they had to overcome adversity to create order in the world. In effect, Wu had turned the discussion of calamities and inauspicious events inside out. They became tests of greatness rather than harbingers of the intervention of the supernatural on earth. Flood and drought demonstrated the sagely credentials of Yao and T'ang.[145]

This policy question and its answer, typical of the cosmological outlook favored in written examinations, were pervaded by a distancing orientation to natural calamities and were clearly opposed to what were called "disjoined" (*pu-ho* 不合) interpretations of nature. Limitations in the human understanding of the cosmos, according to both the examiners and candidate, had to be recognized. Otherwise, to impute human meaning and intent to calamities, as prognostication and the mantic arts presumed, was to humanize heaven and translate human knowledge into human fear and ignorance. Furthermore, the candidate's appeal to sage-kings as men who confronted the events of their time and rectified them indicated that notions of fate implying resignation in the face of calamities were unacceptable for orthodox literati operating in the public domain. What mattered was not the symbolic meaning of floods or droughts but rather what concrete policies were followed to deal with them. Governance by men took precedence in a world in which the complete workings of heaven were beyond one's understanding.

### Ch'ing Views of Fate Prediction in the Examinations

The tension between an ideal cosmos, in which the natural and political worlds were acceptable though distant reflections of each other, and the popular mantic arts, which brought such theories dangerously down to earth in the forms of religious and popular communication with the other

144. Ibid., 2.27a–28b.
145. Ibid., 2.28b–29b.

world, were never successfully resolved in the late empire. Although increasingly evident in the Ch'ing, literati dissatisfaction with the inroads that popular religion and the mantic world of diviners, fortune-tellers, and Taoist priests had made in Ming examination life was already foreshadowed during the sixteenth century.

The Che-chiang scholar-bibliophile Hu Ying-lin 胡應麟 (1551–1602), for example, became a *chü-jen* degree-holder in 1576, but between 1577 and 1598 he failed the metropolitan examination eight times. His distaste for the examination system carried over into his private life, during which he read widely and began writing fiction at the age of fifteen. In 1594–95, while he stayed in Peking preparing for his seventh attempt at the *chin-shih* degree in spring 1595, Hu recorded one of his dreams, which in effect became a parody of the dream-visions so popular among examination candidates.[146]

Under the heading "Examiners in Heaven" ("T'ien-shang chu-ssu" 天上主司), Hu Ying-lin related that the night before the 1595 metropolitan examination he had dreamed of an officially dressed man sitting above him in the palace, who invited him to enter and take the examination. When Hu entered the palace examination, he found that a man named I-shui sheng (易水生, lit., "Master Change-Water") was already seated. When only one sheet of paper with the examination questions on it floated down from the examiner, Hu struggled with the other man to catch it. Master Change-Water succeeded in catching the paper, although Hu could make out seven characters on the sheet. After falling short on the heavenly examination, Hu awoke angrily and remained ill at ease. When the first session of the actual metropolitan examination commenced, Hu was surprised to see that the seven characters he had glimpsed in his dream, if properly interpreted, would have correctly predicted the first quotation.

Nevertheless, when Hu saw the official rankings posted, he learned that he had failed a seventh time. When he saw the name of the 1595 metropolitan *hui-yuan*, Hu noted that the surname of T'ang Pin-yin 湯賓尹 (b. 1568) bore a striking resemblance to the two characters of "Change-Water" in Hu's dream, the man with whom he had struggled to catch the examination paper. The character for *i* 易 (change) made up the right side of T'ang's surname, while the character for *shui* 水 formed the left-side water radical 氵 in T'ang. So far, Hu's story was a straightforward account of fate and the reason why one man lost and another won.

146. See Hu Ying-lin, *Chia-i sheng-yen* 甲乙剩言 (Leftover words from heavenly stems one and two), *Pai-pu ts'ung-shu* 百部叢書 edition (reprint, Taipei: I-wen Press), pp. 4b–5b.

Hu went on to note, however, that the heavenly examiner must have been "illiterate" (*pu-shih tzu* 不識字) because the character for "change" was missing the middle line contained in the graph *yang* 易. In other words, the heavenly examiner had not understood the rules for character formation, whereby the left-side radical for water 氵 provided the correct meaning of "soup" for T'ang Pin-yin's surname, but the right-side character for "change" was the wrong phonetic element. Instead of the sound of *i*, the correct phonetic should have rhymed with the sound of [*y*]*ang* 易. Such a backhanded critique of the heavenly examiner permitted Hu to conclude: "If the heavenly examiner was illiterate, how much better could the earthly examiners be?"[147]

Hu Ying-lin effectively turned the typical Ming dream interpretation inside out and cast doubt on the credibility of the other world. His parody of the dream satirized the mantic arts, which had given the other world precedence over the human realm. In the end, all Hu could do, however, was to throw up his hands in disgust and retire to private life. Nevertheless, his views echoed sentiments among many Ming literati that the degree of belief in fate and examination success had gone too far. It took a mortal such as Hu to recognize that the heavenly examiner was poorly grounded in the linguistic foundations of the classical language that most young boys had mastered in childhood.

Resistance to the mantic arts in examination life probably increased during the Ch'ing, but given the deluge of candidates taking the civil examinations after 1700 (see Chapter 4), it is unlikely that such resistance had much effect in practice. Tai Ming-shih 戴名世 (1653–1713), who became a popular writer of classical essays and as an outside observer frequently criticized the official examination rankings, ridiculed the popular belief in the role of fate in these rankings. In his 1702 preface to his collection of the best provincial examination essays from that year, Tai pointedly attacked those who attributed their success or failure to fate, ghosts, or the mantic arts. In Tai's view, the hard work required to learn how to write proper eight-legged essays, outlined in Chapter 4, was the key to success or failure. In this regard, "individuals had to accept responsibility because ghosts had no role to play" (人有權，而鬼為無權矣). Tai Ming-shih restored the years of childhood memorization and thousands of practice essays that had been elided in the rush to grant fate the final say.[148]

In the eighteenth century, Wu Ching-tzu, for example, relied on geomancy early in his quest for an examination degree, but as his failures

---

147. Ibid., pp. 4b–5b.
148. See Tai Ming-shih, "Jen-wu mo-chüan hsu" 壬午墨卷序 (Preface for examination essays from 1702), in *Ch'ing-tai ch'ien-ch'i chiao-yü lun-chu hsuan*, 2/238.

mounted Wu ridiculed the practice in his famous novel *The Scholars*. His lineage had attributed their early Ch'ing literary prominence to an auspicious gravesite chosen by a geomancer. In the famous chapter 44 of his novel, Wu had a character say:

> Nothing enrages me more than the way geomancers nowadays, who quote Kuo [P'u 郭璞, 276–324] as an authority to say: "This plot will ensure that your descendants come first in the palace examination and are Number One Palace Graduates." I ask you, sir: Since the rank of Number One Palace Graduate was instituted in the T'ang dynasty, how could Kuo P'u, who lived in the Chin dynasty [265–419], know of this T'ang title and decree that a certain type of ground would produce this rank? This is absolutely ridiculous! If the ancients could foretell high honors and rank from the soil, how is it that Han Hsin 韓信 [d. 196 B.C.], who chose a high and spacious burial ground for his mother, first became a noble and then had three branches of his lineage wiped out? Was that site good or bad?[149]

This Ch'ing backlash against such religious avenues for fate prediction, however considerable, should not cloud our conclusions about their popular role in the examination market. We can certainly see in Wu Ching-tzu's satire the voice of the literatus ideal enunciated since Confucius that "to keep one's distance from the gods and spirits while showing them reverence can be called wisdom."[150] Nevertheless, the literati mastery, in theory, of the high-minded areligiosity in the Four Books did not eliminate the inroads of popular religion or its mantic resources in literati life. At best, classical aloofness and literary satire could only curtail the public affirmation of popular religion and try to keep it in its secondary place. Even the Ch'ien-lung emperor was bedeviled by the mass hysteria in 1768 resulting from rumors that sorcerers were practicing magical arts by stealing the souls of their owners. They used the technique of cutting off the queues worn by Han Chinese men, which had symbolized their submission to the Manchu dynasty since the fall of the Ming.[151]

Dream interpretation, for example, remained an important feature of literati life in the Ch'ing dynasty, but its historical significance when compared to the Ming elite craze for dreams diminished and was transposed to general works on popular lore. In the late Ch'ing, the *Tien-shih-chai hua-pao* 點石齋畫報 (The Tien-shih Pavilion's pictorial), a popular periodical,

149. See Wu Ching-tzu, *The Scholars*, pp. 490–91. See also Richard Smith, *Fortune-Tellers and Philosophers*, pp. 160–71.

150. *Lun-yü yin-te*, 11/6/22. Cf. Lau, ed., *Confucius: The Analects*, p. 84.

151. See Philip Kuhn, *Soulstealers*, pp. 94–118.

FIGURE 6.13.  Dreaming of an Auspicious Meeting at the Local
Wen-ch'ang Temple in 1822. *Source: Tien-shih-chai hua-pao* 點石
齋畫報 (The Tien-shih Pavilion's pictorial), serial 2, vol. 11
(1897), *hsu* 戌 12, pp. 91b–92a. Reprinted, Yang-chou: Chiang-
su Rare Books, 1983.

also presented accounts of preordained examination success, which included illustrations of the "dream visions" of Ch'ing literati fated to succeed.
In Figure 6.13, for instance, we see a youth from the Huang 黃 family
napping in his bookish study within an elegant garden. In his daydream,
which takes place before the 1822 Shan-hsi provincial examination, the

young man is received in the local Wen-ch'ang Temple, where he meets the patron deity of the literary arts. The meeting is later read as an omen of his future success (*teng-k'o yu-chao* 登科有兆) as the *chieh-yuan* on the provincial examination.[152]

The popularity of such collections indicated that the "distancing" of heaven in the civil examination compound was always resisted even when the candidate's examination essay correctly reproduced the required literati critique of fate and anomaly interpretation. The *Ming chuang-yuan t'u-k'ao*, for example, was also enlarged to include lists of Ch'ing *optimi*. But such lists gave only the barest of examination information and career success each *optimus* had attained. Not one mini-account mentioned any Ch'ing *optimus* who had premonitions and dreams of their imminent success in the examination competition similar to Ming *chuang-yuan*. Nor were any illustrations of dream-visions included. Sketchy accounts were added about the second- and third-place finishers on the palace and the top graduate from the metropolitan examinations.

Moreover, the brief accounts stopped in 1682, indicating that support for such an elite record of the role of mantic techniques and dreams among the most heralded Ch'ing literati empirewide was not as acceptable for gentry publications as in the late Ming. Titled the *Chuang-yuan t'u-k'ao*, the Ming-Ch'ing accounts covered *chuang-yuan* from 1371 to 1682, some three hundred years in the heyday of the late imperial civil examination machinery and its cultural efflorescence, but a sharp break in the acceptability of dream narratives had occurred after 1644. No subsequent publication attempted to paint dreams and the mantic arts as positively as the Ming account of *chuang-yuan* had.[153]

Instead, the narratives of dreams continued in popular works of literature, such as those by P'u Sung-ling,[154] in *i-wen lu* 異聞錄 (records of unusual matters) accounts of the examination compounds, and in late-Ch'ing periodicals such as the *Tien-shih-chai hua-pao*. The *Kuo-ch'ao k'o-ch'ang i-wen lu* 國朝科場異聞錄 (Recording unusual matters heard in the Ch'ing examination grounds) in particular became a rich depository of civil examination lore up to the Taiping Rebellion and paralleled earlier *chih-kuai* collections during the Sung and Ming dynasties. Such popular elements were also incorporated in two influential works on Ming and

152. See *Tien-shih-chai hua-pao* 點石齋畫報 (The Tien-shih Pavilion's pictorial), serial 2, vol. 11 (1897), *hsu* 戌 12, pp. 91b–92a (reprint, Yang-chou: Chiang-su Rare Books, 1983). My thanks to Meng Yue for pointing out this source for Ch'ing dreams of examination success.

153. *Chuang-yuan t'u-k'ao*, 4.23a–32a. See also Richard Smith, *Fortune-Tellers and Philosophers*, p. 251.

154. For discussion, see Zeitlin, *Historian of the Strange*, pp. 164–81.

Ch'ing civil examinations: the *Chih-i ts'ung-hua* 制義叢話 (Collected comments on the crafting of eight-legged civil examination essays), compiled by Liang Chang-chü 梁章鉅 and published in 1843, and the *Chih-i k'o-so chi* 制義科瑣記 (Collection of fragments about the crafted eight-legged essays for civil examinations), by Li T'iao-yuan 李調元.

This trend to reclassify and thereby redomesticate the oddities of the civil examination experience shared much in kind with the T'ang-Sung evolution of the *chih-kuai* genre overall, which had evolved in medieval times into an acceptable elite record of unusual phenomena and human fortune. The late Ming passion for dream interpretation never really waned in the Ch'ing, but its official portrait became more scholarly and aloof, perhaps under the influence of a more sober-minded elite increasingly oriented toward evidential research (see Chapter 9). Many Sung literati, such as Ou-yang Hsiu, had distanced themselves from the mantic practices of their times, and many Ming-Ch'ing followers of the Ch'eng-Chu orthodoxy or Han Learning followed their lead.[155]

By the late Ch'ing and early Republic, this elite view of popular custom was reconfigured in modernist terms, a trend that culminated with Hsu K'o's *Ch'ing-pai lei-ch'ao* 清稗類鈔 (Classified jottings on Ch'ing dynasty unofficial history). In Hsu's collection, examination lore was divided up and reclassified into the categories of "civil examinations," "magicians and shamans" (*fang-chi* 方伎), and "confused beliefs" (*mi-hsin* 迷信). Hsu K'o intended his collection of lore, published in 1917, as a sequel to the Sung *T'ai-p'ing kuang-chi*, but the new cultural context ensured that such lore was publicly acceptable among modernist literati only if it could be pigeonholed as superstition.[156] Here we see that Ch'ing literati views of mantic techniques and the later "May Fourth" hostility toward imperial Chinese "superstitions" were homologous.

## ALTERNATIVE RESPONSES TO FAILURE

To conclude this account of the examination life and its late imperial popular forms of cultural expression, I shall briefly look at psychological portraits of students and examination candidates during the Ming and Ch'ing dynasties. The internalization of public failure, which became the lot of

155. Campany, *Strange Writing*, pp. 116–19, 122–29. See also Smith, *Fortune-Tellers*, pp. 160–71. On evidential research, see my *From Philosophy to Philology*, pp. 27–36.

156. See Zwia Lipkin, "Soothsayers, Clients and the State in Republican Canton," presented at the Graduate Student Conference on Modern Chinese History, University of California, San Diego, spring 1996, for the survival of late-imperial mantic practices despite these modernizing tendencies.

almost all young men who competed in the examination market, was usually rationalized according to the therapeutic regimes offered candidates and their families by religion and popular mantic techniques. Such therapies when accepted and effectively applied kept male anxiety within the acceptable social boundaries of personal mental well-being and prevented dreams and hallucinations from losing their links to acceptable standards of cultural health during the Ming and Ch'ing. But this was an inherently unstable balance of outer public pressure and inner emotional resources that each individual had to navigate successfully for himself.

### P'u Sung-ling on Alienation and the Examination Life

P'u Sung-ling, a failure many times himself, immortalized the travails of the vast majority trapped in the relentless machinery of late imperial civil examinations in his many stories that parodied the examination system. In his most famous portrait of the candidate as a young man, P'u realistically sketched "The Seven Likenesses of a Candidate" ("Hsiu-ts'ai ju-wei yu ch'i-ssu yen" 秀才入闈有七似焉):

> A licentiate taking the provincial examination may be likened to seven things. When entering the examination hall, bare-footed and carrying a basket, he is like a beggar. At roll-call time, being shouted at by officials and abused by their subordinates, he is like a prisoner. When writing in his cell, with his head and feet sticking out of the booth, he is like a cold bee late in autumn. Upon leaving the examination hall, being in a daze and seeing a changed universe, he is like a sick bird out of a cage. When anticipating the results, he is on pins and needles; one moment he fantasizes success and magnificent mansions are instantly built; another moment he fears failure and his body is reduced to a corpse. At this point he is like a chimpanzee in captivity. Finally the messengers come on galloping horses and confirm the absence of his name on the list of successful candidates. His complexion becomes ashen and his body stiffens like a poisoned fly no longer able to move. Disappointed and discouraged, he vilifies the examiners for their blindness and blames the unfairness of the system. Thereupon he collects all his books and papers from his desk and sets them on fire; unsatisfied, he tramples over the ashes; still unsatisfied, he throws the ashes into a filthy gutter. He is determined to abandon the world by going into the mountains, and he is resolved to drive away any person who dares speak to him about examination essays. With the passage of time, his anger subsides and his aspiration rises. Like a turtle dove just hatched, he rebuilds his nest and starts the process once again.[157]

---

157. See *Ch'ing-pai lei-ch'ao*, 21.62–63, for a version of the original. This famous passage is narrated in Sheang [Shang] Yen-liu, "Memories of the Chinese Imperial Civil Service

This account is of course fiction, but its realistically constructed cultural content lays out in full relief the massive psychological strain that candidates like P'u Sung-ling experienced in and outside the cultural prisons of the Ch'ing government. Writing in the late Ch'ing, Shang Yen-liu noted that P'u's phrase "like a cold bee in late autumn" may have been accurate for Shan-tung, but that in Kuang-chou, where Shang took his *chü-jen*, it was more like "an ant in a hot pot."[158] For our purposes, P'u Sung-ling's literary version of male anxiety circa 1700 reflects how his society and his time described the examination experience for most young men who traversed the rites of passage from youthful hope to adult disappointment and then to elderly maturity. P'u's account thus tells us a great deal about his views of the examinations and the toll they took on him and his fellow failures who tried to cope with the social pressure to succeed. Their narratives of examination failure stand in sharp relief against the reassuring woodblock prints carved by Huang Ying-ch'eng of Ming *optimi* daydreaming in the midst of their studies.

Read autobiographically, the account of the "seven transformations" tells us how P'u Sung-ling channeled his experiences and transformed them into cultural significance as fictional stories that appealed to others for their realism and maturity. As Allan Barr correctly notes, through the ironic exploration of fancy, fate, and gods, P'u Sung-ling had successfully turned his disappointments into a series of therapeutic versions of Ch'ing daily life. He did not seek to overthrow the examination regime, despite his sharp satire. Rather, P'u learned to come to grips with his failures inside the system and coped with it by turning his energies to literature instead. In the process, P'u achieved a level of therapeutic distance that must have been emotionally common in a land filled with so many examination failures and so few daydreaming *chuang-yuan*. As indicated in Chapter 5, even *optimi* had to fail several times before their predestined success was successfully rationalized.[159]

In the psychological narrative that P'u Sung-ling depicted, the examination candidate, typically a young man from a gentry family who had spent ten or more years preparing for local licensing examinations and

---

Examination System," pp. 67–68, and translated in C. T. Hu, "The Historical Background: Examinations and Control in Pre-Modern China," *Comparative Education* 20, 1 (1984): 16, and incompletely in Miyazaki, *China's Examination Hell*, pp. 57–58. See also P'u's [Pu] *Strange Tales of Liaozhai*. For discussion, see Barr, "Pu Songling and the Qing Examination System," pp. 87–111.

158. Sheang [Shang] Yen-liu, "Memories of the Chinese Imperial Civil Service Examination System," p. 68.

159. See Barr, "Pu Songling and the Qing Examination System," pp. 107–08.

another five to ten competing in provincial examination halls (see Chapter 5), is transformed into a supplicant begging for admission into the cultural prisons of the dynasty. Once inside, his status as a prisoner subject to constant surveillance and abuse as he prepares his essays inside his assigned examination cell isolates him from his fellow candidates and identifies him in that isolation as a lonely individual caught in a system of political power to which he has sought admission.

After leaving the compound, the psychological toll of the brief imprisonment leads to moments of flight and fancy as hopes for success are balanced by fears of failure in the subsequent days of nervously waiting for the examination rolls to be announced. Elation is assumed for the 1% who see their names on the list. P'u Sung-ling, however, tells us the emotional costs for the 99% who failed. Their faces become white; their bodies are immobilized; their hopes are dashed. Here we see the psychological and physical symptoms of the examination life, and its manifest imagery in the literature inscribed by P'u Sung-ling's own historical circumstances.

Failure quickly turns to discouragement, but P'u Sung-ling details how such emotions can be quickly channeled into anger at the examiners and criticism of the examination system itself. In the extreme, the candidate renounces his studies, burns his books, and not satisfied with that, further reveals the obsessive nature of his emotional reaction to failure by trampling on the ashes of the physical traces of his years of sacrifice and hard work and then gathering them up to throw away as garbage. In the accepted psychology of late imperial times, failure and religion go hand in hand. Escape from the regime of examinations is culturally narrated by P'u Sung-ling in light of Taoist and Buddhist notions of leaving this world and entering the world of pure nature where human artifice does not intervene. The candidate, who competed alone in the examination cell, now seeks to live alone in the forest, away from friends and family.

P'u's account is formulaic in many ways, even for successful graduates. Arthur Waley, for example, has described the T'ang roots of such dreams of escapism in his gloss on a poem by the eighteenth-century poet and stylist Yuan Mei 袁枚 (1716–98), who in 1765 came across a chair-carrier who looked familiar to him. Yuan's poem captured the pain of remembrance:

> The chair-carrier wiped his eyes and looked,
> And looked again, and heaved a deep sigh.
> He told me that on the day of my wedding
> He was one of those that carried the bridegroom's chair.
> "Brisk you were, a little Hanlin academician,
> Your young cheeks rosy as a morning glow.

Why have we not seen you for so long
That then you were a boy and now an old man?"
He broke off; but before he had finished speaking
A great depression suddenly came upon me.
It was like meeting an aged T'ien-pao era [742–55] person
Telling again the yellow millet dream.

Yuan Mei's poetic reference to the "yellow-millet dream" (*Han-tan meng-chueh* 邯鄲夢覺) and the glories of the T'ang before the An Lu-shan Rebellion of 756 (see Chapter 1) contained a parable that Waley succinctly summarizes:

A young man going up to the capital to try his fortune orders supper at an inn. While he is waiting for the millet to be cooked he falls asleep, his head propped on a pillow given to him by another guest. He dreams that he comes to the Capital, takes his degree, is promoted from one high post to another, gets into trouble and is degraded, is recalled to office, endures the hardship of distant campaigns, is accused of treason, condemned to death, saved at the last moment, and finally dies at a great old age. Awakening from his dream he discovers that the millet is not yet cooked. In a moment's sleep he has lived through the vicissitudes of a great public career. Convinced that in the world "honors are followed by disgrace and praise by calumny" he turns back towards the village from which he came. The pillow was a magic pillow, and the other guest a Taoist magician.[160]

Whether for failure or graduate, the therapeutic role of religious awakening and dreams of an unencumbered life were available to both as an escape from the examination life and its subsequent careerist ordeals.

Though his parody of the anger felt by the examination failure is the part of the narrative that most current readers of P'u Sung-ling's tale focus on, the more important part comes at the end, for it was this part that told examination candidates that they could cope with their failures. P'u's clinical depiction of the failure as an emotional wreck is not the final story for him or for them. Rehabilitation, the return to mental peace of mind and the restoration of personal confidence, is the final lesson. Here P'u wisely tells us how and why the 99% who failed healed their mental and physical wounds and in time returned to the examination cell to compete again and again, not much wiser perhaps, but surely emotionally stronger, more mature, and experienced in the ways of the examination market and the difficult paths to fame and fortune in the late empire.

160. Waley, *Yuan Mei: Eighteenth Century Chinese Poet* (Stanford: Stanford University Press, 1956), pp. 103–04. See also Yuan Mei, *Shih-hua* 詩話 (Poetry talks), 3.7b, in *Sui-yuan ch'üan-chi* 隨園全集 (Complete works of Yuan Mei) (Shanghai: Wen-ming Bookstore, 1918). My thanks to Tony Wang, then of the Fulbright Foundation in Taiwan, for directing my attention to this passage.

Accordingly, P'u Sung-ling's realism is therapeutic in intent. Rebellion and iconoclasm were among the responses that examination failures often entertained, but in the end they persevered and became part of the vast pool of residual manpower who repeatedly took examinations while they got on with their lives. In P'u's own case, this meant turning to writing stories as an alternative means of cultural life and livelihood. Some could channel their frustrations into compiling examination editions for local printers or become local printers themselves, as did the Mas 馬 and Tsous 鄒 in the Ssu-pao 四堡, Fu-chien, publishing industries. Others would crack under the pressure, as did the northern literatus Yen Yuan 顏元 (1635–1704), when he failed to cope with his personal family crisis and with his continual failures on local examinations. Yen successfully transformed his emotional crisis into a virulent attack on Ch'eng-Chu teachings as bookish and the examinations as unmanly.[161] Similarly, a Che-chiang licentiate, when deprived of his local degree and expelled by his father in 1819, was arrested by authorities in the Temple of Confucius, where he had damaged the tablet of Confucius while wailing and complaining.[162] P'u Sung-ling's therapeutic response, which falls far short of rebellion against the civil examinations, was typical but not unique. Not infrequently, failures would take that extra emotional step and strike out at the dynasty and its coercive examination regime.[163]

It has long been taken for granted in accounts of late imperial history that local troublemakers frequently came from the pool of local licentiates who sought in vain to gain the coveted *chü-jen* and *chin-shih* degrees. Indeed, some of the leaders of the northwest revolt, whose forces had captured Peking in 1644 and brought down the dynasty in north China, were local examination candidates who had repeatedly failed to gain high office. Though the late Ming economic crisis, exacerbated by famine, corruption, and war, was the primary cause for the weakness of the Ming after the Tung-lin debacle (see Chapter 4), the willingness of some disgruntled examination candidates, such as Li Tzu-ch'eng 李自成 (1605?–45), to take up arms at a time of dynastic crisis was predictable within an examination regime that could produce such high levels of emotional disappointment and anger among so many failures.[164]

161. See Jui-sung Yang, "A New Interpretation of Yen Yuan (1635–1704) and Early Ch'ing Confucianism in North China" (Ph.D. diss., UCLA, History, 1997), chapters 2 and 3.

162. For this case, see Bodde and Morris, *Law in Imperial China*, pp. 271–72.

163. Barr, "Pu Songling and the Qing Examination System," pp. 88–91. See also Nivison, "Protest against Conventions and Conventions of Protest," pp. 198–201; and Brokaw, "Commercial Publishing in Late Imperial China," pp. 62–65.

164. On the late-Ming economic crisis, see William Atwell, "The T'ai-ch'ang, T'ien-ch'i, and Ch'ung-chen Reigns, 1620–1644," in Frederick W. Mote and Denis Twitchett,

## Hung Hsiu-ch'üan and Examination Countervisions

Men like P'u Sung-ling, who transformed their bitter examination failures into "healthy," apolitical forms of cultural production, were the rule during the Ming and Ch'ing dynasties. Some, however, crossed the political and cultural boundaries of what their society and dynasty could consider acceptable. Chapter 4 described how the Ch'ing court in particular vainly tried to keep the pool of local licentiates and candidates in political and legal line. The Ch'ien-lung emperor feared that plots against Manchu rule would emerge from the pool of men who had failed the civil examinations.[165]

The hallucinations and countervisions of Hung Hsiu-ch'üan 洪秀全 (1813–64), whose religious visions were the ideological foundations for the Taiping Rebellion, are a case in point. Many like the future Taiping leader, who had a complete mental breakdown after repeatedly failing to pass local examinations in Canton, were left bereft of any hope of competing successfully for political office. Atypical in his use of Christian themes in the mid-nineteenth century to augment his views, Hung nevertheless appealed to long-standing religious forms of protest to contest the Ch'ing dynasty's examination regime and its cultural legitimacy under Manchu rulers.[166]

At the age of thirteen *sui* in 1827, under his registered name of Huo-hsiu 火秀, Hung Hsiu-ch'üan traveled from his village in Kuang-tung province to take the qualifying examination in Hua county 花縣. Since the age of seven he had studied in his Hakka village school, and by all accounts he had been fond of learning for the five years he attended. There were high hopes for him. His teacher and family thought his literary talent would enable Hung Hsiu-ch'üan to gain high office, and perhaps even enter the Hanlin Academy. Hung passed the county qualifying examination on his first try. When he traveled to Kuang-chou prefecture 廣州 (Canton) to take the licensing examination, he failed, however. It is assumed that Hung first came into contact with a new world of trade, foreigners, and perhaps even Christian literature when he went for the pre-

---

eds., *The Cambridge History of China*, vol. 7, part 1, *The Ming Dynasty, 1368–1644*, pp. 615–40. On examination candidates who became rebels, see Ku Kung-hsieh, *Hsiao-hsia hsien-chi chai-ch'ao*, B.3a–3b. Cf. Miyazaki, *China's Examination Hell*, pp. 121–24.

165. Philip Kuhn, *Soulstealers*, p. 227.

166. Wang Ch'ing-ch'eng 王慶成, "Lun Hung Hsiu-ch'üan te tsao-ch'i ssu-hsiang chi ch'i fa-chan" 論洪秀全的早期思想及其發展 (On Hung Hsiu-ch'üan's early thought and its development), in *T'ai-p'ing t'ien-kuo-shih hsüeh-shu t'ao-lun-hui lun-wen hsüan-chi* 太平天國史學術討論會論文選集 (Peking: Hsin-hua Bookstore, 1981), pp. 244–49.

fectural examinations to the only port in Ch'ing China legally open to foreign trade and contact.[167]

To prepare for the next round of local examinations, Hung became a village teacher, based on his success in the county examination. His teaching allowed him the leisure to continue preparing for the civil examinations. In 1836, at the age of twenty-four, already a bit old among the many younger candidates, Hung traveled a second time to Canton to take the prefectural examination. Again he failed. He also failed in 1837. After the third failure, Hung returned home and became seriously ill. Ill for four days (later Taiping accounts said he was ill for forty days, to accord with Jesus' forty days of fasting) and in the midst of a delirium, Hung had a fantastic dream.[168]

Fearing his own imminent death, Hung asked his parents' forgiveness for his examination failures before visions began to appear to him. He first saw a dragon, a tiger, and a rooster. Then a group of men playing music approached in a beautiful sedan and carried him away. They reached a land of distinguished-looking men and women who greeted him. An old woman took Hung to a river and, while washing him, admonished him not to defile himself again among the people below. Hung then entered a large hall, where an esteemed elderly man of the heavens (天上至尊的老人) asked Hung to venerate him because the man sustained all worldly life (世界人類皆我所生). The man presented Hung with a sword to overcome all demons and to protect his brothers and sisters, a seal to overcome evil spirits, and a golden fruit that was sweet to the taste. These represented imperial regalia, and Hung immediately began to admonish all around him to honor the venerable man who had presented him with these three marks of future power.[169]

---

167. See Jonathan Spence, *God's Chinese Son: The Taiping Heavenly Kingdom of Hong Xiuquan* (New York: W. W. Norton, 1996), passim. Spence argues that Hung was given a missionary tract by an American missionary that he later used to unravel the meaning of his subsequent illness and dream.

168. See Su Shuang-p'i 蘇雙碧, *Hung Hsiu-ch'üan chuan* 洪秀全傳 (Biography of Hung Hsiu-ch'üan) (Peking: Ta-ti Press, 1989), pp. 13–15; and Ch'en Hua-hsin 陳華新 et al., *Hung Hsiu-ch'üan ssu-hsiang yen-chiu* 洪秀全思想研究 (Research on the thought of Hung Hsiu-ch'üan) (Canton: Kuang-tung People's Press, 1991), pp. 9–11. See also Franz Michael and Chung-li Chang, *The Taiping Rebellion*, vol. 1, *History* (Seattle: University of Washington, 1966), pp. 22–23; and Jen Yu-wen (Chien Yu-wen), *The Taiping Revolutionary Movement* (New Haven: Yale University Press, 1973), pp. 15–19.

169. For the dream, see Su Shuang-p'i, *Hung Hsiu-ch'üan chuan*, pp. 17–18. For a different version, see Jen Yu-wen, *The Taiping Revolutionary Movement*, pp. 15–16, which is based on Theodore Hamberg's 1854 account in *The Visions of Hung-siu-tshuen, and Origin of the Kwang-si Insurrection* (reprint, Peking: Yenching University Library, 1935), pp. 9–11. Because the accounts of the dreams were manipulated under Taiping rule, some later scholars have dis-

Typically this series of fantastic visions that Hung had in 1837 have been dissected by later Western or westernized scholars as evidence of Hung Hsiu-ch'üan's "madness" or religious conversion. In the former view, Hung was a victim of acute paranoia, "a form of psychosis in which there are delusions of grandeur, hallucinations, and feelings of untoward pride and hatred, all of which are logically systematized so that the individual actually believes his disordered perceptions." Following the latter view, scholars contend that Hung had been decisively influenced by Christianity in his visits to Canton, and that these experiences "served as a catalyst, transforming his disordered and frustrated mind through the impact of the idea of salvation and the concept of a 'Man-God.'" Alternatively, scholars in China have demystified Hung's religious visions and rationalized them as premonitions of a new political order in China that would replace the imperial system.[170]

The discussion of the mantic arts and dreams in imperial Chinese examination lore earlier in this chapter reveals how inadequate such modernist, psychohistorical, and sociohistorical accounts of Hung Hsiu-ch'üan's initial dreams are. When placed within the historical context of Chinese dream interpretation during the Ming and Ch'ing dynasties, Hung's visions are less evidence of an individual Han Chinese man's paranoia then they are comprehensible narratives drawing on the rich symbolic traditions of Chinese religious and cultural life, which well-adjusted Ming *chuang-yuan* and Ch'ing literati equally engaged in and which were deemed socially acceptable among upper elites until the late seventeenth century. The cultural boundaries of mental health were drawn differently in late imperial China than in early modern Europe, and Hung Hsiu-ch'üan's delirium was an acute response to the examination pressures he faced and the high expectations his family and teacher had placed in him. Unlike most literati, such as P'u Sung-ling, who coped, Hung had cracked.

For the Taipings and for Hung himself, who both benefited from hindsight, Hung Hsiu-ch'üan's strange, "anomalous dream" (*i-meng* 異夢) be-

---

missed them as fabrications. For our purposes, however, Hung Hsiu-ch'üan's dreams, even if historical fabrications, are useful historical constructions that reveal how human experience was ordered, altered, and reshaped in the mid-nineteenth century. For discussion, see Ch'en Hua-hsin et al., *Hung Hsiu-ch'üan ssu-hsiang yen-chiu*, pp. 10–12.

170. See P. M. Yap, "The Mental Illness of Hung Hsiu-ch'üan, Leader of the Taiping Rebellion," *Far Eastern Quarterly* 13, 3 (May 1954): 287–304; and Hamberg, *The Visions of Hung-siu-tshuen*. See also Vincent Shih, *The Taiping Ideology*, pp. 448–49. For a political reading of Hung's dream, see Ch'en Hua-hsin et al., *Hung Hsiu-ch'üan ssu-hsiang yen-chiu*, pp. 12–13.

came a sign of his special future and confirmed his fate as the anointed leader of the Taipings. Along with the rich repertoire of traditional Chinese religious and mantic symbolism, which included immortals, gods, demons, and fairies, Hung initially had unconsciously added Christian notions of a single old man in power in the heavens to the pluralist menagerie of Taoist and Buddhist powers in the other world that intervened in this world on behalf of young men who were trapped in the examination life. As therapeutic as these visions were (Hung recovered on his own without any successful medical treatment), they contained ominous elements that threatened to go beyond the usual limits of literati critiques and spoofs of the examiners and the civil examination system.

Rather than offering guarantees of examination success or even premonitions that Hung would become an *optimus,* as Ming dreams formulaically depicted, the old man above had presented Hung Hsiu-ch'üan with imperial regalia and a call to purify the world below. The Hung lineage called in local doctors to treat the illness and also asked a mantic expert to interpret Hung's visions and exorcise the demon possessing him, but we have no record of how the latter handled these disturbing aspects of the dream. We know only that Hung rebuked the exorcist brought in to cure him. In Ch'ing times, under Manchu rulers, the crime of lèse-majesté was just below the surface of Hung Hsiu-ch'üan's manifest dreams.[171]

After recovering, Hung appeared more sure of himself, but his life was relatively uneventful for several more years. Based on his dream, however, Hung changed his name from Huo-hsiu to Hsiu-ch'üan, thinking, according to some scholars, that the two parts of the graph for *ch'üan* 全 symbolized the people's (*jen* 人) ruler (*wang* 王). Following the traditional art of character analysis and glyphomancy described above, Hung had responded to his dream by renaming himself in accordance with his dream. In the spring of 1843, Hung tried again for the coveted status of local licentiate. To this point, his emotional recovery followed the same pattern P'u Sung-ling had described in the examination candidate who had rebuilt his nest and started over. Hung had returned to the examination life.

When he failed a fourth time, however, Hung's reaction was rage not delirium. While returning by boat from Canton, he cursed the examiners and composed a poem intimating a revolt against the Manchu dynasty. After arriving home, Hung's fury had not relented. Denouncing the dynasty and its officials, Hung threw his books out and apparently cried out: "Let me give examinations to select the literati of the empire" (等我 自己來開科取天下士罷). Hung's threat to become the examiner was realized when, as we shall see in Chapter 11, he radically revised the

171. Jen Yu-wen, *The Taiping Revolutionary Movement,* p. 17.

Ch'ing examination curriculum to conform with Taiping ideology and Christian doctrine and in 1851 ordered civil examinations under the Heavenly Kingdom to commence.[172]

By rejecting the psychological mold that had in Nivison's words conventionalized literati protest against the civil examinations since the T'ang dynasty, Hung Hsiu-ch'üan was revolutionary in the content of his protest, but the institutional forms his examination protest took were still conventional. After 1843, Hung's "anomalous dream" was used by him and his God Worshipers Society (*Pai shang-ti chiao* 拜上帝教) to demonstrate that Hung had ascended to heaven and met with God and Jesus Christ. Their instructions to purify the earth meant that the Manchus had to be removed, the Ch'ing dynasty overturned, and the teachings of Confucius and Mencius eliminated. Hung had found his calling as the new emperor of the Heavenly Kingdom of Eternal Peace (*T'ai-p'ing t'ien-kuo* 太平天國), which would establish an examination regime for young men in the Yangtzu delta based on Sino-Christian Taiping truth. Whether they admitted it or not, late Ch'ing reformers who decanonized the official literati orthodoxy (see Chapter 11) used in the civil examinations since the early Ming dynasty were following in Hung Hsiu-ch'üan's rebellious wake.[173]

The popular, nonofficial dimensions of the civil examinations described in this chapter affected the lives of elites and commoners in remarkable ways. Popular culture permeated the examination venues of the dynasty, while Hanlin examiners vainly struggled to keep the mantic arts out of the examination compound. Although such attempts failed, their efforts succeeded in setting limits to the scope of religion and popular culture in the orthodox content of the civil examination papers until the eruption of Taiping religiosity and its penetration of examinations in the 1850s (see Chapter 11). The next chapter further examines elite aspects of the cultural scope of the civil examinations and the classical essays produced during the Ming dynasty. Chapters 8 and 9 then turn to the standards used to measure success and failure on the examinations before 1800.

172. Ibid., pp. 19–20; Su Shuang-p'i, *Hung Hsiu-ch'üan chuan*, pp. 13–14; and Ch'en Hua-hsin et al., *Hung Hsiu-ch'üan ssu-hsiang yen-chiu*, pp. 20–21.

173. Su Shuang-p'i, *Hung Hsiu-ch'üan chuan*, pp. 21–34; and Ch'en Hua-hsin et al., *Hung Hsiu-ch'üan ssu-hsiang yen-chiu*, pp. 14–37. See also Michael and Chang, *The Taiping Rebellion*, pp. 24–37.

# CHAPTER SEVEN

# The Cultural Scope
# of Civil Examinations and
# the Eight-Legged Essay among Elites

The public ceremonies that accompanied the testing and selection of candidates for public office accorded local *sheng-yuan*, provincial *chü-jen*, and palace *chin-shih* graduates with both sociopolitical status and cultural prestige. Classical literacy, the mastery of *Tao-hsueh* learning, and the ability to write terse but elegant examination essays together publicly marked the educated literati whose names appeared on the final lists of graduates. In addition to its political and social functions (described in previous chapters), the civil service competition successfully created a dynastic curriculum that consolidated gentry, military, and merchant families empirewide into a culturally defined status group of degree-holders sharing a common classical language and memorization of a mutual canon of Classics.

The internalization of a literary culture that was in part defined by the civil examination curriculum also influenced the literatus' public and private definition of his moral character and social conscience.[1] A view of government, society, and the individual's role as an elite servant of the dynasty was continually reinforced in the memorization process leading up to the examinations themselves. The moral cultivation of the literatus (*shih-hsi* 士習; see Tables 8.5 and 8.6) was a perennial concern of the imperial court as it sought to ensure that the officials it chose in the examination market would serve the people in the name of the ruling family. Literati, as the highest social group, were expected to be partners of the dynasty and serve as models (*ssu-min chih shou* 四民之首) for those beneath them politically and socially. For the literatus, it was important that the dynasty conformed to classical ideals and upheld the Ch'eng-Chu orthodoxy that literati themselves had formulated in the Sung-Yuan-Ming tran-

---

1. Rieff, *The Feeling Intellect*, pp. 233–35, citing Durkheim.

sition (see Chapter 1). The cultural reproduction of Tao Learning, thus, was also about the cultural transformation of the literatus into a political servant of the people and the ruler.

## LANGUAGE, CLASSICISM, CALLIGRAPHY, AND CULTURAL REPRODUCTION

When we consider the linguistic aspects of classical Chinese as an empowering language in political selection, we discover that our stress on the moral meaning and philosophical significance of Ch'eng-Chu *Tao-hsueh* should be accompanied by discussion of the social value and political power resulting from mastery of the classical language of imperial orthodoxy by candidates for officialdom. In other words, bringing language into the discussion of civil examinations enables us to analyze an authorized classical language as a linguistic instrument of social and political policy, which also functioned as the lingua franca of a classically educated literati elite.[2]

Given the absence of public schools in late imperial China before 1898, most male commoners (particularly rural peasants, artisans, and traders) were linguistically and thus culturally excluded from the examination market. Unequal social distribution of linguistic and cultural resources meant that those from families with limited traditions of literacy were unlikely to compete successfully in the degree market with those whose family traditions included classical literacy (see Chapter 5).[3] Indeed, the civil examinations were meant to be exclusive by choosing members of the local elite to join with the dynasty to maintain order in society.

Moral values such as filial piety and ancestor worship certainly transcended class and cultural barriers in imperial China. Even the *Thousand Character Text, Hundred Surnames,* and *Three Character Classic* reading primers, which almost all families and local schools used to train children to read and write the 1,500 different characters needed for functional literacy, were encoded with classical values that the society upheld. Popular literacy in vernacular Chinese was widely prevalent among non-elites,[4] but such cultural levels were not as politically empowering as full, classical literacy.

---

2. Waltner, "Building on the Ladder of Success," pp. 30–36, presents a literature generally devoid of linguistic awareness. Cf. Pierre Bourdieu, "The Economics of Linguistic Exchanges," translated by Richard Nice, *Social Science Information* 16, 6 (1977): 645–68.

3. David Johnson, "Communication, Class, and Consciousness in Late Imperial China," p. 59, estimates there were at least 5 million classically educated male commoners in Ch'ing times, or roughly 5% of the adult male population in 1800, 10% in 1700.

4. Angela Ki Che Leung, "Elementary Education in the Lower Yangtzu Region," pp. 391–96. See also Rawski, *Education and Popular Literacy in Ch'ing China,* pp. 140–54.

Since the early and middle empires in China, the linguistic chasms between vernacular, semiclassical, and classical Chinese ensured that fully classically literate scholar-officials were entering a world of written discourse that few in local society could understand or participate in.[5]

Similar to the Latin-vernacular divide that demarcated secondary from primary education in early modern Europe,[6] the spoken (Mandarin) and written (classical) languages of higher education in late imperial China differed from everyday speech outside of north China after 1415–21 and were taught to a minority as elite disciplines. As we have seen, after 1787 over 500,000 characters of textual material had to be memorized to master the examination curriculum of the Four Books and Five Classics. This count does not include the voluminous pages of the Dynastic Histories (by the Sung there were seventeen, by the Ch'ing twenty-two "legitimate" dynasties) and, after 1756, T'ang poetry, mastery of which was also expected of examination candidates. Frederic Wakeman has noted: "A better-than-average apprenticeship for the examinations meant beginning to learn to write characters at the age of 5, memorizing the Four Books and the Five Classics by the age of 11, mastering poetry composition at age 12, and studying *pa-ku* [eight-legged] essay style thereafter."[7]

Beginning in the early Ming, the dominant values, ideas, questions, and debates that prevailed in court and among officials were translated into a terse classical language whose pronunciation was based on the standard Mandarin dialect of the court (*kuan-hua* 官話) in the capital region in north China (after the Mongol invasion and after the Ming transfer of the primary capital from Nanking in 1415–21) and not on the dialects of the more populous and prosperous south, although a form of "southern" *kuan-hua* remained in use during the Ming in the parallel ministries that were maintained in Nanking as the southern capital. This policy represented a precocious form of "linguistic gerrymandering," whereby after 1425 China was divided into geographical *cum* linguistic units to try to limit the economic advantages of the south (see Chapter 2). The authorized official languages under the Ming, known as "northern" and "southern" *kuan-hua*, required written and spoken forms of discourse that only privileged outsiders, who through education and social contacts were more likely to be masters of several dialects, could fully grasp after years of training. Even later, when during the Ch'ing dynasty, Manchu and Mongolian were

5. Ridley, "Educational Theory and Practice in Late Imperial China," pp. 369–90, discusses the technical aspects of the classical language that made it different from the vernacular. See also Rawski, *Education and Popular Literacy in Ch'ing China*, pp. 1–23.

6. Houston, *Literacy in Early Modern Europe*, pp. 23–24.

7. Miyazaki, *China's Examination Hell*, pp. 16–17; and Wakeman, *The Fall of Imperial China*, p. 23.

374 / THE CULTURAL SCOPE

added as the official languages of warrior elites, the classical language of literati remained the dominant public voice of the bureaucracy. Without a competing capital such as Nanking, Peking alone during the Ch'ing dynasty provided the standard language for officials.[8]

Such policies condemned most commoners—who traveled little, spoke only local or regional dialects outside the capital(s), or were "primer-literate"— to classical illiteracy. They could perhaps become scribes, woodblock carvers, and even writers of local legal plaints, but as non-degree-holding primer-literates, they were not eligible to enter the civil examination compounds, where the political elite was chosen from the social elite.[9] To acquire the legitimate cultural training necessary to qualify for the civil service, most students preparing for the examinations (especially those in the south) were essentially mastering a new spoken dialect (northern or southern Mandarin) as a second language and a written language (classical Chinese) whose linguistic terseness, thousands of unusual written graphs, and archaic grammatical forms required memorization and constant attention from childhood to adulthood.[10]

The mastery of literati learning that was required of elites for political success reproduced a shared spoken and written language for officialdom in the dual capitals of the Ming. Southern and southeastern Chinese, whose native dialects differed from the dominant, official language of Pekinese Mandarin during the Ch'ing, were able to overcome their initial linguistic disadvantages vis-à-vis northern spoken Chinese through the translation of their greater wealth into wider social contacts and superior educational resources and facilities, but at the price of admitting the limitations of their native tongue and identifying with a broader, empirewide linguistic elite. Reproduction of classical values and historical mind-sets among candidates for public office meant that gentry, military, and merchant families from all over the empire had more in common culturally

8. See Pamela Kyle Crossley, "Manchu Education," in Elman and Woodside, eds., *Education and Society in Late Imperial China*, pp. 340–48. See also Man-kam Leung, "Mongolian Language and Examinations," pp. 29–44. Cf. Boettcher, "'To Make Them Ready for Official Employment.'"

9. See Fuma Susumu 夫馬進, "Sōshi hihon no sekai" 訟師秘本の世紀 (The world of the secret handbooks of pettifoggers), in Ono Kazuko 小野和子, ed., *Mimmatsu Shinsho no shakai to bunka* 明末清初の社會と文化 (Kyoto: Meibun Press, 1996), pp. 189–238, who contends that most plaints were written by local licentiates. The latter's position could be strengthened if he took into account those who were candidates for local examinations, and not simply those who became dynastic school students or licentiates. Yasuhiko Karasawa, a graduate student in Chinese history at UCLA, is working on a dissertation that will revise some of Fuma's views.

10. Hsiao-tung Fei, *China's Gentry: Essays on Rural-Urban Relations* (Chicago: University of Chicago Press, 1953), pp. 71–72.

and linguistically with each other than did lower social groups in their native areas, who remained tied to local traditions, temples, and dialects that did not transcend local life. Elites therefore could move effectively in local, provincial, and capital circles, while non-elites were limited to local groups that spoke the same dialect and shared the same traditions. Preparation for the civil service thus entailed mental mastery of orthodox and regionalized schemes of classical language, thought, perception, appreciation, and action. In class and individual terms, social and political reproduction influenced the character of both "literati culture" and the literatus as a "man of culture" (wen-jen 文人) to some degree, although we have seen that the civil examinations themselves existed in a world of local and regional, religious and intellectual, life that humanized and individualized the literatus.

After years of classical training, for instance, Cantonese literati from southeast China shared decisive linguistic—Mandarin—and discursive—classical—commonalities with other literati all over the empire, whether from Shan-tung in the north, Ssu-ch'uan in the southwest, or any other area whose native spoken dialect was distinctively different from that of Kuang-tung. In unforeseen ways, the institutionalization of the Mandarin dialect used in the Peking court after 1415 to 1421 as the official spoken language and the requirement of ancient classical texts in the civil service examination process had generated linguistic cleavages between classically literate, Mandarin-speaking elites, who served as "outsider" officials in counties, townships, prefectures, and provinces where the non-elite, sometimes semiliterate, natives spoke a different dialect. Gentry and merchants were conceptually operating in diverse, although often overlapping, linguistic traditions, one local, rich in popular culture and lineage traditions, and one empirewide, embodying the written classical language and the official tongue of political power. A literatus from Shan-hsi in the northwest would have little trouble bridging the vernacular gap with his southeastern Cantonese colleague, even if spoken communication between them was possible only in written form using a brush (pi-hua 筆畫).[11]

Political and social reproduction through the civil service examinations entailed a degree of cultural and linguistic uniformity among elites that only a classical education could provide. Such general linguistic uniformity, however, permitted a wide range of regional textual traditions and local "schools" of scholarship, which could use the civil examinations to wage ideological and political battles at home and in the bureaucracy.[12]

11. Teng Ssu-yü, Chung-kuo k'ao-shih chih-tu shih, pp. 343–47; and DeFrancis, The Chinese Language, pp. 53–66.

12. For such regional diversity in classical learning, see my "Ch'ing Schools of Scholarship," Ch'ing-shih wen-t'i 4, 6 (December 1979): 51–82.

Nevertheless, the Tao Learning curriculum chosen by the literati for the Ming and Ch'ing civil service represented a cultural repertoire of linguistic signs (over 500,000 repeating graphs), stylistic categories (eight-legged essay rhetorical forms), and moral concepts (Tao Learning theory) that ensured that elite political power and social status throughout the late imperial period would be defined in shared terms acceptable to the government and its literati. For good or bad, unintentionally or not, Sung Tao Learning became the classical guideline for political and cultural legitimation of the dynasty and enhancement of the social prestige of its dominant status group. Literati had been full participants in the cultural construction of the classical canon, and because they remained involved in its reform and operation, the civil examination system had both political and social support for its maintenance as an educational institution.

Proficiency in spoken Mandarin and classical literacy was a vital element for elite kinship strategies, as was "primer-literacy" for many other commoners. Compilation of genealogies, preparation of deeds or legal pleas, and settlements for adoption contracts and mortgages required linguistic expertise and political contacts that only the elite within a descent group could provide. A classical education became a seal of cultural approval. Like European elites in the fifteenth and sixteenth centuries, who crossed over from their vernacular to classical Latin as the language of instruction in secondary education, most Ming and Ch'ing Chinese, Manchus, and Mongols subordinated their native tongues in favor of Mandarin and classical Chinese if they entered higher education and passed on to the examination halls.[13]

Merchants, like gentry families in late imperial China, also became cultured patrons of classical scholarship. In fact, such merchants were almost indistinguishable from the gentry elite, although Ming hereditary designations as "merchant families" (see Chapter 5) remained in use if not in practice. In the Yangtzu delta, for instance, they supplied resources for establishing local schools and private academies.[14] The result was a merging of literati and merchant social strategies and interests. Merchant success in local society, particularly in urban centers, pointed to the correlation between profits from trade and high social status. Classical scholar-

13. Houston, *Literacy in Early Modern Europe*, p. 31; and James Watson, "Chinese Kinship Reconsidered: Anthropological Perspectives on Historical Research," *China Quarterly* 92 (1982): 601.

14. Angela Ki Che Leung, "Elementary Education in the Lower Yangtzu Region," pp. 381–91. Cf. Harriet Zurndorfer, "Chinese Merchants and Commerce in Sixteenth Century China," in Wilt Idema, ed., *Leiden Studies in Sinology* (Leiden: E. J. Brill, 1981).

ship flourished due to merchant patronage, and books were printed and collected in larger numbers than ever before.[15]

During the Ming and Ch'ing, subordination of the content of the civil service examinations to elite literary culture was further cemented through strict enforcement of requirements that all candidates' essays be composed in what eventually became the rigid parallel-prose styles known as "eight-legged essays," a genre infamous among examination candidates and baffling for "primer-literate" merchants, peasants, and artisans unschooled in elite discourse.[16] Such cultural expectations were heightened by the gentlemanly requirement that candidates be adept in the art of calligraphy (shu-fa 書法), one of the most esoteric and characteristic cultural forms of training, to master written classical Chinese.

The well-publicized rituals for properly writing Chinese graphs, learned from childhood as students traced the characters in their primers over and over again, included cultural paraphernalia long associated with literati culture: the writing brush, ink-stick, ink-slab, stone monuments, fine silk, and special paper (see Figure 7.1). The brush, ink, inkstone, and paper were known as the "four treasures of the scholar's studio" (wen-fang ssu-pao 文房四寶). Chinese high culture demanded both mastery of literary forms and artistic training to write those forms beautifully.[17]

State examinations required acceptably written "regular" calligraphy (k'ai-shu 楷書) on special paper free of smudges or cut-and-paste graphs. In local examinations, a student's papers were not anonymous, and the county, township, and prefectural examiners evaluated a t'ung-sheng candidate's penmanship as well as his essays. Similarly, in the palace and court (since 1723) examinations, where there were no copyists, calligraphy was an important element in the final ranking of chin-shih, a procedure that continued for the evaluation of those few who entered the Hanlin

---

15. Ōkubo Eiko, Min-Shin jidai shoin no kenkyū, pp. 221–361; and Ping-ti Ho, The Ladder of Success in Imperial China, pp. 130–68. See also Ōki Yasushi 大木康, "Minmatsu Kōnan ni okeru shuppan bunka no kenkyū" 明末江南における出版文化の研究 (A study of print culture in Chiang-nan in the late Ming), Hiroshima daigaku bungakubu kiyō 廣島大學文學部紀要 50, 1 (1991).

16. Teng Ssu-yü, Chung-kuo k'ao-shih chih-tu shih, pp. 281–82; Ching-i Tu, "The Chinese Examination Essay: Some Literary Considerations," Monumenta Serica 31 (1974–75): 393–406; and Woodside, "Some Mid-Qing Theorists of Popular Schools," pp. 11–18.

17. Lothar Ledderose, Mi Fu and the Classical Tradition of Chinese Calligraphy (Princeton: Princeton University Press, 1979); and Ledderose, "An Approach to Chinese Calligraphy," National Palace Museum Bulletin 7, 1 (1972): 1–14. See also Marilyn and Shen Fu, Studies in Connoisseurship: Chinese Paintings from the Arthur M. Sackler Collections in New York, Princeton, and Washington, D.C. (Princeton: Princeton University Press, 1973), p. 9. Brushes and ink-sticks from An-hui province near Mt. Huang, where the giant pines there provided the soot to be pressed into ink-sticks, were highly prized among literati.

FIGURE 7.1.   Writing Paraphernalia of the 1388 *Optimus*.
*Source: Ming chuang-yuan t'u-k'ao* 明狀元圖考 (Illustrated survey
of *optimi* during the Ming dynasty). Compiled by Ku Ting-
ch'en 顧鼎臣 and Ku Tsu-hsun 顧祖訓. 1607 edition.

Academy, where literary examinations for compilers were regularly held.[18]
In the 1850 palace examination, for example, the distinguished Han Learning scholar Yü Yueh 俞樾 (1821–1906) was deemed deficient in his "small

18. On the role of calligraphy in Ch'ing civil examinations, see *Ch'ing-pai lei-ch'ao*, 21.117,
21.135–36. See also Chiang An-fu 江安傅, *Ch'ing-tai tien-shih k'ao-lueh* 清代殿試考略 (Survey
of Ch'ing period palace examinations) (T'ien-chin: Ta-kung Press, 1933), pp. 9b–11b, which
indicates that after 1760 calligraphy became the major ranking aspect of the palace examinations, replacing style and content (*wen-li* 文理).

character" calligraphy (*hsiao-t'i* 小體), although he passed and entered the Hanlin Academy. In 1851 this style of calligraphy was dropped as a measure of court talent.[19]

Students prepared calligraphically acceptable answers using the officially recognized "regular" script, but the man of culture also mastered "cursive" (*ts'ao-shu* 草書), "running" (*hsing-shu* 行書), and by the Ch'ing dynasty even ancient "seal" (*chuan-shu* 篆書) forms of writing. Seal and cursive script were unintelligible to all but the most erudite. Accordingly, at the higher levels, reading and writing classical Chinese were further mystified by the time-honored rituals of calligraphy. Sun Hsing-yen 孫星衍 (1753–1818), for example, gained reverse prestige from his literati friends when the Manchu official Ho-shen 和珅 (1750–99) failed him—on a court examination to determine the level of Sun's appointment to the Bureau of Punishments—for using, correctly, a seal character that Ho-shen did not recognize.[20]

Although this feature should not be overemphasized, an "amateur" literati ideal (and an "ideal" is all it was!), which equated classical, literary, and calligraphic forms of cultural expression with social status, did take rhetorical precedence among elites, particularly when young men were students and had not yet held public office.[21] This much-heralded ideal of the "gentleman" and his literary and aesthetic sensibilities precluded somewhat non-elite participation in the ways of conspicuous leisure (painting, calligraphy, poetry, etc.) as defined in higher culture.

Although legal, medical, institutional, and fiscal specialties were tested as policy questions on Ming civil examinations (see Chapters 8 and 9), the end of most specialty examinations in the civil service selection process after the Southern Sung marked the imperial withdrawal of social and political prestige from technical subjects.[22] This turn of events did not automatically doom these technical fields to oblivion, as Joseph Levenson incorrectly suggested, but thereafter, training in law, medicine, astronomy, and fiscal affairs frequently became the preserve of commoner clerks, yamen secretaries, official aides, and even Muslims and Europeans, who staffed the technically oriented yamens of the Ming-Ch'ing bureaucracy. Only when faced with alien rule under the Manchus in the seventeenth

19. Calligraphy had remained an important aspect of the examination system, even when anonymous testing took place. During the T'ang and Sung, calligraphy examinations were given; in the Sung a calligraphy *po-shih* was selected. In 1706 a candidate was granted the *chin-shih* degree because of his calligraphy. See *Ch'ang-t'an*, pp. 28–29. See also *Ch'ing-pai lei-ch'ao*, 21.112, 21.116–131.

20. See my *From Philosophy to Philology*, pp. 191–97; and Hummel, ed., *Eminent Chinese of the Ch'ing Period*, p. 676.

21. On the "professional" aspects of literati as officials, see Dardess, *Confucianism and Autocracy*, pp. 13–84, which although overstated does make the valid observation that literati were responsible for public service and were rewarded accordingly.

22. See, however, Chang Hung-sheng 張鴻聲, "Ch'ing-tai i-kuan k'ao-shih chi t'i-li" 清

century, demographic revolution in the eighteenth, and Western capital-
ism in the nineteenth did significant numbers of literati again turn to
occupations outside the civil service, as they had under the Mongols during the Yuan dynasty.[23]

During the Ming and Ch'ing dynasties in particular, cultural reproduction conveniently supported the political aims of the government, although
such reproduction was voluntarily monopolized by social elites and not
the dynasty itself. Rote memorization of the Four Books and one of the
Five Classics (before 1787) in Mandarin pronunciation by examination
candidates, constantly deplored but never resolved, was a cultural act of
great meaning for Han Chinese. As in early modern Europe, where stress
on order and conformity ensured that rote learning (e.g., the catechism)
played a fundamental role in the educational process,[24] in late imperial
China educators prized orthodoxy and the rote reception of that orthodoxy. The civil examinations were a fundamental factor, among many
others, in influencing cultural consensus and conditioning the forms of
reasoning and rhetoric that prevailed in elite society.[25]

## THE EIGHT-LEGGED ESSAY AND
## INCREASED LITERARY FORMALISM AFTER 1475

Most accounts of the development of the late imperial examination essay
begin with modernist apologies. The twentieth-century cultural assault on
the infamous eight-legged essay ( pa-ku-wen 八股文), as the classical essay
on the Four Books and Five Classics was called since mid-Ming times, has
included accusations that the eight-legged essay became a "byword for
petrification" in Chinese literature or that the essay itself was one of the
reasons for China's cultural stagnation and economic backwardness in the
nineteenth century. Consequently, most works on the history of Chinese
literature have ignored the examination essay as a literary form or written
about it with unconcealed modern contempt.[26]

---

代醫官考試及題例 (Ch'ing dynasty examinations for medical officials with examples),
*Chung-hua i-shih tsa-chih* 中華醫史雜誌 25, 2 (April 1995): 95–96, which documents the continuation of medical specialty examinations in the Ming and Ch'ing.

23. Chaffee, *The Thorny Gates of Learning in Sung China*, pp. 70–71; and Joseph Levenson,
"The Amateur Ideal in Ming and Early Ch'ing Society: Evidence from Painting," in John
Fairbank, ed., *Chinese Thought and Institutions* (Chicago: University of Chicago Press, 1957),
pp. 320–41. In the eighteenth and nineteenth centuries, when demographic pressure meant
that even provincial and metropolitan examination graduates were not guaranteed official
appointments, many literati turned to teaching and scholarship as alternative careers. See
my *From Philosophy to Philology*, pp. 67–137.

24. Houston, *Literacy in Early Modern Europe*, pp. 56–58.

25. Bourdieu, "Systems of Education and Systems of Thought," pp. 189–207.

26. For discussions that gainsay this twentieth-century view of eight-legged essays as a

Whatever the literary verdict, the late imperial examination essay had its most immediate roots conceptually in the epochal transition from T'ang-Sung belles lettres to the classical essay (*ching-i*) championed by Wang An-shih in the eleventh century, which was documented in Chapter 1. The classical essay, however, was not firmly in place in civil examinations as the key literary form empirewide until the early Ming. When the eight-legged essay was still the rage, before 1850, there were many efforts to trace a history of ideas on its literary pedigree.

Most Ming-Ch'ing literati traced the essay form back to the 1057–71 Northern Sung debates for and against replacing poetry and rhyme-prose (*shih-fu* 詩賦) on civil examinations with *ching-i* essays.[27] Some simply saw the form as the equivalent of applying the literary rules of regulated verse (*lü-fu* 律賦) in T'ang dynasty civil examinations to the new essay form. Others thought the selection of quotations for an essay was indirectly derived from the *t'ieh-ching* 帖經 tradition in T'ang times, when candidates had to recite a classical passage from memory after seeing only one phrase from it. Still others saw the style influenced by the development of a dramatic persona (*k'ou-ch'i* 口氣) in Chin and Yuan dynasty theatrical writings.[28]

There is some truth in each position, but the history of the classical essay form in examinations actually dates from the policy essay used in Han times, the parallel prose (*p'ien-t'i-wen* 駢體文) of T'ang essays for the *ming-ching* degree, and the ancient-style prose (*ku-wen* 古文) styles of the Northern Sung that Ou-yang Hsiu and Wang An-shih championed in different ways. In fact, when it was still fashionable to do so, champions of both parallel- and ancient-style prose essays each claimed the eight-legged essay as a kindred genre to legitimate their competing literary traditions in the late eighteenth and early nineteenth centuries. Indeed, the "legs" (*ku* 股, lit., "bones") of the classical essay were thought to refer to the parallel and balanced lines structuring both literary genres (see Ku Yen-wu below).

The Ch'ing Han Learning scholars Li Chao-lo 李兆洛 (1769–1849) and Juan Yuan 阮元 (1764–1849), for instance, both claimed that the "contem-

---

literary malaise, see Teng Yun-hsiang 鄧云鄉, *Ch'ing-tai pa-ku-wen* 清代八股文 (Ch'ing dynasty eight-legged essays) (Peking: People's University Press, 1994), pp. 277–301; Ching-i Tu, "The Chinese Examination Essay," pp. 393–94; and Andrew Lo, trans., "Four Examination Essays of the Ming Dynasty," pp. 167–68 ("Editor's Introduction"). For the stock view, which gives the essay some credit as an "objective standard of measurement," see Ch'ien Mu, *Traditional Government in Imperial China: A Critical Analysis*, trans. Chün-tu Hsueh and George Totten (Hong Kong: Chinese University Press, 1982), pp. 112–13.

27. See *Wu-li t'ung-k'ao*, 174.14a–b.

28. On the origins of the genre, see Ch'en Te-yun 陳德芸, "Pa-ku wen-hsueh" 八股文學 (eight-legged essay literature), *Ling-nan hsueh-pao* 領南學報 6, 4 (June 1941): 17–21, who outlines six different positions and the Ming-Ch'ing literati who held each position.

porary-style essay" in eight-legged form derived directly from parallel prose styles requiring balanced phrases and arguments in a series of four and six characters (*ssu-liu chih liu-p'ai* 四六之流派). To gainsay this Han Learning position, T'ung-ch'eng scholars such as Fang Pao 方苞 (1668–1749), who compiled the *Ch'in-ting ssu-shu wen* 欽定四書文 (Imperially authorized essays on the Four Books) collection of model eight-legged essays for the Ch'ien-lung emperor, and Yao Nai 姚鼐 (1731–1815) linked the eight-legged essay to ancient-style prose and Ch'eng-Chu Sung Learning.[29]

It remains the case historically, however, that the examination essay style that was specifically called the "eight-legged" style appeared for the first time in the early years of the Ming Ch'eng-hua reign, 1465–87. Consequently, the tendency to construct the historical genealogy of the eight-legged essay backwards from the Han, T'ang, or Sung dynasties usually elides its sudden appearance in the 1480s as the accepted form for an examination essay. Without denying that the eight-legged form had its roots in earlier dynasties, this chapter nonetheless focuses on its first conscious appearance in the mid-Ming and tries to unravel the cultural significance of the form among literati writers. Indeed, claims that the form derived from earlier styles served to legitimate the eight-legged essay as the proper harvest of past literature and classical learning. And, as in earlier such cases, the literati themselves, not the imperial court, initially produced this new trend in classical writing.

While detractors of the eight-legged essay genre have received a more sympathetic hearing in the twentieth century, its late imperial advocates were numerous and came from a broad spectrum of Ming-Ch'ing literati. Li Chih 李贄 (1527–1602), a late Ming iconoclast on so many issues,[30] saw in the evolution of classical essay genres a cultural dynamic that was commentary to the ongoing literati search for values in antiquity. The contemporary-style essay, for Li, was a bona-fide genre that had proven its worth in producing famous officials. Their moral achievements, he thought, were due to its use as the orthodox genre for the classical essay in civil examinations.[31]

---

29. Ch'en Te-yun 陳德芸, "Pa-ku wen-hsueh," pp. 20–21. For discussion, see my *Classicism, Politics, and Kinship*, pp. 290–95. See also *Li Shen-ch'i nien-p'u* 李申耆年譜 (Chronological biography of Li Chao-lo) (Nan-lin: Chia-yeh-t'ang 嘉業堂, ca. 1831), 2.7a–7b.

30. See William Theodore de Bary, "Individualism and Humanitarianism in Late Ming Thought," in de Bary et al., *Self and Society in Ming Thought* (New York: Columbia University Press, 1970), pp. 188–222.

31. See Li Chih, "Shih-wen hou-hsu" 時文後序 (Afterword for contemporary-style essays), in *Fen-shu* 焚書 (A book to be burned) (Peking: Chung-hua Bookstore, 1975), p. 117.

Similarly, late Ming literati such as Yuan Hung-tao 袁宏道 (1568–1610) and Li Yü 李玉 (1611–80), known for their unconventional literary traditions, viewed eight-legged essays as reliable mirrors of the literary currents in their times. For such writers, the eight-legged essay had transcended its requirement as a formal exercise and become an important literary genre of prose writing in its own right. Not merely an examination requirement, it was a cultural form that existed inside and outside the examination compound and was written by all classically literate men, young and old.[32]

The Hanlin academician Liang Chang-chü's 梁章鉅 (1775–1849) early nineteenth-century work entitled *Chih-i-ts'ung-hua* 制義叢話 (Collected comments on the crafting of eight-legged civil examination essays), while mentioning the accruing flaws in the selection process, praised the artistic and cultural levels the examination essays fostered in Chinese life. Liang noted that no one to date had come up with an acceptable alternative.[33] Ch'ing literati who prepared prefaces for the work, which was designed to place the examination essay in full cultural relief, wrote in praise of Ch'ing contributions to the further evolution of the Ming genre.[34]

## *Origins of the Eight-Legged Essay "Grid"*

In his preface to Liang Chang-chü's influential collection *Chih-i-ts'ung-hua*, Yang Wen-sun 楊文蓀 (1782–1853), a Che-chiang bibliophile, noted that the eight-legged genre dated from the Sung classical essay but took its final form in the early Ming, when the *chih-i* essay irrevocably replaced poetry and rhyme-prose.[35] This claim is not unreasonable because the tradition of belles lettres as literary questions in civil examinations had continued in the Sung, Chin, and Yuan dynasties (see Chapter 1). *Ching-i* style essays began in 1071 reforms, when poetry was briefly reduced in importance in civil examinations. Works such as *Ku-wen kuan-chien* 古文關鍵 (Pivotal points in ancient-style prose) by Lü Tsu-ch'ien 呂祖謙 (1137–81) were widely used after the Sung to study prose technique.[36]

32. See Andrew Plaks, "*Pa-ku wen* 八股文," in William Nienhauser, ed., *Indiana Companion to Traditional Chinese Literature* (Bloomington: Indiana University Press, 1986), pp. 641–43. See also Plaks, "The Prose of Our Time," in *The Power of Culture: Studies in Chinese Cultural History*, edited by W. J. Peterson, A. H. Plaks, and Y. S. Yu (Hong Kong: Chinese University Press, 1994), pp. 206–17.

33. Liang Chang-chü, "Li-yen" 例言 (Outline of contents), in *Chih-i ts'ung-hua*, pp. 1a–4a, and 1.4b–5a. On the use of the term *chih-i* 制義, see note 82 below.

34. See the 1843 prefaces included in the *Chih-i ts'ung-hua*.

35. See Yang's "Hsu" 序 (Preface), p. 3a, in ibid.

36. Ridley, "Educational Theory and Practice in Late Imperial China," pp. 419–24.

Unraveling the evolution of the eight-legged essay form certainly is complicated, but the discussion suggests some significant continuities between Sung and Ming dynasty examination essay styles. Aspects of the Ming structure were in evidence during the Sung.[37] To claim, however, that the eight-legged essay itself took its final form in the early Ming is excessive. There are two opposite views on the Ming origins of the genre that became known as *pa-ku-wen*. The authors of the *Ming-shih* 明史 (Dynastic history of the Ming) dated it from the early Ming reign of Emperor T'ai-tsu: "The essay for the examination curriculum was generally patterned on the Sung classical essay. However, it now had to be articulated in words in the name of the sages, and its literary form had to be strictly parallel. Hence it was called 'eight-legged' or more generally 'crafted essays' (*chih-i*)."[38]

Following this somewhat premature view, as Ching-i Tu does, scholars have singled out the classical essays of Huang Tzu-ch'eng 黄子澄 (d. 1402) for the 1385 metropolitan examination, on which he finished first (he was third on the palace examination), particularly his first essay on the quotation from the *Analects*, "When the Way prevails in the empire, the rites and music and punitive expeditions are initiated by the emperor" (天下有道，則禮樂征伐，自天子出。), as the first essays to embody some of the structural parts and rhetorical style of the eight-legged essay format.[39] Writing his account of Ming examinations in the late seventeenth century, Ku Yen-wu, however, dated the eight-legged essay with more historical precision to the late fifteenth century:

> The popular tradition of calling classical essays "eight-legged" probably began from the Ch'eng-hua emperor's reign (1465–88). The term "leg" (*ku* 股, lit. "bone") is the term for "parallel wording" (*tui-ou* 對偶). Before the T'ien-shun emperor's reign (1457–65), writing in the classical essay was nothing more than an extension of classical scholia. They were sometimes parallel, sometimes varied, but without any fixed form.... In the 1487 metropolitan examination, the essay topic was "He who delights in heaven will continue to possess the empire" (樂天者保天下).[40] The essay for this quotation began with three sentences on the topic (*ch'i-chiang* 起講), which were

37. *Ch'ang-t'an*, pp. 16–17, shows that some of the terms for eight-legged essay sections, such as the *p'o-t'i* 破題 (opening), *chieh-t'i* 接題 (connecting), etc., were used in the Sung.

38. *Ming-shih*, 3/1693.

39. See *Ming-tai wei-k'o hsing-shih lu*, A.1b; and Ch'ien Chi-po 錢基伯, *Ming-tai wen-hsueh* 明代文學 (Ming dynasty literature) (Shanghai: Commercial Press, 1939), pp. 109–10. See also *Lun-yü yin-te*, 33/16/2; and Lau, trans., *Confucius: The Analects*, p. 139. Cf. Ching-i Tu, "The Chinese Examination Essay," p. 396. Tu mistakenly gives 1386 for this metropolitan examination.

40. *Meng-tzu yin-te*, 5/1B/1; and Lau, trans., *Mencius*, p. 62.

followed by four legs on "delights in heaven." The next four sentences served as a middle transition, while the final four legs dealt with "possess the empire." Another four sentences recapitulated, and then the candidate wrote a conclusion (*ta-chieh* 大結).

In the 1496 metropolitan examination, the essay on the passage "To take one's prince to task is respect" (責難于君謂之恭)[41] began with three sentences, and then presented the passage "to take one's prince to task" in four legs. In the middle transition there were two sentences followed by four legs on "respect." After a two-sentence recapitulation, the writer presented his conclusion. In every four legs there were two balanced propositions, one empty, the other solid, one shallow, one deep. Thus in each section there were four legs, which all followed in strict order. Consequently, people called this form "eight-legged." ... Since the Chia-ching emperor's reign (1522–67), the essay style has continually changed, and if you ask a *Ju* 儒 candidate, none of them know why such essays are called "eight-legged."[42]

### Wang Ao's Formative Role

What is interesting about Ku Yen-wu's account is his dating of the first eight-legged essay in the Ch'eng-hua reign, and his failure to attribute the form to any particular literatus writer. One of the most renowned early composers of eight-legged essays was the distinguished scholar-official Wang Ao 王鏊 (1450–1524), who passed the Ying-t'ien provincial examination ranked number one out of 2,300 candidates and 135 graduates in 1474.[43] Ao then passed the 1477 metropolitan examination also ranked number one.[44] Both examinations were held during the Ch'eng-hua reign.

In the palace examination, however, Wang Ao had the misfortune of having as his chief reader Shang Lu 商輅 (1414–86), who was at that point the only Ming literatus who had achieved "three firsts" (*san-yuan* 三元) on the Ming civil examinations. He made sure that Wang would not be the second by ranking Ao's final policy answer third overall, after others had initially ranked it first.[45] Shang Lu could identify Wang Ao's

---

41. *Meng-tzu yin-te*, 26/4A/1; and Lau, trans., *Mencius*, p. 118.

42. Ku Yen-wu, *Jih-chih lu*, pp. 479–80 (*chüan* 卷 19) on "Shih-wen ko-shih" 時文格式 (the form for contemporary-style essays).

43. See *Chin-shih teng-k'o lu*, 1475: unpaginated manuscript.

44. See *Hui-shih lu*, 1475: 18a.

45. *Chih-i ts'ung-hua*, 4.6a–b. The *Chin-shih teng-k'o lu*, 1475, gives information that Liu Chien 劉戩, who finished second on the palace examination, had also finished first on an earlier Ying-t'ien provincial examination and an earlier metropolitan examination. Shang Lu was thus preventing two Chiang-nan men from duplicating his achievement. Li T'iao-yuan, *Chih-i k'o-so-chi*, 2.46, notes that Huang Kuan 黃觀 had achieved "three firsts" in 1391, counting both his Yuan and Ming rankings. He had changed his surname to "Hsu" 徐 during the Ming.

paper because the palace examination, unlike the provincial and metropolitan examinations, was not graded anonymously. Hsieh Ch'ien 謝遷
(1450–1531), who had also finished first on the 1474 Che-chiang provincial
examination, Shang Lu's home province, was chosen the 1475 *optimus*. In
this way, Wang Ao's achievement was also overshadowed by the eight
Ming "two firsts" (*erh-yuan* 二元), who had finished first on the metropolitan and palace examinations, and the *erh-yuan*, such as Hsieh Ch'ien, on
the provincial and palace examinations. Wang Ao's "two firsts" on only
the provincial and metropolitan examinations placed him in the third
tier.[46]

| Ming: 8 "Two Firsts" (Erh-yuan 二元)[47] | Ch'ing: 10 "Two Firsts" (Erh-yuan 二元)[48] |
|---|---|
| 1391: Hsu Kuan (Metro and Palace #1) | 1673: Han Chiao (Metro and Palace #1) |
| 1472: Wu K'uan 會元 and 狀元 | 1676: P'eng Ting-ch'iu 會元 and 狀元 |
| 1490: Ch'ien Fu 會元 and 狀元 | 1685: Lu K'en-t'ang 會元 and 狀元 |
| 1499: Lun Wen-shu 會元 and 狀元 | 1703: Wang Shih-tan 會元 and 狀元 |
| 1604: Yang Shou-ch'in 會元 and 狀元 | 1727: P'eng Ch'i-feng 會元 and 狀元 |
| 1610: Han Ching 會元 and 狀元 | 1733: Ch'en T'an 會元 and 狀元 |
| 1613: Chou T'ing-ju 會元 and 狀元 | 1742: Chin Shen 會元 and 狀元 |
| 1619: Chuang Chi-ch'ang 會元 and 狀元 | 1757: Ts'ai I-t'ai 會元 and 狀元 |
| | 1780: Wang Ju-hsiang 會元 and 狀元 |
| | 1802: Wu T'ing-shen 會元 and 狀元 |

| Ming: 1 "Three Firsts" (san-yuan 三元) | Ch'ing: 2 "Three Firsts" (san-yuan 三元) |
|---|---|
| 1445: Shang Lu, San-yuan 三元 | 1781: Ch'ien Ch'i, San-yuan 三元 |
| 1 Yuan-Ming 三元: 1391 | 1820: Ch'en Chi-ch'ang 三元 |

NOTE: There were altogether 45 *erh-yuan* 二元 and 14 *san-yuan* 三元 from the T'ang
through Ch'ing dynasties. Of these Su-chou in particular had 8 *erh-yuan* 二元 (18%) and
1 *san-yuan* 三元 (7%).

46. See *Nan-kuo hsien-shu*, 1.6b; and Wang Yang-ming, *Yang-ming ch'üan-shu* 陽明全書
(Complete works of Wang Yang-ming), *Ssu-pu pei-yao* edition (Taipei: Chung-hua Bookstore,
1979), 25.12b. See also *Huang-Ming san-yuan k'ao*, 4.13a; and *Chuang-yuan ts'e*, A.6a–13a.

47. *Ming Chuang-yuan t'u-k'ao*, 1607 edition; and Huang Kuang-liang, *Ch'ing-tai k'o-chü
chih-tu chih yen-chiu*, pp. 166–185.

48. See *Kuo-ch'ao kung-chü k'ao-lueh*, 1825 edition.

Despite this down-classing, Wang Ao's classical essays won the day outside the examination compound and beyond the reach of the Hanlin Academy. It was said that "in terms of essays, victory was conceded Wang Ao; in terms of appearances, victory was conceded Hsieh Ch'ien" (文讓王鏊，貌讓謝遷). Although official rankings could be tampered with by jealous men such as Shang Lu, the latter's writings never measured up to Wang Ao's in the evolution of the genre that would be become the "eight-legged" essay grid.[49]

Although from Che-chiang, Wang Yang-ming, for example, greatly admired Wang Ao's essay on "nature" (*hsing* 性), which was based on his metropolitan policy answer, which had been selected as the best essay for the second metropolitan policy question in 1475. In Wang Yang-ming's biography of Wang Ao, he noted that the Nanking provincial examiners had been astonished at Ao's 1474 provincial examination essays, which they compared to those of the great Sung *litterateur* Su Shih. The provincial examiners recorded Ao's discourse and policy essays verbatim in the final report, not daring to change a single character.[50]

Moreover, Wang Ao, unlike Shang Lu, who retired in 1477, frequently served as a metropolitan examiner in the late fifteenth century, occasions on which his classical essays served as models for thousands of candidates in the compounds he supervised. Indeed, Wang Ao was an associate examiner for the 1487 metropolitan (with 4,000 candidates) and one of the two chief examiners for the 1496 metropolitan examinations. Ku Yen-wu has contended that the eight-legged model was first consciously used to rank examination essays in these two examinations. In 1490 Wang Ao was also an associate metropolitan examiner, and he was appointed chief metropolitan examiner again in 1508.[51] In fact, on the 1759 Ho-nan provincial examination, the third policy question on examination essays (*chih-i* 制藝) pointedly asked if Wang Ao's essays were the forerunners of the eight-legged essay.[52]

Accordingly, the first glimpse we have of the early emergence of the eight-legged form of the classical essay, before its explicit declaration as

49. For Shang Lu's examination essays, see *Hui-shih lu*, 1445: 45a–47a, which contains his discourse answer on sincerity (*ch'eng* 誠). For his palace examination policy answer, see *Huang-Ming chuang-yuan ch'üan-ts'e*, 4.18a–24a. See also *Chih-i ts'ung-hua*, 4.6b.

50. *Hui-shih lu*, 1475: 49a. See also *Yang-ming ch'üan-shu*, 25.12a–14b.

51. *Hui-shih lu*, 1487: 3a–4a; 1490: unpaginated manuscript; 1496: 2.12a. See also *Hui-shih lu*, 1508, for the "Hsu" 序 (Preface) by Wang Ao; and *Huang-Ming ch'eng-shih tien-yao lu* 皇明程世典要錄 (Digest of records of metropolitan examinations during the Ming dynasty), late Ming edition, 2.31b.

52. *Ho-nan hsiang-shih lu*, 1759.

the official examination style in 1487, can be traced to Wang Ao's 1475 *ching-i* essay on a session one passage from the *Mencius:* "The Duke of Chou subjugated the northern and southern barbarians, drove away the wild animals, and brought security to the people" (周公兼夷狄，驅猛獸，而百姓寧).[53] In that metropolitan examination, Wang's classical essays on two of the three quotations from the *Poetry Classic,* his memorial (*piao* 表), and two of his policy answers were also singled out by the examiners for their literary style and substantive excellence (*li-ming tz'u-ta* 理明辭達). Ch'iu Chün 丘濬 (1420–95), one of the chief examiners and a distinguished Hanlin academician since 1454, described Wang Ao's essay on the *Mencius* as "profoundly crafted and to the point" (*hsiu-tz'u shen erh i-ta* 修辭深而意達). Wang's session-three policy essays were also praised for their "basis in what can be ascertained" (*yu k'ao-chü* 有考據), a telling examiner comment that is discussed in more detail in Chapter 8.[54]

Wang Ao's central role in the formation of the eight-legged essay style was recognized in the Ch'ing by Yü Ch'ang-ch'eng 俞長城, who compared Wang's position to that of Ssu-ma Ch'ien 司馬遷 (145–90? B.C.) in history, Tu Fu 杜甫 (712–70) in poetry, and Wang Hsi-chih 王羲之 (307–65) in calligraphy. Yü added: "Before Wang's time the eight-legged essay had not developed fully, but his essays contained everything that had not appeared earlier. After his time, the eight-legged essay went through many changes, but Wang's essays had already included what came later."[55]

We will look at two of Wang Ao's eight-legged essays, which were later cited in Ch'ing collections as models for the form. Based on a passage in the *Analects* "When the people have enough, how can the ruler alone have too little?" (百姓足，君孰不足？), the first essay deals with the ruler's responsibilities to provide a livelihood for his people.[56] The second, based on the famous opening passage from the *Analects* "Is it not a joy to have friends come from afar?" (有朋自遠方來，不亦樂乎？), focused on moral cultivation in Tao Learning terms.[57] Each was copied, printed, and studied by generations of civil examination candidates.[58]

53. *Hui-shih lu,* 1475: 6b–8b. See also *Meng-tzu yin-te,* 25/3B/9; and Lau, trans., *Mencius,* p. 115.

54. *Hui-shih lu,* 1475: 6b–7a, 21a–b, 40a, 48a–52b, 62b–69a.

55. Yü's *Pai-er-shih ming-chia chi* 百二十明家集 (Collection of 120 famous writers) is cited in Ching-i Tu, "The Chinese Examination Essay," p. 403.

56. *Lun-yü yin-te,* 23/12/9; and Lau, trans., *Confucius,* p. 114.

57. *Lun-yü yin-te,* 1/1/1; and Lau, trans., *Confucius,* p. 59.

58. The first essay can be found in Fang Pao's *Ch'in-ting Ssu-shu wen* 欽定四書文 (Imperially authorized essays on the Four Books) (1738; reprint, Taipei: Commercial Press, 1979), vol. 1, 3.3a–4a. See also Sung P'ei-wei 宋佩韋, *Ming wen-hsueh shih* 明文學史 (History of Ming literature) (Shanghai: Commercial Press, 1934), pp. 228–30, which is the source for

[1. *Break open the topic* (*p'o-t'i* 破題)]: 百姓足，君孰不足？

When the people below are prosperous, the ruler above will be prosperous.

民即富於下，君自富於上。

[2. *Receiving the topic* (*ch'eng-t'i* 承題)]:

The wealth of the ruler is stored among the people. If the people are prosperous, why should the ruler alone be poor?

蓋君之富藏於民者也。民即富矣，君豈有獨貧之理哉？

[3. *Beginning discussion* (*ch'i-chiang* 起講)]:

In giving advice to Duke Ai, Yu Jo said profoundly that the people and the ruler were one.[59] He implied that the Duke had increased taxation because he lacked resources. To ensure his resources, the Duke should have first satisfied his people.

有若深言君民一體之意以告哀公，蓋謂公之加賦以用之不足也。欲足其用，蓋先足其民乎。

[4. *Initial leg* (*ch'i-ku* 起股)]:

If one can honestly

> tithe one hundred *mou* with a mind to stay frugal and love the people,
> and the one-tenth tax is not levied so the people provide his livelihood,

then

> what the people would produce would not be for tax levies,
> what resources they have would not all be for tax collection,
> there would be accumulation and surplus in village households,
>> and no worries in caring for parents or raising children,
> there would be abundant grain and millet in the fields,
>> and no anxiety about nurturing the living or seeing off the dead.

誠能
> 百畝而徹，恒存節用愛人之心，
> 什一而征，不為厲民自養之計，

則
> 民力所出，不因於征求，
> 民財所有，不盡於聚斂。
> 閭閻之內，乃積乃倉，

---

the English translation in Ching-i Tu, "The Chinese Examination Essay," pp. 400–02, which has some mistaken characters. Tu follows Ch'en Shou-yi, *Chinese Literature: A Historical Introduction* (New York: Ronald Press, 1961), pp. 506–08. The second essay was included in *Ming-wen ch'ao* 明文鈔 (Copies of Ming writing), compiled by Kao T'ang 高嵣 (1781 edition), "Shang-lun" 上論, and is translated in Plaks, "The Prose of Our Time," pp. 206–17. I have given my own translations below.

59. See *Li-chi yin-te*, 4/48, 49; and *Ch'un-ch'iu ching-chuan yin-te* 春秋經傳引得 (Combined concordances to the *Spring and Autumn Annals* and commentaries) (Taipei: Ch'eng-wen Publishing Co., 1966), 478/Ai 哀 8/2 Tso 左. Yu Jo was one of Confucius' immediate disciples.

而所謂仰事俯育者無憂矣。
田野之間，如茨如梁，
而所謂養生送死者無憾矣。

[5. *Transition leg* (*hsu-ku* 續股)]:

If the people have enough, how can the ruler alone be poor?

百姓既足，君何為而獨貧乎？

[6. *Middle leg* (*chung-ku* 中股)]:

I know that

The ruler could have everything if it were stored in village households,
with no need to hoard it in his treasury as his goods.

The ruler could use everything if it were placed in the fields,
with no need to accumulate it in his vaults as his possessions.

With unlimited access, why worry that requests would not be honored?
With unlimited resources, why fret over unpreparedness in an emergency?

吾知
藏諸閭閻者，君皆得而有之，
不必歸之府庫而後為吾財也。
畜諸田野者，君皆得而用之，
不必積之倉廩而後為吾有也。
取之無窮，何憂乎有求而不得？
用之不竭，何患乎有事而無備？

[7. *Later leg* (*hou-ku* 後股)]:

Sacrificial animals and ritual grains would be sufficient for religious offerings; jades and silks would be abundant as gifts for tribute and audiences.

Even if insufficient, the people would supply what they have, so what
shortage would there be?

Foods and delicacies, beef and drinks would be sufficient for the needs of
official guests; carriages and horses, weapons and armor would be sufficient for wartime preparations.

Even if insufficient, the people would respond with what they have, so
what shortage would there be?

犧牲粢盛，足以為祭祀之供；玉帛筐篚，足以資朝聘之費。
借曰不足，百姓自有以給之也，其孰與不足乎？
饔飧牢醴，足以供賓客之需；車馬器械，足以備征伐之用。
借曰不足，百姓自有以應之也，又孰與不足乎？

[8. *Conclusion* (*ta-chieh* 大結)]:

Oh! Tithing originally was for the benefit of the people, and the suf-
ficiency of the dynasty's resources arose in this way. Why should one raise
taxes to seek prosperity?

吁！徹法之立，本以為民，而國用之足乃由於此，何必加賦以求富哉？

Wang's essay was included in Fang Pao's early Ch'ien-lung era collection of outstanding Ming-Ch'ing eight-legged essays, entitled *Imperially
Authorized Essays on the Four Books*. Fang said of this Wang Ao piece: "The

levels and sequence are refined and clear, moving from the shallow to the profound. When the meaning of the passage is completed, the essay's form also ends. This shows how our predecessors were truthful, concrete, and showed the way themselves. Those that came later, although their openings and closings, followings and reflections, were brought to completion and included ingenious changes, none could carry on the task."[60]

## Cognitive Issues in Eight-Legged Essays

What is immediately striking about Wang Ao's first essay is its exaggerated structural commitment to formal parallelism and thinking by analogy. Strict adherence to balanced clauses (tui-chü 對句) and balanced pairs of characters (shu-tui 屬對) was required throughout the essay, but this feature becomes particularly rule-like in Wang's framing of the argument by building the three major legs of his essay.[61] As the classical essay's length requirement increased from the five hundred characters common in late Ming times to over seven hundred during the mid-Ch'ing, the basic structure of the essay remained unchanged. During the Chia-ching emperor's reign, however, a dispute in the 1543 Shan-tung provincial examination over the veiled criticism of the throne in the "conclusion" in an eight-legged essay led to a decline in the practice of ending the essay with rhetorical flourish.[62] In the K'ang-hsi era, the ta-chieh section was dropped from the essay form and replaced by a lesser summary (shou-chieh 收結 or lo-hsia 落下).[63] An additional leg was frequently added to the Ch'ing essay, which meant there could be four perfectly parallel and numerically balanced paragraphs building the theme of the quotation assigned.[64]

The chain arguments used in such essays were built around pairs of complementary propositions, which derived their cogency from rich literary traditions that over the centuries had drawn on both the parallel and ancient-style prose traditions of early and medieval China.[65] Balanced prose presupposed that an argument should advance via pairs of comple-

60. See Fang Pao, Ch'in-ting Ssu-shu wen, vol. 1, 3.3a–4a. For Wang Ao's other essays included in this collection, see vol. 1, 2.21a–22a, 3.7a–8b, 4.9a–10b, 6.3a–6b, 6.9a–12b, 6.19a–20b. See also Ching-i Tu, "The Chinese Examination Essay," p. 402.

61. Plaks, "The Prose of Our Time," pp. 206–10.

62. Chih-i k'o-so-chi, 1.37–38.

63. See Shang Yen-liu, Ch'ing-tai k'o-chü k'ao-shih shu-lu, pp. 234, 257.

64. See Chih-i ts'ung-hua, 2.8a–b; and Ridley, "Educational Theory and Practice in Late Imperial China," pp. 459–69. On the changing length of eight-legged essays, see Ch'en Te-yun, "Pa-ku wen-hsüeh," pp. 48–49.

65. See Yu-shih Chen, Images and Ideas in Chinese Classical Prose: Studies of Four Masters (Stanford: Stanford University Press, 1988), pp. 1–13, 109–14.

mentary clauses and sections, which, when formalized and disciplined by analogies, avoided a wandering, unfocused narrative. Accordingly, the eight-legged essay represented an effort to confirm the vision of the sages in the Four Books and Five Classics from a "double angle of vision" that strictly correlated with the parallel syntax of the legs of the examination essay.[66]

In the first leg of Wang Ao's above essay, the ruler's actions were directly related to a series of economic consequences that would ensue if he followed the way of sagely governance. In the middle leg, Wang Ao's personal assessment was delivered within a balanced sequence that analogized the households of farmers to the prince's treasury in the first half, and compared the farmers' fields to the prince's vaults in the second half. The final leg presented the same conclusion in light of the lord's ritual and culinary needs, all the while stressing the priority of the people in any equation between taxes and wealth. From these three balanced legs, it therefore followed that raising taxes of itself was not the sage's method for governance.

The first leg was almost Aristotelian in its explicit rhetorical linkage of cause (low taxes) and effect (the people's prosperity).[67] Leg two elaborated on the first by showing how low taxes would increase the overall wealth of the realm, if wealth remained in the hands of the people. And the final leg clinched the argument by responding to questions of how low taxes would directly benefit the dynasty and not just the people. In this manner, a conclusion that ran counterintuitively to statist discourse about the wealth and power of the dynasty, which drew on Legalist traditions (see Chapter 2), was successfully channeled into a literati discourse built around Confucius' vision of a polity pegged to the interests of the people.

A great deal of print has been wasted on the role (or "lack") of reason in Chinese cultural history.[68] Here, I do not wish to beat a dead horse. Understanding the cognitive aspects of a literary genre as fundamental and as widely used as the eight-legged essay allows us to see the rhetorical forms of argumentation that millions of elite Chinese males empirewide learned as young adults while preparing for local civil examinations. Whether the eight-legged essay can be compared to the Aristotelian syllogism, deductive or inductive in form, is an exercise for armchair philosophers. It is more useful historically to engage in what E. R. Hughes has

---

66. See E. R. Hughes, "Epistemological Methods in Chinese Philosophy," in Charles Moore, ed., *The Chinese Mind* (Honolulu: University of Hawaii Press, 1967), pp. 28–56.

67. Cf. Chung-ying Cheng, "On Implication (*tse* 則) and Inference (*ku* 故) in Chinese Grammar," *Journal of Chinese Philosophy* 2, 3 (June 1975): 225–43.

68. For discussion, see Hart, "Proof, Propaganda, and Patronage," chap. 1.

called "comparative epistemology"[69] and thereby to grasp the "legs" of the late imperial classical essay as a rhetorical style of persuasion that had evolved since antiquity in China. In the proper climate of full classical literacy, the classical essay detailed how literati organized, presented, and defended their views within the context of civil examinations, in public literary discourse, and in related fields such as law.[70] Late imperial medical examinations required the eight-legged format, as did the Taiping examinations when the Taipings changed the topics of the essays to Sino-Christian themes (see Chapter 11).[71]

Catholic missionaries teaching in China in the nineteenth century clearly saw the rhetorical properties of the eight-legged essay in light of medieval and Renaissance forms of reasoning prominent in Latin discourse in Europe before the rise of vernaculars there. Hence, when they translated such essays into Latin, they respected the literary devices in them and explored how those devices persuaded literati of conclusions that derived from the oratorical and poetic skills required in classical Chinese.[72]

While their 1882 views are subject to the obvious cultural limits of equating Latin and classical Chinese rhetoric, their "premodernist" analysis, ironically, turns out to be far superior to twentieth-century studies composed in a "post–May Fourth" era when enlightened "modernists" in China and the West surgically elided the cultural sophistication of the eight-legged essay and translated its lifeless residues into a mindless literary genre. Below I give the latinized versions of the rhetorical forms in the eight-legged essay to restore some of the respect the eight-legged genre had among earlier Westerners who were more fluent in classical Chinese than most scholars today:[73]

---

69. See Hughes, "Epistemological Methods in Chinese Philosophy," p. 92.

70. For the carryover of parallelism and analogy from literary prose to legal writing, see Fu-mei Chang Chen, "On Analogy in Ch'ing Law," *Harvard Journal of Asiatic Studies* 30 (1970): 212–24. See also Wang Yin-t'ing 王蔭庭, "Pan-an yao-lueh" 辦案要略 (Outline for handling legal cases), in *Ju-mu hsu-chih* 入幕須知, compiled by Chang T'ing-hsiang 張廷驤 (Che-chiang Bookstore, 1892), pp. 36a–38a, which describes the explicit overlap in preparing legal documents by legal secretaries and eight-legged essays. At the lower end of the legal process, however, it is likely that "primer literacy" sufficed for the plaints of commoners and rural folk who were not classically literate. For discussion, see Wejen Chang, "Legal Education in Ch'ing China," pp. 309–310. Yasuhiko Karasawa is currently preparing a dissertation at UCLA that will touch on this topic.

71. *Ch'ing-pai lei-ch'ao*, 21.165–66, 21.173.

72. See Jacques Le Goff, *Intellectuals in the Middle Ages* (Cambridge and Oxford: Blackwell, 1993), pp. 88–92, on scholastic disputation.

73. See P. Angelo Zottoli, S.J., *Cursus Litteraturae Sinicae*, Vol. V: *Pro Rhetorices Classe pars Oratoria et Poetica* (Shanghai: Catholic Mission, 1882), pp. 12–44. This work contains the largest number of eight-legged essays ever translated into a foreign language.

1. *Break open the topic* ( *p'o-t'i* 破題): *Apertura*
2. *Receiving the topic* (*ch'eng-t'i* 承題): *Continuatio*
3. *Beginning discussion* (*ch'i-chiang* 起講): *Exordium*
4. *Initial leg* (*ch'i-ku* 起股): *Anterior pars*
5. *Transition leg* (*hsu-ku* 續股): *Propositio*
6. *Middle leg* (*chung-ku* 中股): *Media pars*
7. *Later leg* (*hou-ku* 後股): *Posterior pars*
8. *Conclusion* (*ta-chieh* 大結): *Conclusio*

The epistemological significance of strict parallelism in a Chinese classical essay, whether *p'ien-t'i, ku-wen,* or *pa-ku,* must be recognized if we are to grasp the historical significance of a cognitive system as long-lived in literati cultural life as that of the eight-legged essay. Literature, rhetoric, and argumentation were all of a piece in the formalized eight-legged "grid" that emerged in the 1470s, and that unity yielded a precise literary measure of the linguistic talents of thousands of men physically locked into the examination compounds and cognitively locked into the eight-legged essay. I use "grid" here rather than "genre," which assumes continuities in examination essays since the Sung dynasty, to describe the more formalized eight-legged categories of rhetoric during the Ming and Ch'ing dynasties after 1475. The notion of a grid allows us to see how earlier literary "genres" for examination essays had changed over time and were then formalized in the fifteenth century into the technical rhetorical features used by Ming-Ch'ing examiners to grade and rank actual examination essays. Provincial and metropolitan examiners scrutinized such anonymous products for their power of abstract thinking, persuasiveness, and prosodic form.[74]

Based on the specific "eight-legged grid" of formal parallelism, examiners and tutors would literally follow the number of legs and count the number of characters in an essay based on the requirements of balanced clauses, phrases, and characters. In marked-up examination essays that have survived, we always find numerous small circles marking exactly the balanced and antithetical clauses in each leg of the essay.[75] Even in third-session policy answers on the metropolitan and provincial civil examinations, which were not required to follow the eight-legged essay grid, exam-

---

74. Hughes, "Epistemological Methods in Chinese Philosophy," pp. 92, 99. For discussion of "genre," see Campany, *Strange Writing*, pp. 21–24.

75. See the eight-legged essays included in *Ming-wen ch'ao*, which include punctuation markings and internal notes to mark the stages in an eight-legged essay. See also the academy essays marked up in T. C. Lai, *A Scholar in Imperial China* (Hong Kong: Kelly & Walsh Ltd., 1970), pp. 16–18.

iners used a set pattern of markings to demarcate the main points (*ta-chih* 大旨: long, double lines 字字), ends of sections (*tuan-luo* 段落: 一 or 亅), important characters (*yao-tzu* 要字: small triangles △ △ △), and parallel clauses (*t'iao-tui* 條對: small circles ○○○ and filled in drop-like markings ' ' ').[76]

This classical grid provided examiners with a simple, impartial standard for ranking essays, which Ch'ien Mu has rightly labeled "a kind of stylistically formalized classicism."[77] The grid also included rules for presentation of the essay form on paper that necessitated proper spacing of characters from top to bottom and left to right. References to the reigning emperor, for instance, had to be highlighted by raising that column of characters higher and avoiding taboo names, while the body of the essay began at a lower level in each column. Essay drafts that survive from the early Ch'ing reveal that eight-legged essays were copied onto paper that was divided into columns and rows to make it easier for examiners to keep track of the rule-like grid for the parallel legs of the essay (see Figure 4.10).[78]

If a candidate could not follow these strict rules of length, balance, and complementarity, then his essay was judged inferior.[79] One misplaced character, or one character too many or too few, in building a clause in one of the legs of the essay could result in failure. Given the tens of thousands of civil candidates in the yamens and compounds where local and provincial examinations were held, the official examiners rightly felt that with a stylized and formulaic eight-legged grid as a requirement, their job of reading and evaluating thousands of essays in a brief time was made easier and more impartial.

Such requirements could backfire, however. The 1745 *secundus* Chuang Ts'un-yü 莊存與 (1719–88), when he served as the Hanlin provincial examiner in Che-chiang in 1756, for example, favored short eight-legged essays modeled on the early Ming dynasty, but he made the mistake of

---

76. *Chin-k'o ch'üan-t'i hsin-ts'e fa-ch'eng* 近科全題新策法程 (Models of complete answers for new policy questions in recent provincial civil examinations), compiled and annotated by Liu T'an-chih 劉坦之, 1764 edition, "Fan-li" 凡例 (Overview), pp. 1a–2a.

77. Ch'ien Mu, *Traditional Government in Imperial China*, p. 113.

78. On the style-format of writing essays down on paper, see *Lin-wen pien-lan* 臨文便覽, 1875 edition, *t'iao-li* 條例 (regulations), pp. 1a–5b. See also the session one eight-legged essays in *chu-chüan* 硃卷 (vermillion papers) form from the 1661, 1664, 1667, and 1685 metropolitan examinations that survive in the Ming-Ch'ing Archives, Academia Sinica, Taiwan. Copies are in the UCLA East Asian Library.

79. For detailed analysis of the structural parts of an eight-legged essay, see Ch'en Te-yun, "Pa-ku wen-hsueh," pp. 23–48; and Shang Yen-liu, *Ch'ing-tai k'o-chü k'ao-shih shu-lu*, pp. 231–38.

choosing as the top paper one that had only two of the required legs. When the final rankings were announced, it became clear that the essay had been prepared by a dynastic school student whose classical literacy and essay-writing ability were limited.[80] By the late Ming, many literati felt as Ku Yen-wu and Fang I-chih 方以智 (1611–71) did that, despite the stiff requirements, candidates could study the essays of recent graduates and produce passable essays on almost any quotation. In 1637 Fang wrote in his "Seven Solutions" ("Ch'i-chieh" 七解), which presented career options for a young man from a family of means: "One may have mumbled only one chapter and memorized several thousand examination essays, but after a year goes by these essays become unsuited. Then once again one must collect and memorize the essays of those who have newly achieved rank."[81]

What was fascinating about this eight-legged grid, however, was that although its structure was limited to 500 characters in the Ming and 700 in the Ch'ing, the parallel form required candidates rhetorically to "speak in the place of the sages" (tai sheng-jen li-yen 代聖人立言).[82] This well-known appeal to literati as voices of orthodoxy contrasted with parallel appeals in policy questions to Ming and Ch'ing emperors as the inheritors of the political mantle of the sage-kings (see Chapter 2). Even if literati could repossess the "orthodox transmission of the Tao" (tao-t'ung 道統 through their eight-legged essays, it was still left to the emperor to reestablish his "political legitimacy" (chih-t'ung 治統, lit, "legitimate transmission of governance") by empowering literati who shared this vision of cultural authority.

Without resorting to mediating commentaries and erudition, candidates were expected to interpret a passage as if each spoke for the sage who had authored the canon. This "speaking in the place of a sage" form reminded Ch'ing scholars such as Ch'ien Ta-hsin 錢大昕 (1728–1804) and Chiao Hsun 焦循 (1763–1820) of Chin and Yuan dynasty vernacular drama (tsa-chü 雜劇 or ch'ü-chü 曲劇). The rhetorical form of the essay also

80. See Tan-mo lu, 13.12b–13b; and Ch'en Te-yun, "Pa-ku wen-hsueh," p. 48.

81. Ku Yen-wu, Jih-chih lu, pp. 386–87. Cf. Lung-chang Young, "Ku Yen-wu's Views," p. 51. See also Willard Peterson, Bitter Gourd, p. 47.

82. Chih-i ts'ung-hua, 1.10b. Interestingly, the locus classicus for this ideal is the Kung-yang 公羊 Commentary to the last passage in the Spring and Autumn Annals, in which Confucius is purported to have announced the capture of a fabulous animal called the lin 麟 (lit., "horned doe," usually translated as "unicorn"). In this commentary, Confucius is said to have compiled the Annals to "await a later sage" (制春秋之義以俟聖人). See Ch'un-ch'iu ching-chuan yin-te, vol. 1, p. 487 (哀 14). This sentence is also the source for the use of chih-i 制義 to mean "writing an eight-legged essay" to emulate sages like Confucius.

required the use of exclamatory particles and single-character conjunctions (called *hsu-yen* 虛言), which captured the supposed diction and emotive force of the ancient sages. In other words, the written essay was encoded with oratorical elements, which also played out in the tonal musicality of the parallel phrases and clauses (see Chapter 10 on poetry).[83]

In the first essay, on "When the people have enough, how can the ruler alone have too little?," Wang Ao was able to use the rigorous parallel structures in his essay to chide the ruler about raising taxes by invoking the name of Confucius' disciple Yu Jo, who had spoken of the unity between the interests of the people and the lord. This pre-Mencian voice of the priority of the people over the ruler (see Chapter 2) allowed Wang Ao to frame the dramatic legs of the argument in such a way that the ruler was repeatedly told to think counterintuitively. If the people are prosperous, then the ruler has no lack, no want, no worries. Raising taxes, the intuitive thing to do if the ruler sought to enhance imperial wealth, was rhetorically defeated in favor of improving the people's benefit. Within a formulaic eight-legged grid, Wang Ao had presented in his essay the long-standing literati (read as "sages") role of remonstrating with the ruler.

The second essay, on "Is it not a joy to have friends come from afar?," allowed Wang Ao to transmit Ch'eng-Chu views of human commonality (*t'ung-lei* 同類 = *p'eng* 朋)[84] through the voice of Confucius in the *Analects* and celebrate the literati intellectual community. Again, the eight-legged essay grid, far from constricting such views into a lifeless collection of empty words (the usual view of such essays), permitted Wang Ao to play out the piece as a musician plays out the notes of a required score with virtuoso force and power.[85]

[1. *Break open the topic* (*p'o-t'i* 破題)]: 有朋自遠方來，不亦樂乎？
Believing in and then studying commonalities, we can know how things are brought to completion.
即同類之信，從而學之，成物可知矣。

[2. *Receiving the topic* (*ch'eng-t'i* 承題)]:
Study is the way to complete ourselves and to complete things. When

83. For discussion, see Ch'en Te-yun, "Pa-ku wen-hsueh," pp. 19–20; Shang Yen-liu, *Ch'ing-tai k'o-chü*, p. 230; and Ching-i Tu, "The Chinese Examination Essay," p. 405. On the tonal quality of an eight-legged essay, see Ch'i-kung 啓功, "Shuo pa-ku" 説八股 (On the eight-legged essay), *Pei-ching shih-fan ta-hsueh hsueh-pao* 北京師範大學學報 3 (1991): 56–58.

84. See Chu Hsi, *Lun-yü chi-chu* 論語集注 (Collected notes on the Analects), p. 47, in Chu's *Ssu-shu chang-chü chi-chu* 四書章句集注 (Taipei: Ch'ang-an Press, 1991).

85. Plaks, "The Prose of Our Time," pp. 211–17, successfully captures the degree of subtle intricacy in this essay, although I differ considerably with his translation.

friends come from afar and we gather with them, can we not authenticate their accomplishments?

夫學所以成己而成物也。遠方之朋而有以來之，不可以驗其所得乎？

[3. *Beginning discussion* (*ch'i-chiang* 起講)]:

Moreover, virtue in the world by definition does not stand alone. Our studies contain the impulses of commonality. When after study we reach happiness, then we achieve self-completion. Is this not also the way things are brought to completion?

且天下之德無孤立之理。吾人之學有類應之機。

學而至於說，則所以成己者至矣。豈無所以及物者乎？

[4. *Initial leg* (*ch'i-ku* 起股)]:

Indeed

> There are many in the world who have humbly and earnestly respond-ed to the times. Their thoughts of those enlightened earlier are similar to mine. It is just that they cannot illuminate them and have no way to express the ardor of their faith and commitment.

> There are many in the world who bravely follow the Way. Their search for like-minded people is similar to mine. It is just that they can-not complete this in themselves and lack the heart to motivate them-selves to return to the Way.

蓋

> 天下之遜志時敏者眾矣。其先覺之思猶之吾也。

> 惟不能自淑斯，無以發其信從之志耳。

> 天下之勇往從道者多矣。其同志之求猶之吾也。

> 惟不能自成斯，無以動其歸向之心耳。

[5. *Transition leg* (*hsu-ku* 續股)]:

Now, to discuss it only in light of study, then

> Those who study what I study, and whose ardor for emulation has no thought of distance, come and share the same feelings with me.

> Those who say what I say, and who do not leave far behind the sounds of the drum-dance, come and share the same response.

今唯學而說也，則

> 意氣之所招徠不禦於遠，而學吾之學者，自相感而來焉。

> 風聲之所鼓舞不遺於遠，而說吾之說者，自相應而來焉。

[6. *Middle leg* (*chung-ku* 中股)]:

Although living as if fenced off in a far frontier, he can still make light of it if buoyed by the presence of those enlightened earlier and if moved by memories of warm intimacy and the ardor of solidarity.

Although hemmed in by the danger of peaks and gorges, he can still yearn for return if he calls for help from like-minded people, and if he harbors the hope for reunion.

雖封疆之界若有以域之也，然彼方幸先覺之有

> 人，而興親炙之念涉履之勞，固其所輕者矣。

雖山谿之險若有以限之也，然彼方謂同志之多
　助，而有聚首之思往還之煩，固其所願者矣。

[7. *Later leg* (*hou-ku* 後股)]:

This is not a matter of my seeking something from them. The goodness of
human nature resides in my friend as it does in me. I make sincerity clear
for myself. Even those living a hundred generations later will still be
moved by this. How much more so those that live in this age!

Nor is it a matter of someone else gaining selfishly from me. The same-
ness of peoples' minds holds when they are far off just as when they were
close by. My sincerity is completed by myself. Even those who lived a
hundred generations earlier are still revered as friends. How much more
so those that live in this age!

是非吾之有求於彼也。人性之善在朋也，
　猶夫己也。吾誠自淑矣。雖在百世之下，
　猶興起焉，而況生同斯世者乎。
亦非彼之有私於吾也。人心之同其遠也，
　猶夫近也。吾誠自成矣。雖在百世之上，
　將尚友焉。而況生同斯世者乎。

[8. *Conclusion* (*ta-chieh* 大結)]:

Oh! When study reaches this point,
　then it reaches many people,
　　and one can authenticate the achievement of their self-completion.

Those who were happy with this in the past all have been joyous and
pleased. Can a student afford not to apply himself in study?

吁！學至於此，
則即其及人之眾，
而驗其成己之功。
向之説者，有不能不暢然而樂矣。學者可不勉哉。

A celebration of contemporary literati and their solidarity with past
sages, even though some now lived on the borders or in exile, was a key
element in Wang Ao's essay. It suggests the degree to which Ming literati
remained committed to the Tao Learning dicta that the human mind was
the same for all literati and that human nature was in its original form
good for everyone. This sort of universalist moral vision was even more
germane under conquest dynasties such as the Yuan and Ch'ing and helps
us to understand why both the Mongols and Manchus could approve of
an educational regime that was based on classical literacy and the production of eight-legged essays that only a few in society, mainly Han Chinese
elites, fully mastered. That it remained orthodox under the Ming, when
Han Chinese were the masters of their fate, is all the more remarkable.

## PRINTING AND PUBLISHING EXAMINATION ESSAYS

Ming civil examination papers (*mo-chüan* 墨卷) were first compiled in the publishing rooms inside the provincial and metropolitan examination compounds, where a host of copyists, woodblock carvers, and printers worked under the examiners. Essays were printed out giving examiner comments for the papers of examination graduates, and bound according to rank. These editions were known as "*wei-mo*" (闈墨, lit., "hall essays"[86]). Such official collections of civil examination essays inside provincial and metropolitan compounds were also called "*chu-chüan*" 硃卷 (vermilion papers), even though they were printed in black ink (*mo-chüan* 墨卷), because they were based on the recopied (in red ink) anonymous essays that the examiners actually had read. The originals were returned to candidates who requested them after the examination. The *wei-mo, chu-chüan,* and *mo-chüan* collections included the comments of the associate examiners in the specialty wards, which were divided according to the Five Classics (see Chapter 4), not just the chief examiners. Hence, they were also called "ward papers" (*fang-kao* 房稿) when such classical essays on each Classic were published outside the examination compound. In addition, the best essay on each quotation or question in all three sessions of both provincial and metropolitan examinations was included in the official examiners' report (*Lu* 錄) that was sent to the court for review by Hanlin academicians.[87]

Widespread public collections of essays were first compiled in the Ming, although their prominence increased during the late Ming publishing boom, when the commodification of culture intensified.[88] In the Sung, models for *ching-i* essays had also been available, many of which were later included in Southern Sung encyclopedias (*lei-shu* 類書) such as the *Ku-chin yüan-liu chih-lun* 古今源流至論 (The best discourse essays past and present),[89] which was reprinted in the late Yuan and early Ming.[90] Liu

86. During the T'ang, *wei* 闈 were the palace halls where the *chin-shih* and *ming-ching* examinations were taken.

87. Such printouts of eight-legged essays ranked in order by quotation for internal use in the examination compound are preserved in the Ming-Ch'ing Archives, Academia Sinica, for the 1699 and 1702 Chiang-hsi provincial examinations, the 1699 Chiang-nan, and the 1702 Shan-hsi, Ho-nan, and Che-chiang provincial examinations. The UCLA East Asian Library has copies of these materials.

88. Craig Clunas, *Superfluous Things: Material Culture and Social Status in Early Modern China* (Urbana: University of Illinois Press, 1991), p. 118.

89. Compiled by Lin Chiung 林駉 and Huang Lü-weng 黃履翁, early Ming edition (reprint, Taipei: Hsin-hsing Bookstore, 1970).

90. *Ch'ang-t'an*, pp. 18–19. According to the *Chih-i k'o-so-chi*, 4.133, there were breaks in examination records in the K'ang-hsi reign. The tradition of examination records goes back

Hsiang-kwang rightly attributes the mid-Ming increase in private, commercial collections of examination essays to the formalization of the eight-legged essay during the Ch'eng-hua era as the official essay style. The expansion of the examination market, which during the Ming and Ch'ing added a third tier of regular local county and prefectural examinations, and thus dramatically increased the empirewide pool of candidates who would be interested in such collections (see Chapter 3) from one (in Ming times) to two or three million (in Ch'ing times), must also be taken into account. During the T'ang, there were about 60,000 registered students eligible for the capital examination. In Sung, only provincial and metropolitan examinations were held regularly for some 400,000 candidates.[91]

Liang Chang-chü's *Chih-i ts'ung-hua* documents the increasing number of model essay writers from the late Ming, with 33 authors listed for the Chia-ching reign (1522–66), 41 for the Wan-li reign (1573–1619), and 47 for the combined T'ien-ch'i and Ch'ung-chen reigns (1621–43).[92] In addition to the "ward papers" popular during the Wan-li reign (1573–1619), an imperial assortment of eight-legged essays on the Four Books first appeared in 1587; it collected various essays from the Hung-chih, Cheng-te, and Chia-ching reigns. This was the beginning of the publication of "contemporary-style essays" known as *hsuan-pen* 選本 (selections), which included examples of the best eight-legged examinations then current. Another *hsuan-pen* collection was issued in 1592. Popular editions of a single author's eight-legged essays, known as *kao-pen* 稿本 (drafts), which often were not from the examinations themselves, began in the Hung-chih

---

to T'ang precedents. See also Lucille Chia, "The Development of the Jianyang Book Trade, Song-Yuan," *Late Imperial China* 17, 1 (June 1996): 38.

91. See Liu Hsiang-kwang 劉祥光, "Shih-wen kao: K'o-chü shih-tai te k'ao-sheng pi-tu" 時文稿：科舉時代的考生必讀 (Examination essay compilations: required reading for examination students), *Newsletter for Modern Chinese History* (Academia Sinica, Taiwan) 22 (1996): 49–68; and his "Examination Essays: Timely and Indispensable Reading for Students in the Ming," paper presented at the 1997 Annual Meeting of the Association for Asian Studies (Chicago, March 13–16, 1997). Liu attributes the increase in Ming personal essay collections to increasing competition for degrees, but he is puzzled that the Sung, which also had high levels of competition for degrees, lacked such compilations. The answer lies in the difference between the one-level T'ang, two-level Sung and three-level Ming-Ch'ing examinations. Cf. Peter Bol, "The Examination System and Sung Literati Culture," in Léon Vandermeersch, ed., *La société civile face à l'État* (Paris: École Française d'extrème-orient, 1994), p. 55. In Sung times, from four to ten or more thousand candidates might take a prefectural examination, while ten or more thousand candidates were common for departmental examinations. See Chaffee, *The Thorny Gates of Learning in Sung China*, pp. 33–36. This pool was significantly smaller than the number of candidates for local Ming-Ch'ing licensing examinations.

92. Liang Chang-chü, *Chih-i ts'ung-hua, chüan* 卷 4–6. See also Liu Hsiang-kwang, "Shih-wen kao," p. 54.

reign (1488–1505). Wang Ao's eight-legged essays, for instance, were first published under the title *Shou-hsi wen-kao* 守溪文稿 (Draft essays of [Wang] Shou-hsi [Ao]) and were frequently reprinted.[93]

Many other examination publications date from the late Ming and early Ch'ing period. The expansion of commercial printing in Fu-chien and the Yangtzu delta provinces in particular made examination essays more widely available there than during the Sung or Yuan dynasties. While we know examination essay publications were not the chief product of those printing shops and publishing houses that have received increased attention in recent research, cumulatively such essays—and the digests, almanacs, and popular literature that were also coming out in increasing numbers—point to an increase in vernacular and classical literacy (at least in absolute numbers) in the sixteenth and seventeenth centuries.[94] By the late Ch'ing, it was noted that although the Classics and Dynastic histories still did not sell as well as more popular collections of eight-legged essays, the latter fared a poor second to sales of vernacular fiction.[95]

In addition to "society collections" known as *hsing-chüan* 行卷 that were compiled by late Ming literary *cum* political societies such as the Fu-she (see Chapter 4) to rectify literary style,[96] the publications of examination essays by the most recent *chü-jen* and *chin-shih* graduates were very successful financially, albeit short-lived. The essays of Wang Shih-chen 王世貞 (1526–90), who was a child prodigy (see Chapter 5), were widely emulated.[97] As a Hanlin academician who had excelled on the examinations, his essays and views represented the Hanlin insiders in the court, which tried to influence literati taste based on their public success. His son, Wang Shih-su 王士驌 (1566–1601), although he never attained high

93. Shang Yen-liu, *Ch'ing-tai k'o-chü k'ao-shih shu-lu*, pp. 244–45.

94. See Ōki Yasushi, "Minmatsu Kōnan ni okeru shuppan bunka no kenkyū"; and Ellen Widmer, "The Huanduzhai of Hangzhou and Suzhou: A Study in Seventeenth-Century Publishing," *Harvard Journal of Asiatic Studies* 56, 1 (June 1996): 77–122, especially 118–19. See also Lucille Chia, "The Development of the Jianyang Book Trade, Song-Yuan," pp. 10–48; and Brokaw, "Commercial Publishing in Late Imperial China," pp. 49–92, both published in *Late Imperial China* 17, 1 (June 1996). See also Lucille Chia, "Commercial Publishing in Ming China: New Developments in a Very Old Industry," paper presented at the 49th Annual Meeting of the Association for Asian Studies (Chicago, March 15, 1997), pp. 11–12.

95. See K'ang Yu-wei 康有為, "Hsu" 序 (Preface), to his *Jih-pen shu-mu chih shih-yü* 日本書目之識語 (Guide to Japanese bibliography), reprinted in Ch'en P'ing-yuan 陳平原 et al., *Erh-shih shih-chi chung-kuo hsiao-shuo li-lun tzu-liao ti-i chüan* 二十世紀中國小說理論資料第一卷 (Peking: Peking University Press, 1989), p. 13, where K'ang relates his conversation with a Shanghai lithographer in 1897.

96. See Liu Hsiang-kwang, "Shih-wen kao," pp. 62–65.

97. *Dictionary of Ming Biography*, pp. 1399–1400.

office, was the first to compile an edition of examination essays that included critical comments.[98]

*Competing Literati Opinions outside the Examination Compound*

The growth of a "writing" *cum* reading public (see Chapter 5) catered to by private publishing enterprises created intellectual space for others, less successful in the examination process, to publish their own essays and gain public recognition.[99] For example, Kuei Yu-kuang 歸有光 (1506–71), who failed the provincial examinations six times before finally passing in 1540, built a wide reputation during this time for his ancient-style prose essays, enough so that he developed a bitter rivalry with Wang Shih-chen, even though Kuei did not receive his *chin-shih* degree until the age of sixty in 1565, and then only ranked near the bottom of the 394 graduates.[100]

Ai Nan-ying, whose controversial eight-legged essay at the 1624 Chiang-hsi provincial examination, containing a veiled attack on eunuch power, barred him from the metropolitan examinations for nine years (see Chapter 4), became an acknowledged master of the eight-legged essay style despite never gaining the *chin-shih* degree. His annotated collection of his own examination essays was the most widely heralded of the late Ming and became the model for late Ming and early Ch'ing collections.[101] Later, many of his essays, including a politically charged essay on the "The people should be valued most" (*min wei kuei* 民為貴) from the *Mencius,* were included in Fang Pao's imperially authorized collection.[102] Because it belies the usual image of an eight-legged essay as a politically innocuous work (most were!), and because it should remind us of the censorship the *Mencius* faced in the early Ming (see Chapter 2), I focus on it as another example of the interesting directions an essay in eight-legged grid form could take.

98. See Tai Ming-shih 戴名世, "Keng-ch'en hui-shih mo-chüan hsu" 庚辰會試墨卷序 (Preface for the collection of examination essays from the 1700 metropolitan examination), in *Ch'ing-tai ch'ien-ch'i chiao-yü lun-chu hsuan* 清代前期教育論著選 (Selections of writings on education from the early Ch'ing period), Li Kuo-chün 李國鈞, ed. (Peking: People's Education Press, 1990, 3 vols.), 2/223.

99. See Kai-wing Chow, "Writing for Success."

100. For Kuei's eight-legged examination essays, see *Kuei Yu-kuang ch'üan-chi* 歸有光全集 (Complete essays of Kuei Yu-kuang) (Taipei: P'an-keng Press, 1979), pp. 375–81. Cf. *Dictionary of Ming Biography,* pp. 759–61; and Willard Peterson, *Bitter Gourd,* pp. 53–54.

101. See Ai Nan-ying, *Ai Ch'ien-tzu hsien-sheng ch'üan-kao* 艾千子先生全稿 (Complete drafts of examination essays by Ai Nan-ying), early Ch'ing edition (reprint, Taipei: Wei-wen t'u-shu Press, 1977).

102. Fang Pao, *Ch'in-ting Ssu-shu wen,* vol. 9, 9.34a–36a. See also Andrew Lo, trans., "Four Examination Essays of the Ming Dynasty," pp. 176–78.

1. *Break open the topic* (*p'o-t'i* 破題): *min wei kuei* 民為貴

    One can reflect upon the honored statement that the people should be valued and how the ruler should treat the people.

    極論民之所為貴，而君之所以待民者可思已。

2. *Receiving the topic* (*ch'eng-t'i* 承題):

    A comparison between the ruler and the altars to earth and grain cannot be given as much weight as a comparison with the people. Hence, how can the people be thought of lightly?

    夫君與社稷，至不能與民比重，而顧可輕其民哉？

3. *Beginning discussion* (*ch'i-chiang* 起講):

    Moreover, for the sake of the people, heaven raises an outstanding talent to lead them and be their ruler, and then follows this with feudal lords, councilors, and ministers to support him and make known his power. Heaven will also set up for the people altars to the gods of earth and grain. In the spring, sacrifices are offered in the hope of a bountiful harvest, and in the autumn, sacrifices are made to thank the gods for the harvest. Through these, signs are sought from the dark unknown.

    且夫天之為夫民也，必使出類之才，首而君長之，而後承以諸候大夫師長以宣其力。又為之壇壝社稷。春祈秋報，以求其相於冥漠之表。

4. *Initial leg* (*ch'i-ku* 起股):

    Accordingly,

    Are the people, the altars, or the ruler most important? I say, the people should be valued most, the altars next, and the ruler least.

    Originally, when people first appeared, they could not by themselves set up a local leader.

    One with great virtue had to appear before the people within a hundred *li* would follow and obey his orders.

    Then arose the states of the local lords, and neither could the states by themselves set up a leader to unify them.

    Again, the states turned to one with greater virtue before the people of the four seas would follow and obey his orders.

    然則

    民之與社稷與君，其輕重何如哉？吾謂民為貴，而社稷次之，君為輕。

    原夫生民之初，不能自君長也。

    　必有德之大者，而後百里之民從而聽命焉。

    於是有諸侯之國，合諸侯之國又不能自君長也。

    　又就其德之愈大者，而後四海之民從而聽命焉。

5. *Middle leg* (*chung-ku* 中股):

    As a result,

    the son of heaven derives his role from the masses of people.

    However,

    after becoming the son of heaven,

he will of necessity create the dynasty,

and the lords will by necessity establish family domains.

The greatest will control the domains around the capital or protect the frontiers.

The lowest will assist in lesser domains or become imperial servants.

As a result,

the lords derive their positions from the son of heaven and the grandees derive theirs from the lords.

However,

none of them compare with gaining the support of the people and becoming the son of heaven.

Still, this is insufficient to understand the people as the most valued.

於是乎

為天子，是得乎丘民而為天子也。

然既為天子矣，

　天子必建國，

　諸侯必立家，

　大為侯甸藩衛，

　小為亞圉陪隸，

於是

有得乎天子而為諸侯，

得乎諸侯而為大夫者，

然

皆不若得乎丘民者，而遂為天子，

雖然猶未足以見民之貴也。

6. *Later leg* (*hou-ku* 後股):

Someone who derives his position as lord from the son of heaven,

relies on the aura of the son of heaven above, and grandees pay homage below.

Still, the son of heaven has power from above as chief minister to carry out nine kinds of punitive campaigns,

and the grandees as royal stock have the power from below to depose a lord.

This occurs when he loses the people's heart and endangers the altars to earth and grain.

Accordingly, to replace a lord for the sake of the altars,

is really this for the sake of the altars?

It is done because the lord has lost the people and no more.

彼得乎天子而為諸侯矣，

　上憑天子之威而下有大夫之奉。

　然上則天子有大司馬九伐之權。

　而下則大夫有貴戚卿易位之柄。

為其失民心而危社稷也，

　然則為社稷而變置諸侯，

　　豈為社稷哉？

　　為失民而已矣。

7. *Fourth leg (ssu-ku* 四股):

Why is this so?

Those altars can still replace these. The altars are valuable and given priority. The public respect accorded them compares to that given the lord.

And since the altars are in charge of floods, droughts, and famines,

then their position is like a lord who shares responsibility over a territory.

Because the altars enjoy the sacrifices of animals and millet,

then their position is like a lord who receives tribute from a vassal.

If the people place heavy responsibilities on lords and light responsibilities on the altars,

then heaven would not have established the altars for the people.

The son of heaven uses the altars to appoint the hundred gods and offers sacrifices to control their promotion and demotion.

Therefore,

during droughts and floods the altars are replaced.

When the harvest fails the *cha* sacrifices are not done,

instead drums are beaten at the altar,

red silk is wound around the god of earth to threaten and rebuke him.

It is clear that if the altars cannot guard people against calamities,

then the altar cannot sit idly by and enjoy rewards for no merit.

How much more so when the lords lose the peoples' hearts!

何也?

彼社稷者尚未能免夫此也。

社稷貴為上,公尊比諸侯,

而所司者水旱凶荒之事,

　　則既有分藩之職,

所享者犧牲粢盛之薦,

　　則又有侯國之奉,

使斯民之責獨重繩諸侯而輕繩社稷,

　　則非天為民而立。

天子使之百神受職,而祭祀以馭其黜陟之意。

故

　　旱乾水溢,則變置社稷。

　　所謂年不順成,八蜡不通而伐鼓於社。

　　朱絲脅之皆有責譴之意。

明乎社稷不能為民捍災禦患,

　　則不能無功而坐食其報。

　　況於諸侯之失民心乎?

8. *Conclusion (shou-chieh* 收結):

Nevertheless, why speak of the lords and the altars but not the son of heaven?

When the people lose faith,

and the lords revolt,

the son of heaven has nowhere to stand.

Those who cannot bear speaking of this seek to exalt the heavenly king and emphasize the grand unity.

However,

> when the ministers go to the southern suburbs, call out to heaven and lament,
>
> it is a subtle measure of the need to replace the altars.

雖然

言諸侯社稷而不及天子，何也。

民心既散，

諸侯皆叛，

天子將無與立而不忍言之者，所以尊天王大一統也。

然而

群臣至於南郊稱天而誅之，

則以變置之微權也。

When compared to the rule-like, perfect parallelism in Wang Ao's beautifully crafted essays, Ai Nan-ying's politically charged essay reveals that, as the eight-legged essay increased in length from 500 to over 600 characters in the late Ming, its strict balance and symmetrical structure were compromised in practice if not in literary spirit. Perhaps that was why Ai's essay was not ranked very high by the examiners even though they certainly sympathized (they had chosen the quotation, after all) with his Mencian political critique (see Chapter 4). Fang Pao said of Ai's essay: "Ai Nan-ying's natural talent was limited,...but the essay comes from wide reading and hard work" (艾之天分有限，...則讀書多用功深之效。)[103] Its political message was unequivocal in tone and seriousness, and its historical account was prophetic. The "altars" were indeed changed twenty years later.

The Ming loyalist Lü Liu-liang's 呂留良 (1629–83) editions of eight-legged essays eventually surpassed Ai Nan-ying's in popularity among literati in the early Ch'ing, although Lü first annotated Ai's own collection of essays. Lü was said to be able to write eight-legged essays at the age of eight *sui*, but he never could get past the formidable hurdle of the Che-chiang provincial examination and withdrew in 1666 to become a physician. In addition, he became an editor of popular collections of eight-legged essays, to which he added his own views of the official rankings by examiners and at times included disparaging comments on barbarian rule in China, which posthumously caused a scandal during the succeeding Yung-cheng reign.[104]

103. Fang Pao, *Ch'in-ting Ssu-shu wen*, volume 9, 9.35b–36a.

104. See Jung Chao-tsu 容肇祖, *Lü Liu-liang chi ch'i ssu-hsiang* 呂留良及其思想 (The thought of Lü Liu-liang) (Hong Kong: Ch'ung-wen Bookstore, 1974), pp. 1–18; and Hummel, ed., *Eminent Chinese of the Ch'ing Period*, p. 551. See also Tai Ming-shih's 戴名世 assessment of Ai's and Lü's collections in Tai's "Chiu-k'o ta-t'i-wen hsu" 九科大題文序 (Preface to essays on long quotations in nine examinations), in *Ch'ing-tai ch'ien-ch'i chiao-yü lun-chu hsuan*, 2/226–28.

Lü Liu-liang's classical scholarship was widely recognized despite his examination failures, and he was invited by the K'ang-hsi emperor to take the special 1679 *po-hsueh hung-tz'u* examination in Peking, but he declined to do so. Such autonomy permitted Lü to write critically about current examination trends and to gainsay the standards used by the official examiners who passed and failed men like him. In a 1658 preface to a bookstore collection of essays, for instance, Lü charged that official corruption was the real reason why the civil examinations had become purely literary exercises and were no longer a real measure of literati talent. Rather than blame the eight-legged essay for the sterile intellectual climate, as so many of his contemporaries such as Ku Yen-wu and Huang Tsung-hsi did (see Chapter 4), Lü defended the genre and supplemented his living by preparing collections of outstanding essays that he thought fulfilled the ideals of Tao Learning.[105]

Similarly, Tai Ming-shih 戴名世 (1653–1713) made a reputation for himself as an expert writer of classical essays, despite his initial examination failures in the 1680s on the Chiang-nan provincial examination. His editions of eight-legged essays, complete with comments and analysis, were widely read and emulated, even though he failed the provincial examination several times again. His own essays on a wide variety of subjects were published in 1701, four years before he finally took his *chü-jen* degree. Normally, a scholar of note achieved examination success first, before his own essays were published. When Tai passed the metropolitan examination in 1709 ranked first and the palace examination ranked second, he entered the Hanlin Academy as a compiler. Such success confirmed his reputation as a great essayist, but he lost his cultural autonomy by entering the court. Accused of sedition in 1711 for using late Ming reign titles in his writings on the history of the Southern Ming dynasty after 1644, Tai was executed in 1713 and all his work destroyed.[106]

In his prefaces to several bookstore publications of examination essays, Tai presented his public evaluation of examination essays. Tai blamed the examiners for the decline of the eight-legged essay. Outside the petty competitions in the examination compound, where only careerism mattered for most of the candidates, the essay, he thought, could still retain its central role as an arbiter of culture and Tao Learning ideals. Tai saw his task as restoring the examination essay to its cultural roots in the great ancient-style prose styles of T'ang and Sung. As a native of T'ung-ch'eng

105. See Lü's 1658 preface and other comments in *Ch'ing-tai ch'ien-ch'i chiao-yü lun-chu hsuan*, 2/11–16.

106. On Tai Ming-shih's career, see the excellent study by Pierre-Henri Durand, *Lettrés et pouvoirs: Un procès littéraire dans la Chine impériale* (Paris: École des Hautes Études en Sciences Sociales, 1992). Cf. Hummel, ed., *Eminent Chinese of the Ch'ing Period*, p. 701.

in An-hui province, Tai Ming-shih was effectively retracing the tradition of *ku-wen* writing, which would be championed by Fang Pao (who was later implicated in Tai's sedition) and later Yao Nai in northern An-hui. To Tai, the split between the Ming eight-legged essay and Sung ancient-style prose was the cause for the decline of literati writing (文章風氣之衰也，由於區古文時文而二之也。).[107]

Lü Liu-liang, Tai Ming-shih, and others such as Li Fu 李紱 (1673–1750) effectively turned the official rankings of eight-legged essays by the examiners inside out. In effect, there were now two public tribunals for the genre. One derived from the official rankings of candidates. The other represented the views of literati outside the official compounds, whose criticisms of both successful essays and the examiners reflected the more pervasive public taste for the eight-legged essay in literati life and the fact that there were many times more losers than winners. Losers tended to sympathize with the views of literati posing as cultural arbiters outside examination compounds, which usually condemned the examiners as poor judges of the eight-legged essay genre. Tai Ming-shih, writing in 1702 about examination essays ranked that year, said as much: "Those who set the standards are out there in the empire; those who do not set the standards are there among the examiners!" (有定者在天下，而無定者則在主司而已矣).[108]

Such criticisms of examiner standards, however, were not the work of "professional critics." The "professionalization" of literati cultural pursuits certainly included those who made a living by compiling, editing, and commenting on prize-winning examination essays, but their diffuse occupational concerns were not yet established as formalized positions in the cultural economy of premodern China.[109]

### The Evolution of Studies of the Four Books

Sano Kōji 佐野公治 in his important study has described in detail how Four Books studies (*Ssu-shu-hsueh* 四書學) during the Ming and Ch'ing dynasties became oriented to contemporary-style examination essays.

---

107. See Tai's forewords and comments from his 1694, 1697, 1699, 1700, and 1702 examination collections, in *Ch'ing-tai ch'ien-ch'i chiao-yü lun-chu hsuan*, 2/213–40. Cf. my "Ch'ing Schools of Scholarship," pp. 15–17.

108. See Tai Ming-shih, "Jen-wu mo-chüan hsu," in *Ch'ing-tai ch'ien-ch'i chiao-yü lun-chu hsuan*, 2/238. On Li Fu, see *Ch'ing-tai ch'ien-ch'i chiao-yü lun-chu hsuan*, 2/330–33.

109. See my *From Philosophy to Philology*, pp. 88–137, for discussion of academic professionalization in late imperial China. Cf. Chow, "Writing for Success," pp. 128–130, which leaps to many unsubstantiated claims about "professional critics" in the late Ming.

Previously, before they became part of the official curriculum, the Four Books had been constructed as a unit by Chu Hsi and other Southern Sung Tao Learning scholars to serve as a vehicle for a new vision of antiquity to replace the Han-T'ang scholia on the Five Classics, which had been canonical to that time. After becoming a canon in its own right, however, the Four Books became the source for examination essays first under the Yuan and then again under the Ming.[110]

We have seen that Sung dynasty interpretations of the Four Books and Five Classics were chosen by the Hung-wu emperor and his Ming successors as the orthodox curriculum. On the Four Books, candidates were expected to have mastered the relevant materials in Chu Hsi's *Chu-tzu chi-chu* 朱子集注 (Collected notes by Chu Hsi). For the Five Classics, Chu Hsi's views were also favored. On the *Change Classic*, Ch'eng I's commentary and Chu Hsi's "Original Meanings" (*Pen-i* 本義) were required. Ts'ai Shen's 蔡沈 (1167–1230) commentary to the *Documents Classic*, which Chu Hsi had directed Ts'ai to compile, was emphasized. Similarly, for the *Poetry Classic*, Chu's "Collected Commentaries" (*Chi-chuan* 集傳) were requirements.

For the *Spring and Autumn Annals* and *Record of Rites*, on which Chu Hsi had not prepared commentaries, the views of other Sung Confucians were used for examination standards. In addition to the ancient "three commentaries" (*san-chuan* 三傳), that is, the *Tso* 左, *Kung-yang* 公羊, and *Ku-liang* 穀梁 commentaries, for the *Spring and Autumn Annals*, commentaries by Hu An-kuo 胡安國 (1074–1138) and Chang Hsia 張洽 (1161–1237) were also chosen for testing (Chang's was later dropped). Like Ts'ai Shen, Chang had studied under Chu Hsi. For the *Record of Rites*, ancient Han commentaries and T'ang sub-commentaries (*ku chu-shu* 古注疏) were at first required, although, later in the Ming, Ch'en Hao's 陳澔 (1261–1341) work entitled "Collected Annotations" (*Chi-shuo* 集説) was singled out for attention.

The Ming, in contrast to the Ch'ing, was a period when the more accessible moral philosophy of the Four Books in particular took precedence over the difficult classicism of the Five Classics in civil examinations and literati culture. Such precedence was due in part to the specialty privilege, which allowed candidates to master only one of the Classics (see Chapter 5).[111] Few literati mastered all the Classics, but all were required to memorize the Four Books, which were the heart of the Ch'eng-Chu inspired moral and philosophical orthodoxy. Every phrase and clause in

110. See Sano, *Shisho gakushi no kenkyū* 四書學史の研究 (Research on Four Books studies) (Tokyo: Sōbunsha, 1988), pp. 103–55, and 365–68.

111. On the differences between the Four Books and Five Classics, see my *From Philosophy to Philology*, pp. 46–49.

the Four Books was pored over, discussed by students, tutors, examiners, and essayists, and included in collections of examination essays.

Such collections of examination essays usually were focused on the Four Books and divided into sections dealing with passages from the *Analects*, *Mencius*, *Great Learning*, and *Doctrine of the Mean*. Fang Pao's *Ch'in-ting Ssu-shu wen* thus represented an imperial version of collections on the Four Books that had proliferated widely by author and region since the sixteenth century. Many such late Ming works were attributed to famous scholars such as the Fu-she activist Chang P'u 張溥 (1602–41), who noted that bookstores were filled with works naming him as compiler.[112]

### Struggles over Imperial Orthodoxy

Noted literary stylists such as the ancient-style prose writer Li P'an-lung 李攀龍 (1514–70)—who along with Li Meng-yang 李夢陽 (1473–1529) and others were known as the "Former Seven Masters" of the Ming because they tried to emulate Han and T'ang styles of prose writing—compiled works on the Four Books to spread their views. The Four Books, after all, were seen as quintessentially Han literary works, whose terseness and balance were the sine qua non of *ku-wen* prose. Li P'an-lung's *Ssu-shu cheng-pien* 四書正辯 (Corrections and defenses of the Four Books), for instance, appeared in an era when Wang Yang-ming had refuted Chu Hsi's views of the *Great Learning*, and forgeries by Feng Fang 豐坊 (1523 *chin-shih*) and others were appearing on the purported "Old Text" versions of the *Great Learning* allegedly derived from recently discovered stone relics.[113]

In addition, Buddhism and Taoism were influential in this period, and literati-scholars such as Wang Yang-ming were increasingly sympathetic to the popular "three teachings are one" (*san-chiao ho-i* 三教合一) tenor of the time. Lin Chao-en 林兆恩 (1517–98), for instance, turned his back on examination studies in 1551 and, although he was a licentiate, sought to teach students his own method of mind cultivation. Yuan Huang 袁黃 (1533–1606), one of the leaders of late Ming syncretic tendencies, thought his use of moral ledger books (*shan-shu* 善書) compatible with Ch'eng-Chu studies. To this end he compiled the *Ssu-shu shan-cheng* 四書刪正 (Cutting to the correct in the Four Books). Buddhism and Taoism were creeping into the civil examinations.[114]

112. See Chow, "Writing for Success," pp. 130–32.

113. See Sano, *Shisho gakushi no kenkyū*, pp. 371–73; and James J. Y. Liu, *Chinese Theories of Literature* (Chicago: University of Chicago Press, 1975), pp. 90–92.

114. Yuan Huang, "Fan-li" 凡例 (Overview), in *Ssu-shu shan-cheng* (n.d.), p. 1b; and *Huang-Ming Che-shih teng-k'o k'ao*, "chao-ling" 詔令 (patents and orders), pp. 20a–23a. For

The degree to which Wang Yang-ming's views on the *Great Learning* had influenced literati life is clear from both collections on the Four Books and examination essays that reflected his teachings. In his own reconstitution of the "Old Text" version of the *Great Learning*, Wang claimed that Chu Hsi had misrepresented the original version of the *Great Learning* by adding Chu's own commentary to the "investigation of things" (*ko-wu* 格物) passage and passing it off as canonical because the original commentaries had not stressed this passage. As Chapter 8 demonstrates, this textual debate, as Yü Ying-shih has rightly argued, would become one of the sources in late Ming times for the popularity of philology and evidential research to resolve such puzzles.[115]

During the 1516 Che-chiang provincial examination in Wang Yang-ming's home province, where he received the *chü-jen* degree in 1492 (see Chapter 5), 2,200 candidates were directed to deal on their second policy answer with the "orthodox transmission of the Way" (*tao-t'ung* 道統) and the role of the "transmission of the mind" (*hsin-fa chih ch'uan* 心法之傳). The best policy answer by Wu Chin 吾謹 (fl. ca. 1516–17) effectively did this (see Chapter 8), but his essay concluded with a twin assault on the Taoist doctrine of "emptiness" (*hsu-wu* 虛無) and the Buddhist notion of "extinction" (*chi-mieh* 寂滅). In addition, the literati's scholarly predilection for the arid textual fields of etymology (*hsun-ku* 訓詁) and grammar-punctuation exercises (*tz'u-chang* 詞章) was singled out. Wu's attack on Buddhism, Taoism, and classical philology indicated that literati trends counter to the Ch'eng-Chu persuasion were already brewing in Hang-chou early in the sixteenth century.[116]

As Ai Nan-ying, a staunch defender of Ch'eng-Chu orthodoxy in the last years of the Ming, noted in his introduction to a collection of essays entitled *Li-k'o Ssu-shu ch'eng-mo hsuan* 歷科四書程墨選 (Selections from model essays on the Four Books from several examinations), Wang Yang-ming's views had not yet taken hold among examination candidates before the Chia-ching reign commenced in 1522. Essays might indirectly

discussion, see also Brokaw, *The Ledgers of Merit and Demerit*, pp. 17–27, 231–32; Judith Berling, *The Syncretic Religion of Lin Chao-en* (New York: Columbia University Press, 1980), pp. 49–61, 73–74; and Wei-ming Tu, *Neo-Confucian Thought in Action: Wang Yang-ming's Youth* (Berkeley: University of California Press, 1976).

115. Sano, *Shisho gakushi no kenkyū*, pp. 375–78. See also Yü Ying-shih, "Some Preliminary Observations on the Rise of Ch'ing Confucian Intellectualism," *Tsing Hua Journal of Chinese Studies*, n.s., 11, 1 and 2 (December 1975): 125; and Lin Ch'ing-chang, *Ch'ing-ch'u te ch'ün-ching pien-wei hsueh*, pp. 359–68. Cf. Bruce Rusk, "Chen Que (1604–77) and the *Critique of the Great Learning*" (B.A. Graduating Essay, Department of History, University of British Columbia, 1996), pp. 46–60.

116. *Che-chiang hsiang-shih lu*, 1516: 5/2679–81, and 5/2787–94, in *Ming-tai teng-k'o lu hui-pien*.

attack such positions, as in 1516, but their affirmation was still anathema to the examiners. In the 1523 metropolitan examination, however, examiners composed a policy question meant to be critical of Wang Yang-ming's teachings, and several of Wang's many disciples from Chiang-hsi province who took the examination walked out of the hall in protest. Another of them, Ou-yang Te 歐陽德 (1496–1554), used the occasion to celebrate his master's teachings and was rewarded with a *chin-shih* degree. Other graduates were duly impressed with Ou-yang's essays on Wang Yang-ming's teachings, especially the eventual third-place finisher on the palace examination, Hsu Chieh 徐階 (1503–83), who entered the Hanlin Academy and later became a grand secretary. The anti-Wang atmosphere among examiners thus lessened during Hsu's period of service. According to Ai Nan-ying, during the Lung-ch'ing reign (1567–72) the 1568 examiners for the metropolitan examination actually were disciples of Wang Yang-ming and passed eight-legged essays on the *Analects* quotations that favored Wang's interpretations. Thereafter, what Ai and others considered "heterodox studies" (*hsieh-hsueh* 邪學) steadily penetrated the civil examinations.[117]

Chia-ching era commentaries on the Four Books also reveal this partial turn from orthodox Ch'eng-Chu interpretations to newer views drawn from Wang Yang-ming and his disciples.[118] A 1563 compilation entitled *Ssu-shu ch'u-wen* 四書初聞 (Preliminary questions on the Four Books) by Hsu Kuang 徐曠, for example, highlighted Wang Yang-ming's interpretations as guides to the canon. Wang's doctrine of innate moral knowledge (*liang-chih* 良知) became the key to the Four Books, in Hsu Kuang's commentary. The doctrine of "transmission of the mind" was explained by drawing on what was then called Wang's "school of mind" (*hsin-hsueh* 心學): "The mind equals the way, the way equals the mind. Mind is the ruler of this way" (心即道，道即心。心是道之主宰。).[119]

117. Ai Nan-ying, *T'ien-yung-tzu chi*, 1.28a–30a. See also Li T'iao-yuan, *Chih-i k'o-so chi*, 2.61; and *Dictionary of Ming Biography*, p. 1103.

118. I have relied here on the collection of late Ming and early Ch'ing Four Books' commentaries housed in the National Central Library, Center for Chinese Studies, Taipei, Taiwan. Although the opinions contained in these collections were certainly diverse, and new intellectual trends were clearly apparent, they do not represent, overall, the triumph of "open and pluralistic interpretations of the Confucian Canon" that Chow Kai-wing overstates in his "Writing for Success," pp. 122, 130–44, which is also based on same collection. Chow fails to take into account Sano Kōji's 1988 work on Ming Four Books editions, which presents a more nuanced account of the new intellectual trends in late Ming examination essays.

119. *Ssu-shu ch'u-wen* 四書初聞, 3.98b. See also the preface by Chiang Ying-k'uei 蔣應奎, pp. 1b–3a, where he equates the school system of Confucius with "studies of the mind."

In the same vein, Chiao Hung 焦竑 (1541–1620), who was the 1589 *opti-mus* and entered the Hanlin Academy, was ecumenical in his classical scholarship. In a 1594 collection on the Four Books honoring the best one hundred Ming literati-scholars, Chiao included both Wang Yang-ming and his followers, as well as those who upheld the Ch'eng-Chu orthodoxy, to highlight Ming interpretations of moral principle.[120] Such ecumenism was not unusual even among Ch'eng-Chu loyalists such as the Tung-lin founder Ku Hsien-ch'eng, who were more critical of Wang Yang-ming's most radical disciples in the early seventeenth century than of Wang him-self. Classical ecumenism in a collection also drew a larger audience of buyers and readers in the examination market.[121]

Tao Learning orthodoxy was generally upheld by most of the Four Books compilations that have survived, such as *Ssu-shu yen-ming chi-chu* 四書衍明集註 (Collected notes amplifying the Four Books) by T'ang Pin-yin 湯賓尹 (b. 1568; 1595 *chin-shih* and *hui-yuan*), in which T'ang claimed to include what Chu Hsi would have included if he were still alive, and *Ssu-shu ch'ung-Hsi chu-chieh* 四書崇熹註解 (Notes to the Four Books honoring Chu Hsi) by Hsu Hsieh 許獬 (1601 *chin-shih* and *hui-yuan*).[122] But few were left unaffected by the Wang Yang-ming movement. The Ch'eng-Chu school of the late Ming and early Ch'ing was in many respects a post–Wang Yang-ming revival of Ch'eng-Chu learning that affected the interpretation of Tao Learning in examinations and in collections on the Four Books. As more and more such collections publicly incorporated Wang's views in the Wan-li era (1573–1619), the door was also opened to examination essays and commentaries that included Buddhist or Taoist interpretations.[123]

Looking back at Ming eight-legged essays from the vantage of the Ch'ing dynasty, Yü Ch'ang-ch'eng (T'ung-ch'uan 俞桐川), for example,

---

120. See Chiao Hung's *Hsin-ch'ieh huang-Ming pai-ming-chia Ssu-shu li-chieh chi* 新鍥皇明百名家四書理解集 (Newly carved collection of commentary on moral principle in the Four Books by one hundred famous writers of the august Ming) (ca. 1594), A.8b. See also Edward Ch'ien, *Chiao Hung and the Restructuring of Neo-Confucianism in the Late Ming* (New York: Columbia University Press, 1986), pp. 67–113.

121. See my *Classicism, Politics, and Kinship*, pp. 76–77, 104–05.

122. See the "Fan-li" 凡例 (Overview) to T'ang Pin-yin, *Ssu-shu yen-ming chi-chu* (n.d.). In 1619, T'ang also prepared the *Ssu-shu mo chiang-i* 四書脈講意 (Lectures on the pulse of the Four Books). Hsu Hsieh was a co-compiler of the *Ssu-shu ch'ung-Hsi chu-chieh* (1602 edition), which was designed to cash in on his fame as the metropolitan *optimus* the previous year.

123. See also the *Ssu-shu chu-i hsin-te chieh* 四書主心得解 (Main new ideas in the Four Books), compiled by Chou Yen-ju 周延儒 (1588–1644) and Chu Chiang-ch'un 朱長春, who was the *optimus* in 1613, and others (ca. 1613). Kai-wing Chow notes that it is impossible to verify whether such figures were the actual compilers. See Chow, "Writing for Success," p. 132.

blamed Wang Chi 王畿 (1498–1583), a direct disciple of Wang Yang-ming, for the beginning of Ch'an Buddhist doctrine entering literati thought, and traced the first such eight-legged essay to Yang Ch'i-yuan 楊起元 (1547–99). As his source, Yü cited Ai Nan-ying, who in the late Ming wrote that Yang's Ch'an influence came from his teacher Lo Ju-fang 羅汝芳 (1515–88). In his quest for enlightenment, Lo had sought refuge in both Taoism and Buddhism before passing the 1543 provincial examination in Chiang-hsi and the palace examination in 1553. Yang Ch'i-yuan himself took his *chü-jen* degree in Kuang-tung and his *chin-shih* in 1577. Both Ai Nan-ying and Ku Yen-wu attacked Yang's 1577 metropolitan examination eight-legged essays for being filled with Ch'an doctrine.[124]

In addition to heterodox elements entering the eight-legged essays on the Four Books written by literati influenced by Taoism and Buddhism, another scholarly trend in such studies in the late Ming was the revival of Han and T'ang dynasty scholia, which had been dropped from the official classical curriculum in the early Ming. Some Ming scholars were increasingly critical of the *Ta-ch'üan* trilogy compiled in the Yung-lo era and sought instead to revive classical studies by combining evidential research with studies of the Four Books. Already in the 1516 Che-chiang provincial examination, one of the policy essays had criticized this trend, and Chapter 8 will examine in more detail the penetration of "learning based on what can be ascertained" (*k'ao-chü-hsueh* 考據學) in Ming civil examinations, which began in the fifteenth century. We have already seen that even Fang Pao was critical of mid-Ming eight-legged essays for their weak grasp of Han-T'ang commentaries.[125]

In this vein, Chang P'u's *Ssu-shu k'ao-pei* 四書考備 (Search for completeness in the Four Books), which he completed while heading the Fu-she in the last years of the Ming, was an evidential study of persons (*jen-wu* 人物) mentioned in or associated with the Four Books. It represented a 1642 follow-up to *Ssu-shu jen-wu k'ao* 四書人物考 (Study of persons in the Four Books) by Hsueh Ying-ch'i 薛應旂 (1500–73?), published in 1557. Later in the early Ch'ing, the evidential research scholar Yen Jo-chü 閻若璩 (1636–1704) prepared a geographical study entitled *Ssu-shu shih-ti* 四書釋地 (Explanations of place-names in the Four Books).[126] Evidence and analysis were now applied to the canonical Four Books.

124. See Liang Chang-chü, *Chih-i ts'ung-hua*, 5.10b. See also *Chih-i k'o-so-chi*, 1.40, on the 1448 palace examination. Cf. Sano, *Shisho gakushi no kenkyū*, pp. 406–18. Cf. *Dictionary of Ming Biography*, pp. 975–78. For further Ch'an impact on examinations, see *Yang-ch'eng T'ien T'ai-shih ch'üan-kao*, by T'ien Tsung-tien, 2.14a; and Ku Yen-wu, *Jih-chih lu*, 3.111–12.

125. See Sano, *Shisho gakushi no kenkyū*, pp. 379–80, 420–24.

126. See the "Hsu" 序 (Preface) to Chang P'u's 張溥, in *Ssu-shu k'ao-pei* (ca. 1642), p. 1a. For discussion see my *From Philosophy to Philology*, pp. 47, 103, and 187.

Looking back on these Ming to Ch'ing developments in Four Books' studies, the 1780s editors of the *Ssu-k'u ch'üan-shu* 四庫全書 (Complete collection of the Four Treasuries) commented on how much had changed since the sixteenth century: "In the Ming period, literati emphasized the eight-legged essays. These essays in turn stressed the Four Books. As a result, we have authoritative works like this one [that is, the *Ssu-shu jen-wu k'ao* by Hsueh Ying-ch'i]. They patch together and rip apart sources to allow candidates to impress examiners. This approach represents an extreme in the corruption of classical techniques."[127] Such Ch'ing haughtiness described, if little else, how far studies of the Four Books were moving in their Ming drift away from Ch'eng-Chu orthodoxy toward first Wang Yang-ming studies and then evidential research.

Early Ch'ing commentaries to the Four Books followed this late Ming current. In 1645 the Ch'ing decreed the order of the three quotations from the Four Books on provincial and metropolitan examinations. Either the *Great Learning* or the *Doctrine of the Mean* had to be the source of one of the three quotations. The other two were mandated from the *Analects* and the *Mencius*. In 1658 the emperor himself selected the Four Books quotations for the metropolitan examination.[128] The collections prepared by Lü Liu-liang and Tai Ming-shih, cited above, differed from those of Ai Nan-ying, for example, because of the former's care in supplementing Ch'eng-Chu studies with Han and T'ang scholia. In the eighteenth century, during the height of Han Learning, the use of pre-Sung scholia in eight-legged essays peaked. For example, in 1779 the Ch'ien-lung emperor personally reviewed essays on a quotation from the *Analects* in the Shun-t'ien provincial examinations and accused them of being at variance with Han and T'ang classical commentaries.[129]

The turn to "ancient studies" (*ku-hsueh* 古學), begun in the Ming but climaxing in the Ch'ing, affected both classical studies and the civil examination essays. Mao Ch'i-ling 毛奇齡 (1623–1716) and others who emphasized the importance of Han-T'ang scholia for Four Books' studies influenced later literati such as Tai Chen 戴震 (1724–77), who would gainsay Ch'eng-Chu Tao Learning interpretations (see Chapter 8). Subsequently, Juan Yuan, a distinguished Han Learning scholar, compiled a definitive work on the history of the Four Books and its commentaries in the civil examinations. Entitled *Ssu-shu wen-hua* 四書文話 (Comments on examination essays on the Four Books), Juan's collection paralleled the 1843 publication of the influential *Chih-i ts'ung-hua* 制義叢話 (Collected

---

127. *Ssu-k'u ch'üan-shu tsung-mu*, 37.14a–b.
128. See *Ch'ang-t'an*, pp. 33, 35.
129. See Sano, *Shisho gakushi no kenkyū*, pp. 420–22.

comments on the crafting of eight-legged civil examination essays), compiled by Liang Chang-chü, which also detailed the literary content and institutional machinery of the eight-legged essay for a wider audience of scholar-literati and officials.[130]

## Officializing Literary Taste

Ch'ing imperial collections of examination essays were modeled on the Ming. Ming and early Ch'ing models for such essays based on ancient-style prose (ku-wen 古文) principles were collected together under imperial auspices in 1737 by the Sung Learning (Sung-hsueh 宋學) partisan and T'ung-ch'eng classicist Fang Pao and entitled Ch'in-ting Ssu-shu wen. Kai-wing Chow has noted that between 1704 and 1750, numerous anthologies of ancient-style prose had already been published. Fang Pao, himself implicated in the Tai Ming-shih treason case, sought after his political rehabilitation to unify Ch'eng-Chu learning with the ku-wen literary tradition and reinvigorate the eight-legged essay with new life and relevance in an age of increasing Han Learning–oriented evidential research.[131]

R. Kent Guy has described how Fang Pao's collection was subdivided into four collections of Ming essays (486 total) and one collection of Ch'ing essays (297 total) through the end of the preceding Yung-cheng reign. In addition, Fang Pao delineated in his preface a brief literary account of how the eight-legged essay had evolved during the Ming dynasty after 1465. During the Ch'eng-hua and Hung-chih reigns (1465–1506), in a tradition that dated from the early Ming, examination candidates, according to Fang Pao, stayed close to the text of the Four Books and Five Classics and followed the commentaries. Their language was constrained and followed the rules of the form exactly, but they often misconstrued the commentaries in their writings.[132]

130. See Yang I-k'un 楊一崑, Ssu-shu chiao-tzu tsun-ching ch'iu-t'ung lu 四書教子尊經求通錄 (Record of honoring the classics and seeking comprehensiveness from the Four Books to teach children) (n.d.), B.17a–b, which cites Mao Ch'i-ling's views. See also Mao Ch'i-ling, Ssu-shu kai-ts'o 四書改錯 (Changes in the Four Books) (Shanghai: Commercial Press, Ts'ung-shu chi-ch'eng ch'u-pien, 1936), p. 19. Cf. Shang Yen-liu, Ch'ing-tai k'o-chü k'ao-shih shu-lueh, p. 248.

131. See R. Kent Guy, "Fang Pao and the Ch'in-ting Ssu-shu wen," pp. 168–75; and Kai-wing Chow, "Discourse, Examination, and Local Elite," p. 187, both in Elman and Woodside, eds., Education and Society in Late Imperial China.

132. Fang Pao, Ch'in-ting Ssu-shu wen, "Fan-li" 凡例 (Overview), pp. 1a–2a. Fang failed to mention, however, that the commentaries used in the Ming derived from the Yung-lo era Ta-ch'üan trilogy and not directly from the Han-T'ang scholia themselves. See Chapter 2. For discussion see Cheng Pang-chen 鄭邦鎮, "Pa-ku-wen 'shou-ching tsun-chu' te k'ao-

In the second age, from 1506 to 1567, which encompassed the Cheng-te and Chia-ching reigns, Fang Pao contended that outstanding writers such as T'ang Shun-chih 唐順之 (1507–60) and Kuei Yu-kuang were able to equate ancient-style prose with contemporary-style essays (以古文為時文) and thereby brought Ming essays to their height. Fang believed that during the third period, covering the Lung-ch'ing and Wan-li reigns (1567–1620), the eight-legged essay declined because writers became overly concerned with literary devices and as a consequence classical substance was lost. Similarly, according to Fang, the essays from the fourth period, covering the T'ien-ch'i and Ch'ung-chen reigns (1621–44), declined into a subjective account of personal concerns that were then read into the quotations (凡胸中所欲者皆借題以發之). Despite these caveats, Fang included more essays from the fourth period in his collection than from any other.[133]

Fang Pao was more discreet about rating the Ch'ing essays he included. His own experiences of exile under Manchu rule taught him that literature and politics were an explosive mix. To include Ming essays such as Ai Nan-ying's critique of the T'ien-ch'i reign (1621–28) was as far as he dared go within the limits of his time. Instead, for the Ch'ing essays, Fang appealed rhetorically to their synthesis of the finest points in Ming essays of all four periods and concluded his account with the summation that all Ch'ing essays included in the collection "illuminated the meanings and principles" (*fa-ming i-li* 發明義理) of "orthodox learning" (*cheng-hsueh* 正學), which of course was a reference to Tao Learning. His intent, after all, was to draw the examination essay into a defense of Sung Learning at a time when Han Learning and parallel prose were challenging such pretensions by associating the eight-legged essay with pre-Sung forms of *p'ien-t'i-wen* (see above).[134]

What Fang Pao succeeded in doing, however, was to augment the eight-legged essay's distinguished place in China's literary history beyond what Kuei Yu-kuang and other Ming literati, as official outsiders but mas-

---

ch'a: chü Ch'in-ting Ssu-shu wen ssu-t'i pa-p'ien wei li" 八股文'守經遵注'的考察：舉欽定四書文四題八篇為例 (Analysis of the eight-legged essay in terms of 'preserving the Classics and honoring the commentaries': Using eight essays on four quotations in the *Ch'in-ting Ssu-shu wen* as examples), *Ch'ing-tai hsueh-shu yen-t'ao-hui* 清代學術研討會 (Kao-hsiung: Chung-shan University, first volume, 1989), pp. 219–43. See also Ching-i Tu, "The Chinese Examination Essay," pp. 403–04.

133. Fang Pao, *Ch'in-ting Ssu-shu wen*, "Fan-li," pp. 1a–2a. On T'ang Shun-chih and Kuei Yu-kuang, see vol. 2, 2.9a.

134. Fang, *Ch'in-ting Ssu-shu wen*, "Fan-li," pp. 2b–3a. For discussion, see Guy, "Fang Pao and the *Ch'in-ting Ssu-shu wen*," pp. 167–68; and Chow, "Discourse, Examination, and Local Elite," pp. 188–90.

ters of the genre, had already done. To that point, individuals such as Ai Nan-ying, Lü Liu-liang, and Tai Ming-shih had rescued the eight-legged essay grid from its dismal cultural prisons and made it into a viable genre that could stand on its own in the publishing world. Their literary pedigree was limited to literati life outside the official examinations, which gained the grid a measure of literary autonomy. Fang Pao brought that pedigree into the Ch'ing imperial court and gave the essay an encomium that balanced and challenged the ongoing machinery in the biennial and triennial civil examinations. Some whose essays had been included in Fang's collection, for instance, had not been successes in the examinations.[135] The grid now encompassed civil examinations and literati taste in genres, both of which the Manchu dynasty was happy to co-opt.

Moreover, Fang Pao's collection opposed the Ming-Ch'ing tradition of criticism of the eight-legged essay by seventeenth-century literati such as Ku Yen-wu, which modern scholarship mistakenly cites as the rule rather than the exception. In the midst of a period of significant reform of the examination curriculum that lasted from 1740 to 1793 (see Chapter 10), Fang Pao's collection was granted imperial support. The eight-legged essay thereby survived its critics and became an accepted genre for both civil examinations and literati collections of writings (chi-pu 集部). In 1781 and again in 1814, officials asked that model examination essays prepared since Fang Pao's collection be reissued to the public.[136] Late-Ch'ing attacks on the eight-legged essay, which climaxed in the 1898 reforms (see Chapter 11), conveniently elided this cultural pedigree and stripped the genre of its meaning and significance in literati life.

Writing in the late eighteenth century, Li T'iao-yuan 李調元 (1734–1803), for example, spoke in praise of the longevity and the vital role played by the civil examination process in selecting officials for over five centuries from the early Ming. Li's pioneering study of Ming-Ch'ing civil examinations entitled Chih-i k'o-so-chi 制義科瑣記 (Collection of items about the crafted eight-legged essays for civil examinations) took stock of their influence on the daily lives of the people and represented the late-eighteenth-century view of the examinations as a positive influence overall, despite the many inadequacies he also described.

135. Guy, "Fang Pao and the Ch'in-ting Ssu-shu wen," pp. 166–67. Guy notes, however, that 98 of 122 Ch'ing authors held the chin-shih degree and that Fang's choice of Ch'ing essays did reflect those who were early Ch'ing models of examination success.

136. See Li-pu t'i-pen, 1781, 2nd month, for the memorial by Fu-chien censor Tung Chih-ming 董之銘 proposing that a sequel to Fang's earlier collection be compiled. Tung wanted Hanlin compilers to select more Ch'ing examination papers for inclusion than Fang Pao had. This request was repeated in the 3rd month.

This positive assessment carried over to the literati role as examiners. Serving on such staffs, they shared responsibility with the court for setting the literary and scholarly standards acceptable in examination essays and for periodically changing the scope of knowledge tested in the official curriculum. Chapter 8 explores further how literati examination life was influenced by the examination regime and how the same literati when appointed as examiners could set and revise the range of policy issues that candidates for office were expected to master. Literati examiners were partners of the dynasty in gauging the examination market.

# CHAPTER EIGHT

# Examiner Standards, Literati Interpretation, and Limits to the Dynastic Control of Knowledge

This chapter addresses which examination standards were established and how successfully examiners enforced the dynasty's conception of Tao Learning orthodoxy during the Ming and Ch'ing dynasties. The bureaucracy made an enormous financial commitment to staffing and operating the empirewide examination regime. Ironically, the chief consequence was that beginning in the late Ming, and exacerbated in the late eighteenth century, examiners could no longer take the time to read each individual essay carefully. Final rankings, even for the eight-legged essay, appeared haphazard. While acknowledging the educational impact of the curriculum in force, we must guard against overinterpreting the classical standards of weary examiners inside examination halls as a consistent or coherent attempt to impose orthodoxy from above. Although the civil examinations did play a role in defending the official canon, increasingly the examiners' role in upholding the standards used in the final rankings resembled a complicated guessing game.

An interpretive community, canonical standards, and institutional control of formal knowledge were key features of the civil examination system and its examination halls empirewide. But public political power did not translate into a closed intellectual world of "literary taste" or an unchanging "*Tao-hsüeh* orthodoxy." Instead, close scrutiny of the continuities and changes in linguistic structures and syllogistic chains of moral argument in the examination system since the early Ming reveals an explicit logic for the formulation of questions and answers and an implicit logic for building semantic and thematic categories of learning. These enabled examiners and students to mark and divide their cognitive world according to the moral attitudes, social dispositions, and political compulsions of their day. The analytic framework for moral reasoning in imperial examinations pre-

supposed influential linguistic assumptions about the behavioral consequences of examinations testing moral categories and literary distinctions,
which were invariably disproved in practice. Nevertheless, examiners
served as officials and agents of literati knowledge. Their judgments were
the licensing interpretation for all licentiates, *chü-jen,* and *chin-shih* in the
late empire.

Civil examiners served the court as a community of classical and literary specialists; they interpreted the classical canon, prescribed institutionally how it would be tested, and determined the literary standards that
would be applied to rank candidates. Through these cultural and institutional mechanisms, examiners controlled, in theory, access to most important political appointments in the bureaucracy. The historical integrity of
the classical canon had been finalized in the early Ming (see Chapter 2),
and it would remain largely unaltered until the eighteenth century, when
Manchu rulers were persuaded by their literati advisors to initiate an era
of major curricular reform (see Chapter 11).

The intertextual classical assemblage of the Four Books, Five Classics,
and Dynastic Histories was overseen since the Ming by examiners, who,
as members of the gentry-merchant elite, had once been examination candidates and had passed the civil examinations they were now supervising.
As successful graduates, they were in effect licensed practitioners of classical learning. Their possession of interpretive power helped reproduce and
alter the canon. Examiners transmitted the authority of the orthodox Tao
Learning persuasion in the examination compound. Their efforts to control interpretations in classical essays ensured that the dynasty's cultural
conservatism was based on the authority of a fixed canon. Such canonical
authority, however, could not always dictate the hermeneutic procedures
candidates would apply in their essays. Novelty and literary creativity
could not be legislated against. Moreover, as we saw in Chapter 7, new
styles and new interpretations allowed the classical essays to evolve into an
important genre in literati life outside examination halls.[1]

The grammar, rhetoric, and balanced phraseology of the examination
essay contained rules of prosody that turned classical learning into a literary contest. Both the orthodox interpretation of Tao Learning and the
prescribed chain-argument for moral rhetoric were screened through the
classical style favored by examiners, who were not only representatives of
the court and its bureaucracy but also participants in literati culture and
in tune with its vicissitudes. The interpretive style then in effect often nar-

---

1. Cf. Frank Kermode, "The Canon," in Robert Alter and Kermode, eds., *The Literary
Guide to the Bible* (Cambridge: Harvard University Press, 1987), pp. 600–10. See also
Kermode, "Institutional Control of Interpretation," *Salmagundi* 43 (1979): 72–86.

rowed the classical language, filtered the prescribed conceptualization, and constricted the stylistic genres that were favored and left some like poetry out altogether (before 1756).[2]

The required symbolic reconstruction of antiquity by candidates for examiners demanded elegant and formulaic language to transmit the vision of the ancients in written words. That symbolic reconstruction of antiquity was based on the Ch'eng-Chu reconstruction of the classical canon. Before the fall of the Ming dynasty, after which new currents in classical studies appeared among literati scholars, the most compelling ideal that appealed to the greatest scholars was sagehood. Although inevitably diluted for many candidates by their rote mastery of *Tao-hsueh* for the examinations, the emphasis in Tao Learning was placed on the cultivation of moral perfection as the fundamental ethos of the literatus. If every literatus became an exemplar of virtue, the dynasty, its elites, and its vast peasantry would prosper. In Wang Yang-ming's hands, moral knowledge and human action were equated during the late Ming. For both Wang and Ch'eng-Chu learning, political, social, and cultural harmony depended on the moral rigor of each individual.

In examination writings, whether the eight-legged composition, discourse questions, or policy essays, candidates were expected to articulate an elaborate and systematic account of the interaction between heaven and earth. Through such meditations on the role of cosmological patterns of differentiation and organization in creating all things in the world, candidates demonstrated that they understood the place of human life and civilization in an empire of orderly and determinable change. As we shall see in essays presented below, moral self-cultivation based on one's individual mental capacities enabled the literatus to reach the Tao Learning vision of the highest good in which each was a pivotal part of a morally just and rational cosmos.

Examiner standards were the accepted forms of distinction in official circles. The outside dissent and popular world of religion and the mantic arts discussed earlier challenged but never overturned these classical foundations for examination essays. Reified as a set of cultural genres (ancient-style prose, parallel prose, etc.) and expressed through the eight-legged grid, the classical essay became a meeting ground where the dynasty chose its officials and literati expressed the classical vision of the sage-kings. In Wang Ao's time, circa 1475, and thereafter until 1900, stylistic answers written in eight-legged essay forms, which were selected as models for emulation (*chün-tse* 準則), were expected of all candidates.

2. Cf. Kenneth Burke, *On Symbols and Society* (Chicago: University of Chicago Press, 1989), pp. 63–70.

## THE FOUR BOOKS AND FINAL RANKINGS

Institutionalization, however, required substantial modification of the literary formalism practiced in the civil examinations.[3] In practice, the scope and magnitude of the Ming civil examinations were already daunting (see Chapter 3). The chief examiner for the 1523 metropolitan examination noted, for example, that in selecting 400 graduates the 17 associate examiners and 2 chief examiners were divided into 15 wards (see Table 4.3) and had gone through some 3,600 separate rolls (*chüan* 卷) of essays, almost one roll for each of the 3,800 candidates, for all three sessions. Each of the 55 examination officials had to handle approximately 69 candidates (see Table 3.15) and 65 rolls. The associate examiners had to read over 220 rolls each.[4]

By the Ch'ing dynasty, the number of candidates in local and provincial examinations had increased so much that the examiners, even though their ranks were increased, had trouble keeping up with the number of examination papers that were produced. For instance, the chief examiner of the 1742 metropolitan examination, O-erh-t'ai 鄂爾泰 (1680–1745), reported that the 4 chief examiners and 18 associate examiners had read through 5,073 rolls of papers produced by 5,913 candidates, from which they had selected 22 essays from 319 graduates to include in the official record. Each associate examiner had to read approximately 282 rolls for 328 candidates.[5]

Despite extended deadlines that began in 1711, the chief examiner for the 1729 Kuang-tung provincial examination described in the preface for his official report that it had taken twenty days of grading papers by some 9,000 candidates to select only 78 graduates (.9%) and the top 22 essays.[6] Ch'ien Ta-hsin 錢大昕 (1728–1804), who supervised four provincial examinations between 1759 and 1774, laid out realistically the difficulties the examiners faced in maintaining high standards in the face of such numbers, when he prepared the report for the 1762 Hu-nan provincial examination:

> Over 4,000 literati took the Hu-nan examination. The three sessions produced a total of 12,000 rolls of answers. If you separately count the papers on the [Five] Classics, [Four] Books, poetry, discourse, and policy questions, then there were no less than 56,000 compositions. From the time we began to read the [essays on the] rolls until we made the final selections, my fel-

3. Cf. Eliot Freidson, *Professional Powers: A Study of the Institutionalization of Formal Knowledge* (Chicago: University of Chicago Press, 1986), pp. 1–17.

4. *Hui-shih lu*, 1523: "Hsu" 序 (Preface), p. 1b.

5. *Hui-shih lu*, 1742: "Hsu" 序 (Preface), p. 1a.

6. *Kuang-tung hsiang-shih lu*, 1729: "Hsu" 序 (Preface), pp. 5a–b.

low examiners and I spent eighteen days and nights on them. The number of the rolls of essays was huge, and the time [to grade them] was limited. If we were to say that those we chose were always correct, or that even one man of talent was not overlooked, then, sincerely, I would not dare to believe this myself. We did our best, however, to open the path for selection widely and to evaluate the papers impartially.[7]

The increasing number of examiners per examination from the Ming to the Ch'ing is outlined in Chapter 3. During both the Ming and the Ch'ing, the essays that dealt with quotations from the Four Books were usually read with extreme care, and frequently the remaining questions during sessions two and three of the examination were used to confirm the initial standings of the candidates after the papers from session one were graded. Important changes in the grading of essays on the Four Books did occur in the transition from the Ming to the Ch'ing dynasty, however (see Table 8.1).

During the Ming dynasty, examiners tended to rank several of the top candidates according to the caliber of their eight-legged essays on the Four Books. After 1465, the top three finishers on the provincial and metropolitan examination were usually those who composed the best essay on one of the three quotations. In other words, the number-one finisher normally ranked first on one of the essays, number two on another, and number three on the one remaining. They were then distinguished from each other by their rank on the classical essays, the discourse question in session two (see Table 10.1), or by their rank on the policy questions in session three (see Table 8.2). Recall that before 1787 the top five finishers were also selected on the basis of the best specialization essay on each of the Five Classics. Ming examiners, thus, still had their hands full grading papers, even though the eight-legged essays on the Four Books took precedence.

During the early Ch'ing, however, this evaluation tactic decisively changed, presumably at the discretion of the examiners. Table 8.1 also reveals that from 1654, when we have reliable records, until the 1890s, civil examiners in both the provincial and metropolitan examinations tended to rank a single candidate's three essays on the Four Books as uniformly superior to all others, thereby justifying his higher rank. In other words, the rule was to select one candidate as the top Four Books essay writer. This procedural change made a great difference, and candidates

7. See Ch'ien Ta-hsin 錢大昕, "Hu-nan hsiang-shih lu hsu" 湖南鄉試錄序 (Preface to the Hunan provincial examination), in *Ch'ien-yen-t'ang wen-chi* 潛研堂文集 (Collected essays from the Hall of Subtle Research), *Kuo-hsueh chi-pen ts'ung-shu* edition (Taipei: Commercial Press, 1968), 23.327–28.

were aware of it from the final rankings and official reports. It meant that during the Ch'ing dynasty examiners could rely almost exclusively on the Four Books to make their final top rankings, without the need to break the tie among three finalists by expending precious reading time ranking other parts of the examination, as was the practice during the Ming. This focus on a candidate's essays on the Four Books meant that examiners could use the essays on the Five Classics, discourse quotation, and policy question to corroborate rankings based on the Four Books.

This change was confirmed by a significant decrease in the length of examiner comments on prize essays from the Ming to the Ch'ing. During the Ming, examiners typically wrote several sentences of evaluation in the final report (see below). By the Ch'ing, examiners barely had enough time to write short phrases in eight characters in 1788 (e.g., "deep thoughts, rich in force, sufficient life, and perspicacious," *ssu-shen li-hou ch'i-tsu shen-chiu* 思深力厚氣足神究),[8] four characters in 1831 (e.g., "studies that have a base" *hsueh yu pen-yuan* 學有本原),[9] or single characters in 1882 (e.g., "selected" *chü* 取 or "hit the mark" *chung* 中).[10] These brief comments gave no sign of how the essays had been distinguished from each other. As the Ch'ing dynasty progressed, the length of examiner comments decreased from eight to one character evaluations.[11]

In the Ming, the court had already begun to complain that policy questions were not taken seriously enough. In 1527, and again in 1564, the Chia-ching emperor demanded that examiners stress the policy questions, and ordered that all those whose answers were worthless should fail, regardless of the caliber of their Four Books or classical essays.[12] Table 8.2 reveals that, although less important, policy questions during most of the Ming were still taken seriously (see also Chapter 9). That the best essays in both provincial and metropolitan examinations were usually written by the top five candidates helped examiners to make their final choices of the candidates' rankings. Indeed, in 1445, when Shang Lu became the *chuang-yuan, hui-yuan,* and *chieh-yuan* ("three firsts"), none of his eight-legged essays on the metropolitan examination, for example, was deemed the best.

8. *Shun-t'ien hsiang-shih lu,* 1788: 1a (answers).

9. *Shun-t'ien hsiang-shih lu,* 1831: 45a.

10. *Shun-t'ien hsiang-shih lu,* 1882: 33a.

11. See *Ming-tai teng-k'o lun hui-pien,* passim, for the comments by Ming examiners; and the section "*K'ao-chü-hsueh* and the Use of Evidence in Ming Policy Questions" below. For the Ch'ing, see *Ch'ing-tai chu-chüan chi-ch'eng* 清代硃卷集成 (Ch'ing examination essays) (reprint, 420 vols., Taipei: Ch'eng-wen Publishing in cooperation with the Shanghai Library, 1993–94), passim.

12. *Huang-Ming kung-chü k'ao,* 1.25a. See also *Ming-shih,* 3/1685, 1688–89, 1693–94, 1698–99.

Rather, he was made number one on the basis of his outstanding classical, discourse, memorial, and policy essays on sessions one, two, and three.[13]

As a consequence of the Ch'ing change in the evaluation of the essays on the Four Books, however, policy questions during session three became increasingly undervalued in the grading process, although they remained an important clue to the changes in intellectual trends among examiners who posed long essay questions in provincial and metropolitan examinations (see Chapter 9). Table 8.2 also discloses that after 1654 those candidates whose policy essays were classed as the best and included in the official record of the provincial or metropolitan examination were increasingly ranked below the top ten graduates. Except for a brief revival of importance during the seventeenth century and again in the late nineteenth century, graduates who ranked as low as 88th (1693) or 90th (1852) could have their policy essay chosen as the best.

In fact, in 1825 the graduate who ranked 68th on the Shun-t'ien provincial examination wrote the best essays for all five of the policy questions on the third session, a practice that was unheard of during the Ming. Increasingly, harried examiners in the Ch'ing would choose one person's policy essays as the best, thus obviating the need to choose someone different on each of the five questions to rank as the best. What had happened to the evaluation of the Four Books in the early Ch'ing now repeated itself for the policy questions in the late Ch'ing.

The result in Ch'ing times was that many students merely went through the motions when preparing session two or three answers, knowing from others' experiences that the rankings had pretty much been determined based on the first sessions. Despite the sophisticated forms of literary genre formation that had undergirded the eight-legged essay and the classical curriculum in theory, the logistics of grading papers and ranking candidates had deflected examiners and candidates alike from a purely "classical map" of moral and literary distinction. Formal, classical knowledge for each question had not been applied as expected. The examiners, who were the cultural agents of the dynasty and represented the literary and classical trends of each reign, selectively influenced the way in which Tao Learning, classical erudition, historical knowledge, and literary flair were mastered by the candidates. Their situational judgments, pressured by limited time and vast numbers of papers to grade, tended to outweigh in practice the formalistic classical standards on which the curriculum rested. This development became more conspicuous in the Ch'ing.[14]

13. *Hui-shih lu*, 1445, in *Ming-tai teng-k'o lu hui-pien*, 2/369–441.

14. See *Ch'ing-shih kao*, 11/3149, 3152, for unsuccessful efforts to correct these problems. Cf. Freidson, *Professional Powers*, pp. 209–30.

## HAPHAZARD RANKINGS FROM TEST TO TEST

Over the long run, what seriously undercut the authority of civil examiners and the credibility of the classical curriculum in the examination market and allowed the mantic arts and notions of fate to infiltrate widely the minds and hearts of those grading or taking the examinations was the lack of consistency in the rankings from test to test, or from lower level to higher level of examination. So few repeatedly ranked at the top of each examination they took that it was taken as a given that on any particular examination almost anyone could finish first and that someone who had finished first before could also finish last.

Part of the reason for this was examiner incompetence or corruption (see Chapter 4), but, more important, the increasing number of candidates even in Ming times had created a vast pool of classically literate males at the local level, many of whom were as competitive in terms of formal education as anyone else empirewide in the examination market. Once the classical illiterates, primer-literates, and semiliterates had been weeded out in the local qualifying and licensing examinations, the provincial examinations weeded out 99% of the rest, with generally only the repeaters able to pass this *chü-jen* hurdle and move on to the capital for the *chin-shih* degree.[15]

As Table 8.3 demonstrates, even in the results of the Ming metropolitan and palace examinations there were few correlations in rankings from one test to the next. In fact, the renowned *optimus* could finish 240th on the 1469 metropolitan examination and rank only 83rd on the provincial. In 1568 the *chuang-yuan* ranked 84th on his provincial examination and 351st (out of 410 graduates) on the metropolitan. Going through the list, close correlations in results were rare. That is why Shang Lu, who had "three firsts" in 1445, was so honored, and perhaps also why he prevented others from emulating his feat in 1475 (see Chapter 7). Records from the 1586 metropolitan examination, which also give the final rankings on the palace examination that year, confirm this lack of correlation for the top two levels of final rankings.[16]

Table 8.4 shows that this haphazard ranking trend continued throughout the Ch'ing dynasty. Other than Ch'en Chi-ch'ang (see Chapter 7), who achieved "three firsts" in 1820, or Lu K'en-t'ang 陸肯堂 (1650–96) who had "two firsts" in 1685, few of the rankings of Ch'ing dynasty *chuang-yuan* on the provincial, metropolitan, or palace examination correlated. Twenty-one (35% of sample) ranked below number 100, while seven

15. Man-cheong, "Fair Fraud and Fraudulent Fairness," stresses the corruption aspects.
16. See *Hui-shih lu*, 1586: 20/11135–74, in *Ming-tai teng-k'o lu hui-pien*.

(12%) ranked below number 200 on the metropolitan examination. Only sixteen *optimi* (29%) ranked in the top ten on the metropolitan examination; fewer (15, or 25%) finished in the top ten on the provincial examination. A total of only five *chuang-yuan* in this sample (8%) managed to finish in the top ten on both the provincial and metropolitan examinations.

As Chapter 10 demonstrates, the addition of a poetry question after 1756 and the elimination of the discourse question in 1793 further changed the standards by which the examiners weighed individual essays and ranked the candidates who produced them. The requirement that candidates memorize all Five Classics, which was promulgated after 1786, also changed the dynamics favoring the Four Books over the Classics in the examination halls. In short, our brief contextualization of examiner interpretation during the Ming and Ch'ing (elaborated further in Chapter 9) reveals the degree to which the civil examiners' standards, their classical interpretations, and their control of formal knowledge were successfully compromised from within the examination compound by the sheer magnitude of the examination regime and frequently contested from without by literati opinion, popular religion, and the mantic arts.

The stock interpretation in Ming and Ch'ing popular literature of the examiner as a bumbling idiot drew on these realities to paint a comic background to the selection process. Even a powerful and influential Hanlin academician and imperial secretary such as Chuang Ts'un-yü (see Chapter 7) could become the brunt of jokes by candidates who ridiculed him as an examiner notorious for his "preference for short essays" (*hao tuan-wen* 好短文). It was said that whenever Chuang was an examiner, anyone who could avoid writing more than 300 characters in an eight-legged essay (550 were the mid-Ch'ing norm) had a chance to rank among the highest graduates. They had little sympathy for Chuang's dilemma as he faced the insuperable task of reading thousands of examination papers.[17]

## CIVIL EXAMINATIONS
## AND MING-CH'ING CLASSICAL ORTHODOXY

In the examination hall, orthodoxy and standards in theory went hand in hand. Outside, those standards were frequently challenged. Moreover, during periods of intense intellectual ferment, such as the rise of Wang Yang-ming learning in the sixteenth century and the challenge of Han Learning in the eighteenth, such challenges to orthodox standards also

17. *Tan-mo lu*, 13.12b–13b.

penetrated examination halls, where new views contended with old interpretations. Orthodox interpretations did not prevent Ming or Ch'ing literati from writing about the rule of feelings and sentiments in human affairs, for example, which challenged Ch'eng-Chu teachings. Examination questions and answers that were graded by examiners can be contrasted with the way leading scholars were actually debating classical issues.

### "Overcoming the Self" in Examination Questions

One of the most telling classical passages for both orthodox *Tao-hsueh* philosophy and late imperial ideology was drawn from Confucius' response to his disciple Yen Yuan's 顏淵 query concerning the moral doctrine of benevolence (*jen* 仁). Confucius had responded: "*To return to the observance of the rites through overcoming the self constitutes benevolence* [*k'o-chi fu-li wei-jen* 克己復禮為仁]. If for a single day a man could return to the observance of the rites through overcoming himself, then the whole Empire would consider benevolence to be his. However, *the practice of benevolence depends on oneself alone* [*wei-jen yu-chi* 為仁由己], and not on others."[18]

In his commentary to this passage, Chu Hsi gave the following glosses: "K'o" 克 means to conquer [*sheng* 勝]. *Chi* 己 refers to "one's selfish desires." According to Chu Hsi, this meant that "to practice benevolence, one must conquer one's selfish desires and return to the observance of the rites." In this manner, the "perfect virtue of the original mind" (*pen-hsin chih ch'üan-te* 本心之全德), which Chu equated with heavenly principle, could be attained.[19]

Outside the precincts of civil examinations, however, many late Ming literati-scholars had objected to Chu Hsi's gloss "to conquer one's selfish desires" for Confucius' notion of "overcoming the self." Members of the T'ai-chou 泰州 school (in Yang-chou prefecture), a radical group of Wang Yang-ming's followers, saw in this gloss confirmation of what they considered Chu Hsi's absolute bifurcation of human desires from heavenly principle. Chu Hsi, they thought, was in effect reading into this passage from the *Analects* Chu's distinction between *li* 理 (moral principles) and *ch'i* 氣 (variously rendered as "material force," "ether", "stuff," "energy," "matter").

Despite such disagreements in interpretation during the Ming, however, Chu Hsi's views generally prevailed in the important arena of provincial and metropolitan examinations, which frequently picked the benevolence passage for quotations from the Four Books in the first session. In the six-

18. Emphasis added. See *Lun-yü yin-te*, 22/12/1; and the translation by Lau, *Confucius: The Analects*, p. 112. For discussion, see my "Criticism as Philosophy," pp. 165–98.

19. See Chu Hsi, *Lun-yü chi-chu*, 6.10b–11a.

teenth century, as we have seen in Chapter 7, Wang Yang-ming's positions penetrated the examinations via both candidates and examiners. Later in the eighteenth century, the views of evidential research scholars so influenced literati classical learning that philological interpretations of classical passages were entertained in policy essays.[20]

The 1465 Shan-tung provincial civil examination, held before the rise in popularity of Yang-ming learning, demonstrates how prominent orthodox views could be when they appeared on civil examinations. The first quotation from the Four Books for session one of the Shan-tung examination proceedings, which was drawn from the passage in the *Analects* cited above, required that all candidates have mastered Chu Hsi's views on the practice of benevolence and the return to ritual. Ranked second of all candidates in Shan-tung who took the 1465 examination, Wang Lun 王綸 (fl. ca. 1465–87) had his essay for this passage from the *Analects* judged the best, and it was included in the official records of the proceedings. One of the examiners wrote that "the words in this essay were well-ordered and comprehensive, indeed they were worthy of revealing the essential thread in [Confucius'] teachings."[21] Beneath the rhetoric lurked deep political waters, however.

Earlier in 1456, Wang had taken the equivalent of the provincial examinations in the capital region, where his father, Wang Wen 王文 (1393–1457), was a grand secretary in the court. When Wang Lun failed, his father charged the chief examiner with corruption, but Wang Wen's charges were dismissed after an investigation. The 1456 provincial examination had taken place in the aftermath of the T'u-mu Affair (see Chapter 1), and Wang Wen had been a collaborator with Yü Ch'ien (see Chapter 6) in resisting Mongol efforts to ransom the Cheng-t'ung emperor when he was captured by the Oirats in 1449. When the ransomed emperor returned and took power again in 1457 as the T'ien-shun emperor, both Yü and Wang were executed as traitors. As a result, Wang Lun could not take the provincial examination again until the Ch'eng-hua emperor (r. 1465–87) took power and restored Wang's father's name to a place of imperial honor in 1465. The next year Wang Lun changed his name to Tsung-i 宗彝 and passed the metropolitan and palace examinations, eventually rising to become a Minister of Personnel.[22]

20. Mizoguchi Yūzō 溝口雄三, "Mōshi jigi soshō no rekishi teki kō satsu" 孟子字義疏證の歷史的考察 (Historical analysis of the Evidential Analysis of the Meaning of Terms in the Mencius), *Tōyō bunka kenkyū jo kiyō* 東洋文化研究所紀要 48 (1969): 144–45, 163–65.

21. *Shan-tung hsiang-shih lu*, 1465: 2/685, 719, in *Ming-tai teng-k'o-lu hui-pien*.

22. See *Ming-shih*, 7/4515–18; and *Dictionary of Ming Biography*, pp. 970, 1610.

432 / LIMITS TO DYNASTIC CONTROL OF KNOWLEDGE

In his 1465 classical essay, Wang Lun emphasized Chu Hsi's gloss for the benevolence passage, in which Chu claimed that the "perfect virtue of the original mind" did not derive from external forms but emanated instead from the "heavenly principles of the individual mind." In the essay, Wang neatly reproduced for the examiners the orthodox bifurcation of heavenly principles from human desires, contending that the doctrine of the "sagely transmission of the mind" was the key to their vision. Confucius' "theory of the four renunciations" was defended by Wang Lun in light of the constant struggle required to enable heavenly principles to prevail over wayward desires. Eight years after his father had fallen from grace, Wang Lun successfully translated Ch'eng-Chu orthodoxy into personal and family vindication on the civil examination in Shan-tung.

Immediately following the benevolence passage in the *Analects*, Confucius had said: "Do not look unless it is in accordance with the rites; do not listen unless it accords with the rites; do not speak unless it accords with the rites; do not move unless it is in accordance with the rites." Because Chu Hsi's interpretation of this passage was at least publicly orthodox, candidates like Wang Lun were expected to demonstrate that they had mastered what Confucius had meant about benevolence and the four renunciations by reproducing the essentials of Chu Hsi's dualistic position on the antagonism between moral principles and human desires. Although some leeway was permitted to question whether Chu Hsi's views were entirely appropriate to the passage in question, the more radical views of Wang Yang-ming had not yet appeared. In the pages of fifteenth-century examination questions and answers, students such as Wang Lun confirmed correct views and did not stray into textual debates that might cloud the moral issues at stake in the passage.[23]

Questions dealing with the benevolence passage in the *Analects* were also popular early in the Ch'ing dynasty. In the 1685 metropolitan examination, which occurred during an early Ch'ing era of anti–Wang Yang-ming literati trends,[24] the first quotation selected from the Four Books was this passage recording the exchange between Yen Yuan and Confucius. The prize essay, which was rated as "orthodox principles" by the examiner Wang Hung-hsu 王鴻緒 (1645-1723), was prepared by the eventual *optimus* on the palace examination, Lu K'en-t'ang, who also finished first as *hui-yuan* 會元 on the metropolitan examination. He had come in among the top five (*ching-k'uei* 經魁) in the 1681 Chiang-nan provincial examination. Lu's eight-legged essay presented the orthodox Ch'eng-Chu position on the importance of "overcoming the self" and "returning to the rites" out-

23. *Shan-tung hsiang-shih lu*, 1465: 2/719–22. For the translation, see Lau, *Confucius: The Analects*, p. 112.
24. See my *From Philosophy to Philology*, pp. 42–56.

lined above. The 1685 answer restored intact the acceptable interpretation of this passage as given earlier in 1465. It was not so much that classical interpretation had not changed between 1465 and 1685. Rather, the challenge of Yang-ming learning had peaked in the late Ming, and the early Ch'ing saw a restoration of Ch'eng-Chu learning, particularly in examination essays.[25]

Lu K'en-t'ang's essay on "benevolence" emphasized the tension between human desires and moral principles. To "bring order to one's selfish interests," Lu noted, one had to "recognize that the inception of selfishness began in desires." If personal desires could be overcome, there were no limits to what could be achieved. To manifest benevolence in one's behavior demanded that "each affair be cleansed by principles." The most admired essay for the entire examination, this eight-legged masterpiece affirmed the cultural values of Sung Tao Learning and divided the world according to orthodox philosophical categories acceptable to the political authorities.[26]

Differing interpretations of this celebrated passage reemerged among literati in the late seventeenth and eighteenth centuries, however, when the ritualist scholars Yen Yuan 顏元 (1635–1704) and Li Kung 李塨 (1659–1733) explicitly attacked the orthodox position, although little impact was felt in the examination process itself until the eighteenth century. Chu Hsi's rigorous definition of human desires as evil was the key issue for both Yen and Li. They favored an interpretation of the *Analects* that emphasized the role of rituals to control the self (*yueh chih i-li* 約之以禮) rather than eliminating selfish desires (*ch'ü-ssu* 去私).[27]

When Han Learning and evidential research (*k'ao-cheng-hsueh* 考證學) became popular among Ch'ing scholars in the eighteenth century, such critical views of orthodoxy began to make their way into the civil examinations. In his discussion of the *Analects* passage, the polymath Tai Chen 戴震 (1724–77) noted: "Lao-tzu, Chuang-tzu, and the Buddha [spoke of] 'having no desires,' not of 'having no selfishness.' The way of the sages and worthies was 'to have no selfishness' and not 'to have no desires.' To equate [the self] with selfish desires is therefore a notion the sages totally lacked."[28]

---

25. See Kai-wing Chow, *The Rise of Confucian Ritualism in Late Imperial China* (Stanford: Stanford University Press, 1994), pp. 50–53.

26. *Hui-shih lu,* 1685: 7a, 32a–34b. See also *Ch'ing-tai chuang-yuan p'u* 清代狀元譜 (Accounts of Ch'ing dynasty *optimi*), compiled by Chou La-sheng 周臘生 (Peking: Forbidden City Press, 1994), p. 237.

27. See *Yen-Li ts'ung-shu* 顏李叢書 (Collectanea of Yen Yuan and Li Kung) (reprint, Taipei: Kuang-wen Bookstore, 1965), 1/70, 3/904.

28. Tai Chen, *Meng-tzu tzu-i shu-cheng* 孟子字義疏證 (Evidential analysis of meaning of terms in the Mencius) (Peking: Chung-hua Bookstore, 1961), p. 56.

The theoretical debate was drawn over the affirmation or negation of human desires. For Tai Chen, the Chu Hsi line of inquiry had scorned the essential characteristics of humanity in favor of attention to heavenly principles: "The sages ordered the world by giving an outlet to people's feelings and by making it possible for them to realize their desires.... With regard to the Sung literati, however, [the people] believe in them, thinking that they are the equivalent of the sages. Everyone can talk about the distinction between moral principles and human desires. Therefore, those who control the people today pay no attention to the sages giving an outlet to people's feelings and making it possible for them to realize their desires."[29] Tai's political criticism of the way in which classical values had been used to stifle the interests of the people was a direct result of his revaluation of the Chu Hsi interpretation of classical terms such as benevolence.

### The "Human Mind and the Mind of Tao" in Examination Questions

In addition to the passage in the *Analects* in which Confucius called for "overcoming the self," two passages from the *Documents Classic* added fuel to the orthodox Ch'eng-Chu position. In the chapter entitled "Offices of Chou" ("Chou kuan" 周官), the Chou dynasty king announced: "Oh, all my officials and superior men, pay reverent attention to your charges, and be careful of the commands you issue. Once issued, commands must be put into effect and cannot be retracted. By your public-mindedness extinguish all selfish aims, and the people will have confidence."[30] This was the locus classicus for the priority of the "public" domain over the "private" in literati and imperial discourse.[31]

In another chapter, entitled "Counsels of Yü the Great" ("Ta Yü mo" 大禹謨), the distinction between the "human and mind of the Tao" was enunciated for the first time. The sage-king Shun 舜 admonished the soon-to-be-crowned Yü 禹: "The human mind is precarious. The mind of the Tao is subtle. Have absolute refinement and singleness of purpose. Hold fast the mean."[32]

29. Tai Chen, *Meng-tzu tzu-i shu-cheng*, pp. 9–10. For discussion, see my "Criticism as Philosophy," pp. 173–74.

30. *Shang-shu t'ung-chien*, 40/0281–0313 (p. 21). Cf. Legge, *The Chinese Classics*, vol. 3, *The Shoo King*, p. 531.

31. See Mizoguchi Yūzō, *Chūgoku no kō to shi* 中國の公と私 (Public and private in China) (Tokyo: Kembun Press, 1995), pp. 21–28.

32. *Shang-shu t'ung-chien*, 03/0517–0532 (p. 2). I have followed, with minor changes, the translation in Wing-tsit Chan, "Chu Hsi's Completion of Neo-Confucianism," *Études Song-Sung Studies* 2, 1 (1973): 79.

Taken together, these two passages from the *Documents Classic* became key pillars of the orthodox position during the Yuan, Ming, and Ch'ing dynasties. In a culture that drew its ideals from a past golden age populated by sage-kings of unquestioned wisdom, orthodoxy expected classical verifications for its present articulation. Accordingly, Ch'eng I had drawn the explicit bifurcation between the human mind (*jen-hsin* 人心) as uncontrolled desire and the mind of the Tao (*tao-hsin* 道心) as heavenly principle: "The human mind equals human desires; therefore it is very precarious. The mind of the Tao equals heavenly principle; therefore it is extremely subtle. Only through refinement can the [mind of the Tao] be observed. Only through singleness of purpose can it be preserved. In this manner only can one hold to the mean."[33]

Chu Hsi, building on Ch'eng I's Northern Sung interpretation, gave the *jen-hsin tao-hsin* 人心道心 passage a new theoretical twist in the Southern Sung by subsuming the distinction into his own philosophy of principle: "Those who speak of the precariousness of the human mind mean that it is the sprout of human desires. The subtlety of the mind of the Tao conveys heavenly principle."[34] Chu was suggesting that his bifurcation between *li* and *ch'i* had its counterpart in Shun's declaration of the distinction between the mind of Tao and the human mind. The former could be described as moral, that is, the source of moral principles, and the latter as human, that is, the source of desires and hence of evil as well. To the degree that Chu Hsi's concepts of *li* and *ch'i* were mutually exclusive, and thus mutually irreducible, his position could be interpreted as introducing an antagonism between moral principles and the material world of human desires.

In his famous 1189 preface to his *Chung-yung chang-chü* 中庸章句 (Phrases and sentences in the *Doctrine of the Mean*), which became required reading for all young men preparing for civil examinations (see Chapter 5), Chu made more explicit his reason for linking the distinction between the moral and human mind to his philosophy of *li-hsueh*. Moreover, he added to the distinction of the mind of Tao and the human mind the parallel distinction between "public" (*kung* 公) and "private" (*ssu* 私) enunciated in the "Offices of Chou" chapter: "If one does not know how to control the mind, then it is precarious. The more precarious [the human mind becomes] the more subtle the subtle [mind of the Tao] becomes.

33. *Erh-Ch'eng ch'üan-shu* 二程全書 (Complete writings of Ch'eng Hao and Ch'eng I), in *Ho-nan Ch'eng-shih i-shu* 河南程氏遺書 (Bequeathed writings of Ch'eng I), *Ssu-pu pei-yao* edition (Shanghai: Chung-hua Bookstore, 1927–35), 19.7a–7b.

34. Chu Hsi, *Chu-tzu ta-ch'üan* 朱子大全 (Master Chu [Hsi's] Great Compendium), *Ssu-pu pei-yao* edition (Shanghai: Chung-hua Bookstore, 1927–35), 67.19a. Cf. Chu Hsi's answers about the passage to inquiring students in the *Chu-tzu yü-lei*, 78.26b–34a.

The public-mindedness of [universal] principles thus has no way to overcome the personal concerns of one's human desires. One must cause the mind of the Tao always to be the master of the person and the human mind always to obey it."[35]

Chu Hsi moved freely between the Four Books and Five Classics, treating them holistically as the basis for the thought-world of the classical age. Chu's efforts culminated with Ts'ai Shen 蔡沈 (1167–1230), his student, who used the "human and mind of the Tao" passage for a holistic interpretation of all the chapters in the *Documents*, a view that became required in the Ming examination curriculum. In the 1209 preface to his annotation of the *Documents*, Ts'ai wrote: "The world-ordering of the two emperors and three kings drew its roots from the Way. The Way of the two emperors and three kings drew its roots from the mind. If one recaptures their thought-world, the Way and world order can be gotten and articulated. What is [this mind]? It is 'absolute refinement and singleness of purpose [thereby] holding the mean.' These are the methods of mental discipline, which [the sage-kings] Yao, Shun, and Yü transmitted to each other."[36]

Referring specifically to the *jen-hsin tao-hsin* passage in the "Counsels of Yü the Great," and the "public versus private" distinction in the "Offices of Chou" chapter, Ts'ai made his point even more explicit. Mental discipline was the essence of the tension between the moral and human mind. The sage-king became master of himself and forced his desires to obey his will: "The human mind easily becomes selfish and is hard to keep public-minded. Therefore, it is precarious. The mind of the Tao is hard to illuminate but easy to cloud over. Therefore, it is subtle. ... If the mind of the Tao is always made the master and the human mind obeys it, then the precarious [human mind] is pacified and the subtle [mind of the Tao] manifests itself. ... Probably, when the ancient sages were about to hand the empire over to a successor, they always brought together and transmitted their methods of world-ordering to [him]."[37]

In addition, Ts'ai Shen made clear that the moral and human mind reflected the bifurcation between public and private. Commenting on the passage "By your public-mindedness extinguish all selfish aims" in the "Offices of Chou" chapter, Ts'ai Shen wrote: "One uses public-minded principles in the world to extinguish selfish feelings."[38] In his discussions with his students concerning the need "to overcome oneself," Chu Hsi

---

35. *Chu-tzu ta-ch'üan*, 76.21a–22a.

36. Ts'ai Shen, "Hsu" 序 (Preface) to the *Shu chi-chuan* 書集傳 (Collected commentaries to the Documents) (Taipei: World Bookstore, 1969), pp. 1–2.

37. Ibid., p. 14.

38. Ibid., p. 121.

had earlier put the final touches on his vision of human nature, in which benevolence was the product of personal control through overcoming the self, of public-minded behavior, and of the elimination of selfish motives and desires: "Public-mindedness is the way of practicing benevolence. Man is the raw material for benevolence. When you have a [public-spirited] man, then you also have benevolence.... If there were no selfish interests, then the entire physical existence of man would exhibit such benevolence.... The reason men are not benevolent is their selfish interests."[39]

By equating public-mindedness with the chief virtue of benevolence, Confucius' admonition "to overcome the self" was placed within a moral framework in which personal emotions and aspirations were designated as selfish desires that required elimination. Furthermore, the public domain of benevolence included the practice of love and reciprocity precisely to the degree that the private domain of the self was curtailed. In his effort to wed classical passages to his analysis of the public domain of heavenly principle and the private domain of human desires, Chu Hsi successfully developed a classical sanction for his philosophical ideas. In the early fifteenth century, however, Chu's humanistic philosophy was hardened by Ming scholar-officials into the Ch'eng-Chu school of *li-hsueh*, which readily served as the theoretical underpinnings for the dynasty and its examination curriculum (see Chapter 2).

Sung *Tao-hsueh* ideals of the priority of "public" over "private" overlapped with appeals to the throne as the representative of public virtue and virtuous succession. Except among the late Ming followers of Wang Yang-ming, the Tao Learning interpretation of "public" left little room for appeals to individual desires or private interests. Employing the image of "master" and "slave" in his theory of the mind and desires, Chu Hsi created sufficient ideological space in his political philosophy for unintended interpretive consequences that Ming spokesmen for the emperor would find useful to legitimate imperial authority as the sage-king protector of Ch'eng-Chu learning.

For example, during the 1516 Che-chiang provincial examination, the second policy question for session three focused on the issue of the "orthodox transmission of the Way" and the role of the "transmission of the mind" in enabling the mind of the Tao to reach its goals of "absolute refinement, singleness of purpose, and allegiance to the mean." The examiners stressed in their question that spiritual and mental subtlety were the keys to unraveling the ties between individual self-cultivation of the mind of the Tao and public mastery of the comprehensive handles of gov-

39. *Chu-tzu yü-lei*, 95.32b–33a.

ernment. Study of nature and principle was presented as the Sung dynasty reconstruction of the mind-set of the sage-king Yao, who had passed on the lesson of the middle way of governance to his chosen successor Shun. The 2,200 candidates were asked to reconcile Chu Hsi's views with the classical doctrines of absolute refinement, singleness of purpose, and allegiance to the mean.[40]

Examiners chose as the most outstanding essay for this policy question the answer prepared by Wu Chin 吾謹 (fl. ca. 1516–17), who finished third in the overall competition. One examiner rated Wu's essay as an exemplar for Tao Learning and the explication of the *tao-t'ung*. Another remarked that Wu was "one with whom one could discuss the Way." Wu's essay indeed confirmed the orthodox position on the nature of the mind and its transmission since the sage-kings of antiquity: "From antiquity to the present, through different periods, this mind-set has been unaltered." Chu Hsi's views, and Ts'ai Shen's elaborations of them, were defended in the strongest terms; their efforts to encompass both morality and learning were praised. "Morality depended on the *Doctrine of the Mean* for its efficacy," Wu Chin wrote, and "learning must seek out benevolence as its goal."

To complete the exercise, Wu Chin brought into his answer the "benevolence" passage (see above) from the *Analects* to demonstrate the inner consistency between the restraint of desires (associated with the human mind) and the mastery of moral principles (in the mind of the Tao). "Different epochs all shared the same mind. Different [historical] traces all shared the same principles." The goal, according to Wu, was to "complete the original power" and "recapture the natural essence of one's mind."

Wu Chin's prize essay concluded with an attack on Buddhist and Taoist doctrines as well as a critique of the literati's predilection for etymology and punctuation exercises (see Chapter 7). By these pursuits, the "human mind was daily buried and the Way was daily distanced," according to Wu. Such attacks on Wang Yang-ming style heterodoxy (see Chapter 6), at a time in the early sixteenth century when Wang's more generous views of Taoism and Buddhism were influential empirewide, clarified for the examiners the doctrinal ground upon which Chu Hsi's orthodox position was constructed.[41]

Wu Chin's written abilities carried him successfully through the metropolitan examination hurdle in 1517, when he received his *chin-shih* degree in the third tier of graduates. Interestingly, however, Wu early on retired

---

40. *Che-chiang hsiang-shih lu,* 1516: 5/2679–81, in *Ming-tai teng-k'o lu hui-pien.*
41. Ibid., 5/2787–94. See also Lü Miaw-fen, "Practice as Knowledge."

to a life of scholarship, poetry, prose, and leisure, associating with many of the leading literary figures of his day, such as Li Meng-yang 李夢陽 (1473–1529). Wu's well-thought-out attack on such pursuits in his youthful examination essay seemed to carry little weight in practice. Candidates such as Wu knew what they were supposed to say in examination essays, but this did not mean they believed it. Perhaps Wu changed his mind, perhaps the examination was a mere exercise for him, or perhaps he became disenchanted with the harsh realities of the Cheng-te and Chia-ching reigns, particularly the Great Ritual Debate that rocked the court in 1522–24. Li Meng-yang, for instance, served the Ming court but was deprived of his official status in 1521–22. Earlier in 1514 he had been thrown into prison in Chiang-hsi after charges were brought against him for his activities as an educational commissioner there.[42]

Sung Tao Learning, although frequently criticized outside the examination cubicles, survived the Yang-ming challenge intact as orthodoxy into the seventeenth century. During the late Ming, Ku Hsien-ch'eng, the influential leader of the privately endowed Tung-lin Academy in Wu-hsi county, agreed with Chu Hsi that evil was due to the inherent instability of the human mind, which, if left unchecked, could cloud the mind of the Tao: "The mind of the Tao has a master; the human mind does not. If there is a master [in charge], then everything in the world through its activity will be the epitome of sacred. This is called the gate of numerous subtleties. If there is no master, then everything in the world through its activity will reach extreme danger. This is the gate of numerous calamities." By appealing to the "commanding presence" of the mind of the Tao, Ku was reaffirming in political terms the authority of the Ch'eng-Chu orthodoxy for classical discourse and gainsaying the views of Wang Yang-ming.[43]

Similarly, the Ch'ang-chou Tung-lin partisan Ch'ien I-pen 錢一本 (1539–1610) accepted Chu Hsi's bifurcation of the mind, but with an important political twist: he equated the mind of the Tao with the ruler and the human mind with the subject. Just as the mind of the Tao was master in Chu Hsi's theory of mind, so the ruler was master of his sub-

---

42. *Che-chiang hsiang-shih lu*, 1516: 5/2787–94. See also *Ming-jen chuan-chi tzu-liao suo-yin* 明人傳記資料索引 (Index to Ming persons in biographical sources) (Taipei: Central Library, 1965), p. 187; and Carney Fisher, "The Great Ritual Controversy in the Age of Ming Shih-tsung," *Society for the Study of Chinese Religions Bulletin* 7 (fall 1979): 71–87.

43. See Ku Hsien-ch'eng's paraphrase of Chu Hsi's position in "Hsiao-hsin-chai cha-chi" 小心齋劄記 (Random notes from the Pavilion of Watchfulness), 5.7a, in *Ku Tuan-wen kung i-shu* 顧端文公遺書 (Bequeathed writings of Ku Hsien-ch'eng), K'ang-hsi reign edition.

jects, in Ch'ien I-pen's late Ming gloss of Ch'eng-Chu orthodoxy. The "descending" view of political power now operated in moral theory as well.[44] Such interpretations in the hands of dogmatic literati moralists and formalistic political hacks provided political autocrats with the ideological weapons they would require to maintain the perennial goals of short-term gains based on political opportunism and long-term preservation of imperial power and prestige. But they usually could not dictate to local literati what the latter should say or write inside or outside the precincts of the government.

After the Ch'ing triumph, Manchu rulers still accorded Ch'eng-Chu orthodoxy eminence of place in imperial ideology and examination requirements. During the 1685 metropolitan examination in Peking, the "mind of the Tao" passage was raised in the first policy question for session three. Referring to the passage in the *Documents* where the distinction between the human and mind of the Tao occurred, the examiners summarized Chu Hsi's and Ts'ai Shen's interpretations: "The rule of the ancient emperors and kings was based on the Way. The Way was grounded in the mind. After Yao instructed Shun to hold fast to the mean, Shun then expanded this lesson and passed it on to Yü."[45] In essence, the examiners contended that the doctrines of "preserving sincerity" and "investigating things" depended on the "learning of the mind." Lu K'en-t'ang's prize essay opened with a summary of the centrality of the mind that corroborated the examiners' position: "All emperors and kings [of old] were men who through study governed effectively. Accordingly, they were all men who learned through the mind."[46]

During both the regular 1730 and special 1737 metropolitan examinations, policy questions raised in the third session dealt with the "human mind and mind of the Tao" passage. For the first policy question of 1730, examiners explicitly brought up the distinction between the moral and human mind while asking candidates to discuss the metaphysical attributes of the Supreme Ultimate (*t'ai-chi* 太極). The answer prepared by Shen Ch'ang-yü 沈昌宇 (1700-44), the *hui-yuan* on the metropolitan and *secundus* on the palace examination, was reprinted in the official record and was rated by one of the chief examiners as "learning having a basis." Shen's exemplary essay presented the Sung literati view of cosmology whereby the Supreme Ultimate gave rise to yin and yang, which in turn produced the five evolutive phases and the world of myriad things.

---

44. See also Ch'ien I-pen, *Kuei-chi* 龜記 (Records on tortoise shells), ca. 1613 edition, 1.11a; and his *Fan-yen* 範衍 (Exposition of models), ca. 1606 edition, 1.9a-9b.

45. *Hui-shih lu,* 1685: 11a.

46. *Hui-shih lu,* 1685: 71a.

Discussion of cosmology served as a prelude for explication of the metaphysical foundations of the "mind and nature." Nature, according to Shen Ch'ang-yü, "served as a standard for the mind." The essay then explored how the relation between nature and the mind corroborated the Ch'eng-Chu distinction between the human mind and mind of the Tao. Without the moral categories derived from nature, the mind remained unaffected by its roots in the Supreme Ultimate. The practice of benevolence required "nurturing one's nature" by "having singleness of purpose and holding fast to the mean." Otherwise, Shen concluded, the "human mind" would reign, and one's heavenly nature containing moral principles would be lost. Rhetorically presenting his answer to the Yung-cheng emperor, Shen appealed to the "orthodox studies" (cheng-hsueh 正學) upon which his essay was based.[47]

For the first policy question prepared during the 1737 special examination, which commemorated the recent enthronement of the Ch'ien-lung emperor (r. 1736–95), the examiners repeated almost verbatim earlier questions dealing with correspondences between the doctrines of "orthodox statecraft" (chih-t'ung, i.e., "political legitimacy") and "orthodox transmission of the Way" (tao-t'ung, i.e., "cultural legitimacy"), which correlated with the distinction between "methods of governance" (chih-fa 治法) and "methods of the mind" (hsin-fa 心法). Claiming that these concepts together formed the "unified Way" of governance, the examiners asked candidates to demonstrate their understanding of the Ch'eng-Chu agenda for "mental discipline" (hsin-fa) and "singleness of purpose and holding to the mean," which derived from the distinction between the mind of Tao and human mind.[48]

Ho Ch'i-jui 何其睿 from Chiang-hsi, who finished sixth on the palace examination, prepared an answer that was selected as the best essay for this policy question. Although Ho was ranked first on the metropolitan examination, the Ch'ien-lung emperor, exercising his imperial prerogative, later had him demoted to the top of the second tier of graduates after the palace examination was held. Understandably, Ho's essay recapitulated the orthodox bifurcation between threatening human desires and saving moral principles derived from heaven. The Ch'eng-Chu program for mental discipline required allegiance to the doctrine of the mean and to the "esoteric words and great meanings" bequeathed by the sages. Mind and body correlated with the Tao and governance (身心無二法，道治無二統。).[49]

47. *Hui-shih lu,* 1730: 41a–43a.
48. *Hui-shih lu,* 1737: 4a–5a.
49. *Hui-shih lu,* 1737: 40a.

The heart of Ho's essay defended the chief doctrines Chu Hsi had championed in the latter's quest to provide a framework for moral cultivation of the mind of the Tao. "The extension of knowledge" (*chih-chih* 致知) and "residing in seriousness" (*chü-ching* 居敬) are examples of Chu's doctrines that Ho Ch'i-jui covered. According to Ho, the goal Chu had demarcated was to "save people so they could become sages." Sageliness and benevolence went hand in hand in orthodox moral theory. Self-cultivation based on mental discipline was the prerequisite for political order. Such policy answers were also reflections of eight-legged essays that focused on elucidating the passage in the *Documents Classic*: "The human mind is precarious, the mind of Tao is subtle; have absolute refinement and singleness of purpose; hold fast the mean" (人心惟危，道心惟微，惟精惟一，允執厥中), which was used as a quotation for the required classical essay in the 1797 Ho-nan provincial examination.[50]

## The Contested Uniformity of Classical Essays

The student essays examined above demonstrate the overall uniformity of public views that reappeared in the civil service selection process from the late Ming to the mid-Ch'ing. This uniformity contrasted sharply with the diversity of opinions in the private domain of literati debate that had influenced examinations in the sixteenth and seventeenth centuries. During both dynasties, a wide range of scholarly opinions and classical positions were variously defended by literati. In the precincts of the examination system, however, diversity of opinion was for the most part not tolerated, except for periods of literati ferment such as occurred in the sixteenth and late eighteenth centuries. Unintentionally, the Ch'eng-Chu school's appeal to absolute and universal principles provided the Ming and Ch'ing imperiums with a system of theoretical devices, that is, an "ideology," to combat perceived threats to the political and moral status quo by Wang Yang-ming and others.

Chu Hsi's views on the priority of public values over private interests dovetailed in theoretical terms with his negative view of factional alignments in politics. The ideal of personal behavior and political action reduced to the same formula: affirm the public-minded principles of the mind of the Tao and oppose the selfish tendencies of the human mind. To join a political faction was to follow one's personal interests, which would in the end be based on one's selfish desires. A faction or party conformed to the wayward tendencies of the "human mind"—in this case a

50. *Hui-shih lu*, 1737: 38a–40a. See also *Ho-nan hsiang-shih lu* 河南鄉試錄 (Record of the Ho-nan provincial examination), 1798: 31b–34a.

number of human minds horizontally joined together—against the universal standards of the mind of the Tao, exemplified hierarchically by a steadfast minister who served the emperor with unswerving loyalty.[51]

As Chapter 9 reveals, however, the distance between official orthodoxy tested in civil examinations and research findings in Ch'ing dynasty classical and historical studies began to widen so much in the seventeenth and eighteenth centuries that the controversy over Sung Learning versus Han Learning as competing classical orthodoxies began to affect the questions and answers administered in the provincial and metropolitan examinations. Sagehood in light of Ch'eng-Chu learning might remain an orthodox ideal in eight-legged essays, but among empirically minded evidential research scholars, the Sung and Ming classical program for self-cultivation was increasingly deemed naive and impractical.

## EXAMINER STANDARDS
## AND THE TYPOLOGY OF POLICY QUESTIONS

As we have seen above, one of the major problems in evaluating policy questions prepared by examiners for the provincial and metropolitan examinations during the Ming and Ch'ing was their obvious subordination to the eight-legged essays on the Four Books required for session one of the tests. Such subordination has led historians to overlook the importance of policy questions and to miss the long-term evolution of such questions from the Former Han dynasty to the end of the civil examinations in 1905. Policy questions should be evaluated over this historical continuum of two millennia. Study of examination essays that began in the Sung or the eight-legged essay grid that lasted just over four hundred years is insufficient to elucidate the full examination curriculum.

Historically, the study of policy questions clarifies the intellectual vicissitudes between late imperial Chinese examinations and those from the early and middle empires (addressed in Chapter 1). Policy questions during the late empire frequently did not involve current government "policy." Instead, such questions were often defined by examiners according to issues drawn from the Classics and the Dynastic Histories that shed light on classical learning, literary matters, nonphilosophical issues, and

---

51. *Chu-tzu ta-ch'üan*, 11.9b–10a, 12.4b, and 12.8b. The early *Tao-hsueh* movement had some characteristics of a horizontal peer group association of like-minded gentry and was condemned by its opponents for such behavior. Yet Chu Hsi's own theories were later appropriated against forms of gentry solidarity he himself had engaged in, but had never legitimated in his political theories. See James T. C. Liu, "How Did a Neo-Confucian School Become the Imperial Orthodoxy," pp. 483–505.

practical affairs (*ching-shih shih-wu ts'e* 經史時務策).[52] The policy answers of
an influential Former Han erudite, Tung Chung-shu, for example, also
became stylistically praised and emulated. During the Ming, for instance,
T'ang Shun-chih 唐順之 (1507–60), a leading literary stylist, included
Tung's policy answers as model essays of "ancient-style prose" in T'ang's
literary compilation known as the *Wen-pien* 文編 (Compilation of essays).[53]

Consequently, in addition to their content, policy essays, like eight-
legged essays, were valued during the Ming for their aesthetic and literary
standards. In fact, Tung's Han policy essays were the lead writings that
T'ang chose for his volume, not contemporary examination essays (*shih-
wen* 時文). The policy question thus has survived since the Han as a measure of talent in the selection process, even if it was made subordinate to
the eight-legged essay for final rankings in late imperial times. Particularly
heralded have been the policy answers prepared by the *optimus, secundus,*
and *tertius* for the triennial palace examinations, which are included in
many Ming and Ch'ing dynasty collections.[54] In addition to the policy
question on the palace examination, candidates were required to answer
five policy questions during the third session of both the provincial and
the metropolitan examinations. Perhaps the most famous single policy
essay ever written in Chinese history was the answer, 10,000 characters
(actually about 9,600 characters) long, composed by the celebrated
Southern Sung loyalist Wen T'ien-hsiang in the 1256 palace examination
(see Chapter 1). Wen's essay was written when the Southern Sung capital
of Hang-chou was increasingly threatened by the Mongol invasion of
south China, explaining perhaps why the emperor's question was on *Tao-
hsueh* views of eternity rather than the present.[55]

Beginning in the Yuan dynasty, when poetry and rhyme-prose were
partially eliminated from the civil examinations because of their alleged

52. On the historical importance of policy questions see *Ch'ang-t'an*, pp. 21–24.

53. T'ang Shun-chih's *Wen-pien* was included in the 1780s in the *Ssu-k'u ch'üan-shu* 四庫
全書 (Complete Collection of the Four Treasuries) (reprint, Taipei: Commercial Press),
1377/101–117.

54. See, for example, *Huang-Ming chuang-yuan ch'üan-ts'e, Chuang-yuan ts'e,* 1733 Huai-te-
t'ang edition; and *Chuang-yuan ts'e,* Chia-ch'ing edition. Many modern collections are now
also available. See, for example, *Li-tai chin-tien tien-shih ting-chia chu-chüan.*

55. See the 1522 edition of the *Pao-yu ssu-nien teng-k'o-lu* 寶祐四年登科錄 (Record of the
ascension to *chin-shih* rank on the 1256 palace civil examination), pp. 1a–7a, 104a–129b. An
incomplete version of the answer appears in *Nan-Sung teng-k'o-lu liang-chung* 南宋登科錄兩種
(Two types of records of ascension to the *chin-shih* degree in the Southern Sung) (reprint,
Taipei: Wen-hai Press, 1981), pp. 301–49. Wen's answer has been reproduced in many
Ming-Ch'ing collectanea and in the *Ssu-k'u ch'üan-shu*. For an account of his career, see *Sung
li-k'o chuang-yuan lu* 宋歷科狀元錄 (Record of *optimi* from palace examinations of the Sung),
compiled by Chu Hsi-chao 朱希召, Ming edition (reprint, Taipei: Wen-hai Press), 8.10a–15b.

frivolity (see Chapter 1), essays on the Four Books and Five Classics became the mainstay of the late imperial examinations to test classical models for world-ordering. The policy question was retained to test "classical and historical knowledge to be applied in contemporary affairs."[56] Although subordinate to questions on the Four Books and Five Classics over the long run, policy questions were frequently deemed essential and thus were highly prized by examiners and scholars as markers of the confluence between classical theory and practical affairs.

The prestige of policy questions increased during the late Ming Chia-ching (1522–66) and Wan-li (1573–1619) reigns, when policy answers often reached over 3,500 characters in length.[57] During this period, two compilations of outstanding policy questions and answers were undertaken. The first, completed in 1604, was entitled *Huang-Ming ts'e-heng* 皇明策衡 (Balancing of civil policy examination essays during the Ming dynasty).[58] Arranged by reign period and topic, it contained samples of metropolitan and provincial policy questions between 1504 and 1604. The collection was enlarged in 1633 to include questions from sessions two and three of the civil examinations from 1504 to 1631 under the title *Huang-Ming hsiang-hui-shih erh-san-ch'ang ch'eng-wen hsuan* 皇明鄉會試二三場程文選 (Selection of model examination essays from the second and third sessions of the provincial and metropolitan civil examinations during the Ming dynasty).[59]

Usually the metropolitan examination policy questions were chosen by the emperor, although by Ch'ing times Hanlin examination officials generally sent a list of topics to the ruler and asked him to circle the topics he wanted on the provincial and metropolitan examinations.[60] The palace

56. Yuan dynasty policy questions can be found in Huang Chin 黃溍, *Chin-hua Huang hsien-sheng wen-chi* 金華黃先生文集 (Collected essays of Huang Chin from Chin-hua) (Shanghai: Commercial Press, *Ssu-pu ts'ung-k'an*, 1919–37), pp. 191–200. Early Ming policy questions prepared by Su Po-heng 蘇伯衡 (1329–92?) in 1385 can be found in *Huang-Ming wen-heng* 皇明文衡 (Balancing of essays from the Ming dynasty) (Shanghai: Commercial Press, *Ssu-pu ts'ung-k'an*, 1919–1937), 23.220–222. See also the 1370–71 provincial, metropolitan, and palace policy answers by the first Ming *optimus* Wu Po-tsung (see Chapter 1) in the *Ssu-k'u ch'üan-shu*, 1233/217–236.

57. For examples, see *Chü-yeh cheng-shih* 舉業正式 (Correct models for examinations), Chia-ching edition, pp. 1a–58b, which gives examples from 1529–53 policy questions; and *Ming Wan-li chih Ch'ung-chen chien hsiang-shih-lu hui-shih-lu hui-chi* 明萬曆至崇禎間鄉試錄會試錄彙集 (Digest of provincial and metropolitan civil examination records from the Wan-li and Ch'ung-chen reigns of the Ming dynasty), late Ming edition.

58. *Huang-Ming ts'e-heng.*

59. *Huang-Ming hsiang-hui-shih erh-san-ch'ang ch'eng-wen hsuan,* compiled by Ch'en Jen-hsi 陳仁錫 1633 *Pai-sung-t'ang* edition.

60. See the memorial composed in 1757, 10th month, 6th day, by the Grand Secretary Ch'en Shih-kuan 陳世倌 (1680–1758), requesting the Ch'ien-lung emperor to choose the

policy question was by then also broken down into four separate topics. In addition to composing the palace examination policy question, Ming and Ch'ing emperors as a rule read the top ten policy essays on the palace examination and determined their final rankings, leaving the rest in the second and third tier to be ranked by the palace readers.[61] Often, however, Ch'ing emperors read only the top three papers on the palace examination.[62]

During the early reigns of the Ch'ing dynasty, Manchu emperors continually criticized examiners and candidates alike for relegating policy questions to relative obscurity. As Chapter 10 relates, the Yung-cheng and Ch'ien-lung emperors frequently lamented the overly literary focus in examination essays and tried to encourage attention to more practical matters.[63] In fact, a review of the 1760 provincial examinations by the Hanlin Academy revealed that in Shan-hsi the examiners had not even graded the policy questions from session three. The academicians speculated that other provinces might be guilty of similar lapses.[64]

Such concerns were transmitted by examiners in the examinations themselves. The Hanlin academician Wu Sheng-ch'in 吳省欽 (1729–1803), for instance, headed the staffs of several provincial examinations during the Ch'ien-lung reign. In 1771 he prepared a policy question for the Hu-pei provincial examination in which he asked candidates to review the history of policy questions on civil examinations and to assess the length of such questions. How examiners were using policy questions to reflect their

policy question topics for the *Wu hui-shih* 武會試 (Metropolitan military examination), in the Ch'ing dynasty examination materials from the Ming-Ch'ing Archives, Academia Sinica, Taiwan. Emperors as a rule were too busy to formulate their own questions; in some cases formulating a long classical question may have been beyond their intellectual reach.

61. See the memorial composed in 1757, 5th month, 9th day, by the Grand Secretary Lai-pao 來保, requesting the Ch'ien-lung emperor to rank the top ten policy essays for the palace examination (*tien-shih* 殿試), in the Ming-Ch'ing Archives, Academia Sinica, Taiwan. See the similar request in 1768, 7th month, 26th day, by the chief minister of rites Kuan-pao 觀保 (d. 1776), in *Li-pu t'i-pen*.

62. See the 1775, 4th month, memorial by the palace examination reader, which indicates the change, in the Ming-Ch'ing Archives, Academia Sinica, Taiwan. On the four parts of an imperial policy question for the palace examination, see the 220 palace examination papers from 1646 to 1904, in the Han Yü-shan Collection, in the UCLA Department of Special Collections. Professor Hanchao Lu helped me classify the four parts of each Ch'ing palace examination in the collection.

63. See *Ch'in-ting mo-k'an t'iao-li*, 2.7b–13b, and 2.21b–25a.

64. See the 1760, 10th month, 15th day, report by the Hanlin Academy, in *Li-pu t'i-pen*, which indicates that only the eight-legged essays on session one were graded in Shan-hsi province that year.

own views was becoming problematic, and attention no longer focused on the poor quality of the graduates' answers alone.[65]

Many officials were upset that policy questions set by the examiners were frequently over 300 characters in length, while the policy answers, because they mattered less in the final rankings, were not much longer. Indeed, some argued that the examiners were merely prompting the candidates to parrot the examiners' views. This was called "repeating familiar questions" (*shu-hsi t'i* 熟習題) and "asking a question and answering it" (*tzu-wen tzu-ta* 自問自答).[66] To keep the answers from becoming shorter than the questions, a requirement was added in 1786 that the minimum length of a policy answer had to be 300 characters (see Chapter 10). In the eighteenth century, policy questions became a bone of contention between the court and its Hanlin examiners. The court feared unauthorized policy questions, while the examiners tried to impress candidates with their classical and historical erudition and thereby influence classical and literary taste.

The decline in importance of policy questions during the Ming and Ch'ing dynasties curiously was compensated for when examiners used the third session of both provincial and metropolitan civil examinations as an opportunity to express their own views in a series of relatively long essay questions on a wide range of classical, historical, and practical topics. For our purposes, the examiners' questions represent important cultural artifacts that are as interesting historically as the candidates' answers. As answers by candidates grew shorter, the examiners' policy questions grew in length. In sessions one and two, examiners selected only classical quotations for candidates to write essays about. The policy questions permitted examiners to lead candidates into a variety of directions, and these questions tell us a great deal about examiner intellectual concerns and changing historical contexts.

Fortunately, complete records exist that allow us to reconstruct the range of policy questions prepared by examiners in Ying-t'ien prefecture during the Ming dynasty and in Che-chiang province during the Ch'ing dynasty. For Ying-t'ien provincial examinations, there are complete records covering questions for forty-seven provincial examinations over the 126 years from 1474 to 1600, and for Che-chiang provincial examinations, complete lists of policy questions for ninety-two examinations covering 213

65. See Wu Shen-ch'in, "Ch'ien-lung san-shih-liu nien Hu-pei hsiang-shih ts'e-wen erh shou" 乾隆三十六年湖北鄉試策問二首 (Two policy questions from the 1771 Hu-pei provincial examination), in *Ch'ing-tai ch'ien-ch'i chiao-yü lun-chu hsuan,* 3/167.

66. See Wejen Chang, "Legal Education in Ch'ing China," pp. 294–95, 234–35n17–20.

years from 1646 to 1859. The range and probability of policy questions during the Ming and Ch'ing in these two southern regions are summarized in Tables 8.5 and 8.6.

These results can be read in different ways, but they reveal a number of historical trends. First, classical studies increased in frequency (from 4.3% to 14.1%) and in probability (from 19.4% to 63.7%) as policy questions from the Ming to the Ch'ing, ranking seventh overall in Ming Ying-t'ien and first in Ch'ing Che-chiang. Slipping noticeably in frequency of occurrence and probability from the Ming to the Ch'ing were questions concerning "Tao Learning," which moved from second to sixth. By the eighteenth century, both classical and historical studies had eclipsed *Tao-hsueh* as topics for policy questions, a finding that is not surprising considering the popularity of Han Learning and *k'ao-cheng* 考證 ("evidential research") during the Ch'ien-lung (1736–95) and Chia-ch'ing (1796–1820) reigns.[67]

Second, questions on history in the third session moved from thirteenth in frequency (2.6%) and probability (11.8%) in Ying-t'ien during the Ming dynasty to fifth in Che-chiang (7.4% in frequency; 33.4% probability) during the Ch'ing. Moreover, 73% of the history questions on the Che-chiang examinations were prepared from 1777 on, thus confirming the late-eighteenth-century rise in popularity of historical studies among scholars (see Chapter 9). In other words, of the thirty-three policy questions devoted to history in the Che-chiang examinations for which we have records during the Ch'ing dynasty, only nine were asked between 1646 and 1777; twenty-four were asked between 1777 and 1859, when the records stop because of the Taiping Rebellion. Indeed, history questions rank a close second in frequency, after classical studies, for the period 1777–1859.

Third, policy questions on natural studies in the civil examinations moved from eleventh in frequency (3%) in Ying-t'ien during the Ming dynasty to a much lower rank (below the top fifteen, only 0.9% of all policy questions) in Che-chiang during the Ch'ing. Clearly, the frequency and probability of questions dealing with the natural world declined markedly from the Ming to the Ch'ing, suggesting that the usual image of the seventeenth century in China as a time when through Jesuit influence Chinese literati became more interested in the European sciences and their own native traditions in the Chinese sciences has been overdrawn and is not reflected here (see Chapter 9).

This change from Ming to Ch'ing was not a matter of changing monarchic tastes. The K'ang-hsi emperor (r. 1662–1722), for example, was enthusiastic about natural studies and mathematics. Considering his fasci-

67. See my "The Unravelling of Neo-Confucianism," pp. 67–89.

nation with Jesuit science and the fact that he strongly encouraged scholars close to him to study the technical fields of astronomy and mathematics associated with what the Jesuits called in Chinese *ko-chih-hsueh* 格致學 (*scientia*), it is peculiar that these developments had little impact on civil examinations. We shall explore this puzzle further in Chapter 9.[68]

These initial findings should be qualified, however, by two caveats: (1) we have complete evidence from only two adjacent provinces in the Yangtzu delta and (2) we are considering only the questions given on the third and last session of the provincial examinations. Regarding the first caveat: even if Chiang-su (where Ying-t'ien was located) and Che-chiang provinces may not be representative of all other provinces, they are representative of the wealthiest provinces in south and southeast China, such as Fu-chien and Kuang-tung. There the frequency of elite families possessing the financial and cultural resources required to prepare students for the civil examinations far exceeded provinces in north China and elsewhere.

Concerning the second caveat: bear in mind that from 1475 on, policy questions were unquestionably considered less important than the eight-legged essays on the Four Books for the provincial and metropolitan civil examinations. During the late Ming, such essays were usually 500 characters in length, increasing to 700 and then 800 in the Ch'ing, while the length of policy answers declined. Consequently, even as the nature of the policy questions on session three changed, Tao Learning remained the core curriculum of the first session. Both examiners and students knew very well that questions on the first session were the key to the final ranking of graduates. Examiners framed long policy questions to express their views and to solicit opinion about problems of the day (see Chapter 10).

Even with these important caveats in mind, we can see that Table 8.7, which gives the range and frequency of policy questions during the Ch'ien-lung emperor's efforts to revive the civil examination standing of the third session in the 1750s and 1760s (see Chapter 10), reveals a general pattern that is repeated in Table 8.8, dealing with late Ch'ing policy questions. In general, questions on political economy, classical studies, literature, geography, and history became the top five questions in the mid-Ch'ien-lung period.

The scholar-official and Han Learning advocate Sun Hsing-yen 孫星衍 (1753–1818), for example, recommended early in the nineteenth century that the five topics for provincial and metropolitan policy questions be set

68. See Catherine Jami, "Learning Mathematical Sciences during the Early and Mid-Ch'ing," in Elman and Woodside, eds., *Education and Society in Late Imperial China, 1600–1900*, pp. 223–56; and Willard Peterson, "Fang I-chih: Western Learning and the 'Investigation of Things,'" in William Theodore de Bary et al., *The Unfolding of Neo-Confucianism* (New York: Columbia University Press, 1975), pp. 399–400.

so that "practical learning" (*shih-hsueh* 實學), a code for "evidential research" in the late eighteenth century, would prevail among degree candidates. Sun advocated a series of policy questions that would stress literati techniques for governance (*ju-shu* 儒術), classical studies, ancient pre-Han learning (*chu-tzu pai-chia* 諸子百家), local geography, and material resources.[69] By the nineteenth century, the evolution of policy questions, both in terms of format and content, had a fluid but still discernible pattern.

Table 8.8 (based on a study of nineteenth-century provincial examinations held in the No. 1 Historical Archives in Beijing and the Ming-Ch'ing Archives in Academia Sinica, Taipei) shows that for nine provinces in 1840 and for fifteen in 1849 the most frequent policy questions prepared by examiners generally followed the frequencies and probabilities outlined in Tables 8.6 and 8.7. Based on these results, we can arrive at the following arrangement for the five policy questions on provincial examinations in the late Ch'ing: (1) classical studies 經學, (2) historical studies 史學, (3) literature 詩文, (4) institutions and economy 法度理材, and (5) local geography 地理. This is not to say that the order was obligatory, or that these five types of questions were always included, but a reading of nineteenth-century provincial policy questions and answers shows these terms and this order to be generally in use.

Overall, during the Ming and Ch'ing, questions on learning, statecraft, and world-ordering remained the most common policy questions when measured in terms of the changing frequencies of policy questions. Moreover, institutional questions remained a dominant concern among examiners preparing the policy questions for session three. And with hindsight we know that Han Learning classicism was destined to surpass the Sung Learning focus on "Tao Learning" as the dominant scholarly discourse in the late Ch'ing, which was also reflected in changes in the late Ch'ing examination curriculum.

Turning now to actual policy questions and answers concerning *k'ao-chü* 考據 (lit., "learning based on what can be ascertained") on the provincial examinations in Ming China, we shall investigate the importance of this new field of study for Ming candidates preparing for the civil examinations. As the next chapter shows, such changes in the fields of learning, when tested as policy questions, affected historical and natural studies; the result was an increased probability of history and a decrease in frequency of astronomy and calendrical studies in policy questions during the Ch'ing.

69. See Sun Hsing-yen, "Kuan-feng shih-shih ts'e-wen wu-t'iao yu-hsu" 觀風試士策問 五條有序 (Preface for observations on trends in five policy questions for testing literati), in *Ch'ing-tai ch'ien-ch'i chiao-yü lun-chu hsuan,* 3/285–86.

## *K'AO-CHÜ-HSUEH* AND THE USE OF EVIDENCE IN MING POLICY QUESTIONS

Investigation of Ming policy questions suggests that the conceptual roots of Ch'ing dynasty "evidential research" (*k'ao-cheng-hsueh* 考證學) as a formal category of learning began in the mid-Ming, and that earlier efforts to date its beginnings to the seventeenth-century Ming-Ch'ing transition are unsatisfactory.[70] Adam Schorr's recent study of Yang Shen's 楊慎 (1488–1559) scholarship demonstrates that earlier claims for the Ming-Ch'ing roots of *k'ao-cheng* discourse are overstated and teleological.[71] Yü Ying-shih's 余英時 long-standing claim that the turn toward precise philology in classical studies can be traced to sixteenth-century debates surrounding the Old Text version of the *Great Learning* (*Ta-hsueh ku-pen* 大學古本), which Wang Yang-ming restored to contest Chu Hsi's "externalist" views of the "investigation of things" (*ko-wu* 格物) in the Four Books, deserves follow-up.[72]

Since the mid-Ming, examiners had been using the term *k'ao-chü-hsueh* 考據學 to mean "learning based on what can be ascertained" and to describe a field of learning requiring evidence in the policy questions on provincial and metropolitan civil examinations. As early as the 1445 civil metropolitan examination, for instance, examiners used the term to describe the fifth policy answer, which dealt with the issue of selecting talented men as officials. Ma Yü 馬愉 (1395–1447), a Hanlin lecturer then serving as one of the chief examiners, evaluated (*p'i* 批) the best answer

70. See, for example, Chow, *The Rise of Confucian Ritualism in Late Imperial China*, pp. 15–43, for an account of the late Ming genesis of Han Learning based on what Chow calls "ritualist ethics." See also Huang Chin-shing, *Philosophy, Philology, and Politics in Eighteenth-Century China*, pp. 32–46, which deals with Wang Yang-ming's impact and shows the limitations in Chow's reading of late Ming evidential scholarship. More recently, however, Chow has maintained that late Ming printing and its production of "interpretive frenzy and confusion" touched off the *k'ao-cheng* movement. See Chow, "Writing for Success," p. 46. On Ming evidential research, see Lin Ch'ing-chang 林慶彰, *Ming-tai k'ao-cheng-hsueh yen-chiu* 明代考證學研究 (Study of Ming dynasty evidential research) (Taipei: Student Bookstore, 1984).

71. See Schorr, "The Trap of Words," passim. See also Schorr, "Connoisseurship and the Defense against Vulgarity: Yang Shen (1488–1559) and His Work," *Monumenta Serica* 41 (1993): 89–128.

72. See Yü Ying-shih, "Some Preliminary Observations on the Rise of Ch'ing Confucian Intellectualism," p. 125, for discussion of Wang Yang-ming's critique of Chu Hsi's elucidation of the *Great Learning*, which created a textual crisis in the sixteenth century that Yü links to the emergence of evidential research in the late Ming. On the debate over the authenticity of new versions of the *Great Learning* in the late Ming, see Lin Ch'ing-chang, *Ch'ing-ch'u te ch'ün-ching pien-wei hsueh*, pp. 369–86. Cf. Rusk, "Chen Que (1604–77) and the *Critique of the Great Learning*," pp. 46–60.

for the fifth policy question, which was written by Li Yung-hsiu 李庸脩 from Chiang-hsi province. Li finished thirteenth on the metropolitan examination and twenty-fourth on the palace. Ma wrote in the official report: "This policy answer contains learning based on what can be ascertained; it is very good at answering what was asked for; this is a literatus who deliberates."[73]

For the 1465 Shan-tung examination, provincial examiners used *k'ao-chü* to describe the first policy answer prepared by the *chieh-yuan* Wang Lun, whose eight-legged essay on benevolence was discussed above. The associate examiner Lo Hsuan 羅絢, an education official serving in Hu-kuang who had received his *chü-jen* degree in 1453 from Chiang-hsi province, evaluated the answer on penal law: "learning based on what can be ascertained that is detailed and clear (考據詳明); replied to each item in the question very well; suitable to be placed at the top rank." On session one, Wang Lun had written a model essay on Ch'eng-Chu learning. For session three, he was equally adept at what the Ming examiners called *k'ao-chü*.[74]

In the Kuang-hsi provincial examination of 1471, *k'ao-chü* was a guidepost for the evaluations of both documentary and policy questions. The best memorial, in which the candidates were asked to write a memorial of thanks (*hsieh-piao* 謝表) in the name of Ou-yang Hsiu serving in the Sung Ministry of Punishments, was prepared by Huang Chin 黃晉, who finished thirty-second out of fifty-five graduates. The associate examiner, Tung Chueh 董珏, a 1450 *chü-jen* from Che-chiang serving as an education official in Fu-chien, wrote about Huang's memorial that "the memorial shows learning based on what can be ascertained" (表有考據).[75]

Four of the five policy answers selected in 1471 as the best essays were evaluated in light of *k'ao-chü* criteria. In each case the Kuang-hsi examiners stressed that the best answers were based on research and careful sifting of information. The five questions were drawn from a variety of fields: (1) the works of Ming emperors on governance, (2) literati officials, (3) local geography, (4) mind and nature (*hsin-hsing* 心性), and (5) the monetary system (*ch'ien-fa* 錢法).[76] All but the fourth, which stressed Tao Learning, were consciously referred to in light of "learning based on what can be ascertained." On the first, an essay by Ch'in Wu 秦武, who finished fourth, the examiner Shan Kao 單睾, a *chü-jen* education official from Kuang-tung, wrote: "This policy answer shows learning based on what

73. *Hui-shih lu*, 1445: 1/347–49, 438–41, in *Ming-tai teng-ko-lu hui-pien*.
74. *Shan-tung hsiang-shih lu*, 1465: 2/771–76.
75. *Kuang-hsi hsiang-shih lu*, 1471: 3/1097–98, in *Ming-tai teng-k'o-lu hui-pien*.
76. Ibid., 3/1033–42.

can be ascertained; it can be lauded!" On the second, the examiners Yuan Ching 袁敬 and Chang Hsuan 張瑄, both *chü-jen* education officials (Yuan in Hu-kuang, Chang in Che-chiang), wrote lengthy evaluations of Li Teng's 李澄 (Li finished as *chieh-yuan*) policy answer:[77]

*Yuan:* For the policy question on literati trends, all the candidates got it right here but missed it there; only this essay shows learning based on what can be ascertained; the words cover institutions in a fine essay; it is suitable as a model answer.

*Chang:* This policy question was asked to evaluate precisely the mind-heart of the literati. This essay is an example of learning based on what can be ascertained that is detailed and clear; its arguments are orthodox and accurate (考據詳明，議論正當); it is good at showing the greater meaning of the question.

On the third policy question, the examiner Tung Chueh wrote of the essay on local geography by the number-two-ranked *chü-jen* Wang Shih 王時: "This policy answer is clear in its use of evidence (考據明白); its words and style are so straightforward as if the writer bows before earlier examples of orthodoxy in the temple. How can we not respect it?"[78] Monetary policy as a statecraft issue on policy questions was a significant example of *k'ao-chü* on the 1471 Kuang-hsi provincial examination. The three examiners who evaluated the best essay by Kuo Hung 郭弘 (fifth in rank) clearly outlined the practical and institutional aspects of Kuo's answer:[79]

*Wu Hsiang* 鄔祥 (Hu-kuang education official): Those who answered this policy question for the most part had views that merely skimmed the surface and revealed nothing; only this answer's learning based on what can be ascertained was focused and detailed (考據精詳); it was good at reviewing institutions; a scholar who has sincerity.

*Chang Hsuan:* In researching the ancient monetary system (考究古之錢法) and in tracing the successes and failures of reform efforts (沿革得失), every knot in the argument is clear; the arrangement is suitable; an answer to select.

*Shan Kao:* On this question dealing with monetary policy, the candidates in the session were mostly baffled by it; only this essay could examine antiquity as the standard for the present (考古准今) and trace the

77. Ibid., 3/1107.
78. Ibid., 3/1111–12.
79. Ibid., 3/1120–21.

reason why [ancient monetary policies] had not been revived; an especially accurate answer.

In the 1475 metropolitan examination, the chief examiners Hsu P'u 徐浦 (1428–99) and Ch'iu Chün 丘濬 (1421–95), both Hanlin academicians, used *k'ao-chü* to classify the five policy questions they had chosen for the proceedings. The five topics chosen in 1475 were: (1) rulers and officials (*chün-ch'en* 君臣), (2) human nature (*hsing* 性), (3) resources (*li-ts'ai yung-ren* 理材用人), (4) customs (*feng-su* 風俗), and (5) geography (*ti-li* 地理). In his evaluation remarks (*p'i* 批) for the best answer to the second policy question by Wang Ao, who finished first on the metropolitan and second on the palace examination and became one of the most distinguished officials of his day (see Chapter 7), Hsu P'u noted: "The five policy questions are divided between *k'ao-chü* and judgments of institutional history (有考據有斷制). The question on nature allows us to see how profound [Wang Ao's] understanding of *li-hsueh* is."[80]

Similarly, Ch'iu Chün's comments for the best answer to the third policy question by Hsieh Ch'ien 謝遷 (1450–1531), who finished as the *optimus* on the palace examination, ahead of Wang Ao, stressed that Hsieh's essay on material and human resources "comprehended ancient learning" (*t'ung ku-hsueh* 通古學) and revealed him as "a talent who exhibits evidence and practice" (*yu-chü yu-yung chih ts'ai* 有據有用之才).[81] Ch'iu's official career and his influential writings on statecraft also influenced literati learning in the fifteenth century, which was beginning to reassess the *Tao-hsueh* classical learning exalted since the Yung-lo reign (see Chapter 2).[82]

In 1508 the policy questions in metropolitan examinations were again appraised according to the standards of *k'ao-chü*. The second policy question on civil and military institutions and the fifth on practical statecraft (*shih-wu ts'e ching-shih chih hsueh* 時務策經世之學) were evaluated according to evidence and practical information. In his comments on the best answer to the fifth policy question by Chiang Hsiao 江曉 (1482–1553), who finished fourth on the metropolitan and ninth on the palace examination, the associate examiner Lin T'ing-ang 林庭㭿 (1472–1541) wrote in the final report: "In each of the papers on the five policy questions by this candidate there were usually one thousand graphs. Over and over the essays left nothing out. They contained more than enough learning based

---

80. *Hui-shih lu*, 1475: 9b–17b, and 48b.
81. Ibid., p. 53a.
82. See Hung-lam Chu, "Ch'iu Chün (1421–95) and the 'Ta-hsueh yen-i pu': Statecraft Thought in Fifteenth-Century China" (Ph.D. diss., Princeton University, East Asian Studies, 1983), pp. 225–28. See also Chu's "Intellectual Trends in the Fifteenth Century," *Ming Studies* 27 (1989): 1–16.

on what can be ascertained, judgments of institutional history, and rhetorical phrases that flowed copiously. We see that this student has stored a wealth [of knowledge] that is profound."[83]

This sixteenth-century trend can also be documented empirewide for the 1519 provincial examination in Shan-tung; the 1520, 1544, and 1619 metropolitan examinations in Peking; the 1522 and 1540 Ying-t'ien provincial examinations in Nanking; the 1528 Che-chiang provincial examination; the 1537 Shan-hsi provincial examination; the 1552 provincial examination in Fu-chien; and the 1558 Che-chiang provincial examination.[84] In many of these examination proceedings, the telling phrases "learning based on what can be ascertained that is detailed and clear" (考據詳明) or "learning based on what can be ascertained that is focused and detailed" (考據精詳) became the Ming civil examiner's formulas to explain to the court and the candidates the merits of the best policy essay on the topic.

A final example showing the scope of k'ao-chü in Ming policy questions comes from the 1535 metropolitan examination, in which the distinguished Ch'ang-chou literatus Hsueh Ying-ch'i 薛應旂 (1500–73?) took his chin-shih degree in the third tier of palace examination graduates, even though he had ranked second on the metropolitan. Although one of Hsueh's eight-legged essays was singled out as the best of its kind on a quotation from the Mencius, and another was chosen a model essay on a quotation from the Poetry Classic,[85] Ying-ch'i was versatile enough as a scholar to have his policy essay on paleography (wen-tzu-hsueh 文字學) selected as the best answer to the third policy question. Because paleography, along with etymology (hsun-ku-hsueh 訓詁學) and ancient phonology (ku-yin-hsueh 古音學), became the three major fields in Ch'ing dynasty evidential research, it is worth looking at this Ming dynasty question on paleography to appraise

83. *Hui-shih lu,* 1508: 43b, 57a.

84. *Shan-tung hsiang-shih lu,* 1519: 6/2957, 2965, in *Ming-tai teng-k'o-lu hui-pien. Hui-shih lu,* 1520: 50b, and 1544: 49b, 53a (see also the *Hui-shih lu,* 1619: 73a–b, in *Ming Wan-li chih Ch'ung-chen chien hsiang-shih lu hui-shih lu hui-chi). Ying-t'ien fu hsiang-shih lu,* 1522: 6/3391, 3401, and 1540: 9/4974, both in *Ming-tai teng-k'o-lu hui-pien. Che-chiang hsiang-shih lu,* 1528: 7/3585, 3605, in *Ming-tai teng-k'o-lu hui-pien. Shan-hsi hsiang-shih lu,* 1537, in the Rare Books Collection of the Fu Ssu-nien Library, Academia Sinica, Taiwan. *Fu-chien hsiang-shih lu,* 1552: 12/6126, 6142, in *Ming-tai teng-k'o-lu hui-pien. Che-chiang hsiang-shih lu,* 1558: 13a–14a. The examiner's comments in this last examination used the phrase *yu so k'ao-cheng* 有所考證 (contains evidential research, lit., "the search for evidence"). *K'ao-cheng* replaced *k'ao-chü* as the most common term for evidential studies during the Ch'ing dynasty, although both were interchangeable in the Ch'ing. See, for example, Hamaguchi Fujio, *Shindai kokyogaku no shisō shi teki kenkyū;* and Kinoshita Tetsuya, *Shindai koshōgaku to sono jidai.*

85. *Hui-shih lu,* 1535: 4b–6b, 14b–16b.

the nature of *k'ao-chü-hsueh* in Ming civil examinations and its difference from Ch'ing "evidential research."[86]

The four other topics chosen for the 1535 policy questions were: (1) heavenly admonishments (*t'ien-chieh* 天戒), (2) social rules and political regulations (*chi-kang* 紀綱), (3) astronomy officials (*hsing-kuan* 星官), and (4) resources and taxes (*ts'ai-fu* 財賦).[87] Again the main distinction in the five policy questions was between those that stressed the history of institutions and those that stressed practical knowledge (*shih-wu* 時務) based on *k'ao-chü* and statecraft (*ching-chi* 經濟). In their policy question on paleography, the examiners described the Classics as the repository of the statecraft ideals of the ancient emperors and kings (六經萬古帝王經世之典). They asked the candidates to distinguish the transmission of the Classics from higher antiquity to middle antiquity and the written forms that were then used. The question assumed that the "return to the beginning" (*huan ch'i ch'u* 還其初) of the written forms of the Classics would enable literati to "restore antiquity" (*fu-ku* 復古).[88]

In his model policy answer, Hsueh Ying-ch'i was able to associate different calligraphic styles with the different ages of antiquity, although his answer had an uninformed aspect (tadpole script did not come before large seal script) when compared with Ch'ing paleography. In higher antiquity, according to Hsueh, characters had looked like tadpoles (*k'o-tou* 蝌蚪). In middle antiquity, the written forms of characters had evolved into large seal (*ta-chuan* 大篆) characters, which by the time the Classics had taken form in the Han dynasty were written down in "old text" (*ku-wen* 古文), or clerical-style script (*li-shu* 隸書). To recover the ancient forms, Hsueh contended, Hsu Shen's pioneering paleographic dictionary, the *Shuo-wen chieh-tzu* (see Chapter 5), was essential. The six rules of character formation that Hsu Shen had elaborated were the keys to fathoming the textual history of the Classics.[89]

This technical discussion, based probably on earlier discussions of paleography included in Ming encyclopedias, was needed, Hsueh argued, in order for literati of the sixteenth century to comprehend how the history of calligraphy enabled them to unravel the history of the Classics and, by extension, their original content and the original intentions of the sage-kings who had authored them. Hsueh concluded: "People all rely on the Classics to seek the Way. Writing must be linked to antiquity in order to provide proof for the present (*cheng-chin* 證今), and paleography can corroborate that. If the paleography is correct, then we need not worry about

---

86. See my *From Philosophy to Philology*, pp. 165–66.
87. *Hui-shih lu*, 1535: 9a–13b.
88. Ibid., 11a–12a.
89. Ibid., 46a–48a.

the techniques in the Classics remaining unclear. If those techniques are clear, then we need not worry that the Way and morality remain disunified. If the Way and morality are unified, then customs will be solidified." Paleography was a form of statecraft, according to Hsueh Ying-ch'i.[90]

The seven examiners who commented on Hsueh's model answer were unanimous in their assessment that Ying-ch'i's essay demonstrated his "intent to restore antiquity" (*yu chih hu fu-ku che i* 有志乎復古者矣). The associate examiner Chou Wen-chu 周文燭, a Hanlin academician and *chin-shih* of 1526 from Che-chiang, made explicit the link between the question on paleography and a sixteenth-century Ming notion of "evidence": "This candidate is really able to focus his mind on the paleography of the ancients. He is able to bring learning based on what can be ascertained to bear on each item of the answer. Hasn't he practiced the [calligraphic] arts and gotten to the heart of things!"[91] Little did the examiners know that Hsueh, like many others, had rehearsed answering such questions on the role of ancient-style script in the evolution of the Classics in practice examinations at his lineage school in Wu-chin county.[92]

Similar philological concerns were also raised in 1537 when Hsueh Ying-ch'i, then serving as magistrate in Tz'u-ch'i 慈谿 county near Ning-po prefecture, Che-chiang, was assigned to help supervise the Fu-chien provincial examination. One of the policy questions that Hsueh prepared for that civil examination focused on the textual issues needed to grasp the transmission of the Classics since the Ch'in dynasty's (221–207 B.C.) infamous "burning of the books." How, Hsueh asked the candidates, could one unravel the authenticity of the Classics under such circumstances? The forms of writing were again made the vehicle to "restore the past."[93] Here we can observe how the assignment of examiners could influence the content of the civil examinations, a trend that was repeated in the Ch'ing dynasty during the eighteenth century (see Chapter 9).[94]

By 1500, then, we can demarcate a clear standard of *k'ao-chü-hsueh* in Ming civil examinations, which was regularly employed by examiners in the provincial and metropolitan examinations to grade policy questions.[95]

90. Ibid., 49a.

91. Ibid., 45a–b.

92. Hsueh Ying-ch'i, *Fang-shan hsien-sheng wen-lu* 方山先生文錄 (Recorded writings of Hsueh Ying-ch'i), Su-chou edition (1553), 20.12a–15b.

93. Ibid., 20.16b–21a.

94. Hsueh Ying-ch'i, for example, also supervised the 1552 Che-chiang provincial examination.

95. See also the *Shan-tung hsiang-shih lu,* 1489: 3/1460, 1478, for two policy questions evaluated according to the standards of *k'ao-chü;* and *Hu-kuang hsiang-shih lu,* 1489: 3/1628. Both are in the *Ming-tai teng-k'o lu hui-pien.*

Such classical standards deployed in session three paralleled the literary criteria used to rank eight-legged essays in session one (see Chapter 7). Although the third session was less important than the first in the final rankings of candidates, as the detailed comments of Ming examiners show, the policy questions were taken seriously and were an integral part of civil examination rankings. Policy questions were important enough in mid-Ming examinations to be equated with "ancient-style prose" (*ku-wen* 古文) essays in Sung examinations, and late Ming policy answers were at times over 1,500 characters long. Some essays in late Ming collections of model policy answers are over 3,000 characters long.[96]

These Ming forms of *kao-chü* research standards for policy questions can be compared fruitfully to the linguistic self-consciousness of "evidential," *k'ao-cheng* 考證 evaluation in the tacit standards used by the *Ssu-k'u ch'üan-shu* 四庫全書 (Complete collection of the four treasuries) editors to evaluate works turned in to the commission in the 1770s and 1780s for possible inclusion in the Imperial Library. Their criteria for evaluation of classical scholarship were based on the proper use of sources and verification, stress on precise scholarship, and deployment of philological methods. To be labeled "worthy of consideration as a work in evidential research" (*k'ao-cheng chih tzu* 考證之資) meant that the *Ssu-k'u ch'üan-shu* editors were pleased to include the work in the Imperial Library.[97]

There were important differences between Ming *k'ao-chü*, which after all remained secondary to Ch'eng-Chu moral philosophy, and Ch'ing *k'ao-cheng*, which challenged Tao Learning as the model for classical learning. Perhaps the most obvious aspect in Ming times was the tie between state-craft and evidential studies. *K'ao-chü* in the Ming did not yet refer specifically to philology or textual studies, which would be the focus of *k'ao-cheng* in the Ch'ing. The textual focus on paleography in Ming policy questions, for example, placed classical philology within the context of statecraft studies.

In the Ming view of the place of textual studies in *k'ao-chü* research, writing—that is, the changing forms of characters as analyzed in the *Shuo-wen chieh-tzu* dictionary—was the key to research on the past (*k'ao-ku* 考古).[98] This Ming textual stress on written characters was at times also

96. The *Ming Wan-li chih Ch'ung-chen chien hsiang-shih lu hui-shih lu hui-chi* contains civil examinations from 1595 to 1628. See, for example, Ch'ien Ch'ien-i's policy answer on human and material resources (用人理材) from the 1606 Ying-t'ien provincial examination, which is included in the collection. We have noted above how *ts'e* 策 were collected in late Ming publications for wider dissemination.

97. See my *From Philosophy to Philology*, pp. 65–66.

98. See also the policy question and answer on paleography in the 1561 provincial examination in Ying-t'ien, which is included in the *Huang-Ming ts'e-heng*, 1.48–53a.

complemented by the use of etymology (*hsun-ku*) to trace the meanings of characters over time. What was new in Ch'ing *k'ao-cheng*, however, was the discovery that the classification of the changing sounds, especially in poetic rhymes, of written characters was most reliable for reconstructing the ancient meanings of classical writings.

Emergence of ancient phonology as a discrete textual field began in the late Ming, to be sure, but the field matured and prospered in the eighteenth century to become the queen of evidential studies, with paleography and etymology downgraded as ancillary disciplines.[99] Ming policy questions rarely broached ancient phonology as a classical discipline; when the subject of sound was raised, it was quickly skimmed over to focus on writing. In Ch'ing policy questions, phonology was the more common topic, although when the Old versus New Text (*chin-wen ku-wen* 今文古文) debate peaked in the nineteenth century, paleography returned to prominence in classical studies.[100] Nevertheless, the role of *k'ao-chü* as a standard of evaluation in Ming policy questions represented the first stage of the penetration of specialized knowledge in the civil examinations and later was called evidential research.

The next chapter traces the evolution of policy questions in late imperial civil examinations, complementing the discussion of the eight-legged essay. As we shall see, the fields of knowledge tested in the policy questions underwent changes reflective of larger changes in literati concerns from the Ming to the Ch'ing. The fields of history, natural studies, and evidential studies evolved in ways that reveal how pervasive the shift from Sung Learning to Han Learning among literati elites in the eighteenth and nineteenth centuries really was. As before, the court and the bureaucracy managed to keep up with the times and incorporated the views and interests of the dynasty's leading elites.

99. See my *From Philosophy to Philology*, pp. 216–21. Cf. Hamaguchi Fujio, *Shindai kokyo-gaku no shisō shi teki kenkyū*, pp. 175–217, for how phonology correlated to paleography.

100. See my *Classicism, Politics, and Kinship*, pp. xxv–xxx, 188–203.

# CHAPTER NINE

# Natural Studies, History, and Han Learning in Civil Examinations

Both the Ming and Ch'ing dynasties encouraged the widespread publication and circulation of acceptable materials dealing with the Four Books, Five Classics, and Dynastic Histories because the latter were the basis of the civil service curriculum and literati learning throughout the empire. During all of the Ming and Ch'ing dynasties, classically literate Chinese read or had ready access to the literati canon.[1] As we saw in Chapter 8, in the discussion of policy questions on session three, the scholarly orientation of Ming and Ch'ing examiners toward classical studies underwent an interesting change, with an increasing focus on *k'ao-chü* essays for the best policy answers.

This chapter reveals that literati fields of learning in late imperial China, such as natural studies and history, were also represented in late imperial civil examinations. Such inclusion reflected the influence of both the imperial court, which for political reasons could widen or limit the scope of policy questions on provincial and metropolitan examinations, and the literati examiners assigned to supervise the examination halls, whose classical knowledge echoed the intellectual trends of their time. Examination topics were not fully representative of literati scholarship in any particular period, but they did represent the standards used by examiners at a particular examination site at a particular time. Such "local knowledge," when repeated in several provincial examinations and in the capital, was usually tied to changes in literati opinion over time. The per-

---

1. Perhaps more Han elites read the Classics than literate Europeans had access to the Bible's Old and New Testaments. Cf. Stephen Ozment, *The Age of Reform, 1250–1550* (New Haven: Yale University Press, 1980), p. 202; and my *From Philosophy to Philology*, pp. 140–69.

sonal interests of individual examiners mattered, as the case of the rise of Han Learning in civil examinations clearly demonstrates.

In the late eighteenth century, the examination curriculum started to conform with Han Learning and evidential research currents popular among southern literati during the Ch'ien-lung and Chia-ch'ing reigns. The scope and content of the policy questions on session three increasingly reflected the academic inroads of Ming and Ch'ing classical scholarship among examiners. The Ch'eng-Chu orthodoxy was increasingly subjected to careful textual scrutiny and precise scholarship.[2] The tension between Tao Learning and Han Learning yielded competing constituencies in the examination regime, which the court tried to ameliorate in the eighteenth and nineteenth centuries.

## NATURAL STUDIES IN MING POLICY QUESTIONS

One of the most common generalizations scholars make about the role of science in late imperial China is that studies of astronomy and mathematics were in steady decline there until the arrival of Jesuit missionaries in the sixteenth century.[3] When Matteo Ricci (1552–1610), founder of the first Catholic missions in China, described the scientific prowess of the Chinese, he noted that they "have not only made considerable progress in moral philosophy but in astronomy and in many branches of mathematics as well. At one time they were quite proficient in arithmetic and geometry, but in the study and teaching of these branches of learning they labored with more or less confusion." Arguing that some of their knowledge of mathematics was derived from the Saracens, Ricci described Chinese imperial schools for mathematics and the Nanking observatory. However, Ricci concluded:

> It is evident to everyone here that no one will labor to attain proficiency in mathematics or in medicine who has any hope of becoming prominent in the field of philosophy. The result is that scarcely anyone devotes himself to

2. See my *From Philosophy to Philology,* pp. 57–85.

3. Keizō Hashimoto, *Hsu Kuang-ch'i and Astronomical Reform* (Osaka: Kansai University Press, 1988), p. 17. Most policy question "topics" discussed in this section are based on actual Chinese categories. I have added the category of "natural studies," i.e., *ko-chih-hsueh* 格致 學, which is based on combining "astrology," "calendrical studies," and "mathematical harmonics." See Tables 8.5 and 8.6. For discussion of the "quantitative" and "qualitative" sciences in imperial China, see Nathan Sivin, "Introduction," in Sivin, ed., *Science and Technology in East Asia* (New York: Science History Publications, 1977), pp. xii–xiii. According to Sivin, although there was no unified notion of "science" in imperial China, calendrical studies and mathematical harmonics were "quantitative" in nature, while the related field of astrology was qualitative.

these studies, unless he is deterred from the pursuit of what are considered to be the higher studies, either by reason of family affairs or by mediocrity of talent. The study of mathematics and that of medicine are held in low esteem, because they are not fostered by honors as is the study of philosophy, to which students are attracted by the hope of the glory and the rewards attached to it. This may be readily seen in the interest taken in the study of moral philosophy. The man who is promoted to the higher degrees in this field, prides himself on the fact that he has in truth attained to the pinnacle of Chinese happiness.[4]

Chinese mathematics and astronomy, according to this view, had reached their pinnacle of success during the Sung and Yuan dynasties but had declined precipitously during the Ming.[5] This long-standing perspective has been challenged by recent studies that indicate that mathematics and calendar reform were important concerns among Ming literati before the arrival of the Jesuits in China.[6] Moreover, Nathan Sivin has demonstrated that the Jesuits consciously misrepresented their knowledge of contemporary European astronomy to suit their religious objectives in Ming China. Such self-serving tactics, which produced contradictory information about new trends in European astronomy, lessened their success among late Ming literati in transmitting the European sciences to late imperial China.[7] From this new perspective, late Ming scholars were not lifted out of their scientific "decline" by their contact via the Jesuits with European astronomy. Rather, they themselves reevaluated their astronomical legacy, successfully taking into account pertinent features of the European sciences introduced by the Jesuits.[8]

4. *China in the Sixteenth Century: The Journals of Matteo Ricci: 1583–1610*, translated into Latin by Father Nicolas Trigault and into English by Louis J. Gallagher, S.J. (New York: Random House, 1953), pp. 31–33.

5. For the conventional perspective, see Needham, *Science and Civilisation in China*, vol. 3, pp. 173, 209; and Ho Peng Yoke, *Li, Qi, and Shu: An Introduction to Science and Civilization in China* (Hong Kong: Hong Kong University Press, 1985), p. 169.

6. See Hart, "Proof, Propaganda, and Patronage," passim. See also Willard Peterson, "Calendar Reform Prior to the Arrival of Missionaries at the Ming Court," *Ming Studies* 21 (1986): 45–61; and my *Classicism, Politics, and Kinship*, pp. 78–79. The latter discusses the calendrical interests of T'ang Shun-chih 唐順之 (1507–60) and his efforts to reintegrate calendrical studies with literati learning in the mid-sixteenth century.

7. Sivin, "Copernicus in China," in *Colloquia Copernica II: Études sur l'audience de la théorie héliocentrique* (Warsaw: Union Internationale d'Histoire et Philosophie des Sciences, 1973), pp. 63–114.

8. Jacques Gernet, *China and the Christian Impact*, translated by Janet Lloyd (Cambridge: Cambridge University Press, 1985), pp. 15–24. See also Sivin's "Wang Hsi-shan (1628–1682)," in *Dictionary of Scientific Biography*, vol. 14 (New York: Scribner's Sons, 1970–78), pp. 159–68.

Views that Ming literati, unlike their Sung and Yuan predecessors, were participants in a strictly humanist civilization whose elite participants were trapped in a literary ideal that eschewed interest in the natural world have been common since the Jesuits.[9] Historians have typically appealed for corroboration to the imperial civil examination system. Matteo Ricci, for example, wrote:

> In concluding this account of degrees awarded among the Chinese, the following should not be omitted, which to Europeans might seem to be a rather strange and perhaps a somewhat inefficient method. The judges and the proctors of all examinations, whether they be in military science, in mathematics, or in medicine, and particularly so with examinations in philosophy, are always chosen from the senate of philosophy, nor is ever a military expert, a mathematician, or a medical doctor added to their number. The wisdom of those who excel in the profession of ethics is held in such high esteem that they would seem to be competent to express a proper judgment on any subject, though it be far afield from their own particular profession.[10]

Catholic scholars were acutely aware of the role played by political and social institutions in Chinese cultural matters, and the Jesuits realized that the civil service recruitment system achieved for Ming education a degree of standardization and importance unprecedented by early modern European standards.[11] Later Europeans would seek to emulate the Chinese civil examinations.[12]

The examination ethos carried over for a time into the domains of medicine, law, fiscal policy, and military affairs during the Northern Sung dynasty. For example, Shen Kua 沈括 (1031–95) wrote that during the Huang-yu reign (1049–53) civil examination candidates were asked to prepare essays on astronomical instruments. The essays were so confused

9. See Michael Adas, *Machines as the Measure of Men: Science, Technology, and Ideologies of Western Dominance* (Ithaca: Cornell University Press, 1989), pp. 41–68, 79–95.

10. Ricci, *China in the Sixteenth Century*, p. 41.

11. Donald F. Lach, *China in the Eyes of Europe: The Sixteenth Century* (Chicago: Phoenix Books, 1968), pp. 780–83, 804.

12. Cf. Kiyosi Yabuuti, "Chinese Astronomy: Development and Limiting Factors," in Shigeru Nakayama and Nathan Sivin, eds., *Chinese Science: Explorations of an Ancient Tradition* (Cambridge: MIT Press, 1973), pp. 98–99. See also George H. Dunne, S.J., *Generation of Giants: The Story of the Jesuits in China in the Last Decades of the Ming Dynasty* (Notre Dame: University of Notre Dame Press, 1962), pp. 129–30; and Elman and Woodside, eds., *Education and Society in Late Imperial China, 1600–1900*, passim. On the Chinese system's role in the origin of European civil service examinations, see Ssu-yü Teng, "China's Examination System and the West," in Harley Farnsworth, ed., *China* (Berkeley: University of California Press, 1946), pp. 441–51.

about the celestial sphere, however, and the examiners were themselves so ignorant of the subject, that all candidates were passed with distinction.[13] After the Southern Sung dynasty, only military examinations remained institutional fixtures parallel to the civil service.[14] According to this view, Ming civil examinations had in effect refocused elite attention on a Tao Learning curriculum stressing moral philosophy and literary values (see Chapter 2) and away from earlier more specialized or technical studies. Conventional scholarship still contends that technical fields such as law, medicine, and mathematics, common in T'ang and Sung examinations, were not replicated in Ming examinations.[15]

Such assessments are generally correct in the broad strokes they paint of literati intellectual life after 1400. Chapter 1 pointed out, for example, that when faced with foreign rule (first under the Mongols and later briefly under the Manchus), significant numbers of literati, in addition to the usual number of those who failed in the biennial and triennial competitions, did turn to occupations outside the civil service such as medicine. In the eighteenth and nineteenth centuries, when demographic pressure meant that even provincial and metropolitan examination graduates were not likely to receive official appointments, many literati turned to teaching and scholarship as alternative careers. But, as Chapter 6 indicated, Ming examiners used policy questions on natural events and anomalies to keep the widespread penetration of popular religion and the mantic arts among examination candidates out of politics.[16]

### Ming Interest in Natural Studies

Careful scrutiny of the Ming dynasty civil examination records that survive in archives and libraries in China, Taiwan, and Japan reveals that

13. See Needham, *Science and Civilisation in China*, vol. 3, p. 192. My thanks to David Schaberg for this information.

14. See Joseph Needham, "China and the Origins of Qualifying Examinations in Medicine," in Needham, *Clerks and Craftsmen in China and the West* (Cambridge: Cambridge University Press, 1970), pp. 379–95; Hartwell, "Financial Expertise, Examinations, and the Formulation of Economic Policy in Northern Sung China," pp. 281–314; McKnight, "Mandarins as Legal Experts," pp. 493–516.

15. See, however, Chang Hung-sheng, "Ch'ing-tai i-kuan k'ao-shih chi t'i-li," pp. 95–96, on Ch'ing examinations to choose a limited number of medical officials, which were based on Ming precedents. See also Liang Chün 梁峻, *Chung-kuo ku-tai i-cheng shih lueh* 中國古代醫政史略 (Historical summary of medicine and government in ancient China) (Huhehot: Inner Mongolia People's Press, 1995).

16. Hymes, "Not Quite Gentlemen?" pp. 11–85; Jonathan Spence, *To Change China: Western Advisers in China, 1620–1960* (Middlesex: Penguin Books, 1980); and Levenson, "The Amateur Ideal in Ming and Early Ch'ing Society," pp. 320–41. See also my *From Philosophy to Philology*, pp. 67–137.

the examinations themselves actually tested the candidates' knowledge of astronomy, the calendar, and other aspects of the natural world that we call the "Chinese sciences" (*tzu-jan chih hsueh* 自然之學) today.[17] "Natural studies" in China had since the Yuan dynasty often been classified under the term *ko-chih* 格致 (lit., "inquiring into and extending knowledge"), a term that was retained until its replacement by *k'o-hsueh* 科學 as "modern science" in the early twentieth century.[18] Early Jesuit translations of Aristotle's theory of the four elements (*K'ung-chi ko-chih* 空際格致, 1633) and Agricola's *De Re Metallica* (*K'un-yü ko-chih* 崑崙格致, 1640) into classical Chinese, for example, had used the term *ko-chih* 格致 as a general word for the Latin *scientia* in their titles.[19]

Such titles suggest our image of literati intellectual life before the arrival of the Jesuits has been one-sided.[20] The preeminent position of the Four Books and Five Classics was left unchallenged in the orthodox curriculum, but Ming candidates for both the provincial and metropolitan examinations, unlike their Sung counterparts, were expected to grasp many of the technicalities of the calendar, astronomy, and music. Indeed, during the Sung, T'ang and Sung works on mathematics and astrology had been banned from publication for security reasons. Only dynastic specialists working on the calendar in the astronomy bureau were allowed such knowledge, even though in practice popularly printed calendars and almanacs were widely available.[21]

In the early Ming, for example, the Yung-lo emperor put calendrical and practical studies near the top of what counted for official, literati scholarship. He ordered Hsieh Chin (see Chapter 2), the chief examiner

17. Nathan Sivin, "Introduction," in Sivin, ed., *Science and Technology in East Asia*, pp. xi–xv. See also Sivin, "Max Weber, Joseph Needham, Benjamin Nelson: The Question of Chinese Science," in E. Victor Walter, ed., *Civilizations East and West: A Memorial Volume for Benjamin Nelson* (Atlantic Highlands, N.J.: Humanities Press, 1985), p. 45.

18. See, for example, the Yuan work on medicine by Chu Chen-heng 朱震亨 (1282–1358) entitled *Ko-chih yü-lun* 格致餘論 (Views on extending medical knowledge), in the *Ssu-ku ch'üan-shu*, vol. 746–637. Angela Leung, in her article "Transmission of Medical Knowledge from the Sung to the Ming," paper presented at the Song-Yuan-Ming Transitions Conference (Lake Arrowhead, Calif., June 5–11, 1997), p. 10, notes that Chu opposed Sung medical prescriptions.

19. See Pan Jixing, "The Spread of Georgius Agricola's *De Re Metallica* in Late Ming China," *T'oung Pao* 57 (1991): 108–18; and James Reardon-Anderson, *The Study of Change: Chemistry in China, 1840–1949* (Cambridge: Cambridge University Press, 1991), pp. 30–36, 82–88.

20. See Roger Hart, "Local Knowledges, Local Contexts: Mathematics in Yuan and Ming China," paper presented at the Song-Yuan-Ming Transitions Conference (Lake Arrowhead, Calif., June 5–11, 1997).

21. See Lucille Chia, "*Mashaben*," pp. 4–5.

for the 1404 metropolitan examination (on which 472 graduates drawn from over 1,000 candidates were selected and appointed to high offices) to include questions that tested a candidate's "broad learning" (*po-hsueh* 博學). Hsieh selected policy questions (*ts'e* 策) dealing with astronomy, law, medicine, ritual, music, and institutions, and the emperor was especially pleased with the top policy answer that year. More important, the emperor had legitimated "natural studies." Thereafter, such questions regularly appeared on Ming civil examinations.[22]

During the Ming dynasty, then, although the perennial relationship between classical and historical studies remained the most important consideration among literati, the importance of "natural studies" as part of the "broad learning" required of an official also received imperial support. The demarcation between the universality of classical studies and specialization in practical studies was not called into question, however. Astronomy and calendrical studies, nevertheless, successfully penetrated the Ming imperial civil service in that they were required periodically as policy questions on session three of the provincial and metropolitan examinations.

In Chapter 2 we saw that, in general, most Ming provincial and metropolitan candidates, usually around 60% to 65%, chose to specialize on either the *Change Classic* (30–35%) or the *Poetry Classic* (30%). Only around 20% chose the *Documents Classic,* and only 6% to 7% usually selected the *Spring and Autumn Annals* or the *Record of Rites* for their specialization. If we include the *Change Classic* as a possible source for questions dealing with the cosmology of "natural studies," then the frequency of some questions dealing with some aspect of the "natural world" on session one of the civil examinations was also fairly high. One should not overstate this aspect of the classical essay on the *Change Classic,* however, because such compositions remained literary in form and were measured by the eight-legged "grid," and not *ko-chih.*

To understand the full range of influence natural studies had on the civil examinations, we must consider the role of examinations in creating a broad class of classically literate and historically knowledgeable males that encompassed all who competed in the selection process, including the failures. We can assume that the ratio of 25% for graduates choosing for their specialization classical historical texts that contained information on astronomy and the calendar (the *Documents Classic* or the *Annals*) and another 30% choosing the *Change Classic,* with its cosmological passages, roughly held for those who failed the examination.

22. See *Huang-Ming san-yuan k'ao,* 2.3b; and *Chuang-yuan ts'e,* 1733 *Huai-te-t'ang* edition, "Tsung-k'ao" 總考 (General overview), p. 15a. For the political background to the 1404 examination, see Chapter 2.

This assumption is strengthened by the fact that in provincial and metropolitan examinations all candidates were divided equally into wards according to the Classic chosen for specialization. During the Ming in 1580 and 1583, Ku Yen-wu tells us there were eighteen wards: five each for the *Change* and *Poetry*, four for the *Documents*, and two each for the *Annals* and *Rites*.[23] In the Ch'ing, until the specialization requirement was dropped in 1787, usually five or six wards of students specialized on the *Change*, four wards on the *Documents*, five or six wards on the *Poetry*, and one ward each on the *Annals* and *Rites* Classics.[24] Thus, the historical Classics constituted during the late Ming 33% and during the Ch'ing 28% to 31% of the total number of wards in the examinations. The *Change* had 28% to 33% of all wards (see also Chapter 4).

We can extrapolate that every three years in late Ming Ying-t'ien prefecture, for example, about 1,250 to 1,875 candidates chose either the *Documents* or *Annals* for their specialization for the triennial tests. About the same number chose the *Change*. Similarly, for Ch'ing Chiang-nan in the seventeenth and eighteenth centuries, 2,500 to 4,250 candidates chose historical Classics to specialize on, and a similar number probably chose the *Change*. Given the magnitude of population growth from the late Ming to Ch'ing, we see that examination rules and quotas influenced a growing number of students to study important aspects of natural studies in the historical Classics and the *Change Classic* to prepare for the seventeen triennial provincial tests. Again, caution is needed, because such awareness was not really a sign of increased interest in *ko-chih*. Nor can we demonstrate that candidates who prepared eight-legged essays on the *Change* knew much more than the most perfunctory aspects of ancient cosmology as filtered through the required Sung Tao Learning commentaries.

What we can surmise, nevertheless, is that candidates for the provincial examinations during the Ming dynasty could reasonably expect a required policy question on astronomy, for instance. During any cycle of triennial provincial examinations, a large number of the 50,000 to over 75,000 candidates empirewide probably were prepared to answer them (see Table 8.5), although we usually only have the best answers. In the Ch'ing, curiously, the likelihood of such policy questions was negligible (see Table 8.6), as candidates increasingly had to answer questions dealing with textual issues growing out of the evidential research studies that peaked in the late eighteenth century. It should be added, however, that the ability

---

23. See Ku Yen-wu, "Shih-pa-fang" 十八房 (The 18 examination wards), in *Jih-chih lu chi-shih*, 16.382–83.

24. See *Chin-shih san-tai lü-li pien-lan* 進士三代履歷便覽 (Overview by region of backgrounds to three generations of civil *chin-shih* graduates from 1646 to 1721), n.d.

to deal with astronomical, medical, mathematical, and other technical questions was an essential tool of the new classical studies emerging in the late Ming and early Ch'ing. It just was not tested in the Ch'ing civil service before 1860.[25] Below I give a sequence of questions and answers from Ming civil examinations to explain what happened in practice in policy questions on natural studies.

### Calendrical Studies

For the 1525 Chiang-hsi provincial examination, one of the policy questions prepared by the examiners dealt with "calendrical methods" (*li-fa* 曆法). In the first part of their question, the examiners asked the candidates for the *chü-jen* degree to elaborate on the methods employed by the ancients to order the calendar, which they noted "had been the immediate priority of all ancient kings and emperors in bringing order to the empire."[26] Next the examiners noted that the astronomical systems established by the Han, T'ang, and Sung dynasties all followed the precedent of the Triple Concordance system (*San-t'ung li* 三統曆) of 104 B.C. in basing computation on a Day Divisor (*jih-fa* 日法) and Accumulated Years (*chi-nien* 積年) counted from a set epoch. They asked: (1) Why did the calendar frequently have to be revised? (2) Why did the current system introduce an Annual Difference (*sui-ch'a* 歲差) constant in addition to the old method of periodically inserting extra lunar months? And (3) why was the current system, which employed no epoch, accurate enough to have been used for two centuries without revision?

To answer these questions one needed a sound knowledge of both mathematical astronomy and its history, which was available to candidates in the Dynastic Histories, particularly those of the Chin and Yuan dynasties, and statecraft-oriented encyclopedias. The point was: when the Triple Concordance system adopted a Day Divisor of 81, which amounted to setting the length of a lunar month as 29 43/81 days, and counted Accumulated Days from an epoch 143,727 years in the past, it was inevitable that the small discrepancy in the constant of 29.53086 minus the modern value of 29.53059 days, which equaled an error of only one

25. See Yuan-ling Chao, "Medicine and Society in Late Imperial China: A Study of Physicians in Suzhou" (Ph.D. diss., UCLA, History, 1995); and Chu Ping-yi, "Technical Knowledge, Cultural Practices and Social Boundaries." Cf. my *From Philosophy to Philology*, pp. 61–64, 79–85, 180–84.

26. *Huang-Ming ts'e-heng*, 1.19a. A similar policy question and answer on the calendar appeared on the 1594 Kuei-chou provincial examination. See *Huang-Ming ts'e-heng*, 4.32a. My thanks to Nathan Sivin for his guidance on the technical aspects of this question and answer.

day per 310 years, would accumulate over such a great span of time to become appreciable.[27]

Succeeding computational systems simply adjusted the Day Divisor and Accumulated Days without realizing that they unavoidably led to errors. Finally, the Yuan Season-Granting system (*Shou-shih li* 授時曆), which the Ming's Great Concordance system (*Ta-t'ung li* 大統曆) closely followed, rejected this approach entirely. The Triple Concordance system and its successors had been improved upon in the *Shou-shih* calendar developed in 1280 during the Yuan dynasty by Kuo Shou-ching 郭守敬 (1231–1316) to give more precise measurements of the length of a solar year. The Yuan system adopted precise decimal constants and counted from the solstice of December 1279 rather than an ancient epoch. Without the earlier sources of error, revision of the system became unnecessary.

The Annual Difference was a constant used to compensate for the slight difference between the tropical or "solar" year (the time it takes the sun moving along the ecliptic to pass the same point twice, for instance, the interval between two winter solstices) and the sidereal year (the time it takes for the sun to line up twice with the same star, related to the celestial equator). Functionally (but only functionally), the Annual Difference corresponds to the precession of the equinoxes in Western astronomy. It first appeared in the Yuan system because the latter used what roughly amounts to spherical trigonometry, and thus had to deal in new ways with the discrepancy between motion along the equator and that along the ecliptic of the celestial sphere.

Candidates were then reminded that the celestial orbits were invisible and could be known only through phenomena such as conjunctions of the sun and moon, and asked a fourth part of the policy question: Why do solar eclipses recorded in the *Documents Classic*, the *Poetry Classic*, and *Spring and Autumn Annals* occur only on the first day of the month (by definition, the day of conjunction), while those set down from the Han dynasty on sometimes fall on the last day of the month? Records of eclipses not on the first day, despite the impression the examiners gave, did not postdate the Han, and many such records in Han sources refer to pre-Han eclipses. The reason is, first, that times associated with records in the Classics were not precise and, second, that until the Han neither observation nor calculation could yield precise timings of either conjunctions (the true new moon) or eclipses.

The fifth part of the policy question had to do with various proposals to alter the Yuan-Ming system because, like its predecessors, it was bound

27. *Huang-Ming ts'e-heng*, 1.19b–23a. See the detailed explanation in Sivin, "Cosmos and Computation," pp. 1–73, esp. pp. 12, 19. The candidate gave the period from the epoch as 144,511 years, probably due to a difference in endpoint rather than an error.

eventually to show accreted errors. "Of those who have discoursed on the calendar from antiquity to today, some say that there can be a determinate method [that is, a theory]. Some deny it on grounds that all one can do is periodically adduce observations to keep the computational system in accord with the phenomena. But if there actually can be a determinate method, it will always be possible to make predictions on the basis of constants, and techniques of observation to track the orbits are not [comparably] dependable. These arguments are all recorded in historical documents and are open to scrutiny."[28] The question, unlike the preceding four, had no correct answer. But it raised a perennial issue of Chinese astronomy, the tension between prediction based on continual observation, interpolation, and extrapolation, on the one hand, and, on the other, forecasts derived from rigorous mathematical techniques that did not require continual infusions of new data.[29]

One of the answers (by an unknown candidate but one of the highest finishers) focused immediately on the chief theoretical question. His response was impeccable from the literary point of view, formally stereotyped, and astronomically well informed. It is unclear, however, how many other such essays were as knowledgeable. The candidate began with a neat antithesis: Because there has been no change in the sky as we have known it from antiquity on, "I don't believe the declaration that there is no definite method" (曰無一定之法，吾不信也). Because of the undeniable irregularities in the orbital motions of the sun, moon, and planets, "I don't believe the declaration that there is a definite method" (曰有一定之法，吾不信也). He quoted verbatim the early Classics enumerated in the question, with glosses for each difficult word, to summarize what was known about the astronomy of antiquity, and he gave precise Han dynasty values for the Day Divisor and Accumulated Years. He also quoted historical critiques, including a maxim of the astronomer-geographer and classicist Tu Yü 杜預 (222–84): "Creating an astronomical system is a matter of conforming celestial phenomena [lit., 'the sky'] to find what [techniques] accord with them, not forcing accord (wei-ho 為合) so that predictions will be validated [by phenomena]." This exhibition of learning lead him naturally to his answer. "The orbits in the sky are not uniform, but astronomy [between Han and Sung] was restricted to set methods, because they were not aware of 'conforming to the sky to find what accords with it' (shun-t'ien i ch'iu-ho 順天以求合)."[30]

28. *Huang-Ming ts'e-heng*, 1.19a.

29. See the discussion of a particular crisis in Sivin, "Cosmos and Computation," p. 63, which speaks of "a commitment to continued observation, which Chinese calendrical astronomy was dedicated to transcend."

30. For his source see *Yuan-shih*, 52.1130–31, where Yü the Great and his successors are identified as precursors of the Yuan technique.

The answer to the second question is extraordinary in its recall of techniques and its ability to relate them. The response noted that the discrepancy was too small to be noted in antiquity. Although the Season-Granting system was the first to master it, a succession of astronomers from Yü Hsi 虞喜 (ca. A.D. early fourth century) on worked out simple empirical corrections that minimized precessional error. The candidate listed them and accurately summarized the techniques used by each. It took considerable understanding to see that these adjustments anticipated the Annual Difference; the candidate had obviously digested the account in the *Yuan History* of the Season-Granting system's predecessors.[31] He finally gave a succinct account of the Yuan innovation, closing with a literary conceit of his own: "In antiquity there was no intercalation of months until the time of [Emperor] Yao. Once [this practice] was established, the calendrical intervals of the seasons were regularized. In antiquity there was no Annual Difference until the time of Yü Hsi and his colleagues. Once it was established, the anomalous motions of the Seven Governors [the sun, moon, and five planets] became clear. Both [techniques] have become so interdependently useful that neither can be dispensed with."[32]

The combined responses to the third and fourth questions were similar. The author did not delve into principles but rather summarized successive improvements in determining the time of conjunction and eclipse. These improvements had combined with the substitution of true (actual and varying) solar and lunar motions for mean (average) motions to yield precision that could avoid error for more than 150 years. The candidate did not entirely depend on the account in the *Yuan History*, citing changes in the Ming period.[33]

In the final question the candidate made short work of current debates: "In my ignorant opinion, if you have the right people [to manage astronomical computation, discussion of cumulative errors] is permissible; if not, I fear that superficial discussion is best not permitted." Here he explicitly cited Li Ch'ien's 李謙 report included in the *Yuan History*, which made it clear that the Season-Granting system had been meticulously tested against records covering more than two millennia of phenomena and extending even beyond the borders of China. The author concluded, not altogether correctly, that remarks about the limits of its precision must be badly informed. Periodic divergences in the Annual Difference did not compromise the basic reliability of the computational system, so long as errors when no longer negligible were corrected by observation. He even

31. *Huang-Ming ts'e-heng*, 1.21a–21b.
32. Ibid., 1.21a–21b.
33. Ibid., 1.21b–22a.

noted that the refined instruments used in the Yuan calendar reform were fully documented, and could be reconstructed for this purpose (he was unaware that they had in fact been reconstructed in 1421 and were extant).[34] Writing a generation before the arrival of the Jesuits, the candidate recommended reviving the instruments bequeathed to the astronomical bureau since Kuo Shou-ching's reforms of 1280.[35]

This remarkable call for calendar reform and rebuilding instruments some fifty years before the arrival of the Jesuits was just as quickly framed in orthodox Ch'eng-Chu *Tao-hsueh* rhetoric, however. The answer closed with a flourish, a quotation from Chu Hsi that, however irrelevant to mathematical astronomy, moved the focus back to the imperial throne: "The kingly ruler uses his virtue to govern, and uses worthy [subordinates] to get rid of treacherous ones. If he is able to make yang predominant so as to ensure its victory over yin, then the [yin] moon will avoid the [yang] sun, so there can be no eclipses." The candidate conventionally declared that "as a rustic scholar of the lowest sort who has never received transmission from a [qualified] teacher, I merely set out what has been recorded in the Classics and Histories, without daring to assert that it is true."[36]

The candidate's ability to recall technical data from ancient sources and quote them accurately from memory would be impressive in a historian of Chinese astronomy today. In addition, the candidate's appeal to Yuan instrumentation as a corrective measure in the sixteenth century suggests that the policy question had been formulated as a way for the dynasty to get some response about what to do with the Ming Grand Concordance (*Ta-t'ung* 大統) Calendar that was now increasingly out of whack. Accordingly, the candidate argued that the dynasty should rely on expert instrumentation to reform the calendar. Rather than technical manuals, however, the candidate cited dynastic histories as his sources of information, which indicates that what the examiners also expected was knowledge of the role of the calendar in political life and awareness of the difficulties in keeping the official calendar accurate and up-to-date.

And it is clear that the examiners did not grade this essay so high

34. See the illustration of one of them in Sivin, "Science and Medicine in Chinese History," in Paul S. Ropp, ed., *Heritage of China: Contemporary Perspectives on Chinese Civilization* (Berkeley: University of California Press, 1990), pp. 164–96, esp., p. 175; and for a detailed account, P'an Nai 潘鼐, "Nan-ching te liang-t'ai ku-tai ts'e-t'ien i-ch'i—Ming chih hun-i ho chien-i" 南京的兩台古代測天儀器—明制渾儀和簡儀 (Nanking's two ancient instruments for astronomical observation, the armillary sphere and the simplified instrument of the Ming), *Wen-wu* 文物 7 (1975): 84–89.

35. *Huang-Ming ts'e-heng*, 1.23a.

36. Ibid., 1.22b–23a.

solely because of the details in its answers. They were not only astronomically informed but high-minded, unimpeachably orthodox (thus the citation from Chu Hsi), compounded of conventional sentiments culled from broad reading, and estimable for their rhetorical structure and balance. They represented, in other words, astronomical counterparts of what made a good essay on morality or governance. The fact that there were astronomical counterparts adds to the evidence that has been accumulating for decades to prove that the humanistic bias of imperial orthodoxy, as it affected the educations of civil service careerists, did not effectively discourage knowledge of science, medicine, technology, statistics, finance, and so on. To the contrary, passing this 1525 civil examination demanded thorough study and general recall of highly technical material.

### Celestial Counterparts

Next we turn to a representative policy question on "celestial luminaries as counterparts to matters in the human world" (*t'ien-hsiang* 天象) that appeared on the 1561 Che-chiang provincial examination.[37] Initially, the examiners queried candidates about the order given by the sage-king Yao to his ministers Hsi 羲 and Ho 和 to delineate the motion of the sun, moon, planets, and stars and thereby clearly establish the seasons. In later times, the examiners continued, men relied on the celestial counterparts (*hsiang-wei* 象緯) to predict the future. Subsequently, the official post of Grand Historian was established to observe patterns in the heavens (*t'ien-wen* 天文) and record the seasons. The examiners asked why the astrological and political functions of the Grand Historian had been separated.[38]

Again, we do not know the name of the high-ranking candidate whose policy answer was chosen, but what is interesting about the 1561 essay that survives is the equation between astrological "regularities" (*shu* 數) and heavenly principles (*li* 理) that the candidate made in his opening statement: "Regularities capture the wonder of revolving changes [in the heavens]. They are equivalent to principles. That which fathoms the wonder of the changes is the mind. The record of the changes themselves is not [enough]. Principles avail themselves of regularities. The mind is completed in principles."[39]

37. Typically such policy questions were titled "celestial portents" (*t'ien-wen* 天文) when they appeared. See, for example, policy questions from the 1573 Hu-kuang and the 1603 Fu-chien provincial examinations in *Huang-Ming ts'e-heng*, 4.49a, and 21.7a. See also Edward Schafer, *Pacing the Void: T'ang Approaches to the Stars* (Berkeley: University of California Press, 1977), pp. 63ff.

38. *Huang-Ming ts'e-heng*, 2.54a.

39. Ibid., 2.54a–54b.

Correctly citing the "Canon of Yao" (*Yao-tien* 堯典) in the *Documents Classic,* on which the examiners had based their question, the graduate pointed out that the revolutions of the sun, moon, planets, and stars were also dependent on the action of *ch'i.* Only men's mind could penetrate to the principles underlying observed correspondences, because the individual mind was already complete with principles. The Che-chiang graduate's policy answer had accepted the priority of the mind that his famous landsman Wang Yang-ming had preached in the sixteenth century as the central slogan of his philosophy, the phrase "the mind equals principle" (*hsin chi li* 心即理).[40]

The principles of nature (*tzu-jan chih li* 自然之理), according to the answer, were known to the ancients. They thereby understood heaven, bequeathing diagrams in the *Change Classic* for later generations to study. The candidate's paper in essence recapitulated the historical record, best summarized in the *Chin-shu* 金書 (History of the Chin dynasty, 1115–1234), whereby the legendary Fu Hsi 伏羲 had observed the heavenly counterparts and studied their regularity. Similarly, the Yellow Emperor, when he received the "River Chart" (*Ho-t'u* 河圖), found in it celestial counterparts and predicted events based on the position of the stars. The essay thus reproduced the Yuan dynasty narrative of ancient astronomy from Fu Hsi through the ministers of the Hsia, Shang, and Chou dynasties, who had been charged with observing celestial phenomena.[41] The answer then clarified the astronomical bureau's role in previous dynasties and discussed Kuo Shou-ching's tables based on data from the astronomical instruments Kuo had constructed in the thirteenth century.[42]

Next the policy essay turned to the origins of the universe out of the unity of *ch'i* (*i-yuan chih ch'i* 一元之氣). In the "great vacuity" (*t'ai-hsu* 太虛) that existed before the bifurcation of heaven and earth, there was only water and fire. When fire reached its greatest intensity the products were heaven, the sun, stars (including planets), wind, and thunder. When water reached its extreme, mountains, rain, and snow were formed. The visible was composed of *ch'i.* What remained invisible were spirits (*shen* 神). Heavenly principles (*t'ien-li* 天理) were acted on by the forces of yin and yang and produced different densities of *ch'i* in all heavenly and earthly things.

40. Ibid., 2.54b. For discussion, see Willliam Theodore de Bary et al., *Self and Society in Ming Thought* (New York: Columbia University Press, 1970), passim.

41. *Huang-Ming ts'e-heng,* 2.54b–55a. See also Ho Peng Yoke, *The Astronomical Chapters of Chin Shu* (Paris: Mouton, 1966); and summarized in his *Li, Qi, and Shu,* pp. 115–16.

42. *Huang-Ming ts'e-heng,* 2.55a.

The motions of the sun and moon were set in place following regular paths on the celestial sphere. Eclipses resulted whenever their paths crossed. In addition, the policy answer linked the change in seasons to interaction between the sun and moon as they traversed the fixed polestar, the twenty-eight lunar mansions, and the planets.[43] In turn, the answer described the motions of the five planets, focusing on the congruence in the paths of the sun, moon, and Mercury, and the relation between the motions of Mercury and Venus. Venus traversed the heavens yearly by following the sun. It took Mars two years to do the same, Jupiter twelve years, and Saturn twenty-four years. The relative speed of planetary motions was conjoined with the polestar, which was the referent point for measuring the distances of other stars because of its fixed position around which the other stars and planets moved.[44]

According to the essay, ancient officials had recognized the importance of celestial portents for governance. The Hall of Enlightened Rule (*Ming-t'ang* 明堂), a symbol of dynastic legitimacy, and the Spiritual Pavilion (*Ling-t'ai* 靈臺) had been designed as observation sites to view celestial counterparts to events on earth. Through the years, however, the ancient cosmological systems had been lost. Because the theories that the sky had a cover (*kai-t'ien* 蓋天) or that it contained unlimited space (*hsuan-yeh* 宣夜) had not been transmitted in detail, they had little relevance to practical problems in seeking celestial counterparts or revising the calendar. The lack of a definite theory (*ting-lun* 定論) resulted in a fixation on empirical regularities (*ni yü shu* 泥於數) among astrologers in the imperial bureau, who took no account of the principles underlying them (*i ch'i li* 遺其理). "Without the informing power of the mind, how could one grasp the spiritual workings of heaven?" (弗通以心又何足以上達天載之神也), the essay reasoned.[45]

In conclusion, the policy question turned to instrumentation, in particular the armillary sphere. Based on a view of the cosmos as a celestial sphere (*hun-t'ien* 渾天), which became the underlying theory for explanations of celestial motions, such instruments measured the regular movements of the sun, moon, stars, and planets on the sphere. The *hsuan-chi* 璿璣 and *yü-heng* 玉衡 instruments were presented in the policy essay as the tools used by the ancient sage-kings to chart the skies. The essay accepted Later Han dynasty annotations by Ma Jung 馬融 (A.D. 79–166) and others that the *hsuan-chi* was an astronomical instrument improved upon by emperors Yao and Shun that served as a model for the armillary sphere,

---

43. Ibid., 2.55a–56a.
44. Ibid., 2.56a–56b. My thanks to Nathan Sivin for his help on this issue.
45. *Huang-Ming ts'e-heng*, 2.56b–57b.

which the Yellow Emperor and his successors used to determine the calendar.[46]

According to the policy answer, such instrumentation had survived until the Yuan, when Kuo Shou-ching constructed his simplified armillary sphere (*chien-i* 簡儀), hemispherical sundial (*yang-i* 仰儀), and his celestial tables, which improved the precision of astronomical observations and measurements far beyond the existing but dated instruments of antiquity. Such methods were recorded in the *History of the Yuan Dynasty* and had been used until the present, the essay claimed. The Dynastic Histories thus were very important for anyone studying the history of Chinese astronomy or for Ming civil examination candidates answering policy questions such as this one.[47]

Because the Son of Heaven represented the link between heaven and earth, his imperial virtue was reflected in the movements of the sun, moon, planets, and stars. Imperial legitimacy was corroborated by proper grasp of celestial phenomena and their periodic motions. Unpredicted solar and lunar eclipses were thought to be moral reflections of limitations in imperial virtue and penal decisions. Similarly, the five planets influenced the four seasons and, along with the sun and moon, acted as celestial counterparts to the imperial bureaucracy. In a rhetorical flourish that emphasized the role of the mind in comprehending the linkages between heaven and earth, the candidate concluded: "Observing heaven using the mind, observing the mind using the mind of Yao and Shun, this is being good at observing heaven" (觀天而觀之以心，觀心而觀之以堯舜之心，斯其為善觀天者矣).[48]

In addition to covering very capably the technical ground undergirding the Ming dynasty's need to fathom celestial events, the policy answer also had the air of a literati generalist dealing with planetary motion in light of the mind-centered philosophy of Wang Yang-ming. Reference to *hsin-fa* (methods of the mind; see Chapter 2) theory when addressing astronomical issues allowed the author to demonstrate how the Tao Learning doctrines of the *tao-t'ung* (orthodox transmission of the Tao) and *chih-t'ung* (political legitimacy) operated in natural philosophy. Principles took prece-

46. Ibid., 2.56b–58a. On the controversy concerning the *hsuan-chi* as an astronomical instrument, see Christopher Cullen and Anne Farrer, "On the Term *hsuan chi* and the Flanged Trilobate Discs," *Bulletin of the School of Oriental and African Studies* 46, 1 (1983): 52–76, which argues that originally the term *hsuan-chi* had nothing to do with astronomical observation until Han dynasty glosses of a passage in the *Documents Classic*, which claimed that the term *hsuan-chi* referred to an astronomical instrument akin to a circumpolar constellation template and the *yü-heng* either as a sighting tube or a constellation. See also Ho Peng Yoke, *Li, Qi, and Shu*, pp. 117–18.

47. *Huang-Ming ts'e-heng*, 2.58a–58b.

48. Ibid., 2.58a–59b.

dence over observation in framing the rhetoric about heavenly bodies in motion. The essay's successful combination of astronomical knowledge and Tao Learning moral philosophy, despite the classical hierarchy favoring the latter, suggests that both were viewed by the examiners and candidate as overlapping domains.

## Mathematical Harmonics and Musical Theory

Theories about the role and function of music in late imperial China were inseparable from governance. In most dynastic histories, discussions of mathematical harmonics and astronomy were combined because both embodied the same natural principles.[49] Since the early empire of Ch'in and Han, the Office of Music in the Bureau of Weights and Measures had been an essential part of every dynasty's efforts to use court and popular music to enhance public virtue and to set the basis for all official measurements. As a quantifiable discipline, music was defined in light of twelve pitches and their symbolic interpretations, which depended on the use of numbers, measurements, and equations. The court used a single pitch known as the *huang-chung* (黃鐘, lit., "yellow bell") pitch pipe as the official standard for length, volume, and weight measurements. With this standard in hand, the ratios inherent in a pitch series also became a matter of dynastic standardization and regulation.[50]

Mathematical harmonics, in Nathan Sivin's words, "was concerned primarily with number and its application to physical reality." Music as a harmonic system important for imperial governance and official measures, like astrological portents, appeared frequently as a policy question in Ming civil examinations.[51] In the third policy question in the 1567 Ying-t'ien

49. See Needham, *Science and Civilisation in China*, vol. 4, part 1, pp. 126–228; Kenneth DeWoskin, *A Song for One or Two: Music and the Concept of Art in Early China* (Ann Arbor: University of Michigan Center for Chinese Studies, 1982), pp. 29–39; and John Henderson, *The Development and Decline of Chinese Cosmology* (New York: Columbia University Press, 1984), pp. 22–23.

50. Needham, *Science and Civilisation in China*, vol. 4, part 1, pp. 157–76.

51. In addition to the 1567 music question discussed below, see the 1579 policy question on music from the Chiang-hsi provincial examination in *Huang-Ming ts'e-heng*, *chüan* 6; and one from the 1582 Che-chiang provincial examination in *Huang-Ming ts'e-heng*, *chüan* 7. See also Sivin, "Introduction," in Sivin, ed., *Science and Technology in East Asia*, p. xiii; Willy Hartner, "Some Notes on the Chinese Musical Art," in Sivin, ed., *Science and Technology in East Asia*, pp. 32–54; R. H. Van Gulik, *The Lore of the Chinese Lute* (Tokyo: Charles Tuttle Co., 1961), pp. 23–27; and Gene J. Cho, *Lu-Lu: A Study of Its Historical, Acoustical, and Symbolic Signification* (Taipei: Caves Books, 1989), pp. 1–18. The pioneering study remains Joseph Marie Amiot's *Mémoire sur la musique des chinois, tant anciens que modernes*, published in Paris in 1776, which was based on Li Kuang-ti's 李光地 (1642–1718) *Ku yueh-ching chuan* 古樂經傳 (Commentary to the ancient Music Classic).

provincial examination, for example, the chief examiners asked candidates to answer a question dealing with the twelve-pitch musical series (*yueh-lü* 樂律) dating from antiquity.[52] The question presumed technical knowledge of the system of twelve chromatic semitones, that is, the twelve half-steps of the chromatic scale within an octave, that underlay tones in Chinese music.

Because pitch standards were used to define musical tones (and weights and measures) rather than serving as musical notes themselves,[53] the examiners first cited Sung literati who had contended that in using instruments to produce sound, it was the sound that mattered and not the instrument itself. Others had argued that "the difficulty in discerning tones lay not in determining the sound but rather in determining the six yang pitches." "Determination of tone," from this perspective, "also depended on the Yellow Bell [pitch pipe] and not on the six yin pitches." Candidates were asked to reconcile these conflicting positions.[54]

Second, the examiners required students to comment on the various recorded lengths of the Yellow Bell pitch pipe in ancient texts. Over the millennia, just as the dynasties had to clarify the starting point for the calendar, they also had to ascertain the correct length for this standard pitch for use in imperial ritual and orthodox music. Some records measured the Yellow Bell pitch pipe as nine *ts'un* 寸 (inches) long; others described it as three *ts'un* by nine *fen* 分 (one-tenth of a *ts'un*). The determination of the standard pitch had been continuously modified up to the Ming, and the candidates were asked to clarify how one could verify the correct length of the pitch pipe used to produce the Yellow Bell pitch. In addition, candidates were asked to discuss Ts'ai Yuan-ting's 蔡元定 (1135–1198) *Lü-lü hsin-shu* 律呂新書 (New treatise on the twelve-pitch system), which had added six "altered tones" of flat tones and semitones to the original pitch system to resolve inconsistencies and imperfections in earlier interpretations of the ancient pitch system.[55]

52. On the musical series, see Needham, *Science and Civilisation in China*, vol. 4, part 1, pp. 165–71. See also Lothar von Falkenhausen's recent findings in *Suspended Music: Chime-Bells in the Culture of Bronze Age China* (Berkeley: University of California Press, 1993), pp. 310–24.

53. Lothar von Falkenhausen, "On the Early Development of Chinese Musical Theory: The Rise of Pitch Standards," *Journal of the American Oriental Society* 112, 3 (1992): 433–39; and Hartner, "Some Notes on the Chinese Musical Art," p. 38.

54. *Huang-Ming ts'e-heng*, 3.1a. See also *Nan-kuo hsien-shu*, 4.7a–12a. On Sung musical theory, see Rulan Chao Pian, *Song Dynasty Musical Sources and Their Interpretation* (Cambridge: Harvard University Press, 1967); and Kojima Tsuyoshi 小島毅, "Sōdai no gakuritsu ron" 宋代の樂律論 (Theories of musical pitch in Sung times), *Tōyō bunka kenkyūjo kiyō* 東洋文化研究所紀要 109 (1989): 273–305.

55. *Huang-Ming ts'e-heng*, 3.1a. See also Cho, *Lu-Lu*, pp. 41–42, 65–71; Pian, *Song Dynasty Musical Sources*, pp. 7–9. Chu Hsi had written the preface to Ts'ai's study.

The best student policy answer (again the candidate remains anonymous) began by distinguishing between the "basis for making music" and the "instrument used to produce music." Drawing on the musical theory of the "Yueh-chi" 樂記 (Record of music) in the *Record of Rites*, one of the Five Classics, the essay argued that music grew out of the nature and feelings inherent in the world, extended into the cardinal social relationships, and was embodied in human customs. Music thus transcended its instrumental origins by improving customs and morals.[56] The answer added, however, that the technical aspects of music required the proper harmonization of pitch and sound achieved through accurate musical instruments. Otherwise, the pitch system would remain in error. Without accurate instruments, even a sage like Confucius could not produce music that harmonized.[57]

The policy answer continued by noting that because the records and books about the sound rules (for music) had not been transmitted, very little was known about them. "Many people could talk about the rules, but it was rare for someone to follow them as models." Even the greatest Sung scholars understood little of the ancient pitch system for music. Only Chu Hsi, whom the candidate correctly cited as the source for one of the examiners' quotations, had said that "the difficulty in discerning tones lay not in determining the sound but rather in determining the six yang pitches" and that "determination of tone also depended on the Yellow Bell [pitch pipe] and not on the six yin pitches." Chu Hsi had correctly realized that the key to ancient music was constructing an accurate pitch pipe that corresponded to the fundamental symbolic pitch.[58]

Starting with the official historian of the Former Han, Ssu-ma Ch'ien 司馬遷 (145–86? B.C.), the candidate described various views on calculating the complete twelve-pitch series. The division between six yang pitches and six yin pitches based on a nine *ts'un* Yellow Bell pitch pipe as the fundamental pitch, which Ssu-ma had articulated in the music treatise in the *Shih-chi* 史記 (Record of the official historian), was revived in the Sung by Ts'ai Yuan-ting in his *Lü-lü hsin-shu*. The twelve-pitch series, as the policy answer indicated, was part of a correspondence system in which the acoustical position also had cosmological significance. The hexagrams in the *Changes Classic*, according to the candidate, were produced through numerical procedures similar to those used in the production of the pitch system.

Pitch correspondences to the calendar, the seasons, and celestial phe-

---

56. *Huang-Ming ts'e-heng*, 3.1a–1b. See also Van Gulik, *The Lore of the Chinese Lute*, pp. 23–27.

57. *Huang-Ming ts'e-heng*, 3.1b–2a.

58. Ibid., 3.1b–2a.

nomena were also part of the cosmic score. Certain pitches were assigned to each of the twelve months, the twelve hours of the day, in addition to other official measures. The essay also noted that pitch was dependent on the *ch'i* that arose from the earth at the beginning of the tropical year during the winter solstice.[59] Such changes in *ch'i* could influence the absolute pitch. Consequently, efforts to determine the correct pitch series also employed a technique known as "waiting for the *ch'i*" (*hou-ch'i* 候氣) that tied the pitch series to putative monthly emanations of *ch'i* from the earth. This technique was difficult and often unworkable because the resonances between the pitch pipes and the emanation of *ch'i* were barely discernible—confirmation of Joseph Needham's observation on the *hou-ch'i* technique that "by the Ming period, however, skepticism was rampant."[60]

On alternative measurements for the pitch series, the candidate reviewed evidence in Ssu-ma Kuang's *Tzu-chih t'ung-chien* 資治通鑒 (Comprehensive mirror for aid in government) that the Yellow Emperor had ordered construction of a bamboo wind instrument three *ts'un* by nine *fen*, which became an alternative basis for measuring absolute pitch. Recent scholars had used these measurements to compute the "fundamental pitch" (*yuan-sheng* 元聲) and the corresponding six yang and six yin tones in the series. Using this length for absolute pitch, the complete twelve-pitch series was explained in terms of the *san-fen sun-i* 三分損益 (increase and decrease by one-third) theory of pitch generation, whereby the final tone generated would be the fundamental pitch.

This mathematical formula for successive pitch generation was expressed through ratios such as 4:3 or 2:3, which represented the addition or subtraction of one-third to or from a whole number. By this process of pitch generation, the alternate multiplication of the preceding pitch length by two-thirds and four-thirds would yield the length of the succeeding pitches. Determined in this way, the pitch pipe producing the seventh pitch was nine *ts'un* in length while that for the fundamental pitch was three *ts'un* by nine *fen*, the starting number. Accordingly, the answer concluded that Ssu-ma Ch'ien's claim that the length of the Yellow Bell was nine *ts'un* was erroneous, because only the seventh pitch could be generated this way.[61]

59. Derk Bodde, "The Chinese Cosmic Magic Known as Watching for the Ethers," in S. Egerod and E. Glahn, eds., *Studia Serica: Bernhard Karlgren Dedicata* (Copenhagen: Ejnar Munksgaard, 1959), pp. 14–35.

60. *Huang-Ming ts'e-heng*, 3.2b–3a. See also Needham, *Science and Civilisation in China*, vol. 4, part 1, pp. 186–92; Cho, *Lu-Lu*, pp. 8–9; Hartner, "Some Notes on the Chinese Musical Art," p. 38; and Henderson, *The Development and Decline of Chinese Cosmology*, pp. 163, 188.

61. *Huang-Ming ts'e-heng*, 3.2b–4a. Recent research suggests that the superimposition of yin and yang on musical pitch came in the late Chou dynasty after the pitch-series had

To corroborate his claim, the candidate cited other authorities. Chu Hsi in particular was cited for his doubts about using existing records to ascertain ancient sounds. Chu had argued that contemporary scholars would have to defer to better-informed scholars in later ages who would have more knowledge about ancient music. In this sense, the candidate writing in 1567 contended that scholars in the sixteenth century had a better grasp of the ancient musical pitch series. Indeed, with hindsight we know that the mathematician and musician Chu Tsai-yü 朱載堉 (1536–1611), whose pioneering studies on the twelve-pitch system in the late sixteenth century were submitted to the court in 1606 to correct discrepancies in the pitch series, successfully elaborated the mathematically correct formula for an equal-tempered musical pitch system. Chu's research definitively demonstrated that the Yellow Bell pitch pipe could not have been nine *ts'un* in length.[62]

This policy answer on the twelve-pitch musical series was remarkably technical both in conception and in its use of mathematics to define the twelve steps in the pitch series. Given its frequency as a question on the civil examinations, provincial and metropolitan candidates had to master the principles of music to be adequately prepared. Moreover, the high frequency of such policy questions indicates how important mathematical harmonics were to the dynasty.

### The Elimination of Natural Studies in Early Ch'ing Examinations

Future research should help balance our one-sided views about the cultural status of natural studies during the late empire. The three examples given above demonstrate, however, how dangerous it is to read back into the Ming dynasty the view that Tao Learning moral philosophy and natural studies were already opposed to technical learning, as they came to be in the Ch'ing under Manchu rulers. We should acknowledge that specialized knowledge about astronomy, the calendar, and musical harmonics required in the civil examinations made some difference in the cultural prestige and social status of literati-officials vis-à-vis experts employed in the Astronomy Bureau or the Office of Music. As moral generalists versed in the classical orthodoxy that granted them the highest social, political,

---

been developed. See Lothar von Falkenhausen, "On the Early Development of Chinese Musical Theory," pp. 436–37.

62. *Huang-Ming ts'e-heng*, 3.5a–5b. Cf. *Dictionary of Ming Biography*, pp. 367–70; and Cho, pp. 73–88. It is interesting that Ch'ing emperors adopted instead the ancient pitch system for units of measure.

and cultural prestige, Ming civil officials were required to know how astronomy, mathematics, calendrical studies, and musical harmonics fit into the orthodox apparatus of ritual. They were not licensed to become "scientists," but neither were they hostile to understanding the role of natural phenomena in governance.

Moreover, the long-standing political raison d'être for the literatus had been his official status as a moral paragon who made his classical degree, earned by examination, relevant to his bureaucratic position. Classical statecraft had always been premised on the linkage between classical learning and political competence. That competence was not measured by the literatus's status as an expert in "natural studies." Part of it, however, involved using his knowledge of the Classics to understand the role of the calendar or music in governance. In the policy questions discussed above, technical learning was not the ultimate object of the question. Rather, the examiners expected candidates to place technical learning within the classical narrative of world-ordering bequeathed by the sage-kings.

Accordingly, the policy questions on "natural studies" were restricted to fields relevant to bureaucratic governance and discussed in the basic Classics, or at least read into them by the early commentaries. Other fields such as medicine and alchemy were not deemed appropriate for the examination curriculum. It was important that astronomy and mathematics were discussed in the early Classics, while medicine and alchemy were not. The "five phases" and "inauspicious calamities" were cosmological interpretations of the workings of nature within which political governance was rationalized according to the imperial synthesis of classical learning. The "wrong" answer to such policy questions would indicate that the candidate had failed to grasp the heterodox implications of any effort to observe phenomena in the heavens or on earth in ways that challenged the dynasty in power (see Chapter 6).

As a public event, the policy question and answer delivered in the precincts of an examination compound made "natural studies" part of (or a hostage to) the orthodox system by placing them, during the Ming, within the civil service examination curriculum. By promoting technical knowledge, the examiners successfully domesticated astronomy, music, and the calendar. Literati were chosen for officialdom in this way precisely because they knew that the moral terms of their political success presupposed the subordination of expert knowledge to Tao Learning cultural knowledge that translated via civil examinations into bureaucratic power.

Looking at "natural studies" in late imperial China from the angle of this cultural hierarchy, which paralleled the social and political hierarchies, we see that such learning was justified as the proper concern of the moral generalist exactly because it could thereby be brought within the orthodox system. Experts, as long as they were subordinate to dynastic orthodoxy and its legal representatives, were necessary parts of the cultural, political, and social hierarchies. The literatus-official coexisted with the calendrical expert in the bureaucratic apparatus but at higher levels of political status, cultural prominence, and social prestige. The Ming civil examinations, therefore, were not remarkable because they included policy questions on natural studies. They were remarkable because they successfully encapsulated natural studies within a system of political, social, and cultural reproduction that guaranteed the long-term dominance of the dynasty, its literati, and the Ch'eng-Chu orthodoxy. Hence, literati did not become "scientists," but they did learn the terms of their reliance on experts.[63]

We are left partially in the dark, however, about why in the Ch'ing period such policy questions on natural studies were so rare and uninformed when compared to the Ming dynasty. In the 1660s, for example, a policy question on astrological portents was given on the Shan-tung civil provincial examination. One of the candidates who was ignorant about the subject tried to disguise his answer by discussing geography instead. Thinking he had failed, the candidate was so surprised to see his name on the list of graduates that he read through the examiner's comments on his answer: "The question was on astrological portents, and the answer combined this with discussion of geography. The candidate can be praised as a learned and refined literatus."[64] Geography and astrological studies had been overlapping fields in earlier dynasties, but during the early Ch'ing this linkage was broken when, as shown below, the court banned policy questions on the calendar and celestial studies. Thereafter, geography, particularly local geography, flourished as a source for provincial and metropolitan policy questions (see Chapter 8).[65]

Given our present understanding of how the Jesuits used astronomy to take over the Bureau of Astronomy, and the interest early Manchu emperors had in astronomy, we would expect that such influence, as in the Ming, would have carried over to the civil examinations. It is likely that we are here captive of an assumption that natural studies ought to be progressive, and we therefore overlook the likelihood that the Manchu throne sought to monopolize this potentially volatile area of expertise. The

63. In this sense Ming literati had much in common with contemporary historians of science who lack credentials as scientists themselves but are able to ascertain and critique the social, political, and cultural uses of science in government and society.

64. See Hsu K'o, *Ch'ing-pai lei-ch'ao*, 21.65.

65. See Shen Hsin-chou 沈新周, "Hsu" 序 (Preface), in *Ti-hsueh* 地學 (Shanghai: Sao-yeh shan-fang lithograph, 1910). My thanks to Ping-tzu Chu of Harvard University for this source.

early Manchu manipulation of the civil examinations in the 1650s and 1660s (for example, the civil examinations were drastically reformed in 1664 and then unreformed in 1667; see Chapter 10) and the contemporary calendrical debates between Jesuits and literati-officials, which challenged the orthodox cultural system during the Ming-Ch'ing transition, were probably connected and gave the Manchu court pause about allowing possibly divisive questions on the calendar to appear in civil examinations.[66]

The collapse of the Ming dynasty and its Ch'ing successor under non-Han rule created opportunities until 1685 for experts in astronomy and music to break out of their subordinate positions and to challenge a discredited Ming elite for political power under a new Manchu ruling elite. The increased cultural importance of astronomical expertise when the new dynasty had to reformulate in expert terms its calendrical and musical raison d'être as quickly as possible probably outweighed, or at least challenged for a time, the cultural distinction accumulated by literati via mastery of classical studies.

Not until the 1680s, when the Manchu dynasty had mastered its political and military enemies, did the social fluidity of the early decades of the Ch'ing begin to disappear, leaving Han literati and Manchu elites in a precarious balance at the top (and calendar specialists again in the middle or near the bottom) of the political and social hierarchies, which lasted into the eighteenth century. In the process, policy questions on the third session of the provincial and metropolitan examinations virtually ceased to include natural studies. Perhaps the hard-fought court victory of Tao Learning by the 1680s, manipulated by a shrewd Manchu emperor, precluded in civil examinations the successful literati accommodation with the natural studies that had marked Ming civil examinations.

What we do know is that by 1715, the K'ang-hsi emperor (r. 1662–1722) had banned the public study of astronomical portents and the calendar because they pertained to Ch'ing dynastic legitimacy. The emperor, for example, decreed in 1713 that thereafter all examiners assigned to serve in

66. See Jonathan Spence, *Emperor of China: Self-Portrait of K'ang-hsi* (New York: Vintage Books, 1974), pp. xvii–xix, 15–16, 74–75; and Catherine Jami, "Western Influence and Chinese Tradition in an Eighteenth Century Chinese Mathematical Work," *Historia Mathematica* 15 (1988): 311–31. On the Yang Kuang-hsien 楊光先 (1597–1669) anti-Jesuit affair in K'ang-hsi court life in the 1660s, see Chu Ping-yi, "Scientific Dispute in the Imperial Court: The 1664 Calendar Case," *Chinese Science* 14 (1997): 7–34, which also summarizes many of the important new findings by Professor Huang Yi-long 黃一農 of Tsing Hua University in Taiwan. See, for example, Huang Yi-long, "Ch'ing-ch'u t'ien-chu-chiao yü hui-chiao t'ien-wen-chia te cheng-tou" 清初天主教與回教天文家的爭鬥 (The struggle between Catholic and Muslim astronomers in the early Ch'ing), *Chiu-chou hsueh-k'an* 九州學刊 5, 3 (1993): 47–69.

provincial and metropolitan civil examinations were forbidden to prepare policy questions on astronomical portents, musical harmonics, or calculation methods (朕常講易及修定天文律呂算法註書，爾等考試官斷不可以此註書出題). The latest works in Ch'ing natural studies, court projects on which the K'ang-hsi emperor had employed Jesuit experts, were put off limits to examiners and examination candidates. The ban on natural studies was stipulated within a general effort by the court to keep the mantic arts and discussion of auspicious versus inauspicious portents out of public discussion.[67]

This Ch'ing ban on Chinese literati studying astronomy, astrology, and music openly was noted at the time in Shen Hsin-chou's 沈新周 1712 preface to his study entitled *Ti-hsueh* 地學 (Studies of geography). Shen indicated that all discussions of astronomical portents (*yen t'ien-wen* 言天文) were forbidden during the K'ang-hsi reign. In this public acknowledgment of Ch'ing imperial policy, we see by way of contrast how important the Yung-lo emperor's early Ming decree had been in encouraging natural studies when he demanded such policy questions on examinations in 1404. Likewise, we can understand how the K'ang-hsi emperor's ban affected Ch'ing intellectual life. What seems counterintuitive—namely, that the Ming dynasty encouraged while the Ch'ing discouraged natural studies among its literati elites—makes historical sense. In place of the banned natural studies, historical geography in particular prospered as an acceptable field of Ch'ing scholarship, although map-making was kept secret by the throne. The Yung-cheng emperor also changed the K'ang-hsi emperor's policy a bit by admitting imperial students with specializations in astrology (*t'ien-wen-sheng* 天文生) into the dynastic schools.[68] As we shall see in Chapters 10 and 11, both emperors and their literati officials were responsible for curricular changes in civil examinations, emperors through their private concerns and examiners through their scholarly interests.

## THE CHANGING ROLE OF HISTORICAL KNOWLEDGE IN MING-CH'ING POLICY QUESTIONS

In the middle of the Ch'ing dynasty, the Che-chiang literatus Chang Hsueh-ch'eng 章學誠 (1738–1801) enunciated what became one of the

---

67. See *Huang-ch'ao cheng-tien lei-tsuan* 皇朝政典類纂 (Classified materials on Ch'ing dynasty government regulations), compiled by Hsi Yü-fu 席裕福 (reprint, Taipei: Shen-wu Press, 1969), 191.7b–8a. For discussion of these court compilations, see my *From Philosophy to Philology*, pp. 79–80.

68. See Shen, "Hsu" 序 (Preface), in *Ti-hsueh*; also *Ch'ing-ch'ao t'ung-tien* 清朝通典 (Complete institutions of the Ch'ing dynasty) (Shanghai: Commercial Press, 1936), 18.2131. Literati remained students of the sciences outside of the examination market, however.

most commented upon slogans in late imperial and modern Chinese intellectual circles: "The Six Classics are all Histories" (*liu-ching chieh shih yeh* 六經皆史也). Since the Han dynasties, the Classics had been referred to as the "sacred Classics" (*sheng-ching* 聖經), and along with the Four Books had become the basis for a classical education in schools and at home. To become an official, study of the Five Classics was obligatory, and their importance increased after 1787, when the classical specialization was dropped on civil examinations in favor of mastery of all the Classics (see Chapter 10).

In Chang Hsueh-ch'eng's time, however, the preeminent position of the Classics was somewhat challenged. In its place, eminent eighteenth-century literati-scholars from the Yangtzu delta such as Chang Hsueh-ch'eng, Ch'ien Ta-hsin 錢大昕 (1728–1804), Wang Ming-sheng 王鳴盛 (1722–98), and Chao I 趙翼 (1727–1814), among others, attempted to restore historical studies (*shih-hsueh* 史學) at the top of what counted for literati learning. In the early Ch'ing, Ku Yen-wu 顧炎武 (1613–82) had already complained that historical studies had declined during the Sung and Ming dynasties because of excessive concern on civil examinations for literary talent. He urged restoration of T'ang-dynasty-style examination essays devoted solely to history.[69]

Chang's famous slogan accordingly reflected the changing intellectual trajectories between classical studies and historical studies in the eighteenth century. During the late Ch'ing, historical studies gradually replaced classical studies as the dominant framework for scholarly research. In the early twentieth century, the eclipse of classical studies was complete. Ku Chieh-kang 顧頡剛 and others who participated in the *Ku-shih-pien* 古史辨 (debates concerning ancient Chinese history) in the 1920s made the Classics the object of historical study, not the premise for historical studies.[70]

In the eighteenth century, for example, although the perennial relationship between classical and historical studies remained an important consideration among orthodox literati, with the rise in status of historical studies almost to parity with classical studies, the demarcation between the

69. Ku Yen-wu, "San-ch'ang" 三場 (The three examination sessions), in *Jih-chih lu chi-shih*, 16.385–86; and "Shih-hsueh" 史學 (Historical studies), in *Jih-chih lu chi-shih*, 16.391–92. For discussion, see Inoue Susumu 井上進, "Rikkyō mina shi setsu no keifu" 六經皆史説の系譜 (The descent of the thesis that the "Six Classics are all histories"), in Ono Kazuko, ed., *Mimmatsu Shinsho no shakai to bunka*, pp. 535–85, which presents Ming precedents.

70. Tu Wei-yun 杜維運, *Ch'ing Ch'ien-Chia shih-tai chih shih-hsueh yü shih-chia* 清乾嘉時代之史學與史家 (Historians and historical studies in the Ch'ing Ch'ien-lung and Chia-ch'ing eras) (Taipei: Wen-shih ts'ung-k'an, 1962), pp. 13–48, 99–121.

universality of the Classics and the particularity of the Dynastic Histories was called into question. Such doubts penetrated the imperial civil service examinations. The noted evidential research scholar Lu Wen-ch'ao 盧文弨 (1717–96), while serving as a senior examination official at the 1767 Hunan provincial examination, prepared one of the five policy questions in which he pointedly asked the *chü-jen* candidates to reconsider the relationship between the Classics and Histories: "The Histories have different uses from the Classics, but they derive from the same sources. The *Documents Classic* and *Spring and Autumn Annals* are the historical records of the sages, which have become Classics. Later ages honored the latter and divided [the Histories and Classics] into two genres. Can you grasp [how this happened] and then explain it?"[71]

Others went even further when they claimed that there was no difference between the Classics and Dynastic Histories. This artificial division of genres, Ch'ien Ta-hsin contended, had not existed in the classical era. Rather, the demarcation of genres had been first used in the *ssu-pu* 四部 (four divisions) system of classification after the fall of the Later Han dynasty, when the Classics for the first time were demarcated from history, philosophy, and literature. On these grounds, Ch'ien rejected the priority given the Classics over History and concluded that both were essential historical sources for retrieving from antiquity the wisdom of the sages. Placed in its own proper historical context, then, Chang Hsueh-ch'eng's often cited claim that "the Six Classics are all Histories" reflected the growing historicization of literati learning in the eighteenth century.[72]

The changing role of historical knowledge vis-à-vis classical studies is for the most part confirmed when we examine the nature of the policy questions and answers found in the civil service examinations during the Ming and Ch'ing dynasties. Based on Tables 8.5 and 8.6, we can generally conclude that late imperial examiners who prepared the policy questions devoted a substantial proportion of them to the study of history, a trend that increased under Ch'ing rule. In addition, most policy questions that did not take history as an object of scholarly focus presumed that candidates would prepare a historical account on whatever topic was asked, whether dealing with institutions, Classics, flood control, local governance, or the like.

In addition, two of the Five Classics (the *Documents Classic* and the *Spring and Autumn Annals*) were essentially historical in format and content. Be-

71. Lu Wen-ch'ao, *Pao-ching-t'ang wen-chi* 抱經堂文集 (Collected essays from the Hall for Cherishing the Classics) (Shanghai: Commercial Press, 1937), 4:327.

72. Ch'ien Ta-hsin, "Hsu" 序 (Preface), in *Nien-erh-shih k'ao-i* 廿二史考異 (Examination of variances in the Twenty-two Dynastic Histories) (Shanghai: Commercial Press, 1935–37), p. 1.

cause candidates before 1787 chose to specialize on either the *Documents* or the *Annals* in relatively large numbers (25–27%), we can also conclude that history was an important part of the first session of the civil examinations, even while the frequency of policy questions focusing on history was increasing from the Ming to the Ch'ing. Around 20% chose the *Documents Classic*, and another 6% to 7% usually selected the *Spring and Autumn Annals* for their specialization (see Chapter 5). Consequently, about 25% of the provincial examination graduates chose a Classic dealing with history for their specialization. Certainly, this number is not minimal, but it does lag behind the number who chose the metaphysics and cosmology of the *Change Classic* (30–35%) or the literature of the *Poetry Classic* (30–35%).

If the ratio of 25% for graduates choosing history texts for their specialization roughly held for those who failed the examination, then in late Ming Ying-t'ien prefecture, for example, about 1,250 to 1,875 candidates chose either the *Documents* or *Annals* for their specialization. Similarly, for An-hui and Chiang-su provinces in the seventeenth and eighteenth centuries, 2,500 to 4,250 provincial candidates in Chiang-nan chose historical Classics to specialize on (see Chapter 3). With the increase in the overall examination pool, the number of candidates who were studying the historical Classics or answering history policy questions to prepare for the seventeen triennial provincial tests was increasing during the Ch'ing dynasty.

The next section addresses those policy questions on examinations in several provinces that focused on history as a discipline and historiography as a scholarly problem. But we should keep in mind that few policy questions remained untouched by the overall literati concern for moral truth and historical change and development. Moral philosophy and history were virtually inseparable in the policy questions.

### Tao Learning History in 1516 Che-chiang Policy Questions

As the third policy question on session three of the 1516 Che-chiang provincial examination, the one on history followed two earlier questions: the first on the sage-kings model of rulership and the second on the "orthodox transmission of the Way" (*tao-t'ung*) and the role of the mind (*hsin-fa*) in the emperor's personal cultivation. I will first examine the question on history and then compare it with the other policy questions prepared in 1516 to further elaborate on the nature of historical knowledge required in the Che-chiang provincial examination. It is unclear how representative the 1516 policy question was. In the 1489 Shan-tung provincial examination, for example, a policy question on history there did not raise any of the *Tao-hsueh* issues discussed below, whereas one policy question on the 1489 Hu-kuang provincial examination did inquire about the Sung roles of Ssu-ma Kuang and Chu Hsi as historians in determining dynastic legitimacy, as did a policy question in the 1502 metropolitan examination.[73]

The examiners' 1516 question (of some 345 characters) on history opened by defining the chief genres that made up history: "Chu Wen-kung [Hsi] has said that the forms of ancient history can best be seen in the *Documents* [Classic] and the *Spring and Autumn Annals*. The *Annals* is a chronicle that comprehensively reveals the chronology of events. The *Documents* records each matter separately in order to grasp its beginning and end."[74] History was divided according to the long-standing distinction between pure chronologies (*pien-nien* 編年), that is "annalistic history," which used the *Annals* as their model, and topical accounts (*chi-chuan* 紀傳, lit., "imperial reigns and official biographies") based on the *Documents Classic*.

Hence, lurking within the assumptions that the examiners presented in their question was the view that historical studies could be approached in terms of pure chronology (i.e., in an annalistic format) or discrete topics (i.e., in a topical format). "Process versus structure" is an overly modern interpretation of how Ming literati viewed the genres of historiography, but it is clear that in Ming times, scholars and candidates thought about history in light of the nature of change and the role of continuity.[75]

For the 1516 examiners, both Ssu-ma Ch'ien's *Records of the Official Historian* and Pan Ku's 班固 (A.D. 32–92) *History of the Former Han Dynasty* represented outstanding historical works, but because neither followed exactly the classical genres that had preceded them they were criticized by later generations. Implicitly, the examiners suggested that Han historians had not lived up to classical models. This suggestion became explicit when the examiners described how some considered the *San-kuo-chih* 三國志 (History of the Three States period) that followed the Han histories as "the betrayer of the *Spring and Autumn Annals*." Candidates were asked to identify the author of the latter and discuss whether such charges were right.[76]

73. *Che-chiang hsiang-shih lu*, 1516: 5/2643–830, in *Ming-tai teng-k'o-lu hui-pien*, vol. 5. See also *Shan-tung hsiang-shih lu*, 1489: 2/1370–72 (question), 2/1460–67 (answer); *Hu-kuang hsiang-shih lu*, 1489: 2/1531–33 (question), 2/1628–33 (answer); and *Hui-shih lu*, 1502: 5/2236–38 (question), 5/2361–70 (answer), all in *Ming-tai teng-k'o lu hui-pien*, vols. 2–5.

74. *Che-chiang hsiang-shih lu*, 1516: 5/2681.

75. Political institutions, social family histories, and economic processes described in Chinese topical histories were never presented in purely structural terms and still stressed the role of human agency in historical change.

76. *Che-chiang hsiang-shih lu*, 1516: 5/2682. The Han histories as examinable texts had been the mainstay of the T'ang civil examination questions on history, thus putting these Ming examiners at odds with their T'ang predecessors; see McMullen, *State and Scholars in T'ang China*, pp. 197–99.

Next the examiners brought up T'ang through Sung dynasty histories, criticism of which candidates were also asked to evaluate. Actually, these questions turned out to be simply a prelude to what the examiners were really getting at in their question, for they then turned to Ssu-ma Kuang's *Comprehensive Mirror of History* and Chu Hsi's condensed version known as the *T'ung-chien kang-mu* 通鑒綱目 (Condensation of the comprehensive mirror) as historical works. Ssu-ma Kuang's work was likened to the *Tso chuan* 左傳 (Tso's commentary to the *Spring and Autumn Annals*), while Chu Hsi's condensation was said by some "to have gotten the essential meaning of the *Annals*."

In closing, the examiners brought up for evaluation Hu An-kuo 胡安國 (1074–1138), who had written an authoritative commentary to the *Annals* during the Northern Sung (see Chapter 1), which was part of the examination curriculum from 1313 until 1793. The examiners also cited prominently later historians who had filled in lacunae in the *Comprehensive Mirror*, such as Chin Lü-hsiang 金履祥 (1232–1303). They asked candidates to elaborate on Hu An-kuo's claim that the *Annals* was an "important canon on the transmission of the mind" (*ch'uan-hsin yao-tien* 傳心要典). Finally, the examiners asked: "Today in order to produce outstanding history that aspires to the sages' important canon on the transmission of the mind [that is, the *Annals*], what should those whose minds are set on history follow?"[77]

In effect, the examiners had dissolved a question on history into a classical framework that equated Confucius' *Spring and Autumn Annals* with the Sung "Tao Learning" stress on the "transmission of the mind." Moreover, Han and post-Han histories were criticized, while Sung histories were praised. Just as Han and T'ang literati had failed to transmit the essential moral teachings of the sages, that is, the *tao-t'ung*, they had also failed in their histories to transmit the proper legacy of Confucius' *Annals*. History served philosophy, and Chu Hsi became the historian who had best captured the legacy of the *Annals*.

It did not matter to the examiners that Chu Hsi had at times belittled the *Annals* as an irrelevant record of ancient facts and details. Nor were they deterred by a fact, frequently pointed out by later *k'ao-cheng* scholars, that the terms usually associated with Sung dynasty theories of the mind did not occur anywhere in the *Annals* but were derived from the Four Books as well as Buddhist and Taoist sources. Moreover, Chu Hsi had compiled only a brief *T'ung-chien t'i-yao* 通鑒提要 (Essentials of the *Comprehensive Mirror*), in which he set the overall guidelines for his followers to compile the detailed *Kang-mu*. As in the case of the *Chia-li* 家禮 (Family

77. *Che-chiang hsiang-shih lu*, 1516: 5/2682–4.

rituals) and *Hsiao-hsueh* 小學 (Elementary education), during the Ming dynasty Chu Hsi received credit for works such as the *Kang-mu*, which were substantially completed by his later followers.[78]

The best policy answer to the history question was written (in about 960 characters) by Kung Hui 龔輝, a student from the Yü-yao county school who had specialized on the *Poetry Classic* and ranked second overall on the 1516 provincial examination. Over 2,200 candidates had competed for the 90 places on the Che-chiang provincial *chü-jen* quota, a ratio of 24 to 1. Of those who passed, 34.4% had concentrated on the *Change Classic*, 17.8% on the *Documents*, 34.4% on the *Poetry*, 7.8% on the *Annals*, and only 6.6% on the *Rites Classic*. Kung Hui was an example, then, of a typical candidate who, although he had not chosen to specialize on one of the historical Classics, still had enough of a general knowledge of them to compose the best history policy answer.

One of the associate examiners commented that "in testing candidates on history one wanted to ascertain the breadth of their knowledge." One of the two chief examiners noted that this candidate "recorded his knowledge broadly and in harmony; his argumentation was precise and correct [such that it was clear that] he was one who was well-versed in historical studies." Consequently, the best students studied history, regardless of what Classic they had chosen to specialize on and regardless of how well they had mastered eight-legged essays on the Four Books.[79]

First, Kung Hui enunciated the underlying principles governing history using a circular argument: "If first one takes the public good of the empire (*t'ien-hsia chih kung* 天下之公) to write history, then one's writings will be transmitted. If first one takes the public good of the empire to criticize history, then the debate will be settled. History is defined as the measure of right and wrong; it is the great model for making the empire serve the public good." These principles gave history an important role in assessing the present in light of the past. Moreover, Kung's essay stressed at the outset that the *Documents* and *Annals*, the first compiled by and the second written by Confucius, represented the greatest public good imaginable: "Therefore, we can say that the *Documents* is a history included as a Classic. The *Annals* is a Classic included as a history. Later historians all

---

78. See *Chu Wen-kung wen-chi, hsu chi* 朱文公文集續集 (Continuation to the collected essays of Chu Hsi), *Ssu-pu ts'ung-k'an* edition (Shanghai: Commercial Press, 1934–35), 2.6b. On Chu's limited role in compiling the *Kang-mu*, see Sung Lien, *Sung Wen-hsien kung ch'üan-chi*, 12.14b–15a. See also Patricia Ebrey, *Confucianism and Family Rituals in Imperial China: A Social History of Writing about Rules* (Princeton: Princeton University Press, 1991), pp. 102–44, 167–87; and M. Theresa Kelleher, "Back to Basics," pp. 221–24.

79. *Che-chiang hsiang-shih lu*, 1516: 5/2794–95.

have been classified according to the authority of the *Documents* and *Annals*."[80]

When measuring Ssu-ma Ch'ien's *Shih-chi* and Pan Ku's *Han-shu* against these orthodox standards, Kung found that because both had given priority to the Taoist teachings of the Yellow Emperor and Lao-tzu and relegated the Six Classics, their works had immoral implications. Similarly, Ch'en Shou's 陳壽 (A.D. 233–297) *San-kuo-chih* had failed to measure properly the political legitimacy (*cheng-t'ung* 正統) of the competing dynasties, thus bequeathing moral confusion to posterity and deserving the epithet of "the betrayer of the *Spring and Autumn Annals*."[81]

Coming to the Sung historical works by Ssu-ma Kuang and Chu Hsi, prominently identified by the examiners, Kung Hui's essay described how both had been composed to continue Confucius' *Annals* for the 1,362 years (403 B.C. to A.D. 959) up to the Northern Sung. Moreover, because Chu Hsi had faithfully modeled his condensed history on the moral principles of the *Annals*, Chu deserved to be known as the successor to Confucius as model historian. Chu Hsi's predecessor Hu An-kuo had correctly perceived that the "praise and blame" ( *pao-pien* 褒貶) judgments in the *Annals* were equivalent to the heavenly principles and that, accordingly, the *Annals* was indeed an "important canon on the transmission of the mind." In choosing the best models for writing history, Kung Hui contended that Chu Hsi, after Confucius, was the "Grand Historian," not Ssu-ma Ch'ien.[82]

It is intriguing that Chu Hsi, whom we normally associate with the "Tao Learning" moral and philosophic orthodoxy of late imperial times, was also considered by the 1516 examiners to have been equally important as a historian. But this surprise is lessened by the fact that the sort of history the examiners were testing candidates on was akin to what we would today call "moralizing historiography." The historiographic differences between narrative and topical history initially raised in the question were quickly relegated to the background.

We shall see in later policy questions on history that the division of history into two different genres would itself become the issue, not just whether both genres served as "mirrors" for moral and political governance. In the 1516 history question, the only "Histories" that really mattered were "Classics." Thus, the *Shih-chi* and *Han-shu* were mere histories reflecting their time; the *Annals* and *Kang-mu* were histories for the ages. In the 1516 provincial examination, which may or may not have been repre-

---

80. Ibid., 5/2795–7.
81. Ibid., 5/2797–8.
82. Ibid., 5/2799–2802. For discussion, see Hervouet, ed., *A Sung Bibliography*, pp. 75–76.

sentative, the examiners in Che-chiang were still a long way from granting historical studies an independent status equal to classical studies. The Classics were still sacred and paramount, a position that does reflect Ming literati thought.

If we compare the history policy question to the second policy question immediately preceding it, which focused on the issue of the "orthodox transmission of the Way" and the role of the "transmission of the mind" in enabling the moral mind (tao-hsin 道心) to reach its goals of "absolute refinement, singleness of purpose, and allegiance to the mean" (ching-i chih-chung 精一執中), we find similarities in the content and phraseology of the two policy questions. One was devoted to "Tao Learning;" the other to history. Yet, because history was dissolved by the examiners into "Tao Learning," both questions wound up reflecting similar moral and philosophic concerns. The examiners stressed in their second policy question, for example, that spiritual and mental subtlety were the keys to unraveling the ties between individual self-cultivation of the moral mind and public mastery of the comprehensive handles of government. Study of human nature and principle was presented as the Sung dynasty reconstruction of the mind-set of the sage-king Yao, who had passed on the lesson of the middle way of governance to his chosen successor, Shun.[83]

To complete our discussion of the 1516 civil examination, I will look at the first policy question on rulership, since this was, in the eyes of the examiners, the most important question. It was standard in a Ming civil service examination that the political authority of the ruler should be confirmed in the manner policy questions were presented. The first policy question, for example, asked students to comment on the way the sagely two emperors and three kings of antiquity took upon themselves the concerns of the empire. The question stressed that such concerns could be seen in the present ruler's own mindful efforts to cultivate his virtue, which was based on his seriousness of purpose.

The examiners noted that these ideals had been realized in antiquity, but in subsequent dynasties, such as the Sung, few emperors had lived up to them. Earlier T'ang dynasty rulers had been especially negligent in their duties, the examiners pointed out. The rhetorical flourish at the end of their question, which took the form of a historical narrative of the early Ming dynasty, quickly dispelled any likelihood that the examiner's impartial political criticism would be directed at the present dynasty as well: "Our nation has endured for over one hundred years from the Hung-hsi [r. 1425] to Hung-chih reigns. Five imperial ancestors have successively embodied the realm, and all have preserved seriousness of purpose and

83. *Che-chiang hsiang-shih lu,* 1516: 5/2679–81.

imperial majesty. None has been remiss in his concerns for the empire, nor have any failed to preserve and protect the law-models of their predecessors. It is likely that they have matched the [achievements of the] Three Dynasties [of antiquity] in recreating for today the glorious peace and prosperity [of yore]."[84]

In asking students, who of course "were more filial and respectful of their ruler than even the examiners," for their opinions, they had successfully narrowed the terms of reply for this policy essay to a literary form of an oath of allegiance to the dynasty. Renowned in later literati-inspired accounts for his alleged profligacy, dabblings in esoteric Buddhism, and lechery, however, the Cheng-te emperor (r. 1506–1521) seemed an unlikely candidate for such pompous praise. His reign was dominated by powerful eunuchs such as Liu Chin 劉瑾 (d. 1510), against whom literati such as Wang Yang-ming had unsuccessfully mobilized (Wang was jailed, beaten, and exiled in 1506 for his efforts). Eunuch cliques thereafter remained a powerful element in court politics.[85]

Moreover, Wang Yang-ming was a native son of Che-chiang province, who had resided most of his life in Shao-hsing and passed the provincial examination in Hang-chou in 1492. Both the provincial examiners and local candidates for the 1516 Che-chiang examinations probably were aware of how far the first policy question overpraising Ming emperors had strayed from reality. Was the inflated rhetoric a form of disguised criticism? If so, then under the circumstances in 1516 the stakes were very high. Punishment awaited anyone caught at even veiled criticism of his imperial majesty. If we judge by the top answer to the first policy question prepared by Chang Huai 張懷 (1486–1561), also from Yü-yao county and a specialist in the *Change*, for which the examiners spared no praise, no examination candidate dared to read into the question any explicit suggestion of contemporary imperial impropriety—certainly not the number-one-ranked *chü-jen*, as Chang turned out to be.[86]

In summary, then, Chang Huai's carefully crafted opening policy essay typified the expectations that students fulfilled in the first three 1516 policy answers. The student's job in the first question was to affirm in the clear-

84. Ibid., 5/2676–79.

85. *Dictionary of Ming Biography*, pp. 308–09, 1409–10.

86. *Che-chiang hsiang-shih lu*, 1516: 5/2778–80. See also *Ming-Ch'ing chin-shih t'i-ming pei-lu so-yin* 明清進士題名碑錄索引 (Index to the stelae rosters of Ming and Ch'ing *chin-shih*) (Taipei: Wen-shih-che Press, 1982), 3/2504. Curiously, however, the fourth policy question raised the issue of official remonstrance (*chien* 諫): "the official shows his loyalty through good remonstrance; the ruler shows his sageliness by obeying [such] remonstrance." See *Che-chiang hsiang-shih lu*, 5/2684–86. This question indicates that examiners were not imperial lackeys and could use the policy questions to invoke the official's moral high ground vis-à-vis the ruler, even one like the Cheng-te emperor.

est terms possible his personal loyalty to the political system devised by the ancients and replicated in the present. In the second, the student acknowledged his commitment to the moral philosophy of the "Tao Learning" orthodoxy. For the third, the student followed the examiners' lead in linking historical studies to imperial orthodoxy. The first three policy questions and answers in the Che-chiang proceedings were in essence a ritualized exchange of orthodox political, classical, and historical beliefs that legitimated the dynasty and extracted a written oath of loyalty from the student. Given this ceremonial duet between the examiner, appealing to imperial majesty, and the student, affirming that majesty, political criticism was best left implicit. The function of the history policy question was to affirm the classical underpinnings of imperial orthodoxy. If the ruler was presented in the questions as both sage to his subjects and teacher to his examination candidates, Chu Hsi was both moral philosopher and historian without compare.

### Moralizing Historiography in 1594 Fu-chien Policy Questions

In the 1594 provincial examinations, examiners in Fu-chien province prepared a policy question on *shih-hsueh*, whose answer in over 3,000 characters was selected for inclusion in the *Huang-Ming ts'e-heng*. Unfortunately, we have no information concerning the examiners or the student who composed the policy answer. Nevertheless, the question and answer both show continuity and consistency with the 1516 policy question just discussed. In addition to Fu-chien, similar policy questions on history were also prepared for other 1594 provincial examinations, including those in Shun-t'ien, Shen-hsi, and Ssu-ch'uan.[87]

As the third policy question in Fu-chien, the 1594 history question was preceded by two questions, one on the proper use of talented men for governance (*yung-jen* 用人) and the other on ways to end natural disasters (*mi-tsai* 弭災). It was then followed by a fourth question on the equal-field system as a basis for military organization and a fifth on dealing with Japanese pirates. It is interesting that not a single policy question was framed in terms of Tao Learning or classical studies. In fact, all five of the policy questions in Fu-chien dealt directly or indirectly with the historical aspects of contemporary issues.

The policy question on history opened by broaching the difference between annalistic and topical history and then asked candidates to "point out the strengths and weaknesses of the two genres." Ssu-ma Ch'ien was brought up as the historian who had led the change in ancient historiog-

---

87. *Huang-Ming ts'e-heng*, "Mu-lu" 目錄 (Table of contents), pp. 10a–12a.

raphy from chronicles to topical histories. So much so, the examiners noted, that Ssu-ma Ch'ien's favored genre had become "orthodox history," while chronicles in the style of the *Annals* had virtually died out. Candidates were asked to comment on the aftereffects of this reversal in historical genres.

Revival of annalistic history by Ssu-ma Kuang, according to the examiners, had reversed the earlier trend that had favored topical histories. What advantages did Ssu-ma Kuang's *pien-nien*, the examiners asked, have over Ssu-ma Ch'ien's *chi-chuan*? Finally, the candidates had to discuss what improvements Chu Hsi had brought to Ssu-ma Kuang's *Comprehensive Mirror*. As an afterthought, or so it may have seemed, the examiners ended by writing that although the chronicles were the most ancient form of historiography, there were many "who today groundlessly contend that besides [Ssu]-ma Ch'ien's [*Shih-chi*] there is no history." The intent behind the 1594 policy question on history was to debunk Ssu-ma Ch'ien as the "Grand Historian." Ssu-ma Ch'ien, for all of his strengths using the *chi-chuan* genre, was taken to task by the examiners and candidates for his moral heterodoxy and his fascination with historical persons of questionable repute.[88]

The policy answer opened by embellishing on the importance of history for the ruler. The ruler had the power to demote the unworthy and promote the worthy, but he relied on history to weigh right and wrong. While the ruler's power had limits, the rights and wrongs of history extended in all directions and provided the ruler with a guide for his policies. "History contained both words and meanings. Meanings harbored both right and wrong." All good historians can use vivid and flowery language to write history, but the words were insufficient in and of themselves. Only sages could capture the "pattern of meanings" (*i-fa* 義法) and "scales" (*ch'üan-heng* 權衡) of right and wrong revealed through words.[89]

As in the policy question of 1516, a clear distinction was made between historical Classics and mere histories. Sages, according to the 1594 policy answer, had enunciated the principles of history in three Classics: (1) the *Documents*, (2) the *Poetry*, and (3) the *Annals*. The first contained the directives and instructions of the sage-kings, but was incomplete. The second supplemented the *Documents* with the songs and chants of ancient people that had reversed trends in immorality. Confucius' explication of the rights and wrongs of history in his account of the history of the state of Lu in the *Annals* had captured the "methods of the mind" (*hsin-fa*) of the sage-kings.[90]

88. Ibid., 13.17a. See also 7.54a–59a for the policy question and answer in the 1582 Kwangtung provincial examination that focused on the *Shih-chi*.

89. *Huang-Ming ts'e-heng*, 13.17b.

90. Ibid.

Although this point was not yet explicitly stated, the author of the answer had placed Confucius' chronicles on a higher historical plane than mere histories, such as Ssu-ma Ch'ien's topical history. The answer then praised Tso Ch'iu-ming, who had aided Confucius by compiling an authoritative commentary to the *Annals* that enabled later ages to grasp the "affairs" (*shih* 事) and "meanings" (*i* 義) encoded in the chronicle of events, Tso thereby becoming the "loyal official of the 'uncrowned king' and the drummer who spread the word of the 'Unicorn Classic.'" The *Annals*, as annalistic history, exemplified the most ancient ideal of historiography.[91]

According to the candidate, this ancient historiographical tradition had been overturned when Ssu-ma Ch'ien created the topical history as an alternative to the chronicle. In so doing, Ssu-ma Ch'ien's *Shih-chi* had become the model for orthodox history from the Han dynasty onward. Following the lead of the examiners, the student answer rejected this tradition by pointing out that Ssu-ma Ch'ien himself had been guilty of heterodoxy when he had granted the Yellow Emperor and Lao-tzu intellectual priority over Han literati loyal to Confucius and the Six Classics. In addition, he had included in his history accounts of immoral adventurers and tricksters that served to delude rather than edify his readers. The rights and wrongs of history were no longer apparent. More important, however, this genre of history had focused on the strengths and weaknesses of individuals and delineated the ins and outs of historical events without correctly divining the reasons for the rise and fall of the dynasty (*kuo-yun* 國運).[92]

After the Former Han dynasty, the essay continued, historians such as Pan Ku and Ch'en Shou had emulated Ssu-ma Ch'ien. Annalistic history almost disappeared, but there had been some who had kept the genre alive by producing limited chronicles based on a single dynasty, enough so that the author of the policy answer rejected claims made by earlier literati that "after [Tso] Ch'iu-ming there was no history." Nonetheless, it was not until Ssu-ma Kuang completed his *Comprehensive Mirror* in the eleventh century that the *pien-nien* genre revived, thereby illuminating the history of sixteen dynasties over 1,362 years and earning Chu Hsi's praise for being the most important history since the Han dynasties.[93]

Though Ssu-ma Kuang had followed the model of Confucius' *Annals*, his massive historical compilation had confused the vital historical issue of

91. Ibid., 13.18a–b. Reference to Confucius as an "uncrowned king" (*su-wang* 素王) and the *Annals* as the "Unicorn Classic" (*lin-ching* 麟經) derive from the *Kung-yang Commentary*, not the *Tso chuan*, which the essay in a curious way has rhetorically elided. For discussion see my *Classicism, Politics, and Kinship*, chaps. 4–7.

92. *Huang-Ming ts'e-heng*, 13.19a–b.

93. Ibid., 13.19b–22a.

the political legitimacy of dynasties during the periods of disunity before the rise of the Han dynasty. The policy answer noted that such an oversight, according to some, demonstrated that Ssu-ma Kuang was morally deficient in his historical analysis and was unclear about the difference between a legitimate king (the Chou dynastic ruler) and illegitimate usurpers (*wang-pa chih pien* 王霸之辨).

Accordingly, the historian who saved the *Comprehensive Mirror* from its flaws was Chu Hsi. With a penetrating understanding of the classical principles of political legitimacy bequeathed by Confucius' *Annals*, Chu Hsi prepared guidelines (*fan li* 凡例) for the *Kang-mu* condensation of Ssu-ma Kuang's work that eventually made it into a textbook of political ethics replete with *Annals*-like "praise and blame" historiography: "I dare to say that Ssu-ma Kuang used the methods of the *Annals* and at times captured its intent. Chu Hsi got the [full] intent of the *Annals* and also was marvelous in employing its methods. Since the 'Unicorn Classic,' this is the only compilation that counts."[94]

The essay ended by giving a brief account of historiography after the Sung dynasties. Later historians had produced continuations to the *Comprehensive Mirror* that kept it up-to-date and carried it further back in time. Moreover, during the Ch'eng-hua reign (1465–87) the emperor authorized an imperial supplement that included the Sung and Yuan dynasties and brought the *Comprehensive Mirror* up to 1367. The model for the twenty-two dynastic histories up to the Ming remained the *Annals*, but the essay reached a conciliatory conclusion concerning the two genres of annalistic and topical histories. According to the candidate, the distinction was a product of Ssu-ma Ch'ien's misguided historiography. Previously the two genres had been unified. Consequently, "it was wrong to honor topical history at the expense of annalistic history. But it was equally mistaken to prepare annalistic history and overlook topical history." What was required of contemporary historians was for them to reunite the two genres and recapture the classical model for historiography that preceded Ssu-ma Ch'ien.[95]

Overall, the 1516 and 1594 policy answers resonated. Ssu-ma Ch'ien and his topical historiography were attacked on moral grounds. The *chi-chuan* genre of historiography placed a premium on style and language, but its authors had missed the forest for the trees. Uninformed by moral vision, historical events became meaningless. Although separated by seventy-eight years, both policy essays stressed that moralizing historiography was the key. And both answers contended that after Confucius only Chu Hsi

94. Ibid., 13.22a–23a.
95. Ibid., 13.23a–25a.

had recaptured the *cheng-t'ung* of the rise and fall of dynasties. "Political legitimacy" was the historical correlate to the "orthodox transmission of the Way" (*tao-t'ung*), which Tao Learning, leaping over T'ang and Han literati, traced back to Confucius and Mencius. In both philosophy and history, then, literati after the Han had lost their way. Not until the Sung was the moral vision of antiquity restored in classical and historical studies.[96] As a continuator of the Sung vision, the Ming confirmed through such questions and answers that the Sung legacy remained orthodox.

## Han Dynasty Style History in 1654 and 1685

Turning to early Ch'ing policy questions on history, we should first recall the earlier discussion of the changing trajectories of historical vis-à-vis classical studies in the eighteenth century. In mid- and late Ch'ing policy questions on history, the earlier focus on Tao Learning historiography increasingly receded into the background and moralizing historiography became less important. In the process, Ssu-ma Ch'ien and Pan Ku reemerged as historical models who exemplified the best Han models of historiography. Just as Ch'ing dynasty Han Learning classicists stressed Han dynasty classical studies over now-suspect Sung and Ming Tao Learning, so too eighteenth- and nineteenth-century Han Learning historians emphasized Ssu-ma Ch'ien and Pan Ku, rather than Chu Hsi, as exemplary historians.[97]

In the 1654 Kuang-tung provincial examination, for instance, the second policy question addressed the relationship between the Classics and the Dynastic Histories. We know that over 2,600 candidates took this examination, of whom only 86 (3.6%) passed. Of the latter, 25.8% specialized on the *Change Classic*, 17.2% on the *Documents*, 43% on the *Poetry*, 6.5% on the *Annals*, and 7.5% on the *Record of Rites*. As estimated above, we find that roughly 25% of the graduates and candidates mastered one of the historical Classics in their preparations for the Kuang-tung provincial examination of 1654. In addition, all students had to answer the policy question raising the issue of the boundaries between historical and classical studies.[98]

96. If one compares the 1594 Fu-chien policy question and answer on history with the ones in Shun-t'ien and Shen-hsi the same year, the chief difference one finds among them is that the latter two paid more attention to the two genres of annalistic versus topical histories per se and focused much less or hardly at all on Tao Learning moralizing historiography. See ibid., 12.13a–18b, 13.83a–90a.

97. See for example the *Shun-t'ien hsiang-shih-lu*, 1831: 4a–5a, pp. 64a–66b; and *Hui-shih lu*, 1685: 13a–15a, 74b–77a. On the latter, see further below.

98. *Kuang-tung hsiang-shih lu*, 1654: "Hsu" 序 (Preface), pp. 1a–5a, and pp. 15a–20a of the record.

In his introduction to the official record of the examination proceedings, chief examiner Chang Feng-pao 張鳳抱, a 1643 *chin-shih* from Tientsin, noted that during the Ming dynasty Kuang-tung had produced an outstanding scholar of Tao Learning in Ch'en Hsien-chang 陳獻章 (1428–1500) and a historian of major stature in Ch'en Chien 陳建 (1497–1567), suggesting the centrality of classical and historical studies among literati scholars. Ch'en Chien had passed the Kuang-tung provincial examination in 1528 but failed twice in the metropolitan examinations. Ironically, his annalistic history of the Ming dynasty up to 1521, entitled *Huang-Ming t'ung-chi* 皇明通紀 (Comprehensive records of the Ming dynasty), became a handy reference book for examination candidates, first published in 1555 and in several later editions. In this vein, I should add that all five of the policy questions prepared by Chang Feng-pao and his associates assumed a historical understanding of various policy matters: (1) education for the present young ruler, (2) classics and histories, (3) creating and employing talented men, (4) military structure and agricultural labor, (5) the need for reform to keep pace with change. As in 1594, no policy question directly questioned students about Tao Learning.[99]

The 1654 policy question was quite different from the earlier Ming dynasty questions we looked at. Students were asked to discuss in detail the "origins and development" (*yuan-liu* 源流) of the Classics and the "core and branches" (*pen-mo* 本末) of the Histories. In other words, candidates were to delineate the evolutionary pattern of the Classics from the original six in number to thirteen by the Sung dynasty. This completed, they were asked to take up the evolution of historical writing from Tso Ch'iu-ming to Ssu-ma Ch'ien and Pan Ku. Historical and classical studies in effect stood on equal ground, as the examiners noted: "Earlier literati have said that classical studies focused on matters of the mind (*hsin-shu* 心術); historical studies have stressed actual achievements (*shih-kung* 事功)." Ssu-ma Kuang and Chu Hsi were no longer the focus of attention.[100]

Chosen as the best policy answer for this question was Ch'en I-hsiung's 陳一熊 essay in some 2,300 characters. The examiners rated it as "penetrating," "comprehensive," and "elegant," suggesting that they valued both historical knowledge and narrative style. The policy essay opened with the usual general discussion of the importance of history that we have seen in earlier policy answers, but Ch'en noted that the Classics and the Histories taken together represented the proper standard for public

99. *Kuang-tung hsiang-shih lu*, 1654: "Hsu," 序 p. 10a, and pp. 8b–14b of the record. Cf. *Dictionary of Ming Biography*, pp. 148–51 and 153–56.

100. *Kuang-tung hsiang-shih lu*, 1654: 10a–11a.

well-being: "The Classics are the stars, planets, sun, and moon in the human realm; the Histories are the lofty peaks and the Yangtzu and Yellow rivers of our human realm." By advancing our knowledge through the penetration of things (*chih-chih ko-wu* 致知格物), one could master the Classics. The *Spring and Autumn Annals* should be mastered, for it contained the "rights and wrongs" essential for public well-being.[101]

Classical studies were still the provenance of Tao Learning, as the pat appeal to the doctrine of *ko-wu* demonstrates. Similarly, the *Annals* remained the core of the orthodox moralizing historiography. In this regard, Ch'en's essay was in essential agreement with those of his Ming predecessors. Moreover, Ch'en contended that while historical circumstances changed, the principles underlying those changes remained eternal, a reassuring theme in a time of dynastic change. The Classics already contained the essentials of the Histories, whereas the Histories were based on the unified vision informing classical studies. This vision, however, had been lost during the period of disunity after the fall of the Later Han dynasty and not recovered until the great Tao Learning masters of the Sung, best represented by the "original meanings" (*pen-i* 本義) elucidated by Chu Hsi.[102]

In theory, Ch'en I-hsiung's essay diverged very little from earlier essays that dissolved history into the classical philosophy of Tao Learning. But in practice, there were some important differences. First of all, Ch'en was forced by the examiners to detail Han and T'ang dynasty vicissitudes in classical and historical studies, which had been undervalued during the Ming. More important, however, Ch'en's essay, although it prominently displayed Confucius' *Annals,* made no significant mention of Ssu-ma Kuang's *Comprehensive Mirror* or of Chu Hsi's condensation, which Ming examiners and candidates had virtually worshiped as the model for orthodox historiography. The Chu Hsi that appeared in Ch'en's 1654 policy essay was circumscribed. Chu was hailed for his classical studies but ignored for his history. In effect, the question on classical and historical studies revealed a rudimentary but still noticeable distance that the examiners had placed between the two disciplines.[103]

In concluding remarks, Ch'en emphasized that historians should base themselves on the "methods of the mind" (*hsin-fa*) of the *Annals,* but this was more formulaic than substantive. In Ming essays, those "methods" had been articulated in light of Ssu-ma Kuang's and Chu Hsi's revitalization of the genre of annalistic history as a textbook for political ethics.

101. Ibid., 1654: 61b–63b.
102. Ibid., 1654: 63b–64b.
103. Ibid., 1654: 64b–69b.

Without the latter guidelines, or the earlier premeditated attacks on Han and post-Han historians for their heterodox views, Ch'en's use of the stock terminology of Tao Learning had lost some of its normative power. Ch'en's answer had lost the self-righteous conviction that informed Ming essays.[104]

To conclude this account of the changes in historical studies during the seventeenth century, I refer for comparative purposes to the 1685 metropolitan examination. By this time the K'ang-hsi emperor had established an office to compile the history of the Ming dynasty, which probably affected thinking about historiographical formats. As part of the 1685 examination, the second policy question also tested candidates on the distinction between classical and historical studies. As in 1654, the examiners asked candidates to describe in detail the evolution of the Thirteen Classics and Twenty-one Dynastic Histories. Along the way the examiners expressed what was then a common position among Ch'ing literati concerning the provenance of the Histories: "The *Annals* is a Classic of history; [Ssu-ma] Ch'ien and [Pan] Ku are the patriarchs of history." The late Ming exclusion of Han historians from the lineage of orthodox historiography was effectively over.[105]

What concerned the examiners was not the disjunction between annalistic and topical history. Rather, they asked students to discuss how orthodox history (*cheng-shih* 正史) had rightly been modeled on the histories by Ssu-ma Ch'ien and Pan Ku. Han and post-Han dynastic historians were now offered to candidates as respectable scholars. This relative openness, when compared to the rather "closed" Ming policy questions on history, allowed graduates such as Chin Chü-ching 金居敬, whose essay was selected as the best policy answer for the 1685 question on classical and historical studies, to itemize the Twenty-one Dynastic Histories as individual works. He thereby could exclude such comprehensive histories as Ssu-ma Kuang's *Tzu-chih t'ung-chien* from mention. Chin's model essay also criticized individual histories by T'ang scholars such as Liu Chih-chi 劉知幾 (661–721) (conspicuously missing in the 1516 and 1594 and most Ming policy questions), but the aim of such criticism was not to exclude the Dynastic Histories from consideration. Instead, the criticism was meant simply to correct or reconsider earlier accounts.[106]

Chu Hsi was discussed in light of the Classics and not the Histories. Both the examiners and Chin Chü-ching made clear that the distinction between annalistic and topical histories was part of the classical legacy

104. Ibid., 1654: 69a–70a.
105. *Hui-shih lu,* 1685: 13a–15a.
106. Ibid., 1685: 74a–76a.

itself and not the invention of Ssu-ma Ch'ien. As Chin noted at the outset of his prize essay, "Ancient histories were also Classics. The *Documents Classic* followed the genre of topically recording [history]. The *Annals* followed the genre of chronicling events." In the process, topical history had evolved into the accepted form for "dynastic history" (*kuo-shih* 國史). Countering the Ming views of historiography already analyzed, the Ch'ing examiners did not think that chronicles should take precedence, as Ssu-ma Kuang and Chu Hsi had wanted it, over topical histories. In the early Ch'ing, the genre of *chi-chuan* was preferred over *pien-nien*.[107]

The 1685 metropolitan examination question on history had also gone one step further than the 1658 Kuang-tung policy question by dropping all mention of the Tao Learning "methods of the mind" that were still part of the 1658 question and answer on history. Instead, the 1685 examiners gave the "doctrines of the mind" (*hsin-hsueh* 心學) prominence of place in the first policy question, devoted solely to the "orthodox transmission of the Way." There, separate from questions of history, Tao Learning orthodoxy still held sway.

In the policy question on classical and historical studies, however, the scope of Tao Learning had been curtailed. There had been a clear diminution of Chu Hsi as a historian. No longer was history automatically reduced to the Classics. No longer was historiography simply a question of the proper moralizing historiography. But neither were any of the Classics themselves yet reduced to history. Nor were the historical Classics denied their priority. Changes were brewing, but another century would pass before late eighteenth-century literati such as Chang Hsueh-ch'eng would begin to gainsay the priority of the Classics and dissolve classicism into historical studies. Overall, Ch'ing dynasty policy questions on history increasingly reflected the views the examiners enunciated in 1685.[108]

## HAN VERSUS SUNG LEARNING
## IN CH'ING POLICY QUESTIONS

In the seventeenth and eighteenth centuries, the Classics and the Dynastic Histories were carefully scrutinized by a growing community of textual scholars in Yangtzu delta urban centers. The slow but steady emergence of evidential research studies in the delta as a self-conscious field of academic discourse was predicated on the centrality of philological research to (1) determine the authenticity of classical and historical texts, (2) unravel the etymologies of ancient classical terms, (3) reconstruct the phonology of

107. Ibid., 1685: 74b.
108. Ibid., 1685: 11a–13a.

ancient Chinese, and (4) clarify the paleography of Chinese characters. These trends, as we have seen, began in the late Ming, but they climaxed under the Ch'ing.

The Ming *k'ao-chü* (see Chapter 8) and Ch'ing *k'ao-cheng* evidential research agendas for accumulating verifiable knowledge represented a major reorientation in thought and epistemology among classical scholars in the Yangtzu delta. Evidential scholars there favored a return to the most ancient sources available, usually from the Han and T'ang dynasties, to reconstruct the classical tradition. Because the Han was closer in time to the actual compilation of the Classics, Ch'ing scholars increasingly utilized Han works (hence called "Han Learning") to reevaluate the Classics. Frequently, this change in emphasis also entailed a rejection of Sung sources (hence called "Sung Learning") to study the Classics because the latter were separated by over 1,500 years from the classical era, and because many Ch'ing scholars were convinced that the Tao Learning schools of Chu Hsi and Wang Yang-ming had unwittingly incorporated heterodox Taoist and Buddhist doctrines and theories into the literati canon.[109]

### *The Old Text Documents Controversy*

As a representative example of the overall direction in Ch'ing evidential studies, many *k'ao-cheng* scholars claimed, for instance, that the Old Text portions of the *Documents Classic* were forgeries from the third century A.D., and not the work of the sage-kings of antiquity. This textual controversy became a cause célèbre among Han Learning scholars, at the same time that the civil examination system used Old Text passages on the "human mind and the mind of the Way" to test candidates' knowledge of the Sung Learning orthodoxy. Students were expected to memorize the Ch'eng-Chu position on the Classics and elaborate on it for imperial examiners, but even the examiners increasingly recognized that many orthodox views were philologically suspect.

Since the Sung dynasty, doubts had been expressed concerning the provenance of the Old Text chapters of the *Documents,* but it was not until Yen Jo-chü's 閻若璩 (1636–1704) research and the definitive conclusions he drew in his unpublished but widely distributed manuscript entitled *Evidential Analysis of the Old Text Documents (Shang-shu ku-wen shu-cheng* 尚書古

109. See my *From Philosophy to Philology,* pp. 26–36. See also Ping-yi Chu, "Ch'eng-Chu Orthodoxy, Evidential Studies and Correlative Cosmology: Chiang Yung and Western Astronomy," *Philosophy and the History of Science: A Taiwanese Journal* 4, 2 (October 1995): 71–108.

文疏證) that the question was considered settled.[110] Based on Yen's demonstrations that the Old Text portion was not authentic, some officials sent memorials to the throne in the 1690s and again in the 1740s, calling for elimination of the Old Text chapters from the official text used in the civil examinations. Each time the proposals were set aside. Hui Tung 惠 棟 (1697–1758), the doyen of Han Learning in Su-chou, had renewed Yen Jo-chü's attack on the Old Text chapters in the 1740s. Hui noted that it had taken several centuries for suspicions concerning the Old Text *Documents* to lead anywhere conclusive. Hui Tung's Han Learning followers continued research on the Old Text chapters, picking up where their mentor had left off. Ch'ang-chou's Sun Hsing-yen 孫星衍 (1753–1818), with his definitive study of the variances between the Old and New Text *Documents* brought to completion the attack on the spurious Old Text chapters. Sun's analysis of Later and Former Han sources marked one of the high points of Han Learning prestige during the Ch'ing dynasty.[111]

At the confluence of classical studies, legitimation of imperial power, and public policy, the conservative position vis-à-vis the Classics taken by Sung Learning advocates represented their cultural solidarity with the imperial orthodoxy of the Ming and Ch'ing dynasties. The Han Learning threat to the orthodox Old Text Classics threatened the shared consensus enshrined since the early Ming in the civil examination curriculum. Many refused to accept the textual findings of evidential research scholars.

For example, Chuang Ts'un-yü, a Hanlin academician frequently assigned to supervise provincial examinations and later a leader in the reemergence of New Text classicism in Ch'ang-chou, noted while serving as a court secretary to the Ch'ien-lung emperor in the 1740s that if the long-accepted Old Text chapter known as the "Counsels of Yü the Great" were impugned, then the cardinal doctrine of the "human mind and mind of the Tao," as well as Kao Yao's (minister to Emperor Shun) legal injunction, which stated "rather than put to death an innocent person, you [Shun] would rather run the risk of irregularity," would be subverted. These were teachings, Chuang contended, that depended on their classical sanction. Accordingly, on ideological grounds, Chuang Ts'un-yü attempted to set limits to the accruing *k'ao-cheng* research in the Han Learning mainstream by insulating the Classics from such criticism.[112]

---

110. For recent research, see Liu Jen-p'eng 劉人鵬, "Lun Chu-tzu wei-ch'ang i ku-wen shang-shu wei-tso" 論朱子未嘗疑古文尚書偽作 (Chu Hsi never doubted the authenticity of the Old Text *Documents*), *Ch'ing-hua hsueh-pao* 清華學報 n.s., 22, 4 (December 1992): 399–430.

111. For discussion, see my "Philosophy (*I-li*) versus Philology (*K'ao-cheng*)," pp. 175–222.

112. See my *Classicism, Politics, and Kinship*, chaps. 3–5.

Yet, as noted in Chapter 8, the metropolitan examinations of 1685, 1730, and 1737 continued to cite the passage on the human mind and mind of the Tao from the Old Text "Counsels of Yü the Great" with no indication of the philological controversy surrounding its authenticity. Similarly, we have seen that Ming student answers, even when such students wrote policy answers on *kao-chü* issues, never mentioned such textual debates. They faithfully recapitulated the Ch'eng-Chu interpretation of the transmission of the mind of the sage-kings.

Whether as an act of cultural loyalty to the reigning dynasty or as confirmation of orthodox literati values, the eight-legged examination essay was not designed conceptually for rigorous textual analysis. To bring up philological issues in a literary exercise would run the risk of failing the dual cultural and political litmus tests the classical essay was designed to measure. Policy questions on session three of the provincial and metropolitan examinations were the proper venue for the philological analysis of the Classics, but during the Ming such questions and answers were usually linked to statecraft and had not yet become critical of the textual basis of the Ch'eng-Chu orthodoxy.

Classical predispositions began to change in the late eighteenth century, however, when in session-three policy questions in the provincial and metropolitan examinations, examiners at times tested technical *k'ao-cheng* topics previously outside the civil curriculum. In chronological terms, however, policy questions based on Han Learning crested in the nineteenth century, a generation after its intellectual triumph among southern literati during the last twenty years of the Ch'ien-lung reign. In the 1810 Chiang-nan provincial examination for candidates from An-hui and Chiang-su, for instance, the first of the third session's policy questions straightforwardly raised the issue of the authenticity of portions of the *Documents Classic*.

The examiners opened their query by immediately raising the debate concerning the relation of the "Preface" ("Hsu" 序) to the original 100-chapter version of the *Documents*, which had long been attributed to Confucius. The examiners asked: "Why wasn't the preface included in the [original] listing of the hundred chapters?" Next, candidates were asked to explain why during the Former Han dynasty there were discrepancies over how many chapters (28 or 29) of the New Text version of the *Documents* text had survived the Ch'in "burning of the books" policy. Following this, the candidates were required to explicate the perplexing circumstances whereby K'ung An-kuo 孔安國 (156–74? B.C.), a descendant of Confucius and a Han Erudite of the Classics, had prepared his own "preface" for a version of the *Documents* that added 29 more Old Text chapters from a recently discovered text of the *Documents* to the earlier New Text version. "Why," the examiners asked, "were 59 chapters listed for this version when there should have been only 58?"

After dealing with Former Han sources, the examiners turned to the Later Han dynasty classicist Cheng Hsuan 鄭玄 (A.D. 127–200), the "patron-saint" of Ch'ing dynasty Han Learning, whose scholia listed the 100 chapters in the original but lost *Documents* in a different order from K'ung An-kuo's version. "Why this discrepancy?" the candidates were asked. Subsequently, issues related to T'ang and Sung handling of the *Documents* text were raised. Why had K'ung Ying-ta 孔穎達 (574–648), then in charge of T'ang efforts to settle on authoritative texts for the classical examination curriculum (see Chapter 1), labeled a third version of the *Documents* from the Han dynasty a forgery? Why had Chu Hsi voiced suspicions concerning the unusual phraseology (for Han dynasty writings) of K'ung An-kuo's commentary and preface to the *Documents*?[113]

The organization and content of this query reveal the degree to which the philological discoveries associated with Han Learning and evidential research had begun to filter into the civil examination system. Although still a test of cultural and political loyalty, whereby the Ch'ing reign was praised by the examiners for its nourishing classical studies, this exploration of the textual vicissitudes surrounding the *Documents Classic* required precise information that would demonstrate to the examiners that the candidate was aware of the authenticity controversy surrounding this particular Classic. Rather than testing cultural orthodoxy, however, the question raised potentially corrosive issues that could challenge orthodox "truths." One of the key Old Text chapters now thought by many literati to be a forgery was the "Ta Yü mo," which contained classical lessons on the basis of which the theories of "orthodox statecraft" and "orthodox transmission of the Way" had been constructed.[114]

Such textual concerns might be considered unique to the Yangtzu delta because the academic community there had been pioneers in reviving Han Learning concerns and appropriating *k'ao-cheng* research techniques for classical and historical studies. On the contrary, however, changes in civil examination questioning were occurring throughout the empire, principally as a result of the Ch'ing appointments of provincial examiners, who frequently came from the Yangtzu delta and thus were conversant with the latest research findings of classical scholars there. Yangtzu delta

113. *Chiang-nan hsiang-shih t'i-ming lu* 江南鄉試題名錄 (Record of successful candidates in the Chiang-nan provincial examination), 1810: 9a–9b, in the archives of the No. 1 Historical Archives, Peking. For purposes of focus, I have not described other important debates, which I have done elsewhere. See, for example, my "Ming Politics and Confucian Classics," pp. 93–171. I have chosen the relatively well-known and representative Old Text versus New Text *Documents* debate to summarize the changes in examination questions in the eighteenth and nineteenth centuries.

114. For discussion, see my *From Philosophy to Philology*, pp. 177–80, 200–02, 207–12.

scholars had long been the most successful on the metropolitan and palace examinations in Peking (see Chapter 5) and thus were the most likely to gain appointment to the Hanlin Academy and the Ministry of Rites. Most who served as provincial examination officials were chosen from the latter two overlapping institutions in the metropolitan bureaucracy. Examinations held in the culturally peripheral provinces of Shan-tung in the north, Ssu-ch'uan in the southwest, and Shan-hsi in the northwest all reveal the magnitude and scope of the scholarly changes promoted by literati examiners that were appearing after 1750.

### Civil Examinations in Shan-tung

Although not as directly stated as in the above 1810 question, the first policy question in the Shan-tung provincial examination of 1771 dealt with the philology of the Classics. For the policy question in Shan-tung dealing with the Classics, examiners explored textual issues, even though themes pertaining to moral philosophy remained more common. The 1771 policy question, for example, brought up the complicated divisions between the Old and New Text versions of the *Documents* in order to elicit from candidates the lack of unanimity about the Classics and what sort of consensus was possible based on differing viewpoints. Why had even Chu Hsi and Ch'eng I failed to agree on certain issues?[115]

Other technical aspects of *k'ao-cheng* were also tested. In the 1807 provincial examinations held in Shan-tung, for example, the third policy question dealt with the technical field of ancient phonology (*yin-yun chih hsueh* 音韻之學). Inclusion of this question was due to the presence of Sun Hsing-yen as examiner. As a distinguished *k'ao-cheng* scholar from Ch'ang-chou prefecture in the Yangtzu delta, Sun made his influence felt among candidates preparing for the Shan-tung examinations. The examination question stressed the priority of ancient rhyme schemes in the *Poetry Classic* for the reconstruction of ancient phonology. Students were also expected to take into account the linguistic factor of the development of four tones in their explication of the classification of rhymes.[116]

---

115. *Shan-tung hsiang-shih t'i-ming lu* 山東鄉試題名錄 (Record of successful candidates in the Shan-tung provincial examination), 1771: unpaginated manuscript, in the archives of the No. 1 Historical Archives, Peking. Policy questions for the 1783, 1807, 1808, 1810, 1813, 1819, 1831, 1832, 1855, 1859, 1885, 1893, and 1894 Shan-tung examinations also contain significant philological queries.

116. *Shan-tung hsiang-shih t'i-ming lu*, 1807: unpaginated manuscript. For examples of other examination policy questions Sun Hsing-yen prepared in private academies and as an official examiner, see *Ch'ing-tai ch'ien-ch'i chiao-yü lun-chu hsuan*, 3/279–81, 285–88.

During the 1819 Shan-tung examination, the examiners specifically asked in the first policy question that candidates engage in a *k'ao-cheng* analysis of the New Text–Old Text provenance of the Classics:

Wang Po-hou 王伯厚 [Ying-lin 應鄰, 1223–96] claimed that the "Offices of Chou" 周官 [chapter of the *Documents*] belonged to the New Text version, but he added that within the Classic many Old Text portions remained. Moreover, in his annotation Wang used New Text [sources] to change the latter. Why? Notes to the *Decorum Ritual* [*I-li* 儀禮] in some cases follow Old Text [views], in others they follow New Text [views], and in still other cases they combine New and Old Text [views]. Can you separate out these issues for clarification?

Later, during the 1831 examination, Shan-tung students were required to answer two policy questions dealing with philology. The first asked specific information about the Old and New Text *Documents;* the second tested the students' knowledge of the paleographical origins of the distinction between Old and New Text script. Students who had only mastered Ch'eng-Chu moral philosophy for sessions one and two would now be hard-pressed to pass session three of the provincial examinations in Shan-tung.[117]

In 1741, in another northern provincial examination, the Shun-t'ien provincial examiner's comments on Liang Kuo-chih's 梁國治 (1723–87) top essay for the second policy question on the historical development of classical commentaries linked Liang's answer directly to evidential research: *k'ao-cheng ching-hsiang* 考證精詳 (evidential research that is focused and detailed). Liang finished seventh on the 1741 provincial examination and later was the *optimus* in the palace examination of 1748 when he received his *chin-shih* degree. The emergence of paleography, etymology, and phonology as the key tools in classical studies was explicitly cited in 1795 by examiners in Shun-t'ien prefecture. In the query on *hsiao-hsueh* 小學 philology, the candidates were required to review the major works in its three areas of specialization, which conceptually went well beyond the boundaries of *k'ao-chü* in the Ming.[118]

### Civil Examinations in Ssu-ch'uan

In Ssu-ch'uan province, on the other hand, the 1738 examination there revealed that Sung Learning orthodoxy remained intact as the mind-set of provincial examiners. Since the fourteenth century, Ssu-ch'uan had de-

---

117. *Shan-tung hsiang-shih t'i-ming lu*, 1819 and 1831: both unpaginated manuscripts.
118. *Shun-t'ien hsiang-shih lu*, 1741: 36a, 39a; 1759: unpaginated.

clined in economic and cultural prominence. With this long-term secular decline came the eclipse of classical learning there until the early eighteenth century, when the Ch'eng-Chu learning undergirding the civil examinations penetrated dynastic schools in the province.[119] Students in 1738 were asked, for example, to prepare a policy question essay dealing with the Ch'eng-Chu agenda for mental discipline, which duplicated almost verbatim earlier questions on the metropolitan examinations (analyzed above). The first policy question of 1738 thus assumed a unified classical vision for the "orthodox transmission of the Way," which was based on the long-accepted distinction between the "human mind and mind of the Tao" and the Ch'eng-Chu agenda for "absolute refinement, singleness of purpose, and allegiance to the mean."[120]

Philological issues were raised in policy questions prepared for the Ssu-ch'uan provincial examinations of 1741 and 1747, for instance, but Sung Learning remained the dominant mind-set for questioning through the eighteenth century. In the 1800 provincial examinations, however, Han Learning issues were raised in policy questions. For the second policy question, students were asked to compare Han-T'ang scholia (chu-shu 注疏) with Sung "meanings and principles" (i-li 義理) and determine where the Ch'eng-Chu school differed from Han and T'ang literati. Examiners required for the third policy question an explicit "evidential" (k'ao-chü 考據) analysis to assess the accuracy of historical studies to date. To answer the fourth policy question, candidates had to demonstrate their understanding of the fields of ancient etymology, ancient phonology, and paleography, which the examiners defined as the key subdisciplines of philology (hsiao-hsueh 小學).[121]

In subsequent Ssu-ch'uan examinations, Han and Sung Learning issues

119. Yu Li, "Social Change during the Ming-Qing Transition and the Decline of Sichuan Classical Learning in the Early Qing," Late Imperial China 19, 1 (June 1998): 26–55. This otherwise useful article places the revival in the late nineteenth century, a view I modify here. Yu claims that "there has been no empirical evidence found to support the idea that these policy questions ... actually diverted Sichuan scholars' attention to evidential studies" (pp. 41–42). Apparently, the 3,400 to 5,000 candidates per provincial examination in Ch'eng-tu during the eighteenth century (see Table 3.6) do not consistute sufficient evidence. Yu also claims that policy questions were "relatively unimportant" and that "the Ming dynasty candidates who participated in provincial examinations attached no importance to policy questions." Yu's position, which I have gainsaid in Chapter 8 and here, is not based on any archival research and simply reiterates, uncritically, the rhetoric of late Ming examination critics discussed earlier in Chapter 4.

120. Ssu-ch'uan hsiang-shih t'i-ming lu 四川鄉試題名錄 (Record of successful candidates in the Ssu-ch'uan provincial examination), 1738: unpaginated manuscript, in the archives of the No. 1 Historical Archives, Peking.

121. Ibid., 1800: unpaginated manuscript.

were frequently raised. In the first policy question of 1832, for instance, examiners prepared a question focusing on the history of calligraphy and how Old Text (lit., "ancient script") forms of writing pertained to the Four Books. Later, in 1846, the third policy question flatly granted one of the linguistic premises of evidential research studies: "The starting point for mastering the Classics is the knowledge of written graphs. To understand written graphs, nothing takes priority over the *Shuo-wen* (Explication of writing)." The question and answer remind us of Hsueh Ying-ch'i's discussion of paleography in a policy question on *k'ao-chü* three centuries earlier.

In the lead policy question of 1859, candidates were asked about doubts concerning the Old Text *Documents:* "Many who are fond of antiquity have supposed that the twenty-five Old Text chapters of the *Documents,* such as the 'Counsels of Yü the Great,' are forgeries. From what period do they come? Who transmitted them? Who were the first to question them?" By 1860, then, the very texts upon which orthodox interpretation of the human mind and the mind of Tao that we traced earlier had been based were openly questioned in the precincts of provincial civil service examinations.

Such developments were cumulative but not irrevocable, however, given the ties between conservatism and orthodox learning after the Taiping Rebellion (see Chapter 11). In 1885 the examiners raised issues pertaining to New and Old Text philology in the first policy question, but for the second question they prepared a typical query testing the student's knowledge of Sung Learning "orthodox studies." In fact, the juxtaposition of Han and Sung Learning on the same examination but in different questions reflected the synthesis of the two competing schools that became an important characteristic of the last century of classical thought.[122]

### Civil Examinations in Shen-hsi

Similarly in Shen-hsi province, provincial examination questions remained focused on Sung Ch'eng-Chu themes and issues for most of the first century of Ch'ing rule. In 1756, for example, examiners prepared the first policy question as a test of the student's knowledge of the by-now-standard doctrine of the "transmission of the mind-set of the sages and worthies," referring specifically to the passage in the "Counsels of Yü the Great" on the distinction between the human mind and mind of the Tao. This question was repeated almost verbatim in 1788 when the centrality of

---

122. Ibid., 1832, 1846, 1859, 1885: all unpaginated manuscripts. In the 1885 examination, examiners faithful to Sung Learning were clearly in charge. On Han-Sung syncretism. see my *From Philosophy to Philology,* pp. 245–48.

the "Counsels" chapter was affirmed without any questioning of its Old Text provenance.

In 1759, however, the tenor of questions had changed somewhat. The first policy question for the 1759 proceedings emphasized pre-T'ang classical traditions dating back to the "schools system" (*chia-fa* 家法) used in the Han dynasty Imperial Academy to teach the Classics. Students were asked to summarize the history of the transmission of the *Documents Classic* as well as the other Classics. In the first policy questions for both 1795 and 1800, examiners focused their query dealing with the Classics specifically on the Han Learning of Cheng Hsuan.

Students were asked in 1795 to discuss the exemplary position held by Cheng Hsuan in the "classical studies of Han literati." In 1800 the examiners again stressed Cheng Hsuan's contributions to classical studies and tested candidates about Cheng's explication of the *Chou-i* 周易 (Chou dynasty *Change Classic*), among other issues. For the third policy question of 1800, archaeology and paleography were presented as fields of expertise when the examiners asked students to demonstrate their knowledge of the characteristics of engraved monoliths from the Han dynasty that contained the "Classics carved on stone tablets" (*shih-ching* 石經). Similarly for the fourth policy question, philological issues concerning the relationship between the present 300-chapter version of the *Poetry Classic* and its numerous "missing poems" were tested.

Thereafter, Han Learning and *k'ao-cheng* themes became a regular feature of the Shen-hsi examinations. In the 1825 examination, the first policy question queried students on the antiquity of the Five Classics. With regard to the *Documents,* for example, the examiners asked students to comment on the possible forgery of K'ung An-kuo's preface. Similar philological points were raised concerning the *Change* and *Poetry* Classics. In 1831, the Han dynasty "schools system" was tested in the first policy question. By the 1833 provincial examination held in Shen-hsi, examiners were openly skeptical of the authenticity of the Old Text *Documents* and proudly announced in the first policy question that "classical studies under the sagely [Ch'ing] dynasty had been greatly illumined, doubts investigated, and forgeries ferreted out."

Political legitimacy was now transmitted through evidential research, as well as through the Ch'eng-Chu orthodoxy, indicating that students could demonstrate their loyalty to the dynasty by mastering *k'ao-cheng* techniques.[123]

123. *Shen-hsi hsiang-shih t'i-ming lu* 陝西鄉試題名錄 (Record of successful candidates in the Shan-hsi provincial examination), 1690, 1741, 1756, 1759, 1788, 1795, 1800, 1825, 1831, and 1833: all unpaginated manuscripts, in the archives of the No. 1 Historical Archives, Peking.

*Changes in Metropolitan Examination Questions*

As might be expected of a dynasty that used Sung Tao Learning rhetoric to defend its cultural legitimacy, changes in policy questions for the metropolitan and palace examinations were slower in coming than in their provincial counterparts. Here, we witness dynamic intellectual changes, which began in the urban centers of the Yangtzu delta and first influenced local provincial examinations before appearing in the capital selection process. Ch'ing emperors unilaterally decreed from above that "natural studies" were inappropriate at all examinations, even as Ch'ing currents of classical scholarship were ascending the examination ladder on the strength of those Han Learning and *k'ao-cheng* scholars who as examiners were themselves moving up the civil service ladder of success.

As we have seen, the 1685 metropolitan examination was administered by officials who prepared questions that required mastery of Sung moral and political theory. Although classical issues dealing with texts and their transmission were tested, the overall Sung Learning mind-set did not change. In the metropolitan examination of 1730, for instance, we have seen that the 1685 question on the "human mind and the mind of the Tao" was repeated almost verbatim. In 1737, the question appeared again.

In the metropolitan examinations of 1739, 1742, 1748, 1751, and 1752, the first policy question for each characteristically dealt with the topic of "orthodox statecraft" and the "orthodox transmission of the Way." Examiners in Peking seemed intent on making sure that students got the message: the doctrine of "mental discipline," which enabled students to "grasp the fundamentals of moral principles," was the sine qua non for discussing the "methods of governance of the [Three] Emperors and [Five] Kings." Ch'en Chin 陳晉, a native of the Yangtzu delta, prepared the model answer for the 1739 policy question, which emphasized the dual roles of "external kingship" (*wai-wang* 外王) and "inner sagehood" (*nei-sheng* 內聖).[124]

In 1742 policy questions, the examiners expressly asked students to treat the Ch'eng-Chu position on human nature. The prize answer by Chin Shen 金甡 (1702–82) from Hang-chou focused on "principles of the mind and nature," which Chin equated with the primacy of the "mind of the Tao" over the "human mind." The "mind of the sages" was the key subject for the policy questions of the 1748 proceedings. Examiners asked: "Do the teachings of Confucius stress sincerity and seriousness? Before Confucius, in what Classic did the principle of sincerity first appear?" The most outstanding essay was prepared by Li Chung-chien 李中簡 (ca.

---

124. *Hui-shih lu*, 1739: 4a–4b, 36a–38b.

1713–74), who traced the linkage between orthodox statecraft and the orthodox transmission of the Way to the teachings transmitted from Yao to Shun, and from Shun to Yü.[125]

The first policy question in 1751 presented the view that "nature originated in the heavenly mind." To "return to one's nature" entailed "holding to the mean" and grasping the superiority of the "mind of the Tao." Unlike earlier questions, however, here the examiners asked candidates to compare the different positions Chu Hsi and Wang Yang-ming held concerning the polarity between "honoring one's moral nature" (*tsun te-hsing* 尊德性) and "inquiring into culture and study" (*tao wen-hsueh* 道問學). In his answer, the Che-chiang litcratus Chou Li 周澧 (1709–53) summarized the orthodox position in which Chu Hsi's equation of human nature and principle (*hsing chi li* 性即理) took precedence over Wang Yang-ming's equation of the moral mind (*liang-hsin* 良心) with principle (*hsin chi li* 心即理).[126]

Again in 1752, the "human mind and mind of the Tao" passage was the focus of the first policy question. "Mental discipline," according to the prize essay prepared by Chi Fu-hsiang 紀復享 (n.d.), was equated with "methods of governance." To perfect one's discipline, Chi contended, one had to "grasp the learning of the Way." Such training was premised on "residing in seriousness" and "fathoming principles" (*chü-ching ch'iung-li* 居敬窮理).[127]

Although questions dealing with textual aspects of the Classics were presented in some of these metropolitan examinations, the mind-set the examiners sought to reproduce among the candidates was decidedly in favor of the Sung Learning orthodoxy—so much so that in the 1754 metropolitan examination, which became famous as the examination passed by five of the greatest Han Learning scholars of the late eighteenth century (Ch'ien Ta-hsin; Chi Yun 紀昀, 1724–1805; Wang Ch'ang 王昶, 1725–1806; Wang Ming-sheng; and Chu Yun 朱筠, 1729–81), only one of the policy questions dealt with textual issues at all. The first policy question in fact required an orthodox restatement of the premises of the Ch'eng-Chu "school of principle," which the Han Learning scholars-to-be would later attack as "empty and unverifiable" rhetoric (*k'ung-t'an* 空談).[128]

Ch'ien Ta-hsin's 1754 examination essay for the second policy question, which dealt with textual issues concerning the transmission of the Four Books and Five Classics, was selected as the outstanding answer to the

125. Ibid., 1742: 4a–5b, 35b–39a, 1748: 4b–6a, 33a–35a.
126. Ibid., 1751: 4a–6a, 37a–41a.
127. Ibid., 1752: 4a–6a, 33b–36a.
128. Ibid., 1739: 6a–6b, 1748: 6a–7b, 1751: 6a–8a, 1754: 4a–5a.

question. Although the examiners had stressed the importance of Chu Hsi's place in classical studies, particularly with regard to arranging the proper order of chapters in the *Great Learning* (one of the Four Books), their question did address technical issues surrounding the Four Books. Ch'ien Ta-hsin's extremely long model answer (indicating that unlike most other candidates in the mid-eighteenth century he took this policy question on session three very seriously) deftly maneuvered through the complexities of the classical issues.

Without directly impugning the Sung Learning orthodoxy, Ch'ien pointed out that the Four Books were never referred to as the "Four Books" until the Sung dynasty, when Chu Hsi and his followers had brought the *Analects,* the *Mencius, Great Learning,* and *Doctrine of the Mean* together as a special repository of classical teachings. Although the Four Books had since 1384 taken precedence over the Five Classics, Ch'ien Ta-hsin noted that originally the Four Books had been secondary to and a derivative of the Five Classics. According to Ch'ien, "the six Classics were all definitively compiled by the sages," thus suggesting that the later Four Books had less classical authority because they were only authorized by recent Sung literati. In his essay, Ch'ien also raised doubts about the authenticity of the Old Text portions of the *Documents Classic.*[129] Later Ch'ien also attacked Fang Pao for his efforts to legitimate eight-legged essays as examples of Sung dynasty ancient-style prose (see Chapter 7).[130]

Policy questions dealing with the classical Canon increasingly moved from obligatory requests of candidates to reproduce Sung Ch'eng-Chu moral discourse to tests of their mastery of classical information. In the 1766 metropolitan examination, for example, candidates were asked a policy question requiring mastery of the Han Learning field of phonology. The examiners pointed out in their question that "because the Han was not very far separated in time from antiquity," the initials and finals (*sheng-yun* 聲韻) in Han versions of the *Poetry Classic* were likely to be the most accurate ancient pronunciations available.[131]

Later policy questions prepared during the 1793 and 1823 metropolitan examinations reveal the degree to which Ch'ing classical studies were penetrating the civil examination process. In 1793 students were asked to deal with the controversies surrounding the three orthodox commentaries to Confucius' *Spring and Autumn Annals,* particularly the debate over the reliability of the *Tso chuan,* whose author, Tso Ch'iu-ming, had been regarded as one of Confucius' direct disciples, although this Old Text claim had

129. Ibid., 1754: 39b–45b.
130. *Ch'ing-tai ch'ien-ch'i chiao-yü lun-chu hsuan,* 3/148–50.
131. *Hui-shih lu,* 1766: 3a–4b, 50a–53b.

been challenged by eighteenth-century New Text scholars. In 1792, for instance, Chi Yun had memorialized the throne concerning the various commentaries to the *Annals*, which had included since the Ming dynasty the Hu An-kuo commentary as one of four required commentaries in dynastic schools. Chi requested that this Sung commentary should be removed from the school curriculum because of its distance of more than 1,500 years from the date of the Classic itself. Chi's request was granted, which symbolized the victory of Han Learning at court. Thereafter, only the three Han commentaries were regarded as orthodox, and the Hu commentary fell into oblivion.[132] Later, as chief examiner for the 1796 metropolitan examination, Chi Yun wrote in his preface to the final report that the civil examiners "should make Sung Learning the main line of transmission but where it was lacking they should supplement it with Han Learning" (以宋學為宗，而以漢學補萱其所遺).[133]

Earlier in 1758 the Hu commentary on the *Annals* had already been attacked as arbitrary. In its place, Han Learning scholars, following Ku Yen-wu's lead, recommended that Tu Yü's commentary to the *Tso chuan* should be used to "recover ancient studies."[134] In addition to removing one of the Sung dynasty commentaries to the Five Classics, Han Learning scholar-officials such as Hung Liang-chi 洪亮吉 (1746–1809) stressed Han masters for each Classic, thus seeking to restore the teacher-disciple model (*chia-fa* 家法) of the early empire and replace the mind-to-mind *tao-t'ung* transmission associated with Tao Learning (see Chapter 1). Hung regarded Confucius, not Chu Hsi, as the model example for *chia-fa*.[135]

In addition, Ch'ing literati in the late eighteenth century attacked the early Ming *Ta-ch'üan* 大全 (Great collection) trilogy, which the Yung-lo emperor had established as the key repository of Sung-Yuan commentaries required in the civil examinations for the Four Books and Five Classics (see Chapter 2). Sun Hsing-yen, for instance, drafted a memorial to the emperor requesting that the Han-T'ang scholia in the *Shih-san ching chu-shu* 十三經注疏 (Scholia for the Thirteen Classics), compiled in the Sung, replace the *Ta-ch'üan* trilogy, which, according to Sun, had elided the true face of antiquity: "In the [current] atmosphere inside examination compounds, all that matters is the rise and fall of human talent. If we compel everyone to read the scholia, then the literati will all master the Classics. If the Classics are mastered, then they will also master the dynasty's

132. Ibid., 1793: 15a–17a, 46a–50, and *Huang-ch'ao hsu wen-hsien t'ung-kao*, p. 8429. See also my *Classicism, Politics, and Kinship*, chaps. 5–8.

133. See Chi's preface in *Ch'ing-tai ch'ien-ch'i chiao-yü lun-chu hsuan*, 3/114–18.

134. See *Ch'ang-t'an*, pp. 14–15; and, for discussion, my *Classicism, Politics, and Kinship*, pp. 156–57, 166–68.

135. For Hung's views, see *Ch'ing-tai ch'ien-ch'i chiao-yü lun-chu hsuan*, 3/269.

rules and regulations. The meaning of the Classics will then be translated into useful knowledge."[136]

In the same vein, Chang Hai-shan 張海珊 (1782–1821) sent a letter to Sun Hsing-yen, when Sun was leaving to supervise a provincial examination, in which Chang bemoaned the decline in literati learning during the Ming after the Yung-lo emperor had established his classical trilogy as the examination curriculum. Much of the Han and T'ang classical legacy, Chang contended, had been set aside in the process.[137] Liu K'ai 劉開 (1784–1824), a follower of the T'ung-ch'eng ancient-prose tradition that stressed Ch'eng-Chu Learning, was critical of Ming Ch'eng-Chu learning for its superficiality, which Liu attributed to the limits established in the early Ming on the full scope of Sung *Tao-hsueh*.[138] Han Learning scholars revived early Ch'ing attacks on the Ming trilogy, attacks that had been set aside after the failure of the 1664–67 Oboi examination reforms.

Although eighteenth-century evidential scholars as an academic community in the Yangtzu delta were somewhat insulated from the civil examination system by their specialized work as researchers, compilers, and teachers,[139] in the late eighteenth and early nineteenth centuries their classical views had become mainstream. Many were successful in the changing format of the provincial and metropolitan examinations, which after 1756 and 1787 favored the erudition of *k'ao-cheng* scholars.[140] In addition to the authenticity of the Old Text *Documents*, mid-Ch'ing examiners also raised other important textual puzzles. In the 1795 Hu-nan provincial examination, for instance, the second policy question honed in on the delicate issue of the late Ming appearance of an "ancient version of the Great Learning" (*ku-pen ta-hsueh* 古本大學), which reopened the Wang Yang-ming claim that Chu Hsi had manipulated the original text in Sung times to validate his interpretation of the "investigation of things" as its key passage.[141]

The 1823 metropolitan examination, for which the distinguished *k'ao-cheng* scholar Wang Yin-chih 王引之 (1766–1834) served as examiner, included three policy questions that queried students about classical stud-

---

136. Sun's draft memorial is in ibid., 3/278–79.

137. See ibid., 3/453.

138. See ibid., 3/476. On the T'ung-ch'eng school, see my *Classicism, Politics, and Kinship*, pp. 290–95.

139. See my *From Philosophy to Philology*, pp. 88–137, on the professionalization process.

140. On this phenomenon and how it favored Yangtzu delta scholars, see Chow, "Discourse, Examination, and Local Elite," pp. 195–205. Chow fails to note the changes in the examination curriculum that produced these changes, however.

141. See *Hu-nan hsiang-shih lu*, 1795: second policy question.

ies. In the first, examiners asked candidates about the historical transmission of the Classics. The model answer by Chou K'ai-ch'i 周開麒, who finished fifty-sixth in the metropolitan examination but moved up to third in the palace examination, focused on the role Cheng Hsuan had played during the Later Han dynasty as the key transmitter of the meaning of the Classics to posterity.

For the second policy question, students were asked to describe the origins, evolution, and content of lectures to the emperor by prominent literati since the Han dynasties. Again, the best essay was by Chou K'ai-ch'i. The third policy question tested the role of literati ( *ju* 儒) in the imperial system. In his prize essay, Lin Chao-t'ang 林召棠 (n.d.), twenty-sixth on the metropolitan but *optimus* for the palace examination, noted how emperors had variously promoted the teachings of notable literati. Lin described how in 1242 the Ch'eng-Chu school was patronized, whereas Ming T'ai-tsu (r. 1368–98) had for a time promoted the teachings of the Former Han literatus Tung Chung-shu, who had advised Emperor Wu.[142]

A Han Learning bent to policy questions was solidified in session three of the 1847 and 1852 metropolitan examinations. Prize essays for the initial policy questions by Hsu P'eng-shou 許彭壽, first on the 1847 metropolitan examinations, covered the fields of classical studies, with an emphasis on etymology in the first question and on poetic rhymes and cadences in the second. In 1852 examiners who prepared the first policy question for session three asked students to present evidence (*cheng* 證) concerning textual issues related to the Classics. In his prize essay Hsu Ho-ch'ing 徐河清, who was ranked in the third tier of graduates after the palace examination, summarized the contributions made by earlier Han and T'ang literati to the study of the Classics. In a closing rhetorical flourish, however, Hsu reveled in the "research" ( *yen-chiu* 研究) "exhausting the Classics" (*ch'iung-ching* 窮經) by Ch'ing scholars, which candidates should emulate. Similarly, in 1894 the chief Chiang-nan provincial examiners exalted the richness of the Ch'ing *k'ao-cheng* tradition in the Yangtzu delta in both the preface and afterword of their official report sent to the court in Peking.[143]

Consequently, policy questions during the late eighteenth and early nineteenth centuries increasingly reflected the changing intellectual context within which the imperial civil service examinations were administered. Although the quotations from the Four Books and Five Classics presented

142. *Hui-shih lu*, 1823: 16a–19b, 61a–72a.

143. Ibid., 1847: 17a–20a, 62a–70b; 1852: 17a–18a, 62a–65b. See also *Chiang-nan hsiang-shih lu*, 1894: "Hsu" 序 (Preface), pp. 2b–3a, and "Hou-hsu" 後序 (Afterword), pp. 2a–b.

during sessions one and two of the metropolitan examinations remained, for the most part, unchanged in content and governed by orthodox Ch'eng-Chu interpretations (there were stylistic developments as the length of eight-legged essays increased, however), Han Learning trends and *k'ao-cheng* issues had successfully penetrated both provincial and metropolitan examinations through the policy questions of session three.

Before the Western impact and the Taiping Rebellion, many literati began to reevaluate their cultural tradition and the forms of education through which native values were transmitted from the past and repro-duced in the present. The cumulative effects of these new scholarly and educational initiatives eventually made themselves felt in private acade-mies and imperial examinations at the provincial and national levels. Although the attitude-forming role of civil examinations remained central even after reforms were initiated, its content-expressing function increas-ingly took on more significance and emphasis after 1750.[144]

Candidates were still asked to demonstrate both their political loyalty to the reigning emperor and their allegiance to the moral orthodoxy that legitimated the political status quo. Visible cracks that appeared in the moral orthodoxy, brought on by the eighteenth-century *k'ao-cheng* move-ment, surfaced during the nineteenth century and were worked into the civil examinations. The political implications of these classical tremors, however, were not felt fully until the late nineteenth century (see Chapter 11). If session one of the civil examinations remained centered on ortho-dox moral reasoning drawn from the Ch'eng-Chu school of *li-hsueh*, session-three policy questions reveal that official examiners in the late eighteenth and early nineteenth centuries had become very conscious of Han Learning contributions to Ch'ing classical and historical studies. Mirroring their larger community of scholar-officials, they tried to bring Han and Sung Learning together in the nineteenth century and thereby achieve a balance between moral training and classical erudition. Curricular reform, which we shall focus on next, became one of the key differences between the Ming and Ch'ing dynasties.

Han Learning criticism of Ming-style civil examinations peaked during the Ch'ien-lung reign. Classical knowledge in sessions one and two had changed little between 1384, when Ming civil examinations took their final form, and the period 1756–93, when, as we shall see in Chapter 10, the reformed Ch'ing curriculum began to take final shape. The Ch'ing dynasty continued to employ the civil service examinations to legitimate

---

144. Cf. Chad D. Hansen, "Ancient Chinese Theories of Language," *Journal of Chinese Philosophy* 2 (1975): 245–80.

itself politically and culturally. The cultural dimension, however, increasingly reflected the Han versus Sung Learning debate then prominent among Ch'ing literati, neither of which the Manchu rulers saw as politically corrosive. Before the Taiping Rebellion, then, we have evidence that the civil examination system was itself undergoing slow but nonetheless important internal changes in content and direction, even as it remained the key governmental institution for political and social reproduction of gentry-officials.

When criticized before 1850, civil examinations were still considered superior by most literate Chinese to alternative systems of recommendation for public office. Chapter 10 reveals that the Ch'ing dynasty was able to keep pace with the times by carrying out a series of important curriculum changes in the eighteenth century that reinvigorated the civil examination system during the Ch'ien-lung era. At no time since the Northern Sung Wang An-shih reforms of the eleventh century had so much effort been spent on reforming the classical curriculum for the civil examinations.[145]

145. Li Tiao-yuan, "Hsu" 序 (Introduction), in *Chih-i k'o-so-chi*, pp. 1a–2a.

# CHAPTER TEN

# Acceleration of Curricular Reform under Ch'ing Rule before 1800

In Chapter 9 we saw the degree to which Han Learning and evidential research had penetrated civil examinations throughout the empire beginning in the late eighteenth century. This penetration initially occurred through the individual choices made by examiners who were tied to the Yangtzu delta and its literati community, which had during the Ch'ienlung reign (1736–95) embraced *k'ao-cheng* as the legitimate textual means to restore classical learning to eminence of place.[1] This chapter shows that Han Learning guidelines were also applied to the civil examination curriculum as a whole. Beginning in the 1740s, officials in the Hanlin Academy and the Ministry of Rites debated a series of new initiatives that challenged the classical curriculum in place since the early Ming. As a result, the *Tao-hsueh* rejection of T'ang-Sung belles lettres in civil examinations, documented in Chapter 1, was turned back. Ch'ing officials decided to restore pre-Sung aspects of the civil examinations that had been eliminated in the Yuan and Ming dynasties.

## MING AND EARLY CH'ING CURRICULAR CONTINUITY

The Ming-Ch'ing format for civil examinations presented in Chapter 3 reminds us of the remarkable continuity in the classical curriculum from

---

1. Readers sympathetic with recent views linking the rise of Han Learning to "ritualism" are advised to read the Japanese scholarship on the subject before they uncritically accept the conclusions found in Chow, *The Rise of Confucian Ritualism in Late Imperial China*, passim. For recent reevaluation of Ch'ing evidential studies, see the studies by Hamaguchi Fujio, *Shindai kokyogaku no shisō shi teki kenkyū*, and Kinoshita Tetsuya, *Shindai koshōgaku to sono*

1384 to 1756, when compared with the constant debates and frequent changes that marked civil examinations from the T'ang through Sung dynasties, roughly 650–1250 (see Chapter 1). Since the early Ming, the classical curriculum for dynastic schools and public examinations continued to emphasize the Four Books, Five Classics, and Dynastic Histories. In addition to the *Complete Collection [of Commentaries] for the Four Books and Five Classics* and *Great Collection of Works on Nature and Principle* used since the Yung-lo reign (see Chapter 2), the Ch'ing government during the K'ang-hsi reign (1662–1722) also promoted the compilation of the *Hsing-li ching-i* 性理精義 (Essential meanings of nature and principle) as a convenient compendium of orthodox *Tao-hsueh* philosophical and moral teachings.[2]

FORMAT OF PROVINCIAL AND METROPOLITAN CIVIL EXAMINATIONS, 1384–1756

| Session One | Session Two | Session Three |
|---|---|---|
| 1. Four Books 四書 three quotations | 1. Discourse 論 | 1. Five policy questions 經史時務策五道 |
| 2. Five Classics 五經 four quotations each | 2. Documents 詔誥表 [imperial mandates, admonitions, memorials] | |
| | 3. Judicial terms 判語 [reasons for conferring decisions] | |

NOTE:  The requirement that all candidates specialized (*chuan-ching* 專經) on one of the Five Classics was maintained until 1787.

Essays for the examinations were still required in eight-legged essay form. In the early Ch'ing, a maximum of 550 graphs were required for each of the first-session examination essays dealing with the Four Books and Five Classics. The maximum was raised to 650 in 1681 and again raised to 700 graphs in 1778, a number that remained in effect until the end of the dynasty.[3] As a result of these increases in maximum essay length, however, the task of grading papers by readers and examiners increased proportionally. Despite a substantial increase of personnel from the mid-Ming to the Ch'ing (see Chapter 4) and further requests for added numbers of examiners, their massive reading load prevented them

---

*jidai.* The studies by Yamanoi Yū 山井湧, Shimada Kenji 島田虔次, and Mizoguchi Yūzō 溝口雄三, published in the 1960s and 1970s, should also be referred to.

2. *Ch'ing-shih kao,* 11/3101, 3147.

3. Cf. the discussion in Liang Chang-chü, *Chih-i ts'ung-hua,* 1.5b–6a.

from paying adequate attention to essays prepared during the second and third sessions.

Typically overlooked were the last session's five policy questions. By 1786, regulations had to be enforced requiring a minimum of 300 graphs for each answer to a policy question, indicating that candidates were preparing short replies to the questions. In many cases, the policy questions themselves contained some 500 to 600 graphs, frequently double those in the answer, although in 1735 examiners were asked to curtail their rhetoric.[4] Review officials in the capital were told to check to see that examiners did not write out long policy questions, which invariably included the answer or reflected the examiner's biases. A limit of 200 graphs was set for the question.[5] Examiners were also asked in 1771 to broaden their selection of quotations for sessions one and two of the provincial and metropolitan examinations, which were based on texts selected and published by the government, because the questions had become too predictable.[6]

As in the Ming, Ch'ing civil examination candidates were expected to master the orthodox interpretations of the Ch'eng-Chu Tao Learning school for their essays. This persuasion had been reiterated as imperial orthodoxy (*li-hsueh wei t'ien-hsia tsung-chu* 理學為天下宗著) by 1652 examination graduates entering the Hanlin Academy such as T'ang Pin 湯斌 (1627–87), who took his *chü-jen* degree in 1648 in Ho-nan province. Classical lectures on imperial orthodoxy to the emperor were reinstated in 1655, and Manchu/Han quotas for such lecturers were discussed.[7] Until the K'ang-hsi reign, then, the Ch'ing dynasty reproduced verbatim the Ming civil examination regime.

What did change from the start of the Ch'ing, however, was the increased frequency of metropolitan, provincial, and local examinations. There were eighty-four Ch'ing "regular metropolitan examinations" (*cheng-k'o* 正科), somewhat fewer than the eighty-nine under the Ming. Beginning in 1659, the Manchus periodically added "grace examinations" (*en-k'o* 恩科), which celebrated imperial enthronements or special birthdays for both emperors and empress dowagers. Most of the twenty-seven *en-k'o* were added after 1736, with the Ch'ien-lung emperor favoring his literati with seven "grace examinations" during his sixty-year reign, the most of any ruler. These privileges, when appropriate, were also extended to

4. *Ch'ing-shih kao*, 11/3101, 3115, 3152–53. See also *Huang-ch'ao hsu wen-hsien t'ung-k'ao*, 1/8442.

5. *Ch'in-ting mo-k'an t'iao-li*, 1.14a.

6. See *Li-pu t'i-pen*, 1771, 3rd month, 1st day, for the memorial by the censor Chao Ying 趙瑛 (b. 1678) to the *Nei-ko*.

7. See *Tan-mo lu*, 1.18b–19a, 2.3a, 2.3b–4b.

provincial and local examinations. Of the 112 Ch'ing metropolitan examinations, 24% were "grace examinations," which helped to produce a total
of 26,747 *chin-shih*, some 2,153 (or 8.7%) more than in Ming times (see
Table 1.1).[8]

LITERATI AND OFFICIAL DEBATES
ON EXAMINATION REFORM, 1645–1750

As early in the Ch'ing as 1645, Han literati had already appealed to the
Manchu throne to reduce the emphasis on eight-legged essays for the metropolitan and provincial civil examinations. Kung Chih-li 龔芝麗, then a
supervising secretary and originally from Ho-fei in An-hui province,
requested that the Shun-chih emperor (r. 1644–61) lessen the Ming eight-
legged essay requirements on session one from seven (three on the Four
Books, and four on one of the Five Classics) to five separate essays. Kung
also asked that a poetry question be added to session two and that the
policy questions be eliminated on session three in favor of a memorial to
complement the other documentary questions on session two. The regents,
speaking for the young emperor, chose instead to follow to the letter the
Ming curriculum, with its stress on Ch'eng-Chu school commentaries to
the Four Books and Five Classics.[9]

Similarly, early Ch'ing examiners assigned by the court appealed to
early Ming rhetoric to justify the existing format for civil examinations. In
the 1657 provincial examination in Shun-t'ien prefecture, for example, the
chief examiners each stressed in their report that the revival of Ch'eng-
Chu learning and the role of the Five Classics and Four Books, if properly
heeded, would bring order to the world. In his afterword to the 1657
report, the Hanlin compiler Sung Chih-sheng 宋之繩 (1579–1668), *secundus*
on the last Ming palace examination in 1643, linked the emperor's search

---

8. In addition, there were two "added" (*chia-k'o* 加科) Ch'ing metropolitan examinations. Metropolitan "grace examinations" were held in 1659, 1713, 1723, 1737, 1752, 1761,
1771, 1780, 1790, 1795, 1796, 1801, 1809, 1819, 1822, 1832, 1836, 1841, 1845, 1852, 1860, 1863,
1876, 1890, 1894, 1901–1902 (held in 1903), and 1904. Seven were promulgated during the
Ch'ien-lung reign, and five each in the Tao-kuang and Kuang-hsu reigns. The latter represented a higher frequency than under the Ch'ien-lung emperor. Provincial "grace examinations" that we can document were held in 1736, 1752, 1760, 1770, 1789, 1794, 1795, 1797,
1816, 1819, 1831, 1835, 1851, 1859, 1862, 1875, 1893, and 1900–1901. See Huang Kuang-
liang, *Ch'ing-tai k'o-chü chih-tu chih yen-chiu*, pp. 137–52. Man-cheong, "The Class of 1761: The
Politics of a Metropolitan Examination," pp. 329–30, gives 25 grace examinations during
the Ch'ing, with 5,555 *chin-shih* degrees granted, or 21% of the total number of Ch'ing *chin-
shih*.

9. See Hsu K'o, *Ch'ing-pai lei-ch'ao*, 20.52–53.

for men of talent (*ch'iu-jen* 求人) to the examiner's search for outstanding writing (*ch'iu-wen* 求文). Sung's link between talent and classical writing was based on the early Ming formula enunciated in Ming examinations by its first *optimus* Wu Po-tsung in 1371 (see Chapter 2). Like Wu, Sung Chih-sheng appealed to Yang Hsiung's Han dynasty equation: "words are the sound of the mind." Sung concluded: "We examiners feel that to clarify the Classics, principles must first be clarified; to rectify learning, the mind must first be rectified."[10]

In the 1660 Shun-t'ien provincial examination, examiners repeated the formulaic link between talent and classical writing. In his preface to the report of results, Chuang Ch'ao-sheng 莊朝生, a 1649 *chin-shih* and scion of the distinguished Yangtzu delta Chuang lineage in Ch'ang-chou prefecture, wrote that the search for talent (*ch'iu-ts'ai* 求才) correlated exactly to the search for outstanding essays on the civil examinations. Essay writing, Chuang maintained, was based on the "techniques of the mind" (*hsin-shu* 心術), and thus was an accurate measure of literati talent. In Chuang's view, the teachings of Ch'eng-Chu *li-hsueh*, which were the principles enunciated in essays, equated with the ability to deal with practical matters of statecraft (*ching-chi* 經濟). The afterword by Hsiung Ssu-fu 熊賜覆 (1635–1709), a recent 1658 *chin-shih*, repeated Chuang Ch'ao-sheng's analogy between the mind of the literatus (*shih-hsin* 士心) and the ability to construct essays (*chih-wen* 治文).[11] In the 1659 metropolitan examination, chief examiner Liu Cheng-tsung 劉正宗, a Ming *chin-shih* degree-holder since 1628, stated in his report to the court that during the Yuan and Ming dynasties "the selection of literati had lasted for more than three hundred years without changing." The Ch'ing therefore could rely on its efficacy, Liu concluded.[12]

Despite the Ch'ing court's initial conservatism, however, the views of dissenting Ming literati (see Chapter 4), who were unhappy with the civil examinations (which had not changed in content since 1384), were increasingly heard during the early Ch'ing. The fourth policy question in the 1657 Shun-t'ien provincial examination, for example, asked students to write an essay on the history of literary examinations in China and to evaluate the vicissitudes in literary genres. Although both the question and the answer stressed the linkage between classical essays and the mind of the literatus (文者天地之心也), which the examiner Sung Chih-sheng

10. *Shun-t'ien fu hsiang-shih lu*, 1657: "Hou-hsu" 後序 (Afterword), pp. 1a–8a.
11. *Shun-t'ien fu hsiang-shih lu*, 1660: "Hsu" 序 (Foreword), pp. 1a–10a, and "Hou-hsu" 後序 (Afterword), pp. 1a–8a. See also *Hui-shih lu*, 1655: "Hsu," pp. 1a–8a; 1658: "Hsu," pp. 1a–10a, for similar views expressed by the chief examiners on early Ch'ing metropolitan examinations.
12. *Hui-shih lu*, 1659: "Hsu," pp. 1a–10a.

parroted in his afterword to the official report, it was made clear that the classical curriculum had changed considerably over time. Since the Yuan and Ming, however, the examiners pointedly remarked, the curriculum had remained unchanged and thus had become more and more irrelevant to contemporary issues and themes. Lurking within its conservative cast, the question posed by the examiners represented a preliminary discussion of what needed to be done to reform the examination curriculum. Later Manchu rulers, especially during the Ch'ien-lung reign, were able to initiate successful curricular reforms that had only been talked about in the Ming.[13]

### Early Ch'ing Private Views of Examination Essays

Also in 1645, the Yangtzu delta literatus Lu Shih-i 陸世儀 (1611–72) prepared his "Chih-k'o i" 制科議 (Proposals for eight-legged essay examinations). Lu and the late Ming examination critic Huang Ch'un-yao (see Chapter 4) had been in contact with each other. In fact, Huang had prepared a preface for Lu Shih-i's views on examination essays, and Lu praised Huang's ability to combine *li-hsueh* moral philosophy with statecraft concerns.[14] By the early Ch'ing, literati concerned about civil examinations included many Ming loyalists who opposed the Manchus but were powerless to prevent the Ch'ing court from co-opting Ming examinations to select Han Chinese officials loyal to the new dynasty. Literati such as Lu Shih-i, who favored Ch'eng-Chu Tao Learning, appealed in their private writings for changes in the examination questions and format rather than a wholesale overhaul.

Lu's basic position was that the Ming civil examinations had focused too much on eight-legged, classical essays (*ching-i*) and not enough on discourse and policy questions. During the late Ming, examiners, who were forced by circumstances to grade thousands of papers in a few days, mainly read papers from the first session dealing with the Four Books and generally overlooked questions from later sessions on morality (such as discourse essays on the *Classic of Filial Piety*) and policy. The "contemporary-style essay" (*shih-wen* 時文), as *ching-i* were called, became the route to the *chin-shih* degree. Book learning became secondary to literary flair in producing formalistic essays that would catch the examiners' attention. Erudition, according to Lu, was now limited to memorization of passages

13. *Shun-t'ien fu hsiang-shih lu*, 1657: 9b–11b (for the question), and 62a–67b (for the answer).

14. See Huang Ch'un-yao, *T'ao-yan chi*, 2.40b–42a; and Lu Shih-i, *Ssu-pien lu chi-yao* 思辨錄輯要 (Collection of essentials in the record of thoughts for clarification) (Chiang-su Bookstore, 1877), 5.7a.

likely to be themes for the civil examinations, while examiners even resorted to giving partial quotations to try to confuse some candidates.[15]

Lu, who in 1657 had been invited to assist the Chiang-su provincial education commissioner to grade local examinations in Chin-chiang prefecture, proposed in his writings that all levels of the civil examinations be revamped. For local examinations, Lu asked that candidates be tested in a single session on the Four Books, on one of the Classics, and on a policy question, rather than in the numerous sessions that students now faced. Lu further suggested that for the provincial and metropolitan examinations two instead of three sessions would suffice, because previous session-two questions on documentary style and legal terms had long since proven useless. Although the first session should emphasize essays on the Four Books and Classics to "clarify the principles of the Way," the second session should reestablish policy questions on "contemporary affairs" as a major determinant of the final rankings. In particular, Lu advocated three policy questions for the metropolitan examinations, two of which would be drawn from basic institutional encyclopedias such as the *Wen-hsien t'ung-k'ao* 文獻通考 (Comprehensive examination of civil institutions), compiled by Ma Tuan-lin 馬端臨 (1254–1325) in the Yuan. In this way, the rankings would not privilege the first session's classical essays. Book learning would again become the key to examination success, and more knowledgeable graduates would be the result.[16]

Another late Ming literatus, Tiao Pao 刁包 (1603–69), who had received a *chü-jen* degree in 1627, lived in isolation after the Manchu conquest. Addressing the literati community in his private writings, Tiao attributed the decline of "true studies" (*chen-hsueh* 真學) in the Ming to the pervasive influence of examination essays. Their eight-legged form had wasted generations of talented men, Tiao contended. The essays had survived only because they were based on teachings in the Four Books and Five Classics, but the consequences had been that "the Four Books and Five Classics had been lost because the eight-legged essay had caused them to be lost." "True studies," according to Tiao, were based on "true writing." Without the later, the "true statecraft" (*chen ching-chi* 真經濟) of the Four Books and Five Classics were discarded in favor of flowery prose of little relevance to actual conditions. As a solution, Tiao called for the complete elimination of eight-legged essays and a stress on the Four Books

15. Lu Shih-i, *Lu-tzu i-shu* 陸子遺書 (Bequeathed writings of Master Lu), Yang-hu edition (ca. 1900), vol. 18, 1.1a–2b.

16. Ibid., 1.3a–5b. Although a Ch'eng-Chu scholar, Lu stressed that specialized fields such as water control and astronomy should also be part of the curriculum. See 5.8a. Astronomy questions had been included in Ming civil examinations but were dropped in the Ch'ing. See Chapter 9.

and Five Classics as "true learning." But Tiao's call left open what form "true essays" should take or how they would be graded by examiners.[17]

Ming loyalists such as those associated with Ku Yen-wu (1613–82) or Huang Tsung-hsi (1610–95) also exemplified the carryover from Ming to Ch'ing of concerns over the educational defects in civil examinations, which were given an added poignancy by the Ming fall. A host of early Ch'ing literati such as the mathematician Mei Wen-ting 梅文鼎 (1633–1721) blamed Ming literary examinations for the failure of the dynasty.[18] Ku Yen-wu spent two chapters in his acclaimed *Jih-chih lu* 日知錄 (Record of knowledge earned day by day), first printed in 1670, on technical aspects of the Ming examinations and was generally critical of their operation.[19] In addition to blaming the emphasis on eight-legged essays over discourse and policy questions in the civil examinations for the decline in classical studies during the Ming, Ku also painted a picture of a selection system rife with inequities, cheating, and favoritism (cited in Chapter 4). The system's primary feature was its police-like surveillance of candidates, which fostered intimidation rather than learning: "The error in today's examinations is that the way of seeking talent is insufficient, while the methods of preventing criminal acts are excessive."[20]

In his 1663 *Ming-i tai-fang lu* 明夷待訪錄 (Record of a wait for an enlightened ruler in a time of darkness), which was passed around privately, Huang Tsung-hsi exclaimed that "the errors in the examination system had never been as serious as today." Citing Chu Hsi's Southern Sung critique of *ching-i* style essays (see Chapter 1), Huang also called for a reevaluation of the three sessions of the testing process so that the policy questions on session three would receive equal consideration in a candidate's final standing. "Real talent," as Chu Hsi had noted, could not be measured by literary exercises. In addition, Huang pointed out that since the T'ang dynasty the route to officialdom had for the most part been restricted to the single road of examinations. To select talent from millions of men in this manner was too restrictive. The problem lay in restricting the path and not relying on earlier forms of recommendation used during the Han

---

17. See Tiao's "Fei pa-ku hsing ssu-tzu wu-ching shuo" 廢八股興四子五經說 (Get rid of eight-legged essays and promote the Four Books and Five Classics), in *Ch'ing-tai ch'ien-ch'i chiao-yü lun-chu hsuan*, 1/14–16.

18. For early Ch'ing critiques, see Mei Wen-ting, "Wang hsien-sheng pa-shih-shou hsu" 王先生八十壽序 (Preface to the 80th anniversary of Mr. Wang), *Ch'ing-tai ch'ien-ch'i chiao-yü lun-chu hsuan*, 2/73–74. See also 2/172–74 (comments by Wan Ssu-t'ung 萬斯同, 1643–1703), 2/183–85 (remarks by P'an Lei 潘耒, 1646–1708), in *Ch'ing-tai ch'ien-ch'i chiao-yü lun-chu hsuan*. Cf. *Huang-ch'ao ching-shih wen-pien*, pp. 7.1a–13a.

19. Ku Yen-wu, *Jih-chih lu chi-shih*, pp. 376–418 (*chüan* 16–17).

20. Ibid., pp. 383–84, 385–86, 406–07 (*chüan* 16–17).

to bring in talent. Men of talent could bring honor to the civil examinations, but the examinations themselves were of questionable value, Huang concluded.[21]

Other early Ch'ing literati such as Shao Ch'ang-heng 邵長蘅 (1637–1704) reciprocated such feelings about the civil examinations in their writings. Barred from taking examinations (until 1684) because of his family's tax arrears in 1662, Shao advocated discourse and policy questions in place of literary essays to select men of talent for the bureaucracy. Shao felt that during the late Ming, eight-legged examination essays had deteriorated into a formalist exercise.[22] In an essay in two parts entitled "Chih-k'o ts'e" 制科策 (Examination questions on policy) initiated in 1645 and completed in 1663, Wei Hsi 魏禧 (1624–81), who since the age of twenty-four in 1647 had refused to write eight-legged essays, advocated that the policy questions take precedence over all other questions in the examinations. He proposed accomplishing this goal by moving the policy questions from the third to first session and eliminating the eight-legged essay from the test entirely. In one fell swoop, which Wei termed a "change of models" (*pien-fa* 變法), candidates for office would be forced to master political affairs and their historical vicissitudes. Practical learning would replace empty literary exercises. When national emergencies occurred, scholars and officials would be prepared to deal with them and find solutions. Since this claim was written in 1645, we can assume that Wei Hsi thought the officials chosen through the late Ming civil service had failed in their responsibilities to the Ming dynasty.[23]

A literati brouhaha concerning the eight-legged essay was evident in their private writings during the early decades of the Ch'ing dynasty. Early Ch'ing attacks on early Ming examination policies, particularly those of the Yung-lo emperor, by literati such as Lü Liu-liang, Lu Lung-ch'i, and Liu Hsien-t'ing 劉獻廷 (1648–95), would be revived in the late eighteenth century.[24]

21. *Huang-ch'ao ching-shih wen-pien*, 7.1a–1b, 8a–8b. See also Franke, *The Reform and Abolition of the Traditional Chinese Examination System*, pp. 20–22. On the *Ming-i tai-fang lu*, see William Theodore de Bary, "Chinese Despotism and the Confucian Ideal: A Seventeenth-Century View," in John K. Fairbank, ed., *Chinese Thought and Institutions* (Chicago: University of Chicago Press, 1957); and de Bary, trans., *A Plan for the Prince*.

22. See Shao's "Ni Chiang-hsi shih-ts'e i shih-wen" 擬江西試策一時文 (Drafting the first policy question on contemporary-style essays for Chiang-hsi), in *Ch'ing-tai ch'ien-ch'i chiao-yü lun-chu hsuan*, 2/144–46.

23. *Huang-ch'ao ching-shih wen-pien*, 7.4b–6a. See also Hummel, ed., *Eminent Chinese of the Ch'ing Period*, pp. 847–48.

24. See *Ch'ing-tai ch'ien-ch'i chiao-yü lun-chu hsuan*, 2/15, 2/21, 2/187.

*The Oboi Reforms*

Early Ch'ing examination debates among literati that carried over from the Ming turned out to be more than just Ming loyalist rhetoric. After six cycles of triennial provincial and metropolitan examinations dating from 1645, which had followed to the letter the Ming model of three sessions with the eight-legged essay as its frontispiece and policy questions as its end, the Manchu court, then under the Oboi Regents ruling in the name of the child-emperor K'ang-hsi (r. 1662–1722), took up the call for examination reform in 1663. It was a sign of the times that Wei Hsi completed his essay "Examination Questions on Policy" that same year. In 1663, the court suddenly announced the abrogation of the infamous *pa-ku* essay, which was to go into effect for the next local, provincial, and metropolitan examinations. In local licensing, renewal, and qualifying examinations, which had only one format, the policy and discourse questions replaced quotations from the Four Books and Five Classics.[25]

The 1657 examination scandal in the Shun-t'ien provincial examination and numerous examination corruption and tax evasion cases in the south (see Chapter 4) had soured the regents on the reliability of civil examinations. Their efforts to control Yangtzu delta literati through the 1661 tax case certainly paralleled the first Ming emperor Chu Yuan-chang's efforts to control his Su-chou enemies and the ensuing northern versus southern quotas issue of the early Ming (see Chapter 2).

The Oboi Regents, as Manchu military men, were also skeptical of the efficacy of purely literary qualifications for office. Their reform, however, by following closely the substantive proposals made by dissenting literati who had survived the Ming-Ch'ing transition, suggests that their Han advisors were well aware of the literati brouhaha over the eight-legged essay, and that such initial support made extensive changes in the format of the civil examinations possible. The requirement that all examination essays be prepared in rigorous eight-legged essay form was rescinded to devalue literary exercises. The number of questions based on the Four Books and Five Classics was significantly reduced to one each and relegated to the second session, effectively ending the educational regime, in place since 1384, of at least a decade of childhood memorization in preparation for classical examinations (see Chapter 5). In effect, the entire first session of Ming and early Ch'ing provincial and metropolitan examina-

---

25. *T'ung-hsiang t'i-ming lu,* 2.6a, gives the changed format for local examinations in T'ung-chou in 1668. The eight-legged essays based on the Four Books and Five Classics were restored there in the jointly held 1672 *sui* and *k'o* examinations. See also the *Yü-yang k'o-ming lu,* 4A.16a, where the new format in 1667 for local examinations in Ch'ang-shu took the form of two discourse questions. In 1670 the eight-legged essay was restored.

tions, which had been the most important determinant in the final rankings of candidates, was transformed.

To stress practical questions of government policy and concrete themes dealing with political institutions, the Oboi Regents approved a proposal from the Ministry of Rites, which was still in charge of the civil examinations, to move the five policy questions from the third session of the civil examination proceedings to the first. Session three was still needed, the regents thought, but it was subsequently dropped. When the provincial and metropolitan examinations were held, for instance, they did not include a third session. The documentary question and five legal terms from the penal code were added to the second session, which indicated a slight change of heart in the court about the format. The discourse question was dropped completely.[26] As the format below reveals, the second session was shortened and simplified to include a single essay based on a quotation from the Four Books, and a quotation from the Five Classics. Preparation of a document and five legal terms to identify were supposed to be included in session three, but these were moved up to session two when the examinations were given. The reforms took effect for the 1664 and 1667 metropolitan and for the 1666 provincial examinations.[27]

FORMAT OF PROVINCIAL AND METROPOLITAN CIVIL SERVICE
EXAMINATIONS DURING THE EARLY CH'ING DYNASTY REFORM OF
1663 (RESCINDED IN 1667)

| *Session No.* | *No. of Questions* |
| --- | --- |
| ONE | |
| 1. Policy questions 經史時務策 | 5 essays |
| TWO | |
| 1. Four Books 四書 | 1 quotation |
| 2. Five Classics 五經 | 1 quotation |
| THREE | |
| 1. Documentary style 表 | 1 document |
| 2. Judicial terms 判語 | 5 terms |

NOTE: The requirement that all candidates specialized (*chuan-ching* 專經) on one of the Five Classics was dropped. In addition, such essays no longer had to follow the "eight-legged" style. In the actual examination documents, session two and three were conflated. There was no *lun* 論 (discourse) question.

26. The 1664 and 1667 *chu-chüan* 硃卷 (anonymous vermillion papers) from the reformed metropolitan examinations given those years indicate that a third session was not tested. These papers are housed in the Ming-Ch'ing Archives, Academia Sinica, Taiwan. Copies are available in the UCLA East Asian Library.

27. *Ch'ang-t'an*, p. 36.

These innovations, by lessening the importance of the requirement of memorization of the Five Classics and Four Books in the core of skills tested in the selection process, produced an uproar among Han Chinese more conservative than the Ming loyalist dissenters discussed above. The reforms were quickly rescinded in 1667–68, in time for the 1669 provincial examinations by the K'ang-hsi emperor, who was then in the midst of wresting power from his regents. Understandably, many Chinese preparing for the rigorous Ming-style examinations, who were less concerned with dissenting issues, felt that their financial sacrifices and memorization efforts had been compromised. Others, like Li Yin-tu 李因篤 (1631–92), who was invited to participate in the 1679 special examination, took a balanced position; Li contended in his private writing that any examination system based on "words" (*yen* 言) and "names" (*ming* 名) rather than "deeds" (*hsing* 行) and "reality" (*shih* 實) was imperfect. What was needed, Li argued, was not elimination of the essay format but a widening of the selection process so that "deeds" could be better assessed in raising men to high office.[28]

Moreover, in an era when Ming loyalism was still a potent political and military force in the Yangtzu delta and on Taiwan, many dissenters could point to these examination reforms as an example of the betrayal of the long-standing Ch'eng-Chu *Tao-hsueh* orthodoxy by the Manchu conquest elite. It did not matter that the Oboi Regents were in effect following the suggestions of the most learned of the Han Chinese loyalists such as Ku Yen-wu, Huang Tsung-hsi, and Wei Hsi, who initially had the ear of officials in the Ministry of Rites. Their ideas clearly did not represent the literati mainstream, whom the young emperor sought to appease. In 1665 Huang Chi 黃機 (d. 1686), then vice minister of the Ministry of Rites, memorialized for a return to the rigorous Ming three-session format for the selection process. He contended: "Today, the use of only policy questions and a discourse essay, and the elimination of the first session entirely, appears to have made the examinations too easy. Moreover, if the Classics and Histories are not required for the essays, people will no longer discuss the teachings of the sages and worthies. Please restore the three sessions [of the examinations] to their old form."[29]

To avoid a potentially damaging cultural clash between Chinese and Manchus, which the palace examinations of 1646 and 1649 had expressly addressed (see Chapter 3), the K'ang-hsi emperor, who now opposed his regents, yielded to Huang's earlier request and granted the Han Chinese

28. See Li Yin-tu, "Yung-jen" 用人 (Employing people), 2/57–58, in *Ch'ing-tai ch'ien-ch'i chiao-yü lun-chu hsuan.*

29. *Ch'ing-shih kao*, 11/3149. See also *Tan-mo lu*, 1.10a–b.

request for the reinstitution of eight-legged essays. After two metropolitan and one provincial examinations, the reformed format was ended, and the Ming three-session format stressing memorization and literary style was restored. Although the literati reformers had been persuasive enough for the regents in the Manchu court, they had not been persuasive enough for their own literati community, with whom the emperor sided. Literary men whom the K'ang-hsi emperor patronized, such as Wang Shih-chen 王士 禎 (1634–1711) and Ho Cho 何焯 (1661–1722), for example, were still avid proponents of eight-legged essays as the correct measure of cultural attainment. The career of Ho Cho, a well-known eight-legged essay stylist who had received his *chin-shih* degree in 1703 despite never passing any provincial or metropolitan civil examination, reflected the residual importance of literature in early Ch'ing literati life.[30]

Clearly, the examinations, for all their faults, successfully performed political, social, and cultural functions that seventeenth-century critics had underestimated, and which the K'ang-hsi emperor astutely exploited. Political selection of talent was only one piece in the examination puzzle. Two others were corroboration of local social status and cultural maintenance of Ch'eng-Chu orthodoxy, neither of which most local gentry, merchant, or military families wanted to see challenged. Under the K'ang-hsi emperor, the Ch'ing court quickly caught on to the long-term strengths of the cultural system in place, which could ameliorate Manchu-Han relations.[31]

It was ironic that vocal Ming loyalists had wanted to establish the priority of policy questions over literary essays in the selection process, and that when the Ch'ing court tried to oblige them, the difficulties proved insuperable.[32] The failure of the 1664–67 reforms cuts against the argument that the Manchus from the start used the civil examinations and the eight-legged essay to control the Han Chinese, a criticism frequently voiced by Chinese nationalists in the twentieth century. In fact the Manchus were much more reform-minded than Ming dynasty rulers had been. By letting Han Chinese elites expend their energies in eight-legged essay competitions, the Manchus were no different from earlier Han

30. See Wang's preface for the 1671 Ssu-ch'uan provincial examination and afterword for the 1691 metropolitan civil examinations, in *Ch'ing-tai ch'ien-ch'i chiao-yü lun-chu hsuan*, 2/81–83, 85–86. See also Ho's prefaces to collections of examination essays, in ibid., 2/279–80. Cf. Hummel, ed., *Eminent Chinese of the Ch'ing Period*, 283–85.

31. See *Tan-mo lu*, 1.10a–10b.

32. Northern Sung literati had also appealed to the emperor to prioritize policy questions but in vain. See Feng Meng-chen 馮夢禎, *Li-tai kung-chü chih* 歷代貢舉志 (Accounts of the civil examinations over several dynasties) (Shanghai: Commercial Press, 1936), p. 5. See also Chapter 1.

Chinese, Jurchen, and Mongol rulers who were savvy enough to understand how useful the competitive nucleation of literati candidates was for political and social control, even if the intellectual results were stultifying. Perhaps that was the point.[33]

The vast majority of literati remained obsessed with preparing for the literary competition itself. Others such as Lü Liu-liang 呂留良 (1629–1683), Lu Lung-ch'i 陸隴其 (1630–1693), and Tai Ming-shih 戴名世 (1653–1713) noted the limitations of literary examinations but still defended examination essays as worthy forms to present Ch'eng-Chu orthodoxy. What had happened in the late Ming, they argued, was that the classical essay had been corrupted by careerism and subverted by heterodox teachings, which was not the fault of the essay form itself. If Chu Hsi's model for literati moral practice were heightened, Lu Lung-ch'i wrote, then the examination essay would again fulfill its role as a vehicle for testing a candidate's ability to present the Tao Learning vision of moral cultivation as the beginning point for political action. As a Chu Hsi loyalist, Lü Liu-liang feared that abolishing the eight-legged essay would diminish the impact of Ch'eng-Chu learning, which was the strength of a form requiring students to present themselves as spokesmen for the sages. Tai Ming-shih combined a distaste for civil examinations with a literary career premised on teaching and writing about the style and content of eight-legged essays (see Chapter 8). After 1685, when Manchu rule was no longer actively challenged, many Ch'eng-Chu followers such as Chang Po-hsing 張伯行 (1652–1725) were no longer critical of examination essays. Instead they recognized their role in affirming "Tao Learning" orthodoxy.[34]

Few in high position after 1690, for example, took the northern ritualist Yen Yuan 顏元 (1635–1704) seriously when he commented that literary writings were not the mark of the literatus scholar, but rather were merely the products of "stylists" (wen-jen 文人) who were divorced from moral practice and "concrete affairs" (shih-hsueh 實學).[35] In the late seventeenth

33. Nevertheless we still should take into account Tsou Jung's 鄒容 (1885–1905) late Ch'ing charge that Manchus kept the most important positions for themselves and forced Chinese into a cutthroat examination system before appointing them to the few positions remaining. See Ch'ien Mu, *Traditional Government in Imperial China*, pp. 134–37.

34. See Lü Liu-liang, "Wu-hsu fang-shu hsu" 戊戌房書序 (Preface to the 1658 examination ward essays), 2/11–13; Lu Lung-ch'i, "Huang T'ao-an hsien-sheng chih-i hsu" 黃陶菴先生制義序 (Preface to a Collection of Huang T'ao-an's examination essays), 2/25–27; Tai Ming-shih's numerous prefaces to Ch'ing examination essay collections, 2/213–40; and Chang Po-hsing, "Tzu-yang shu-yuan shih chu-sheng" 紫陽書院示諸生 (Informing students at the Tzu-yang Academy) 2/193–96, all in *Ch'ing-tai ch'ien-ch'i chiao-yü lun-chu hsuan*.

35. See Yen's "Ta Ho Ch'ien-li" 答何千里 (Response to Ho Ch'ien-li), 2/101, in *Ch'ing-tai ch'ien-ch'i chiao-yü lun-chu hsuan*. For discussion, see Jui-sung Yang, "A New Interpretation of Yen Yuan (1635–1704) and Early Ch'ing Confucianism in North China."

century, Yen Yuan, whose influence in north China as a ritualist had spread somewhat to the south via his disciple Li Kung 李塨 (1659–1733), blamed the written examinations used to select officials as the reason that learning had declined in China. Prophetically he called for a revival of schools to take the place of examinations as the means to select men of moral character and useful talents. Literary qualifications had produced ineffectual administrators, he argued. Yen Yuan and Li Kung both harked back to the days when morality and behavior as measured by the "six arts" (*liu-i* 六藝) had been the basis for selecting men of talent. The views of Yen, a poor scholar who had labored through lower-level examinations but never got any further, were no doubt still shared by many, but Chang Po-hsing and others in positions of power dismissed them because they were tied to disparagement of Ch'eng-Chu orthodoxy.[36]

After the K'ang-hsi emperor himself took full control of his reign in the 1670s, however, further efforts to reform the examination process were made. In his official writings, the emperor made it clear that he considered the present selection process inadequate but he also understood that "circumstances beyond his control" (*shih* 勢) made it impossible to "get rid of civil examinations completely."[37] In 1687, for example, the requirements to prepare imperial documents in the forms of *chao* 詔 (imperial proclamations or announcement of posts) and *kao* 誥 (imperial patents or bestowal of titles) were dropped by the Ministry of Rites, as Lu Shih-i had earlier recommended. This change was initiated to encourage study of the Five Classics. Again, because of literati protests, the change was short-lived. Not until 1756 were these changes reintroduced. The epochal shift during the Sung-Yuan-Ming transition from poetry and belles lettres to examination essays and documentary and legal questions (see Chapter 1) was running its course after four centuries.

The discourse essay was also subjected to changes. In 1690, because of the limited number of quotations examiners had to choose from, other possible sources besides the *Hsiao-ching* 孝經 (Classic of Filial Piety) were added by the Ministry of Rites. "Tao Learning" tracts such as the *Hsing-li ching-i* 性理精義 (Essential meanings of nature and principle) and the *T'ai-chi t'u shuo* 太極圖説 (Theories of the Great Ultimate in diagram form) by Chou Tun-i 周敦頤 (1017–73), among other collections of Sung writings, were also made canonical sources for quotations requiring discourse essays. In 1718 the *Essential Meanings* was alone designated for discourse essays, and all other sources were dropped. In 1723, however, uproar over

---

36. *Yen-Li ts'ung-shu*, vol. 1, pp. 176–77. On Li Kung, see "Ch'ü shih" 取士 (Selecting literati) in *Ch'ing-tai ch'ien-ch'i chiao-yü lun-chu hsuan*, 2/270–71.

37. See the K'ang-hsi emperor's "Hsiang-chü li-hsuan chieh" 鄉舉里選解 (Explication for selecting local talent), 2/244–45, in *Ch'ing-tai ch'ien-ch'i chiao-yü lun-chu hsuan*.

dropping the *Classic of Filial Piety* forced the Ministry of Rites to reinstate it as the source for the discourse question. Indeed, in his 1736 memorial, the censor Li Hui 李徽 recommended that the *Classic of Filial Piety* should be added to the Four Books, bringing them to five and thus balancing the Five Classics. This memorial was set aside because of the authenticity debates lingering over the Old Text and New Text versions of the *Hsiao-ching*. Nevertheless, until 1757, when debate over the discourse question recurred (see below), the *Classic of Filial Piety* and *Essential Meanings* were equally stressed.[38]

### Reform Efforts during the Yung-cheng and Early Ch'ien-lung Reigns

Neither the Yung-cheng emperor (r. 1723–35) nor his successor was satisfied with the literary focus of the civil examinations, however. In 1728 the Yung-cheng emperor approved a Ministry of Rites proposal to select candidates based on the second- and third-session essays, and added that examiners should stop emphasizing the first session's eight-legged essays at the expense of the last session's policy questions. In fact, it was during his reign that the earlier Oboi era abrogation of eight-legged essays was again entertained.[39] Later in 1732, the emperor complained that questions on the last two sessions of the examinations were devoted to important statecraft and practical issues, but literati paid them no mind because the examiners stressed essays from the first session. As in his efforts to reform local education officials (see Chapter 4), the Yung-cheng emperor tried but failed to redress the literary focus of the examinations.[40]

With the support of the Hanlin Academy, the Yung-cheng emperor succeeded in creating, however, another layer of examinations for those who passed the *chin-shih* degree. To the metropolitan and palace examinations, the Hanlin Academy added in 1723 the *ch'ao-k'ao* 朝考 (court examination), which tested only the top-ranked *chin-shih* from the palace examination and ranked them for entry into the Hanlin Academy. Previously, examinations for Hanlin probationers (*shu-chi-shih* 庶吉士) were held after a select group of *chin-shih* graduates were accepted into the Academy. From 1724 until the late Ch'ing, however, a court examination was required before a *chin-shih* degree-holder entered the Hanlin.[41]

38. *Ch'ing-shih kao*, 11/3149–50. See also Kutcher, "Death and Mourning in China, 1550–1800."

39. *Ch'ing-pai lei-ch'ao*, 21.11.

40. *Ch'in-ting mo-k'an t'iao-li*, 2.7b–10b.

41. For discussion, see *Ch'ang-t'an*, p. 25; and Yang Hsueh-wei 楊學為 et al., comps., *Chung-kuo k'ao-shih chih-tu shih tzu-liao hsuan-pien*, p. 351. For examples, see *Ch'in-ch'ü ch'ao-k'ao chüan* 欽取朝考卷 (Imperially selected court examination papers), in the Kyoto University,

In contrast to the format of the civil metropolitan and palace examinations, the Yung-cheng emperor required for the court examination that potential Hanlin probationers be tested in four literary genres: (1) a discourse essay (*lun* 論), (2) an imperial proclamation (*chao* 詔), (3) a memorial (*shu* 疏), and (4) a poem (*shih* 詩) composed in eight-rhyme five-word regulated meters. Even after being dropped from the provincial and metropolitan examinations in 1793, a discourse essay, for example, remained a requirement on the court examination. This was also the first time since the Yuan dynasty that a poetry question had been included in public civil examinations, and it foreshadowed this question's reappearance in 1757 in provincial and metropolitan examinations. Later, the Chia-ch'ing emperor (1796–1820) reduced to three the number of essays required on the court examination by removing the *chao* requirement. Ironically, the Yung-cheng emperor succeeded in defining the Hanlin Academy as a literary institute that provided the court with able writers. This renewed focus on poetry, for example, reminded many of the T'ang Hanlin Academy.[42]

Although private and public attacks on examination essays increased (see Chapter 4), little was actually done to answer the charges that "contemporary-style essays" were "non-innovative" (*wu so fa-ming* 無所發明) and "impractical" (*ch'üan wu shih-yung* 全無實用). As always, there were frequent calls to emphasize the policy questions in session three and to increase attention paid to current affairs. In 1738, however, during the early years of the Ch'ien-lung reign, the rhetoric took a new turn.[43] Rather than Han Chinese literati privately debating the uses and abuses of the civil examinations, two well-placed Manchu court officials, O-erh-tai 鄂爾泰 (1680–1745), then a grand secretary, and Shu-ho-te 舒赫德 (1711–77), then vice minister of military personnel, took different political sides over whether the civil examinations should be abolished.[44]

Well-versed in the Classics, Shu-ho-te presented a 1744 memorial to the

Oriental Library. See also *Li-k'o ch'ao-yuan chüan* 歷科朝元卷 (Examination papers from court examinations over several cycles), which are preserved in the Tokyo University, Oriental Library.

42. See Chang Chung-ju, *Ch'ing-tai k'ao-shih chih-tu*, pp. 38–41. Chang notes that court examinations had also been established for special examination graduates (*pa-kung-sheng* 拔貢生) and senior tribute students (*yu-kung-sheng* 優 [or 憂] 貢生).

43. See the 1738 memorial by Huo Pei 霍備 calling for "literary reform to correct literati behavior" (正文體以端士風), in *Huang-Ch'ing ming-ch'en tsou-i* 皇清名臣奏議 (Memorials of famous officials during the August Ch'ing), ca. 1796–1820 edition, 35.20a–22a.

44. *Huang-ch'ao ching-shih wen-pien*, 7.13a–14a. Franke, *The Reform and Abolition of the Traditional Chinese Examination System*, pp. 29–30, gives 1744 for this debate. This is when it ended. See also Huang Kuang-liang, *Ch'ing-tai k'o-chü chih-tu chih yen-chiu*, pp. 308–09; and Hummel, ed., *Eminent Chinese of the Ch'ing Period*, pp. 601–03, 559–51.

emperor in which he gave four reasons why the entire examination process should immediately be abrogated (*fei k'o-mu* 廢科目). He explained: "Today's contemporary-style essays are nothing but empty words and cannot be applied to any use (今之時文徒空言而不適於用). This is the first reason why the civil examinations are inadequate to select men." Shu-ho-te then enumerated the other factors involved. He complained about the process of copying candidates' papers to ensure they would be graded anonymously, which inevitably meant that the papers took a circuitous route through the wards of the examination compound and were given ingenious but empty evaluations by the examiners who passed them around. Third, Shu-ho-te explained that because the sons of literati specialized on a single Classic, they could easily master all the possible quotations from the shortest Classic in several months and prepare classical essays for them in advance.[45] Finally, Shu-ho-te complained that many of the questions, particularly the documentary questions on session two, could be answered perfunctorily and were "non-innovative" (無所發明). Changes were needed in the "way to recruit men of true talent and practical learning."[46]

O-erh-t'ai, also a member of the Grand Council (*Chün-chi-ch'u* 軍機處), supervised the 1742 civil metropolitan examination and defended its stress on examination essays in the preface for the official report.[47] As a chief minister in 1744, he admitted to the Ch'ien-lung emperor that everyone knew what the problems were and that reforms in the selection system were needed, but he added that no one had an adequate replacement for the present system or a solution to improve it without losing its benefits. O-erh-t'ai then reviewed the litany of attacks since Chao K'uang's 趙匡 famous T'ang dynasty criticisms of the sterility of the examination essays and the educational poverty induced by examination studies. O-erh-t'ai also summarized the Three Dynasties, Han, Wei-Chin, and Sui-T'ang mechanisms for selection of talent. Literary examinations, he concluded, were the Sui-T'ang solution for selecting officials that was followed by later empires. O-erh-t'ai handled Chao K'uang's denigration of examinations for their break between "learning" (*hsueh* 學) and "practice" (*hsi* 習) by realistically admitting that all subsequent dynasties had recognized the problem but none had provided an adequate solution.[48]

45. Ku Yen-wu also noted this problem. See *Jih-chih lu chi-shih*, 16.386–87; and the discussion in Chapter 5.

46. See *Tan-mo lu*, 13.7a–7b; Liang Chang-chü, *Chih-i ts'ung-hua*, 1.4a–b; and *Huang-ch'ao ching-shih wen-pien*, 7.13a–14a.

47. *Hui-shih lu*, 1742: "Hsu" 序 (Preface), pp. 1a–4a.

48. *Tan-mo lu*, 13.7b–10b; Liang Chang-chü, *Chih-i ts'ung-hua*, 1.4b–5b; and *Huang-ch'ao ching-shih wen-pien*, 7.14a.

The reform issue was then raised by civil examiners for the thirteen thousand candidates taking the 1744 Chiang-nan provincial examination in Nanking to consider. In the fifth policy question on session three, the examiners asked the candidates to ponder the history of examination essays and their role on the three sessions of the metropolitan and civil examination since the early Ming. In effect, within the context of an examination, examiners ingeniously solicited literati opinion about the format of the examination the candidates themselves were taking. The question asked for a summary of the vicissitudes and success and failure (*yuan-liu te-shih* 源流得失) of the format used since 1384.[49]

The best answer by one of the 126 *chü-jen* graduates (less than 1% passed!) was that of Hu Ch'eng-fu 胡承福, a second-class tribute student from Ching 涇 county in An-hui province, and it was included in the final record sent to Peking. In his answer, Hu focused on the role of eight-legged essays (called *chih-i* 制藝) in Ming civil examinations and presented the position of those who supported the eight-legged essay. He added, however, that there was another, darker side to their rhetoric:

> Although people know that in the *chih-i* essay "prose is a vehicle for the Way" (*wen i tsai-tao* 文以載道),[50] they do not know that such prose can also obscure the Way (*wen i hui-tao* 文以晦道). Similarly, people know that the *chih-i* essay is a form of writing that establishes sincerity (*hsiu-tz'u li-ch'eng* 修辭立誠), but they do not realize that the essay also is a form for writing falsehoods (*hsiu-tz'u tso-wei* 修辭作偽). Isn't it clear that the principles and models may be correct, but in the examination compound such intentions for selecting literati can be betrayed?

Hu Ch'eng-fu concluded, however, that the eight-legged essay could not be blamed for all the faults in the civil examinations. The questions on the second and third sessions also had to stress "concrete learning" (*shih-hsueh* 實學), he added.[51]

The 1745 policy question for the palace examination, which was either prepared by the Ch'ien-lung emperor or by those who spoke for him, also concentrated on the historical evolution of civil examinations, which indicated that in the Grand Council the 1744 disagreement between Shu-ho-te and O-erh-t'ai carried over to the next year. Using the 313 candidates on the palace examination as a forum about the examination, the emperor asked the *chin-shih* finalists to tell him if he was unrealistic to expect that

49. See *Chiang-nan hsiang-shih lu*, 1744: 22a–23b, for the fifth policy question.
50. This ideal had been formulated by Chou Tun-i (1017–73). For discussion, see James J. Y. Liu, *Chinese Theories of Literature*, pp. 114, 128.
51. *Chiang-nan hsiang-shih lu*, 1744: 74a–76a.

those whose essays were chosen as best were appropriate for political appointments. The emperor wanted confirmation that "public office and scholarship were not two separate paths" (夫政務與學問非二途).[52]

In his answer, the 1745 *optimus*, Ch'ien Wei-ch'eng 錢維城 (1720–72), clothed his position with the garments of orthodox Tao Learning: "Your servant has heard that the empire is ordered by the Way, and the Way is most complete in the Classics." Learning and cultivation of the mind must go hand in hand, Ch'ien contended. The selection of literati for office must be based on their mastery of classical techniques (*ching-shu* 經術).[53] Chuang Ts'un-yü, as *secundus* in 1745, emphasized in his recorded palace essay that long-term peace was "always based on training literati and choosing the best of them for the [dynasty's] foundation" (以造士為本，得賢為基). Neither Ch'ien nor Chuang attributed their own success to fate, as had more popular accounts of the 1745 palace examination (see Chapter 6). After reviewing Sung debates about the literary content of civil examinations, in which Chuang cited Su Shih's and Chu Hsi's positions on the role of belles lettres in examination essays, Chuang Ts'un-yü concluded that even Chu Hsi had only sought to reform the system and had never intended that such a permanent institution (*ch'ang-fa* 常法) should be eliminated. Chuang was clearly taking O-erh-t'ai's side in the court debate.[54]

The Ch'ien-lung emperor heard out both sides and concluded:

> We will see if after several years literati still throw themselves into the midst of the *Poetry Classic* [to master it for their specialization on the examinations]. If [instead] they diligently study the learning of substance and use, then the literary tide will daily become more glorious, and more true talents will daily arise. In the end, however, these endeavors are devoted simply to literature. It is doubtful written characters can show whether or not a person is outstanding or stupid. Consequently, in establishing models to select literati we can do no more than this. Moreover, the origins of imperial order versus chaos or dynastic rising versus declining do not come from this. There is nothing we can do about changing established institutions. The memorials have not provided us with any useful proposals.[55]

Despite the political tensions between O-erh-t'ai and Chang T'ing-yü 張廷玉 (1672–1755) when both were ministers in the Grand Council early in the Ch'ien-lung reign, Chang (who in the name of Ch'eng-Chu "mean-

52. *Chuang-yuan ts'e*, 1733 edition, vol. 8, pp. 503a–b.
53. Ibid., pp. 504a–509a.
54. Ibid., pp. 509a–513a, especially 511a–512a.
55. *Huang-ch'ao ching-shih wen-pien*, 7.14a.

ings and principles" had opposed dropping the eight-legged essay during the Yung-cheng reign) joined O-erh-t'ai in 1743 and opposed Shu-ho-te's efforts to drop the civil examinations entirely. When as a member of the Grand Council he was asked by the Ch'ien-lung emperor to consider the merits of Shu-ho-te's request, Chang also conceded that Shu-ho-te was right about the accumulated faults in the present examination system, but Chang felt that the reform proposals were too drastic. What was needed was reform of the system so that the civil examinations would fulfill the ideals established in earlier dynasties.[56] Because the former regent Oboi had tried to abolish eight-legged essays in 1664, it was not without irony that during the early years of the Ch'ien-lung reign O-erh-t'ai defended an examination process based on literary essays that his Manchu predecessors had unsuccessfully tried to reform. O-erh-t'ai had carried the day. Civil examinations remained in place throughout the empire.

### The Aftermath of the 1740s Debate

The Ch'ien-lung emperor, however, did not let the matter rest. His officials continually made recommendations through the Ministry of Rites for improving the civil examination selection process, many of which he enacted. The Ch'ien-lung reign was the most active period of civil examination reform from the early Ming until the end of the Ch'ing dynasty.[57] The emperor issued several edicts between 1736 and 1755 intended to address the literary, classical, and social problems that the civil examinations had engendered. Moving on many fronts, he tactfully tried to balance the requirements of the Ch'eng-Chu li-hsueh orthodoxy with the rising current of evidential research studies of the Classics (see Chapter 7). In addition, the Ch'ien-lung emperor addressed the "empty rhetoric" (hsu-wen 虛文) of examination essays, which he felt corrupted both Han literati and Manchu bannermen.[58]

56. See Kuo-ch'ao Chang T'ing-yü hsien-sheng nien-p'u 國朝張廷玉先生年譜 (Chronological biography of the Ch'ing dynasty's Chang T'ing-yü), in Li-tai nien-p'u ta-ch'eng 歷代年譜大成 (Compendium of chronological biographies over the ages), compiled by Liu Shih-p'ei 劉師培 (late Ch'ing manuscript), unpaginated. Chang's rejoinder to Shu-ho-te's proposals are in Ch'ing-tai ch'ien-ch'i chiao-yü lun-chu hsuan, 2/315–17. See also Hsu K'o's Ch'ing-pai lei-ch'ao, 21.11; and Franke, The Reform and Abolition of the Traditional Chinese Examination System, p. 29.

57. See, for example, Ch'ien-lung era memorials in 1738 and 1750 favoring examination reform collected in Huang-Ch'ing ming-ch'en tsou-i, 35.20a–22a, 46.5a–11a, 46.1a–4a.

58. See the Ch'ien-lung emperor's 1736–88 edicts on education and the civil examinations, in Ch'ing-tai ch'ien-ch'i chiao-yü lun-chu hsuan, 3/2–17. See Ch'ing-pai lei-ch'ao, 21.41, on the rise of Han Learning and examinations.

The emperor was trying to please all sides in the examination debates in the Council of State during the 1740s and 1750s, debates that became increasingly polarized between followers of Ch'eng-Chu "Sung Learning" and champions of "Han Learning." In the late 1730s, for example, the emperor's stress on moral practice over literary form was mitigated when he approved Fang Pao's request to select, edit, and print a collection of eight-legged essays on the Four Books written during the Ming and early Ch'ing to serve as ancient-prose style models for examination candidates (see Chapter 7).[59] In 1742, however, the emperor addressed the need to get away from purely literary evaluation of examination papers and to focus more on the practical aspects of moral character.[60]

Later in 1751, he selected fifty outstanding candidates for office via the guaranteed recommendation route and stressed the importance of classical over literary qualifications.[61] Moreover, the Ch'ien-lung emperor quickly approved when the Ministry of Rites added a special examination in 1769 for candidates of high moral character recommended by provincial education commissioners after they completed their three-year terms in office.[62] Throughout the 1750s, the Ch'ien-lung emperor had bemoaned the overly literary focus in examination essays and tried to encourage attention to more practical matters.[63]

The reform issues were first broached more widely in the policy questions on the civil examinations themselves. For the 1754 palace examination, for example, the Ch'ien-lung emperor raised the issue as the next to last of the five major points in his imperial question to the metropolitan graduates. The *optimus* that year was Chuang P'ei-yin 莊培因 (1723–59), whose policy answer to this part of the imperial question built on the emperor's contention that classical essays should be based on the Six Classics. There was no hint in the question or answer that major changes in the curriculum were being planned, but Chuang's answer did suggest that both Ming-style classical essays and Sung-style belles lettres could be used to satisfy this classical prerequisite.[64]

59. Hummel, ed., *Eminent Chinese of the Ch'ing Period*, p. 236. See also the Ch'ien-lung emperor's edict ordering Fang Pao's collection, in *Ch'ing-tai ch'ien-ch'i chiao-yü lun-chu hsuan*, 3/2–3.

60. *Ch'in-ting Ta-Ch'ing hui-tien shih-li*, 383.19a.

61. *Tan-mo lu*, 14.1a.

62. *Ch'in-ting Ta-Ch'ing hui-tien shih-li*, 383.23a. A quota also was established for such candidates.

63. See *Ch'in-ting mo-k'an t'iao-li*, 2.7b–13b, and 2.21b–25a. See also *Wen-wei hsiang-shih li-an* 文闈鄉試例案 (Case-examples of essays from the provincial examinations), 1832 edition, pp. 4a–5a, 20a–22b, on other eighteenth-century efforts to make policy questions more important.

64. *Chuang-yuan ts'e*, pp. 569a–576b. See also *Pen-ch'ao Che-wei san-ch'ang ch'üan-t'i pei-k'ao*, "Hsu" 續 (Continuation), pp. 5a–b, on the 1756 reforms.

The 1754 *secundus*, Wang Ming-sheng 王鳴盛 (1722–98), also wrote on this issue in his policy answer, in which he profiled the literary forms the classical essay had taken since its inception during the Sung and Yuan dynasties. Wang, who became a distinguished Han Learning scholar, stressed that during the T'ang and Sung dynasties, whenever the literary form of the civil examinations had become overly faddish and new styles had overshadowed ancient substance, concerned literati such as Ou-yang Hsiu had redirected corrupt literary currents toward more substantive issues. The implication was that the current eight-legged essay also needed to be brought back to its roots as a classical essay elucidating "orthodox studies" (*cheng-hsueh* 正學) via an "orthodox literary style" (*cheng wen-t'i* 正文體). Already in 1754 there were currents in the court suggesting that major changes in the curriculum, picked up from the 1740s debates, would not be far off.[65]

First, in 1756, the discourse essay, whose content had been changed in 1718 and then restored to its original form in 1723 (see above), was dropped from the curriculum, along with the documentary forms and legal terms that had been the core of session two since the early Ming dynasty. After a year, however, the discourse requirement was quickly reinstated when opposition memorials came in. The surviving routine memorials from 1757–58 about these changes reveal that in 1758 the Shan-hsi circuit investigating censor, Wu Lung-chien 吳龍見 (1694–1773), called for reinstatement of the discourse essay because of its importance to Ch'eng-Chu Sung Learning and imperial orthodoxy.

Wu's explicit linkage of the *lun* 論 question to Sung Learning suggested that removing it was part of a general pattern in favor of the more ancient Five Classics popular among Han Learning scholars during the Ch'ien-lung emperor's reign. During the Ming and early Ch'ing, the candidate who wrote the best discourse essay on provincial or metropolitan examinations had usually been the one whose essays on the Four Books were also highly ranked. As Table 10.1 demonstrates, the correlation between high ranking on the discourse essay and the final rankings had begun to decrease in the Ch'ing after 1654. The Tao Learning linkage between the Four Books essays and discourse essay had been challenged.[66]

Gainsaying claims that the discourse essay was useless, Wu countered that the moral basis of the dynasty was at stake. If the discourse essay, which required candidates to study the *Essential Meanings of Works on Nature and Principles* prepared under the auspices of the K'ang-hsi emperor and issued in 1715, were dropped, then the orthodox "Tao Learning" of Sung

---

65. *Chuang-yuan ts'e*, pp. 579b–580a.

66. *Li-pu t'i-pen*, 1758, 4th month, 26th day. These unpaginated documents are in the Ming-Ch'ing Archives, Academia Sinica, Taiwan, awaiting publication.

literati transmitted as the *tao-t'ung* (orthodox transmission of the Way) from Chou Tun-i to Chu Hsi would be lost and the sovereignty of the dynasty imperiled. Wu Lung-chien urged the emperor to show his support for Ch'eng-Chu learning by making the discourse essay part of the shortened first session, where it would receive even more attention than before. In effect, Wu was going along with the emperor's wish to reform the examination system, but he was making sure that Tao Learning would remain an important part of the curriculum. The Ch'ien-lung emperor agreed and placed the discourse essay stressing the *Essential Meanings* on the first session.[67]

## CHANGES IN THE LATE CH'IEN-LUNG PERIOD

Beginning in 1756–57, the provincial and metropolitan format for *chü-jen* and *chin-shih* degrees, which had lasted unchanged for 372 years, was dramatically transformed, although the initial changes were not put into effect permanently until 1759.[68] As we have seen, many early Ch'ing literati such as Ku Yen-wu had complained that the Five Classics had declined in importance during the Yuan and Ming dynasties because of the stress on the Four Books in civil examinations, a decline that in turn had precipitated a serious decline in classical studies.

Quotations from the Four Books remained on the first session, but in deference to the popularity of Han Learning, and because of the problems in the quotas for classical specialization already outlined, the Five Classics were moved from session one to become the core of session two. The Classics were replaced in the first session by the discourse essay, which was moved up from the second session.[69] Along with quotations from the Classics, students were also expected to compose during session two a poem in eight-rhyme regulated poetry (*pa-yun lü-shih* 八韻律詩), indicating the revival of interest in T'ang-Sung poetry as a testable measure of cultural attainment. As before, however, the policy questions remained relegated to the last session.[70]

In the 1760s, when efforts to reemphasize the policy questions on a par with eight-legged essays were unsuccessful, the Ch'ien-lung emperor had

---

67. *Li-pu t'i-pen*, 1758, 4th month, 26th day.

68. *Che-chiang hsiang-shih lu*, 1759: 7a–8a. See also the 1760 special examination in *Pen-ch'ao Che-wei san-ch'ang ch'üan-t'i pei-k'ao*, "Hsu" 續 (Continuation), pp. 1a–4b.

69. See the remarks by Chu I-tsun 朱彝尊 (1629–1709) in *Huang-ch'ao ching-shih wen-pien*, 7.10a. Cf. my *From Philosophy to Philology*, pp. 46–49. See also Lung-chang Young, "Ku Yen-wu's Views," pp. 50–52.

70. *Tan-mo lu*, 14.12a.

examiners publish a collection of the best policy answers prepared during the provincial examinations of 1756, 1759, 1760, and 1762. The work was entitled *Chin-k'o ch'üan-t'i hsin-ts'e fa-ch'eng* 近科全題新策法程 (Models of complete answers for new policy questions in recent provincial civil examinations). Patterned after Fang Pao's imperial collections of "contemporary-style essays," this mid-century collection of policy questions included questions and answers, as well as comments in the margins to highlight the strengths of the policy essays (see Chapter 8).[71]

FORMAT OF PROVINCIAL AND METROPOLITAN CIVIL SERVICE
EXAMINATIONS DURING THE MID-CH'ING DYNASTY, 1757–87

| *Session No.* | *No. of Questions* |
| --- | --- |
| ONE | |
| 1. Four Books 四書 | 3 quotations |
| 2. Discourse 論 | 1 quotation |
| TWO | |
| 1. Change 易經 | 4 quotations |
| 2. Documents 書經 | 4 quotations |
| 3. Poetry 詩經 | 4 quotations |
| 4. Annals 春秋 | 4 quotations |
| 5. Rites 禮記 | 4 quotations |
| 6. Poetry question 詩題 | 1 poetic model |
| THREE | |
| 1. Policy questions 經史時務策 | 5 essays |

The documentary and legal questions on session two since the Yuan dynasty were summarily removed, their symbolic role in the transition from T'ang-Sung belles lettres to Sung-Yuan classical essays all but forgotten (see Chapter 1). As a trade-off, the documentary and legal questions were replaced on session two by the revival for the first time since the Yuan dynasty of a T'ang-style poetry question for all candidates. This trade-off reflected, however, the resurgence of interest in literary expression and a pre–Sung Learning sensibility among Ch'ien-lung era literati. In effect, mid-Ch'ing reformers were tampering with a curriculum that had been the mainstay of Ch'eng-Chu Tao Learning since Yuan and Ming times. They restored pre-Sung elements to the curriculum.[72]

---

71. *Chin-k'o ch'üan-t'i hsin-ts'e fa-ch'eng*, 1764 edition.
72. *Kuo-ch'ao liang-Che k'o-ming lu*, p. 128b; *Ch'ing-pai lei-ch'ao*, 21.59, 21.97, 21.99.

## The Revival of a Poetry Question

Despite some misgivings, the emperor looked favorably on ministry requests in the 1750s to increase the use of poetry in the examinations, and in 1760 he permitted rhymed poetry to become part of the dynastic school curriculum and be tested monthly.[73] The late Ch'ien-lung era would witness in the revival of T'ang poetry one of the great reversals of the Yuan-Ming civil examination regime stressing the classical essay. Revival of ancient learning (see Chapter 7), particularly pre-Sung forms of literati writing and commentaries, brought in its wake an increased awareness by Ch'ing literati of the role of poetry and belles lettres in T'ang and Sung civil examinations.[74]

The epochal shift toward the examination essay—which began in the Sung, continued in the Yuan, and climaxed in the early Ming, when poetry was finally eliminated from civil examinations—had run its course. Slowly but surely, the Ch'ing court approved requests to roll back key elements in the Yuan-Ming examination curriculum. First the discourse, documentary, and legal judgment questions were challenged by reform-minded officials in the K'ang-hsi, Yung-cheng, and early Ch'ien-lung courts. Then poetry was reconsidered as a proper measure of literati talent for officialdom. The ruling Manchus, who saw themselves as heirs of the Jurchen Chin dynasty, perhaps saw in the revival of poetry a return to Chin belles lettres (see Chapter 1).[75]

Many Ch'ing traditionalists who favored Ch'eng-Chu orthodoxy over Han Learning, such as Chang Hsueh-ch'eng, looked back to the 1756–57 reforms favoring poetry as the beginning of a forty-year process that turned the civil examinations into a trendy contest (科場有名無實之弊) of literary taste, where the most recent fads (日新月異) in classical prose and poetry held sway. The earlier stress on "solid learning" (*shih-hsueh* 實學) in the civil examinations, according to Chang, had been displaced.[76] Oddly, this revival of poetry in Ch'ing civil examinations, which Chang Hsueh-ch'eng and others viewed as a betrayal of the Tao Learning legacy, has been generally overlooked by cultural historians and the few literary scholars who study Ch'ing poetry.[77]

73. *Ch'in-ting Ta-Ch'ing hui-tien shih-li*, 382.6b.

74. See *Ch'ang-t'an*, pp. 26–27.

75. See ibid., pp. 24–25.

76. See Chang Hsueh-ch'eng 章學城, *Chang-shih i-shu* 章氏遺書 (Bequeathed works of Mr. Chang Hsueh-ch'eng) (reprint, Shanghai: Commercial Press, 1936), 29.54a.

77. See, for example, the elegant introduction of Ch'ing cultural life by Kondo Mitsuo 近藤光男, from whom I have learned much, in his *Shinshi sen* 清詩選 (Selections of Ch'ing poetry) (Tokyo: Shūeisha, 1967), pp. 9–35; and Wang Chen-yuan 王鎮遠, *Ch'ing-shih hsuan* 清詩選 (Selections of Ch'ing poetry) (Taipei: Lo-chün wen-hua, 1991). Neither mentions the change in civil examination curriculum.

Poetry was the key to the T'ang selection process for *chin-shih*, privileging it as a written form among literati. Pauline Yu notes that its "fidelity to prosodic regulations" appealed to T'ang examiners, who used the form as a grid to evaluate examination papers much as the eight-legged essay grid was used since 1475. After the T'ang, both ancient-style poetry (*ku-shih* 古詩) and regulated verse (*lü-shih* 律詩) lost their "privileged positions," as Yu puts it, in both civil examinations and literati life. For Ch'ing literati, however, it was precisely its loss of privilege in the Yuan-Ming age of Ch'eng-Chu Tao Learning that, in Yu's words, guaranteed T'ang poetry "aesthetic incorruptibility," because the T'ang era was closer to antiquity and unaffected by the Buddhist infiltration of literati thought in Sung times.[78]

The Yuan (though only partially) and Ming had gotten rid of a poetry question on the civil examinations, a policy that was observed by the Ch'ing until a poetry question was reinstated in 1757 and prioritized in civil examinations after 1786. Nevertheless, T'ang and Sung poetic forms still thrived among Ming and Ch'ing literati. Their passion for poetry was not merely private, however. As long as the *Poetry Classic* remained the most popular Classic among examination candidates (see Chapter 5), its styles of language and canonical phrases were memorized by over 30% of all provincial and metropolitan examination candidates. With the rise of ancient studies in the late Ming, ancient-style prose writers such as Li P'an-lung proclaimed: "Prose must be of Ch'in and Han; poetry must be of high T'ang."[79]

Poetry questions were not used on local, provincial, metropolitan, and palace examinations during the Ming and early Ch'ing, but they were used in the higher and lower levels of the civil examinations. We have noted earlier that written examinations for Hanlin academicians included poetry in both the Ming and Ch'ing periods.[80] *Fu* 賦 (rhyme-prose) remained an important form of testing within the Hanlin Academy, where literary tests were periodically administered. Designated special examina-

---

78. Pauline Yu, in her essay "Canon Formation in Late Imperial China," in Theodore Huters et al., eds., *Culture and State in Chinese History: Conventions, Accommodations, and Critiques* (Stanford: Stanford University Press, 1997), pp. 83–104, has begun to explore these issues from a literary point of view. See also Stephen Owen, *The Great Age of Chinese Poetry*, pp. 5–26, for the vicissitudes in T'ang poetry.

79. On the early Ch'ing revival of the lyric (*tz'u* 詞), see David Mc Craw, *Chinese Lyricists of the Seventeenth Century* (Honolulu: University of Hawaii Press, 1990), pp. 1–9. For discussion, see also Richard Lynn, "Orthodoxy and Enlightenment: Wang Shih-chen's Theory of Poetry and Its Antecedents," in William Theodore de Bary et al., *The Unfolding of Neo-Confucianism* (New York: Columbia University Press, 1975), pp. 217–19, 232–41. On the Ch'ing, see my *Classicism, Politics, and Kinship*, pp. 291–93.

80. See *Tan-mo lu*, 3.18a–b, for Hanlin chosen by poetry; and *Ch'ing-pai lei-ch'ao*, 21.142, for 1694 Hanlin poetry tests.

tions, such as the *po-hsueh hung-tz'u*, also tested poetry and rhyme-prose on special occasions. In 1679, for example, the K'ang-hsi emperor chose as the topic for a special examination a *fu* on the *hsuan-chi* 璿璣 and *yü-heng* 玉衡, instruments that were then thought to be part of the astronomical system used by the ancient sage-kings to chart the skies (see Chapter 9).[81]

Moreover, in the 1658 repeat examination for the provincial examination in Nanking, which earlier had been troubled by corruption (see Chapter 4), the imperial examiners changed the usual format and instead used a poetry and rhyme-prose question (*ku-wen shih-fu* 古文詩賦) to retest all the candidates in the Chiang-nan provincial examination.[82] Poetry in regulated verse, along with policy questions, was also used on translation examinations (*fan-i* 翻譯) for Manchu bannermen.[83] In 1723 the *ch'ao-k'ao* court examination, which would test only the top-ranked *chin-shih* from the palace examination and rank them for entry into the Hanlin Academy, was added and included a poem *shih* composed in eight-rhyme five-word meters. In 1749 a poetry question in regulated verse, ancient-style prose, or lyric form (律詩，古文，詞) was used on *pa-kung* 拔貢 special examinations for the first time.[84]

In 1756 regulated verse in five words (or syllables; i.e., "pentasyllabic") and eight rhymes (*wu-yen pa-yun* 五言八韻) was formally reintroduced as a required literary form; it took effect first in the 1757 metropolitan examination and then was extended to the 1759 provincial examinations.[85] Initially the poetry question was added to the second session of examinations, fittingly replacing the documentary and legal judgment questions that had four centuries earlier symbolically replaced poetry during the high tide of Tao Learning. In 1758 the requirement of literati to be examined in regulated verse was extended to local qualifying examinations, and then included the renewal and licensing examinations in 1760. For example, the new renewal examinations required first an essay on a passage from the Four Books, second an essay on a passage from the Classics, and

---

81. See *Ch'ang-t'an*, pp. 26–27. Copies of the famous rhyme-prose question on astronomical instruments asked in 1679 survive in the Ming-Ch'ing Archives, Academia Sinica, Taiwan.

82. *Chih-i k'o-so-chi*, 4.123.

83. See the translation examination paper by Shih Piao-ku 史彪古 in the Ming-Ch'ing Archives, Academia Sinica, Taiwan.

84. On the court examination, see *Ch'ang-t'an*, p. 25. See also Ridley, "Educational Theory and Practice in Late Imperial China," p. 217. *Pa-kung* examinations were given once every six years until 1742 and once every twelve years thereafter. See Chang Chung-ju, *Ch'ing-tai k'ao-shih chih-tu*, pp. 40–41.

85. *Tan-mo lu*, 14.11b–12b. See also James J. Y. Liu, *The Art of Chinese Poetry*, pp. 26–29, and Eva Shan Chou, *Reconsidering Tu Fu*, pp. 56–59.

third a poem. On qualifying examinations, licentiates first prepared an essay on the Four Books, then a policy essay, and finally a poem.[86]

To facilitate the transition to the new mechanical details stressing form and adherence to rules of prosody, a book of rhymes was officially printed and distributed. In 1762, for example, a sample of poetic models entitled *Ying-shih p'ai-lü ching-hsuan* 應試排律精選 (Selection of outstanding models of regulated verse for taking examinations) was compiled by Chou Ta-shu 周大樞, which included T'ang, Sung, Yuan, Ming, and Ch'ing poems deemed to be appropriate for students to emulate.[87] Young boys (and girls) learned how to balance five- or seven-word lines in regulated verse by referring to several poetry primers such as the *Sheng-lü ch'i-meng* 聲律啟蒙 (Primer for sound rules), which consisted of lessons for matching characters and phrases of varying lengths.[88]

That candidates were expected to compose a poem in eight-syllable regulated verse (*pa-yun lü-shih* 八韻律詩), along with eight-legged essays on quotations from the Four Books and Five Classics, was a clear marker of revival of interest in T'ang-Sung poetry as a testable measure of cultural attainment. Within ten years, private publication and republication of T'ang and Sung poetry anthologies flourished.[89] Other anthologies of "poetry discussions" (*shih-hua* 詩話) from the Ming were reprinted, and Ch'ing scholars such as Weng Fang-kang 翁方綱 (1733–1818) and Yuan Mei 袁枚 (1716–95) compiled several new ones. Kuo Shao-yü 郭紹虞 estimates that altogether Ch'ing literati produced 300 to 400 such "poetry discussions."[90] Weng Fang-kang, for instance, described how in 1765–68,

86. Shang Yen-liu, *Ch'ing-tai k'o-chü k'ao-shih shu-lueh*, p. 251, argues that for local examinations, the examiners only required six rhyming lines (五言六韻). In the licentiate records I have looked at, local candidates were required to prepare eight rhyming lines, just like *chü-jen* and *chin-shih*. For a 1761 example, see *Yü-yang k'o-ming lu*, 4B.19b. In other places only six rhymes were required. For a 1760 example, see *Tung-hsiang t'i-ming lu*, "Li-yen" 例言 (Overview), p. 1b. On the change in local licensing and qualifying examinations, see *Yü-yang k'o-ming lu*, 4B.19a–b, where the change to poetry was effected for qualifying examinations in 1761 and renewal examinations in 1763. See also *Ch'in-ting Ta-Ch'ing hui-tien shih-li*, 382.6b; and *Ch'ing-ch'ao t'ung-tien*, 18.2133.

87. See *Ying-shih p'ai-lü ching-hsuan* (1762 manuscript), which is in the Rare Books Room of the National Central Library, Taiwan.

88. Ridley, "Educational Theory and Practice in Late Imperial China," pp. 400–01, 437n73. On the techniques teachers used to teach poetic composition, see pp. 409–15.

89. Ibid., pp. 416–25.

90. See Kuo Shao-yü, comp., *Ch'ing shih-hua* 清詩話 (Ch'ing works on poetry discussions) (Shanghai: Ku-chi Press, 1963), which includes Weng Fang-kang's "Wu-yen-shih p'ing-tse chü-yü" 五言詩平仄舉隅 (Pairs in level and deflected tones for five-word poetry), pp. 261–68, among several poetic works by Wang Shih-chen 王士禎 (1634–1711) and other Ch'ing poets. See also Kuo Shao-yü's preface to his *Ch'ing shih-hua hsu-pien* 清詩話續編

when serving as provincial examiner and education commissioner, he frequently discussed the addition of poetry to the curriculum with all county yamen staffs. As one of the chief examiners on four provincial examinations in 1759 (Chiang-hsi), 1762 (Hu-pei), 1779 (Chiang-nan), and 1783 (Shun-t'ien), Weng Fang-kang's influence on *chü-jen* candidates was considerable, an indication that the initiative was supported by literati as well as the throne.[91]

Shen Te-ch'ien 沈德潛 (1673–1769), famous for his poetry and literary writings, had great influence in Su-chou in the 1750s, when he was head of the prestigious Tzu-yang 紫陽 Academy there—despite the fact that he received his *chü-jen* degree at the advanced age of sixty-six after failing the provincial examination seventeen times! Famous from childhood as a poetic genius, Shen received his *chin-shih* degree in 1739, entered the Hanlin Academy, and became an imperial favorite and possibly influenced the court's new initiatives in poetry. When poetry became required on civil examinations, Shen's influence spread throughout the empire. The Ch'ien-lung emperor honored Shen's collected works of prose and poetry with a 1752 preface, and Shen produced several collections of T'ang and pre-T'ang poetry for students. Particularly important were anthologies Shen Te-ch'ien compiled after the poetry question in regulated verse was made mandatory in 1756.[92]

By 1800, ancient poetry was a common feature at dynastic schools and private academies. Juan Yuan, for example, required Sung-style essays and regulated verse (*ching ku-shih* 經古試) at the Ku-ching ching-she 詁經精舍 (Refined study for the explication of the classics) Academy in Hangchou, a center for Han Learning studies that Juan had founded in 1801 when he was governor of Che-chiang province. In nineteenth-century local examinations, officials and candidates usually referred to the essay and poetry question as "*ching-ku*" 經古 (classical essay and ancient-style poetry), "*t'ung-ku*" 童古 (essay and ancient-style poem for school candidates), or "*sheng-ku*" 生古 (essay and ancient-style poem for licentiates).[93]

(Ch'ing works on poetry discussions, continuation) (Shanghai: Ku-chi Press, 1983), p. 1. Cf. Waley, *Yuan Mei*, pp. 166–204; and Pauline Yu, "Canon Formation in Late Imperial China," pp. 83–104.

91. See Weng's "Tzu-hsu" (Personal preface) to his *Shih-chou shih-hua*, in *Ch'ing shih-hua hsu-pien*, p. 1363. See also *Kuo-ch'ao kung-chü k'ao-lueh*, 1.9a.

92. See *Ch'ing shih-hua*, pp. 22–23, which discusses Shen Te-ch'ien's "Shuo-shih sui-yü" 說詩晬語 (Words on poetry in the past year of my life), published in 1731. See also Hummel, ed., *Eminent Chinese of the Ch'ing Period*, pp. 645–46, for Shen's poetry anthologies; and Waley, *Yuan Mei*, pp. 168–71.

93. *Ch'ing-pai lei-ch'ao*, 21.43. See also *Ssu-ch'uan sheng tang-an-kuan Pa-hsien tang-an*, "Wen-wei," Kuang-hsu 四川省檔案館巴縣檔案，文衛 microfilm reel 56, document no. 6231 (1901), for poetry on local examinations before the late-Ch'ing reforms.

The early anthology *Ch'ien-chia shih* 千家詩 (Poems by a thousand authors), later annotated by Li Hsun 黎恂 (1785–1863), became one of the key collections students and candidates referred to to learn regulated verse.[94]

As in the case of other changes in the examination curriculum, the court had its examiners "test" the new stress on regulated verse by asking the first candidates for the revised *chü-jen* degree empirewide to discuss the reform in answers to policy questions in the third session of the 1759 and 1760 provincial examinations that addressed the poetry requirement (*shih-hsueh* 詩學) and examination essays (*chih-i* 制藝).[95] Thereafter, this procedure of examiners eliciting candidates' opinions about the very examinations the latter were taking was frequently used by the Ministry of Rites and Hanlin Academy to size up literati opinion, and it prepared the way to further upgrade poetry to a position of eminence by moving the question to the first session of provincial and metropolitan examinations in 1787.

For instance, in the 1759 Shen-hsi provincial examination, 4,000 candidates, of whom only 61 would graduate (1.5%), were tested under the reformed format, with the Four Books and discourse (*lun* 論) questions on session one, and the Five Classics and poetry (*shih-t'i* 詩題) on session two. Among the five policy questions on session three, the topics were mixed: (1) classical studies 經學, (2) historical form 史體, (3) the history of poetry studies 歷代詩學, (4) bureaucratic evaluation 吏治考績, and (5) storage of agrarian surplus 倉法儲蓄. The Shen-hsi question reflected the policy questions on poetry in the examinations that were asked in other provinces clearly enough that we can see a unified attempt by the examiners to influence imperial policy.[96]

In the third policy question, the Shen-hsi examiners asked students to comment first on the importance the sages had placed in poetry by compiling what eventually became the *Poetry Classic*, which included some three hundred poems from antiquity. Then, the examiners asked the candidates to evaluate the poetry of each dynasty, particularly focusing on the

---

94. Ridley, "Educational Theory and Practice in Late Imperial China," p. 398. The authorship of the *Ch'ien-chia shih* is disputed.

95. The *Chin-k'o ch'üan-t'i hsin-ts'e fa-ch'eng* gives an example of a question and answer on "the vicissitudes of poetry studies" (*shih-hsueh yuan-liu* 詩學源流) on pp. 9a–11b. I have also found such policy questions on the new poetry question in the 1759 *Hsiang-shih lu* 鄉試錄 (civil provincial examination records) of the following provinces: Che-chiang, Chiang-hsi, Chiang-nan, Ho-nan, Kuang-tung, Shan-tung, Shen-hsi, Shun-t'ien, Ssu-ch'uan, and Yun-nan. Similar policy questions were asked in Kuang-tung in 1760 and Hu-kuang in 1762.

96. See *Shen-hsi hsiang-shih lu*, 1759: 8a–12b (policy questions), and pp. 42b–55b (answers).

great poets of the T'ang, Chin, Yuan, and Ming. The Sung dynasty was elided here, and two conquest dynasties were alluded to in light of the popularity of poetry before the Sung classical essay became influential.

Then the examiners raised the issue of rhyme and phonology, about which candidates were asked to comment in terms of "rhyme books" (*yun-shu* 韻書) in use during the Sung, Chin, Yuan, and Ming dynasties. This aspect suggested that the new poetry question was linked to the currents of phonology then prominent in eighteenth-century evidential research. Proudly, the examiners heralded the Ch'ing dynasty's completion of the *P'ei-wen yun-fu* 佩文韻府 (Thesaurus arranged by rhymes), which the K'ang-hsi emperor had ordered compiled in 1704 (it was published in 1711) to revise and correct earlier, Yuan and Ming works on rhyming phrases, as the greatest work of its kind in Chinese history (足以超越千古). And finally, the examiners noted that the Ch'ien-lung emperor had decreed that T'ang regulated verse in eight rhymes would be tested on the second session of such civil examinations to fashion and nurture human talent (陶育人材), and that the present candidates were the first to benefit from the emperor's largesse.[97]

The best answer to this policy question was by Wang Hsun 王勳, who finished as the *chieh-yuan* (number-one *chü-jen*). Wang began with a discussion of the link between the evolution of music and poetry in antiquity, which reflected the human heart (*jen-hsin* 人心) and encoded by the sages in the *Poetry Classic*. Then, Wang Hsun surveyed the great poetry of each dynasty, including the Sung in his account. The final part of Wang's policy answer listed without discussion the various works on rhyme compiled since the fall of the Han dynasty to the Ch'ing and affirmed the greatness of the *P'ei-wen yun-fu* by repeating the words the examiners themselves had used to describe it. Wang Hsun was no protester of the new poetry regime, and he clearly told the examiners what they wanted to hear.[98]

The best poem prepared for the poetry question, however, was by Li Chia-lin 李家麟, who finished only number seventeen out of sixty-one. Table 10.2 shows that after 1759, however, the top ranks in civil provincial and metropolitan examinations were no longer held simply by those whose examination essays, discourse essay, or policy answers were the best (see Chapter 8). When compared with Table 10.1, which traces the decline in importance of the discourse essay for final rankings since the late Ming, Table 10.2 confirms the rise of poetry as an exercise that complemented the essays on the Four Books to determine high rank for *chü-jen* and *chin-*

97. *Shen-hsi hsiang-shih lu,* 1759: 8a–12b. See also the "Hou-hsu" 後序 (Afterword), p. 1a.
98. *Shen-hsi hsiang-shih lu,* 1759: 42b–55b.

*shih* degrees. It is possible that Ch'ing examiners were simply making sure that the top-ranked poem was also by one of the top-ranked graduates on session one's Four Books essays, but the formalistic nature of the brief fifty-character poetry grid suggests that examiners now had a new and efficient grading tool for ranking thousands of candidates, which they effectively utilized to complement the eight-legged grid in place since 1475. During the late Ch'ing, then, regulated verse probably rivaled the eight-legged essay as a genre that marked the cultured literatus.[99]

Li's poem in regulated verse was composed in sixteen lines of eight-rhyme and five-word meter (*wu-yen pa-yun* 五言八韻). This form required that each of the sixteen lines (i.e., 80 total characters) in two refrains should have five syllables (i.e., characters), and that every second line (i.e., the 2nd, 4th, 6th, 8th, 10th, 12th, 14th, and 16th) should rhyme without repeating the same character. A more variable tone pattern (that is, a "tune" for the poem) was also expected in regulated verse, along with antithetical couplets (*shu-tui* 屬對) spaced in the middle.[100] A typical quatrain of five characters for each line in regulated verse was organized into a sequence of two-character/three-character cadences as follows:

$$-- / -++ \qquad (- \text{ means level tone; } / \text{ means a pause;}$$
$$+ \text{ means deflected tone)}$$
$$++ / +--R \quad (\text{R means rhyme})$$
$$++ / --+$$
$$-- / ++-R$$

In addition, the rhyme scheme was dictated by the examiners, who chose a specific character to set the rhyme. In the final stanza, Li was required to "acclaim the sages" (*sung-sheng* 頌聖).[101]

The 1759 examiners in Shen-hsi chose the line "Bright moon born of the sea" (賦得『海上生明月』) from the first line of an eight-line poem by Chang Chiu-ling 張九齡 (673–740); of course, they did not identify it for the candidates. The examiners also appropriately chose the character *kuang* 光 (brilliant) for the required rhyme scheme (underlined in translation below), which was different from that in Chang's original regulated

---

99. Ibid., 14a–b.

100. Ridley, "Educational Theory and Practice in Late Imperial China," pp. 399–403.

101. See Wang Shih-chen 王士禛 (1634–1711), "Lü-shih ting-t'i" 律詩定體 (Fixed style of regulated verse), in *Ch'ing shih-hua*, pp. 113–15. On the form of regulated verse in the civil examinations, see Ch'i-kung, "Shuo pa-ku," pp. 61–62. Cf. James J. Y. Liu, *The Art of Chinese Poetry*, pp. 26–27; and Hsiao Ch'ih 蕭馳, "Lun Chung-kuo ku-tien shih-ko lü-hua kuo-ch'eng te kai-nien pei-ching" 論中國古典詩歌律化過程的概念背景 (The conceptual context for the process of the formation of classical regulated verse), *Chung-kuo wen-che yen-chiu chi-k'an* 中國文哲研究集刊 9 (1996): 131–62.

verse.[102] Li Chia-lin's sixteen-line poem in comparable regulated verse follows. I have chosen to present the translation character by character to better represent the structure of the poem:[103]

| 皓月當秋夜 | *hao yueh tang ch'iu yeh*[104] | "white moon midst autumn night" |
|---|---|---|
| 圓靈漸吐光 | *yuan ling chien t'u kuang*[105] | "round spirit gradually spits light" |
| 重輪離海嶠 | *ch'ung lun li hai ch'iao* | "double wheel leaving sea and peaks" |
| 一鑒印中央 | *i chien yin chung yang* | "single mirror inscribes the center" |
| 蟾影丹霄度 | *ch'an ying tan hsiao tu*[106] | "moon-toad reflection is red in sky passing" |
| 冰壺碧落張 | *ping hu pi lo chang*[107] | "ice jug emerald sky displays" |
| 金波初泛彩 | *chin po ch'u fan ts'ai* | "gold waves first float colors" |
| 玉宇乍生涼 | *yü yü cha sheng liang* | "jade world abruptly produces chill" |
| 始起蓬瀛窟 | *shih ch'i p'eng ying k'u*[108] | "starts rise from P'eng Ying cave" |
| 旋符雲漢章 | *hsuan fu yun han chang* | "rotates and matches Milky Way display" |

102. See *Hsin-i T'ang-shih san-pai-shou* 新譯唐詩三百首 (New translations of 300 T'ang poems), compiled by Ch'iu Hsieh-yu 邱燮友 (Taipei: San-min Bookstore, 1976), p. 175. For the tonal pattern of Chang's T'ang poem, see pp. 170–72. For a translation of Chang's poem, entitled "Watching the Moon with Thoughts of Far Away" (望月懷遠), see Burton Watson, ed. and trans., *The Columbia Book of Chinese Poetry* (New York: Columbia University Press, 1984), p. 273.

103. *Shen-hsi hsiang-shih lu*, 1759: 7b–8a.

104. By using 皓月, Li was paraphrasing the expression in the *Poetry Classic* 月出皓兮 (a moon rising white). See *Shih-ching chin-chu chin-yi* 詩經今註今譯, compiled by Ma Ch'ih-ying 馬持盈 (Taipei: Commercial Press, 1971), p. 197. See also *The Book of Songs*, translated by Arthur Waley (New York: Grove Press, 1937), p. 41. In addition, this and subsequent lines made clear references to Li Po's 李白 (701–62) poems with moon themes: (1) "Yu-jen hui-su shih" 友人會宿詩 (Poem on lodging a friend), in which Li Po wrote: *hao-yueh shui-ying ruo fu-t'ien* 皓月水影若浮天 (white moon reflecting in the water as if floating to heaven); (2) "Kuan shan-yueh" 關山月 (Pass with mountains and moon), in which the first line read "The bright moon appears from the Heavenly Mountains" (*ming yueh ch'u t'ien shan* 明月出天山). See *Hsin-i T'ang-shih san-pai-shou*, pp. 52–53.

105. The image evokes Tu Fu's 杜甫 T'ang poem on the moon in which "the mountains spit forth a moon" (山吐月). My thanks to David Schaberg for this citation.

106. The reflection of the thousand-year-old toad from which a magic medicine is made is "red" because it has cinnabar-colored markings (丹書) on its belly. Again, my thanks for David Schaberg's help here in locating the image in the *Pao-p'u-tzu* 抱朴子.

107. "Ice jug" was a frequent theme in T'ang and Sung poetry as a theme of a "white, frozen moon in the fall sky," *ping-hu ch'iu-yueh* 冰壺秋月. See, for example, Su Shih's poem "Tseng P'an Ku shih" 贈潘古詩 (Poem presented to P'an Ku).

108. This line refers to the mythical domains of P'eng-lai 蓬萊 and Ying-chou 瀛州.

| | | |
|---|---|---|
| 菱花浮貝闕 | *ling hua fu pei ch'ueh*[109] | "caltrop flowers float on jade palace" |
| 桂子落龍堂 | *kuei tzu lo lung t'ang* | "cassia buds fall on dragon hall" |
| 上下清規合 | *shang hsia ch'ing kuei ho* | "above and below pure and regular join" |
| 高卑素色長 | *kao pei su se chang* | "high and low white color expands" |
| 文明欽聖治 | *wen ming ch'in sheng chih* | "culture is bright as imperial sage orders" |
| 水鏡照遐方 | *shui ching chao hsia fang* | "water mirror illumines distant place" |

As the romanization above shows, Li produced the required eight-rhyme scheme, one of the principal reasons his poem was ranked number one. One missed rhyme (*ch'u-yun* 出韻), and he would have been ranked much lower for not meeting the standard.[110] His tone pattern and use of antithesis were acceptable, and the two-character/three-character cadences in his five-word lines were, as the examiners noted in their comments, an "elegant matching of the rules of prosody" (*yin-chieh ho-ya* 音節和雅). Second, Li Chia-lin made an allusion to a poem on the moon in the *Poetry Classic*, and alluded to a reference to that poem by the great T'ang poet Li Po 李白 (701–62). There were many other phrases in Li Chia-lin's piece that echoed other T'ang and Sung poems using the imagery of the moon. Chia-lin's poem was thus a clever re-creation of well-known metaphors from the literary canon. It was not very creative, but it was a signal to the examiners that he knew his poetic models. His technical proficiency and aesthetic appreciation were clearly demonstrated. Finally, the overall meaning of the poem in the final two lines reminded the readers that the brightness of the moon and its many reflections and allusions corresponded with the culture of a glorious age when sages ordered the world. Such words were an expression of safe conservatism, and the earlier T'ang-Sung tradition that poetry should express the feelings of those below to admonish those above was not evident. The current age was

---

109. "Pei-ch'ueh" is a frequent poetic allusion to the jade hall or pearl office, source of the waters of the Yangtzu or the god of the Yellow River. See Su Shih's poem "Teng chou hai shih shih" 登州海市詩 (Poem on climbing to the city on the sea's sand bank).

110. For an example of poetry answers that were outside the required rhyme, see *Ch'ing-pai lei-ch'ao*, 74.11, which records that in the 1870s a Hanlin candidate for a regular bureaucratic appointment forgot to use the required character *hsin* 心字 for the rhyme in the poetry question. See also *Hsu-tseng k'o-ch'ang t'iao-li* 續增科場條例, p. 3b, for the wrong tone in a character used for the poetry question in the 1852 metropolitan examination. The candidate, who passed the *hui-shih* due to the negligence of the examiners, was not permitted by the court to take the palace examination.

being metaphorized in terms of sagely culture, and this metaphor likely was a reference to the great achievements of the Ch'ien-lung emperor.

Reading over this answer, we can also see why examiners welcomed another grid, this one poetic, to their repertoire for measurably testing and ranking the ability of candidates for office to write well and think under pressure. Unquestionably, the new poetry question, by replacing the long-since-perfunctory documentary and legal judgment questions, enhanced the degree of difficulty in local, provincial, and metropolitan examinations at a time when the number of candidates was increasing precipitously (see Chapter 4). Those not fully classically literate were now at a further disadvantage once the poetry canon was added to the curriculum.[111]

In other provinces, the 1759 policy question on the new poetry requirement was presented in similar ways. At Shun-t'ien, the capital region, examiners stressed the Ch'ien-lung emperor's love for T'ang and Sung poetry as the background for his efforts to revive T'ang regulated verse among literati.[112] This reference reminded everyone that earlier in the eighteenth century, the dynasty had compiled a definitive edition of the *Ch'üan T'ang-shih* 全唐詩 (Complete T'ang poems) that had been released in 1707.[113] In Chiang-nan, candidates were asked to outline the great schools of regulated verse from antiquity through the Ming.[114] Examiners in Che-chiang asked candidates to evaluate prose writing in one policy question and poetry composition in another, suggesting that ancient-style prose was another aspect of the return to T'ang-Sung belles lettres.[115] In all provincial examinations, the policy question and answer clearly linked poetry and the dynasty's efforts to regulate and transform society (*chih-hua* 治化). Just as the sages had compiled the *Poetry Classic* to record human feelings, so the current dynasty wanted to be in touch with the mood of its people.[116]

111. Pauline Yu, "Canon Formation in Late Imperial China," pp. 83–104.

112. *Shun-t'ien fu t'i-ming hsiang-shih lu*, 1759: unpaginated manuscript.

113. For discussion, see Chou Hsun-ch'u 周勛初, "K'ang-hsi yü-ting Ch'üan T'ang-shih te shih-tai yin-chi yü chü-hsien" 康熙御定全唐詩的時代印記與局限 (The setting and limitations of the K'ang-hsi emperor's edition of the Compete T'ang Poems), *Chung-kuo wen-che yen-chiu t'ung-hsun* 中國文哲研究通訊 (Academia Sinica, Taiwan) 5, 2 (June 1995): 1–12, which overstates the impact of the Han "civilizing process" on the Manchus.

114. *Chiang-nan hsiang-shih lu*, 1759: 17b–18a.

115. *Che-chiang hsiang-shih lu*, 1759: 9b–13a. See Huters, "From Writing to Literature."

116. See also the *Chiang-hsi hsiang-shih lu*, 1759, fifth policy question; *Ssu-ch'uan hsiang-shih lu*, 1759, third policy question; *Kuang-hsi hsiang-shih t'i-ming lu*, 1759, second policy question; and the *Yun-nan hsiang-shih lu*, 1759, second policy question, in which this linkage is made explicit.

In the "grace" (*en-k'o* 恩科) Shen-hsi provincial examination in 1760, again 4,000 candidates competed for 61 official *chü-jen* places and 12 second-class (*fu-pang* 副榜) slots. The new format as in 1759 was in effect, and for the poetry question, the Shen-hsi examiners chose the theme: "In the eighth month the harvest is gathered" ("Pa-yueh ch'i huo" 八月其穫), which was a line from the poem "Seventh Month" ("Ch'i-yueh" 七月) in the *Poetry Classic*,[117] and they stipulated that the rhyme must follow the character *shih* 時 (time). The third policy question on session three again raised the issue of examination essays and the new poetry requirement. This time, the question was balanced in asking candidates to appraise both the eight-legged essay as an example of ancient-style prose (Fang Pao's influence was clear here) and the role of regulated verse in testing a candidate's knowledge of rhyme schemes.[118]

By extension, the examiners also tested the candidates' knowledge of how recent phonological studies had enabled the Ch'ing to improve on earlier rhyming books, philologically inferior to those of the present age. This time the best answer to the poetry in regulated verse question was produced by the candidate who finished first, Lei Erh-chieh 雷爾杰, and the best answer to the third policy question on eight-legged essays and regulated verse was prepared by Chiang Te-fu 江得符, who finished only sixteenth. The best writer of eight-legged essays on this examination was also singled out as the best author of regulated verse.[119]

Chiang Te-fu's policy answer began with paraphrases of the two most famous slogans in Chinese literary history: "Prose is a vehicle for the way" (*wen i tsai tao yeh* 文以載道也) by Chou Tun-i 周敦頤 (1017–73); and "Poetry expresses intent" (*shih yen chih* 詩言志) from the *Documents Classic*, later elaborated in the "Major Preface" (*Ta-hsu* 大序) to the *Poetry Classic*. These phrases were thereafter cited by candidates over and over in their policy questions on literature. Chiang meant by this to show how both prose and poetry had been stressed in Tao Learning and classical studies. He then traced the literary evolution of regulated verse and its use in T'ang civil examinations, before turning to Wang An-shih and the Sung stress on the classical essay, which Chiang saw as the roots of the eight-legged essay. Styles changed according to the times, Chiang argued.[120]

117. See *Shih-ching chin-chu chin-i*, p. 214; and Waley, trans., *The Book of Songs*, p. 165. My thanks to Pauline Yu for identifying the line.

118. *Shen-hsi hsiang-shih lu*, 1760: 7b, 11a–12a.

119. Ibid., 15a–21b, 44b–45a, 52b–53a.

120. Ibid., 52b–53a. See also the *Hu-kuang Hu-pei hsiang-shih lu*, 1762: 14a–15a, in which the phrases *wen i tsai tao* and *shih yen chih* were raised by the examiners in their policy question on prose and poetry. For discussion, see James J. Y. Liu, *Chinese Theories of Literature*, pp. 69, 114.

For T'ang styles of poetry, particularly regulated verse, Chiang Te-fu cited the Sung collection of T'ang literature entitled *Wen-yuan ying-hua* 文苑英華 (A gathering of masterpieces of literature), compiled by Li Fang 李昉 (925–96), which by the mid-Ch'ing candidates were going through very carefully if they hoped to pass civil examinations. In his conclusion, Chiang praised the ecumenical tone that the Ch'ien-lung emperor had struck by emphasizing both T'ang-style poetry that "expressed intent" and Sung-style prose that "was a vehicle for the Way." Particularly poetry, Chiang thought, was a means "to return to antiquity" (*fu-ku* 復古) and recapture T'ang, Han, and ancient ideals.[121]

In the 1766 metropolitan examination, the Hanlin examiners affirmed the new wedding between prose and poetry in the civil examinations. Their first policy question contended that ancient-style prose derived from the *Documents*, while rhyming sounds (*sheng-yun* 聲韻) came from the *Poetry Classic* (書經為古文之祖，三百篇為聲韻之祖). Their fifth policy question addressed the eight-legged essay and cited Ming writers such as Kuei Yu-kuang for equating ancient-style prose with the contemporary-style examination essay. Clearly, the Hanlin academicians were trying to have it both ways by strategically ignoring the animosities that had bedeviled T'ang and Sung literati, who warred culturally over belles lettres versus essay form as the proper measure of the scholar-official (see Chapter 1). The war was over. T'ang regulated verse and the Sung essay were both declared orthodox.[122]

Subsequently, the examination reformers began to square off between those who favored upgrading the new poetry question, which had vanquished the documentary and legal judgment questions on session two, and those who favored continuing the emphasis on the discourse question, which had been moved to session one after 1756. Variations were tried. In 1777, for instance, the poetry question was tested on the first session in Ho-nan but was still on session two in Che-chiang province.[123] In this curriculum struggle, fought among examiners in the precincts of the Ministry of Rites, the discourse question became a Sung Learning cause. Han Learning scholars tended to favor highlighting T'ang regulated prose on the civil examinations because of its pre-Sung ties to ancient learning, and they sought first to diminish and ultimately to eliminate the discourse question entirely.

121. *Shen-hsi hsiang-shih lu*, 1760: 53a–54b. Cf. Owen, *The Great Age of Chinese Poetry*, pp. 4, 64–65, 225–46, 253–56.

122. *Hui-shih lu*, 1766: 3a–b, 9a–10a.

123. See *Ho-nan hsiang-shih lu*, 1777: 45a; and *Che-chiang hsiang-shih lu*, 1777: 6a–8a.

*Phonology and Poetry in the Ch'ien-lung Reign*

Further provincial and metropolitan examination reforms were initiated in the 1780s, and the final form of the civil service examinations took shape in 1787 and 1793. The court approved the Ministry of Rites' 1782 recommendation to move the poetry requirement from session two to the first session, immediately after quotations from the Four Books, and this was to take effect in time for the 1783 provincial and 1784 metropolitan examinations. Dropped again in 1784 but then reinstated in 1785, the discourse essay based on the *Essential Meanings* was moved to the second session, following quotations from each of the Five Classics. Policy questions remained last and still least important.[124]

To counter this Han Learning trend, one of the ministers of rites, Yao Ch'eng-lieh 姚成烈 (1716–86), sent a memorial to the emperor in 1785 proposing to move the poetry question to session three and to replace it on the first session with the discourse essay stressing the *Classic of Filial Piety*. Instead, the Grand Council recommended a compromise that would restore the discourse to session two but leave regulated verse on the first session right after the Four Books quotations.[125] In 1788 eight-legged essays on the Four Books, which had sporadically been replaced in some counties by examination essays on the Five Classics since 1761, when the poetry requirement had been added, were restored on local examinations, as the court tried to sort out a complicated compromise that would satisfy both Han and Sung Learning advocates.[126]

In fact, the decision made after 1787 to remove the "discourse" question, which had stressed Ch'eng-Chu moral philosophy, upset eighteenth-century followers of Tao Learning, who complained bitterly about its removal in favor of T'ang regulated verse. The Yuan-Ming triumph of Tao Learning via the classical essay had been mitigated by the revival of Han Learning in the mid-Ch'ing. By testing both poetry and essays after 1756, the Ch'ien-lung court was taking a position reminiscent of the wedding of belles lettres and the *ching-i* essay in Sung times, before the final triumph of Tao Learning views in the Ming civil examinations (see Chapter 1).[127]

124. *Kuo-ch'ao Yü-yang k'o-ming lu*, 1.39b, notes that in 1782 the poetry question was moved to session one, the discourse was moved to second. The *Pen-ch'ao Che-wei san-ch'ang ch'üan-t'i pei-k'ao*, 1783: 3a, records that in Che-chiang the change took effect in 1783.

125. See the memorial by Yao in *Li-pu t'i-pen*, 9th month, 10th day.

126. *Kuo-ch'ao Yü-yang k'o-ming lu*, 4B.38a.

127. See the memorial to the emperor, 1758, 4th month, 25th day, in the *Li-pu t'i-pen*, complaining about the changes.

Again, the court tested its 1787 reform proposals by asking candidates on provincial examinations to comment on policy questions prepared by examiners to discuss the new changes. In the 1788 Chiang-hsi provincial examination, examiners devised the first policy question to focus on Chu Hsi's views on the examination essay and asked candidates why Chu's private proposals had not been enacted in his own time. The examiners then asked about the Ming policy of classical specialization, which had made the *Poetry Classic* the most popular for candidates and left the other Classics often unread. This question was clearly meant to invoke the correctness of the court's policy to remove classical specialization and require all the Classics for all candidates. In the fourth policy question, the Chiang-hsi examiners stressed how *wen* 文 as forms of writing surpassed any distinction between ancient and present (*wen wu ku-chin* 文無古今) and were themselves of utmost use when properly composed in the standards appropriate to that age.[128]

Provincial examiners for the 1788 Shen-hsi civil examinations put together a fourth policy question that questioned candidates about the role of belles lettres in T'ang civil examinations and asked them to compare this format with the Han dynasty use of classical techniques (*ching-shu* 經術) to select literati for office. The point here was to emphasize that moral behavior mattered more than the literary form chosen for testing literati.[129] The 1788 and 1793 Shun-t'ien provincial examiners also prepared policy questions about the civil examinations. In 1788 the examiners used the second policy question to query candidates about poetry and its links to rhyme and music. In 1793 the examiners' third policy question raised the issue of *wen* as an emblem of the dynasty's commitment to high culture and asked candidates to describe how prose had evolved since antiquity.[130]

Analogously, in the 1789 Ho-nan examination, provincial examiners prepared five policy questions on (1) Classics (經傳), (2) history (史學), (3) poetry (詩學), (4) selection (取士), and (5) paleography (六書). By the late eighteenth century, reflecting the Han Learning scholarly trends of the Ch'ien-lung era, the third session's policy questions for provincial examinations began to exhibit an irregular but somewhat common five-way division of topics: (1) Classics, (2) histories, (3) literature, (4) statecraft, and (5) local geography. The 1789 Ho-nan policy question on poetry asked candidates to describe the prosodic rules for different styles of poetry and then tied such rules to the ancient role of song and music in the *Poetry*

128. *Chiang-hsi hsiang-shih lu,* 1788.
129. *Shen-hsi hsiang-shih lu,* 1788.
130. *Shun-t'ien hsiang-shih t'i-ming lu,* 1788: 3a–4a (question), 23a–27b (answer); 1793: unpaginated manuscript.

*Classic.* The fourth query on selection tested candidates on their knowledge of the forms of civil selection practiced since the T'ang dynasty.[131]

For the best answer to the policy question on poetry, the examiners selected the one by Ko Ang 葛昂, who finished eighth out of the seventy-one graduates (altogether 4,700 candidates took part). The examiners particularly liked Ko's linkage of poetry and music, which Ko elaborated in light of the phonology of the three hundred poems in the *Poetry Classic,* and from which the five-word and seven-word line traditions in ancient poetry had derived. Considered in light of Ko Ang's answer to the fourth question on selection, and the fifth question on paleography, which the examiners also chose as the best policy answers, the 1789 questions and answers in Ho-nan seem devised to explain how prose, poetry, and philology had served as cultural markers and selection tools for different dynasties. The Ch'ing dynasty, with its stress on essays, poetry, and policy questions on philology (see Chapter 9), was thus ecumenical in its selection of the best precedents for its own selection process.[132]

Such changes occurred because of the logistical need for a simple grid to grade the ever-growing numbers of examination papers. Cutting the lengthy discourse essay in favor of a short poem, when tied to the elimination of the three documentary styles and five judicial terms required before 1756, meant a significant decrease in papers examiners had to read. They also required new fields of learning, such as T'ang-Sung belles lettres and mastery of all Five Classics, to make the curriculum more difficult for the expanding population of candidates. What was also fueling the popularity of the poetry question on session one and the policy questions on poetry in session three was the link between the rules of rhyming in regulated verse and the rise of phonology as the queen of philology in evidential research during the Ch'ien-lung reign.

Interestingly, the role of phonology in evidential research studies was paying poetic dividends by improving literati knowledge of classical sounds and rhymes throughout the empire. We should recall the rhyming and pronunciation dictionaries that were produced as examination aids during both the T'ang and the Sung dynasties, when belles lettres was required (see Chapter 5). By integrating the Ch'ing dynasty evolution of evidential research studies outside the examination market with the story of the revival of poetry and prose inside examination halls, we can pinpoint the scholarly context within which Ch'ing examiners asked candidates to add poetry and phonology to classical learning.[133]

Hamaguchi Fujio's 濱口富士雄 recent analysis of the exact steps forward in textual research made by evidential research scholars during the

131. *Ho-nan hsiang-shih lu,* 1789: 7b–13a.
132. Ibid., 41b–44b.
133. For discussion, see my *From Philosophy to Philology,* pp. 212–21.

eighteenth and nineteenth centuries describes how philological studies developed and evolved during the Ch'ing dynasty. Hamaguchi has shown that Ch'ing dynasty evidential scholars sought to restore the textual legacy of antiquity. Literati such as Tai Chen 戴震 (1724–77) had in mind a systematic research agenda that built on paleography and phonology to reconstruct the "meaning" (*i yin ch'iu-i* 以音求義) of Chinese words in the Classics and Four Books.[134]

Later Wang Nien-sun 王念孫 (1744–1832), and his son Yin-chih 王引之 (1766–1834), extended Tai's approach and attempted to use the "meanings" of Chinese words as a method to reconstruct the "intentions" of the sages, the farsighted authors of those words. Moreover, technical phonology became the measuring stick of evidential research as the study of the history of the classical language reached unprecedented precision and exactness in the eighteenth and nineteenth centuries. To achieve this end, evidential scholars chose philological means, principally the application of phonology (音韻學/古音學), paleography (文字學), and etymology (訓詁學), to study the Classics.[135]

One by-product of these philological tools was the full realization of how important poetry, particularly regulated verse, was for the reconstruction of antiquity via phonology, paleography, and etymology. For example, Liang Chang-chü, who prepared one of the first studies of the civil examinations, also compiled a collection on poetry studies in which he outlined the study of poetry (*hsueh-shih* 學詩) and the rules of regulated verse. As he explored the history of poetic studies, Liang discussed earlier Sung and Yuan anthologies of poetry that he thought could serve as contemporary models. In the conclusion, Liang Chang-chü tracked how Ch'ing classical scholars had unraveled the rhyme system in the *Poetry Classic*. They had illuminated the technical rules in regulated verse and made major advances in the study of phonology.[136] Examiner needs and literati scholarly currents had worked together to transform the examination curriculum.

134. Note how Chow, in *The Rise of Confucian Ritualism in Late Imperial China*, pp. 188–91, elides this aspect of Tai Chen's scholarship by incorrectly tying him to "Sung Confucians" on ritual. The passage on ritual from Tai's writings that Chow cites is in fact a direct attack on Chu Hsi's ritualism. See *Tai Chen chi* 戴震集 (Tai Chen's collected essays) (Shanghai: Ku-chi Press, 1980), pp. 317–19.

135. See Hamaguchi Fujio, *Shindai kokyogaku no shisō shi teki kenkyū*, pp. 175–575. His discussion emphasizes the work of Tai Chen, Ch'ien Ta-hsin 錢大昕 (1728–1804), Tuan Yü-ts'ai 段玉裁 (1735–1815), Wang Nien-sun, Wang Yin-chih, Chiao Hsun 焦循 (1763–1820), and Juan Yuan 阮元 (1764–1849). While ritual was an important object of their research, ritualism per se did not motivate their studies. Cf. my *From Philosophy to Philology*, p. 116.

136. See Liang Chang-chü, "T'ui-an sui-pi" 退庵隨筆 (Random writings by Liang Chang-chü), in *Ch'ing shih-hua hsu-pien*, pp. 1949–97. Liang compiled a work entitled *Shih-lü*

## *Abrogating Classical Specialization*

Classical specialization as an examination requirement had remained intact since 1756, even though the four quotations from each classic were given eminence of place on session two, instead of their previously subordinate position to the Four Books on the first session. Candidates still mastered mainly the *Poetry* and *Change* classics, however, leaving the others, particularly the *Annals* and *Rites*, unstudied. In 1765, for example, the Manchu governor-general in Ssu-ch'uan in a memorial to the court described the distribution of specialization for the sixty candidates on the Classics in the Ssu-ch'uan provincial examination: fourteen (23%) on the *Change;* thirteen (22%) on the *Documents;* twenty-one (35%) on the *Poetry;* nine (15%) on the *Rites* and *Annals;* three (5%) on the Five Classics. The memorial and attached materials suggested that the problem of encouraging students to specialize on the less popular Classics remained, despite the 1756 reforms, which had moved the Five Classics to session two. The 1765 Ssu-ch'uan figures were roughly the same as those for the distribution of the classical specialization before 1750 presented in Chapter 5.[137]

As with the new poetry question, described above, imperial examiners assigned to the 1788 Shun-t'ien provincial examination also devised a policy question on the merits of classical specialization. The first policy question that year in Shun-t'ien asked students to describe the role of the Classics in civil examinations over time and to present the various positions by literati such as Chu Hsi on how many Classics should be tested.[138] The best policy answer by Wang Te-ch'eng 汪德鉞, who finished seventieth out of 232 graduates, obliged the examiners by tracing the specialization policy (*chuan-ching* 專經) versus the policy of mastering all the classics (*chien-ching* 兼經) in imperial history.

In addition, Wang profiled how many Classics had been tested during the T'ang and Sung dynasties, when there were "Nine Classics" and "Thirteen Classics," which were further subdivided into "greater" (*ta-ching* 大經) and "lesser classics" (*hsiao-ching* 小經). Wang showed how the Ming had limited the number to the "Five Classics" and chosen the specialization policy based on earlier precedents. In his conclusion, Wang Te-ch'eng affirmed the new Ch'ing policy of testing all the Classics: "Those who do not master the Five Classics, certainly cannot master just one. Therefore, the rule of specialization is not bad, but literati candidates of

---

*ts'ung-hua* 試律叢話 (Collected comments on testing regulated verse) to complement his *Chih-i ts'ung-hua.*

137. See *Li-pu t'i-pen,* 1765, 9th month, 5th day, for the memorial in this Ssu-ch'uan case.

138. *Shun-t'ien hsiang-shih lu,* 1788: 2a–3a.

low character take advantage and concentrate on just one Classic and lose the others. Consequently, the policy of mastering all the Classics is required to improve the situation so that all the Classics will actually be learned."[139]

To resolve such difficulties, the specialization requirement initially was altered to allow examiners, not candidates, to choose which of the Classics they would require for the triennial local qualifying, provincial, and metropolitan examinations. Degree candidates were expected to master all of the Five Classics, but the provincial and metropolitan examiners themselves would now preselect on a revolving basis a different one of the Five Classics as the source of quotations for students to write essays. In 1788 the *Poetry Classic* was announced as the source of quotations on the second session of all provincial examinations; in the 1789 metropolitan examination it was the *Documents;* in the 1790 "grace" (*en-k'o* 恩科) provincial examinations, the *Change* was chosen; for the 1790 metropolitan examination, the *Li-chi* was required on session two. In the 1792 Che-chiang provincial examination, all candidates had to write essays on the four quotations selected from the *Spring and Autumn Annals,* the most formidable of all the Five Classics because of its long commentaries. Moreover, records were no longer kept concerning classical specialization.[140]

FORMAT OF PROVINCIAL AND METROPOLITAN CIVIL SERVICE
EXAMINATIONS DURING THE CH'ING DYNASTY, 1787–92

| Session No. | No. of Questions |
| --- | --- |
| ONE | |
| 1. Four Books 四書 | 3 quotations |
| 2. Poetry question 詩題 | 1 poetic model |
| TWO | |
| 1. *Change* 易經 | 4 quotations |
| 2. *Documents* 書經 | 4 quotations |
| 3. *Poetry* 詩經 | 4 quotations |
| 4. *Annals* 春秋 | 4 quotations |
| 5. *Rites* 禮記 | 4 quotations |
| 6. Discourse 論 | 1 quotation (dropped in 1793) |
| THREE | |
| 1. Policy questions 經史時務策 | 5 essays |

NOTE: The Classics on session two were selected by examiners on a revolving basis.

139. Ibid., pp. 18a–22b.
140. *Che-chiang hsiang-shih lu,* 1792: 6a. See also *Kuo-ch'ao liang-Che k'o-ming lu,* p. 139a.

The final step in changing the specialization requirement began in 1792, after the last of the Five Classics, the *Annals*, had been tested on a revolving basis in the provincial and metropolitan examinations between 1787 and 1792. This dramatic increase in classical requirements (see Chapter 5) paralleled the increase in human competition on Ch'ing examinations (see Chapter 4). China's demographic realities, to which the reform of examination requirements was in part addressed, meant that as the civil examinations became more difficult in content, the odds against passing them because of the increasing number of competing candidates became prohibitive. The results are outlined below in the format for civil examinations from 1793 to 1898. Not until after the Taiping Rebellion did the court consider increasing the quotas (see Chapter 11).[141]

FORMAT OF PROVINCIAL AND METROPOLITAN CIVIL SERVICE
EXAMINATIONS DURING THE CH'ING DYNASTY, 1793–1898

| *Session No.* | *No. of Questions* |
| --- | --- |
| ONE | |
| 1. Four Books 四書 | 3 quotations |
| 2. Poetry question 詩題 | 1 poetic model |
| TWO | |
| 1. *Change* 易經 | 1 quotation |
| 2. *Documents* 書經 | 1 quotation |
| 3. *Poetry* 詩經 | 1 quotation |
| 4. *Annals* 春秋 | 1 quotation |
| 5. *Rites* 禮記 | 1 quotation |
| THREE | |
| 1. Policy questions 經史時務策 | 5 essays |

Beginning in 1793, for both the provincial and metropolitan examinations, examiners chose a single quotation from each of the Five Classics for all candidates to answer on the second session. Again, examiners prepared policy questions to review the changes and solicit reactions. In the 1794 Kuang-tung provincial examination, for instance, the second policy question stressed the changes in the classical curriculum since Han and T'ang times in an effort to show that the new changes followed the pre-Sung accent on the Five Classics as a whole. In the best policy answer included in the official record, Yen Yueh 顏樾, the thirteenth-place finisher, accepted the Han Learning slant of the new stress on the Five Classics and documented how Later Han scholars such as Cheng Hsuan

141. See Li T'iao-yuan, *Tan-mo lu,* 16.10a–12a.

had mastered all the Classics and not simply specialized on one of them.[142]

In 1788, however, the Ch'ien-lung emperor had already complained that the new poetry questions were further corrupting literati by creating a fad that, like the eight-legged essay, favored literary technique over practical governance, but he made no effort to push the clock back to the earlier format.[143] Even after finally being dropped—Sung Learning protests notwithstanding—from the provincial and metropolitan examinations in 1787, discourse essays remained required on the special *ch'ao-k'ao* (court examination), although such discourse questions were now more literary than substantive. By 1787, sentiments favoring Sung Learning (see above) in civil examinations were strategically dismissed.

Nor were Han Learning advocates completely satisfied. Ch'ien Ta-hsin, one of the leading evidential research scholars of the Ch'ien-lung reign, recommended in his private writings that the Four Books—not the Five Classics—should be moved back to session two, thereby giving the Five Classics priority on session one. After four centuries of use for essays on local, provincial, and metropolitan examinations, Ch'ien contended, there were essays on every possible quotation in the Four Books an examiner might choose.[144] Consequently, candidates could read such essays, which were widely circulated by printers, and avoid reading any of the Four Books themselves. The Five Classics were too extensive and difficult for an adequate number of essays on quotations selected from them to be available, Ch'ien maintained.

Similarly, Sun Hsing-yen 孫星衍 (1753–1818), also a leading advocate of Han Learning, was particularly critical of the early Ming removal of Han-T'ang scholia from the civil examination curriculum, which, following Ku Yen-wu, he associated with the decline of classical studies during the Ming. In a memorial to the emperor, Sun called for a revival of Han classical commentaries and T'ang subcommentaries to the Ch'ing examination curriculum to supplement the Sung scholia included in the early Ming *Ta-chüan* trilogy (see Chapter 2). This request was not acted upon, and Sun could only include the memorial in his collected works.[145]

142. *Kuang-tung hsiang-shih lu*, 1794: 9a–10b, 36a–39b.

143. See the Ch'ien-lung emperor's 1788 edict decrying literary fads in *Ch'ing-tai ch'ien-ch'i chiao-yü lun-chu hsuan*, 1/15–17. See also *Pen-ch'ao Che-wei san-ch'ang ch'üan-t'i pei-yao*, 1788: 1a–2b.

144. Ch'ien Ta-hsin, *Shih-chia-chai yang-hsin lu* 十駕齋養新錄 (Record of self-renewal from the Ten Yokes Study), 1804 edition (reprint, Taipei: Kuang-wen Bookstore), 18.15b–16a.

145. See Sun Hsing-yen, "Ni k'o-ch'ang shih-shih ch'ing chien-yung chu-shu che" 擬科場試士請兼用註疏摺 (Memorial recommending the use of scholia in examination compounds testing literati), in *Ch'ing-tai ch'ien-ch'i chiao-yü lun-chu hsuan*, 3/278–79.

In one area, however, the Han Learning group was able to change the examination curriculum with surprising ease. In 1792 Chi Yun 紀昀 (1724–1805), then a minister of rites, requested abandoning the Hu An-kuo commentary to the *Spring and Autumn Annals* in the examination curriculum. This Northern Sung commentary, discussed in Chapters 1 and 9, had enunciated Sung Learning themes that Han Learning scholars such as Chi Yun thought were anachronistic. Chi contended that Hu An-kuo had used the *Annals* as a foil to express his own opinions about the fall of the Northern Sung and the move of the dynastic court to the south. Chi preferred the three Han commentaries to the *Annals,* which had duly informed the K'ang-hsi era *Ch'in-ting ch'un-ch'iu chuan-shuo hui-tsuan* 欽定春秋傳説彙纂 (Imperially prescribed commentaries and explications of the *Annals*), and had on many points refuted the Hu version. The Ch'ien-lung emperor responded by immediately ordering that beginning in 1793 with local examinations the Hu commentary would no longer be used in the civil examinations.[146]

Chi Yun's victory was incomplete, however. Table 10.3 reveals that except for the beginning period in 1794, the best essays on the Five Classics were usually less important than those on the Four Books in determining a candidate's final rank. The Han Learning challenge to the Four Books had been successful in authorizing the Five Classics for all candidates, but the Four Books monopoly on the highest ranks in the local, provincial, and metropolitan civil examinations had been maintained. Indeed, the examiners' tendency to grade each candidate's essays on the Five Classics uniformly undermined their significance individually in the rankings. Such essays, as in the case of Ch'ing examination essays on the Four Books (see Table 8.1) were evaluated as a group. Again, the court's penchant for compromise had enabled the Ch'ien-lung reforms to take hold successfully within the bureaucracy and mollify its Sung versus Han Learning advocates.

Although the Chia-ch'ing (r. 1796–1820) and Tao-kuang (r. 1820–50) courts did little about the curriculum of civil examinations and focused instead on procedural problems, literati opinion in the early nineteenth century began to retrace many of the debates that had marked earlier dissatisfaction with the examination system (see Chapter 4). If the Ch'ien-lung emperor had succeeded in keeping pace with literati opinion concerning the literary versus practical aspects of the tests, his successors quickly fell behind. Both the Chia-ch'ing and Tao-kuang courts were satisfied with nitty-gritty responses to specific, noncurricular irregularities in the selection process, such as selection of quotations, grading, and what

---

146. See *Ch'ing-ch'ao hsu wen-hsien t'ung-k'ao*, 84.8429–30.

to do with failed examination papers. They failed to recognize that an important aspect of the civil examinations was the periodic questioning of the system from within that gave it credibility from without, a theme that is developed more fully in the next and final chapter.[147]

147. See *Chung-kuo chin-tai chiao-yü-shih tzu-liao hui-pien* 中國近代教育史資料匯編 (Compendium of sources on the history of Chinese modern education) (Shanghai: Education Press, 1990), pp. 57–76, on nineteenth-century official responses, and pp. 414–34, on literati opinion. These debates are discussed in Chapter 11.

# CHAPTER ELEVEN

# Delegitimation and Decanonization: The Pitfalls of Late Ch'ing Examination Reform

One of the conditions for the fluid functioning of the late imperial civil service examinations was the dynasty's constant attention to its improvement and reform. Past accounts of education and modernization in China have generally underestimated the degree to which imperial institutions were subjected to internal criticism and reform before the processes of westernization were initiated after 1860. We have seen in earlier chapters that although many in and outside the bureaucracy viewed the examination road to success as a detestable solution, they also admitted that realistically there was no alternative to the regimented process of anonymously examining young men to enter the civil service. During the Ming and Ch'ing dynasties, civil examinations held from the county yamen to the imperial palace were considered self-evident as impartial means for commoners to achieve elite status and wield political power.[1]

In this satisfactory, "natural" form of selection that produced graduates in biennial and triennial competitions, the criteria of selection were often scrutinized. Such scrutiny frequently dissolved into literati rhetoric; meanwhile the dynasty's unrelenting examination regime remained in place, enticing millions of men to compete with each other to memorize the classical curriculum. In the last years of the Ch'ing dynasty, the civil examinations lost their cultural luster and became instead the object of ridicule by literati-officials as an "unnatural" educational regime that should be discarded. This decisive intellectual turn among leading late-Ch'ing literati has in past scholarship been viewed as inevitable. This chapter, however, reverses the usual interpretation of the inevitable decline of the imperial examination regime in the face of Western power

1. Cf. Foucault, *Discipline and Punish*, pp. 231, 272.

and influence in China. As we shall see, the transformation in literati perception from "natural" imperial examinations to "unnatural" education followed a historical sequence that was neither inevitable nor uncontested. Indeed, many dissenting literati, followers of Tao Learning included, had contended since the Sung dynasties that the examination regime had ruined classical educational ideals.

Until 1904–5, calls for reform or abrogation of late imperial civil examinations never threatened the inexorable pace and rhythm of the examination compound, where since the early Ming the "best and brightest" literati publicly proved their educational mettle.[2] What purpose, then, lay behind the ritual-like protests that accompanied the relentless gears of examination selection?[3] What goals were served by overlooking or simply co-opting the complaints of the critics and keeping the examination system running in place? And, finally, what were the consequences when literati critics won out and convinced the imperial court that its interests would be best served by abrogating the civil and military examinations and instituting in their place a European-style school system with new forms of examination for selecting men for the government?[4] The story of educational reform in late imperial China is an old one, but this chapter adds new pieces to the analysis that problematize past conclusions about the modernization story line within which civil examinations became a straw man in the plot.

## CALLS FOR EXAMINATION REFORM IN THE EARLY NINETEENTH CENTURY

Although the Chia-ch'ing (r. 1796–1820) and Tao-kuang (r. 1820–50) courts did little beyond keeping the civil examinations running on schedule, no small feat in itself, literati began to retrace many of the debates that had marked Sung (see Chapter 1), late Ming (see Chapter 4) and early Ch'ing dissatisfaction (see Chapter 10) with the examination curriculum. The Ch'ien-lung emperor had maintained a reformist policy between

2. Wolfgang Franke, *The Reform and Abolition of the Traditional Chinese Examination System*, pp. 28–47, gives a good, general overview.

3. Nivison, "Protest against Conventions and Conventions of Protest," pp. 177–201.

4. See Sally Borthwick, *Education and Social Change in China: The Beginnings of the Modern Era* (Stanford: Hoover Institution Press, 1983), pp. 4–6, 38–64, 153–54; Marianne Bastid, *Educational Reform in Early 20th-Century China*, translated by Paul J. Bailey (Ann Arbor: University of Michigan China Center, 1988), pp. 10–13; and Satō Shin'ichi 佐藤慎一, *Kindai Chūgoku no chishikijin to bunmei* 近代中國の知識人と文明 (Intellectuals and civilization in modern China) (Tokyo: University of Tokyo Press, 1996), pp. 19–26.

1740 and 1793, but his successors failed to heed minority opinions about the increasing corruption in the examination compounds and the need to improve classical studies raised by their literati elites.[5]

In the early nineteenth century, many literati were caught up in the Han versus Sung Learning debate, and some called for a comprehensive classical synthesis. Ch'en Keng-huan 陳庚煥 (1757–1820), a local Fu-chien literatus, proposed turning Han classicism and Sung theory into complementary standards for policy questions on the civil examinations. Since the 1787–93 reforms, examiners had frequently prepared policy questions reflecting either Han or Sung Learning (see Chapter 9), but there had been little effort at synthesis. Similarly, Wang T'ing-chen 王廷珍 (1757–1827), while serving as a Hanlin academician and examiner, called for eight-legged essays that would reflect both Ch'eng-Chu learning and Han Learning.[6]

There were others such as Ch'en Shou-ch'i 陳壽祺 (1771–1834), a Fu-chien scholar with Han Learning sympathies, who nevertheless, when serving as one of the two chief examiners for the 1807 Ho-nan provincial examination, made clear in the afterword for the official report that Han classical schools and Sung Tao Learning together were the foundations of classical models for governance.[7] Chang Hai-shan 張海珊 (1782–1821), on the other hand, favored Sung Learning, but he admitted in his writings on the examinations that the achievements of both traditions were significant. Hu P'ei-hui 胡培翬 (1782–1849) from An-hui, an 1819 chin-shih who rose to high office, openly called on literati to adopt Han-Sung syncretism as a means to overcome the battle lines between them.[8]

Liu K'ai 劉開 (1784–1824), a follower of Yao Nai 姚鼐 (1731–1815) and the T'ung-ch'eng tradition of Tao Learning in An-hui province, demonstrated the degree to which Sung Learning advocates in the early nineteenth century were willing to compromise: he equated Cheng Hsuan, the patron scholar of Han Learning, and Chu Hsi, the sage of Sung Learning (且朱子之與康成，固異世相需者也). As a local Chiang-hsi senior tribute student, Shang Jung 尚鎔 (1785–?) composed an essay entitled "Ching-hsueh pien" 經學辨 (Discerning classical studies) in which he criticized

5. See *Chung-kuo chin-tai chiao-yü-shih tzu-liao hui-pien: ya-p'ien chan-cheng shih-ch'i chiao-yü* 中國近代教育史資料匯編：鴉片戰爭時期教育 (Compendium of sources on the history of Chinese modern education: Opium War education), compiled by Chen Yuan-hui 陳元暉 (Shanghai: Education Press, 1990), pp. 57–76, on official responses, and pp. 414–34, on literati opinion.

6. See *Ch'ing-tai ch'ien-ch'i chiao-yü lun-chu hsuan*, 3/305–07, 3/326–27.

7. See Ch'en's 1807 afterword in ibid., 3/392–93.

8. Ibid., 3/455–56, 3/459–60.

efforts by literati to champion only one side of the Han-Sung controversy. Shang favored accepting the strengths of both classical traditions.[9]

We have already seen the widespread influence of Liang Chang-chü's famous *Collected Comments on the Crafting of Eight-legged Civil Examination Essays*.[10] Liang's entries were later included in Hsu K'o's *Ch'ing-pai lei-ch'ao* 清稗類鈔 (Classified jottings on Ch'ing dynasty unofficial history). Such painstaking accounts of actual examination experiences presented Ch'ing literati with the harsh realities of the examination compounds (fires, riots, etc.) and the arbitrariness of many examiners.[11]

Ch'en Shou-ch'i, for example, also prepared an influential essay entitled *K'o-chü lun* 科舉論 (On the civil examinations), in which he blasted the impractical focus of the curriculum. Citing Chu Hsi and the late Ming writer Kuei Yu-kuang 歸有光 (1506–71) as precedents, Ch'en recounted how generations of literati had buried themselves in literary pursuits for careerist goals. For a millennium, the error had been to link civil service selection to literary talent. Interestingly, Ch'en made no mention of such misgivings in his "afterwords" ("Hou-hsu" 後序) for the 1804 Kuang-tung or 1807 Ho-nan provincial examinations, nor did he publicly recommend any major reforms.[12]

Many Tao-kuang literati such as Pao Shih-ch'en 包世臣 (1775–1855), Kung Tzu-chen 龔自珍 (1792–1841), and Wei Yuan 魏源 (1794–1856) increasingly perceived that more activist statecraft initiatives were required if the Ch'ing government hoped to cope with its administrative decline.[13] Within their overall reformist strategies, they included criticism of the role that the civil examinations played in creating a sterile academic environment in which literati paid little attention to the actual problems facing the dynasty. A poor scholar who unsuccessfully competed for *chin-shih* status over twelve times and eventually settled for a provincial *chü-jen* degree, Pao Shih-ch'en noted that the examination system was supposed to attract men of talent to government service. Instead, it stressed literary and classical erudition of dubious use. In his private writings, Pao called for changes that would drop the eight-legged essay and emphasize instead historical and practical affairs tested by policy questions based on encyclopedias from the Sung dynasty down to the present.[14]

9. Ibid., 3/472, 3/515–17.

10. See Liang Chang-chü, *Chih-i ts'ung-hua*, 22.1a–18a. The *Chung-kuo chin-tai chiao-yü-shih tzu-liao hui-pien* frequently cites his work.

11. See *Ch'ing-pai lei-ch'ao*, 1.1–178.

12. Ch'en Shou-ch'i, *Tso-hai wen-chi* 左海文集 (Collected essays of Ch'en Shou-ch'i), Ch'ing edition (ca. 1796–1849), 3.22a–25a, 1.25a–28b.

13. For discussion, see my *Classicism, Politics, and Kinship*, pp. 275–306.

14. See *Chung-kuo chin-tai chiao-yü-shih tzu-liao hui-pien*, pp. 414–17. Cf. Hummel, ed., *Eminent Chinese of the Ch'ing Period*, pp. 610–11.

Also unsuccessful in the metropolitan examinations, Kung Tzu-chen blamed the pettiness of the selection process for his failures. Wei Yuan, who achieved the *chin-shih* degree late in life at the age of fifty, complained privately that the civil service lacked men with any practical talent because the selection process made little effort to stress administrative concerns. Literature and classicism were the pillars of literati life, but these were of no avail when the dynasty faced unprecedented threats to its governing capacities.[15]

Despite these dissatisfactions, however, the Tao-kuang court made no move to build on earlier reforms. For example, an 1835 memorial by an imperial censor to the Tao-kuang emperor asking that legal expertise be tested regularly as one of the five policy questions administered during the third session was not enacted, although policy questions on law did sometimes appear on provincial and metropolitan examinations.[16] As the Ch'ing dynasty lost the initiative to reform the civil selection process in the early nineteenth century, some men, such as the future leader of the Taiping Rebellion, Hung Hsiu-ch'üan, bereft of hope in the examination market (see Chapter 6), took more radical positions than mere reform and called for overthrow of the Ch'ing dynasty.

## THE TAIPINGS AND NEW EXAMINATIONS

During the Taiping Rebellion (1850–64), local and provincial examinations under Ch'ing auspices in many provinces were brought to a halt. In Hunan, for example, as early as 1852, officials loyal to the Manchus asked that the provincial examinations be postponed because of the Taiping military threat.[17] Particularly hard hit, because the Taiping rebels made Nanking their capital, the Yangtzu delta provinces ceased holding Ch'ing examinations in 1859. Candidates from Chiang-su province who could do so were asked to travel to Che-chiang for Ch'ing provincial examinations, while An-hui students took the examinations in unaffected areas of the province. In Hang-chou, the capital of Che-chiang, local examinations were stopped for three cycles in 1860 and not resumed until 1865. Local examinations there were not fully back on track until 1869.[18] The Yangtzu delta had dominated imperial examinations since the Ming dynasty (see Chapter 5), but after the devastation of the Taiping Rebellion, sons of Chiang-

15. See *Chung-kuo chin-tai chiao-yü-shih tzu-liao hui-pien*, pp. 417–30.
16. *Ch'ing-shih kao*, 11/3151–52; and *Huang-ch'ao hsu wen-hsien t'ung-k'ao*, 1/8448.
17. *Ch'ing cheng-fu chen-ya T'ai-p'ing t'ien-kuo tang-an shih-liao* 清政府鎮壓太平天國檔案史料 (Archival historical documents on the Qing government suppression of the Taiping Heavenly Kingdom) (Peking: She-hui k'o-hsueh wen-hsien Press, 1992), vol. 3, pp. 318, 334.
18. See *Ch'ing li-ch'ao hsiu-ts'ai lu*, pp. 48a–55a.

nan families were no longer unchallenged in the empirewide examination competition. Provinces such as Hu-nan in the central Yangtzu and Kuang-tung in the southeast increasingly placed their candidates among metro-politan graduates.

It is an important clue to the local importance of examinations, howev-er, that areas under Taiping control held civil and military examinations devised by the new rulers and supervised by military officials assigned to govern local areas.[19] Hung Hsiu-ch'üan and his top leaders, many of whom had been rejected for the Ch'ing civil service, recognized the importance of civil examinations for augmenting Taiping political legiti-macy and for opening the doors of officialdom to local literati.[20] Beginning in 1851–53, the Taipings initiated periodic local, provincial, and capital examinations, which included a number of changes from the Ch'ing ver-sions. There were no quotas for the Taiping examinations, for example, and, when compared with the Ch'ing, the likelihood of passing was con-siderably higher. Nor were candidates asked to report their family back-grounds in applications to take the Heavenly Kingdom's examinations. In an 1854 Hu-pei examination, over 800 of the 1,000 candidates passed, compared with a normal passing rate of 1% to 5% for Ch'ing provincial examinations. Moreover, the Taipings at first held yearly metropolitan examinations in contrast to those of the Ch'ing, which were triennial—presumably to replace local Ch'ing officials with their own.[21]

According to some sources, civil examinations for the first time were also held for women. If true, this change would have been unprece-dented.[22] But scholars of the examinations such as Shang Yen-liu 商衍鎏 and Li Ch'un 酈純 have contested such records because they are not mentioned in most Taiping sources and because the alleged examination for women was only a high-level examination and that would presuppose lower examinations for women, for which there are no records. Nevertheless, Shang Yen-liu and Li Ch'un do acknowledge Taiping efforts to augment education for women.[23]

19. See Hsu K'o, *Ch'ing-pai lei-ch'ao*, 21.171–78; and Shang Yen-liu, *T'ai-p'ing t'ien-kuo k'o-chü k'ao-shih chi-lueh* 太平天國科舉考試紀略 (Survey of civil examinations under the Heavenly Kingdom of the Taipings) (Peking: Chung-hua Bookstore, 1961), pp. 24–25.

20. Vincent Shih, *The Taiping Ideology*, pp. 42–43.

21. Chien Yu-wen 簡又文, *T'ai-p'ing t'ien-kuo tien-chih t'ung-k'ao* 太平天國典制通考 (Comprehensive study of the Taiping Heavenly Kingdom's ordinances and institutions) (Hong Kong: Chi-cheng Book Co., 1958), pp. 263–78; and Vincent Shih, *The Taiping Ideology*, pp. 98–99.

22. Hsu K'o, *Ch'ing-pai lei-ch'ao*, 21.177–78.

23. Shang Yen-liu, *T'ai-p'ing t'ien-kuo k'o-chü k'ao-shih chi-lueh*, pp. 74–80; and Li Ch'un, *T'ai-p'ing t'ien-kuo chih-tu ch'u-t'an hsia* 太平天國制度初探下 (Preliminary analysis of the

At first Hung Hsiu-ch'üan was not sure what format the curriculum should follow. He sent an imperial decree to the chief examiner for the special examination to celebrate Hung's birthday seeking his advice:

> The selection of officials through examinations is beset with dangers, and it has never pleased me. Now at the beginning of the establishment of the nation, there are a hundred things to be done. Apparently the only way to cope with the situation is to select as many men of learning as possible to do the job. This is the reason for taking the occasion of my birthday to give this examination as a temporary measure. However, the *Analects* and *Mencius* should most certainly not be used, because of the fact that the doctrines contained in them are contrary to our sacred teachings. Do you have any good way to handle this situation?[24]

The examiner recommended using Hung Hsiu-ch'üan's "Heavenly Commandments" (*T'ien-t'iao shu* 天條書) and other Taiping religious decrees for the special examination, which pleased the "Heavenly King." This solution mimicked Ming T'ai-tsu's *Sheng-yü liu-yen* 聖諭六言 (Sacred edict in six maxims), which Ming emperors had used on the civil examinations.[25] Hung Hsiu-ch'üan's maxims thus supplanted the K'ang-hsi emperor's 1670 *Sacred Edict* and the Yung-cheng emperor's 1724 *Amplified Instructions for the Sacred Edict,* which Ch'ing *sheng-yuan* had to write from memory for licensing examinations.[26]

Efforts to use Christian "Classics" to legitimate the Taipings paralleled earlier efforts to use Tao Learning and the Five Classics to uphold Ming and Ch'ing rulers. The Four Books and Five Classics, for example, were replaced on the Taiping examination curriculum by Chinese versions of the Old and New Testaments of the Judeo-Christian Bible, as well as Taiping texts attributed to Hung Hsiu-ch'üan. For example, the "Eastern King" of the Taipings, Yang Hsiu-ch'ing 楊秀清 (d. 1856), set the quotation for the discourse question in 1853 as: "Is the true Way the same as the worldly Way?" (真道豈與世道相同). The quotation for the literary

---

Taiping Heavenly Kingdom's institutions, vol. 2) (Peking: Chung-hua Bookstore, 1990), pp. 574–75, 632–40. See also Chien Yu-wen, *T'ai-p'ing t'ien-kuo tien-chih t'ung-k'ao*, pp. 263–78. Vincent Shih, *The Taiping Ideology*, pp. 62–65, uncritically accepts the evidence for women's examinations originally presented by Lo Erh-kang 羅爾綱 in 1933.

24. Cited and translated in Vincent Shih, *The Taiping Ideology*, p. 42.

25. See Omura Kōdō, "Shinchō kyōiku shisō shi ni okeru Seigo kōkun no ichi ni cuite," pp. 233–46. See also Su Shuang-p'i, *Hung Hsiu-ch'üan chuan*, pp. 83–88.

26. Vincent Shih, *The Taiping Ideology*, pp. 110–33, discusses Taiping maxims and their textual basis.

essay was: "God is the great parent of all countries. He has produced and nourished all people." (皇上帝是邦國大父母，人人是其所生，人人是其所養). And the poetry question that Yang set was clearly an effort to claim political legitimacy for himself: "Everywhere within the four seas there is the Eastern King." (四海之內有東王).[27]

Although the Bible had been translated into a semi-colloquial form (see the literary question above), the literary and institutional forms of Taiping examinations were nevertheless consistent with Ming and Ch'ing examinations. For instance, Taiping candidates were still expected to write essays on the biblical quotations selected by the examiners using the eight-legged essay grid. In addition, answers to poetry questions were required to use the same standard Ch'ing rhyming requirements initiated in 1756, that is, T'ang dynasty–style regulated verse. A single policy question was usually also required with a minimum answer of 300 characters.[28] Form did not concern Hung Hsiu-ch'üan and the Taipings as much as content, which suggests that the long-standing stylistic requirements for essay, poetry, and policy questions and their division into separate testing sessions, whether Ch'ing or Taiping, were not irrevocably wedded to the classical curriculum but had a cultural life of their own as testable signs of a candidate's intelligence.[29]

Curiously, a Taiping quotation on the ruler's "true spirit" (chen-shen 真神) chosen for an eight-legged examination essay effectively legitimated Hung Hsiu-chüan in ways parallel to earlier efforts to use the Tao Leaning notion of the pure "mind of Tao" to legitimate Ming and Ch'ing rulers. Some candidates in the Yangtzu delta had little trouble passing both Taiping and Ch'ing civil examinations. In fact, many scholars afterward were accused by the Ch'ing of supporting the Taipings. Wang T'ao 王韜 (1828–?), later a collaborator with James Legge in Hong Kong and Scotland in the 1860s in the translation of the Chinese Classics into English, was accused of being the chuang-yuan on a Taiping palace examination under the alias of Huang Wan 黃畹, although such claims have been refuted by Shang Yen-liu and others. Wang did, however, support

---

27. Shang Yen-liu, T'ai-p'ing t'ien-kuo k'o-chü k'ao-shih chi-lueh, pp. 19–20.

28. Hsu K'o, Ch'ing-pai lei-ch'ao, 21.173–74. Shang Yen-liu, T'ai-p'ing t'ien-kuo k'o-chü k'ao-shih chi-lueh, pp. 53–54, gives an example of a model Taiping eight-legged essay for the 1859 metropolitan examination in their capital at Nanking based on a quotation about God, the Heavenly Father (t'ien-fu shang-ti 天父上帝).

29. Shang Yen-liu, T'ai-p'ing t'ien-kuo k'o-chü k'ao-shih chi-lueh, pp. 51–52, 58–59. See also Chung-kuo chin-tai chiao-yü-shih tzu-liao hui-pien, pp. 461–79; and Li Ch'un, T'ai-p'ing t'ien-kuo chih-tu ch'u-t'an, pp. 617–30.

the Taiping governor of Su-chou, and he later was protected from arrest by the British in Shanghai when Ch'ing authorities sought Wang as a traitor.[30]

In political reforms initiated by Hung Jen-kan 洪仁玕 (1822–64) beginning in 1859, the Taiping civil and military examinations were adjusted, despite changes in nomenclature, to correspond more closely to the Ch'ing models from which they were derived.[31] In an 1861 introduction to Taiping regulations concerning recruitment of literati, Hung Jen-kan and others established triennial provincial and metropolitan examinations, although they dropped the privilege that earlier *chü-jen* who failed the metropolitan examination had enjoyed since the Ming dynasty—namely, not having to repeat the provincial *hsiang-shih* tests before they could compete again for the *chin-shih* degree (see Chapter 3). Thus, as in Sung times, *chü-jen* under the Taipings would not have constituted their own status group.[32] Taiping examiners also had to be selected by special tests before being assigned.

In addition, Hung Jen-kan's new regulations stressed that morality and talent went hand in hand in the selection process. To this end, the Taipings now permitted portions of Confucius' *Analects* and the *Mencius* to be used to select suitable quotations for candidates to write essays about. Revised versions of the Four Books and Five Classics were prepared by Taiping authorities to complement earlier Christian texts. Although Hung Jen-kan had been critical of eight-legged essays, they remained the literary form for the reformed Taiping examinations until the Heavenly Kingdom was eradicated in 1864.[33] We can see in such efforts that the examination regime could and did serve the educational purposes of different dynasties and different ideologies over time, from belles lettres during the T'ang and Sung, *Tao-hsueh* in the Ming and Ch'ing, to Taiping Christianity in the 1860s.

30. Shang Yen-liu, *T'ai-p'ing t'ien-kuo k'o-chü k'ao-shih chi-lueh*, pp. 82–93, rejects the claim that Wang T'ao was a Taiping *optimus*. See also Hummel, ed., *Eminent Chinese of the Ch'ing Period*, pp. 836–37. The question and answer on "spirit" are cited in Hsu K'o, *Ch'ing-pai lei-ch'ao*, 21.174–75.

31. Li Ch'un, *T'ai-p'ing t'ien-kuo chih-tu ch'u-t'an*, pp. 641–48; and Vincent Shih, *The Taiping Ideology*, pp. 268–71.

32. Before the Ming, if a candidate failed the equivalent of the regional, middle-level examination, then he returned to his home area as a licentiate and was usually required to start over with the regional examination. See Wada, "Mindai kyojinzō no keisei katei ni kan suru ichi kōsatsu," pp. 36–71.

33. Chien Yu-wen, *T'ai-p'ing t'ien-kuo tien-chih t'ung-k'ao*, pp. 285–302. See also *Chung-kuo chin-tai chiao-yü-shih tzu-liao hui-pien*, pp. 448–61; and Li Ch'un, *T'ai-p'ing t'ien-kuo chih-tu ch'u-t'an*, p. 596.

## POST-TAIPING EXAMINATION REFORM

In the aftermath of the bloody defeat of the Taipings, a weakened Ch'ing dynasty and its literati-officials began to face up to the new educational requirements that the civil service would have to fulfill to survive in a world increasingly filled with menacing industrializing nations. Whereas the Opium War (1839–42) had not provoked any important calls for introduction of "Western learning" into the civil service curriculum, the situation after the fall of the Taipings was remarkably different. After 1865 Western schools and Japanese education policies served literati reformers as concrete models for delivering changes that would improve or replace the prestigious civil service examinations. In addition, earlier Sung, Ming, and Ch'ing critics of the civil service selection process had also presented viable reform proposals that the dynasty could take seriously (see Chapters 1, 4, and 10).

Both Feng Kuei-fen 馮桂芬 (1809–74), a Hanlin academician who later played a major role in the post-Taiping restoration movement between 1862 and 1874, and Hsueh Fu-ch'eng 薛福成 (1838–94), who was prevented by the Taiping wars from taking civil examinations, became administrative experts and advisors to many of the chief ministers of the late Ch'ing, including Tseng Kuo-fan 曾國藩 (1811–72) and Li Hung-chang 李鴻章 (1823–1901), the leaders of the post-Taiping turn toward foreign studies (*yang-wu yun-tung* 洋務運動). In their capacity as agents for change, both Feng and Hsueh used their private writings to attack the civil examinations from a new standpoint. The classical curriculum needed to adapt more to Western learning to be viable, they claimed. Western models became a legitimate object of concern and debate to reform the civil examinations. Li Hung-chang, for example, proposed establishing eight categories for civil examination (*pa-k'o ch'ü-shih* 八科取士) in 1867, in which "mathematical science" (*suan-shu ko-chih* 算數格致) and "technical science" (*chi-ch'i chih-tso* 機器制作) were included as a single category.[34]

To attain the goal of "wealth and power" (*fu-ch'iang* 富強), with which Ch'ing literati and officials became obsessed in the last decades of the dynasty, Feng Kuei-fen, for example, while living in the treaty port of Shanghai to avoid the Taipings, had prepared an essay around 1861 entitled "Kai k'o-chü i" 改科舉議 (Proposal for reforming the civil examinations) in which he attempted to balance the strengths of the selection

34. *Chung-kuo chin-tai chiao-yü-shih tzu-liao hui-pien*, pp. 431–34. See also "Yang-wu yun-tung ta-shih chi" 洋務運動大事記 (Record of important matters during the foreign studies movement), in Hsu T'ai-lai 徐泰來, ed., *Yang-wu yun-tung hsin-lun* 洋務運動新論 (Ch'angsha: Hu-nan People's Press, 1986), pp. 349–448; and Hummel, ed., *Eminent Chinese of the Ch'ing Period*, pp. 240–43, 331–33.

process to date with the needs of the future. Feng began by reviewing earlier proposals for reforming the civil examinations, which had frequently called for getting rid of the contemporary-style eight-legged examination essay because of its uselessness. Such efforts were partially misguided, Feng thought, because they didn't take into account why the eight-legged essay had been used for so long. The classical essay, as it had evolved since the time of Wang An-shih, was a test of the teachings of Confucius and Mencius that measured the intelligence (*ts'ung-ming* 聰明) and knowledge (*chih-ch'iao* 智巧) of candidates. The problem, as Feng saw it, was that the essay had become so much a part of literati life that it was too easy for candidates to prepare and too hard for examiners to discern which essays were superior. Hence, the examinations were failing to select men of talent. Poetry questions of the T'ang and Sung had met the same fate during the Yuan-Ming transition and therefore were later dropped.[35]

Building on earlier critiques by Ku Yen-wu, Feng Kuei-fen contended that the examinations had to become more difficult to be useful as a means of selection. Hence, what was now needed was a revamped civil examination that would test more challenging knowledge than poetry or prose writing. Feng proposed three new sessions for the provincial and metropolitan examinations: (1) explication of the Classics, (2) policy and discourse questions, and (3) ancient studies. At first sight, these recommendations seem recondite and traditional, but Feng was aware that he had to sell the changes to opponents who would be against any blatant effort to introduce Western learning into the examination curriculum. Instead, Feng altered the content of native traditional fields. What Feng meant by classical studies, for instance, included evidential research (*k'ao-chü* 考據) and philology (*hsiao-hsueh* 小學), already included in provincial and metropolitan policy questions. In addition, he added mathematics to the field of classical studies and quietly relegated the literary essay and poetry question to the last session.[36]

Feng also recommended changes for both local examinations and the palace examination that would turn them into three-session tests using the same format as the provincial and metropolitan examinations. In addition, he called for widening the selection process for officials to include recommendations and the promotion of clerks who demonstrated their adminis-

---

35. Feng, *Chiao-pin-lu k'ang-i* 校邠廬抗議 (Protests from the cottage of Feng Kuei-fen), 1897 edition (reprint, Taipei: Wen-hai Press), B.55a–56b.

36. Feng Kuei-fen, *Chiao-pin-lu k'ang-i*, B.56b–57a. Cheng Kuan-ying 鄭觀應 (1842–1923) also was an early advocate of including Western topics in the examination framework. See below and Borthwick, *Education and Social Change in China*, pp. 40–42. Unlike most of his contemporaries, Cheng early on advocated schools as the solution to China's problems.

trative abilities to their superiors. This proposal was presented as a return to Han precedents for broadening the paths to officialdom. One way to do this, according to Feng, was to divide the civil examination system in two, with the new group required to master machinery and physics (*chih-ch'i shang hsiang* 制器尚象). Finally, Feng called for abrogating the military examinations because the best way to select men of real talent was to have them all compete in a single examination process without the arbitrary distinction between civil and military paths. Based on such reforms, "our China [*Chung-hua* 中華] can begin to rise in the world." Otherwise, Feng presciently predicted, China would become a victim of native militarists hiding behind the slogan of "self-strengthening" (*tzu-ch'iang* 自強).[37]

These were remarkable proposals from a man who had been honored with an immediate appointment into the Hanlin Academy after distinguishing himself by finishing second on the 1840 palace examination. Moreover, he had served as an imperially selected examiner on several occasions. In other essays composed circa 1861, Feng also called for increased specialization of knowledge among officials and more attention to Western studies. These points were not explicitly part of his examination reforms, but Feng made clear that the world had changed so drastically that models from antiquity were no longer appropriate. And one of the strengths of Western learning, he noted, was its mastery of mathematics, which Feng wished to incorporate into the civil examinations. Geography and calendrical studies, the latter banned in dynastic schools and civil examinations since the K'ang-hsi reign (see Chapter 9), were also essential fields for literati, Feng contended. Not until 1887, however, were candidates specializing in mathematics allowed to pass the provincial examinations under a special quota, although they also had to fulfill the classical requirements.[38]

Even though Li Hung-chang and other key Ch'ing dynasty officials initially failed to convince the court to implement most of these proposed changes, the late Ch'ing literati world increasingly was shaped by such debates. Hsueh Fu-ch'eng's proposals for reform to Li Hung-chang and others appeared in 1864 and 1873 in a three-part essay entitled "Hsuan-chü lun" 選舉論 (On the selection and promotion of officials). In the first part, Hsueh addressed the classical essay requirement, which he contended had reduced the talents of millions of literati to literary pursuits.

37. Feng Kuei-fen, *Chiao-pin-lu k'ang-i*, B.57a–64a, 72b–74b.

38. Ibid., B.66a–70a; and Wolfgang Franke, *The Reform and Abolition of the Traditional Chinese Examination System*, p. 31. See also *Kuang-hsu cheng-yao* 光緒政要 (Important issues of governance in the Kuang-hsu reign), compiled by Shen T'ung-sheng 沈桐生 (Shanghai: Ch'ung-i-t'ang, 1909), vol. 10, 13.18a–20a.

Ignorant of classical models, lacking historical perspective, and fixated on distinguishing the subtle words of nature and principles (i.e., Ch'eng-Chu "Tao Learning"), contemporary literati had abdicated their statecraft responsibilities. It was just as Ku Yen-wu had earlier claimed: "When the eight-legged essay became popular, then the Six Classics declined; when the eighteen civil examination wards appeared, then the Twenty-one Histories were discarded." Examination essays were originally intended to exhibit practical learning, Hsueh added, but now they were "outside the domain of practical studies." The solution according the Hsueh was to change the examinations. After five hundred years of classical essays, it was time to turn back to practical studies for testing.[39]

Again building on Ku Yen-wu's early Ch'ing observations, Hsueh argued in part two of his essay that the bureaucracy spent too much time and effort trying to prevent corruption and cheating in the examination compounds. Because of the many rules and regulations and efforts to enforce them, examiners had forgotten the core reason for the examinations: to select men of talent. Instead, they had become a device to monitor fraud. Of the one in ten who made it through the monitoring mechanisms, which included the examinations, only one in ten were men of virtue or practical learning. Consequently, even when the monitoring mechanisms were successful, the dynasty got only one man of talent out of a hundred.

Hsueh proposed that the examination route should be reduced and the selection process broadened to include other avenues for entry into officialdom. If Han dynasty recommendation procedures were again put in place, he maintained, then the government could expect that four or five of every ten candidates would be men of talent. In addition, Hsueh suggested that regular and special examinations be instituted. Regular examinations would stress policy and discourse questions. For the latter, questions would come from the Four Books and Five Classics. Policy answers would require knowledge of ancient and contemporary matters. Special examinations every few years would be administered by the emperor, who would himself test and select outstanding men whom local officials had highly recommended. These would be modeled on earlier po-hsueh hung-tz'u 博學鴻詞 tests of the K'ang-hsi and Ch'ien-lung eras, which went back to Sung times (see Chapter 1).[40]

In the third part of his essay, Hsueh again attacked the sterility of the examination essay. In addition to its formalistic content, Hsueh pointed

39. See *Hsueh Fu-ch'eng hsuan-chi* 薛福成選集 (Selected writings of Hsueh Fu-ch'eng) (Shanghai: People's Press, 1987), pp. 1–2.

40. See ibid., pp. 3–5.

out, since the mid-Ch'ien-lung era, small-style regular script calligraphy (*hsiao-k'ai* 小楷) had become the rage among examination candidates, which made the essay an even more dubious mechanism for selecting talented men with practical training. According to Hsueh, Chao K'uang of the T'ang dynasty had been right all along about literary tests: candidates "study things they will never use and later use what they have never studied." Hanlin academicians, for example, depended on their talents in the latest styles of calligraphy for promotions. All their adult careers they were like children standing before a strict master. Then they were sent out as examiners to act as masters themselves. Hsueh wryly added, however, that the mid-century wars had brought forward a generation of military heroes who tried to correct civilian problems. What was now needed was to get rid of calligraphy tests for Hanlin academicians and to replace classical essays with policy and discourse questions on regular civil examinations.[41]

Further reform ideas were published for general literati consideration in the early 1880s by the comprador-scholar Cheng Kuan-ying 鄭觀應 (1842–1923) and the Cantonese literatus Ch'en Li 陳澧 (1810–82). During his teaching career at the Hsueh-hai T'ang 學海堂 (Sea of learning) Academy in Canton, Ch'en Li had influenced a generation of local students, as well as later scholars such as Liang Ch'i-ch'ao 梁啓超 (1873–1929) and K'ang Yu-wei 康有為 (1858–1927). Cheng Kuan-ying proposed in 1884 that the government finance academies in every province to teach Western studies and that such studies should form a separate part of the civil examination curriculum. In favor of specialization, Cheng was the first reformer to advocate a plan for revamping the existing private and dynastic schools into a system of primary and secondary schools.[42]

Ch'en Li's essay "K'o-ch'ang i" 科場議 (On the civil examinations) was a tour de force, addressing the precise limitations in the examinations and suggesting numerous concrete reforms. First Ch'en pointed out two limitations in the eight-legged essay. Because it was based on the premise that candidates "take the place of the sages and worthies" (*tai sheng-hsien li-yen*) in enunciating moral truths, the essay could not include any reference to post-Han works, which made the essay out-of-date. Next, Ch'en explained that the eight-legged format of the essay was a formalistic exercise that imprisoned the minds and hearts of candidates. Accordingly, Ch'en argued that the essay should be changed into a discussion of classical and historical topics.[43]

41. See ibid., pp. 3–5.

42. Paul J. Bailey, *Reform the People: Changing Attitudes towards Popular Education in Early Twentieth Century China* (Edinburgh: Edinburgh University Press, 1990), p. 21.

43. *Chung-kuo chin-tai chiao-yü-shih tzu-liao hui-pien*, p. 96. See also Hummel, ed., *Eminent Chinese of the Ch'ing Period*, pp. 90–92.

In part two of the essay, Ch'en Li adumbrated a revised order and content for the traditional three sessions of the tests. He brought up five changes that he thought would correct current problems. Perhaps borrowing from Feng Kuei-fen, Ch'en Li wished that candidates be required first to present "explications of the Classics" in place of eight-legged essays. Second, the earlier requirement that students specialize on a single Classic (dropped in 1787) should be revived because, Ch'en contended, realistically no one could master all of the Five Classics. Third, the policy questions should be changed into history questions that would be based on an imperially approved continuation and digest of Ssu-ma Kuang's *Comprehensive Mirror of History* and Chu Hsi's condensed version, known as the *Tung-chien kang-mu* (see Chapter 9). Fourth, the poetry question should be changed to a question on rhyme-prose (*fu* 賦). Finally, Ch'en advocated changing the order of the sessions. The Classics should be given priority and placed on session one. Questions on the Four Books would be moved down to session two. Session three would test history questions and rhyme-prose.[44]

Part three of Ch'en Li's essay took up Ou-yang Hsiu's Sung dynasty proposal that candidates should be first tested on policy questions. Those that passed this first step would then move on to the literary questions, on which their final ranks would be based. In this way, Ou-yang had thought, both practical learning and literary talent could be given special attention. In addition, this procedure would permit examiners to eliminate candidates along the way, instead of having to read all the papers produced by thousands of candidates on all three sessions. Ch'en thought this an ideal proposal, which would make the provincial and metropolitan examinations similar in format to the current county, township, and prefectural tests, where candidates were eliminated after every question. Examiners would be able to read all papers if this change were made, as opposed to giving attention currently only to the first session's eight-legged essays.[45]

Despite the increasing appeal of civil examination reform for literati after the Taiping Rebellion, which drew in part on Northern Sung and early Ch'ing reform ideas, the Ministry of Rites did not act on any concrete curricular proposals. The priority of the Hanlin Academy during the T'ung-chih reign was to restore the scope and magnitude of civil examinations to their pre-Taiping levels, a policy that was generally successful in increasing the total number of local licentiates and academies. Prefaces and afterwords to examination reports prepared by the chief examiners

44. *Chung-kuo chin-tai chiao-yü-shih tzu-liao hui-pien*, pp. 97–98.
45. Ibid., pp. 98–99.

generally spelled out a commitment to maintaining the civil examination status quo.[46] As Chapter 4 indicates (see Tables 4.8 and 4.9), the total number of degreed literati after the Taiping Rebellion was almost 1.5 million, an increase of 36% over pre-Taiping estimates, although the general population had increased by about 50%.

Table 11.1 shows the magnitude of this increase in total degreed gentry at all levels of the examination regime. In particular, it should be stressed that the total number of gentry with regular degrees had increased from 750,000 to 920,000, an increase of almost 23%. The total number of upper- and lower-degree graduates represented a sizable pool of local literati who would be directly affected by any changes in the curriculum or the process of selection. Moreover, the much larger pool of candidates for the biennial qualifying examinations, which probably reached 3 million after 1850 (assuming 2,000 candidates per county and 1,500 counties on the *t'ung-shih*), when added to the 1.5 million local, provincial, and palace graduates, means that over 4 million men were part of the huge constituency that the imperial examination regime mobilized.

The price of holding fast to the status quo, however, was to miss an important opportunity to influence the civil examination pool as a whole and to follow up on the reformist policies of the Ch'ien-lung reign, after fifty years of little change during the Chia-ch'ing and Tao-kuang eras. Not until the ill-fated 1898 reformers brought forward many of the ideas already proposed and in one fell swoop tried to shove them down the throats of the stubborn bureaucracy did the court finally respond to literati pressure for change. Many literati inside and outside the bureaucracy still felt after 1865 that what was now called "Chinese learning" (*Chung-hsueh* 中學), to distinguish native learning from Western studies (*hsi-hsueh* 西學), should remain dominant in the examination curriculum. Others continued to praise the examination system for having produced so many outstanding officials over the centuries. Substantial reform, they argued, was not needed. And the dynasty was still convinced that the tight quotas and strict curriculum of the examinations were important tools to maintain local political, social, and cultural control.[47]

---

46. See Mary Wright, *The Last Stand of Chinese Conservatism*, pp. 79–84, 127–33; and Barry Keenan, *Imperial China's Last Classical Academies: Social Change in the Lower Yangzi, 1864–1911* (Berkeley: Institute of East Asian Studies, University of California, Berkeley, 1994), pp. 9–28. See also note 47.

47. See the chief examiners' "Preface" and "Afterword" to the *Ssu-ch'uan wen hsiang-shih lu*, 1893: 4a–4b and 69a, which defend the integrity of the civil examinations. See also *Chung-kuo chin-tai chiao-yü-shih tzu-liao hui-pien*, pp. 435–45; and Wolfgang Franke, *The Reform and Abolition of the Traditional Chinese Examination System*, p. 32.

## FROM 1895 TO THE 1898 REFORM PROPOSALS

By 1895 the Ch'ing dynasty had lost the Sino-Japanese War, and literati increasingly felt they faced a bleak political future. Reforms initiated in the post-Taiping decades seemed to have failed to stem the tide of Ch'ing decline. Indeed, many now thought that earlier efforts to achieve "wealth and power" through "self-strengthening" had failed because the educational system, which had not been properly addressed since 1865, was deficient. One of the four chief examiners for the 1890 metropolitan examination, on which the future chancellor of Peking University and Shao-hsing literatus Ts'ai Yuan-p'ei 蔡元培 (1868–1940) finished eighty-first, referred to Ku Yen-wu's attack on the eight-legged essay but defended its use. Clearly, however, the genre was under attack.[48] In a 1934 reminiscence of his early education, Ts'ai Yuan-p'ei wrote, for example, that the eight-legged essay of his time had already been curtailed to "six legs" (liu-ku 六股), and he poked fun at it as an out-of-date form of writing that at age seventeen he quickly discarded in favor of evidential research and literary works.[49]

Yen Fu 嚴復 (1853–1921), whose poor prospects in the civil examination system caused him to enter the School of Navigation of the Fu-chou Shipyard in 1866, expressed long pent-up bitterness toward the civil examinations and the eight-legged essay when he became a publicist and prepared articles for the reformist press that emerged after 1895. Since 1885, Yen had failed the provincial examinations four times.[50] Many like Yen Fu began in the 1890s to link the weakness of Ch'ing China to the infamous eight-legged examination essay, which allegedly had wasted the minds of generations. Moreover, Yen and the reformist voices associated the power of the West with modern schools where students were trained in modern subjects requiring practical training. Where earlier reformers had suggested getting rid of civil examinations and replacing them with Han dynasty–style recommendation procedures, late Ch'ing reformers began to offer schools instead of examinations as the panacea for China's ills.[51]

48. *Hui-shih lu,* 1890: "Hou-hsu" 後序, pp. 86a–b.

49. See *Ts'ai Yuan-p'ei hsuan-chi* 蔡元培選集 (Selected works of Ts'ai Yuan-p'ei) (Taipei: Wen-hsing Bookstore, 1967), pp. 462–63.

50. See Yen's "Chiu-wang chueh-lun" 救亡決論 (On what determines rescue or perishing), in *Wu-hsu pien-fa tsu-liao* 戊戌變法資料 (Sources on the 1898 reform movement) (Peking: Shen-chou kuo-kuang she, 1953), 3/60–71. See also Benjamin Schwartz, *In Search of Wealth and Power: Yen Fu and the West* (New York: Harper Torchbooks, 1969), pp. 22–41.

51. Bastid, *Educational Reform in Early 20th-Century China,* pp. 12–13; and Borthwick, *Education and Social Change in China,* pp. 38–64. See also Y. C. Wang, *Chinese Intellectuals and the West, 1872–1949* (Chapel Hill: University of North Carolina Press, 1966), pp. 52–59.

For Yen Fu and the reformers, Western schools and Westernized
Japanese education were examples that the Ch'ing dynasty must emulate.
The extension of mass schooling within a standardized classroom system
and homogeneous or equalized groupings of students seemed to promise a
way out of the quagmire of the imperial examination regime, whose educational efficiency was now, in the 1890s, suspect. Uncritical presentations
of Western schools and Japanese education as success stories were widely
accepted.[52] Interestingly, such calls for Western-style schools usually failed
to address the classical versus vernacular language problem in any con-
templated program for education and examination reform (see below).[53]
The twin problems of the alleged unsuitability of a classically trained elite
for modern government and the lack of a system for mass education were
analytically distinct. As we shall see, however, competition between financial costs for maintaining an empirewide network of examinations and
funds for new schools became keen.

Those involved with the 1898 Reform Movement (戊戌變法) contended that political reform required fundamental educational change, and
educational change was possible only if the civil examinations were
reformed. When reforms that had been called for since the late Ming
were finally promulgated in the late nineteenth and early twentieth centuries, however, they were both too early, for there was nothing comparable to replace the civil examinations with, and too late, because the
changes could not keep pace with the demands of the times. It took six
years of debate and controversy before the civil examinations were unceremoniously dropped in 1904–5 by the very men who had short-circuited
the reforms of 1898. In another seven years the dynasty itself collapsed.

But the story of the demise of civil examinations and the rise of modern schools in China is more complicated than just the demise of imperial
examinations and the rise of modern education, which subordinated
examinations to schooling. A social, political, and cultural nexus of classical literati values, dynastic imperial power, and elite gentry status was
unraveling before everyone's eyes.[54] Remarkably, the Ch'ing bureaucracy
unwittingly was made party to its own delegitimation. By first decanoniz-
ing the content of civil examinations, a process that began in the eigh-

52. Paula Harrell, *Sowing the Seeds of Change: Chinese Students, Japanese Teachers, 1895–1905*
(Stanford: Stanford University Press, 1992), pp. 11–60.

53. Bailey, *Reform the People*, pp. 73–75, discusses the use of the vernacular in education
from 1899 to 1909.

54. For the concept of "cultural nexus," see Duara, *Culture, Power, and the State*, pp. 5–6,
38–41, 247–48. Curiously, on pp. 38–39 Duara rejects consideration of the examination
regime as part of the cultural nexus that linked Chinese society organizationally to the government.

teenth century with the Han Learning attack on Ch'eng-Chu Tao Learning, late-nineteenth-century literati hoped to free themselves from the imperatives of the sterile "examination life" that their predecessors had strained against but remained ensnared in. From the dynasty's point of view, however, if civil examinations survived even in a decanonized form, they would still be an avenue for candidates—and there were still millions of them—to march obediently into the examination compounds to the drums of the dynasty.[55]

During the chaos of the Boxer Rebellion of 1900 in Peking, the Ch'ing dynasty court under the Empress Dowager forgot the lessons that earlier emperors had understood very well. The delegitimation of the civil examinations, once complete, eventually had consequences that went beyond what the court and many literati expected.[56] The race to establish new institutions was a consequence of the occupation of the capital by Western and Japanese troops in 1900. The Boxer popular rebellion and the response of the Western powers and Japan to it had unbalanced the power structure in the capital so much that foreigners were able to put considerable pressure on provincial and national leaders. Foreign support of reform thus strengthened the political fortunes of provincial reformers such as Yuan Shih-k'ai 袁世凱 (1859–1916) and Chang Chih-tung 張之洞 (1837–1909), who opposed the Boxers. The Empress Dowager became dependent on Yuan, for example, because of his expertise in dealing with the foreign powers after the Boxer debacle.[57]

After the civil examinations were abrogated, the Manchus quickly lost one of their most loyal, if recalcitrant, constituencies, the examination candidates. The political consequences of this loss were to be expected

55. Cf. Chuzo Ichiko, "The Role of the Gentry: An Hypothesis," in Mary Wright, ed., *China in Revolution: The First Phase, 1900–13* (New Haven: Yale University Press, 1968), p. 299; Ernest P. Young, *The Presidency of Yuan Shih-k'ai: Liberalism and Dictatorship in Early Republican China* (Ann Arbor: University of Michigan Press, 1977), pp. 7–8; and Helen R. Chauncey, *Schoolhouse Politicians: Locality and State during the Chinese Republic* (Honolulu: University of Hawaii Press, 1992), pp. 10–11.

56. See *Ta-Ch'ing Te-tsung shih-lu* 大清德宗實錄 (Veritable records of the Te-tsung reign during the great Ch'ing) (reprint, Taipei: Hua-wen Bookstore, 1964), 476.4378–79 (vol. 79). See also Bailey, *Reform the People*, pp. 26–27, who stresses the Boxer Rebellion as the "turning point in the court's attitude towards reform."

57. See Stephen R. MacKinnon, *Power and Politics in Late Imperial China: Yuan Shi-kai in Beijing and Tianjin, 1901–1908* (Berkeley: University of California Press, 1980), pp. 3–4, 216–17. On the impact on the urban elite in Hu-nan and Hu-pei, see Joseph W. Esherick, *Reform and Revolution in China: The 1911 Revolution in Hunan and Hubei* (Berkeley: University of California Press, 1976), pp. 40–52. For Che-chiang province, see Mary B. Rankin, *Elite Activism and Political Transformation in China: Zhejiang Province, 1865–1911* (Stanford: Stanford University Press, 1986), pp. 172–88.

when the Ch'ing bureaucracy meekly gave up one of its major weapons of cultural control, which had for centuries successfully induced literati acceptance of the imperial system. Some have already noted that the post-Boxer reforms were so radical that they helped precipitate the downfall of the dynasty.[58] What should be added, however, is that the radical reforms in favor of new schools initially failed because they could not readily replace public institutions for mobilizing millions of literati in examination compounds that had existed since the early Ming.

The march toward this suicidal cataclysm (from the standpoint of the Ch'ing dynasty) began in earnest during the spring 1895 metropolitan examinations, the first after the Sino-Japanese War. K'ang Yu-wei, then a candidate for the *chin-shih* degree, was in Peking in the spring of 1895. He and some of his Kuang-tung followers tried to use the gathering of candidates for the metropolitan examination to influence the court to adopt a more activist response toward the postwar crisis. K'ang participated in candidate demonstrations and passed around petitions concerning political policy.[59] K'ang finished fifth on the metropolitan examination, and for the palace examination policy question, on which he finished fifty-first overall, K'ang offered the Kuang-hsu emperor (r. 1875–1908) a vision of reform in which he made modifications of the civil examinations a high priority. All his examination reform proposals, however, built on ideas presented by earlier literati, which the court had not heeded since the late eighteenth century.[60]

Employing the post-Taiping rhetoric of "self-strengthening," K'ang appealed in his policy answer for the emperor to adopt a more practical and specialized curriculum for selecting officials through examinations and

58. Cf. MacKinnon, *Power and Politics in Late Imperial China*, p. 4. See also Joseph Esherick's *The Origins of the Boxer Uprising* (Berkeley: University of California Press, 1987), pp. 271–313, which notes that the rebellion "thoroughly discredited the conservative policies which had reversed the 1898 reforms."

59. See K'ang Yu-wei, "Chronological Autobiography," in Jung-pao Lo, ed. and trans., *K'ang Yu-wei: A Biography and a Symposium* (Tucson: University of Arizona Press, 1967), pp. 63–65. Wolfgang Franke, *The Reform and Abolition of the Traditional Chinese Examination System*, pp. 32–33. Franke assumed K'ang's early memorials were authentic but many were not. See Tang Zhijun and Elman, "The 1898 Reform Movement Revisited," *Late Imperial China* 8, 1 (June 1987): 205–213.

60. See *Hui-shih t'ung-nien ch'ih-lu*, 1895: 1a–3a. See also *K'ang Yu-wei cheng-lun chi* 康有為政論集 (Collection of K'ang Yu-wei's political writings), compiled by T'ang Chih-chün 湯志鈞 (Peking: Chung-hua Bookstore, 1981), pp. 106–09. Cf. Luke S. K. Kwong's *A Mosaic of the Hundred Days: Personalities, Politics, and Ideas of 1898* (Cambridge: Harvard University Press, 1984), pp. 90–93. Kwong claims K'ang finished 49th on the palace examination. K'ang himself claimed he had initially been ranked first on the metropolitan and palace examinations but had been victimized by his political enemies. See K'ang Yu-wei, "Chronological Autobiography," p. 66.

thereby avoiding Chao K'uang's by-now-haunting refrain that literati "study things they will never use and later use what they have never studied." K'ang's model was the classical fields of examinations that Ssu-ma Kuang had advocated in the Northern Sung (see Chapter 1). In addition, K'ang asked that the ineffectual military examinations be stopped. Here he was basically taking the same position that Feng Kuei-fen had enunciated more than three decades earlier. An examination essay is an unlikely place to expect more than platitudes, but K'ang's program for changing the civil examinations was little more than evocations of the past, rather than a new educational vision for the future.[61]

In 1896 K'ang's disciple Liang Ch'i-ch'ao prepared a sober but not particularly radical assessment of the civil examination system entitled "Lun k'o-chü" 論科舉 (On civil examinations), which was intended for a literati audience. Couched in a detailed historical account of the strengths and failures of the examinations, Liang's evaluation made it clear that even if the system now needed changing, it had played an important role in earlier dynasties by providing talented officials. As long as schools and the selection process were unified, the examination process was balanced by attention to learning. After the failure of Wang An-shih's school reforms in the Northern Sung, Liang argued, examinations took precedence in the civil service and schools precipitously declined, taking down with them literati learning. Thereafter, preparing for the examinations was all that mattered for most literati.[62]

Liang pointed out the deleterious influence of the civil examinations on learning. Most candidates would master whatever curriculum was set on the examinations, whether the six fields of examinations during the T'ang, the multiple examinations of the Sung, or the classical essay of the Ming and Ch'ing. Hence, curricular reform was mandatory to change the learning habits of literati who sought public office. To this end Liang recommended three changes. First and foremost, the dynasty should combine the civil examinations with schools using both ancient Chinese and modern Western models as guides. Next, the multiple examination procedures

---

61. See *K'ang Yu-wei cheng-lun chi*, p. 107. Given the authenticity problems in K'ang's memorials, it is going a bit too far to claim that in 1895 K'ang articulated "a true vision of modern education which would subordinate examinations to schools." See Bastid, *Educational Reform in Early 20th-Century China*, p. 12. See also Wolfgang Franke, *The Reform and Abolition of the Traditional Chinese Examination System*, pp. 37–40, for discussion of Li Tuan-fen's 李端棻 (1863–1907) 1896 memorial explicitly linking examination reform to establishment of schools. Cf. Harrell, *Sowing the Seeds of Change*, pp. 23–29.

62. Liang Ch'i-ch'ao, *Yin-ping-shih wen-chi* 飲冰室文集 (Collected writings from the Ice-Drinker's Studio) (Taipei: Chung-hua Bookstore, 1970), 1.21–23. Cf. Wolfgang Franke, *The Reform and Abolition of the Traditional Chinese Examination System*, p. 40.

of the Han and T'ang dynasties should be reestablished to encourage classical, philological, mathematical, and legal studies. Third, the three sessions of the civil examinations should be revamped and equal attention paid to all sessions, particularly those devoted to new learning. Session one would remain devoted to the Four Books and Five Classics, but session two would include questions on Chinese and foreign history, while session three would test astronomy, geography, and other natural sciences.[63]

Liang deemed the school program the key to his proposals. The other two options were presented because he expected that the more radical schooling initiative would be difficult to carry out. In another 1906 essay, "Hsueh-hsiao tsung-lun" 學校總論 (General remarks on schools), he linked the decline of imperial China to the decline of schools. To revive schools and thereby revive China, examinations must be reformed, teaching schools must be established, and specialized learning should be promoted. By 1896 Liang and others had taken the important step of calling for the "subordination of civil examinations to schools." Vice Minister of Punishments Li Tuan-fen 李端棻, in his 1896 memorial, made the telling point that if civil examinations remained unchanged, then the new schools would never take root.[64]

Schools and examination reform continued to be debated until 1898 when the reformers who gathered around the Kuang-hsu emperor during the "Hundred Days of Reform" tackled the problems of the examination system, although only on paper. One of the more moderate voices for reform was that of Chang Chih-tung, whose influential *Ch'üan-hsueh p'ien* 勸學篇 (A plea for learning) was presented to the throne in mid-1898. It included an extensive critique of civil examinations, on which Chang had excelled as a young prodigy (see Chapter 5) and which he had supervised throughout his distinguished career as a provincial education commissioner, head of many academies, governor-general, and court official. It was through his intervention that many reformers were in the court in 1898, even though he was among the few who survived the fall coup d'état.

Chang took many of his ideas from earlier criticisms of the examination system, most notably Ou-yang Hsiu's stress on policy questions rather than classical essays as the key to testing the practical abilities of candidates. Based on Ou-yang Hsiu's proposals, Chang advocated, as had Ch'en Li earlier in the nineteenth century, that candidates be eliminated

---

63. Liang Ch'i-ch'ao, *Yin-ping-shih wen-chi*, 1.24–29.

64. Ibid., pp. 1.14–21, 1.27–28. See also Wolfgang Franke, *The Reform and Abolition of the Traditional Chinese Examination System*, p. 38; and Bastid, *Educational Reform in Early 20th-Century China*, p. 12.

at each stage of the three official sessions. Chang went further, however, by adding that policy questions should test Chinese and Western subjects, particularly those dealing with institutions and political affairs. In addition, Chang favored establishing schools, but he did not envision them as replacing or encompassing the civil examination system. Rather, he wanted examinations and schools to balance each other, while maintaining the degree system as it was.[65]

In many of the 1898 proposals prepared by K'ang Yu-wei for his superiors, K'ang, like Chang Chih-tung, reviewed the criticisms of the eight-legged essays made by earlier Ming and Ch'ing literati. The proposals made it clear that earlier scholars such as Ch'en Li had influenced K'ang's recommendations. For example, abolishing the eight-legged essay requirement became one of the major themes of the 1898 "paper" reforms. In June 1898 K'ang averred that if the ruler favored practical learning and real talent, then the starting point was to correct the essay style required of literati. Over and over again, K'ang and his cohorts bemoaned the pernicious influence the contemporary-style essay had on tens of millions of young students. Initially, however, the change called for in civil examinations was in style rather than content. K'ang in effect thought that Yuan and early Ming examinations were the example for the present, since they had preceded the eight-legged essay requirement of the late empire. The Four Books, however, should remain the heart of the selection process, K'ang added.[66]

K'ang and the reformers seem to have genuinely believed that change in the form of the examinations when tied to the establishment of schools would do the trick, that is, turn the dynasty down the road of "wealth and power." Also, in June 1898, K'ang offered another reform that had been frequently voiced since the late Ming, namely, to replace the eight-legged essay with policy questions. For instance, K'ang appealed to the short-lived abrogation of the eight-legged essay in 1663, a policy that he cleverly, but wrongly, attributed to the sagacity of the K'ang-hsi emperor, as a precedent for the 1898 reforms (see Chapter 10). But K'ang used the policy question as a wedge to introduce aspects of Western learning, such as mathematics, geography, astronomy, and electricity, into the content of the examinations, not knowing or not bothering to mention that astronomy had been eliminated from the examinations by the K'ang-hsi emperor. For this change, which Feng Kuei-fen had also advocated, K'ang

65. See Wolfgang Franke, *The Reform and Abolition of the Traditional Chinese Examination System*, pp. 41–43; and Harrell, *Sowing the Seeds of Change*, pp. 26–28. See also Ayers, *Chang Chih-tung and Educational Reform in China*, pp. 44–50; and Hummel, ed., *Eminent Chinese of the Ch'ing Period*, p. 30.

66. *K'ang Yu-wei cheng-lun chi*, pp. 247–49, 285–87.

appealed to the Kuang-hsu emperor's earlier edict that declared that the teachings of the sages would be the core of the dynasty but Western studies of practical use would also be promoted. The policy essay (and its new content) should be used, K'ang requested, in all local, provincial, and metropolitan examinations.[67]

The reason for the continued stress on civil examination reform by both K'ang Yu-wei and Liang Ch'i-ch'ao was made clear in another of K'ang's proposals. Even if establishment of new schools was the ideal solution, there were not yet enough of them to make any significant contribution to educational reform or the production of a new elite. Hence, K'ang argued that with millions of candidates still studying for the examinations it was impossible to abrogate them. All that could be done was to change their form and content so that they would accord with practical learning and the current needs of the dynasty. For K'ang and Liang, then, it was essential that policy questions immediately replace the eight-legged essay.

With one million licentiates from 1,500 counties (using the county quota method for estimating the total number of licentiates, K'ang's figures doubled Ku Yen-wu's early Ch'ing estimate)[68] repeatedly taking the examinations, the waste in talent over the last thirty years had been enormous. The dynastic passion for useless eight-legged essays disgusted K'ang. They had to go if the dynasty was to have any chance to turn itself around. Once new schools were established, the examination system itself could be abrogated. Although he recognized the civil examinations' role as vestiges in the present, K'ang Yu-wei underestimated the degree to which their social, political, and cultural uses would also be lost if they were abolished. Things would automatically fall into place, he naively believed, once schools were established.[69]

In addition to changes in the civil examinations, K'ang called on the court to stop the military examinations immediately and establish military schools instead. Again, this proposal was tied to the reformers' views on the evils of the traditional examination system, a perspective that was probably strengthened by the dubious discovery that Western nations had never developed a national examination system. Little did K'ang realize how quickly national examinations would be set up in Western Europe based on Chinese models.[70] Again, schools were the panacea for everything.

Reformers like K'ang were not trying to replace civil and military examinations with schools, however, because they thought schools would be havens for dissent and pluralism. They wanted schools to serve as new

67. Ibid., pp. 264–65, 315–16. See pp. 305–10 for his views on schools.
68. Ku Yen-wu, *Jih-chih lu chi-shih*, 16.392–96.
69. *K'ang Yu-wei cheng-lun chi*, pp. 268–71.
70. See Teng Ssu-yü, "China's Examination System and the West," pp. 441–51.

mechanisms for social, political, and cultural reproduction and control in Chinese society. Examinations had failed the dynasty. Schools, they maintained, could do everything the civil examinations had done and more. These were untested assumptions that had dimly perceived implications.[71]

In June 1898 K'ang also called on the court to "honor the sage Confucius by creating an official religion, to establish a Ministry of Religion (Chiao-pu 教部) and a Religion Association (Chiao-hui 教會) to commemorate Confucius, and to extinguish all heterodox religions." Such proposals for the invention of "Confucianism" (Kung-chiao 孔教) were based on Confucius' New Text classical writings, although the Jesuits had already invented "Confucianism" in sixteenth- and seventeenth-century European discourse.[72] The self-serving rhetoric was directed toward enhancing imperial power by invoking the New Text strand of Han Learning orthodoxy. What K'ang wanted was a national unification modeled in part on the 1867 Meiji Restoration in Japan that would quickly transform the Ch'ing dynasty into a "modern" nation-state. Even before the establishment of a Ministry of Education (Hsueh-pu 學部), which was to take place in 1905 after the abrogation of the civil examinations,[73] K'ang saw orthodoxy based on a new religion of New Text "Confucianism" as the only way to focus education in the right direction. In the same vein, K'ang betrayed his xenophobia toward native popular religion by asking the court to "change all provincial academies and evil shrines into new schools" stressing both Chinese and Western learning.[74] Chang Chih-tung had made similar proposals about Buddhist and Taoist temples. Neither K'ang nor Chang comprehended the degree to which the Ch'ing dynasty had already patronized the religious cults abounding in Ch'ing China and the degree to which such religious policies had further strengthened the legitimation of the dynasty in local communities.[75] By betraying the religious beliefs of commoners, the dynasty paid a heavy price for its appeasement of literati reformers. Again, elite anti-religious

71. K'ang Yu-wei cheng-lun chi, pp. 272–74.

72. See Lionel Jensen, "The Invention of 'Confucius' and His Chinese Other, 'Kong Fuzi'," positions: east asia cultures critique 1, 2 (fall 1993): 414–49.

73. See Borthwick, Education and Social Change in China, p. 73.

74. Perhaps the "xenophobia" on K'ang's part was a calculated position. He had dabbled in attaining Buddhist enlightenment and had retreated into seclusion for a time before his rise to fame in Peking in the late 1890s.

75. K'ang Yu-wei cheng-lun chi, pp. 279–83, 311–13. On Chang, see Wolfgang Franke, The Reform and Abolition of the Traditional Chinese Examination System, p. 43. Huang Tsung-hsi had made such proposals in the early Ch'ing (see Chapter 4). On K'ang's New Text writings and efforts to invent Confucianism as a religion, see Hsiao Kung-chuan, A Modern China and a New World: K'ang Yu-wei, Reformer and Utopian, 1858–1927 (Seattle: University of Washington Press, 1975), pp. 41–136. On the dynasty's role in local religion during the Ming and Ch'ing, see Chapter 6; and Duara, "Subscribing Symbols," pp. 778–95.

elements homologous with subsequent May Fourth era iconoclasm were evident.

K'ang Yu-wei's efforts to reinvent "Confucianism" in 1898 represented a form of "symbolic compensation" paid to classical literati thought (*ju-hsueh* 儒學) by unilaterally declaring its eternal moral superiority as a reward for its historical failure. Such "modern" forms of cultural compensation also remind us of the high moral value placed on Sung Tao Learning after the fall of the Southern Sung to the Mongols, which began the apotheosis of the idealized "Sung dynasty" among surviving Han Chinese literati during the Sung-Yuan-Ming transition (see Chapter 1). K'ang Yu-wei's invention of "Confucianism" was completed in the twentieth century despite the decline of classical learning in public schools after 1905. In China and the West, "Confucianism" became instead a venue for academic scholarship, when the "modern Chinese intellectual" irrevocably replaced the late Ch'ing literatus in the early Republic.[76]

## FROM THE 1901 REFORMS TO THE 1905 ABROGATION

The 1898 Reforms were never carried out, and the coup d'état that restored the Empress Dowager Tz'u-hsi to power sent many reformers into exile. From 1898 until 1900 civil examinations in counties, townships, prefectures, provinces, and the capital went on as they always had. In fact, not even the spring 1898 metropolitan examination had been affected by the reformers.[77] Wang Hsien-ch'ien 王先謙 (1842–1918), an erstwhile supporter of the education reforms advocated by the 1898 reformers, tried in vain to salvage them by first repudiating in his private writings the Kang Yu-wei "clique," which had fled to Japan, and then tying the reforms to earlier 1664 and 1740s Ch'ing efforts at examination reform. In an 1899 follow-up essay on the civil examinations, Wang also appealed to 1875 calls for examination reform—that is, getting rid of eight-legged essays, which he had opposed when he was a provincial examiner in the 1870s. Rather than stressing them as the sudden brainstorm of political radicals such as K'ang Yu-wei, Wang Hsien-ch'ien tried to present the 1898 proposals in light of the long-standing interest in civil service reform exemplified by the court during the K'ang-hsi and Ch'ien-lung reigns.[78]

76. Charlton M. Lewis, *Prologue to the Chinese Revolution: The Transformation of Ideas and Institutions in Hunan Province, 1891–1907* (Cambridge: Harvard East Asian Research Center, 1976), pp. 152–53.

77. See the *Kuang-hsu wu-hsu k'o hui-shih ti-chiu-fang chu-chüan* 光緒戊戌科會試第九房硃卷 (Examination papers from the ninth ward of the 1898 metropolitan examination) (unpaginated 1898 manuscripts).

78. See Wang's *Hsu-shou-t'ang wen-chi* 虛受堂文集 (Collected writings from Wang Hsien-ch'ien's studio) (Taipei: Wen-hua Press, 1966), 1.1a–6a, 2.4a–8b.

Only after the dislocation in all aspects of governance in north China, including the 1900–1901 civil examinations, produced by the Boxer Rebellion and the foreign occupation of Peking, did the issue of education reform again come up in court.[79] In January 1901, while in refuge in Hsian (Sian), the court sent out an urgent plea asking all high officials to submit proposals for reform.[80] Then serving as Hu-kuang governor-general, Chang Chih-tung took this opportunity in July 1901 to submit a memorial coauthored with the Chiang-nan governor-general, Liu K'un-i 劉坤一 (1830–1902). Both of these men had opposed the court's ill-fated alliance with the Boxers, and their memorial strongly encouraged overhaul of the content of the civil examinations and outlined a school system modeled after Japanese elementary, middle, and higher education.[81]

In addition, Chang and Liu urged the court to begin the integration of schools with the examination system, which they saw as the first step toward the eventual elimination of the latter in ten years. Official quotas for degrees would favor school graduates for dynastic positions at the expense of examination graduates. All private and official academies, they suggested, should be turned into new schools as soon as possible. They also advocated abolition of all military examinations and sending students abroad to study.[82]

Most of the details of the reforms had been argued for centuries, and the 1898 reformers had unsuccessfully tried to put most of them in effect as a package of changes. But in August 1901, for the first time since 1664–67, the abolition of eight-legged essays was approved by the court and obeyed by the Ministry of Rites. Local examiners could now expect *t'ung-sheng* and *sheng-yuan* candidates on licensing and qualifying examinations to answer questions dealing with both Chinese and Western learning. In addition, the format of the provincial and metropolitan civil examinations would thereafter emphasize discourse and policy questions on the first and second sessions.[83]

79. David D. Buck, "Educational Modernization in Tsinan, 1899–1937," in Mark Elvin and G. William Skinner, eds., *The Chinese City between Two Worlds* (Stanford: Stanford University Press, 1974), pp. 173–77.

80. Wolfgang Franke, *The Reform and Abolition of the Traditional Chinese Examination System*, p. 48.

81. On Japanese models for education reform in China, see Harrell, *Sowing the Seeds of Change*, pp. 40–106. See also Y. C. Wang, *Chinese Intellectuals and the West*, pp. 59–61.

82. Wolfgang Franke, *The Reform and Abolition of the Traditional Chinese Examination System*, pp. 49–54, discusses this memorial in detail.

83. See *Ching-hsiang t'i-ming lu*, 2.21b–24a, for examples of the reformed local examinations.

FORMAT OF PROVINCIAL AND METROPOLITAN CIVIL SERVICE
EXAMINATIONS DURING THE LATE CH'ING DYNASTY, AFTER
THE 1901 REFORM (ABOLISHED IN 1905)

| Session No. | No. of Questions |
|---|---|
| ONE | |
| 1. Discourses on the history of Chinese politics 中國政治史事論 | 5 essays |
| TWO | |
| 1. Policy questions on world politics 各國政治藝學策 | 5 essays |
| THREE | |
| 1. Four Books 四書義 | 2 essays |
| 2. Five Classics 五經義 | 1 essay |

NOTE: The requirement that all candidates specialize (*chuan-ching* 專經) on one of the Five Classics was dropped in 1787. In addition, such essays no longer had to follonger had to follow the "eight-legged" style.

In session one candidates were expected to answer five discourse questions dealing with Chinese institutions and politics. Session two included five policy questions on Western institutions and politics. The last session required three classical essays, two on quotations from the Four Books and one from the Five Classics. In theory, all three sessions were expected to count equally for the final rankings, but how this would work out in practice remained unknown. Would examiners really relegate classical essays to last and give priority to discourse and policy answers?[84]

In 1902 the first civil examinations since enactment of the reforms took place in K'ai-feng, the capital of Ho-nan province. Because the provincial examination halls in Shun-t'ien, where the metropolitan examinations in Peking had also been held, had been burned down by the foreign troops sent in to relieve the Boxer siege of the international legations, this metropolitan examination could not be held in Peking. On the 1902 metropolitan examination held in K'ai-feng, the five discourse questions on session one dealt with (1) the military policies of Kuan-tzu 管子, (2) the policies of Han Wen-ti 漢文帝 (r. 179–156 B.C.) toward Nan-yueh 南越, (3) imperial use of laws, (4) evaluation procedures for officials, and (5) the proposals of Liu Kuang-tsu 劉光祖 (1142–1222) for stabilizing the Southern Sung dynasty. On session two, the five policy questions concerned (1) the Western stress on travel as part of studying, (2) the Japanese use of Western

84. For a conventional account of the 1903 provincial examinations in Hu-nan, see Lewis, *Prologue to the Chinese Revolution*, pp. 148–49.

models for educational institutions, (3) the banking policies of various countries, (4) the police and laws, and (5) the industrial basis of wealth and power. For session three, three passages, one each from the *Analects, Great Learning,* and *Change Classic,* were chosen for essays of 500 to 550 characters.[85]

At first sight the reforms seem to have been effective, even though the classical essays on session three still resembled the tight format of an eight-legged essay.[86] Oddly enough, however, the examiners, who were apointed in the traditional way by the Ministry of Rites and Hanlin Academy, still presented their final evaluations of the candidates' papers in the traditional order. That is, they first presented the outstanding essays on the Four Books and the Five Classics, without even mentioning that this was the third session. Next, they presented the discourse answers, even though these were on session one. And, finally the best policy answers were included at the end, as if they were still on session three.

In other words, despite the revised order in which the examination of 1902 was given, which followed the imperial reforms decreed in 1901, the examiners persisted in reporting the results in terms of the traditional order of (1) classical essay, (2) discourse essay, and (3) policy question. Consequently, the examiners betrayed in practice what they accepted in theory, namely the new format for the civil examinations. Their forms of "local resistance" could not undo what the reformers had wanted, but they certainly could mitigate the final outcome of the reforms. This secretive resistance by the 1902 examiners indicates that not all literati, particularly those who served as examiners, supported the reformers. The court, however, had reluctantly sided with them.[87]

The answers that were later printed for the second policy question dealing with the Japanese use of Western models for educational institu-

85. *Kuang-hsu hsin-ch'ou jen-yin en-cheng ping-k'o hui-shih wei-mo* 光緒辛丑壬寅恩正併科會試闈墨 (Compositions of graduates in the 1901/1902 combined special and regular metropolitan civil examination), 1902: 1a–26a.

86. Shu Hsin-ch'eng 舒新城, *Wo ho chiao-yü* 我和教育 (Education and I) (Taipei: Lung-wen Press, 1990), pp. 29–32, noted that as late as 1904, local private schools still required students to master eight-legged essays and regulated verse with eight-rhymes. Fan P'ei-wei's 范沛濰 "Ch'ing-mo kuei-mao chia-ch'en hui-shih shu-lun" 清末癸卯甲辰會試述論 (Account of the 1903–04 metropolitan examinations at the end of the Ch'ing), *Chung-kuo chin-tai shih* 中國近代史 (1993.3): 81–86, gives a positive assessment of the reformed civil examinations.

87. See *Kuang-hsu hsin-ch'ou jen-yin en-cheng ping-k'o hui-shih wei-mo,* pp. 1a, 7a, 17a. See also *Kuang-hsu hsin-ch'ou jen-yin en-cheng ping-k'o hui-shih mo-chüan* 光緒辛丑壬寅恩正併科會試墨卷 (Compositions of graduates in the 1901/1902 combined special and regular metropolitan civil examination), 1903: 9th examination ward papers, not consecutively paginated.

tions give us a taste of what kind of policy answers the examiners favored. The answer prepared by the top-ranked metropolitan graduate, Chou Yun-liang 周蘊良, was cautionary. Japan, Chou noted, had honored *Han-hsueh* 漢學 (lit., "Han Learning"), which now stood for "Chinese learning" and not evidential research, but since the Meiji Restoration the Japanese began almost exclusively to follow Western models for taxes, laws, and education. Men like Fukuzawa Yukichi 福澤諭吉 (1835–1901) advocated complete "Europeanization" (*Ou-hua chu-i* 歐化主義) of Japan. Later, a reaction set in against this emulation of all things European, Chou went on, and other Japanese advocated instead a return to native purity (*kuo-ts'ui chu-i* 國粹主義). China, Chou concluded, should learn from Japan's mistakes and not rush headlong into a wild emulation of all things European. She should be selective in her adoption of foreign models and ideas.[88]

Others who passed the 1902 examination took a similar tack on this policy question. Hsieh Mu-han 謝慕韓 (b. 1864) from Chiang-hsi, who finished 103rd out of a total of 315 graduates, began his answer by arguing that schools were the basis for nurturing talent. Since education in schools should be a balance of moral, mental, and physical training, Hsieh maintained, there really was no difference between Chinese or Western, ancient or modern, education. When it came to educational institutions, however, everyone today in China spoke of Japan as a model. But during the T'ang dynasty, Hsieh pointed out, Japan had established Buddhist schools. Later during the Ming dynasty, she adopted the Four Books and Five Classics of China for study.

During the Meiji Restoration, Hsieh went on, Japanese emulated Europe in establishing schools, claiming that Western learning stressed practical studies necessary for a nation's wealth and power. Chinese learning was denigrated for its vacuousness and dropped. Statesmen like Itō Hirobumi 伊藤博文 (1841–1909) sent students abroad to Europe and the United States to learn about their political institutions. In turn the Japanese established their own teaching, elementary, and higher schools, as well as Tokyo Imperial University. Students of finance, politics, and the sciences arose in abundance, which began Japan's march to wealth and power.

But then Hsieh turned cautionary as well. Japan's haste to emulate Europe also created problems. The Japanese sank into a drunken craze of

88. See *Kuang-hsu hsin-ch'ou jen-yin en-cheng ping-k'o hui-shih wei-mo*, pp. 19a–20a; and *Kuang-hsu hsin-ch'ou jen-yin en-cheng ping-k'o hui-shih mo-chüan*, pp. 7a–8a, pp. 5a–6b (separate manuscripts). See also *Chung-wai shih-wu ts'e-wen lei-pien ta-ch'eng* 中外時務策問類編 (Great compendium of policy questions on Chinese and foreign affairs classified topically), 1903 edition, 7.11b–13a. Cf. Harrell, *Sowing the Seeds of Change*, pp. 65–66.

Western learning and disdain for "Chinese learning." They overstressed mental and physical training, thereby overlooking the importance of moral training. Such a bias in education damaged Japanese customs and values, Hsieh contended. Nevertheless, in 1889, when the Japanese government established a constitution, it also affirmed the four virtues of loyalty, filial piety, trust, and propriety associated with "Chinese learning." Moral education again became a priority among Japanese. The examiners in the ninth ward evaluated Hsieh's paper as a good assessment of scholarly vicissitudes in Japan, but they were especially pleased with his demonstration that "Chinese learning" was the key to moral education.[89]

Yuan Chia-ku 袁嘉穀 (b. 1872) from Yun-nan, who ranked 135th in the 1902 metropolitan examination, began his essay on the same policy question by describing the Japanese fascination with machinery, which lead them to study Western learning and follow Western laws. But Japan's rapid transformation, however dramatic, also depended, Yuan maintained, on the efficacy of the Japanese people's minds. Their minds, he maintained, drew strength from Chinese moral teachings, as was clear from their reverence for their emperor, which Yuan argued had derived from Confucius' *Spring and Autumn Annals*. The latter had established the precedent that the key to quelling revolt and expelling outsiders was to honor the ruler. For Yuan, the moral was that in establishing schools as the precursor to a constitution and self-strengthening, the emperor of China should also make "Chinese learning" (i.e., the replacement of Ch'eng-Chu Tao Learning) the core of education and emphasize morality and respect for the nation.

Yuan continued to focus on China rather than Japan throughout his essay. Building on earlier formulations of "Chinese learning as the basis and Western learning as practice," Yuan admitted that "Chinese learning" now needed to be buttressed by Western learning to become complete. "Chinese learning" in recent times, according to Yuan, had become limited to three major areas: evidential research, literary style, and calligraphy. The ancient ideal of "comprehensive sages" (*t'ung-sheng* 通聖) resurrected by "Sung Learning" had been left behind, bequeathing a corrupted version of "Chinese learning" (i.e., "Han Learning") that stressed only profit and status. People now had more trust in Western learning and found "Chinese learning" wanting.

Yuan proposed that rediscovering the true merit of Chinese learning as moral teachings should take precedence over copying Japan's emulation of Europe. Chinese human values and relationships, when complemented

89. *Kuang-hsu hsin-ch'ou jen-yin en-cheng ping-k'o hui-shih mo-chüan*, pp. 7a–8a (separate manuscript).

by Western practical learning, Yuan concluded, should be the core of Chinese education. The examiners agreed with the general thrust of what they called Yuan's affirmation of "Eastern learning" (*tung-hsueh* 東學), although they probably graded him lower than Chou or Hsieh because Yuan knew little about Japan.[90]

Other answers to this policy question followed a similar pattern of defending "Chinese learning" while criticizing Japan's flirtation with Western learning. Rather than enter into a detailed account of Japanese educational institutions, as the reformers of the examination system likely intended by making international policy questions a requirement, candidates could get by simply mouthing platitudes that stressed the utility of Western learning but glorified the centrality of "Chinese learning." Ranging in length from 480 to 600 characters, the policy answers candidates wrote for the 1902 examination were about the same length as their classical essays and thus very difficult to rank in terms of substance. The only demarcation seemed to be how much the candidate knew about the Meiji Reforms and how much he showed knowledge of Japan's recent actions and some appreciation of the benefits.[91]

Understandably, perhaps, the examiners felt more at ease with final rankings that stressed the classical essays. In a typical final assessment, one of the chief examiners wrote of Shih Pao-an 史寶安 (b. 1876) from Honan, who ranked fifth, that "his classical essays were refined and pure, while his discourse and policy essays were outstanding and extraordinary." Ward assessments of Shih for each session were also included, with the classical essays listed in the report as "session one," discourse essays as "session two," and policy essays as "session three."[92]

The rise of "Chinese learning" as a counterpart to "Western learning" in policy essays, moreover, indicated that the divisive nineteenth-century dichotomy between Han and Sung Learning had been translated into a new form of native studies that amalgamated both under the banner of *Han-hsueh* 漢學 (lit., "Han Learning"). The latter now was equivalent to *Chung-hsueh* 中學 (lit., "Chinese learning"), as the reference to "Han" was transformed from the "Han dynasty" to the "Han people." The English translation that resulted from this linguistic change was "sinology," which

90. Ibid., pp. 5a–6b (separate manuscript).

91. For how students learned about Meiji Japan, see Hu Shih 胡適, "Ssu-shih tzu-shu" 四十自述 (Autobiography at age forty), in *Hu Shih tzu-chuan* 胡適自傳 (Autobiography of Hu Shih) (Ho-fei: Hsin-hua Bookstore, 1986), pp. 43–44.

92. See *Chung-wai shih-wu ts'e-wen lei-pien ta-ch'eng*, 7.12a–13a, for other answers. See *Kuang-hsu hsin-ch'ou jen-yin en-cheng ping-k'o hui-shih mo-chüan*, pp. 1a–1b, for the examiners' final comments and ward assessments of Shih Pao-an.

became the standard term referring to a "China specialist." Increasingly, the Manchus and their dynasty were disappearing from within.[93]

If the 1902 examination reforms failed in the short run to accomplish their goals because of the examiners' tenacity, nevertheless the overall scope of the examinations became decidedly more institutional and international in focus.[94] A catalog, compiled in 1903, of policy questions used in the examinations after the reforms identified thirty-two categories that were used:[95]

| | |
|---|---|
| Way of ordering 治道 | Mathematics 算學 |
| Scholarship 學術 | Sciences (I) 格致（上） |
| Domestic government 內政 | Sciences (II) 格致（下） |
| Foreign relations 外交 | State finance 財政 |
| Current affairs 時事 | Monetary system 幣制 |
| Civil examinations 科舉 | Military system (I) 軍政（上） |
| Schools 學校 | Military system (II) 軍政（下） |
| Official institutions 官制 | Defense matters 防務 |
| Assemblies 議院 | Agriculture system (I) 農政（上） |
| State organization 政體 | Agriculture system (II) 農政（下） |
| Public laws 公治 | Public works 工政 |
| Penal laws 刑律 | Commercial system 商政 |
| Education affairs 教務 | Roads and mines 路礦 |
| Astronomy 天學 | Topography 輿地 |
| Geography 地學 | History 史學 |
| Calendrical studies 曆學 | Foreign history 外史 |

The examiners' biases toward "Chinese learning" pervaded many of these fields, however. For example, five of the eight questions on the natural sciences were phrased as follows:

1. Much of European science originates from China (*Chung-kuo* 中國); we need to stress what became a lost learning as the basis for wealth and power.
2. In the sciences China and the West (*T'ai-hsi* 泰西) are different; use Chinese learning (*Chung-hsueh* 中學) to critique Western learning (*Hsi-hsueh* 西學).

93. See the discussion in Levenson, *Confucian China and Its Modern Fate*, 1/100–08.
94. For the impact on family schools, see Kuo Mo-jo 郭沫若, *Kuo Mo-jo hsuan-chi* 選集 (Selected writings of Kuo Mo-jo) (Ch'eng-tu: Ssu-ch'uan People's Press, 1979), p. 38.
95. See *Chung-wai shih-wu ts'e-wen lei-pien ta-ch'eng, mu-lu* 目錄 (Table of contents), pp. 1a–28b.

3. Substantiate in detail the theory that Western methods all originate from China.

6. Prove in detail that Western science studies mainly were based on the theories of China's pre-Han masters.

7. Itemize and demonstrate using scholia that theories from the Mohist Canon preceded Western theories of calendrical studies, light, and pressure.[96]

Other questions and answers on the civil examinations and schools for the most part confirmed in rhetoric at least the reformers' conviction that policy and discourse questions should take precedence over classical essays and that schools should take precedence over examinations. But given the difficulties in establishing schools after 1902 and the reluctance of many to destroy the examination system's monopoly in awarding degrees, the idealistic argument that schools and examinations could complement each other had to be reassessed. Officials now convinced themselves that Li Tuan-fen and Liang Ch'i-ch'ao had been right in 1896 when they contended that new schools would never develop very far or receive popular support as long as civil examinations monopolized higher degrees.[97]

Chang Chih-tung and Yuan Shih-k'ai, the latter serving as a court official involved in military and educational reform, proposed early in 1903 that degree quotas for examinations should be gradually reduced in favor of school degrees as the basis for civil appointments. Otherwise, most degree candidates would continue to choose the examination path over schools as the best way to status and public esteem. They cited as a precedent for such action a 1744 Ch'ien-lung edict that had ordered provincial quotas to be dropped, but critics quickly pointed out that the Ch'ien-lung emperor had wanted only to reform the civil examinations, not abolish them, and called for Chang's and Yuan's impeachment instead. Although temporarily tabled due to the impeachment charges, the Chang and Yuan memorial admitted that getting rid of the eight-legged essay had not been the panacea everyone had expected: "Even though the eight-legged essay has been abolished and replaced by essays on current policies and classical principles, yet, after all, one's writings are based on the strength of one day and these empty words cannot be compared with actual achievements."[98]

96. See ibid., pp. 13a–13b.

97. See *Chung-wai shih-wu ts'e-wen lei-pien ta-ch'eng*, 6.1a–6b, 7.1a–17a. See also Wolfgang Franke, *The Reform and Abolition of the Traditional Chinese Examination System*, pp. 54–56.

98. On Yuan's role in educational reform, see MacKinnon, *Power and Politics in Late Imperial China*, pp. 138–51. On Chang, see Daniel H. Bays, *China Enters the Twentieth Century:*

Chang Chih-tung and Yuan Shih-k'ai exposed the false hopes of those who had thought getting rid of the eight-legged essay would suffice to create a new and less literary elite. Now policy essays were presented as empty exercises in formal rhetoric as well, something Su Shih, living in Northern Sung times, already knew (see Chapter 1). The strengths of the civil examinations, which assured the court's cultural control over its elites, and the "natural" constituency for the examinations, who numbered over four million, were forgotten. School degrees became the new panacea for the production of government officials for dynastic service.

A Committee on Education was established in 1903, which in 1904 presented the throne with new policies to replace examinations with schools as the road to officialdom. This proposal became known as the "memorial requesting the gradual reduction of the civil examinations as an experiment and that stress be placed on new schools." Still facing conservative opposition, however, the full abrogation of the examinations was put off until 1912, when the school system presumably would be in place, but the quotas for all examinations from 1906 on would be reduced by one-third.[99]

A powerful consensus had emerged: in Chang's and Yuan's words, "unless schools are established there will be no way to bring forward men of ability to avert the dangers of these times." In the midst of crisis, many high officials now saw civil examinations as the fundamental problem in the way of further educational reform rather than the institutional means to control literati elites that earlier rulers had perceived. The imperial edict of January 13, 1904, agreed with the new view: "Present conditions are very difficult. The improving of learning and the training of men of ability are pressing tasks." This heralded memorial was presented in the inaugural 1904 issue of Shanghai Commercial Press' *Tung-fang tsa-chih* 東方雜誌 (Eastern miscellany), which made the case even more compelling for all those engaged in educational reform of the civil service.[100]

Shu Hsin-ch'eng 舒新城 (1892–1960), then an editor for the *Tz'u-hai* 辭海 (Sea of words) dictionary for the Shanghai Commercial Press and later an early Republican educator and historian, recalled the pressure of the

---

*Chang Chih-tung and the Issues of a New Age, 1895–1909* (Ann Arbor: University of Michigan Press, 1978), pp. 108–24. Cf. Wolfgang Franke, *The Reform and Abolition of the Traditional Chinese Examination System*, pp. 56–57; and Ssu-yü Teng and John Fairbank, *China's Response to the West: A Documentary Survey, 1839–1923* (New York: Atheneum, 1967), pp. 206–07, for translation of parts of the memorial.

99. The 1904 memorial is translated in Wolfgang Franke, *The Reform and Abolition of the Traditional Chinese Examination System*, pp. 59–64, along with the imperial edict that followed.

100. See *Tung-fang tsa-chih* 1 (1904), *chiao-yü* 教育 (education section), pp. 7–10.

times to change: "The changeover to a new system of education at the end of the Ch'ing appeared on the surface to be a voluntary move by educational circles, but in reality what happened was that foreign relations and domestic pressures were everywhere running up against dead ends. Unless reforms were undertaken, China would have no basis for survival. Education simply happened to be caught up in a situation in which there was no choice."[101]

An article in the eighth issue of *Eastern Miscellany* in 1904, which was drawn from a Cantonese daily, contended, for example, that the "examination system as a whole had poisoned the Chinese people for one thousand and several hundred years." The sort of emotional rhetoric that dissenting literati had for centuries directed against the infamous eight-legged essay was now directed against the civil examinations *sans* the eight-legged essay by a newly emerging Han Chinese intelligentsia.[102] Later in 1904 the imperial court issued school regulations making schools and school examinations a formal part of the civil examinations by granting such students civil degrees. Gradual transformation of the venerable procedures and institutions of the late imperial civil examination system into a system of school examinations was by 1904 irrevocable.[103]

The floodgates broke wide open in 1905, however, in the aftermath of the Russo-Japanese War of 1904–5, which was largely fought on Chinese soil in Manchuria. Given the frantic political climate of the time, the hoary imperial examination system was by 1905 a convenient scapegoat for the war. Now joined by a host of court officials, governor-generals, and governors, Chang Chih-tung and Yuan Shih-k'ai submitted a common memorial on August 31, 1905, calling for the immediate abolition of the civil examinations at all levels. Examinations were an insuperable obstacle to new schools, they contended, because civil examination degrees still outnumbered their equivalent school degrees and prevented the ideal of universal education.

---

101. Shu Hsin-ch'eng, *Chin-tai Chung-kuo chiao-yü ssu-hsiang-shih* 近代中國教育思想史 (Intellectual history of modern Chinese education) (Shanghai: Chung-hua Bookstore, 1932), pp. 6–7. Translated in Borthwick, *Education and Social Change in China*, p. 38.

102. *Tung-fang tsa-chih* 8 (1904), *chiao-yü*, pp. 178–80.

103. Chuzo Ichiko, "Political and Institutional Reform, 1901–11," in John K. Fairbank and Kwang-ching Liu, eds., *The Cambridge History of China*, vol. 11, part 2 (Cambridge: Cambridge University Press, 1980), pp. 376–83; and Wolfgang Franke, *The Reform and Abolition of the Traditional Chinese Examination System*, pp. 65–67. On the rise of an autonomous Chinese press in Japan and China, see Esherick, *Reform and Revolution in China*, pp. 45–46; Leo Ou-fan Lee and Andrew J. Nathan, "The Beginnings of Mass Culture: Journalism and Fiction in the Late Ch'ing and Beyond," in David Johnson, Andrew Nathan, and Evelyn Rawski, eds., *Popular Culture in Late Imperial China*, pp. 361–78; and Harrell, *Sowing the Seeds of Change*, pp. 102ff.

The Empress Dowager quickly approved the memorial on September 2 by issuing an edict that, beginning in 1906, all degrees qualifying a student for civil office could be earned only by graduating from the new schools according to the regulations for schools established in 1904. Unexpectedly, the 1903 provincial examinations became the last of their kind; the last metropolitan examination had already been held in 1904; and the 1905 local qualifying and licensing examinations were the unheralded finale of an institution that had lasted over five hundred years in its late imperial form.[104] Suddenly, millions of local candidates, licentiates, and dynastic school students who had been eligible for government degrees were told to enroll in the new public schools for degrees leading to an official appointment. Remarkably, even among the vast number of licentiates, there were few protests, perhaps because many of them expected to become students or teachers in the new education system.[105]

## SCHOOL REFORMS AND EXAMINATIONS

New schools (*hsueh-t'ang* 學堂) became the focus of educational and political reformers after 1905, but examinations remained an important feature of a student's life. The pages of *Eastern Miscellany* from 1905 to 1909 were filled with articles about improving public and private schools.[106] Others, however, saw the shift from civil examinations to new schools as simply a displacement from the late imperial form of examination control to school-based examinations. Or, to put it another way, some maintained that the emerging public school system was simply a new form of civil examinations to select men for the civil service.[107]

An article reprinted from the *Chung-wai jih-pao* 中外日報 (China and the outside daily), entitled "Ways to rectify matters since the abolition of the civil examinations," appeared late in 1905 in *Eastern Miscellany*. It put the matter straightforwardly before the fluid but slowly evolving local and

104. See *Ching-hsiang t'i-ming lu*, 2.24a, for an example of the last township examination in 1905.

105. Wolfgang Franke, *The Reform and Abolition of the Traditional Chinese Examination System*, pp. 69–71. See also Cyrus Peake, *Nationalism and Education in Modern China* (New York: Columbia University Press, 1970), p. 71. Xiaping Cong is working on a UCLA history dissertation that discusses this tradition in terms of new teachers' colleges.

106. See, for example, *Tung-fang tsa-chih* 2, 2 (1905), *chiao-yü*, pp. 23–217; 2, 11 (1905), pp. 283–87. See also Abe Yō 阿部洋, "Tōhō zasshi ni mirareru Shimmatsu kyōikushi shiryō ni tsuite, jō ge" 東方雑誌にみられる清末教育史資料について上下 (Materials on late Ch'ing educational history appearing in *Eastern Miscellany*, parts 1 and 2), *Rekishi hyōron* 歴史評論 (historical criticism) 137, 1 (1962): 23–33; 137, 2 (1962): 23–33.

107. See Kuo Mo-jo, *Kuo Mo-jo hsuan-chi*, p. 61. Cf. Abe Yō, "Tōhō zasshi ni mirareru Shimmatsu kyōikushi shiryō ni tsuite, jō," p. 27.

provincial gentry educational establishment of late Ch'ing China. The essayist noted that it had taken twenty years for protests against civil examinations to have their effect. Meanwhile, the society had over the last thousand years become acclimated to civil examinations. The writer went on: "Now in one day they have been abolished, and the result is sure to be that society will be greatly inconvenienced." Long-standing aspirations of examination candidates had been dashed, but such aspirations should not be left to fester into dissatisfaction, he added.

The solution during the period of transition from an old educational system to a new one, according to the article, was to create more elementary schools where students who would normally have prepared for the civil examinations could study the new learning. Private schools in particular could serve as a haven for so many examination candidates left hanging after 1905. The new path to officialdom would then pass through the new schools, the article concluded. In fact, local licentiates did seek teaching positions in the expanding school system, which slowly were becoming centers for local elite cultural and political activities, an unintended consequence of the new educational policies.[108]

Stephen Averill has claimed that such schools "constituted the last best hope of social and cultural survival for many rural local elites."[109] By 1910, according to government figures, there were over 35,000 *hsueh-t'ang* empirewide, almost 64,000 teachers, and about 875,000 students in the new schools. With an estimated total population of 406 million in 1910, however, this meant that less than 1% of the population attended schools. Moreover, regional and provincial examination quotas, which had ensured that Ming and Ch'ing elites were more evenly distributed geographically, also ended with the last civil examinations in 1905. The new school system did not take into account problems facing culturally and educationally disadvantaged areas.[110]

But many of the new schools, intended to function as a nested hierarchy of elementary, middle, and advanced *hsueh-t'ang*, foundered initially because students could not afford the fees to attend them. Sally Borthwick

108. See "Lun fei k'o-chü hou pu-chiu chih fa" 論廢科舉後補救治法, in *Tung-fang tsa-chih* 2, 11 (1905), *chiao-yü*, pp. 251–254.

109. On late Ch'ing gentry-merchant elites and their new forms of public opinion, see Joan Judge, "Public Opinion and the New Politics of Contestation in the Late Qing, 1904–1911," *Modern China* 20, 1 (January 1994): 64–91. On educational associations, see Stephen Averill, "Education and Local Elite Politics in Early Twentieth Century China," paper presented at the Association of Asian Studies Annual Meeting in Honolulu, Hawaii, April 1996.

110. The figures were published in *Chiao-yü tsa-chih* 教育雜誌 (Journal of education), 2, 7 (1910): 1861–62.

has explained: "Lack of money had not hampered the examination system which had determined the objective and course of study for students throughout the empire by simply setting standards and rewarding achievement." Although Borthwick's view overlooks the cultural resources that Ming and Ch'ing candidates required to prepare for civil examinations, the new school system, particularly the higher schools, did reverse the costs by requiring fees for fixed and continuous attendance in schools, unlike the self-regulating civil examination system, which placed the burden for preparation on the individual and his family. Having raised expectations that schools were a panacea for mass education and production of talent, the Ch'ing government now discovered that few could afford the school fees, particularly poorer scholars who earlier would have financed their examination studies through tutoring and other means. Imperial school students paid for their success before passing licensing examinations and entering dynastic schools subject to a quota. If they failed, they could still teach in private homes and schools. New school students, however, first paid school fees and were entitled to teach only after graduating from that school, although initially those with lower civil examination degrees could be appointed teachers in such schools. A new school student thus had fewer teaching opportunities than a failed examination candidate. Joseph Esherick has noted that in Hu-pei, many holders of the lowest civil examination degree joined the army after 1905, "discarding the brush to follow the army."[111]

Recruiting students into the new schools remained difficult even after the civil examinations had been abolished. This situation prompted discussion over how to fund the new schools properly. Many proposed that the old stipends set aside to encourage local candidates to travel to take pre-1905 provincial and metropolitan civil examinations should now be turned over to students attending schools. Earlier fees charged candidates for taking examinations could also be used to establish new schools.[112] By spring 1906, however, Yen Fu, in an article entitled "Lun chiao-yü yü kuo-chia chih kuan-hsi" 論教育與國家之關係 (On the relation between schools and the nation), admitted that many, including himself, were now having second thoughts about getting rid of the civil examinations so precipitously.[113] Similarly, Hu Ssu-ching 胡思敬 (1869–1922), who received his

111. *Tung-fang tsa-chih* 2, 12 (1905), *chiao-yü*, pp. 301–09. See also Borthwick, *Education and Social Change in China*, pp. 77, 105–08; and Esherick, *Reform and Revolution in China*, pp. 147–48.

112. See *Shinkoku gyōseihō* 清國行政法 (Ch'ing executive institutions) (Tokyo: Rinji Taiwan kyūkan chōsankai, 1910–14), III/521–31.

113. *Tung-fang tsa-chih* 3, 3 (1906), *chiao-yü*, pp. 29–34; and 3.1 (1906), pp. 1–3. See also Yen's "Chiu-wang chueh-lun," 3/60–71.

*chin-shih* degree in 1895 along with K'ang Yu-wei, became disillusioned with late Ch'ing reform efforts and attacked the new Western-style schools. In a memorial to the court, Hu urged restoration of the imperial examination system. Others followed suit. After the 1911 Revolution, Hu Ssu-ching abandoned official life and retired to his home in Chiang-hsi province.[114]

After several years of dynastic support, the new schools had failed, many contended, to provide either the talent or the results that had been expected. Yen Fu, who earlier expressed some bitterness toward the civil examinations, which he had never qualified for, still stressed the new education as the hope of the nation and called on all Chinese to shoulder the burden of the new aspects of moral, mental, and physical education. Others called on educators to provide a unified vision for the new educational system comparable to that of the Ch'eng-Chu orthodoxy of the civil examinations, which had provided a clear marker for all who competed in them.[115]

## THE LEGACY OF DECANONIZATION AND DELEGITIMATION

Not only had the abolition of the civil examinations destabilized the dynasty's "natural" constituency of degree candidates, but its delegitimation also left a cultural void, namely the decanonization of classical studies in favor of new, Western learning and the challenging of "Chinese learning" (whether Ch'eng-Chu Tao Learning or New Text Han Learning) as orthodoxy. New schools eventually became an effective means of connecting urbanites with rural elites. The hierarchical networks of new schools, according to Averill, transmitted the new cultural and political currents of the late Ch'ing to local society. New textbooks also emerged that changed the reading requirements for the children of elites.[116]

---

114. Averill, "Education and Local Elite Politics in Early Twentieth Century China," pp. 23–24. See also Joan Judge, *Print and Politics: 'Shibao' and the Culture of Reform in Late Qing China* (Stanford: Stanford University Press, 1996), pp. 151–52.

115. See Saito Akio 齋藤秋男, "Chūgoku gakusei kaikaku no shisō to genjitsu" 中國學制改革の思想と現實 (Ideas and reality in the reform of China's education system), *Senshū jimbun ronshū* 專修人文論集 4 (December 1969): 1–25, which focuses on the new schools just before and after the 1911 Revolution.

116. Mark Elvin, "The Collapse of Scriptural Confucianism," *Papers on Far Eastern History* 41 (1990): 45–76. Harrell, *Sowing the Seeds of Change*, p. 214, notes that 90% of the foreign trained students who entered the Ch'ing civil service after 1905 graduated from Japanese schools. On this see Y. C. Wang, *Chinese Intellectuals and the West*, p. 64. See also Averill, "Education and Local Elite Politics in Early Twentieth Century China," pp. 35, 43;

A separate Education Board (*Hsueh-pu* 學部) had been established in December 1905 to administer the new schools and oversee the many semi-official educational associations (*chiao-yü hui* 教育會; also called *hsueh-hui* 學會) that had emerged at the local, provincial, and regional levels. The board reflected the increasing influence of Han Chinese provincial officials such as Yuan Shih-k'ai, who as governor-general of the northern metropolitan region had already in 1903 created an Education Bureau (*Hsueh-wu-ch'u* 學務處) in Chih-li, the northern metropolitan region. The diminution of central education power, which had been maintained through appointments to the Ministry of Rites, whose examiners were in charge of the civil examinations before 1905, climaxed in 1906 when the court decreed that the Education Board should be in charge of general education and supersede the Ministry of Rites and Hanlin Academy in the administrative hierarchy.[117]

In early issues of the new Shanghai Commercial Press journal *Chiao-yü tsa-chih* 教育雜誌 (Journal of education), which from 1909 on took over responsibility from *Eastern Miscellany* for presenting an empirewide forum on educational matters,[118] Chinese educators began to debate whether elementary students should be required to study the classical canon any longer. Writing in the April 1909 issue, Ku Shih 顧實 protested the Education Board's recent reduction of the number of hours students should study the Classics. Ku appealed to the dynasty's 1904 regulation that one of the subjects required of children was "*tu-ching*" 讀經 (reading the Classics). He noted that the board had been swayed by foreign criticisms of Chinese schools: "Educators from all over the world have different opinions. For example, a certain Japanese criticized our new schools as merely a disguise for the examination system because it still employed corrupt and outdated teachers [hired from among examination degree-holders]."[119]

Ku Shih called on the Education Board to reject the misguided views of foreigners and maintain a commitment to serious study of the Classics. In a typical lineage school of the 1890s, for example, students like Shu Hsin-ch'eng, Kuo Mo-jo 郭沫若 (b. 1892), and Li Tsung-huang 李宗黃 (b. 1886) still read primers such as the *Three Character Classic* and *Thousand*

and Wang Chien-chün 王建軍, *Chung-kuo chin-tai chiao-k'o-shu fa-chan yen-chiu* 中國近代教科書發展研究 (Research on the development of modern textbooks in China) (Kuang-chou: Kuang-tung Education Press, 1996), passim.

117. See Bailey, *Reform the People*, pp. 37–48; and David Buck, "Educational Modernization in Tsinan," pp. 178–86.

118. Abe, "Tōhō zasshi ni mirareru Shimmatsu kyōikushi shiryō ni tsuite, jō," p. 23; and Bailey, *Reform the People*, pp. 64–67.

119. *Chiao-yü tsa-chih* 1, 4 (1909), *yen-lun* 言論, pp. 58–62.

610 / DELEGITIMATION AND DECANONIZATION

Character Primer before turning to poetry and classical texts such as the Four Books, which they mastered—that is, memorized—by the age of ten or so (see also Chapter 5). Ma I-ch'u 馬夷初 (b. 1884), later a professor at Peking University, noted that as a child he didn't understand what was written in the texts he studied until he was fifteen, although he was praised for his calligraphy. Hu Shih 胡適 (1891–1962) reminisced that he could recognize one thousand characters at age three and began memorizing regulated verse thereafter, which he hardly understood. Kuo Mo-jo saw poetic drills as "the penalty of poetry" but was spared the misery of eight-legged essays.[120]

After six or more years of classical instruction, students who could afford it moved at about age fifteen to a private academy for more advanced instruction and lectures on the Four Books and Five Classics, which usually included study of Chu Hsi's (or his follower's) orthodox commentaries. Half the time in such an academy had been devoted to preparing eight-legged essays, as well as policy and discourse essays. With the demise of civil examinations, however, the raison d'être for memorizing the Four Books and Five Classics lost its appeal, and most of the rigor of a classical education drawn from Ch'eng-Chu Tao Learning was lost. Remnants of what passed for classical literacy in early twentieth-century schools were what Ku Shih was trying to protect in 1909. Indeed, the role of moral cultivation for character building remained a perennial theme in twentieth-century educational circles.[121]

A subsequent article in the *Journal of Education* took issue with Ku Shih's conservative views, and the author concluded that "an unlearned and unreasonable form of education would result" if classical texts were forced down the throats of students. Later, in 1911, Ho Ching 何勁 prepared an article entitled "Shuo liang-teng hsiao-hsueh tu-ching chiang-ching k'o chih hai" 説兩等小學讀經講經科之害 (On the harm done by classes on reading and lecturing about the Classics in the two levels of elementary school). As a result of those who promoted theories of "national essence"

120. See Shu Hsin-ch'eng, *Wo ho chiao-yü*, pp. 14–18; Kuo Mo-jo, *Kuo Mo-jo hsuan-chi*, pp. 32–37; and Li Tsung-huang, *Li Tsung-huang hui-i lu* 李宗黃回憶錄 (Recollections of Li Tsung-huang) (Taipei: Chinese Educational Society for Local Autonomy, 1972), p. 41. See also Ma I-ch'u, *Wo tsai liu-shih-sui i-ch'ien* 我在六十歲以前 (My life before I was sixty) (Shanghai: Sheng-huo Bookstore, 1947), pp. 2–8; and Hu Shih, "Ssu-shih tzu-shu," pp. 20–25. Hu never had to write examination essays until after the 1901 reforms and thus avoided the eight-legged essay. See pp. 27, 43–44.

121. Shu Hsin-ch'eng, *Wo ho chiao-yü*, pp. 39–45; and Li Tsung-huang, *Li Tsung-huang hui-i lu*, pp. 50–52. Cf. Bailey, *Reform the People*, pp. 116–17; and Xiaoqing C. Lin, "Social Science and Social Control: Empirical Scientific Theories and Chinese Uses," *Chinese Science* 14 (1997).

(*kuo-ts'ui* 國粹) and others who were deluded by their reverence for the Classics (*tsun-ching* 尊經), Ho thought, many schools were promoting classical studies and writing classical essays in the schools.

Such classical instruction, Ho contended, not only was of no practical use but actually did harm to the students. The teachings in the *Great Learning* and *Doctrine of the Mean* were too abstruse and their classical language too difficult, Ho argued, for thirteen- or fourteen-year-old students to grasp. Furthermore, to expect eight- or nine-year-olds to master the *Classic of Filial Piety* and the *Analects* was, according to Ho Ching, preposterous. A deep educational chasm was emerging between literati traditionalists and new educators about the role of classical learning in twentieth-century China. Increasingly, the Education Board served the interests of the modernists in first forgetting the carefully formulated cultural foundations of late imperial childhood education in the Classics (discussed in detail in Chapter 5) and then undoing the schooling mechanisms under which classical literacy and essay writing had been achieved.[122]

Literati discussion generally still showed a lack of concern about elite classical versus popular vernacular language in education reform, although the opening issue of *Chiao-yü tsa-chih* in 1909 announced that articles written in vernacular Chinese were acceptable for the literary section.[123] A vital component was still missing, however: the need to address the role of classical versus vernacular language in school instruction and in written examinations. Full-scale educational reform still required champions of a "literary revolution" that became vocal during the early Republic. Not until the Republican Ministry of Education began to move on the written language of education could popular education move from ideal to practical reality.

In the spring of 1911, Chuang Yü 莊俞 (1879–1939?), a member of the Shanghai editorial staff of the *Journal of Education* and a product of a nearby Ch'ang-chou lineage that for ten generations had produced an illustrious list of imperial officials and scholars,[124] described the Education Board's 1910 instructions for reforming elementary education and compared them to earlier reforms in 1903 and 1909. In addition to dropping

122. *Chiao-yü tsa-chih* 1, 5 (1909), *yen-lun*, pp. 67–70, and 3.5 (1911), *yen-lun*, pp. 52–54.

123. Bailey, *Reform the People*, pp. 73–75, discusses the use of the vernacular in education from 1899–1909. See also M. Dolezelova-Velingeroova, "The Origins of Modern Chinese Literature," in Merle Goldman, ed., *Modern Chinese Literature in the May Fourth Era* (Cambridge: Harvard University Press, 1977), pp. 19–20.

124. See *P'i-ling Chuang-shih tseng-hsiu tsu-p'u* 毘陵莊氏增修族譜 (Revised genealogy of the Chuang lineage in Ch'ang-chou), 1935 edition (Ch'ang-chou), 7B.26a. Cf. Elman, *Classicism, Politics, and Kinship*, chap. 2.

Chinese history, geography, and biology from the daily curriculum of grades one to five, as the 1909 reforms had already done, in 1910 the Board also changed the requirements for the texts to be used in the classes for "moral cultivation" (hsiu-shen 修身) and for "reading and lecturing on the Classics."

Chu Hsi's "Hsiao-hsueh" 小學 (Elementary learning), which had been condensed into a book of illustrations and drawings in 1909 for first-grade classes on moral cultivation, was dropped in 1910 in favor of a new Board textbook on morality for grades one to four. While the Four Books and the Classic of Filial Piety had been variously required in elementary classes on the classics in 1903, only a simplified version of the Record of Rites had been required (for fifth graders only) in 1903. In 1909 and 1910, however, only the Classic of Filial Piety, Analects, and a simplified version of the Li-chi were required of third- to fifth-year students. First and second graders no longer had to read the Classics.[125]

In addition to the decline of classical learning in the schools, particularly the overnight jettisoning of the Ch'eng-Chu Tao Learning orthodoxy as the core framework for reading classical texts such as the Four Books and Five Classics (where were the Ch'eng-Chu partisans in 1910—isolated and irrelevant in the Ministry of Rites?), the Education Board was faced with problems of keeping track of the progress made by the more than 13,000 chin-shih (now college graduates), 66,960 chü-jen (high school graduates), and 353,380 kung-sheng (elementary teaching and lowest school degree-holders) who had received degrees every year since new schools had been established. Although the board was proud that the yearly number of chin-shih had increased 124 times, the number of chü-jen 125 times, and the number of kung-sheng 346 times over yearly levels of graduates when the civil examinations were held, it still faced a massive problem in confirming that the education in all the schools was comparable and that the skills of graduates were all equal.[126]

To confirm a school's performance and to measure a student's abilities according to a national standard, the Education Board from the beginning used examinations to test all levels of schools. Private and public school entrance examinations were already ubiquitous, as were graduation examinations. Moreover, the board used standard examinations to test the ever-increasing numbers of graduated students who still were floating around as yu-hsueh-sheng 游學生 (lit., "wandering students") looking for

125. Chiao-yü tsa-chih 3, 2 (1911), yen-lun, pp. 21–32. The Mencius, Great Learning, and Doctrine of the Mean were still required for upper-level elementary classes. See 3.2 (1911), "fa-ling" 法令, pp. 9–13. Cf. Bailey, Reform the People, pp. 140–41.

126. For the figures, see table 3 in Chiao-yü tsa-chih 2, 1 (1910), p'ing-lun, pp. 3–4.

positions. Repeat examinations were required to confirm earlier results; these reminded many of the "repeat examinations" (*fu-shih* 覆試) used during the Ch'ing dynasty to crack down on cheating and fraud among candidates (see Chapter 4). Credentials, requirements, grading, rewards, and punishments for fraud were spelled out in great detail before each such board-sponsored national examination. Those who passed were called *wen-k'o* 文科 (course of letters) *chü-jen* and *chin-shih*.[127]

A test in economics had already been given in July 1903 as a "special examination" to discover talent.[128] In addition, the late Ch'ing bureaucracy for the first time since the Sung dynasty used "special examinations" to select legal officials in 1910. The top examiners were *chin-shih* degree-holders, but some of the candidates were returned students from Japan and Europe.[129] Finally, we should note that the court still held special examinations in 1907, 1909, and 1910 for recommended pre-1905 civil examination candidates; for the most part they were symbolic exercises, although some candidates were chosen for office.[130]

Ironically, a Chinese bannerman, Shang Yen-liu 商衍鎏, who was the last *tertius* but the third Han bannerman *t'an-hua* in the regular civil examinations in 1904, was appointed one of the chief examiners for the 1909 T'ang and Sung dynasty style *ming-ching* 明經 (clarify the Classics; see Chapter 1) examination in Peking, which was held for bannermen still fixated on the old curriculum.[131] Shang later prepared for posterity a definitive account of the Ch'ing and Taiping civil examinations.[132] Similarly, the first chancellor of Yen-ching University, Wu Lei-ch'uan 吳

127. See Education Board announcements concerning such examinations in *Chiao-yü tsa-chih* 1, 8 (1909), *fa-ling*, pp. 51–54; 1, 11 (1909), *fa-ling*, pp. 63–67. See also Hsu K'o's *Ch'ing-pai lei-ch'ao*, 21.61–62.

128. See Fang Tu Lien-che 房杜聯喆, "Ching-chi t'e-k'o" 經濟特科 (Special examination in economics), *Chung-kuo hsien-tai-shih ts'ung-k'an* 中國現代史叢刊 3 (1969): 1–44. See also Ernest Young, *The Presidency of Yuan Shih-k'ai*, p. 67, 270n38.

129. See *Hsuan-t'ung keng-hsu k'o ti-i-tz'u k'ao-shih fa-kuan t'ung-nien lu* 宣統庚戌科第一次考試法官同年錄 (Record of graduates of the first examination for legal officials in 1910), 1910 edition, passim.

130. See *Kuang-hsu san-shih-san nien ting-wei k'o chü-kung k'ao-chih t'ung-nien ch'ih-lu* 光緒三十三年丁未科舉貢考職同年齒錄 (Record of the recommendees for office in the 1907 civil examination), 1907 edition; and *Hsuan-t'ung erh-nien keng-hsu k'o chih-sheng chü-kung hui-k'ao ch'ih-lu* 宣統二年庚戌科直省舉貢會考齒錄 (Record of recommendees from each province in the 1910 metropolitan civil examination), 1910 edition. See also Meribeth Cameron, *The Reform Movement in China, 1898–1912* (Stanford: Stanford University Press, 1931), pp. 82–83.

131. See *Hsuan-t'ung chi-yu k'o chien-i ming-ching t'ung-p'u* 宣統己酉科簡易明經通譜 (Record of graduates of the 1909 simplified examination to clarify the Classics), 1909 edition, passim.

132. See Shang Yen-liu, *Ch'ing-tai k'o-chü k'ao-shih shu-lu*, cited in earlier chapters. Shang's study of the Taiping civil examinations has been cited above in this chapter.

雷川 (1870–1944), the last Christian and only Protestant to hold an imperial *chin-shih* degree (which he received in 1898), was admitted to the newly established Court of *Chin-shih* (*Chin-shih kuan* 進士館) in 1909. While he waited for an official appointment, Wu became involved in provincial education.[133]

School examinations to measure student progress began to receive so much attention that teachers increasingly spent class time just before an examination preparing students for the test. Some like Chiang Wei-ch'iao 蔣維喬, later a scholar of Buddhism and Chinese philosophy, bitterly complained in the winter of 1910 about how much in-class time was taken up by teachers preparing their students for examinations. Chiang felt this time could be better spent in actual instruction. More time devoted to instruction, Chiang thought, would also decrease the obsessive concern for competition among students, which was counterproductive.

An extended debate ensued in the pages of the *Journal of Education* over the usefulness of school examinations and the amount of preparation that teachers should devote to such tests. Many saw the examinations as the only impartial way to measure the actual achievements of students and their schools on a national basis. Most educators had by 1910 forgotten that obsession with standard examinations had been the educational logic that had turned dynastic schools during the Ming and Ch'ing dynasties into "testing centers" for the civil examinations.[134]

The irony of what had happened to the new schools was clear, however, to Chiang Wei-lung 江為龍, who, using the pen name "Wo i" 我一 ("I alone"), prepared a scathing editorial entitled "K'ao-shih kan-yen" 考試感言 (Moving words on examinations) for the winter 1910 *Journal of Education*. "I alone" began by reviewing the reasons why the civil examinations had been dropped in 1905 and why new schools had been established in their place. In order to nurture men of real talent, worthless literary talent promoted by the civil examinations was replaced by practical studies in schools. What had been the results, however? New schools had been in existence for ten years, "I alone" pointed out, yet the results were astonishing: "The achievements of schools were still imperceptible, and the old apparition of civil examinations was alive once more."

The Education Board, "I alone" continued, considered teachers' evaluations and grades for students unreliable. Tests administered by local education officials and governors general were also deemed insufficient. Instead, the board preferred a national, standard examination to measure

---

133. Sin-Jan Chu, *Wu Leichuan: A Confucian-Christian in Republican China* (New York: Peter Lang, 1995), pp. 5–6.

134. *Chiao-yü tsa-chih* 2, 8 (1910), *chu-chang* 主張 (advocacy), pp. 3–4; 2, 10 (1910), *chih-i wen-ta* 質疑問答 (questions and answers), pp. 23–32. Chiang Wei-ch'ao, like Chuang Yü, was from Ch'ang-chou.

the strengths and weaknesses of all students. Repeat examinations were continually required of those who failed the first tests. "I alone" then sarcastically added: "If for a long time this does not change, then what are called colleges, high schools, and middle schools can be completely done away with. We can encourage all those who wish to do so to stay at home and study by themselves to prepare for examinations. Everything can be just as it was during the time of civil examinations!"[135]

"I alone" also acidly commented on the standard examinations required of students who had returned from studying abroad.[136] Some were away three to four, others eight to ten years. Yet, unless they passed the special examination set up by the board to test students who studied abroad, they were told that they didn't have the credentials for a civil appointment in the bureaucracy. According to the logic of this system, all the college teachers in all the nations of the world could not compare with the several days of examinations devised by the Education Board. "I alone" asked: "Could it really be the case that a Ph.D. degree from abroad was inferior to an examination paper read by the Ministry?"

Next "I alone" turned to the examination and reexamination of "roaming" school graduates who congregated in the capital like *chin-shih* candidates of old each time the Board held its national examination for them. The cost in fees and supplies alone made the attendance of such examinations prohibitively expensive for most school graduates from the provinces. These sort of inequities had certainly dampened the future of education in China, "I alone" added.[137]

It used to be the case that literati were deluded by the glory of achieving a civil examination degree and gaining the office of a magistrate or entering the Hanlin Academy. "They were intoxicated with the civil examinations until their death and refused to change," "I alone" explained. After the Sino-Japanese War and the Boxers, however, civil examinations were blamed for the dynasty's weaknesses and abolished. New schools were established and students were encouraged to study abroad. But looking back on it now, "I alone" concluded, the civil examinations were really still in place. Chao K'uang of the T'ang remained right: "Candidates still

135. *Chiao-yü tsa-chih* 2, 5 (1910), *p'ing-lun,* p. 13.

136. Y. C. Wang, *Chinese Intellectuals and the West,* pp. 68–71, discusses examinations for returning students. They are implicit in the 1903 regulations, but such tests were not initiated until 1905, when fourteen students returning from Japan were tested. In 1907 the Chinese essay was made compulsory for such examinations. In 1908 the examination was divided into two stages: first by the *Hsueh-pu;* the second by the emperor, which then led to an appointment. The Chinese Classics were not compulsory for science students, but rankings were biased toward them. The increase in such returned graduates was as follows: 38 (1907), 107 (1908), 400 (1911).

137. *Chiao-yü tsa-chih* 2, 5 (1910), *p'ing-lun,* pp. 13–15.

study things they will never use." Schools were again simply a front for examinations, "I alone" explained, but he did not note that they were now also a front for a new Chinese-dominated nation-state emerging within the ruins of the Manchu regime.[138]

Via these new school-based national examinations, the Manchu court tried in vain to maintain control over the delegitimated remnants of the older examination constituencies and at the same time to gain control over education in the new schools. The Ch'ing dynasty never reestablished its control of the provincial and local educational systems, which it had irrevocably lost in 1905. Power had shifted to the new schools and, more important, to the Han Chinese gentry constituencies they served.[139] This weakness of the dynasty was also apparent in its loss of civil judicial power, which shifted to nongovernment agencies such as chambers of commerce (shang-hui 商會) in local counties and prefectures. In fact, the interlocking committees of gentry and merchants who oversaw both the local and provincial education associations (hsueh-hui) and the chambers of commerce meant that education was part of a general process lessening dynastic power and influence in the provinces.[140]

Many unofficial organizations and groups had entered the fray of education and school reform at all levels, thus further eroding the Manchu court's control over education policy. Increasingly, the dynasty lost its monopoly over educational institutions to unofficial elites who gained the upper hand in determining the future of education after 1905.[141] Through the portal of local education, local official and unofficial elites took over the educational domains of the central bureaucracy. As the Ch'ing court and its upper levels of bureaucratic power grew weaker, regional and local tiers of power began to create the educational institutions that would accelerate the demise of the dynasty and form the educational pillars of the Republic after 1911.[142] A fundamental change in the recruitment and training of county magistrates was but one important result.[143]

138. Ibid., pp. 15–16.

139. David Buck, "Educational Modernization in Tsinan," pp. 173, 182–85.

140. See Ma Min and Li Yandan, "Judicial Authority and the Chamber of Commerce: Merchant Dispute Mediation and Adjudication in Suzhou City in the Late Qing," paper presented at the Conference on Law and Society in Late Imperial China, sponsored by the Center for Chinese Studies at UCLA, August 8–10, 1993.

141. See Bailey, Reform the People, pp. 136–39; Borthwick, Education and Social Change in China, pp. 93–103; and Chauncey, Schoolhouse Politicians, pp. 22–24, 59–64.

142. John Fincher, "Political Provincialism and the National Revolution," in Mary Wright, ed., China in Revolution: The First Phase, 1900–13 (New Haven: Yale University Press, 1968), pp. 188–89. Cf. Chuzo, "The Role of the Gentry," p. 302; and Ernest Young, The Presidency of Yuan Shih-k'ai, pp. 9–14.

143. Odoric Wou, "The District Magistrate Profession in the Early Republican Period," Modern Asian Studies 8, 2 (April 1974): 217–45.

Moreover, the Education Board established in 1905 continued into the Republican period, although renamed as a "ministry," and it remained on the side of new schools and a new curriculum. The educational institutions of the Republic of China after 1911 were the direct legacy of the late Ch'ing reforms.[144] The creation by Sun Yat-sen 孫中山 (1866–1925) of the *k'ao-shih yuan* 考試院 (examination bureau) as part of the Republic's "five-power constitution" of the 1920s was also a twentieth-century echo of Ch'ing institutions. The twentieth-century "examination life," which became associated with university and public school entrance examinations in China and later in Taiwan, is the cultural heir of life under the Ming-Ch'ing examination regime.[145]

For example, in December 1913, the Republic of China stipulated that all present and future magistrates would have to pass an examination specially designed for them before they could be officially appointed. A candidate for the magistrates' examination, which was held in the capital, was required to sit for four sessions of tests: (1) essay writing, (2) legal procedure and international law, (3) local administration, and (4) oral questions on local customs and past experience. The 1913 policy was based on the magistrates' examination first given under Ch'ing auspices in 1909. In fact, up to 1917 over 73% of all magistrates still held traditional degrees; in 1923 almost 63% were also Ch'ing degree-holders.[146]

Despite these important continuities, however, between 1898 and 1911 a complete break occurred in the concordance between long-standing, internalized expectations of Chinese families for power, wealth, and prestige based on traditional preparation of sons for local, provincial, and metropolitan examinations and the Ch'ing dynasty's objective political institutions, increasingly reformed based on Western and Japanese models. The devaluation of classical civil examination degrees when compared with graduation from new schools in China or from foreign schools precipitated a generalized down-classing of most traditional examination candidates and the Ch'eng-Chu curriculum, complemented by Han Learning, that they had mastered. Growing disparity between old expectations and new

144. See Mary Wright, "Introduction: The Rising Tide of Change," in Wright, ed., *China in Revolution: The First Phase, 1900–13*, pp. 30–44, on a "new society in the making." See also David Buck, "Educational Modernization in Tsinan," pp. 179–81.

145. Julia Strauss, "Symbol and Reflection of the Reconstituting State: The Examination Yuan in the 1930s," *Modern China* 20, 2 (April 1994): 211–38. Cf. Roland Depierre, "Maoism in Recent French Educational Thought and Practice," in Ruth Hayhoe and Marianne Bastid, eds., *China's Education and the Industrialized World: Studies in Cultural Transfer* (Armonk, N.Y.: M. E. Sharpe, 1987), pp. 199–224.

146. Odoric Wou, "The District Magistrate Profession in the Early Republican Period," pp. 219–24.

objective opportunities increasingly meant the failure of many conservative families to convert their inherited educational and literary cultural resources into new academic degrees for their children.[147] A revolutionary transformation in student dispositions toward education accompanied the radical change in the conditions of recruitment of public officials after 1905.[148] The Ch'ing dynasty in effect became a party to its own political dismantling by losing control of national, provincial, and local cultural and educational institutions.

## FINAL COMMENTS

Because late imperial civil examinations from 1400 to 1900 represented a carefully worked-out partnership between the dynasty in power and its gentry-merchant elites, imperial interests and literati values were equally served through the institutions that enforced local, provincial, and metropolitan examinations empirewide. Each chapter in this book has illustrated that the examination regime was a viable educational and cultural institution, which through its continuities and changes served the political, social, and intellectual needs of those in the state and society who participated in its precincts. Its demise, therefore, brought with it consequences that the last rulers of imperial China and reformist gentry underestimated.

Chapters 1 and 2 examined the historical conditions within which native and conquest dynasties appropriated the civil service and literati teachings during the Sung-Yuan-Ming transition. We discovered that although early Ming rulers carried out political purges that established Ming "autocracy," and although the partnership between the state and society was challenged by the growth of the Ming court's power over the bureaucracy, literati still enhanced the role of Ch'eng-Chu Tao Learning in late imperial governance. Precisely because they were collaborators, early Ming literati ensured that the dynasty would maintain a political balance between the court and the bureaucracy and use Ch'eng-Chu learning as the standard to select officials.

Because of commercialization and demographic growth, the reach of the Ming civil service selection process expanded for the first time from metropolitan and provincial capitals to all 1,200 counties. In addition, the

147. See my *Classicism, Politics, and Kinship*, pp. 22–25, for discussion of how family and lineage cultural resources had translated via examination success into social status and political power before 1900.

148. Cf. Pierre Bourdieu, *Homo Academicus* (Stanford: Stanford University Press, 1988), pp. 156–65.

upsurge in numbers of candidates in the Ming and the Ch'ing was marked by the dominance of *chin-shih* degree-holders over the increasing number of local degree-holders and provincial graduates. Starting in the late sixteenth century, the most prestigious positions in metropolitan, provincial, and local government were monopolized by *chin-shih*. The limits of dynastic power, however, were also revealed through the examination regime. Forms of resistance emerged among examiners, and dissatisfaction and corruption among the candidates at times mitigated the goals of the dynasty. The examination hall became a contested site, where the political interests of the dynasty, the social interests of its elites, and the cultural ideals of Tao Learning were all compromised in practice.

The civil service process also represented the social selection of elites, as educational requirements to master nonvernacular classical texts created a linguistic barrier between those licensed to compete in examination compounds and those who were classically illiterate. In this way, the partnership between the court and the bureaucracy was monopolized by gentry-merchant literati who organized into lineages and clans to maximize their cultural resources. Such resources via superior classical educations usually translated into some level of degree success.

In Chapters 1 to 5, discussion of the sociohistorical consequences of the Ming-Ch'ing selection of elites for the civil service was limited to the examination regime itself. Later chapters described the interaction between the examination marketplace and elite cultural history. Literati regularly turned to religion and the mantic arts in their efforts to understand and rationalize their emotional responses to the competitive local, provincial, and metropolitan examinations. As we have seen, the civil service competition created a dynastic curriculum that consolidated gentry, military, and merchant families into a culturally defined status group of degree-holders that shared (1) a common classical language, (2) memorization of a shared canon of Classics, and (3) a literary style of writing known as the eight-legged essay. Internalization of elite literary culture was in part defined by the civil examination curriculum, but that curriculum also showed the impact of literati opinion on imperial interests. The moral cultivation of the literatus was a perennial concern of the imperial court as it sought to ensure that the officials it chose in the examination market would serve the ruling family.

The bureaucracy was financially committed to operating the examination regime, but the chief consequence since the late Ming was that examiners could not carefully read each of the thousands of individual essays. Final rankings, even for the eight-legged essay, became haphazard. Hence, classical standards inside examination halls did not represent, in practice, a consistent or coherent orthodoxy. To meet these challenges, the Ch'ing dynasty began in the mid-eighteenth century a series of Han Learning curricular reforms to make the examinations more difficult for the increasing numbers of candidates. A poetry question was added in 1756 and all Five Classics were required in 1787. In addition, the formalistic requirements of the poetry question gave examiners an additional tool, along with the eight-legged essay "grid," to grade papers more efficiently. After 1860, however, more radical reforms were initiated to meet the challenges of the Taiping Rebellion and Western imperialism.

Examination topics chosen for policy questions were not representative of literati scholarship as a whole, but they did represent the intellectual standards used at a particular site at a particular time. Literati fields of learning in late imperial China, such as natural studies and history, were also represented in late imperial civil examinations. This inclusion showed the influence of the court, which for political reasons widened or limited the scope of policy questions on examinations, and the assigned examiners, whose classical knowledge echoed the intellectual trends of their time. In the eighteenth century, Han Learning guidelines were also applied to the civil examination curriculum. As a result, the *Tao-hsueh* rejection of T'ang-Sung belles lettres in civil examinations, documented in Chapter 1, was turned back. Mid-Ch'ing officials decided to restore pre-Sung aspects of the civil examinations that had been eliminated in the Yuan and Ming dynasties.

Educational, cultural, and religious institutions in late imperial China generally reflected the complex order of authority by which literati culture became operative, that is, practiced within a hierarchy of values and statuses in social, religious, and political life.[149] When that hierarchy was destroyed, more than intellectual change was involved. Classical texts in premodern China depended for their intellectual authority in practice on the orthodox status of the Classics and the social, political, economic, and cultural enhancements that accrued when they were properly mastered. When that status was challenged, so was its authority, and the classical Canon no longer provided a reliable haven for those seeking ancient knowledge, which the society and the dynasty, working in partnership, together had prioritized and rewarded.

The textual monuments of literati classical learning, like an archaeological site, were never really refuted by their critics or successors after 1900. Simply put, when the Chinese Classics no longer were intellectually inhabited by those in high places, they became the target rather than the basis for analysis. As we are outsiders in a postclassical world, our interpretive strategies cannot reproduce in practice what was once taken for

149. Cf. Rieff, *The Feeling Intellect*, pp. 221–22, 247–48.

granted and is now probably gone forever—namely, the timeless authority of the classical Canon and its instantiation in premodern social and political norms. Because of its empirewide reach, the examination marketplace was the principal imperial venue for reproducing that authority, but the Classics and *Tao-hsueh* were also taught in literati schools and private academies in the provinces where dynastic authority was more distant.

Reform of education and examinations in China after 1900 was tied to newly defined national goals of Western-style change that superseded conservative imperial goals during the Ming and Ch'ing dynasties of reproducing dynastic power, granting gentry prestige, and affirming Tao Learning orthodoxy. The ideal of national unity replaced dynastic solidarity, as the sprawling, multi-ethnic Manchu empire became a struggling Han Chinese Republican state, which was later refashioned as a multiethnic communist nation. Since the Sung-Yuan-Ming transition, as we saw in Chapter 1, the struggle between insiders and outsiders in "China" to unite the empire had resulted in what was now clearly defined as more than four hundred years of "barbarian rule" over the Han Chinese. With the Republican Revolution of 1911–12, that dynastic narrative ended. Manchus, Mongols, and those formerly called *se-mu* peoples have receded into the background of the twentieth-century Chinese republics.

During the transition from the Ch'ing dynasty to the Republic of China, new political, institutional, and cultural forms emerged that challenged the creedal system of the late empire and refracted the latter's political institutions. The emperor, his bureaucracy, and literati cultural forms quickly became symbols of backwardness. Traditional forms of knowledge about the natural world, for example, were uncritically labeled as "superstition" (*mi-hsin* 迷信, lit. "confused belief"), while "modern science" in its European and American forms was championed by new intellectuals as the path to knowledge, enlightenment, and national power.[150] Perhaps the most representative change occurred in the dismantling of the political, social, and cultural functions of the Ming-Ch'ing civil examination regime that had lasted from 1370 to 1905.

By dismantling imperial institutions such as the civil examination system so rapidly, before they provided suitable alternatives or replacements, the late Ch'ing reformers and early Republican revolutionaries underestimated the public reach of historical institutions that had taken two dynasties and five hundred years to build. When they delegitimated them all within the space of two decades starting in 1890, Han Chinese literati helped bring down both the Manchu Ch'ing dynasty and the imperial

---

150. See Peter Buck, *American Science and Modern China* (Cambridge: Cambridge University Press, 1980), pp. 91–121.

system of governance. Although he does not choose to include the examination system in his notion of a "cultural nexus," Prasenjit Duara, along with others who have studied the colonial experience in India, has perceptively noted that emerging nations such as the Republic of China were in a "race to nurture new forms of legitimation before they [were] overwhelmed by the forces of delegitimation that they themselves [had] unleashed."[151] The precipitous end of the civil examinations in 1905 was a case in point.

Its fall concluded a millennium of elite belief in literati values and five hundred years of an empirewide Ch'eng-Chu orthodoxy. The legacy of destroying that cultural *cum* creedal system and the centering frames for human experience it enforced should not be miscalculated or underestimated. The political, social, and cultural utility of symbolic illusions about imperial power, because that utility had become natural and accepted in the daily ritual practice of the civil examinations, was more apparent than the unrealistic school reforms promoted by well-intentioned radicals who no longer understood the full implications of what they were doing. In this regard, at least, the Yung-lo and K'ang-hsi emperors were far more insightful than Empress Tz'u-hsi and her court when the former consolidated their power through military campaigns and civil bureaucracy and the latter relinquished almost all educational power to Han Chinese elites.

What fell in 1905, however, was not only an educational regime based on what I have called "cultural prisons." Socially, examination credentials no longer confirmed gentry status, so sons of gentry turned to other avenues of learning and careers outside officialdom. The Chuangs of Ch'ang-chou, to cite but one example, quickly changed from a distinguished literati super-lineage, which since the sixteenth century had invested heavily in the imperial examinations to maintain its high status, to a weakened group of families whose sons, such as Chuang Yü and Chuang Shih 莊適 (1885–1960?), increasingly traveled to Shanghai to seek their fortunes as members of a new gentry-based Chinese intelligentsia that would be the seed for modern Chinese intellectuals.[152]

Culturally, the long-standing affinity between literati status and Tao Learning was also severed in 1905. In other words, the linguistic monop-

151. See Duara, *Culture, Power, and the State*, pp. 242–43. Elsewhere, on pp. 38–39, for example, Duara prefers to include the examination regime in the earlier historical paradigm of imperial power in China, which he argues was superseded by the "gentry society" paradigm. The latter, Duara contends, should now be replaced by the "cultural nexus" paradigm. Unfortunately, his notion of paradigm change fails to take into account that as new explanations supersede older ones, they should explain what the older explanations could explain and more. Consequently, although Duara leaves out the civil examinations in his discussion of the late imperial cultural nexus, I have tried in this book to show how any formulation of late imperial power must take into account the cultural role of the civil examinations for both urban gentry-merchant elites and rural commoners.

152. See *P'i-ling Chuang-shih tseng-hsiu tsu-p'u*, 1.27a, 7B.26a.

FIGURE 11.1. Peasants Trashing a New School. *Source: Hsing-ch'i hua-pao* 星期華報 (Chinese weekly), no. 1 (1906).

oly of that official, classical knowledge by cultural elites no longer mattered so much socially or politically. As elites turned to Western studies and modern science, fewer remained to continue the traditions of classical learning (Han Learning) and Ch'eng-Chu moral philosophy (Sung Learning) that had been the basis for imperial orthodoxy and literati debate before 1900. Thereafter, classical studies, "Confucianism," and "Neo-Confucianism" have survived as vestiges in the public schools established by the Ministry of Education and have endured as contested scholarly fields taught in the vernacular in universities. The millennial hierarchy of literati learning, based on memorization of the Four Books and Five Classics, study of the Dynastic Histories, and mastery of T'ang poetry, was demolished, although remnants of what is today called a "Confucian repertoire" of skills and habits survive and may be revived in the future.[153]

Riots by commoners and peasants (see Figure 11.1) against the new

153. See the essays in Wei-ming Tu, ed., *Confucian Traditions in East Asian Modernity* (Cambridge: Harvard University Press, 1996), passim.

schools established by urbanized, modernizing elites also represented the end of the elite "Chinese dream" of success in the examination life and its concomitant ties to popular culture and religion.[154] As temples and shrines were forcibly changed into *hsueh-t'ang*, the cultural significance of those sites for examination candidates and local people was belittled by Westernizing elites who were overly confident they were overturning religious and mantic folly. Both Lu Hsun 鲁迅 (1881–1936) and Mao Tsetung 毛澤東 (1893–1976) realized how resistant peasants were to the imposition of impractical Western learning from the outside by the "Imitation Foreign Devil." Mao wrote:

> The "foreign-style schools" were always unpopular with the peasants. In my student days I used to stand up for the "foreign-style schools" when, upon returning to my native place, I found peasants objecting to them.... The teaching materials used in the rural primary schools all dealt with city matters and were in no way adapted to the needs of the rural areas. Besides, the primary school teachers behaved badly towards the peasants, who, far from finding them helpful, grew to dislike them. As a result, the peasants wanted old-style rather than modern schools—"Chinese classes," as they called them, rather than "foreign classes"—and they preferred the masters of the old-style school to the teachers in the primary schools.[155]

Lu Hsun's simultaneously comic and tragic portrait of the surviving examination candidates in his story "K'ung I-chi" 孔乙己 was a stinging reminder of what had happened to so many of the over four million local *t'ung-sheng* and *sheng-yuan* who had been abandoned to their own devices after 1905. Now a petty criminal, K'ung I-chi frequented a tavern before his legs were broken when he was caught for thievery. There, until he disappeared, the long-gowned examination candidate, named after Confucius, earned ridicule rather than the respect once due him:

> "K'ung I-chi, do you really know how to read?" When K'ung looked as if such a question were beneath contempt, they would continue: "How is it you never passed even the lowest official examination?" At that K'ung would look disconsolate and ill at ease. His face would turn pale and his

---

154. See Borthwick, *Education and Social Change in China,* pp. 105–18.

155. See Lu Hsun, "The True Story of Ah Q," in *Lu Hsun: Selected Stories,* translated by Yang Hsien-yi and Gladys Yang (New York: Norton, 1977), pp. 65–112; and Mao, "Report on an Investigation of the Hunan Peasant Movement," in William Theodore de Bary et al., eds., *Sources of Chinese Tradition* (New York: Columbia University Press, 1960), 2/214–15.

lips move, but only to utter those unintelligible classical expressions. Then everyone would laugh heartily again, and the whole tavern would be merry.[156]

A vast institutional apparatus of compounds and buildings populated by examiners, candidates, copyists, proofreaders, and guards had vanished. Gone were the hopes and dreams of millions of young and old men from villages, towns, and cities who had sought official fame and fortune. A cultural regime that had thrived in its late imperial form since 1450 perished. Also lost in the demise of the civil examinations was the cultural confidence that the dynasty and its elites were united in their efforts to maintain public order, imperial prestige, and literati learning. The remarkable partnership between the Ming and Ch'ing dynasties and their gentry, military, and merchant elites, which I have documented in earlier chapters, was unceremoniously scrapped in 1905. Despite a living legacy in modern civil service and college-entrance examinations in China after 1911, the end of the Ch'ing dynasty marked the end of the cultural history of civil service examinations in imperial China.

156. Lu Hsun, "K'ung Yi-chi," in *Lu Hsun: Selected Stories*, p. 21.

# Civil Examination Primary Sources, 1148–1904 (1,042 Reports)

1148, *Shao-hsing shih-pa-nien t'ung-nien hsiao-lu* 紹興十八年同年小錄 (Minutiae for graduates of the 1148 civil examination). *Chin-shih* 進士 roll. Ming edition with 1491, 1595, and 1835 afterwords.

1256, *Pao-yu ssu-nien teng-k'o lu* 寶祐四年登科錄 (1256 Palace Chin-shih roll)

See also:

*Chung-kuo chuang-yuan ch'üan-chuan* 中國狀元全傳 (Complete biographies of Chinese *optimi*), compiled by Ch'e Chi-hsin 車吉心 and Liu Te-tseng 劉德增. Chi-nan: Shan-tung Arts Press, 1993.

*Li-tai chin-tien tien-shih ting-chia chu-chüan* 歷代金殿殿試鼎甲硃卷 (Examination essays of the top three graduates of civil and palace examinations of several dynasties), compiled by Chung Kuang-chün 仲光軍 et al. 2 vols. Shih-chia-chuang: Hua-shan Arts Press, 1995.

*Li-tai kung-chü chih* 歷代貢舉志 (Accounts of the civil examinations over several dynasties), compiled by Feng Meng-chen 馮夢禎. Shanghai: Commercial Press, 1936.

*Sung hui-yao chi-kao* 宋會要輯稿 (Draft compendium of Sung collected statutes). Taipei: Shih-chieh Bookstore reprint, 1964.

*Sung li-k'o chuang-yuan lu* 宋歷科狀元錄 (Record of optimi from palace examinations of the Sung), compiled by Chu Hsi-chao 朱希召. Ming 嘉靖 edition. Taipei: Wen-hai Press reprint.

*Sung-Yuan k'o-chü san-lu* 宋元科舉三錄 (Three records of Sung-Yuan civil examinations). Collated by Hsu Nai-ch'ang. 1923 reissue based on earlier editions.

*T'ai-p'ing yü-lan* 太平御覽, compiled by Li Fang 李昉 et al. Taipei, Commercial Press reprint, 1968 edition.

*T'ang-Sung k'o-ch'ang i-wen-lu* 唐宋科場異聞錄 (Recording unusual matters heard in the T'ang and Sung examination grounds). Canton, Wei-ching-t'ang shu-fang 味經堂書坊 edition. Ch'ien-t'ang, 1873 reprint.

*Yun-lueh t'iao-shih* 韻略條式, Southern Sung manual for civil examinations.

*Wen-hsien t'ung-k'ao* 文獻通考 (Comprehensive analysis of civil institutions), compiled by Ma Tuan-lin 馬端臨, in *Shih-t'ung* 十通 (Ten comprehensive encyclopedias). Shanghai: Commercial Press, 1936.

*Wu-li t'ung-k'ao* 五禮通考 (Comprehensive analysis of the five ritual texts). Compiled by Ch'in Hui-t'ien 秦蕙田. 1761 edition.

*Yü-hai* 玉海 (Jade sea), compiled by Wang Ying-lin 王應麟, Taipei: Hua-wen shu-chü reprint, 1964 edition.

## II. YUAN DYNASTY (1280–1367) CIVIL EXAMINATIONS: EIGHTEEN REPORTS

1314, *Chiang-hsi hsiang-shih-lu* 江西鄉試錄 (Chiang-hsi civil provincial roll)

1315, *Hui-shih lu* 會試錄 (Civil metropolitan roll)

1315, *T'ing-shih chin-shih wen* 廷試進士問 (Civil palace question)

1317, *Hui-shih lu* 會試錄 (Metropolitan roll)

1318, *T'ing-shih chin-shih wen* 廷試進士問 (Civil palace question)

1321, *Hui-shih lu* 會試錄 (Civil metropolitan roll)

1324, *Hui-shih lu* 會試錄 (Civil metropolitan roll)

1327, *Hui-shih lu* 會試錄 (Civil metropolitan roll)

1330, *Hui-shih lu* 會試錄 (Civil metropolitan roll)

1333, *Hui-shih lu* 會試錄 (Civil metropolitan roll)

1333, *Yuan-t'ung yuan-nien chin-shih lu* 元統元年進士錄 (Civil palace *chin-shih* roll)

1334, *Yü-shih ts'e* 御試策 (Civil palace question and answers)

1335, *Hu-kuang hsiang-shih lu* 湖廣鄉試錄 (Hu-kuang civil provincial roll)

1350, *Shan-tung hsiang-shih-t'i-ming-chi* 山東鄉試題名記 (Civil provincial roll)

1351, *Chin-shih t'i-ming-chi* 進士題名記 (Civil *chin-shih* roll)

1360, *Kuo-tzu-chien kung-shih t'i-ming-chi* 國子監貢士題名記 (Civil *chin-shih* roll)

1362, *Shan-tung hsiang-shih t'i-ming pei-chi* 山東鄉試題名碑記 (Civil provincial roll)

1366, *Kuo-tzu-chien kung-shih t'i-ming-chi* 國子監貢士題名記 (Civil *chin-shih* roll)

See also:

*Ch'eng-shih chia-shu tu-shu fen-nien jih-ch'eng* 程氏家塾讀書分年日程年日程 (Daily and yearly reading schedule in the Ch'eng clan school), compiled by Ch'eng Tuan-li 程端禮, 1315 preface, Ch'ing edition (reprint, Taipei: I-wen Press).

*Hsu wen-hsien t'ung-k'ao* 續文獻通考 (Comprehensive analysis of civil institutions, continuation), compiled by Wang Ch'i 王圻, in *Shih-t'ung* 十通 (Ten comprehensive encyclopedias). Shanghai Commercial Press, 1936.

*Li-tai chin-tien tien-shih ting-chia chu-chüan* 歷代金殿殿試鼎甲硃卷 (Examination essays of the top three graduates of civil and palace examinations of several dynasties), compiled by Chung Kuang-chün 仲光軍 et al. 2 vols. Shih-chia-chuang: Hua-shan Arts Press, 1995.

*Sung-Yuan-Ming san-ch'ao chuang-yuan chi-ti* 宋元明三朝狀元及第 (Ascent of Sung, Yuan, Ming *optimi*), Ming edition.

*Yuan chin-shih k'ao* 元進士考 (Study of Yuan dynasty *chin-shih*), compiled by Ch'ien Ta-hsin 錢大昕. Ch'ing draft in the Beijing Library Rare Books Collection.

III. MING DYNASTY (1368–1643) CIVIL EXAMINATION REPORTS: 153 CAPITAL AND PROVINCIAL RECORDS

(1) *Palace Examinations* 明代殿試登科錄 等: 54/48 種 records/years [T'ien-i-ko 天一閣: 50+ 種 records; 56 extant elsewhere in China and Taiwan]

1371 年, 1400, 1411, 1412, 1433, 1436, 1457, 1466, 1469, 1472, 1475, 1490, 1493, 1496, 1499, 1504, 1505, 1508, 1517, 1521, 1529, 1535, 1538, 1541, 1544, 1547, 1553, 1556, 1559, 1562, 1568, 1571, 1577, 1580 (2), 1583 (2), 1586 (2), 1595, 1598 (2), 1599, 1601 (2), 1604, 1607, 1610 (2), 1622, 1634, 1637, 1640, 1643

See also:

*Chuang-yuan chuan* 狀元傳 (Biographies of *optimi*), compiled by Ts'ao Chi-p'ing 曹濟平. Ho-nan People's Press, n.d.

*Chuang-yuan ts'e* 狀元策 (Policy answers of optimi), compiled by Chiao Hung 焦竑 and Wu Tao-nan 吳道南. 1484–1640, palace examination essays, late-Ming edition; and 1478–1637, palace examination essays, Ch'ing 1733 edition.

*Chuang-yuan t'u-k'ao* 狀元圖考 (Illustrated survey of *optimi* during the Ming and early Ching dynasty), compiled by Ku Ting-ch'en 顧鼎臣, and others, and originally called *Ming Chuang-yuan t'u-k'ao* (see below); Ch'en Mei 陳枚 and Chien Hou-fu 簡侯甫 later added materials covering 1631–82 to the Ming collection.

*Chung-kuo chuang-yuan ch'üan-chuan* 中國狀元全傳 (Complete biographies of Chinese *optimi*), compiled by Ch'e Chi-hsin 車吉心 and Liu Te-tseng 劉德增. Chi-nan: Shan-tung Arts Press, 1993.

*Huang-Ming chin-shih teng-k'o k'ao* 皇明進士登科考 (Study of Ming *chin-shih* degree-holders), compiled by Yü Hsien 俞憲. Ming, Chia-ching 嘉靖 edition.

*Huang-Ming chuang-yuan ch'üan-ts'e* 皇明狀元全策 (Complete set of policy questions prepared during the Ming dynasty by *optimi* for the palace civil examination), compiled by Chiang I-k'ui 蔣一葵. Palace examinations from 1371 until 1589. 1591 edition.

*Huang-Ming li-k'o chuang-yuan lu* 皇明歷科狀元錄 (Record of Ming *optimi* over several examinations), compiled by Ch'en Liu 陳鎏. Ming edition.

*Huang-Ming san-yuan k'ao* 皇明三元考 (Study of the provincial, metropolitan, and palace civil examination *optimi* during the Ming dynasty), compiled by Chang Hung-tao 張弘道 and Chang Ning-tao 張凝道. Late Ming edition, after 1618.

*K'o-ming sheng-shih lu* 科名盛事錄 (Record of examination success), compiled by Chang Hung-tao 張弘道 and Chang Ning-tao 張凝道. Ming edition.

*Kuang-tung li-tai chuang-yuan* 廣東歷代狀元 (*Optimi* from Kuang-tung over the ages), compiled by Ch'en Kuang-chieh 陳廣杰 and Teng Ch'ang-chü 鄧長琚. Kuang-chou: Kuang-chou Cultural Press, 1989.

*Li-k'o t'ing-shih chuang-yuan ts'e* 歷科廷試狀元策 (Policy examination essays for the palace civil examination by *optimi* during scheduled examinations), compiled by Chiao Hung 焦竑 and Wu Tao-nan 吳道南. Examinations from 1478 until 1640. Late Ming edition.

*Li-tai chin-tien tien-shih ting-chia chu-chüan* 歷代金殿殿試鼎甲硃卷 (Examination essays of the top three graduates of civil and palace examinations of several dynasties), compiled by Chung Kuang-chün 仲光軍 et al. 2 vols. Shih-chia-chuang: Hua-shan Arts Press, 1995.

*Mindai tokaroku sakuin kō* 明登科錄索引稿, compiled at Kyoto University by the Institute of Humanistic Studies. Published by the "Late-Ming Early-Ch'ing Society and Culture Research Group," 1995.

*Ming chuang-yuan t'u-k'ao* 明狀元圖考 (Illustrated survey of *optimi* during the Ming dynasty), compiled by Ku Ting-ch'en 顧鼎臣 and continued by his grandson Ku Tsu-hsun 顧祖訓. Covers Ming *chuang-yuan* from 1371 to 1571. For the 1607 edition, Wu Ch'eng-en 吳承恩 and Ch'eng I-chen 程一楨 added materials that brought it up to 1604. Materials for 1607–28 were later added by unknown compilers.

*Su-chou chuang-yuan* 蘇州狀元 (*Optimi* from Su-chou), compiled by Li Chia-ch'iu 李嘉球. Shanghai: Shanghai Social Science Press, 1993.

(2) *Metropolitan Examinations* 明代會試錄等: 32 種 records by year
[T'ien-i-ko 天一閣: 40 種 records; 54 extant elsewhere in China and Taiwan]

1371 年, 1400, 1415, 1445, 1469, 1472, 1475, 1478, 1481, 1484, 1487, 1490, 1496, 1499, 1502, 1508, 1520, 1523, 1535, 1541, 1544, 1547, 1559, 1562, 1568, 1571, 1583, 1586, 1598, 1601, 1619, 1622
See also:

*Ch'ien-Ming k'o-ch'ang i-wen-lu* 前明科場異聞錄. (Recording unusual matters heard in the earlier Ming examination grounds). Canton: Wei-ching-t'ang shu-fang 味經堂書坊 edition. Ch'ien-t'ang, 1873 reprint.

*Ch'ien-Ming kung-chü k'ao-lueh* 前明貢舉考略 (Brief study of civil examinations in the earlier Ming dynasty), compiled by Huang Ch'ung-lan 黃崇蘭. 1370–1643, metropolitan and provincial examinations. 1834 edition.

*Chih-i k'o-so-chi* 制義科瑣記 (Collection of fragments about the crafted eight-legged essays for civil examinations), by Li T'iao-yuan 李調元. On Ming and Ch'ing civil examinations. *Ts'ung-shu chi-ch'eng ch'i-pien* 叢書集成初編 edition, 1935–37.

*Chü-yeh cheng-shih* 舉業正式 (Formal models for policy questions). 1529–1553 metropolitan examinations. Chia-ching edition, ca. 1553.

*Huang-Ming ch'eng-shih lu* 皇明程世錄 (Records of metropolitan examinations during the Ming dynasty), 1469–1499, metropolitan examinations. Late Ming Wan-li 萬曆 edition.

*Huang-Ming ch'eng-shih tien-yao lu* 皇明程世典要錄 (Digest of records of metropolitan examinations during the Ming dynasty), 1371–1625, metropolitan examinations. Late Ming edition.

*Huang-Ming hsiang-hui-shih erh-san-ch'ang ch'eng-wen hsuan* 皇明鄉會試二三場程文選 (Selection of model examination essays from the second and third sessions of the provincial and metropolitan civil examinations during the Ming dynasty). 1504–1633 policy questions and answers. 1633 edition.

*Huang-Ming kung-chü k'ao* 皇明貢舉考 (Survey of civil examinations during the Ming dynasty), compiled by Chang Ch'ao-jui 張朝瑞. 1371–1577 metropolitan examinations. Ming 萬曆 edition.

*Huang-Ming ts'e-heng* 皇明策衡 (Balancing civil policy examination essays during the Ming dynasty), compiled by Mao Wei 茅維. 1504–1604, policy questions and answers. Wu-hsing, 1605 edition.

*Ming-tai teng-k'o-lu hui-pien* 明代登科錄彙編. (Compendium of Ming dynasty civil and military examination records). 22 vols. Taipei: Hsueh-sheng Bookstore, 1969.

*Ming-tai wei-k'o hsing-shih lu* 明代魏科姓氏錄 (Name roll for the highest rankings on Ming dynasty examinations), compiled by Chang Wei-hsiang 張惟驤. 1371–1643, metropolitan and palace examinations. Ch'ing edition, Taipei, Ming-wen Bookstore, 1991 reprint, in *Ming-tai chuan-chi ts'ung-k'an* 明代傳記叢刊 (Collectanea of Ming dynasty biographical materials). Taipei: Ming-wen Bookstore, 1991.

*Ming Wan-li chih Ch'ung-chen chien hsiang-shih lu hui-shih lu hui-chi* 明萬曆至崇禎間鄉試錄會試錄彙輯 (Compiled collection of provincial and metropolitan examinations during the Ming from the Wan-li to the Ch'ung-chen reigns). Civil examinations from 1595 to 1628. Late Ming edition.

*Nan-yung chih* 南雍志 (Gazetteer of the Southern Dynastic School), compiled by Huang Tso 黃佐 (1490–1566). Reprint of Ming edition in 8 vols. Taipei: Wei-wen Books, 1976.

(3) *Provincial Examinations* 明代鄉試錄等: 67/43 種 records/years
[T'ien-i-ko 天一閣: 280 種 records; 324 extant elsewhere in China and Taiwan]

1399 年, 1465, 1468, 1471, 1489 (2), 1492 (2), 1501, 1504, 1507, 1516, 1519, 1522 (2), 1525, 1528, 1531 (4), 1532, 1534, 1537 (2), 1540, 1544, 1546, 1549 (2), 1552 (3), 1555, 1558 (4), 1561, 1564, 1567 (3), 1573 (2), 1576, 1579 (2), 1582, 1585, 1591, 1594 (2), 1597, 1600 (4), 1606 (2), 1618, 1624, 1627, 1630, 1639 (3)
See also:

*Chü-yeh cheng-shih* 舉業正式 (Formal models for policy questions). 1534–1543 provincial examinations. Chia-ching edition, ca. 1553.

*Huang-Ming hsiang-hui-shih erh-san-ch'ang ch'eng-wen hsuan* 皇明鄉會試二三

場程文選. 1504–1633, policy questions and answers, 1633 edition.

*Huang-Ming kung-chü k'ao* 皇明貢舉考, 1370–1579 provincial examinations.

*Huang-Ming ts'e-heng* 皇明策衡 (Balancing civil policy examination essays during the Ming dynasty), compiled by Mao Wei. Provincial policy questions and answers, 1504–1604. Wu-hsing, 1605 edition.

*Ming Wan-li chih Ch'ung-chen chien hsiang-shih lu hui-shih lu hui-chi* 明萬曆至崇禎間鄉試錄會試錄彙輯. Contains civil examinations from 1595 to 1628. Late Ming edition.

*T'ai-hsueh wen-hsien ta-ch'eng* 太學文獻大成 (Compendium of sources on the Imperial Academy). 20 vols. Peking: Hsueh-yuan Press, 1996.

A. *Che-chiang Provincial Examinations* 浙江鄉試錄等: 18 種 records
1468, 1492, 1507, 1516, 1522, 1525, 1528, 1546, 1549, 1555, 1558, 1567, 1576, 1582, 1591, 1600, 1606, 1618
See also:

> *Huang-Ming Che-shih teng-k'o k'ao* 皇明浙士登科考 (Study of Che-chiang examination graduates during the Ming dynasty). 1370–1619 Che-chiang examinations. Ca. 1621 edition.

B. *Ying-t'ien Provincial Examinations* 應天府鄉試錄等: 9 種 records
1399, 1492, 1501, 1522, 1532, 1540, 1549, 1597, 1630
See also:

> *Nan-kuo hsien-shu* 南國賢書 (Book about civil provincial examination worthies in Ying-t'ien 應天 prefecture), compiled by Chang Ch'ao-jui 張朝瑞. Digest of 1370–1600 triennial provincial civil examinations. 1633 edition.
>
> *Nan-kuo hsien-shu* 南國賢書, ca. 1600 edition, 1474–1600, 43 Ying-t'ien examinations.

C. *Shan-tung Provincial Examinations* 山東鄉試錄等: 10 種 records
1465, 1489, 1504, 1519, 1544, 1552, 1561, 1585, 1594, 1639
See also:

> *Huang-Ming Shan-tung li-k'o hsiang-shih lu* 皇明山東歷科鄉試錄 (Record of Shan-tung provincial civil examinations during the Ming dynasty). 1369–1643 Shan-tung examinations. Ca. 1642 edition.

D. *Shun-t'ien Provincial Examinations* 順天鄉試錄等: 6 種 records
1531, 1537, 1552, 1558, 1600, 1609

E. *Yun-nan Kuei-chou Provincial Examinations* 雲貴鄉試錄等: 5 種 records
1531 (Y-K), 1537 (K), 1573 (Y), 1573 (K), 1579 (Y)

F. *Chiang-hsi Provincial Examinations* 江西鄉試錄等: 4 種 records
1558, 1567, 1609, 1627

G. *Ho-nan Provincial Examinations* 河南鄉試錄等: 3 種 records
1531, 1579, 1606

H. *Shan-hsi Provincial Examinations* 山西鄉試錄等: 3 種 records
1531, 1537, 1639

I. *Fu-chien Provincial Examinations* 福建鄉試錄等: 2 種 records
1552, 1600
See also:

> *Fu-ch'eng hsiang-chin-shih t'i-ming chi* 福城鄉進士題名記 (Record of graduates of local, provincial, and palace examinations from Fu-ch'eng, Fu-chien) 1370 to 1546 Fu-chien examinations. Ca. 1546 ms.

> *Min-sheng hsien-shu* 閩省賢書 (Book about civil provincial examination worthies in Fu-chien). Compiled by Shao Chieh-ch'un 邵捷春. Digest of 88 Fu-chien 1370–1636 triennial provincial civil examinations. Printed ca. 1636.

J. *Shen-hsi Provincial Examinations* 陝西鄉試錄等: 2 種 records
1567, 1639
K. *Kuang-hsi Provincial Examinations* 廣西鄉試錄等: 2 種 records
1471, 1624
L. *Hu-kuang Provincial Examinations* 湖廣鄉試錄等: 1 種 record
1489
M. *Kuang-tung Provincial Examinations* 廣東鄉試錄等: 1 種 record
1558
N. *Ssu-ch'uan Provincial Examinations* 四川鄉試錄等: 1 種 record
1564

IV. CH'ING DYNASTY (1644–1911) CIVIL EXAMINATION REPORTS: 869 CAPITAL, PROVINCIAL, AND LOCAL RECORDS (EXCLUDING RUSSIAN AND MUSLIM MATERIALS)

(1) *Palace Examinations* 清代殿試登科錄等: 56 種 records
1649, 1651, 1652, 1655, 1658, 1659, 1661, 1664, 1667, 1670, 1673, 1685, 1697, 1700, 1703, 1706, 1712, 1713, 1718, 1724, 1730, 1733, 1739, 1748, 1751, 1752, 1754, 1757, 1760, 1761, 1763, 1766, 1769, 1780, 1796, 1801, 1802, 1805, 1818, 1819, 1820, 1823, 1829, 1835, 1836, 1838, 1841, 1852, 1853, 1859, 1860, 1868, 1874, 1892, 1901–1902, 1903
See also:

> *Ch'in-ting ting-chia ts'e* 欽定鼎甲策 (Imperially prescribed palace civil examination policy essays by the top three graduates). Essays from 1853 to 1883. N.d.

> *Ch'ing-ch'ao te chuang-yuan* 清朝的狀元 (*Optimi* of the Ch'ing dynasty), compiled by Sung Yuan-ch'iang 宋元強. Ch'ang-ch'un: Chi-lin Wen-shih Press, 1992.

> *Ch'ing-tai chuang-yuan ch'i-t'an* 清代狀元奇談 (Strange accounts of Ch'ing dynasty *optimi*), compiled by Chou La-sheng 周腊生. Peking: Forbidden City Press, 1994.

> *Ch'ing-tai chuang-yuan p'u* 清代狀元譜 (Accounts of Ch'ing dynasty *optimi*), compiled by Chou La-sheng 周腊生. Peking: Forbidden City Press, 1994.

*Chuang-yuan ts'e* 狀元策 (Policy essays by *optimi)*. Chia-ch'ing edition. 1646–1769, palace examination essays.

*Chung-kuo li-tai chuang-yuan lu* 中國歷代狀元錄 (Record of *optimi* in China over the ages). Shen-yang: Shen-yang Press, 1993.

*Chung-kuo li-tai tien-shih chüan* 中國歷代殿試卷 (Palace examination papers in China over the ages), compiled by Teng Hung-p'o 鄧洪波 et al. Hai-nan: Hai-nan Press, 1993.

College de France, East Asian Library, Paris. 34 original palace examinations, 1684–1904.

Fudan University Rare Books Collection, Shanghai: Ch'ing dynasty Palace and Hanlin examination papers (殿試考卷 and 翰林散館試卷)

*Kuang-tung li-tai chuang-yuan* 廣東歷代狀元 (*Optimi* from Kuang-tung over the ages), compiled by Ch'en Kuang-chieh 陳廣杰 and Teng Ch'ang-chü 鄧長琚. Kuang-chou: Kuang-chou Cultural Press, 1989.

*Kuo-ch'ao Yü-yang k'o-ming-lu* 國朝虞陽科名錄 (Record of civil service graduates in Yü-yang under the Ch'ing dynasty), compiled by Wang Yuan-chung 王元種. Ch'ing *chin-shih* rolls 1647–1850. 1850 edition.

*Li-k'o chuang-yuan ts'e* 歷科狀元策 (Policy examination essays by *optimi* during scheduled civil examinations). Taipei: Kuang-wen Bookstore reprint of late Ch'ing edition, 1976. Policy examination essays from 1808 until 1876.

*Li-tai chin-tien tien-shih ting-chia chu-chüan* 歷代金殿殿試鼎甲砵卷 (Examination essays of the top three graduates of civil and palace examinations of several dynasties), compiled by Chung Kuang-chün 仲光軍 et al. 2 vols. Shih-chia-chuang: Hua-shan Arts Press, 1995.

*Su-chou chuang-yuan* 蘇州狀元 (*Optimi* from Su-chou), compiled by Li Chia-ch'iu 李嘉球. Shanghai: Shanghai Social Science Press, 1993.

*Ting-chia cheng-hsin lu* 鼎甲徵信錄 (Record of verified and reliable information concerning the top three candidates for the civil examinations), compiled by Yen Hsiang-hui 閻湘蕙. 1864 edition.

UCLA, University Research Library, Dept. of Special Collections, Han Yü-shan Collection of 221 Ch'ing Dynasty Palace Civil Examination Papers, 1646–1904.

(2) Chin-pang *Rolls* 金榜 *of* Chin-shih 進士 *Rankings*: 56 種 records
1667, 1673, 1676, 1703, 1712, 1718, 1724, 1727, 1736, 1737, 1739, 1742, 1745, 1748, 1752, 1754, 1757, 1760, 1763, 1766, 1769, 1771, 1772, 1775, 1778, 1780, 1784, 1787, 1789, 1790, 1796, 1799, 1801, 1805, 1809, 1817, 1820, 1822, 1826, 1832, 1835, 1838, 1841, 1845, 1847, 1852, 1856, 1876, 1877, 1880, 1883, 1886, 1890, 1892, 1894, 1895
See also:

*Chin-shih san-tai lü-li pien-lan* 進士三代履歷便覽 (Overview by region of backgrounds to three generations of civil *chin-shih*). Graduates from 1646 to 1721. N.d.

(3) *Metropolitan Examinations* 清代會試錄題名錄等: 64/62 種/年 records/ years

1647, 1652, 1655, 1658, 1659, 1664, 1667, 1679, 1682, 1685, 1691, 1694, 1700, 1703, 1710, 1720, 1724, 1729, 1730, 1734, 1737, 1739, 1742, 1748, 1751, 1752, 1754, 1760, 1763, 1766, 1793, 1796, 1802, 1808, 1811, 1823, 1832, 1835, 1838, 1842, 1844, 1845 (2), 1847, 1850, 1852, 1859, 1860, 1862, 1865, 1868, 1874, 1883, 1886, 1889, 1890, 1892, 1894, 1895, 1898, 1901–1902, 1902–1903, 1904 (2)

See also:

*Chih-i ts'ung-hua* 制義叢話 (Collected comments on the crafting of eight-legged civil examination essays), compiled by Liang Chang-chü 梁章鉅. 1843 edition. Reprint: Taipei: Kuang-wen Bookstore, 1976.

*Ch'in-ting k'o-ch'ang t'iao-li* 欽定科場條例 (Imperially prescribed guidelines for the civil examination grounds). 1832, 1887 editions.

*Ch'in-ting mo-k'an t'iao-li* 欽定磨勘條例 (Imperially prescribed guidelines for post-examination review of civil examination papers). Ch'ing dynasty, late Ch'ien-lung (r. 1736–95) edition.

*Ch'ing-tai chu-chüan chi-ch'eng* 清代硃卷集成 (Collection of Ch'ing examination essays). Taipei: Ch'eng-wen Publishing Co. reprint, published in 420 volumes in cooperation with the Shanghai Library, 1993–94.

*Hsu-tseng k'o-ch'ang t'iao-li* 續增科場條例 (Continuation to the Imperially prescribed guidelines for the civil examination grounds). 1855 edition.

*Hsuan-chü chih shih-chi* 選舉志事蹟, Palace Museum, Taiwan. Materials from Ch'ing civil examination sections.

*Kuo-ch'ao k'o-ch'ang i-wen lu* 國朝科場異聞錄 (Recording unusual matters heard in the Ch'ing examination grounds). Canton: Wei-ching-t'ang shu-fang 味經堂書坊 edition. Ch'ien-t'ang, 1873 reprint.

*Kuo-ch'ao kung-chü k'ao-lueh* 國朝貢舉考略 (Summary of Ch'ing civil examinations), compiled by Huang Ch'ung-lan 黃崇蘭. Metropolitan and provincial examinations, 1645–1826. 1834 edition.

Ming-Ch'ing Archives 明清檔案, Academia Sinica, Taiwan, 1655–1903, metropolitan, palace, and provincial examinations.

No. 1 Historical Archives 第一歷史檔案, Palace Museum, Beijing, 1646–1904, metropolitan, palace, and provincial examinations.

*Tan-mo lu* 淡墨錄 (Record of skilled civil examination papers), by Li T'iao-yuan 李調元, in *Han-hai* 函海 (Seas of writings). 1881 collectanea compiled by Li T'iao-yuan.

(4) *Provincial Examinations* 清代鄉試錄題名錄等: 623/109 種 records/years [1645–1903 = 258 years; every 2.22 years (258/116); 5.67 records per examination year]

[Missing: 1663, 1666, 1669, 1675, 1687, 1717, 1804]

1645, 1646, 1648, 1651, 1654, 1657, 1660, 1672, 1678, 1681, 1684, 1690, 1693, 1696, 1699, 1700, 1702, 1705, 1708, 1711, 1713, 1720, 1723, 1726, 1729, 1732, 1735, 1736, 1738, 1741, 1744, 1747, 1750, 1752, 1753, 1754, 1756, 1759, 1760, 1762, 1765, 1768, 1770, 1771, 1774, 1777, 1779, 1780, 1783, 1786, 1788, 1789, 1792, 1794, 1795, 1798, 1799, 1800, 1801, 1807, 1808, 1810, 1813, 1816, 1818, 1819, 1821, 1822, 1825, 1828, 1831, 1832, 1833, 1834, 1835, 1836, 1837,

1839, 1840, 1843, 1844, 1846, 1849, 1851, 1852, 1855, 1856, 1858, 1859, 1861–1862, 1864, 1867, 1870, 1873, 1875, 1876, 1879, 1882, 1885, 1888, 1889, 1891, 1893, 1894, 1897, 1900, 1901, 1902, 1903

See also:

*Chin-k'o ch'üan-t'i hsin-ts'e fa-ch'eng* 近科全題新策法程 (Complete models for answers for new policy questions in recent provincial civil examinations), compiled and annotated by Liu T'an-chih 劉坦之. 1764 edition.

*Kuo-ch'ao Hai-ning chü-kung piao* 國朝海寧舉貢表 (Tables of provincial and local degree-holders in Ning-po). 1646–1903 provincial lists. Late Ch'ing manuscript.

*Kuo-ch'ao Yü-yang k'o-ming-lu* 國朝虞陽科名錄 (Records of examination graduates in Yü-yang during the Ch'ing dynasty). Provincial rolls 1645–1851.

*T'ai-hsueh wen-hsien ta-ch'eng* 太學文獻大成 (Compendium of sources on the Imperial Academy). 20 vols. Peking: Hsueh-yuan Press, 1996.

A. *Shun-t'ien Provincial Examinations* 順天鄉試錄等: 70 種 records

1654, 1657, 1660, 1684, 1693, 1702, 1705, 1708, 1723, 1726, 1729, 1732, 1735, 1736, 1738, 1741, 1744, 1747, 1750, 1752, 1753, 1754, 1756, 1759, 1768, 1779, 1780, 1788, 1789, 1795, 1801, 1807, 1808, 1810, 1813, 1816, 1818, 1819, 1821, 1822, 1825, 1828, 1831, 1832, 1835, 1837, 1838, 1844, 1849, 1851, 1852, 1855, 1858, 1859, 1861, 1864, 1867, 1870, 1873, 1875, 1879, 1882, 1885, 1888, 1889, 1891, 1893, 1894, 1897, 1900

B. *Chiang-nan Provincial Examinations* 清代江南鄉試錄等: 51 種 records

1648, 1651, 1657, 1672, 1678, 1681, 1684, 1687, 1690, 1696, 1699, 1702, 1711, 1713, 1714, 1720, 1729, 1735, 1738, 1741, 1744, 1747, 1750, 1753, 1756, 1759, 1760, 1770, 1807, 1810, 1813, 1816, 1822, 1825, 1831, 1832, 1835, 1839, 1843, 1849, 1851, 1852, 1859, 1864, 1885, 1889, 1893, 1894, 1897, 1902, 1903

C. *Ssu-ch'uan Provincial Examinations* 四川鄉試錄等: 59 種 records

1684, 1687, 1689, 1690, 1696, 1699, 1702, 1705, 1708, 1711, 1713, 1729, 1732, 1735, 1736, 1738, 1741, 1744, 1747, 1750, 1752, 1753, 1756, 1759, 1760, 1768, 1770, 1771, 1786, 1800, 1807, 1810, 1816, 1821, 1822, 1825, 1828, 1831, 1832, 1834, 1835, 1844, 1846, 1849, 1851, 1855, 1858, 1859, 1870, 1875, 1879, 1882, 1885, 1888, 1893, 1894, 1900, 1902, 1903

D. *Che-chiang Provincial Examinations* 浙江鄉試錄: 41 種 records

1699, 1702, 1705, 1711, 1723, 1735, 1747, 1750, 1753, 1759, 1762, 1765, 1768, 1770, 1771, 1777, 1792, 1807, 1813, 1816, 1819, 1831, 1834, 1835, 1837, 1839, 1840, 1844, 1846, 1849, 1851, 1852, 1855, 1858, 1882, 1885, 1893, 1894, 1897, 1900–1901, 1902

See also:

*Che-tung k'o-shih lu* 浙東課士錄 (Record of literati civil examination essays in Eastern Che-chiang), compiled by Hsueh Fu-ch'eng 薛福成. 1894 edition.

*Kuo-ch'ao liang-Che k'o-ming lu* 國朝兩浙科名錄 (Record of examinations in Che-chiang during the Ch'ing dynasty), 1646–1858 provincial examinations. Peking, 1857 edition.

*Pen-ch'ao Che-wei san-ch'ang ch'üan-t'i pei-k'ao* 本朝浙闈三場全題備考 (Complete examination of all questions on the three sessions of the Che-chiang provincial examinations during the Ch'ing dynasty). Covers examinations from 1646 to 1859. Late Ch'ing edition.

E. *Shan-tung Provincial Examinations* 山東鄉試錄等: 42 種 records
1648, 1651, 1672, 1678, 1687, 1702, 1711, 1713, 1724, 1738, 1747, 1753, 1759, 1762, 1768, 1771, 1783, 1795, 1807, 1808, 1810, 1813, 1818, 1819, 1822, 1831, 1832, 1839, 1851, 1855, 1858, 1859, 1861–1862, 1870, 1873, 1875, 1879, 1885, 1888, 1893, 1894, 1897
See also:

*Kuo-ch'ao Shan-tung li-k'o hsiang-shih lu* 國朝山東歷科鄉試錄 (Record of Shan-tung provincial civil examinations during the Ch'ing dynasty). 1645–1777 Shan-tung examinations. Ca. 1777 edition.

F. *Fu-chien Provincial Examinations* 福建鄉試錄等: 26 種 records
1684, 1690, 1708, 1711, 1741, 1752, 1753, 1755, 1756, 1758, 1759, 1765, 1798, 1807, 1822, 1831, 1849, 1851, 1852, 1855, 1875, 1885, 1891, 1893, 1897, 1902
See also:

*Chih-i ts'ung-hua* 制義叢話, *chüan* 卷 16–17.

G. *Shen-hsi Provincial Examinations* 陝西鄉試錄等: 35 種 records
1645, 1646, 1651, 1672, 1684, 1687, 1690, 1700?, 1741, 1744, 1750, 1756, 1759, 1760, 1765, 1788, 1795, 1800, 1807, 1810, 1822, 1825, 1831, 1833, 1834, 1835, 1836?, 1843, 1851, 1861, 1885, 1893, 1894, 1897, 1903

H. *Kuang-hsi Provincial Examinations* 廣西鄉試錄等: 44 種 records
1701, 1723, 1724, 1735, 1738, 1741, 1747, 1753, 1759, 1760, 1765, 1768, 1770, 1771, 1779, 1783, 1795, 1799, 1804, 1807, 1808, 1810, 1813, 1816, 1818, 1819, 1822, 1828, 1831, 1839, 1843, 1844, 1846, 1849, 1856, 1861, 1862, 1864, 1867, 1870, 1875, 1893, 1894, 1897

I. *Kuang-tung Provincial Examinations* 廣東鄉試錄等: 44 種 records
1651, 1654, 1699, 1702, 1705, 1729, 1735, 1737, 1738, 1741, 1747, 1759, 1760, 1762, 1765, 1768, 1770, 1794, 1795, 1807, 1808, 1810, 1813, 1816, 1818, 1819, 1822, 1825, 1831, 1832, 1837, 1844, 1849, 1851, 1856, 1862, 1856, 1875, 1882, 1885, 1893, 1894, 1897, 1900

J. *Ho-nan Provincial Examinations* 河南鄉試錄等: 32 種 records
1702, 1705, 1723, 1735, 1738, 1741, 1760, 1762, 1774, 1777, 1780, 1789, 1795, 1798, 1807, 1808, 1810, 1813, 1819, 1822, 1831, 1843, 1849, 1851, 1858, 1875, 1885, 1891, 1893, 1894, 1897, 1902–1903

K. *Yun-nan Provincial Examinations* 雲南鄉試錄 等: 38 種 records
1672, 1684, 1687, 1699, 1705, 1711, 1726, 1729, 1735, 1736, 1738, 1741, 1744, 1747, 1750, 1756, 1759, 1760, 1762, 1768, 1770, 1807, 1810, 1813, 1816, 1819, 1821, 1831, 1851, 1855, 1864, 1882, 1885, 1891, 1893, 1894, 1897, 1903

L. *Kuei-chou Provincial Examinations* 貴州鄉試錄 等: 30 種 records
1693, 1699, 1705, 1711, 1736, 1741, 1750, 1759, 1760, 1762, 1771, 1795, 1797, 1801, 1807, 1811, 1813, 1818, 1819, 1822, 1828, 1831, 1832, 1835, 1840, 1846, 1851, 1873, 1885, 1893

M. *Chiang-hsi Provincial Examinations* 江西鄉試錄 等: 32 種 records
1672, 1693, 1696, 1699, 1702, 1708, 1724, 1735, 1736, 1741, 1750, 1756, 1759, 1762, 1768, 1788, 1807, 1808, 1813, 1822, 1831, 1851, 1862, 1875, 1876, 1882, 1885, 1891, 1893, 1897, 1900, 1903

N. *Shan-hsi Provincial Examinations* 山西鄉試錄 等: 26 種 records
1702, 1708, 1711, 1729, 1735, 1741, 1744, 1760, 1762, 1794, 1795, 1807, 1808, 1816, 1818, 1819, 1831, 1840, 1849, 1851, 1862, 1885, 1893, 1894, 1900, 1903

O. *Hu-kuang and Hu-pei Provincial Examinations* 湖廣湖北鄉試錄 等: 9 種 records
1684, 1690, 1702, 1756 (H-P), 1762 (H-P), 1765 (H-P), 1768 (H-P), 1795 (H-P), 1807 (H-P)

P. *Hu-nan Provincial Examinations* 湖南鄉試錄 等: 26 種 records
1738, 1746, 1747, 1753, 1762, 1767, 1777, 1795, 1788, 1807, 1813, 1816, 1819, 1822, 1825, 1831, 1832, 1839, 1851, 1858, 1862, 1882, 1885, 1893, 1894, 1903

Q. *Hu-pei Provincial Examinations* 湖北鄉試錄 等: 12 種 records
1759, 1831, 1849, 1851, 1858, 1873, 1876, 1882, 1885, 1891, 1893, 1897

R. *Kan-su Provincial Examinations* 甘肅鄉試錄 等: 6 種 records
1882, 1885, 1893, 1894, 1900–1901, 1903

(5) *Court Examinations* 清代朝考等: 25 種 records
1852, 1853, 1856, 1858, 1859, 1860, 1862, 1863, 1864, 1865, 1867, 1868, 1870, 1871, 1873, 1874, 1875, 1876, 1877, 1879, 1880, 1883, 1889, 1890, 1909
See also:

Li-k'o ch'ao-yuan chüan 歷科朝院卷 (Court examination papers from scheduled civil examinations). 1868–1886 *chin-shih* court examination papers.

(6) *Special Tribute Examinations* 清代拔貢等: 10 種 records
Usually once every 12 years after 1742; once every six years before that.
1789, 1801, 1813, 1837, 1849, 1870, 1873, 1881, 1885, 1909
See also:

An-hui hsuan-pa-kung chüan 安徽選拔貢卷 (An-hui tribute examination papers). 1909.

Kuo-ch'ao Yü-yang k'o-ming-lu 國朝虞陽科名錄, tribute *pa-kung* 拔貢 rolls, 1644–1790.

*Pa-hsien tang-an wen-wei tzu-liao* 巴縣檔案文衛資料 (Pa-hsien Archives, Education and Health Section), late-Ch'ing *pa-kung* 拔貢 materials.

(7) *Local County Licensing and Prefectural Qualifying Examinations* 清代歲科考 等: 12 種 records

1656, 1708, 1712, 1843, 1844, 1867, 1875, 1888, 1891, 1902, 1904, 1905 See also:

*Ch'ang-hsing hsien-hsueh wen-tu* 長興縣學文牘 (Local civil examinations in the Ch'ang-hsing county school). Compiled by Sun Te-tsu. Shan-yin, 1890 edition.

*Che-chiang k'ao-chüan* 浙江考卷 (Che-chiang county and prefecture civil examination essays), emended by education commissioner Juan Yuan 阮元. Tsai-tao-t'ing 再到亭 edition, ca. 1795–98.

*Che-chiang shih-k'o* 浙江詩科 (Che-chiang poetry examinations), emended by education commissioner Juan Yuan 阮元. Tsai-tao-t'ing edition.

*Che-shih chieh-ching lu* 浙士解經錄 (Record of explications of the classics by Che-chiang literati), emended by education commissioner Juan Yuan 阮元. Tsai-tao-t'ing edition.

*Chiang-hsi shih-tu* 江西試牘 (Local civil examinations from Chiang-hsi province), compiled by Lung Chan-lin 龍湛霖. Ca. 1891 edition.

*Ch'ing li-ch'ao hsiu-ts'ai lu* 清歷朝秀才錄 (Record of local licentiates [in Su-chou 蘇州] during Ch'ing reign periods). 1645–1905 local examinations. Late Ch'ing manuscript.

*Hsi-Chin k'o-ti k'ao* 錫金科第考 (Examination rolls in Wu-hsi and Ch'in-k'uei). 1646–1903 local examinations. Ca. 1910.

*Hsiao-shih i-wen-lu* 小試異問錄 (Recording unusual matters heard in the local examination grounds). Ch'ien-t'ang, 1873 edition.

*Kuang-tung chiao-shih lu* 廣東校士錄 (Record of Kung-tung literati). Kuang-tung local examinations. 1904.

*Kuo-ch'ao Hai-ning chü-kung piao* 國朝海寧舉貢表 (Tables of provincial and local degree-holders in Ning-po). Late Ch'ing manuscript.

*Kuo-ch'ao Hang-chün hsiu-ts'ai lu* 國朝杭郡秀才錄 (Record of licentiates in Hang-chou prefecture). 1772–1899 local records. Late Ch'ing manuscript.

*Kuo-ch'ao Yü-yang k'o-ming-lu* 國朝虞陽科名錄. Local *sheng-yuan* 生員 rolls, 1645–1850.

*Pa-hsien tang-an chiao-wei tzu-liao* 巴縣檔案教衛資料 (Pa-hsien Archives, Education and Health Section). Late-Ch'ing local examination materials for Pa-hsien county.

*P'i-ling k'o-ti k'ao* 毗陵科第考 (Study of those from Ch'ang-chou 常州 prefecture on examination rosters), compiled by Chao Hsi-hung, Chuang Chu 莊柱, and others. 1868 edition.

*Shen-Kan hsueh-lu* 陝甘學錄 (Record of examination studies in Shen-hsi and Kan-su). Shensi-Kansu local examinations. Ch'ing Tao-kuang unpaginated edition, ca. 1820–50.

*Su-chou ch'ang-yuan-wu san-i k'o-ti p'u* 蘇州長元吳三邑科第譜 (Records of examination rosters in the three cities of Su-chou: Ch'ang-chou, Yuan-ho, and Wu-hsien), compiled by Lu Mao-hsiu 陸懋修 et al. 1645–1904 civil and military examinations. 1906 edition.

*Sung-chiang fu-shu li-k'o ts'ai-ch'in lu* 松江府屬歷科采芹錄, 1645–1904 Sung-chiang local examinations. Shanghai: Kuo-kuang Press photolithograph, 1939.

*Tung san-sheng shih-tu* 東三省試牘 (Local civil examinations from the eastern three provinces), compiled by Wang Chia-pi. Ca. 1879 edition.

*T'ung-Hsiang t'i-ming-lu* 通庠題名錄 (Record of civil service graduates in T'ung-chou 通州 and Ching-hsiang), compiled by Ku Chin-nan 顧金楠. Local *sheng-yuan* 生員 rolls, 1645–1906. 1931 edition.

*Wu-chiang hsien-hsueh ts'e* 吳江縣學冊 (Wu-chiang county school papers), 1645–1794 examinations. N.d.

*Wu-hsing k'o-ti piao* 吳興科第表 (Table of examination rosters in Wu-hsing). Local examination rolls 1646–1873. Ca. 1872–73.

*Yueh-yu ts'ai-feng lu* 越輶采風錄 (Selection of local civil examinations in Yueh-yu), compiled by Ch'ü Hung-chi 瞿鴻禨. Che-chiang local examinations. 1888 edition.

(8) *Fan-i Translation Examinations* 清代翻譯考卷等: 23 種 records
A. *Provincial Translation Examinations: Fan-i hsiang-shih* 翻譯鄉試
1816, 1818, 1832, 1843 (2), 1858, 1859, 1861, 1891, 1893, 1894, 1897
B. *Metropolitan Translation Examinations: Fan-i hui-shih-lu* 翻譯會試錄
1739, 1809, 1811, 1832, 1856, 1883, 1892, 1894, 1895, 1898
C. *Russian Language Examinations:* 俄羅斯文館試卷
1861, others with no dates
D. *Muslim Language Examinations:* 回回館試卷
No dates

APPENDIX TWO

# Civil Examination Primary Sources in the Mormon Genealogical Library

Compiled with the help of Cong Xiaoping and Sam Gilbert

Microfilms of civil examination reports from the *Ti-i li-shih tang-an-kuan* 第一歷史檔案 (No. 1 Historical Archives) in Peking:

I. HUI-SHIH LU 會試錄 (RECORDS OF METROPOLITAN EXAMINATIONS) [1208751–753]

(Reel: 751)

1647, 1682, 1685, 1694, 1703, 1737, 1739, 1742, 1748, 1751, 1752, 1754, 1766, 1793, 1811, 1823, 1832, 1847, 1852, 1859, 1860, 1862, 1886, 1890, 1892, 1898, 1901, 1902, 1904.

II. TENG-K'O LU 登科錄 (RECORDS OF PALACE EXAMINATIONS)

(Reel: 752)

1673, 1700, 1706, 1712, 1713, 1718, 1730, 1739, 1748, 1751, 1752, 1757, 1760, 1761, 1780, 1801, 1805, 1819, 1820, 1823, 1829, 1835, 1836, 1841, 1852, 1859.

(Reel: 753)

1892, 1894, 1895, 1898

III. CHIN-PANG 金榜 (CHIN-SHIH 進士 rolls) [1357550–551]

(Reel: 550)

1667, 1673, 1676, 1703, 1712, 1718, 1724, 1727, 1736, 1737, 1739, 1742, 1745, 1748, 1752, 1754, 1757, 1760, 1763, 1766, 1769, 1771, 1772, 1775, 1778, 1780, 1784, 1787, 1789, 1790, 1796, 1799, 1801, 1805, 1809, 1817, 1820, 1822, 1826, 1832, 1835, 1838, 1841, 1845, 1847, 1852, 1856, 1876, 1877, 1880, 1883, 1886, 1890, 1892, 1894, 1895

IV. WEN-HSIANG-SHIH LU 文鄉試錄 (PROVINCIAL EXAMINATIONS) [1357533–549]

1. *Che-chiang hsiang-shih t'i-ming-lu* 浙江鄉試題名錄 (Che-chiang provincial examinations)

(Reel: 543)

1699, 1702, 1705, 1711, 1723, 1735, 1747, 1750, 1759, 1768, 1770, 1771, 1807, 1813, 1816, 1831, 1834, 1835, 1837, 1839, 1840, 1844, 1846, 1849, 1851, 1852

641

(Reel: 544)
1855, 1858, 1893, 1894, 1897

2. *Chiang-hsi hsiang-shih t'i-ming-lu* 江西鄉試題名錄 (Chiang-hsi provincial examinations)

(Reel: 534)
1894, 1897
(Reel: 546)
1672, 1696, 1702, 1708, 1724, 1735, 1736, 1741, 1750
(Reel: 547)
1756, 1759, 1762, 1768, 1788, 1807, 1808, 1813, 1822, 1831, 1851, 1862, 1885, 1893, 1903

3. *Chiang-nan hsiang-shih t'i-ming-lu* 江南鄉試題名錄 (Chiang-nan provincial examinations)

(Reel: 534)
1672, 1696, 1714, 1735, 1738, 1750, 1770, 1807, 1810, 1813, 1816, 1831, 1832, 1835, 1849, 1852, 1859, 1893, 1894, 1897
(Reel: 542)
1672, 1687, 1690, 1702, 1711, 1729, 1738, 1741, 1744, 1747, 1753, 1756, 1759, 1760, 1807, 1813, 1816, 1822, 1831, 1843, 1849, 1851, 1864, 1885, 1893, 1894, 1897

4. *Fu-chien hsiang-shih t'i-ming-lu* 福建鄉試題名錄 (Fu-chien provincial examinations)

(Reel: 541)
1684, 1690, 1708, 1711, 1741, 1752, 1755, 1758, 1765, 1798, 1807, 1822, 1831, 1849, 1851
(Reel: 542)
1855, 1885, 1893, 1897, 1902

5. *Ho-nan hsiang-shih t'i-ming-lu* 河南鄉試題名錄 (Ho-nan provincial examinations)

(Reel: 544)
1705, 1723, 1725, 1738, 1741, 1760, 1795, 1798, 1807, 1808, 1810, 1813
(Reel: 545)
1819, 1822, 1831, 1849, 1851, 1858, damaged, 1875, 1891, 1893, 1894, 1897, 1902

6. *Hu-kuang hsiang-shih t'i-ming-lu* 湖廣鄉試題名錄 (Hu-kuang provincial examinations)

(Reel: 534)
1684, 1690
(Reel: 547)
1702

7. *Hu-nan hsiang-shih t'i-ming-lu* 湖南鄉試題名錄 (Hu-nan provincial examinations)

(Reel: 545)
1738, 1747
(Reel: 546)
1788, 1807, 1813, 1816, 1819, 1822, 1825, 1831, 1832, 1839, 1851, 1858, 1862, 1882, 1885, 1893, 1894, 1903

8. *Hu-kuang Hu-pei hsiang-shih t'i-ming-lu* 湖廣湖北鄉試題名錄 (Hu-kuang and Hu-pei provincial examinations)

(Reel: 546)
1756, 1762, 1765, 1768, 1795, 1807, 1831

9. *Hu-pei hsiang-shih t'i-ming-lu* 湖北鄉試題名錄 (Hu-pei provincial examinations)

(Reel: 546)
1759, 1847, 1858, 1873, 1882, 1885, 1891, 1893

10. *Kan-su hsiang-shih t'i-ming-lu* 甘肅鄉試題名錄 (Kan-su provincial examinations)

(Reel: 534)
1882, 1893, 1894
(Reel: 546)
1885, 1893, 1894

11. *Kuang-tung hsiang-shih t'i-ming-lu* 廣東鄉試題名錄 (Kuang-tung provincial examinations)

(Reel: 534)
1735, 1760, 1762, 1765, 1770, 1807, 1808, 1810, 1816, 1818, 1819, 1825, 1831, 1832, 1844, 1849, 1893, 1894
(Reel: 544)
1651, 1699, 1702, 1705, 1737, 1741, 1747, 1759, 1760, 1762, 1768, 1770, 1795, 1807, 1808, 1816, 1818, 1822, 1825, 1831, 1851, 1875, 1894, 1897

12. *Kuang-hsi hsiang-shih t'i-ming-lu* 廣西鄉試題名錄 (Kuang-hsi provincial examinations)

(Reel: 534)
1738, 1741, 1747, 1753, 1779, 1807, 1808, 1810, 1819, 1831, 1832, 1839, 1856, 1861, 1893, 1894
(Reel: 545)
1701, 1723, 1724, 1735, 1747, 1759, 1760, 1768, 1770, 1771, 1783, 1795, 1804, 1808, 1810, 1813, 1816, 1818, 1819, 1822, 1831, 1843, 1844, 1846, 1849, 1861, 1862, 1864, 1867, 1870, 1893, 1897

13. *Kuei-chou hsiang-shih t'i-ming-lu* 貴州鄉試題名錄 (Kuei-chou provincial examinations)

(Reel: 534)
1699, 1759, 1807, 1811, 1813, 1818, 1819, 1828, 1832, 1835, 1846, 1893
(Reel: 548)
1693, 1699, 1705, 1711, 1736, 1741, 1750, 1759, 1760, 1762, 1771, 1807, 1813, 1818, 1822, 1831, 1840, 1851, 1885, 1893
(Reel: 549)
1894, 1897, 1903

14. *Shan-tung hsiang-shih t'i-ming-lu* 山東鄉試題名錄 (Shan-tung provincial examinations)

(Reel: 547)
1651, 1672, 1687, 1702, 1711, 1713
(Reel: 548)
1724, 1738, 1747, 1753, 1759, 1762, 1768, 1795, 1807, 1810, 1819, 1839, 1851, 1855, 1858, 1859, 1885, 1893, 1894, 1897
(Reel: 753)
1678, 1771, 1783, 1807, 1808, 1810, 1813, 1818, 1819, 1831, 1832, 1855, 1859, 1861, 1862, 1885, 1893, 1894

15. *Shan-hsi hsiang-shih t'i-ming-lu* 山西鄉試題名錄 (Shan-hsi provincial examinations)

(Reel: 547)
1702, 1708, 1711, 1729, 1744, 1760, 1795, 1807, 1808, 1819, 1831, 1840, 1849, 1851, 1885, 1893, 1894

16. *Shen-hsi hsiang-shih t'i-ming-lu* 陝西鄉試題名錄 (Shen-hsi provincial examinations)

(Reel: 542)
1645, 1672, 1684, 1687
(Reel: 543)
1744, 1750, 1760, 1765, 1807, 1822, 1825, 1831, 1834, 1851, 1861, 1885, 1893, 1894, 1897
(Reel: 753)
1690, 1741, 1756, 1759, 1788, 1795, 1800, 1825, 1831, 1843

17. *Shun-t'ien hsiang-shih t'i-ming-lu* 順天鄉試題名錄 (Shun-t'ien provincial examinations)

(Reel: 540)
1684, 1705, 1708, 1723, 1726, 1729, 1732, 1735, 1736, 1738, 1741, 1747, 1750, 1752, 1759, 1768, 1789, 1801, 1810, 1813, 1821, 1822, 1828, 1831, 1832, 1835, 1837, 1855, 1859, 1861, 1864, 1885, 1889, 1891, 1894

(Reel: 534)

1735, 1780, 1808, 1810, 1816, 1818, 1819, 1831, 1832, 1838, 1844, 1861, 1864

18. *Ssu-ch'uan hsiang-shih t'i-ming-lu* 四川鄉試題名錄 (Ssu-ch'uan provincial examinations)

(Reel: 539)

1684, 1687, 1690, 1699, 1702, 1705, 1708, 1711, 1713, 1729, 1732, 1735, 1736, 1738, 1741, 1744, 1747, 1750, 1752, 1753, 1756, 1759, 1760, 1768, 1770, 1771, 1807, 1816, 1821, 1822, 1831, 1835, 1844, 1849, 1851, 1855, 1870, 1875, 1885, 1888, 1893, 1897, 1903

(Reel: 753)

1696, 1699, 1736, 1738, 1741, 1747, 1759, 1760, 1770, 1786, 1800, 1810, 1816, 1825, 1832, 1834, 1846, 1855, 1859, 1885, 1893, 1894

19. *Yun-nan hsiang-shih t'i-ming-lu* 雲南鄉試題名錄 (Yun-nan provincial examinations)

(Reel: 534)

1735, 1738, 1747, 1760, 1762, 1768, 1770, 1807, 1810, 1813, 1816, 1819, 1864, 1851, 1893, 1894

(Reel: 541)

1672, 1684, 1687, 1699, 1705, 1711, 1729, 1735, 1736, 1747, 1750, 1756, 1759, 1762, 1807, 1810, 1813, 1831, 1851, 1855, 1893, 1894, 1897, 1903

V. FAN-I 翻譯 (TRANSLATION EXAMINATIONS)

1. *Fan-i hsiang-shih lu* 翻譯鄉試錄 (provincial translation examination records)

(Reel: 549)

1816, 1818, 1832, 1843 (2), 1849, 1858, 1859, 1861, 1891, 1893, 1894, 1897

2. *Fan-i hui-shih-lu* 翻譯會試錄 (metropolitan translation examination records)

(Reel: 751)

1832, 1856, 1883, 1892, 1894, 1895, 1898

# Tables

TABLE 1.1. Yuan *Chin-shih* 進士 Degrees by Year,
1315–1366

| *Year* | Chin-shih | *Year* | Chin-shih |
|--------|-----------|--------|-----------|
| 1315 | 56 | 1345 | 78 |
| 1318 | 50 | 1348 | 78 |
| 1321 | 64 | 1351 | 83 |
| 1324 | 84[a] | 1354 | 62 |
| 1327 | 85[a] | 1357 | 51 |
| 1330 | 97 | 1360 | 35 |
| 1333 | 100 | 1363 | 62 |
| 1342 | 78 | 1366 | 73 |
| Total: | | | 1,136 |

SOURCE: *Yuan chin-shih k'ao* 元進士考 (Study of Yuan *chin-shih*), compiled by Ch'ien Ta-hsin 錢大昕 (Ch'ing draft). See also Huang Kuang-liang 黃光亮, *Ch'ing-tai k'o-chü chih-tu chih yen-chiu* 清代科舉制度之研究 (Research on the Ch'ing dynasty civil examination system) (Taipei: Chia-hsin Cement Co. Cultural Foundation, 1976), pp. 60–61.

[a]Yang Shu-fan 楊樹藩, "Yuan-tai k'o-chü chih-tu" 元代科舉制度 (Yuan dynasty civil service system), in *Sung-shih yen-chiu chi* 宋史研究集 14 (1983): 208, gives 86 *chin-shih* for both 1324 and 1327, with a total of 1,139 *chin-shih* during the Yuan.

TABLE 1.2. Annual Number of *Chü-jen* and *Chin-shih* in the Sung, Chin, Yuan, and
Ming Dynasties

| Dynasty / Years | Chü-jen *per Year* | Chin-shih *per Year* | | |
|---|---|---|---|---|
| *Yuan* | | | | |
| 1315–33 | 116 | 30 | | |
| 1315–68 | — | 21 | | |
| 1280–1368 | — | 13 | | |
| *Ming* | | | | |
| 1368–98 | 100 | 31 | | |
| 1399–1401 | 167 | 37 | | |
| 1402–25 | 167 | 76 | | |
| 1388–1448 | 190 | 50 | | |
| 1451–1505 | 385 | 97 | | |
| 1508–1643 | 400 | 110 | | |
| | | | (Total *Chin-shih*) | |
| Total: Sung | — | 124[a] | (39,711) | = 36% |
| Total: Chin | — | 149 | (16,484) | = 15% |
| Total: Yuan | — | 13 | (1,136) | = 1% |
| Total: Ming | — | 89 | (24,594)[b] | = 23% |
| 1368–1450 | — | 44 | | |
| 1451–1644 | — | 109 | | |
| Total: Ch'ing | 416 | 100 | (26,747) | = 25% |
| Total: 960–1911 | | 114 | (108,672) | = 100% |

SOURCES: John Chaffee, *The Thorny Gates of Learning in Sung China* (Cambridge: Cambridge University Press, 1985; New edition, Albany: SUNY Press, 1995), pp. 132–33, gives 39,605 total *chin-shih* during the Sung dynasties and presents them by circuit and by overlapping reigns. On pp. 192–95 he presents the annual number of Sung *chin-shih* degrees, which totals 39,711 degrees. See also Wolfgang Franke, "Historical Writing during the Ming," in *The Cambridge History of China*. Volume 7, Part 1: *The Ming Dynasty, 1368–1644* (Cambridge: Cambridge University Press, 1988), p. 726; Ho Ping-ti, *The Ladder of Success in Imperial China* (New York: Columbia University Press, 1962), p. 189, and Chung-li Chang, *The Chinese Gentry: Studies on Their Role in Nineteenth-Century Chinese Society* (Seattle: University of Washington Press, 1955), pp. 157–59. Huang Kuang-liang 黃光亮, *Ch'ing-tai k'o-chü chih-tu chih yen-chiu* 清代科舉制度之研究 (Research on the Ch'ing dynasty civil examination system) (Taipei: Chia-hsin Cement Co. Cultural Foundation, 1976), also gives T'ang, Sung, Yuan, and Ming-Ch'ing *chin-shih* figures. He derives his Sung figures from the *Ku-chin t'u-shu chi-ch'eng* 古今圖書集成 (Synthesis of books and illustrations past and present) encyclopedia (1728 edition) *chüan* 71. I have calculated 42,852 total *chin-shih* from Huang's Sung reign figures (his own Sung totals do not match his reign figures). Of these, some 4,335 are facilitated degrees granted during the Li-tsung reign. Subtracting them yields 38,517 regular *chin-shih* degrees awarded during the Sung. Although neither Huang (except for the years between 1241–62) nor Chaffee includes facilitated degree-holders (*t'e-tsou-ming chin-shih* 特奏名進士) in their counts of Sung *chin-shih*, because the facilitated degree did not automatically carry official status with it, their figures for regular *chin-shih* are roughly comparable in aggregate and by reign.

[a]Tao Ching-shen estimates the Northern Sung average *chin-shih* per annum at 194 and that of the Southern Sung at 149. See Tao, "Political Recruitment in the Chin Dynasty," *Journal of the American Oriental Society* 94, 1 (January–March 1974): 28. John Chaffee, *The Thorny Gates of Learning in Sung China*, pp. 132–33, gives 39,605 total *chin-shih* during the Sung dynasties.

[b]Huang Kuang-liang, *Ch'ing-tai k'o-chü chih-tu chih yen-chiu*, pp. 72–81, gives 24,480 for the total number of Ming *chin-shih*. I have followed Ping-ti Ho's figures here.

TABLE 1.3. *Chin-shih* by Reign Period during the Sung Dynasties

| Ruler Title | Years | Duration in Years | No. of Exams | No. of Chin-shih Chaffee | (Huang) | Chin-shih by Year |
|---|---|---|---|---|---|---|
| T'ai-tsu | 960–75 | 15 | 15 | 188 | (173) | 13 |
| T'ai-tsung | 976–97 | 21 | 8 | 1,400 | (1,368) | 67 |
| Chen-tsung | 998–1022 | 24 | 12 | 1,651 | (1,675) | 69 |
| Jen-tsung | 1023–63 | 40 | 13 | 4,555 | (4,255)[a] | 114 |
| Ying-tsung | 1064–67 | 3 | 2 | 450 | (450) | 150 |
| Shen-tsung | 1068–85 | 17 | 6 | 2,395 | (2,395) | 141 |
| Che-tsung | 1086–1100 | 14 | 5 | 2,679 | (2,679) | 191 |
| Hui-tsung | 1101–1125 | 24 | 8 | 5,831 | (5,495) | 243 |
| Ch'in-tsung | 1126 | 1 | 0 | 0 | (0) | 0 |
| N. Sung | 960–1126 | 166 | 69 | 19,149 | (18,490) | 115 |
| Kao-tsung | 1127–62 | 35 | 11 | 3,246 | (3,697) | 93 |
| Hsiao-tsung | 1163–89 | 26 | 9 | 4,066 | (4,066) | 156 |
| Kuang-tsung | 1190–94 | 4 | 2 | 953 | (953) | 238 |
| Ning-tsung | 1195–1224 | 29 | 10 | 4,727 | (4,352) | 163 |
| Li-tsung | 1225–64 | 39 | 13 | 6,404 | (6,294)[b] | 164[b] |
| Tu-tsung | 1265–74 | 9 | 4 | 1,166 | (665)[c] | 129[c] |
| Kung-tsung | 1275 | 1 | 0 | 0 | (0) | 0 |
| Tuan-tsung | 1276–77 | 2 | 0 | 0 | (0) | 0 |
| Ti-ping | 1278–79 | 2 | 0 | 0 | (0) | 0 |
| S. Sung | 1127–1279 | 152 | 49 | 20,562 | (20,027) | 135 |
| Total | 960–1279 | 319 | 118 | 39,711 | (38,517) | 124 |

SOURCE: On the Sung, John Chaffee, *The Thorny Gates of Learning in Sung China* (Cambridge: Cambridge University Press, 1985; new edition, Albany: SUNY Press, 1995), pp. 132–33, gives 39,605 total *chin-shih* during the Sung dynasties and presents them by circuit and by overlapping reigns. On pp. 192–95 he presents the annual number of Sung *chin-shih* degrees, which totals 39,711 degrees. See also *Wen-hsien t'ung-k'ao* 文獻通考 (Comprehensive analysis of civil institutions), compiled by Ma Tuan-lin 馬端臨 in *Shih-t'ung* 十通 (Ten comprehensive encyclopedias) (Shanghai Commercial Press, 1936), 30.284; and Huang Kuang-liang 黃光亮, *Ch'ing-tai k'o-chü chih-tu chih yen-chiu* 清代科舉制度之研究 (Research on the Ch'ing dynasty civil examination system) (Taipei: Chia-hsin Cement Co. Cultural Foundation, 1976), pp. 41–51. Huang derives his Sung figures from the *Ku-chin t'u-shu chi-ch'eng* 古今圖書集成 (Synthesis of books and illustrations past and present) encyclopedia (1728 edition) *chüan* 71. I have calculated 42,852 total *chin-shih* from Huang's Sung reign figures (his own Sung totals do not match his reign figures). Of these, some 4,335 are facilitated degrees granted during the Li-tsung reign. Subtraction yields 38,517 regular *chin-shih* degrees awarded during the Sung. Although neither Huang (except for the years 1241–62)

TABLE 1.3 (*continued*)

nor Chaffee includes facilitated degree-holders (*t'e-tsou-ming chin-shih* 特奏名進士) in their counts of Sung *chin-shih*, because the facilitated degree did not automatically carry official status with it, their figures for regular *chin-shih* are roughly comparable in aggregate and by reign.

[a] *Sung-shih* 宋史 (History of the Sung dynasty), compiled by Toghto (T'o T'o) 脫脫 (1314–55) et al. (Taipei: Ting-wen Bookstore, 1980), 5/3616 (*chüan* 卷 155), gives 4,570 *chin-shih* during the Jen-tsung era.

[b] In the Li-tsung reign, there are no figures for the number of *chin-shih* in 1253.

[c] In the Tu-tsung reign, there are no figures for the number of *chin-shih* in 1265 or 1274. Assuming an additional 500 *chin-shih* for each of those years (there were 664 in 1268 and 502 in 1271), the annual average for the Tu-tsung reign was likely over 200 *chin-shih*. John Chaffee, *The Thorny Gates of Learning*, p. 133, estimates 500 each for the years 1253 and 1265.

TABLE 1.4. *Chin-shih* by Reign Period during the Yuan Dynasty

| Ruler Title | Years | Duration in Years | No. of Exams | No. of Chin-shih | Chin-shih by Year |
|---|---|---|---|---|---|
| Jen-tung | 1312–20 | 8 | 2 | 106 | 13 |
| Ying-tsung | 1321–23 | 2 | 1 | 64 | 32 |
| T'ai-ting | 1324–28 | 4 | 2 | 169 | 42 |
| Wen-tsung | 1328–32 | 4 | 1 | 97 | 24 |
| Ning-tsung | 1332–67 | 25 | 10 | 700 | 28 |
| Total | 1315–1368 | 53 | 16 | 1,136 | 21 |
| | 1280–1368 | 88 | 16 | 1,136 | 13 |

SOURCE: *Yuan chin-shih k'ao* 元進士考 (Study of Yuan *chin-shih*), compiled by Ch'ien Ta-hsin 錢大昕, Ch'ing draft. Cf. Huang Kuang-liang 黃光亮, *Ch'ing-tai k'o-chü chih-tu chih yen-chiu* 清代科舉制度之研究 (Research on the Ch'ing dynasty civil examination system) (Taipei: Chia-hsin Cement Co. Cultural Foundation, 1976), pp. 60–61.

TABLE 1.5. *Chin-shih* by Reign Period during the Ming Dynasty

| Reign Name | Reign Years | Duration in Years | No. of Exams | No. of Chin-shih | Chin-shih by Year |
|---|---|---|---|---|---|
| Hung-wu | 1368–99 | 31 | 6 | 933 | 30 |
| Chian-wen | 1399–1402 | 3 | 1 | 110 | 37 |
| Yung-lo | 1403–25 | 22 | 8 | 1,849 | 84 |
| Hung-hsi | 1425–26 | 1 | 0 | 0 | 0 |
| Hsuan-te | 1426–36 | 10 | 3 | 300 | 30 |
| Cheng-t'ung | 1436–50 | 14 | 5 | 650 | 46 |
| Ching-t'ai | 1450–57 | 7 | 2 | 549 | 78 |
| T'ien-shun | 1457–65 | 8 | 3 | 694 | 87 |
| Ch'eng-hua | 1465–88 | 23 | 8 | 2,398 | 104 |
| Hung-chih | 1488–1506 | 18 | 6 | 1,798 | 100 |
| Ch'eng-te | 1506–22 | 16 | 5 | 1,800 | 113 |
| Chia-ching | 1522–67 | 45 | 15 | 4,924 | 105 |
| Lung-ch'ing | 1567–73 | 6 | 2 | 799 | 133 |
| Wan-li | 1573–1620 | 47 | 16 | 5,082 | 108 |
| Kuang-tsung | 1620–21 | 1 | 0 | 0 | 0 |
| T'ien-ch'i | 1621–28 | 7 | 2 | 700 | 100 |
| Ch'ung-chen | 1628–45 | 17 | 6 | 1,950 | 115 |
| Early Ming | 1368–1450 | 82 | 23 | 3,636 | 44 |
| Later Ming | 1451–1644 | 193 | 65 | 20,958 | 109 |
| Total | 1368–1644 | 276 | 89[a] | 24,594 (24,536)[b] | 89 |

SOURCE: Huang Kuang-liang 黃光亮, *Ch'ing-tai k'o-chü chih-tu chih yen-chiu* 清代科舉制度之研究 (Research on the Ch'ing dynasty civil examination system) (Taipei: Chia-hsin Cement Co. Cultural Foundation, 1976), pp. 72–81. Cf. Ping-ti Ho, *The Ladder of Success in Imperial China* (New York: Columbia University Press, 1962), p. 189.

[a]There were two palace examinations in 1397.

[b]Revising Huang's *chin-shih* figures from supplementary data, we can increase his total to 24,536 *chin-shih* during the Ming dynasty. Ping-ti Ho gives 24,594.

TABLE 1.6. Establishment of Private Academies during the Sung
and Ming Dynasties

| Dynasty | No. of Academies | Years | Annual Index |
|---|---|---|---|
| N. Sung | 56 | 166 | .33 |
| (Pai) | (73)[a] | (166) | (.44) |
| S. Sung | 261 | 153 | 1.64 |
| (Pai) | (317)[a] | (153) | (2.07) |
| Undated Sung | 108 | — | — |
| (Pai) | (125)[a] | — | — |
| Total: Sung | 425 | 320 | 1.33 |
| (Pai) | (515)[a] | (320) | (1.61) |
| Yuan | 320 | 88 | 3.64 |
| (Pai) | (406)[a] | (88) | (4.61) |
| Ming | | | |
| 1370–1470 | 90 | 100 | .90 |
| 1470–1505 | 120 | 35 | 3.43 |
| 1506–1572 | 495 | 66 | 7.50 |
| 1573–1620 | 221 | 47 | 4.70 |
| Total: Ming | 926 | 250 | 3.70 |
| (Pai) | (1,962)[a] | (250) | (7.85) |
| Total: Ch'ing (Pai) | (4,365) | (267) | (16.35) |

NOTE: Figures not in parentheses are approximate and vary by source. See Linda Walton-Vargo, "Education, Social Change, and Neo-Confucianism in Sung-Yuan China: Academies and the Local Elite in Ming Prefecture (Ningpo)" (University of Pennsylvania, Ph.D. diss., History, 1978), pp. 244–45, John Chaffee, *The Thorny Gates of Learning in Sung China* (Cambridge: Cambridge University Press, 1985), p. 89; and John Meskill, *Academies in Ming China: A Historical Essay* (Tucson: University of Arizona Press, 1982), pp. 28, 66. Cf. Chu Han-min 朱漢民, *Chung-kuo te shu-yuan* 中國的書院 (China's academies) (Taipei: Commercial Press, 1993); Ting Kang 丁鋼, *Shu-yuan yü Chung-kuo wen-hua* 書院與中國文化 (Academies and Chinese culture) (Shanghai: Education Press, 1992); Sheng Lang-hsi 盛朗西, *Chung-kuo shu-yuan chih-tu* 中國書院制度 (Chinese academy system) (Taipei: Hua-shih Press, 1977 reprint of 1934 edition).

[a]Figures in parentheses are from Pai Hsin-liang 白新良 in his *Chung-kuo ku-tai shu-yuan fa-chan shih* 中國古代書院發展史 (History of academy development in ancient China) (T'ien-chin: T'ien-chin University Press, 1995), pp. 271–73. Pai counts 73 new and old academies in the Northern Sung, 317 academy projects in the Southern Sung, 125 academies belonging to either the Northern or Southern Sung, 406 in Yuan, and 1,962 during the Ming. In addition, Pai counts 4,365 (one of Pai's tables gives 4,355 by mistake) academies during the Ch'ing dynasty.

TABLE 2.1. Provincial *Chü-jen* Quotas during the Ming Dynasty, 1370–1630

| Place | Year | | | | | | |
|---|---|---|---|---|---|---|---|
| | 1370 | 1384 | 1440 | 1453 | 1550 | 1600 | 1630 |
| Pei Chih-li | 40 | 50 | 80 | 135 | 135 | 135 | 140 |
| Nan Chih-li | 100 | 80 | 100 | 135 | 135 | 135 | 150 |
| Che-chiang | 40 | 50 | 60 | 90 | 90 | 90 | 98 |
| Chiang-hsi | 40 | 50 | 65 | 95 | 95 | 95 | 102 |
| Fu-chien | 40 | 45 | 60 | 90[a] | 90 | 90 | 95 |
| Ho-nan | 40 | 35 | 50 | 80 | 80 | 80 | 85 |
| Hu-kuang | 40 | 40 | 55 | 85 | 90 | 90 | 95 |
| Shan-tung | 40 | 30 | 45 | 75 | 75 | 75 | 82 |
| Shan-hsi | 40 | 30 | 40 | 65 | 65 | 65 | 70 |
| Shen-hsi | 40 | 30 | 40 | 65 | 65 | 65 | 71 |
| Kuang-tung | 25 | 40 | 50 | 75 | 75 | 75 | 80 |
| Kuang-hsi | 25 | 20 | 30 | 55 | 55 | 55 | 60 |
| Ssu-ch'uan | — | 35 | 45 | 70 | 70 | 70 | 75 |
| Yun-nan | — | 10 | 20 | 30 | 30 | 40 | 45 |
| Kuei-chou | — | — | — | — | 25 | 25 | 30 |
| Total | 510 | 545 | 740 | 1,055 | 1,175 | 1,185 | 1,278 |

[a]There were 137 actual *chü-jen* in 1453, despite the quota of 90 in Fu-chien.

TABLE 2.2. Ming Dynasty Ratio of Graduates to Candidates in Metropolitan
Examinations, 1371–1601, with Comparisons to T'ang and Sung Ratios

| Year | Candidates | Graduates | % |
|---|---|---|---|
| T'ang *chin-shih* | 1,000 | 10–20 | 1–2 |
| T'ang *ming-ching* | 2,000 | 20–40 | 1–2 |
| 977 | 5,200 | 500 | 9.6 |
| 1044 | South | | 100:1 ratios |
| | North | | 10:1 ratios |
| 1124 | 15,000 | 800 | 5.3 |
| 1371 | 200 | 120 | 60.0 |
| 1409 | 3,000 | 350 | 11.7 |
| 1439 | 1,000 | 100 | 10.0 |
| 1451 | 2,200 | 200 | 9.1 |
| 1475 | 4,000 | 300 | 7.5 |
| 1499 | 3,500 | 300 | 8.6 |
| 1520 | 3,600 | 350 | 9.7 |
| 1526 | 3,800 | 300 | 7.9 |
| 1549 | 4,500 | 320 | 7.1 |
| 1574 | 4,500 | 300 | 6.7 |
| 1601 | 4,700 | 300 | 6.4 |

SOURCES: *Wen-hsien t'ung-k'ao* 文獻通考 (Comprehensive analysis of civil institutions), compiled by Ma Tuan-lin 馬端臨, in *Shih-t'ung* 十通 (Ten comprehensive encyclopedias) (Shanghai
Commercial Press, 1936), 30.284; *Huang-Ming ch'eng-shih tien-yao lu* 皇明程世典要錄 (Digest of
records of metropolitan examinations during the Ming dynasty) (late Ming edition); *Hui-shih lu* 會
試錄, 1559, 1562, 1568.

TABLE 2.3. Ming Dynasty Frequency of Specialization (%) on One of the Five Classics in Civil Metropolitan Examinations, 1371–1637

| Classic | Year | | | | | | | | | |
|---|---|---|---|---|---|---|---|---|---|---|
| | 1371 | 1400 | 1415 | 1433 | 1466 | 1508 | 1544 | 1571 | 1601 | 1637 |
| Change | 18% | 17% | 16% | 22% | 19% | 25% | 28% | 31% | 30% | 30% |
| Documents | 20 | 32 | 36 | 30 | 27 | 23 | 21 | 19 | 21 | 21 |
| Poetry | 23 | 30 | 30 | 26 | 33 | 37 | 36 | 36 | 34 | 34 |
| Annals | 33 | 16 | 11 | 10 | 11 | 7 | 8 | 8 | 8 | 8 |
| Rites | 6 | 5 | 6 | 12 | 10 | 8 | 6 | 6 | 7 | 7 |
| Graduates | 120 | 110 | 350 | 99 | 353 | 350 | 320 | 399 | 300 | 300 |

SOURCE: *Hui-shih lu* 會試錄 (Record of the metropolitan civil examination), 1371, 1400, 1415, 1433, 1466, 1508, 1544, 1571, 1601, 1637.

TABLE 2.4. Ming Dynasty Frequency of Specialization (%) on One of the Five Classics in Ying-t'ien Prefecture, 1399–1630

| Classic | Year | | | | | | | | |
|---|---|---|---|---|---|---|---|---|---|
| | 1399 | 1450 | 1474 | 1501 | 1525 | 1549 | 1576 | 1600 | 1630 |
| Change | 10.5% | 20.5% | 17.8% | 20.7% | 29.6% | 30.3% | 32.6% | 33.6% | 33.3% |
| Documents | 30.6 | 28.5 | 25.9 | 24.4 | 20.7 | 18.5 | 20.7 | 21.4 | 22.0 |
| Poetry | 39.5 | 33.0 | 39.3 | 43.7 | 40.0 | 37.8 | 34.8 | 32.1 | 31.3 |
| Annals | 17.6 | 11.0 | 9.6 | 5.2 | 5.2 | 7.4 | 5.9 | 6.4 | 6.7 |
| Rites | 1.7 | 7.0 | 7.4 | 5.2 | 4.4 | 5.9 | 5.9 | 6.4 | 6.0 |

SOURCES: *Nan-kuo hsien-shu* 南國賢書 (Record of civil examination success in the Southern Capital Region). Compiled by Chang Ch'ao-jui 張朝瑞 (ca. 1600 and 1633 editions); *Chien-wen yuan-nien ching-wei hsiao-lu* 建文元年京闈小錄 (Small record of 1399 provincial examination in the capital) (unpaginated ms.); *Ying-t'ien-fu hsiang-shih lu* 應天府鄉試錄 (Record of the provincial civil examination administered in Ying-t'ien prefecture), 1630 edition.

NOTE: From 1370 to 1440 the quota for *chü-jen* in Ying-t'ien ranged from 80 to 100, with exceptions such as 200 in 1450; from 1474 until 1588 there were 135 graduates. In 1600 the quota increased to 140; in 1630 there were 150 graduates.

TABLE 2.5. Ratios (%) of Southern versus Northern
Graduates on Early Ming *Chin-shih*
Examinations

| Year | Graduates | South (%) | North (%) |
|---|---|---|---|
| 1371 | 120[c] | 89 (74.2) | 31 (25.8) |
| 1385 | 472 | 340 (72.0) | 132 (28.0) |
| 1388 | 95 | 80 (84.2) | 15 (15.8) |
| 1391 | 31 | 22 (71.0) | 9 (29.0) |
| 1394 | 100 | 78 (78.0) | 22 (22.0) |
| 1397[a] | 51 | 51 (100) | 0 (0.0) |
| 1397[a] | 61 | 0 (0.0) | 61 (100) |
| 1400 | 110 | 96 (87.3) | 14 (12.7) |
| 1404 | 470[d] | 427 (90.9) | 43 (9.1) |
| 1406 | 219 | 195 (89.0) | 24 (11.0) |
| 1411 | 84 | 79 (94.0) | 5 (6.0) |
| 1412 | 106 | 96 (90.1) | 10 (9.9) |
| 1415 | 351 | 311 (88.6) | 40 (11.4) |
| 1418 | 250 | 207 (82.8) | 43 (17.2) |
| 1421 | 201 | 170 (84.6) | 31 (15.4) |
| 1424 | 148 | 133 (89.9) | 15 (10.1) |
| 1427[b] | 101 | 70 (69.3) | 31 (30.7) |
| 1430 | 100 | 72 (72.0) | 28 (28.0) |
| 1433 | 99 | 67 (67.6) | 32 (33.4) |
| Total | 3,169 | 2,583 (81.5) | 586 (18.5) |

SOURCES: *Huang-Ming kung-chü k'ao, chüan* 2. Cf. Danjō, "Mindai
kakyo kaikaku," p. 514; and Ikoma Shō 生駒晶, "Minsho kakyo
gokakusha no shushin ni kan suru ichi kōsatsu" 明初科舉合格者
の出身に關する一考察 (A study of birthplaces of successful examination candidates during the early Ming), in *Yamane Yukio kyōju
taikyuō kinen Mindaishi ronshū jō* 山根幸夫教授退休紀念明代史論
叢上 (Tokyo: Kyoko shoin, 1990), p. 48. Danjō's and Ikoma's figures differ slightly.

[a] In 1397 two *chin-shih* examinations were held, one in the spring
and one in the summer.

[b] In 1425, quotas of 60% for the south and 40% for the north
were established. In the 1427 metropolitan examination, this policy
for quotas was amended to 55% for the south, 35% for the north,
and 10% for the central region. In the figures above, the totals for
the central region from 1427 to 1433 have been included in the
total of the southern region. For the *South*: Nan-chih-li, Che-
chiang, Chiang-hsi, Hu-kuang, Fu-chien, Kuang-tung, Kuang-hsi,
Ssu-ch'uan, Yun-nan, Kuei-chou; For the *North*: Pei-chih-li, Ho-
nan, Shan-tung, Shan-hsi, Shen-hsi. The *Central* region included:
Kuang-hsi, Kuei-chou, Yun-nan, Ssu-ch'uan, and portions of
Nan-chih-li.

[c] In 1371, one Korean received the *chin-shih* degree.

[d] Some sources give 472.

TABLE 2.6. Ranking of Prefectures Producing *Chü-jen* and *Chin-shih* during the Early and Mid-Ming Dynasty

| Prefecture | Total No. of Chü-jen | Total No. of Chin-shih |
|---|---|---|
| Chi-an, Chiang-hsi | 2,197 | 744 |
| Su-chou, Nan-chih-li | 1,273 | 574 |
| Shao-hsing, Che-chiang | 1,303 | 552 |
| Fu-chou, Fu-chien | 1,852 | 479 |
| Hsing-hua, Fu-chien | 1,096 | 349 |
| Nan-ch'ang, Chiang-hsi | 1,085 | 338 |
| Sung-chiang, Nan-chih-li | 642 | 234 |
| P'ing-yang, Shan-hsi | 1,260 | 169 |
| T'ai-yuan, Shan-hsi | 1,083 | 160 |

SOURCES: Chien Chin-sung 簡錦松, *Ming-tai wen-hsueh p'i-p'ing yen-chiu* 明代文學批評研究 (Research on Ming dynasty literary criticism) (Taipei: Student Bookstore, 1989), pp. 115–19. Chien's figures are generally based on sixteenth-century sources. Cf. Ping-ti Ho, *The Ladder of Success in Imperial China* (New York: Columbia University Press, 1962), pp. 246–47, for Ming and Ch'ing *chin-shih* figures.

TABLE 2.7. Ming-Ch'ing Provincial Quotas and Ch'ing *Chin-shih* Totals by Province

| Province | Quota % | Total No. of Chin-shih | % of Total Chin-shih |
|---|---|---|---|
| Nan-chih-li | 10.8 | 4,119 | 16.3 |
| Che-chiang | 8.0 | 2,798 | 11.1 |
| Pei-chih-li | 11.6 | 2,702 | 10.7 |
| Shan-tung | 5.9 | 2,250 | 8.9 |
| Hu-kuang | 8.0 | 1,954 | 7.7 |
| Chiang-hsi | 8.0 | 1,887 | 7.5 |
| Ho-nan | 6.3 | 1,691 | 6.7 |
| Shan-hsi | 5.4 | 1,438 | 5.6 |
| Fu-chien | 7.7 | 1,400 | 5.5 |
| Shen-hsi | 5.3 | 1,387 | 5.5 |
| Kuang-tung | 6.4 | 971 | 3.8 |
| Ssu-ch'uan | 5.7 | 798 | 3.2 |
| Kuang-hsi | 4.0 | 573 | 2.3 |
| Kuei-chou | 2.8 | 604 | 2.4 |
| Yun-nan | 4.0 | 696 | 2.7 |
| Total | 100 | 25,260[a] | 100 |

SOURCE: Lin Ch'i-hsien 林奇賢, "K'o-chü chih-tu te Ming-Ch'ing chih-shih fen-tzu" 科舉制度的明清知識分子 (Ming-Ch'ing intellectuals of the civil service examinations), *Chiao-yü yen-chiu-so chi-k'an* 教育研究所集刊 (National Taiwan Teachers College) 32 (1990): 52–53.

[a] Ping-ti Ho gives 26,747 total *chin-shih* in the Ch'ing.

TABLE 2.8. Regional Breakdown of Top Three Finishers on Civil Palace
Examinations and Top Finisher on Metropolitan Examinations
during the Ming and Ch'ing Dynasties

| Province | Ming (1370–1643) | | | | | Ch'ing (1646–1905) | | | | |
|---|---|---|---|---|---|---|---|---|---|---|
| | No. 1 | No. 2 | No. 3 | Metro | Total | No. 1 | No. 2 | No. 3 | Metro | Total |
| Nan-chih-li[a] | 23 | 19 | 20 | 23 | 85 | 58 | 34 | 46 | 49 | 187 |
| Che-chiang | 20 | 18 | 14 | 20 | 72 | 20 | 29 | 26 | 32 | 107 |
| Chiang-hsi | 16 | 11 | 22 | 17 | 66 | 3 | 10 | 5 | 2 | 20 |
| Fu-chien | 10 | 12 | 9 | 9 | 40 | 3 | 6 | 1 | 2 | 12 |
| Hu-kuang | 3 | 3 | 3 | 5 | 14 | 5 | 10 | 11 | 4 | 30 |
| Pei Chih-li | 3 | 4 | 2 | 4 | 13 | 3 | 2 | 3 | 11 | 19 |
| Kuang-tung | 3 | 2 | 2 | 4 | 11 | 3 | 4 | 4 | 2 | 13 |
| Ssu-ch'uan | 1 | 3 | 2 | 0 | 6 | 1 | 1 | 1 | 0 | 3 |
| Shen-hsi | 2 | 2 | 2 | 3 | 9 | 1 | 2 | 0 | 1 | 4 |
| Ho-nan | 2 | 3 | 2 | 0 | 7 | 1 | 2 | 2 | 1 | 6 |
| Shan-tung | 3 | 1 | 2 | 1 | 7 | 6 | 5 | 3 | 6 | 20 |
| Shan-hsi | 0 | 2 | 3 | 0 | 5 | 0 | 1 | 3 | 0 | 4 |
| Kuang-hsi | 0 | 1 | 1 | 0 | 2 | 4 | 1 | 0 | 1 | 6 |
| Yun-nan | 0 | 0 | 0 | 0 | 0 | 0 | 0 | 0 | 0 | 0 |
| Kuei-chou | 0 | 0 | 0 | 0 | 0 | 1 | 0 | 0 | 0 | 1 |

SOURCES: *Chuang-yuan t'u-k'ao* 狀元圖考 (Illustrated survey of *optimi* during the Ming dynasty),
compiled by Ku Tsu-hsun 顧祖訓 and Wu Ch'eng-en 吳承恩 (1607 edition), 6.30a–37b; Sung
Yuan-ch'iang 宋元強, *Ch'ing-ch'ao te chuang-yuan* 清朝的狀元 (*Optimi* of the Ch'ing dynasty)
(Ch'ang-ch'un: Chi-lin Wen-shih Press, 1992), p. 109. Sung gives different figures for the Ming
dynasty. See also Liu Chao-pin 劉兆璸, *Ch'ing-tai k'o-chü* 清代科舉 (Civil service examinations
during the Ch'ing dynasty) (Taipei: Tung-ta t'u-shu kung-ssu, 1979), pp. 89–96.

[a]Nan-chih-li during the Ch'ing was called "Chiang-*nan*," which included Chiang-su and An-
hui provinces. Ch'ing figures are given for them together, although they were separated in the
eighteenth century. Chiang-su province alone had 49 Ch'ing *optimi* and 40 metropolitan number
ones, for example.

TABLE 2.9. Ratios (%) of Early Ming Southern *Chin-shih*
Graduates from Chiang-hsi and Che-chiang

| Year | Graduates | Chiang-hsi (%) | Che-chiang (%) |
|------|-----------|----------------|----------------|
| 1371 | 120 | 27 (20.0) | 31 (26.0) |
| 1385 | 472 | 59 (12.5) | 97 (20.5) |
| 1388 | 95 | 18 (19.9) | 23 (24.2) |
| 1391 | 31 | 5 (16.1) | 8 (25.8) |
| 1394 | 100 | 14 (14.0) | 24 (24.0) |
| 1397 | 51 | 18 (35.3) | 17 (33.3) |
| 1397 | 61 | 0 (0.0) | 0 (0.0) |
| 1400 | 110 | 23 (20.9) | 20 (18.2) |
| 1404 | 470[a] | 112 (23.8) | 86 (18.3) |
| 1406 | 219 | 54 (24.7) | 41 (18.7) |
| 1411 | 84 | 27 (32.1) | 18 (21.4) |
| 1412 | 106 | 28 (26.4) | 16 (15.1) |
| 1415 | 351 | 94 (26.8) | 60 (17.1) |
| 1418 | 250 | 65 (26.0) | 38 (15.2) |
| 1421 | 201 | 73 (36.3) | 27 (13.4) |
| 1424 | 148 | 42 (28.4) | 24 (16.2) |
| 1427 | 101 | 31 (30.7) | 10 (9.9) |
| 1430 | 100 | 18 (18.0) | 21 (21.0) |
| 1433 | 99 | 22 (22.2) | 17 (17.2) |
| Total | 3,169 | 730 (23.0) | 578 (18.4) |

SOURCES: *Huang-Ming kung-chü k'ao, chüan* 2; and *Huang-Ming chin-shih teng-k'o k'ao, chüan* 3. Cf. Danjō, "Mindai kakyo kaikaku," p. 514; and Ikoma Shō, "Minsho kakyo gokakusha no shusshō ni kan suru ichi kōsatsu," p. 48.

[a]Some sources give 472.

TABLE 3.1. Flow Chart of Civil Examinations and Degrees during the Ming and Ch'ing Dynasties

*T'ung-sheng* 童生 Apprentice Tests
(Pre-school apprentice students educated at home)
↓
County, Department, and Prefectural Licensing Examinations, (*T'ung-shih* 童試)
(*Hsien-k'ao* 縣考, *Chou-k'ao* 州考, *Fu-k'ao* 府考, and *Yuan-k'ao* 院考)
↓
*Sheng-yuan* 生員 (*Hsiu-ts'ai* 秀才)
(Licentiate = county/prefecture/town school student)
(Includes biennial local exams for renewal of status, *Sui-shih* 歲試 or *Sui-k'ao* 歲考)
↓
Triennial Qualifying Examination, *K'o-shih* 科試 or *K'o-k'ao* 科考
↓

| *Kung-sheng* 貢生 Tribute Student: → | ↓ ← *Chien-sheng* 監生 State Student: |
|---|---|
| *Sui-kung* 歲貢 → | ← *Li-chien* 例監 |
| (Annual tribute student) | (State student by purchase) |
| *Pa-kung* 拔貢 → | ← *Tseng-chien* 增監 |
| (Special exam student) | (2nd class purchase) |
| *En-kung* 恩貢 → | ← *Fu-chien* 附監 |
| (Grace student) | (3rd class purchase) |
| *Yu-kung* 優貢 → | ← *Yu-chien* 優監 |
| (Senior tribute student) | (Senior licentiate) |
| *Fu-kung* 副貢 → | ← *Yin-chien* 蔭監 |
| (2nd class *Chü-jen* list; 副榜) | (Student by inheritance) |
| *Fu-sheng* 附生 and *lin-sheng* 廩生 → | ← *En-chien* 恩監 |
| (Supplementary students and stipendiaries) | (Grace student) |
| | ← *Pa-kung sheng* 拔貢生 (Special test) |

↓
Triennial Provincial Examinations in fall, *Chih-sheng hsiang-shih* 直省鄉試
↓
*Chü-jen* 舉人 (Raised candidate degree; also called *Kung-shih* 貢士 in Ming)
(No. 1 in each province = *Chieh-yuan* 解元)
↓
Triennial Metropolitan examination in spring, *Hui-shih* 會試
(No. 1 = *Hui-yuan* 會元)
↓
*Kung-shih* 貢士 (Tribute literatus status; Ch'ing term for "all but palace exam")
↓
Palace examination 殿試
↓
*Chin-shih* 進士 (literatus presented to emperor for appointment)
↓
*Chuang-yuan* 狀元 (*Optimus*)
*T'an-hua* 探花 → ↓ ← *Pang-yen* 榜眼
(*Tertius*) (*Secundus*)
↓
Court Placement Examination for Hanlin Academy 朝考 (after 1723)
↓
Palace (內府), capital (六部), provincial (省), or local (府縣州) appointment by rank

TABLE 3.2. Local Civil Licentiate Quotas in T'ung-chou 通州 and Ching-hsiang 靜庠, Chiang-su, 1645–95

| Year | Type | Licentiates in T'ung-chou | Licentiates in Ching-hsiang |
|---|---|---|---|
| 1645 | 科 *K'o-k'ao* | 27 | 2 |
| 1646 | 歲 *Sui-k'ao* | 28 | 3 |
| 1648 | 科 *K'o-k'ao* | 28 | 1 |
| 1649 | 歲 *Sui-k'ao* | 26 | 2 |
| 1650 | 科 *K'o-k'ao* | 29 | 8 |
| 1651 | 歲 *Sui-k'ao* | 28 | 6 |
| 1654 | 科 *K'o-k'ao* | 30 | 6 |
| 1655 | 歲 *Sui-k'ao* | 33 | 6 |
| 1656 | 科 *K'o-k'ao* | 31 | 6 |
| 1659 | 歲 *Sui-k'ao* | 10 | 7 (歲科 *Sui* and *K'o*) |
| 1661 | 歲科 *Sui* and *K'o* | 15 | |
| 1662 | 歲科 *Sui* and *K'o* | 15 | |
| 1668 | 歲科 *Sui* and *K'o* | 15 | |
| 1672 | 歲科 *Sui* and *K'o* | 15 | |
| 1674 | 歲科 *Sui* and *K'o* | 15 | |
| 1676 | 歲科 *Sui* and *K'o* | 15 | |
| 1677–78 | 歲科 *Sui* and *K'o* | 8 | |
| 1680–81 | 歲科 *Sui* and *K'o* | 19 | |
| 1682 | 歲 *Sui-k'ao* | 15 | |
| 1683 | 科 *K'o-k'ao* | 15 | |
| 1686–87 | 歲科 *Sui* and *K'o* | 30 | |
| 1689 | 歲 *Sui-k'ao* | 20 | |
| 1690 | 科 *K'o-k'ao* | 20 | |
| 1691 | 歲 *Sui-k'ao* | 20 | |
| 1692 | 科 *K'o-k'ao* | 20 | |
| 1695 | 歲 *Sui-k'ao* | 20 | |

SOURCES: *Tung-Hsiang t'i-ming lu* 通庠題名錄 (Record of civil service graduates in T'ung-chou 通州 and Ching-hsiang 靜庠), compiled by Ku Chin-nan 顧金楠 (1931 edition). Local *sheng-yuan* 生員 rolls, 1645–1906. See also *Shen-Kan hsueh-lu* 陝甘學錄 (Record of examination studies in Shen-hsi and Kan-su) (Tao-kuang edition) for a schedule of 1843 and 1844 local exams for *t'ung-sheng* 童生 and *sheng-yuan* 生員; and *Ssu-ch'uan sheng tang-an-kuan Pa-hsien tang-an*, "Wen-wei" 四川省檔案館巴縣檔案 ，"文衛" (Cultural and health materials in the Ssu-ch'uan Provincial Archives, Pa-hsien County Archives), Kuang-hsu 光緒 microfilm reel 55, document nos. 6207–6230 (1891–96), for confirmation.

NOTE: Before 1725, T'ung-chou and Ching-hsiang were combined.

TABLE 3.3. Ming Dynasty Ratio of Graduates to
Candidates in Ying-t'ien Prefecture
(Chiang-nan) Provincial Examinations

| Year | Candidates | Graduates | % |
|---|---|---|---|
| 1393 | 800 | 88 | 11.0 |
| 1396 | 1,000 | 300 | 30.0 |
| 1399 | 1,500 | 214 | 14.3 |
| 1453 | 1,900 | 205 | 10.8 |
| 1465 | 2,000 | 135 | 6.8 |
| 1477 | 2,500 | 135 | 5.4 |
| 1480 | 2,700 | 135 | 5.0 |
| 1492 | 2,300 | 135 | 5.9 |
| 1519 | 2,000 | 135 | 6.8 |
| 1549 | 4,500 | 135 | 3.0 |
| 1555 | 4,911 | 135 | 2.7 |
| 1561 | 5,400 | 135 | 2.5 |
| 1630 | 7,500 | 150 | 2.0 |
| 1684 | 10,000 | 73 | 0.7 |
| 1738 | 17,000 | 126 | 0.7 |
| 1744 | 13,000 | 126 | 0.9 |
| 1747 | 9,800 | 114 | 1.2 |
| 1864 | 16,000[a] | 114 | 0.7 |
| 1893 | 17,000 | 145 | 0.8 |

SOURCES: *Nan-kuo hsien-shu* 南國賢書 (Record of civil examination
success in the Southern Capital Region), compiled by Chang Ch'ao-jui
張朝瑞 (ca. 1600 and 1633 editions); *Ying-t'ien-fu hsiang-shih lu* 應天府鄉
試錄 (Record of the provincial civil examination administered in Ying-
t'ien prefecture), 1555, 1630 editions, and *Chiang-nan hsiang-shih lu* 江南鄉
試錄 (see Appendix 1).

[a] Cells, or examination cubicles.

TABLE 3.4. Ming-Ch'ing Dynasty Ratio of Graduates
to Candidates in Che-chiang Provincial
Examinations

| Year | Candidates | Graduates | % |
|------|-----------|-----------|------|
| 1468 | 1,800 | 90 | 5.0 |
| 1492 | 2,200 | 90 | 4.1 |
| 1516 | 2,200 | 90 | 4.1 |
| 1528 | 2,800 | 90 | 3.2 |
| 1546 | 3,000 | 90 | 3.0 |
| 1558 | 4,000 | 90 | 2.3 |
| 1582 | 2,700 | 90 | 3.3 |
| 1607 | 3,800 | 90 | 2.4 |
| 1859 | 12,000[a] | 94 | 0.8 |
| 1865 | 10,000 | 94 | 0.9 |
| 1870 | 11,000 | 112 | 1.0 |

SOURCES: *Che-chiang hsiang-shih lu* 浙江鄉試錄 (see Appendix 1);
*Huang-Ming Che-shih teng-k'o k'ao* 皇明浙士登科考 (Study of Che-chiang
examination graduates during the Ming dynasty) (ca. 1621 edition). Cf.
G. E. Moule, "Notes on the Provincial Examination of Chekeang of
1870, with a version of one of the essays," *Journal of the Royal Asiatic Society,
North-China Branch* 6 (1869–70): 129–37; and Chung-li Chang, *The Chinese
Gentry: Studies on Their Role in Nineteenth-Century Chinese Society* (Seattle:
University of Washington Press, 1955), pp. 167–70.

[a] Cells, or examination cubicles.

TABLE 3.5. Ming-Ch'ing Dynasty Ratio of Graduates to Candidates in Shun-t'ien and Shan-tung Provincial Examinations

| Place | Year | Candidates | Graduates | % |
|---|---|---|---|---|
| Shun-t'ien | 1531 | 1,900 | 135 | 7.1 |
| | 1558 | 3,500 | 135 | 3.9 |
| | 1609 | 4,600 | 140 | 3.0 |
| | 1654 | 6,000 | 276 | 4.6 |
| | 1657 | 6,000 | 206 | 3.4 |
| | 1660 | 4,000 | 105 | 2.6 |
| | 1748 | 10,000 cells | 229 | 2.3 |
| | 1874 | 13,000 | 229 | 1.8 |
| Shan-tung | 1465 | 1,000 | 75 | 7.5 |
| | 1504 | 1,400 | 75 | 5.4 |
| | 1585 | 2,000 | 75 | 3.8 |
| | 1747 | 4,000 | 69 | 1.7 |
| | 1759 | 4,800 | 69 | 1.4 |
| | 1873 | 12,900 | 69 | 0.5 |

SOURCES: *Shun-t'ien hsiang-shih lu* 順天鄉試錄; and *Shan-tung hsiang-shih lu* 山東鄉試錄 (see Appendix 1).

TABLE 3.6. Ming-Ch'ing Dynasty Ratio of Graduates to
Candidates in Other Provincial Examinations
(Alphabetically Arranged)

| Place | Year | Candidates | Graduates | % |
|-------|------|-----------|-----------|---|
| Chiang-hsi | 1456 | 2,000 | 65 | 3.3 |
| | 1534 | 3,000 | 95 | 3.2 |
| | 1558 | 4,300 | 95 | 2.2 |
| | 1571 | 4,000 | 95 | 2.4 |
| | 1609 | 4,400 | 95 | 2.2 |
| | 1627 | 5,300 | 102 | 1.9 |
| Fu-chien | 1552 | 3,000 | 90 | 3.0 |
| | 1753 | 7,400 | 85 | 1.1 |
| Ho-nan | 1579 | 2,400 | 80 | 3.3 |
| Hu-kuang | 1489 | 1,600 | 85 | 5.3 |
| Hu-nan | 1762 | 4,000 | 46 | 1.1 |
| | 1795 | 4,000 | 45 | 1.1 |
| Kuang-hsi | 1816 | 2,400 | 45 | 1.9 |
| | 1819 | 2,900 | 45 | 1.6 |
| | 1844 | 2,400 | 45 | 1.9 |
| | 1862 | 2,700 | 102 | 3.8 |
| | 1864 | 3,900 | 92 | 2.4 |
| | 1867 | 4,500 | 52 | 1.2 |
| Kuang-tung | 1558 | 2,700 | 75 | 2.8 |
| | 1729 | 9,000 | 78 | 0.9 |
| | 1794 | 4,600 | 71 | 1.5 |
| | 1813 | 4,600 | 71 | 1.5 |
| | 1822 | 7,600[a] | 71 | 0.9 |
| | 1844 | 7,500 | 72 | 1.0 |
| | 1846 | 8,000 | 72 | 0.9 |
| | 1861 | 8,154[a] | 72 | 0.9 |
| | 1863 | 8,654[a] | 72 | 0.8 |
| | 1867 | 11,708[a] | 109 | 0.9 |
| | 1870 | 9,000 | 72 | 0.8 |
| Kuei-chou | 1537 | 800 | 25 | 3.1 |
| Shan-hsi | 1531 | 1,400 | 65 | 4.6 |

TABLE 3.6 (*continued*)

| Place | Year | Candidates | Graduates | % |
|---|---|---|---|---|
| Shen-hsi | 1567 | 2,000 | 65 | 3.3 |
| | 1759 | 4,000 | 61 | 1.5 |
| | 1760 | 4,000 | 61 | 1.5 |
| | 1894 | 5,000 | 66 | 1.3 |
| Ssu-ch'uan | 1564 | 1,750 | 70 | 4.0 |
| | 1735 | 5,070 | 66 | 1.3 |
| | 1750 | 3,900 | 60 | 1.5 |
| | 1768 | 3,900 | 60 | 1.5 |
| | 1770 | 3,400 | 60 | 1.8 |
| | 1844 | 7,700 | 60 | 0.8 |
| | 1882 | 14,000 | 98 | 0.7 |
| | 1888 | 14,000 | 103 | 0.7 |
| Yun-Kuei | 1531 | 1,400 | 55 | 3.9 |
| Yun-nan | 1540 | 2,000 | 40 | 2.0 |
| | 1573 | 1,300 | 45 | 3.5 |
| | 1579 | 1,300 | 45 | 3.5 |
| | 1736 | 5,000 | 69 | 1.4 |

SOURCES:  Provincial *Hsiang-shih lu* 鄉試錄 (see Appendix 1). See also Chung-li Chang, *The Chinese Gentry: Studies on Their Role in Nineteenth-Century Chinese Society* (Seattle: University of Washington Press, 1955), pp. 167–70.

[a] Cells, or examination cubicles.

TABLE 3.7. Careers of Provincial *Chü-jen* Graduates from Shan-tung during the Ming Dynasty

| Year | No. of Chü-jen | Those Becoming Officials | | Those Becoming Chin-shih | |
|------|------|------|------|------|------|
| | | No. | % | No. | % |
| 1369 | 15 | 4 | 27 | 4 | 27 |
| 1384 | 45 | 8 | 18 | 16 | 36 |
| 1400 | 41 | 15 | 37 | 5 | 12 |
| 1403 | 61 | 16 | 26 | 12 | 20 |
| 1417 | 203 | 88 | 43 | 1 | 0.5 |
| 1426 | 42 | 12 | 29 | 6 | 14 |
| 1450 | 109 | 43 | 39 | 11 | 10 |
| 1474 | 71 | 35 | 49 | 14 | 20 |
| 1501 | 79 | 37 | 47 | 23 | 29 |
| 1525 | 73 | 31 | 42 | 19 | 26 |
| 1549 | 81 | 27 | 33 | 35 | 43 |
| 1576 | 78 | 24 | 31 | 30 | 38 |
| 1600 | 76 | 25 | 33 | 33 | 43 |
| 1624 | 87 | 15 | 17 | 33 | 38 |
| 1642 | 90 | 17 | 19 | 41 | 46 |

SOURCE: *Huang-Ming Shan-tung li-k'o hsiang-shih lu* 皇明山東歷科鄉試錄 (Record of Shan-tung provincial civil examinations during the Ming dynasty) (ca. 1642 edition).

TABLE 3.8. Official Positions of *Chü-jen* Graduates from Shan-tung during the
Ming Dynasty

| *Year* | Chü-jen | *Magistrate* | *Prefect* | *Subprefects* | *Judge* | *Total* | % |
|--------|---------|-----------|---------|------------|-------|-------|-----|
| 1369 | 15 | 1 | 0 | 1 | 0 | 2 | 13 |
| 1400 | 41 | 3 | 1 | 2 | 4 | 10 | 24 |
| 1426 | 42 | 4 | 0 | 2 | 0 | 6 | 14 |
| 1450 | 109 | 20 | 7 | 5 | 3 | 35 | 32 |
| 1474 | 71 | 24 | 5 | 1 | 3 | 33 | 46 |
| 1501 | 79 | 21 | 6 | 4 | 4 | 35 | 44 |
| 1525 | 73 | 13 | 6 | 1 | 5 | 25 | 34 |
| 1549 | 81 | 14 | 1 | 2 | 7 | 24 | 30 |
| 1576 | 78 | 11 | 4 ? | 5 | 3 | 23 | 29 |
| 1600 | 76 | 14 | 4 | 2 | 1 | 21 | 28 |
| 1624 | 87 | 8 | 1 | 2 | 1 | 12 | 14 |
| 1642 | 90 | 14 | 2 | 0 | 0 | 16 | 18 |
| Total | 842 | 147 | 37 | 27 | 31 | 242 | 29 |

SOURCE: *Huang-Ming Shan-tung li-k'o hsiang-shih lu* 皇明山東歷科鄉試錄 (Record of Shan-tung provincial civil examinations during the Ming dynasty) (ca. 1642 edition); *Kuo-ch'ao Shan-tung li-k'o hsiang-shih lu* 國朝山東歷科鄉試錄 (Record of Shan-tung provincial civil examinations during the Ch'ing dynasty) (ca. 1777 edition).

TABLE 3.9. Career Patterns of *Chin-shih* Graduates from Shan-tung during the Ming Dynasty

| Position | 1404 (N=17) | 1427 (N=6) | 1451 (N=6) | 1475 (N=21) | 1502 (N=19) | 1526 (N=30) | 1550 (N=24) | 1574 (N=23) | 1601 (N=35) | 1625 (N=36) | 1643 (N=24) |
|---|---|---|---|---|---|---|---|---|---|---|---|
| Minister | 1 | 0 | 1 | 1 | 1 | 1 | 2 | 0 | 5 | 2 | 2 |
| Governor-General | 0 | 0 | 0 | 0 | 0 | 0 | 0 | 0 | 1 | 0 | 0 |
| Governor | 0 | 0 | 0 | 0 | 0 | 2 | 1 | 2 | 3 | 3 | 0 |
| Censor | 3 | 1 | 3 | 3 | 4 | 2 | 5 | 4 | 2 | 6 | 6 |
| Director | 0 | 1 | 0 | 1 | 0 | 2 | 1 | 1 | 2 | 1 | 0 |
| Commissioner | 2 | 1 | 1 | 2 | 1 | 0 | 0 | 0 | 2 | 2 | 0 |
| Secretary | 0 | 0 | 0 | 0 | 0 | 0 | 1 | 2 | 2 | 5 | 1 |
| Circuit | 0 | 0 | 0 | 1 | 0 | 0 | 1 | 1 | 1 | 1 | 0 |
| Assistant | 0 | 1 | 0 | 0 | 0 | 0 | 0 | 4 | 2 | 3 | 1 |
| Magistrate | 2 | 0 | 0 | 1 | 0 | 3 | 0 | 4 | 4 | 7 | 1 |
| Prefect | 2 | 0 | 0 | 1 | 4 | 0 | 2 | 2 | 2 | 0 | 3 |
| Aide | 1 | 0 | 0 | 0 | 0 | 0 | 0 | 1 | 0 | 2 | 0 |
| Judge | 0 | 0 | 0 | 0 | 1 | 0 | 0 | 1 | 0 | 0 | 2 |
| Legal aide | 0 | 0 | 0 | 2 | 3 | 0 | 1 | 0 | 1 | 0 | 4 |
| Messenger | 1 | 1 | 0 | 0 | 0 | 0 | 0 | 0 | 0 | 0 | 0 |

SOURCE: *Huang-Ming Shan-tung li-k'o hui-shih lu* 皇明山東歷科會試錄 (Record of Shan-tung candidates in metropolitan civil examinations during the Ming dynasty) (ca. 1643 edition).

NOTE: In some cases the position for *chin-shih* is not given.

TABLE 3.10. Civil Examination Officials on the 1465 Shan-tung Provincial Examination

| Official Title | No. | Chü-jen 舉人 | Chiao-kuan 教官 | Chin-shih 進士 | Chien-sheng 監生 |
|---|---|---|---|---|---|
| Presiding Examiners 監臨官 | 1 | 1 | 0 | 0 | 0 |
| Education Commissioners 提調 | 2 | 0 | 0 | 2 | 0 |
| Proctors 監試官 | 2 | 0 | 0 | 2 | 0 |
| Examiners 考官 | 2 | 2 | 2 | 0 | 0 |
| Associate Examiners 同考 | 5 | 5 | 5 | 0 | 0 |
| Printers 印卷官 | 1 | 0 | 0 | 0 | 1 |
| Clerks 收掌試卷官 | 2 | 1 | 0 | 0 | 1 |
| Collectors 受卷官 | 2 | 1 | 0 | 0 | 1 |
| Sealers 彌封官 | 2 | 2 | 0 | 0 | 0 |
| Copyists 謄錄官 | 2 | 2 | 0 | 0 | 0 |
| Proofreaders 對讀官 | 2 | 0 | 0 | 0 | 2 |
| Guards 巡綽官 | 2 | 0 | 0 | 0 | 0 |
| Inspectors 搜檢官 | 4 | 0 | 0 | 0 | 0 |
| Suppliers 供給官 | 3 | 1 | 0 | 0 | 1 |
| Total | 32 | 15 | 7 | 4 | 6 |

SOURCE: *Shan-tung hsiang-shih lu* 山東鄉試錄, 1465: 7a–9b.

NOTE: The *chü-jen* degree-holder during the Ming dynasty was usually referred to as a *kung-shih* 貢士 (tribute literatus). In the Ch'ing, the term referred to metropolitan graduates who had not yet taken the palace examination. See Liang Chang-chü 梁章鉅, *Ch'eng-wei lu* 稱謂錄 (Record of terms) (1875 edition), 24.21b.

TABLE 3.11. Civil Examination Officials on the 1594 Shan-tung Provincial Examination

| Official Title | No. | Chü-jen 舉人 | Chiao-kuan 教官 | Chin-shih 進士 | Chien-sheng 監生 |
|---|---|---|---|---|---|
| Presiding Examiners 監臨官 | 1 | 0 | 0 | 1 | 0 |
| Education Commissioners 提調 | 2 | 0 | 0 | 2 | 0 |
| Proctors 監試官 | 2 | 0 | 0 | 2 | 0 |
| Examiners 考官 | 2 | 0 | 0 | 2 | 0 |
| Associate Examiners 同考 | 12 | 8 | 8 | 4 | 0 |
| Printers 印卷官 | 2 | 0 | 0 | 0 | 2 |
| Clerks 收掌試卷官 | 3 | 1 | 0 | 0 | 2 |
| Collectors 受卷官 | 3 | 0 | 0 | 0 | 3 |
| Sealers 彌封官 | 3 | 1 | 0 | 0 | 2 |
| Copyists 謄錄官 | 3 | 2 | 0 | 0 | 1 |
| Proofreaders 對讀官 | 3 | 1 | 0 | 0 | 2 |
| Guards 巡綽官 | 5 | 0 | 0 | 0 | 0 |
| Inspectors 搜檢官 | 5 | 0 | 0 | 0 | 0 |
| Suppliers 供給官 | 26 | 3 | 0 | 0 | 12 |
| Total | 72 | 16 | 8 | 11 | 24 |

SOURCE: *Shan-tung hsiang-shih lu* 山東鄉試錄, 1594: 1a–5b.
NOTE: Thirteen cases were not degreed.

TABLE 3.12. Examination Status of Chief and Associate Provincial Examiners during the Ming Dynasty, 1465–1639

| Year/Place | *Type of Official* | | | | |
|---|---|---|---|---|---|
| | Chief/Associate 主考／同考 | Hanlin 翰林 | Chin-shih 進士 | Chü-jen 舉人 | Education Official 儒學教官 |
| 1465 Shan-tung | 2/5 | 0 | 0 | 6 | 6 |
| 1489 山東 | 2/7 | 0 | 0 | 9 | 9 |
| 1504 山東 | 2/7 | 0 | 1 | 8 | 8 |
| 1519 山東 | 2/7 | 0 | 0 | 9 | 9 |
| 1552 山東 | 2/5 | 0 | 1 | 6 | 7 |
| 1585 山東 | 2/14 | 0 | 7 | 9 | 9 |
| 1594 山東 | 2/12 | 0 | 6 | 8 | 8 |
| 1468 Che-chiang | 2/6 | 0 | 0 | 8 | 8 |

TABLE 3.12 (*continued*)

| Year/Place | Chief/Associate 主考/同考 | Hanlin 翰林 | Chin-shih 進士 | Chü-jen 舉人 | Education Official 儒學教官 |
|---|---|---|---|---|---|
| 1507 浙江 | 2/6 | 0 | 0 | 8 | 8 |
| 1516 浙江 | 2/8 | 0 | 0 | 10 | 10 |
| 1525 浙江 | 2/7 | 0 | 0 | 7 | 9 |
| 1528 浙江 | 2/10 | 2 | 2 | 10 | 10 |
| 1549 浙江 | 2/8 | 0 | 0 | 10 | 10 |
| 1576 浙江 | 2/6 | 0 | 0 | 8 | 8 |
| 1582 浙江 | 2/5 | 0 | 0 | 7 | 7 |
| 1492 Ying-t'ien | 2/7 | 0 | 2 | 7 | 7 |
| 1501 應天 | 2/9 | 1 | 2 | 9 | 9 |
| 1522 應天 | 2/9 | 2 | 2 | 9 | 9 |
| 1540 應天 | 2/9 | 2 | 2 | 9 | 9 |
| 1549 應天 | 2/9 | 2 | 2 | 9 | 9 |
| 1555 應天 | 2/8 | 1 | 2 | 8 | 8 |
| 1558 Chiang-hsi | 2/9 | 0 | 0 | 11 | 11 |
| 1567 江西 | 2/10 | 0 | 0 | 12 | 12 |
| 1627 江西 | 2/15 | 1 | 17 | 0 | 0 |
| 1531 Shun-t'ien | 2/9 | 1 | 8 | 3 | 4 |
| 1537 順天 | 2/9 | 1 | 3 | 7 | 8 |
| 1600 順天 | 2/13 | 2 | 12 | 3 | 3 |
| 1609 順天 | 2/14 | 2 | 15 | 1 | 1 |
| 1567 Shen-hsi | 2/5 | 0 | 0 | 7 | 7 |
| 1639 陝西 | 2/12 | 0 | 11 | 3 | 3 |

SOURCES: *Che-chiang hsiang-shih lu* 浙江鄉試錄, 1468, 1507, 1516, 1525, 1528, 1549, 1576, 1582; *Chiang-hsi hsiang-shih lu* 江西鄉試錄, 1558, 1567, 1627; *Fu-chien hsiang-shih lu* 福建鄉試錄, 1552; *Henan hsiang-shih lu* 河南鄉試錄, 1579; *Hu-kuang hsiang-shih lu* 湖廣鄉試錄, 1489; *Kuang-tung hsiang-shih lu* 廣東鄉試錄, 1558; *Kuang-hsi hsiang-shih lu* 廣西鄉試錄, 1471; *Kuei-chou hsiang-shih lu* 貴州鄉試錄, 1537, 1573; *Shan-hsi hsiang-shih lu* 山西鄉試錄, 1531; *Shan-tung hsiang-shih lu* 山東鄉試錄, 1465, 1489, 1504, 1519, 1537, 1552, 1594; *Shen-hsi hsiang-shih lu* 陝西鄉試錄, 1567, 1639; *Shun-t'ien hsiang-shih lu* 順天鄉試錄, 1531, 1600, 1609; *Ssu-ch'uan hsiang-shih lu* 四川鄉試錄, 1564; *Ying-t'ien hsiang-shih lu* 應天鄉試錄, 1492, 1501, 1522, 1540, 1549, 1555; *Yun-kuei hsiang-shih lu* 雲貴鄉試錄, 1531; *Yun-nan hsiang-shih lu* 雲南鄉試錄, 1573, 1579.

NOTE: The *chü-jen* degree-holder during the Ming dynasty was usually referred to as a *kung-shih* 貢士 (tribute literatus). In the Ch'ing, the term referred to metropolitan graduates who had not yet taken the palace examination. See Liang Chang-chü 梁章鉅, *Ch'eng-wei lu* 稱謂錄 (Record of terms) (1875 edition), 24.21b.

Hanlin were usually also *chin-shih*. *Chü-jen* usually were *chiao-kuan*.

TABLE 3.13. Provincial Civil Examination Officials in Che-chiang during the Ming Dynasty

| Official Title | No. in Year | | | | Notes |
|---|---|---|---|---|---|
| | 1492 (2,200 candidates) | 1522 (2,800 candidates) | 1567 (3,000 candidates) | 1582 (2,700 candidates) | |
| Presiding Examiners | 1 | 1 | 1 | 1 | All chin-shih |
| Education Commissioners | 2 | 2 | 2 | 2 | All chin-shih |
| Proctors | 2 | 2 | 2 | 2 | All chin-shih |
| Examiners | 2 | 2 | 2 | 2 | Chü-jen in 1492–1522; chin-shih in 1567–82 |
| Associate Examiners | 8 | 8 | 6 | 7 | All chü-jen |
| Clerks | 2 | 2 | 6 | 9 | All chin-shih |
| Printers | 2 | 2 | 2 | 2 | Chü-jen, chien-sheng |
| Collectors | 3 | 5 | 6 | 9 | All chin-shih |
| Sealers | 3 | 5 | 8 | 10 | All chin-shih |
| Copyists | 3 | 5 | 9 | 11 | All chin-shih |
| Proofreaders | 3 | 5 | 9 | 11 | All chin-shih |
| Guards | 2 | 4 | 8 | 6 | Locals |
| Inspectors | 8 | 6 | 8 | 6 | Locals |
| Suppliers | 10 | 14 | 18 | 25 | Chü-jen, chien-sheng |
| Total | 51 | 63 | 87 | 103 | |
| Ratio (Candidates per Examiner) | 43 | 44 | 34 | 26 | |

TABLE 3.14. Examination Status of Chief and Associate Metropolitan Examiners during the Ming Dynasty

| Year | Chief/Associates 主考/同考 | Hanlin 翰林 | Chin-shih 進士 | Kung-shih 貢士 | Education Official 儒學教官 |
|---|---|---|---|---|---|
| 1371 | 2/4 | 0 | 0 | 0 | 0 |
| 1400 | 2/6 | 1 | 1 | 0 | 0 |
| 1415 | 2/8 | 2 | 9 | 0 | 0 |
| 1478 | 2/12 | 10 | 14 | 0 | 0 |
| 1499 | 2/14 | 10 | 16 | 0 | 0 |
| 1502 | 2/14 | 11 | 16 | 0 | 0 |
| 1541 | 2/17 | 13 | 19 | 0 | 0 |
| 1547 | 2/17 | ? | 19 | 0 | 0 |
| 1556 | 2/17 | 11 | 19 | 0 | 0 |
| 1559 | 2/17 | 15 | 19 | 0 | 0 |
| 1562 | 2/17 | 11 | 19 | 0 | 0 |
| 1568 | 2/17 | 12 | 19 | 0 | 0 |
| 1586 | 2/18 | 13 | 20 | 0 | 0 |
| 1598 | 2/18 | ? | 20 | 0 | 0 |
| 1601 | 2/18 | 14 | 20 | 0 | 0 |
| 1619 | 2/20 | 14 | 22 | 0 | 0 |
| 1622 | 2/20 | ? | 22 | 0 | 0 |

SOURCE: *Hui-shih lu* 會試錄. See Appendix 1.

NOTE: The *chü-jen* degree-holder during the Ming dynasty was usually referred to as a *kung-shih* 貢士 (tribute literatus). In the Ch'ing, the term referred to metropolitan graduates who had not yet taken the palace examination. See Liang Chang-chü 梁章鉅, *Ch'eng-wei lu* 稱謂錄 (Record of terms) (1875 edition), 24.21b.

Hanlin were usually also *chin-shih*.

TABLE 3.15. Metropolitan Civil Examination Officials during the Ming Dynasty

| Official Title | No. in Year | | | | | | Notes |
|---|---|---|---|---|---|---|---|
| | 1371 (200 candidates; 120 graduates) | 1400 (1,000 candidates; 110 graduates) | 1415 (3,000 candidates; 351 graduates) | 1523 (3,800 candidates; 400 graduates) | 1547 (4,300 candidates; 301 graduates) | 1598 (4,600 candidates; 300 graduates) | |
| Chief Administrator 知貢舉事 | 2 | 1 | 2 | 2 | 2 | 2 | Chih-shih after 1523 |
| Essay Officials 主文官 | 2 | — | — | — | — | — | None were chin-shih |
| Education Commissioners 提調官 | 3 | 1 | 2 | 2 | 2 | 2 | All chin-shih |
| Presiding Examiners 監試官 | 2 | 2 | 2 | 2 | 2 | 2 | Chin-shih after 1415 |
| Examiners 考試官 | 4 | 2 | 2 | 2 | 2 | 2 | Chin-shih after 1415 |
| Associate Examiners 同考官 | — | 6 | 8 | 17 (11 Hanlin) | 17 | 17 | Chin-shih after 1523 |
| Clerks 收掌試卷官 | 1 | 2 | 2 | 2 | 2 | 2 | Most were chin-shih |
| Printers 印卷官 | 2 | 1 | 1 | 2 | 2 | 2 | Chin-shih after 1415 |
| Collectors 受卷官 | 1 | 2 | 2 | 4 | 4 | 4 | Chin-shih 1400–15; chü-jen from 1523 |

| | 1371 | 1400 | 1415 | 1523 | 1547 | 1598 | |
|---|---|---|---|---|---|---|---|
| Sealers 彌封官 | 1 | 2 | 2 | 4 | 4 | 4 | *Chü-jen* from 1523 |
| Copyists 謄錄官 | 1 | 2 | 4 | 4 | 4 | 4 | *Chü-jen* from 1523 |
| Proofreaders 對讀官 | 2 | 5 | 8 | 4 | 4 | 4 | Locals and *chü-jen* 對讀官 from 1523 |
| Guards 巡綽官 | 1 | 2 | 4 | 6 | 6 | 6 | Locals |
| Inspectors 搜檢官 | 1 | 2 | — | — | — | — | Locals |
| Gatekeepers 監門官 | 2 | 2 | 6 | 0 | 0 | 0 | Locals |
| Suppliers 供給官 | 1 | 3 | 6 | 4 | 6 | 6 | Locals and *chü-jen* from 1523 |
| Woodblock carvers 掌行文字 | 9 | — | — | — | — | — | |
| Total | 35 | 35 | 51 | 55 | 57 | 57 | |
| Ratio (Candidates per Examiner) | 6 | 29 | 59 | 69 | 75 | 81 | |

SOURCE: *Hui-shih lu* 會試錄 (Records of the metropolitan civil examination), 1371, 1400, 1415, 1523, 1547, 1598.

TABLE 3.16. Palace Civil Examination Officials during the Ming Dynasty

| Official Title | No. in Year | | | | | Notes |
|---|---|---|---|---|---|---|
| | 1400 (110 graduates) | 1411 (84 graduates) | 1499 (300 graduates) | 1541 (300 graduates) | 1580 (300 graduates) | |
| Readers 讀卷官 | 10 | 8 | 15 | 16 | 13 | All *chin-shih* from 1499; some Hanlin from 1400 |
| Education Commission 提調官 | — | 2 | 3 | 2 | 3 | All *chin-shih* from 1499 |
| Presiding Examiners 監試官 | — | 2 | 2 | 2 | 2 | All *chin-shih* from 1499 |
| Collectors 受卷官 | 2 | 4 | 4 | 4 | 4 | Most are *chin-shih* |
| Sealers 彌封官 | 2 | 4 | 10 | 14 | 14 | Most are *chin-shih*; some are *chü-jen* |
| Clerks 掌卷官 | 2 | 3 | 5 | 4 | 6 | Most are *chin-shih*; some are Hanlin and *chü-jen* |
| Guards 巡綽官 | 2 | 4 | 9 | 12 | 9 | Locals |
| Administrators 知貢舉官 | 2 | — | — | — | — | |
| Printers 印卷官 | 1 | 2 | 4 | 4 | 3 | *Chin-shih* after 1499 |
| Suppliers 供給官 | 2 | 3 | 5 | 8 | 4 | *Chin-shih* and *chü-jen* |
| Total | 23 | 32 | 57 | 66 | 58 | |
| Ratio (Graduates per Examiner) | 4.8 | 2.6 | 5.3 | 4.5 | 5.2 | |

SOURCE: *Teng-k'o lu* 登科錄 (Records of the palace civil examination), 1400, 1411, 1499, 1541, 1580.

TABLE 3.17. Total Number of Fu-chien *Chü-jen* and *Chin-shih* by Prefecture, 1370–1634

| Prefecture | Chü-jen | Chin-shih | % Becoming Chin-shih |
|---|---|---|---|
| Fu-chou 福州 | 2,554 | 637 | 24.9 |
| Ch'üan-chou 泉州 | 1,961 | 558 | 28.5 |
| Hsing-hua 興化 | 1,860 | 522 | 28.1 |
| Chang-chou 漳州 | 1,055 | 320 | 30.3 |
| Chien-ning 建寧 | 558 | 138 | 24.7 |
| T'ing-chou 汀州 | 248 | 49 | 19.8 |
| Yen-p'ing 延平 | 247 | 38 | 15.4 |
| Shao-wu 邵武 | 177 | 32 | 18.1 |
| Fu-ning 福寧 | 148 | 33 | 22.3 |
| Total | 8,808 | 2,327 | 26.4 |

SOURCE: *Min-sheng hsien-shu* 閩省賢書 (Book about civil provincial examination worthies in Fu-chien province). Compiled by Shao Chieh-ch'un 邵捷春 (ca. 1636).

TABLE 3.18. *Chü-jen* Who Became *Chin-shih* from Fu-ch'eng 福城, Fu-chien, 1370–1546

| Year | Chin-shih | Year | Chin-shih | Year | Chin-shih |
|------|------|------|------|------|------|
| 1370 | 8 | 1384 | 8 | 1387 | 4 |
| 1390 | 0 | 1393 | 4 | 1396 | 1 |
| 1399 | 5 | 1403 | 10 | 1405 | 9 |
| 1408 | 1 | 1411 | 11 | 1414 | 13 |
| 1417 | 6 | 1420 | 6 | 1423 | 3 |
| 1426 | 6 | 1429 | 2 | 1432 | 0 |
| 1435 | 3 | 1438 | 3 | 1441 | 3 |
| 1444 | 1 | 1447 | 8 | 1450 | 10 |
| 1453 | 7 | 1456 | 2 | 1459 | 4 |
| 1462 | 5 | 1465 | 9 | 1468 | 8 |
| 1471 | 4 | 1474 | 7 | 1477 | 7 |
| 1480 | 9 | 1483 | 7 | 1486 | 4 |
| 1489 | 3 | 1492 | 5 | 1495 | 4 |
| 1498 | 1 | 1501 | 0 | 1504 | 7 |
| 1507 | 4 | 1510 | 8 | 1513 | 5 |
| 1516 | 10 | 1519 | 4 | 1522 | 12 |
| 1525 | 9 | 1528 | 5 | 1531 | 5 |
| 1534 | 15 | 1537 | 2 | 1540 | 4 |
| 1543 | 2 | 1546 | 3 | | |

Total: 306 *Chin-shih* 進士

Total per year: 1.74

SOURCE: *Fu-ch'eng hsiang-chin-shih t'i-ming chi* 福城鄉進士題名記 (Record of graduates of local, provincial, and palace examinations from Fu-ch'eng, Fu-chien) (ca. 1546 ms.).

TABLE 3.19. Profile of Civil Examination
Success in Fu-chien during the
Ming Dynasty, 1370–1636

| | |
|---|---|
| Hanlin members from Fu-chien | 92 |
| Fu-chou 福州 | 33 |
| Hsing-hua 興化 | 20 |
| Ch'üan-chou 泉州 | 11 |
| Chien-ning 建寧 | 12 |
| Chang-chou 漳州 | 7 |
| Metropolitan top three | 33 |
| 1391, 1406, 1412, 1415, 1592: | |
| two of top three from Fu-chien | |
| 1430: top three from Fu-chien | |
| No. 1 on metropolitan exam | 12 |
| Metropolitan top five | 53 |
| No. 1 on provincial exams | |
| Hsing-hua 興化 | 32 |
| Fu-chou 福州 | 23 |
| Ch'üan-chou 泉州 | 22 |
| Chang-chou 漳州 | 11 |
| Seven generations of success | 2 |
| Six generations of success | 4 |
| Five generations of success | 8 |
| Four generations of success | 13 |
| Five generations of *chin-shih* | 1 |
| Four generations of *chin-shih* | 2 |
| Three generations of *chin-shih* | 6 |
| Father-son *chin-shih* | 96 |
| Father-son no. 1 in Fu-chien | 1 |
| Grandfather-grandson *chin-shih* | 56 |
| Brothers *chin-shih* | 65 |
| Five brothers pass exams | 1 |
| Four brothers pass exams | 2 |
| Three brothers pass exams | 18 |
| Three generations no. 1 in Fu-chien | 1 |
| Youths 13–19 *sui* pass exams | 43 |
| Elderly 80–104 *sui* pass exams | 84 |

SOURCE: *Min-sheng hsien-shu* 閩省賢書 (Book about civil provincial examination worthies in Fu-chien province), compiled by Shao Chieh-ch'un 邵捷春 (ca. 1636).

TABLE 3.20. Ch'ing Dynasty Ratio of Graduates to Candidates
in Metropolitan Examinations, 1691–1850

| Year | Candidates | Graduates | % |
|---|---|---|---|
| 1691 | 2,500 | 156 | 6.2 |
| 1742 | 5,993 | 319 | 5.3 |
| 1761 | 5,059 | 217 | 4.3 |
| 1850 | 6,000 | 209 | 3.5 |

SOURCE: *Hui-shih lu* 會試錄, 1691, 1742, 1761.

TABLE 3.21. Late Ming and Early Ch'ing *Chü-jen* in Shan-tung Who Received
*Chin-shih* Degrees under Ch'ing Rule

| Year (No.) Chü-jen | Year Chin-shih | | | | | | | | |
|---|---|---|---|---|---|---|---|---|---|
| | 1646 | 1647 | 1649 | 1652 | 1655 | 1658 | 1659 | 1661 | 1664 |
| 1639 (85) | 13 | — | 3 | 0 | 2 | 0 | 0 | — | 1 |
| 1642 (90) | 14 | — | 6 | 5 | 4 | 1 | 1 | — | 0 |
| 1645 (95) | 50 | 2 | 8 | 4 | 2 | — | 1 | 2 | — |
| 1646 (96) | — | 10 | 19 | 7 | 7 | 2 | — | 2 | 1 |
| 1648 (95) | — | — | 24 | 12 | 5 | 5 | 9 | 5 | 2 |

SOURCE: *Huang-Ming Shan-tung li-k'o hsiang-shih lu* 皇明山東歷科鄉試錄 (Record of Shan-tung provincial civil examinations during the Ming dynasty) (ca. 1642 edition).

TABLE 3.22. Date of *Chin-shih* Degree for High Civil Examination Officials during the Early Ch'ing Dynasty

| | Chief/ Associate | Chief | Year of Chin-shih | Associate | Year of Chin-shih |
|---|---|---|---|---|---|
| 1645 (Shun-t'ien) | 2/? | 1 Shan-hsi | 1622 | n.a. | n.a. |
| | | 1 Chiang-hsi | 1643 | | |
| 1645 (Chiang-nan) | 2/? | 1 Hu-kuang | 1643 | n.a. | n.a. |
| | | 1 Chih-li | 1643 | | |
| 1646 (Metropolitan) | 4/20 | 2 Han banner | | 12 | 1643 |
| | | 1 Manchu | | 3 | 1622 |
| | | 1 Shun-t'ien | 1613 | 2 | 1628 |
| 1647 (Metropolitan) | 5/17 | 1 Manchu | | 11 | 1646 |
| | | 2 Han banner | | 2 | 1637 |
| | | 1 Shun-t'ien | 1613 | 4 | 1621–43 |
| | | 1 | 1634 Manchu (*chü-jen*) | | |
| | | 1 Ho-nan | 1625 | | |
| 1648 (Shan-tung) | 2/15 | 1 Chiang-nan | 1631 | 8 | 1646 |
| | | 1 Chih-li | 1643 | 7 | 1647 |
| 1649 (Metro) | 5/20[a] | 1 Manchu | | 1 | 1640 |
| | | 1 | 1638 Manchu (*chü-jen*) | | |
| | | 1 Ho-nan | 1625 | 4 | 1643 |
| | | 2 Han banner | | 15 | 1646 |
| 1651 (Metro) | 2/12 | 1 Manchu | 1646 | 1 | 1646 |
| | | 1 Manchu | 1649 | 7 | 1649 |
| | | | | 4 | 1647 |
| 1654 (Kuang-tung) | 2/13 | 1 Chih-li | 1642 | 1 | 1639 (*chü-jen*) |
| | | 1 Chiang-nan | 1649 | 3 | 1642 |
| | | | | 1 | 1643 |
| | | | | 2 | 1646 |
| | | | | 1 | 1649 |
| | | | | 1 | 1652 |
| 1655 (Metro) | 4/27 | 2 Manchu | | 6 | Manchu |
| | | 1 Chiang-nan | 1619 | 1 | 1631 |
| | | 1 Shun-t'ien | 1646 | 1 | 1643 |
| | | | | 19 | Ch'ing (*chin-shih*) |
| 1658 (Metro) | 2/20 | 1 Shan-tung | 1628 | 13 | 1655 |
| | | 1 Chih-li | 1646 | | |

SOURCES: *Hui-shih san-tai lü-li pien-lan* 會試三代履歷便覽 (Overview by region of backgrounds of civil metropolitan graduates), 1649; *Hui-shih lu* 會試錄, 1651, 1655, 1658; *Shan-tung hsiang-shih lu* 山東鄉試錄, 1648; *Kuang-tung hsiang-shih lu*, 1654; *Kuo-ch'ao Yü-yang k'o-ming lu* 國朝虞陽科名錄; *Ch'ing-mi shu-wen* 清秘述聞 (Gleanings on Ch'ing secrets), compiled by Fa-shih-shan 法式善 (1753–1813) (Peking: Chung-hua Bookstore, 1982).

[a] 18 associate examiners in the 1649 metropolitan examination were from north China.

TABLE 3.23. Provincial *Chü-jen* Quotas during the Ch'ing Dynasty, 1645–1900

| Place | 1645 | 1660 | 1700 | 1750 | 1800 | 1850 | 1881 | 1900 |
|---|---|---|---|---|---|---|---|---|
| | | | | | Year | | | |
| Chih-li | 168 | 105 | 217 | 229 | 233 | 239 | 229 | 400 |
| Chiang-nan | 163 | 63 | 83 | 114 | 114 | 114 | 114 | 290 |
| Che-chiang | 107 | 66 (1677) | 81 | 94 | 94 | 94 | 94 | 214 |
| Chiang-hsi | 113 | 57 (1672) | 75 | 94 | 94 | 94 | 104 | 104 (1897) |
| Fu-chien | 105 | 63 | 74 | 85 | 85 | 85 | 133 | 192 |
| Ho-nan | 94 | 47 | 72 | 71 | 71 | 73 | 71 | 82 (1897) |
| Hu-kuang | 106 | 63 (1684) | 53 | — | — | — | — | — |
| Hu-nan | — | — | — | 45 | 45 | 47 | 45 | 56 (1897) |
| Hu-pei | — | — | — | 47 | 47 | 47 | 51 | 75 (1894) |
| Shan-tung | 90 | 53 | 60 | 69 | 69 | 69 | 69 | 94 |
| Shan-hsi | 79 | 40 | 53 | 60 | 60 | 60 | 60 | 91 (1894) |
| Shen-hsi | 79 | 40 | 40 | 61 | 61 | 61 | 61 | 66 |
| Kan-su | — | — | — | 30 | 30 | 30 | — | 84 (1897) |
| Kuang-tung | 86 | 71 | 64 | 71 | 71 | 71 | 72 | 88 (1897) |
| Ssu-ch'uan | 84 | 49 (1684) | 53 | 60 | 60 | 60 | 60 | 108 |
| Yun-nan | 54 | 29 (1672) | 45 | 54 | 54 | 54 | 54 | 64 (1897) |
| Kuang-hsi | 60 | 30 | 43 | 45 | 45 | 45 | 45 | 51 (1897) |
| Kuei-chou | 40 | 20 | 33 | 40 | 40 | 40 | 40 | 50 (1897) |
| Total | 1,428 | 796 | 1,046 | 1,269 | 1,273 | 1,283 | 1,302 | 2,109 |

SOURCE: *Ch'in-ting k'o-ch'ang t'iao-li* 欽定科場條例 (Imperially prescribed guidelines for the civil examination grounds), 1832, 1887 editions. See also Chang Chung-li, *The Chinese Gentry: Studies on Their Role in Nineteenth-Century Chinese Society* (Seattle: University of Washington Press, 1955), pp. 124, 167–68.

NOTE: Joint Shen-hsi and Kan-su examinations were held from 1795 through 1875.

Some sample numbers of *chü-jen* degrees in the nineteenth century follow—1834: 1,371 *chü-jen*; 1840: 1,246; 1851: 1,770, 1881: 1,302 (includes 133 graduates in Fu-chien in 1875); 1885: 1,521; 1891: 1,529. The norm was 1,439 *chü-jen* degrees, but there was substantial variation in the actual number of graduates because the quotas could be increased or lessened.

TABLE 4.1. Ming Dynasty Provincial Civil Examination Officials

| Official Title | Shan-tung, 1465 (1,000 candidates, 75 graduates, 7.5% passing) No. | Shun-t'ien, 1609 (4,600 candidates, 140 graduates, 3% passing) No. |
|---|---|---|
| Presiding Examiners 監臨官 | 1 | — |
| Education Commissioners 提調 | 2 | 2 |
| Proctors 監試官 | 2 | 2 |
| Examiners 考官 | 2 | 2 |
| Associate Examiners 同考 | 5 | 14 |
| Printers 印卷官 | 1 | 1 |
| Clerks 收掌試卷官 | 2 | 2 |
| Collectors 受卷官 | 2 | 2 |
| Sealers 彌封官 | 2 | 2 |
| Copyists 謄錄官 | 2 | 2 |
| Proofreaders 對讀官 | 2 | 2 |
| Guards 巡綽官 | 2 | 4 |
| Gatekeepers 監們官 | — | 4 |
| Inspectors 搜檢官 | 4 | 6 |
| Suppliers 供給官 | 3 | 19 |
| Total | 32 | 64 |
| Ratio (Candidates per Examiner) | 31 | 72 |

SOURCE: *Shan-tung hsiang-shih lu* 山東鄉試錄, 1465: 7a–9b; *Shun-t'ien hsiang-shih lu* 順天鄉試錄, 1609: 1a–5a.

TABLE 4.2. Ming Dynasty Metropolitan Civil Examination Officials

| Official Title | No. in 1415 (3,000 candidates, 351 graduates, 12% passing) | No. in 1598 (4,600 candidates, 300 graduates, 6.5% passing) |
|---|---|---|
| Chief Administrators 知貢舉事 | 2 | 2 |
| Education Commissioners 提調官 | 2 | 2 |
| Presiding Examiner 監試官 | 2 | 2 |
| Examiners 考試官 | 2 | 2 |
| Associate Examiners 同考官 | 8 | 17 |
| Clerks 收掌試卷官 | 2 | 2 |
| Printers 印卷官 | 1 | 2 |
| Collectors 受卷官 | 2 | 4 |
| Sealers 彌封官 | 2 | 4 |
| Copyists 謄錄官 | 4 | 4 |
| Proofreaders 對讀官 | 8 | 4 |
| Guards 巡綽官 | 4 | 6 |
| Inspectors 搜檢官 | — | — |
| Gatekeepers 監門官 | 6 | 0 |
| Suppliers 供給官 | 6 | 6 |
| Total | 51 | 57 |
| Ratio (Candidates per Examiner) | 59 | 81 |

SOURCE: *Hui-shih lu* 會試錄 (Records of the metroplitan civil examination), 1415, 1598.

TABLE 4.3. Number of Wards by Classic in Ming Dynasty
Civil Metropolitan Examinations

| Classic | No. of Wards in Year | | | | | |
|---|---|---|---|---|---|---|
| | 1415 | 1481 | 1523 | 1547 | 1598 | 1622 |
| Change | 2 | 4 | 5 | 5 | 6 | 6 |
| Documents | 2 | 4 | 3 | 3 | 4 | 4 |
| Poetry | 2 | 4 | 5 | 5 | 6 | 6 |
| Annals | 1 | 1 | 1 | 1 | 1 | 2 |
| Rites | 1 | 1 | 1 | 1 | 1 | 2 |
| Total | 8 | 14 | 15 | 15 | 18 | 20 |

SOURCE: *Wu-li t'ung-k'ao* 五禮通考, by Ch'in Hui-t'ien 秦蕙田 et al.; *Chin-shih san-tai lü-li tsung-k'ao* 進士三代履歷總考; *Chin-shih lü-li pien-lan* 進士履歷便覽; *Hui-shih lu* 會試錄, 1415, 1481, 1523, 1547, 1598, 1622.

TABLE 4.4. Number of Wards by Classic in Ch'ing Dynasty
Civil Metropolitan Examinations

| Classic | No. of Wards in Year | | | | | |
|---|---|---|---|---|---|---|
| | 1646 | 1679 | 1703 | 1725 | 1747 | 1802 |
| Change | 6 | 5 | 5 | 5 | 5 | 6 |
| Documents | 4 | 4 | 4 | 4 | 4 | 4 |
| Poetry | 6 | 5 | 5 | 5 | 5 | 6 |
| Annals | 1 | 1 | 1 | 1 | 1 | 1 |
| Rites | 1 | 1 | 1 | 1 | 1 | 1 |
| Total | 18 | 16 | 16 | 16 | 16 | 18 |

SOURCE: *Chin-shih lü-li pien-lan* 進士履歷便覽, 1646–1713; *Hui-shih lu* 會試錄, 1747; *Hui-shih ch'ih-lu* 會試齒錄, 1703, 1802.

NOTE: The division of candidates by wards based on classical specialization ended in 1786, but wards remained the unit of associate examiner supervision. Usually two associate examiners were assigned to the *Annals* and *Rites* wards, one associate examiner for each of the other wards. Hence, if there were 18 wards, there were 20 associate examiners, and 18 associate examiners if there were 16 wards.

TABLE 4.5. Metropolitan Civil Examination Officials during the Ch'ing Dynasty

| | No. of Officials in Year | | | | |
|---|---|---|---|---|---|
| Official Title | 1691 (2,500 candidates, 154 graduates, 6% passing) | 1737 (5,000 candidates, 321 graduates, 6.4% passing) | 1742 (5,993 candidates, 310 graduates, 5.2% passing) | 1850 (6,000? candidates, 209 graduates, 3.5% passing) | 1890 (6,000? candidates, 328 graduates, 5.5% passing) |
| Chief Administrators | 1 | 1 | 1 | 2 | 2 |
| Ranking Officials | 0 | 0 | 0 | 1 | 1 |
| Examiners | 4 | 2 | 4 | 4 | 4 |
| Associates | 18 | 18 | 18 | 17 | 18 |
| Chief Supervisors | 0 | 8 | 6 | 9 | 10 |
| Presiding Examiners | 0 | 0 | 0 | 0 | 0 |
| Proctors | 12 | 7 | 6 | 10 | 10 |
| Surveillance Officials | 0 | 6 | 6 | 12 | 12 |
| Education Commissioners | 2 | 2 | 2 | 2 | 2 |
| Printers | 2 | 2 | 2 | 6 | 6 |
| Suppliers | 4 | 4 | 5 | 5 | 7 |
| Clerks | 2 | 2 | 2 | 3 | 2 |
| Collectors | 6 | 4 | 4 | 8 | 8 |
| Sealers | 5 | 4 | 4 | 4 | 4 |
| Copyists | 7 | 4 | 4 | 4 | 4 |
| Proofreaders | 4 | 4 | 4 | 4 | 4 |
| Gatekeepers | 2 | 2 | 2 | 2 | 2 |
| Guards | 2 | 2 | 2 | 7 | 7 |
| Inspectors | 2 | 2 | 2 | 0 | 0 |
| Special Assignments | 0 | 6 | 5 | 38 | 43 |
| Provisioners | 4 | 8 | 8 | 0 | 0 |
| Physicians | 0 | 2 | 2 | 2 | 2 |
| Total | 77 | 90 | 89 | 140 | 148 |
| Ratio (Candidates per Examiner) | 32 | 56 | 67 | 43? | 41? |

SOURCE: *Hui-shih lu* 會試錄 (Records of the metropolitan civil examination), 1691, 1737, 1742, 1850, 1890. Cf. Iona Man-cheong, "The Class of 1761: The Politics of a Metropolitan Examination" (Yale University, Ph.D. diss., History, 1991), pp. 98–99.

TABLE 4.6. Percentage of Officials Becoming Local Officials through Civil Examinations, *Yin* Privilege, or Purchase during the Ch'ing Dynasty

| Year | No. of Officials | Examination | Yin 蔭 | Purchase | Other |
|------|------------------|-------------|--------|----------|-------|
| 1764 | 2,071 | 72.5% | 1.1% | 22.4% | 4% |
| 1840 | 1,949 | 65.7 | 1.0 | 29.3 | 4 |
| 1871 | 1,790 | 43.8 | 0.8 | 51.2 | 4.2 |
| 1895 | 1,975 | 47.9 | 1.2 | 49.4 | 1.5 |
| Increase/Decrease | | − 24.6% | | + 27.0% | |

SOURCES: Ping-ti Ho, *The Ladder of Success in Imperial China* (New York: Columbia University Press 1962), p. 49, table 2. Cf. Li T'ieh 李鐵, *Chung-kuo wen-kuan chih-tu* 中國文官制度 (The Chinese civil service system) (Peking: Chinese Political University, 1989), p. 171.

TABLE 4.7. Number of *Chien-sheng* 監生 Degrees Purchased and Amount Collected during the Tao-kuang Reign, 1821–50, by Province

| Province | 1821–1835 | | 1836–1850 | | Total | | |
|---|---|---|---|---|---|---|---|
| | Amount (*Taels*) | Degrees | Amount (*Taels*) | Degrees | Amount (*Taels*) | Degrees | % |
| Chiang-hsi | 2,383,790 | 22,368 | 1,757,290 | 16,184 | 4,141,080 | 38,552 | 12.3 |
| Kuang-tung | 2,667,061 | 24,950 | 1,436,082 | 13,314 | 4,103,143 | 38,264 | 12.2 |
| Chiang-su | 2,548,746 | 23,956 | 1,174,364 | 10,513 | 3,723,110 | 34,469 | 11.0 |
| Che-chiang | 2,080,258 | 19,474 | 1,464,856 | 14,395 | 3,545,114 | 33,869 | 10.5 |
| Hu-nan | 1,865,732 | 17,117 | 1,158,266 | 10,596 | 3,023,998 | 27,713 | 9.0 |
| Ho-nan | 1,332,410 | 12,629 | 1,083,558 | 10,134 | 2,415,968 | 22,763 | 7.2 |
| Fu-chien | 1,200,582 | 11,450 | 939,932 | 8,685 | 2,140,514 | 20,135 | 6.4 |
| Hu-pei | 1,401,990 | 13,220 | 727,290 | 6,740 | 2,129,280 | 19,960 | 6.3 |
| An-hui | 874,682 | 8,241 | 722,268 | 7,443 | 1,596,950 | 15,684 | 4.7 |
| Ssu-ch'uan | 1,093,950 | 10,314 | 502,440 | 4,653 | 1,596,390 | 14,967 | 4.7 |
| Shen-hsi | 940,976 | 8,850 | 316,062 | 2,927 | 1,257,038 | 11,777 | 3.7 |
| Shan-tung | 680,716 | 6,409 | 491,131 | 4,550 | 1,171,847 | 10,959 | 3.5 |
| Kuang-hsi | 591,198 | 5,535 | 436,716 | 4,044 | 1,027,914 | 9,579 | 3.0 |
| Shan-hsi | 475,794 | 4,545 | 162,846 | 1,505 | 638,640 | 6,050 | 1.9 |
| Yun-nan | 199,332 | 1,868 | 238,798 | 2,214 | 438,130 | 4,082 | 1.3 |
| Kan-su | 287,196 | 2,520 | 123,528 | 957 | 410,724 | 3,477 | 1.2 |
| Kuei-chou | 179,540 | 1,687 | 166,266 | 1,548 | 345,806 | 3,235 | 1.0 |
| Total | 20,803,953 | 195,133 | 12,901,693 | 120,402 | 33,705,646 | 315,535 | 100 |

SOURCE: Chung-li Chang, *The Chinese Gentry: Studies on Their Role in Nineteenth-Century Chinese Society* (Seattle: University of Washington Press, 1955), p. 153, table 23. Chang's table has been rearranged.

TABLE 4.8. Quotas and Geographical Distribution of *Sheng-yuan* by Province before 1850

| Province | Civil Quota | Civil Sheng-yuan | Military Quota | Military Sheng-yuan | Total Sheng-yuan | % |
|---|---|---|---|---|---|---|
| Chih-li | 2,845 | 59,745 | 2,418 | 24,180 | 83,925 | 11.4 |
| Shen-hsi | 1,865 | 39,165 | 1,585 | 15,850 | 55,015 | 7.4 |
| Shan-tung | 1,830 | 38,430 | 1,556 | 15,560 | 53,990 | 7.3 |
| Che-chiang | 1,800 | 37,800 | 1,530 | 15,300 | 53,100 | 7.2 |
| Ho-nan | 1,631 | 34,251 | 1,386 | 13,860 | 48,111 | 6.5 |
| Shan-hsi | 1,536 | 32,256 | 1,306 | 13,060 | 45,316 | 6.1 |
| Chiang-su | 1,402 | 29,442 | 1,192 | 11,920 | 41,362 | 5.6 |
| Ssu-ch'uan | 1,366 | 28,686 | 1,161 | 11,610 | 40,296 | 5.4 |
| Chiang-hsi | 1,350 | 28,350 | 1,148 | 11,480 | 39,830 | 5.4 |
| Kuang-tung | 1,326 | 27,846 | 1,127 | 11,270 | 39,116 | 5.3 |
| Yun-nan | 1,323 | 27,783 | 1,130 | 11,300 | 39,083 | 5.3 |
| An-hui | 1,289 | 27,069 | 1,096 | 10,960 | 38,029 | 5.1 |
| Hu-nan | 1,219 | 25,599 | 1,006 | 10,060 | 35,659 | 4.8 |
| Fu-chien | 1,187 | 24,927 | 1,009 | 10,090 | 35,017 | 4.8 |
| Hu-pei | 1,087 | 22,827 | 924 | 9,240 | 32,067 | 4.3 |
| Kuang-hsi | 1,019 | 21,399 | 866 | 8,660 | 30,059 | 4.0 |
| Kuei-chou | 753 | 15,813 | 640 | 6,400 | 22,213 | 3.0 |
| Banners | 109 | 2,289 | 93 | 930 | 3,219 | 0.4 |
| Feng-t'ien | 71 | 1,491 | 60 | 600 | 2,091 | 0.3 |
| Merchants | 81 | 1,701 | — | — | 1,701 | 0.3 |
| Total | 25,089 | 526,869 | 21,233 | 212,330 | 739,199 | 100 |
| *Sheng-yuan* | | | | | 739,199 | 68 |
| *Chien-sheng* | | | | | 355,535 | 32 |
| Total degreed gentry | | | | | 1,094,734 | 100 |

SOURCES: Chung-li Chang, *The Chinese Gentry: Studies on Their Role in Nineteenth-Century Chinese Society* (Seattle: University of Washington Press, 1955), p. 150, table 20, and p. 111, table 8. Chang's tables have been rearranged and errors have been corrected. See also Huang Kuang-liang 黃光亮, *Ch'ing-tai k'o-chü chih-tu chih yen-chiu* 清代科舉制度之研究 (Research on the Ch'ing dynasty civil examination system) (Taipei: Chia-hsin Cement Co. Cultural Foundation, 1976), pp. 377–425.

NOTE: Shen-hsi includes Kan-su figures.

TABLE 4.9. Quotas and Geographical Distribution of Civil *Sheng-yuan* by Province after 1850

| Province | Civil Quota | Increased Quota | Civil Sheng-yuan | Military Quota | Military Sheng-yuan | Total Sheng-yuan | % |
|---|---|---|---|---|---|---|---|
| Chih-li | 2,888 | 2,892 | 60,732 | 2,545 | 25,450 | 86,182 | 9.4 |
| Che-chiang | 2,177 | 2,214 | 46,494 | 1,948 | 19,480 | 65,974 | 7.2 |
| Chiang-hsi | 2,020 | 2,087 | 43,827 | 1,837 | 18,370 | 62,197 | 6.8 |
| Ssu-ch'uan | 1,918 | 1,972 | 41,412 | 1,735 | 17,350 | 58,762 | 6.5 |
| Shan-tung | 1,953 | 1,965 | 41,265 | 1,730 | 17,300 | 58,565 | 6.5 |
| Ho-nan | 1,868 | 1,892 | 39,732 | 1,665 | 16,650 | 56,382 | 6.2 |
| Chiang-su | 1,768 | 1,804 | 37,884 | 1,587 | 15,870 | 53,754 | 6.0 |
| Kuang-tung | 1,748 | 1,789 | 37,569 | 1,574 | 15,740 | 53,309 | 5.9 |
| Hu-nan | 1,647 | 1,689 | 35,469 | 1,486 | 14,860 | 50,329 | 5.5 |
| Shan-hsi | 1,626 | 1,634 | 34,314 | 1,438 | 14,380 | 48,694 | 5.3 |
| An-hui | 1,604 | 1,636 | 34,356 | 1,440 | 14,400 | 48,756 | 5.3 |
| Fu-chien | 1,555 | 1,590 | 33,390 | 1,399 | 13,990 | 47,380 | 5.2 |
| Hu-pei | 1,534 | 1,577 | 33,117 | 1,388 | 13,880 | 46,997 | 5.2 |
| Yun-nan | 1,372 | 1,372 | 28,812 | 1,207 | 12,070 | 40,882 | 4.5 |
| Shen-hsi | 1,236 | 1,246 | 26,166 | 1,096 | 10,960 | 37,126 | 4.1 |
| Kuang-hsi | 1,132 | 1,143 | 24,003 | 1,006 | 10,060 | 34,063 | 3.7 |
| Kan-su | 889 | 890 | 18,690 | 783 | 7,830 | 26,520 | 2.9 |
| Kuei-chou | 767 | 767 | 16,107 | 671 | 6,710 | 22,817 | 2.5 |
| Feng-t'ien | 159 | 162 | 3,402 | 143 | 1,430 | 4,832 | 0.5 |
| Banners | 142 | 145 | 3,045 | 128 | 1,280 | 4,325 | 0.5 |
| Merchants | 110 | 131 | 2,751 | — | — | 2,751 | 0.3 |
| Total | 30,113 | 30,597 | 642,537 | 26,806 | 268,060 | 910,597 | 100 |
| *Sheng-yuan* | | | | | | 910,597 | 63 |
| *Chien-sheng* | | | | | | 533,303 | 37 |
| Total degreed gentry | | | | | | 1,443,900 | 100 |

SOURCES: Chung-li Chang, *The Chinese Gentry: Studies on Their Role in Nineteenth-Century Chinese Society* (Seattle: University of Washington Press, 1955), p. 152, table 22, and p. 111, table 8. Chang's tables have been rearranged. See also Huang Kuang-liang 黃光亮, *Ch'ing-tai k'o-chü chih-tu chih yen-chiu* 清代科舉制度之研究 (Research on the Ch'ing dynasty civil examination system) (Taipei: Chia-hsin Cement Co. Cultural Foundation, 1976), pp. 377–425.

TABLE 5.1. Social Origins of Candidates in Ming-Ch'ing Provincial Civil Examinations

| Year/Exam | Status Total | Commoner No. | % | Military No. | % | Official[a] No. | % | Special, etc.[b] No. | % |
|---|---|---|---|---|---|---|---|---|---|
| 1552/Shun-t'ien | 135[c] | 67 | 50 | 26 | 19 | 8 | 6 | 5 | 4 |
| 1591/Che-chiang | 110 | 73 | 66 | 11 | 10 | 1 | 1 | 18 | 16 |
| 1600/Shun-t'ien | 153 | 87 | 57 | 22 | 14 | 10 | 7 | 8 | 5 |
| 1618/Che-chiang | 98 | 44 | 45 | 20 | 20 | 0 | 0 | 8 | 8 |
| 1639/Shan-tung | 82 | 46 | 56 | 24 | 29 | 4 | 5 | 3 | 4 |
| 1648/Shan-tung | 89 | 45 | 51 | 14 | 16 | 2 | 2 | 2 | 2 |

SOURCES: *Che-chiang t'ung-nien ch'ih-lu* 浙江同年齒錄, 1591, 1600; *Pei-chi jen-tzu t'ung-nien lu* 北畿壬子同年錄, 1552; *Shan-tung hsiang-shih lu* 山東鄉試錄, 1639, 1648; *Shun-t'ien hsiang-shih t'ung-nien lu* 順天鄉試同年錄, 1600.

[a]"Official" (*kuan* 官) as a status in the Ming dynasty applied to military officers and their families. See Ping-ti Ho, *The Ladder of Success*, pp. 68–69.

[b]"Special" includes: medical (*i* 醫), salt (*yen-tsao* 鹽灶), and artisan (*chiang* 匠) households.

[c]For the entries under "Status Total" the information is incomplete. For example, of the 135 graduates in 1552, 29 do not give sufficient information to determine social background.

TABLE 5.2. Social Origins of Candidates for Ming-Ch'ing Metropolitan (M) and Palace (P) Civil Examinations

| Year/Exam | Status Total | Commoner No. | % | Military No. | % | Official[a] No. | % | Special, etc.[b] No. | % |
|---|---|---|---|---|---|---|---|---|---|
| 1411/ 殿試 P | 84[c] | 70 | 83 | 10 | 12 | 1 | 1 | 2 | 2 |
| 1436/ 殿試 P | 100 | 76 | 76 | 19 | 19 | 2 | 2 | 1 | 1 |
| 1499/ 殿試 P | 300 | 165 | 55 | 88 | 29 | 15 | 5 | 19 | 6 |
| 1508/ 殿試 P | 349 | 196 | 56 | 89 | 25 | 21 | 6 | 31 | 9 |
| 1541/ 殿試 P | 298 | 177 | 59 | 77 | 26 | 11 | 4 | 26 | 9 |
| 1547/ 殿試 P | 300 | 181 | 60 | 79 | 26 | 11 | 4 | 22 | 7 |
| 1598/ 殿試 P | 292 | 186 | 64 | 80 | 27 | 10 | 3 | 14 | 5 |
| 1604/ 殿試 P | 308 | 188 | 61 | 82 | 27 | 10 | 3 | 23 | 7 |
| 1622/ 會試 M | 412 | 245 | 59 | 80 | 19 | 15 | 4 | 17 | 4 |
| 1649/ 殿試 P | 143 | 114 | 80 | 18 | 13 | 4 | 3 | 6 | 4 |
| 1651/ 殿試 P | 57 | 35 | 61 | 5 | 9 | 0 | 0 | 0 | 0 |

SOURCES: *Hui-shih t'ung-nien ch'ih-lu* 會試同年齒錄, 1622; *Teng-k'o lu* 登科錄, 1411, 1436, 1499, 1508, 1541, 1547, 1598, 1604, 1649; *T'ing-shih ch'ih-lu* 廷試齒錄, 1651.

[a]"Official" (*kuan* 官) as a status in the Ming dynasty applied to military officers and their families. See Ho, *The Ladder of Success*, pp. 68–69.

[b]"Special" includes: medical (*i* 醫), salt (*yen-tsao* 鹽灶), and artisan (*chiang* 匠) households.

[c]For the entries under "Status Total" the information is incomplete. For example, of the 84 graduates in 1411, one does not give sufficient information to determine social background.

TABLE 5.3. *Chin-shih* from Special Statuses, 1371–1643

| Status | 1371–1445 | 1448–1484 | 1487–1523 | 1526–1562 | 1565–1604 | 1607–1643 | Total |
|---|---|---|---|---|---|---|---|
| Military 軍 | 250 | 1,010 | 1,339 | 1,149 | 1,185 | 676 | 5,609 |
| Official (army) | 18 | 165 | 222 | 197 | 204 | 99 | 905 |
| Artisan 匠 | 29 | 161 | 198 | 211 | 189 | 66 | 854 |
| Salt producer | 7 | 51 | 82 | 79 | 94 | 75 | 388 |
| Scholar 儒 | 79 | 34 | 18 | 15 | 7 | 7 | 160 |
| Private doctor | 3 | 17 | 18 | 7 | 4 | 2 | 51 |
| Medical official | 0 | 10 | 8 | 8 | 4 | 2 | 32 |
| Rich household | 5 | 15 | 4 | 3 | 1 | 0 | 28 |
| Postal worker | 3 | 3 | 9 | 6 | 0 | 1 | 22 |
| Horse breeder | 0 | 0 | 0 | 4 | 2 | 2 | 8 |
| Official cook | 0 | 1 | 0 | 4 | 1 | 0 | 6 |
| Astronomer | 0 | 2 | 3 | 0 | 0 | 0 | 5 |
| Imperial clan | 0 | 0 | 0 | 0 | 0 | 4 | 4 |
| Astrologer | 0 | 0 | 1 | 0 | 0 | 0 | 1 |
| Hunter | 0 | 0 | 0 | 1 | 0 | 0 | 1 |
| Merchant | 0 | 0 | 0 | 0 | 0 | 1 | 1 |
| Total (Special) | 394 | 1,469 | 1,902 | 1,684 | 1,691 | 935 | 8,075 |
| All *chin-shih* | 1,465 | 3,588 | 4,311 | 3,999 | 4,674 | 4,567 | 22,604 |
| % Special | 27 | 41 | 44 | 42 | 36 | 20 | 36 |
| % Military | 17 | 28 | 31 | 29 | 25 | 15 | 25 |

SOURCE: Ping-ti Ho, *The Ladder of Success in Imperial China* (New York: Columbia University Press, 1962), p. 68, table 4. Ho notes that family status information was unavailable in the *Kuo-ch'ao li-k'o t'i-ming pei-lu ch'u-chi* 國朝歷科題名碑錄初集 (Preliminary Record of *chin-shih* civil service graduates in Ming civil examinations) (1746 edition) for the 1418, 1421, and 1427 palace examinations. Ho gives 22,577 for all *chin-shih*, but his figures add up to 22,604.

TABLE 5.4. Geographical Distribution of *Chü-jen* Graduates by Examination in Ying-t'ien Prefecture (Nanking) during the Ming Dynasty

| | 1501 | | 1525 | | 1549 | | 1576 | | 1600 | | 1630 | |
|---|---|---|---|---|---|---|---|---|---|---|---|---|
| *Prefecture/ Province* | *No.* | *%* | *No.* | *%* | *No.* | *%* | *No.* | *%* | *No.* | *%* | *No.* | *%* |
| Su-chou 蘇州 | 21 | 16 | 21 | 16 | 23 | 17 | 20 | 15 | 26 | 19 | 30 | 20 |
| Ch'ang-chou 常州 | 18 | 13 | 12 | 9 | 13 | 10 | 17 | 13 | 27 | 19 | 27 | 18 |
| Sung-chiang 松江 | 15 | 11 | 13 | 10 | 12 | 9 | 5 | 4 | 9 | 6 | 6 | 4 |
| Ying-t'ien 應天 | 12 | 9 | 9 | 7 | 6 | 4 | 4 | 3 | 3 | 2 | 6 | 4 |
| Hui-chou 徽州 | 5 | 4 | 13 | 10 | 10 | 7 | 11 | 8 | 5 | 4 | 7 | 5 |
| Yang-chou 揚州 | 5 | 4 | 7 | 5 | 2 | 1 | 5 | 4 | 4 | 3 | 2 | 1 |
| T'ai-p'ing 太平 | 3 | 2 | 5 | 4 | 1 | 1 | 1 | 1 | 3 | 2 | 4 | 3 |
| T'ung-ch'eng 桐城 | 0 | 0 | 2 | 1 | 1 | 1 | 4 | 3 | 7 | 5 | 2 | 1 |
| Che-chiang 浙江 | 5 | 4 | 1 | 1 | 1 | 1 | 7 | 5 | 5 | 4 | 4 | 3 |
| Fu-chien 福建 | 1 | 1 | 1 | 1 | 1 | 1 | 1 | 1 | 4 | 3 | 1 | 1 |
| Chiang-hsi 江西 | 0 | 0 | 2 | 1 | 1 | 1 | 2 | 1 | 5 | 4 | 3 | 2 |
| Hu-kuang 湖廣 | 0 | 0 | 1 | 1 | 1 | 1 | 2 | 1 | 0 | 0 | 0 | 0 |
| Total | 135 | | 135 | | 135 | | 135 | | 140 | | 150 | |

SOURCES: *Nan-kuo hsien-shu* 南國賢書 (Record of civil examination success in the Southern Capital Region), compiled by Chang Ch'ao-jui 張朝瑞 (ca. 1600 edition); *Ying-t'ien hsiang-shih lu* 應天鄉試錄 (Record of the provincial civil examination administered in Ying-t'ien prefecture), 1630.

NOTE: During the Ming, candidates from other provinces were permitted to take the provincial examination in the Southern Capital Region, if their father served in Nanking rather than Peking. The origins of many *chü-jen* from lesser places are not given here. Some could not be determined.

TABLE 5.5. Su-chou *Optimi* by Dynasty, 869–1874

| *Dynasty* | *No. of* Optimi | *% of Total (50)* *Su-chou* Optimi |
|---|---|---|
| T'ang (869–905) | 7 | 14 |
| Northern Sung | 0 | 0 |
| Southern Sung (1172–1265) | 8 | 16 |
| Yuan | 0 | 0 |
| Ming (1439–1622) | 9 | 18 |
| Ch'ing (1658–1874) | 26 | 52 |

SOURCE: *Su-chou chuang-yuan* 蘇州狀元 (*Optimi* from Su-chou), compiled by Li Chia-ch'iu 李嘉球 (Shanghai: Shanghai Social Science Press, 1993), pp. 259–60. See also *Su-chou Ch'ang-Yuan-Wu san-i k'o-ti p'u* 蘇州長元吳三邑科譜 (Records of examination rosters in the three cities of Su-chou: Ch'ang-chou, Yuan-ho, and Wu-hsien), compiled by Lu Mao-hsiu 陸懋修 et al. (1906 edition).

TABLE 5.6. Geographical Distribution of *Chü-jen* Graduates in the Shun-t'ien
Capital Region during the Early Ch'ing Dynasty by Examination

| Prefecture/Province | 1654 | | 1657 | | 1660 | |
|---|---|---|---|---|---|---|
| | No. | % | No. | % | No. | % |
| Chih-li | 103 | 37 | 87 | 42 | 60 | 57 |
| Shun-t'ien | 96 | 35 | 40 | 19 | 14 | 13 |
| Chiang-nan | 37 | 13 | 32 | 16 | 13 | 12 |
| Che-chiang | 17 | 6 | 20 | 10 | 4 | 4 |
| Fu-chien | 2 | 1 | 5 | 2 | 3 | 3 |
| Shen-hsi | 5 | 2 | 3 | 1 | 1 | 1 |
| Shan-tung | 7 | 3 | 7 | 3 | 4 | 4 |
| Liao-tung | 2 | 1 | 2 | 1 | 0 | 0 |
| Ho-nan | 2 | 1 | 3 | 1 | 0 | 0 |
| Hu-kuang | 2 | 1 | 3 | 1 | 1 | 1 |
| Hsuan-chen | 3 | 1 | 3 | 1 | 2 | 2 |
| Feng-t'ien | 0 | 0 | 1 | 1 | 2 | 2 |
| Banners[a] | (59) | (21) | 0 | 0 | 0 | 0 |
| Total | 276 | 100 | 206 | 100 | 104 | 100 |
| Examiners | 69 | | 56 | | 57 | |
| Candidates | 6,000 | | 6,000 | | 4,000 | |
| % Passing | | 4.6 | | 3.4 | | 2.6 |
| Candidates per Examiner | 87 | | 107 | | 70 | |

SOURCE: *Shun-t'ien-fu hsiang-shih-lu* 順天府鄉試錄, 1654, 1657, 1660.

[a]Bannermen were included in the 1654 examination but under a separate quota and not counted as part of the graduates as a whole. They were not included as a category in 1657 or 1660.

TABLE 5.7. *Optimi* during the Ch'ing Dynasty by Province

| Province | No. | % |
|---|---|---|
| Chiang-su | 49 | 42.9 |
| (Su-chou prefecture) | (26[a]) | (22.8[a]) |
| Che-chiang | 20 | 17.5 |
| An-hui | 9 | 7.9 |
| Shan-tung | 6 | 5.3 |
| Kuang-hsi | 4 | 3.5 |
| Chih-li | 4 | 3.5 |
| Chiang-hsi | 3 | 2.6 |
| Hu-pei | 3 | 2.6 |
| Fu-chien | 3 | 2.6 |
| Kuang-tung | 3 | 2.6 |
| Bannermen | 3[b] | 2.6 |
| Hu-nan | 2 | 2.6 |
| Kuei-chou | 2 | 1.8 |
| Ho-nan | 1 | 0.8 |
| Shensi | 1 | 0.8 |
| Ssu-chuan | 1 | 0.8 |
| Total | 114[b] | 100 |

SOURCES: Sung Yuan-ch'iang 宋元強, *Ch'ing-tai te chuang-yuan* 清代 的狀元 (Ch'ing dynasty *optimi*) (Ch'ang-ch'un: Chi-lin wen-shih ch'u-pan-she, 1992), pp. 105–9. See also *Su-chou chuang-yuan* 蘇州狀元 (*Optimi* from Su-chou), compiled by Li Chia-ch'iu 李嘉球 (Shanghai: Shanghai Social Science Press, 1993); *Ch'ing-tai chuang-yuan ch'i-t'an* 清代狀元奇談 (Strange accounts of Ch'ing dynasty *optimi*), compiled by Chou La-sheng 周腊生 (Peking: Forbidden City Press, 1994), p. 188.

[a]Su-chou prefecture had 53% of all *optimi* from Chiang-su province, Ch'ang-shu county had 12%.

[b]Two *optimi* after passing the metropolitan examination took later palace examinations: 1649/1652, and 1697/1700. These were two Manchu *optimi*, one each in 1652 and 1655 special examinations, and one Mongol *optimus* in 1865.

TABLE 5.8. Geographic Distribution of *Chin-shih* in Ming Times

| Province | 1371–1472 | 1473–1571 | 1572–1644 | Total | Rank | % |
|---|---|---|---|---|---|---|
| Chiang-nan | 663 | 1,728 | 1,366 | 3,757 | 1 | 16 |
| (Chiang-su) | (478) | (1,235) | (1,008) | (2,721) | (2) | (12) |
| (An-hui) | (185) | (493) | (358) | (1,036) | (11) | (4.5) |
| Che-chiang | 653 | 1,581 | 1,046 | 3,280 | 2 | 14 |
| Chiang-hsi | 706 | 1,078 | 616 | 2,400 | 3 | 10 |
| Fu-chien | 448 | 895 | 773 | 2,116 | 4 | 9 |
| Shun-t'ien | 323 | 1,022 | 553 | 1,898 | 5 | 8 |
| Shan-tung | 177 | 814 | 732 | 1,723 | 6 | 7.5 |
| Ho-nan | 272 | 690 | 636 | 1,598 | 7 | 7 |
| Hu-kuang | 192 | 640 | 562 | 1,394 | 8 | 6 |
| Kuang-tung | 241 | 699 | 337 | 1,277 | 9 | 5.5 |
| Shan-hsi | 137 | 551 | 421 | 1,109 | 10 | 5 |
| Shen-hsi | 122 | 476 | 383 | 981 | 11 | 4 |
| Ssu-ch'uan | 144 | 390 | 257 | 791 | 12 | 3 |
| Yun-nan | 17 | 107 | 217 | 341 | 13 | 1.4 |
| Kuang-hsi | 26 | 101 | 46 | 173 | 14 | 0.7 |
| Kuei-chou | 7 | 31 | 47 | 85 | 15 | 0.3 |
| Liao-ning | 10 | 36 | 11 | 57 | 16 | 0.2 |
| Total | 4,138 | 10,839 | 8,003 | 22,980 | | |

SOURCE: Ping-ti Ho, *The Ladder of Success in Imperial China* (New York: Columbia University Press, 1962), p. 227. Ho noted that for certain years no information on the geographic origins of graduates was available; in addition, Ho omitted Korean and Vietnamese graduates. Mistakes in Ho's table 27 have been corrected and the unintended omission of figures for Kuang-tung province rectified. Chiang-nan has been calculated as a single province and not divided between Chiang-su and Au-hui, but the figures for the latter are shown in parentheses.

TABLE 5.9. Provincial Distribution of *Chin-shih* during the Ming Dynasty by Year, 1385–1622

| Province | 1385 No. | 1385 % | 1442 No. | 1442 % | 1517 No. | 1517 % | 1523 No. | 1523 % |
|---|---|---|---|---|---|---|---|---|
| N. Chih-li | 25 | 5 | 18 | 13 | 38 | 11 | 35 | 11 |
| Chiang-nan | 41 | 9 | 12 | 8 | 56 | 16 | 56 | 17 |
| Che-chiang | 97 | 21 | 29 | 20 | 45 | 13 | 30 | 9 |
| Chiang-hsi | 59 | 13 | 33 | 23 | 26 | 7 | 29 | 9 |
| Fu-chien | 55 | 12 | 11 | 8 | 40 | 11 | 37 | 11 |
| Hu-kuang | 55 | 12 | 6 | 4 | 13 | 4 | 20 | 6 |
| Ssu-ch'uan | 2 | 0.4 | 9 | 6 | 23 | 7 | 18 | 6 |
| Shan-tung | 15 | 3 | 5 | 3 | 22 | 6 | 30 | 9 |
| Shan-hsi | 42 | 8 | 3 | 2 | 10 | 3 | 14 | 4 |
| Shen-hsi | 17 | 4 | 5 | 3 | 22 | 6 | 18 | 6 |
| Ho-nan | 33 | 7 | 10 | 7 | 31 | 9 | 19 | 6 |
| Kuang-tung | 23 | 5 | 3 | 2 | 15 | 4 | 14 | 4 |
| Kuang-hsi | 8 | 2 | 0 | 0 | 5 | 1 | 5 | 2 |
| Yun-nan | 0 | 0 | 0 | 0 | 3 | 1 | 3 | 1 |
| Kuei-chou | — | 0 | — | 0 | — | — | — | — |
| Total | 472 | 100 | 144 | 100 | 349 | 100 | 328 | 100 |

| Province | 1547 No. | 1547 % | 1580 No. | 1580 % | 1607 No. | 1607 % | 1622 No. | 1622 % |
|---|---|---|---|---|---|---|---|---|
| N. Chih-li | 33 | 11 | 27 | 9 | 19 | 6 | 35 | 8 |
| Chiang-nan | 48 | 16 | 44 | 14 | 49 | 16 | 73 | 18 |
| Che-chiang | 52 | 18 | 46 | 15 | 37 | 12 | 53 | 13 |
| Chiang-hsi | 29 | 10 | 26 | 8 | 27 | 9 | 34 | 8 |
| Fu-chien | 27 | 9 | 34 | 11 | 33 | 11 | 26 | 6 |
| Hu-kuang | 14 | 5 | 26 | 8 | 18 | 6 | 36 | 9 |
| Ssu-ch'uan | 16 | 5 | 15 | 5 | 15 | 5 | 15 | 4 |
| Shan-tung | 23 | 8 | 31 | 10 | 33 | 11 | 38 | 9 |
| Shan-hsi | 22 | 8 | 8 | 3 | 17 | 6 | 26 | 6 |
| Shen-hsi | 10 | 3 | 12 | 4 | 19 | 6 | 24 | 6 |
| Ho-nan | 12 | 4 | 28 | 9 | 17 | 6 | 23 | 6 |
| Kuang-tung | 4 | 1 | 4 | 1 | 7 | 2 | 13 | 3 |
| Kuang-hsi | 5 | 2 | 0 | 0 | 2 | 1 | 5 | 1 |
| Yun-nan | — | — | 5 | 2 | 3 | 1 | 9 | 2 |
| Kuei-chou | — | — | 3 | 1 | 4 | 1 | 2 | 0.5 |
| Total | 295 | 100 | 309 | 100 | 300 | 100 | 412 | 100 |

SOURCE: *Chin-shih t'ung-nien ch'ih-lu* 進士同年齒錄, 1442, 1523, 1547, 1622; *Chin-shih lü-li pien-lan* 進士履歷便覽, 1607.

TABLE 5.10. Quotas and Actual Numbers of *Chin-shih* in Late Ch'ing Examinations

| Province | 1889 | | 1890 | | 1892 | | 1894 | |
|---|---|---|---|---|---|---|---|---|
| | Quota | Actual | Quota | Actual | Quota | Actual | Quota | Actual |
| Chiang-nan | 42 | 43 | 43 | 42 | 42 | 40 | 42 | 45 |
| Che-chiang | 24 | 23 | 25 | 22 | 24 | 23 | 25 | 25 |
| Chih-li | 23 | 20 | 24 | 25 | 23 | 23 | 24 | 16 |
| Shan-tung | 21 | 19 | 22 | 22 | 21 | 22 | 22 | 22 |
| Chiang-hsi | 22 | 19 | 22 | 22 | 21 | 21 | 22 | 22 |
| Fu-chien | 20 | 17 | 20 | 23 | 20 | 17 | 20 | 15 |
| Banners | 17 | 18 | 20 | 15 | 18 | 25 | 17 | 22 |
| Ho-nan | 17 | 15 | 17 | 16 | 17 | 20 | 17 | 16 |
| Kuang-tung | 16 | 13 | 17 | 18 | 16 | 19 | 16 | 16 |
| Hu-nan | 14 | 14 | 14 | 13 | 14 | 11 | 13 | 14 |
| Hu-pei | 14 | 16 | 15 | 14 | 14 | 14 | 14 | 14 |
| Ssu-ch'uan | 14 | 13 | 14 | 14 | 13 | 15 | 14 | 14 |
| Shen-hsi | 14 | 14 | 14 | 15 | 14 | 15 | 14 | 11 |
| Kuang-hsi | 13 | 11 | 13 | 14 | 13 | 9 | 13 | 15 |
| Yun-nan | 12 | 11 | 12 | 13 | 12 | 10 | 12 | 13 |
| Kuei-chou | 11 | 10 | 11 | 12 | 11 | 11 | 11 | 10 |
| Shan-hsi | 10 | 9 | 10 | 11 | 10 | 9 | 10 | 9 |
| Kan-su | 9 | 8 | 9 | 9 | 9 | 10 | 9 | 9 |
| Feng-t'ien | 3 | 2 | 4 | 5 | 3 | 3 | 3 | 3 |
| T'ai-wan | 2 | 1 | 2 | 1 | 2 | 1 | 2 | 3 |
| Total | 318 | 296 | 328 | 326 | 317 | 317 | 320 | 314 |

SOURCES: Etienne Zi, S.J., *Pratique des Examens Litteraires en Chine* (Shanghai: Imprimerie de la Mission Catholique, 1894), p. 179; Hans Bielenstein, "The Regional Provenance of *Chin-shih* during Ch'ing," *Bulletin of the Museum of Far Eastern Antiquities* (Stockholm) 64 (1992): 13.

TABLE 5.11. Regional Distribution of *Chin-shih* in Early and Late Ch'ing

| 1646–1775 | | | 1776–1904 | | |
|---|---|---|---|---|---|
| Province | Total | % | Province | Total | % |
| Chiang-nan | 2,208 | 17.8 | Chiang-nan | 1,904 | 14.6 |
| Che-chiang | 1,601 | 12.9 | Chih-li | 1,239 | 9.5 |
| Chih-li | 1,450 | 11.7 | Che-chiang | 1,204 | 9.2 |
| Shan-tung | 1,201 | 9.7 | Chiang-hsi | 1,055 | 8.1 |
| Ho-nan | 930 | 7.5 | Shan-tung | 1,042 | 8.0 |
| Shan-hsi | 843 | 6.8 | Ho-nan | 785 | 6.0 |
| Chiang-hsi | 821 | 6.6 | Fu-chien | 756 | 5.8 |
| Fu-chien | 643 | 5.2 | Kuang-tung | 596 | 4.6 |
| Hu-pei | 641 | 5.2 | Hu-pei | 589 | 4.5 |
| Shen-hsi | 539 | 4.4 | Shan-hsi | 581 | 4.4 |
| Kuang-tung | 417 | 3.4 | Hu-nan | 521 | 4.0 |
| Ssu-ch'uan | 237 | 1.9 | Ssu-ch'uan | 522 | 4.0 |
| Yun-nan | 205 | 1.7 | Shen-hsi | 504 | 3.9 |
| Hu-nan | 202 | 1.6 | Yun-nan | 488 | 3.7 |
| Kuei-chou | 175 | 1.4 | Kuang-hsi | 437 | 3.4 |
| Kuang-hsi | 129 | 1.1 | Kuei-chou | 425 | 3.3 |
| Kan-su | 79 | 0.6 | Kan-su | 258 | 2.0 |
| Feng-t'ien | 59 | 0.5 | Feng-t'ien | 126 | 1.0 |
| Unidentified | 18 | | Unidentified | 11 | |
| Total | 12,398 | 100 | Total | 13,043 | 100 |

SOURCE: Hans Bielenstein, "The Regional Provenance of *Chin-shih* during Ch'ing," *Bulletin of the Museum of Far Eastern Antiquities* (Stockholm) 64 (1992): 16.

TABLE 5.12. Number of *Chin-shih* by Province per Million
Mean Population

| Province | Ming Dynasty | | Ch'ing Dynasty | |
|---|---|---|---|---|
| | No. | Rank | No. | Rank |
| Fu-chien | 428 | 1 | 117 | 3 |
| Chiang-nan | 354 | 2 | 134 | 1 |
| Che-chiang | 307 | 3 | 130 | 2 |
| Chih-li | 283 | 4 | 117 | 3 |
| Chiang-hsi | 260 | 5 | 99 | 9 |
| Ho-nan | 258 | 6 | 81 | 13 |
| Hu-kuang | 246 | 7 | 109 | 6 |
| Shan-hsi | 209 | 8 | 108 | 7 |
| Shan-tung | 205 | 9 | 100 | 8 |
| Ssu-ch'uan | 172 | 10 | 38 | 16 |
| Kuang-tung | 144 | 11 | 63 | 14 |
| Shen-hsi | 144 | 11 | 59 | 15 |
| Yun-nan | 120 | 13 | 94 | 10 |
| Liao-ning | 57 | 14 | 91 | 11 |
| Kuei-chou | 42 | 15 | 116 | 5 |
| Kuang-hsi | 40 | 16 | 90 | 12 |

SOURCE: Ping-ti Ho, *The Ladder of Success in Imperial China* (New York: Columbia University Press, 1962), p. 229. Ho's figures for bannermen in table 29 have not been included because they are based on arbitrary estimates. Chiang-nan has been calculated as a single province and not divided between Chiang-su and An-hui. See table 25 on p. 223 for the population figures on which Ho's computations are based.

TABLE 5.13. Ming Dynasty Frequency of Specialization (%) on One of the Five Classics in Che-chiang Province, 1370–1600

| Classic | Year | | | | | | | | | |
|---|---|---|---|---|---|---|---|---|---|---|
| | 1370 | 1399 | 1403 | 1423 | 1450 | 1474 | 1501 | 1549 | 1576 | 1600 |
| Change | 21.9% | 15.6 | 10.3 | 14.8 | 15.1 | 22.2 | 31.1 | 37.8 | 41.6 | 38.9 |
| Documents | 15.6 | 26.6 | 36.8 | 38.1 | 27.6 | 25.6 | 18.9 | 18.9 | 18.0 | 20.0 |
| Poetry | 31.3 | 34.4 | 34.6 | 23.3 | 30.0 | 33.3 | 35.6 | 26.7 | 25.8 | 26.7 |
| Annals | 28.1 | 18.8 | 14.0 | 9.5 | 13.8 | 7.8 | 5.6 | 10.0 | 7.9 | 7.8 |
| Rites | 3.1 | 4.7 | 4.4 | 14.3 | 16.4 | 11.1 | 8.9 | 6.7 | 6.7 | 6.7 |
| Graduates | 32 | 64 | 136 | 189 | 152 | 90 | 90 | 90 | 90 | 90 |

SOURCE: *Huang-Ming Che-shih teng-k'o k'ao* 皇明浙士登科考 (Study of Che-chiang examination graduates during the Ming dynasty) (ca. 1621 edition).

NOTE: From 1370 until 1440 the quota for *chü-jen* in Che-chiang generally ranged from 40 to 60 graduates. There were major exceptions until 1426, however. In 1403 there were 136 graduates; in 1414, 168; in 1420, 205; 1423, 189. In 1453 the quota increased to 90; in 1621 there were 100 graduates.

TABLE 5.14. Ming Dynasty Frequency of Specialization (%) on One of the Five Classics in Fu-chien Province, 1399–1636

| Classic | Year | | | | | | |
|---|---|---|---|---|---|---|---|
| | 1399 | 1453 | 1501 | 1549 | 1600 | 1624 | 1636 |
| Change | 17.5% | 16.8 | 33.3 | 36.7 | 33.3 | 32.6 | 32.6 |
| Documents | 36.8 | 25.6 | 16.7 | 20.0 | 18.9 | 20.0 | 20.0 |
| Poetry | 29.8 | 31.4 | 33.3 | 28.9 | 34.4 | 33.7 | 33.7 |
| Annals | 12.3 | 11.7 | 6.7 | 7.8 | 6.7 | 6.3 | 6.3 |
| Rites | 3.5 | 14.6 | 8.9 | 6.7 | 6.7 | 7.4 | 7.4 |

SOURCE: *Min-sheng hsien-shu* 閩省賢書 (Book about civil provincial examination worthies in Fu-chien). Compiled by Shao Chieh-ch'un 邵捷春.

NOTE: From 1399 to 1453 the quota for *chü-jen* in Fu-chien ranged between 46 and 128 graduates. In 1465 the quota was set at 90, which lasted until 1624, when it increased to 95.

TABLE 5.15. Ch'ing Dynasty Frequency of Specialization (%) on One of the Five Classics in Shun-t'ien Prefecture, 1654–1759

| Classic | Year | | | | | | |
|---|---|---|---|---|---|---|---|
| | 1654 | 1657 | 1660 | 1729 | 1735 | 1756 | 1759 |
| Change | 28.3% | 29.6% | 29.5% | 29.7% | 31.4% | 29.6% | 27.9% |
| Documents | 20.3 | 20.4 | 20.9 | 22.3 | 20.8 | 22.9 | 19.7 |
| Poetry | 38.0 | 35.4 | 34.3 | 31.4 | 26.1 | 30.4 | 33.2 |
| Annals | 7.3 | 8.3 | 7.6 | 11.4 | 8.9 | 11.9 | 13.9 |
| Rites | 6.2 | 6.3 | 7.6 | 4.9 | 8.2 | 5.1 | 4.8 |
| Five Classics | — | — | — | 0.4 | 8.2 | — | — |

SOURCE: *Shun-t'ien-fu hsiang-shih lu* 順天府鄉試錄 (Record of the provincial civil examinations administered in Shun-t'ien prefecture), 1654, 1657, 1660, 1729, 1735, 1756, 1759. Shun-t'ien prefecture handled the provincial examinations for the Metropolitan Region.

NOTE: In 1654 the quota for *chü-jen* in Shun-t'ien was set at 276 graduates. In the 1657 and 1660 provincial examinations the quota was reduced first to 206 and then 105 graduates. From 1729 to 1759, the quota ranged between 229 and 253 names.

TABLE 5.16. Ch'ing Dynasty Frequency of Specialization (%) on One of the Five Classics in Chiang-nan, 1678–1747

| Classic | Year | | | | | | |
|---|---|---|---|---|---|---|---|
| | 1678 | 1684 | 1720 | 1738 | 1741 | 1744 | 1747 |
| Change | 31.5% | 31.5% | 35.2% | 31.7% | 29.4% | 30.9% | 31.6% |
| Documents | 23.3 | 23.3 | 17.0 | 23.0 | 22.2 | 19.0 | 18.4 |
| Poetry | 31.5 | 31.5 | 30.7 | 29.4 | 30.2 | 31.8 | 34.2 |
| Annals | 6.8 | 6.8 | 11.4 | 5.6 | 6.3 | 6.3 | 7.0 |
| Rites | 6.8 | 6.8 | 5.7 | 5.6 | 7.1 | 7.1 | 4.4 |
| Five Classics | — | — | — | 4.8 | 4.8 | 4.8 | 4.4 |

SOURCE: *Chiang-nan hsiang-shih lu* 江南鄉試錄 (Record of the Chiang-nan provincial civil examinations), 1678, 1684, 1720, 1738, 1741, 1744, 1747. Chiang-nan provincial examinations included candidates from Chiang-su and An-hui provinces.

NOTE: In 1678 and 1684 the quota for *chü-jen* in Chiang-nan was set at 73 graduates. In the 1720 provincial examination the quota was 99, but the names of 11 of those graduates are missing. From 1738 to 1747, the quota was set at 126, although in 1744 the quota dipped to 114. During the Ch'ien-lung reign, in addition to one of the Five Classics, students were also allowed to answer questions for all of the Classics, thereby obviating the requirements to answer questions from other parts of the examination.

TABLE 5.17. Ch'ing Dynasty Frequency of Specialization (%) on One of the Five Classics in Civil Metropolitan Examinations, 1655–1760

| Classic | Year | | | | | |
|---|---|---|---|---|---|---|
| | *1655* | *1659* | *1691* | *1742* | *1754* | *1760* |
| Change | 30% | 31% | 30% | 28% | 27% | 26% |
| Documents | 21 | 20 | 20 | 27 | 25 | 24 |
| Poetry | 36 | 35 | 35 | 25 | 35 | 30 |
| Annals | 7 | 7 | 8 | 7 | 7 | 13 |
| Rites | 6 | 6 | 7 | 9 | 7 | 7 |
| Five Classics | — | — | — | 4 | — | — |
| Graduates | 385 | 350 | 156 | 319 | 241 | 191 |

NOTE: The specialization requirement was revised in 1787, when the court chose the required Classic on a revolving basis, and then was dropped for both metropolitan and provincial civil examinations in 1793.

TABLE 5.18. Age of *Chü-jen* on Provincial Examinations during the Ming Dynasty

| Age | 1531 Ying-t'ien 應天 | |
|---|---|---|
| | *No.* | *%* |
| 20 *sui* and under | 5 | 3.7 |
| 21–25 *sui* | 29 | 21.5 |
| 26–30 *sui* | 56 | 41.5 |
| 31–35 *sui* | 24 | 17.8 |
| 36–40 *sui* | 11 | 8.1 |
| 41–45 *sui* | 8 | 5.9 |
| 46–50 *sui* | 2 | 1.5 |
| Over 50 *sui* | 0 | 0.0 |
| Total | 135 | 100 |

SOURCE: *Nan-chi t'ung-nien fang ch'ih-lu* 南畿同年方齒錄 (Record of graduates of the southern capital region) (1531 edition).

TABLE 5.19. Age of *Chü-jen* on Provincial Examinations during the Ch'ing Dynasty

| Age | 1834 | | 1851 | |
|---|---|---|---|---|
| | *No.* | *%* | *No.* | *%* |
| 20 *sui* and under | 51 | 3.7 | 78 | 4.4 |
| 21–25 *sui* | 212 | 15.5 | 324 | 18.3 |
| 26–30 *sui* | 365 | 26.6 | 426 | 24.1 |
| 31–35 *sui* | 301 | 22.0 | 401 | 22.6 |
| 36–40 *sui* | 234 | 17.1 | 242 | 13.7 |
| 41–45 *sui* | 112 | 8.2 | 163 | 9.2 |
| 46–50 *sui* | 51 | 3.7 | 72 | 4.1 |
| Over 50 *sui* | 45 | 3.2 | 64 | 3.6 |
| Total | 1,371 | 100 | 1,770 | 100 |

SOURCE: *Chih-sheng t'ung-nien ch'üan-lu* 直省同年全錄 (Complete record of provincial graduates), 1834, 1851. See also Chung-li Chang, *The Chinese Gentry: Studies on Their Role in Nineteenth-Century Chinese Society* (Seattle: University of Washington Press, 1955), p. 126.

TABLE 5.20. Age (in *Sui*) of 47 (53% of Total 88) Ming *Optimi* Attaining *Chin-shih* Degree

| Year | Age | Year | Age | Year | Age | Year | Age |
|---|---|---|---|---|---|---|---|
| 1391 | 28 | 1487 | 19 | 1535 | 38 | 1577 | 44 |
| 1400 | 36 | 1490 | 30 | 1538 | 30 | 1583 | 25 |
| 1404 | 32 | 1493 | 34 | 1541 | 35 | 1586 | 38 |
| 1442 | 49 | 1499 | 33 | 1544 | 27 | 1589 | 51 |
| 1445 | 32 | 1502 | 28 | 1547 | 38 | 1595 | 35 |
| 1451 | 22 | 1505 | 33 | 1556 | 34 | 1607 | 31 |
| 1457 | 34 | 1508 | 34 | 1559 | 39 | 1610 | 31 |
| 1463 | 27 | 1511 | 24 | 1562 | 28 | 1616 | 41 |
| 1466 | 36 | 1517 | 34 | 1565 | 39 | 1637 | 40 |
| 1472 | 38 | 1523 | 36 | 1568 | 33 | 1640 | 40 |
| 1481 | 28 | 1526 | 26 | 1571 | 34 | 1643 | 30 |
| 1484 | 39 | 1532 | 22 | 1574 | 25 | | |

SOURCE: *Ming chuang-yuan t'u-k'ao* 明狀元圖考 (Illustrated survey of optimi during the Ming dynasty), compiled by Ku Ting-ch'en 顧鼎臣 et al. (1607 edition).

Average age in *sui*: 33 sui.

Range: 19–51 *sui*; 19 = youngest; 51 = oldest. No. 25 *sui* or under: 6 = 12.8%. No. 26–35 *sui*: 25 = 53.2%. No. 36–45 *sui*: 14 = 29.8%. No. 46–55 *sui*: 2 = 4.3%. No. over 55 *sui*: 0 = 0%. No. under 30 *sui*: 16 = 34%.

TABLE 5.21. Age (in *Sui*) of 67 (60% of Total 112) Ch'ing *Optimi* Attaining *Chin-shih* Degree

| Year | Age | Year | Age | Year | Age | Year | Age |
|------|-----|------|-----|------|-----|------|-----|
| 1646 | 37 | 1724 | 28 | 1790 | 35 | 1847 | 37 |
| 1647 | 44 | 1727 | 27 | 1793 | 25 | 1850 | 35 |
| 1649 | 40 | 1733 | 38 | 1795 | 35 | 1856 | 27 |
| 1652 | 30 | 1736 | 35 | 1799 | 42 | 1859 | 33 |
| 1655 | 35 | 1737 | 24 | 1801 | 39 | 1868 | 30 |
| 1659 | 26 | 1739 | 27 | 1802 | 30 | 1871 | 40 |
| 1667 | 41 | 1742 | 41 | 1811 | 30 | 1874 | 34 |
| 1670 | 52 | 1745 | 26 | 1817 | 28 | 1877 | 30 |
| 1673 | 37 | 1748 | 26 | 1819 | 35 | 1880 | 39 |
| 1676 | 32 | 1752 | 38 | 1820 | 31 | 1883 | 25 |
| 1679 | 38 | 1754 | 32 | 1822 | 42 | 1886 | 30 |
| 1682 | 31 | 1760 | 31 | 1832 | 35 | 1890 | 46 |
| 1685 | 36 | 1761 | 37 | 1835 | 39 | 1894 | 42 |
| 1703 | 59 | 1769 | 33 | 1836 | 32 | 1895 | 31 |
| 1706 | 50 | 1772 | 38 | 1840 | 38 | 1903 | 30 |
| 1709 | 47 | 1778 | 24 | 1841 | 28 | 1904 | 33 |
| 1713 | 45 | 1780 | 26 | 1845 | 43 | | |

SOURCE: Sung Yuan-ch'iang 宋元強, *Ch'ing-ch'ao te chuang-yuan* 清朝的狀元 (Optimi of the Ch'ing dynasty) (Ch'ang-ch'un: Chi-lin Ken-shih Press, 1992), pp. 186–88; *Ch'ing-tai chuang-yuan ch'i-t'an* 清代狀元奇談 (Strange accounts of Ch'ing dynasty *optimi*), compiled by Chou La-sheng 周臘生 (Peking: Forbidden City Press, 1994), pp. 184–85. Chou's figures are given in parentheses below.

Average age in *sui*: 36 sui (Chou La-sheng: out of 75 = 34%).

Range: 24–59 *sui*; 24 = youngest; 59 = oldest (Chou, out of 75: 17–84 sui). No. 25 *sui* or under: 4 = 6.1% (Chou, under 30 *sui*: 18 = 24%). No. 26–35 *sui*: 34 = 51.5% (Chou, 30–40 *sui*: 43 = 57%). No. 36–45 *sui*: 23 = 34.8% (Chou, 40+ *sui*: 12 = 19%). No. 46–55 *sui*: 4 = 6.1%. No. over 55 *sui*: 1 = 1.5%. No. under 30 *sui*: 14 = 21%.

TABLE 5.22. Age of *Chin-shih* on Palace Examination during the Ming Dynasty

| Age | 1472 | | 1529 | |
|---|---|---|---|---|
| | *No.* | *%* | *No.* | *%* |
| Under 20 *sui* | 1 | 0.4 | 6 | 1.9 |
| 21–25 *sui* | 10 | 4.0 | 45 | 13.9 |
| 26–30 *sui* | 47 | 18.8 | 67 | 20.7 |
| 31–35 *sui* | 97 | 38.8 | 101 | 31.2 |
| 36–40 *sui* | 72 | 28.8 | 67 | 20.7 |
| 41–45 *sui* | 20 | 8.0 | 31 | 9.6 |
| 46–50 *sui* | 3 | 1.2 | 6 | 1.8 |
| Over 50 *sui* | 0 | 0.0 | 0 | 0.0 |
| Total | 250 | 100 | 323 | 100 |

SOURCE: Chien-Chin-sung 簡錦松, *Ming-tai wen-hsueh p'i-p'ing yen-chiu* 明代文學批評研究 (Research on Ming dynasty literary criticism) (Taipei: Student Bookstore, 1989), p. 44; *Chin-shih t'ung-nien pien-lan lu* 進士同年便覽錄, 1529.

TABLE 5.23. Age of *Chin-shih* on Palace Examinations during the Ch'ing Dynasty

| Age | 1835 | | 1868 | | 1894 | |
|---|---|---|---|---|---|---|
| | *No.* | *%* | *No.* | *%* | *No.* | *%* |
| Under 20 *sui* | 3 | 1.1 | 4 | 1.8 | 1 | 0.4 |
| 21–25 *sui* | 17 | 6.1 | 29 | 12.8 | 26 | 10.6 |
| 26–30 *sui* | 45 | 16.1 | 48 | 21.2 | 54 | 22.0 |
| 31–35 *sui* | 59 | 21.1 | 51 | 22.5 | 64 | 26.1 |
| 36–40 *sui* | 63 | 22.6 | 49 | 21.6 | 63 | 25.8 |
| 41–45 *sui* | 44 | 15.8 | 33 | 14.5 | 29 | 11.9 |
| 46–50 *sui* | 35 | 12.6 | 9 | 3.9 | 6 | 2.4 |
| Over 50 *sui* | 13 | 4.6 | 4 | 1.7 | 2 | 0.8 |
| Total | 279 | 100 | 227 | 100 | 245 | 100 |

SOURCE: *Hui-shih t'ung-nien ch'ih-lu* 會試同年齒錄 (Record of graduates of metropolitan civil examination), 1835, 1868, 1894. See also Chung-li Chang, *The Chinese Gentry: Studies on Their Role in Nineteenth-Century Chinese Society* (Seattle: University of Washington Press, 1955), p. 122.

TABLE 8.1. Importance of the Four Books for Final Rankings during the Ming and Ch'ing Dynasties

| Year | Examination | Place | Four Books Essay | Final Rank of Top Essayist |
|---|---|---|---|---|
| 1400 | Metropolitan | Peking | First | 1 |
| | | | Second | 3 |
| | | | Third | 32 |
| 1445 | Metropolitan | Peking | First | 3 |
| | (Shang Lu No. 1) | | Second | 13 |
| | | | Third | n.a. |
| 1465 | Provincial | Shan-tung | First | 2 |
| | | | Second | 4 |
| | | | Third | 3 |
| 1468 | Provincial | Che-chiang | First | 1 |
| | | | Second | 6 |
| | | | Third | 2 |
| 1475 | Metropolitan | Peking | First | 5 |
| | | | Second | 3 |
| | | | Third | 1 |
| 1489 | Provincial | Shan-tung | First | 2 |
| | | | Second | 1 |
| | | | Third | 3 |
| 1516 | Provincial | Che-chiang | First | 1 |
| | | | Second | 3 |
| | | | Third | 2 |
| 1535 | Metropolitan | Peking | First | 3 |
| | | | Second | 1 |
| | | | Third | 2 |
| 1558 | Provincial | Shun-t'ien | First | 1 |
| | | | Second | 3 |
| | | | Third | 2 |
| 1562 | Metropolitan | Peking | First | 2 |
| | | | Second | 3 |
| | | | Third | 1 |
| 1579 | Provincial | Yun-nan | First | 1 |
| | | | Second | 2 |
| | | | Third | 3 |
| 1586 | Metropolitan | Peking | First | 1 |
| | | | Second | 2 |
| | | | Third | 1 |

TABLE 8.1 (*continued*)

| Year | Examination | Place | Four Books Essay | Final Rank of Top Essayist |
|------|-------------|-------|------------------|----------------------------|
| 1594 | Provincial | Shan-tung | First | 1 |
| | | | Second | 4 |
| | | | Third | 8 |
| 1604 | Provincial | Shun-t'ien | First | 1 |
| | | | Second | 3 |
| | | | Third | 2 |
| 1627 | Provincial | Chiang-hsi | First | 1 |
| | | | Second | 11 |
| | | | Third | 28 |
| 1630 | Provincial | Ying-t'ien | First | 1 |
| | | | Second | 2 |
| | | | Third | 3 |
| 1648 | Provincial | Chiang-nan | First | 1 |
| | | | Second | 3 |
| | | | Third | 2 |
| 1654 | Provincial | Shun-t'ien | First | 1 |
| | | | Second | 1 |
| | | | Third | 1 |
| 1654 | Provincial | Kuang-tung | First | 1 |
| | | | Second | 3 |
| | | | Third | 4 |
| 1655 | Metropolitan | Peking | First | 1 |
| | | | Second | 1 |
| | | | Third | 1 |
| 1660 | Provincial | Shun-t'ien | First | 1 |
| | | | Second | 1 |
| | | | Third | 1 |
| 1684 | Provincial | Chiang-nan | First | 1 |
| | | | Second | 1 |
| | | | Third | 3 |
| 1691 | Metropolitan | Peking | First | 1 |
| | | | Second | 1 |
| | | | Third | 1 |
| 1703 | Metropolitan | Peking | First | 1 |
| | | | Second | 1 |
| | | | Third | 1 |

TABLE 8.1 (*continued*)

| Year | Examination | Place | Four Books Essay | Final Rank of Top Essayist |
|---|---|---|---|---|
| 1735 | Provincial | Shun-t'ien | First | 1 |
| | | | Second | 1 |
| | | | Third | 8 |
| 1742 | Metropolitan | Peking | First | 1 |
| | | | Second | 1 |
| | | | Third | 1 |
| 1747 | Provincial | Chiang-nan | First | 1 |
| | | | Second | 1 |
| | | | Third | 2 |
| 1759 | Provincial | Che-chiang | First | 1 |
| | | | Second | 1 |
| | | | Third | 1 |
| 1770 | Provincial | Ssu-ch'uan | First | 1 |
| | | | Second | 1 |
| | | | Third | 1 |
| 1788 | Provincial (Top Classics: no. 8) | Shun-t'ien | First | 1 |
| | | | Second | 1 |
| | | | Third | 1 |
| 1825 | Provincial | Shun-t'ien | First | 1 |
| | | | Second | 1 |
| | | | Third | 1 |
| 1843 | Provincial | Chiang-nan | First | 1 |
| | | | Second | 1 |
| | | | Third | 1 |
| 1852 | Provincial (Chang Chih-tung: no. 1 張之洞) | Shun-t'ien | First | 1 |
| | | | Second | 1 |
| | | | Third | 1 |
| 1875 | Provincial | Fu-chien | First | 1 |
| | | | Second | 1 |
| | | | Third | 1 |
| 1890 | Metropolitan (Hsia Tseng-yu: no. 1 夏曾佑) | Peking | First | 1 |
| | | | Second | 1 |
| | | | Third | 1 |

sources: Provincial *Hsiang-shih lu* and metropolitan *Hui-shih lu*.

TABLE 8.2. Importance of Policy Questions for Final Rankings during the Ming and Early Ch'ing Dynasties

| Year | Examination | Place | Policy Essay | Final Rank of Top Essayist |
|------|-------------|-------|--------------|----------------------------|
| 1399 | Provincial | Ying-t'ien | First | 34 |
|  |  |  | Second | 7 |
|  |  |  | Third | 1 |
|  |  |  | Fourth | 2 |
|  |  |  | Fifth | 20 |
| 1400 | Metropolitan | Ying-t'ien | First | 8 |
|  |  |  | Second | n.a. |
|  |  |  | Third | n.a. |
|  |  |  | Fourth | 1 |
|  |  |  | Fifth | n.a. |
| 1445 | Metropolitan | Peking | First | 1 (Shang Lu) |
|  |  |  | Second | 8 |
|  |  |  | Third | n.a. |
|  |  |  | Fourth | 15 |
|  |  |  | Fifth | n.a. |
| 1465 | Provincial | Shan-tung | First | 2 |
|  |  |  | Second | 1 |
|  |  |  | Third | 3 |
|  |  |  | Fourth | 1 |
|  |  |  | Fifth | 10 |
| 1489 | Provincial | Shan-tung | First | 4 |
|  |  |  | Second | 1 |
|  |  |  | Third | 5 |
|  |  |  | Fourth | 2 |
|  |  |  | Fifth | 3 |
| 1507 | Provincial | Che-chiang | First | 3 |
|  |  |  | Second | 4 |
|  |  |  | Third | 1 |
|  |  |  | Fourth | 2 |
|  |  |  | Fifth | 5 |
| 1516 | Provincial | Che-chiang | First | 1 |
|  |  |  | Second | 3 |
|  |  |  | Third | 2 |
|  |  |  | Fourth | 6 |
|  |  |  | Fifth | 5 |

TABLE 8.2 (*continued*)

| Year | Examination | Place | Policy Essay | Final Rank of Top Essayist |
|------|-------------|-------|--------------|----------------------------|
| 1535 | Metropolitan | Peking | First | 3 |
| | | | Second | 1 |
| | | | Third | 2 |
| | | | Fourth | 5 |
| | | | Fifth | 4 |
| 1558 | Provincial | Shun-t'ien | First | 2 |
| | | | Second | 5 |
| | | | Third | 1 |
| | | | Fourth | 3 |
| | | | Fifth | n.a. |
| 1562 | Metropolitan | Peking | First | 2 |
| | | | Second | 3 |
| | | | Third | 5 |
| | | | Fourth | 1 |
| | | | Fifth | 4 |
| 1579 | Provincial | Yun-nan | First | 1 |
| | | | Second | 2 |
| | | | Third | 3 |
| | | | Fourth | 4 |
| | | | Fifth | 5 |
| 1586 | Metropolitan | Peking | First | 2 |
| | | | Second | 16 |
| | | | Third | 3 |
| | | | Fourth | 5 |
| | | | Fifth | 13 |
| 1594 | Provincial | Shan-tung | First | 1 |
| | | | Second | 52 |
| | | | Third | 3 |
| | | | Fourth | 2 |
| | | | Fifth | 5 |
| 1604 | Provincial | Shun-t'ien | First | 1 |
| | | | Second | 3 |
| | | | Third | 2 |
| | | | Fourth | 4 |
| | | | Fifth | 7 |

TABLE 8.2 (*continued*)

| Year | Examination | Place | Policy Essay | Final Rank of Top Essayist |
|------|-------------|-------|--------------|----------------------------|
| 1627 | Provincial | Chiang-hsi | First | 16 |
| | | | Second | 24 |
| | | | Third | 17 |
| | | | Fourth | 14 |
| | | | Fifth | n.a. |
| 1630 | Provincial | Ying-t'ien | First | 17 |
| | | | Second | 13 |
| | | | Third | 9 |
| | | | Fourth | 16 |
| | | | Fifth | 15 |
| 1648 | Provincial | Chiang-nan | First | 1 |
| | | | Second | 13 |
| | | | Third | 14 |
| | | | Fourth | 15 |
| | | | Fifth | 16 |
| 1654 | Provincial | Shun-t'ien | First | 22 |
| | | | Second | 16 |
| | | | Third | 46 |
| | | | Fourth | 8 |
| | | | Fifth | 77 |
| 1654 | Provincial | Kuang-tung | First | 11 |
| | | | Second | 2 |
| | | | Third | 9 |
| | | | Fourth | 21 |
| | | | Fifth | 19 |
| 1655 | Metropolitan | Peking | First | 19 |
| | | | Second | 7 |
| | | | Third | 11 |
| | | | Fourth | 2 |
| | | | Fifth | 16 |
| 1660 | Provincial | Shun-t'ien | First | 7 |
| | | | Second | 18 |
| | | | Third | 6 |
| | | | Fourth | 15 |
| | | | Fifth | 15 |

TABLE 8.2 (continued)

| Year | Examination | Place | Policy Essay | Final Rank of Top Essayist |
|------|-------------|-------|--------------|----------------------------|
| 1682 | Provincial | Chiang-nan | First | 7 |
| | | | Second | 18 |
| | | | Third | 8 |
| | | | Fourth | 7 |
| | | | Fifth | 14 |
| 1693 | Metropolitan | Peking | First | 88 |
| | | | Second | 3 |
| | | | Third | 12 |
| | | | Fourth | 6 |
| | | | Fifth | 28 |
| 1703 | Metropolitan | Peking | First | 1 |
| | | | Second | 1 |
| | | | Third | 1 |
| | | | Fourth | 1 |
| | | | Fifth | 1 |
| 1735 | Provincial | Shun-t'ien | First | 1 |
| | | | Second | 41 |
| | | | Third | 9 |
| | | | Fourth | 2 |
| | | | Fifth | 8 |
| 1742 | Metropolitan | Peking | First | 1 |
| | | | Second | 2 |
| | | | Third | 3 |
| | | | Fourth | 3 |
| | | | Fifth | 2 |
| 1747 | Provincial | Chiang-nan | First | 7 |
| | | | Second | 7 |
| | | | Third | 7 |
| | | | Fourth | 7 |
| | | | Fifth | 6 |
| 1759 | Provincial | Che-chiang | First | 30 |
| | | | Second | 30 |
| | | | Third | 30 |
| | | | Fourth | 30 |
| | | | Fifth | 30 |

TABLE 8.2 (*continued*)

| Year | Examination | Place | Policy Essay | Final Rank of Top Essayist |
|------|-------------|-------|--------------|----------------------------|
| 1770 | Provincial | Ssu-ch'uan | First | 1 |
| | | | Second | 5 |
| | | | Third | 23 |
| | | | Fourth | 23 |
| | | | Fifth | 23 |
| 1788 | Provincial | Shun-t'ien | First | 70 |
| | (Wang Te-ch'eng: | | Second | 70 |
| | no. 70 汪德鉞) | | Third | 2 |
| | | | Fourth | 70 |
| | | | Fifth | 2 |
| 1794 | Provincial | Kuang-tung | First | 1 |
| | | | Second | 13 |
| | | | Third | 33 |
| | | | Fourth | 11 |
| | | | Fifth | 29 |
| 1795 | Provincial | Hu-nan | First | 21 |
| | | | Second | 1 |
| | | | Third | 21 |
| | | | Fourth | 41 |
| | | | Fifth | 27 |
| 1825 | Provincial | Shun-t'ien | First | 68 |
| | | | Second | 68 |
| | | | Third | 68 |
| | | | Fourth | 68 |
| | | | Fifth | 68 |
| 1843 | Provincial | Chiang-nan | First | 28 |
| | | | Second | 28 |
| | | | Third | 28 |
| | | | Fourth | 28 |
| | | | Fifth | 28 |
| 1852 | Provincial | Shun-t'ien | First | 1 |
| | | | Second | 90 |
| | | | Third | 90 |
| | | | Fourth | 90 |
| | | | Fifth | 90 |

TABLE 8.2 (*continued*)

| Year | Examination | Place | Policy Essay | Final Rank of Top Essayist |
|------|-------------|-------|--------------|----------------------------|
| 1882 | Provincial | Shun-t'ien | First | 3 |
| | | | Second | 3 |
| | | | Third | 3 |
| | | | Fourth | 3 |
| | | | Fifth | 3 |
| 1890 | Metropolitan (Hsia Tseng-yu: no. 1 夏曾佑) | Peking | First | 1 |
| | | | Second | 1 |
| | | | Third | 1 |
| | | | Fourth | 1 |
| | | | Fifth | 1 |
| 1894 | Provincial | Shen-hsi | First | 8 |
| | | | Second | 8 |
| | | | Third | 8 |
| | | | Fourth | 8 |
| | | | Fifth | 8 |

SOURCES: Provincial *Hsiang-shih lu* and metropolitan *Hui-shih lu*.

TABLE 8.3. Sample of Rankings of 47 (53% of Total 89) Palace Examination *Optimi* on Metropolitan and Provincial Civil Examinations during the Ming Dynasty, 1371–1610

| Name | Chin-shih *Year* | Metropolitan Rank | Provincial Rank |
|------|------------------|-------------------|-----------------|
| Wo Po-tsung | 1371 | 24 | 1 |
| Hu Kuang | 1400 | 8 | 2 |
| Ma Tuo | 1412 | 40 | 18 |
| Ch'en Hsun | 1415 | — | 1 |
| Li Ch'i | 1418 | — | 1 |
| Lin Chen | 1430 | 15 | — |
| Chou Hsuan | 1436 | 95 | — |
| Shih P'an | 1439 | — | 10 |
| Shang Lu | 1445 | 1 | 1 |
| P'eng Shih | 1448 | 3 | — |
| Li Ch'un | 1457 | 25 | 24 |
| Wang I-kuei | 1460 | 2 | — |
| P'eng Chiao | 1464 | 2 | 1 |
| Lo Lun | 1466 | 3 | — |

TABLE 8.3. (continued)

| Name | Chin-shih Year | Metropolitan Rank | Provincial Rank |
|---|---|---|---|
| Chang Sheng | 1469 | 240 | 83 |
| Wu K'uan | 1472 | 1 | 3 |
| Hsieh Ch'ien | 1475 | 3 | 1 |
| Li Min | 1484 | — | 1 |
| Fei Hung | 1487 | 16 | 20 |
| Mao Teng | 1493 | 25 | — |
| Chu Hsi-chou | 1496 | 107 | 95 |
| K'ang Hai | 1502 | 179 | — |
| Ku Ting-ch'en | 1505 | 55 | 86 |
| Lü Jan | 1508 | 6 | 10 |
| Yang Shen | 1511 | 2 | 2 |
| T'ang Kao | 1514 | 4 | — |
| Shu Fen | 1517 | 11 | 23 |
| Yang Wei-ts'ung | 1521 | 10 | 1 |
| Yao Lai | 1523 | 2 | 7 |
| Lin Ta-ch'in | 1532 | — | 6 |
| Mao Tsan | 1538 | 244 | 22 |
| Shen K'un | 1541 | 210 | — |
| Ch'in Lei-ming | 1544 | 107 | 80 |
| Li Ch'un-fang | 1547 | 10 | — |
| T'ang Ju-chi | 1550 | 10 | — |
| Ch'en Chin | 1553 | 24 | — |
| Chu Ta-shou | 1556 | 2 | 16 |
| Ting Shih-mei | 1559 | 267 | 19 |
| Shen Shih-hsing | 1562 | 28 | 3 |
| Lo Wan-hua | 1568 | 351 | 84 |
| Chang Mao-hsiu | 1580 | 13 | 12 |
| Chu Kuo-tso | 1583 | 81 | 19 |
| T'ang Wen-hsien | 1586 | 149 | 47 |
| Chiao Hung | 1589 | 7 | 79 |
| Weng Cheng-ch'un | 1592 | — | 35 |
| Chang I-ch'eng | 1601 | 37 | 8 |
| Han Ching | 1610 | 1 | 8 |

SOURCE: *Ming chuang-yuan t'u-k'ao*. This collection initially covered Ming *chuang-yuan* from 1371 to 1571. Wu Ch'eng-en 吳承恩 and Ch'eng I-chen 程一楨 added materials that brought it up to 1604. Materials for 1607–28 were later also added by unknown compilers. I have benefited from the research paper on the collection prepared by Chiang Chu-shan 蔣竹山 for my winter 1990 seminar at Tsing Hua University, Hsin-chu, Taiwan. See also *Huang-Ming san-yuan k'ao*; *Ming-tai teng-ko lu hui-pien*; *Hui-shih lu*; and *Chung-kuo chuang-yuan ch'üan-chuan* 中國狀元全傳 (Complete biographies of Chinese *optimi*), compiled by Ch'e Chi-hsin 車吉心 and Liu Te-tseng 劉德增 (Chi-nan: Shan-tung Arts Press, 1993), pp. 487–722.

TABLE 8.4. Sample of Rankings of 60 (53% of Total 114) Palace Examination
*Optimi* on Metropolitan and Provincial Civil Examinations during the
Ch'ing Dynasty, 1664–1852

| Name | Chin-shih *Year* | *Metropolitan Rank* | *Provincial Rank* |
|---|---|---|---|
| Yen Wo-ssu | 1664 | 286 | 91 |
| Miu T'ung | 1667 | 36 | 44 |
| Ts'ai-Ch'i-ch'uan | 1670 | 205 | 111 |
| Han Chiao | 1673 | 1 | 16 |
| P'eng Ting-ch'iu | 1676 | 1 | 22 |
| Kuei Yun-su | 1679 | 46 | 24 |
| Ts'ai Sheng-yuan | 1682 | 163 | 52 |
| Lu K'en-t'ang | 1685 | 1 | 5 |
| Shen T'ing-wen | 1688 | 118 | 46 |
| Tai Yu-ch'i | 1691 | 126 | 7 |
| Hu Jen-yu | 1694 | 7 | 1 |
| Li P'an | 1697 | 27 | 46 |
| Wang I | 1700 | 2 | 56 |
| Wang Shih-tan | 1703 | 1 | 6 |
| Wang Yun-chin | 1706 | 260 | 14 |
| Chao Hsiung-chao | 1709 | 27 | 57 |
| Wang Shih-ch'en | 1712 | 77 | 90 |
| Wang Ching-ming | 1713 | 21 | 219 |
| Hsu T'ao-chang | 1715 | 86 | 8 |
| Wang Ying-ch'üan | 1718 | 64 | 4 |
| Teng Chung-yueh | 1721 | 129 | 102 |
| Yu Chen | 1723 | 29 | 5 |
| Ch'en Te-hua | 1724 | 115 | 26 |
| P'eng Ch'i-feng | 1727 | 1 | 74 |
| Chou Shu | 1730 | 136 | 29 |
| Ch'en T'an | 1733 | 1 | 42 |
| Chin Te-ying | 1736 | 241 | 7 |
| Yu Min-chung | 1737 | 33 | 72 |
| Chuang Yu-kung | 1739 | 36 | 21 |
| Chin Shen | 1742 | 1 | 118 |
| Ch'ien Wei-ch'eng | 1745 | 41 | 15 |
| Liang Kuo-chih | 1748 | 123 | 7 |
| Wu Hung | 1751 | 20 | 1 |
| Ch'in Ta-shih | 1752 | 15 | 18 |

TABLE 8.4 (*continued*)

| Name | Chin-shih *Year* | *Metropolitan Rank* | *Provincial Rank* |
|---|---|---|---|
| Chuang P'ei-yin | 1754 | 3 | 79 |
| Ts'ai I-t'ai | 1757 | 1 | 204[a] |
| Pi Yuan | 1760 | 2 | 29 |
| Wang Chieh | 1761 | 10 | 7 |
| Ch'in Ta-ch'eng | 1763 | 3 | 39 |
| Chang Shu-tung | 1766 | 120 | 56 |
| Ch'en Ch'u-che | 1769 | 54 | 43 |
| Lung Ju-yen | 1814 | 67 | — |
| Wu Ch'i-chün | 1817 | 231 | — |
| Ch'en Hang | 1819 | 189 | 6 |
| Ch'en Chi-ch'ang | 1820 | 1 | 1 |
| Tai Lan-fen | 1822 | 192 | 45 |
| Lin Chao-t'ang | 1823 | 26 | 226 |
| Chu Ch'ang-i | 1826 | 12 | 85 |
| Li Chen-chün | 1829 | 204 | 43 |
| Wu Chung-chün | 1832 | 85 | 28 |
| Wang Ming-hsiang | 1833 | 160 | 36 |
| Liu I | 1835 | 14 | 31 |
| Lin Hung-nien | 1836 | 64 | 26 |
| Niu Fu-pao | 1838 | 91 | 46 |
| Li Ch'eng-lin | 1840 | 2 | 10 |
| Lung Ch'i-jui | 1841 | 57 | 2 |
| Sun Yü-huai | 1844 | 104 | 13 |
| Hsiao Chin-chung | 1845 | 166 | 9 |
| Chang Chih-wan | 1847 | 112 | 23 |
| Chang Chün | 1852 | 242 | 27 |

SOURCE: *Chuang-yuan ts'e* 狀元策 (Palace examination essays) (Ch'ien-lung edition), unpaginated manuscript; *Li-k'o chuang-yuan ts'e* 歷科狀元策 (Policy examination essays by *optimi* during scheduled civil examinations) (Taipei: Kuang-wen Bookstore reprint of late Ch'ing edition, 1976); *Kuo-ch'ao kung-chü k'ao-lueh* 國朝貢舉考略 (Brief examination of Ch'ing dynasty civil examinations), compiled by Huang Ch'ung-lan 黃崇蘭 (1825 edition); *Chung-kuo chuang-yuan ch'üan-chuan* 中國狀元全傳 (Complete biographies of Chinese *optimi*), compiled by Ch'e Chi-hsin 車吉心 and Liu Te-tseng 劉德增 (Chi-nan: Shan-tung Arts Press, 1993), pp. 735–1013.

[a]Some candidates such as Ts'ai I-t'ai from Che-chiang took the Shun-t'ien provincial examination although they were from other provinces.

TABLE 8.5. Ming Dynasty Policy Questions Classified by Topic: Ying-t'ien Prefecture, 1474–1600 (230 Questions, Top 15 Ranks Only)

| Rank | Topic | % of Total | Selection Probability (%) |
|------|-------|------------|---------------------------|
| 1 | Learning/Selection 養才/用人 | 9.6 | 43.4 |
| 2 | Tao-hsueh 道學 | 8.3 | 37.5 |
| 3 | Ming rulers 太祖，成祖 | 7.4 | 33.5 |
| 4 | World-ordering 治國 | 7.0 | 31.6 |
| 5 | Economy/Statecraft 理財 | 5.7 | 25.8 |
| 6 | Ruler-official 君臣 | 5.2 | 23.5 |
| 7 | National defense 國防 | 4.3 | 19.4 |
| 7 | Classical studies 經學 | 4.3 | 19.4 |
| 9 | Law 法/刑 | 3.5 | 15.8 |
| 9 | Military matters 兵事 | 3.5 | 15.8 |
| 11 | Literature/Poetry 詩文 | 3.0 | 13.6 |
| 11 | Natural studies 自然 | 3.0 | 13.6 |
| 13 | History 史學 | 2.6 | 11.8 |
| 13 | Agriculture 農政 | 2.6 | 11.8 |
| 13 | Customs/Values 風俗 | 2.6 | 11.8 |

SOURCE: *Nan-kuo hsien-shu* 南國賢書 (Record of civil examination success in the Southern Capital Region). Compiled by Chang Ch'ao-jui 張朝瑞. Ca. 1600 edition.

NOTE: The probability for each policy question is calculated based on the assumption that each of the five selections is mutually independent. If the selection of five questions were mutually dependent, then the probability for each type would be slightly higher. Most "topics" above and below are based on actual Chinese categories. I have added a few, such as "natural studies," which are based on combining categories, such as "astrology," "calendrical studies," and "mathematical harmonics." In the case of "classical studies" versus "philology," which of course are overlapping fields, I have separated them to show the increasing importance of the latter in Ch'ing times (see Table 8.6).

TABLE 8.6. Ch'ing Dynasty Policy Questions Classified by Topic: Che-chiang Province, 1646–1859 (460 Questions, Top 15 Ranks Only)

| Rank | Topic | % of Total | Selection Probability (%) |
|------|-------|-----------|---------------------------|
| 1 | Classical studies 經學 | 14.1 | 63.7 |
| 2 | Learning/Selection 養才/用人 | 10.7 | 48.4 |
| 3 | Economy/Statecraft 理財 | 9.6 | 43.4 |
| 4 | World-ordering 治國 | 7.8 | 35.3 |
| 5 | History 史學 | 7.4 | 33.4 |
| 6 | *Tao-hsueh* 道學 | 6.1 | 27.6 |
| 7 | Literature/Poetry 詩文 | 5.1 | 23.1 |
| 7 | Local governance 吏治 | 5.1 | 23.1 |
| 9 | Philology 小學 | 4.2 | 18.9 |
| 10 | National defense 國防 | 3.8 | 17.2 |
| 11 | Law 法/刑 | 3.1 | 14.0 |
| 11 | Literati training 士習 | 3.1 | 14.0 |
| 13 | Agriculture 農政 | 2.7 | 12.2 |
| 13 | Military matters 兵事 | 2.7 | 12.2 |
| 15 | People's livelihood 民生 | 2.2 | 9.9 |

SOURCE: *Pen-ch'ao Che-wei san-ch'ang ch'üan-t'i pei-k'ao* 本朝浙闈三場全題備考 (Complete listing of all questions from the three sessions of the Che-chiang provincial civil examinations during the Ch'ing dynasty). Compiled ca. 1860.

NOTE: The probability for each policy question is calculated based on the assumption that each of the five selections is mutually independent. If the selection of five policy questions were mutually dependent, then the probability for each type would be slightly higher. Most "topics" above and below are based on actual Chinese categories. I have added a few, such as "natural studies," which are based on combining categories, such as "astrology," "calendrical studies," and "mathematical harmonics." In the case of "classical studies" versus "philology," which of course are overlapping fields, I have separated them to show the increasing importance of the latter in Ch'ing times (see Table 8.5).

TABLE 8.7. Breakdown of 70 Imperially Selected Policy Questions for 1756–1762 Provincial Civil Examinations

| Category | 1756 No. | 1759 No. | 1760 No. | 1762 No. | Sup.[a] No. | Total No. | % |
|---|---|---|---|---|---|---|---|
| Economy/Statecraft 理財 | 1 | 2 | 5 | 3 | 3 | 14 | 20 |
| Classical studies 經學 | 2 | 0 | 2 | 2 | 2 | 8 | 11 |
| Literature/Poetry 詩文 | 2 | 3 | 3 | 0 | 0 | 8 | 11 |
| Geography 地理 | 1 | 1 | 3 | 0 | 1 | 6 | 9 |
| History 史學 | 2 | 1 | 1 | 1 | 0 | 5 | 7 |
| Local Governance 吏治 | 2 | 1 | 3 | 0 | 0 | 5 | 7 |
| Learning/Selection 養才/用人 | 1 | 1 | 1 | 1 | 0 | 4 | 6 |
| Tao-hsueh 道學 | 1 | 1 | 2 | 0 | 0 | 4 | 6 |
| Ritual 禮教 | 1 | 0 | 0 | 0 | 2 | 3 | 4 |
| Nature 格致 | 0 | 1 | 0 | 1 | 0 | 2 | 3 |
| World-ordering 治國 | 0 | 0 | 2 | 0 | 0 | 2 | 3 |
| Philology 小學 | 0 | 0 | 1 | 1 | 0 | 2 | 3 |
| National defense 國防 | 0 | 0 | 1 | 0 | 1 | 2 | 3 |
| Military matters 兵事 | 0 | 2 | 0 | 0 | 0 | 2 | 3 |
| Law 法/刑 | 0 | 0 | 0 | 0 | 1 | 1 | 1 |
| Literati training 士習 | 1 | 0 | 0 | 0 | 0 | 1 | 1 |
| Agriculture 農政 | 0 | 0 | 0 | 0 | 0 | 0 | 0 |
| People's livelihood 民生 | 0 | 0 | 0 | 0 | 0 | 0 | 0 |
| Total | 14 | 13 | 24 | 9 | 10 | 70 | 100 |

SOURCE: *Chin-k'o ch'üan-t'i hsin-ts'e fa-ch'eng* 近科全題新策法程 (Complete models for answers for new policy questions in recent provincial civil examinations), compiled and annotated by Liu T'an-chih 劉坦之. 1764 edition.

[a] "Sup." means "supplementary questions."

TABLE 8.8. Summary of Policy Questions for 1840 and 1849 Provincial Civil Examinations

| Category | 1840 | | 1849 | |
|---|---|---|---|---|
| | *No. of Provinces* | *% Exams* | *No. of Provinces* | *% Exams* |
| Classical studies 經學 | 7 | 78 | 15 | 100 |
| History 史學 | 7 | 78 | 14 | 93 |
| Learning/Selection 養才/用人 | 7 | 78 | 6 | 40 |
| Literature/Poetry 詩文 | 5 | 56 | 4 | 27 |
| Geography 地理 | 5 | 56 | 8 | 53 |
| Economy/Statecraft 理財 | 4 | 44 | 11 | 73 |
| Philology 小學 | 4 | 44 | 6 | 40 |
| Agriculture 農政 | 2 | 22 | 1 | 1 |
| World-ordering 治國 | 1 | 11 | 1 | 1 |
| Law 法/刑 | 1 | 11 | 2 | 13 |
| Military matters 兵事 | 1 | 11 | 1 | 1 |
| Pre-Han masters 諸子 | 1 | 11 | 1 | 1 |
| Nature 格致 | 0 | 0 | 1 | 1 |
| *Tao-hsueh* 道學 | 0 | 0 | 0 | 0 |
| Local governance 吏治 | 0 | 0 | 4 | 0 |
| National defense 國防 | 0 | 0 | 0 | 0 |
| Literati training 士習 | 0 | 0 | 0 | 0 |
| People's livelihood 民生 | 0 | 0 | 0 | 0 |
| Total | 45 | 100 | 75 | 100 |

SOURCES: *Chih-sheng t'ung-nien lu* 直省同年錄 (Record of graduates of each provincial civil examination), 1840, 1849.

NOTE: For 1840 we have the policy questions from nine provincial examinations, yielding 45 questions. For 1849 we have fifteen provincial examinations yielding a total of 75 policy questions.

TABLE 10.1. Importance of Discourse Questions for Final Rankings during the Ming and Early Ch'ing Dynasties

| Year | Examination | Place | Discourse Essay | Final Rank of Top Essayist |
|------|-------------|-------|-----------------|----------------------------|
| 1399 | Provincial | Ying-t'ien | Top | 12 |
| 1400 | Metropolitan | Ying-t'ien | Top | 1 |
| 1445 | Metropolitan | Peking | Top | 1 (Shang Lu) |
| 1465 | Provincial | Shan-tung | Top | 1 |
| 1489 | Provincial | Shan-tung | Top | 1 |
| 1516 | Provincial | Che-chiang | Top | 1 |
| 1520 | Metropolitan | Peking | Top | 2 |
| 1535 | Metropolitan | Peking | Top | 1 |
| 1558 | Provincial | Shun-t'ien | Top | 1 |
| 1562 | Metropolitan | Peking | Top | 1 |
| 1579 | Provincial | Yun-nan | Top | 2 |
| 1586 | Metropolitan | Peking | Top | 1 |
| 1594 | Provincial | Shan-tung | Top | 2 |
| 1597 | Provincial | Ying-t'ien | Top | 2 |
| 1604 | Provincial | Shun-t'ien | Top | 1 |
| 1627 | Provincial | Chiang-hsi | Top | 11 |
| 1630 | Provincial | Ying-t'ien | Top | 12 |
| 1648 | Provincial | Chiang-nan | Top | 1 |
| 1654 | Provincial | Shun-t'ien | Top | 1 |
| 1654 | Provincial | Kuang-tung | Top | 8 |
| 1655 | Metropolitan | Peking | Top | 10 |
| 1660 | Provincial | Shun-t'ien | Top | 17 |
| 1684 | Provincial | Chiang-nan | Top | 14 |
| 1691 | Metropolitan | Peking | Top | 106 |
| 1703 | Metropolitan | Peking | Top | 2 |
| 1735 | Provincial | Shun-t'ien | Top | 41 |
| 1742 | Metropolitan | Peking | Top | 3 |
| 1747 | Provincial | Chiang-nan | Top | 7 |
| 1759 | Provincial | Che-chiang | Top | 6 |
| 1770 | Provincial | Ssu-ch'uan | Top | 1 |
| 1788 | Provincial | Shun-t'ien | Top | 9 |
| 1789 | Provincial | Ho-nan | Top | 1 |
| 1792 | Provincial | Che-chiang | Top | 11 |

SOURCE: Provincial *Hsiang-shih lu* and metropolitan *Hui-shih lu*.

NOTE: Discourse questions were eliminated in 1793. Except for some specific candidates here and there, it is impossible to know systematically how candidates did in all fields. Hence, it is possible that Ming examiners were simply making sure that the top-ranked discourse essay was also by one of the top-ranked graduates on session one's Four Books essays.

TABLE 10.2. Importance of Poetry Questions for Final Rankings during the Late Ch'ing Dynasty

| Year | Examination | Place | Poetry Question | Final Rank of Top Poet |
|------|-------------|-------|-----------------|------------------------|
| 1759 | Provincial | Che-chiang | Top | 1 |
| 1759 | Provincial | Shen-hsi | Top | 17 |
| 1760 | Provincial | Shen-hsi | Top | 1 |
| 1770 | Provincial | Ssu-ch'uan | Top | 1 |
| 1788 | Provincial | Sh'un-t'ien | Top | 9 |
| 1789 | Provincial | Ho-nan | Top | 2 |
| 1792 | Provincial | Che-chiang | Top | 1 |
| 1794 | Provincial | Shan-hsi | Top | 1 |
| 1794 | Provincial | Kuang-tung | Top | 11 |
| 1795 | Provincial | Kuei-chou | Top | 1 |
| 1795 | Provincial | Hu-nan | Top | 3 |
| 1799 | Provincial | Kuang-hsi | Top | 6 |
| 1825 | Provincial | Shun-t'ien | Top | 1 |
| 1835 | Provincial | Che-chiang | Top | 1 |
| 1843 | Provincial | Chiang-nan | Top | 1 |
| 1849 | Provincial | Che-chiang | Top | 1 |
| 1852 | Provincial | Shun-t'ien | Top (Chang Chih-tung) | 1 |
| 1867 | Provincial | Kuang-hsi | Top | 1 |
| 1875 | Provincial | Fu-chien | Top | 1 |
| 1882 | Provincial | Shun-t'ien | Top | 1 |
| 1885 | Provincial | Che-chiang | Top | 2 |
| 1888 | Provincial | Ssu-ch'uan | Top | 1 |
| 1894 | Provincial | Shen-hsi | Top | 1 |

SOURCE: Provincial *Hsiang-shih lu* and metropolitan *Hui-shih lu.*

NOTE: Discourse questions were eliminated in 1793. Except for five specific candidates, such as in 1759, 1770, 1788, 1789, and 1792, which overlap in tables 10.1 and 10.2, it is impossible to know systematically how candidates did in all fields and whether ranks in one area corresponded to ranks in another field.

TABLE 10.3. Importance of Five Classics Questions for Final Rankings during the Late Ch'ing Dynasty

| Year | Examination | Place | Classics Question | Final Rank of Essayist |
|------|-------------|-------|-------------------|------------------------|
| 1794 | Provincial | Shan-hsi | First (*I* 易) | 1 |
| | | | Second (*Shu* 書) | 1 |
| | | | Third (*Shih* 詩) | 1 |
| | | | Fourth (*Ch'un-ch'iu* 春秋) | 1 |
| | | | Fifth (*Li* 禮) | 1 |
| 1794 | Provincial | Kuang-tung | First | 1 |
| | | | Second | 1 |
| | | | Third | 1 |
| | | | Fourth | 1 |
| | | | Fifth | 1 |
| 1795 | Provincial | Kuei-chou | First | 20 |
| | | | Second | 20 |
| | | | Third | 20 |
| | | | Fourth | 20 |
| | | | Fifth | 20 |
| 1795 | Provincial | Hu-nan | First | 10 |
| | | | Second | 13 |
| | | | Third | 13 |
| | | | Fourth | 10 |
| | | | Fifth | 24 |
| 1799 | Provincial | Kuang-hsi | First | 1 |
| | | | Second | 1 |
| | | | Third | 11 |
| | | | Fourth | 1 |
| | | | Fifth | 5 |
| 1825 | Provincial | Shun-t'ien | First | 64 |
| | | | Second | 28 |
| | | | Third | 26 |
| | | | Fourth | 11 |
| | | | Fifth | 52 |
| 1835 | Provincial | Che-chiang | First | 45 |
| | | | Second | 45 |
| | | | Third | 1 |
| | | | Fourth | 3 |
| | | | Fifth | 3 |

TABLE 10.3 *(continued)*

| Year | Examination | Place | Classics Question | Final Rank of Essayist |
|------|-------------|-------|-------------------|------------------------|
| 1843 | Provincial | Chiang-nan | First | 20 |
|  |  |  | Second | 45 |
|  |  |  | Third | 31 |
|  |  |  | Fourth | 20 |
|  |  |  | Fifth | 31 |
| 1849 | Provincial | Che-chiang | First | 14 |
|  |  |  | Second | 14 |
|  |  |  | Third | 14 |
|  |  |  | Fourth | 14 |
|  |  |  | Fifth | 14 |
| 1852 | Provincial | Shun-t'ien | First | 3 |
|  |  |  | Second | 3 |
|  |  |  | Third | 3 |
|  |  |  | Fourth | 3 |
|  |  |  | Fifth | 3 |
| 1867 | Provincial | Kuang-hsi | First | 4 |
|  |  |  | Second | 4 |
|  |  |  | Third | 4 |
|  |  |  | Fourth | 4 |
|  |  |  | Fifth | 4 |
| 1875 | Provincial | Fu-chien | First | 87 |
|  |  |  | Second | 1 |
|  |  |  | Third | 1 |
|  |  |  | Fourth | 1 |
|  |  |  | Fifth | 5 |
| 1882 | Provincial | Shun-t'ien | First | 3 |
|  |  |  | Second | 3 |
|  |  |  | Third | 3 |
|  |  |  | Fourth | 3 |
|  |  |  | Fifth | 3 |
| 1885 | Provincial | Che-chiang | First | 32 |
|  |  |  | Second | 32 |
|  |  |  | Third | 44 |
|  |  |  | Fourth | 6 |
|  |  |  | Fifth | 38 |

TABLE 10.3 (continued)

| Year | Examination | Place | Classics Question | Final Rank of Essayist |
|---|---|---|---|---|
| 1888 | Provincial | Ssu-ch'uan | First | 15 |
| | | | Second | 15 |
| | | | Third | 15 |
| | | | Fourth | 15 |
| | | | Fifth | 15 |
| 1894 | Provincial | Shen-hsi | First | 33 |
| | | | Second | 33 |
| | | | Third | 33 |
| | | | Fourth | 33 |
| | | | Fifth | 33 |

SOURCES: Provincial *Hsiang-shih lu* and metropolitan *Hui-shih lu*.

TABLE 11.1. Total Upper and Lower Ch'ing Civil Examination Degree Graduates before and after the Taiping Rebellion

| Degree | Before 1850 | | After Taiping | |
|---|---|---|---|---|
| | *No.* | *% of Total* | *No.* | *% of Total* |
| *Upper* | | | | |
| Civil *Chin-shih* | 2,500 | 23.8 | 2,600 | 20.6 |
| (Hanlin) | (650) | | (750) | |
| (Military *Chin-shih*) | (1,500) | | (1,500) | |
| *Chü-jen* | 8,000 | 76.2 | 10,000 | 79.4 |
| (Military *Chü-jen*) | (13,000) | | (13,500) | |
| Total (Civil only) | 10,500 | 100 | 12,600 | 100 |
| | | | | |
| *Kung-sheng* (Tribute Students) | | | | |
| Annual tribute | 20,000 | 61 | 20,000 | 50 |
| Grace student | 5,000 | 15 | 12,000 | 30 |
| Special exam | 3,500 | 11 | 3,600 | 9 |
| Senior | 500 | 2 | 500 | 2 |
| 2nd class | 3,600 | 11 | 3,800 | 9 |
| Total | 32,600 | 100 | 39,900 | 100 |
| | | | | |
| *Sheng-yuan* (Licentiates) | | | | |
| Civil | 460,330 | 68 | 549,698 | 67 |
| 2nd class purchase | 37,153 | 5.5 | 37,337 | 4.5 |
| 3rd class purchase | 386,000 | 57 | 475,000 | 58 |
| Supplementary | 37,177 | 5.5 | 37,361 | 4.5 |
| Military | 212,000 | 32 | 268,000 | 33 |
| Total (Civil and Military) | 672,330 | 100 | 817,698 | 100 |
| | | | | |
| *Chien-sheng* (Irregular) | 310,000 | 89 | 430,000 | 81 |
| Upper group | 40,000 | 11 | 100,000 | 19 |
| Total (Irregular) | 350,000 | 100 | 530,000 | 100 |
| | | | | |
| Total Gentry | 1,100,000 | 100 | 1,450,000 | 100 |
| Regular | 750,000 | 68 | 920,000 | 64 |
| Upper | 80,000 | 7 | 100,000 | 7 |
| Lower | 670,000 | 61 | 820,000 | 57 |
| Irregular | 350,000 | 32 | 530,000 | 36 |
| | | | | |
| Upper Gentry (est.) | 120,000 | 11 | 200,000 | 14 |

SOURCE: Chung-li Chang, *The Chinese Gentry: Studies on Their Role in Nineteenth-Century Chinese Society* (Seattle: University of Washington Press, 1955), pp. 122–41.

# Timelines for Civil Examination Curriculum Change, 650–1905

*1. Formats of T'ang Civil Examinations for* Chin-shih 進士 *and* Ming-ching 明經 *Degrees*

| Year | Sessions of Types of Examinations | No. of Items |
|---|---|---|
| Early T'ang *ming-ching* | 1: Essays 經文大義<br>2: Policy 時務策 | 10<br>3 |
| 675–733 | Taoist policy questions 老子策 | |
| 680–681 *chin-shih*<br>(first belles lettres 雜文) | 1: Poetry and/or rhyme-prose 詩賦<br>2: Policy 策 | 1 each? |
| 680s | Palace exam begins under Empress Wu | |
| 713–722 *chin-shih* | Rhyme-prose or eulogy 頌 questions most<br>common belles lettrres | |
| 720s | Neglect of Nine Classics | |
| 724 *chin-shih* | Poetry question becomes common belles lettres | |
| 734 *chin-shih* | Poetry and rhyme-prose belles lettres questions | 1 each |
| 741–763 | Call for abolition in 763–64 | |
| 752 *chin-shih* | 1: Classics 帖經<br>2: Poetry and rhyme-prose 詩賦<br>3: Policy 策 | |
| 754 | Use of poetry and rhyme-prose 詩賦<br>  in decree examinations such as the<br>  *po-hsueh hung-tz'u* 博學宏詞 | |
| 760s–770s | Calls for elimination of poetry and<br>  rhyme-prose 詩賦 fail | 1 each<br>as rule |
| 787 *chin-shih* | 1: Poetry and rhyme-prose 詩賦<br>2: Discourse essay 論<br>3: Policy 策<br>4: Classics 帖經 (added) | 1 each<br>1 |
| 786–89 *ming-ching* | Examinations on 732 K'ai-yuan 開元 Ritual Code<br>Lasted until 993 when Sung used own code | |

| Year | Sessions of Types of Examinations | No. of Items |
|------|-----------------------------------|--------------|
| 789 | Special decree examinations in Ritual: 三禮 (禮記, 儀禮, 周禮) and Ritual Code | |
| 805 | Failure to reform poetry and rhyme-prose 詩賦 examinations | |
| 822 | Regular examination in History: 三史 (史記, 漢書, 後漢書) | |
| 823 | Proposal for *Annals* special examination 春秋三傳 (Unpopular texts among candidates) | |
| 833–34 | Poetry and rhyme-prose 詩賦 briefly dropped for 雜文 examination | |

SOURCES: *Wu-li t'ung-k'ao* 五禮通考 (Comprehensive analysis of the five ritual texts), compiled by Ch'in Hui-t'ien 秦蕙田 (1761 edition); *Wen-hsien t'ung-k'ao* 文獻通考 (Comprehensive analysis of civil institutions), compiled by Ma Tuan-lin 馬端臨, in *Shih-t'ung* 十通 (Ten comprehensive encyclopedias) (Shanghai Commercial Press, 1936); David McMullen, *State and Scholars in T'ang China* (Cambridge: Cambridge University Press, 1988); Arthur Waley, *The Life and Times of Po Chü-i* (London: Allen & Unwin, 1949); Robert des Rotours, *Le traité des examens traduit de la nouvelle histoire des T'ang* (Paris: Librairie Ernest Leroux, 1932); Lo Lien-t'ien 羅聯添, *T'ang-tai wen-hsueh lun-chi* 唐代文學論集 (Collected essays on T'ang dynasty literature) (Taipei: Student Bookstore, 1989), pp. 379–95.

NOTE: In the T'ang, failures could not retake examinations.

*2. Formats of Northern Sung Dynasty Civil Examinations for* Chin-shih 進士 *and* Ming-ching 明經 *Degrees*

| Year | Sessions or Types of Examinations | No. of Items |
|------|-----------------------------------|--------------|
| Early Sung *chin-shih* (帖經墨義) | 1: Poetry, rhyme-prose, and discourse 詩賦論 | 1 each |
| | 2: Policy 策 | 5 |
| | 3: *Analects* 帖論語 | 10 |
| | 4: *Annals* or *Rites* 春秋或禮記墨義 | 10 |
| 963 | Retaking of exams permitted | |
| 975 | Separate departmental 省試 and palace 殿試 examinations | |
| 978 *chin-shih* | 1: Discourse essay 論 added | |
| 1029 *chin-shih* | Poetry and rhyme-prose 詩賦 vs. Discourse and policy 論策 debates | |
| 1044 *chin-shih* Ou-yang Hsiu (歐陽修) | 1. Policy 策 (2): Classics/history 經 and contemporary affairs 時務 | 2 |
| | 2. Discourse 論 | 1 |
| | 3. Institutions 通考 | 1 |
| 1044–45 *chin-shih* Ou-yang Hsiu (proposal) | 1. Policy 策 (3): 經旨 and 時務 | 3 |
| | 2. Discourse 論 | 1 |
| | 3. 詩賦 (Poetry/rhyme-prose for final rank) | 2 |

| | | |
|---|---|---|
| 1057 *ming-ching* | Eight sessions | |
| | Three Classics 三經帖義 (大中小經) | 6 questions |
| | Policy 時務策 | 3 questions |
| 1065 | Triennial examinations begin | |
| | (annual 960–1057; biennial 1057–1063) | |
| 1070–71 *chin-shih* | 1: Classical essay 專五經之一：經義 | 10 (specialty only) |
| Wang An-shih | 2: Discourse 論 | 1 |
| (王安石) | 3: Policy 策 | 3 |
| | 4: Later: *Analects and Mencius* 論語孟子 | 3 each |
| 1070–71 palace | Single policy question 策 replaces three on poetry/rhyme-prose/discourse 詩賦論三題 | 1 |
| 1071 | Specialty exams in law 新科明法 | |
| 1078 | Classical specialty 專經 quotas set: | |
| | Before 1078: *Poetry* 詩 40–50%, | |
| | *Documents* 書 10% | |
| | After 1078: *Poetry* 詩, *Change* 易 each 30%, | |
| | *Documents* 書 20%, *Chou-li* 周禮, | |
| | *Li-chi* 禮記 together 20% | |
| 1080 | Taoist special examinations begin | |
| 1081 | Legal questions added | |
| 1086 | Legal questions dropped | |
| 1087 | Ban on use of Buddhist or Legalist texts | |
| 1089 *chin-shih* | 1: Classics 專經義 (3) and *Analects* 論語 (1) | 4 |
| Classics | 2: Classics (3) and *Mencius* 孟子 (1) | 4 |
| 專經進士 | 3: Policy 策 | 3 |
| 1089 *chin-shih* | 1: Classical essay 經義 and *Annals/Mencius* | 3 |
| Belles lettres | 2: Poetry and rhyme-prose 詩賦 | |
| 詩賦進士 | (restored in 1086 by Ssu-ma Kuang) | 1 |
| | 3: Discourse 論 | 1 |
| | 4: Policy 時務策 | 2 |
| 1090s | Efforts to balance essays 經義 and belles lettres 詩賦 | |
| 1110 | Classical essay 經義 in parallel prose 對偶 and lyric style 詞學 evolves | |
| 1120 | Taoist special examination stopped | |

SOURCES: *Sung-shih* 宋史 (History of the Sung dynasty), complied by Toghto (T'o T'o) 脫脫 (1314–55) et al. (Taipei: Ting-wen Bookstore, 1980); *Sung hui-yao chi-kao* 宋會要輯稿 (Draft compendium of Sung collected statutes) (reprint, Taipei: Shih-chieh Bookstore, 1964), *ce* 冊 108; *Yun-lueh t'iao-shih* 韻略條式 (Southern Sung manual for civil exams) (photolithograph of Sung ms., ca. 1134–1223); *Wen-hsien t'ung-k'ao* 文獻通考 (Comprehensive analysis of civil institutions), compiled by Ma Tuan-lin 馬端臨, in *Shih-t'ung* 十通 (Ten comprehensive encyclopedias) (Shanghai Commercial Press, 1936); *Wu-li t'ung-k'ao* 五禮通考 (Comprehensive analysis of the five ritual texts), compiled by Ch'in Hui-t'ien 秦蕙田 (1761 edition). See also Araki Toshikazu 荒木敏一, *Sōdai kakyo seido kenkyū* 宋代科舉制度研究 (Study of the Sung dynasty civil service examination system) (Kyoto: Dobosha Press, 1969), pp. 357, 450–56; and Thomas H. C. Lee, *Government Education and Examinations in Sung China* (New York: St. Martin's Press, 1985), pp. 145–54.

*3. Format of Provincial and Metropolitan Civil Service Examinations during the Liao* 遼, *988–1114, and Chin* 金 *Dynasties, 1115–1234*

| Year | Type | Sessions No. or Types of Examinations | No. of Questions |
|---|---|---|---|
| 977–83 (Liao) | All | 1: Classics 帖經<br>2: Poetry and rhyme-prose 詩賦<br>3: Policy 策 | |
| 988–1030 (Liao) | All | 1: Poetry and rhyme-prose 詩賦<br>2: Law 法律<br>3: Policy 策 | 1 each |
| 1115–39 (Chin, irregular) | All | 1: Lyric and rhyme-prose 詞賦 or classical essay 經義<br>2: Policy 策 | 1 each |
| 1139–50 (Chin, North) | All | 1: Poetry and rhyme prose 詩賦<br>2: Policy 策 | 1 each |
| 1139–50 (Chin, South) | All | 1: Classical essay 經義<br>2: Policy 策 | |
| 1151–58 (Chin) | All | 1: Poetry and rhyme-prose 詩賦 only<br>2: Policy 策 dropped | 1 each |
| 1171 (Chin) | All | Policy 策 and discourse 論 added | |
| 1188–1234 (Chin) | All | 1: Poetry and rhyme prose 詩賦 or classical essay 經義<br>2: Policy 策 | |

SOURCES: *Chin-shih* 金史 (History of the Chin dynasty), compiled by Toghto (T'o T'o) 脫脫 (1314–55) et al. (Peking: Chunghua Bookstore, 1965), 51/1129–55; Karl Wittfogel, "Public Office in the Liao Dynasty and the Chinese Examination System," *Harvard Journal of Asiatic Studies* 10 (1947): 13–40; Tao Ching-shen, "Political Recruitment in the Chin Dynasty," *Journal of the American Oriental Society* 94, 1 (January–March 1974): 24–34; Peter Bol, "Seeking Common Ground: Han Literati under Jurchen Rule," *Harvard Journal of Asiatic Studies* 47, 2 (1987): 461–538; Hoyt Tillman and Stephan West, eds., *China under Jurchen Rule* (Albany: SUNY Press, 1995).

*4. Formats of Southern Sung Dynasty Civil Examinations for* Chin-shih 進士 *Degrees*

| Year | Sessions or Types of Examinations | No. of Items |
|---|---|---|
| 1128–32 | 1. Poetry and rhyme prose 詩賦<br>2. Discourse 論<br>3. Policy 策 | 2<br>1<br>3 |
| 1143–45 | 1. Dual exams in Classics and poetry and rhyme prose 經義 and 詩賦：兩科.<br>Prose 經義：論語 or 孟子<br>Poetry 詩賦：(1) 360 字 and (1) 五言六音<br>2. Discourse 論<br>3. Policy 策：子 and 時務 | 2 each=4<br><br>2<br>2<br><br>1<br>2 |

| | | |
|---|---|---|
| or | 1. Classical essay 經義 | 3 |
| | 2. Discourse 論 | 1 |
| | 3. Policy 策 | 3 |

ca. 1187–95 — Private recommendations by Chu Hsi 朱熹：Examinations on Classics and specialty exams 治經 and 諸科

| | | |
|---|---|---|
| Over 10 years based on 12 branch cycle: | A. Classical *Ching-i* 經義 Essay: | 3 tests |
| 1st 子 and 7th 午 year: | 1: *Change, Poetry, Documents* 易詩書 | 2 questions |
| 4th year 卯: | 2: *Rites* Classics 周禮儀禮二戴之禮 | 2 questions |
| 10th year 酉: | 3: *Annals* and Commentaries 春秋三傳 | 2 questions |
| | B. Various Classics 諸經 (i.e., the "Four Books") | |
| | 4: 大學論語中庸孟子 | 1 question each |
| Divide by year: 分年 | C. Discourse *Lun* 論 Essays 四科 | 4 parts |
| | 5. Questions on pre-Han philosophers 諸子 | |
| Divide by year: | D. Policy *Ts'e* 策 Essays | |
| | 6. Questions on Dynastic Histories 諸史 | 5 tests |
| |    1) Ancient history | |
| |    2) Post-Han histories | |
| |    3) Tang histories | |
| |    4) Five Dynasties | |
| |    5) *Comprehensive Mirror* 通鑒 | |
| | 7. Policy questions 時務 | 4 tests |
| |    1) Music and calendar | 2 parts |
| |    2) Ritual and protocol | 2 parts |
| |    3) Military matters and law | 2 parts |
| |    4) *T'ung-tien* 通典 encyclopedia | 2 parts |
| 1220s | *Tao-hsueh* views impact *Lun* 論 questions | |
| 1230s–50s | *Tao-hsueh* increasingly impacts *Lun* and *Ts'e* 策 Policy questions | |
| 1260s | *Tao-hsueh* views achieve substantial influence on *Lun* and *Ts'e* questions | |

SOURCES: *Sung hui-yao chi-kao* 宋會要輯稿 (Draft compendium of Sung collected statutes) (Taipei: Shih-chieh Bookstore reprint, 1964), *ce* 冊 108; *Yun-lueh t'iao-shih* 韻略條式 (Southern Sung manual for civil exams) (Photolithograph of Sung ms., ca. 1134–1223); *Wen-hsien t'ung-k'ao* 文獻通考 (Comprehensive analysis of civil institutions), compiled by Ma Tuan-lin 馬端臨, in *Shih-t'ung* 十通 (Ten comprehensive encyclopedias) (Shanghai Commercial Press, 1936); *Wu-li t'ung-k'ao* 五禮通考 (Comprehensive analysis of the five ritual texts), compiled by Ch'in Hui-t'ien 秦蕙田 (1761 edition); *Chu-tzu ta-ch'üan* 朱子大全 (Complete collection of Master Chu Hsi) (SPPY), 69.18A–26a. See also Araki Toshikazu 荒木敏一, *Sōdai kakyo seido kenkyū* 宋代科舉制度研究 (Study of the Sung dynasty civil service examination system) (Kyoto: Dobosha Press, 1969), and Hilde De Weerdt, "The Composition of Examination Standards: *Daoxue* and Southern Sung Dynasty Examination Culture" (Harvard University Ph.D. diss., in East Asian Civilizations and Cultures, 1998).

*5. Format of Provincial and Metropolitan Civil Service Examinations during the Yuan (1237, 1314–66) and Early Ming (1370–71) Dynasties*

| Year | Type | Sessions No. or Types of Examinations | No. of Questions |
|---|---|---|---|
| 1237–38 Literatus (儒戶) | Metropolitan 會試 | 1: Discourse 論<br>2: Classical essay 經義<br>3: Poetry and rhyme-prose 詩賦 | 1<br>1<br>1 each |
| 1260s | | *Tao-hsueh* opposition to literary exams | |
| 1275 (proposal) | all | Replace belles lettres with classical essay | |
| 1284 (proposal) | all | 1. Stop poetry and rhyme-prose questions 罷詩賦<br>2. Stress classical studies 重經學 | |
| 1313 (proposal) | all | 1: Test classical techniques 經術 and<br>2: Literary composition 詞章 | |
| 1314 | Provincial 鄉試 | 2: Rhyme-prose 賦 | 1 |
| 1315 (Mongols) | Metropolitan 會試 | 1: Classics and Four Books 經問 and 四書<br>2: Policy 時務策 | 5 types 條<br>1 question 問<br>1 question 道 |
| 1315 (Han) | Metropolitan 會試 | 1: Classics and composite essay 明經經疑 (四書，專經義)<br>2: ancient-style rhyme-prose 古賦 (律賦不用詩)<br>2: Documents 詔誥表<br>3: Policy 經史時務策 | 2 questions 問<br>1 each<br>1<br><br>1 question 道<br>1 question 道 |
| 1333 (Han) | Metropolitan 會試 | 1: Classical essay 經義<br>2: Rhyme-prose 賦 | 1 |
| 1333 (All) | Palace 殿試 | 1: Policy 策 | 1 question |
| 1335 (Han) | Provincial 鄉試 | 2: Rhyme-prose 賦 | 1 |
| 1370–71 (Ming) | Provincial 鄉試 and Metropolitan 會試 | 1: Classical composite 經疑 (四書)<br>1: Classical essay 專經義<br>2: Discourse 論<br>3: Policy 策<br>4: Five arts: 騎射書算律 (Riding, archery, calligraphy, calculations, penal code) | 1<br>1<br>1<br>1<br>5 matters 事 |

SOURCE: *Yuan chin-shih k'ao* 元進士考 (Study of Yuan dynasty *chin-shih*), compiled by Ch'ien Ta-hsin 錢大昕 (Ch'ing draft); *Yuan-t'ung yuan-nian chin-shih lu* 元統元年進士錄 (1333 Palace *Chin-shih* roll). Cf. *Wu-li t'ung-k'ao* 五禮通考 (Comprehensive analysis of the five ritual texts), compiled by Ch'in Hui-t'ien 秦蕙田 (1761 edition); Wu Po-tsung 吳伯宗, *Jung-chin chi* 榮進集 (Collection from the glorious *chin-shih*), in *Ssu-k'u ch'üan-shu* 四庫全書, 1233.218–21; Abe Takeo 阿部建夫, "Gendai chishikijin to kakyo" 元代知識人と科舉 (Yuan dynasty intellectuals and the civil service examination), in Abe, *Gendaishi no kenkyū* 元代史の研究 (Research on the history of the Yuan dynasty) (Tokyo: Sōbunsha, 1972), pp. 3–53.

*6. Format of Provincial and Metropolitan Civil Service Examinations during the Ming and Early Ch'ing Dynasties, 1384–1756*

| Session No. | No. of Questions |
| --- | --- |
| *One* | |
| 1. Four Books 四書 | 3 quotations |
| 2. Change 易經 | 4 quotations |
| 3. Documents 書經 | 4 quotations |
| 4. Poetry 詩經 | 4 quotations |
| 5. Annals 春秋 | 4 quotations |
| 6. Rites 禮記 | 4 quotations |
| *Two* | |
| 1. Discourse 論 | 1 quotations |
| 2. Documentary style 詔誥表 | 3 documents |
| 3. Judicial terms 判語 | 5 terms |
| *Three* | |
| 1. Policy questions 經史時務策 | 5 essays |

NOTE:  On session one, all candidates were expected to specialize (*chuan-ching* 專經) on one of the Five Classics and write essays for only that Classic.

*7. Format of Provincial and Metropolitan Civil Service Examinations during the Early Ch'ing Dynasty Reform of 1663 (Rescinded in 1667)*

| Session No. | No. of Questions |
| --- | --- |
| *One* | |
| 1. Policy questions 經史時務策 | 5 essays |
| *Two* | |
| 1. Four Books 四書 | 1 quotation |
| 2. Five Classics 五經 | 1 quotation |
| *Three* | |
| 1. Documentary style 表 | 1 document |
| 2. Judicial terms 判語 | 5 terms |

NOTE:  The requirement that all candidates specialized (*chuan-ching* 專經) on one of the Five Classics was dropped. In addition, such essays no longer had to follow the eight-legged style. In the actual examination documents, sessions two and three were conflated. There was no *lun* 論 (discourse) question.

*8. Format of Provincial and Metropolitan Civil Service Examinations during the Mid-Ch'ing Dynasty, 1757–87*

| Session No. | No. of Questions |
|---|---|
| *One* | |
| 1. Four Books 四書 | 3 quotations |
| 2. Discourse 論 | 1 quotation |
| *Two* | |
| 1. Change 易經 | 4 quotations |
| 2. Documents 書經 | 4 quotations |
| 3. Poetry 詩經 | 4 quotations |
| 4. Annals 春秋 | 4 quotations |
| 5. Rites 禮記 | 4 quotations |
| 6. Poetry question 詩題 | 1 poetic model |
| *Three* | |
| 1. Policy questions 經史時務策 | 5 essays |

*9. Format of Provincial and Metropolitan Civil Service Examinations during the Ch'ing Dynasty, 1787–92*

| Session No. | No. of Questions |
|---|---|
| *One* | |
| 1. Four Books 四書 | 3 quotations |
| 2. Poetry question 詩題 | 1 poetic model |
| *Two* | |
| 1. Change 易經 | 4 quotations |
| 2. Documents 書經 | 4 quotations |
| 3. Poetry 詩經 | 4 quotations |
| 4. Annals 春秋 | 4 quotations |
| 5. Rites 禮記 | 4 quotations |
| 6. Discourse 論 | 1 quotation (dropped in 1793) |
| *Three* | |
| 1. Policy questions 經史時務策 | 5 essays |

NOTE: The Classics on session two were selected by examiners on a revolving basis.

*10. Format of Provincial and Metropolitan Civil Service Examinations during the Late Ch'ing Dynasty, 1793–1898*

| Session No. | No. of Questions |
|---|---|
| *One* | |
|     1. Four Books 四書 | 3 quotations |
|     2. Poetry question 詩題 | 1 poetic model |
| *Two* | |
|     1. Change 易經 | 1 quotation |
|     2. Documents 書經 | 1 quotation |
|     3. Poetry 詩經 | 1 quotation |
|     4. Annals 春秋 | 1 quotation |
|     5. Rites 禮記 | 1 quotation |
| *Three* | |
|     1. Policy questions 經史時務策 | 5 essays |

*11. Format of Provincial and Metropolitan Civil Service Examinations during the Late Ch'ing Dynasty, after the 1901 Reform (Abolished in 1905)*

| Session No. | No. of Questions |
|---|---|
| *One* | |
|     1. Discourses on the history of Chinese politics 中國政治史事論 | 5 essays |
| *Two* | |
|     1. Policy questions on world politics 各國政治藝學策 | 5 essays |
| *Three* | |
|     1. Four Books 四書義 | 2 essays |
|     2. Five Classics 五經義 | 1 essay |

NOTE: The requirement that all candidates specialized (*chuan-ching* 專經) on one of the Five Classics was dropped in 1787. After 1901, such essays no longer had to follow the eight-legged style.

# Major Types of Civil Examination
# Sources besides Gazetteers

1. Local examinations, *Sui-k'ao* 歲考 (biennial renewal of status examination) and *K'o-k'ao* 科考 (triennial qualifying examination). These were also often called *T'ung-shih* 童試 (first-time capping examination; see Chapter 3), *Hsien-k'ao* 縣考 (county licensing examination), *Chou-k'ao* 州考 (department licensing examination), *Fu-k'ao* 府考 (prefecture licensing examination), and *Yuan-k'ao* 院考 (provincial educational commissioner's licensing examination). Given in one session, typically three questions in succession on the Four Books, Five Classics, and, after 1756, poetry.

    Sources about Local Examinations besides Gazetteers

        *Hsiu-ts'ai lu* 秀才錄 (record of licentiates)

        *Kung-chü lu* 貢舉錄 (record of examination candidates)

        *Shih-tu* 試牘 (examination documents that include local civil
        examination records)

2. Tribute examinations, *Pa-kung* 拔貢: given once every six years up to 1742, once every twelve years after 1742; two sessions. They were an irregular route to lower political positions.

    *Hsuan pa-kung chüan* 撰拔貢卷 (provincial and metropolitan tribute examination papers)

    *Ko-sheng pa-kung lu hsiang-shih lu* 各省拔貢錄鄉試錄 (record of graduates of the *pa-kung* and *chü-jen* civil examinations in all provinces)

    *Ko-sheng hsuan-pa ming-ching t'ung-p'u* 各省選拔明經同譜 (record of *pa-kung* classicists selected in civil examinations in all provinces)

    *Ko-sheng hsuan-pa t'ung-nien ch'ih-lu* 各省選拔同年齒錄 (record of *pa-kung* graduates selected in civil examinations in all provinces)

    *Kuo-tzu-chien ch'ing k'ao-hsuan pa-kung wen* 國子監請考選拔貢文 (local tribute examination papers requested by the Dynastic School [Imperial Academy])

3. Triennial provincial examinations, *Hsiang-shih* 鄉試, 1399–1639, 1645–1903
   Regular (*Cheng-k'o* 正科) or grace (*En-k'o* 恩科) examinations: three sessions
   *Hsiang-shih lu* 鄉試錄 (record of the provincial civil examination)
   *Hsiang-shih t'i-ming-lu* 鄉試題名錄 (record of the ranking of graduates of the provincial civil examination)
   *Hsiang-shih t'ung-nien ch'ih-lu* 鄉試同年齒錄 (record of graduates of the civil provincial examination): gives social and geographic information
   *Hsiang-shih t'ung-nien lü-li pien-lan* 鄉試同年履歷便覽 (overview by region of backgrounds of civil provincial graduates): gives social and geographic information

4. Triennial metropolitan examinations, *Hui-shih* 會試, 1371–1622, 1647–1904
   Regular (*Cheng-k'o* 正科) or grace (*En-k'o* 恩科) examinations: three sessions
   *Hui-shih lu* 會試錄 (record of the metropolitan civil examination)
   *Hui-shih t'i-ming-lu* 會試題名錄 (record of the ranking of graduates of the metropolitan civil examination)
   *Hui-shih t'ung-nien ch'ih-lu* 會試同年齒錄 (record of graduates of the metropolitan civil examination): gives social and geographic information
   *Hui-shih t'ung-nien lü-li pien-lan* 會試同年履歷便覽 (overview by region of backgrounds of civil metropolitan graduates): gives social and geographic information

5. Triennial palace examinations, *Tien-shih* 殿試, 1371–1643, 1652–1903
   Regular (*Cheng-k'o* 正科) or grace (*En-k'o* 恩科) examinations: one session
   *Chin-shih teng-k'o lu* 進士登科錄 (record of the ascension to *chin-shih* ["literatus presented to the emperor for appointment"] rank on the civil palace examination)
   *Chin-shih t'ung-nien ch'ih-lu* 進士同年齒錄 (record of *chin-shih* graduates of the civil palace examination): gives social and geographic information
   *Chin-shih lü-li pien-lan* 進士履歷便覽 (overview by region of backgrounds of civil *chin-shih*); gives social and geographic information

6. Triennial court examinations (*Ch'ao-k'ao* 朝考): special Hanlin Academy appointment examination given after 1723. There were also separate court examinations for tribute students (see above).
   *Ch'in-ch'ü ch'ao-k'ao chüan* 欽取朝考卷 (imperially selected civil court examination papers): one session; three questions—*lun* 論 (discourse), *shu* 疏 (memorial), *shih* 詩 (poetry)

7. Ch'ing translation examinations, *Fan-i k'ao-shih* 翻譯考試 for Manchus, Mongolians, etc.
   *Fan-i hsiang-shih lu* 翻譯鄉試錄 (record of the provincial civil translation examination)
   *Fan-i hui-shih lu* 翻譯會試錄 (record of the metropolitan civil translation examination)
   *O-luo-ssu wen-kuan shih* 俄羅斯文館試 (Russian-language examination)
   *Hui-hui-kuan shih* 回回館試 (Muslim-language examination)

8. Imperially invited special examinations, *Po-hsueh hung-tz'u* 博學鴻詞: one session; poetry, discourse, and policy questions 賦論策

    *Po-hsueh hung-ju* 博學鴻儒 (search for those of wide learning and illustrious literati)

    *Po-hsueh hung-tz'u* 博學鴻詞 (search for those of wide learning and illustrious words)

# BIBLIOGRAPHY OF PRIMARY
# AND SECONDARY SOURCES

Abe Takeo 阿部建夫. "Gendai chishikijin to kakyo" 元代知識人と科舉 (Yuan dynasty intellectuals and the civil service examination). In *Gendaishi no kenkyū* 元代史 の 研究 (Research on the history of the Yuan dynasty). Tokyo: Sōbunsha, 1972.

Abe Yō 阿部洋. "Tōyō zasshi ni mirareru Shimmatsu kyōikushi shiryō ni tsuite, jō ge" 東方雜誌にみられろ清末教育史資料について上下 (Materials on late Ch'ing educational history appearing in *Eastern Miscellany*, parts 1 and 2). *Rekishi hyōron* 歷史評 論 137, 1 (1962): 23–33; 137, 2 (1962): 23–33.

Abell, Walter. *The Collective Dream in Art*. Cambridge: Harvard University Press, 1957.

Adas, Michael. *Machines as the Measure of Men: Science, Technology, and Ideologies of Western Dominance*. Ithaca: Cornell University Press, 1989.

Ai Nan-ying 艾南英. *Ai Ch'ien-tzu hsien-sheng ch'üan-kao* 艾千子先生全稿 (Complete drafts of examination essays by Ai Nan-ying). Early Ch'ing edition. Reprint, Taipei: Wei-wen t'u-shu Press, 1977.

———. *T'ien-yung-tzu chi* 天傭子集 (Collection of the Heavenly Hired Hand). 1699 edition. Reprint, Taipei: I-wen Press, 1980.

Amano, Ikuo. *Education and Examination in Modern Japan*. Translated by William K. Cummings and Fumiko Cummings. Tokyo: Tokyo University Press, 1990.

"An-hui hsueh-cheng t'i-pen" 安徽學政題本 (Memorial of the An-hui education commissioner). 1765, 7th month, 26th day. In the Ming-Ch'ing Archives, Academia Sinica, Taiwan.

Appleby, Joyce, et al. *Telling the Truth about History*. New York: Norton, 1994.

Araki Toshikazu 荒木敏一. "Yōsei ninen no hikō jiken to Ten Bunkei" 雍正二年の罷 考事件と田文鏡 (T'ien Wen-ching and the 1725 examination boycott). *Tōyōshi kenkyū* 東洋史研究 15, 4 (March 1957): 100–104.

———. *Sōdai kakyo seido kenkyū* 宋代科舉制度研究 (Study of the Sung dynasty civil service examination system). Kyoto: Dōbōsha, 1969.

———. "Chokusho kyōgaku no sei o tsujite kantaru Yōsei chika no bunkyō seisaku" 直省教學の制を通じて 觀たる 雍正治下の 文教政策 (Yung-cheng era educational

---

See also Appendices 1 and 2 for primary examination sources, which are not in the bibliography.

policies viewed through the provincial education system). In *Yōsei jidai no kenkyū* 雍正時代の研究, pp. 284–308. Kyoto: Tōmeisha, 1986.

———. "Yōsei jidai ni okeru gakuchin sei no kaikaku" 雍正時代に於ける學臣制の改革 (The reform of education officials in the Yung-cheng age). In *Yōsei jidai no kenkyū* 雍正時代の研究, pp. 503–18. Kyoto: Tōmeisha, 1986.

Aramiya Manabu 新宮學. "Nankei kando" 南京還都 (Restoring the capital to Nanking). In *Wada Hakutoku kyōju koki kinen: Minshin jidai no hō to shakai* 和田博德教授古稀記念：明清時代の法と社會. Tokyo: Kyuko shoin, 1993.

Atwell, William S. "From Education to Politics: The Fu She." In William Theodore de Bary, ed., *The Unfolding of Neo-Confucianism*. New York: Columbia University Press, 1975.

———. "The T'ai-ch'ang, T'ien-ch'i, and Ch'ung-chen Reigns, 1620–1644." In Frederick W. Mote and Denis Twitchett, eds., *The Cambridge History of China*, vol. 7, part 1, *The Ming Dynasty, 1368–1644*. Cambridge: Cambridge University Press, 1988.

Averill, Stephen. "Education and Local Elite Politics in Early Twentieth Century China." Paper presented at the annual meeting of the Association of Asian Studies, Honolulu, Hawaii, April 1996.

Ayers, William. *Chang Chih-tung and Educational Reform in China*. Cambridge: Harvard University Press, 1971.

Backus, Robert. "The Relationship of Confucianism to the Tokugawa Bakufu As Revealed in the Kansei Educational Reform." *Harvard Journal of Asiatic Studies* 34 (1974): 97–162.

Bailey, Paul J. *Reform the People: Changing Attitudes towards Popular Education in Early Twentieth Century China*. Edinburgh: Edinburgh University Press, 1990.

Balazs, Etienne. *Chinese Civilization and Bureaucracy*. Translated by H. M. Wright. New Haven: Yale University Press, 1964.

Barfield, Thomas. *The Perilous Frontier: Nomadic Empires and China, 221 B.C. to A.D. 1757*. Cambridge: Blackwell Publishers, 1989.

Barr, Allan. "Pu Songling and the Qing Examination System." *Late Imperial China* 7, 1 (1986): 92–103.

Bartlett, Beatrice S. *Monarchs and Ministers: The Grand Council in Mid-Ch'ing China, 1723–1820*. Berkeley: University of California Press, 1991.

Bastid, Marianne. *Educational Reform in Early 20th-Century China*. Translated by Paul J. Bailey. Ann Arbor: University of Michigan China Center, 1988.

Bauer, Wolfgang. "Chinese Glyphomancy." In Sarah Allan and Alvin Cohen, eds., *Legend, Lore, and Religion in China*. San Francisco: Chinese Materials Center, 1979.

Bays, Daniel H. *China Enters the Twentieth Century: Chang Chih-tung and the Issues of a New Age, 1895–1909*. Ann Arbor: University of Michigan Press, 1978.

Beattie, Hilary. *Land and Lineage in China: A Study of T'ung-ch'eng County, Anhui, in the Ming and Ch'ing Dynasties*. Cambridge: Cambridge University Press, 1979.

Bendix, Richard. *Higher Civil Servants in American Society*. Boulder: University of Colorado Press, 1949.

Berling, Judith. *The Syncretic Religion of Lin Chao-en*. New York: Columbia University Press, 1980.

———. "Religion and Popular Culture: The Management of Moral Capital in *The Romance of the Three Teachings*." In David Johnson, Andrew Nathan, and Evelyn

Rawski, eds., *Popular Culture in Late Imperial China*. Berkeley: University of California Press, 1985.

Bielenstein, Hans. "Chinese Historical Demography, A.D. 2–1982." *Bulletin of the Museum of Far Eastern Antiquities* 59 (1967).

———. "The Regional Provenance of *Chin-shih* during Ch'ing." *Bulletin of the Museum of Far Eastern Antiquities* (Stockholm) 64 (1992): 6–178.

Birch, Cyril, trans. *Scenes for Mandarins: The Elite Theater of the Ming*. New York: Columbia University Press, 1995.

Birge, Bettine. *Holding Her Own: Women, Property and Confucian Reaction in Sung and Yuan China (960–1368)*. Cambridge: Cambridge University Press, 1997.

Bodde, Derk. "'The Chinese Cosmic Magic Known as Watching for the Ethers." In S. Egerod and E. Glahn, eds., *Studia Serica: Bernhard Karlgren Dedicata*. Copenhagen: Ejnar Munksgaard, 1959.

———. "Prison Life in Eighteenth Century Peking." *Journal of the American Oriental Society* 89 (April–June 1969): 311–33.

Bodde, Derk, and Clarence Morris. *Law in Imperial China*. Philadelphia: University of Pennsylvania Press, 1973.

Boettcher, Cheryl M. "'To Make Them Ready for Official Employment': Literacy in Manchu and the Hanlin Cohort of 1655." Seminar paper, UCLA History Department, winter–spring 1993.

Bol, Peter. "Seeking Common Ground: Han Literati under Jurchen Rule." *Harvard Journal of Asiatic Studies* 47, 2 (1987): 461–538.

———. "Chu Hsi's Redefinition of Literati Learning." In William Theodore de Bary and John Chaffee, eds., *Neo-Confucian Education: The Formative Stage*. Berkeley: University of California Press, 1989.

———. "The Sung Examination System and the *Shih*." *Asia Major*, 3rd ser., 3, 2 (1990): 149–71.

———. *"This Culture of Ours": Intellectual Transitions in T'ang and Sung China*. Stanford: Stanford University Press, 1992.

———. "The Examination System and Sung Literati Culture." In Léon Vandermeersch, ed., *La société civile face à l'État*. Paris: École Française d'Extrême-Orient, 1994.

———. "Chao Ping-wen (1159–1232): Foundations for Literati Learning." In Hoyt Tillman and Stephen West, eds., *China under Jurchen Rule*. Albany: SUNY Press, 1995.

———. "The Neo-Confucian Position in Chinese History, 1200–1600." Paper presented at the Song-Yuan-Ming Transitions Conference, Lake Arrowhead, Calif., June 5–11, 1997.

Boorman, Howard, and Richard Howard, eds. *Biographical Dictionary of Republican China*. New York: Columbia University Press, 1967.

Borthwick, Sally. *Education and Social Change in China: The Beginnings of the Modern Era*. Stanford: Hoover Institution Press, 1983.

Bossler, Beverly. "Women's Literacy in Song Dynasty China: Preliminary Inquiries." Paper presented at the Song-Yuan-Ming Transitions Conference, Lake Arrowhead, Calif., June 5–11, 1997.

Boudon. *The Analysis of Ideology*. Translated by Malcolm Slater. Chicago: University of Chicago Press, 1989.

Bourdieu, Pierre. "Systems of Education and Systems of Thought." In Michael Young, ed., *Knowledge and Control: New Directions for the Sociology of Education.* London: Collier Macmillan, 1971.

———. "The Economics of Linguistic Exchanges." Translated by Richard Nice. *Social Science Information* 16, 6 (1977): 645–68.

———. *Distinction: A Social Critique of the Judgement of Taste.* Cambridge: Harvard University Press, 1984.

———. *Homo Academicus.* Stanford: Stanford University Press, 1988.

Bourdieu, Pierre, and Monique de Saint-Martin. "Scholastic Values and the Values of the Educational System." In J. Eggleston, ed., *Contemporary Research in the Sociology of Education.* London: Metheun, 1974.

Bourdieu, Pierre, and Jean-Claude Passeron. *Reproduction in Education, Society, and Culture.* Translated by Richard Nice. Beverly Hills, Calif.: Sage Publications, 1977.

Brokaw, Cynthia. *The Ledgers of Merit and Demerit: Social Change and Moral Order in Late Imperial China.* Princeton: Princeton University Press, 1991.

———. "Commercial Publishing in Late Imperial China: The Zou and Ma Family Businesses of Sibao, Fujian." *Late Imperial China* 17, 1 (June 1996): 49–92.

Brook, Timothy. *Praying for Power: Buddhism and the Formation of Gentry Society in Late-Ming China.* Cambridge: Harvard-Yenching Institute Monograph Series, 1993.

———. "Edifying Knowledge: The Building of School Libraries in Ming China." *Late Imperial China* 17, 1 (June 1996): 93–119.

Brose, Michael. "Uighur Elites in Yuan and Ming: A Case of Negotiated Identity." Paper presented at the Song-Yuan-Ming Transitions Conference, Lake Arrowhead, Calif., June 5–11, 1997.

Brown, Carolyn, ed. *Psycho-Sinology: The Universe of Dreams in Chinese Culture.* Lantham, Md.: University Press of America, 1988.

Buck, David D. "Educational Modernization in Tsinan, 1899–1937." In Mark Elvin and G. William Skinner, eds., *The Chinese City between Two Worlds.* Stanford: Stanford University Press, 1974.

Buck, Mary. "Justice for All: The Application of Law by Analogy in the Case of Zhou Fuqing." *Journal of Chinese Law* 7, 2 (fall 1993): 113–43.

Buck, Peter. *American Science and Modern China.* Cambridge: Cambridge University Press, 1980.

Bullock, T. L. "Competitive Examinations in China." In James Knowles, ed., *Nineteenth Century* (London) 36 (July 1894): 87–99.

Burke, Kenneth. *On Symbols and Society.* Chicago: University of Chicago Press, 1989.

Busch, Heinrich. "The Tung-lin Academy and Its Political and Philosophical Significance." *Monumenta Serica* 14 (1949–55): 1–163.

Cahill, James. *Hills beyond a River: Chinese Painting of the Yuan Period, 1279–1368.* New York: Weatherhill, 1976.

———. *Parting at the Shore: Chinese Painting of the Early and Middle Ming Dynasty, 1368–1580.* New York: Weatherhill, 1978.

Cameron, Meribeth. *The Reform Movement in China, 1898–1912.* Stanford: Stanford University Press, 1931.

Campany, Robert F. *Strange Writing: Anomaly Accounts in Early Medieval China.* Albany: SUNY Press, 1996.

Carnoy, Martin. "Education, Economy, and the State." In Michael Apple, ed., *Cultural and Economic Reproduction in Education*. London: Routledge & Kegan Paul, 1982.

Chaffee, John. "Chu Hsi and the Revival of the White Deer Grotto Academy, 1179–81." *T'oung Pao* 71 (1985).

———. *The Thorny Gates of Learning in Sung China*. Cambridge: Cambridge University Press, 1985. 2nd edition, Albany: SUNY Press, 1995.

Chan, Hok-lam. "The Rise of Ming T'ai-tsu (1368–98): Facts and Fictions in Early Ming Historiography." *Journal of the American Oriental Society* 95 (1975): 679–715.

———. "Chinese Official Historiography at the Yuan Court: The Composition of the Liao, Chin, and Sung Histories." In John D. Langlois, Jr., ed., *China under Mongol Rule*. Princeton: Princeton University Press, 1981.

———. *Theories of Legitimacy in Imperial China*. Seattle: University of Washington Press, 1982.

———. "The Chien-wen, Yung-lo, Hung-hsi, and Hsuan-te Reigns, 1399–1435." In Frederick W. Mote and Denis Twitchett, eds., *The Cambridge History of China*, vol. 7, part 1, *The Ming Dynasty, 1368–1644*. Cambridge: Cambridge University Press, 1988.

Chan, Wing-tsit. "The Ch'eng-Chu School of Early Ming." In William Theodore de Bary et al., *Self and Society in Ming Thought*. New York: Columbia University Press, 1970.

———. "Chu Hsi's Completion of Neo-Confucianism." *Études Song-Sung Studies* 2, 1 (1973).

———, trans. *Instructions for Practical Living and Other Neo-Confucian Writings by Wang Yang-ming*. New York: Columbia University Press, 1963.

———. *Reflections on Things at Hand. The Neo-Confucian Anthology Compiled by Chu Hsi and Lü Tsu-ch'ien*. New York: Columbia University Press, 1967.

Chang Ch'en-shih 張忱石. "Yung-lo ta-tien shih-hua" 永樂大典史話 (Historical remarks on the Great compendium of the Yung-lo era). In *Ku-tai yao-chi kai-shu* 古代要籍概述, pp. 187–92. Peking: Chung-hua Bookstore, 1987.

Chang Chieh-pin 張介賓. *Ching-yueh ch'üan-shu* 景岳全書 (Complete works of physician Chang). Shanghai: Science & Technology Press, 1984.

Chang Chien-jen 張健仁. *Ming-tai chiao-yü kuan-li chih-tu yen-chiu* 明代教育管理制度研究 (Research on the educational review system of the Ming dynasty). Taipei: Wen-chin Press, 1991.

Chang Chih-kung 張志公. *Ch'uan-t'ung yü-wen chiao-yü ch'u-t'an* 傳統語文教育初探 (Preliminary inquiry into traditional language education). Shanghai: Education Press, 1962.

Chang, Chun-shu. "Emperorship in Eighteenth-Century China." *Journal of the Institute of Chinese Studies of the Chinese University of Hong Kong* 7, 2 (December 1974).

Chang Chung-ju 章中如. *Ch'ing-tai k'ao-shih chih-tu* 清代考試制度 (Ch'ing civil examination system). Shanghai: Li-ming Bookstore, 1931.

Chang, Chung-li. *The Chinese Gentry*. Seattle: University of Washington Press, 1955.

———. *The Income of the Chinese Gentry*. Seattle: University of Washington Press, 1962.

Chang Feng-i 張鳳翼. *Meng-chan lei-k'ao* 夢占類考 (Classified studies of dream interpretations). Late Ming edition.

Chang Hsueh-ch'eng 章學城. *Chang-shih i-shu* 章氏遺書. (Bequeathed works of Mr. Chang Hsueh-ch'eng). Reprint, Shanghai: Commercial Press, 1936.

———. *Wen-shih t'ung-i* 文史通義 (General meaning of literature and history). Taipei: Han-shang Press, 1973.

———. "Lun k'o-meng hsueh wen-fa" 論科蒙學文法 (On teaching students to write). In Chang Hsueh-ch'eng *Chang-shih i-shu*, 章氏遺書, "Pu-i" 補遺 (Supplement).

Chang Hung-sheng 張鴻聲. "Ch'ing-tai i-kuan k'ao-shih chi t'i-li" 清代醫官考試及題例 (Ch'ing dynasty examinations for medical officials with examples). *Chung-hua i-shih tsa-chih* 中華醫史雜誌 25, 2 (April 1995): 95–96.

Chang I-shan 張奕善. *Chu-Ming wang-ch'ao shih-lun wen-chi—T'ai-tsu, T'ai-tsung p'ien* 朱明王朝史論文輯—太祖太宗篇 (Collected historical essays on the Chu's Ming dynasty—Emperors T'ai-tsu and T'ai-tsung). Taipei: Kuo-li pien-i kuan, 1991.

Chang Po-hsing 張伯行. "Tzu-yang shu-yuan shih chu-sheng" 紫陽書院示諸生 (Informing students at the Tzu-yang Academy). In *Ch'ing-tai ch'ien-ch'i chiao-yü lun-chu hsuan* 清代前期教育論著選 (Selections of writings on education from the early Ch'ing period), edited by Li Kuo-chün et al., 3 vols. Peking: People's Education Press, 1990.

Chang P'u 張溥. *Ssu-shu k'ao-pei* 四書考備 (Search for completeness in the Four Books). Ca. 1642.

Chang, Wejen. "Legal Education in Ch'ing China." In Benjamin Elman and Alexander Woodside, eds., *Education and Society in Late Imperial China, 1600–1900*. Berkeley: University of California Press, 1994.

*Ch'ang-chou fu-chih hsu-chih* 常州府誌續志 (Continuation of the gazetteer of Ch'ang-chou Prefecture). 1513 edition.

*Ch'ang-t'an* 常談 (Everyday discussions on the civil examinations). Compiled by T'ao Fu-lü 陶福履. In *Ts'ung-shu chi-ch'eng ch'u-pien* 叢書集成初編. Shanghai: Commercial Press, 1936.

Chao Hsin-i. "Daoist Examinations and Daoist Schools during the Northern Sung Dynasty." Seminar paper, UCLA History Department, 1994.

Chao I 趙翼. *Nien-erh shih cha-chi* 廿二史劄記 (Reading notes to the twenty-two dynastic histories). Taipei: Kuang-wen Bookstore, 1974.

Chao, Wei-pang. "The Chinese Science of Fate-Calculation." *Folklore Studies* 5 (1946).

Chao, Yuan-ling. "Medicine and Society in Late Imperial China: A Study of Physicians in Suzhou." Ph.D. diss., UCLA, History, 1995.

Chartier, Roger. "Gutenberg Revisited from the East." *Late Imperial China* 17, 1 (1996): 1–9.

Chauncey, Helen R. *Schoolhouse Politicians: Locality and State during the Chinese Republic*. Honolulu: University of Hawaii Press, 1992.

Chen, Fu-mei Chang. "On Analogy in Ch'ing Law." *Harvard Journal of Asiatic Studies* 30 (1970): 212–24.

Chen, Min-sun. "Three Contemporary Western Sources on the History of the Late Ming and the Manchu Conquest of China." Ph.D. diss., University of Chicago, History, 1971.

Chen, Yu-shih. *Images and Ideas in Chinese Classical Prose: Studies of Four Masters*. Stanford: Stanford University Press, 1988.

Ch'en Chen-ch'eng 陳真晟. "Ch'eng-shih hsueh-chih" 程氏學制 (Study system of Master Ch'eng). In *Ming-tai chiao-yü lun-chu hsuan* 明代教育論著選 (Selections from writings on education during the Ming dynasty). Peking: People's Education Press, 1990.

Ch'en Ch'ing-hsin 陳慶新. "Sung-ju Ch'un-ch'iu tsun-wang yao-i te fa-wei yü ch'i cheng-chih ssu-hsiang" 宋儒春秋遵王要義的發微與其政治思想 (Propagation of the key meaning to honor the ruler in the Spring and Autumn Annals by Sung Confucians and their political thought). *Hsin-Ya hsueh-pao* 新亞學報 1A (December 1971): 269–368.

Ch'en Heng-sung 陳恆嵩. "Shu-chuan ta-ch'üan ch'ü-ts'ai lai-yuan t'an-chiu" 書傳大全取材來源探究 (Inquiry into the sources selected for the *Complete Collection of Commentaries for the Documents Classic*). In Lin Ch'ing-chang 林慶彰, ed., *Ming-tai ching-hsueh kuo-chi yen-t'ao-hui lun-wen chi* 明代經學國際研討會論文集. Taipei: Academia Sinica, 1996.

Ch'en Hua-hsin 陳華新 et al. *Hung Hsiu-ch'üan ssu-hsiang yen-chiu* 洪秀全思想研究 (Research on the thought of Hung Hsiu-ch'üan). Canton: Kuang-tung People's Press, 1991.

Ch'en Liang 陳亮. *Lung-ch'uan wen-chi* 龍川文集 (Collected essays of Ch'en Liang). *Ssu-pu pei-yao* 四部備要 edition. Shanghai: Chung-hua Bookstore, 1927–35.

Ch'en Shih-kuan 陳世倌. "Tsou-che" 奏摺 (Memorial), 1757, 10th month, 6th day. Ch'ing dynasty examination materials in the Ming-Ch'ing Archives, Academia Sinica, Taiwan.

Ch'en Shih-yuan 陳士元. *Meng-chan i-chih* 夢占逸旨 (Remaining points on dream interpretation). *Pai-pu ts'ung-shu* 百部叢書 edition. Reprint, Taipei: I-wen Publishing, 1968.

Ch'en Shou-ch'i 陳壽祺. *Tso-hai wen-chi* 左海文集 (Collected essays of Ch'en Shou-ch'i). Ch'ing edition ca. 1796–1849.

Ch'en, Shou-yi. *Chinese Literature: A Historical Introduction*. New York: Ronald Press, 1961.

Ch'en Te-yun 陳德芸. "Pa-ku wen-hsueh" 八股文學 (Eight-legged essay literature). *Ling-nan hsueh-pao* 嶺南學報 6, 4 (June 1941): 17–21.

Ch'en Wu-t'ung 陳梧桐. *Chu Yuan-chang yen-chiu* 朱元璋研究 (Study of Chu Yuan-chang). T'ien-chin: People's Press, 1993.

Cheng, Chung-ying. "On Implication (*tse* 則) and Inference (*ku* 故) in Chinese Grammar." *Journal of Chinese Philosophy* 2, 3 (June 1975): 225–43.

Cheng K'o-ch'eng 鄭克晟. *Ming-tai cheng-cheng t'an-yuan* 明代政爭探源 (Inquiry into the origins of political struggle during the Ming dynasty). T'ien-chin: T'ien-chin ku-chi Press, 1988.

Cheng Pang-chen 鄭邦鎮. "Pa-ku-wen 'shou-ching tsun-chu' te k'ao-ch'a: Chü Ch'in-ting Ssu-shu wen ssu-t'i pa-p'ien wei li" 八股文守經遵注的考察：舉欽定四書文四題八篇為例 (Analysis of the eight-legged essay in terms of 'preserving the Classics and honoring the commentaries': Using eight essays on four quotations in the *Ch'in-ting Ssu-shu wen* as examples). In *Ch'ing-tai hsueh-shu yen-t'ao-hui* 清代學術研討會, vol. 1. Kao-hsiung: Chung-shan University, 1989.

Ch'eng Hao 程顥. "Ch'ing hsiu hsueh-hsiao tsun shih-ju ch'ü-shih cha-tzu" 請修學校尊師儒取士箚子 (A directive for building schools and honoring teachers and scholars to select literati). In *Erh Ch'eng wen-chi* 二程文集 (Collected essays of the Ch'eng brothers). Taipei: I-wen Press, n.d.

Ch'eng I 程頤. *Ho-nan Ch'eng-shih i-shu* 河南程氏遺書 (Bequeathed writings of Ch'eng I). In *Erh-Ch'eng ch'üan-shu* 二程全書. Shanghai, 1927–35.

Ch'eng Tuan-li 程端禮. *Ch'eng-shih chia-shu tu-shu fen-nien jih-ch'eng* 程氏家塾讀書分年日程 (Daily and yearly reading schedule in the Cheng clan school). *Pai-pu ts'ung-shu* 百部叢書 edition. Reprint, Taipei: I-wen Press.

Cherniack, Susan. "Book Culture and Textual Transmission in Sung China." *Harvard Journal of Asiatic Studies* 54, 1 (1994): 5–125.

Chi Yun 紀昀. *Yueh-wei ts'ao-t'ang pi-chi* 閱微草堂筆記 (Note-form writings from the straw hut for reading subtleties). Shanghai: Ku-chi Press, 1980.

Ch'i-kung 啟功. "Shuo pa-ku" 說八股 (On the eight-legged essay). *Pei-ching shih-fan ta-hsueh hsueh-pao* 北京師範大學學報 3 (1991): 56–58.

Chia, Lucille. "The Development of the Jianyang Book Trade, Song-Yuan." *Late Imperial China* 17, 1 (June 1996): 10–48.

———. "Commercial Publishing in Ming China: New Developments in a Very Old Industry." Paper presented at the 49th annual meeting of the Association for Asian Studies, Chicago, March 15, 1997.

———. "*Mashaben:* Commercial Publishing in Jianyang, Song-Ming." Paper presented at the Song-Yuan-Ming Transitions Conference, Lake Arrowhead, Calif., June 5–11, 1997.

Chia Nai-lien 賈乃謙. "Ts'ung Meng-tzu chieh-wen chih Ch'ien-shu" 從孟子節文致潛書 (From the Abridged text of the Mencius to the Submerged writings). *Tung-pei shih-ta hsueh-pao* 東北師大學報 2 (1987): 43–44.

Chiang An-fu 江安傅. *Ch'ing-tai tien-shih k'ao-lueh* 清代殿試考略 (Survey of Ch'ing period palace examinations). T'ien-chin: Ta-kung Press, 1933.

Chiang Chu-shan 蔣竹山. "Seminar Paper on the *Chuang-yuan t'u-k'ao* 狀元圖考. Tsing Hua University, Hsin-chu, Taiwan, 1990.

Chiao Hung 焦竑. *Hsin-ch'ieh huang-Ming pai-ming-chia Ssu-shu li-chieh chi* 新鍥皇明百名家四書理解集 (Newly carved collection of commentary on moral principle in the Four Books by one hundred famous writers of the august Ming). Ca. 1594.

———. *Kuo-ch'ao hsien-cheng lu* 國朝獻徵錄 (Record of verified documents during the Ming dynasty). 1616 Wan-li edition. Reprint, Taipei: Student Bookstore, 1984.

Ch'iao Kuo-chang 喬國章. "Lun T'ung-ch'eng-p'ai ku-wen ho Ch'ing-ch'ao te wen-hua t'ung-chih" 論桐城派古文和清朝的文化統治 (On the ancient-style prose of the T'ung-ch'eng school and Ch'ing dynasty cultural control). In *T'ung-ch'eng-p'ai yen-chiu lun-wen chi* 桐城派研究論文集. Ho-fei: An-hui People's Press, 1963.

Chieh Hsi-ssu 揭傒斯. *Chieh Wen-an kung ch'üan-chi* 揭文安公全集 (Complete collection of Chieh Hsi-ssu). *Ssu-pu ts'ung-k'an* 四部叢刊 edition. Shanghai: Commercial Press, 1920–22.

Chien Chin-sung 簡錦松. *Ming-tai wen-hsueh p'i-p'ing yen-chiu* 明代文學批評研究 (Research on Ming dynasty literary criticism). Taipei: Student Bookstore, 1989.

*Chien-wen ch'ao-yeh hui-pien* 建文朝野彙編 (Compendium of unofficial records on the Chien-wen reign). Compiled by T'u Shu-fang 屠叔方. Wan-li edition. Reprinted in *Pei-ching t'u-shu-kuan ku-chi chen-pen ts'ung-k'an*, vol. 11. Peking: Shu-mu Press, 1988.

Chien Yu-wen 簡又文. *T'ai-p'ing t'ien-kuo tien-chih t'ung-k'ao* 太平天國典制通考 (Comprehensive study of the Taiping Heavenly Kingdom's ordinances and institutions). Hong Kong: Chi-cheng Book, 1958.

Ch'ien Chi-po 錢基伯. *Ming-tai wen-hsueh* 明代文學 (Ming dynasty literature). Shanghai: Commercial Press, 1939.

Ch'ien Chung-lien 錢仲聯. "T'ung-ch'eng-p'ai ku-wen yü shih-wen te kuan-hsi wen-t'i" 桐城派古文與時文的關係問題 (Concerning the question of the relation between ancient-style prose of the T'ung-ch'eng school and contemporary-style [examination] essays). In *T'ung-ch'eng-p'ai yen-chiu lun-wen chi* 桐城派研究論文集. Ho-fei: An-hui People's Press, 1963.

Ch'ien, Edward. *Chiao Hung and the Restructuring of Neo-Confucianism in the Late Ming*. New York: Columbia University Press, 1986.

Ch'ien I-pen 錢一本. *Fan-yen* 範衍 (Exposition of models). Ca. 1606 edition.

———. *Kuei-chi* 龜記 (Records on tortoise shells). Ca. 1613 edition.

Ch'ien-lung 乾隆 emperor. "1788 edict decrying literary fads." In *Ch'ing-tai ch'ien-ch'i chiao-yü lun-chu hsuan* 清代前期教育論著選 (Selections of writings on education from the early Ch'ing period), edited by Li Kuo-chün et al., 3 vols. Peking: People's Education Press, 1990.

*Ch'ien-Ming k'o-ch'ang i-wen-lu* 前明科場異聞錄 (Recording unusual matters heard in the earlier Ming examination grounds). Wei-ching-t'ang shu-fang 味經堂書坊 edition. Canton; reprint, Ch'ien-t'ang, 1873.

*Ch'ien-Ming kung-chü k'ao-lueh* 前明貢舉考略 (Brief study of civil examinations in the earlier Ming dynasty). Compiled by Huang Ch'ung-lan 黃崇蘭. 1834 edition.

Ch'ien, Mu. *Traditional Government in Imperial China: A Critical Analysis*. Translated by Chün-tu Hsueh and George Totten. Hong Kong: Chinese University Press, 1982.

Ch'ien Ta-hsin 錢大昕. *Shih-chia-chai yang-hsin lu* 十駕齋養新錄 (Record of self-renewal from the Ten Yokes Study). 1804 edition. Reprint, Taipei: Kuang-wen Bookstore.

———. "Hsu" 序 (Preface). In *Nien-erh-shih k'ao-i* 廿二史考異 (Examination of variances in the twenty-two dynastic histories). Shanghai: Commercial Press, 1935–37.

———. "Hu-nan hsiang-shih lu hsu" 湖南鄉試錄序 (Preface to the Hunan provincial examination). In *Ch'ien-yen-t'ang wen-chi* 潛研堂文集 (Collected essays from the Hall of Subtle Research), 8 vols. *Kuo-hsueh chi-pen ts'ung-shu* edition. Taipei: Commercial Press, 1968.

Chin Chung-shu 金中樞. "Pei Sung k'o-chü chih-tu yen-chiu" 北宋科舉制度研究 (Research on the Northern Sung civil examination system). *Sung-shih yen-chiu chi* 宋史研究集 (Taiwan) 11 (1979): 1–72; 13 (1981): 61–188; 14 (1983): 53–189; 15 (1984): 125–88; 16 (1986): 1–125.

Chin Jih-sheng 金日升. *Sung-t'ien lu-pi* 松天臚筆 (Display of writings in praise of heaven). 1633 edition.

*Chin-k'o ch'üan-t'i hsin-ts'e fa-ch'eng* 近科全題新策法程 (Models of complete answers for new policy questions in recent provincial civil examinations). Compiled and annotated by Liu T'an-chih 劉坦之. 1764 edition.

*Chin-shih* 金史 (History of the Chin dynasty). Compiled by Toghto (T'o T'o) 脫脫 (1314–55) et al. Peking: Chung-hua Bookstore, 1965.

*Chin-shih san-tai lü-li pien-lan* 進士三代履歷便覽 (Overview by region of backgrounds to three generations of civil *chin-shih* graduates from 1646 to 1721). N.d.

*Chin-shih t'ung-nien hsu-ch'ih pien-lan* 進士同年序齒便覽 (Overview of *chin-shih* graduates in the same year), 1595.

*Ch'in-ch'ü ch'ao-k'ao chüan* 欽取朝考卷 (Imperially selected [Ch'ing] court examination papers). In the Kyoto University Oriental Library.

*Ch'in-ting hsueh-cheng ch'üan-shu* 欽定學政全書 (Imperially sponsored collection of writings by education commissioners). Ca. 1773 edition.

*Ch'in-ting k'o-ch'ang t'iao-li* 欽定科場條例 (Imperially prescribed guidelines for the civil examination grounds). 1832 edition.

*Ch'in-ting mo-k'an t'iao-li* 欽定磨勘條例 (Imperially prescribed guidelines for post-examination review of civil examination papers). Late Ch'ien-lung (r. 1736–95) edition.

*Ch'in-ting Ta-Ch'ing hui-tien shih-li* 欽定大清會典事例 (Collected statutes and precedents in the great Ch'ing). Taipei: Chung-hua Bookstore, 1968.

*Ching-hsiang t'i-ming lu* 靜庠題名錄 (Record of civil service graduates in Ching-hsiang). Compiled by Li Yun-hui 李芸暉. 1895 edition.

Ching, Julia. "Truth and Ideology: The Confucian Way (Tao) and Its Transmission (Tao-t'ung)." *Journal of the History of Ideas* 35, 3 (July–September 1974): 371–88.

*Ch'ing-ch'ao hsu wen-hsien t'ung-k'ao* 清朝續文獻通考 (Comprehensive analysis of civil institutions of the Ch'ing dynasty, continuation). Compiled by Wang Ch'i 王圻. In *Shih-t'ung* 十通 (Ten comprehensive encyclopedias). Shanghai: Commercial Press, 1936.

*Ch'ing-ch'ao t'ung-tien* 清朝通典 (Complete institutions of the Ch'ing dynasty). In *Shih-t'ung* 十通 (Ten comprehensive encyclopedias). Shanghai: Commercial Press, 1936.

*Ch'ing cheng-fu chen-ya T'ai-p'ing t'ien-kuo tang-an shih-liao* 清政府鎮壓太平天國檔案史料 (Archival historical documents on the Qing government suppression of the Taiping Heavenly Kingdom). Beijing: She-hui k'o-hsueh wen-hsien Press, 1992.

*Ch'ing li-ch'ao hsiu-ts'ai lu* 清歷朝秀才錄 (Record of local licentiates [in Su-chou] during Ch'ing reign periods). Manuscript, late Ch'ing.

*Ch'ing-shih kao* 清史稿 (Draft history of the Ch'ing dynasty). Compiled by Chao Erh-hsun 趙爾巽 et al. Chung-hua Press edition, 40 vols. Peking, 1977.

*Ch'ing-tai ch'ien-ch'i chiao-yü lun-chu hsuan* 清代前期教育論著選 (Selections of writings on education from the early Ch'ing period). Edited by Li Kuo-chün 李國鈞 et al. 3 vols. Peking: People's Education Press, 1990.

*Ch'ing-tai chu-chüan chi-ch'eng* 清代硃卷集成 (Ch'ing examination essays). Reprint, 420 vols., Taipei: Ch'eng-wen, published in cooperation with the Shanghai Library, 1993–94.

*Ch'ing-tai chuang-yuan p'u* 清代狀元譜 (Accounts of Ch'ing dynasty *optimi*). Compiled by Chou La-sheng 周腊生. Peking: Forbidden City Press, 1994.

Ch'iu Han-sheng 邱漢生. "Ming-ch'u Chu-hsueh te t'ung-chih ti-wei" 明初朱學的統治地位 (The hegemony of Chu Hsi learning in the early Ming). *Chung-kuo che-hsueh* 中國哲學 14 (1988): 142–43.

Cho, Gene J. *Lu-Lu: A Study of Its Historical, Acoustical, and Symbolic Signification*. Taipei: Caves Books, 1989.

Chou, Eva Shan. *Reconsidering Tu Fu: Literary Greatness and Cultural Context*. Cambridge: Cambridge University Press, 1995.

Chou Hsun-ch'u 周勛初. "K'ang-hsi yü-ting Ch'üan T'ang-shih te shih-tai yin-chi yü chü-hsien" 康熙御定全唐詩的時代印記與局限 (The setting and limitations of the K'ang-hsi emperor's edition of the Compete T'ang Poems). *Chung-kuo wen-che yen-chiu t'ung-hsun* 中國文哲研究通訊 (Academia Sinica, Taiwan) 5, 2 (June 1995): 1–12.

Chou Yen-wen 周彥文. "Lun li-tai shu-mu chung te chih-chü lei-shu-chi" 論歷代書目中的制舉類書籍 (On examination encyclopedias in book catalogs over the dynasties). *Shu-mu chi-k'an* 書目季刊 31 (June 1997): 1–13.

Chow, Kai-wing. "Discourse, Examination, and Local Elite: The Invention of the T'ung-ch'eng School in Ch'ing China." In Benjamin Elman and Alexander Woodside, eds., *Education and Society in Late Imperial China*. Berkeley: University of California Press, 1994.

———. *The Rise of Confucian Ritualism in Late Imperial China*. Stanford: Stanford University Press, 1994.

———. "Writing for Success: Printing, Examinations, and Intellectual Change in Late Ming China." *Late Imperial China* 17, 1 (June 1996): 120–57.

Chu Chen-heng 朱震亨. *Ko-chih yü-lun* 格致餘論 (Views on extending knowledge). In *Ssu-k'u ch'üan-shu* 四庫全書 (Complete collection of the four treasuries). Reprint, Taipei: Commercial Press, 1983–86.

*Chu-chüan* 硃卷 1661–85 (Anonymous vermillion papers from the [Ch'ing] metropolitan examinations). In the Ming-Ch'ing Archives, Academia Sinica, Taiwan. Copies available in UCLA East Asian Library.

Chu Hsi 朱熹. *Chu-tzu yü-lei* 朱子語類 (Conversations with Master Chu [Hsi] classified topically). 1473 edition. Reprint, Taipei: Chung-cheng Bookstore.

———. *Chu Wen-kung wen-chi* 朱文公文集 (Chu Hsi's collected essays). Ming edition (ca. 1522–66). *Ssu-pu ts'ung-k'an* 四部叢刊 photolithograph, Shanghai: Commercial Press, 1934–35.

———. *Chu-tzu ta-ch'üan* 朱子大全 (Master Chu [Hsi's] Great Compendium). *Ssu-pu ts'ung-k'an* edition. Shanghai: Commercial Press, 1920–22.

———. "Hsueh-hsiao kung-chü ssu-i" 學校貢舉私議 (Personal proposals for schools and civil examinations). In *Chu-tzu ta-ch'üan* 朱子大全 (Complete collection of Master Chu Hsi). Shanghai: Commercial Press, 1920–22.

———. *Chu-tzu ta-ch'üan* 朱子大全 (Master Chu [Hsi's] Great Compendium). *Ssu-pu pei-yao* 四部備要 edition. Shanghai: Chung-hua Bookstore, 1927–35.

———. *Chu Wen-kung wen-chi, hsu chi* 朱文公文集續集 (Continuation to the collected essays of Chu Hsi). *Ssu-pu ts'ung-k'an* edition. Shanghai: Commercial Press, 1934–35.

———. *Chung-yung chang-chü* 中庸章句 (Parsing of phrases and sentences in the *Doctrine of the Mean*). Ming edition. Reprint, Taipei: Commercial Press, 1980.

———. *Lun-yü chi-chu* 論語集注 (Collected notes on the Analects). In Chu's *Ssu-shu chang-chü chi-chu* 四書章句集注. Taipei: Ch'ang-an Press, 1991.

Chu Hung 朱鴻. *Ming Ch'eng-tsu yü Yung-lo cheng-chih* 明成祖與永樂政治 (The Ming Emperor Ch'eng-tsu and politics in the Yung-lo reign). Teacher's College Institute of History Monograph. Taipei, 1988.

Chu, Hung-lam. "Ch'iu Chün (1421–95) and the 'Ta-hsüeh yen-i pu': Statecraft Thought in Fifteenth-Century China." Ph.D. diss., Princeton University, East Asian Studies, 1983.

———. "Intellectual Trends in the Fifteenth Century." *Ming Studies* 27 (1989): 1–16.

Chu I-tsun 朱彝尊. *P'u-shu-t'ing chi* 曝書亭集 (Collection from the Pavilion for Honoring Books). *Ssu-pu ts'ung-k'an* edition. Shanghai: Commercial Press, 1919–37.

———. *Ching-i k'ao* 經義考 (Analysis of meanings in the Classics). Shanghai: Chung-hua Press, 1927–35.

———. *P'u-shu t'ing-chi* 曝書亭集. *Ssu-pu pei-yao* 四部備要 edition.

Chu Ping-yi 祝平一. *Han-tai te hsiang-jen shu* 漢代的相人術 (The technique of physiognomy in the Han period). Taipei: Hsueh-sheng Bookstore, 1990.

———. "Technical Knowledge, Cultural Practices and Social Boundaries: Wan-nan Scholars and Recasting of Jesuit Astronomy, 1600–1800." Ph.D. diss., UCLA, History, 1994.

———. "Ch'eng-Chu Orthodoxy, Evidential Studies and Correlative Cosmology: Chiang Yung and Western Astronomy." *Philosophy and the History of Science: A Taiwanese Journal* 4, 2 (October 1995): 71–108.

———. "Scientific Dispute in the Imperial Court: The 1664 Calendar Case." *Chinese Science* 14 (1997): 7–34.

Chu Ron-Guey 朱榮貴. "Ts'ung Liu San-wu Meng-tzu chieh-wen lun chün-ch'üan te hsien-chih yü chih-shih fen-tzu chih tzu-chu-hsing" 從劉三梧孟子節文論君權的限制與知識分子之自主性 (Limits on the ruler's power and the autonomy of intellectuals as viewed from Liu San-wu's Abridged text of the Mencius). *Chung-kuo wen-che yen-chiu chi-k'an* 中國文哲研究集刊 6 (1995): 173–95.

Chu, Sin-Jan. *Wu Leichuan: A Confucian-Christian in Republican China*. New York: Peter Lang, 1995.

Chu T'an 朱倓. *Ming-chi she-tang yen-chiu* 明季社黨研究 (Research on Ming dynasty societies and parties). Ch'ung-ch'ing: Commercial Press, 1945.

Chu Ti 朱棣. *Sheng-hsueh hsin-fa* 聖學心法 (The method of the mind in the sages' teachings). 1409; *Chung-kuo tzu-hsueh ming-chu chi-ch'eng* 中國子學名著集成 reprint, Taipei, 1978.

———. "Yü-chih Hsing-li ta-ch'üan hsu" 御製性理大全序 (Imperial preface to the official presentation of the *Great Collection of Works on Nature and Principle*). In *Hsing-li ta-ch'üan* 性理大全. 1415 edition. Reprint, Kyoto: Chūbun Press.

Ch'u, T'ung-tsu. *Law and Society in Traditional China*. Paris: Mouton, 1961.

———. *Local Government in China under the Ch'ing*. Stanford: Stanford University Press, 1962.

*Chü-yeh cheng-shih* 舉業正式 (Correct models for examinations). Chia-ching edition.

Ch'üan Te-yü 權德輿. *Ch'üan Tsai-chih wen-chi* 權載之文集 (Collected essays of Ch'üan Te-yü). *Ssu-pu ts'ung-k'an* 四部叢刊 edition. Shanghai: Commercial Press, 1919–37.

Chuang Chi-fa 莊吉發. "Ch'ing Kao-tsung Ch'ien-lung shih-tai te hsiang-shih" 清高宗乾隆時代的鄉試 (Provincial examinations during the reign period of the Ch'ien-lung Emperor of the Ch'ing dynasty). *Ta-lu tsa-chih* 大陸雜誌 52, 4 (December 1975).

Chuang Chu 莊柱. *P'i-ling k'o-ti k'ao* 毘陵科第考 (Record of examination success in Ch'ang-chou). 1868 edition.

*Chuang-yuan ts'e* 狀元策 (Policy answers of *optimi*). Compiled by Chiao Hung 焦竑 and Wu Tao-nan 吳道南. Late Ming edition.

*Chuang-yuan ts'e* 狀元策 (Policy essays by *optimi)*. Compiled by Chiao Hung 焦竑, Wu Tao-nan 吳道南, et al. 1733 edition.

*Chuang-yuan t'u-k'ao* 狀元圖考 (Illustrated survey of *optimi* during the Ming dynasty). Compiled by Ku Tsu-hsun 顧祖訓 and Wu Ch'eng-en 吳承恩. 1607 edition. (See also *Ming chuang-yuan t'u-k'ao*.)

*Ch'un-ch'iu ching-chuan yin-te* 春秋經傳引得 (Combined concordances to the *Spring and Autumn Annals* and commentaries). Taipei: Ch'eng-wen Publishing, 1966.

*Ch'un-ch'iu fan-lu i-cheng* 春秋繁露義證 (Proofs of meanings in [Tung Chung-shu's] The Spring and Autumn's Radiant Dew). Compiled by Su Yü 蘇輿. Kyoto: Chūbun Press, 1973.

*Chung-kuo chin-tai chiao-yü-shih tzu-liao hui-pien* 中國近代教育史資料匯編 (Compendium of sources on the history of Chinese modern education). Shanghai: Education Press, 1990.

*Chung-kuo chin-tai chiao-yü-shih tzu-liao hui-pien: ya-p'ien chan-cheng shih-ch'i chiao-yü* 中國近代教育史資料匯編：鴉片戰爭時期教育 (Compendium of sources on the history of Chinese modern education: Opium War education). Compiled by Chen Yuan-hui 陳元暉. Shanghai: Education Press, 1990.

*Chung-kuo li-tai chuang-yuan tien-shih chüan* 中國歷代狀元殿試卷 (Palace examination papers over the dynasties in China). Compiled by Teng Hung-p'o 鄧洪波 et al. Hai-nan: Hai-nan Press, 1993.

*Chung-wai shih-wu ts'e-wen lei-pien ta-ch'eng* 中外時務策問類編大成 (Great compendium of policy questions on Chinese and foreign affairs classified topically). 1903 edition.

*Ch'ung-chen shih-lu* 崇禎實錄 (Veritable records of the Ch'ung-chen reign). Reprint, Taipei: Academia Sinica Institute of History and Philology, 1967.

Chuzo, Ichiko. "The Role of the Gentry: An Hypothesis." In Mary Wright, ed., *China in Revolution: The First Phase, 1900–13.* New Haven: Yale University Press, 1968.

———. "Political and Institutional Reform, 1901–11." In John K. Fairbank and Kwang-ching Liu, eds., *The Cambridge History of China,* vol. 11, part 2. Cambridge: Cambridge University Press, 1980.

Cleverley, John. *The Schooling of China: Tradition and Modernity in Chinese Education.* London: Allen & Unwin, 1985.

Clunas, Craig. *Superfluous Things: Material Culture and Social Status in Early Modern China.* Urbana: University of Illinois Press, 1991.

Cole, James. *Shaohsing: Competition and Cooperation in Nineteenth-Century China.* Tucson: University of Arizona Press, 1986.

Collins, Randall. *The Credential Society: An Historical Sociology of Education and Stratification.* Orlando: Academic Press, 1979.

"Competitive Examinations in China: A Chapter of Chinese Travel." *Edinburgh Magazine* (London) 138 (July–December 1885).

Crawford, Robert. "The Biography of Juan Ta-ch'eng." *Chinese Culture* 6 (1965): 28–105.

———. "Chang Chü-cheng's Confucian Legalism." In William Theodore de Bary et al., *Self and Society in Ming Thought.* New York: Columbia University Press, 1970.

Crawford, Robert, Harry Lamley, and Albert Mann. "Fang Hsiao-ju in Light of Early Ming Society." *Monumenta Serica* 15 (1956): 305–07.

Creel, Herrlee. *Confucius and the Chinese Way.* New York: Harper & Row, 1960.

Crossley, Pamela K. *Orphan Warriors: Three Manchu Generations and the End of the Ch'ing World.* Princeton: Princeton University Press, 1990.

———. "Structure and Symbol in the Role of the Ming-Qing Foreign Translation Bureaus" (*Siyiguan*). *Central and Inner Asian Studies* 5 (1991): 38–70.

———. "Manchu Education." In Benjamin Elman and Alexander Woodside, eds., *Education and Society in Late Imperial China.* Berkeley: University of California Press, 1994.

Cullen, Christopher, and Anne Farrer. "On the Term *hsuan chi* and the Flanged Trilobate Discs." *Bulletin of the School of Oriental and African Studies* 46, 1 (1983): 52–76.

Dale, H. E. *The Higher Civil Service of Great Britain.* London: Oxford University Press, 1941.

Danjō Hiroshi 檀上寬. "Mindai kakyo kaikaku no seijiteki haikei—nanbokuken no sō setsu o megutte" 明代科舉改革の政治的背景—南北卷の創設をめぐって (The political background to Ming dynasty reform of the civil service examination—concerning the establishment of quotas for northern and southern candidates). *Tōhō gakuhō* 東方學報 58 (1986): 499–524.

———. "Mindai nanbokuken no shisō haikei" 明代南北卷の思想的背景 (The intellectual background to the northern versus southern examination papers case during the Ming dynasty). In Kotani Nakao 小谷仲男 et al., *Higashi Ajiashi ni okeru bunka denpa to chihōsa no shosō* 東アジア史における文化傳播と地方差の諸相, pp. 55–67. Fuyama University, 1988.

———. "Minsho Kenbunchō no rekishi teki ichi" 明初建文朝の歴史的位置 (The historical position of the Chien-wen court in the early Ming). *Chūgoku—bunka to shakai* 中國—文化と社會 7 (1992): 167–75.

Dardess, John W. "The Transformation of Messianic Revolt and the Founding of the Ming Dynasty." *Journal of Asian Studies* 29, 3 (1970): 539–58.

———. *Conquerors and Confucians: Aspects of Political Change in Late Yuan China*. New York: Columbia University Press, 1973.

———. "The Cheng Communal Family: Social Organization and Neo-Confucianism in Yuan and Early Ming China." *Harvard Journal of Asiatic Studies* 34 (1974): 7–53.

———. "Ming T'ai-tsu on the Yuan: An Autocrat's Assessment of the Mongol Dynasty." *Bulletin of Sung and Yuan Studies* 14 (1978).

———. *Confucianism and Autocracy: Professional Elites in the Founding of the Ming Dynasty*. Stanford: Stanford University Press, 1983.

———. "The Management of Children and Youth in Upper-Class Households in Late Imperial China." Paper presented at the meetings of the Pacific Coast Branch of the American Historical Association, Occidental College, Pasadena, Calif., summer 1987.

———. *A Ming Society: T'ai-ho County, Kiangsi, in the Fourteenth to Seventeenth Centuries*. Berkeley: University of California Press, 1996.

Davis, Richard L. "Historiography as Politics in Yang Wei-chen's 'Polemic on Legitimate Succession.'" *T'oung Pao* 69, 1–3 (1983): 33–72.

———. *Wind against the Mountain: The Crisis of Politics and Culture in Thirteenth-Century China*. Cambridge: Harvard University Council on East Asian Studies, 1996.

de Bary, William Theodore. "Chinese Despotism and the Confucian Ideal: A Seventeenth-Century View." In John K. Fairbank, ed., *Chinese Thought and Institutions*. Chicago: University of Chicago Press, 1957.

———. "Individualism and Humanitarianism in Late Ming Thought." In William Theodore de Bary et al., *Self and Society in Ming Thought*. New York: Columbia University Press, 1970.

———. *Neo-Confucian Orthodoxy and the Learning of the Mind-and-Heart*. New York: Columbia University Press, 1981.

———. "Chu Hsi's Aims as an Educator." In de Bary and John W. Chaffee, eds., *Neo-Confucian Education: The Formative Stage*. Berkeley: University of California Press, 1989.

———. "Confucian Education in Premodern East Asia." In Wei-ming Tu, ed., *Confucian Traditions in East Asian Modernity*. Cambridge: Harvard University Press, 1996.

———, ed. *The Unfolding of Neo-Confucianism*. New York: Columbia University Press, 1975.

———, trans. *A Plan for the Prince: Huang Tsung-hsi's Ming-i tai-fang lu*. New York: Columbia University Press, 1993.

de Bary, William Theodore, and John W. Chaffee, eds. *Neo-Confucian Education: The Formative Stage*. Berkeley: University of California Press, 1989.

de Crespigny, Rafe. "The Recruitment System of the Imperial Bureaucracy of Later Han." *Chung Chi Journal* 6, 1 (November 1966).

DeFrancis, John. *The Chinese Language: Fact and Fantasy*. Honolulu: University of Hawaii Press, 1984.

de Heer, Philip. *The Care-Taker Emperor: Aspects of the Imperial Institution in Fifteenth-Century China As Reflected in the Political History of the Reign of Chu Ch'i-yü*. Leiden: E. J. Brill, 1986.

d'Elia, Pasquale M., S.J., ed. *Fonti Ricciane: Documenti originali concernenti Matteo Ricci e la storia delle relazioni tra l'Europa e la Cina*. Vol. 1. Rome: Libreria dello Stato, 1942.

Dennerline, Jerry. *The Chia-ting Loyalists: Confucian Leadership and Social Change in Seventeenth-Century China*. New Haven: Yale University Press, 1981.

Depierre, Roland. "Maoism in Recent French Educational Thought and Practice." In Ruth Hayhoe and Marianne Bastid, eds., *China's Education and the Industrialized World: Studies in Cultural Transfer*. Armonk, N.Y.: M. E. Sharpe, 1987.

de Rachewiltz, Igor. "Yeh-lü Ch'u-ts'ai (1189–1243): Buddhist Idealist and Confucian Statesman." In Arthur Wright and Denis Twitchett, eds., *Confucian Personalities*. Stanford: Stanford University Press, 1962.

———. "Personnel and Personalities in North China in the Early Mongol Period." *Journal of the Economic and Social History of the Orient* 9, 1–2 (1966): 88–144.

des Rotours, Robert. *Le traite des examens traduit de la nouvelle histoire des T'ang*. Paris: Librairie Ernest Leroux, 1932.

De Weerdt, Hilde. "Aspects of Song Intellectual Life: A Preliminary Inquiry into Some Southern Song Encyclopedias." *Papers on China* (Harvard University) 3 (1994): 1–27.

———. "The Composition of Examination Standards: *Daoxue* and Southern Sung Dynasty Examination Culture." Ph.D. diss., Harvard University, East Asian Civilizations and Cultures, 1998.

DeWoskin, Kenneth. "The Six Dynasties *Chih-kuai* and the Birth of Fiction." In Andrew Plaks, ed., *Chinese Narrative*. Princeton: Princeton University Press, 1977.

———. *A Song for One or Two: Music and the Concept of Art in Early China*. Ann Arbor: University of Michigan Center for Chinese Studies, 1982.

*Dictionary of Ming Biography*. Edited by L. Carrington Goodrich et al. 2 vols. New York: Columbia University Press, 1976.

Dirks, Nicholas. *The Hollow Crown: Ethnohistory of an Indian Kingdom*. Cambridge: Cambridge University Press, 1987.

Ditmanson, Peter. "Intellectual Lineages and the Early Ming Court." *Papers on Chinese History* (Harvard University) 5 (1996): 1–17.

Dolezelova-Velingeroova, M. "The Origins of Modern Chinese Literature." In Merle Goldman, ed., *Modern Chinese Literature in the May Fourth Era*. Cambridge: Harvard University Press, 1977.

Doolittle, Justus. *Social Life of the Chinese*. New York: Harper & Brothers, 1865.

Duara, Prasenjit. *Culture, Power, and the State: Rural North China, 1900–1942*. Stanford: Stanford University Press, 1988.

———. "Superscribing Symbols: The Myth of Guandi, Chinese God of War." *Journal of Asian Studies* 47, 4 (November 1988): 783–85.

Dudbridge, Glen. *Religious Experience and Lay Society in T'ang China*. Cambridge: Cambridge University Press, 1995.

Dull, Jack. "A Historical Introduction to the Apocryphal (*Ch'an-wei*) Texts of the Han Dynasty." Ph.D. diss., University of Washington, 1966.

Dunne, George H., S.J. *Generation of Giants: The Story of the Jesuits in China in the Last*

*Decades of the Ming Dynasty*. Notre Dame, Ind.: University of Notre Dame Press, 1962.

Dunnell, Ruth. *The Great State of White and High: Buddhism and State Formation in Eleventh-Century Xia*. Honolulu: University of Hawaii Press, 1996.

Durand, Pierre-Henri. *Lettrés et pouvoirs: Un procès littéraire dans la Chine impériale*. Paris: École des Hautes Études en Sciences Sociales, 1992.

Durkheim, Emile. *Education and Sociology*. Translated by Sherwood Fox. Glencoe, Ill.: Free Press, 1956.

Dutton, Michael. *Policing and Punishment in China*. Cambridge: Cambridge University Press, 1992.

Eberhard, Wolfram. "The Political Function of Astronomy and Astronomers in Han China." In John K. Fairbank, ed., *Chinese Thought and Institutions*. Chicago: University of Chicago Press, 1957.

———. *Social Mobility in Traditional China*. Leiden: E. J. Brill, 1962.

———. *Lexikon chinesischer Symbole*. Cologne: Eugen Diederichs Verlag, 1983.

Ebrey, Patricia Buckley. "Patron-Client Relations in the Later Han." *Journal of the American Oriental Society* 103, 3 (1983): 533–42.

———. "Conceptions of the Family in the Sung Dynasty." *Journal of Asian Studies* 43, 2 (February 1984): 219–43.

———. *Confucianism and Family Rituals in Imperial China: A Social History of Writing about Rules*. Princeton: Princeton University Press, 1991.

———. *The Inner Quarters: Marriage and the Lives of Chinese Women in the Sung Period*. Berkeley: Universty of California Press, 1993.

Ebrey, Patricia Buckley, and James L. Watson, eds. *Kinship Organization in Late Imperial China, 1000–1940*. Berkeley: University of California Press, 1986.

Egan, Ronald C. *The Literary Works of Ou-yang Hsiu (1007–72)*. Cambridge: Cambridge University Press, 1984.

———. *Word, Image, and Deed in the Life of Su Shi*. Harvard-Yenching Institute Monograph Series, no. 39. Cambridge: Harvard University Council on East Asian Studies, 1994.

Elias, Norbert. *The Civilizing Process: The History of Manners*. Oxford: Blackwell, 1994.

Elman, Benjamin. "Ch'ing Schools of Scholarship." *Ch'ing-shih wen-t'i* 4, 6 (December 1979).

———. "Philosophy (*I-li*) versus Philology (*K'ao-cheng*): The *Jen-hsin Tao-hsin* Debate." *T'oung Pao* 59, 4–5 (1983): 175–222.

———. "The Unravelling of Neo-Confucianism: From Philosophy to Philology in Late Imperial China." *Tsing Hua Journal of Chinese Studies*, n.s., 15 (1983): 67–89.

———. *From Philosophy to Philology: Social and Intellectual Aspects of Change in Late Imperial China*. Cambridge: Harvard University Council on East Asian Studies, 1984.

———. "Criticism as Philosophy: Conceptual Change in Ch'ing Dynasty Evidential Research." *Tsing Hua Journal of Chinese Studies*, n.s., 17 (1985): 165–98.

———. "Imperial Politics and Confucian Societies in Late Imperial China: The Hanlin and Donglin Academies." *Modern China* 15, 4 (1989): 379–418.

———. "Ch'ing Dynasty Education Materials in the Department of Special Collections, UCLA." *Late Imperial China* 10, 2 (December 1989): 139–140.

———. *Classicism, Politics, and Kinship: The Ch'ang-chou School of New Text Confucianism in Late Imperial China*. Berkeley: University of California Press, 1990.

———. "Education in Sung China." *Journal of the American Oriental Society* III, 1 (January–March 1991): 83–93.

———. "Social, Political, and Cultural Reproduction via Civil Service Examinations in Late Imperial China." *Journal of Asian Studies* 51, 1 (February 1991): 7–28.

———. "Where Is King Ch'eng? Civil Examinations and Confucian Ideology during the Early Ming, 1368–1415." *T'oung Pao* 79 (1993): 23–68.

———. "Ming Politics and Confucian Classics: The Duke of Chou Serves King Ch'eng" 明代政治與經學：周公相成王. In *International Conference Volume on Ming Dynasty Classical Studies* 明代經學國際研討會論文集. Nankang, Taiwan: Institute of Chinese Literature and Philosophy, Academia Sinica, 1996.

Elman, Benjamin, and Alexander Woodside, eds. *Education and Society in Late Imperial China, 1600–1900.* Berkeley: University of California Press, 1994.

Elvin, Mark. "The Collapse of Scriptural Confucianism." *Papers on Far Eastern History* 41 (1990): 45–76.

*Erh-Ch'eng ch'üan-shu* 二程全書 (Complete writings of Ch'eng Hao and Ch'eng I). In *Ho-nan Ch'eng-shih i-shu* 河南程氏遺書 (Bequeathed writings of Ch'eng I). *Ssu-pu pei-yao* 四部備要 edition. Taipei : Chung-hua Bookstore, 1927–35.

Esherick, Joseph W. *Reform and Revolution in China: The 1911 Revolution in Hunan and Hubei.* Berkeley: University of California Press, 1976.

———. *The Origins of the Boxer Uprising.* Berkeley: University of California Press, 1987.

Esherick, Joseph W., and Mary Rankin, eds. *Chinese Local Elites and Patterns of Dominance.* Berkeley: University of California Press, 1990.

Fa-shih-shan 法式善. *Ch'ing-mi shu-wen* 清秘述聞 (Gleanings on Ch'ing secrets). Peking: Chung-hua Bookstore, 1982.

Fairbank, John K. *Trade and Diplomacy on the China Coast: The Opening of the Treaty Ports, 1842–1854.* Stanford: Stanford University Press, 1969.

Fan P'ei-wei 范沛潍. "Ch'ing-mo kuei-mao chia-ch'en hui-shih shu-lun" 清末癸卯甲辰會試述論 (Account of the 1903–04 metropolitan examinations at the end of the Ch'ing). *Chung-kuo chin-tai shih* 中國近代史 (1993.3): 81–86.

Fang Pao 方苞. *Fang Pao chi* 集 (Collected writings of Fang Pao). Shanghai: Rare Books Press, 1983.

———, comp. *Ch'in-ting Ssu-shu wen* 欽定四書文 (Imperially authorized essays on the Four Books). 1738; reprint, Taipei, Commercial Press, 1979.

Fang Tu Lien-che 房杜聯喆. "Ching-chi t'e-k'o" 經濟特科 (Special examination in economics). *Chung-kuo hsien-tai-shih ts'ung-k'an* 中國現代史叢刊 3 (1969): 1–44.

——— [Lien-che Tu Fang]. "Ming Dreams." *Tsing Hua Journal of Chinese Studies*, n.s., 10, 1 (June 1973): 61–70.

Farmer, Edward. "Social Order in Early Ming China: Some Norms Codified in the Hung-wu Period." In Brian McKnight, ed., *Law and the State in Traditional East Asia.* Honolulu: University of Hawaii Press, 1987.

———. "Social Regulations of the First Ming Emperor: Orthodoxy as a Function of Authority." In Kwang-Ching Liu, ed., *Orthodoxy in Late Imperial China.* Berkeley: University of California Press, 1990.

Fei, Hsiao-tung. *China's Gentry: Essays on Rural-Urban Relations.* Chicago: University of Chicago Press, 1953.

Feng Kuei-fen 馮桂芬. *Chiao-pin-lu k'ang-i* 校邠盧抗議 (Protests from the cottage of Feng Kuei-fen). 1897 edition. Reprint, Taipei: Wen-hai Press.

Feng Meng-chen 馮夢禎. *Li-tai kung-chü chih* 歷代貢舉志 (Accounts of the civil examinations over several dynasties). Shanghai: Commercial Press, 1936.

Fincher, John. "Political Provincialism and the National Revolution." In Mary Wright, ed., *China in Revolution: The First Phase, 1900–13*. New Haven: Yale University Press, 1968.

Fish, Michael. "Bibliographical Notes on the *San Tzu Ching* and Related Texts." Master's thesis, Indiana University, 1968.

Fisher, Carney. "The Great Ritual Controversy in the Age of Ming Shih-tsung." *Society for the Study of Chinese Religions Bulletin* 7 (fall 1979): 71–87.

———. *The Chosen One: Succession and Adoption in the Court of Ming Shizong*. Sydney: Allen & Unwin, 1990.

Foucault, Michel. *Discipline and Punish: The Birth of the Prison*. Translated by Alan Sheridan. New York: Vintage Books, 1979.

Franke, Herbert. "Tibetans in Yuan China." In John D. Langlois, Jr., ed., *China under Mongol Rule*. Princeton: Princeton University Press, 1981.

———. "The Role of the State as a Structural Element in Polyethnic Societies." In S. R. Schram, ed., *Foundations and Limits of State Power in China*. London: University of London, 1987.

Franke, Herbert, and Denis Twitchett, eds. *The Cambridge History of China*. Vol. 6, *Alien Regimes and Border States, 907–1368*. Cambridge: Cambridge University Press, 1994.

Franke, Wolfgang. *The Reform and Abolition of the Traditional Chinese Examination System*. Harvard University East Asian Monograph. Cambridge, 1960.

———. "The Veritable Records of the Ming Dynasty." In W. G. Beasley and E. G. Pulleyblank, eds., *Historians of China and Japan*. Oxford: Oxford University Press, 1961.

———. "Historical Writing during the Ming." In Frederick W. Mote and Denis Twitchett, eds., *The Cambridge History of China*, vol. 7, part 1, *The Ming Dynasty, 1368–1644*. Cambridge: Cambridge University Press, 1988.

Freedman, Maurice. *Chinese Lineage and Society: Fukien and Kwangtung*. London: Athlone Press, 1966.

———. *The Study of Chinese Society*. Edited by G. William Skinner. Stanford: Stanford University Press, 1979.

Freidson, Eliot. *Professional Powers: A Study of the Institutionalization of Formal Knowledge*. Chicago: University of Chicago Press, 1986.

Freud, Sigmund. *New Introductory Lectures on Psychoanalysis*. Translated by James Strachey. New York: Norton, 1964.

*Fu-ch'eng hsiang-chin-shih t'i-ming chi* 福城鄉進士題名記 (Record of graduates of local, provincial, and palace examinations from Fu-ch'eng, Fu-chien). Manuscript, ca. 1546.

Fu, Daiwie. "A Contextual and Taxonomic Study of the 'Divine Marvels' and 'Strange Occurrences' in the *Mengxi bitan*." *Chinese Science* 11 (1993–94): 3–35.

Fu I-ling 傅衣凌. *Ming-tai Chiang-nan shih-min ching-chi shih-t'an* 明代江南市民經濟試探 (Exploration of the urbanite economy in Chiang-nan during the Ming period). Shanghai: People's Press, 1957.

Fu, Marilyn Wong. "The Impact of the Re-unification: Northern Elements in the Life and Art of Hsien-yu Shu (1257?–1302) and Their Relation to Early Yuan Literati Culture." In John D. Langlois, Jr., ed., *China under Mongol Rule*. Princeton: Princeton University Press, 1981.

Fu, Marilyn Wong, and Shen Fu. *Studies in Connoisseurship: Chinese Paintings from the Arthur M. Sackler Collections in New York, Princeton, and Washington, D.C.* Princeton: Princeton University Press, 1973.

*Fu-she chi-lueh* 復社紀略 (Abridged records of the Return to Antiquity Society). Unpaginated manuscript, late Ming.

Fuma Susumu 夫馬進. "Sōshi hihon no sekai" 訟師秘本の世紀 (The world of the secret handbooks of pettifoggers). In Ono Kazuko 小野和子, ed., *Mimmatsu Shinsho no shakai to bunka* 明末清初の社會と文化. Kyoto: Meibun Press, 1996.

Gardner, Daniel. "Principle and Pedagogy: Chu Hsi and the Four Books." *Harvard Journal of Asiatic Studies* 44, 1 (June 1984): 57–81.

———. "Transmitting the Way: Chu Hsi and His Program of Learning." *Harvard Journal of Asiatic Studies* 49, 1 (June 1989): 141–72.

Garrett, Valery M. *Mandarin Squares: Mandarins and Their Insignia.* Oxford: Oxford University Press, 1990.

Gernet, Jacques. *Daily Life in China on the Eve of the Mongol Invasion, 1250–1276.* Stanford: Stanford University Press, 1962.

———. *China and the Christian Impact.* Translated by Janet Lloyd. Cambridge: Cambridge University Press, 1985.

———. *Buddhism in Chinese Society: An Economic History from the Fifth to the Tenth Centuries.* Translated by Franciscus Verellen. New York: Columbia University Press, 1995.

Giles, Herbert, trans. *San Tzu Ching: Elementary Chinese.* 1910; reprint, Taipei: Wen-chih Press, 1984.

Goodrich, L. Carrington. *The Literary Inquisition of Ch'ien-lung.* Baltimore: Waverly Press, 1935.

———. "Prisons in Peking, *circa* 1500." *Tsing-hua hsueh-pao* 清華學報, n.s., 10 (1973): 45–53.

———. "Who Was T'an-hua in 1385." *Ming Studies* 3 (1976): 9–10.

Goody, Jack. *The Interface between the Written and the Oral.* Cambridge: Cambridge University Press, 1987.

Graff, Harvey. *The Legacies of Literacy: Continuities and Contradictions in Western Culture and Society.* Bloomington: Indiana University Press, 1987.

Grafflin, Dennis. "The Great Families of Medieval South China." *Harvard Journal of Asiatic Studies* 41 (1981): 65–74.

Grafton, Anthony, and Lisa Jardine. *From Humanism to the Humanities: Education and the Liberal Arts in Fifteenth- and Sixteenth-Century Europe.* Cambridge: Harvard University Press, 1986.

Gray, John Henry. *China: A History of the Laws, Manners, and Customs of the People.* London: Macmillan, 1878.

Grimm, Tilemann. *Erziehung und Politik in konfuzianischen China der Ming-Zeit.* Hamburg: Gesellschaft für Natur- und Volkerkunde Ostasiens e.V., 1960.

———. "Ming Education Intendants." In Charles Hucker, ed., *Chinese Government in Ming Times: Seven Studies.* New York: Columbia University Press, 1969.

———. "Academies and Urban Systems in Kwangtung." In G. William Skinner, ed., *The City in Late Imperial China.* Stanford: Stanford University Press, 1977.

———. "State and Power in Juxtaposition: An Assessment of Ming Despotism." In S. R. Schram, ed., *The Scope of State Power in China.* London: School of Oriental and African Studies, 1985.

Grove, Linda, and Christian Daniels, eds. *State and Society in China: Japanese Perspectives on Ming-Qing Social and Economic History*. Tokyo: Tokyo University Press, 1984.

Guy, R. Kent. *The Emperor's Four Treasuries: Scholars and the State in the Late Ch'ien-lung Era*. Cambridge: Harvard University Council on East Asian Studies, 1987.

———. "Fang Pao and the *Ch'in-ting Ssu-shu wen*." In Benjamin Elman and Alexander Woodside, eds., *Education and Society in Late Imperial China*. Berkeley: University of California Press, 1994.

Haeger, John W. "1126–27: Political Crisis and the Integrity of Culture." In Haeger, ed., *Crisis and Prosperity in Sung China*. Tucson: University of Arizona Press, 1975.

Hamaguchi Fujio 濱口富士雄. *Shindai kokyogaku no shisō shi teki kenkyū* 清代考據學の思想史的研究 (Research on the intellectual history of Ch'ing dynasty evidential studies). Tokyo: Kokusho kankōkai, 1994.

Hamberg, Theodore. *The Visions of Hung-siu-tshuen, and Origin of the Kwang-si Insurrection*. Reprint, Peking: Yenching University Library, 1935.

Hamilton, David. *Towards a Theory of Schooling*. New York: Falmer Press, 1989.

*Han-shu* 漢書 (History of the Former Han dynasty). Compiled by Pan Ku 班固. 7 vols. Peking, Chung-hua Bookstore, 1962; Taipei: Shih-hsueh ch'u-pan-she, 1974.

Hansen, Chad D. "Ancient Chinese Theories of Language." *Journal of Chinese Philosophy* 2 (1975): 245–80.

Hansen, Valerie. *Changing Gods in Medieval China, 1127–1276*. Princeton: Princeton University Press, 1990.

Harrell, Paula. *Sowing the Seeds of Change: Chinese Students, Japanese Teachers, 1895–1905*. Stanford: Stanford University Press, 1992.

Hart, Roger. "Proof, Propaganda, and Patronage: A Cultural History of the Dissemination of Western Studies in Seventeenth-Century China." Ph.D. diss., UCLA, History, 1997.

———. "Local Knowledges, Local Contexts: Mathematics in Yuan and Ming China." Paper presented at the Song-Yuan-Ming Transitions Conference. Lake Arrowhead, Calif., June 5–11, 1997.

Hartner, Willy. "Some Notes on the Chinese Musical Art." In Nathan Sivin, ed., *Science and Technology in East Asia*. New York: Science History Publications, 1977.

Hartwell, Robert. "Financial Expertise, Examinations, and the Formulation of Economic Policy in Northern Sung China." *Journal of Asian Studies* 30, 2 (1971): 281–314.

———. "Historical-Analogism, Public Policy, and Social Science in Eleventh- and Twelfth-Century China." *American Historical Review* 76, 3 (June 1971): 690–727.

———. "Demographic, Political, and Social Transformations of China, 750–1550." *Harvard Journal of Asiatic Studies* 42, 2 (1982): 365–442.

Hashimoto, Keizō. *Hsu Kuang-ch'i and Astronomical Reform*. Osaka: Kansai University Press, 1988.

Hashimoto Mantarō 橋本萬太郎. "Hoppogo" 北方語 (Northern Chinese language). In *Gengogaku daijiten* 現語學大辭典, vol. 3, *Sekai gengo hen* 世界語言編, part 2-1. Tokyo: Sanseido Press, 1992.

Hayashi Tomoharu 林友春, ed., *Kinsei Chūgoku kyōikushi kenkyū* 近世中國教育研究 (Research on education in early modern China). Tokyo: Kokutosha, 1958.

Hegel, Robert. *The Novel in Seventeenth-Century China*. New York: Columbia University Press, 1981.

————. "Distinguishing Levels of Audiences for Ming-Ch'ing Vernacular Literature: A Case Study." In David Johnson, Andrew Nathan, and Evelyn Rawski, eds., *Popular Culture in Late Imperial China*. Berkeley: University of California Press, 1985.

————. "Heavens and Hells in Chinese Fictional Dreams." In Carolyn Brown, ed., *Psycho-Sinology: The Universe of Dreams in Chinese Culture*. Lantham, Md.: University Press of America, 1988.

Henderson, John. *The Development and Decline of Chinese Cosmology*. New York: Columbia University Press, 1984.

Herbert, P. A. "Civil Service Recruitment in Early T'ang China: Ideal and Reality." *Chūgoku kankei ronsetsu shiryō* 中國關係論説資料 28, 3B, I (1986): 30–36.

————. "T'ang Objections to Centralised Civil Service Selection." *Papers on Far Eastern History* 33 (1986): 81–112.

————. *Examine the Honest, Appraise the Able: Contemporary Assessments of Civil Service Selection in Early T'ang China*. Canberra: Australian National University, 1988.

Hervouet, Yves, ed. *A Sung Bibliography*. Hong Kong: Chinese University Press, 1978.

Hevia, James L. *Cherishing Men from Afar: Qing Guest Ritual and the Macartney Embassy of 1793*. Durham and London: Duke University Press, 1995.

Hexter, J. H. *Reappraisals in History: New Views on History and Society in Early Modern Europe*. Chicago: University of Chicago Press, 1979.

Ho, Peng Yoke. *The Astronomical Chapters of Chin Shu*. Paris: Mouton, 1966.

————. *Li, Qi, and Shu: An Introduction to Science and Civilization in China*. Hong Kong: Hong Kong University Press, 1985.

Ho, Ping-ti. "The Salt Merchants of Yang-chou." *Harvard Journal of Asiatic Studies* 17 (1954): 130–68.

————. *The Ladder of Success in Imperial China*. New York: Wiley & Sons, 1962.

————. "An Estimate of Total Population of Sung-Chin China." In Francoise Aubin, ed., *Études Sung en Memorium Etienne Balazs*. Paris, 1970.

Ho, Yun-yi. "Ideological Implications of Ming Sacrifices in Early Ming." *Ming Studies* 6 (spring 1978): 55–67.

————. *The Ministry of Rites and Suburban Sacrifices in Early Ming*. Taipei: Shuang-yeh Bookstore, 1980.

Holcombe, Charles. *In the Shadow of the Han: Literati Thought and Society at the Beginning of the Southern Dynasties*. Honolulu: University of Hawaii Press, 1994.

Houn, Franklin. "The Civil Service Recruitment System of the Han Dynasty." *Tsing-hua hsueh-pao* 清華學報, n.s., 1 (1956): 138–64.

Houston, R. A. *Literacy in Early Modern Europe: Culture and Education, 1500–1800*. New York: Longman, 1988.

Hsiao Ch'i-ch'ing 蕭啟慶. "Yuan-tai te ju-hu—ju-shih ti-wei yen-chin shih-shang te i-chang" 元代的儒戶—儒士地位演進史上的一章 (Yuan dynasty literati households—a chapter in the historical change in status of literati). *Tung-fang wen-hua* 東方文化 16, 1–2 (1978): 151–70.

————. "Yuan-tai k'o-chü yü ching-ying liu-tung" 元代科舉與菁英流動 (Yuan dynasty civil examinations and elite mobility). *Han-hsueh yen-chiu* 漢學研究 5, 1 (June 1987): 129–60.

Hsiao Ch'ih 蕭馳. "Lun Chung-kuo ku-tien shih-ko lü-hua kuo-ch'eng te kai-nien pei-ching" 論中國古典詩歌律化過程的概念背景 (The conceptual context for the process of the formation of classical regulated verse). *Chung-kuo wen-che yen-chiu chi-*

*k'an* 中國文哲研究集刊 9 (1996): 131–62.

Hsiao, Kung-chuan. *Rural China: Imperial Control in the Nineteenth-Century*. Seattle: University of Washington Press, 1960.

———. *A Modern China and a New World: K'ang Yu-wei, Reformer and Utopian, 1858–1927*. Seattle: University of Washington Press, 1975.

*Hsiao-shih i-wen-lu* 小試異聞錄 (Recording unusual matters heard in the local examination grounds). 1873 edition. Ch'ien-t'ang.

Hsieh Ch'ing 謝青 et al., eds. *Ching-kuo k'ao-shih chih-tu shih* 中國考試制度史 (History of the Chinese examination system). Ho-fei: Huang-shan Press, 1995.

*Hsin-i T'ang-shih san-pai-shou* 新譯唐詩三百首 (New translations of 300 T'ang poems). Compiled by Ch'iu Hsieh-yu 邱燮友. Taipei: San-min Bookstore, 1976.

Hsiung Ping-chen. "Constructed Emotions: The Bond between Mothers and Sons in Late Imperial China." *Late Imperial China* 15, 1 (June 1994): 87–117.

Hsu Hsieh 許獬. *Ssu-shu ch'ung-Hsi chu-chieh* 四書崇熹註解 (Notes to the Four Books honoring Chu Hsi). 1602 edition.

Hsu K'o 徐珂. *Ch'ing-pai lei-ch'ao* 清稗類鈔 (Classified jottings on Ch'ing dynasty unofficial history). Shanghai: Commercial Press, 1920.

Hsu Tao-lin 徐道鄰. *Chung-kuo fa-chih-shih lun-chi* 中國法制史論集 (Collected essays on China's legal-institutional history). Taipei: Cheng-chung Bookstore, 1961.

Hsu Ti-shan 許地山. *Fu-chi mi-hsin te yen-chiu* 扶乩迷信的研究 (Research on spirit-writing superstition). Ch'ang-sha, 1941.

*Hsu-tseng k'o-ch'ang t'iao-li* 續增科場條例 (Continuation to the Imperially prescribed guidelines for the civil examination grounds). 1855 edition.

*Hsu wen-hsien t'ung-k'ao* 續文獻通考 (Comprehensive analysis of civil institutions, continuation). Compiled by Wang Ch'i 王圻. In *Shih-t'ung* 十通 (Ten comprehensive encyclopedias). Shanghai: Commercial Press, 1936.

Hsu Yang 徐揚. "Ku-Su fan-hua t'u" 姑蘇繁華圖 (Painting of prosperous Su-chou) (1759). Hong Kong: Commercial Press, 1988, 1990.

*Hsuan-t'ung chi-yu k'o chien-i ming-ching t'ung-p'u* 宣統己酉科簡易明經通譜 (Record of graduates of the 1909 simplified examination to clarify the Classics). 1909 edition.

*Hsuan-t'ung erh-nien keng-hsu k'o chih-sheng chü-kung hui-k'ao ch'ih-lu* 宣統二年庚戌科直省舉貢會考齒錄 (Record of recommendees from each province in the 1910 metropolitan civil examination). 1910 edition.

*Hsuan-t'ung keng-hsu k'o ti-i-tz'u k'ao-shih fa-kuan t'ung-nien lu* 宣統庚戌科第一次考試法官同年錄 (Record of graduates of the first examination for legal officials in 1910). 1910 edition.

*Hsueh Fu-ch'eng hsuan-chi* 薛福成選集 (Selected writings of Hsueh Fu-ch'eng). Shanghai: People's Press, 1987.

*Hsueh-hai-t'ang chi* 學海堂集 (Collected writings from the Hsueh-hai Academy). Compiled by Juan Yuan et al. 4 series. Canton: Hsueh-hai-t'ang, 1825–86.

Hsueh Ying-ch'i 薛應旂. *Fang-shan hsien-sheng wen-lu* 方山先生文錄 (Recorded writings of Hsueh Ying-ch'i). Su-chou edition. 1553.

*Hsun-tzu chi-chieh* 荀子集解 (Collected notes to the Hsun-tzu). Taipei: Hua-cheng Bookstore, 1979.

Hu, C. T. "The Historical Background: Examinations and Control in Pre-Modern China." *Comparative Education* 20, 1 (1984).

Hu Chü-jen 胡居仁. *Chü-yeh-lu* 居業錄 (Record of the enterprise of sitting in reverence). In *Ssu-k'u ch'üan-shu* 四庫全書 (Complete collection of the four treasuries). Reprint, Taipei: Commercial Press, 1983–86.

Hu Kuang 胡廣 et al. "Chin-shu piao" 進書表 (Words on presenting the [three] books). In *Hsing-li ta-ch'üan* 性理大全. 1415 edition. Reprint, Kyoto: Chūbun Press.

Hu Kuang 胡廣 et al. *Lun-yü chi-chu ta-ch'üan* 論語集注大全 (Great collection of the collected notes to the *Analects*). In *Ssu-shu ta-ch'üan* 四書大全.

Hu Shih 胡適. "Ssu-shih tzu-shu" 四十自述 (Autobiography at age forty). In *Hu Shih tzu-chuan* 胡適自傳 (Autobiography of Hu Shih). Ho-fei: Hsin-hua Bookstore, 1986.

Hu Ying-lin 胡應麟. *Chia-i sheng-yen* 甲乙剩言 (Leftover words from heavenly stems one and two). *Pai-pu ts'ung-shu* 百部叢書 edition. Reprint, Taipei: I-wen Press.

*Huang-ch'ao cheng-tien lei-tsuan* 皇朝政典類纂 (Classified materials on Ch'ing dynasty government regulations). Compiled by Hsi Yü-fu 席裕福. Reprint, Taipei: Shen-wu Press, 1969.

*Huang-ch'ao ching-shih wen-pien* 皇朝經世文編 (Collected writings on statecraft from the Ch'ing dynasty). Edited by Wei Yuan 魏源. 1827 and 1873 editions. Reprint, Taipei: World Bookstore, 1964.

*Huang-ch'ao hsu wen-hsien t'ung-kao* 皇朝續文獻通考 (Comprehensive survey of state documents during the Ch'ing dynasty, continuation). Compiled by Liu Chin-tsao 劉錦藻. Shanghai: Commercial Press, 1936.

Huang Chin 黃溍. *Chin-hua Huang hsien-sheng wen-chi* 金華黃先生文集 (Collected essays of Huang Chin from Chin-hua). *Ssu-pu ts'ung-k'an* edition. Shanghai: Commercial Press, 1919–37.

Huang, Chin-shing. *Philosophy, Philology, and Politics in Eighteenth-Century China*. Cambridge: Cambridge University Press, 1995.

Huang Ch'ing-lien. "The *Li-chia* System in Ming Times and Its Operation in Ying-t'ien Prefecture." *Bulletin of the Institute of History and Philology* (Academia Sinica, Taiwan) 54 (1983): 103–155.

———. "The Recruitment and Assessment of Civil Officials under the T'ang Dynasty." Ph.D. diss., Princeton University, East Asian Studies, 1986.

*Huang-Ch'ing ming-ch'en tsou-i* 皇清名臣奏議 (Memorials of famous officials during the August Ch'ing). Ca. 1796–1820 edition.

Huang Ch'un-yao 黃淳耀. *Tao-an chi* 陶菴集 (Collection of Huang Ch'un-yao). Chia-ting edition. 1676.

Huang I-long 黃一農. "Ch'ing-ch'u t'ien-chu-chiao yü hui-chiao t'ien-wen-chia te cheng-tou" 清初天主教與回教天文家的爭鬥 (The struggle between Catholic and Muslim astronomers in the early Ch'ing). *Chiu-chou hsueh-k'an* 九州學刊 5, 3 (1993): 47–69.

Huang Kuang-liang 黃光亮. *Ch'ing-tai k'o-chü chih-tu chih yen-chiu* 清代科舉制度之研究 (Research on the Ch'ing dynasty civil examination system). Taipei: Chia-hsin Cement Co. Cultural Foundation, 1976.

Huang, Martin. *Literati and Self-Re/Presentation: Autobiographical Sensibility in the Eighteenth-Century Chinese Novel*. Stanford: Stanford University Press, 1995.

*Huang-Ming ch'eng-shih tien-yao lu* 皇明程世典要錄 (Digest of records of metropolitan examinations during the Ming dynasty). Late Ming edition.

*Huang-Ming chin-shih teng-k'o k'ao* 皇明進士登科考 (Study of the accession to *chin-shih* status during the august Ming dynasty). Compiled by Yü Hsien 俞憲. 1548 edition. In *Ming-tai teng-k'o lu hui-pien*, vols. 1–2.

*Huang-Ming chuang-yuan ch'üan-ts'e* 皇明狀元全策 (Complete set of policy questions prepared during the Ming dynasty by *optimi* for the palace civil examination). Compiled by Chiang I-k'ui 蔣一葵. 1591 edition.

*Huang-Ming hsiang-hui-shih erh-san-ch'ang ch'eng-wen hsuan* 皇明鄉會試二三場程文選 (Selection of model examination essays from the second and third sessions of the provincial and metropolitan civil examinations during the Ming dynasty). Compiled by Ch'en Jen-hsi 陳仁錫. 1633 *Pai-sung-t'ang* edition.

*Huang Ming kung-chü k'ao* 皇明貢舉考 (Survey of civil examinations during the Ming dynasty). Compiled by Chang Ch'ao-jui 張朝瑞. Ming Wan-li edition.

*Huang-Ming san-yuan k'ao* 皇明三元考 (Study of the provincial, metropolitan, and palace civil examination *optimi* during the Ming dynasty). Compiled by Chang Hung-tao 張弘道 and Chang Ning-tao 張凝道. Late Ming edition. After 1618.

*Huang-Ming ts'e-heng* 皇明策衡 (Weighing civil policy examination essays during the Ming dynasty). Compiled by Mao Wei 茅維. Wu-hsing edition. 1605.

*Huang Ming t'ung-chi chi-yao* 皇明通紀集要 (Collection of essentials to the Comprehensive Accounts of the August Ming dynasty). Compiled by Ch'en Chien 陳建, and appended by Chiang Hsu-ch'i 江旭奇. Late Ming edition. Reprint, Taipei: Wen-hai Press.

*Huang-Ming t'ung-chi shu-i* 皇明通紀述遺 (Additions to the Comprehensive Accounts of the August Ming dynasty). Compiled by Ch'en Chien 陳建, and appended by P'u Shih-ch'ang 卜世昌 and T'u Heng 屠衡. 1605 edition. Reprint, Taipei: Student Bookstore, 1972.

*Huang-Ming wen-heng* 皇明文衡 (Balancing of essays from the Ming dynasty). *Ssu-pu ts'ung-k'an* edition. Shanghai: Commercial Press, 1919–37.

Huang, Philip. *The Peasant Economy and Social Change in North China*. Stanford: Stanford University Press, 1985.

———. *The Peasant Family and Rural Development in the Yangzi Delta, 1350–1988*. Stanford: Stanford University Press, 1990.

Huang, Ray. *Taxation and Governmental Finance in Sixteenth-Century Ming China*. Cambridge: Cambridge University Press, 1974.

———. *1587: A Year of No Significance*. New Haven: Yale University Press, 1981.

Huang Tsung-hsi. *The Record of Ming Scholars*. Edited by Julia Ching. Honolulu: University of Hawaii Press, 1987.

Hucker, Charles O. "Confucianism and the Chinese Censorial System." In David S. Nivison and Arthur Wright, eds., *Confucianism in Action*. Stanford: Stanford University Press, 1969.

———. "The Tung-lin Movement of the Late Ming Period." In John K. Fairbank, ed., *Chinese Thought and Institutions*. Chicago: University of Chicago Press, 1973.

———. *The Ming Dynasty: Its Origins and Evolving Institutions*. Ann Arbor: University of Michigan Center for Chinese Studies, 1978.

———, ed. *Chinese Government in Ming Times: Seven Studies*. New York: Columbia University Press, 1969.

Hughes, E. R. "Epistemological Methods in Chinese Philosophy." In Charles Moore, ed., *The Chinese Mind*. Honolulu: University of Hawaii Press, 1967.

*Hui-shih chu-chüan* 會試硃卷 ([Ch'ing] metropolitan examination essays). Ming-Ch'ing Archives, Academia Sinica, Taiwan.

*Hui-shih t'ung-nien ch'ih-lu* 會試同年齒錄 (Record of same year metropolitan graduates). 1895, 1904.

*Hui-shih t'ung-nien shih-chiang lu* 會試同年世講錄 (Record of same year metropolitan graduates). 1556. In *Ming-tai teng-k'o-lu hui-pien* 明代登科錄彙編 (Compendium of Ming dynasty civil and military examination records), 22 vols. Taipei: Hsueh-sheng Bookstore, 1969.

Hummel, Arthur, et al., eds. *Eminent Chinese of the Ch'ing Period.* Reprint, Taipei: Ch'eng-wen Bookstore, 1972.

Hung Mai 洪邁. *Jung-chai sui-pi* 容齋隨筆 (Miscellaneous jottings from Jung Studio). Shanghai: Ku-chi Press, 1978.

Huters, Theodore. "From Writing to Literature: The Development of Late Qing Theories of Prose." *Harvard Journal of Asiatic Studies* 47, 1 (June 1987).

Hymes, Robert. "Marriage, Kin Groups, and the Localist Strategy in Sung and Yuan Fu-chou." In Patricia Buckley Ebrey and James L. Watson, eds., *Kinship Organization in Late Imperial China.* Berkeley: University of California Press, 1986.

———. "Not Quite Gentlemen? Doctors in Sung and Yuan." *Chinese Science* 7 (1986): 11–85.

———. *Statesmen and Gentlemen: The Elite of Fu-chou, Chiang-hsi, in Northern and Southern Sung.* Cambridge: Cambridge University Press, 1987.

———. "Some Thoughts on Plague, Population, and the Sung-Yuan-Ming Transition: The McNeill Thesis after Twenty Years." Paper presented at the Sung-Yuan-Ming Transitions Conference, Lake Arrowhead, Calif., June 5–11, 1997.

Hymes, Robert, and Conrad Schirokauer, eds. *Ordering the World: Approaches to State and Society in Sung Dynasty China.* Berkeley: University of California Press, 1993.

*I-hsing hsien-chih* 宜興縣志 (Gazetteer of I-hsing county). 1869.

Ihara Hiroshi 井原弘. "Chūgoku chishikijin no kisō shakai—Sōdai Onshū Yōka gakuha o rei to shite" 中國知識人の基層社會—宋代溫州永嘉學派を例として (The social basis of Chinese intellectuals: The Sung dynasty Wen-chou and Yung-chia scholarly traditions as examples). *Shisō* 思想 802 (April 1991): 82–103.

Ikoma Shō 生駒晶. "Minsho kakyo gokakusha no shushin ni kan suru ichi kōsatsu" 明初科舉合格者の出身に關する一考察 (A study of birthplaces of successful examination candidates during the early Ming). In *Yamane Yukio kyōju taikyū kinen Mindaishi ronshū jō* 山根幸夫教授退休紀念明代史論叢上. Tokyo: Kyoko shoin, 1990.

Inoue Susumu 井上進. "Rikkyō mina shi setsu no keifu" 六經皆史説の系譜 (The descent of the thesis that the "Six Classics are all histories"). In Ono Kazuko, ed., *Mimmatsu Shinsho no shakai to bunka.* Kyoto: Meibun Press, 1996.

Jami, Catherine. "Western Influence and Chinese Tradition in an Eighteenth Century Chinese Mathematical Work." *Historia Mathematica* 15 (1988): 311–31.

———. "Learning Mathematical Sciences during the Early and Mid-Ch'ing." In Benjamin Elman and Alexander Woodside, eds., *Education and Society in Late Imperial China, 1600–1900.* Berkeley: University of California Press, 1994.

Jen Yu-wen (Chien Yu-wen). *The Taiping Revolutionary Movement.* New Haven: Yale University Press, 1973.

Jensen, Lionel. "The Invention of 'Confucius' and His Chinese Other, 'Kong Fuzi.'" *positions: east asia cultures critique* 1, 2 (fall 1993): 414–49.

Jin, Qicong. "Jurchen Literature under the Chin." In Hoyt Tillman and Stephen West, eds., *China under Jurchen Rule.* Albany: SUNY Press, 1995.

Johnson, David. "Communication, Class, and Consciousness in Late Imperial China." In David Johnson, Andrew Nathan, and Evelyn Rawski, eds., *Popular Culture in Late Imperial China.* Berkeley: University of California Press, 1985.

Johnston, Alastair. *Cultural Realism: Strategic Culture and Grand Strategy in Chinese History*. Princeton: Princeton University Press, 1995.

Juan Yuan 阮元. *Ssu-shu wen-hua* 四書文話 (Comments on examination essays on the Four Books). N.d.

Judge, Joan. "Public Opinion and the New Politics of Contestation in the Late Qing, 1904–1911." *Modern China* 20, 1 (January 1994): 64–91.

———. *Print and Politics: "Shibao" and the Culture of Reform in Late Qing China*. Stanford: Stanford University Press, 1996.

Jung, C. G. *Dreams*. Princeton: Princeton University Press, 1974.

Jung Chao-tsu 容肇祖. "Hsueh-hai-t'ang k'ao" 學海堂集 (Study of the Hsueh-hai Academy). *Ling-nan hsueh-pao* 領南學報 3, 4 (June 1934): 1–147.

———. *Lü Liu liang chi ch'i ssu-hsiang* 呂留良及其思想 (The thought of Lü Liu-liang). Hong Kong: Ch'ung-wen Bookstore, 1974.

Kahn, Harold. "The Education of a Prince: The Emperor Learns His Roles." In Albert Feuerwerker et al., eds., *Approaches to Modern Chinese History*. Berkeley: University of California Press, 1967.

———. *Monarchy in the Emperor's Eyes: Image and Reality in the Ch'ien-lung Reign*. Cambridge: Harvard University Press, 1971.

Kamo Naoki 狩野直喜. *Shinchō no seido to bungaku* 清朝の制度と文學 (Ch'ing institutions and literature). Tokyo: Misuzu Bookstore, 1984.

K'ang-hsi 康熙 emperor. "Hsiang-chü li-hsuan chieh" 鄉舉里選解 (Explication for selecting local talent). In *Ch'ing-tai ch'ien-ch'i chiao-yü lun-chu hsuan* 清代前期教育論著選 (Selections of writings on education from the early Ch'ing period), edited by Li Kuo-chün et al., 3 vols. Peking: People's Education Press, 1990.

K'ang Yu-wei 康有為. "Chronological Autobiography." In Jung-pao Lo, ed. and trans., *K'ang Yu-wei: A Biography and a Symposium*. Tucson: University of Arizona Press, 1967.

———. *K'ang Yu-wei cheng-lun chi* 康有為政論集 (Collection of K'ang Yu-wei's political writings). Compiled by T'ang Chih-chün 湯志鈞. Peking: Chung-hua Bookstore, 1981.

———. "Hsu" 序 (Preface), to his *Jih-pen shu-mu chih shih-yü* 日本書目之識語 (Guide to Japanese bibliography). Reprinted in Ch'en P'ing-yuan 陳平原 et al., *Erh-shih shih-chi chung-kuo hsiao-shuo li-lun tzu-liao ti-i chüan* 二十世紀中國小説理論資料第一卷. Peking: Peking University Press, 1989.

Katsumata Kenjirō 勝又憲治郎. "Hokukei no kakyo jidai to kōin" 北京の科舉時代と貢院 (The examination hall and Peking in the age of civil examinations). *Tōhō gakuhō* 東方學報 (Tokyo) 6 (1936): 203–39.

Katz, Paul. *Demon Hordes and Burning Boats: The Cult of Marshall Wen in Late Imperial Chekiang*. Albany: SUNY Press, 1995.

Kelleher, Kathleen. "Seems Taking a Final Exam Is Everyone's Worst Nightmare." *Los Angeles Times*, May 28, 1996.

Kelleher, M. Theresa. "Back to Basics: Chu Hsi's *Elementary Learning (Hsiao-hsueh)*. In William Theodore de Bary and John Chaffee, eds., *Neo-Confucian Education: The Formative Stage*. Berkeley: University of California Press, 1989.

Keenan, Barry. *Imperial China's Last Classical Academies: Social Change in the Lower Yangzi, 1864–1911*. Berkeley: Institute of East Asian Studies, University of California, 1994.

Kermode, Frank. "Institutional Control of Interpretation." *Salmagundi* 43 (1979): 72–86.

———. "The Canon." In Robert Alter and Kermode, eds., *The Literary Guide to the Bible*. Cambridge: Harvard University Press, 1987.

Kessler, Lawrence. *K'ang-hsi and the Consolidation of Ch'ing Rule, 1661–1684*. Chicago: University of Chicago Press, 1976.

Kim, Yung Sik. "The World-View of Chu Hsi (1130–1200): Knowledge about the Natural World in 'Chu-tzu ch'üan-shu.'" Ph.D. diss., Princeton University, History, 1980.

Kinoshita Tetsuya 木下鉄矢. *Shindai koshōgaku to sono jidai* 清代考證學とその時代 (Ch'ing dynasty evidential research and its times). Tokyo: Sōbunsha, 1995.

Kleeman, Terry, trans. *A God's Own Tale: The Book of Transformations of Wenchang, the Divine Lord of Zitong*. Albany: SUNY Press, 1994.

Knowles, James. "Competitive Examinations in China." *The Nineteenth Century: A Monthly Review* 36 (July–December 1894): 87–99.

Ko, Dorothy. *Teachers of the Inner Chambers: Women and Culture in Seventeenth-Century China*. Stanford: Stanford University Press, 1994.

———. "The Written Word and the Bound Foot: A History of the Courtesan's Aura." In Ellen Widmer and Kang-i Sun Chang, eds., *Writing Women in Late Imperial China*. Stanford: Stanford University Press, 1997.

Kobayashi Kazumi 小林一美. "Shū Genchō no kobu seiji" 朱元璋の恐怖政治 (Chu Yuan-chang's reign of terror). In *Yamane Yukio kyōju taikyū kinen Mindaishi ronshū jō* 山根幸夫教授退休紀念明代史論叢上. Tokyo: Kyoko shoin, 1990.

Kojima Tsuyoshi 小島毅. "Sōdai no gakuritsu ron" 宋代の樂律論 (Theories of musical pitch in Sung times). *Tōyō bunka kenkyūjo kiyo* 東洋文化研究所紀要 109 (1989): 273–305.

Kondo Mitsuo 近藤光男. *Shinshi sen* 清詩選 (Selections of Ch'ing poetry). Tokyo: Shūeisha, 1967.

*Koryō sa* 高麗史 (History of the Koryō dynasty). Seoul: Yonsei University, 1955.

Kracke, E. A. "Family vs. Merit in Chinese Civil Service Examinations during the Empire." *Harvard Journal of Asiatic Studies* 10 (1947): 103–23.

———. *Civil Service in Early Sung China*. Cambridge: Harvard-Yenching Institute, 1968.

Ku Chieh-kang. "A Study of Literary Persecution during the Ming." Translated by L. Carrington Goodrich. *Harvard Journal of Asiatic Studies* 3 (1938): 282–85.

*Ku-chin t'u-shu chi-ch'eng* 古今圖書集成 (Synthesis of books and illustrations past and present). 1728 edition.

*Ku-chin yuan-liu chih-lun* 古今源流至論 (The best discourse essays past and present). Compiled by Lin Chiung 林駉 and Huang Lü-weng 黃履翁. Early Ming edition. Reprint, Taipei: Hsin-hsing Bookstore, 1970.

*Ku-ching ching-she wen-chi* 詁經精舍文集 (Collected essays from the Ku-ching ching-she Academy). Edited by Juan Yuan 阮元 et al. Taipei: Commercial Press, 1966.

Ku Hsien-ch'eng 顧憲成. "Ching-cheng-t'ang shang-yü" 經正堂商語 (Discussions at the Hall of Classical Correctness). In *Ku Tuan-wen kung i-shu* 顧端文公遺書 (Bequeathed writings of Ku Hsien-ch'eng). Ch'ing dynasty K'ang-hsi edition.

———. "Hsiao-hsin-chai cha-chi" 小心齋箚記 (Random notes from the Pavilion of Watchfulness). In *Ku Tuan-wen kung i-shu* 顧端文公遺書 (Bequeathed writings of Ku Hsien-ch'eng). Ch'ing dynasty K'ang-hsi edition.

———. "Tung-lin hui-yueh fu" 東林會約附 (Addition to the statutes for meetings at the Tung-lin). In *Ku Tuan-wen kung i-shu* 顧端文公遺書 (Bequeathed writings of Ku Hsien-ch'eng). Ch'ing dynasty K'ang-hsi edition.

Ku Hung-ting. "Upward Career Mobility Patterns of High-Ranking Officials in Ch'ing China, 1730–1796." *Papers on Far Eastern History* (Australia) 29 (1984): 45–66.

Ku Kung-hsieh 顧公燮. *Hsiao-hsia hsien-chi chai-ch'ao* 消夏閑記摘抄 (Selected notes jotted in leisure to pass the summer). Ca. 1797 edition. In *Han-fen-lou mi-chi* 涵芬樓秘笈. Shanghai: Commercial Press, 1917, *erh-chi* 二集.

*Ku-kung wen-wu yueh-k'an* 故宮文物月刊 (Palace Museum Monthly) 88 (July 1990).

Ku Yen-wu 顧炎武. *Jih-chih lu* 日知錄 (Record of knowledge gained day by day). 1780s manuscript, included in *Ssu-k'u ch'üan-shu* 四庫全書 (Complete collection of the four treasuries). Taipei: Commercial Press, 1983–86. Reprint, punctuated version, Taipei: P'ing-p'ing Press, 1974.

———. *Jih-chih lu chi-shih* 日知錄集釋 (Record of knowledge gained day by day, collected notes). Taipei: Shih-chieh Bookstore, 1962.

———. *Ku T'ing-lin shih-wen chi* 顧亭林詩文集 (Collected essays and poetry of Ku Yen-wu). Hong Kong: Chung-hua Bookstore, 1976.

*Kuang-hsu cheng-yao* 光緒政要 (Important issues of governance in the Kuang-hsu reign). Compiled by Shen T'ung-sheng 沈桐生. Shanghai: Ch'ung-i-t'ang, 1909.

*Kuang-hsu hsin-ch'ou jen-yin en-cheng ping-k'o hui-shih mo-chüan* 光緒辛丑壬寅恩正併科會試墨卷 (Compositions of graduates in the 1901/1902 combined special and regular metropolitan civil examination). 1903 edition.

*Kuang-hsu hsin-ch'ou jen-yin en-cheng ping-k'o hui-shih wei-mo* 光緒辛丑壬寅恩正併科會試闈墨 (Compositions of graduates in the 1901/1902 combined special and regular metropolitan civil examination). 1902 edition.

*Kuang-hsu san-shih-san nien ting-wei k'o chü-kung k'ao-chih t'ung-nien ch'ih-lu* 光緒三十三年丁未科舉貢考職同年齒錄 (Record of the recommendees for office in the 1907 civil examination). 1907 edition.

*Kuang-hsu wu-hsu k'o hui-shih ti-chiu-fang chu-chüan* 光緒戊戌科會試第九房硃卷 (Examination papers from the ninth ward of the 1898 metropolitan examination). Manuscript, 1898.

Kuei Yu-kuang 歸有光. *Kuei Yu-kuang ch'üan-chi* 全集 (Complete essays of Kuei Yu-kuang). Taipei: P'an-keng Press, 1979.

Kuhn, Philip. *Soulstealers: The Chinese Sorcery Scare of 1768*. Cambridge: Harvard University Press, 1990.

Kuhn, Thomas. *The Essential Tension: Selected Studies in Scientific Tradition and Change*. Chicago: University of Chicago Press, 1970.

———. *The Structure of Scientific Revolutions*. 2nd edition. Chicago: University of Chicago Press, 1970.

*K'un-shan hsien-chih* 昆山縣志 (K'un-shan county gazetteer). 1538 edition. Ning-po: T'ien-i-ko.

*Kung-pu t'i-pen* 工部題本 (Memoranda including memorials from the Ministry of Works). In the Ming-Ch'ing Archives, Academia Sinica, Taiwan.

Kung Tzu-chen 龔自珍. *Kung Tzu-chen ch'üan-chi* 全集 (Complete writings of Kung Tzu-chen). Shanghai: Shanghai People's Press, 1975.

*Kuo-ch'ao Chang T'ing-yü hsien-sheng nien-p'u* 國朝張廷玉先生年譜 (Chronological biography of the Ch'ing dynasty's Chang T'ing-yü). In *Li-tai nien-p'u ta-ch'eng* 歷代年譜大成 (Compendium of chronological biographies over the ages), compiled by Liu Shih-p'ei 劉師培. Manuscript, late Ch'ing.

*Kuo-ch'ao k'o-ch'ang i-wen lü* 國朝科場異聞錄 (Recording unusual matters heard in the Ch'ing examination grounds). Wei-ching-t'ang shu-fang 味經堂書坊 edition. Canton; reprint, Ch'ien-t'ang, 1873.

*Kuo-ch'ao kung-chü k'ao-lueh* 國朝貢舉考略 (Summary of Ch'ing civil examinations). Compiled by Huang Ch'ung-lan 黃崇蘭. 1834 edition.

*Kuo-ch'ao li-k'o Han-lin kuan k'o* 國朝歷科翰林館課 (Series of examinations for Ming dynasty Hanlin academicians). 1603 edition.

*Kuo-ch'ao liang-Che k'o-ming lu* 國朝兩浙科名錄 (Record of examinations in Che-chiang during the Ch'ing dynasty). 1857 edition. Peking.

*Kuo-ch'ao Yü-yang k'o-ming-lu* 國朝虞陽科名錄 (Record of civil service graduates in Yü-yang under the Ch'ing dynasty). Compiled by Wang Yuan-chung 王元種. 1850 edition.

Kuo Mo-jo 郭沫若. *Kuo Mo-jo hsuan-chi* 選集 (Selected writings of Kuo Mo-jo). Ch'eng-tu: Ssu-ch'uan People's Press, 1979.

Kuo Shao-yü 郭紹虞, comp. *Ch'ing shih-hua* 清詩話 (Ch'ing works on poetry discussions). Shanghai: Ku-chi Press, 1963.

———. *Ch'ing shih-hua hsu-pien* 清詩話續編 (Ch'ing works on poetry discussions, continuation). Shanghai: Ku-chi Press, 1983.

Kutcher, Norman. "Death and Mourning in China, 1550–1800." Ph.D. diss., Yale University, History, 1991.

Kwong, Luke S. K. *A Mosaic of the Hundred Days: Personalities, Politics, and Ideas of 1898.* Cambridge: Harvard University Council on East Asian Studies, 1984.

Lach, Donald F. *China in the Eyes of Europe: The Sixteenth Century.* Chicago: Phoenix Books, 1968.

Lach, Donald F., and Edwin J. Van Kley. *Asia in the Making of Europe.* Vol. 3, *A Century of Advance,* book 4, *East Asia.* Chicago: University of Chicago Press, 1993.

Lai-pao 來保. "Tsou-che" 奏摺 (Memorial), 1757, 5th month, 9th day. In the Ch'ing dynasty examination materials from the Ming-Ch'ing Archives, Academia Sinica, Taiwan.

Lai, T. C. *A Scholar in Imperial China.* Hong Kong: Kelly & Walsh, 1970.

Lam, Yuan-chu. "On Yuan Examination System: The Role of Northern Ch'eng-Chu Pioneering Scholars." *Journal of Turkish Studies* 9 (1985): 197–203.

Langley, Charles B. "Wang Yinglin (1223–1296): A Study in the Political and Intellectual History of the Demise of the Sung." Ph.D. diss., Indiana University, East Asian Languages and Cultures, 1980.

Langlois, John D., Jr. "Chinese Culturalism and the Yuan Analogy: Seventeenth-Century Perspectives." *Harvard Journal of Asiatic Studies,* 40, 2 (December 1980): 355–97.

———. "Political Thought in Chin-hua under Mongol Rule." In Langlois, ed., *China under Mongol Rule.* Princeton: Princeton University Press, 1981.

———. "Law, Statecraft, and *The Spring and Autumn Annals* in Yuan Political Thought." In Hok-lam Chan and William Theodore de Bary, eds., *Yuan Thought: Chinese Thought and Religion under the Mongols.* New York: Columbia University Press, 1982.

———. "The Hung-wu Reign." In Frederick W. Mote and Denis Twitchett, eds., *The Cambridge History of China.* Vol. 7, part 1, *The Ming Dynasty, 1368–1644.* Cambridge: Cambridge University Press, 1988.

———, ed. *China under Mongol Rule.* Princeton: Princeton University Press, 1981.

Lao, Yan-shuan. "Southern Chinese Scholars and Educational Institutions in Early

Yuan: Some Preliminary Remarks." In John D. Langlois, Jr., ed., *China under Mongol Rule*. Princeton: Princeton University Press, 1981.

Latham, Ronald, trans. *The Travels of Marco Polo*. Harmondsworth: Penguin Books, 1958.

Lau, D. C., trans. *Mencius*. New York: Penguin Books, 1976.

———. *Confucius: The Analects*. Harmondsworth: Penguin Books, 1979.

Ledderose, Lothar. "An Approach to Chinese Calligraphy." *National Palace Museum Bulletin* 7, 1 (1972): 1–14.

———. *Mi Fu and the Classical Tradition of Chinese Calligraphy*. Princeton: Princeton University Press, 1979.

Lee, Cheuk-yin 李焯然. "Chih-kuo chih Tao—Ming Ch'eng-tsu chi ch'i Sheng-hsueh hsin-fa" 治國之道—明成祖及其聖學心法 (The art of rulership—the Ming Emperor Ch'eng-tsu and his *The Method of the Mind in the Sages' Teachings*). *Han-hsueh yen-chiu* 漢學研究 17 (1991): 211–25.

Lee, John. "The Dragons and Tigers of 792: The Examination in T'ang History." *T'ang Studies* 6 (1988): 25–47.

Lee, Leo Ou-fan, and Andrew J. Nathan. "The Beginnings of Mass Culture: Journalism and Fiction in the Late Ch'ing and Beyond." In David Johnson, Andrew Nathan, and Evelyn Rawski, eds., *Popular Culture in Late Imperial China*. Berkeley: University of California Press, 1985.

Lee, Thomas H. C. *Government Education and Examinations in Sung China*. Hong Kong: Chinese University, 1982.

———. "The Social Significance of the Quota System in Sung Civil Service Examinations." *Journal of the Institute of Chinese Studies* (Chinese University of Hong Kong) 13 (1982): 287–318.

———. "Sung Schools and Education before Chu Hsi." In William Theodore de Bary and John Chaffee, eds., *Neo-Confucian Education: The Formative Stage*. Berkeley: University of California Press, 1989.

Legge, James, trans. *The Four Books*. Reprint, New York: Paragon, 1966.

———. *The Chinese Classics*. Vol. 5, *The Ch'un Ts'ew with the Tso Chuan*. Reprint, Taipei: Wen-shih-che Press, 1971.

———. *The Chinese Classics*. Vol. 3, *The Shoo King or The Book of Historical Documents*. Reprint, Taipei: Wen-shih-che Press, 1972.

Le Goff, Jacques. *Intellectuals in the Middle Ages*. Cambridge and Oxford: Blackwell, 1993.

Leung, Angela Ki Che. "Elementary Education in the Lower Yangtzu Region in the Seventeenth and Eighteenth Centuries." In Benjamin Elman and Alexander Woodside, eds., *Education and Society in Late Imperial China*. Berkeley: University of California Press, 1994.

——— (Liang Ch'i-tzu 梁其姿). "Ch'ing-tai te hsi-tzu hui" 清代的惜字會 (Societies for cherishing written characters during the Ch'ing dynasty). *Hsin shih-hsueh* 新史學 (Taiwan) 5, 2 (June 1994): 83–113.

———. *Shih-shan yü chiao-hua: Ming-Ch'ing te tz'u-shan tsu-chih* 施善與教化：明清的慈善組織 (Performing merit and transforming through culture: Charitable institutions in Ming and Ch'ing). Taipei: Lien-ching Press, 1997.

———. "Transmission of Medical Knowledge from the Sung to the Ming." Paper presented at the Song-Yuan-Ming Transitions Conference, Lake Arrowhead, Calif., June 5–11, 1997.

Leung, Man-kam. "Mongolian Language and Examinations in Peking and Other Metropolitan Areas during the Manchu Dynasty in China (1644–1911)." *Canada-Mongolia Review* 1 (1975): 29–44.

Levenson, Joseph. "The Amateur Ideal in Ming and Early Ch'ing Society: Evidence from Painting." In John Fairbank, ed., *Chinese Thought and Institutions*. Chicago: University of Chicago Press, 1957.

———. *Confucian China and Its Modern Fate: A Trilogy*. 3 vols. Berkeley: University of California Press, 1968.

Lewis, Charlton M. *Prologue to the Chinese Revolution: The Transformation of Ideas and Institutions in Hunan Province, 1891–1907*. Cambridge: Harvard University East Asian Research Center, 1976.

*Li-chi chin-chu chin-i* 禮記今註今譯 (Modern notes and translations for the Record of Rites). Annotated by Wang Meng-ou 王夢鷗. 2 vols. Taipei: Commercial Press, 1974.

*Li-chi yin-te* 禮記引得 (Concordance to the Record of Rites). Reprint, Shanghai: Ku-chi Press, 1983.

Li Chih 李贄. *Hsu ts'ang-shu* 續藏書 (A book to be hidden away, continuation). Taipei: Chung-hua Bookstore, 1974.

———. *Hsu fen-shu* 續焚書 (Continuation to a book destined to be burned). Peking: Chung-hua Bookstore, 1975.

———. "Shih-wen hou-hsu" 時文後序 (Afterword for contemporary-style essays). In *Fen-shu* 焚書 (A book to be burned). Peking: Chung-hua Bookstore, 1975.

Li Ch'un 酈純. *T'ai-p'ing t'ien-kuo chih-tu ch'u-t'an hsia* 太平天國制度初探下 (Preliminary analysis of the Taiping Heavenly Kingdom's institutions, vol. 2). Peking: Chung-hua Bookstore, 1990.

Li Hsin-ta 李新達. *Chung-kuo k'o-chü chih-tu shih* 中國科舉制度史 (History of the civil service examination system). Taipei: Wen-chin Press, 1995.

*Li-k'o ch'ao-yuan chüan* 歷科朝元卷 (Examination papers from court examinations over several cycles). In Tokyo University, Oriental Library.

Li Kung 李塨. "Ch'ü-shih" 取士 (Selecting literati). In *Ch'ing-tai ch'ien-ch'i chiao-yü lun-chu hsuan* 清代前期教育論著選 (Selections of writings on education from the early Ch'ing period), edited by Li Kuo-chün et al., 3 vols. Peking: People's Education Press, 1990.

*Li-pu t'i-pen* 禮部題本 (Memoranda including memorials from the Ministry of Rites). Collected in the Ming-Ch'ing Archives, Academia Sinica, Taiwan.

*Li Shen-ch'i nien-p'u* 李申耆年譜 (Chronological biography of Li Chao-lo). Nan-lin: Chia-yeh-t'ang 嘉業堂, ca. 1831.

*Li-tai chin-tien tien-shih ting-chia chu-chüan* 歷代金殿殿試鼎甲硃卷 (Examination essays of the top three graduates of civil and palace examinations of several dynasties). Compiled by Chung Kuang-chün 仲光軍 et al., 2 vols. Shih-chia-chuang: Hua-shan Arts Press, 1995.

*Li-tai kung-chü chih* 歷代貢舉志 (Accounts of the civil examinations over several dynasties). Compiled by Feng Meng-chen 馮夢禎. Shanghai: Commercial Press, 1936.

Li T'iao-yuan 李調元. *Tan-mo lu* 淡墨錄 (Record of skilled civil examination papers). In *Han-hai* 函海 (Seas of writings), by Li T'iao-yuan 李調元. 1881 collectanea.

———. *Chih-i k'o-so chi* 制義科瑣記 (Collection of fragments about the crafted eight-legged essays for civil examinations). *Ts'ung-shu chi-ch'eng ch'u-pien* 叢書集成初編. Shanghai: Commercial Press, 1936.

Li Tse-fen 李則芬. *Yuan-shih hsin-chiang* 元史新講 (New lectures on Yuan history). 5 vols. Taipei: Chung-hua Bookstore, 1978.

Li Tsung-huang 李宗黃. *Li Tsung-huang hui-i lu* 回憶錄 (Recollections of Li Tsung-huang). Taipei: Chinese Educational Society for Local Autonomy, 1972.

Li Yin-tu 李因篤. "Yung-jen" 用人 (Employing people). In *Ch'ing-tai ch'ien-ch'i chiao-yü lun-chu hsuan* 清代前期教育論著選 (Selections of writings on education from the early Ch'ing period), edited by Li Kuo-chün et al., 3 vols. Peking: People's Education Press, 1990.

Liang Chang-chü 梁章鉅. *Chih-i ts'ung-hua* 制藝叢話 (Collected comments on the crafting of eight-legged civil examination essays). 1859 edition. Reprint, Taipei: Kuang-wen Bookstore, 1976.

*Liang-Che hsueh-cheng* 兩浙學政 (Education commissioners in western and eastern Che-chiang). 1610 edition.

Liang Ch'i-ch'ao 梁啟超. *Intellectual Trends in the Ch'ing Period*. Translated by Immanuel Hsu. Cambridge: Harvard University Press, 1959.

———. *Yin-ping-shih wen-chi* 飲冰室文集 (Collected writings from the Ice-Drinker's Studio). 8 vols. Taipei: Chung-hua Bookstore, 1970.

Liang Chün 梁峻. *Chung-kuo ku-tai i-cheng shih lueh* 中國古代醫政史略 (Historical summary of medicine and government in ancient China). Huhehot: Inner Mongolia People's Press, 1995.

Lien Tzu-ning 練子寧. *Lien Chung-ch'eng Chin-ch'uan chi* 練中丞金川集 (Collection of Lien Tzu-ning from Chin-ch'uan). 1762 edition.

———. *Lien Chung-ch'eng kung wen-chi* 練中丞公文集 (Collected writings of Lien Tzu-ning). Late Ming Wan-li edition.

Lin Ch'ing-chang 林慶彰. *Ming-tai k'ao-cheng-hsueh yen-chiu* 明代考證學研究 (Study of Ming dynasty evidential research). Taipei: Student Bookstore, 1984.

———. *Ch'ing-ch'u te ch'ün-ching pien-wei hsueh* 清初的群經辨偽學 (Study of forged classics in the early Ch'ing). Taipei: Wen-chin Press, 1990.

———. "Wu-ching ta-ch'üan chih hsiu-tsuan chi ch'i hsiang-kuan wen-t'i t'an-chiu" 五經大全之修纂及其相關問題探究 (Inquiry into the compilation of the Complete Collection [of commentaries] for the Five Classics and related issues). *Chung-kuo wen-che yen-chiu chi-k'an* 中國文哲研究集刊 1 (1991): 366–67.

———, ed. *Ming-tai ching-hsueh kuo-chi yen-t'ao-hui lun-wen chi* 明代經學國際研討會論文集 (Conference volume for the International Conference on Ming Dynasty Classical Studies). Taipei: Academia Sinica, 1996.

*Lin-wen pien-lan* 臨文便覽 (Overview for writing down essays). 1875 edition.

Lin, Xiaoqing C. "Social Science and Social Control: Empirical Scientific Theories and Chinese Uses." *Chinese Science* 14 (1997).

Lipkin, Zwia. "Soothsayers, Clients and the State in Republican Canton." Paper presented at the Graduate Student Conference on Modern Chinese History, University of California at San Diego, spring 1996.

Lipset, Seymour M., and Richard Bendix. *Social Mobility in Industrial Society*. Berkeley: University of California Press, 1960.

Liu Chao-pin 劉兆濱. *Ch'ing-tai k'o-chü* 清代科舉 (Examination system during the Ch'ing period). Taipei: Tung-ta Books, 1979.

Liu Hsiang-kwang 劉祥光. "Shih-wen kao: K'o-chü shih-tai te k'ao-sheng pi-tu" 時文稿：科舉時代的考生必讀 (Examination essay compilations: Required reading for examination students). *Newsletter for Modern Chinese History* (Academia Sinica, Taiwan) 22 (1996): 49–68.

———. "Education and Society Development of Public and Private Institutions in Hui-chou, 960–1800." Ph.D. diss., Columbia University, History, 1997.

———. "Examination Essays: Timely and Indispensable Reading for Students in the Ming." Paper presented at the 1997 Annual Meeting of the Association for Asian Studies, Chicago, March 13–16, 1997.

Liu I-cheng 柳詒徵. "Chiang-su shu-yuan chih ch'u-kao" 江蘇書院志初稿 (Preliminary draft of a gazetteer for Chiang-su academies). *Kuo-hsueh t'u-shu-kuan nien-k'an* 國學圖書館年刊 4 (1931): 1–112.

Liu, James J. Y. *The Art of Chinese Poetry.* Chicago: University of Chicago Press, 1962.

———. *Chinese Theories of Literature.* Chicago: University of Chicago Press, 1975.

Liu, James T. C. *Reform in Sung China.* Cambridge: Harvard East Asian Center, 1959.

———. *Ou-yang Hsiu: An Eleventh-Century Neo-Confucianist.* Stanford: Stanford University Press, 1967.

———. "Yueh Fei (1103–1141) and China's Heritage of Loyalty." *Journal of Asian Studies* 31 (1972): 291–97.

———. "How Did a Neo-Confucian School Become the State Orthodoxy?" *Philosophy East and West* 23, 4 (1973): 483–505.

Liu, James T. C., and Peter Golas, eds. *Change in Sung China: Innovation or Renovation?* Lexington, Mass.: D. C. Heath, 1969.

Liu Jen-p'eng 劉人鵬. "Lun Chu-tzu wei-ch'ang i ku-wen shang-shu wei-tso" 論朱子未嘗疑古文尚書偽作 (Chu Hsi never doubted the authenticity of the Old Text Documents). *Ch'ing-hua hsueh-pao* 清華學報 n.s., 22, 4 (December 1992): 399–430.

Liu, Kwang-Ching, ed., *Orthodoxy in Late Imperial China.* Berkeley: University of California Press, 1990.

Liu Wen-ying 劉文英. *Chung-kuo ku-tai te meng-shu* 中國古代的夢書 (Dream books from ancient China). Peking: Chung-hua Bookstore, 1990.

Lo, Andrew, trans. "Four Examination Essays of the Ming Dynasty." *Renditions* 33 and 34 (1990): 176–78.

Lo, Jung-pang. "The Decline of the Early Ming Navy." *Oriens Extremus* 5, 2 (1958): 147–68.

Lo Lien-t'ien 羅聯添. *T'ang-tai wen-hsueh lun-chi* 唐代文學論集 (Collected essays on the T'ang dynasty literature). Taipei: Student Bookstore, 1989.

Lo, Winston. "A New Perspective on the Sung Civil Service." *Journal of Asian History* 17 (1983): 121–35.

———. *An Introduction to the Civil Service of Sung China.* Honolulu: University of Hawaii Press, 1987.

———. "Wan-yen Tsung-han: Jurchen General as Sinologist." *Journal of Sung-Yuan Studies* 26 (1996): 87–112.

Loch, Henry Brougham. *Personal Narrative of Occurrences during Lord Elgin's Second Embassy to China in 1860.* London, 1900.

Lockridge, Kenneth. *Literacy in Colonial New England: An Enquiry into the Social Context of Literacy in the Early Modern West.* New York: Norton, 1974.

Lu Chiu-yuan 陸九淵. *Lu Chiu-yuan chi* 集 (Collected writings of Lu Chiu-yuan). Taipei: Ch'i-hai Press, 1981.

Lu Hsun. "The True Story of Ah Q." In *Lu Hsun: Selected Stories,* translated by Yang Hsien-yi and Gladys Yang. New York: Norton, 1977.

Lu Lung-ch'i 陸隴其. "Huang T'ao-an hsien-sheng chih-i hsu" 黃陶菴先生制義序 (Preface to a Collection of Huang T'ao-an's examination essays). In *Ch'ing-tai ch'ien-ch'i chiao-yü lun-chu hsuan* 清代前期教育論著選 (Selections of writings on education from the early Ch'ing period), edited by Li Kuo-chün et al., 3 vols. Peking: People's Education Press, 1990.

Lu Shen 陸深. *K'o-ch'ang t'iao-kuan* 科場條貫 (Rules in the examination compound). In *Chi-lu hui-pien* 紀錄彙編, compiled by Shen Chieh-fu 沈節甫. Ming Wan-li edition. Lithograph, Shanghai: Commercial Press, 1938. Also in *Yen-shan wai-chi* 儼山外集, Ming Chia-ching edition; and *Huang-Ming kung-chü-k'ao.*

Lu Shih-i 陸世儀. *Ssu-pien lu chi-yao* 思辨錄輯要 (Collection of essentials in the record of thoughts for clarification). Chiang-su Bookstore, 1877.

———. *Lu-tzu i-shu* 陸子遺書 (Bequeathed writings of Master Lu). Yang-hu edition ca. 1900.

Lu Wen-ch'ao 盧文弨. *Pao-ching-t'ang wen-chi* 抱經堂文集 (Collected essays from the Hall for Cherishing the Classics). Shanghai: Commercial Press, 1937.

Lü K'un 呂坤. "Chiao-kuan chih chih" 教官之制 (The institution of education officials). In *Ming-tai chiao-yü lun-chu hsuan* 明代教育論著選, compiled by Kao Shih-liang 高時良. Peking: People's Press, 1990.

Lü Liu-liang 呂留良. "Wu-hsu fang-shu hsu" 戊戌房書序 (Preface to the 1658 examination ward essays). In *Ch'ing-tai ch'ien-ch'i chiao-yü lun-chu hsuan* 清代前期教育論著選 (Selections of writings on education from the early Ch'ing period), edited by Li Kuo-chün et al., 3 vols. Peking: People's Education Press, 1990.

Lü Miaw-fen. "Practice as Knowledge: Yang-ming Learning and *Chiang-hui* in Sixteenth Century China." Ph.D. diss., UCLA, History, 1997.

Lui, Adam Y. C. *The Hanlin Academy: Training Ground for the Ambitious, 1644–1850.* Hamden, Conn.: Shoe String Press, Archon Books, 1981.

———. *Two Rulers in One Reign: Dorgon and Shun-chih, 1644–1660.* Canberra: Faculty of Asian Studies, Australian National University, 1989.

———. *Ch'ing Institutions and Society (1644–1795).* Hong Kong: Centre of Asian Studies, University of Hong Kong, 1990.

"Lun fei k'o-chü hou pu-chiu chih fa" 論廢科舉後補救治法 (Ways to rectify matters since the abolition of the civil examinations). *Tung-fang tsa-chih* 東方雜誌 2, 11 (1905), *chiao-yü* 教育, pp. 251–254.

*Lun-yü yin-te* 論語引得 (Concordance to the Analects). Reprint, Taipei: Chinese Materials and Research Aids Service Center, 1966.

*Lung-ch'eng shu-yuan k'o-i* 龍城書院科藝 (Instruction at the Lung-ch'eng Academy). Compiled by Hua Miu 華繆. 1901 edition.

Lynn, Richard. "Orthodoxy and Enlightenment: Wang Shih-chen's Theory of Poetry and Its Antecedents." In William Theodore de Bary, ed., *The Unfolding of Neo-Confucianism.* New York: Columbia University Press, 1975.

Ma I-ch'u 馬夷初. *Wo tsai liu-shih-sui i-ch'ien* 我在六十歲以前 (My life before I was sixty). Shanghai: Sheng-huo Bookstore, 1947.

Ma Min and Li Yandan. "Judicial Authority and the Chamber of Commerce: Merchant

Dispute Mediation and Adjudication in Suzhou City in the late Qing." Paper presented at the Conference on Law and Society in Late Imperial China, sponsored by the Center for Chinese Studies, UCLA, August 8–10, 1993.

Ma, Tai-loi. "The Local Education Officials of Ming China, 1368–1644." *Oriens Extremus* 22, 1 (1975): 11–27.

MacKinnon, Stephen R. *Power and Politics in Late Imperial China: Yuan Shi-kai in Beijing and Tianjin, 1901–1908.* Berkeley: University of California Press, 1980.

Mair, Victor. "Language and Ideology in the Written Popularizations of the *Sacred Edict*." In David Johnson, Andrew Nathan, and Evelyn Rawski, eds., *Popular Culture in Late Imperial Culture.* Berkeley: University of California Press, 1985.

Makino Tatsumi 牧野巽. "Ko Enbu no seiin ron" 顧炎武の生員論 (Ku Yen-wu's "Essay on Licentiates"). In Hayashi Tomoharu, ed., *Kinsei Chūgoku kyōikushi kenkyū.* Tokyo: Kokutosha, 1958.

Man-cheong, Iona. "The Class of 1761: The Politics of a Metropolitan Examination." Ph.D. diss., Yale University, History, 1991.

———. "Fair Fraud and Fraudulent Fairness: The 1761 Examination Case." *Late Imperial China,* 18, 2 (December 1997).

Manguel, Alberto. *A History of Reading.* New York: Viking Press, 1996.

Mann, Susan. *Precious Records: Women in China's Long Eighteenth Century.* Stanford: Stanford University Press, 1997.

Mao Ch'i-ling 毛奇齡. *Ssu-shu kai-ts'o* 四書改錯 (Changes in the Four Books). *Ts'ung-shu chi-ch'eng ch'u-pien* 叢書集成初編. Shanghai: Commercial Press, 1936.

Mao P'ei-chi 毛佩琦. "Ts'ung Sheng-hsueh hsin-fa k'an Ming Ch'eng-tsu Chu Ti te chih-kuo li-hsiang" 從聖學心法看明成祖朱棣的治國理想 (A view of Ming Ch'eng-tsu Chu Ti's ideals of ordering the dynasty from his *The Method of the Mind in the Sages' Teachings*). *Ming-shih yen-chiu* 明史研究 1 (1991): 119–30.

Mao Tse-tung. "Report on an Investigation of the Hunan Peasant Movement." Translated in William Theodore de Bary et al., eds., *Sources of Chinese Tradition.* New York: Columbia University Press, 1960.

Massey, Thomas. "Chu Yuan-chang, the Hu-Lan Cases, and Early Ming Confucianism." Paper presented at the Columbia University Neo-Confucian Seminar, New York City.

McClelland, Charles E. "The Aristocracy and University Reform in Eighteenth-Century Germany." In Lawrence Stone, ed., *Schooling and Society. Studies in the History of Education.* Baltimore: Johns Hopkins University Press, 1976.

Mc Craw, David. *Chinese Lyricists of the Seventeenth Century.* Honolulu: University of Hawaii Press, 1990.

McDermott, Joseph. "Land, Labor, and Lineage in Southeast China." Paper presented at the Song-Yuan-Ming Transitions Conference, Lake Arrowhead, Calif., June 5–11, 1997.

McKnight, Brian. "Mandarins as Legal Experts: Professional Learning in Sung China." In William Theodore de Bary and John Chaffee, eds., *Neo-Confucian Education: The Formative Period.* Berkeley: University of California Press, 1989.

McMullen, David. *State and Scholars in T'ang China.* Cambridge: Cambridge University Press, 1988.

McNeill, William H. *The Pursuit of Power: Technology, Armed Force, and Society since A.D. 1000.* Chicago: University of Chicago Press, 1982.

Mei Wen-ting 梅文鼎. "Wang hsien-sheng pa-shih-shou hsu" 王先生八十壽序 (Preface to the 80th anniversary of Mr. Wang). In *Ch'ing-tai ch'ien-ch'i chiao-yü lun-chu hsuan* 清代前期教育論著選 (Selections of writings on education from the early Ch'ing period), edited by Li Kuo-chün et al., 3 vols. Peking: People's Education Press, 1990.

Menegon, Eugenio. "The Catholic Four-Character Classic (*Tianzhu Shengjiao Sizijing*): A Confucian Pattern to Spread a Foreign Faith in Late Ming China." Seminar paper, University of California at Berkeley, fall 1992.

Meng Sen 孟森. *Ming-Ch'ing-shih lun-chu chi-k'an* 明清史論著季刊 (Collection of articles on Ming-Ch'ing history). Taipei: World Bookstore, 1965.

———. *Ming-tai shih* 明代史 (History of the Ming period). Taipei: Chung-hua ts'ung-shu wei-yuan-hui, 1967.

*Meng-tzu chi-chu ta-ch'üan* 孟子集注大全 (Great collection of the collected notes to the Mencius). In *Ssu-shu ta-ch'üan* 四書大全. In *Ssu-k'u ch'üan-shu* 四庫全書 (Complete collection of the four treasuries). Reprint, Taipei: Commercial Press, 1983–86.

*Meng-tzu chieh-wen* 孟子節文 (Abridged text of the Mencius). In *Pei-ching t'u-shu-kuan ku-chi chen-pen ts'ung-k'an* 北京圖書館古籍珍本叢刊. Peking: Shu-mu Press, 1988.

*Meng-tzu yin-te* 孟子引得 (Concordance to the Mencius). Peking: Harvard-Yenching Publication, 1941.

Meskill, John. "A Conferral of the Degree of *Chin-shih*." *Monumenta Serica* 23 (1964): 351–71.

———. "Academies and Politics in the Ming Dynasty." In Charles O. Hucker, ed., *Chinese Government in Ming Times: Seven Studies*. New York: Columbia University Press, 1969.

———. *Academies in Ming China: A Historical Essay*. Tucson: University of Arizona Press, 1982.

Metzger, Thomas. *The Internal Organization of Ch'ing Bureaucracy*. Cambridge: Harvard University Press, 1973.

Michael, Franz, and Chung-li Chang. *The Taiping Rebellion*. Vol. 1, *History*. Seattle: University of Washington, 1966.

*Min-sheng hsien-shu* 閩省賢書 (Book about civil provincial examination worthies in Fu-chien). Compiled by Shao Chieh-ch'un 邵捷春. Late Ming edition.

*Ming-Ch'ing chin-shih t'i-ming pei-lu so-yin* 明清進士題名碑錄索引 (Index to the stelae rosters of Ming and Ch'ing *chin-shih*). Taipei: Wen-shih-che Press, 1982.

*Ming chuang-yuan t'u-k'ao* 明狀元圖考 (Illustrated survey of *optimi* during the Ming dynasty). Compiled by Ku Ting-ch'en 顧鼎臣 and Ku Tsu-hsun 顧祖訓. 1607 edition. (Wu Ch'eng-en 吳承恩 and Ch'eng I-chen 程一楨 added materials that brought it up to 1604. Materials for 1607–28 were later added by unknown compilers. See also *Chuang-yuan t'u-k'ao*.)

*Ming-jen chuan-chi tzu-liao so-yin* 明人傳記資料索引 (Index to Ming persons in biographical sources). Taipei: Central Library, 1965.

*Ming ming-ch'en yen-hsing-lu* 明名臣言行錄 (Record of words and actions of famous Ming officials). Compiled by Hsu K'ai-jen 徐開任. Ch'ing edition. Reprint, Taipei: Ming-wen Bookstore, 1991.

*Ming-shih* 明史 (Ming history). Taipei: Ting-wen Bookstore, 1982.

*Ming-shih chi-shih pen-mo* 明史紀事本末 (Record of the beginning and end of recorded events in Ming history). Compiled by Ku Ying-t'ai谷應泰. San-min Bookstore version of the 1658 edition. Taipei, 1969.

*Ming Shih-tsung shih-lu* 明世宗實錄 (Veritable records of the Ming dynasty Shih-ts'ung reign). Reprint. Taipei: Academia Sinica, 1965.

*Ming-tai chiao-yü lun-chu hsuan* 明代教育論著選 (Selections from Ming dynasty educational writings). Compiled by Kao Shih-liang 高時良. Peking: People's Press, 1990.

*Ming-tai teng-k'o-lu hui-pien* 明代登科錄彙編 (Compendium of Ming dynasty civil and military examination records). 22 vols. Taipei: Hsueh-sheng Bookstore, 1969.

*Ming-tai wei-k'o hsing-shih lu* 明代巍科姓氏錄 (Record of names on the highest examinations during the Ming dynasty). Compiled by Chang Wei-hsiang 張惟驤. Ch'ing edition. *Ming-tai chuan-chi ts'ung-k'an* reprint, Taipei: Ming-wen Bookstore, 1991.

*Ming T'ai-tsu shih-lu* 明太祖實錄 (Veritable records of Ming T'ai-tsu). In *Ming shih-lu* 明實錄. Taipei: Academia Sinica, Institute of History and Philology, 1962.

*Ming T'ai-tsu yü-chih wen-chi* 明太祖御製文集 (Collected writings of Chu Yuan-chang). Reprint, Taipei: Student Bookstore, 1965.

*Ming Wan-li chih Ch'ung-chen chien hsiang-shih-lu hui-shih-lu hui-chi* 明萬曆至崇禎間鄉試錄會試錄彙集 (Digest of provincial and metropolitan civil examination records from the Wan-li and Ch'ung-chen reigns of the Ming dynasty). Late Ming edition.

*Ming-wen ch'ao* 明文鈔 (Copies of Ming writing). Compiled by Kao Tang 高嶝. 1781 edition.

Miu T'ung 繆彤. *Lu-chuan chi-shih* 臚傳紀事 (Autobiography and record of occurrences). *Ts'ung-shu chi-ch'eng ch'u-pien* 叢書集成初編. Shanghai: Commercial Press, 1936.

Miyakawa, Hisayuki. "An Outline of the Naito Hypothesis and Its Effects on Japanese Studies of China." *Far Eastern Quarterly* 14 (1954–55): 533–52.

Miyazaki Ichisada 宮崎市定. *Kakyoshi* 科舉史 (History of the civil examination system). Revision of 1946 edition. Tokyo: Heibonsha, 1987.

———. *Kyūhin kan jinhō no kenkyū: Kakyo zenshi* 九品官人法の研究：科舉前史 (Research on the nine grades of civil officials: The early history of the civil examinations). Kyoto: Dōbōsha, 1956.

———. *China's Examination Hell*. Translated by Conrad Schirokauer. New Haven: Yale University Press, 1981.

Mizoguchi Yūzō 溝口雄三. "Mōshi jigi soshō no rekishi teki kō satsu" 孟子字義疏證の歷史的考察 (Historical analysis of the Evidential Analysis of the Meaning of Terms in the Mencius). *Tōyō bunka kenkyūjo kiyo* 東洋文化研究所紀要 48 (1969): 144–65.

———. "Iwayuru Tōrinha jinshi no shisō" いわゆる東林派人士の思想 (The thought of the members of the so-called Tung-lin faction). *Tōyō bunka kenkyūjo kiyo* 東洋文化研究所紀要 75 (March 1978): 111–341.

———. *Chūgoku no kō to shi* 中國の公と私 (Public and private in China). Tokyo: Kembun Press, 1995.

Moore, Oliver. "The Ceremony of Gratitude." In Joseph P. McDermott, ed., *Court and State Ritual in China*. Cambridge: Cambridge University Press, 1998.

Mote, F. W. "Confucian Eremitism in the Yuan Period." In Arthur Wright, ed., *The Confucian Persuasion*. Stanford: Stanford University Press, 1960.

———. "The Growth of Chinese Despotism." *Oriens Extremus* 8, 1 (August 1961): 1–41.

———. "The T'u-mu Incident of 1449." In Frank Kierman, Jr., and John Fairbank, eds., *Chinese Ways in Warfare*. Cambridge: Harvard University Press, 1974.

————. "Introduction." In Mote and Twitchett, eds., *The Cambridge History of China*, vol. 7, *The Ming Dynasty*. Cambridge: Cambridge University Press, 1988.

Mote, F. W., and Denis Twitchett, eds. *The Cambridge History of China*. Vol. 7, part 1, *The Ming Dynasty, 1368–1644*. Cambridge: Cambridge University Press, 1988.

Mou Jun-sun 牟潤孫. "Liang-Sung Ch'un-ch'iu-hsueh chih chu-liu, shang hsia" 兩宋春秋學之主流上下 (Main currents in studies of the Spring and Autumn Annals during the two Sung dynasties, parts 1 and 2). *Ta-lu tsa-chih* 大陸雜志 5, no. 4 (Aug. 1952): 113–15; no. 5 (September. 1952) 170–72.

Murakami Masatsugu 村上正二. *Chūgoku no rekishi 6: Yuboku minzoku kokka: Gen* 中國の歷史 6: 游牧民族國家：元 (Chinese history 6: Nomadic tribal nations: The Yuan). Tokyo: Kodansha, 1977.

Murphy, Raymond. *Social Closure: The Theory of Monopolization and Exclusion*. Oxford: Clarendon Press, 1988.

Murray, Julia K. "The Temple of Confucius and Pictorial Biographies of the Sage." *Journal of Asian Studies* 55, 2 (May 1996): 269–300.

*Nan-kuo hsien-shu* 南國賢書 (Book about civil provincial examination worthies in Ying-t'ien 應天 prefecture). Compiled by Chang Ch'ao-jui 張朝瑞. 1633 edition.

*Nan-Sung teng-k'o-lu liang-chung* 南宋登科錄兩種 (Two types of records of ascension to the *chin-shih* degree in the Southern Sung). Reprint, Taipei: Wen-hai Press, 1981.

Naquin, Susan, and Evelyn Rawski. *Chinese Society in the Eighteenth Century*. New Haven: Yale University Press, 1987.

Needham, Joseph. *Science and Civilisation in China*. Multiple vols. Cambridge: Cambridge University Press, 1954–.

————. "China and the Origins of Qualifying Examinations in Medicine." In Needham, *Clerks and Craftsmen in China and the West*. Cambridge: Cambridge University Press, 1970.

Neskar, Ellen. "The Cult of Confucian Worthies." Ph.D. diss., Columbia University, East Asian Languages and Cultures, 1994.

Nietzsche, Friedrich. *On the Genealogy of Morals*. Translated by Francis Golffing. Garden City, N.Y.: Anchor Books, 1956.

————. "Preface." In *Beyond Good and Evil*. Translated by Walter Kaufmann. New York: Vintage Books, 1966.

Nivison, David S. "Protest against Conventions and Conventions of Protest." In Arthur Wright, ed., *The Confucian Persuasion*. Stanford: Stanford University Press, 1960.

————. *The Life and Thought of Chang Hsueh-ch'eng (1738–1801)*. Stanford: Stanford University Press, 1966.

Nylan, Michael. "The *Chin Wen/Ku Wen* Controversy in Han Times." *T'oung Pao* 80 (1994): 83–136.

Ojima Sukema 小島祐馬. *Chūgoku no shakai shisō* 中國の社會思想 (Social thought in China). Tokyo: Chikuma Bookstore, 1967.

Ōki Yasushi 大木康. "Minmatsu Kōnan ni okeru shuppan bunka no kenkyū" 明末江南における出版文化の研究 (A study of print culture in Chiang-nan in the late Ming). *Hiroshima daigaku bungakubu kiyō* 廣島大學文學部紀要 50, 1 (1991).

Ōkubo Eiko 大久保英子. *Min-Shin jidai shoin no kenkyū* 明清時代書院の研究 (Research on academies in the Ming-Ch'ing period). Tokyo: Kokusho kankōkai, 1976.

Omura Kōdō 大村興道, "Shinchō kyōiku shisōshi ni okeru Seigo kōkun ni tsuite" 清

朝教育思想史に於ける聖諭廣訓について (Concerning the Amplified Instructions of the Sacred Edict in the history of educational thought in the Ch'ing dynasty). In Hayashi Tomoharu, ed., *Kinsei Chūgoku kyōikushi kenkyū*. Tokyo: Kokutosha, 1958.

Ong, Roberto. *The Interpretation of Dreams in Ancient China*. Bochum: Studienverlag Brockmeyer, 1985.

Ono Kazuko 小野和子. "Tōrin tō kō (ichi)" 東林黨考一 (Study of the Tung-lin party, part 1). *Tōhō gakuhō* 東方學報 52 (1980): 563–594.

———. "Tōrin tō kō (ni)" 東林黨考二 (Study of the Tung-lin party, part 2). *Tōhō gakuhō* 東方學報 55 (1983): 307–15.

———. *Minki dōsha kō* 明季黨社考 (Study of Ming dynasty factions and societies). Kyoto: Dōbō sha, 1996.

———, ed. *Mimmatsu Shinsho no shakai to bunka* 明末清初の社會と文化 (Late-Ming early-Ch'ing society and culture). Kyoto: Meibun Press, 1996.

Ou-yang Hsiu 歐陽修. *Ou-yang Wen-chung kung chi* 歐陽文忠公集 (Collection of Duke Ou-yang Hsiu). Taipei: Commercial Press, 1967.

Ou-yang Hsiu 歐陽修 and Sung Ch'i 宋祁. *Hsin T'ang-shu* 新唐書 (New history of the T'ang dynasty). Peking: Chung-hua Bookstore, 1971.

Overmyer, Daniel. "Values in Chinese Sectarian Literature: Ming and Ch'ing *Pao-chüan*." In David Johnson, Andrew Nathan, and Evelyn Rawski, eds., *Popular Culture in Late Imperial China*. Berkeley: University of California Press, 1985.

Owen, Stephen. *The Great Age of Chinese Poetry: The High T'ang*. New Haven: Yale University Press, 1981.

Oxenham, E. L. "Ages of Candidates at Chinese Examinations; Tabular Statement." *Journal of the China Branch of the Royal Asiatic Society*, n.s., 23 (1888): 286–87.

Oxnam, Robert. *Ruling from Horseback: Manchu Politics in the Oboi Regency*. Chicago: University of Chicago Press, 1975.

Ozment, Stephen. *The Age of Reform, 1250–1550*. New Haven: Yale University Press, 1980.

Pai Hsin-liang 白新良. *Chung-kuo ku-tai shu-yuan fa-chan shih* 中國古代書院發展史 (History of academy development in ancient China). T'ien-chin: T'ien-chin University Press, 1995.

Pan, Jixing. "The Spread of Georgius Agricola's *De Re Metallica* in Late Ming China." *T'oung Pao* 57 (1991): 108–18.

Pan Ku. See under *Han-shu*.

P'an Nai 潘鼐. "Nan-ching te liang-t'ai ku-tai ts'e-t'ien i-ch'i—Ming chih hun-i ho chien-i" 南京的兩台古代測天儀器—明制渾儀和簡儀 (Nanking's two ancient instruments for astronomical observation, the armillary sphere and the simplified instrument of the Ming). *Wen-wu* 文物 7 (1975): 84–89.

*Pao-yu ssu-nien teng-k'o-lu* 寶祐四年登科錄 (Record of the ascension to *chin-shih* rank on the 1256 palace civil examination). Ming edition.

Parker, Franklin. "Civil Service Examinations in China: Annotated Bibliography." *Chinese Culture* (Taiwan) 27, 2 (June 1986): 103–110.

Parsons, James. "The Ming Bureaucracy: Aspects of Background Forces." In Charles O. Hucker, ed., *Chinese Government in Ming Times: Seven Studies*. New York: Columbia University Press, 1969.

Peake, Cyrus. *Nationalism and Education in Modern China*. New York: Columbia University Press, 1970.

Peterson, Charles. "First Sung Reactions to the Mongol Invasion of the North, 1211–17." In John Haeger, ed., *Crisis and Prosperity in Sung China*. Tucson: University of Arizona Press, 1975.

———. "Old Illusions and New Realities: Sung Foreign Policy, 1217–1234." In Morris Rossabi, ed., *China among Equals: The Middle Kingdom and Its Northern Neighbors, 10th–14th Centuries*. Berkeley: University of California Press, 1983.

Peterson, Willard. "Fang I-chih: Western Learning and the 'Investigation of Things.' " In William Theodore de Bary, ed., *The Unfolding of Neo-Confucianism*. New York: Columbia University Press, 1975.

———. *Bitter Gourd: Fang I-chih and the Impetus for Intellectual Change*. New Haven: Yale University Press, 1979.

———. "Calendar Reform Prior to the Arrival of Missionaries at the Ming Court." *Ming Studies* 21 (spring 1986): 45–61.

*P'i-ling Chuang-shih tseng-hsiu tsu-p'u* 毘陵莊氏增修族譜 (Revised genealogy of the Chuang lineage in Ch'ang-chou). 1935 edition. Ch'ang-chou.

Pian, Rulan Chao. *Song Dynasty Musical Sources and Their Interpretation*. Cambridge: Harvard University Press, 1967.

*Ping-pu t'i-pen* 兵部題本 (Memoranda including memorials from the Ministry of Military Personnel). In the Ming-Ch'ing Archives, Academia Sinica, Taiwan.

Plaks, Andrew. "*Pa-ku wen* 八股文." In William Nienhauser, ed., *Indiana Companion to Traditional Chinese Literature*. Bloomington: Indiana University Press, 1986.

———. "The Prose of Our Time." In W. J. Peterson, A. H. Plaks, and Y. S. Yu, eds., *The Power of Culture: Studies in Chinese Cultural History*. Hong Kong: Chinese University Press, 1994.

Po Chü-i 白居易. *Po Chü-i chi-chien chiao* 集箋校 (Collated notes to the collected writings of Po Chü-i). Shanghai: Ku-chi Press, 1988.

P'u Sung-ling 蒲松齡. *Liao-chai chih-i* 聊齋志異 (Strange tales of Liao-chai). Shanghai: Ku-chi Press, 1962.

———. *Strange Tales of Liaozhai*. Translated by Lu Yunzhong, Chen Tifang, Yang Liyi, and Yang Zhihong. Hong Kong: Commercial Press, 1988.

Pulleyblank, Edwin. "Neo-Confucianism and Neo-Legalism in T'ang Intellectual Life, 755–805." In Arthur Wright, ed., *The Confucian Persuasion*, pp. 77–114. Stanford: Stanford University Press, 1960.

Purcell, Victor. *Problems of Chinese Education*. London: Kegan, Paul, Trench, Trubner, 1936.

Ramsey, S. Robert. *The Languages of China*. Princeton: Princeton University Press, 1987.

Rankin, Mary. " 'Public Opinion' and Political Power: *Qingyi* in Late Nineteenth-Century China." *Journal of Asian Studies* 41, 3 (May 1982): 453–84.

———. *Elite Activism and Political Transformation in China: Zhejiang Province, 1865–1911*. Stanford: Stanford University Press, 1986.

Rawski, Evelyn. *Education and Popular Literacy in Ch'ing China*. Ann Arbor: University of Michigan Press, 1979.

Reardon-Anderson, James. *The Study of Change: Chemistry in China, 1840–1949*. Cambridge: Cambridge University Press, 1991.

Reed, Bradly. "Scoundrels and Civil Servants: Clerks, Runners, and County Administration in Late Imperial China." Ph.D. diss., History, UCLA, 1994.

Ricci, Matteo. *China in the Sixteenth Century: The Journals of Matteo Ricci: 1583–1610*.

Translated into Latin by Father Nicholas Trigault and into English by Louis J. Gallagher, S.J. New York: Random House, 1953.

Ridley, Charles. "Educational Theory and Practice in Late Imperial China: The Teaching of Writing as a Specific Case." Ph.D. diss., Stanford University, Education, 1973.

Rieff, Philip. *The Triumph of the Therapeutic.* New York: Harper & Row, 1968.

———. *The Feeling Intellect: Selected Writings.* Chicago: University of Chicago Press, 1990.

Roddy, Stephen. *Literati Identity and Its Fictional Representations in Late Imperial China.* Stanford: Stanford University Press, 1998.

Rogers, Michael. "Foreign Relations during the Koryŏ Dynasty." In John Duncan, ed., *The Cambridge History of Korea,* vol. 2. Cambridge: Cambridge University Press, forthcoming.

Ropp, Paul. *Dissent in Early Modern China.* Ann Arbor: University of Michigan Press, 1981.

———. "Review of *Male Anxiety and Female Chastity.*" *Journal of Asian Studies* 48, 3 (August 1989).

Rossabi, Morris. "The Muslims in the Early Yuan Dynasty." In John D. Langlois, Jr., ed., *China under Mongol Rule.* Princeton: Princeton University Press, 1981.

———. *Khubilai Khan.* Berkeley: University of California Press, 1988.

———, ed. *China among Equals: The Middle Kingdom and Its Neighbors, 10th–14th Centuries.* Berkeley: University of California Press, 1983.

Rowe, William. "Success Stories: Lineage and Elite Status in Hanyang County, Hupeh, c. 1368–1949." In Joseph Esherick and Mary Rankin, eds., *Chinese Local Elites and Patterns of Dominance.* Berkeley: University of California Press, 1990.

———. "Education and Empire in Southwest China: Ch'en Hung-mou in Yunnan, 1733–38." In Benjamin Elman and Alexander Woodside, eds., *Education and Society in Late Imperial China.* Berkeley: University of California Press, 1994.

Rusk, Bruce. "Chen Que (1604–77) and the *Critique of the Great Learning.*" A.B. graduating essay, Department of History, University of British Columbia, 1996.

Russell, Terence. "Chen Tuan at Mount Huangbo: A Spirit-writing Cult in Late Ming China." *Asiatische Studien* 44, 1 (1990): 107–40.

Saito Akio 齋藤秋男. "Chūgoku gakusei kaikaku no shisō to genjitsu" 中國學制改革の思想と現實 (Ideas and reality in the reform of China's education system). *Senshū jimbun ronshū* 專修人文論集 4 (December 1969): 1–25.

Sakai, Naoki. "Modernity and Its Critique: The Problem of Universalism and Particularism." *South Atlantic Quarterly* 87, 3 (summer 1988): 475–504.

Sano Kōji 佐野公治. *Shisho gakushi no kenkyū* 四書學史の研究 (Research on Four Books studies). Tokyo: Sōbunsha, 1988.

Sariti, Anthony W. "Monarchy, Bureaucracy, and Absolutism in the Political Thought of Ssu-ma Kuang." *Journal of Asian Studies* 32, no. 1 (November 1972): 53–76.

Satō Shin'ichi 佐藤慎一. *Kindai Chūgoku no chishikijin to bunmei* 近代中國の知識人と文明 (Intellectuals and civilization in modern China). Tokyo: University of Tokyo Press, 1996.

Sawyer, Ralph, trans. *The Seven Military Classics of Ancient China.* Boulder, Colo.: Westview Press, 1993.

Schafer, Edward. *Pacing the Void: T'ang Approaches to the Stars.* Berkeley: University of California Press, 1977.

Schirokauer, Conrad. "Neo-Confucians under Attack: The Condemnation of *Wei-hsueh*." In John Haeger, ed., *Crisis and Prosperity in Sung China.* Tucson: University of Arizona Press, 1975.

Schorr, Adam. "Connoisseurship and the Defense against Vulgarity: Yang Shen (1488–1559) and His Work." *Monumenta Serica* 41 (1993): 89–128.

———. "The Trap of Words: Political Power, Cultural Authority, and Language Debates in Ming Dynasty China." Ph.D. diss., UCLA, East Asian Languages and Culture, 1994.

Schram, S. R., ed. *Foundations and Limits of State Power in China.* London: University of London, 1987.

Schwartz, Benjamin. *In Search of Wealth and Power: Yen Fu and the West.* New York: Harper Torchbooks, 1969.

Senor, Denis, ed. *The Cambridge History of Early Inner Asia.* Cambridge: Cambridge University Press, 1990.

Seo Tatsuhiko 妹尾達彦. "Tōdai no kakyo seido to Chōan no gokaku giri" 唐代の科舉制度と長安の合格儀禮 (The Tang civil service system and graduate rituals in Ch'ang-an). In *Ryūreisei—Chūgoku Chōsen no hō to kokka* 律令制—中國朝鮮の法と國家. Tokyo: Kyūko shoin, 1986.

Serruys, Henry. *Sino-Mongol Relations during the Ming.* In *Mélanges chinois et bouddhiques.* Vol. 1, *The Mongols in China during the Hung-wu Period, 1368–1398.* Vol. 2, *The Tribute System and the Diplomatic Missions.* Brussels: Institut Belge des Hautes Études Chinoises, 1959 and 1967.

Shang Ch'uan 商傳. *Yung-lo huang-ti* 永樂皇帝 (The Yung-lo emperor). Peking: Peking Press, 1989.

*Shang-shu cheng-i* 尚書正義 (Orthodox ·meanings in the Documents Classic). Compiled by K'ung Ying-ta 孔穎達 (547–648) et al. In *Shang-shu lei-chü ch'u-chi* 尚書類聚初集. Taipei: Hsin-wen-feng Press, 1984.

*Shang-shu t'ung-chien* 尚書通檢 (Concordance to the Documents Classic). Reprint, Peking: Ch'ao-jih wen-hsien Press, 1982.

Shang Yen-liu 商衍鎏. *Ch'ing-tai k'o-chü k'ao-shih shu-lueh* 清代科舉考試述略 (Summary of civil examinations during the Ch'ing period). Peking: San-lien Bookstore, 1958.

———. *T'ai-p'ing t'ien-kuo k'o-chü k'ao-shih chi-lueh* 太平天國科舉考試紀略 (Survey of civil examinations under the Heavenly Kingdom of the Taipings). Peking: Chung-hua Bookstore, 1961.

——— (Sheang Yen-liu). "Memories of the Chinese Imperial Civil Service Examination System." Translated by Ellen Klempner. *American Asian Review* 3, 1 (spring 1985): 48–83.

*Shang-yü tang* 上諭檔 (Imperial edict record book). Ch'ing dynasty archives preserved in the Palace Museum, Taiwan.

Shao Ch'ang-heng 邵長蘅. "Ni Chiang-hsi shih-ts'e i shih-wen" 擬江西試策一時文 (Drafting the first policy question on contemporary-style essays for Chiang-hsi). In *Ch'ing-tai ch'ien-ch'i chiao-yü lun-chu hsuan* 清代前期教育論著選 (Selections of writings on education from the early Ch'ing period), edited by Li Kuo-chün et al., 3 vols. Peking: People's Education Press, 1990.

Shen Hsin-chou 沈新周. "Hsu" 序 (Preface). In *Ti-hsueh* 地學 (Geographical studies). Lithograph, Shanghai: Sao-yeh shan-fang, 1910.

Shen Te-ch'ien 沈德潛. "Shuo-shih sui-yü" 說詩晬語 (Words on poetry in the past year of my life). 1731 edition.

*Shih-ching chin-chu chin-i* 詩經今註今譯 (New notes and meanings for the Poetry Classic). Compiled by Ma Ch'ih-ying 馬持盈. Taipei: Commercial Press, 1971.

*Shih-ching yin-te* 詩經引得 (Index to the Poetry Classic). Reprint, Taipei: Ch'eng-wen Bookstore, 1972.

Shih Piao-ku 史彪古. "Translation examination paper." In the Ming-Ch'ing Archives, Academia Sinica, Taiwan.

*Shih-san-ching chu-shu* 十三經注疏 (Notes and commentaries to the Thirteen Classics). 1797. Reprint, Taipei: Hsin wen-feng Press, n.d.

Shih, Vincent. *The Taiping Ideology: Its Sources, Interpretations, and Influences*. Seattle: University of Washington Press, 1967.

*Shinkoku gyōseihō* 清國行政法 (Ch'ing executive institutions). Tokyo: Rinji Taiwan kyū kan chōsankai, 1910–14.

Shu Hsin-ch'eng 舒新城. *Chin-tai Chung-kuo chiao-yü ssu-hsiang-shih* 近代中國教育思想史 (Intellectual history of modern Chinese education). Shanghai: Chung-hua Bookstore, 1932.

———. *Wo ho chiao-yü* 我和教育 (Education and I). Taipei: Lung-wen Press, 1990.

"Shun-t'ien fu t'i-pen" 順天府題本 (Memorials from Shun-t'ien prefecture). In the Ming-Ch'ing Archives, Academia Sinica, Taiwan.

Sivin, Nathan. "Cosmos and Computation in Early Chinese Mathematical Astronomy." *T'oung Pao* 55 (1969).

———. "Wang Hsi-shan (1628–1682)." In *Dictionary of Scientific Biography*, vol. 14. New York: Scribner's Sons, 1970–78.

———. "Copernicus in China." In *Colloquia Copernica II: Études sur l'audience de la théorie héliocentrique*. Warsaw: Union Internationale d'Histoire et Philosophie des Sciences, 1973.

———. "Introduction." In Nathan Sivin, ed., *Science and Technology in East Asia*. New York: Science History Publications, 1977.

———. "Max Weber, Joseph Needham, Benjamin Nelson: The Question of Chinese Science." In E. Victor Walter, ed., *Civilizations East and West: A Memorial Volume for Benjamin Nelson*. Atlantic Highlands, N.J.: Humanities Press, 1985.

———. "Science and Medicine in Chinese History." In Paul S. Ropp, ed., *Heritage of China: Contemporary Perspectives on Chinese Civilization*. Berkeley: University of California Press, 1990.

———, ed. *Science and Technology in East Asia*. New York: Science History Publications, 1977.

Skinner, G. William. "Cities and the Hierarchy of Local Systems." In Skinner, ed., *The City in Late Imperial China*. Stanford: Stanford University Press, 1977.

———. "Introduction: Urban and Rural in Chinese Society." In Skinner, ed., *The City in Late Imperial China*. Stanford: Stanford University Press, 1977.

———. "Introduction: Urban Development in Imperial China." In Skinner, ed., *The City in Late Imperial China*. Stanford: Stanford University Press, 1977.

Smith, Arthur H. *Chinese Characteristics*. Port Washington, N.Y.: Kennikat Press, 1894.

Smith, Joanna Handlin. "Benevolent Societies: The Reshaping of Charity during the Late Ming and Early Ch'ing." *Journal of Asian Studies* 46, 2 (May 1987): 309–31.

Smith, Richard. *Fortune-Tellers and Philosophers: Divination in Traditional Chinese Society.* Boulder, Colo.: Westview Press, 1991.

———. *Chinese Almanacs.* Hong Kong and Oxford: Oxford University Press, 1992.

Sommer, Deborah. "Confucianism's Encounter with the Evil Arts of Herodoxy: Ch'iu Chün's (1421–1495) Visions of Ritual Reform." Paper presented at the University Seminar on Neo-Confucian Studies, Columbia University, December 7, 1990.

Spence, Jonathan. *Emperor of China: Self-Portrait of K'ang-hsi.* New York: Vintage Books, 1974.

———. *To Change China: Western Advisers in China, 1620–1960.* Middlesex: Penguin Books, 1980.

———. *The Memory Palace of Matteo Ricci.* New York: Viking Penguin, 1985.

———. *God's Chinese Son: The Taiping Heavenly Kingdom of Hong Xiuquan.* New York: W. W. Norton, 1996.

*Ssu-ch'uan sheng tang-an-kuan Pa-hsien tang-an, "Wen-wei"* 四川省檔案館巴縣檔案, "文衛" ("Cultural and health materials" in the Ssu-ch'uan Provincial Archives, Pa-hsien County Archives). Tao-kuang 道光 through Kuang-hsu 光緒 microfilms.

*Ssu-k'u ch'üan-shu* 四庫全書 (Complete collection of the four treasuries). Reprint, Taipei: Commercial Press, 1983–86.

*Ssu-k'u ch'üan-shu tsung-mu* 四庫全書總目 (Catalog of the complete collection of the four treasuries). Compiled by Chi Yun 紀昀 et al. Reprint, Taipei: I-wen Press, 1974.

Ssu-ma Ch'ien 司馬遷. *Shih-chi* 史記 (Records of the official historian). Peking: Chung-hua Press, 1972.

Ssu-ma Kuang 司馬光. "Ch'i i shih-k'o chü-shih cha-tzu" 乞以十科舉士劄子 (Directive for using ten types of examinations to select literati). In *Wen-kuo Wen-cheng Ssu-ma kung wen-chi* 溫國文正司馬公文集 (Collected essays of Duke Ssu-ma Kuang). Shanghai: Commercial Press, 1920–22.

———. *Tzu-chih t'ung-chien* 資治通鑑 (Comprehensive mirror for aid in government). 11 vols. Taipei: Hung-shih Press, 1980.

*Ssu-shu chu-i hsin-te chieh* 四書主意心得解 (Main new ideas in the Four Books). Compiled by Chou Yen-ju 周延儒 and Chu Ch'ang-ch'un 朱長春. Ca. 1613.

*Ssu-shu ch'u-wen* 四書初問 (Preliminary questions on the Four Books). Compiled by Hsu Kuang 徐曠. 1563 edition.

*Ssu-shu ta-ch'üan* 四書大全 (Complete collection of the Four Books). Wen-yuan-k'o edition. Peking, 1776.

Stone, Lawrence. "The Educational Revolution in England, 1560–1640." *Past & Present* 28 (1964): 41–80.

———. "Literacy and Education in England 1640–1900." *Past & Present* 42 (1969): 69–139.

Strauss, Julia. "Symbol and Reflection of the Reconstituting State: The Examination Yuan in the 1930s." *Modern China* 20, 2 (April 1994): 211–38.

Strickmann, Michel. "Dreamwork of Psycho-Sinologists: Doctors, Taoists, Monks." In Carolyn Brown, ed., *Psycho-Sinology: The Universe of Dreams in Chinese Culture.* Lantham, Md.: University Press of America, 1988.

Su Shih 蘇軾. "I hsueh-hsiao kung-chü chuang" 議學校貢舉狀 (Debates on schools and civil examinations). In *Tung-p'o ch'üan-chi* 東坡全集 (Complete collection of Su Shih). In *Ssu-k'u ch'üan-shu* 四庫全書 (Complete collection of the four treasuries). Reprint, Taipei: Commercial Press, 1983–86.

Su Shuang-p'i 蘇雙碧. *Hung Hsiu-ch'üan chuan* 洪秀全傳 (Biography of Hung Hsiu-ch'üan). Peking: Ta-ti Press, 1989.

Su Yü. See *Ch'un-ch'iu fan-lu i-cheng.*

Sun Fu 孫復. *Ch'un-ch'iu tsun-wang fa-wei* 春秋尊王發微 (Bringing to light the honoring of the ruler in the *Annals*). In *T'ung-chih-t'ang ching-chieh* 通志堂經解. 1676; reprint, Kuang-chou: Yueh-tung, 1873.

Sun Hsing-yen 孫星衍. "Kuan-feng shih-shih ts'e-wen wu-t'iao yu-hsu" 觀風試士策問五條有序 (Preface for observations on trends in five policy questions for testing literati). In *Ch'ing-tai ch'ien-ch'i chiao-yü lun-chu hsuan* 清代前期教育論著選 (Selections of writings on education from the early Ch'ing period), edited by Li Kuo-chün et al., 3 vols. Peking: People's Education Press, 1990.

———. "Ni k'o-ch'ang shih-shih ch'ing chien-yung chu-shu che" 擬科場試士請兼用注疏摺 (Memorial recommending the use of scholia in examination compounds testing literati). In *Ch'ing-tai ch'ien-ch'i chiao-yü lun-chu hsuan* 清代前期教育論著選 (Selections of writings on education from the early Ch'ing period), edited by Li Kuo-chün et al., 3 vols. Peking: People's Education Press, 1990.

Sun, K'o-k'uan. "Yü Chi and Southern Taoism during the Yuan Period." In John D. Langlois, Jr., ed., *China under Mongol Rule*. Princeton: Princeton University Press, 1981.

Sun Shen-hsing 孫慎行. *En-hsu chu-kung chih lueh* 恩卹諸公志略 (Brief account of several dukes whose blood flowed as tribute). In *Ching-t'o i-shih* 荊駝遺史, compiled by Ch'en Hu 陳湖. Tao-kuang edition (1820–49).

*Sung Biographies.* Edited by Herbert Franke. Wiesbaden: Franz Steiner Verlag, 1976.

*Sung-chiang-fu shu li-k'o ts'ai-ch'in lu ch'u-pien* 松江府屬歷科采芹錄初編 (Preliminary compilation of the record of civil selection over several examinations in Sung-chiang prefecture). Photolithograph, Shanghai: Kuo-kuang, 1939.

*Sung li-k'o chuang-yuan lu* 宋歷科狀元錄 (Record of *optimi* from palace examinations of the Sung). Compiled by Chu Hsi-chao 朱希召. Ming edition. Reprint, Taipei: Wen-hai Press.

Sung Lien 宋濂. "Hui-shih chi-lu t'i-tz'u" 會試紀錄題辭 (Remarks on records of the metropolitan examination). In *Sung Wen-hsien kung ch'üan-chi* 宋文憲公全集. *Ssu-pu pei-yao* 四部備要 edition. Shanghai: Chung-hua Bookstore, 1927–37.

Sung P'ei-wei 宋佩韋. *Ming wen-hsueh shih* 明文學史 (History of Ming literature). Shanghai: Commercial Press, 1934.

*Sung-shih* 宋史 (History of the Sung dynasty). Compiled by T'o T'o 脫脫 (1313–55) et al. Taipei: Ting-wen Bookstore, 1980.

Sung Ting-tsung 宋鼎宗. "Sung-ju Ch'un-ch'iu jang-i shuo" 宋儒春秋攘夷説 (The Sung literati theory of repelling the barbarians in the Spring and Autumn Annals). *Ch'eng-kung ta-hsueh hsueh-pao* 成功大學學報 18 (March 1983): 7–20.

Sung Yuan-ch'iang 宋元強. *Ch'ing-tai te chuang-yuan* 清代的狀元 (Ch'ing dynasty *optimi*). Ch'ang-ch'un: Chi-lin ch'u-pan-she, 1992.

*Ta-Ch'ing hui-tien shih-li* 大清會典事例 (Collected statutes and precedents in the great Ch'ing). Shanghai: Commercial Press, 1908.

*Ta-Ch'ing Jen-tsung Jui (Chia-ch'ing) huang-ti shih-lu* 大清仁宗睿（嘉慶）皇帝實錄 (Veritable records of the great Ch'ing Chia-ch'ing Emperor). Reprint, Taipei, 1964.

*Ta-Ch'ing Kao-tsung Ch'un-huang-ti sheng-hsun* 大清高宗純皇帝聖訓 (Sacred edicts of the great Ch'ing Ch'ien-lung Emperor). Peking, n.d.

*Ta-Ch'ing Kao-tsung Ch'un (Ch'ien-lung) huang-ti shih-lu* 大清高宗純（乾隆）皇帝實錄 (Veritable records of the great Ch'ing Ch'ien-lung Emperor). Reprint, 30 vols., Taipei: Hua-wen Bookstore, 1964.

*Ta-Ch'ing Shih-tsung Hsien (Yung-cheng) huang-ti shih-lu* 大清世宗憲（雍正）皇帝實錄 (Veritable records of the Great Ch'ing dynasty Yung-cheng emperor Hsien's reign). Reprint, Taipei: Hua-wen Bookstore, 1964.

*Ta-Ch'ing Te-tsung shih-lu* 大清德宗實錄 (Veritable records of the Te-tsung reign during the great Ch'ing). Reprint, Taipei: Hua-wen Bookstore, 1964.

*Ta-Ming T'ai-tsung Wen huang-ti shih-lu* 大明太宗文皇帝實錄 (Veritable records of the Yung-lo emperor). Ming edition. Reprint, Taipei: Academia Sinica.

Tai Chen 戴震. *Meng-tzu tzu-i shu-cheng* 孟子字義疏證 (Evidential analysis of meaning of terms in the Mencius). Peking: Chung-hua Bookstore, 1961.

———. *Tai Chen wen-chi* 文集 (Tai Chen's collected essays). Hong Kong: Chung-hua Bookstore, 1974.

———. *Tai Chen chi* 集 (Tai Chen's collected essays). Shanghai: Ku-chi Press, 1980.

Tai Ming-shih 戴名世. "Keng-ch'en hui-shih mo-chüan hsu" 庚辰會試墨卷序 (Preface for the collection of examination essays from the 1700 metropolitan examination). In *Ch'ing-tai ch'ien-ch'i chiao-yü lun-chu hsuan* 清代前期教育論著選 (Selections of writings on education from the early Ch'ing period), edited by Li Kuo-chün et al., 3 vols. Peking: People's Education Press, 1990.

———. "Jen-wu mo-chüan hsu" 壬午墨卷序 (Preface for examination essays from 1702). In *Ch'ing-tai ch'ien-ch'i chiao-yü lun-chu hsuan* 清代前期教育論著選 (Selections of writings on education from the early Ch'ing period), edited by Li Kuo-chün et al., 3 vols. Peking: People's Education Press, 1990.

———. "Chiu-k'o ta-t'i-wen hsu" 九科大題文序 (Preface to essays on long quotations in nine examinations). In *Ch'ing-tai ch'ien-ch'i chiao-yü lun-chu hsuan* 清代前期教育論著選 (Selections of writings on education from the early Ch'ing period), edited by Li Kuo-chün et al., 3 vols. Peking: People's Education Press, 1990.

T'ang Chih-chün (Tang Zhijun) 湯志鈞 and Benjamin A. Elman. "The 1898 Reforms Revisited: A Review of Luke S. K. Kwong's *A Mosaic of the Hundred Days: Personalities, Politics, and Ideas of 1898.*" *Late Imperial China* 8, 1 (June 1987): 205–13.

T'ang Chih-chün (Tang Zhijun) 湯志鈞 et al. *Hsi-Han ching-hsueh yü cheng-chih* 西漢經學與政治 (Classicism and politics in the Western Han). Shanghai: Ku-chi Press, 1994.

T'ang Pin-yin 湯賓尹. *Ssu-shu mo chiang-i* 四書脈講意 (Lectures on the pulse of the Four Books). 1619 edition.

———. *Ssu-shu yen-ming chi-chu* 四書衍明集註 (Collected notes amplifying the Four Books). N.d.

T'ang Shun-chih 唐順之. *Wen-pien* 文編. In *Ssu-k'u ch'üan-shu* 四庫全書 (Complete Collection of the Four Treasuries). Reprint, Taipei: Commercial Press.

*T'ang-Sung k'o-ch'ang i-wen-lu* 唐宋科場異聞錄 (Recording unusual matters heard in the T'ang and Sung examination grounds). Wei-ching-t'ang shu-fang 味經堂書坊 edition. Canton; reprint, Ch'ien-t'ang, 1873.

Tanigawa Michio 谷川道雄. *Medieval Chinese Society and the "Local Community."* Translated by Joshua Fogel. Berkeley: University of California Press, 1985.

Tao, Ching-shen. "The Influence of Jurchen Rule on Chinese Political Institutions." *Journal of Asian Studies* 30, 1 (1970): 121–30.

————. "Political Recruitment in the Chin Dynasty." *Journal of the American Oriental Society* 94, 1 (January–March 1974): 24–33.

Taylor, Romeyn. "The Social Origins of the Ming Dynasty (1351–1360)." *Monumenta Serica* 22 (1963): 1–78.

————. "Ming T'ai-tsu's Story of a Dream." *Monumenta Serica* 32 (1976): 1–20.

————. "Official and Popular Religion and the Political Organization of Chinese Society in the Ming." In Kwang-ching Liu, ed., *Orthodoxy in Late Imperial China*. Berkeley: University of California Press, 1990.

————, trans. *Basic Annals of Ming T'ai-tsu*. San Francisco: Chinese Materials Center, 1975.

*Teng-k'o chi-k'ao* 登科記考 (Study of the records of ascension to civil degrees [during the T'ang]). Compiled by Hsu Sung 徐松 (1781–1848). Reprint, Kyoto: Chūbun Press, 1982.

*Teng-k'o lu* 登科錄 (Record of the ascension to *chin-shih* rank), 1371 palace civil examination. In *I-hai chu-ch'en* 藝海珠麈 (Dust from pearls of writing in the literary world). Ch'ing edition.

Teng Ssu-yü 鄧嗣禹. "China's Examination System and the West." In Harley Farnsworth, ed., *China*. Berkeley: University of California Press, 1946.

————. *Chung-kuo k'ao-shih chih-tu shih* 中國考試制度史 (History of Chinese examination institutions). Taipei: Student Bookstore, 1967.

Teng Ssu-yü 鄧嗣禹 and Knight Biggerstaff, comps. *An Annotated Bibliography of Selected Chinese Reference Works*. 2nd edition. Cambridge: Harvard University Press, 1971.

Teng Ssu-yü 鄧嗣禹 and John Fairbank. *China's Response to the West: A Documentary Survey, 1839–1923*. New York: Atheneum, 1967.

Teng Yun-hsiang 鄧云鄉. *Ch'ing-tai pa-ku-wen* 清代八股文 (Ch'ing dynasty eight-legged essays). Peking: People's University Press, 1994.

Thatcher, Melvin. "Selected Sources for Late Imperial China on Microfilm at the Genealogical Society of Utah." *Late Imperial China* 19, 2 (December 1998): 111–29.

*Ti-mu* 題目 (Question posters). In the Ming-Ch'ing Archives, Academia Sinica, Taiwan.

Tiao Pao 刁包 "Fei pa-ku hsing ssu-tzu wu-ching shuo" 廢八股興四子五經説 (Get rid of eight-legged essays and promote the Four Books and Five Classics). In *Ch'ing-tai ch'ien-ch'i chiao-yü lun-chu hsuan* 清代前期教育論著選 (Selections of writings on education from the early Ch'ing period), edited by Li Kuo-chün et al., 3 vols. Peking: People's Education Press, 1990.

*Tien-shih-chai hua-pao* 點石齋畫報 (The Tien-shih Pavilion's pictorial). Serial 2, vol. 11. 1897; reprint, Yang-chou: Chiang-su Rare Books, 1983.

T'ien, Ju-k'ang. *Male Anxiety and Female Chastity: A Comparative Study of Chinese Ethical Values in Ming-Ch'ing Times*. Leiden: E. J. Brill, 1988.

Tillman, Hoyt. "Proto-Nationalism in Twelfth-Century China? The Case of Ch'en Liang." *Harvard Journal of Asiatic Studies* 39, 2 (December 1979): 403–28.

————. *Utilitarian Confucianism: Ch'en Liang's Challenge to Chu Hsi*. Cambridge: Harvard University Council on East Asian Studies, 1982.

————. "Encyclopedias, Polymaths, and *Tao-hsueh* Confucians." *Journal of Sung-Yuan Studies* 22 (1990–92): 89–108.

————. *Confucian Discourse and Chu Hsi's Ascendancy*. Honolulu: University of Hawaii Press, 1992.

————. "Confucianism under the Chin and the Impact of Sung Confucian Tao-hsueh." In Hoyt Tillman and Stephen West, eds., *China under Jurchen Rule*. Albany: SUNY Press, 1995.

————. "An Overview of Chin History and Institutions." In Hoyt Tillman and Stephen West, eds., *China under Jurchen Rule*. Albany: SUNY Press, 1995.

*Ting-chia cheng-hsin lu* 鼎甲徵信錄 (Record of verified and reliable information concerning the top three candidates for the civil examinations). Compiled by Yen Hsiang-hui 閻湘慧. 1864 edition.

Trauzettel, Rolf. "Sung Patriotism as a First Step toward Chinese Nationalism." In John Haeger, ed., *Crisis and Prosperity in Sung China*. Tucson: University of Arizona Press, 1978.

Ts'ai Shen 蔡沈. "Hsu" 序 (Preface). In the *Shu chi-chuan* 書集傳 (Collected commentaries to the Documents). Taipei: World Bookstore, 1969.

Ts'ai Yuan-p'ei 蔡元培. *Ts'ai Yuan-p'ei hsuan-chi* 選集 (Selected works of Ts'ai Yuan-p'ei). Taipei: Wen-hsing Bookstore, 1967.

————. *Ts'ai Yuan-p'ei ch'üan-chi* 蔡元培全集 (Complete works of Ts'ai Yuan-p'ei). T'ai-nan: Wang-chia Press, 1968.

Tsien, T. H. *Written on Bamboo and Silk*. Chicago: University of Chicago Press, 1962.

Tsou Shao-chih 鄒紹志 and Kuei Sheng 桂勝. *Chung-kuo chuang-yuan ch'ü-wen* 中國狀元趣聞 (Interesting things heard about Chinese *optimi*). Taipei: Han-hsin Cultural Enterprises, 1993.

Tu, Ching-i. "The Chinese Examination Essay: Some Literary Considerations." *Monumenta Serica* 31 (1974–75): 393–406.

Tu, Wei-ming. *Neo-Confucian Thought in Action: Wang Yang-ming's Youth*. Berkeley: University of California Press, 1976.

————, ed. *Confucian Traditions in East Asian Modernity*. Cambridge: Harvard University Press, 1996.

Tu Wei-yun 杜維運. *Ch'ing Ch'ien-Chia shih-tai chih shih-hsueh yü shih-chia* 清乾嘉時代之史學與史家 (Historians and historical studies in the Ch'ing Ch'ien-lung and Chia-ch'ing eras). Taipei: Wen-shih ts'ung-k'an, 1962.

Tu Yu 杜佑. *T'ung-tien* 通典 (Comprehensive institutions). In *Shih-t'ung* 十通 (Ten Comprehensive Encyclopedias). Shanghai: Commercial Press, 1936.

T'u Shan 涂山. *Ming-cheng t'ung-tsung* 明政統宗 (Chronicle of Ming government). Ca. 1615 edition. Reprint, Taipei: Ch'eng-wen Bookstore, 1971.

Tung Ch'i-ch'ang 董其昌. *Hsueh-k'o k'ao-lueh* 學科考略 (Brief overview of civil examination studies). *Ts'ung-shu chi-ch'eng ch'u-pien* 叢書集成初編. Shanghai: Commercial Press, 1936.

"Tung-lin pieh-sheng" 東林別乘 (Separate records of Tung-lin). Transcribed list from an old manuscript in the provincial Chung-shan Library. Kuang-chou, 1958.

*T'ung-Hsiang t'i-ming lu* 通庠題名錄 (Record of civil service graduates in T'ung-chou and Ching-hsiang). Compiled by Li Yun-hui 李芸暉. 1895 edition.

Twitchett, Denis. "The Fan Clan's Charitable Estate, 1050–1760." In David S. Nivison and Arthur Wright, eds., *Confucianism in Action*. Stanford: Stanford University Press, 1959.

————. "The Birth of the Chinese Meritocracy: Bureaucrats and Examinations in T'ang China." *China Society Occasional Papers* (London) 18 (1974).

Uno Seiichi 宇野精一. *Chūgoku kotengaku no tenkai* (The development of classical studies in China). Tokyo: Hokuryūkan, 1949.

———. "Gokyō kara Shisho e: keigakushi oboegaki" 五經から四書へ：經學史覺書 (From the Five Classics to the Four Books: Notes on the history of classical studies). *Tōyō no bunka to shakai* 東洋の文化と社會 2 (1952): 1–14.

Van Gulik, R. H. *The Lore of the Chinese Lute.* Tokyo: Charles Tuttle, 1961.

von der Sprenkel, Otto Berkelbach. "High Officials of the Ming: A Note on the Ch'i Ch'ing Nien Piao of the Ming History." *Bulletin of the School of Oriental and African Studies* 14 (1952): 83–114.

von Falkenhausen, Lothar. "On the Early Development of Chinese Musical Theory: The Rise of Pitch Standards." *Journal of the American Oriental Society* 112, 3 (1992): 433–39.

———. *Suspended Music: Chime-Bells in the Culture of Bronze Age China.* Berkeley: University of California Press, 1993.

von Glahn, Richard. "Municipal Reform and Urban Social Conflict in Late Ming China." *Journal of Asian Studies* 50, 2 (1991).

———. "The Enchantment of Wealth: The God Wutong in the Social History of Jiangnan." *Harvard Journal of Asiatic Studies* 51, 2 (December 1991): 651–714.

———. *Fountain of Fortune: Money and Monetary Policy in China, 1000–1700.* Berkeley: University of California Press, 1996.

Wada Masahiro 和田正廣. "Mindai kyojinzō no keisei katei ni kan suru ichi kōsatsu" 明代舉人層の形成過程にする一考察 (A study of the formative process of the *chü-jen* class in the Ming dynasty). *Shigaku zasshi* 史學雜志 83, 3 (March 1978): 36–71.

———. "Mindai kakyo seido no kamoku no tokushoku: bengo no donyū o megutte" 明代科舉制度の科目の特色：判語の導入をめぐって (Special characteristics of the Ming dynasty civil examination curriculum: concerning introduction of legal judgment questions). *Hōseishi kenkyū* 法制史研究 43 (1993): 271–308.

Wagner, Rudolph. "Imperial Dreams in China." In Carolyn Brown, ed., *Psycho-Sinology: The Universe of Dreams in Chinese Culture.* Lantham, Md.: University Press of America, 1988.

———. "Twice Removed from the Truth: Fragment Collection in 18th and 19th Century China." In Glenn W. Most, ed., *Collecting Fragments/Fragmenta sammeln.* Göttingen: Vandenhoeck & Ruprecht, 1997.

Wakefield, David. *Fenjia: Household Division and Inheritance in Qing and Republican China.* Honolulu: University of Hawaii Press, 1998.

Wakeman, Frederic, Jr. "The Price of Autonomy: Intellectuals in Ming and Ch'ing Politics." *Daedalus* 101, 2 (1972): 35–70.

———. *The Fall of Imperial China.* New York: Free Press, 1975.

———. *The Great Enterprise: The Manchu Reconstruction of Imperial Order in Seventeenth-Century China.* 2 vols. Berkeley: University of California Press, 1985.

Waldron, Arthur. *The Great Wall of China: From History to Myth.* Cambridge: Cambridge University Press, 1990.

Waley, Arthur. *Yuan Mei: Eighteenth Century Chinese Poet.* Stanford: Stanford University Press, 1956.

———, trans. *The Book of Songs.* New York: Grove Press, 1937.

Waltner, Ann. "Building on the Ladder of Success: The Ladder of Success in Imperial China and Recent Work on Social Mobility." *Ming Studies* 17 (1983): 30–36.

———. *Getting an Heir: Adoption and the Construction of Kinship in Late Imperial China.* Honolulu: University of Hawaii Press, 1990.

Walton-Vargo, Linda. "Education, Social Change, and Neo-Confucianism in Sung-

Yuan China: Academies and the Local Elite in Ming Prefecture (Ningpo)." Ph.D. diss., University of Pennsylvania, History, 1978.

*Wan-li san-shih-pa-nien keng-hsu k'o-hsu ch'ih-lu* 萬歷三十八年庚戌科序齒錄 (Record of graduates of the 1610 palace examination). In *Ming-tai teng-k'o-lu hui-pien* 明代登科錄彙編 (Compendium of Ming dynasty civil and military examination records), vol. 21. Taipei: Hsueh-hseng Bookstore, 1969.

Wang An-shih 王安石. "Ch'i kai k'o-t'iao chih cha-tzu" 乞改科條制劄子 (Directive to reform the civil curriculum). In *Lin-ch'uan chi* 臨川集 (Collection of Wang An-shih). *Ssu-pu pei-yao* 四部備要 edition. Taipei: Chung-hua Bookstore, 1970.

Wang Ao 王鏊. *Chen-tse ch'ang-yü* 震澤長語 (Common sayings of Wang Ao). Taipei: Commercial Press, 1965.

Wang Ch'ang 王昶. *Ch'un-jung-t'ang chi* 春融堂集 (Collection from the Hall of Cheerful Spring). 1807 edition.

Wang Chen-main. *Hung Ch'eng-chou.* Tucson: University of Arizona Press, 1999.

Wang Chen-yuan 王鎮遠. *Ch'ing-shih hsuan* 清詩選 (Selections of Ch'ing poetry). Taipei: Lo-chün wen-hua, 1991.

Wang Chien-chün 王建軍. *Chung-kuo chin-tai chiao-k'o-shu fa-chan yen-chiu* 中國近代教科書發展研究 (Research on the development of modern textbooks in China). Kuang-chou: Kuang-tung Education Press, 1996.

Wang Chih-tung 王志東. *Chung-kuo k'o-chü ku-shih* 中國科舉故事 (Stories about the Chinese civil examinations). Taipei: Han-hsin Cultural Enterprises, 1993.

Wang Ch'ing-ch'eng 王慶成. "Lun Hung Hsiu-ch'üan te tsao-ch'i ssu-hsiang chi ch'i fa-chan" 論洪秀全的早期思想及其發展 (On Hung Hsiu-ch'üan's early thought and its development). In *T'ai-p'ing t'ien-kuo-shih hsüeh-shu t'ao-lun-hui lun-wen hsuan-chi* 太平天國史學術討論會論文選集. Peking: Hsin-hua Bookstore, 1981.

Wang Fu-chih 王夫之. *Sung-lun* 宋論 (Discussions of the Sung). *Ssu-pu pei-yao* 四部備要 edition. Shanghai: Chung-hua Bookstore, 1927–35.

Wang Gungwu. "The Rhetoric of a Lesser Empire: Early Sung Relations with Its Neighbors." In Morris Rossabi, ed., *China among Equals: The Middle Kingdom and Its Northern Neighbors, 10th–14th Centuries.* Berkeley: University of California Press, 1983.

———. "Pre-Modern History: Some Trends in Writing the History of the Sung (10th–13th Centuries)." In Michael Yahuda, ed., *New Directions in the Social Sciences and Humanities in China.* New York: Macmillan Press, 1987.

———. *Community and Nation: China, Southeast Asia and Australia.* St. Leonards, Australia: Allen & Unwin, 1992.

Wang Hsien-ch'ien 王先謙. *Hsu-shou-t'ang wen-chi* 虛受堂文集 (Collected writings from Wang Hsien-ch'ien's studio). Taipei: Wen-hua Press, 1966.

Wang Ming-hsiung 王明雄. *T'an-t'ien shuo-ming* 談天說命 (On heaven and fate). Taipei: Huang-kuan Magazine Press, 1988.

Wang Shih-chen 王士禎. "Lü-shih ting-t'i" 律詩定體 (Fixed style of regulated verse). In *Ch'ing shih-hua* 清詩話 (Ch'ing works on poetry discussions). Shanghai: Ku-chi Press, 1963.

———. "Preface for the 1671 Ssu-ch'uan provincial examination." In *Ch'ing-tai ch'ien-ch'i chiao-yü lun-chu hsuan* 清代前期教育論著選 (Selections of writings on education from the early Ch'ing period), edited by Li Kuo-chün et al., 3 vols. Peking: People's Education Press, 1990.

————. "Afterword for the 1691 metropolitan civil examinations." In *Ch'ing-tai ch'ien-ch'i chiao-yü lun-chu hsuan* 清代前期教育論著選 (Selections of writings on education from the early Ch'ing period), edited by Li Kuo-chün et al., 3 vols. Peking: People's Education Press, 1990.

Wang, Y. C. *Chinese Intellectuals and the West, 1872–1949.* Chapel Hill: University of North Carolina Press, 1966.

Wang Yang-ming 王陽明. *Wang Yang-ming ch'üan-chi* 王陽明全集 (Complete works of Wang Yang-ming). Hong Kong: Kuang-chi Bookstore, 1959.

————. *Yang-ming ch'üan-shu* 陽明全書 (Complete works of Wang Yang-ming). *Ssu-pu pei-yao* edition. Taipei: Chung-hua Bookstore, 1979.

Wang Yin-t'ing 王蔭庭. "Pan-an yao-lueh" 辦案要略 (Outline for handling legal cases). In *Ju-mu hsu-chih* 入幕須知, compiled by Chang T'ing-hsiang 張廷驤. Che-chiang Bookstore, 1892.

Wang Yun 王筠. "Chiao t'ung-tzu fa" 教童子法 (On teaching youthful students). In *Ch'ing-tai ch'ien-ch'i chiao-yü lun-chu hsuan* 清代前期教育論著選 (Selections of writings on education from the early Ch'ing period), edited by Li Kuo-chün et al., 3 vols. Peking: People's Education Press, 1990.

Wang, Yuquan. "Some Salient Features of the Ming Labor Service System." *Ming Studies* 21 (spring 1986): 1–44.

とWatari Masamitsu 渡昌弘. "Minsho no kakyo fukkatsu to kensei" 明初の科舉復活　監生 (Early Ming revival of the civil service examination system and Imperial School students). *Shūkan tōyōgaku* 集刊東洋學 49 (1983): 19–36.

Watson, Burton, ed. and trans. *The Columbia Book of Chinese Poetry.* New York: Columbia University Press, 1984.

Watson, James. "Chinese Kinship Reconsidered: Anthropological Perspectives on Historical Research." *China Quarterly* 92 (1982).

————. "Standardizing the Gods: The Promotion of T'ien Hou ('Empress of Heaven') along the South China Coast." In David Johnson, Andrew Nathan, and Evelyn Rawski, eds., *Popular Culture in Late Imperial China.* Berkeley: University of California Press, 1985.

Watson, Rubie. *Inequality among Brothers: Class and Kinship in South China.* Cambridge: Cambridge University Press, 1985.

Watt, John. *The District Magistrate in Late Imperial China.* New York: Columbia University Press, 1972.

Weber, Max. *The Religion of China.* Translated by Hans Gerth. New York: Macmillan, 1954.

Wechsler, Howard. *Mirror to the Son of Heaven; Wei Cheng at the Court of T'ang T'ai-tsung.* New Haven: Yale University Press, 1974.

————. "T'ai-tsung (Reign 626–49) the Consolidator." In Denis Twitchett, ed., *The Cambridge History of China,* vol. 3, part 1. Cambridge: Cambridge University Press, 1979.

————. *Offerings of Jade and Silk: Ritual and Symbol in the Legitimation of the T'ang Dynasty.* New Haven: Yale University Press, 1985.

Wei Yuan. See *Huang-ch'ao ching-shih wen-pien.*

*Wen-hsien t'ung-k'ao* 文獻通考 (Comprehensive analysis of civil institutions). Compiled by Ma Tuan-lin 馬端臨. Shanghai: Commercial Press, 1936.

*Wen-wei hsiang-shih li-an* 文闈鄉試例案 (Case-examples of essays from the provincial examinations). 1832 edition.

*Wen-yuan ying-hua* 文苑英華 (A gathering of masterpieces of literature). Compiled by Li Fang 李昉. 1567 edition.

Weng Fang-kang 翁方綱. "Wu-yen-shih p'ing-tse chü-yü" 五言詩平仄舉隅 (Pairs in level and deflected tones for five-word poetry). In Kuo Shao-yü 郭紹虞, comp., *Ch'ing shih-hua* 清詩話 (Ch'ing works on poetry discussions). Shanghai: Ku-chi Press, 1963.

———. "Tzu-hsu" 自序 (Personal preface) to his *Shih-chou shih-hua* 石洲詩話 (Poetry talks from rock islets). In Kuo Shao-yü 郭紹虞, comp., *Ch'ing shih-hua hsu-pien* 清詩話續編 (Ch'ing works on poetry discussions, continuation). Shanghai: Ku-chi Press, 1983.

West, Stephen. "Mongol Influence on the Development of Northern Drama." In John D. Langlois, Jr., ed., *China under Mongol Rule*. Princeton: Princeton University Press, 1981.

———. "Yuan Hao-wen's Poems of Death and Disorder, 1233–1235." In Hoyt Tillman and Stephen West, eds., *China under Jurchen Rule*. Albany: SUNY Press, 1995.

———. "Rewriting Text, Inscribing Ideology: The Case of *Zaju* Comedy." Paper presented at the Song-Yuan-Ming Transitions Conference, Lake Arrowhead, Calif., June 5–11, 1997.

Weston, Tim. "Beijing University and Chinese Political Culture, 1898–1920." Ph.D. diss., University of California at Berkeley, History, 1995.

Widmer, Ellen. "The Huanduzhai of Hangzhou and Suzhou: A Study in Seventeenth-Century Publishing." *Harvard Journal of Asiatic Studies* 56, 1 (June 1996): 77–122.

Wiens, Mi Chu. "Changes in the Fiscal and Rural Control Systems in the Fourteenth and Fifteenth Centuries." *Ming Studies* 3 (1976): 53–69.

———. "Lord and Peasant: The Sixteenth to the Eighteenth Century." *Modern China* 6, 1 (1980).

Wilhelm, Hellmut. "From Myth to Myth: The Case of Yueh Fei's Biography." In Denis Twitchett and Arthur Wright, eds., *Confucian Personalities*. Stanford: Stanford University Press, 1962.

Wilson, Thomas. *Genealogy of the Way: The Construction and Uses of the Confucian Tradition in Late Imperial China*. Stanford: Stanford University Press, 1995.

Wittfogel, Karl. "Public Office in the Liao Dynasty and the Chinese Examination System." *Harvard Journal of Asiatic Studies* 10 (1947): 13–40.

"Wo i" 我一 ("I alone"). "K'ao-shih kan-yen" 考試感言 (Moving words on examinations). *Chiao-yü tsa-chih* 教育雜誌 (Journal of education) 2.5 (1910), *p'ing-lun* 評論.

Wong, R. Bin. "Great Expectations: The Search for Modern Times in Chinese History." *Chūgokushi gaku* 中國史學 (Tokyo) 3 (1993): 7–50.

Wood, Alan. *Limits to Autocracy: From Sung Neo-Confucianism to a Doctrine of Political Rights*. Honolulu: University of Hawaii Press, 1995.

Woodside, Alexander. "Some Mid-Qing Theorists of Popular Schools." *Modern China* 9, 1 (1983): 3–35.

Woodside, Alexander, and Benjamin A. Elman. "The Expansion of Education in Ch'ing China." In Elman and Woodside, eds., *Education and Society in Late Imperial China*. Berkeley: University of California Press, 1994.

Wou, Odoric. "The District Magistrate Profession in the Early Republican Period." *Modern Asian Studies* 8, 2 (April 1974): 217–45.

Wright, David. "Parity, Pedigree, and Peace: Routine Sung Diplomatic Missives to the Liao." *Journal of Sung-Yuan Studies* 26 (1996): 55–85.

Wright, Mary. *The Last Stand of Chinese Conservatism: The T'ung-chih Restoration, 1862–1874.* Stanford: Stanford University Press, 1957.

———. "Introduction: The Rising Tide of Change." In Wright, ed., *China in Revolution: The First Phase, 1900–13.* New Haven: Yale University Press, 1968.

Wu Chih-ho 吳智和. *Ming-tai te ju-hsueh chiao-kuan* 明代的儒學教官 (Education officials in literati schools during Ming times). Taipei: Student Bookstore, 1991.

Wu Ching-tzu. *The Scholars.* Translated by Yang Hsien-yi and Gladys Yang. Peking: Foreign Languages Press, 1957.

Wu Han 吳晗. *Chu Yuan-chang chuan* 朱元璋傳 (Biography of Chu Yuan-chang). Peking: San-lien Bookstore, 1949.

Wu Hung-i 吳宏一. *Ch'ing-tai shih-hsueh ch'u-t'an* 清代詩學初談 (Preliminary analysis of poetry studies in the Ch'ing period). Taipei: Mu-t'ung Press, 1977.

*Wu-li t'ung-k'ao* 五禮通考 (Comprehensive analysis of the five ritual texts). Compiled by Ch'in Hui-t'ien 秦蕙田. 1761 edition.

Wu, Pei-yi. *The Confucian's Progress: Autobiographical Writings in Traditional China.* Princeton: Princeton University Press, 1990.

Wu Ping 吳炳. *Lü mu-tan* 綠牡丹 (The green peony). In Wu Mei 吳梅, ed., *She-mo t'a-shih ch'ü-ts'ung* 奢摩他室曲叢. Shanghai: Commercial Press, 1928.

Wu Po-tsung 吳伯宗. *Jung-chin chi* 榮進集 (Collection from the glorious *chin-shih*). In *Ssu-k'u ch'üan-shu* 四庫全書 (Complete collection of the four treasuries). Reprint, Taipei: Commercial Press, 1983–86.

Wu Sheng-ch'in 吳省欽. "Ch'ien-lung san-shih-liu nien Hu-pei hsiang-shih ts'e-wen erh shou" 乾隆三十六年湖北鄉試策問二首 (Two policy questions from the 1771 Hu-pei provincial examination). In *Ch'ing-tai ch'ien-ch'i chiao-yü lun-chu hsuan* 清代前期教育論著選 (Selections of writings on education from the early Ch'ing period), edited by Li Kuo-chün et al., 3 vols. Peking: People's Education Press, 1990.

Wu, Silas. *Passage to Power: K'ang-hsi and His Heir Apparent, 1661–1722.* Cambridge: Harvard University Press, 1979.

Wu, Yiyi. "Auspicious Omens and Their Consequences: Zhen-ren (1006–1066) Literati's Perception of Astral Anomalies." Ph.D. diss., Princeton University, History, 1990.

Yabuuti, Kiyosi. "Chinese Astronomy: Development and Limiting Factors." In Shigeru Nakayama and Nathan Sivin, eds., *Chinese Science: Explorations of an Ancient Tradition.* Cambridge: MIT Press, 1973.

Yamamoto Takayoshi 山本隆義. "Gendai ni okeru Kanrin gakushi in ni tsuite" 元代に於ける翰林學士院について (Concerning the Hanlin Academy during the Yuan period). *Tōhōgaku* 東方學 11 (1955): 81–99.

Yang, C. K. *Religion in Chinese Society.* Berkeley: University of California Press, 1967.

*Yang-ch'eng T'ien T'ai-shih ch'üan-kao* 陽城田太師全稿 (Complete drafts of T'ien Ts'ung-tien 從典 from Yang-ch'eng). 1722 edition.

Yang Chin-lung 揚晉龍. "Shih-chuan ta-ch'üan ch'ü-ts'ai lai-yuan t'an-chiu" 詩傳大全取材來源探究 (Inquiry into the sources selected for the *Complete Collection of Commentaries for the Poetry Classic*). In Lin Ch'ing-chang 林慶彰, ed., *Ming-tai ching-hsueh kuo-chi yen-t'ao-hui lun-wen chi* 明代經學國際研討會論文集. Taipei: Academia Sinica, 1996.

Yang Hsiung 揚雄. *Fa-yen* 法言 (Model words). In *Yang Tzu-yun chi* 揚子雲集 (Collection of Yang Hsiung). Compiled by Cheng P'u 鄭樸. Late Ming Wan-li edition.

Yang Hsueh-wei 楊學為 et al., comps. *Chung-kuo k'ao-shih chih-tu shih tzu-liao hsuan-pien* 中國考試制度史資料選編 (Selected sources on the history of the Chinese civil service examination system). Ho-fei, An-hui: Huang-shan shu-she, 1992.

Yang I-k'un 楊一崑. *Ssu-shu chiao-tzu tsun-ching ch'iu-t'ung lu* 四書教子尊經求通錄 (Record of honoring the classics and seeking comprehensiveness from the Four Books to teach children). N.d.

Yang, Jui-sung. "A New Interpretation of Yen Yuan (1635–1704) and Early Ch'ing Confucianism in North China." Ph.D. diss., UCLA, History, 1997.

Yang Shu-fan 楊樹藩, "Yuan-tai k'o-chü chih-tu" 元代科舉制度 (The Yuan civil service examination system). *Sung-shih yen-chiu chi* 宋史研究集 14 (1983): 210–16.

"Yang-wu yun-tung ta-shih chi" 洋務運動大事記 (Record of important matters during the foreign studies movement). In Hsu T'ai-lai 徐泰來, ed., *Yang-wu yun-tung hsin-lun* 洋務運動新論 (New views on the foreign studies movement). Ch'ang-sha: Hu-nan People's Press, 1986.

Yao Lo-yeh 姚樂野. "Ming-Ch'ing k'o-chü chih yü chung-yang chi-ch'üan te chuan-chih chu-i" 明清科舉制與中央集權的專制主義 (The Ming-Ch'ing civil examination system and despotism via the centralization of power). *Ssu-ch'uan ta-hsueh hsueh-pao* 四川大學學報 1 (1990): 98–104.

Yao Ta-li 姚大力. "Yuan-tai k'o-chü chih-tu te hsing-fei chi ch'i she-hui pei-ching" 元代科舉制度的行廢及其社會背景 (The social background and promulgation of the civil examination system in the Yuan period). *Yuan-shih chi pei-fang min-tsu shih yen-chiu* 元史及北方民族史研究 5 (1982): 26–59.

———. "Chin-mo Yuan-ch'u li-hsueh tsai pei-fang de ch'uan-po" 金末元初理學在北方的傳播 (The transmission of the school of principle in the north during the late Chin and early Yuan). *Yuan-shih lun-ts'ung* 元史論叢 2 (1983).

Yao Wei-chün 姚偉鈞. *Shen-mi te chan-meng* 神秘的占夢 (Mysteries of dreams). Kuang-hsi: People's Press, 1991.

Yap, P. M. "The Mental Illness of Hung Hsiu-ch'üan, Leader of the Taiping Rebellion." *Far Eastern Quarterly* 13, 3 (May 1954): 287–304.

Yates, Frances. *The Art of Memory*. New York: Penguin, 1969.

Yee, Carsey. "The Shuntian Examination Scandal of 1858: The Legal Defense of Imperial Institutions." Manuscript, n.d.

Yen Chia-yen 嚴家炎. "Wu-ssu, wen-ko, ch'uan-t'ung wen-hua" 五四，文革，傳統文化 (May Fourth, cultural revolution, and traditional culture). *Erh-shih-i shih-chi* 二十一世紀 41 (1997): 11–18.

Yen Fu 嚴復. "Lun chiao-yü yü kuo-chia chih kuan-hsi" 論教育與國家之關係 (On the relation between schools and the nation). *Tung-fang tsa-chih* 東方雜誌 3, 3 (1906), *chiao-yü* 教育, pp. 29–34.

———. "Chiu-wang chueh-lun" 救亡決論 (On what determines rescue or perishing). In *Wu-hsu pien-fa tzu-liao* 戊戌變法資料 (Sources on the 1898 reform movement). Peking: Shen-chou kuo-kuang she, 1953.

*Yen-Li ts'ung-shu* 顏李叢書 (Collectanea of Yen Yuan and Li Kung). Reprint, Taipei: Kuang-wen Bookstore, 1965.

Yen Yuan 顏元. "Ta Ho Ch'ien-li" 答何千里 (Response to Ho Ch'ien-li). In *Ch'ing-tai ch'ien-ch'i chiao-yü lun-chu hsuan* 清代前期教育論著選 (Selections of writings on education from the early Ch'ing period), edited by Li Kuo-chün et al., 3 vols. Peking: People's Education Press, 1990.

———. *Ssu-shu cheng-wu* 四書正誤 (Correction of errors on the Four Books). In Yen Yuan and Li Kung, *Yen-Li ts'ung-shu*. Reprint, Taipei: Kuang-wen Bookstore, 1965.

Yoshikawa Kōjirō 吉川幸次郎. *An Introduction to Sung Poetry*. Translated by Burton Watson. Cambridge: Harvard University Press, 1967.

———. "Shushigaku hokuden zenshi" 朱子學北傳前史 (Early history of the spread north of Chu Hsi studies). In *Uno Tetsuto sensei byakuju shukuga kinen Tōyō gaku ronsō* 于野哲人先生百壽祝賀記念東洋學論叢. Tokyo: Honoring Committee for Uno Tetsuto, 1974.

Young, Ernest P. *The Presidency of Yuan Shih-k'ai: Liberalism and Dictatorship in Early Republican China*. Ann Arbor: University of Michigan Press, 1977.

Young, Lung-chang. "Ku Yen-wu's Views on the Ming Examination System." *Ming Studies* 23 (1987): 48–63.

Young, Michael, ed. *Knowledge and Control: New Directions for the Sociology of Education*. London: Collier Macmillan, 1971.

Yu Li. "Social Change during the Ming-Qing Transition and the Decline of Sichuan Classical Learning in the Early Qing." *Late Imperial China* 19, 2 (June 1998): 26–55.

Yu, Pauline. "Canon Formation in Late Imperial China." In Theodore Huters et al., eds., *Culture and State in Chinese History: Conventions, Accommodations, and Critiques*. Stanford: Stanford University Press, 1997.

Yü Chi 虞集. *Tao-yuan hsueh-ku lu* 道園學古錄 (Record of the study of antiquity in the garden of the Way). *Kuo-hsueh chi-pen ts'ung-shu* 國學基本叢書. Shanghai: Commercial Press, 1929–41.

Yü Chih-chia 于志嘉. "Mindai gunko no shakai teki ni tsuite" 明代軍戶の社會的地位について (The social status of military households in the Ming dynasty). *Tōyō gakuhō* 東洋學報 71, 3 and 4 (March 1990).

*Yü-hai* 玉海 (Sea of jade). Compiled by Wang Ying-lin 王應麟 (1223–1296). 1337 edition. Facsimile, Taipei: Hua-wen Bookstore, 1964.

*Yü-p'i li-tai t'ung-chien chi-lan* 御批歷代通鑑輯覽 (Imperially approved collection of mirrors for aid in government over several dynasties). Ch'ien-lung edition. Reprint, Taipei: n.p., n.d.

Yü, Ying-shih. "Some Preliminary Observations on the Rise of Ch'ing Confucian Intellectualism." *Tsing Hua Journal of Chinese Studies*, n.s., 11, 1 and 2 (December 1975).

Yuan Huang 袁黃. "Fan-li" 凡例 (Overview). In *Ssu-shu shan-cheng* 四書刪正 (Cutting to the Correct in the Four Books). N.d.

Yuan Mei 袁枚. *Shih-hua* 詩話 (Poetry talks). In *Sui-yuan ch'üan-chi* 隨園全集 (Complete works of Yuan Mei). Shanghai: Wen-ming Bookstore, 1918.

*Yuan-shih* 元史 (History of the Yuan dynasty). 7 vols. Reprint, Taipei: Ting-wen Press, 1982.

Yuan, Tsing. "Urban Riots and Disturbances." In Jonathan Spence and John Wills, eds., *From Ming to Ch'ing: Conquest, Region, and Continuity in Seventeenth-Century China*. New Haven: Yale University Press, 1979.

Zeitlin, Judith. *Historian of the Strange: Pu Songling and the Chinese Classical Tale*. Stanford: Stanford University Press, 1993.

———. "Spirit Writing and Performance in the Work of You Tong (1618–1704)." Paper presented at UCLA-USC Southern California China Colloquium, November 1995.

———. "Making the Invisible Visible: Images of Desire and Constructions of the Female Body in Chinese Literature, Medicine, and Art." Manuscript, 1998.

Zhou, Guangyuan. "Illusion and Reality in the Law of the Late Qing." *Modern China* 19, 4 (October 1993).

Zi, Etienne, S.J. *Pratique des examens littéraires en Chine*. Shanghai: Imprimerie de la Mission Catholique, 1894.

Zottoli, P. Angelo, S.J. *Cursus Litteraturae Sinicae*. Vol. 5, *Pro Rhetorices Classe pars Oratoria et Poetica*. Shanghai: Catholic Mission, 1882.

Zurndorfer, Harriet. "Chinese Merchants and Commerce in Sixteenth Century China." In Wilt Idema, ed., *Leiden Studies in Sinology*. Leiden: E. J. Brill, 1981.

———. "Local Lineages and Local Development: A Case Study of the Fan Lineage, Hsiu-ning *hsien*, Hui-chou, 800–1500." *T'oung Pao* 70 (1984) : 18–59.

# INDEX

*Note:* Page numbers in italics refer to illustrations. Chinese characters are usually shown under initial entry in text.

absenteeism (*ch'ueh-k'ao*), 232
academies, 31–32, 58–59, 128, 651
  late imperial, 58–59, 130, 131, 248, 278, 550; in 1890s, 609–10; 1572 imperial edict abolishing, 208; and late Ch'ing education reforms, 519, 595; merchant-financed, 246, 376–77; after 1905, 606; reemergence in 1627, 210; 17th-century imperial denunciation of, 210, 229
  *see also* dynastic schools; imperial schools; Tung-lin Academy
Accumulated Years (*chi-nien*), 468–69, 470
age of candidates and graduates, 261, 286–92, 295, 703–6
agency, human, 331–32, 351, 489n75
agnosticism, Confucian, 312
Agricola, *De Re Metallica,* 465
Ai Nan-ying (1583–1646), 118, 210, 219, 403–7, 412–13, 415, 416, 418–19
almanacs (*t'ung-shu*), 313
*Amplified Instructions for the Sacred Edict (Sheng-yü kuang-hsun),* by Yung-cheng emperor, 135, 221, 222, 575
*Analects,* 16, 116, 267, 272, 275, 515; examination essays on, 320, 388–91, 397–99, 413, 416, 577, 597; passage on moral doctrine of benevolence, 430–34; teaching of in new schools, 611–12
ancestor worship, 243, 372

ancestors, store of merit, and success in examinations, 306–7, 326
An-hui province, 227, 243–44, 258; civil examinations, 170, 257, 488, 573
annalistic history (*pien-nien*), 489, 500–502; vs. topical history, 495–98, 499n96, 502–3
*Annals* (Confucius). See *Spring and Autumn Annals*
Annual Difference (*sui-ch'a*), 468–69, 471–72
anomalies, natural, 346–54, 350–52
anonymity on civil examinations, 17, 188, 207, 248, 386; avoidance of as cheating technique, 196–97, 197n48, 203, 204
antithetical (balanced) clauses (*tui-chü*), 270, 391
anxiety (*ssu-yü*) of examination candidates, 175, 296–98, 298n9, 331; dream-visions as window to, 327–45; means for dealing with, 299–311, 361–70
apparitions of past, inside examination compounds, 308–9
appointment (*ch'üan-hsuan*) of officials, 127, 163, 215
Araki Toshikazu, 8n17
archery, in early Ming examinations, 38, 41
areligiosity: attributed to elite, 312; seen in Classics, 299, 357
Aristotle, 465

armillary sphere (*chien-i*), 475–76
art careers, 30
artisans, 241, 246–47, 249, 250–51, 253, 372
astrology (*chan-hsing; t'ien-wen*), 312–15, *314*, 331, 461n3, 465, 485; in Ming policy question, 473–77; political role in Han, 348–50; portents, 483, 485
astronomy, 348–50, 461–64, 468, 470, 477, 527n16
    as alternative field for literati, 379–80
    changing positions on in Ch'ing, 483–85, 590–91
    instruments, 463–64, 474, 475–76, 476n46
    in Ming civil examinations, 465, 466, 467–68, 481–82; in policy question on calendrical methods, 468–73; in policy question on celestial counterparts, 473–77
    Western, xxvi, 449, 462–63
    *see also* calendrical studies
Astronomy, Directorate of, in Sung, 351
Astronomy Bureau, 474, 481, 483
autocratic power, 66–67, 79, 120
Averill, Stephen, 606, 608
"avoidance laws," 18th-century, 201–2

Bailey, Paul J., 587n56
bamboo: blows with as punishment for examination corruption, 202; slips, questioning and answering by, 6; sticks, used for divination, 303, *315*, 315–16
bannermen: Han, 170, 204; Manchu, 166, 204, 223, 541; Mongol, Fa-shih-shan as, 287–88. *See also* bannermen examinations; military
bannermen examinations, 166, 167n125, 199, 223, 223n138, 613. *See also* military examinations
barbarians (*i*), 46–56, 62, 407, 621. *See also specific groups*
Barr, Allan, 362
Beattie, Hilary, xxix
belles lettres (*tsa-wen*), 8–12, 25, 32–33, 38, 163, 558
    Ch'ing revival of interest in, 545, 546, 556
    in civil examinations, 31, 44–45, 89, 266, 540, 560–61; Ch'ing, 535, 561, 620; in conquest and Southern Sung dynasties, 23, 24–25, 26–29, 32, 561; Han and T'ang, 73, 217; and palace examina-

tions in T'ang and Sung, 8–12, 15, 17, 19; and T'ang-Sung transition to classical essay, 381, 383, 558, 559; and *Tao-hsueh* rejection of, 521
benevolence (*jen*), 430–34, 437–38, 441–42
Berling, Judith, 311
Bible, Judeo-Christian, in Taiping civil examinations, 575–76
Bielenstein, Hans, 259
biology, dropped from elementary education, 612
Birge, Bettine, 63
black ink (*mo-chüan*), 188, 400
Board (Ministry) of Education. *See* Education Board
Bol, Peter, xxi, 1n, 3, 11, 15, 60, 61, 111
Borthwick, Sally, 606–7
Bourdieu, Pierre, xxx, 245
Boxer Rebellion, 587, 587n56, 595, 596, 615
boycott, of local examinations in 1733 and 1851, 231–32, 236
bribery (*kuan-chieh*), in civil examination system, 196–202, 204, 221, 228, 233–34, 297
Brook, Tim, 115n148
brush (*pi-hua*), 375, 377
Buddhism and Buddhists, 45, 60, 103, 247, 307–8, 312, 415
    in civil examinations, 299, 311; influence in late Ming and early Ch'ing, 411–12, 414–15
    in compilation of *Yung-lo ta-tien*, 108–9
    dabbling in, 494, 593n74
    "fatalistic" ideologies, 299n11
    heterodox doctrines and theories seen in literati canon, 504
    Japanese schools, 598
    on leaving this world and entering world of pure nature, 363–64
    link with Taoism and Confucianism, 45, 306, 312
    monks, 193n, 299, 304–5
    priests, 132, 249, 312–15, 327
    privileges in Yuan, 30
    T'ang era poetry seen as unaffected by infiltration of, 547
    temple(s), 194, 304, 593
    temple schools, 239, 246
    terms associated with Sung theories of mind and, 490

vision of good vs. evil seen in Yung-lo era
commentaries, 116–17
Wang Yang-ming's views of, 438
White Lotus sects, 71
worthies and deities, 369; in dream-
visions, 327, 339, 343–45; Kuan-ti
appropriated as deity, 304
Wu Chin's attack on, 438

Cahill, James, 30
calendar: orthodox (*huang-li*), stem-branch
characters in, 313; pitch correspondences to, 479–80; reform as concern
of Ming literati, 462, 462n6, 472
calendrical studies: Ch'ing, 461n3, 483–85,
580; in Ming civil examinations, 465,
466, 468–73, 475, 481–82
calligraphy (*shu-fa*), 7, 14, 30, 276, 456; in
civil examinations, xxxiii n33, 38, 41,
136, 377–79, 379n19, 511, 582; in education in 1890s, 610; memorization of
primers reinforced by, 263–65; writing
paraphernalia for, 377, *378*
candles, at examination compounds, 180,
180n12, 185, 226, 283
capital (department) examinations (*sheng-
shih*), 14, 57, 133–34, 249
"capping" of young boys, as rite of passage,
261, 261n60
Catholic missionaries, 393. *See also* Jesuits
celestial counterparts (*hsiang-wei*), 473–77
celestial phenomena, pitch correspondences
to, 479–80
celestial studies. *See* astronomy
celestial tables, constructed by Kuo Shou-
ching, 476
ceremonies. *See* ritual(s)
Ceremonies, Bureau of, 160
ceremony of gratitude (*hsieh-en*), 194, 205–6
Cha Ssu-t'ing (1664–1727), 211–12
Chaffee, John, xxi, xxvi, 26, 26n70, 144n63
*ch'ai-tzu* (deciphering of written words; *ts'e-
tzu*), 312, 322–24, 328, 339
chain arguments, in eight-legged essay,
391–92
Chan Erh-hsuan (1631 *chin-shih*), 216, 217
*chan-hsing. See* astrology
*chan-meng* (dream interpretation), 312,
326–46, 355–60
Ch'an Buddhism, 415

Chang Chien (Chi-chih) (b. 1853), 274–76,
289, 290, 295
Chang Chih-tung (1837–1909), 213, 228,
288, 587, 590–91, 593, 595, 602–3
Chang Chih-wan (1811–97), 310
Chang Chiu-ling (673–740), 553
Chang-chou prefecture, in Fu-chien
province, 155, 208–9, 225, 677
Chang Chü-cheng (1525–82), 201, 201n64,
207–8, 256
Chang Chung-ju, 537n42
Chang Feng-i (1527–1613), 328
Chang Feng-pao, 500
Chang Hai-shan (1782–1821), 517, 571
Chang Hsia (1161–1237), 410
Chang Hsuan, 453
Chang Hsueh-ch'eng (1738–1801), 277–78,
279, 485–86, 487, 503, 546
Chang Huai (1486–1561), 494–95
Chang Hui-yen (1761–1802), 241n5
Chang Hung-sheng, 464n15
Chang Po-hsing (1652–1725), 198, 534–35
Chang P'u (1602–41), 211, 415
Chang Shih-ch'eng (d. 1367), 90
Chang T'ing-hsiang, 393n70
Chang T'ing-yü (1672–1755), 234, 540–41
Chang Wei-yen, 305–6
Ch'ang-chou prefecture, in Chiang-su
province, 256; Chuang lineage, 241,
242–43, 255, 317–19; P'eng lineage,
318–19
*Change Classic (I-ching)*, 189, 267, 272, 474,
479; commentaries on, 410; in late
imperial civil examinations, 42, 74, 273,
512, 545, 564–65, 597; specialization in,
281, 283, 466–67, 488, 491, 499, 563;
used for examination predictions, 312,
315–16
*chao* (imperial patents/proclamations),
41–42, 285n120, 535, 537
*chao* (sighting of portents), 312, 326–45
Chao I (1727–1814), 195, 316–17, 486
Chao K'uang (fl. ca. 770), 213, 219, 538,
582, 589, 615–16
Chao Meng-fu (1254–1322), 32
Chao Ping-wen (1159–1232), 25
*ch'ao-fa* (copying portions of Classics text),
273
*ch'ao-k'ao* (court examination), 167–68,
536–37, 537n42, 548, 566

characters (graphs; *shih-tzu*), Chinese
  in civil examination questions: effects of
    using taboo, 206, 211; mistakes in as
    cause for protests, 198, 198n52
  divination technique using, 322–24
  evidential research on, 458–59, 504
  memorization and writing of, 373; role in
    classical literacy, 262–66, *264*
  number repeating in Classics, 266–67
  primers used to train children in, 372
  *shu-tui* (balanced pairs of), 391
  styles associated with different ages of
    antiquity, 456
  *see also* calligraphy; paleography
charitable schools (*i-hsueh*), 239, 246
Chartier, Roger, 277n97
cheating, on examinations, xxxii, 195–99,
  202, 206, 224–26, 228; by bannermen,
  167, 223n138; clothing in, 185, *186*, 196;
  prevention of, 177, 184–85, 195–96, 235;
  repeat examinations used to crack
  down on, 613
Che-chiang province, 258
Che-chiang province, late imperial civil
  examinations in, 154, 203–4
  Ch'ing, 151, 212, 212n98, 556, 564; policy
    questions, 447–49, 720; during Taiping
    Rebellion, 573
  Ming, 280–82, 412, 473–77, 488–96,
    498–99, 672; classical specialization
    1370–1600, 701; late Ming *chü-jen*, 253
  number of graduates, 257, 259–60, 658,
    662
*chen-hsueh* (true studies), 527–28
Chen, Min-sun, xxxiii n33
*chen-shen* (true spirit), 576
Ch'en Chen-ch'eng (1411–74), 214
Ch'en Chi-ch'ang (Ch'en Shou-jui), 325,
  327, 428
Ch'en Chien (1415–71), 329
Ch'en Chien (1497–1567), 500
Ch'en Ch'i-hsin (n.d.), 214–16, 217
Ch'en Chin (18th century), 513
Ch'en Chin (1525–66), dream-vision,
  343–45, *345*
Ch'en Hao (1261–1341), 410
Ch'en Hsien-chang (1428–1500), 500
Ch'en Hsun (1385–1462), 207
Ch'en Hung-mou (1696–1771), 169, 174,
  232–33, 316–17

Ch'en I-hsiung, 500–502
Ch'en Keng-huan (1757–1820), 571
Ch'en Li (1810–82), 582–83, 590
Ch'en Liang (1143–94), 49, 50
Ch'en P'eng-nien ( 961–1017), 266
Ch'en Shih-kuan (1680–1758), 445n60
Ch'en Shih-yuan, 329
Ch'en Shou (A.D. 233–297), 489, 492,
  497
Ch'en Shou-ch'i (1771–1834), 571, 572
Ch'en Te-yun, 381n28
Ch'en Yuan-lung, 307
*cheng-chiao. See* education
Cheng Ch'iao (1104–62), 266
Cheng Hsuan (127–200), 121, 507, 512, 518,
  565–66, 571
*cheng-k'o*, 523. *See also* metropolitan examina-
  tions
Cheng Kuan-ying (1842–1923), 579n36, 582
*cheng-ming* (rectification of names), 150
Cheng-te emperor (r. 1505–21), 439, 494,
  494n86
*cheng-t'ung. See* legitimacy, political
Cheng-t'ung (r. 1436–49). *See* Chu Ch'i-chen
*Cheng-t'ung p'ien* (Yang Wei-chen), 52
Ch'eng (r. 1042/35–1006 B.C.), 98–99,
  98n94, 99n97, 105
Ch'eng-Chu *li-hsueh* ("school of principle"),
  3–4, 12, 62, 155, 173, 307, 437, 587
  in early Ming government, 67–70, 80
  Fang Pao's attempt to unify with *ku-wen*
    literary tradition, 417
  in late imperial civil examinations,
    174–75, 429–43, 481–83, 519, 523–26,
    543; commentaries' importance in, 37,
    44–45, 261; criticisms of, 214, 365; cul-
    tural maintenance of in Ch'ing,
    533–34; early Ch'ing reforms seen as
    betrayal of by Manchu conquest elite,
    532; in early Ming, 40–41, 55–56;
    eight-legged essay linked to, 382; 18th-
    and 19th-century policy answers on,
    517, 519; in 18th-century Ssu-ch'uan
    province, 510–11; and 1525 provincial
    examination answer on calendrical
    methods, 472–73; licensing examina-
    tions evaluated in light of, 136; 1742
    metropolitan examination policy ques-
    tion on, 513–14
  in late imperial governance, 618–19

in Ming cultural and political life after
1425, 119–23
orthodoxy, 360, 371–72, 612, 622;
affirmation of from late Ming to mid-
Ch'ing, 434–42; Ch'ien-lung emperor's
efforts to balance with evidential
research studies, 541–42; debates over
among Ming-Ch'ing literati, 429–30 (see
also Han Learning; Wang Yang-ming,
learning); Four Books as heart of,
410–11; turn from in late Ming and
early Ch'ing, 411–17
school of Tao learning, 47, 132, 545;
addressed in Ch'ing reform issues, 540,
542, 543–44, 559; Ch'eng Tuan-li's curriculum for mastery of, 272–73; in early
Ming government, 67–70, 78, 97; ideological function for Yuan, Ming, and
Ch'ing rulers, 104–5; as imperial orthodoxy under Chu Ti, 101, 102–19; and
imperial power in Ming and Ch'ing,
69–70; see also Tao-hsueh
seen as Chinese Learning, 608
under Southern Sung and Yuan, 32–33,
35, 39
in Sung-Yuan-Ming transition, 58–61, 65
view of human commonality in Wang
Ao's essay on Analects, 397–99
Ch'eng Hao (1032–85), 18, 25, 69
Ch'eng-hua emperor (r. 1465–88), 146, 207,
330, 431, 498; examinations under, and
eight-legged essay, 382, 384–85, 401,
417
Ch'eng I (1033–1107), 15–16, 18–19, 25–27,
69, 101; commentaries on Classics, 410,
435, 508. See also Ch'eng-Chu li-hsueh
Ch'eng I-chen, 313n60, 330
ch'eng-t'i (receiving the topic), as section of
eight-legged essay, 389, 394, 397–98,
404
Ch'eng Tuan-li (1271–1345), 31, 265, 271–73,
279
chi-chuan. See topical history
chi-ch'i chih-tso (technical science), 379,
483–84, 578
Chi Fu-hsiang (n.d.), 514
chi-hsing (memory), 263, 268
chi-meng ("auspicious dream"), 334–35
chi-mieh ("extinction"), Buddhist notion of,
412

chi-nien (Accumulated Years), 468–69, 470
Chi Yun (1724–1805), 322–24, 514, 515,
567
ch'i (material/spiritual world of matter and
energy), 474; efforts to control, 353;
influence on pitch, 480; vs. li, 430, 435
ch'i-chiang (beginning discussion topic), section of eight-legged essay, 389, 394,
398, 404
"Ch'i-chieh" ("Seven Solutions") (Fang I-
chih), 295n1, 396
ch'i-ku (initial leg of eight-legged essay),
389–90, 392, 394, 398, 404
ch'i-meng ("pray for dreams"), 328
Ch'i T'ai (d. 1402), 84–85, 85n54
Chia-ching emperor (r. 1522–66), 100, 146,
189, 329; examinations under, 112, 391,
426, 445; reign, 146, 401, 413, 439, 448
Chia-ch'ing emperor (r. 1796–1820), civil
examinations under, 235, 537, 567–68,
570, 584
chia-fa (schools system), 512, 516
chia-k'o (added examinations), 129n10, 524n8
Chia-li (Family rituals) (Chu Hsi), 490–91
Chia-ting massacre of 1645, 219
Chiang-hsi dialect, 310
Chiang-hsi province, 106–10, 151–52, 168,
258–59; late imperial civil examination
graduates, 91–93, 257–58, 259, 658;
provincial examinations, 211, 468–73,
560
Chiang Hsiao (1482–1553), 454–55
Chiang-nan, 90–92, 170, 257, 259
provincial examinations, 506–7; classical
specialization in Ch'ing, 702; 17th- and
18th-century, 198–99, 284–85, 467, 539,
556; 1657 scandal, 204
see also An-hui province; Chiang-su
province
Chiang-su province, 258
civil examinations, 154, 198, 224, 488,
573; late imperial graduates, 256–57;
quotas, 170, 660
see also Ch'ang-chou prefecture; Su-chou
prefecture
Chiang Te-fu, 557–58
Chiang Wei-lung (pen name "Wo i"),
614–16
Chiang Ying-k'uei, 413n119
Chiao Hsun (1763–1820), 396, 562n135

*Chiao-hui* (Religion Association), to commemorate Confucius, 593

Chiao Hung (1541–1620), 203, 414

*chiao-kuan* (*hsueh-kuan*) (Ming local education officials), 148

*Chiao-pu* (Ministry of Religion), to commemorate Confucius, 593

*chiao-shou* (Ming prefectural schools instructors), 148, 150

*chiao-yü* (instructors in Ming county schools), 148, 150, 155

*chiao-yü hui* (educational associations; *hsueh-hui*), 609, 616

*Chiao-yü tsa-chih* (*Journal of Education*), 609, 610, 611–12, 614–16

Chieh Hsi-ssu, 36

*chieh-shih. See* prefecture examinations, Sung

*chieh-t'i* (connecting section of eight-legged essay), 384n37

*chieh-yuan* (dispatched *optimus* in Sung), 133n27, 163

*Ch'ieh-yun* (rhyming dictionary), 266

*chien-ch'en* (traitorous vermin), officials described as, 102

*chien-chü. See* recommendations

*chien-i* (armillary sphere), 475–76

*chien-sheng* (purchasing/Imperial School degrees), 200, 200n60, 292, 297; late Ch'ing, 225n146, 226–28, 233–34, 236, 688; late Ming, 139, 149, 150. 241, 241n8

Chien-wen (emperor, r. 1399–1402), 82, 85, 91–92, 98–100, 102, 105; late Ming rehabilitation of, 118; literati transfer of loyalty from to Chu Ti, 105–10; reign expunged from historical records, 100, 106, 110, 113–16

*Ch'ien-chia shih* (Poems by a thousand authors), 551

Ch'ien Ch'ien-i (1582–1664), 203–4, 255n46, 458n96

*ch'ien-fa* (monetary question), Ming policy questions on, 452–53

Ch'ien I-pen (1539–1610), 439–40

Ch'ien-lung emperor (r. 1736–95), 108, 122, 347n126, 357
    civil examinations under, 167–68, 174, 201, 212, 222, 291, 446, 524n8; Han Learning criticism of, 519–20; *k'ao-cheng* embraced, 521; mastery of all Five Classics advocated, 284–85; policy questions, 441, 445n60, 446–49, 446n61, 539–41; rankings changed by, 316–17; reformist policies, 224–25, 232–35, 537–68, 570–71, 584; return of poetry to, 275, 552; rewards for old men, 290n, 291–92; 1744 edict on quotas, 602

Ch'ien Mu, 395

Ch'ien Ta-hsin (1728–1804), 189, 396, 424–25, 486, 487, 514–15, 562n135, 566

Ch'ien T'ang (fl. ca. 1368–73), 80–81

*Ch'ien-tzu wen* (*Thousand Character Text*), 185, 263, 272, 274–75, 372, 609–10

Ch'ien Wei-ch'eng (1720–72), 168, 317, 540

*chih* (substance), complemented by *wen* (culture), 165

*chih-ch'iao* (knowledge), classical essays seen as test of, 579

*chih-fa* (methods of governance), vs. *hsin-fa* (method of mind), 441

*chih-i*, used to mean "writing an eight-legged essay," 396n82

*Chih-i k'o-so chi* (Collection of fragments about the crafted eight-legged essays) (compiled by Li T'iao-yuan), 360

*Chih-i ts'ung-hua* (Collected comments on the crafting of eight-legged essays) (compiled by Liang Chang-chü), 360, 383, 401, 416–17, 572

*chih-k'o. See* special examinations

"Chih-k'o i" (Proposals for eight-legged essay examinations) (Lu Shih-i), 526–27

"Chih-k'o ts'e" ("Examination Questions on Policy") (Wei Hsi), 529, 530

*chih-kuai* (recording unusual events), 350–51, 359–60

*chih-t'ung. See* legitimacy, political

Chin: as advisors to Mongols, 30–31. *See also* Chin dynasty

Chin Chü-ching, 502–3

Chin dynasty (1115–1234), 3–4, 22, 34, 36, 51–52, 552; civil service examinations (*see* civil service examinations, in conquest dynasties); Dynastic History, 468, 474; Manchus as heirs of, 546. *See also* Jurchen

Chin-hua advisors to Chu Yuan-chang, 74, 79

*Chin-k'o ch'üan-t'i hsin-ts'e fa-ch'eng* (Models of complete answers...), 545

Chin Lü-hsiang (1232–1303), 490

Chin Shen (1702–82), 513

*chin-shih* ("palace graduate") degree, xxvii, 8–10, 42–43, 56–61, 89; calligraphy's importance in ranking of, 377–78; ceremonies for, 191, 371; in conquest dynasties, 23–24, 647; late imperial (*see entry below*); Sung, 15–18, 24, 26–27, 26n70, 34, 56–60, 647, 648; T'ang, 400n86, 547; Yuan, 34–35, 56–58, 96, 646, 647, 649. *See also* metropolitan examinations; palace examinations

*chin-shih* ("palace graduate") degree, late imperial, 141–44, 142n57, 149n77, 157–63, 165–66, 171–72, 293

age at time of degree, 286–92

Ch'ing, 32, 58, 125, 656, 680–81, 700; age of candidates, 705, 706; as college graduate degree after 1905, 612–13; early Ch'ing, 169–71; holders as education officials, 229–30; increase in due to grace examinations, 523; late, 152–53; quotas and numbers 1889–94, 698; regional distribution 1646–1904, 699

classical specialization, 283, 285

court examinations for, 167–68, 536–37, 548, 566

downclassing of degree-holders, 297–98

education trusts for sons seeking, 244–45

geographical ranking of graduates, 256–57, 259–60

Ming, 56–61, 152–53, 215, 647, 650, 655–56, 658, 677–78; age of candidates, 704, 706; careers of graduates, 668; *chü-jen* status outpaced by in degree market, 147–57; early Ming, 74, 76, 93–97, 97n91, 110, 144–45; as education officials and examiners, 147–54; geographic distribution, 696; provincial distribution, 697, 700; from special status 1371–1643, 692

quotas for, 134, 157–58, 256

rankings, 157–58, 428–29, 536

rate of *chü-jen* receiving, 146–47

social origins of holders, 253–55

*Chin-shih kuan* (Court of *Chin-shih*), 614

*Chin-shu* (History of the Chin Dynasty), 468, 474

*chin-wen* (New Text) classical learning, 241, 319, 593, 608; vs. Old Text, 459, 504–9, 512, 515, 517

Chin Yu-tzu (1368–1431), 107, 110, 115

Ch'in dynasty (221–207 B.C.), 75, 83–84, 477; "burning of the books," 216, 457, 506

Ch'in Ming-lei (1518–93), 329; dream-vision, *338*, 338–39

*Ch'in-ting ch'un-ch'iu chuan-shuo hui-tsuan* (Imperially prescribed commentaries...on the *Annals*), 567

*Ch'in-ting Ssu-shu wen* (Imperially authorized essays on the Four Books) (compiled by Fang Pao), 382, 388–91, 388n58, 403–7, 417–19, 545

Ch'in Ying (1743–1821), 189

Chinese Learning (*Chung-hsueh*; *Han-hsueh*), 584, 599–602, 608; Han Learning seen as, 598–99

*ching-chi*. *See* statecraft

Ching Fang (79–37 B.C.), 349, 353

*ching-hsueh*. *See* classical learning

"Ching-hsueh pien" (Discerning classical studies) (Shang Jung), 571–72

*ching-i*. *See* classical essays

*ching-kuan* (classical instruction): in charitable and community schools, 246. *See also* classical curriculum/education

*ching-shu* (classical techniques), 218, 560

Ching-t'ai emperor (r. 1450–56), 53, 303

Ch'ing dynasty (1644–1911), 20, 55n147, 69–70, 103; civil service examinations (*see* civil service examinations, late imperial); collapse in 1911, 586, 617–18; examination compounds, 173–95; Grand Council creation, 161, 162, 317; population increases, 130, 260, 467; Taiping Rebellion (*see* Taiping Rebellion); transition to Republic of China, 621–22. *See also* Manchus; *specific emperors and events*

*Ch'ing-mi shu-wen* (Fa-shih-shan), 287–88

*Ch'ing-pai lei-ch'ao* (Classified jottings...) (Hsu K'o), 360, 36n, 555n110, 572

*ch'ing-pi* (green ink), 188, 188n27

Ch'ing-wen (Manchu language), 166

*chiu-p'in kuan* ("nine-rank system"), 6–7

*chiu-shih chih hsing* ("Awakening the Nine Foods"), presented to Shen K'un in dream-vision, 341–43, *342 ch'iu-ch'ien* (bamboo sticks), used for divination, 303, *315*, 315–16

Ch'iu Chün (1420–95), 85n56, 214, 302, 346n121, 388, 454

*ch'iu-jen* (men of talent), 524–25, 534, 535, 581

*ch'iung-li* ("fathoming the principles"), 352, 514

Chou dynasty (1049–221 B.C.), 6n10, 47, 50, 474

Chou Fu-ch'ing, 201

Chou K'ai-ch'i, 518

*chou-k'ao* (township [department] examinations), 134

Chou K'o-ch'ang, 325–26

Chou Li (1709–53), 514

Chou Shu-jen (Lu Hsun) (1881–1936), 201, 624–25

Chou Ta-chü, 549

Chou Tun-i (1017–73), 69, 535, 544

Chou Wen-chu, 457

Chou Yen-ju (1588–1644), 414n123

Chou Yun-liang, 598, 600

Ch'ou Ying (ca. 1490–1552), 191

Chow, Kai-wing, 413n118, 414n123, 417, 451n70, 517n140, 562n134

Christianity, 270, 366–70, 393, 575–76. See also Jesuits

chronologies. See annalistic history

*chü* (qualifying examinations), T'ang, 7

Chu Ch'i-chen (1427–64): as Cheng-t'ung emperor (r. 1436–49), 53, 142, 303, 329, 431; palace coup of 1457, 93, 303; as T'ien-shun (Ying-tsung) emperor (r. 1457–64), 53, 202, 258, 431

Chu Chin, 307

Chu Ch'üan, 233–34

*chu-chüan* (red ink; vermillion papers), 188, 400, 532n26

Chu Hsi (1130–1200), xxv, 9n20, 19, 112, 156n94, 443n51, 507–8, 571; Ch'ing policy answers concerning, 500–501, 502–3, 514–15, 560; on civil examination curriculum, 26–29, 32–33, 37, 39, 116, 540; commentaries to Five Classics, 410, 434–38; commentaries to Four Books, 85, 410–12, 430–34, 451, 451n72; credited for works completed by later followers, 491; criticism of rote learning, 261; Hsieh Chi-shih's views

seen as impugning commentary of, 212; on musical harmonics, 479, 481; place in Ch'eng Tuan-li's classical curriculum, 272–73; praise for as historian, 488–92, 495, 498–99; seen as having learning but no achievements, 69; seen as successor of Confucius and Mencius, 101. *See also* Ch'eng-Chu *li-hsueh*; *Tzu-chih t'ung-chien kang-mu*

Chu I-tsun (1629–1709), 81n41, 119, 284

*chu-k'ao* (chief examiner), Ming, 151

*chu-k'o* (specialty examinations), 10, 44, 379

Chu Kuo-tso, dream-vision, 335–36, *336*

*chu-shu* tradition. *See* scholia

Chu Ti (Prince of Yen) (1360–1424), 68, 101 as Yung-lo emperor (1402–24), 70, 85, 88, 96, 97–105, 161, 329; civil examinations, 91–92, 97–98, 110–13, 465–66, 485, 529; consolidation of power, 82, 622; domestication of Ch'eng-Chu learning, 105–10; legacy, 119–23; *Ta-chüan* established as repository of Sung-Yuan commentaries, 516–17

Chu Tsai-yü (1536–1611), 481

*Chu-tzu chi-chu* (Collected notes...) (Chu Hsi), 410

*chu-tzu pai-chia* (ancient pre-Han learning), 450

*Chu-tzu pien-lueh* (Discerning the use of particles) (Liu Ch'i), 279

Chu Yuan-chang (1328–98), 38–44, 68, 70, 101, 111, 129, 384 descending view of political power, 78–88 dream recorded in imperial writings, 326–27, 329 Hung-wu reign (r. 1368–98), 39–44, 282, 329, 410, 518, 530; civil examinations during, 71–78, 81, 89–97, 135, 202, 215, 218; executions and torture under, 77, 83, 93, 98; Hanlin Academy's political functions, 159; registration of households, 249–50 *Sheng-yü liu-yen*, 135, 575 support for Tao Learning, 107, 119 "Veritable Records" of whitewashed by Chu Ti, 106, 107–8

Chu Yun (1729–81), 514, 516

*chü-ching* (residing in seriousness), 442, 514

*chü-jen* graduates, late imperial, 134, 141, 149n77, 256, 293, 428–29 age at time of degree, 286–92

candidates: as classically illiterate, 198–99; control of selection taken over by *chin-shih*, 152; examination compounds, 179–80

ceremonies for, 191, 371

changing status, 142–57

Ch'ing, 169–70, 694; age, 704; as high school graduates after 1905, 612–13; provincial quotas 1645–1900, 682; status during Taiping Rebellion, 577

classical specialization, 280–85

as education officials and examiners, 147–54, 229–30

education trusts for sons seeking degree, 244–45

geographic ranking of, 256–57

Ming, 75, 144–46, 647, 656, 677–78; age, 703; careers, 666, 667; geographic distribution, 693; provincial quotas, 652; success of Fu-she members in 1630, 211 social origins, 253

*chü-jen* graduates, pre-Ming, 577n32, 647. *See also* provincial examinations

*ch'ü-chü* (*tsa-chü*; vernacular drama), 396

Ch'ü-fu, Confucius' ancestral temple in, 81, 121

Ch'ü Jung (Chi-chien), 319

Ch'ü Li-chiang, 317, 319

Ch'ü lineage, 319

*chuan-ching. See* classical specialization

*chuan-shu* (seal calligraphy), 379, 456

*ch'uan-hsin yao-tien* (important canon on transmission of the mind), *Annals* seen as, 490, 492. *See also* mind, transmission of

*ch'uan-shou hsin-fa. See* mind, transmission of

*chüan-na* (purchase), late imperial use for appointing officials, 58, 145–46, 687

*ch'üan-hsuan* (appointment), role in reproduction of officials, 127, 163, 215

*Ch'üan-hsueh p'ien* (A plea for learning) (Chang Chih-tung), 590–91

*ch'üan-jou* (dog meat), dreaming about, 322, *323*, 331

*Ch'üan T'ang-shih* (Complete Tang poems), 556

Ch'üan Te-yü (759–818), 11

Chuang Ch'ao-sheng, 525

Chuang Chu (1670–1759), 318

Chuang lineage, 241, 242–43, 255, 317–19, 622

Chuang P'ei-yin (1723–59), 255, 317–19, 542

Chuang Shih (1885–1960?), 622

Chuang Ts'un-yü (1719–88), 199, 255, 291, 317–18, 395–96, 429, 505, 540

Chuang Yü (1879–1939?), 611, 622

*chuang-yuan* (top-ranked civilian *chin-shih*), 166, 166n124, 203, 290, 313, 428–29; age of, 290–91; dreams and aspirations, 330–45; geographic distribution, 257

*Chuang-yuan t'u-k'ao*, 313n60, 359

*ch'ueh-k'ao* (absenteeism), 232

*Ch'un-ch'iu tsun-wang fa-wei* (Sun Fu), 47

*chün-ch'en* (rulers and officials), Ming era policy questions on, 454

*Chün-chi chu* (Grand Council), 161, 162, 317, 538, 539–41, 559

*chün-tse* (emulation), stylistic answers in eight-legged essay as models, 423

*Ch'ün-ching lei-yao* (Classified essentials of the Classics), 107–8

*chung-cheng* ("arbiter's system"), in Sui, 6–7

*Chung-hsueh. See* Chinese Learning

*chung-ku* (middle leg of eight-legged essay), 390, 392, 394, 398–99, 404–5

*Chung-yung chang-chü* (Phrases and sentences in the Doctrine of the Mean) (Chu Hsi), 272, 435–36

Ch'ung-chen emperor (r. 1628–44), 216, 401

civil examination papers (*mo-chüan*), printing and publishing in Ming, 400–403

civil service examinations, xvii–xxxvi
    bureaucracy (*hsuan-chü*), xx, 7, 126–27
    in conquest dynasties, 19–26, 63–64; Chin, 19–26, 32, 57, 60, 71, 163n115, 647; as model for Yuan, 40; as possible precedent for early Ming, 39. *See also below*, Yuan
    curriculum: consolidation of gentry, military, and merchant families into status group, 371; orthodox, 1n; from 650 to 1400, 5–46
    emotional tensions produced by: *see* emotional tensions
    Han, 5–12, 410
    in Japan, limited use of, 23
    late imperial: *see entry below*
    memorization in preparation for: *see* memorization

civil service examinations *(continued)*
  officials: *see* education officials; examiners
    and political groups and organized dis-
    sent before Ming, 205–6
  resistance to regime, 172, 174, 195–205
  Sung, xxiii, 44, 119, 133–34, 213–14,
    401n91, 522; aspects of Ming eight-
    legged essay in, 384, 384n37; candi-
    dates' appeal to local deities, 300;
    cheating and irregularities, 196; classi-
    cal specialization, 284; curriculum,
    5–29; in declining dynasty, 61–65; geo-
    graphic distribution of graduates, 256;
    hiatus in, 20, 71; middle-level degrees,
    144; Northern, 5–19, 34, 43, 106;
    rhyming and pronunciation dictio-
    naries as preparation for, 266; role in
    system for reproduction of officials,
    127; Southern, 19–29, 39, 40, 70–71;
    specialty examinations, 280; on tech-
    nical fields, 464; *yin* privilege, 252
  Sung-Yuan-Ming transition, 31–32, 35–38
  T'ang, 44, 103, 133–34, 213, 266, 299,
    522; candidates' appeal to local deities,
    300, 304; cheating, 196; curriculum,
    5–12, 410; essays devoted to history,
    486; Han histories as mainstay of,
    489n76; literati's fears and emotions
    aroused by, 297; middle-level degrees,
    144; one-level, 401n91; ritual conven-
    tions of and court politics, 205–6; seen
    as supporting emperor, 173; specialty
    examinations, 280; on technical fields,
    464
  Yuan, xxiii, 8, 29–38, 133, 163n115, 547;
    classical specialization, 284; curriculum,
    xxiv–xxv, 19–25, 33–34, 410; elimina-
    tion and restoration, 27, 30–38; middle-
    level degrees, 144; as model for early
    Ming examinations, 39–41, 72, 74–75,
    79, 89, 123; social status of military
    families, 254; specialty examinations, 280
  *see also specific degrees and examinations*
civil service examinations, late imperial,
  125–26, 173–75, 242–47, 292–94, 360,
  421–23, 618–20
  changing status of *chü-jen* and *chin-shih,*
    142–57
  Ch'ing, xxxiii–xxxv, 64–65, 519, 569–70,
    594–605, 622n, 728; abrogation in

1904–5, 443, 586, 587–88, 593, 603–8,
  621–22; absence of age restrictions,
  286–92, 295; curriculum, 44, 409–10,
  273, 487, 505–6, 546; early Ch'ing,
  77–78, 163–71, 484; efforts to control
  local candidates and licentiates
  1650–1850, 220–37; flow chart, 659;
  Han Chinese and Manchu role in,
  163–71; Hung Hsiu-ch'üan's protests
  against, 368–70; literati emotional
  rhetoric against, 604; natural studies
  and history represented in, 460–85;
  passed by Fu-she members, 211; P'u
  Sung-ling's portrayal of, 361–63,
  364–65; reforms *(see* reform); support
  for Ming system of examination halls,
  173; during Taiping Rebellion, 573–77;
  women barred from, 240–41
  and classical orthodoxy late Ming to mid-
    Ch'ing, 429–43
  curriculum, 271–73, 320–21, 460, 521–24;
    Ch'ing, 44, 409–10, 273, 487, 505–6,
    546; Ming, 38–46, 54, 116, 409–11, 547
  de facto elimination of candidates before
    examinations, 248–49
  examination compounds: *see* examination
    compounds
  geographic distribution of graduates,
    256–60, 292, 693–97
  Ming, xxxiii–xxxv, 61, 88, 123–26, 160,
    250, 618–20; "barbarian break"
    between Sung and, 20; cheating and
    irregularities, 196–98; Ch'eng-Chu
    orthodoxy in, 55–56; under Chu Ti,
    106–13, 119; under Chu Yuan-chang,
    41, 43–44, 81, 84–85, 89–90, 93; cur-
    riculum, 38–46, 54, 116, 409–11, 547;
    documentary texts and legal judg-
    ments, 38–46; early Ming, 38–46,
    66–78, 55–56, 78–97, 106–13, 119; flow
    chart, 659; Huang Ch'un-yao's pro-
    posed changes, 217–18; late Ming cri-
    tiques and calls for reform, 213–20;
    literati dissatisfaction with, 120, 213–14;
    and Mencian view of political power,
    78–88; natural studies and history in,
    460–83; Sung-Yuan civil examination
    models elaborated in, 125–26, 173
  natural studies and history represented in,
    460–85

orthodoxy in questions, 429–43
and political groups and organized dissent, 206–13
political and social reproduction through, 119, 126–33, 240, 375–80
social origins of graduates, 249–56, 691
subordination of content to elite literary culture, 372–77
*see also specific degrees and examinations*
clan schools, 263, 271
*Classic of Filial Piety (Hsiao-ching)*, 611–12; discourse essays on in late imperial civil examinations, 37, 41, 516, 531, 535–36, 559; Old Text–New Text controversy over, 536
classical Chinese language, 88, 166–68, 261n60, 372–76; calligraphy, 377–79; Jesuit translations of Aristotle and Agricola into, 465; literacy in, 240, 244; Mandarin as spoken form of, 373–75, 380 (*see also* Mandarin dialect); philological research on, 504, 562; vs. vernacular as problem in education and examination reform, 586, 611
classical curriculum/education, 16, 37–38, 89, 103, 246, 271–76, 570; access to among gentry elite, 240–47; challenged by conquest dynasties, 20–25; decline during Yung-lo era, 113–19; role in social status, 126, 128, 371–76; seen as civilian ideal for literati in Ming and Ch'ing, 174–75; Southern Sung, 26–29; Yuan, 31–32. *See also* classical learning; classical studies
classical essays (*ching-i*), 297, 371, 394, 422; in Chu Hsi's scheme, 28; in conquest and Southern Sung dynasties, 23–25; early Ch'ing private views of, 526–29; Hsueh Fu-ch'eng's views on, 580–81; in licensing examinations, 135–36; Ming, 37, 72–75; Northern Sung, 17–18; printing and publishing of in Ming, 400–403; reforms proposed in late Ming, 217–19; Sung models for, 400–401; transition to from T'ang-Sung belles lettres, 381, 559. *See also* eight-legged essay
classical learning (*ching-hsueh*), 10, 15, 89, 152, 159, 239; decline of in schools after 1905, 608–18; as form of resistance to Ming examination regime, 214; in

Hanlin Academy literary examinations, 163; interwoven with Han nativism in Sung-Yuan-Ming transition, 48–52; New Text (*chin-wen*) tradition, 241, 319, 593, 608; Old vs. New Text tradition, 459, 504–9, 512, 515, 517; role in social status, xvii n, 371–76. *See also* classical curriculum/education; classical literacy
classical literacy (*t'ung wen-li*), 127–28, 297, 372, 372n3, 619; audience for works requiring, 276–80; of bannermen, 223; within lineages, 242; memorization as technology for, 261–70; and social status, xxx–xxxi, 239, 242, 371. *See also* classically illiterate
classically illiterate (*wen-li pu-t'ung*), 293, 374, 619; barrier to competition in civil examinations, 239, 372; as candidates, 198–99, 221, 228, 297, 428. *See also* classical literacy
classical scholarship. *See* classical learning
classical specialization (*chuan-ching*), 37, 74, 189, 214, 280–85, 335, 425, 583
Ch'ing, 544, 685, 702–3; changes during Ch'ien-lung reign, 467, 486, 563–68; dropped in 1663, 531; policy questions on, 284, 560
Ming, 466–67, 654, 685, 701
classical studies
in civil examinations, xvii, xix, xxiv, xxvii n21; Ch'ing, 450, 579; late imperial policy questions on, 448, 499–503; Yuan, 33
late imperial, xxvi, 610; and changing role of historical knowledge, 485–88, 499–503; decanonization of after 1905, 608–20; natural studies as tool of, 466–68
promoted by Chu Ti, 101
in schools after 1905, 608–20, 623–24
Classics, Chinese, 5, 6n10, 27, 266–67, 620–21
Chu Yuan-chang as untutored in, 79; in civil examinations, xxxiii, 502–3; Ming, 38, 456; policy questions drawn from, 38, 443–44, 456, 502–3; Sung, 15–19, 17, 32; T'ang, 9, 10–12, 15–19, 23, 381
18th-century evidential research on, 562
in Ming government's political agenda after 1425, 121

Classics, Chinese (continued)
as object of historical study in 1920s, 486
seen as areligious, 299
seen as Histories, 486, 487, 492–93
translation of into English, 576
universality of questioned, 486–87
works explicating in early Ming, 107–8
see also Five Classics; Four Books; specific
works
clerks, xxvii–xxviii, 31, 197, 199, 199n58,
249; bribery of, 199–200; examinations
taken by sons and grandsons of, 223,
226–27; training in technical subjects,
379–80
clothing, used for cheating, 185, 186, 196
cognition, issues of in eight-legged essays,
391–99
Cole, James, xxvii n22
Collected Comments on the Crafting of Eight-legged
Essays (Chih-i ts'ung-hua) (compiled by
Liang Chang-chü), 360, 383, 401,
416–17, 572
commonality (t'ung-lei p'eng), 397
commoner examination papers (min-chüan),
252
commoners (min-chi), 293; linguistic and cultural exclusion, 246, 372, 374; as official
Ming classification of population,
250–51, 255; riots against new schools,
623, 624; schools for, 246; social mobility, 147–48; as social origins of chü-jen
and chin-shih, 253–54, 255
community schools (she-hsueh), 246
Complete [Great] Collection [of commentaries] for
the Five Classics and Four Books (Wu-ching
Ssu-shu ta-ch'üan), 107, 114, 116, 522
composition (tso-wen), 261–63, 276–80
Comprehensive Mirror for Aid in Government
(Comprehensive Mirror of History) (Tzu-chih
t'ung-chien) (Ssu-ma Kuang), 17, 50–51,
480, 490, 492, 496–98, 501; as basis for
history questions, 583; Chu Hsi's con-
densations of, 50–51, 276, 490, 496,
498, 501, 583; continuations by later
historians, 498
concrete words (shih-tzu), 279
Confucianism (K'ung-chiao), 1, 60, 306, 312,
593; proposed as official religion,
593–94; vestiges of in public schools
after 1905, 623–24

Confucius, 19, 62, 80, 265; sacrificial ceremony for, 80–81, 206; temple honoring, 27, 81, 121. See also Analects;
Confucianism; Spring and Autumn Annals
conquest dynasties, 3, 46–56, 51–52, 66n. See
also Chin; civil service examinations, in
conquest dynasties; Five Dynasties;
Hsi-hsia; Liao; Yuan
constitution, Japanese, 599
corporate estates, local lineages united by,
243, 246
corruption, in examination regime. See
irregularities
corvée labor, 221, 241, 251, 298
cosmology, 423, 440–41, 466, 473–77, 482
"Counsels of Yü the Great" (Old Text
chapter of Documents Classic), 505–6,
511–12
countervisions, 366–70
county examinations (hsien-k'ao), late imperial, 40, 133–34, 140, 143, 249, 401. See
also licensing examinations
county schools, 138–39, 148
court examination (ch'ao-k'ao), 167–68,
536–37, 537n42, 548, 566
Court of Chin-shih (Chin-shih kuan), 614
Court of the Imperial Clan, 161
cover (kai-t'ien), of sky, 475
cranes, in dreams, 327, 329, 339–40,
340n117, 341, 344, 344
crime(s): Ch'ing abrogation of licentiate status for those committing, 229; as factor
in failure in civil examinations, 301,
308; in provincial examination halls in
Ch'ien-lung era, 233
Crossley, Pamela, 167n126
Cullen, Christopher, 476n46
cults, 302–4, 593; in dream-visions, 339, 343;
of Wen-ch'ang, 300–302, 304, 309; of
Yueh Fei, 55
cultural nexus, 586, 586n54, 622, 622n
"cultural prisons": civil examination regime
seen as, 327; examination compounds
seen as, 174–95
culture. See popular culture; wen
cursive calligraphy (ts'ao-shu), 379

Danjō Hiroshi, 90, 91, 109
Dardess, John, 35, 141n54, 147, 242, 258,
258n52

Davis, Richard, 27n73
Day Divisor (*jih-fa*), 468–69, 470
de Bary, William Theodore, 1n
*De Re Metallica* (Agricola), 465
De Weerdt, Hilde, 59
decapitation, in dream-vision, 333–34
deciphering of written words (*ch'ai-tzu; ts'e-tzu*), 312, 322–24, 328, 339
*Decorum Ritual (I-li)*, 267, 272, 276, 509
demonstrations: during 1895 metropolitan examinations, 588. *See also* protests; riots
department examinations: capital (*sheng-shih*), 14, 133; township (*chou-k'ao*), 134
department schools, 138, 148
desires, human, 430–37
dialects, 88, 96, 310, 373–74. *See also* Mandarin dialect
dictionaries: etymological, 268n76, 275, 309; Hsu Shen's paleographical, 266, 322, 456, 458–59; rhyming and pronunciation, 266, 561
disasters, natural: policy questions on, 346–54; in political culture in Han, 348–50
discourse essay (*lun*)
  Ch'ing, 273, 537, 545, 551, 559, 566, 723; additional use recommended by critics of eight-legged essay, 526, 529; emphasis on after 1901 reforms, 595–97; late-18th-century eliminations and restorations, 429, 537, 542, 559, 561, 566; reform efforts involving, 530–31, 530n, 535–36, 543–44, 546, 558, 579, 581, 582; during Taiping Rebellion, 575–76
  Ming, 37, 41–42, 73, 723
  T'ang and Sung, 15–16, 26–27, 28
divination. *See* mantic arts
divining instrument, in spirit-writing, 319–22
doctors (*i-kuan*), 195, 298
*Doctrine of the Mean*, 116, 267, 272, 275, 515; Chu Hsi's *Chung-yung chang-chü* on, 272, 435–36; essays on in early Ming examinations, 73, 85, 416; teaching of in new schools criticized, 611
doctrine of the mean, morality as dependent on, 438, 441
documentary questions: Ch'ing reform efforts involving, 531, 538, 545, 546,

548, 558; *k'ao-chü* used as guidepost for evaluation of, 452
documentary style, 167, 273, 561
*Documents Classic*, 189, 267, 272, 469, 487–89, 496, 503
  Chu Ti's elucidation of "mind of the Tao" passage, 112, 434–42
  in civil examinations: Ch'ing, 273, 545, 564–65; Ming, 42, 74–75, 85, 347; specialization in, 281, 283, 335, 466–67, 488, 491, 499
  Old Text vs. New Text controversy, 504–8; policy questions concerning, 508–9, 511–12, 517
  original 100-chapter version, prefaces to, 506
  on sagely mind, 68–69
  as support for social mobility myth, 230–31
  Ts'ai Shen's commentary on, 410, 436
  *Yao-tien* (Canon of Yao), 474
dog meat (*ch'üan-jou*), dreaming about, 322, *323*, 331
Doolittle, Justus, 264–65
Dorgon (regent) (1612–50), 164
drafts of examination essays, 185, *187*, 401–2
dragons, in dream-visions, 339, 339n115
dramatis persona (*k'ou-ch'i*), influence on eight-legged essay style, 381
dream(s), 86, 318–19, 322, 326–45
  and civil examinations, xxxi, 182, 296, 305–6, 307n30, 309, 368–70; about deities, 302–3; about name changes, 324–25; pressures of failure sublimated into, 153
  as illusion (*huan*), 329
  interpretation of (*chan-meng*), 312, 326–46, 355–60
  of Ming *chuang-yuan*, 330–45
  as prophecy (*chao*), 329–45
  -visions, 331–45, 357–59, *358*; of Hung Hsiu-ch'üan, 367–70; Hu Ying-lin's parody of, 355–56
droughts, Han dynasty interpretations of, 349, 350
Duara, Prasenjit, xxxv, 586n54, 622, 622n
Duke of Chou, 84, 98–99, 98n94, 105
Dynastic Histories, 123, 262, 373, 422, 460, 468; in classical curriculum (1384–1756), 522; and Classics, 486–88, 492–93,

Dynastic Histories *(continued)*
496, 499–503; policy questions on, 38,
443–44, 499–503; T'ang and early
Sung discourse essays on, 15–16
Dynastic School (Imperial Academy; *Kuo-
tzu-chien*; *T'ai-hsueh*), 5, 27, 60, 206, 280,
512
dynastic schools *(hsueh-hsiao)*, 31–32, 127–28,
145, 240
late imperial, 127–28, 130, 131, 141;
Ch'ing, 164, 227, 546, 550; classical
curriculum for (1384–1756), 522;
entrance requirements and quotas, 134,
138–39, 239, 607; Ming, 41, 126–27,
218; Ming education officials for, 148,
151–52
*see also* Dynastic School; imperial schools

earth, interaction with heaven, 423, 476
*Eastern Miscellany* (*Tung-fang tsa-chih*), 603–6,
609
Eberhard, Wolfram, 348–49
eclipses, 469, 475, 476
economic categories, official Ming
classification of population into, 250–51
economics: early Ming policy, political linkage to civil examinations, 90–92; and
late Ming crises, 365; Northern Sung
examinations on fiscal policy, 463; role
in obtaining access to classical education, 242, 243–44; special examination
in (July 1903), 613
ecumenism, among Ch'eng-Chu loyalists in
late Ming, 414
education, xxx, 110, 127
as career path for literati in Sung-Yuan-
Ming transition, 31–32
in conquest dynasties, 21–25
gender differences in, 240–41
Japanese: influence on late Ch'ing reform
proposals, 586, 595; in T'ang and
Ming, 598; use of Western models,
596–600
late imperial: *see entry below*
Lu Shih-i on elementary vs. advanced,
263, 263n63
as marker of social status, 240–47
in Republic, calls for reform, 611
Sung, 15, 16–17, 127, 145
Yuan, 31–32.

*see also* academies; classical
curriculum/education; classical literacy;
schools
Education, Board (Ministry) of. *See*
Education Board
Education, Committee on, 603
education, late imperial, 131–33, 239,
244–45, 292–93, 376–77
Ch'ing, xxxv–xxxvi, 578; early-20th-
century, 570, 596–600, 603–20; late-
19th-century proposal of schools as
solution to problems, 519, 579n36, 582,
585–86, 589–93, 595, 602–5
Ming, 38–39, 41, 124, 145; Chu Ti's use
to legitimize "correcting" historical
record, 113–19; Huang Ch'un-yao's
views on, 218–19; North vs. South,
92
Education, Ministry of: late Ch'ing (*see*
Education Board); in Republic, 611,
617, 623
Education Board (Education Ministry)
(*Hsueh-pu*), xxxvi, 593, 609, 611–12,
615n136; as Ministry in Republican
period, 611, 617, 623; use of examinations to test students of new schools,
612–16
Education Bureau (*Hsueh-wu-ch'u*), 609
education officials, late imperial
Ch'ing, 224–25, 229–30, 681, 686
Ming, 147–55, 162, 202–3, 220; for metropolitan examinations, 147–50, 153–54,
673–75, 684; for palace examinations,
148–49, 153–54, 676; for provincial
examinations, 127, 147–52, 669–72, 683
*see also* examiners
educational associations (*chiao-yü hui*; *hsueh-
hui*), 609, 616
educational trusts, 244–45
eight characters (*pa-tzu*) of one's birth,
312–13
eight-legged essay (*chih-i*; *pa-ku-wen*), 40n113,
381–85, 408–9, 506; cognitive issues in,
391–99; late imperial (*see entry below*);
single-author collections, 401–2; training for writing, 278, 279, 309, 373
eight-legged essay (*chih-i*; *pa-ku-wen*), late
imperial, 18, 45, 190, 217, 376–77, 407,
522
Buddhist and Taoist influences in, 414–15

in Ch'ing, 218, 423, 515, 553, 559, 571, 610; abolished (1901), 595, 602–3; Ai Nan-ying's, 403–7; Ch'a Ssu-t'ing's, 211; early abrogations and reinstatements of, 78, 530, 530n, 533–34, 536; and increased literary formalism after 1475, 380–99; literati opinions on, 403–9, 524–29; policy questions on, 551, 557–5; private school students expected to master (early 1900s), 597n86; problems with as seen by post-Taiping reformers, 579, 582–83; proposals for abolishing, 585, 591–92, 594; in reform efforts of 1700s, 537–41, 543, 544, 572; subordination of policy questions to, 443–45, 449; in Taiping civil examinations, 576, 576n28, 577; 20th-century cultural assault on, 380, 382; Wang Ao's essays as models, 214, 385–91

and examiners' ranking of candidates, 424–27

printing and publishing of, 400–420

T'ang Hsien-tsu's early skill at, 287

elderly, eligibility of for civil examinations, 286–92, 295

elementary schools: creation of after 1905, 606; 1910 reforms, 611–12

elite. See gentry elite; literati

elixir, presented to Shen K'un in dream-vision, 341–43, *342*

emotional stasis (*yü*), 298, 299n9

emotional tensions, produced by civil examination system, 295–98, 317; alternative means for dealing with, 360–70; Hung Hsiu-ch'üan's hallucinations and countervisions, 366–70; religion as factor in efforts to reduce, 299–311; viewed through dream-visions, 327–45

empirical regularities (*ni yu shu*), and celestial counterparts, 475

Empress Dowager (Tz'u-hsi) (1835–1908), 587, 594, 605, 622

*en-k'o*. See grace examinations

enlightenment, Buddhist notion of, 308

epidemics, danger of at examination compounds, 197–98

epistemology: comparative, applied to eight-legged essay, 393–99; evidential research role, 504

equal-field system, policy question on, 495

eremitism, literati, in Yuan, 71–72

*Erh-ya chu-shu* (etymological dictionary), 268n76, 275, 309

escapism, dreams of, 363–64

Esherick, Joseph, 607

essays. See classical essays; discourse essay; eight-legged essay; *ku-wen* essays

*Essential Meanings of Works on Nature and Principles*. See *Hsing-li ching-i*

etymology (*hsun-ku-hsueh*), 412, 438; in Ch'ing evidential research, 455, 459, 503–4, 562; in Ch'ing policy questions, 509, 510, 518; dictionaries, 268n76, 275, 309

eulogies (*shih-fu-sung*), 8

eunuch power, 209–10, 494

Europe, early modern, 368, 460n, 463; scholarly attitudes toward late imperial Chinese science, 461–64; use of Latin language, 373, 376, 393. See also West

*Evidential Analysis of the Old Text Documents* (*Shang-shu ku-wen shu-cheng*) (Yen Jo-chü), 504–5

evidential research (*k'ao-cheng; k'ao-chü*), xxv–xxvi, 412, 415–16, 417, 460, 504, 519

Ch'ing, xxv–xxvi, 433, 461, 510–13, 561–62, 579; aspects of in 18th- and 19th-century policy questions, 508–9, 512, 517, 518; Ch'ien-lung emperor's efforts to balance with Ch'eng-Chu orthodoxy, 541–42; 18th-century influence on literati classical learning, 431, 433; *k'ao-cheng* vs. *k'ao-chü*, 455n84, 456, 458, 490; and Old Text *Documents* controversy, 504–8

Ming, xxxiv, 450–59, 506; *k'ao-chü* vs. *k'ao-cheng*, 456, 458, 490

*shih-hsueh* as 18th-century code for, 449–50

standards used by *Ssu-k'u ch'üan-shu* editors, 458

Yangtzu delta as center of studies in, 503–4

*see also* phonology

examination bureau (*k'ao-shih yuan*), created by Sun Yat-sen, 617

examination cells, 178, *178*, 181–82, *183–84*, 185, 193n, 363; cheating techniques, 196

examination compounds (*kung-yuan*), xxxii, 173–74, *176, 178, 179, 182–84, 186–88, 191, 193*, 571, 572; continuance into late 19th century, 587; as "cultural prisons," 174–95; publishing rooms in, 400; P'u Sung-ling's portrayal of, 363; resistance to procedures, 195–205; spirits and ghosts in, 308–9; surveillance procedures, 194–95, 219–20
examination officials. *See* education officials
"Examination Questions on Policy" ("Chih-k'o ts'e") (Wei Hsi), 529, 530
examination skipping (*pi-k'ao*), 232
examinations: after 1905 abrogation of civil examinations, 605, 612–17; in Republic of China, 617; used to test graduates of new schools after 1905, 612–13, 616–17. *See also* civil service examinations
examiner(s), 177–78, 181, 190, 197, 429, 522–23
    bribery of, 200–202
    in ceremonies celebrating graduates, 205–6
    Ch'ing, 225, 229–30, 551, 553–54, 564; early Ch'ing, 154, 165–66, 525–26; late Ch'ing, 539, 585, 597, 613–14; on metropolitan examinations, 597, 686; during Taiping Rebellion, 577; Yangtzu delta scholars as, 507–8
    helped by spirits, 309
    Hung Hsiu-ch'üan as, 369–70
    increase in numbers needed in late Ming and early Ch'ing, 424–27
    mantic techniques and belief in connections with other world challenged by, 346–54
    Ming, 150–53, 177, 387, 526; collusion with cheaters, 196–97; comments on essays included in printed versions, 400; corruption charges against, 202–5; on metropolitan examinations, 673, 674; on palace examinations, 676; on provincial examinations, 210, 669, 670–72
    ranking methods, 424–28
    standards, 421–23, 443–50, 460–61
    use of eight-legged grid in grading process, 394–95
execution(s), 66; by Chu Ti, 99–100, 103, 105; by Chu Yuan-chang, 77, 83,

93–94, 93n82, 103, 105; as punishment for examination corruption, 202, 204; of Tai Ming-shih, 408; of Yü Ch'ien and Wang Wen in 1457, 431
exile, Fang Pao's period of, 418
exorcism, with Hung Hsiu-ch'üan, 369

Fa-shih-shan (1753–1813), 287–88
facilitated degrees (*t'e-tsou*), Sung, 58; facilitated degree-holders (*t'e-tsou-ming chin-shih*), 26n70
fair labor services, obtaining of in Ming, 250–51
family, 240, 249–56, 296–97, 298, 607
family schools, 287
Fan Chung-yen (989–1052), 15–16, 351
*fan-i hsiang-shih* (translation examinations), 166–67, 223, 548
Fan P'ei-wei, 597n86
*fang-chih* (gazetteers), xx–xxi, xxiii, 149n77
Fang Hsiao-ju (1357–1402), 91, 97–100, 99n97, 118; seen as martyr, 102, 103, 104–6, 113, 120
Fang I-chih (1611–71), 295n1, 396
*fang-kao* ("ward papers"), 400–401
Fang Pao (1668–1749), 382, 390–91, 409, 415, 417n132, 557; Ch'ien Ta-hsin's attack on, 515; *Ch'in-ting Ssu-shu wen*, 382, 388–91, 388n58, 403–7, 417–19, 545
Farrer, Anne, 476n46
fate (*ming*): prediction of (*suan-ming*), 311–25, 328, 330–45, 354–60; success presented in dream as natural outcome of, 334–35; used to explain inequalities at heart of selection process, 299, 304
fees, for new schools, 606–7
Feng Fang (1523 *chin-shih*), forgeries by, 411
Feng Kuei-fen (1809–74), 228, 578–80, 583, 589, 591
*feng-shui* (geomancy), 312, 326, 328, 346, 356–57
*Filial Piety*, 267, 272, 275
filial piety, as value, 240, 286, 372
fire: danger of at examination compounds, 180, 180n12, 182, 184, 197–98, 309; role in origins of universe, 474
Five Classics, 123, 262, 266–67, 275–76, 460, 486, 522

Chu Yuan-chang's presentation of sets to northern schools, 92

in civil examinations: *see entry below*

commentaries on, 212, 417; of Chu Hsi, 410, 436; prepared in Yung-lo era, 107, 114–16

and Dynastic Histories, in Ch'ing, 486–88, 499–502

explications of prepared in early Ming, 107–8

Han-T'ang scholia on, Four Books as replacement for, 410

Japanese use of for study in Ming, 598

memorization and mastery of, 269, 286, 373, 610; emphasized in Ming and early Ch'ing civil examination curriculum, 273; indicated by "capping" of young boy, 261; after 1786 (all five), 262, 266, 268, 284, 288, 429; before 1786 (one), 262, 266, 268, 287

message concerning from Kuan-ti on medium's planchette, 321

reemphasis encouraged by late Ming and early Ch'ing literati, 284

Sung dynasty interpretations of, 410

*Wu-ching cheng-i* on, 103

see also *Change Classic*; *Documents Classic*; *Poetry Classic*; *Record of Rites*; *Spring and Autumn Annals*

Five Classics, in civil examinations, 28

in Ch'ing, 65, 135, 273, 512, 544, 551; place of philology in policy questions, 508; in provincial and metropolitan examinations, 273, 499–502, 514–15, 725–27; reform proposals on in late Ch'ing, 581, 583, 590, 596, 597; 1645 policy question on relationship to Dynastic Histories, 499–502; during Taiping Rebellion, 575, 577; testing all five, 524, 527, 530–32, 563–67, 620

interpretive power of examiners, 422

in Manchu and Mongol translation examinations, 167

in Ming, 40, 273; essays on, 41, 44, 73, 74, 85, 190, 217; in licensing examinations, 135; policy questions as subordinate to, 445

specialization in one of. *See* classical specialization

in Yuan, 33, 35

*see also* classical essays; eight-legged essay

Five Dynasties (907–960), 14, 50, 206. *See also* Liao dynasty

five phases (*wu-hsing*), in heavenly order, 347–48, 347n125

floods, Han dynasty interpretations, 349–50, 354

foreign studies (*yang-wu yun-tung*), 578

forgeries: Old Text portions of *Documents Classic* seen as, 504–8, 511, 512; 16th-century, 411

formalism, literary, increase in after 1475, 380–99, 421–24

"Former Seven Masters," works on Four Books compiled by, 411

fortune-tellers, 312–16, 327

Four Books, 123, 272, 275–76, 415, 460, 522

areligiosity seen in, 357

Chu Yuan-chang's presentation of sets to northern schools, 92

in civil examinations: *see entry below*

collections of examination essays on, 411

commentaries on, 411–17, 417; of Chu Hsi, 27, 410, 436; by "Former Seven Masters," 411; prepared in Yung-lo era, 107, 114–16

in elementary classes in 1903, 612

emergence in Southern Sung as family of canonical texts, 16, 19

evolution of study of, 409–11

explications of prepared in early Ming, 107–8

importance in classical literacy, 262, 266, 486

Japanese use of for study, 598

mastery and memorization of, 273, 286, 373; in 1890s, 610; indicated by "capping" of young boy, 261

and Ming government's political agenda after 1425, 121

Sung dynasty interpretations of, 410, 490

see also *Analects*; *Doctrine of the Mean*; *Great Learning*; *Mencius*

Four Books, in civil examinations

Ch'ing, 65, 135, 417, 511, 707–9; late Ch'ing, 544–45, 548–49, 551, 552–53, 559, 562, 563, 566–67 (reform proposals involving, 581, 583, 590, 591; after 1901 reforms, 596, 597); in provincial and metropolitan examinations, 273,

Four Books, in civil examinations *(continued)*
416, 514–15; reform efforts involving
essays on, 524, 527–28, 530–32, 530n;
during Taiping Rebellion, 575, 577
classical specialization, 280, 283–84. *See
also* classical specialization
essays on: in Ch'ing, 135, 417; in Chu
Hsi's scheme, 28; grading of in late
Ming and early Ch'ing, 425–27; in
Manchu and Mongol translation examinations, 167; in Ming, 37, 41, 42, 44,
73, 85, 135, 190, 217. *See also* eight-
legged essay
interpretive power of examiners, 422
Ming, 37, 40, 135, 190, 217, 707–9; early
Ming, 41, 42, 44, 73, 85; policy questions as subordinate to, 445
quotations from: predicted by spirit medium, 320; techniques for predicting,
311
Yuan, 33, 35
fox-fairy *(hu)*, possession of candidate's body
by, 310
Franke, Wolfgang, 97n91
fraud, in examination regime. *See* irregularities
Freud, Sigmund, 333n108
Fu, Daiwie, 350–51
*fu-chi* (spirit-writing), 312, 319–22, 328
*fu-ch'iang* (wealth and power): industrial basis
of in 1902 metropolitan examination
policy question, 597; obsession with of
late Ch'ing literati and officials, 578,
585; practical learning necessary for,
598
Fu-chien province, 131, 244–45, 402
*chin-shih* and *chü-jen* in Ming, 154–57,
677–78
late imperial civil examinations in, 232,
257, 259–60, 286–87, 679; classical specialization 1399–1636, 701; 1594 provincial examination, 495–99; provincial
examination trends, 282–83
*fu-ch'iu* (revenge), against barbarians called
for, 49
Fu-heng (d. 1770), 252
Fu Hsi, 474
Fu I-chien (1609–65), 164
Fu-k'ang-an (d. 1796), 169

*fu-k'ao* examinations. *See* prefecture examinations
*fu-ku* (restore antiquity), 456; poetry seen as
means to, 558
*fu-pang* (second-class provincial graduates),
144, 149–50, 170, 289–90
Fu-she (Return to antiquity society), 210–11,
214–15, 220, 402
*fu-shih*. *See* reexaminations
Fukuzawa Yukichi (1835–1901), 598
Fuma Susumu, 374n9
funding, of Ch'ing new schools, 607–8

Gali (d. 1714), 198
garrison schools *(wei-hsueh)*, 148
Gate of Heaven, in Ch'in Ming-lei's dream-
vision, *338*, 338–39
gazetteers *(fang-chih)*, xx–xxi, xxiii, 149n77
gender ideology, xxix, 241, 296–97
gentry elite, xvii n, 443n5
changing composition of between 750 and
1100, 12–13;
in conquest dynasties, 20–25
Han, means of entry into, 5–7
late imperial, xix–xx, 66n, 171–72, 239,
312, 371; Ch'ing, 298, 584, 586–87, 616;
classical education as measure of moral
and social worth, 128; effect on of fall
of Ch'ing, 622–23; interest in vernacular literature on civil examinations,
296; invocation of fate to explain failure in examination competition, 299;
linguistic advantages, 372–76; Ming,
104, 139–40, 140–42, 253; pressures of
failure sublimated into dreams and
nightmares, 153; schools serving after
1905, 606, 608, 616; selection for civil
service, 619; social reproduction of,
240–47; status of and civil examinations, 191, 194, 569–70; after Taiping
Rebellion, 584
*see also* merchant elites
gentry-literati. *See* gentry elite; literati
geographical study, of Four Books by Yen
Jo-chü, 415
geography *(ti-li)*, 485, 580, 590; dropped
from elementary education in 1909,
612; policy questions on, 450, 452–53,
454, 483, 560, 591

geomancy (*feng-shui*), 312, 326, 328, 346, 356–57

ghosts, 325–26, 330; inside examination compounds, 308–9

goat's head (*yang-t'ou*), in dream-vision, 339, *340*

God Worshipers Society (*Pai shang-ti chiao*), 370

gods: determination of examination success, belief in, 299; of literature (*k'uei-hsing*), 309; and temple dreams, 328

governance (*ju-shu; yung-jen*), 75, 218, 475; as dual under conquest dynasties, 20; methods of (*chih-fa*), vs. method of mind (*hsin-fa*), 441; policy questions on, 450, 452, 482, 495; theories about role and function of music as inseparable from, 477–81

grace examinations (*en-k'o*), Ch'ing, 129n10, 171n142, 524n8; to celebrate imperial birthdays or auspicious events, 129, 171, 523–24, 564; poetry question in 1760, 557

grammar-punctuation exercises (*tz'u-chang*), 412, 438

grammatical forms, of written classical Chinese, 374

grammatical particles (*hsu-tzu*), in training for writing, 279

Grand Concordance (*Ta-t'ung*) Calendar, 472

Grand Council (*Chün-chi chu*), 161, 162, 317, 538, 539–41, 559

Grand Historian, 473

Grand Secretariat (*Nei-ko*), 159, 161–62

Grand Secretaries (*Ta-hsueh-shih*), 159, 201, 211

graphs, Chinese. *See* characters, Chinese

Gray, John Henry, 124, 265n68

*Great Collection of the Four Books*, 116–17

*Great Collection of Works on Nature and Principle (Hsing-li ta-ch'üan)*, 112, 114, 115–16, 522

Great Concordance system (*Ta-t'ung li*), 469

*Great Learning (Ta-hsueh ku-pen)*, 116, 267, 272, 275, 515

Ch'a Ssu-t'ing's essay on, 211

Chu Hsi's elucidation of, 451, 451n72; Wang Yang-ming's refutation, 411–12, 517

Chu Hsi's role in arrangement of chapters, 515

in civil examinations: early Ming, 73, 85, 416; essays on in 1902 metropolitan examination, 597

Hsieh Chi-shih's annotations on, 212

Old Text versions of: forgeries, 411; Wang Yang-ming's restoration of, 412, 451

teaching of in new schools criticized, 611

green ink (*ch'ing-pi*), 188, 188n27

grid, eight-legged, 394–96. *See also* eight-legged essay

guards, in examination compounds, 185, 195–96

Guy, R. Kent, 417, 419n135

Hall of Enlightened Rule (*Ming-t'ang*), 475

Halley's comet, sighting of, 351

hallucinations, of Hung Hsiu-ch'üan, 366–70

Hamaguchi Fujio, 561–62, 562n135

Han Chinese, xxxv, 1, 3–4, 4, 357; in Ch'ing, 20, 163–71, 532, 609; and civil examinations (early Ch'ing), 163–71, 532; in conquest dynasties, 19–25, 20n51, 34–35, 191; gender ideology, xxix, 241, 296–97; outsiders seen by as "barbarians," 46–56; in Yuan dynasty, 29–38, 71. *See also* gentry elite; literati

Han Ching, 203, 255

Han dynasty (206 B.C.–A.D. 220), 5–7, 75, 268, 347, 477; astronomical system established by, 468–70; civil service, 130, 133; dynastic histories, 489, 489n76; influence on late imperial thought, 444, 504 (*see also* Han Learning); manipulation of calamities as inauspicious political events, 348–50, 352, 353

Han Hsin (d. 196 B.C.), 357

*Han-hsueh. See* Chinese Learning; Han Learning

Han Learning (*Han-hsueh*), xxv, 29, 418, 450, 499, 521

in Ch'ing examination regime, 461, 499, 504–19, 620; in late Ch'ien-lung examinations, 559–61, 565–67; use of pre-Sung scholia in eight-legged essays, 416

Han Learning (*Han-hsüeh*) *(continued)*
  distancing of self from mantic practices by followers of, 360
  as 18th-century challenge to classical orthodoxy, 418, 433, 587
  importance for Yangtzu delta scholars, 504
  Japanese honoring of, 598
  New Text strand of, 593, 608
  after 1905, 623
  and Old Text *Documents Classic* controversy, 504–8
  popularity in Ch'ien-lung and Chia-ch'ing reigns, 448, 544
  scholars as advisors to Oboi Regents, 530
  seen as Chinese Learning in early 1900s, 598, 608
  seen as linked with ritualism, 521n
  vs. Sung Learning, 443, 504–8, 519–20, 558, 571–72; amalgamation under title of Chinese learning, 600–601; in Ch'ing policy questions, 504–19; in Grand Council debates during 1740s and 1750s, 541–42
*Han-shu (History of the Former Han Dynasty)* (Pan Ku), 269, 489, 492
Han Wen-ti (r. 179–156 B.C.), 596
Han Wu-ti (140–87 B.C.), 280
Han Yü (768–824), 11
Hang-chou Dynastic School, 27n73
Hang-chou shrine of Yü Ch'ien, 303, 303n21, 328
Hanlin Academy, 11, 94, 158–63, 162n111, 173, 260, 582
  in Ch'ing, 167–68, 408, 521, 523, 547–48, 551; appointment of examiners for 1902 metropolitan examination, 597; Manchu inner court's 18th-century insulation from, 161; place in educational hierarchy superseded by Education Board, 609; priorities in T'ung-chih reign, 583–84; provincial education commissioners from, 230, 234; support for Yung-cheng reign examination reforms, 536–37
  and court, 158–59
  entry into, 85, 95, 288–89, 508, 536–37, 550; calligraphy's importance in, 377–79; Chu Ti's appointments to, 106, 109; by Chuang lineage members, 255;

in early Ming, 78, 81, 85, 87; examinations for, 167–68, 536–37, 548; Fu-she members selected for in 1629, 211
  Institute of Advanced Studies (*Shu-ch'ang-kuan*), 163
  members as examiners, 151, 153–54, 200–201, 203, 206
  in Ming, 114, 159, 537; reestablished by Chu Yuan-chang, 38
  Tung-lin followers in, 207, 209–10
*hao-wen* ("cult of literary style"), 89
Hart, Sir Robert (1835–1911), xxi, 132
heaven, interaction with earth, 423, 476
Heavenly Kingdom of Eternal Peace (*T'ai-p'ing t'ien-kuo*), 370. *See also* Taiping Rebellion
heavenly principles (*t'ien-li*), 18, 303, 432–34, 474, 492
hemispherical sundial (*yang-i*), 476
hereditary (*yin*) privilege (inheritance), 15, 127, 145–46, 248–49, 249, 252; in Ming and Ch'ing, 127, 249, 251, 292–93, 687; permitted by Liao, 23; transmission of student rankings, 252; under Yuan, confirmation of Mongols and *se-mu* in government positions by, 35–36
heterodoxy, 60, 413, 414–15
"hidden merit" (*yin-kung*), 305–6
hieroglyphics (*ta-tzu*), 24
historical studies (*shih-hsüeh*), 460–61, 485–88, 499–503
  in civil examinations, 590, 620; policy questions on, xxxv, 448, 450, 488–503, 560; as replacement for eight-legged essays advocated by Ch'en Li, 582–83; specialty examinations in during T'ang, 10
  Sung-Ming imperial, treatment of conquest dynasties and Han Chinese, 46–56, 62
Histories. *See* Dynastic Histories
history: Chinese, dropped from elementary education, 612; division into two genres (*see* annalistic history; topical history)
*History of the Former Han Dynasty (Han-shu)* (Pan Ku), 269, 489, 492
*History of the Yuan Dynasty*, 468, 471, 474, 476
Ho Ch'i-jui, 441–42
Ho Ching, 610–11
Ho Cho (1661–1722), 533

Ho-nan province, 231–32, 236, 560–61, 571

Ho, Ping-ti, 126, 128, 158, 171, 254; on social mobility, 247–48, 252n39

Ho Shao-chi (1799–1873), 327

Ho-shen (1750–99), 379

*Ho-t'u* (River Chart), received by Yellow Emperor, 474

horsemanship, on early Ming civil examinations, 38, 41

*hou-ch'i* (waiting for *ch'i*), 480

*hou-ku* (later leg of eight-legged essay), 390, 392, 394, 399, 405

households (*hu-t'ieh*), registration of in Ming, 249–51

*hsi* (practice), break between *hsueh* (learning) and, 538

Hsi-hsia dynasty (990–1227), 3, 4, 19–20, 22. *See also* Tanguts

Hsi-hu Academy, 1851 boycott by students from, 236

Hsiang-shan (Lu Chiu-yuan) (1139–92), 49, 60

*hsiang-shih. See* provincial examinations

*hsiang-wei* (celestial counterparts), 473–77

Hsiao Ch'i-ch'ing, 31

*Hsiao-ching. See Classic of Filial Piety*

*Hsiao-hsueh* (Elementary learning) (Chu Hsi), 272, 491, 612

*hsiao-hsueh* (philology). *See* philology

*hsiao-lien* (moral candidates), promotion of regardless of status advocated by Ch'en Ch'i-hsin, 215–16

*hsiao-tzu* (phonetics), 24

Hsieh Chi-shih (1689–1756), 212

Hsieh Ch'ien (1450–1531), 386, 387, 454

Hsieh Chin (1369–1415), 106, 107–8, 109–10, 113, 465–66

*hsieh-en* ("ceremony of gratitude"), 194, 205–6

Hsieh Mu-han (b. 1864), 598–99, 600

*hsieh-piao* ("memorial of gratitude"), 42, 452

Hsien-feng emperor (r. 1851–61), 236

*hsien-k'ao. See* county examinations

*Hsien-liang san-ts'e* ("Three Policy Answers of One Chosen Wise and Virtuous") (Tung Chung-shu), 6

*hsin chi li* (principle): equated with human nature by Chu Hsi, 514; equated with moral mind in Wang Yang-ming's philosophy, 474, 514

*hsin-fa* (methods of the mind), 68–69, 111–13, 412, 488, 496, 501; and astronomical issues, 473–74, 476–77; vs. *chih-fa* (methods of governance), 441

*hsin-hsueh* (doctrines of the mind), 413, 503

*hsin-shu* (matters of the mind), 500, 525

*Hsin T'ang-shu* (Ou-yang Hsiu), 348

*hsing. See* human nature

*hsing-chüan* ("society collections"), as examination essay collections, 402

*Hsing-li ching-i (Essential Meanings of Works on Nature and Principles)*, 122, 522; discourse essays on in Ch'ing, 535–36, 543–44, 559

*Hsing-li ta-ch'üan (Great Collection of Works on Nature and Principle)*, 112, 114, 115–16, 522

*Hsing-li tzu-hsun* (Glosses of characters on nature and principles), 272

Hsing Shao (d. ca. 560), 268–69

*hsing-shu* (running calligraphy), 379

*hsing-yueh* (local officials), Ch'ing, 135

*hsiu-shen* (moral cultivation), 352, 371–72, 610, 612

Hsiung Ssu-fu (1635–1709), 525

Hsu Chieh (1503–83), 413

Hsu Ch'ien-hsueh (1631–94), 241

Hsu Ho-ch'ing, 518

Hsu Hsieh (1601 *chin-shih* and *hui-yuan*), 414

Hsu K'o, 325, 360, 555n110, 572

*hsu-ku* (transition leg of eight-legged essay), 390, 394, 398

Hsu Kuang, 413

Hsu P'eng-shou, 518

Hsu Ping-i (1633–1711), 241

Hsu P'u (1428–99), 454

Hsu Shen (58–147), paleographical dictionary compiled by, 266, 322, 456, 458–59

*hsu-tzu* (grammatical particles), 279

*hsu-wu* ("emptiness"), Taoist doctrine of, 412

Hsu Yuan-wen (1634–91), 241

*hsuan-chi*, as an astronomical instrument, 475–76, 476n46, 548

"Hsuan-chü lun" (On the selection and promotion of officials) (Hsueh Fu-ch'eng), 580–82

*hsuan-pen* (selections), as Ming era collection of essays, 401–2

Hsuan-te emperor (r. 1426–35), 95, 120–21, 138

*hsuan-yeh* (unlimited space), in sky, 475

*hsueh* (learning), break between *hsi* (practice) and, 538

*Hsueh-cheng* (Ch'ing provincial education commissioner), 136

*hsueh-cheng* (Ming department school instructor), 148, 150

Hsueh Fu-ch'eng (1838–94), 578, 580–82

Hsueh-hai T'ang (Sea of learning) Academy, 582

*hsueh-hsiao. See* dynastic schools

"Hsueh-hsiao tsung-lun" (General remarks on schools) (Liang Ch'i-ch'ao), 590

*hsueh-hui* (*chiao-yü hui*; educational associations), 609, 616

*hsueh-kuan* (*chiao-kuan*) (Ming local education officials), 148

*Hsueh-pu. See* Education Board

*hsueh-t'ang. See* new schools

*Hsueh-wu-ch'u* (Education Bureau), 609

Hsueh Ying-ch'i (1500–73?), 415–16, 455–57, 457n94

*hsun-ku-hsueh. See* etymology

*hsun-tao* (assistant instructors), in Ming prefectural schools, 148

Hsun-tzu, 347, 352

*hu* (fox-fairy), possession of candidate's body by, 310

Hu An-kuo (1074–1138), 48–50; commentary on *Annals*, 282, 410, 490, 492, 516, 567

Hu Cheng-meng, 69

Hu Ch'eng-fu, 539

Hu Chü-jen (1434–84), 120, 214

Hu Kuang (1370–1418), 106–7, 109–10, 113, 114–15, 117

Hu-nan province, Ch'ing civil examinations in, 169, 232, 424–25, 517; halting of during Taiping Rebellion, 573–74

Hu P'ei-hui (1782–1849), 571

Hu Ping-wen, 117

Hu Shih (1891–1962), 610, 610n120

Hu Ssu-ching (1869–1922), 607–8

*hu-t'ieh* (households), registration of in Ming, 249–51

Hu Wei-yung (d. 1380), 82–83, 93, 159

Hu Ying (1375–1463), 153–54

Hu Ying-lin (1551–1602), 355–56

Hu Yuan (993–1059), 28

*Hua-shu* (Book of transformations), of Wen-ch'ang, 300–301

*huan ch'i ch'u* (return to the beginning), of written forms of Classics, 456

Huang Chang-pai, 291

*Huang-ch'ao ching-shih wen-pien*, 179n

Huang Chi (d. 1686), 532–33

Huang Chien (1442 *t'an-hua*), 206

Huang Chin, 452

Huang Chin-shing, 69n7, 451n70

Huang Ch'un-yao (1605–45), 217–20, 526

*huang-chung* (Yellow Bell) pitch pipe, 477–81

Huang family, illustration of youth's dream-vision, *358*, 358–59

*huang-ho* (yellow crane), in dream-vision, 339–40, *341*

Huang Kuan, 385n45

Huang Kuang-liang, 26n70, 190n32

*huang-li* (orthodox calendar), 313

*Huang-Ming hsiang-hui-shih erh-san-ch'ang ch'eng-wen hsuan* (Selection of model examinations...), 445

*Huang-Ming ts'e-heng* (Balancing of civil examination essays...), 445, 495–99

*Huang-Ming t'ung-chi* (Comprehensive records of the Ming dynasty) (Ch'en Chien), 500

*huang-miu pu-t'ung* ("preposterous") examination papers, 221

*Huang-shu* (Wang Fu-chih), 54

*huang-ts'e* (yellow registers), 249–50

Huang Tsung-hsi (1610–95), 219, 284, 408, 528

Huang Tzu-ch'eng (d. 1402), 84–85, 86, 384

Huang Ying-ch'eng, 313; woodblocks, 313, *314, 362*

Huang-yu reign (1049–53), 463–64

Hughes, E. R., 392

Hui-chou lineages, 243

*Hui-min* (Chinese Muslims), 169

*hui-shih. See* metropolitan examinations

*Hui-shih lu* (Record of metropolitan examinations), 281

Hui-tsung (emperor, r. 1101–1125), 24

Hui Tung (1697–1758), 505

human nature (*hsing*), 16, 454; Chu Hsi's vision of, 430–37, 513–14

humanism, xxii–xxiii, 437, 463

Hummel, Arthur, 288n128
humor, in dreams about examinations market, 327
*Hundred Surnames* (*Pai-chia hsing*), 263, 275, 372
Hung Ch'eng-ch'ou (1593–1665), 166
Hung-chih emperor (r. 1488–1505), 121, 401–2, 417
Hung-hsi emperor (r. 1425), 95, 112, 120
Hung Hsiu-ch'üan (Hung Huo-hsiu) (1813–64): hallucinations and countervisions, 366–70; as leader of Taiping Rebellion, 369–70, 573, 574–76
Hung Jen-kan (1822–64), 577
Hung Liang-chi (1746–1809), 516
Hung Mai (1123–1202), 351
Hung-wu emperor. *See* Chu Yuan-chang
Hymes, Robert, xxi
hypnotic arts (*ts'ui-mien-shu*), 328

*i* (barbarians), 46–56, 62, 407, 621. *See also* specific groups
*I-chien chih* (Record of I-chien) (Hung Mai), 351
*I-ching*. See *Change Classic*
I Feng, 349
*i-hsueh* (charitable schools), 239, 246
*i-kuan* (doctors), 195, 208
*I-li (Decorum Ritual)*, 267, 272, 276, 509
*i-tuan chih shuo*. *See* heterodoxy
*i-wen lu* (records of unusual matters), 304, 350, 359
*I-yuan chih ch'i* (unity of *ch'i*), origins of universe out of, 474
idealism, political, of Mencius, 84–85
identity, candidate's: cheating technique and, 196–97, 197n48, 203, 204; difficulty in checking with crossover between Ch'ing civil and military examinations, 222
identity changes, and fate calculations, 324–25
illiteracy, 244. *See also* classically illiterate
Imperial Academy (Dynastic School; *Kuo-tzu-chien*; *T'ai-hsueh*), 5, 27, 60, 206, 280, 512
imperial academy of painting, Sung, 30
imperial grace examinations. *See* grace examinations
Imperial Library, 458

Imperial School (*Kuo-hsueh*; *Kuo-tzu chien*), 38, 109, 144–45, 155, 291–92; degrees (see *chien-sheng*)
imperial school system, 200, 461, 607; Ch'ing, 164, 231; Ming, 146, 160, 217–18. *See also* dynastic schools; Imperial Academy; Imperial School
impersonation, as cheating technique, 196
industrialization, 578–84, 597
inheritance (*yin* privilege). *See* hereditary privilege
ink and inkstone, needed for calligraphy, 377
innate moral knowledge (*liang-chih*), Wang Yang-ming's doctrine of, 413
Institute of Advanced Studies (*Shu-ch'ang-kuan*), of Hanlin Academy, 163
instructors, Ming: *chiao-shou* as in prefectural schools, 148; *chiao-yü* as in county schools, 148, 150, 155; *chü-jen* as, 148–49; *hsueh-cheng* as in department schools, 148
instruments, astronomical, 463–64, 474, 475–76, 476n46
intelligence (*ts'ung-ming*), classical essays seen as test of, 579
intelligentsia, gentry-based, after 1905, 623
intermarriage, between Chuang and Liu lineages, 243
irregularities, in examination regime, 189, 195–207, 288, 297; in Ch'ing, 224–28, 233–35, 530, 571, 613. *See also* cheating
Islam, 45, 167
Itō Hirobumi (1841–1909), 598

Jade Emperor, 308
*jang-i* ("driving out the barbarians"), in Sung interpretation of *Spring and Autumn Annals*, 47–49
Jao Tsung-i, 68n3
Japan: constitution established, 599; education, 586, 595, 598–99, 609; limited use of civil examinations, 23; Meiji Restoration (1867), 593, 598; response to Boxer Rebellion, 587; Sino-Japanese War of 1894–95, 585, 588, 615; warrior elites, 22
Japanese pirates, 1594 policy question on, 495
*jen* (benevolence), 430–34, 437–38, 441–42

*jen-hsin. See* mind, human

*jen-hsin tao-hsin*, 68–69, 433–38

*jen-p'in tuan-fang* (moral behavior), 230. *See also* moral character

*jen-shou san k'o* (three heads), in dream-vision, *332, 333*–35

*jen-tao* ("way of civilized people"), 49

Jen-tsung (r. 1312–20), 122

Jesuits, 270, 465, 483–85, 593; attitude toward science in late imperial China, 461–64; influence on Ch'ing era Chinese literati, 448–49

*Jih-chih lu* (Record of knowledge earned day by day) (Ku Yen-wu), 528

*jih-fa* (Day Divisor), 468–69, 470

Johnson, David, 372n3

*Journal of Education (Chiao-yü tsa-chih)*, 609, 610, 611–12, 614–16

*ju-hsueh* (classical literati thought), 594. *See also* Confucianism

*ju-hu* (official literati households), identification of in Yuan, 31

*Ju-lin wai-shih* (Wu Ching-tzu), 175, 286

*ju shu. See* governance

Juan Yuan (1764–1849), 235, 381–82, 416–17, 550, 562n135

judges, outside (*t'ui-kuan*), as associate examiners, 152

judicial offices, Ch'en Ch'i-hsin's recommendations on, 215–16

judicial terms (*p'an-yü*), in provincial and metropolitan examinations, 42, 43–45, 273, 531

Jupiter (planet), 475

Jurchen, 3, 46, 52, 62, 351; acceptance of Han Chinese culture, 63–65; as ministers under Yuan, 33. *See also* Chin dynasty

Kai-feng prefecture, in Ho-nan province, 1733 boycott of local examinations, 231–32, 236

"Kai k'o-chü i" (Proposal for reforming the civil examinations) (Feng Kuei-fen), 578–79

*kai-t'ien* (cover), of sky, 475

K'ai-feng, as Sung capital, fall of, 17–18, 21n54, 36

Kamo Naoki, 135n31

*k'an-hsiang* (physiognomy), 304–5, 312, 328

*k'an-ming* ("reading fate"), 311–25

K'ang Hai (1475–1541), 313–15

K'ang-hsi emperor (r. 1662–1722), xxxiv–xxxv, 122, 212, 407, 502, 622

ban on study of astronomical portents and calendar, 484–85

civil examinations under, 154, 170, 189, 221–22, 229, 230; reform efforts, 530–36, 546, 591; response to 1711 examination scandal, 198; 1679 special examination, 548

enthusiasm over science and mathematics, 448–49

*Hsing-li ching-i* prepared under, 543

*P'ei-wen yun-fu* compiled under, 269, 552

*Sacred Edict (Sheng-yü)*, 135, 221, 222

translation examinations under, 166–67

*K'ang-hsi tzu-tien* (dictionary), 266

K'ang Yu-wei (1858–1927), 212–13, 582, 588–89, 588n60, 608; 1898 reform proposals, 591–94

*kao* (imperial proclamations), 41–42, 285n120

Kao P'an-lung (1562–1626), 208, 210

*kao-pen* (drafts), 185, *187*, 401–2

Kao-tsu (r. 618–26), 7, 103

*k'ao-cheng* (Ch'ing term for evidential research). *See* evidential research

*k'ao-chü* (Ming term for evidential research). *See* evidential research

"K'ao-shih kan-yen" (Moving words on examinations) (Chiang Wei-lung), 614–16

*k'ao-shih yuan* (examination bureau), created by Sun Yat-sen, 617

karma, 306–7, 308, 312

Khitan, 3, 46, 52, 63–65. *See also* Liao dynasty

Khubilai Khan (r. 1264–94), 63

kinship relationship. *See* lineages

knowledge (*chih-ch'iao*), classical essays seen as test of, 579

Ko Ang, 561

*ko-chih-hsueh. See* natural studies

*ko-chih liu-jen* (probation), 233

*ko-wu* ("investigation of things"), 412, 501

"K'o-ch'ang i" (On the civil examinations) (Ch'en Li), 582–83

K'o Ch'ien (1423–73), dream-vision, 339, *340*

*K'o-chü lun* (On the civil examinations) (Ch'en Shou-ch'i), 572

*k'o-hsing* (supernova), sighting of, 351

*k'o-hsueh* (modern science), 465. *See also* natural studies; science

*k'o-k'ao. See* qualifying examinations

*k'o-mu. See* civil service examinations; military examinations

Kondo Mitsuo, 546n77

Korea, xxii, 22, 23

Koreans, 74; occasional participation in Ming civil examinations, 132

Koryŏ dynasty (918–1392), 23

*k'ou-ch'i* (dramatis persona), influence on eight-legged essay style, 381

Kracke, Edward, xxi, 247–48

Ku Chieh-kang, 486

*Ku-chin t'u-shu chi-ch'eng* (Synthesis of books and illustrations past and present), 122

*Ku-chin yuan-liu chih-lun* (The best discourse essays...), 400

Ku-ching ching-she Academy, in Hangchou, 550

*ku-fu. See* rhyme-prose

Ku Hsien-ch'eng (1550–1612), 208–9, 414, 439

*ku-hsueh* (ancient studies), turn to in late Ming and early Ch'ing, 416–17

*Ku-liang* Commentary, 267, 410; on *Annals*, 410

Ku Shih, 609–10

*ku-shih* (ancient-style poetry), 285

*Ku-shih-pien* debates, in 1920s, 486

Ku Ting-ch'en (1453–1540), 313, 313n60, 330; dream-vision, 339–40, *341*

Ku Tsu-hsun, 313n60, 330

*ku-wen* (prose) essays, 25, 381, 394, 409, 411, 458; importance in Sung, 15–16, 26; as models for Ming and Ch'ing examination essays, 417

*Ku-wen kuan-chien* (Pivotal points...) (Lü Tsu-ch'ien), 383

Ku Yen-wu (1613–82), xxxii–xxxiii, 54, 396, 467, 516, 592; criticism of eight-legged essays, 408, 419, 528, 538n45, 581, 585; criticism of Ming classical learning, 284; critiques built on by Feng Kuei-fen, 579; dating of eight-legged essay origin, 384–85, 387; on decline of historical studies, 114–15, 486; on examination compounds, 179n, 219; on Five Classics' decline in importance, 544, 566

*ku-yin-hsueh. See* phonology, ancient

Ku Yun-ch'eng (1554–1607), 207, 208

*kuan-chieh. See* bribery

*kuan-chüan* (military officer examination papers), 252

*kuan-hua. See* Mandarin dialect

"Kuan-pang t'u" ("Looking at Examination Results") (Ch'ou Ying), 191

Kuan-ti (Kuan Yü) (god of war and sometimes wealth), 302n17, 321, 328; cult of, 302–3, 304; temples (*Kuan-ti miao*), 315

Kuan-tzu, 596

Kuang-chai temple, 299

Kuang-hsi province, 171, 260, 452–53

Kuang-hsu (r. 1875–1908), 132, 524n8, 588–89; and 1898 Reform Movement, 590, 591–92

Kuang-tsung (r. 1190–94), 24

Kuang-tung province, 131, 236; Ch'ing provincial examinations, 424, 499–502, 565; Kuang-chou examination compound, *184*

Kuang-wu emperor (r. A.D. 25–57), 9n20

Kuei-chou province, 131, 171, 259–60, 468n26

Kuei Yu-kuang (1506–71), 403, 418, 558, 572

*k'uei-hsing* (god of literature), 309

*K'un-yü ko-chih*, as translation of Agricola's *De Re Metallica*, 465

*kung* (public domain), vs. private domain, 434–38

Kung Chih-li, 524

Kung Hui, 491–92

*kung-sheng*, after 1905, 612

Kung-sun Ch'ing, 349

Kung-sun Hung (d. 121 B.C.), 349

Kung Tzu-chen (1792–1841), 572–73

*Kung-yang Commentary*, 267, 396n82, 410, 497n91

*kung-yuan. See* examination compounds

K'ung An-kuo (156–74? B.C), version of *Documents Classic*, 506–7, 512

*K'ung-chi ko-chih*, as translation of Aristotle's theory of four elements, 465

*K'ung-chiao. See* Confucianism

*k'ung-ching t'ien-hsia* ("alarm the heavens"), 306

"K'ung I-chi" (Lu Hsun), 624–25
K'ung Ying-ta (574–648), 507
*Kuo-ch'ao k'o-ch'ang i-wen lu,* 359
*Kuo-hsueh. See* Imperial School
Kuo Hung, 453–54
Kuo Mo-jo (b. 1892), 609–10
Kuo P'u (276–324), in Wu Ching-tzu's *The Scholars,* 357
Kuo Shao-yü, 549
Kuo Shou-ching (1231–1316), 469, 472, 474, 476
*kuo-ts'ui* (national essence), theories of, 610–11
*Kuo-tzu-chien. See* Dynastic School; Imperial Academy; Imperial School
Kwong, Luke S. K., 588n60

labor: corvée, 221, 241, 250–51, 298; 18th-century emancipation of, 251, 251n32
labor tax, 30, 241
Lach, Donald F., xxxiii n33
land registers, Ming, 250–51
land surveys, 250
land tax, Ming, 250–51
landed aristocracy, T'ang, 12
Langlois, John D., Jr., 55n147
language(s), 586, 611; in civil examinations, 88, 164, 166–67, 211, 240, 247; dialects, 88, 96, 310, 373–74; Latin, 373, 376, 393; in social and political status, xxx, 239, 372–76; written versions of spoken Khitan and Jurchen, 21 *See also* classical Chinese language; Mandarin dialect; vernacular Chinese
*Lao-tzu,* 10, 492, 497
Latin (language), 373, 376, 393
latrines, in examination compounds, 177, 181
law: degree in *(ming-fa),* 42–43; examinations on *(see* legal questions); linguistic expertise needed for, 376.
Lee, John, 7n14
legal benefits, for passing examinations, xxvi–xxvii, 175, 241, 298
legal code, 63, 76, 202; in civil examinations *(see* legal questions)
legal documents, and eight-legged essays, 393, 393n70
legal questions, in civil examinations: Ch'ing, 44–45, 545–46, 548, 558, 573, 590, 596–97; on judgments *( p'an),*

42–44, 75, 545, 548, 558; on judicial terms *( p'an-yü),* 42–45, 73, 274, 531; Liao, 23; Ming, 44–45, 75–76, 85, 452; T'ang and Sung, 10, 42–44, 463–64
Legalism, 82–84, 87, 392
Legge, James, 576
legitimacy, political *(chih-t'ung),* 51–52, 68, 68n3, 71, 122, 396, 498; *cheng-t'ung* as T'ang and Sung notion of, 68n3, 492, 499; Chu Ti's claims, 97, 112–13; reestablished by Ming emperors, 68, 97, 111–13; Taiping, importance of civil examinations for augmenting, 574–76; and *tao-t'ung,* 68n3, 97, 441–42, 476–77; transmitted through evidential research, 512
legitimate succession of the Way. See *tao-t'ung*
legitimation, of early Ming autocracy by court literati, 67
Lei Erh-chieh, 557
*lei-shu* (encyclopedias), Southern Sung, 400
lèse-majesté: examiners in 1537 Ying-t'ien provincial examination accused of, 206; in Hung Hsiu-ch'üan's dream, 369; of *Mencius* for Chu Yuan-chang, 80–81
Levenson, Joseph, 379
levirate rights, 20–21, 63
*li* (heavenly/moral principles), 430, 435, 473. *See also* moral philosophy
Li Chao-lo (1769–1849), 381–82
*Li-chi. See Record of Rites*
*li-chia* (village-family units) of households, 250
Li Chia-lin, 552–56
Li Ch'ien, 471
Li Chih (1527–1602), 153, 155–56, 382
Li Ch'un, 574
Li Chung-chien (ca. 1713–74), 513–14
*li-fa* (calendrical methods), 468–73. *See also* calendrical studies
Li Fang (925–96), 558
Li Fu (1673–1750), 409
*li-hsueh. See* moral philosophy
Li Hui, 536
Li Hung-chang (1823–1901), 578, 580
Li Kung (1659–1733), 433, 535
Li Meng-yang (1473–1529), 98n95, 411, 439
Li P'an-lung (1514–70), 411, 547
Li Po (701–62), 554n104, 555

*Li-pu* (Ministry of Personnel), 8, 127

Li Shih-min, 103; as T'ang T'ai-tsung (r. 627–50), 7, 103, 107, 122, 129, 173, 269

Li Teng, 301, 453

Li T'iao-yuan (1734–1803), 40, 40n113, 360, 385n45, 419

*li-ts'ai yung-ren* (resources), Ming era policy questions on, 454

Li-tsung (r. 1225–64), 24, 25, 26n70, 27, 122; civil service examinations under, 57–58, 60

Li Tsung-han (1769–1831), 169

Li Tsung-huang (b. 1886), 609

Li Tuan-fen (1863–1907), 589n61, 590, 602

Li Tzu-ch'eng (1605?–45), 219, 365

Li Yin-tu (1631–92), 532

Li Yu (1611–80), 383

Li Yung-hsiu, 452

Liang Chang-chü (1775–1849), 383, 562, 562n136; *Chih-i ts'ung-hua* compiled by, 360, 401, 416–17, 572

Liang Ch'i-ch'ao (1873–1929), 582, 589–90, 592, 602

*liang-chih* (innate moral knowledge), Wang Yang-ming's doctrine of, 413

Liang Kuo-chih (1723–87), 509

Liao dynasty (907–1125), 3–4, 46, 51–52, 63–65; civil examinations, 19–23, 24–25

Liao Hsien-huei, 299n12

licensing examinations (*sui-k'ao*), 123, 175, 177, 239, 242, 288
 late imperial, 133–36, 140, 175, 221–28, 235, 401n91, 530n; corruption in, 224–28; crossover between civil and military examinations, 222–23; final (1905), 605; Huang Ch'un-yao's proposals for, 218–19; levels of competition, 143; overlap with qualifying examinations, 137–38; poetry questions added to, 548; protests over, 232; quotas, 660

licentiates (*sheng-yuan*), 138–40, 145, 153, 221–22, 233, 242–45; candidates, 179–80; ceremonies for, 371; classical specialization, 280, 283; control of 1650–1800, 228–37; in 1890s, 592; eligibility for provincial examinations, 143; eligibility for qualifying examinations, 137; as local education officials, 149–50; local examinations used to renew status

of past, 134; loss of status from cheating, 185; quotas and geographical distribution, 256, 689–90; ratio to population, 140–42; as teachers in new schools, 606

Lien Tzu-ning (d. 1402), 86–88, 97–98, 98n95, 100, 106–7, 118; seen as martyr, 84–85, 99n97, 100, 102–3, 104–5, 113, 120–21

Lin Chao-en (1517–98), 411

Lin Chao-t'ang (n.d.), 518

Lin Huan, 110–11, 322

Lin T'ing-ang (1472–1541), 454–55

lineage, 5; in education and examination success, 240, 242–46, 249, 255, 317–19, 357

lineage schools, 92, 128, 239, 246, 457, 609–10

Ling Shao-wen, 167–68

*Ling-t'ai* (Spiritual Pavilion), 475

linguistics. *See* language

literacy: of Korean aristocracy, 23; oral and written traditions as means for enhancing, 261–62; vernacular, 276, 372–73; of warrior tribes, 21–22; of women, 241. *See also* classical literacy; language

literary examinations: Ch'en Ch'i-hsin's criticism of use to select officials, 215; in court examinations, 537; given by Hanlin Academy, 163; T'ang, 11. *See also* belles lettres

literary (*shih-fu*) requirements: for *chin-shih* degree, in Sung literary culture, 15–16, 26, 32; stressed in Koryŏ dynasty, 23

literary talent (*wen-tz'u*), 90

literary temple (*wen-miao*), 204

literati (gentry-literati; *shih*), xvii, xvii n, xix–xx, xxx–xxxi, 1n, 18–19
 classical learning standards in T'ang, 10
 under conquest dynasties, 30–32, 35–36, 62–64
 late imperial: *see entry below*
 moral values of Tao Learning united with social values of, 104
 *po-shih* (erudite), 5, 280, 379n19
 rank system after fall of Han dynasty, 6–7
 in Sung-Yuan-Ming transition, xxiv, 3; alternative career paths, 31–32, 35–36, 71–72; nativism, 47–52, 54–56

literati (gentry-literati; *shih*) *(continued)*
  transformation of in Sung, 12–15, 18–19,
  24–25
  *see also* gentry elite
literati (gentry-literati; *shih*), late imperial,
  xxix, 126–33, 253, 430–31
  access to civil service examinations, 249,
  293
  Ch'ing: alternative careers, 380, 380n23;
  as officials, civil examinations ridiculed
  by, 569–70; status, connection with
  Tao Learning severed in 1905, 623
  endorsement of *Tao-hsueh* orthodoxy, 1,
  3–4
  Ming, 66–70, 78–88; knowledge of natural studies and reliance on experts, 483,
  483n63; literature, 30, 159, 197, 197n49,
  296, 402, 422, 429, 450 (P'u Sung-ling's
  turn to after examination failures,
  361–63, 364–65); and private academies, 207–10; proposals to remove
  from Ch'ü-fu temple, 121; relations
  with Chu Ti, 97–100, 106–10, 118; relations with Chu Yuan-chang, 38–40,
  71–72, 82, 88
  moral cultivation of as concern of imperial court, 371–72
  values: asymmetrical overlap between
  imperial interests and, 66–70; reflected
  in dynastic school curriculum, 173–74;
  unraveling of in late 19th century,
  586–87
Liu, James, 3–4
Liu Cheng-tsung, 525
Liu Chi (1311–75), 39, 79
Liu Ch'i (early Ching), 279
Liu Chien, 385n45
Liu Chih-chi (661–721), 502
Liu Chin (d. 1510), 494
Liu Feng-lu (1776–1829), 319
Liu Hsiang-kwang, 400–401, 401n91
*Liu Hsiang pao-chüan*, 308
Liu Hsien-t'ing (1648–95), 529
*liu i* (six arts), 73–74, 535
Liu K'ai (1784–1824), 517, 571
Liu Kuang-tsu (1142–1222), 596
Liu K'un-i (1830–1902), 595
Liu lineage, in Ch'ang-chou prefecture,
  Chiang-su province, 242–43
Liu San-wu (1312–99?), 81, 93–94

Liu Tzu-chuang, 164–65
Liu Yen (1394–1457), 206
*lo-chüan* (failing), ranking of examination
  papers according to, 190
*lo-hsia* (concluding section of eight-legged
  essay), as replacement for *ta-chieh*, 391
Lo Hsuan, 452
Lo Ju-fang (1515–88), 287, 415
Lo, Winston, 13
local examinations, 128, 133–42, 145–46,
  205, 205n78, 401, 424
  age of people taking, 288
  Ch'ing, 135n33, 169, 212–13, 220–28,
  523–24; addition of poetry question,
  548, 550; boycotts, 231–32, 236; eight-
  legged essays restored on, 559; halting
  of in Taiping Rebellion, 573; reform
  proposals after Taiping, 579–80
  emotional tensions produced by, 296–98
  Huang Ch'un-yao's proposals for, 218–19
  quotas for, 129–31, 138–39
  testing sites for, 174–75
  *see also* licensing examinations
"Looking at Examination Results" ("Kuan-
  pang t'u") (Ch'ou Ying), 191
lotus flower, in Ch'en Chin's dream-vision,
  343–45, *345*
Lu Chiu-yuan (Hsiang-shan) (1139–92), 49,
  60
Lu Chuang-tao, 269
Lu Fa-yen (fl. ca. A.D. 601), 266
Lu Hsun (Chou Shu-jen) (1881–1936), 201,
  624–25
Lu K'en-t'ang (1650–96), 428, 432–33, 440
Lu Lung-ch'i (1630–1693), 529, 534
Lu Shih-i (1611–72), 263, 263n63, 526–27,
  527n16, 535
Lu Tsu-yü (Lu Hsi-man), 324–25
Lu Wan-kai, 270
Lu Wen-ch'ao (1717–96), 487
Lü K'un (1536–1618), 150
Lü Liu-liang (1629–83), 407–9, 416, 529, 533
*Lü-lü hsin-shu* (New treatise on the twelve-
  pitch system) (Ts'ai Yuan-ting), 478,
  479
*Lü mu-tan* (Wu Ping), 197n49
*lü-shih*. See regulated verse
Lü Tsu-ch'ien (1137–81), 383
Lui, Adam Y. C., 162n111
*lun*. See discourse essay

"Lun k'o-chü" (On civil examinations) (Liang Ch'i-ch'ao), 589–90

*Lun-yü chi-chu* (Collected notes to the Analects) (Chu Hsi), 272

*Lun-yü huo-wen* (Questions on the Analects) (Chu Hsi), 273

lunar month, setting length of, 468–69

Lung-ch'eng Academy, in Wu-chin county, 208, 209

Lung-ch'ing reign (1567–72), 413

Ma I-ch'u (b. 1884), 610

Ma Jung (A.D. 79–166), 475

Ma Tuan-lin (1254–1325), 527

Ma Yü (1395–1447), 451–52

magistrates, 130, 149, 215; bribery of, 200; examinations for, 617; role in examination process, xxvii–xxviii, 152, 220–21

male anxiety, 298, 298n9, 331; means for dealing with, 361–70

*man-t'ou* (steamed rolls), in Ho Shao-chi's dream, 327

Manchu(s), xxxv–xxxvi, 1, 36, 63–65, 621; dyarchy of Han and under Ch'ing dynasty, 20, 55n147; in early Ch'ing civil examinations, 163–71, 534n33; view of selves as heirs of Jurchen Chin dynasty, 546. *See also* Ch'ing dynasty

Manchu dynasty. *See* Ch'ing dynasty

Manchu language: in Ch'ing civil examinations, 167–68; as warrior elites' official language, 373–74;

Manchuria, early-17th-century examinations, 164

Mandarin dialect (*kuan-hua*): as official language of bureaucracy, 239, 240, 244, 373–74; as spoken classical Chinese, 373–75, 380

mantic arts (divination), 485, 624 and civil examinations, 368–70, 464; fate prediction, 354–60; resistance to, 346–60; techniques for predictions, 311–25, 327 therapeutic regime for candidates and families, 295–96, 361, 369, 619

Mao Ch'i-ling (1623–1716), 416

Mao Tse-tung (1893–1976), 624

marriage laws, transformed in 13th and 14th centuries, 63

Mars (planet), 475

mathematical harmonics, 461n3, 477–81, 485

mathematics, xxvi, 449, 461–64, 468, 591; in calendrical systems and astronomy, 469–70; in Ch'ing examination reform proposals, 578–80, 590; in Ming civil examinations, 38, 41, 482; in T'ang and Sung, 10, 464–65; and twelve steps in musical pitch series, 477–81

McDermott, Joseph, 243

medicine, 468; as alternative field for literati, 30, 379–80, 464; examinations on, 463–64, 464n15, 466, 482; Jesuit missionaries on studies of, 461–64

medium, spirit: in *ch'ai-tzu*, 322; in ritual of spirit-writing, 319–22

Mei Li-pen (d. 1767), 168–69

Mei Wen-ting (1633–1721), 528

Meiji Restoration (Japan, 1867), 593, 598

memorial arch (*p'ai-fang*), 191

memorization, 64, 261–70, 276, 293, 371, 610; examination cycle based on, 247; for Han Chinese, 380; importance of lessened by Ch'ing examination reforms, 532, 533; required levels of for civil examinations, 287, 297

memory (*chi-hsing*), 263, 268

*Men-ch'iu* (Search for knowledge by children), 272

Mencius, 19, 78–88, 265; Chu Ti and political philosophy of, 102, 116–17; Chu Yuan-chang's and political philosophy of, 78, 79–88; tablet in Confucius' ancestral temple in Ch'ü-fu, 81, 121

*Mencius*, 16, 116, 267, 272, 275, 515 examination essays on: in early Ming, 73, 416; examples, 388, 403–7, 455; in Taiping civil examinations, 577 expurgated version in Chu Yuan-chang's reign, 81, 102; rehabilitation in 1415, 118–19 inclusion in Chu Ti's *Ta-ch'üan* collections, 116–18

*Meng-chan i-chih* (Remaining points on dream interpretation), compiled by Ch'en Shih-yuan, 329

*Meng-chan lei-k'ao* (Classified studies of dream interpretations), compiled by Chang Feng-i, 328

*Meng-hsi pi-t'an* (Shen Kua), 350–51

*meng-kuan* (beginners curriculum), in charitable and community schools, 246

*Meng-tzu chi-chu* (Collected notes to the Mencius) (Chu Hsi), 272

*Meng-tzu chieh-wen*, as censored version of *Mencius*, 81, 102

*Meng-tzu huo-wen* (Questions on the Mencius) (Chu Hsi), 273

mental health: cultural boundaries of, 368. *See also* emotional tensions

merchant elites, xvii, xix, xxix, 30, 376–77, 422, 616; access to civil service examinations, 249; educational facilities, 246; monopolization of cultural resources, xxx–xxxi, 239. *See also* gentry elite

merchants, xix–xx, 227, 246, 253, 293; exclusion from high office, 241; as official classification of Ming population, 250–51; sons' access to civil service examinations, 251, 252; status, 132, 253, 371. *See also* merchant elites

Mercury (planet), 475

messianic authority, claimed by Ch'eng I, 18

meteorology, political role in Han, 348–50

metrical poetry. *See* regulated verse

metropolitan examinations (*hui-shih*), xxxii, 35, 57, 248; auspicious dreams about, 334–36; emotional tensions from, 296–98; late imperial (*see entry below*). See also *chin-shih* degree; policy questions

metropolitan examinations (*hui-shih*), late imperial, 41–42, 60, 128–29, 129n10, 134, 142, 145–46

age of successful examinees, 287, 289–92

Ch'ing, 416, 440–43, 506, 536, 657, 723; bannermen taking, 223; changes in, 513–19; *chia-k'o* examinations, 129n10, 524n8; classical specialization, 563–68, 685, 703; early Ch'ing, 165–67, 166n124, 170–71, 171n142, 190n32, 273, 531; in 18th century, 531, 564, 565; final (1904), 605; Five Classics mastery in, 284–85; Four Books' importance for final rankings, 708–9; Han vs. Sung Learning as factor in, 513–19; increased frequency of, 523–24; military versions of taken by civil candidates, 222; after 1901 reforms, 595–98, 596; in 1902,

596–601; in 19th century, 585, 588–89, 594; officials, 686; poetry questions in Ch'ien-lung reign, 548, 551, 552–53, 558, 559–62; protests in 1895, 212–13; rankings on of palace examination *optimi* 1664–1852, 717–18; ratio of graduates to candidates (1691–1850), 680; reform efforts, 527, 531, 538, 573, 579–80; in 17th century, 502–3, 513, 525; social origins of candidates, 691; during Taiping Rebellion, 574, 577; transformation of beginning in 1756–57, 544–45

Chu Hsi's views seen as prevailing, 430–43

classical specialization, 280–81

in dynastic schools, as stepping stone to success in, 239

early Ming, 41–45, 74–78, 79, 85–86, 93–95, 144–45; under Chu Ti, 109, 119; place of Chiang-hsi elite, 106–7; regional differences in results, 90

education trusts for sons seeking, 244–45

examination compounds, 178, 195, 400

examiners, corruption charges against, 200–203, 207

format (1384–1756), 522–23

grading of, 188–89

levels of competition, 143

Ming, 144–45, 190, 413, 653, 657, 691; classical specialization, 654, 685; early Ming (*see subentry above*); eight-legged essay examples, 384–85, 388–91; Fu-she members' success in, 211; *Great Collection of Works on Nature and Principle* required for, 116; Hanlin Academy supervision, 159; levels of appointment, 146–47; officials, 147–50, 153–54, 673–75, 684; rankings, 707–8, 710–12, 723, 715–16; reexaminations, 204–5

quotas and rankings, 129–31, 157–58, 424–29

resistance to mantic techniques, 346, 355

social standing of *chin-shih*, 255

success in by those with commoner ancestors, 248

*mi-hsin* (superstition), 360, 621

*mi-tsai*. *See* natural disasters

Miao candidates, quotas for requested in 1807, 169

Miaw-fen Lü, 142
militarists, native, China as victim of predicted by Feng Kuei-fen, 580
military, 3, 174
    Ch'ing, 574, 596, 607; civil examinations for, 222–23; dynastic schools for, 164; sale of local degrees, 227–28; service system of Ming reinstated in, 163–67
    Chu Yuan-chang on, 38–39, 72
    1594 policy question on equal-field system, 495
    and Ming classification of population, 250–51, 253
    social status of families, 254–56, 371
    and T'u-mu Affair, 53–55. see also T'u-mu Affair
Military Classics, xxviii, 222
military degrees: 130, 236–37; education trusts for sons seeking, 244–45
military elites, tribal, under conquest dynasties, 20
military examinations, xxviii, 463–64
    Ch'ing, 163–67, 167n125, 205, 222–24, 226; abrogation of, early 20th century, 570; abrogation of, late Ch'ing proposals for, 580, 589, 592, 595; cheating on, 199; military officer examination papers (kuan-chüan), 252; during Taiping Rebellion, 574
    Ming, 38–40, 250
    overlapping with civil examinations, 137n37, 222–23
    Ricci's view of, 463
min-chi. See commoners
min-chüan (commoner examination papers), 252
mind: cultivation of, 68–69, 411; of emperor, focus on under Chu Ti, 111–12; human (see entry below); matters of (hsin-shu), 500, 525; methods of (see hsin-fa); and nature, Shen Ch'ang-yü on, 441; transmission of (see entry below); Wang Yang-ming teachings on, 474
mind, human ( jen-hsin)
    doctrines of (hsin-hsueh), 413, 503
    in finding principles of celestial counterparts, 473–74, 476
    and mind of Tao (tao-hsin), 68–69, 434–43; "Counsels of Yü the Great" role in doctrine of, 505–6, 511–12;

equated with subject and ruler by Ch'ien I-pen, 439–40; in examination questions late Ming to mid-Ch'ing, 434–43, 437–38, 513–14
    moral (liang-hsin), equation with principle (hsin chi li), 514
    in music-poetry link, 552
mind, transmission of (ch'uan-shou hsin-fa): Annals seen as important canon on, 490, 492; Ch'eng-Chu interpretation of, 506; doctrine of, 413, 432, 438, 511–12; policy questions on, 493, 506; Tao image of used by Chu Ti, 111–12
ming. See fate
ming-ching (clarifying the Classics) examinations, 9–10, 17, 144, 400n86, 613
Ming chuang-yuan t'u-k'ao (Illustrated survey of optimi in Ming dynasty), 313–15, 313n60, 330, 359; woodblocks, 332, 333, 336, 337, 338, 339, 340, 341–43, 342, 343–45, 344, 345
Ming dynasty (1368–1644), xvii, xix; anti-Mongol historiography, 52–56; Ch'eng-Chu school seen as justifying, 69–70; civil service examinations (see civil service examinations, late imperial); examination compounds, 173–95; fall of, 211, 528; palace coup of 1457, 93; Tao-hsueh as orthodoxy in, 29 (see also Tao-hsueh). See also specific emperors and events
ming-fa (degree in law), 42–43
Ming-i tai-fang lu (Huang Tsung-hsi), 528
Ming-shih (Dynastic history of the Ming), 384
Ming-t'ang (Hall of Enlightened Rule), 475
Ming-tao Academy, 209
Miyazaki Ichisada, xxiii, xxxiv n, 8n17, 135n31, 137n37, 173, 299; ahistorical portrait of "examination hell," 285; on "Thirteen Classics," 267–68, 267n76
mnemonic devices, 269–70, 283
mo-chüan (black ink papers), 188, 400
mo-chüan (civil examination papers), printing and publishing in Ming, 400–403
mo-i ("literary meaning"), as testing technique, 10
mobility, social. See social mobility
modernism, 360, 393
modernization in imperial China, civil examinations seen as obstacle to, 126

monetary question (*ch'ien-fa*), Ming policy questions on, 452–53

Mongol dynasty. *See* Yuan dynasty

Mongol language, as official language of Ch'ing warrior elites, 373–74

Mongols, 1, 3, 34n94, 46, 71; degrees under Yuan, 33–35; Ming Han Chinese sentiments against, 53–55; Ming historiography on, 52–56; rule in north China (1234–1271), 25, 27; in T'u-mu Affair, 53–55 (*see also* T'u-mu Affair); 20th-century Chinese republics, 621; written out of Chinese intellectual history, 46. *See also* Yuan dynasty

moon, motion of, 471, 473–76

moral candidates (*hsiao-lien*), promotion of regardless of status advocated by Ch'en Ch'i-hsin, 215–16

moral character of candidates: definition of influenced by literary culture, 371; emphasis on in Ch'ing, 221, 229–37; importance in early Ming civil examinations, 38, 39, 43; rote learning seen as useless for development of, 261

moral cultivation (*hsiu-shen*), 352, 371–72, 610, 612

moral education, seen as priority among Japanese, 599

moral leadership, literati associated with Tung-lin Academy as voice for in late Ming, 209–10

moral orthodoxy, allegiance to expected of Ch'ing candidates, 519

moral perfection, emphasis on in Tao Learning, 423

moral philosophy (moral principles) (*li-hsueh*), 1n, 18–19, 25, 27–28; Ch'eng-Chu, 116–17, 414, 435, 559 (*see also* Ch'eng-Chu *li-hsueh*); Chu Hsi on, 435–36; Chu Yuan-chang on lack in literary criteria for civil service, 89–90; doctrine of benevolence discussed in *Analects*, 430–34; doctrine of innate moral knowledge (*liang-chih*), 413; of Four Books, 410–11; as inseparable from history in Ming and Ch'ing policy questions, 488; Japanese seen as adopting from Chinese, 599–600; and logical framework for reasoning in

Ming and Ch'ing examinations, 421–22; and natural studies in Ming, 481–82; Ricci on Chinese proficiency in, 461–62, 463; in Sung-Yuan-Ming transition, 45–46

moral remonstrance, 118

moral rhetoric, chain-argument for in examination essays, 421–23

morality: in Chu Kuo-tso's dream-vision, 335–36; music seen as improving, 479; public and private, respect for elders as foundation of, 286; in religious discourse on civil examination results, 301, 306–11; and talent, in Taiping selection process, 577. *See also* moral philosophy

morality books (*shan-shu*), 306, 311, 411

Mote, Frederick, 54, 128n9

Murakami Masatsugu, 34n94

Murphy, Raymond, xxix n27

music, 484–85, 552; in Ming civil examinations, 465, 466, 477–82; and poetry, 560–61; theory, and mathematical harmonics, 477–82

Muslims, 19–20, 36, 46, 169

nails (*ting*), dreaming of, 329

Naitō Kōnan, 8n17

name changes as identity changes: in fate calculations, 324–25; use by Hung Hsiu-ch'üan, 369

*nan-chüan* ("southern paper"), 95

Nanking: as capital for Taiping rebels, 573; as capital from 1368 to 1415, 96, 100, 37; as dual capital with Peking, 373–74; examination compound, 178–79, *179, 183*, 198; execution of associate examiners, 204; 1402 massacre, 118; provincial examinations, 142–43, 256

Naquin, Susan, 129n12

national unity, dynastic solidarity replaced by as late Ch'ing ideal, 621

native peoples (*t'u-chi*), attention to in early Ch'ing educational affairs, 168–69

nativism, 48–52, 51, 54–56

natural disasters (*mi-tsai*), policy questions on, 346–54, 346n122, 495

natural sciences, in late Ch'ing civil examinations, 590, 601–2

natural studies (*ko-chih-hsueh*), 461n3, 527n16
in civil examinations, xxxiv–xxxv, 467,
513, 620; policy questions on, 346–54,
448, 461–85; virtual elimination in
early Ch'ing, 483–85
as literati field of learning in Ming and
Ch'ing, 460–61, 464–68
natural world (*tzu-jan*), policy questions on,
347–54
nature: Ming policy questions on, 454; and
mind, Shen Ch'ang-yü on, 441
navy, Ming, and T'u-mu Affair, 53–54
Needham, Joseph, 480
*Nei-ko* (Grand Secretariat), 159, 161–62
*nei-lien kuan* (inner overseers), at examination
compounds, 181
*nei-sheng* (inner sagehood), dual role with
*wai-wang* (external kingship), 513
Neo-Confucianism, xx, xx n, 623–24. *See
also Tao-hsueh*
Neskar, Ellen, 59
new schools (*hsueh-t'ang*), 605–8; curriculum
and examinations, 608–12, 614–17; riots
against, *623*, 624; temples and shrines
changed into, 624
New Text (*chin-wen*) classical learning, 241,
319, 593, 608; vs. Old Text, 459,
504–9, 512, 515, 517, 536
Ni Heng, 268
*ni yu shu* (empirical regularities), and celestial
counterparts, 475
Ni Yueh (1444–1501), 121
Nine Classics, 272n88, 563
"nine-rank system" (*chiu-p'in kuan*), 6–7
nomadic warriors, of steppes, in conquest
dynasties, 19–22
non-elites, 296, 296n4
northern China, 95n; literati, 165; numbers
of civil examination graduates, 257;
performance on metropolitan examinations by candidates from, 131. *See also
specific prefectures and provinces*
Northern Sung dynasty (960–1126), 3, 21,
25, 47–49; civil service examinations
(*see* civil service examinations, Sung);
stability and relations with Khitan and
Jurchen, 48; theories of legitimate succession, 50–52. *See also* Chin dynasty;
Sung dynasties
northwest revolt, 365

O-erh-t'ai (1680–1745), 424, 537, 538, 539–41
Oboi Regents, examination reforms
(1664–67), 65, 77–78, 517, 530–36, 541
Office of Music, in Bureau of Weights and
Measures, 477, 481
"Offices of Chou" (chapter of *Documents*), in
Old Text–New Text controversy, 509
officials, education. *See* education officials;
examiners
officials, reproduction of, 7–12, 15, 127; by
appointment, 127, 163, 215; "arbiter's
system," 6–7; dynastic schools' role in,
126–27; use of purchase, 58, 145–46,
687. *See also* hereditary privilege; recommendations
Oirats, 93, 303; in T'u-mu Affair, 53–55, 432
Old Text–New Text controversy, 459,
504–9, 512, 515, 517; over *Classic of
Filial Piety*, 536; over *Documents Classic*,
504–9, 512, 515, 517
omens, 348, 485; *chao* (sighting of portents),
312, 326–45; in Chu Yuan-chang's
dream, 326–27; in dream-vision, 359;
natural anomalies seen as by Tung
Chung-shu, 347–48; and political culture in Han, 348–50
opium trade, 227
Opium War (1839–42), 578
oral recitation, of classical texts, 261–63,
265, 268, 269
oratory, elements of in eight-legged essay,
396–97
orthodox music, length for standard pitch
used in, 478
orthodox transmission of Tao. See *tao-t'ung*
orthodoxy, 1n. *See also* Ch'eng-Chu *li-hsueh*;
*Tao-hsueh*
Ou-yang Hsiu (1007–72), 15–16, 19, 28,
89–90, 360, 543; *ku-wen* style championed by, 381; on linking events on
earth to heavens, 348, 351–52; memorial of thanks in name of, 452; proposal
on policy questions, 583, 590; theory of
legitimate succession, 50
Ou-yang Te (1496–1554), 413
outsiders. *See* barbarians; *se-mu*
Oxenham, E. L., 292n138

Pa-hsien County Archives, xxviii
*pa-ku-wen. See* eight-legged essay

*pa-kung* (special examinations), 548

*pa-kung-sheng* (special examination graduates), court examinations for, 537n42

*pa-tzu* (eight characters) of one's birth, 312–13

*Pai-chia hsing (Hundred Surnames)*, 166, 263, 372

*Pai shang-ti chiao* (God Worshipers Society), 370

*p'ai-fang* (memorial arch), 191

painting, 30

palace examinations, 8, 14; belles lettres (*tsa-wen*) in, 8–12; calligraphy's importance in, 377–79; ceremonies of cultural prestige at, 177–78; dream-visions about, 337–38; late imperial (*see entry below*); Sung, 9, 60, 134, 177–78. *See also chin-shih*; policy questions

palace examinations, late imperial, 128, 129n10, 134, 157, 255–56, 715–18

age of successful examinees, 287, 289, 290

Ch'ing, 212, 657, 691, 706; bannermen taking, 223, 223n139; during Ch'ien-lung reign, 317–18, 539–40, 542–44; early Ch'ing, 163–68, 166n124, 171, 171n142, 536; Han vs. Sung Learning as factor in, 513; rankings of *optimi*, 717–18; reform proposals after Taiping, 579–80

early Ming, 107, 204; under Chu Ti, 109, 110–11; under Chu Yuan-chang, 84–87, 94–95; in 1404, 69, 109–10, 466

Ming, 159, 211, 259, 657, 691; early Ming (*see subentry above*); officials for, 148–49, 153–54, 676; rankings of *optimi*, 715–16

paleography (*wen-tzu-hsueh*), 10, 455–57, 504, 562; dictionary compiled by Hsu Shen, 266, 322, 456, 458–59; in late imperial policy questions, 456–58, 509–10, 512, 560, 561

Pan Ku (A.D. 32–92), xxxv, 489, 492, 497, 502; as exemplifying Han model of historiography, 499, 500

*p'an* (judgments), in legal questions on civil examinations, 42–44, 175, 545, 548, 558

*p'an-yü* (judicial terms), in legal questions on civil examinations, 42–45, 73, 274, 531

pantheon of worthies and deities, 369

*pao-chü* (guaranteed recommendation), 215

*Pao-chüan* (precious scrolls), 307–8

*pao-jen* (sponsored appointment), 127

*pao-pien* (praise and blame) judgments, in *Annals*, 492

Pao Shih-ch'en (1775–1855), 572

parable(s): about examination market, 305, 311; in Yuan Mei's poem, 363–64

parallel-prose (*p'ien-t'i-wen*) styles, 377, 381–82, 418. *See also* eight-legged essay

parallelism: in eight-legged essays, 384, 391–92, 394–96, 407; in Wang Ao's essays, 391, 397

parodies: of civil examination system by P'u Sung-ling, 296, 359, 361–63, 364–65; of mantic arts by Hu Ying-lin, 355–56

Passeron, Jean-Claude, xxx

peasants, 299n11, 624; exclusion from high office, 241; lack of access to educational facilities, 246, 247, 249, 372; rebellions, 139, 216; riots against new schools, *623*, 624

*pei-chüan* ("northern paper"), 95

*pei ch'üeh* (jade palace), 555, 555n109

*pei-shu* ("backing the book"), 265

*P'ei-wen yun-fu* (Thesaurus arranged by rhymes), 269, 552

Peking (Pei-ching): capital moved to in 1415, 96, 101, 375; as dual capital with Nanking, 142, 373–74; 1895 protest, 213; examination compound, 199; official language, 374, 375; Ta-tu as Yuan capital at, 22

Peking dialect, 96

*pen-hsin chih ch'üan-te* (perfect virtue of the original mind), 430, 432

*pen-i* (original meanings), 501

penal law, in early Ming civil examinations, 41, 43, 452

P'eng Ch'i-feng (1701–84), 318

P'eng lineage, 318–19

P'eng people, incorporated as minority group, 168

P'eng Shih (1416–75), 329

P'eng Ting-ch'iu (1645–1719), 318

Personnel, Ministry of (*Li-pu*), 8, 127

Peterson, Willard, 462n6

philology (*hsiao-hsueh*), 167, 451, 506–7, 579, 590; of Classics, in late Ch'ing policy questions, 431, 508–10, 512, 561; as focus of *k'ao-cheng* in Ch'ing, 458, 561–62; popularity of in late Ming, 412,

457; Yangtzu delta as center of research in, 503–4. *See also* phonology

phonetics (*hsiao-tzu*), 24

phonology, 552, 557, 559–61, 562; ancient (*ku-yin-hsueh; yin-yun chih hsueh*), 455, 459, 503–4, 508–10, 515

physical punishment, exemption from for Yuan literati, 31

physiognomy (*k'an-hsiang*), 304–5, 312, 328

*pi-chi* (note-form literature), anomaly records, 350

*pi-hua* (brush), 375, 377

*pi-k'ao* (examination skipping), 232

*pi-shen* (writing spirit), 320

*piao* (edicts), 41–42

*piao* (posters), 185

*piao* document question, 285n120

*pien-nien. See* annalistic history

*p'ien-t'i-wen* (parallel-prose) styles, 377, 381–82, 418. *See also* eight-legged essay

pitches, twelve (*yueh-lü*), 477–81

Plaks, Andrew, 397n85

planchette, in spirit-writing, 320–22

planets: motions of, 471, 473–76; origin of, 474

*po-hsueh* (broad learning), questions testing, 466

*po-hsueh hung-tz'u* special examination, Ch'ing, 171, 307, 407, 547–48, 581

*po-shih* (erudite; learned literatus), 5, 280, 379n19

*p'o-t'i* (opening of eight-legged essay), 384n37, 389, 394, 397, 404

poetry, 285, 537, 549, 551, 562

in civil examinations. *See entry below*

composed by spirit-mediums, 319–22

popularity among Ming and Yuan literati, 32, 32n88, 37–38, 45

prepared for poetry questions, 552–56, 555n110

T'ang-Sung emphasis on, 19, 547; changed in Ming, 37; revival of in Ch'ing, 546–50

*see also* regulated verse

poetry, in civil examinations, xxxiv, 8–9, 23–24, 42, 44–45, 74, 89, 285, 423

Ch'ing, 135, 524, 535, 544–58, 576, 579, 583, 724; in Ch'ien-lung reign, 373, 423, 429, 518, 544–62, 560–61; restoration after 1756, 37, 266, 269, 275, 287,

291, 537, 547, 620; during Taiping Rebellion, 576

elimination of in Sung-Yuan-Ming transition, 37, 41–42, 383, 444–45

rhyming dictionaries as preparation for, 266

spirit-writing medium's responses to, 321–22

Sung, 17, 19, 26, 29, 57, 59, 266, 381

T'ang, 9–10, 11, 217, 261, 373

*Poetry Classic*, 189, 267, 272, 275, 552, 555–56; Ch'ien-lung emperor on, 540; in Ch'ing civil examinations, 273, 508, 512, 515, 545, 551, 557–58, 560–61, 564–65; Chu Hsi's commentary on, 410; Hsueh Ying-ch'i eight-legged essay on, 455; principles of history seen as enunciated in, 496; solar eclipses recorded in, 469; specialization in, 281, 283, 466–67, 488, 491, 499, 547, 560, 563; Wang Ao's 1475 classical essays on, 388

polestar, 475

police: role in examination compounds, 174, 194–95; as subject of 1902 policy question, 597

policy (*ts'e*) questions, 8–11, 9n20, 23–24; Han, 6, 8, 381, 444; late imperial (*see entry below*); Sung, 16, 60; use by Empress Wu, 8n19; Yuan, 34–35, 444–45

policy (*ts'e*) questions, late imperial, xxxiv–xxxv, 8–11, 135, 425–27, 443–59, 487–89, 506

Ch'ing, 164, 273, 284, 440–43, 504–19, 545, 721–22; on authenticity of portions of *Documents Classic*, 506–7; in Che-chiang province, 447–49; in Ch'ien-lung reign, 560–64; on classical specialization, 563–65; classified by topic 1646–1859, 720; 1895 responses to, 588–89; emphasized after 1901 reforms, 595–603; Han vs. Sung Learning in, 504–19; on history, 499–503; importance for final rankings, 712–15; on natural studies as rare and uninformed, 483–85; reform efforts, 524, 526–27, 529; 530–31, 533, 536–45, 559, 559n124, 571–73, 579, 581, 582–83, 590–92, 620; on regulated verse, 551–58; on relationship between Classics and Histories,

policy (*ts'e*) questions, late imperial
(*continued*)
  487–88; during Taiping Rebellion, 576;
  use of term *k'ao-chü-hsueh,* 451–59
  Ming, 41, 112, 190, 214, 447–49; classified
  by topic 1474–1600, 719; early Ming,
  38–39, 41–42, 44, 73–78, 85–87, 110–11;
  on history, 488–99, 494n86; importance for final rankings, 710–12; on
  interpretation of natural anomalies,
  346–54; on mathematical harmonics
  and musical theory, 477–81; on natural
  studies, 461–85; on transmission of
  Way and mind of Tao, 412, 437–38,
  440–41; use of evidence in and *k'ao-chü-
  hsueh,* 451–59
  natural studies and history in, 312,
  460–61
  not carefully read or not graded by
  examiners, xxxii–xxxiii, 446, 446n64,
  523
  on sage-kings' methods of the mind, 112
  on technical subjects, 379
political order, 16–18, 131
Polo, Marco, 3
popular culture, 3, 296n4; child's ability to
  memorize as highly prized, 268; lore
  about techniques for civil examination
  success, 304–11
population growth, 130, 260, 467
portents: sighting of (*chao*), 312, 326–45. *See
  also* omens
posters (*piao*), 185
power, 245
  autocratic, 66–67, 79, 120
  imperial, 220; unraveling of, 586–87, 622
  military and aristocratic in Northern
  Sung, 13
  political, 5, 260; ascending view of,
  78–80, 84–85, 102, 118–19; civil examinations as route to, 211, 242, 569–70,
  587–88; descending view of, 78–88,
  117–18, 121, 440; early Ming balance of,
  66–70; of Hanlin Academy members,
  159–63, 209
  and wealth, 597, 598; obsession with in
  late Ch'ing, 578, 585
practical knowledge (*shih-wu*), 456, 529, 542
practical learning. See *shih-hsueh* ( practical
  learning)

prediction(s): about examinations, 300–302,
  311–25; through celestial counterparts,
  473–77; spirit-writing, 312, 319–22; *suan-
  ming* (fate prediction), 311–25, 328,
  330–45, 354–60
prefects, xxvii–xxviii, 130, 149, 200, 220, 235
prefectural schools, 138, 148–50, 151
prefecture examinations (*chieh-shih*), Sung,
  133, 133n27, 401n91
prefecture examinations ( *fu-k'ao*), Ming and
  Ch'ing, 40, 133–34, 140, 224, 249, 401;
  examination hall, *176, 177. See also*
  licensing examinations
prime ministers, Chu Yuan-chang's views
  on, 83–84
primer literacy, 374, 376–77, 393n70
primers, 272, 274–75, 372; memorization of
  by children, 185, 263; of poetry, 549;
  used by students in 1890s, 609–10
Prince of Yen. *See* Chu Ti
prisons, penal, vs. examination compounds,
  192–94
private academies (*shu-yuan*). *See* academies
private domain (*ssu*), vs. public domain,
  434–38
private schools, entrance examinations after
  1905, 612–13
probation (*ko-chih liu-jen*), 233
property laws, transformed in 13th and 14th
  centuries, 63
prose: popularity among Yuan literati, 32;
  in Sung civil examinations, 57, 59
prose composition, 279. *See also* classical
  essays; discourse essay; eight-legged
  essay; *ku-wen* essays
prosody, rules of, 555
protection privilege ( *pu-yin*), 127
protests, 207–8, 212–13
  vs. civil examination system, xxxii, 132,
  175, 202–5, 212–13, 413; boycotts of
  local examinations, 231–32, 236; mistakes in characters as cause for, 198,
  198n52
provincial education commissioners, 136,
  147–51, 154, 200, 220; Ch'ien-lung era
  reformism's effects on, 232–35
provincial examinations, xxxii, 219, 248,
  297; dreams and predictions about,
  305–10, 334–36; emotional tensions
  from, 296–98; late imperial (*see entry*

*below*); before Ming, 144; spirits' appearing to candidates and examiners, 309; Sung, 142n57, 144, 144n63; Yuan, 35. See also *chü-jen* graduates; policy questions; *specific provinces*

provincial examinations, late imperial, 41–42, 60, 128–29, 133–34, 142, 145–46
age of candidates, 286–92
Ch'ing, 125, 163, 211, 523–24, 723; classical specialization changes, 563–68; early Ch'ing, 167, 169–70, 190n32, 273, 524–25, 527, 531; 18th-century format, 531, 564, 565; final (1903), 605; Five Classics in, 284–85, 725–27; Han vs. Sung Learning in, 506–12, 517, 518; military versions of taken by civil candidates, 222; outside review reinstated in 1754, 205; poetry questions, 548–58, 559–62, 724; rankings on of palace examination *optimi*, 717–18; ratios of graduates to candidates, 662, 663, 664–65; reform efforts, 232–35, 530–32, 573, 579–80; after reforms of 1901, 595–97; during Taiping Rebellion, 573–77; transformation of beginning, 544–45
Chu Hsi's views seen as prevailing, 430–43
classical specialization, 280–85
and clerks' sons use of false information, 199–200
competition for *chü-jen* and *chin-shih* degrees, 142–44, 142n57
in dynastic schools, as stepping stone to success, 239
education trusts for sons seeking, 244–45
examination compounds, 174–96, 400
examinations for choosing eligible candidates for, 133–34, 137–38. *See also* licensing examinations; qualifying examinations
examiners: accusations against, 206–7; attempts to influence, 200–202; increased number of and ranking methods, 424–29
format from 1384 to 1756, 522–23
levels of appointment, 146–57
levels of competition, 143–44
Ming, 159, 190, 210, 211; in Che-chiang province, 412, 437, 488–95; Chiang-hsi

elite's place, 106–7; *chü-jen* and *chin-shih* as officials for, 147–50; discourse questions' importance, 723; early Ming, 41–45, 72–73, 75–76, 79, 85–86, 89, 93, 95, 106–7, 109n128, 144–45; examiners for, 150–51, 154; in Fu-chien province, 154–57; *Great Collection of Works on Nature and Principle* required for, 116; officials, 669–72, 683; ratios of graduates to candidates, 661, 662, 663, 664–65; Shun-t'ien prefecture (1456), 206–7, 431
quotas for, 129–31, 138–39, 142
rankings on of palace examination *optimi*, 715–16
resistance to mantic techniques, 346–54
riots during, 198
social origins of candidates, 253, 691
testing sites for, 174–75
*pu-chih li-i* (ritual impropriety), 233
*pu erh-ch'en* ("cannot serve two different rulers"), 106, 106n115
*pu-shou* (radicals): divination technique using, 322–24; paleographical dictionary arranged by, 266
*pu-yin* (protection privilege), 127
P'u Sung-ling (1640–1715), 197, 361; Chou K'o-ch'ang story, 325–26; stories parodying examination system, 296, 325–26, 359, 361–63, 364–65
public domain (*kung*), vs. private domain, 434–38
public good of empire (*t'ien-hsia chih kung*), 491–92
public policy (*ts'e*), questions on. *See* policy questions
public schools, Ch'ing, 605; entrance examinations after 1905, 612–13
publishing, 114, 365, 377, 400–411, 460; and growth of "writing elite" and reading public, 403–9; officializing literary taste in Ch'ing, 417–20; of poetry anthologies, 549, 551; and struggles over imperial orthodoxy, 411–17
purchase (*chüan-na*), use for appointing officials, 58, 145–46, 687
purchasing degrees. See *chien-sheng*
purges, political, by early Ming rulers, 66; by Chu Ti, 97–99; by Chu Yuan-chang, 77, 83, 93

qualifying examinations (*k'o-k'ao*), 133, 136–38, 143, 175, 177, 205n78, 288
    Ch'ing, 221, 235, 530n, 548–49, 564; addition of poetry question, 548–49; combined with licensing examinations, 225; final (1905), 605; protests over, 232; after Taiping Rebellion, 584
    *chü* as in T'ang, 7
    Huang Ch'un-yao's proposals for, 218–19
quotas, 96n88, 138–40, 142, 252, 256–57, 259–60, 656; as basis for changing rankings by emperors, 317–18; for candidates of high moral character, 234; for *chin-shih*, 157–58, 698; for *chü-jen*, 652, 682; in early Ch'ing, 164, 166, 168–69, 169–71; end of (1905), effects on distribution of elites, 606; for examination candidates, 129–31, 137; 1567 riot due to reduction in, 198; late Ch'ing proposals for, 595, 602–3; for licentiates, 224, 235, 660, 689–90; not set for Taiping examinations, 574; for official positions, 88, 93, 94–97, 109, 134; 1744 edict on, 602; for specialization, 283; tripartite, 96n88

radicals (*pu-shou*): arrangement by in dictionaries, 266; divination technique using, 322–24
Rawski, Evelyn, 129n12
reading: as ancillary to writing in classical education, 276–77; requirements for new schools, 608–9
reading public, formation of, 276–77
reason, 392–93. *See also* epistemology
Receptions, Bureau of, in Ming, 161
recommendations (*chien-chü*), use of, 58
    Ch'ing, 163, 230, 520, 528–29, 542, 581
    Ming, 92–93, 127, 145–46, 258; abolished after 1459, 146; Ch'en Ch'i-hsin on, 215–16; by Chu Yuan-chang, 71, 81; Huang Ch'un-yao on, 217, 218
    pre-Ming, 5–7; Han and Sui, 5, 133, 217, 218; Sung, 133, 215; Yuan, 35–36
*Record of Rites* (*Li-chi*; *Rites Classic*), 267, 272, 275, 410
    in civil examinations: Ch'ing, 273, 545, 563–65; Ming, 42, 74, 466–67; specialization in, 281, 283, 466–67, 491, 499, 563

in elementary classes, 612
"Yueh-chi" (Record of music), 479
    see also *Doctrine of the Mean*; *Great Learning*
*Records of the Official Historian* (*Shih-chi*) (Ssu-ma Ch'ien), 479, 489, 492, 497
red ink (*chu-chüan*), 188, 400
reexaminations (*fu-shih*; repeat examinations), 154, 204–5, 205n78, 224, 249; Ch'ing, 226, 613, 615; poetry and rhyme-prose question added to, 548–49
reform, of civil examination system, 220, 569–73
    in Ch'ien-lung reign, 224–25, 232–35, 537–68, 570–71, 584, 620
    curriculum, 419, 422, 519–20, 544–45, 569–70
    1898 Reform Movement ("Hundred Days of Reform"), 586, 590–94
    from 1898 to 1905 abrogation, 595–605, 621
    from 1895 to 1898 proposals, 585–94
    late Ming calls for, 213–20
    after Taiping Rebellion, 236, 578–84
    from 1645 to 1750, 484, 524–44; Oboi reforms (1664–67), 530–36; in Yung-cheng and early Ch'ien-lung reigns, 229–32, 536–41
regicide, Mencius' legitimation of, and Chu Ti, 102
regulated verse (*lü-shih*; metrical poetry), 35n98, 276, 285, 297, 321, 381, 547; in Ch'ing poetry questions, 44–45, 275, 548–59, 576; in late Ch'ing, 553, 597n86; and reconstruction of antiquity, 562
reincarnation, literati belief in, 307
religion, xxxi, xxxv, 336–40, 366–70; K'ang Yu-wei on Confucianism as official, 593–94; literati's turn to as aid for emotional tensions, 295–97, 299–326, 361, 619; popular, 104, 346–55, 357, 464, 593; role in Taiping Rebellion, 575–76; Westernizing elites' attempts to overturn, 624. *See also* Buddhism; Taoism
Religion, Ministry of (*chiao-pu*), to commemorate Confucius, proposed, 593
Religion Association (*chiao-hui*), to commemorate Confucius, proposed, 593
repeat examinations. *See* reexaminations

Republic of China, 360, 611, 616–17, 621
Republican Revolution (1911–12), 608, 621
residualism (repeated failures), among candidates, 143–44, 175
retirement trust (*yang-lao*), 245
retribution: as construct for explaining examination market, 306–7; moral, 312, 318–19
revenge (*fu-ch'iu*), against barbarians, called for, 49
Revenue, Ministry of, registration of households in early Ming, 249–50
Revolution of 1911–12, 608, 621
rhyme books (*yun-shu*), 552
rhyme-prose (*ku-fu; shih-fu*)
　in civil examinations, 8–9, 11, 23–24, 266, 583; in Ch'ing *po-hsueh hung-tz'u* special examinations, 548; elimination of in Sung-Yuan-Ming transition, 41–42, 383; in Northern Sung, 17, 381; in Southern Sung, 26, 29, 32; in Yuan, 33, 35, 35n98, 444–45
　in literary examinations of Hanlin Academy, 163
　in writings of Northern Sung literati, 19
rhyme-scheme: in 1579 poetry question, 553–54; in *Poetry Classic*, 562
rhyming and pronunciation dictionaries, 266, 561
Ricci, Matteo (1552–1610), 206, 270, 461–62, 463
Ridley, Charles, xlii, 373n5
riots: over civil examinations, xxxii, 204, 207; in examination compounds, 198, 199, 202; against new schools, *623*, 624
rite of passage, and mastery of classical texts, 260–61
rites. *See* ritual(s)
Rites, Ministry of, xxxvi, 127, 153–54, 160–62, 173, 521, 551
　and Education Board in 1906, 609
　examination bureaucracy, xx, 190, 193, 200–201
　examination bureaucracy in Ch'ing, 234, 536, 595, 597; discourse questions as Sung Learning cause, 558; failure to act on reform proposals after Taiping Rebellion, 583–84; role in reforms, 531, 532, 535–36, 541–42, 559
　in T'ang, 8

Yangtzu delta scholars appointed to, 508
*Rites Classic.* See *Record of Rites*
*Rites (Rituals) of Chou*, 79, 267, 272, 276
ritual(s) (ceremonies; rites), xxvii, 10, 75, 371, 466; celebrating examination graduates, 194, 205–6; music, length for standard pitch in, 478; and natural studies, 482; return to, in Confucius discussion of benevolence, 430–32
ritual impropriety (*pu-chih li-i*), 233
ritualism, 562n135; Han Learning seen as linked with, 521n, 562n134
*Romance of the Three Kingdoms* (novel), 302
rote learning, 64, 261. *See also* memorization
rulership, 1516 policy question on, 488, 493–95
running calligraphy (*hsing-shu*), 379
Russia, ritual communication with in early Ch'ing, 167
Russo-Japanese War of 1904–5, 604

*Sacred Edict (Sheng-yü kuang-hsun)* (K'ang-hsi emperor), 135, 221, 222
Sacrifices, Bureau of, 161
sage-kings, 214, 353–54, 433–38, 440, 490, 496
　Ch'ing emperors seen as, 122
　and *Documents Classic*, Old Text portions seen as not work of, 504
　early Ming cultural idealization of, 103
　mantle of claimed by late imperial rulers, 68–69, 71, 110–11, 115, 157; claimed by Chu Yuan-chang and Chu Ti, 97, 101, 103, 111; in policy questions, 396
　model of rulership, 1516 policy question on, 488, 493–95
　vision of in Four Books and Five Classics, 392
　*see also* Yao
sagehood, 423, 442–43
salvation, in Buddhism, 308
*san-chiao ho-i* ("three teachings are one"), 411
*san-fen sun-i* (increase and decrease by one-third) theory of pitch generation, 480
*San-kuo-chih* (History of the Three States period) (Ch'en Shou), 489, 492, 497
*San-pu ta-ch'üan (Ta-chüan)* (trilogy), 114–17, 119, 159, 415, 417n132, 516, 566. See also *Hsing-li ta-ch'üan; Wu-ching ssu-shu ta-ch'üan*

*San-t'ung li* (Triple Concordance system), 468–69
*San-tzu ching (Three Character Classic)*, 185, 263, 275, 372, 609–10
Sang Yueh, 269
Sano Kōji, 409–10, 413n118
satire: on civil examination system, by P'u Sung-ling, 296, 359, 361–63, 364–65; of mantic arts by Hu Ying-lin, 355–56
Saturn (planet), 475
Schirokauer, Conrad, 3–4
scholar-gentry, xvii n. *See also* literati
*Scholars, The* (Wu Ching-tzu), 296, 357
scholia *(chu-shu)* tradition, 28, 284, 410, 510; Han-T'ang, 410, 415, 416, 417n132, 566
schools, 38, 77, 535
    charitable *(li-hsueh)*, 239, 246
    Ch'ing, 163, 164, 376–77; after 1905, 605–6, 611–13 *(see also* new schools); seen as solution to late-19th-century problems, 579n36, 582, 585–86, 589–93, 595, 602–5
    clan schools, 263, 271
    community schools *(she-hsueh)*, 246
    county and department schools, 138–39, 148
    family schools, 287
    lineage schools, 92, 128, 239, 246, 457, 609–10
    prefectural schools, 138, 148–50, 151
    public schools, absence of, 372
    temple schools, 239, 246, 263
    *see also* academies; dynastic schools; imperial schools
schools system *(chia fa)*, 512, 516
Schorr, Adam, 451
science, xxvi, 448–49, 461–64, 483n63. *See also* natural studies
*scientia*, used by Jesuits, 449, 465
seal calligraphy *(chuan-shu)*, 379, 456
Season-Granting system *(Shou-shih li)*, 469, 471
seasons, pitch correspondences to, 479–80
sedition, accusations of, 211–12, 408–9
self, "overcoming the," in *Analects* discussion of benevolence, 430–34, 437
self-cultivation *(wei-chi chih hsueh)*, 131–32
self-strengthening *(tzu-ch'iang)*, 580, 585, 588
Semedo, Alvarez, xxxiii n33
semiclassical Chinese language, 373

*se-mu* ("categorized") people, 20, 47; interaction with, effect on Chinese dialects, 88; in 20th century, 621; under Yuan, 30, 33–35, 71
senior tribute students *(yu-kung-sheng)*, court examinations for, 537n42
Seven Classics, 268, 272, 272n88
Seven Governors (sun, moon, and five planets): motions of, 471, 473–76; origin of, 474
"Seven Solutions" ("Ch'i-chieh") (Fang I-chih), 295n1, 396
shamans, 22, 327
Shan Kao, 452–54
*shan-shu* (morality books), 306, 311, 411
Shan-tung province, 146–47, 258, 680; careers of *chin-shih* and *chü-jen* graduates in Ming, 165, 666, 667; civil examination officials in Ming, 150–52; provincial examinations in Ch'ing, 197, 508–9, 663; provincial examinations in Ming, 431, 452, 488, 663, 669, 670
*shang-chih* ("emphasis on substance"), 89
Shang Jung (1785–?), 571–72
Shang Lu (1414–86), 385–87, 426–27, 428; dream-vision, *332*, 333–35
*Shang-shu ku-wen shu-cheng (Evidential analysis of the Old Text Documents)* (Yen Jo-chü), 504–5
Shang Yen-liu, 223n139, 268, 296, 549n86, 613–14; on Taiping Rebellion period, 574, 576, 576n28, 577n30
Shanghai Commercial Press: *Eastern Miscellany*, 603–6, 609; *Journal of Education*, 609, 610–12, 614–16
Shao Ch'ang-heng (1637–1704), 529
*she-hsueh* (community schools), 246
*shen* (spirits): in dream-visions, *337*, 337–38; inside examination compounds, 308–9; and origin of universe, 474
Shen Ch'ang-yü (1700–44), 440–41
Shen-hsi province, 151–52, 169, 499n96, 551–58; 18th- and 19th-century policy questions, 511–12, 560
Shen Hsin-chou, 485
Shen I-kuan (1531–1615), 330–31
Shen Kua (1031–95), 350–51, 463–64
Shen K'un (d. 1560?), dream-vision, 341–43, *342*
Shen Te-ch'ien (1673–1769), 550

Shen-tsung emperor (r. 1068–86), 17

*Sheng-hsueh hsin-fa* (Chu Ti), 101, 102, 112, 113

*Sheng-lü ch'i-meng* (Primer for sound rules), 549

*sheng-shih* (capital [department] examinations), 14, 133

*Sheng-yü (Sacred Edict)* (K'ang-hsi emperor), 135, 221, 222

*Sheng-yü kuang-hsun (Amplified Instructions for the Sacred Edict)* (Yung-cheng emperor), 135, 221, 222, 575

*Sheng-yü liu-yen* (Sacred edict in six maxims) (Ming T'ai-tsu), 135, 575

*sheng-yuan. See* licentiates

*shih* (gentry-literati). *See* literati

*Shih-chi (Records of the Official Historian)* (Ssu-ma), 479, 489, 492, 497

*shih-fu. See* rhyme-prose

*shih-fu* (literary) requirements: for civil service *(chin-shih)* degree, in Sung literary culture, 15–16, 26, 32; stressed during Koryŏ dynasty, 23

*shih-hsueh* (historical studies). *See* historical studies

*shih-hsueh* (practical learning), 43, 534; and Ch'ing reforms, 546; in civil examinations, 217, 218, 450, 539, 546; as 18th-century code for "evidential research," 450; Western emphasis on, 598, 599–600

Shih Kuan-min (fl. ca. 1565), 208

*shih-kung* (actual achievements), focus on in historical studies, 500

*shih-li* ("concrete principles"), of heaven, 352

*shih-liu tzu ch'uan* ("sixteen-character transmission"), in *Documents Classic,* 68–69

*Shih-lu (Veritable Records),* from Hung-hsi reign, 95

Shih Pao-an (b. 1876), 600

*Shih-san ching chu-shu* (Scholia for the Thirteen Classics), 516

*shih-shih* ("concrete affairs"), of man, 352

*shih-tzu. See* characters, Chinese

*shih-tzu* (concrete words), 279

*shih-wen* (contemporary-style essay), 526. *See also* eight-legged essay

*shih-wu* (practical knowledge), 456, 529, 542

shops, for examination supplies, 177, 180

*shou-chieh* (concluding section of eight-legged essay), 391, 406–7

*Shou-hsi wen-kao* (Draft essays…) (Wang Ao), 402

*Shou-shih li* (Season-Granting system), 469, 471

shrines: changed into new schools, 624; Hang-chou shrine of Yü Ch'ien, 303, 303n21, 328; "spirit-money" used in, 305

*shu* (astrological "regularities"), 473

*Shu-ch'ang-kuan* (Institute of Advanced Studies), of Hanlin Academy, 163

*shu-chi-shih* (Hanlin probationers), 536

*shu-fa. See* calligraphy

*shu-fa liu-t'iao* (mastery of rules of character formation), 273

Shu-ho-te (1711–77), 537–38, 539, 540

*shu-hsi t'i* (repeating familiar questions), in Ch'ing policy essays, 447

Shu Hsin-ch'eng, 597n86, 603–4, 609

*shu-tui* (balanced pairs of characters), 391

*shu-yuan* (private academies). *See* academies

*shuang-t'ou-jen* (two-headed horseman), in dream-vision, 335–36, *336*

Shun (sage-king), 434–35, 436, 438, 440, 490

Shun-chih emperor (r. 1644–62), 164, 170, 221, 229, 524

Shun-t'ien prefecture, 170, 174, 204, 226, 694, 702

    examination compound, 181, *182*, 198, 202–3

    Ming-Ch'ing dynasty ratio of graduates to candidates, 663

    provincial examinations, Ch'ing, 288, 291; 18th-century, 201, 509, 560, 563; 17th-century, 524–26, 525, 530; specialization, 283

    provincial examinations, Ming, 206–7, 346–54, 431, 499n96

"Shuo liang-teng hsiao-hsueh tu-ching chiang-ching k'o chih hai" (On the harm done…) (Ho Ching), 610–11

*Shuo-wen chieh-tzu* (paleographical dictionary compiled by Hsu Shen), 266, 322, 456, 458–59

Siam, ritual communication with in early Ch'ing, 167

silk thread *(ssu),* dreaming of, 329

silver: as currency in Ming, 242n13, 250–51; used to buy examination success and as "spirit-money," 305

Single Whip Reforms, in late Ming, 250–51

Sino-Japanese War of 1894–95, 585, 588, 615

sinology, 600–601

Sivin, Nathan, 461n3, 462, 477

six arts (*liu i*), 73–74, 535

Six Classics, 492. *See also* Classics, Chinese; Five Classics

Skinner, G. William, 129–30

sleep meditation, 327–28

Smith, Richard, xxxi n, 312

social categories, official classification of Ming population into, 250–51

social mobility, xxix, xxx, 246, 258, 299n11; among gentry, 247–49; myth of, 230–31

social status, xxx–xxxi, 239, 242, 292–93, 371–80, 619; differences in young and elderly licentiates, 286; of families of civil examination candidates, 247–56; governed by rank classification in Sung, 14; late imperial, 131–33, 223, 292–93, 376–80, 533, 586–87; of literati in Yuan, 31; social reproduction of, 240–47

solar eclipses, policy questions on, 469

solar year, measurement of length, 469

Son of Heaven, as link between heaven and earth, 476

sorcerers, during Ch'ien-lung reign, 357

southern China, 88–90, 95n, 131, 165, 256–60. *See also specific prefectures and provinces*

Southern Sung dynasty (1127–1279), 3, 4, 21, 47–49, 300; civil service examinations (*see* civil service examinations, Sung); Han Chinese elites, 31; Tao learning, xxiv–xxv, 410; theories of legitimate succession, 50–52. *See also* Sung dynasties

sovereignty, political, ascending vs. descending view of, 79–80, 84–85, 102

special examinations

  *chih-k'o*, 171, 542, 613, 615

  *pa-kung*, 548; graduates (*pa-kung-sheng*), court examinations for, 537n42

  *po-hsueh hung-tz'u*, 171, 307, 407, 534–48, 581

  Sung, 613

"special" families, *chü-jen* from, 253

specialization examinations, 280. *See also* classical specialization

specialty examinations (*chu-k'o*), 10, 44, 379

Spence, Jonathan, 270, 367n167

spherical trigonometry, in Yuan calendrical system, 469

"spirit-money," gold and silver as form of, 305

spirit-world, dreams as messages from for Han Chinese, 328

spirit-writing (*fu-chi*), 312, 319–22, 328

spirits (*shen*): in dream-visions, 337, 337–38; inside examination compounds, 308–9; and origin of universe, 474

Spiritual Pavilion (*Ling-t'ai*), 475

sponsored appointment (*pao-jen*), 127

*Spring and Autumn Annals* (Confucius), 17, 47–49, 267, 272, 275, 487–89

  approach to natural anomalies, 348, 352–53

  in civil examinations: Ch'ing, 273, 501, 515–16, 545, 563–65; Ming, 42, 74, 490–92; specialization in, 281, 282, 283, 466–67, 488, 491, 499, 563

  commentaries on, 282, 396n82, 410, 490, 496–97, 515–16, 567;

  and Japanese reverence for emperor, 599

  "praise and blame" traditions in, Lien Tzu-ning as student of, 87

  principles of history seen as enunciated in, 496–98

  referred to as "Unicorn Classic," 497, 497n91

  seen as Classic of history, 502

  solar eclipses recorded in, 469

*ssu* (private domain), vs. public domain, 434–38

*ssu* (silk thread), dreaming of, 329

Ssu-ch'uan province, 171, 233–34, 509–11, 563

*ssu-ku* (fourth leg of eight-legged essay), 406

*Ssu-k'u ch'üan-shu* (Complete [Great] collection of the four treasuries), 108, 122, 416, 458

Ssu-ma Ch'ien (145–86? B.C.), xxxv, 388, 479, 495–97, 498–500, 502–3, 589; *Records of the Official Historian*, 479, 489, 492, 497

Ssu-ma Kuang (1019–86), 16–18, 488, 490, 500; and annalistic history revival, 496, 497–98. See also *Comprehensive Mirror for Aid in Government*

Ssu-pao, Fu-chien, publishing industries, 365

*ssu-pu* (four divisions) system of genre classification, 487

*Ssu-shu cheng-pien* (Corrections and defenses …) (Li P'an-lung), 411

*Ssu-shu ch'u-wen* (Preliminary questions…), compiled by Hsu Kuang, 413

*Ssu-shu ch'ung-Hsi chu-chieh* (Notes to the Four Books) (Hsu Hsieh), 414, 414n122

*Ssu-shu jen-wu k'ao* (Study of persons…) (Hsueh Ying-ch'i), 415–16

*Ssu-shu k'ao-pei* (Search for completeness…) (Chang P'u), 415

*Ssu-shu shan-cheng* (Cutting to the correct…) (compiled by Yuan Huang), 411

*Ssu-shu shih-ti* (Yen Jo-chü), 415

*Ssu-shu ta-ch'üan* (Great collection [of commentaries] for the Four Books), 114–15

*Ssu-shu wen-hua* (Juan Yuan), 416–17

*Ssu-shu yen-ming chi-chu* (Collected notes…) (T'ang Pin-yin), 414, 414n133

*ssu-yü. See* anxiety

stars: motion of, 473–74, 476; origin of, 474

statecraft (*ching-chi*), 468, 525, 581; late imperial policy questions on, 454, 456, 458, 513, 536, 560; orthodox, 482, 507, 513–14, 527; paleography as form of for Hsueh Ying-ch'i, 457

steamed rolls (*man-t'ou*), in Ho Shao-chi's dream, 327

stem-branch characters (*t'ien-kan ti-chih*), 313

steppes, 19–22, 53–54

strangulation, as punishment for examination corruption, 202

students sent abroad: examinations for after 1905, 615, 615n136; late-19th-century proposals for, 595, 598

Su-chou prefecture, in Chiang-su province, 91, 210–11, 244, 256, 530; *optimi* by dynasty 869–1874, 693; prefectural examination hall, *176*, 177, 177n6, 198

Su Shih (1036–1101), 16, 18, 25, 540, 603; dream, 340n117

*su-wang* (uncrowned king), reference to Confucius as, 497, 497n91

*suan-ming* (fate prediction), 311–25, 328, 330–45, 354–60

*suan-shu ko-chi* (mathematical science), 578. *See also* mathematics

substance (*chih*), complemented by culture (*wen*), 165

succession, legitimate, 50–52, 55

*sui-ch'a* (Annual Difference), 468–69, 471–72

Sui dynasty (581–618), 6–7, 42, 133, 297

*sui-k'ao. See* licensing examinations

*sui-kung* (tribute students), 145, 150, 153, 200n60

*sui-shih* tests. *See* licensing examinations

sun: eclipses, 469; motions of, 471, 473–76; origin of, 474

Sun Fu (992–1057), 47–48

Sun Hsien, dream-vision, *337*, 337–38

Sun Hsing-yen (1753–1818), 379, 449–50, 505, 508, 516–17, 566

Sun Shen-hsing (1565–1636), 210

Sun Yat-sen (1866–1925), 617

*sung* (eulogies), 8

Sung Chih-sheng (1579–1668), 524–26

Sung dynasties (960–1279), 3, 12–19, 45–46, 84, 130, 360, 499; civil service examinations (*see* civil service examinations, Sung); dynastic histories, policy questions on in Ming provincial examination, 490; education, 127, 127n5, 145, 651; Hanlin Academy relationship to court, 159; intellectual evolution of Tao Learning, 3–4, 5; mathematics and astronomy as field of study, 462–65, 468; memorization of classics, 269; Ming historiography on, 55–56; nativism of literati, 47–52; poetry, 319, 544, 552, 555–56, 558; records of anomalous events, 304, 350–51; "Thirteen Classics," 267–68. *See also* Northern Sung; Southern Sung

Sung Learning (*Sung-hsueh*), xxvi, 29, 437–39, 511, 543, 566

    Fang Pao as partisan of, 417, 418

    vs. Han Learning, 443, 503–8, 519–20, 558, 567; amalgamation under title of Chinese learning, 600–601; in Ch'ing policy questions, 508–19; early-19th-century calls for synthesis, 571–72; in Grand Council debates, 541–42; and Old Text *Documents* controversy, 504–8 after 1905, 623

    surpassed by Han Learning as dominant discourse, 450, 459

    *see also* Ch'eng-Chu *li-hsueh; Tao-hsueh*

Sung Lien (1310–81), 74

*Sung-shih chih* (Wang Chu), 55

supernova (*k'o-hsing*), sighting of, 351

superstition (*mi-hsin*), 360, 621

surveillance, inside examination compounds, 194–96, 219–20

*ta-chieh* (conclusion of eight-legged essay), 385, 390, 394, 399; replaced with *shou-chieh* or *lo-hsia* section, 391

*Ta-ch'üan* (*San-pu ta-ch'üan*) trilogy, 114–17, 119, 159, 415, 417n132, 516, 566. See also *Hsing-li ta-ch'üan*; *Wu-ching ssu-shu ta-ch'üan*

*Ta-hsueh chang-chü* (Parsing of phrases in the Great Learning) (Chu Hsi), 272

*Ta-hsueh ku-pen*. See *Great Learning*

*Ta-hsueh-shih* (Grand Secretaries), 159, 201, 211

*Ta-kao* ("Great Announcement") (Chu Yuan-chang), 135

*Ta-t'ung li* (Great Concordance system), 469; calendar, 472

*ta-tzu* (hieroglyphics), 24

"Ta Yü Mo" (chapter of *Documents Classic*), seen as forgery, 507

Tai Chen (1724–77), 416, 433–34, 562, 562nn134, 135

Tai Ming-shih (1653–1713), 356, 408–9, 416–17, 419, 534

*tai sheng-jen li-yen* ("speaking in the place of the sages"), 396

*t'ai-chi* (Supreme Ultimate), 60, 440–41

*T'ai-chi t'u shuo* (Theories of the Great Ultimate in diagram form) (Chou Tun-i), 535

T'ai-chou school (radical group of Wang Yang-ming's followers), 430

*t'ai-hsu* (great vacuity), before bifurcation of heaven and earth, 474

*T'ai-hsueh* (Dynastic School; Imperial Academy; *Kuo-tzu-chien*), 5, 27, 60, 206, 280, 512

*T'ai-p'ing kuang-chi* (Expanded records of the T'ai-p'ing era), 350; Hsu K'o *Ch'ing-pai lei-ch'ao* as sequel to, 360

*T'ai-p'ing t'ien-kuo* (Heavenly Kingdom of Eternal Peace), Hung Hsiu-ch'üan's calling as emperor of, 370

T'ai-tsu (emperor, r. 960–76), 14, 122

T'ai-tsu (1328–98). *See* Chu Yuan-chang

T'ai-tsung (emperor, r. 627–50), 7, 103, 107, 122, 129, 173, 269

Taiping Rebellion (1850–64), 130, 205, 236, 511, 577

Ch'ing degree graduates before and after, 728

and civil examinations, 237, 448, 573–77, 620; reforms after, 578–84

Hung Hsiu-ch'üan's visions as ideological foundation for, 366, 368–70

Taiwan, 532, 617

talent: and morality, in Taiping selection process, 577; search for (*ch'iu-ts'ai*), 525; search for men of (*ch'iu-jen*), 524–25, 534, 535, 581

T'ang (emperor, tr., r. 2nd mill. B.C.), 349–50, 353, 354

T'ang dynasty (618–907), xxx, 3, 130, 304, 504, 507; astronomical system established by, 468; ceremony of gratitude, 194; civil service examinations (*see* civil service examinations, Tang); dynastic history, 50, 490; Hanlin Academy origins, 158–59; high officials as social equals to emperor, 84; law degree, 42; memorization of classics, 269; officials' selection, 7–12, 15; poetry, 544–47, 552, 555–56, 558; "Thirteen Classics," 267–68

T'ang Hsien-tsu (1550–1616), 287

T'ang Pin (1627–87), 523

T'ang Pin-yin (b. 1568), 203, 355–56, 414, 414n122

*T'ang-shih san-pai-shou* (Three hundred T'ang poems), 285

T'ang Shun-chih (1507–60), 418, 444, 462n6

Tanguts, 3, 19–20, 22, 46, 63–65

*tao* (the Way), 16, 18–19, 25, 61–62, 353; mind of (*see tao-hsin*); relationship to *wen*, 11, 15. See also *tao-t'ung*

Tao Ching-shen, 24

*tao-hsin* (mind of the Tao), 434–43
with *chih-t'ung*, 68–69; *Documents Classic* passage on, 434–38
and human mind (*jen-hsin*), 68–69, 434–43; Ch'ien I-pen's equation with ruler and subject, 439–40; and "Counsels of Yü the Great," 505–6, 511–12; in examination questions, 434–43, 513–14

and transmission of the mind, 493
used to legitimate Ming and Ch'ing
rulers, 576
*Tao-hsueh* ("Tao Learning"), xix–xx,
xxiv–xxvi, xxxv, 1, 3–5, 46, 408,
620–21; absorption of heterodox Taoist
and Buddhist teachings, 504; Ch'eng-
Chu interpretations stressed in, 12; in
conquest dynasties, 24–25, 63–65; horizontal peer group association characteristics seen in, 443n51; ideals of
"public" over "private" virtue, 437;
importance for Ch'eng I and followers,
18–19; late imperial (*see entry below*);
mastery of, relationship to social status,
371; Mencian view of human nature in,
78; in Sung, 15, 24–25, 26–29, 490;
during Sung-Yuan-Ming transition, 5,
37, 44–46, 56–57, 59–61, 285; in Yuan,
30, 33. *See also* Ch'eng-Chu *li-hsueh*;
Han Learning; Sung Learning; *tao-t'ung*
*Tao-hsueh* ("Tao Learning"), late imperial,
in, 103, 132, 421–23
in Ch'ing, 55n147, 437–39, 484, 623; in
civil examinations, 164–65, 501–2, 503,
535–36; revival of poetry questions seen
as betrayal of, 546–47
in civil examinations, 448, 449 (*see also sub*
in Ch'ing, in Ming); curriculum from
1384 to 1756, 522–23
as classical curriculum, 105–19, 376
in Ming, 142, 214, 476–77, 481–83; in civil
examinations, 39, 40–42, 352, 488–95,
493, 495
Tao-kuang emperor (r. 1821–50), 227–28,
235–36, 688; civil examinations under,
226, 524n8, 567–68, 570, 572–73, 584
*tao-t'ung* ("legitimate succession of the Way";
"orthodox transmission of the Tao"),
396, 490, 507, 544; *chia fa* as suggested
replacement for, 516; late imperial policy questions on, 412, 437–38, 488, 493,
503, 510, 513–14; in natural philosophy,
476–77; relationship to political legitimacy, 51–52, 68n3, 97, 441–42, 499;
repossessed by Ming emperors, 68, 97
*tao wen-hsueh* (inquiring into culture and
study), 514
Taoism and Taoists, 45, 104, 247, 306–8,
492, 504

degree in (*Tao-k'o*), 10
in civil examinations, 299; influence in
late Ming and early Ch'ing, 411–12,
414–15; in T'ang, 10, 11; as venue for
parable of, 311
and Confucianism and Buddhism, 45,
306, 312
on leaving this world and entering world
of pure nature, 363–64
monks excluded from examination hall,
299
pantheon of worthies and deities, in
dream-visions, 339, 344
priests, 132, 249, 305, 312–15, 327
privileges under Yuan, 30
temples, 304, 593
and terms associated with Sung dynasty
theories of mind, 490
Wang Yang-ming's views of, 438
Wen-ch'ang cult, 300–302, 304, 309
Wu Chin's attack on, 438
tax(es), xxviii–xxix, 130; benefits, xxvi–xxvii,
138, 175, 241; in Ch'ing, 139, 170, 213,
530; labor, 30, 241; in Ming, 90–92,
139, 250–51; relationship to wealth, 392
tax-exempt land, 243
tax-exempt trusts, 244–45
*t'e-tsou* (facilitated degrees), in Sung, 58; *t'e-
tsou-ming chin-shih* (facilitated degree-
holders), 26n70
technical science (*chi-ch'i chih-tso*), 379,
483–84, 578
temple(s), 305, 315, 328; Buddhist and
Taoist, 304; changed into new schools,
624; honoring Confucius, 81, 121, 299,
365; Kuang-chai, 299; *Wen-ch'ang*,
301–2
temple schools, 239, 246, 263
terror, policies of, enforced by Ming rulers,
66, 82, 210
textbooks, for new schools, 608–9
textual studies: and eight-legged essay, 506;
in 18th-century metropolitan examination policy questions, 514–15; as focus
of *k'ao-cheng* in Ch'ing, 458, 467, 518,
562; in *k'ao-chü* research in Ming, 458
Thirteen Classics, 267–68, 267n76, 272n88,
273, 502, 516, 563
*Thousand Character Text* (*Ch'ien-tzu wen*), 185,
263, 272, 274–75, 372, 609–10

*Three Character Classic* (*San-tzu ching*), 185, 263, 275, 372, 609–10

three heads (*jen-shou san k'o*), in dream-vision, *332*, 333–35

"Three Policy Answers of One Chosen Wise and Virtuous" (*Hsien-liang san-ts'e*) (Tung Chung-shu), 6

*Ti-hsueh* (Studies of geography) (Shen Hsin-chou), preface, 485

*ti-li*. *See* geography

*t'i-hsueh kuan* ("education intendants"; *t'i-tiao kuan*), 136, 148

*t'i-tiao kuan* ("education intendants"; *t'i-hsueh kuan*), 136, 148

Tiao Pao (1603–69), 527–28

Tibetans, 20, 36; written out of Chinese intellectual history, 46

*t'ieh-ching* (identifying passage from Classics), 10–12, 23, 381

*tien-shih* (*t'ing shih*) (written palace examinations), 8

*Tien-shih-chai hua-pao* (periodical), 357–59, *358*, 360

T'ien-ch'i emperor (r. 1621–27), 139, 209–10, 401, 403–7, 418

*T'ien-chu sheng-chiao ssu-tzu ching* (Catholic four-character classic), 270

*t'ien-hsia chih kung* (public good of empire), 491–92

*t'ien-hsiang* (celestial luminaries as counterparts to matters in the world), 473–77

T'ien Ju-k'ang, 298n9

*t'ien-kan ti-chih* (stem-branch characters), 313

*t'ien-li* (heavenly principles), 18, 303, 432–34, 474, 492

*t'ien-pang* ("heavenly rankings"), dreams of, 324

T'ien-shun emperor (r. 1457–64). *See* Chu Ch'i-chen

*T'ien-t'iao shu* (Heavenly Commandments) (Hung Hsiu-ch'üan), 575

*t'ien-wen*. *See* astrology

Tillman, Hoyt, 3, 25, 25n67, 59

*ting* (nails), dreaming of, 329

Ting Hsien, 86, 329

Ting Shih-mei, 342–43, *344*

*t'ing-shih* (*tien-shih*) (written palace examinations), 8

Tokyo Imperial University, 598

tone, in poetry, 555, 555n110

topical history (*chi-chuan*), 489, 489n75; vs. annalistic history, 495–98, 499n96, 502–3

traders, social status, 253, 372

translation bureaus, Ch'ing, 167

translation examinations (*fan-i hsiang-shih*), 166–67, 223, 548

translations, of eight-legged essays into Latin, 393, 393n73

treason, 83, 417, 431

tribute students (*sui-kung*), 145, 150, 153, 200n60

Trigault, Nicholas, xxxiii n33

Triple Concordance system (*San-t'ung li*), 468–69

*tsa-chü* (*ch'ü-chü*; vernacular drama), 396

*tsa-wen*. *See* belles lettres

Ts'ai Shen (1167–1230), 410, 436, 438, 440

Ts'ai Yuan-p'ei (1868–1940), 270, 585

Ts'ai Yuan-ting (1135–98), 478, 479

Ts'ao Nai (1402–44), 149

*ts'ao-shu* (cursive calligraphy), 379

*ts'e* (public policy), civil examination questions on. *See* policy questions

*ts'e-tzu* (*ch'ai-tzu*; deciphering of written words), 312, 322–24, 328, 339

*ts'e-wen* ("questioning by bamboo slips"), 6

Tseng Ch'i (1372–1432), 68–69, 109, 110

Tseng Kuo-fan (1811–72), 578

Tseng Lu (1319–72), 269

Tso Ch'iu-ming, 497, 500

*Tso chuan* (Tso Commentary), 276, 282, 410, 490, 497; character count, 267, 281; debate over reliability of, 515–16

*tso-wen* (composition), 261–63, 276–80

Tsou Chung-i, 303

Tsou Jung (1885–1905), 534n33

*ts'ui-mien-shu* (hypnotic arts), 328

*tsun te-hsing* (honoring one's moral nature), polarity with *tao wen-hsueh*, 514

*tsun-wang* ("honoring the ruler"), in Sung interpretation of *Spring and Autumn Annals*, 47–49

*ts'un* (inches), length for pitch pipe measured in, 478, 480–81

*ts'ung-ming* (intelligence), classical essays seen as test of, 579

Tu Fu (712–70), 29, 388, 554n105

*Tu-hsueh-tao*, as title for provincial education commissioner, 136

Tu Yü (222–84), 470

*t'u-chi* (native peoples), attention to in early Ch'ing educational affairs, 168–69

*t'u-meng* ("map out dreams"), 328

T'u-mu Affair of 1448–49, 46, 53–55, 62, 146, 241n8; 1456 provincial examinations in aftermath of, 431; Yü Ch'ien's role in deposing Cheng-t'ung emperor, 303

Tuan Yü-ts'ai (1735–1815), 562n135

*tui-chü* (antithetical [balanced] clauses), 270, 391

*tui-ou* (parallel wording), 384. *See also* parallelism

*tui-ts'e* ("answering using bamboo slips"), 6

*t'ui-kuan* (outside judges), as associate examiners, 152

*t'ui-suan* (fate extrapolation), 312

Tung Ch'i-ch'ang (1555–1636), 96n88, 136, 203

Tung Chih-ming, 419n136

Tung Chueh, 452–53

Tung Chung-shu (179–104 B.C.), 6, 347–48, 347n126, 444, 518

*Tung-fang tsa-chih (Eastern Miscellany)*, 603–6, 609

Tung-lin Academy, 207, 208–10, 220, 365, 414, 439

T'ung-ch'eng scholarship, 382, 417, 517

*T'ung-chien kang-mu* (Chu Hsi). See *Tzu-chih t'ung-chien kang-mu*

*T'ung-chien t'i-yao* (Essentials of the Comprehensive Mirror) (Chu Hsi), 490–91

*T'ung-chih* (encyclopedia compiled by Cheng Ch'iao), 266

T'ung-chih Restoration (1862–74), 228, 578–84

*t'ung-lei p'eng* (commonality), 397

*t'ung nien* (same year of graduation) reunion, 261

*t'ung-sheng*: candidates, 220–37, 224, 283, 288; as designation for apprentice candidates, 135; as designation for "licentiates," 135n31, 137 (*see also* licentiates); transition from childhood to, 276

*t'ung-shih* (examinations of youths), 133n26

*t'ung-shu* (almanacs), 313

*T'ung-tzu hsu-chih* (What all youthful candidates should know), 272

*t'ung wen-li. See* classical literacy

tutoring, 128, 242, 607

twelve-pitch system (*yueh-lü*), in music, 477–81

Twenty-one Dynastic Histories, 502

Twitchett, Denis, 11–12

two-headed horseman (*shuang-t'ou-ren*), in dream-vision, 335–36, *336*

*tzu-ch'iang* (self-strengthening), 580, 585, 588

*Tzu-chih t'ung-chien* (Ssu-ma Kuang). See *Comprehensive Mirror for Aid in Government*

*Tzu-chih t'ung-chien kang-mu* (Condensation of the Comprehensive Mirror of History) (Chu Hsi), 50–51, 276, 483, 490, 496, 498, 501

*tzu-jan* (natural world), policy questions on, 347–54

*tzu-jan chih hsueh* (Chinese sciences), 465. *See also* natural studies; science

*tzu-jan chih li* (principles of nature), 474

*tzu-wen tzu-ta* (asking a question and answering it), in Ch'ing policy essays, 447

Tzu-yang Academy, 550

*tz'u-chang* (grammar-punctuation exercises), 412, 438

Tz'u-hsi (Empress Dowager) (1835–1908), 587, 594, 605, 622

understanding (*wu-hsing*), 263

"Unicorn Classic." See *Spring and Autumn Annals*

universalist moral vision, 397–99

universe, origin of, in 1561 policy answer, 474

unlimited space (*hsuan-yeh*), contained in sky, 475

Van Kley, Edwin J., xxxiii n34

Venus (planet), 475

*Veritable Records (Shih-lu)*, from the Hung-hsi reign, 95

"Veritable Records of the Hung-wu Reign," revisions of ordered by Chu Ti, 106, 107–8, 109, 114, 120

vermillion papers (*chu-chüan*), 400, 531n26

vernacular Chinese, 88, 373; vs. classical as problem in reform, 586, 611; popular literature in, 296, 372–73, 402; use in teaching classics after 1911, 623–24; vernacular drama (*ch'ü-chü; tsa-chü*), 396

vernacular literacy, 276, 372–73

Vietnam, xxii, 161

Vietnamese, 132

village-family units (*li-chia*) of households, labor service requirements based on, 250

visions. *See* dreams, dream-visions

Wada Masahiro, 44, 141, 143, 144, 158n68

*wai-lien kuan* (outer overseers), 181

*wai-wang* (external kingship), dual role with *nei-sheng* (inner sagehood), 513

Wakefield, David, 244–45

Wakeman, Frederic, Jr., 166, 373

Waley, Arthur, 363–64

Waltner, Ann, 325

Wan-li emperor (r. 1573–1619), 151, 189, 207, 401, 414, 445

wandering students (*yu-hsueh-sheng*), examinations for after 1905, 612–13, 615

Wang, Y. C., 615n136

Wang An-shih (1021–86), 15–19, 28, 121, 351, 381; reform policies, 24, 37, 43, 79, 217, 351, 589

Wang Ao (1450–1524), 214, 334, 423, 454; eight-legged essays, 214, 385–92, 397–99, 402

Wang Ch'ang (1725–1806), 266–67, 268, 514

Wang Chen-yuan, 546n77

Wang Chi (1498–1583), 415

Wang Chieh (1725–1805), 316–17

Wang Chu (fl. ca. 1521), 55

Wang Fu-chih (1619–92), 54

Wang Hsien-ch'ien (1842–1918), 594

Wang Hsun, 552

Wang Hua (1453–1522), 253, 306

Wang Hung-hsu (1645–1723), 432

Wang Jo-hsu (1174–1243), 25

Wang Lun (Wang Tsung-i) (fl. ca. 1465–87), 207, 330, 431–32, 452

Wang Mang interregnum (A.D. 9–23), 79

Wang Ming-sheng (1722–98), 170, 285, 486, 514, 543

Wang Nien-sun (1744–1832), 562, 562n135

*wang-pa chih pien* (illegitimate usurpers), 498

Wang Po-hou (Ying-lin, 1223–96), 509

Wang Shih-chen (1526–90), 287, 402, 403

Wang Shih-chen (1634–1711), 533

Wang Shih-su (1566–1601), 402–3

Wang T'ao (1828–?), 576–77, 577n30

Wang Te-ch'eng, 563–64

Wang T'ing-chen (1757–1827), 571

Wang Tso (1440–1512), 98n95

Wang Wen (1393–1457), 207, 330, 431

Wang Yang-ming (Shou-jen; 1472–1528), 142, 253, 280–82, 287, 387, 494

father's experience with dreams and examinations, 306

learning, 258, 430; 16th-century rise of, 429, 430–31

restoration of Old Text version of *Great Learning*, 451

teachings, 411–15, 432–33, 442, 504, 514; attacks on, 438; equating of moral knowledge and human action, 423; on priority of mind, 474, 476

Wang Yin-chih (1766–1834), 517–18, 562, 562n135

Wang Ying-lin (1223–96), 27, 263, 263n64

Wang Yun (1784–1854), 265, 269, 278–79

Warring States era (403–221 B.C.), 47, 117, 347

warrior elites, 19–25, 36, 223; in Japan, 23

water, role in origins of universe, 474

Watt, John R., xxvii n22

Way, the. *See tao*

wealth, 245; and power, 578, 585, 597, 598; relationship to taxes, 392

*wei-chi chih hsueh* (self-cultivation), 131–32

Wei Chung-hsien (1568–1627), 118, 209–10

*wei-ho* (accord), in astronomy, 470

Wei Hsi (1624–81), 529, 530

*wei-hsueh* (garrison schools), 148

*wei-kuan* ("special assignments"), 195

*wei-mo* (hall essays), printing and publishing in Ming, 400–403

Wei Yuan (1794–1856), 572–73

Wei Yun-ko (Wei Shih-lung), 325

Weights and Measures, Bureau of, Office of Music, 477, 481

weights and measures, pitch standards used to define, 478–81, 481n62

*wen* (culture), 15, 277; in Chin and pre-1240 Sung, 25, 60; complemented by *chih* (substance), 165; in literati discourse, 11, 45; during T'ang-Sung transition, 61–62

Wen-ch'ang: cult of, 300–302, 304, 309, 318; temple, 204; temple dreams, 328, *358*, 358–59

*Wen-hsien ta-ch'eng* (Great collection of written documents), 107–8

*Wen-hsien t'ung-k'ao* (comprehensive examination of civil institutions) (compiled by Ma Tuan-lin), 527

*wen-jen* ("men of culture"), 25, 45, 375, 534

*wen-k'o* (course of letters) *chü-jen* and *chin-shih*, 613

*wen-miao* (literary temple), dedicated to Lord Wen-ch'ang, 204

*Wen-pien* (Compilation of essays), compiled by T'ang Shun-chih, 444, 444n53

Wen T'ien-hsiang (1236–83), 60, 216, 444, 444n55

*wen-tzu-hsueh. See* paleography

*wen-tz'u* (literary talent), 90

*Wen-yuan ying-hua* (A gathering of masterpieces of literature) (compiled by Li Fang), 558

Weng Fang-kang (1733–1818), 234–35, 285n121, 287, 549–50

West
  imperialism, 620
  and learning, 595; adaptation to of late-19th-century classical curriculum, 569, 578–84, 591, 598, 599–600; and decanonization of classical studies after 1905, 608; rise of Chinese Learning as counterpart for, 599–602; stress on practical studies, 592, 598, 599–600
  response to Boxer Rebellion, 587
  school systems, power associated with, 585–86
  *see also* Europe

Wilson, Thomas, xxv, xxvii n21, xxxiv n, 5

wish-fulfillment dreams, 332n, 336–40

"Wo i" (pen name of Chiang Wei-lung), 614–16

Wo-k'ou pirate menace, 54

women, xxix, 249, 288, 298n9; education of, 240–41, 574; role in sons' education, 241, 241n5, 263, 288; as spirits haunting examination candidates, 310

writing elite, formation of, 276–80, 403–9, 525. *See also* publishing

writing paraphernalia, needed for calligraphy, 377, *378*

Wu (emperor, r. 140–87 B.C.), 6, 8, 122

Wu (empress, r. 684–704), 7–8, 8n19

Wu Ch'eng-en, 313n60, 330

*wu-chi* ("Ultimateless"), focus on in 1256 palace examinations, 60

Wu Ch'i (1456 *chin-shih*), 101

Wu Chin (fl. ca. 1516–17), 412, 438–39

*Wu-ching cheng-i*, compilation of authorized by Li Shih-min, 103

*wu-ching po-shih* ("Learned literati of the Five Classics), 280

*Wu-ching ssu-shu ta-ch'üan (Complete [Great] Collection [of commentaries] for the Five Classics and Four Books)*, 107, 114–15, 116, 522

Wu Ching-tzu (1701–54), 175, 286, 296, 356–57

Wu Hsiang, 453

*wu-hsing* (five phases), in heavenly order, 347–48, 347n125

*wu-hsing* (understanding), 263

Wu K'uan (1436–1504), 339

Wu Lei-ch'uan (1870–1944), 613–14

Wu Lung-chien (1694–1773), 543–44

Wu Ping, 197n49

Wu Po-tsung (n.d.), 73–78, 91, 525

Wu P'u (1363–1426), 120

Wu Shao, 352–54

Wu Sheng-ch'in (1729–1803), 446

*wu-shih* (five matters), in human affairs, 347–48

Wu, Yiwi, 351

Wu Yü-pi (1392–1469), 120, 214

xenophobia, of K'ang Yu-wei, 593, 593n74

Yang Ch'i-yuan (1547–99), 302, 415

Yang Hsiu-ch'ing (d. 1856), 575–76

Yang Hsiung, 76–77, 525

*yang-i* (hemispherical sundial), 476

Yang Jung (Tzu-jung) (1371–1440), 105, 107, 110, 115

Yang Kung-i (1225–94), 32

*yang-lao* (retirement trust), 245

*yang-min* ("healthy customs"), 38

yang pitches, in music, 478, 479, 480, 480n61

Yang Shen (1488–1559), 451

*yang-t'ou* (goat's head), in dream-vision, 339, *340*

Yang Wei-chen (1296–1370), 52

Yang Wen-sun (1782–1853), 383

*yang-wu yun-tung* (foreign studies), 578

*yangban* elites, in the Koryŏ dynasty, 23

Yangtzu delta, 170, 258–59, 402; candidates' performance on civil examinations, 131, 256–57, 260; as center of textual scholarship in Ch'ing, 503–4, 507, 513, 517; examinations halted during Taiping Rebellion, 237, 573; Ming loyalism as political and military force in, 532; private academies abolished in, 208; role of economics in access to classical education, 242, 244, 246; Taiping Rebellion centered in, 205. *See also* Anhui province; Che-chiang province; Chiang-su province; Su-chou prefecture

Yao (emperor, tr., r. 3rd mill. B.C.), 349–50, 353, 354, 473; seen as a sage-king, 436, 438, 440, 493

Yao Ch'eng-lieh (1716–86), 559

Yao Kuang-hsiao (1335–1418), 108–9

Yao Nai (1731–1815), 382, 571

*Yao-tien* (Canon of Yao), 474

Yeh-lü Ch'u-ts'ai (1189–1243), 21

Yellow Bell (*huang-chung*) pitch pipe, 477–81

yellow crane (*huang-ho*), in dream-vision, 339–40, *341*

Yellow Emperor (Huang Ti), 474, 476, 480, 492, 497

yellow registers (*huang-ts'e*), 249–50

Yen Fu (1853–1921), 585–86, 607, 608

Yen Jo-chü (1636–1704), 415, 504–5

*yen t'ien-wen* (astronomical portents), 483, 485. *See also* astrology

Yen Yuan (1635–1704), 365, 433, 534–35

Yen Yuan (n.d.) (Confucius' disciple), 430, 432,

Yen Yueh, 565–66

Yi dynasty (Korea; 1392–1910), 23

yin, and yang, 60, 440, 472, 474

*yin-kung* ("hidden merit"), 305–6

yin pitches, in music, 478, 479, 480, 480n61

yin privilege. *See* hereditary privilege

*yin-te* ("hidden virtue"), 305

*yin-tz'u* ("immoral shrines"), attempts to eliminate, 121

*yin-yun chih hsueh. See* phonology, ancient

*Ying-shih p'ai-lü ching-hsuan* (Selection of outstanding models of regulated verse...) (compiled by Chou Ta-chü), 549

Ying-t'ai emperor (r. 1450–56), 207

Ying-t'ien prefecture, provincial examinations, 211, 347n125, 477–81; geographic distribution of *chü-jen* graduates 1501–1630, 693; Ming era policy questions and classical specialties, 447–49, 467, 488; Ming ratio of graduates to candidates in, 661; policy questions classified by topic 1474–1600, 719

Ying-tsung emperor. *See* Chu Ch'i-chen

Yoshikawa Kōjirō, 25n67

*yu-hsueh-sheng* (wandering students), examinations for after 1905, 612–13, 615

Yu Jo, 389, 389n59, 397

*yu-kung-sheng* (senior tribute students), court examinations for, 537n42

Yu Li, 510n119

Yu, Pauline, 547

*yü* (emotional stasis), 298, 299n9

Yü (sage-king), 434–35, 436, 440

Yü Ch'ang-ch'eng (T'ung-ch'uan), 388, 414–15

Yü Chi (1272–1348), 39, 300

Yü Ch'ien (1398–1457), 53, 431; appearance as a ghost, 330; cult devoted to, 303, 304; Hang-chou shrine, 303, 303n21, 328; posthumous title changed to Chung-su, 303

Yü Chih-chia, 254–55

*yü-heng*, as astronomical instrument, 475–76, 476n46, 548

Yü Hsi (ca. A.D. early 4th century), 471

*yü-lin t'u-ts'e* ("fish-scale maps and books"), land surveys in, 250

Yü Ying-shih, 451, 451n72

Yuan Chia-ku (b. 1872), 599–600

Yuan Ching, 453

Yuan dynasty (1280–1368), 3, 71, 130, 146, 159, 165; calendrical system, 469, 471–72; civil service examinations (*see* civil service examinations, Yuan); Dynastic History, 468, 471, 474, 476; issues of legitimate succession, 51–52; literati, construction of Han and barbarian as fixed identities, 47; Ming literati view of, 54–55; success of mathematics and astronomy in, 462–63; *Tao-hsueh* as orthodoxy in, xxiv–xxv, 4, 29, 67; unification of north and south China, 30; Wen-ch'ang cult's recognition, 300

Yuan Hao-wen (1190–1257), 25
Yuan Huang (Yuan Liao-fan) (1533–1606), 306–7, 324, 326, 411
Yuan Hung-tao (1568–1610), 383
Yuan Mei (1716–98), 363–64, 549
*yuan-sheng* (fundamental pitch), 480
Yuan Shih-k'ai (1859–1916), 587, 602–3, 609
Yueh Cheng (1418–72), 329
"Yueh-chi" (Record of music), in *Record of Rites*, 479
Yueh Fei (1103–41), cult of, 55
*yueh-lü* (twelve-pitch system), 477–81
*yun-shu* (rhyme books), 552
Yung-cheng emperor (r. 1723–35), 122, 212, 318, 407

*Amplified Instructions (Sheng-yü kuang-hsun)*, 135, 221, 222, 575
civil examinations under, 283–84, 446; policies on local examinations, 150, 221, 222, 225; reform policies, 229–32, 235, 236, 485, 536–37, 546
*yung-jen. See* governance
Yung-lo reign. *See* Chu Ti
*Yung-lo ta-tien* (Great compendium of the Yung-lo era), 109, 110, 114, 115n148, 122, 159

Zeitlin, Judith, 298, 299n9
Zi, Etienne, xxiii, 135n31, 137n37
Zottoli, P. Angelo, 393n73

Index   Indi-Indexes
Text:   10.5/12.5 Baskerville
Display:   Baskerville
Composition:   Asco Typesetters
Printing and binding:   Edwards Brothers